MW01131221

Phoenicia

Charcoal drawing of J. Brian Peckham by Michael Steinhauser.

Phoenicia

Episodes and Anecdotes from the Ancient Mediterranean

J. Brian Peckham

Winona Lake, Indiana
Eisenbrauns
2014

Library of Congress Cataloging-in-Publication Data

Peckham, Brian, 1934–2008.
    Phoenicia : episodes and anecdotes from the ancient Mediterranean /
    J. Brian Peckham.
        pages   cm
    Includes bibliographical references.
    ISBN 978-1-57506-181-8 (hardback : alk. paper)
    1. Phoenicians—History.   I. Title.
    DS81.P43   2014
    939.4′4—dc23
                                                    2014016961

Contents

List of Illustrations

List of Maps

Note to the reader: The maps are intended to reflect sites mentioned in this book rather than the specific chronology or period of the chapter in which they appear.

Preface

It is not an exaggeration to say that Brian Peckham's dying wish was the publication of this book. As it became clear that his time was very limited, the manuscript was of the utmost concern to him and I am very honored that Brian entrusted me with the task of making sure it came to fruition.

When asked what Brian's book is about, my response in short is that he has managed to document every place that a Phoenician set foot. Brian followed the Phoenicians through time and space as they left their mark on the various places to which they sailed. His expansive knowledge of the history, linguistics, epigraphy, politics, economics, and religions of the ancient Near East makes this work a truly comprehensive examination of the Phoenicians' economic, religious, and social relationships with their neighbors.

In some ways, Brian's scholarship has come full circle. Although his range of expertise was diverse and he published on a number of subjects, his very first and very last book, written some 40 years apart, both concentrate on the Phoenicians.

Brian's death is a major loss to scholarship, to his students, and to his friends. To his students, he was an inspirational teacher, who gave them the confidence to pursue their own insights. To his friends, he was caring, funny, and engaged in their lives. I am very privileged to have known Brian as both teacher and friend, and I sincerely hope that any contribution I have made to this volume reflects the profound influence he had upon me.

The description of the Phoenicians in his introduction as "welcoming waves of newcomers, the displaced and adventurers, by teaching them what [they] learned, and by looking for their learning in return" is an apt description of Brian himself. He was not possessive of his knowledge and ideas but openly shared them and yet often remarked how much he constantly learned from others, his students in particular. He was a dedicated and devoted teacher and friend, whose unique character and selfless giving had an impact on all those around him. His modesty prevented him from readily accepting the accolades and expressions of appreciation that he so deserved. He was a mentor to many and believed in the pursuit of knowledge as being valuable in and of itself. Brian's generosity of spirit will be truly missed.

I am grateful to the people at Eisenbrauns, particularly Jim Eisenbraun, Beverly McCoy, Andrew Knapp, and Gina Hannah, who went to extraordinary lengths to help fulfill Brian's wish for the publication of this book. It is wonderful that both scholars and students who knew Brian and those who have yet to discover his valuable work will have access to his most recent scholarship—scholarship that incorporates a lifetime of study of the Phoenicians.

—Adina Levin

Abbreviations

General

Ag. Ap.	Josephus. *Against Apion*
Diod.	Diodorus. *Histories*
Ph.Byb.	Philo of Byblos. *Phoenician History*

Reference Works

AASOR	Annual of the American Schools of Oriental Research
AB	Anchor Bible
AbrN	*Abr-Nahrain*
ABSA	*Annual of the British School at Athens*
Actas 4	*Actas del IV Congreso Internacional de Estudios Fenicios y Púnicos, Cádiz, 2 al 6 de Octobre de 1995.* 4 vols. Cádiz: University of Cádiz, 2000
Actes 3	M. H. Fantar and M. Ghaki, eds. *Actes du IIIe Congrès International des Études Phéniciennes et Puniques, Tunis, 11–16 novembre 1991.* 2 vols. Tunis: Institut Nationale du Patrimoine, 1995
ADAJ	*Annual of the Department of Antiquities of Jordan*
AfO	*Archiv für Orientforschung*
Ah, Assyria	M. Cogan and I. Eph'al, eds. *Ah, Assyria . . . : Studies in Assyrian History and Ancient Near Eastern Historiography Presented to Hayim Tadmor.* Scripta Hierosolymitana 33. Jerusalem: Magnes, 1991
AHI	G. I. Davies. *Ancient Hebrew Inscriptions: Corpus and Concordance.* Cambridge: Cambridge University Press, 1991
AION	*Annali dell'Istituto Orientale di Napoli*
AJA	*American Journal of Archaeology*
Ammoniter	U. Hübner. *Die Ammoniter: Untersuchungen zur Geschichte, Kultur und Religion einer transjordanischer Volker im 1 . . . Jahrtauend v.-Chr.* Wiesbaden: Harrassowitz, 1992
ANESt	*Ancient Near Eastern Studies*
ANET	J. B. Pritchard, ed. *Ancient Near Eastern Texts Relating to the Old Testament.* 3rd ed. Princeton: Princeton University Press, 1969
ANLM	Atti della Accademia Nazionale del Lincei, Memorie
ANLR	Atti della Accademia Nazionale dei Lincei, Rendiconti
AnSt	*Anatolian Studies*
AoF	*Altorientalische Forschungen*
ArAn	*Archäologischer Anzeiger*
ASKaW	R. Rolle and K. Schmidt, eds. *Archäologische Studien in Kontaktzonen der antiken Welt.* Göttingen: Vandenhoeck & Ruprecht, 1998
ASOR	American Schools of Oriental Research
Atti 1	*Atti del 1 Congresso Internazionale di Studi Fenici e Punici, Roma, 5–10 Novembre 1979.* 3 vols. Collezione di studi fenici 16. Rome: Consiglio Nazionale delle Ricerche, 1983
Atti 2	E. Acquaro, ed. *Atti del II Congresso Internazionale di Studi Fenici e Punici, Roma, 9–14 Novembre 1987.* 3 vols. Collezione di studi fenici 30. Rome: Consiglio Nazionale delle Ricerche, 1991

AuOr	*Aula Orientalis*
BA	*Biblical Archaeologist*
BAR	*Biblical Archaeology Review*
BAR Int. Series	British Archaeological Reports, International Series
BASOR	*Bulletin of the American Schools of Oriental Research*
BATM	N. H. Gale, ed. *Bronze Age Trade in the Mediterranean*. Jonsered: Åström, 1991
Bib	*Biblica*
BCH	*Bulletin de Correspondance Hellénique*
Bierling	M. R. Bierling, ed. *The Phoenicians in Spain: An Archaeological Review of the Eighth–Sixth Centuries B.C.E.—A Collection of Articles Translated from Spanish*. Winona Lake, IN: Eisenbrauns, 2002
BKAT	Biblischer Kommentar: Altes Testament
BaghM	*Baghdader Mitteilungen*
BMB	*Bulletin du Musée de Beyrouth*
BN	*Biblische Notizen*
BPPS	R. Deutsch and A. Lemaire. *Biblical Period Personal Seals in the Shlomo Moussaieff Collection*. Tel Aviv–Jaffa: Archaeological Center, 2000
BSHRDN	P. Bernardini, R. D'Oriano, and P. G. Spanu, eds. *Phoinikes bshrdn: I Fenici in Sardegna. Nuove acquisizioni*. Cagliari: La memoria storica, 1997
BZ	*Biblische Zeitschrift*
CAI	W. E. Aufrecht. *A Corpus of Ammonite Inscriptions*. Lewiston, NY: Edwin Mellen, 1989
Carthago	E. Lipiński, ed. *Carthago*. Studia Phoenicia 5. Louvain: Peeters, 1988
CAT	M. Dietrich, O. Loretz, and J. Sanmartín. *The Cuneiform Alphabetic Texts from Ugarit, Ras Ibn Hani and Other Places*. Münster: Ugarit-Verlag, 1995
CBQ	*Catholic Biblical Quarterly*
CIS	*Corpus Inscriptionum Semiticarum, Pars Prima: Inscriptones Phoenicias Continens*. Paris: Reipublicae Typographeo, 1881–1962
CMP	J. W. Betlyon. *The Coinage and Mints of Phoenicia: The Pre-Alexandrine Period*. Harvard Semitic Monographs 26. Chico, CA: Scholars Press, 1982
COS	W. W. Hallo and K. L. Younger Jr., ed. *The Context of Scripture*. 3 vols. Leiden: Brill, 1997–2003
CPPMR	V. Krings, ed. *La civilisation phénicienne et punique: Manuel de recherche*. Leiden: Brill, 1995
CRAIBL	*Comptes Rendus de l'Académie des Inscriptions et Belles Lettres*
CSOSI	P. Bordreuil. *Catalogue des Sceaux Ouest-Sémitiques Inscrits*. Paris: Bibliothèque Nationale, 1986
Cyprus	G. Hill. *A History of Cyprus, Volume I: To The Conquest by Richard Lion Heart*. Cambridge: Cambridge University Press, 1940
DM	*Damaszener Mitteilungen*
EA	W. L. Moran, ed. and trans. *The Amarna Letters*. Baltimore: John Hopkins University Press, 1992
ErIsr	*Eretz-Israel*
ESC	E. Peltenburg, ed. *Early Society in Cyprus*. Edinburgh: University of Edinburgh Press, 1989
EVO	*Egitto e Vicino Oriente*
FPI	G. del Olmo Lete and M. E. Aubet Semmler, eds. *Los Fenicios en la Península Ibérica, I: Arqueología, cerámica y plástica: II: Epigrafia y lengua Glíptica y numismática. Expansión e interacción cultural*. Sabadell (Barcelona): AUSA, 1986

HAAN	*Histoire et archéologie de l'Afrique du Nord, I: Carthage et son territoire dans l'antiquité.* Paris: Comité des Travaux Historiques et Scientifiques, 1990
HBA	*Hamburger Beiträge zur Archäologie*
HistTyre	H. J. Katzenstein. *The History of Tyre: From the Beginning of the Second Millennium B.C.E. until the Fall of the Neo-Babylonian Empire in 538 B.C.E.* Jerusalem: Schocken Institute for Jewish Research, 1973
HSM	Harvard Semitic Monographs
HSS	Harvard Semitic Studies
HTR	*Harvard Theological Review*
ICS	O. Masson. *Les Inscriptions Chypriotes syllabiques.* Paris: Boccard, 1961
Idalion	L. E. Stager and A. M. Walker, eds. *American Expedition to Idaliion, Cyprus, 1973–1980.* Oriental Institute Communications 24. Chicago: Oriental Institute, 1989
IEJ	*Israel Exploration Journal*
IFPCO	M. G. Amadasi Guzzo. *Le iscrizioni fenici e puniche delle colonie in Occidente.* Studi Semitici 28. Rome: Istituto di Studi del Vicino Oriente, 1967
IJNA	*The International Journal of Nautical Archaeology*
IM	*Istanbuler Mitteilungen*
IOS	Israel Oriental Studies
IPP	B. Delavault and A. Lemaire. "Les inscriptions phéniciennes de Palestine." *RSF* 7 (1979) 1–39, pls. 1–14
JANES	*Journal of the Ancient Near Eastern Society of Columbia University*
JAOS	*Journal of the American Oriental Society*
JARCE	*Journal of the American Research Center in Egypt*
JBL	*Journal of Biblical Literature*
JCS	*Journal of Cuneiform Studies*
JEA	*Journal of Egyptian Archaeology*
JESHO	*Journal of the Economic and Social History of the Orient*
JHS	*Journal of Hellenic Studies*
JJS	*Journal of Jewish Studies*
JMA	*Journal of Mediterranean Archaeology*
JMS	*Journal of Mediterranean Studies*
JNES	*Journal of Near Eastern Studies*
JNSL	*Journal of Northwest Semitic Languages*
JSOT	*Journal for the Study of the Old Testament*
JSOTSup	Journal for the Study of the Old Testament Supplements
JSS	*Journal of Semitic Studies*
KAI	H. Donner and W. Röllig. *Kanaanäische und aramäische Inschriften.* 3 vols. Wiesbaden: Harrassowitz, 1962–64
Kition 3	M. G. Guzzo Amadasi and V. Karageorghis. *Fouilles de Kition, III: Inscriptions Phéniciennes.* Nicosia: Department of Antiquities, 1977
MA	*Mediterranean Archaeology*
MDOG	*Mitteilungen der Deutschen Orient-Gesellschaft*
MEFRA	*Mélanges de l'École Française de Rome—Antiquité*
MHR	*Mediterranean Historical Review*
MM	*Madrider Mitteilungen*
MMJ	*Metropolitcan Museum Journal*
MPT	S. Gitin, A. Mazar, and E. Stern, eds. *Mediterranean Peoples in Transition: Thirteenth to Early Tenth Centuries BCE. In Honor of Professor Trude Dothan.* Jerusalem: Israel Exploration Society, 1998
MRS	Mission de Ras Shamra
Mus	*Le Muséon: Revue des Études Orientales*

MUSJ	*Mélanges de l'Université Saint-Joseph*
ND	Field numbers of tablets excavated at Nimrud (Kalhu)
NEA	*Near Eastern Archaeology*
NEAEHL	E. Stern, ed. *The New Encyclopedia of Archaeological Excavations in the Holy Land.* 4 vols. Jerusalem: Israel Exploration Society, 1993
NSI	G. A. Cooke. *A Text-Book of North-Semitic Inscriptions: Moabite, Hebrew, Phoenician, Aramaic, Nabataean, Palmyrene, Jewish.* Oxford: Clarendon, 1903
OEANE	E. M. Meyers, ed. *The Oxford Encyclopedia of Archaeology in the Near East.* 5 vols. New York: Oxford University Press, 1997
OIP	Oriental Institute Publications
OJA	*Oxford Journal of Archaeology*
OLA	Orientalia Lovaniensia Analecta
OLP	*Orientalia Lovaniensia Periodica*
Or	*Orientalia*
OrAnt	*Oriens Antiquus*
PBSB	G. Markoe. *Phoenician Bronze and Silver Bowls from Cyprus and the Mediterranean.* Berkeley: University of California Press, 1985
PBSR	*Papers of the British School at Rome*
PEQ	*Palestine Exploration Quarterly*
PFPS	S. Moscati, P. Bartoloni, and S. F. Bondì. *La penetrazione fenicia e Punica in Sardegna: Trent'anni dopo.* Atti della Accademia Nazionale dei Lincei, Memorie 9/9, fasc. 1. Rome: Accademia Nazionale dei Lincei, 1997
PhByb	H. W. Attridge and R. A. Oden Jr., eds. *The Phoenician History / Philo of Byblos: Introduction, Critical Text, Translation, Notes.* Catholic Biblical Quarterly Monograph 9. Washington, DC: Catholic Biblical Association, 1981
PhWest	H. G. Niemeyer, ed. *Phönizier im Westen.* Madrider Beiträge 8. Mainz am Rhein: von Zabern, 1982
PRU	Le Palais Royal d'Ugarit
da Pyrgi a Mozia	M. G. Amadasi Guzzo, M. Liverani, and P. Matthiae, eds. *Da Pyrgi a Mozia: Studi sull'archeologia del Mediterraneo in Memoria di Antonia Ciasca.* 2 vols. Vicino Oriente 3/1–2. Rome: Università degli Studi di Roma, "La Sapienza," 2002
QDAP	*Quarterly of the Department of Antiquities of Palestine*
RA	*Revue d'Assyriologie et d'Archéologie Orientale*
RANL	*Rendiconti dell'Accademia Nazionale dei Lincei*
RB	*Revue Biblique*
RDAC	*Report of the Department of Antiquities of Cyprus*
RelPh	C. Bonnet, E. Lipiński, and P. Marchetti, eds. *Religio Phoenicia.* Studia Phoenicia 4. Namur: Société des Études Classiques, 1986
RES	*Répertoire d'Épigraphie Sémitique*
RHR	*Revue de l'Histoire des Religions*
RPC	O. Masson and M. Sznycer. *Recherches sur les Phéniciens à Chypre.* Geneva: Droz, 1972
RSF	*Rivista di Studi Fenici*
RSO	*Rivista degli Studi Orientali*
RSO	Ras Shamra–Ougarit
RSO 7	P. Bordreuil, ed. *Une bibliothèque au sud de la ville: Les texts de la 34e campagne (1973).* Ras Shamra–Ougarit 7. Paris: Editions Recherche sur les Civilisations, 1991
SAA	State Archives of Assyria

SBLDS	Society of Biblical Literature Dissertation Series
SBLWAW	Society of Biblical Literature Writings from the Ancient World
SEL	*Studi Epigrafici e Linguistici*
Sem	*Semitica*
SJOT	*Scandinavian Journal of the Old Testament*
SMEA	*Studi Micenei ed Egeo-Anatolici*
TA	*Tel Aviv*
Tharros	R. D. Barnett and C. Mendleson, eds. *Tharros: A Catalogue of Material in the British Museum from Phoenician and Other Tombs at Tharros, Sardinia.* London: British Museum, 1987
Transeu	*Transeuphratène*
TSSI 1	J. C. L. Gibson. *Textbook of Syrian Semitic Inscriptions, I: Hebrew and Moabite Inscriptions.* Oxford: Clarendon, 1971
TSSI 2	J. C. L. Gibson. *Textbook of Syrian Semitic Inscriptions, II: Aramaic Inscriptions.* Oxford: Clarendon, 1975
TSSI 3	J. C. L. Gibson. *Textbook of Syrian Semitic Inscriptions, III: Phoenician Inscriptions.* Oxford: Clarendon, 1982
UF	*Ugarit-Forschungen*
Ugaritica V	J. Nougayrol et al. *Ugaritica V.* Mission de Ras Shamra 16. Paris: Geuthner, 1968
VO	*Vicino Oriente*
VT	*Vetus Testamentum*
VTSup	Supplement to Vetus Testamentum
WO	*Die Welt des Orients*
WSS	N. Avigad and B. Sass. *Corpus of West Semitic Stamp Seals.* Jerusalem: Israel Exploration Society, 1997
ZA	*Zeitschrift für Assyriologie*
ZÄS	*Zeitschrift für ägyptische Sprache und Altertumskunde*
ZAW	*Zeitschrift für die alttestamentliche Wissenschaft*
ZDMG	*Zeitschrift der deutschen morgenländischen Gesellschaft*
ZDPV	*Zeitschrift des deutschen Palästina-Vereins*
ZPE	*Zeitschrift für Papyrologie und Epigraphik*

Introduction

Time is not a filament of Phoenician history. There are exploits, directions taken, digressions, lifetimes charted, biographical snippets that inform the written and the rough record. There are episodes, partial narratives, or bits of stories leaning against timelines, everything propping the adjacent, casting light on the opposite, waiting on the tangential, like rooms or the ruins of their foundations in a multimansion courtroom palace, ellipses in imaginary beckoning spaces. There are anecdotes, partial pictures, life against life just lingering, meeting, maybe colliding, tales often garbled about people, nations, ethnicities, or personalities. But chronology, because it is scarce—linear sequence, because it is badly broken—is an uneven and unworthy interpreter of this amazing past.

Phoenicia, like all history, is a construct, a product of historiography, an answer to questions, a companion of interest. It comprises research into incontrovertible things such as geography and ethnicity, lingering inquiry into places and spaces, cities and towns and countrysides in their specificity and individuality. It is a search for people, their motives and beliefs, their mentality, spirit, affectivity, their purpose and personality. History is the art of the particular. It is a detailed composition that develops the big picture, singularity that displays the light.

Phoenicia originated in Canaan, a people and a land. It is this origin that counts, the impulsion toward a distinctive constellation of cities in a receptive and productive littoral landscape. This impulse was the Canaanite determination to express its thinking and its way of life in its own language—plainly in its own writing, publicly in a way that evoked and eased response from those with another language and another way of life—and this was the Canaanites' invention of the alphabet. The Canaanite alphabet was not an empty category but came with the words, the glosses and witticisms, with the sentences and conversations and stories that made it live. What distinguished the Phoenicians in their turn was the transmission of the alphabet and literacy to everyone they met. This is how the people were, this was their spirit, this was the spirit of their land. Canaan was a land of immigrants. Phoenicia distinguished itself at home, in its cities and towns spread along the Levantine coast, by welcoming waves of newcomers, the displaced and adventurers, by teaching them what it learned, and by looking for their learning in return. It exceeded its neighbors in not being tied to the land or suspicious of borders and in its intrepid drive—impelled by an empowering religion, an acquired freedom, and a passion for the good life—to explore the boundaries of its world.

Some of the things the Phoenicians learned from their interlocutors were maps of the Mediterranean. Early on, the Sea Peoples brought news of Sardinia, the Aegean, and eastern Anatolia; and what changed the Phoenicians instantly and permanently was meeting the Greeks in Crete, Euboea, and Cyprus. It was immediate inspiration and emulation. On Cyprus, they (the Byblians, Sidonians, and Tyrians) traveled to separate locations, staying out of the way of each other, not interested in competition. There were few of them. They were traders and merchants, the Tyrians especially, thriving in the back-and-forth of barter in copper for Palestinian produce; and artists, notoriously the Sidonians, delighting their hosts with gold and silver masterpieces engraved with scenes from the stories they told, in exchange for iron and eventually steel; and builders, like the Byblians, who taught the alphabet and numbers as elements of their trade. Their inland neighbors—Aram, Israel, Moab, and Judah—tried tribal self-sufficiency and belligerence for awhile, until the new urban civilization caught on, or it was just too late.

When the Greeks went west, the Phoenicians went with them, constant, persistent, but still few in number. Italy was the first destination where the early settlers went with the Greeks congenial to them as free-lancers; unlike the Greeks, they were not dispatched as colonists. Carthage in North Africa, however, was a deliberate Phoenician foundation—the decision of Tyre, Sidon, and Carthage—with the initiative taken by the Tyrian Carthage in Cyprus. The Atlantic Spanish settlements kept their Phoenician character, but the Mediterranean settlements in Spain, Sicily, Sardinia, and Malta were quickly converted into resource centers for the North African colony. The deliberateness of this foundation, the decision to establish another focus in the Phoenician orbit, the unique consensus of the colonizers—these became the defining marks of the western Phoenician, or Punic individual and national spirit.

An emerging independent Western Phoenicia left Tyre free to consolidate its hegemony in the East. It became the sole west-Asiatic agent of the Assyrian Empire in a time of peace and universal accord. It was proud, and praiseworthy, admired and copied by all its neighbors and associates. Everyone shared the same culture, the same belief in a universal divine and political order, the same expectation of lasting happiness, the same world. But then the Babylonians let it all slip away; and the Persians, intent on war and world domination, wasted their own and everyone's time trying to dominate the irascible and indomitable Greeks. The Punic West made the same mistake until it was handed off to the Romans. But Phoenicia had been born in a Greek matrix and in time had the sense and good grace to slip quietly into the dominant and sustaining Occidental culture.

All of this shows up in episodes and anecdotes along a frangible and fractured timeline. There are starting points of sorts, and pieces of progression, but no tyranny of time. Years or centuries are skipped in the twinkling of an eye, sometimes recovered; analogy is as affirmative as linearity, and Phoenicia follows roughly century by century, provided that calendars are taken lightly. Individual men and women come forward in their artifacts, in their words, in the amulets that reveal their fears, or in the personal seals that identify them by name and design. Phoenicia involves Tyre, Sidon, and Byblos but visits and revisits the cities and towns in their dominion, considers their connections and contrasts, and wonders how they fitted into the international cultural network. There are king lists and alliances and politics and petty intrigues, but in its heyday Phoenicia was the individuals, companies, and city assemblies who engineered with bold determination the outreach and prosperity of the great cities, while their governments seemed doomed to routine and relative insignificance.

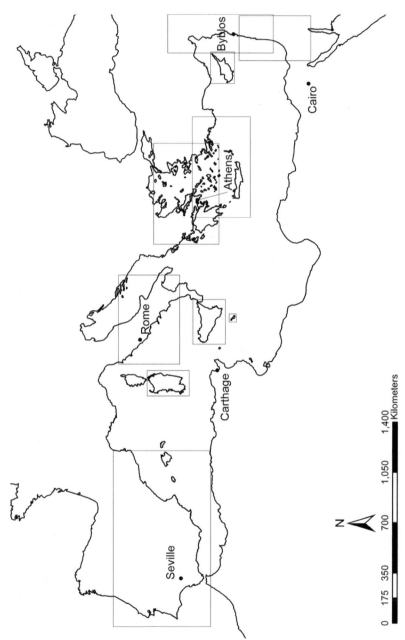

Map 1. The World of the Phoenicians (present-day southern Europe, North Africa, and the Levant; produced by Christopher Brinker).

Chapter 1

Canaan in the Eleventh and Tenth Centuries B.C.E.: The Origin of the Phoenicians

The Canaanites: The Alphabet, Literature, and Literacy

The principal cities of Phoenicia were Tyre, Sidon, and Byblos. They begin to emerge systematically in the material and written record around the middle of the second millennium. Before this time, they are known individually from sporadic bits and pieces of information, but there is little evidence for their interconnection, and the remains of their cultures are generally imported goods or local inscriptions, written either in a foreign language or in the city language but in a script derived from foreign models. At the end of the Late Bronze Age (ca. 1200 B.C.E.), the city-state system was still not firmly in place but waited on the awakening of the Greek world and the emergence of inland kingdoms in Syria and Palestine, from which it derived its stability and purpose. This happened in the Iron Age, in the eleventh and tenth centuries, and it coincided with a radical change in ethnic mix; was swept along in a creative amalgam of urban, rural, and commercial interests; and was cradled in a remarkable awareness of the common origins of their cultures and of belonging to a brand new, outward-looking world.

Inclusiveness was the trademark of the Phoenician cities. Their ancient, erudite, Canaanite cultural consciousness and habits of mind were prepared for the original, or even unexpected; for the curious and the clever. These were welcomed differently in cities that had nourished diversity in civic organization and institutions, foreign relations, religion, language, and art. Their openness to change—more or less enthusiastic or conservative and eclectic—was the incentive and the basic ingredient of their geographical expansion, their political and commercial development; of their brilliant influence on the civilization of Syria and Palestine; and of their role in the formation of a coherent, cultured Mediterranean world. Their splendid achievements, on the analogy of their beliefs in the cycles of life and death, culminated as the first millennium waned in their demise and their separate incorporation into the world they had created.

The history of Phoenicia is the history of its cities in relationship to each other and to the peoples, cities, and kingdoms who nourished their

1

curiosity and their ambition. It is written by deduction and extrapolation, by shaping hard data into malleable evidence, by working from the peripheries of their worlds to the centers where they lived, by trying to uncover their mentalities, plans, beliefs, suppositions, and dreams in the residue of their products and accomplishments; in the things that attracted and inspired them; in the opinions and exploits of those who observed or knew them, who feared and envied, or imitated and admired them. Their history is chronological, often in a rough and relative vein, sometimes linked to the real time of written records, usually running parallel to the typological flow of intuition and the studied guesswork of archaeological analysis and historical reconstruction. The cities, in themselves and in their foreign and colonial enterprises, over time reveal compelling individual, and almost personal, characteristics. They lived on the verge of nations, and on the verge of a glimpsed and projected nationality of their own, and their life can be eked out in the pattern of an evolving cultural map of the world.

Although generalizations about Phoenicia may sometimes be true—because these cities shared ideas and geographical and other advantages—it is the particularity of the individual cities and the specifics of their historical trajectory that call out for recognition. Byblos was the most ancient and long the most renowned, but it began to fade early in the first millennium. Sidon was spectacular in the early parts of the Iron Age (ca. 1200–700 B.C.E.) and brilliant from time to time after that, but succumbed to the animosity of the Assyrian Empire. Tyre managed to get along with the successive waves of overlords and tyrants; and, by managing the inheritance of Egyptian and Syrian and Mesopotamian empires, and by becoming the purveyor of the Mediterranean world, it was the most amazing of all and lasted the longest. What exactly was involved in their stories is what their histories attempt to reconstruct.

The Alphabetization of Canaan

The Late Bronze Age (ca. 1550–1200 B.C.E.) coincides with the Eighteenth and Nineteenth Dynasties in Egypt, which are familiar from the names and achievements of pharaohs such as Tutankhamun and Ramesses. It includes the brilliance of the later Minoan and the Mycenean periods, the stagnation of Babylon and the gradual invigoration of Assyria under the Kassites in Mesopotamia, a resurgence of the Hittite Empire in Anatolia, and the reestablishment of kingdoms such as Alalakh, Ugarit, and Amurru in Syria. Most important, from the perspective of the coastal cities of Phoenicia, during this Egyptian revival were the expulsion of the Hyksos from Egypt and their resettlement in Canaan at the beginning of the Late Bronze Age, and the reaffirmation of Egypt's dominion over the cities and kingdoms of Syria and Palestine during the Amarna period, at the zenith of the Late Bronze Age.

In Canaan itself, what set this period apart was the invention and spread of the alphabet.[1] The invention, apparently, was a Hyksos achievement—

---

1. F. M. Cross, "The Evolution of the Proto-Canaanite Alphabet," *BASOR* 134 (1954) 15–24; idem, "The Origin and Early Evolution of the Alphabet," *ErIsr* 8 (Sukenik Volume; 1967) 8*–24*;

the insight of an individual, such as one of the Hyksos, who knew Canaanite and Egyptian, who was literate and schooled, and who was concerned with promoting the distinctiveness and independence of Canaanite in a world dominated by Egyptian letters and learning. The spread of the alphabet can be traced in Egypt and in Canaan and seems to reflect the movements and interests of merchants and traders and their families who dealt with Egyptians—who themselves, simultaneously, were intrigued by the Canaanite knack for directness and simplicity of expression. The alphabet did not acquire official status at this time, and its use solely as a vernacular is indicative of an upsurge in geographical and ethnic sensibility to which national and international interests, still dominated by the languages of Mesopotamia or their local imitations, were alien.

The Egyptian antecedents of the alphabet are evident in the signs themselves[2] and may be gathered from the pronunciation of the names of the letters. Conversely, the Canaanite origin, of the basic alphabetic insights is evident in the sounds and phonemic realizations of the signs, in their order and their referents, and in their inclusiveness, usefulness, and mnemonic accessibility.

Egyptian, in order to write Canaanite words, had developed a system of syllabic representation in which the simple form of the characters represented one of the Canaanite consonants followed by an /a/ vowel, while the same form, grouped separately with two other characters, represented the same consonant followed by an /i/ or /a/or /u/ vowel.[3] The Canaanite alphabet adopted Egyptian symbols, including some of these characters, to represent its consonants, and like the Egyptian paradigm, gave the consonants names that began with an /a/ vowel in their first syllables—thus producing a uniform, memorable, and repeatable pronunciation of the entire alphabet.

The alphabet, after all, was invented to be easily learned. Its consonants were known to anyone who spoke Canaanite. All its symbols were familiar to anyone who lived in a Canaanite household, and their alphabetic order, which was integral to the alphabetic package from the start, corresponded to what could be seen by a child as it looked from the house to the courtyard. Each consonant was first in the name of the things seen, each name had /a/ in its first syllable, the twenty-three consonants and names were divided into two memorable groups, and both groups could be subdivided for easier retention.

---

idem, "The Invention and Development of the Alphabet," in *Origins of Writing* (ed. W. M. Senner; Lincoln: University of Nebraska Press, 1989) 77–102; B. E. Colless, "Recent Discoveries Illuminating the Origin of the Alphabet," *AbrN* 26 (1988) 30–67; idem, "The Proto-Alphabetic Inscriptions of Canaan," *AbrN* 29 (1991) 18–66; idem, "The Egyptian and Mesopotamian Contributions to the Origins of the Alphabet," *AbrN* Supplement 5 (1995) 67–76; B. Sass, *The Genesis of the Alphabet and Its Development in the Second Millennium* B.C. (Wiesbaden: Harrassowitz, 1988).

2. G. J. Hamilton, *The Origins of the West Semitic Alphabet in Egyptian Scripts* (Catholic Biblical Quarterly Monograph Series 40; Washington, DC: Catholic Biblical Association, 2006).

3. J. E. Hoch, *Semitic Words in Egyptian Texts of the New Kingdom and the Third Intermediate Period* (Princeton: Princeton University Press, 1994) 487–507.

The first group was the A-B-Cs, the "Alpha-Bet"; the second group was the L-M-Ns, the "elements."[4] In Canaanite, the letters were:[5] *'alp*, meaning "ox," whose symbol was an ox-head, and whose pronunciation was [ʔa]; *bayit*, "house," symbolized by an open rectangle with a doorway on the long side, and pronounced [ba]; *gaml*, "staff," was a bent stick looking like a boomerang, pronounced [ga]; *dalt*, "door," was a closed rectangle on a pivot, pronounced [da]. These four letters could easily be learned together because the family ox went with the stick that might be used to guide it, and the house with a doorway belonged with the door. The fifth letter was *halilat*, a "happy woman," shown dancing, with her arms in the air, pronounced [ha]; then *waw*, a "bolt" for the door, seen as a closed hook on the end of a rod, pronounced [wa]; next *zayip*, "eyebrow," two parallel lines representing her eyebrow and her eye shadow, pronounced [za]; then *ḥaṣir*, "courtyard," shown as a house with its door closed in front of a rectangular enclosure, pronounced [ḥa]; then *ṭawat*, "spindle," represented by a slender rod curved at one end with a grip at the other, pronounced [ṭa]. The deliberation involved in the choice and ordering of the signs is evident, once again, in their staggered order, with the alternation of feminine (happy woman, smiling eyes, spindle) and architectural features (door lock and locked door), and in the variant that was found for one of the letters and in the alternative for another: next to the "courtyard" [ḥa] there was another [ḫa] which was represented by a hank of yarn (*ḫayit*) such as the spindle could manage; and the spindle could be represented, not as a spindle, but as the whorl that made it work well. The last two letters in this first A-B-C grouping were *yad*, "hand," a forearm and fingers as seen from the side, pronounced [ya]; and *kap*, "palm," shown as a flat hand and fingers—both of these, of course, being the other essentials in spinning and carding.

The second part of the alphabet, the L-M-Ns, began with *lamd*, "ox goad," represented as such, and pronounced [la]; *mayim*, "water," represented by waves, was pronounced [ma]; *naḥaš*, "snake," drawn like a cobra with lifted head, pronounced [na]; *samk*, "fish," angular and stylized, pronounced [sa]. These four letters represented things that might be found in a typical Egyptian residential courtyard adorned with a pool or water source. The next two letters are *ʿayin*, "eye," and *payh*, "mouth," both represented naturalistically, one pronounced [ʿa], the other [pa]; next were *ṣaror*, "bag," represented as a sack tied in the middle, and *qaw*, the "cord" that tied it, pronounced [ṣa] and [qa]; then *raʾš*, "head," and *šann*, "tooth," looking just so, and pronounced [ra] and [ša]. The last sign *taw*, "mark," was represented by the proverbial X that marks the spot, pronounced [ta], and makes explicit the insight and self-conscious effort to find letters that were obvious abstract symbols of everyday objects in a typical Canaanite household.

That the alphabet was designed to be learned and understood by the whole family and not just by the politically or economically privileged is evident from the pedagogy embodied in it. The first part begins with the sign for the word *'alp*, which means "ox," but which, with a slightly dif-

---

4. M. D. Coogan, "Alphabets and Elements," *BASOR* 216 (1974) 61–63.

5. Colless, "Recent Discoveries Illuminating the Origin of the Alphabet."

ferent pronunciation (*'alap*) can also mean "to teach." The second part begins with *lamd*, which means "oxgoad," but also, with the pronunciation *lamad*, means "to learn." The first part of the alphabet is organized around the woman of the house, shown as happy at home and busy with her household tasks. The second part is the portrait of the man, especially of his face (head, eyes, mouth, and teeth), showing him in the courtyard or homestead engaged in fishing, farming, selling bags of grain, and keeping rudimentary records. Any child could get it.

The alphabet, from the very beginning, contained only 23 consonants out of a possible inventory of 27 consonantal sounds available in various Northwest Semitic languages and dialects and must have been invented by someone in whose language these other values had already been lost by coalescence with similar sounds. The dialects of Tyre and Sidon seem to have had only 22 consonants, without the consonantal sound [ḫa], when they took over the alphabet, and in them the sound [ḫa] may never have been phonemic. Speakers of other languages, such as Judean Hebrew, Ammonite, and Gileadite, are excluded because they had other consonantal phonemes—sounds that were distinctive and significant—for which the alphabet never had any graphic equivalent. It seems, then, at least by elimination, that the 23-letter alphabet was invented by someone from Byblos, or someone living in Egypt or Canaan, who spoke the dialect of Byblos, in which the distinctiveness of (*ḫa*) was maintained at least until the eleventh century.[6] This candidacy, in fact, is supported by the immemorial relations between Byblos and Egypt, by the evidence of the earliest alphabetic inscriptions from Sinai, Egypt, and Canaan, and by the pseudohieroglyphic texts from Byblos.

The alphabetic inscriptions from Sinai can be dated, on the basis of Egyptian monuments in the same place, to the late sixteenth and early fifteenth centuries—that is, approximately 1525–1475 B.C.E.[7] They are dedicatory inscriptions on statuettes and on rough and partially hewn rock faces at Serabit el-Khadem, a mining town in southwestern Sinai on a north–south route near the Red Sea, which was fairly accessible to the Byblian colony at Avaris and to associated sites in the eastern Delta. The town was dominated by the Temple of the Egyptian Goddess Hathor, the patroness of the mines, and the dedications were made mostly by men who supervised the mining and shipment of turquoise. The inscriptions are written either in vertical columns (and sometimes on steles or pillars outlined in the rock, like Egyptian inscriptions) or in horizontal lines inscribed from left to right, or better right-to-left, as became standard in Canaanite and Phoenician inscriptions. One of the texts is bilingual, recording in Egyptian that its author is "Beloved of Hathor," and in Canaanite that he is "Beloved of

---

6. Hoch, *Semitic Words in Egyptian Texts*, 152–53, 240–41, 483–85.

7. W. F. Albright, "The Proto-Sinaitic Inscriptions," *BASOR* 110 (1948) 6–22; idem, *The Proto-Sinaitic Inscriptions and Their Decipherment* (Cambridge: Harvard University Press, 1968); F. M. Cross, "The Origin and Early Evolution of the Alphabet"; B. E. Colless, "The Proto-Alphabetic Inscriptions of Sinai," *AbrN* 28 (1990) 1–52; Sass, *The Genesis of the Alphabet*; idem, *Studia Alphabetica: On the Origin and Early History of the Northwest Semitic, South Semitic, and Greek Alphabets* (OBO 10; Freiburg: Universitätsverlag / Göttingen: Vandenhoeck & Ruprecht, 1991).

Fig. 1.1. Proto-Sinaitic inscription, "Beloved of Baʿalat" (BM 41748). © The Trustees
of the British Museum.

Baʿalat,"[8] the Goddess of Byblos (see fig. 1.1). Because her name, derived
from her title as the "Lady" or "Mistress" (*baʿalat*) of that city, occurs in
almost half the inscriptions (the frequency of its occurrence was the first
clue in the decipherment of the script), it is likely that the Canaanites at
Serabit el-Khadem, or at least the mine operators and the turquoise traders
were from Byblos. There is some support for this in the syntax (at least five
of the inscriptions use the relative pronoun [z], which is peculiar to Byblos
among the Canaanite dialects) and in a dedication to the Goddess ʿAnat,[9]
who was popular outside Syria mainly at Byblos. These bits of evidence
might suggest that the alphabet was invented and spread by Byblians who,
like residents at Serabit el-Khadem, lived among and did business with the
Egyptians and, like the author of the bilingual inscription, knew their language and could use their script.

Some support for this surmise can be gathered from the pseudohieroglyphic inscriptions from Byblos.[10] It was at Byblos, probably at the begin-

8. Colless, "The Proto-Alphabetic Inscriptions of Sinai," 13–15 (Sinai #345).
9. Ibid., 46–47 (Sinai #527).
10. G. E. Mendenhall, *The Syllabic Inscriptions from Byblos* (Beirut: American University of
Beirut, 1985); B. E. Colless, "The Byblos Syllabary and the Proto-Alphabet," *AbrN* 30 (1992)

ning of the second millenium, that there was the first attempt to create a native Canaanite script. True to Mesopotamian models, it was not an alphabet but a syllabary. True to their Egyptian heritage, and influenced by the fact that Byblos at the time was an Egyptian enclave, the Byblian scribes created syllabic signs that were inspired by contemporary Egyptian hieroglyphic and cursive hieratic scripts. The exact number of signs is uncertain, but the system seems to have been designed to represent 23 consonants, each with 3 distinct forms, in order to accommodate combinations with each of the vowels (/a/, /i/, /u/), and an indeterminate number of other symbols. The syllabary's basic insight was the acrophonic principle—that is, the fact that the signs represented the initial sound in the name of the thing symbolized. The system was not perfect and ultimately did not suit the Canaanite genius, but the insight would be critical for the invention of the alphabet; and at least 15 of the signs (usually the sign representing a consonant with an /a/ vowel) would be incorporated into the linear alphabet. The syllabary appears once on a fourteenth-century personal seal[11] but usually was written on bronze and stone tablets and had enough scholarly interest to ensure its preservation through the centuries of alphabetic literacy. It is symbolic of the syllabary's and alphabet's interdependence and of their common derivation from Egyptian learning that the latest example of syllabic writing was erased to make room for an eleventh-century alphabetic text.[12]

Not much time elapsed between the inventions of the Byblian syllabary and the alphabet. There are alphabetic inscriptions from Egypt, carved in a cliffside of the Wadi el-Hol on the ancient road between Abydos and Thebes, that have been dated to the late Egyptian Middle Kingdom (1990–1780 B.C.E.),[13] and clearly one insight followed very quickly on the other. There are some alphabetic inscriptions from southern Canaan that fill in the time before the proto-Sinaitic texts and quite a few from central Canaan that are contemporary with or later than them.[14] The earliest are from the seventeenth or sixteenth centuries and were found at Gezer and Lachish, both of them cities where Egyptian influence was strong. With the exception of Shechem, where there is a fifteenth-century inscription, all the alphabetic texts from central, northern, and coastal Canaan are from the

55–102; idem, "The Syllabic Inscriptions of Byblos," *AbrN* 31 (1993) 1–35; idem, "The Canaanite Syllabary," *AbrN* 35 (1998) 28–46; J. E. Hoch, "The Byblos Syllabary: Bridging the Gap between Egyptian Hieroglyphs and Semitic Alphabets," *The Journal of the Society for the Study of Egyptian Antiquities* 20 (1990) 115–24.

11. G. Garbini, M. M. Luisella, and G. Devoto, *Sigillo die età amariana da Biblo con iscrizione* (ANLR; Rome, 2004) 373–92.

12. M. Dunand, "Spatule de bronze avec épigraphie phénicienne du xiii siècle," *BMB* 2 (1938) 99–107; M. Martin, "A Preliminary Report after Re-Examination of the Byblian Inscriptions," *Or* 30 (1961) 46–78, pls. 6–15; idem, "A Twelfth Century Bronze Palimpsest," *RSO* 37 (1962) 175–97.

13. J. C. Darnell et al., "Two Early Alphabetic Inscriptions from the Wadi el-Ḥôl," *Results of the 2001 Kerak Plateau Early Bronze Age Survey* (AASOR 59; Boston: American Schools of Oriental Research, 2005) 63–124. The Middle Kingdom and early Second Intermediate Period Egyptian texts from the same place were published by J. C. Darnell and D. Darnell, *Theban Desert Road Survey in the Western Desert, Volume 1: Gebel Tjauti Rock Inscriptions 1–45 and Wadi el-Ḥôl Rock Inscriptions 1–45* (OIP 119; Chicago: Oriental Institute, 2002).

14. Colless, "The Proto-Alphabetic Inscriptions of Canaan."

Chapter 1

Fig. 1.2. Shechem inscription, "May waters of the well . . ." (IDAM 38.1201). Reproduced by permission of the Israel Antiquities Authority. Photo by: Miki Koren.

latter part of the Late Bronze Age, that is, ca. 1400–1200 B.C.E. This temporal and geographical distribution suggests that the alphabet was invented in Byblos by Canaanites who lived among Egyptians; that it went to Egypt when they and other Asiatics settled in the Delta; that it functioned there, as it had originally, among aliens in an Egyptian milieu; that it came back to southern Canaan in the seventeenth–sixteenth century, when the Hyksos were expelled from Egypt; and that literacy flourished under Egyptian domination in the south, as it had at Byblos and in Egypt, but then spread northward under the move toward urban and national independence.

The inscriptions provide some information on the contexts in which alphabetic literacy flourished. The proto-Sinaitic inscriptions were dedications to the Goddesses Baʿalat and ʿAnat and to the God El by people who identified themselves by name or by their function in the mining community, and sometimes by drawing pictures of themselves. Individuals with names but without titles may have been merchants from Byblos. A dedication to Tannit, who in later times is known as the Goddess of Tyrian colonists in North African Carthage, might suggest a Tyrian presence; and the six men from Arvad mentioned in another inscription may have been miners or merchants: "This is the camp, beloved of Baʿalat, of six sons of Arvad" (*išknt zt ʾrwdyt.šš bnm mʾhbt bʿlt*).[15]

Of the early inscriptions from Gezer,[16] one is the proper name Caleb, which was written on a cult stand, and the others are single letters incised

---

15. Ibid., 18–19 (Sinai #365).
16. Ibid., 20–32.

on storage jars before firing, which indicated either their contents, their owners, or their place of origin. Lachish provides a variety of inscriptions:[17] the earliest, from around 1600 B.C.E., is a proper name carved into a dagger; there are dedications, apparently all from the thirteenth century, to the God of Night, to the God of Summer and, on a painted and decorated jar, to the Goddess Asherah. Among the more interesting are two, one from the fifteenth and the other from the fourteenth century, specifying that the article on which they are written belongs to the temple: the diphthong in the word temple is uncontracted (*bayt* not *bet*), indicating that the writer spoke a southern dialect, like the dialect of later Judah.

The fifteenth-century inscription from Shechem,[18] which may in fact have been brought there from another place, is written beside the portrait of a man and is a prayer that the well not run dry, "May the waters of the well endure. May they bring comfort" (see fig. 1.2). A sherd from Rehob, near Shechem, was once part of a cultic object, which its inscription identifies as an incense stand.

The most amusing inscription is also one of the longest: it is on a sherd found at Beth Shemesh,[19] between Jerusalem and Lachish, and is about a local entertainer, Hanun, who is "sweet voiced, but too loud after drinking in the tavern with the girls." Most of the other inscriptions from the south are personal names or potters' marks incised on jars. Inscriptions from the coastal cities, similarly, are names of people, sometimes with their place of origin, or are place-names written on jar handles: the most informative are from ʿAkko in the north, where the inscription (*kt*) indicates that the jar came from Kition in Cyprus; and inscriptions from Tell el-ʿAjjul in the south, where one jar is also marked as deriving from Kition (*kt*), and another is said to belong to the "Tyrian" (*ṣry*).

Alphabetic literacy, in short, thrived in business and devotional contexts, among traders, miners, mercenaries, and pilgrims, and among people educated in arts and crafts; but not in government circles, where there were professional scribes to write Egyptian and Akkadian. The alphabet, in this way, began and developed among the people as the instrument of Canaanite identity, the reflection of a basic insight that evolved over the centuries into the common consciousness of people as diverse as the Phoenicians and Israelites and their Transjordanian kin.

The invention of the alphabet was not just a matter of luck. It can be traced to the training of Egyptian scribes who isolated and learned to write down the Canaanite consonantal phonemes—all the consonants that had distinct and significant sounds and could make up different Canaanite words. Next, perhaps, was the idea of representing these sounds separately with pictures of items, the names of which began with these distinct and significant sounds. Because these scholars, presumably at Byblos, were used to writing syllables, they thought of enough names and pictures to represent each of the consonants with one of the three basic vowels.

---

17. Ibid., 35–41.
18. Ibid., 33–35.
19. Ibid., 46–49.

Next, perhaps, was the idea of simplifying the representational system. The things whose names began with these initial Canaanite syllables seem to have belonged to a large number of unrelated contexts. Most were observable, but some were conceptual or abstract: the human body (head, face, eye, mouth, ear; leg, arm, hand, chest, breast) some emotions (weeping and rejoicing); the weather (rain, storm, water); the world (sun, moon, night); secular and religious buildings and furnishings (house, temple, ziggurat, pavilion; door, jar, footstool, altar; scepter, harp); flora, fauna, and natural products (ox, vulture, snake, bee, vine, wine); but also "life" and "kingship."

The simplification consisted of ignoring the world, politics, and religion to concentrate on common folk living in a typical family house. Along with this idea went the negative insight that, because the people for whom the script was being designed already knew the language, knew how to speak it, knew for instance how to say the name of the thing represented and not just the first syllable, the signs did not need to be signs for the pronunciation of words, and writing did not need to mimic or duplicate speech. With this went the positive insight, therefore, that the written letters should be signs that could be combined to make words—not just words representing things that both writer and reader could see, but words with meaning, words that could be used in writing sentences, sentences that could be read by any reader who did not see what the writer observed or thought.

Finally, and perhaps most importantly, because it made the other insights fall into place, was the idea that the alphabet had to be learned and retained, and for this to happen, had to be capable of being pronounced in a fixed order. This then was the alphabet: simple consonantal signs, derived from ordinary things, in an intelligible and memorable order, representing all the familiar sounds, providing the basic patterns of words, a product of thinking and of interest in the common good.

Canaan in the Fourteenth Century and the Amarna Age (ca. 1380–1358 b.c.e.)

In the Amarna age, Canaan was a conglomerate of city kingdoms in political and commercial relations with Egypt. The country was distinguished, in fact and in the opinion of contemporary correspondents, from Amurru to the northwest and from Upi (Damascus), which lay north and east in Syria. The country seems to have been divided temperamentally and practically between cities in the north that had dealings with each other and cities in the south that, apart from their alignment with Egypt, seemed to keep to themselves. Many of these cities survived into the Iron Age, when some of them would thrive as national centers. The country, however, is defined in the Amarna age mainly by its inchoate ethnic consciousness, which facilitated but did not survive the partition of the land into national states.

The names *Canaan* and *Canaanite* are mentioned in the Amarna letters and create the impression of a single land with a cohesive population. The passport issued to the messengers of the king of Mitanni is a

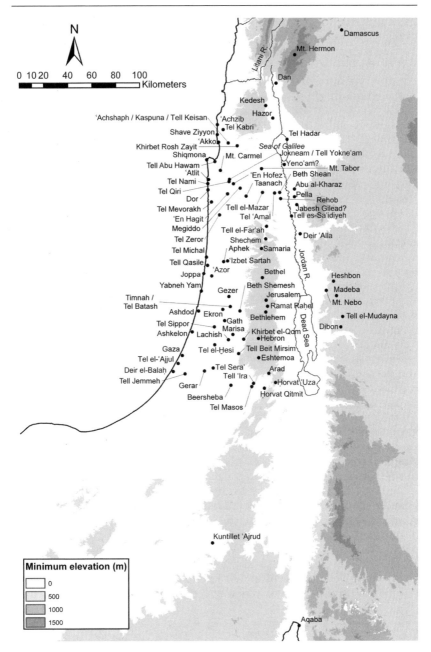

Map 2. Canaan (produced by Christopher Brinker).

letter addressed to "the kings of Canaan."[20] Although Canaan was a land
of many independent kingdoms, the king of Babylon recalls that "all the
Canaanites wrote . . . 'Come to the border of the country so we can revolt
and be allied with you.'"[21] Similarly, when Babylonian merchants on their
way to Egypt are jailed and killed by competitors from the cities of ʿAkko
and neighboring Ḫinnatuna, the king of Babylon refers to this as being de-
tained "in Canaan" and reminds Pharaoh that what happens "in Canaan"
is his responsibility because "Canaan is your country, and its kings are your
servants."[22] The king of Byblos mentions that ships leave Canaan on their
way to Amurru,[23] and the king of Tyre is asked for news from Canaan.[24]
The impression of unity reflects the fact that "all Canaan," "the lands of
Canaan," and "the cities of Canaan"[25] belong to Pharaoh and that the
whole territory is administered by Egyptian officials, but there is an underlying indigenous unity that is not political.

The impression of a cohesive population, on the other hand, masks
a complex and hardly homogeneous society. The population was very
mixed, and Canaan seems to have been a land of immigrants. Personal
names[26] reveal that the population, or at least the ruling population, included indigenous folk with Northwest Semitic names; as well as others
from northern Syria or Asia Minor of Indo-Aryan extraction; and Hurrians
from northern Mesopotamia who had arrived at various times. Among the
indigenous people, including the Hyksos who had returned from Egypt,
some names are Amorite, ultimately from Syria, some are north Canaanite,
and some south Canaanite. The northern coastal cities from Byblos to Tyre
and the southern coastal cities from Joppa to Gaza were governed by kings
with Northwest Semitic names; but in the central coastal region the kings
of ʿAkko, ʿAchshaph, and Sharon had Indo-Aryan names; and the ruler of
Ginti Kirmil was Hurrian. In northern Canaan, at Hazor and Shechem, the
kings' names were Semitic, but Indo-Aryan at Megiddo. In the south, at
Gezer and Lachish, the kings had Semitic names, while the name of the
king of Jerusalem (ʿAbdi-ḫeba) was a combination of Semitic and Hurrian.
In effect, Indo-Aryan and Hurrian kings were grouped in a belt along trade
routes from the Mediterranean to the Jordan, from the Gulf of ʿAkko and
ports south of Carmel to Megiddo and ultimately to Beth Shean and beyond the river.

All in all, however, although more than half of the population was Semitic, almost a third were Indo-Aryan, and about ten percent were Hurrian.
Such then, was Canaanite society, an ethnic group of different racial origins, sharing a country, a culture, and a common cause. Canaan remained a
land of immigrants, and it was new arrivals with their brand new horizons

---

20. *EA* 30.
21. *EA* 9.
22. *EA* 8.
23. *EA* 110.
24. *EA* 151.
25. *EA* 131, 137, 162.
26. R. S. Hess, *Amarna Personal Names* (ASOR Dissertation Series 9; Winona Lake, IN: Eisenbrauns, 1993).

that ultimately distinguished Iron Age Canaan from its Late Bronze Age heritage.

Within this melting pot of kingdoms, there were some alliances, perhaps temporary, and some associations of cities and towns. The king of Jerusalem, for instance, reports that Gezer, along with Lachish and Ashkelon, was nurturing rebellion against Egypt. From other letters, it is clear that the king of Gezer, along with his father-in-law the king of Ginti Kirmil (Carmel), had aligned himself with Shechem, Qiltu, and ʿAyyalon: with Qiltu it had captured the town of Rubute, and with ʿAyyalon it was harassing Jerusalem. Qiltu was also allied with ʿAkko and ʿAchshaph (Kaspuna, Tell Keisan). Shechem, relying on the destabilizing power of the landless and restless ʿApiru, was the great instigator of rebellion in Canaan, and its most famous king, Labʾayu, was a good friend of the kings of Gezer, Ginti Kirmil, and ʿAkko. Their motives were social, political, and commercial, as these various cities resisted their tributary obligations to Egypt, attempted to get control of the trade routes and markets, and tried to integrate or deal with the ʿApiru.[27]

The cities of Tyre, Sidon, and Byblos generally were not involved in the conflicts of these inland cities but were totally taken up with their own brand of dispute and competition. The king of Byblos complained that all his towns along the coast and in the mountains have defected to the ʿApiru. The king of Tyre lost his towns in Galilee to the king of Hazor. Both cities were harassed by Sidon, which also lost its satellite cities on the mainland to the ʿApiru but had allies in the towns north of Byblos, chiefly among the island people of Arvad, and in the coastal towns of Amurru. Tyre was prevented from getting water, wood, clay, straw, and other necessities from the mainland, in particular from the city of Ushu just opposite it. The king of Tyre had married the sister of the king of Byblos, but, when Sidon and Arvad persuaded the people of Tyre to rebel, they killed their king and queen and the entire royal family. The king of Byblos eventually was driven from his throne and had to take refuge in Beirut. This great turmoil, however, seems to have been all in a day's work for these competitive port cities, because all of them continued to prosper—not least Tyre, whose property, according to the king of Byblos, was as great as the sea and whose royal palace might be compared to the palace at Ugarit but had no equal in Canaan.[28]

An image of this prosperity, and some perception of the networks of trade and commerce that produced it can be gathered from a late fourteenth-century shipwreck at Ulu Burun on the coast of Turkey.[29] The ship

27. M. C. Astour, "The Ḫapiru in the Amarna Texts: Basic Points of Controversy," *UF* 31 (1999) 31–50.

28. *EA* 89.

29. G. F. Bass, "Evidence of Trade from Bronze Age Shipwrecks," in *Bronze Age Trade in the Mediterranean* (ed. N. H. Gale; Studies in Mediterranean Archaeology 90; Jonsered: Åström, 1991) 69–82; R. Payton, "The Ulu Burun Writing-Board Set," *AnSt* 41 (1991) 99–106; C. Haldane, "Direct Evidence for Organic Cargoes in the Late Bronze Age," in *World Archaeology* 24 (1993) 348–60; P. T. Nicholson, C. M. Jackson, and K. M. Trott, "The Ulu Burun Glass Ingots, Cylindrical Vessels and Egyptian Glass," *JEA* 83 (1997) 143–53; C. Pulak, "The Uluburun Shipwreck," in *Res Maritimae: Cyprus and the Eastern Mediterranean from Prehistory to Late Antiquity* (ed. S. Swiny, R. L. Hohlfelder, and H. W. Swiny; Atlanta: Scholars Press, 1997) 233–62; idem, "The Uluburun

was heading westward, perhaps to Crete or Mycenean Greece (a nearly contemporary shipwreck from Point Iria east of Tiryns in the Argolic Gulf was carrying Cypriot and Mycenean pottery),[30] possibly to Sardinia, from coastal Canaan. Its cargo was diverse, suggesting that it was a tramp or that it had called in at an emporium at one of the coastal cities or at Kition in Cyprus, where this sort of variety of goods would have been available. It carried gold, silver, faience, and amber jewelry, including a gold scarab that once belonged to Nefertiti, as well as cobalt blue glass ingots that resemble the glass at Amarna and at the Egyptian town of Deir el-Balaḥ, southwest of Gaza. It had copper and tin ingots, probably picked up in Cyprus (a contemporary shipwreck south of Carmel had a similar cargo),[31] and a transport amphora with stacks of Cypriot pottery. It carried raw elephant ivory, perhaps from Syria; and hippopotamus ivory, from Syria or Canaan; an ivory box, ivory scepter heads, and an ivory writing board. There were many transport jars, some with organic goods such as figs, grapes, nuts, and olives, or wheat, barley, and grass seeds—perhaps all from inland cities of Canaan; others, jars with orpiment for staining glass or with fragrances for perfuming oil. There were tools for working metal and ivory, farm implements, weapons, rope and twine, bits of wood for the onboard stove, and lead weights for the fishing nets. There was a scale and weights for doing business, and a wooden writing board that may have contained the ship's inventory or the record of purchases and sales. It might have been a Tyrian ship or could have been from any port on the coast of Canaan, but it clearly testifies to the inner cohesion of the country and the inclusive, outward-looking character of its people.

Through all their competition, and despite all their squabbles and contretemps, these people had an underlying consciousness, evident in their religion and in their language, of their Canaanite identity. The king of Byblos was forever faithful to Baʿalat, mistress of the city, to Adonis, the Lord of the citizens, and to his sister ʿAnat, protectress of the people. The kings of Sidon, like the kings and other people mentioned in the letters, were named for the Gods of Canaan, especially for Baʿal and Astarte. The king of Tyre, a city well known for its eclectic tastes, in composing a hymn to the pharaoh followed the Egyptian precedents in extolling him as God but managed to subsume his divinity into that of the Canaanite Gods Baʿal and Shamash.[32] In the same letter, his excessive fawning on the pharaoh is tempered and undermined by a repeated use of Canaanite glosses (colloquialisms not accessible to the international community

---

Shipwreck: An Overview," *IJNA* 27 (1998) 188–224; C. Bachhuber, "Aegean Interest on the Uluburun Ship," *AJA* 110 (2006) 345–63.

30. Y. Vichos and Y. Lolos, "The Cypro-Mycenaean Wreck at Point Iria in the Argolic Gulf: First Thoughts on the Origin and Nature of the Vessel," in *Res Maritimae: Cyprus and the Eastern Mediterranean from Prehistory to Late Antiquity* (ed. S. Swiny, R. L. Hohlfelder, and H. W. Swiny; Atlanta: Scholars Press, 1997) 321–37.

31. E. Galili, N. Shmueli, and M. Artzy, "Bronze Age Ship's Cargo of Copper and Tin," *IJNA* 15 (1986) 25–37.

32. *EA* 147; W. F. Albright, "The Egyptian Correspondence of Abimilki, Prince of Tyre," *JEA* 23 (1937) 190–203.

trained in Akkadian)[33] meant for the messenger and the Canaanite scribe in Egypt who read the letter, which told them that the hymn was ironic and that Tyrian pride was intact. Most of the other letters from Tyre also have glosses, not necessarily ironic, but emphatic or homey or with a touch of local color to ease the diplomatic strain.

There are similar glosses in the letters from Byblos and Beirut; in those from Sidon, ʿAkko, and some other unnamed places; from Megiddo and Shechem; from Gezer and Ginti Kirmil and Qiltu; and from Jerusalem. In letters from Byblos, the gloss sometimes emphasizes an aphorism: "Like a bird in a trap *ki-lu-bi*\, so am I in Gubla"; but there are also metaphors ("A brick may move from under its mate; still I will not move from the feet of the king, my lord"), similes ("I have become like a bronze pot given in pledge"), and proverbs ("For lack of a cultivator, my field is like a woman without a husband") in letters from Byblos and other cities that are not marked by glosses but that, like the glosses, are part of a scribal subtext and reveal an irrepressible Canaanite spirit.

This Canaanite consciousness was fostered by education and the promotion of alphabetic literacy. A letter from Shechem,[34] written by a woman teacher from a nearby town, complains that she has not been paid but assures her employer that the children, to whom she is like a mother and a father, continue to learn. The employer has an Indo-Aryan name, and this letter on official business is in Akkadian (that is, Babylonian), but she was probably teaching the children how to read and write Canaanite.

An Akkadian letter from Lachish written by an Egyptian administrator to another official in Tel el-Ḥesi, uses a local Canaanite expression to describe the disloyalty of the city's political establishment. Letters from Hebron, Hazor, and Taanach, like letters from El-Amarna, reveal that the scribes were trained in Canaanite grammar, syntax, and style before they graduated to the foreign service and learned Akkadian, because their Akkadian is deliberately and cleverly colored by the forms, word order, and parlance of their own language. Although higher education focused on the classics of Akkadian rather than indigenous literature, and most people learned just the rudiments of social, religious, and economic discourse, there was an underlying Canaanite sensibility residing in a vigorous oral culture that would soon come to expression in the arts and letters that these Canaanites, or specifically the people of the coastal cities, taught their neighbors.

Canaan in the Thirteenth Century B.C.E.

The evidence for the development of Canaanite civilization, culture, and commerce in the thirteenth century is mostly indirect. Various cities are mentioned in the literature and records of Ugarit, a port city on the North Syrian coast, and it is possible to reconstruct the political relations

---

33. S. Izreʾel, "The Amarna Glosses: Who Wrote What for Whom? Some Sociolinguistic Considerations," *IOS* 15 (1995) 101–22; K. van der Toorn, "Cuneiform Documents from Syria–Palestine: Texts, Scribes, and Scholars," *ZDPV* 116 (2000) 97–113.

34. W. F. Albright, "A Teacher to a Man of Shechem about 1400 B.C.," *BASOR* 86 (1942) 28–31; van der Toorn, "Cuneiform Documents," 98 n. 15; W. Horowitz, T. Oshima, and S. Sanders, *Cuneiform in Canaan: Cuneiform Sources from the Land of Israel in Ancient Times* (Jerusalem: Israel Exploration Society/Hebrew University, 2006) 121–23.

and the commercial networks on which they relied. Although Canaan was an Egyptian province, it was relatively autonomous, and its cities independent of each other and of Egyptian authority. The indirect evidence for their culture and civilization, however, is the influence that they, and probably the coastal cities in particular, had on the language, literature, and religion of Ugarit.

Ugarit, already mentioned in the third-millennium texts from Ebla, was an important city in the early second millennium, especially in the eighteenth century when it was part of the great Amorite synergism radiating from Mari and Aleppo. It paid tribute to Egypt in the Amarna age but revived and became prosperous again when Ugarit was incorporated into the Hittite Empire around the middle of the fourteenth century. In the thirteenth century, when Ugarit was still the domain of the Amorite dynasty that had founded it centuries earlier, it was a great cosmopolitan city; the port from which Mesopotamian and North Syrian influence flowed into the Mediterranean; polyglot; the home or refuge of Syrians, Hittites, Hurrians, Cypriots, Myceneans, Assyrians, and Canaanites.

There are hundreds of texts in these various languages, especially in Akkadian and in the local language. In the latter, there are letters, administrative documents, and literary and ritual texts. The language is Northwest Semitic, so it has many affinities with Phoenician and related languages, but its phonology, morphology, and lexicon reveal broad contacts with Arabic. It is not Canaanite, as the city and kingdom are not but, rather, old Syrian, or coastal Amorite.

The Ugaritic letters and administrative texts about Canaan mention only the coastal cities, and the information they provide is always at least laconic and sometimes enigmatic. There is, for instance, a letter from the king of Ugarit to the pharaoh, probably Ramesses II, which refers to the king's settlement of a serious dispute between merchants of Ugarit and the merchants of the land of Canaan by paying 3,500 silver shekels.[35] This letter does not give details of the dispute, but a contemporary letter from the governor of the city of Ugarit to the Egyptian vizier living at Aphek in Canaan[36] may concern the same matter, in which Ugaritic merchants had bought grain and were having it shipped from Joppa but were accused of not paying for the grain or for the ships that were to transport it to Egypt and, probably, to the land of the Hittites.

Of the cities south of Joppa, only Ashdod is known from the Ugaritic records and only as the home of one of the great merchants of Ugarit and as the place of origin of a large number of people who were working in Ugarit, either in the business community or in some unspecified profession. To the north of Joppa, there are important ports that are not mentioned at all, such as Dor, which became a Philistine center in the twelfth century;

35. J. Nougayrol, "Textes suméro-accadiens des archives et bibliothèques privées d'Ugarit," in *Ugaritica V* (ed. J. Nougayrol et al., MRS 16; Paris : Geuthner, 1968) 111–14, #36.

36. D. I. Owen, "An Akkadian Letter from Ugarit at Tel Aphek," *TA* 8 (1981) 1–17; I. Singer, "Takuḫlinu and Ḫaya: Two Governors in the Ugarit Letter from Tel Aphek," *TA* 10 (1983) 3–25; W. Horowitz, T. Oshima, and S. Sanders, *Cuneiform in Canaan: Cuneiform Sources from the Land of Israel in Ancient Times* (Jerusalem: Israel Exploration Society/Hebrew University, 2006) 35–38.

and the anchorage at Tel Nami,[37] which was the gateway to the trade route that led through Megiddo to Beth Shean and to Pella and other places in Transjordan in the thirteenth century. This Tel Nami, one harbor south, along with Tell Abu Hawam, just north of Carmel, may have been ports belonging to ʿAkko, a town that is mentioned often in the Ugaritic archives. A letter to the queen of Ugarit from one of her sons, who was stationed in ʿAkko, acknowledges receipt of her letter and reports that her agent in the town has been involved in some conflict, perhaps in the dispute that occupied the king and the governor of Ugarit, and reports that it is not known whether he is dead or alive.[38] A letter to the king of Ugarit from the king of Tyre reports that the Ugarit ship that was caught in a storm on its way to Egypt is now safe with its cargo intact in the harbor at ʿAkko.[39] Other documents refer to a sea captain from ʿAkko whose ship, which was in the service of Carchemish, has been decommissioned, and to individuals from ʿAkko who have taken up residence in Ugarit. Despite their lack of detail, these documents show that Ugarit was in regular contact with Canaan, at least with its coastal cities, and through them and their various harbors with Egypt and, as archaeological investigation suggests, with Transjordanian and Arabian overland trade routes.

Ugarit's dealings with Tyre, Sidon, Byblos, and Beirut are better documented but can still be somewhat elusive. The documents are letters and administrative texts, and according to them the ties between these cities and Ugarit were sometimes diplomatic but predominantly commercial. Occasionally, however, they reveal a feature of their societies or an aspect of their culture and religion.

Beirut's diplomatic relations with Ugarit are attested in letters from the king of Beirut to the king or the governor of Ugarit. In one letter, he informs the king that a trader from Ashkelon robbed the harbor master in Beirut, fled to Ugarit and then to Enkomi in Cyprus, and is reported to be returning to Ugarit; the king asks that he be arrested and extradited to Beirut.[40] In another he sends his best wishes to the king of Ugarit, who is on a journey, having been summoned before his Hittite overlord at Carchemish

---

37. M. Artzy, "Incense, Camels and Collared Rim Jars: Desert Trade Routes and Maritime Outlets in the Second Millennium," *OJA* 13 (1994) 121–47; idem, "Nami: A Second Millennium International Maritime Trading Center in the Mediterranean," in *Recent Excavations in Israel: A View to the West. Reports on Kabri, Nami, Miqne-Ekron, Dor and Ashkelon* (ed. S. Gitin; Dubuque, IA: Kendall/Hunt, 1995) 17–40; idem, "Routes, Trade, Boats and 'Nomads of the Sea,'" *MPT*, 439–48; idem, "The Carmel Coast during the Second Part of the Late Bronze Age: A Center for Eastern Mediterranean Transshipping," *BASOR* 343 (2006) 45–64.

38. *CAT* 2:82.

39. *CAT* 2:38; D. Pardee, "Ugaritic Letters," *COS* 3.87–114, esp. pp. 93–94 (#8).

40. D. Arnaud and M. Salvini, "Une letter du roi de Beyrouth au roi d'Ougarit de l'époque dite 'd'el-Amarna,'" *SMEA* 42 (2000) 5–17; P. Artzi, J. Klein, and D. Elgavish, "The Letter of the King of Beirut to the King of Ugarit: A Different Interpretation," in *Shlomo: Studies in Epigraphy, Iconography, History and Archaeology in Honor of Shlomo Moussaieff* (ed. R. Deutsch; Tel Aviv-Jaffa: Archaeological Center, 2003) 23–35.

in North Syria or at Ura in Cilicia.[41] In a third letter he asks the governor of Ugarit to welcome the ambassador whom he is sending to Ugarit.[42]

An ambassador (*mâr šipri*) could also head a trade delegation, and there is good evidence for business relations between Ugarit and Beirut. The settlement of a dispute between merchants of Ugarit and merchants of Siyannu, the country south of Ugarit and north of Beirut, over the destruction of a latifundium (*dimtu* or *gat*) and vineyard in Ugaritic territory discloses incidentally that Ugarit used to sell wine to Beirut and that Siyannu was trying to cripple the business.[43]

Ewri-ḫili, a Hurrian merchant from Ugarit living in Beirut, in one transaction sent the king of Ugarit one of his ships loaded with timber[44] and in another, confirmed by the seal of Niqmaddu, king of Ugarit, he paid ransom on behalf of the palace for the men and women of a Ugaritic "family" or commercial house established in Beirut, who had been enslaved because the business went bankrupt. The corporation included two brothers, a third brother with his son and daughter, a young woman from the firm of ʿAbdimilk who was the queen's agent, a wealthy landowner, and a shipping magnate, and another woman who was an independent agent: the company was exempted from property taxes owed to the treasury, until it had repaid Ewri-ḫili.[45]

According to another palace record, Urtenu, the queen's messenger (as well as city librarian and archivist, trader in metals, wool, and dyes with Emar on the Euphrates, with Egypt, and with Beirut)[46] in one transaction received from the palace warehouses a large consignment (4,000 shekels) of copper and tin (600 shekels) for the bronze smiths in Beirut, from whose sale the treasury expected to receive 83 silver shekels;[47] in another transaction he received a small shipment of tunics, rings, and perfume from an individual or consortium in Beirut which were meant for sale in Ugarit.[48]

Close ties between Byblos and Ugarit are suggested by a letter from the king of Byblos to the king of Ugarit that is written, not in Akkadian as usual in foreign correspondence, but in Ugaritic.[49] The letter is fragmentary, and most of its contents are missing, but it is addressed to "my brother" from "your brother," and the usual salutation invoking the blessing of the Gods is expanded to include specific Gods of Byblos and Ugarit. The little that remains of the body of the letter suggests that it was a letter of introduction for the people whom the king of Byblos was sending to Ugarit. The other

---

41. D. Arnaud, "Deux letters de 'Phénicie,'" RSO 7 79–81 (#37).

42. J. Nougayrol, *Textes Accadiens et Hourrites des archives est, ouest et centrales* (PRU 3; Paris: Imprimerie Nationale/Klincksieck, 1955) 12–13 (#11.730).

43. Idem, *Textes Accadiens des Archives Sud* (PRU 4; Paris: Imprimerie Nationale/Klincksieck, 1956) 161–63 (#17.341).

44. D. Arnaud, *Textes Syriens de l'âge de bronze récent* (Barcelona [Sabadell]: AUSA, 1991) 219–20.

45. C. Virolleaud, *Textes en cuneiforms alphabétiques des archives est, ouest et centrales* (PRU 2; Paris: Imprimerie Nationale/Klincksieck, 1957) 18–19 (#6).

46. *CAT* 4:311, 341; F. Malbran-Labat, "Lettres," RSO 7 32–34; D. Arnaud, "Une correspondence d'affaires entre ougaritains et Emariotes," RSO 7 65–78.

47. *CAT* 4:337.

48. *CAT* 4:771.

49. *CAT* 2:44.

texts reveal a fairly vigorous trade between the two cities. This may have been the case in the preceding century as well, because one of the Amarna letters from the king of Byblos mentions that boxwood destined for Egypt was imported from Ugarit.[50]

Regular travel and trade between Ugarit and Byblos is also evident from the Ugaritic archives. For instance, there is a list of resident aliens in Ugarit that includes people from Byblos, Sidon, and ʿAkko.[51] There is a letter from the king of Carchemish to the queen of Ugarit, dealing with her commercial ventures, that advises her not to send ships on long overseas journeys (presumably because of the risk of their encountering marauding Sea Peoples) but only on their usual voyages along the coast to Sidon and Byblos.[52] There is archival evidence for shipwrights in the ports of Ugarit, and there is also a tablet recording a consignment to Abiḫili, the merchant from Ashdod, of seven sails and other textiles destined for Byblos.[53]

But another administrative tablet records a deal with Byblos in which the king of Ugarit loaned 540 shekels to the king of Byblos to build ships, and in turn the king of Byblos bought leather tarpaulins worth 50 shekels from the king of Ugarit to outfit his ships:[54] the loan (ʿrb) is not necessarily the amount that the king of Byblos received but the amount that the king of Ugarit expected to be repaid; the cost of the tarpaulins, on the other hand, was their actual price (ksp mhrhn). The particular interest of this deal with Byblos is that it is just the last item on a tablet recording loans made to other named individuals, none of whom received more than 3 shekels, and the fact that it did not merit special attention might suggest that it was not unusual.

Sidon, according to the Ugaritic *Legend of Keret*, was a pilgrimage center famous for its Temple of Astarte. Its relations with Ugarit are evident in its correspondence. There are four letters from the king of Sidon to the king of Ugarit about a sacrilege, a "great sin" committed by Ugarit merchants in the Temple of the Storm God of Sidon for which they must make reparation—twice daily sacrifices in all the temples of Sidon for four days—or be put to death.[55] This incident provoked a crisis in the normally good relations between the two cities and also caused friction between the palace (the king, his entourage, and the elders), which was trying to accommodate the king of Ugarit, and the assembly of the people of Sidon, who were outraged and demanded satisfaction. The good relations between the two cities, however, are attested in letters sent during the reigns of two other kings of Sidon and in the seals of two more Sidonian kings that were found at Ugarit.

---

50. *EA* 126.

51. J. Nougayrol, *Textes cunéiforms babyloniens des archives du grand palais et du palais sud d'Ugarit* (PRU 6; Paris: Imprimerie Nationale/Klincksieck, 1970) 79–80 (#81).

52. Malbran-Labat, "Lettres," RSO 7 27–64, esp. pp. 32–34 (#9).

53. PRU 6 100 (#126).

54. *CAT* 4:338; Z. R. Ziskind, "Sea Loans at Ugarit," *JAOS* 94 (1974) 134–37; D. Pardee, "The Ugaritic Text 2106: 10–18: A Bottomry Loan?" *JAOS* 95 (1975) 612–19; I. M. Rowe, "Evidence of the Trade between Ugarit and Byblos: Once More on KTU 4. 338: 10–18," *AuOr* 11 (1993) 101–6.

55. D. Arnaud, "Les ports de la 'Phénicie' à la fin de l'Âge du Bronze Récent (XIV–XIII siècles)," *SMEA* 30 (1992) 179–94.

All of these are written in Akkadian, some of them with completely Canaanite syntax,[56] and in all of them the king of Sidon is named first, and
the king of Ugarit is mentioned, but not named, in second place, "Thus
says . . . , king of the land of Sidon, to the king of the land of Ugarit,
my brother," indicating that the king of Sidon considered himself to be
preeminent among the kings of the coastal cities. This sense of superior-
ity is also apparent in Sidon's insistence on direct business dealings with
the Hittites, bypassing Ugaritic intermediaries; and in the authority that it
exercised even in these dealings—in one instance preventing the Hittites
from sailing south of Sidon to do business with Tyre.

There are two letters from the king of Tyre to the king of Ugarit, one in
Babylonian with Canaanite syntax,[57] and the other in Ugaritic. The Ugaritic letter was sent to tell the king of Ugarit that the ship he had sent to
Egypt was caught in a violent storm off Tyre but that its cargo was saved,
and the ship managed to reach the harbor at ʿAkko.[58] The Babylonian letter demands that the king of Ugarit restore the business records of a Tyrian
merchant, Baʿalmišlam, living in Ugarit, that were written on large wooden
tablets and that Šiptibaʿal, a wealthy merchant, son-in-law of the king and
harbor master of Ugarit, had taken from him.[59] In another administrative
document this Baʿalmišlam turns up as one of the witnesses to a series
of transactions in the port of Ugarit,[60] and in another the same Šiptibaʿal
writes to the king of Ugarit that he has been with the king of Tyre, who was
forced to flee to a mainland city and there offered sacrifice.[61] The reason
for this flight may have been the plague which, according to another letter from a Tyrian merchant to his agent in Ugarit, afflicted Tyre for at least
four months. In the second part of this letter, the merchant asks for the
money and goods owed to him by merchants in Ugarit and says that he will
send to Ugarit one blanket, a few linen and purple wool shirts, a talent of
fish, and 30 minas of good-quality wool the color of lapis lazuli.[62] In other
inventories there are references to Tyrian textiles, notably linen robes, and
among them a tunic with rubies on it that was worth 2 shekels.

These casual records of Ugarit's contacts with the principal cities of
coastal Canaan also provide incidental information on their civic and religious constitution. From the Sidonian letters, we know that the king, who
had a residence in the citadel and was surrounded by a coterie of councilors
and elders, always described himself as king of the land rather than of the
city of Sidon and was answerable to the assembly of the people of the city,
who are not referred to as his subjects but simply as "Sidonians." It is also

56. Idem, "Hazor à la fin de l'Âge du Bronze d'après un document méconnu: RS 20. 255,"
AuOr 16 (1988) 27–35, esp. p. 30.

57. Idem, "Une bêche-de-mer antique: La langue des marchands à Tyr à la fin du XIIIe siècle," *AuOr* 17–18 (1999–2000) 143–66.

58. *CAT* 38.

59. D. Arnaud, "Un lettre du roi de Tyr au roi d'Ugarit. Milieux d'affaires et de culture en
Syrie à la fin de l'Âge du Bronze Récent," *Syria* 59 (1982) 101–7.

60. *CAT* 4:782.

61. *CAT* 2:40.

62. Malbran-Labat, "Lettres," RSO 7 57–61 (#25).

of interest, in ascertaining the distinctive character of Sidon, that the diplomatic language of the city was Assyrian rather than peripheral Babylonian and that the theophoric element in the royal names was Akkadian "Hadad" or "Addu" rather than Canaanite "Baʿal."

At Tyre, on the other hand, the few names that are preserved are Northwest Semitic, and the products that it sold, such as fish and beautiful dyed garments and textiles, were those for which it was still famous in the first millennium. In the El-Amarna age, when Pharaoh wanted to know the gossip in Canaan, he wrote to Tyre, and in the Ugaritic archives the report on the vicissitudes of one of its ships that found safe haven at ʿAkko— these facts might suggest that Tyre was still the main source of news along the coast. There is no indication in this limited correspondence that Tyre, Sidon, and Byblos worked together or relied on mutual commercial agreements, but each was politically and fiscally independent. In all these cities there were market places operated by individuals and syndicates, working for themselves or financed by bankers or by the court, who could count on their kings to bail them out when they got into international trouble.

Apart from this documentation that provides snippets of information on various aspects of life in coastal Canaan, there are inferences to be drawn from literacy, literature, and language in Ugarit that can provide a glimpse of Canaan's cultural dynamic. From this perspective Canaan—for whose importance in the contemporary world of trade, travel, and commerce there is not much direct evidence—turns out to have been a brilliant influence on Ugarit and perhaps more generally on Syria and Anatolia in the fourteenth and especially in the thirteenth centuries. This influence was artistic and literary and consisted primarily in the transmission of the alphabet, the legends of the kings, and the developed myth and rituals of Baʿal.

The transmission of the alphabet to people for whom it was a first experiment in reading and writing meant learning the order of the letters and how to remember them. A twelfth-century school exercise from ʿIzbet Sartah, 16 kilometers east of Tel Qasile (Tel Aviv) in Canaanite territory, illustrates both of these pedagogical protocols (see fig. 1.3).[63] There are four practice lines with letters in random order, some of them conceivably words, and the last line is the alphabet in its standard order but with some anomalies that indicate how the student memorized it: the positions of the bilabials /w/ and /m/ are interchanged and it is obvious that, to be misled by their similar sounds, the student must have been pronouncing the alphabet as it was written—when it came time to write /w/ in the place of /m/ the student or teacher realized what had happened and left a blank space instead of perpetuating the mistake; the order of /ḥ/ and /z/ is reversed, and /q/ is written twice instead of /q-r/ (maybe just a graphic

---

63. A. Kochavi, "An Ostracon of the Period of the Judges from Izbet Ṣarṭah," *TA* 4 (1977) 1–13, pl. 1; A. Demsky, "A Proto-Canaanite Abecedary Dating from the Period of the Judges and Its Implications for the History of the Alphabet," *TA* 4 (1977) 14–27; F. M. Cross, "Newly Found Inscriptions in Old Canaanite and Early Phoenician Scripts," *BASOR* 238 (1980) 1–20, esp. pp. 8–15.

Fig. 1.3. Izbet Sartah abecedary (IDAM 80-1). Reproduced by permission of the Israel Antiquities Authority. Photo by: Miki Koren.

mistake); this suggests that the alphabet was being learned in twos, without consideration for rhyming patterns.

About two centuries later, an abecedary from Tel Zayit, north of Lachish, south of Beth Shemesh, and due east of Ashkelon adheres exactly to the standard alphabetic order[64] but is conspicuous for its integration of earlier and later forms of the letters. The abecedary was incised on the bottom of a small, more-or-less ovoid boulder into the upper surface of which a cavity or bowl had been worked, and which was reused in a stone wall—all of this archaeologically well fixed in the tenth century. Four of the letters retain their twelfth- or eleventh-century forms, but one (/m/), typologically, is surprisingly advanced and anticipates ninth-century developments. The likely story is that the abecedary was copied from a table of scripts that recorded the letters in their original, their contemporary, and their developing cursive forms. This accounts for the surprisingly archaic letters and for the precocious /m/, which was included in its proper place in the abecedary: the mason who made the bowl and then adorned it (as Greeks, Etruscans, Judeans, and Phoenicians later did) with the wondrous beauties of the alphabet realized that the cursive /m/ was anomalous; he corrected the mistake by adding two more /m/s at the end of the abecedary that were quite archaic, however, and older than might be expected in the tenth century but more like the twelfth- or eleventh-century forms in his table of scripts. The alphabet, clearly, was a Canaanite heritage, an ongoing lesson; and a sure sign that you were learning was the freedom to correct your mistakes.

64. R. E. Tappy et al., "An Abecedary of the Mid-Tenth Century B.C.E. from the Judaean Shephelah," *BASOR* 344 (2006) 5–46; idem and P. K. McCarter Jr., eds., *Literate Culture and Tenth-Century Canaan: The Tel Zayit Abecedary in Context* (Winona Lake, IN: Eisenbrauns, 2008).

Sometime in the thirteenth century, Ugarit borrowed the alphabet from Canaan,[65] probably from Byblos, with which it had literate and artistic ties and with which it shared an interest in Egyptian culture. The writing at Ugarit until that time had been cuneiform Akkadian, and when the scribes and literati borrowed the alphabet they continued writing with cuneiform signs.[66] They learned the alphabet, as students' abecedaries attest, in its Canaanite (A-B-C) and its South Arabic (H-L-Ḥ)[67] orders, so they must have been familiar with both of these scripts, or languages. They had to expand the alphabet, however, to include five more phonemes, or meaningful signs, and three graphic symbols. The abecedaries generally present this expanded form, but a bilingual abecedary (Ugaritic-alphabetic and Akkadian-syllabic) displays the original short Canaanite alphabet in one column and its syllabic pronunciation in the opposite column.

The Ugaritic cuneiform letters consisted of upright angles, or wedges with a horizontal, vertical, or oblique stance, singly or in creative combinations, and were designed to resemble the contemporary linear alphabetic paradigms—not the items that these signs once represented but just the letters. The resemblances are not always transparent, not least because Ugaritic was written from left to right and the Canaanite model from right to left, so that the stance of the Ugaritic letters could rotate 90 or more degrees. Despite this and despite cuneiform's lack of rounded lines, some of the correspondences are pretty striking: /h/ in both systems is three horizontal prongs, but they face in opposite directions; /w/ is an open semicircle on top of a bar, but the letter has tipped to the left in Ugaritic; /z/ is two vertical wedges, one on top of the other, and approximates alphabetic /z/ which is two horizontal lines and a vertical ligature line. Most of the letters are like this—angular, formal, and static reproductions of a script undergoing lapidary and cursive developments.

The additional five cuneiform alphabetic signs (/ḫ/, /š/, /ḏ/, /ẓ/, /ǵ/) were drawn from archaic forms of the alphabetic letters or by imitating letters in the newly minted cuneiform alphabet that had approximate phonetic or phonemic values. The letter /ḫ/, for instance, is three wedges one above the other and looks like the original braided or woven hank of yarn, which was phonemic at Byblos and at Ugaritic. The letter /š/ is an angle and two oblique wedges arranged to look like the archaic tooth form. The letter /ḏ/, which in late texts is sometimes used instead of /š/, looks almost like it but omits one of the oblique wedges. Two sets of phonemes (/ṭ/ and /ẓ/; /ʿ/ and /ǵ/), similar enough to be written with the same letter and to be distinguished only by a diacritic mark in Classical Arabic, are adaptations of the same Ugaritic sign. The principles governing the insertion of new signs

---

65. A.-S. Dalix, "Suppiluliuma (II?) dans un texte alphabétique d'Ugarit et la date d'apparition de l'alphabet cunéiform," *Sem* 49 (1999) 5–15.

66. M. Dietrich and O. Loretz, *Die Keilalphabete: Die phönizisch-kanaanäischen und altara-bischen Alphabete in Ugarit* (Munster: Ugarit-Verlag, 1988).

67. *Canaanite*: *CAT* 5:6, 8, 19, 20, 25. In *CAT* 5:13, the expanded Ugaritic alphabet is written twice, and in *CAT* 5:9, it is written at the bottom of a form letter. *South Arabic*: *CAT* 5:24; P. Bordreuil and D. Pardee, "Un abécédaire du type sud-sémitique découvert en 1988 dans les fouilles archéologiques françaises de Ras Shamra–Ougarit," *CRAIBL* (1995) 855–60.

seem to have been that the new letters were put in after letters whose shape they resembled or, because the letters were pronounced and the alphabet was recited and learned in segments, they were inserted in the segments in which their pronunciation produced a mnemonic pattern of sound.

The Ugaritic alphabet was manufactured from Canaanite insight and Syrian polyglot expertise. It was a deliberate, studied, and cooperative venture: with the letters themselves, the scribes of Ugarit borrowed their order, perhaps their names, and the idea of learning the alphabet in groupings of letters that had some rhyme or reason and by pronouncing their names. The main difference was that the letters from which they were drawn no longer resembled the things they once represented, and this left the Ugaritic academicians free to devise a cuneiform alphabet. The whole process reflects Ugarit's familiarity with and respect for Canaanite culture and scribal practice, as well as the ability of the Canaanite schools to teach their language and their system, keeping track of the original forms of the letters and of their development, as well as the Old South Arabic system that was adopted at the same time. The addition of the three syllabic signs at the end confirms the alphabetic principle and preempts this position for analogous additions in later alphabets, such as the archaic corrective /m/ at Tel Zayit and the archaic letters that were postscripted to round out the Greek alphabets.

This Canaanite dynamic and the interweaving of its culture with Ugarit's and the proto–South Arabians' is corroborated by other examples of alphabetic literacy. At Ugarit itself, there are thirteenth-century texts that are written in Ugaritic cuneiform alphabetic script, but they are written right to left like Canaanite texts, use the Canaanite 22-letter alphabet, and their language is Canaanite. Three of the texts are scribal exercises, indicating that Canaanite was being taught at Ugarit, but one is a prayer and two others are inventories, and these may imply that learning and writing Canaanite was also becoming common practice.

Canaanite texts written in cuneiform but in the short Canaanite alphabet have been found in other places besides Ugarit and, obviously, when these people learned the language and the script they were eager to share it. One of the texts is from Hala Sultan Tekke, a negligible distance southeast of Kition in Cyprus, but the others are from Syria and Canaan. The Hala Sultan Tekke inscription is on the lip of a small silver bowl and identifies it as belonging to 'Akkuya, son of Yiptah-Addu, who may have been, like the silversmith and engraver who made and inscribed the bowl, a native of Ugarit living in Cyprus in a totally Canaanite milieu.[68] The Syrian example, from Tell Nebi Mend, ancient Qadesh, was written on a huge storage jar to indicate the contents of the jar: these cannot be identified because this part of the text is broken, but its recipient, whose name is Hurrian, was the governor, of Ugarit conceivably, but because the jar was hardly transportable, probably of Qadesh.[69]

---

68. *CAT* 6:68.
69. *CAT* 6:71.

The texts from Canaan in Ugaritic script are from Kumidi, in the Anti-Lebanon; from Sarepta, on the coast between Sidon and Tyre; and from Tabor and Taanach, inland, south of ʿAkko. All except the last, which describes the remedy for an illness, perhaps a hangover ("Kokab harvested sweet wine, unwell he must eat bitter recompense"),[70] identify the owners of the manufactured objects (a blade, jars) or the artisan ("a crater that Yaduʿaʾ made") who created it. These texts are evidence that people of Ugarit settled in Cyprus and Canaan; that natives of Cyprus, Syria, and Canaan spoke Canaanite and wrote alphabetically but experimented with the old-fashioned cuneiform script developed in Ugarit. There is an abecedary from Beth Shemesh in southern Canaan east of Ekron in the hill country west of Jerusalem[71] that was written in the Ugaritic cuneiform alphabet but in its 22-letter Canaanite form and following the south Semitic (HLḤ), rather than the Canaanite (ABC), order of the alphabet.

From all this, it is evident that Canaan had become a clearing house for the alphabet, borrowed first by proto-Arabs or south Semites, then by the Amorites of Ugarit, who seem to have known the alphabet in both orders and both forms, then imported into Canaan by expatriates from Ugarit in their own cuneiform version. It is also clear that this cultural coalescence required regular or extended contact between these peoples and thus travel, trade, and diplomacy; but it is equally apparent that it was a true intellectual exchange requiring not only teaching, study, and memorization but a sense of tradition, or at least an ability to relate contemporary letter forms to the original tables of scripts.

The deliberate and reflective nature of the enterprise was embedded in a broader cultural dissemination: it was not just reading and writing and counting that were shared, the basic easiness of living, but also things remembered that seemed worth repeating—the exotic, amusing, or intriguing tales that came to be loved, the stories fraught with ethnic awareness and pride. This certainly was the situation when Ugarit learned and adapted the alphabet, because the culmination of the process was the appropriation of elements of the myths of life and death that prevailed in Canaan. This in turn is corroborated by the fact that Ugarit's versions of these stories, like its version of alphabetic writing, seem to have found their way back into Canaan, at least into peripheral or inland Canaan if not back to Tyre and Byblos and the cities of coastal Canaan that had been the original instigators of this cultural exchange. It was in learning Canaanite literacy, language, and literature that Ugarit distinguished itself from the other great cities of North Syria and from Hittite and Hurrian imitators with which it had so much else in common.

Literary Relations

The Myth of Baʿal

A key myth of North Syria borrowed from there into surrounding regions was the story of God's defeat of the Sea, or the Sea Monster, or the

---

70. *CAT* 4:767.

71. A. G. Loudine, "L'abécédaire de Beth Shemesh," *Mus* 100 (1987) 243–50.

Seven-Headed Monster. What is peculiar to the Ugaritic version of the myth in the late thirteenth-century form in which it was written is that this great or primordial victory is combined with the myth of God's victory over Death, a story that reflects the beliefs of the cities of coastal Canaan, Tyre, Sidon, and especially Byblos, all of whose city patrons were Gods of Life and Death. The myth exists in only one copy, signed by the scribe Ilimilk,[72] who also wrote the only extant copies of the legends of King Keret and of the noble Daniel, both of which apply the themes of the myth to the problems of mortal existence. Ilimilk, whose distinctive handwriting sets apart the six tablets of the myth, was also the author of the myth, which is communicated with an incomparable humaneness and theological sensitivity. There are other tablets that quote and comment on episodes from the encounter with Death, but they differ from the original myth in being literal, bawdy, disrespectful of the Gods, and unsympathetic to the subject,[73] and there are contemporary ritual texts that deal with death but only as it affects the kings and not as an issue in the world of the Gods.[74]

God's victory over the Sea was celebrated in Syria at least from the eighteenth century b.c.e. on, and this part of the myth may have been recited and celebrated in Ugarit from that time until the days of Ilimilk. But God's victory over Death, although elements of it were available in the stories of Inanna and Tammuz, came to Ugarit in the thirteenth century with the alphabet, and probably from Byblos, where the rites of Adonis were celebrated.

The myth was meant to be recited (there are places where the tablets include instructions for the reader), and it is possible that it was recited at the New Year's festival. Evidence for this might be one of Ilimilk's titles in the colophon to the myth of Baʿal, according to which he is not only a "scribe" or "writer" (*spr*) from the town of Shubbanu (*šbny*) who learned the scribal arts from Attanu (*lmd atn*), a high priest (*rb khnm*) and foreman of the individuals who took care of the herds of sacrificial animals (*rb nqdm*), and a man held in honor by the king (*ʿuty nqmd mlk ugrt*); he is also the reciter or an officiant (*prln*) at the Purullu or New Year's festival. The name Purullu is Hittite and, supposing this interpretation is correct, the festival may have been introduced into Ugarit under the auspices of the kingdom's Hittite suzerains. The festival would have been adapted to local interests by substituting the recitation of the myth of Baʿal for the usual recitation of the myths of the Hittite Weather and Vegetation Gods, with which both its parts have some remarkable thematic parallels.[75] The motive for adopting the Canaanite (specifically Byblian) myth of Adonis that recounts God's

---

72. *CAT* 1:1–6; S. B. Parker, ed., *Ugaritic Narrative Poetry* (SBLWAW 9; Atlanta: Scholars Press, 1997) 81–176; D. Pardee, "Ugaritic Myths," in *COS* 1.241–84; N. Wyatt, *Religious Texts from Ugarit: The Words of Ilimilku and His Colleagues* (Biblical Seminar 53; Sheffield: Sheffield Academic Press, 1998).

73. *CAT* 1:7–12; D. Pardee, *Les textes para-mythologiques de la 24e campagne (1961)* (Paris: Editions Recherche sur les Civilisations, 1988).

74. Idem, *Les Textes Rituels. Fascicule 1: Chapitres 1–53; Fascicule 2: Chapitres 54–83, Appendices et Figures* (RSO 12; Paris: Editions Recherche sur les Civilisations, 2000).

75. V. Haas, *Geschichte der hethitischen Religion* (Handbuch der Orientalistik 1: Der Nahe und Mittlere Osten 15; Leiden: Brill, 1994) 696–747.

victory over Death, therefore, would have been precisely the need to find a congenial Northwest Semitic substitute for the Anatolian myth of the Vegetation God, which could be combined with the story of the God's victory over the Sea, which in itself was an excellent substitute for the Hittite myth of the Weather God.[76]

This victory over the Sea is the first part of the *Ba'al Cycle*. Its presence in the literary repertory of the Amorites, the population group to which the natives of Ugarit originally belonged and a culture with which Byblos was affiliated beginning early in the second millennium, is known from one of the eighteenth-century texts from Mari.[77] This is a letter recording a prophetic oracle for Shamshi Addu, king of Aleppo, that assures him of victory over his enemies, provided he is just in his judgments and seeks the advice of the God before setting out to battle, because Hadad has given him the weapons that were used in his defeat of the Sea. It is this Hadad, the Ba'al of Syria, who was the God of the kingdom of Ugarit, the God of the Weather and of the Storm at sea in particular, and therefore the Warrior God who would save the city. This is made explicit in one of the ritual texts from Ugarit, which begins with the king's sacrificial obligations to Ba'al and then concludes with a prayer to be said by the people:[78]

> When a strong man attacks your gates, a warrior your walls, lift your eyes to Ba'al: Ba'al, drive the strong man from our gates, the warrior from our walls. We will consecrate a bull to you, O Ba'al, our vows we will fulfill, a memorial offering, O Ba'al, we will consecrate, a thanksgiving offering, O Ba'al, we will fulfill, a festival, O Ba'al, we will celebrate, we will ascend to the sanctuary of Ba'al, we will walk in the paths of the house of Ba'al. And Ba'al will hear your plea, will drive the strong man from your gates, the warrior from your walls.

The myth of Ba'al's victory over the Sea, therefore, had a completely practical application at Ugarit, but it was unknown at Byblos and the other cities of the Canaanite coast, except perhaps in an iconic and nonnarrative residue.

The tablets with the first part of the *Ba'al Cycle* are unevenly preserved, but the story line is clear. When the cycle begins, 'Athtar, the God of Wells and springs and irrigation, is the king of the Gods, but the God Yawwu is attempting to replace him, and Haddad is perturbed. At a symposium of the Gods, El renames Yawwu "Yammu" or "Sea" (just as Haddad will assume the title Ba'al in the story) and promises him the kingship, but in the meantime El builds a royal palace for himself as the symbolic center of world order.

The second tablet begins with Sea, whose title is "Prince Sea and Judge River," enthroned, and with Ba'al and his sister 'Anat conspiring against him. Sea sends messengers demanding that El and the assembly of the Gods make Ba'al his slave and, although Ba'al kills the messengers, El yields to the pressure, and Ba'al is imprisoned beneath the throne of Sea. 'Anat

---

76. H. A. Hoffner Jr., *Hittite Myths* (SBLWAW 2; Atlanta: Scholars Press, 1990) 10–20.

77. J.-M. Durand, "Le mythologème du combat entre le dieu de l'orage et la mer en mésopotamie," *Mari* 7 (1993) 41–61.

78. *CAT* 1:119:29–36; Wyatt, *Religious Texts from Ugarit*, 416–22; Pardee, *Les textes rituels*, 1.661–70.

encourages her brother to stand up to Sea, and with the help of weapons designed by the craftsman God, he kills and consumes the Sea and is acknowledged as King of the Gods.

The third tablet is filled with a festival for Baʿal, a celebration of ʿAnat's part in the victory over the Sea by defeating the seven-headed serpent, an account of her defeat of Baʿal's terrestrial enemies, the inauguration of an era of peace, and the description of ʿAnat's journey to El in order to persuade him to build a palace for Baʿal.

In the fourth tablet, Baʿal has the divine craftsman Kothar-and-Hasis ("Crafty and Cunning") make a richly furnished pavilion for Asherah, and these gifts persuade her to ask El to have a temple built for Baʿal. The temple is built, and Baʿal holds a feast for the Gods. In his triumphal tour, Baʿal sees many cities added to his domains and on returning to his temple has the craftsman God install a window in it from which he can hurl lightning bolts on the individuals that are not yet under his dominion. The story, therefore, is about world waters which, for their benefits to humankind, succeed each other as King of the Gods, progressing from the underground waters of the Earth, to the Sea and Rivers, and then to the Sky, culminating in the victory of the Storm God over the Sea.

This last is the story to which the oracle concerning the weapons of Hadad alludes, but there and in the Babylonian *Enūma elish* in which Marduk defeats the Sea to become the King of the Gods, the Sea is the monster Tiamat and a female principle of the world. In the Hittite story of Iluyanka, similarly, as in ʿAnat's defeat of the Sea monster, the threat to the Storm God comes from a serpent which lives underground or in the sea. In Egypt, where the overthrow of the great serpent Apophis was already integral to the myths of creation, the borrowed myth concerns only the victory of Baʿal, or Seth, and freedom from the tyranny of the Sea. The biblical writers know all of these versions: in the simplest version God defeats the seven-headed monster Leviathan (Isa 27:1); in another (Genesis 1; Exodus 14), the world is created by splitting Tiamat into sky and earth, or in a lavish display of magic the Sea is split to reveal dry ground; in the most sophisticated version God becomes King by using the Sea as his weapon against the Egyptians, and the defeated king of Egypt is compared to a Dragon in the river Nile (Exod 15:1–21; Ezek 29:3–5, 32:2–8). In Phoenician lore, as this was recorded by Philo of Byblos,[79] there is some reminiscence of the myth, but it seems to have lost its meaning. Sky (*Ouranos*) did battle with Sea (*Pontos*) and was assisted by Demarous, which at Ugarit was an epithet of Baʿal (*dmrn*), but Demarous was routed by the Sea. This may correspond to Baʿal's initial subjugation to Sea in the Ugaritic myth, not by defeat but by the decree of El, but in the Phoenician story Demarous made a vow in thanksgiving for his escape and never returned to fight, let alone defeat, the Sea. Although Philo says that Demarous is another name for Adad or Haddad, the King of the Gods who ruled over the land, he does not suggest that he became king by a victory over the Sea; on the contrary, he finds this kingship compatible with his defeat by Sea. The myth of Baʿal and the Sea was known, therefore, in Syria (where it seems to have originated), in Ana-

---

79. *PhByb* 1.10.28, 31.

tolia, in Mesopotamia, in inland Canaan (where it is preserved in the traditions of Israel), and in Egypt. But it had another resonance in the religion or literature of coastal Canaan where, as in the legend of Jonah in which the monster and the Sea are victorious but still funny or playful subjects of the God of the Sky, it was adapted to the realities of seafaring.

The second part of the cycle is the account of Ba'al's encounter with Death. This is an addition to the story of the Sea, because it exists independently, and it was probably added and adapted from the legends of coastal Canaan (or of Byblos in particular), around the time that Ugarit borrowed the alphabet from the same source. Its independent existence is known from the myths and rituals of Adonis, as these are attested in later Greek, Phoenician, and Hebrew sources; from comparison with the earlier Tammuz traditions in Babylonia; and from the structure of the *Ba'al Cycle* itself. The special significance of this borrowing—apart from its importance in the reconstruction of the history of Ugarit—is the reflected light that it casts on the culture of thirteenth-century Canaan, which obviously was more than a playground for the great powers; more than an economic hub in the business among Egypt, Syria, and Mesopotamia, and between the Mediterranean world and its inland congeners; and more like a vast differentiated matrix of creativeness and civilization.

Toward the end of the fourth tablet of the *Ba'al Cycle*, after a window has been built in Ba'al's palace, he has hurled his bolts onto the land, and his enemies have escaped to the mountains and forests, Ba'al suddenly realizes that, although he may inspire fear, he is not the king of the world and is unable to protect the people of the earth who cherish him. The ruler of the world, in fact, is death, universal and unwanted. Ba'al recognizes that it is death that prevents him from being king of the world, that death is individual, and that overcoming death is a personal not a political venture—nothing as easy or conventional as hurling thunderbolts out his window. Abruptly, he decides that he must send messengers to Death, go into the jaws of Death, and die, if he is to be king, the one who takes care of and satisfies the Gods and the people of the world.

From the beginning of the cycle, this benevolence and the popular enthusiasm it inspires have been characteristic of Ba'al, and all the while he has seemed destined to have a palace and to be king. But now the cycle presents kingship, at least in its traditional aggressive and insouciant embodiment, as an impediment to popular acceptance. The turn is sudden, and the resolution is unanticipated and unexpected; the breach in the plot may mark a liturgical suture, the place where two myths overlap. In the rituals of the Purullu festival, this was the place where the myth of the Storm God, corresponding more or less with Ba'al's victory over the Sea, merged with the myth of the Vegetation God, which has some of the characters and themes of Ba'al's encounter with Death.

The Ugaritic story, however, is entirely different, most fundamentally in being the myth of a personal encounter with Death; and most importantly in attributing this encounter to the boyish Ba'al, who succumbs to Death, and to his sister 'Anat, called "The Maiden," the perpetual girl, who overcomes Death and orchestrates the return of Life. In the recitation of the Ugaritic cycle, therefore, this is the place where the Syrian myth of the Sea merges with the Canaanite myth of Adonis, where the history of the mighty and insouciant Lord of the stormy sky melds into the story of the gentle youth whom women love, and whose death, disappearance, and revival they orchestrate into ever-present life.

The story of Baʿal's encounter with Death is intricate but fairly clear. At the end of the fourth tablet, Baʿal sends his messengers to Death, who lives in a slimy pit in the underworld. When they enter his realm, the Sun, the lamp of the Gods, who is a main character in this story and in the Hittite myth of the Vegetation God, is extinguished and the heavens collapse. At the beginning of the fifth tablet, the messengers report Death's reply: his appetite is insatiable, he has one lip on the earth and one in the stars, he craves Baʿal, he is the grim harvester; and Baʿal is invited to his feast and must enter his gullet like a withered olive, like fruit falling from the trees. Baʿal is afraid but accepts the invitation and receives detailed instructions about his descent into the underworld with his clouds and rains, his daughters the Dew and the Mist, and his assistants the Boys and the Boars. Before he dies, however, he becomes a Bull, as in his symbolic liturgical representation. He mates with a heifer, who conceives and gives birth to a calf, which is depicted in the realism of the epic mode as a male child whom Baʿal clothes and caresses with love and tenderness. In the last column, El, who has just been told that Baʿal was found lying dead in the pasture, comes down from his throne, rolls in the dust, pours earth on his head, slashes himself in rites of lamentation, and cries out that he too will follow Baʿal into the underworld.

In the last tablet, the scene shifts back and forth between a rural or agricultural setting in which ʿAnat is the main character, and an urban or religious milieu in which El is the main character. It begins with ʿAnat, who has been searching everywhere for Baʿal and just happens upon him, lying dead in the pasture, performing the same rites as El, and crying out that she, all peoples, and the Sun will have to go down into the underworld after Baʿal. But when she has satisfied herself with her tears, she summons the Sun to help her lift Baʿal and carry him to his mountain, Saphon, where they will bury him and offer sacrifices in his honor. Then she travels to El's abode and finds Asherah, his wife, rejoicing because now one of their sons (Baʿal is not the son of El and Asherah but the son of the God Dagon) can become king. She suggests a son who is called "He-Oozes-and-Moistens," but El rejects him as being no match for Baʿal in generative powers. Together they settle on ʿAthtar, who had been king in the beginning. He is too small to occupy Baʿal's throne, however, and has to climb down and resume his role as God of springs, channels, and irrigation.

Then, in a flashback, ʿAnat longs for her brother Baʿal and demands that Death give him to her. Death replies by telling her the story of her brother's death: Death had been out searching for food, hungering for humankind, craving people to eat, when he came upon Baʿal in the pasture and devoured him. Satisfied by the facts but not amused by the story, she takes hold of Death, cuts him with a blade, winnows him, roasts him, grinds him, and plants him in the field so that the birds can eat his flesh and the vultures obliterate his image. Meanwhile, back at his abode, El dreams that the wadis are flowing with honey and that the heavens rain oil, and he rejoices to know that Baʿal is alive, that the Lord of the Earth is and exists. When he asks ʿAnat and the Sun Goddess where Baʿal is, now that the furrows of the fields are damp, the Sun replies that she will search for him, and ʿAnat asks El to protect the Sun wherever she might travel. It turns out that Baʿal is back at El's abode, where he seizes and kills the sons of Asherah—the rollers, breakers, and waves—thus finishing his defeat of the Sea and eliminating any possible pretender to his throne.

Thus, Baʿal reigns for seven years, but in the seventh year, Death pathetically complains to Baʿal about ʿAnat's treatment of him and, still famished, threatens to go on eating people if he does not receive one of Baʿal's brothers to devour. When Baʿal deceives Death by giving him one of his own dead brothers instead, Death challenges Baʿal to a wrestling match. Baʿal gains the upper hand, the Sun intervenes to warn Death that El will not tolerate another challenge to the kingship of Baʿal, and the cycle ends with Death declaring that Baʿal is king and making him offerings of bread and wine.

This part of the *Baʿal Cycle* is not reflected in the Ugaritic ritual and liturgical texts. But at the very end of the last tablet, before the colophon but after the narrative is complete, there is a prayer of praise that sums up the cycle and does reflect current practice as revealed in other texts. "Sun, you are watchful over the Spirits of the dead, Sun, you are watchful over the Godlike. The Gods and the Dead sing of you, Kothar your enchanter sings of you, and Hasis your familiar. In the Sea where Desire and the Dragon lurk, Kothar-and-Hasis tosses, Kothar-and-Hasis travels." The last sentence mentions one of the primordial creatures (the complete list includes Desire, the Beloved of the Gods, Attachment, the calf of El, Fire the bitch of the Gods, and Flame the daughter of El) and one of the monsters, the other being the Twisting Seven-Headed Serpent. These two monsters were subdued by ʿAnat in Baʿal's victory over Sea. The last sentence refers to the voyages of Kothar-and-Hasis, when he was summoned from his home in Crete to do the work of the Gods in Ugarit. Apparently, as in the story of Jonah, the realities of this part of the myth were seafaring, trade, and commerce with exotic places.

The first sentence is an allusion to the Sun's role in Baʿal's victory over Death, but it also indicates that the myth may sustain the cult of the dead ancestors, and in particular of the dead members of the dynasty, over whom the Sun, the Goddess who passes daily through the realms of Life and Death, presides. In the myth, Baʿal dies and goes down into the underworld, but when he is declared to be alive again ("Baʿal Is, Baʿal is Alive"), he is not said to rise or return from the underworld; the myth only indicates that the rains and vegetation have returned. The life of the God is assured in the life of the calf that was born to him before his death and in the life of the peoples over whom Baʿal gained dominion by confronting and overcoming Death. Ugarit's dead ancestors, similarly, do not come back to life, but their life is assured by the individuals who celebrate their cult. Because this cult consists of the joyful invocation of their names in song, it depends on Kothar-and-Hasis, who is the Craftsman God and the muse, the "Enchanter" and "Familiar," of the Sun.

The Hittite myth of the Vegetation God Telepinu which, on the supposition that Ilimilk was cantor at the Purulli festival, was replaced by this local adaptation of the myth of Adonis, is similar in character and theme but entirely different in narrative and liturgical thrust. Telepinu is the son of the Storm God. When the story opens, Telepinu is sulky and withdraws from his house, taking with him grain, fecundity, luxuriance, and growth, with the result that animals and the land are desolate, and the Gods and humans are dying of hunger. The Gods begin to search for Telepinu: the Sun God sends the eagle, the Storm God himself searches for him, and Hannahanna the Mother Goddess sends out the bee to find him, sting him, and stir him from his sleep. When he is found, he must be assuaged, and there are prayers and rituals to remove his sin and relieve his anger and sullenness. At last Telepinu returns to his house, pays attention to the land and to the royal house, and harmony is restored in the vegetation, and among the animals, people, and the Gods.

Some of the characters are the same—the Mother Goddess Hannahanna, who is the rough equivalent of Asherah in the Ugaritic myth; the Sun; the Storm God—but the protagonists and treatment of the basic themes are totally different. Both myths share the theme of searching for the God, and in both the Sun has a part to play in the search, but Telepinu has slipped away out of spite while Baʿal walked boldly into the jaws of Death. Both have the theme of life and death, but in the Hittite myth the God lives and Death is universal; in the Ugaritic myth, death is personal, it is the God who dies, and it is the vivifying effects of his life rather than the dismal effects of his death that are emphasized. The Vegetation God is surly and vindictive, while Baʿal is portrayed as the true friend of all peoples. Both include ritual and liturgical elements that apply the myth to life and experience, but these elements take up almost half of the Hittite myth and are mentioned almost incidentally and in an epilogue at the very end of the Ugaritic myth. It is easy to see how one myth could be used instead of the other, and at the same time impossible to miss the striking differences in the literary, social, psychological, and theological contexts that generated and absorbed them.

The Literary History of the Myth of Baʿal

When Ilimilk took the myth of Baʿal's victory over Death from his Canaanite tutors and combined it with the God's victory over the Sea, he adapted it to the particular sensibilities of Ugarit. A comparison of his creation with later Canaanite versions and with later Canaanite borrowings of his complete composite work gives an appreciation of the creative reworking it underwent at Ugarit and allows an approximation to the original Canaanite composition. The original myth of Adonis must be pieced together from references in Greek literature, from a few allusions in Phoenician inscriptions, and from narrative and poetic texts of the Bible. The latter, which are representative of inland Canaanite culture, have preserved both parts of the cycle separately in different books, and in combination in others, where they become the myth of the origins of Israel.

The Legend of Joseph

The essential plot of the biblical story of Joseph (Genesis 37–50) is that he was taken down into Egypt and died there, but only after he had become the means of survival for the people of Egypt and for his 11 brothers. This is all supposed to have happened in some distant time, during the lifetime of the patriarch Jacob, before the time of Pharaoh Ramesses, when the family lived in Canaan and gained their livelihood as merchants and traders. The story has some historical verisimilitude: trade and commerce between Canaan and Egypt is expected at any time in the Late Bronze Age; there is an analogy between the migration of Canaanites to Egypt, where they gained control of the Delta and lived for hundreds of years, and the Middle-Bronze-Age migration of the Hyksos, who ruled Egypt from the same region and for approximately the same amount of time. However, the story also entertains chronological inconsistencies, digresses into legends, and interweaves an allegory of Joseph (the eponym of the Northern tribes of Israel), who was sold into slavery in Assyria. Joseph himself, the hero of the story, is one of 12 brothers, but he is also specially favored, uncannily perceptive and wise, and at the height of his powers is said to be Adonis, the life-giver who all but takes the place of God. The plot is filled out with multiple allusions to this legend.[80]

At the beginning of the story, Joseph is a young lad, as Adonis was, and is especially loved, not by women as Adonis was, but by his father. This shift in gender roles is perhaps emphasized by the coat of many colors that Israel gave the boy, because another biblical text about Tamar the daughter of David, points out that this was the clothing worn by young princesses (Gen 37:3; 2 Sam 13:18). Adonis, similarly, although very attractive to women, was not particularly masculine.

The boy is a dreamer, in fact a "lord" (*ba'al*) of dreams, and in the dreams that portend his exaltation in Egypt he is worshiped by the grain and by the Sun, the Moon, and the Stars. In the myth, similarly, both the vegetation and the cosmic elements are threatened by Death; and the final exaltation of Ba'al, or the fact that Ba'al is and is alive, is revealed in a dream.

The brothers despise Joseph for his dreams and for tattling on them and, like the council of the Gods who handed Ba'al over to Sea, they sell Joseph to merchants traveling to Egypt. This connivance of overland merchants in the slave trade is attested in Ugaritic administrative texts, but the entire context insists on the connection between his slavery and his death: going down into Egypt is the equivalent of going down into the underworld; selling the boy is literally an alternative to killing him; he is cast into a pit, which is a common biblical symbol of death, but the pit is said to be empty, without water, although in the Ugaritic version Death resides in a slimy pit in the underworld; the caravan from Gilead is carrying gum, balm, and

---

80. The allusions are discussed by J. R. Isaac in unpublished works and in "Here Comes This Dreamer," in *From Babel to Babylon: Essays on Biblical History and Literature in Honour of Brian Peckham* (ed. J. Rilett Wood, J. E. Harvey, and M. Leuchter; New York: T. & T. Clark, 2006) 237–49.

myrrh, the elements of embalming; the brothers soak his robe in the blood
of a goat, and his father recognizes that a wild animal has killed and devoured him, as a wild boar killed Adonis, or as Death in the Ugaritic texts
is likened to a wild animal with a voracious appetite devouring everything
in sight; his father, Israel, as El in the Ugaritic myth, performs mourning
rituals for Joseph and proclaims that he will go down into Death to his son.
This part of the story ends by leaving the allusive realms of myth and ritual
and returning to the reality that Joseph was brought down into Egypt and
sold to Potiphar, the captain of the guard.

At this point the story of Joseph is interrupted by the extraordinary story
of Tamar and Judah (Genesis 38). Judah married the daughter of a Canaanite named Shuaᶜ and had three sons. The oldest son married Tamar, and
when he died his brothers, according to the custom of the time, were supposed to marry her so that she could have children. The second did marry
her, but he also died. The third son was too young, and Judah told her to
return to her father's house and wait until the boy was older. Deceived and
tired of waiting, Tamar disguised herself and waylaid Judah at the entrance
to a town he had to pass on his way to the sheep shearing and he, thinking that she was a prostitute, paid for her services by offering her a lamb,
for which he left in pledge his staff, his signet ring, and the necklace from
which it hung. When he heard some months later that Tamar was pregnant, he decreed that she should be burned to death, but she produced his
pledge, he recognized his fault, and she was exonerated.

Tamar bore twins of this union and died in childbirth. But before she
died she named one Zerah, or "He-Shines," and the other Perez, "He-Split"
because, she said, "What a split you have made!" What is really extraordinary about this story is its remarkable correspondence to the Greek legend
of the birth of Adonis,[81] whose story it interrupts. Adonis was the child of
the incestuous union of Smyrna, or Myrrha, and her father, which was initiated by her when she disguised herself and entered his bed, but instigated
by Aphrodite, the Goddess of Love, or by Helios, the Sun. When her father
discovers her deception, he tries to kill her, but Aphrodite turns her into a
myrrh tree, which is the meaning of both her names, and in due time the
bark splits and Adonis is born.

The parallels are striking: in both stories the woman is a tree, the myrrh
tree, or Tamar the date palm; in both the woman wants a child by any
means, disguises herself, and initiates an illicit affair; in both the father is
too easily duped and self-righteous; in both, either explicitly in the narrative or allusively in the name, the child is literally born of the tree; in
both the woman loses her life, in becoming a tree or in childbirth; in both
cases there are other versions (those about Adonis assigning him different
fathers or taking place in different exotic regions; those about Tamar and
the daughter of Shuaᶜ—that is, of Bathsheba or Batshuaᶜ; being told again
in the time of David and Absalom, when it is the virgin Tamar who wears
the coat of many colors that Joseph once wore; Judah is an older man and

---

81. T. Gantz, *Early Greek Myth: A Guide to Literary and Artistic Sources* (Baltimore: Johns Hopkins University Press, 1993) 729–31.

not the youthful figure that he is in the Joseph story; and the story is spun out of many other threads—genealogy, reflections on sexuality and procreation, ethnography), but it is the legend of the birth of Adonis that holds it all together and fits it into the story that it actually interrupts.

When the story of Joseph resumes, Joseph has been brought down into Egypt, the symbol of Death, but God is with him in this place and pours blessings on the household and the fields of his master. The term "his master" (*'adonayw*) is used twice in a brief text and several times in the later context, and this repetition is probably meant to focus attention on the tale of Adonis. The implication of the story seems to be, in fact, that God has gone down into the realm of Death with Joseph and has countermanded the adverse mythical affects that this usually has on fertility and well-being. Joseph turns out to be the image of Adonis, loved on earth by his father, and in the underworld by God, as Adonis was by Aphrodite on earth and by Persephone in the netherworld.

This connection between Joseph and the agricultural cycle, like the connection between Ba'al's return to life and the fertility of the land in the Ugaritic cycle, will be pursued in the rest of the story, but it is interrupted at this point in order to focus on the personal and sexual expression of the story's general theme of life and death. Joseph was very beautiful, and his master's wife found him irresistible. She begged him to love her, and she kept pestering him every day. When he resisted all her advances, she accused him of trying to seduce her, and he was punished by being thrown into jail. Because in the context of confinement, jail is another metaphor for the realm of death, this tale presages the legend of Aphrodite's passion for Adonis and the time that he had to spend in the underworld with the equally enamored Persephone.

Although this vignette also has a close parallel in the Egyptian *Tale of Two Brothers*, the source of this particular version may be an episode in the *Gilgamesh Epic* and its reuse in the Ugaritic *Legend of Aqhat*. In the Akkadian epic, Ishtar is struck by Gilgamesh's beauty, but he spurns her and reminds her of the sorry fate of her former lovers, among them Tammuz, for whom annual mourning rites were instituted. She retaliates by threatening to upset the cycles of life and death.

This episode was adapted and included by Ilimilk in his *Legend of Aqhat*, which was a retelling in human terms of the myth of Ba'al's encounter with Death. According to the legend, Aqhat, the child of Daniel (and like Ba'al, the perpetual Boy), received a bow and quiver from the Craftsman God Kothar-and-Hasis that were so wonderful that 'Anat promised him eternal life like Ba'al's in return for them. He rejects her plea and scoffs at her pretensions, and she has him killed by vultures. At his death the vegetation withers and, in response to Daniel's curse, Ba'al withholds the rains for seven years. The search for the boy begins, and when his remains are found in one of the vultures, he is buried and lamented. His sister, whose name is Pu'at or "Girl," sets off to avenge his death by killing 'Anat's henchman, who was responsible for it. The story ends, apparently, when the Girl kills death, vegetation has been restored, and the Boy somehow is found alive. The core of the resemblance, therefore, is the theme of the impassioned woman who is spurned and who, by bringing about the downfall of the hero, initiates a cycle of death and life.

In the myths and legends, the cycle revolves around Ishtar and Ereshki-gal, Aphrodite and Persephone, or the Girl and ʿAnat. In the Joseph story, it is the wife of Potiphar who is his downfall, and it is the homophonous daughter of Potipheraʿ (her name, Asnath, associates her with the Goddess Neith, whose symbol was the bow and arrow) who has his children and shares in his exaltation.

In jail Joseph interprets dreams and predicts the cycles of plenty and famine of which he himself is representative. The dreams of Pharaoh's but-ler and baker are cycles of three days that lead to life for the butler and to death for the baker: the three-day cycle is integral to the classical rituals of Adonis, with one day for dying, one for searching for the God, and one to proclaim in a dream or viva voce that he is alive. The pharaoh's dreams concern seven-year cycles of plenty and of famine—the cycles to which the myth of Baʿal and the *Legend of Aqhat* allude. Joseph himself symbolizes the cycles: he is freed from jail in the third year, after interpreting the dreams of the butler and baker; he marries and has children, or as the story puts it, "is fruitful," and is personally responsible for the plenteous crops.

The rest of the story describes the reunion of Joseph and his brothers, revolves around the subplot of international trade, and becomes more and more explicit about its symbolism. When Israel hears that there is grain in Egypt, he sends his sons—on the trade route that Joseph traveled as a slave—to buy some, "so that we may live and not die." Joseph accuses them of being spies, which is reasonable because traders often worked as spies for their kings or syndicates, and after swearing several times "by the life of Pharaoh" sends them to jail for three days. It is on the third day, of course, that he makes them a deal, introducing it with: "Do this and you shall live." He sends them away but includes the money they paid in the sacks of grain they bought, as if they had stolen it, which would not have been unusual in such a deal. When they notice it, they exclaim, "What is this that God has done to us?" leaving it narratively uncertain whether Joseph is God or whether, as the brothers report to their father, he is "Lord of the Land" (ʾadonay ha-ʾareṣ), or as he himself said, just someone who fears God.

In the deal they made, they are supposed to return with Benjamin, but Jacob refuses to part with him because he is convinced that Joseph is dead, and if anything happened to Benjamin on the way, it would be the death of him. Judah persuades him in an exchange that is filled with ref-erences to life and death and with allusions to Joseph's exalted or divine status that Joseph is "the man" whose face, like the face of God, they are not allowed to see unless Benjamin is with them. Joseph had asked if his father was still alive, and Judah argues that they must go down to Egypt in order to live and not die. Jacob finally allows them to go; sends with them articles to trade, including gum and myrrh, the spices of love and death; and invokes on them the blessing of El Shaddai, the God of the Beneficent Spirits of the Dead.

When they arrive in Egypt they are afraid, mainly because of the possible consequences for their business. But Joseph holds a feast in their honor, at which Judah retells the gist of the whole story up to this point—that Joseph is presumed dead and that Israel is inconsolable—and concludes by saying that if Benjamin does not come up out of Egypt Jacob will go down into Sheol. In the recognition scene, Joseph explains the myth: God sent him before them into Egypt to preserve life (or, with reference to the Joseph tribes, the Northern Kingdom of Israel, now in exile in Assyria, in order to establish a remnant), and to give life to the survivors; he is a father to Pharaoh, and lord (*'adon*) of his household, and lord (*'adon*) of all Egypt. He has acquired glory in Egypt, and he will provide for them. Joseph, in short, did what Baʿal did: by dying he became the lord of the land of the living and the benefactor of all peoples. When his brothers go up out of Egypt and return to Canaan, they proclaim, "Joseph is alive," and his father says, "It is enough for me that he is alive; I will go and see him before I die."

And later, when their father is dead and the brothers fear that Joseph might turn against them, he assures them by saying ironically, "Do not be afraid; am I in the place of God?" The final gesture in Joseph's assimilation to Adonis is the preservation of his bones in a coffin that is to be transported back to Canaan—a feature of the second day of the Adonis rituals when his body lay in state, and one of the few elements of these rites that are actually mentioned in Phoenician, and specifically, in Byblian inscriptions.

The Byblos Enactments

Adonis was the God of Byblos. He is mentioned in an Amarna letter in which Rib Hadda, the king of Byblos, begs the Pharaoh to send men to remove from the city the belongings of "my Adonis" lest they fall into the hands of the king of Amurru.[82] He is mentioned, along with the Mistress of the city, in a tenth-century Phoenician inscription that reads simply and without the pronominal suffix, "To the Lord (*li-'adon*) and to the Baʿalat (*wa-li-baʿalat*) of Byblos."[83] A late seventh-century ivory casket that was found at Ur (see fig. 1.4)[84] but that is inscribed in a Byblian hand and in the dialect of Byblos reads: "This coffin 'Amotbaʿal, daughter of Pat'isis, servant of our Lord (*'adônēnû*), gave as a gift to Astarte her Mistress. May she bless her. In his days, behold, our Lord himself lay in state in it (*'adônēnû hû'yasod binû*)." The box is small and clearly was symbolic of the rites of Adonis, specifically of the display of his corpse during the two days ("his

---

82. *EA* 84; T. N. D. Mettinger, "Amarna Letter No. 84: Damu, Adonis, and 'The Living God' at Byblos," in *Sefer Moshe. The Moshe Weinfeld Jubilee Volume: Studies in the Bible and the Ancient Near East, Qumran, and Post-Biblical Judaism* (ed. C. Cohen, A. Hurvitz, and S. M. Paul; Winona Lake, IN: Eisenbrauns, 2004) 361–71.

83. P. Bordreuil, "Un inscription phénicienne champlevée des environs de Byblos," *Sem* 27 (1977) 23–27, pl. 5.

84. R. D. Barnett, *A Catalogue of the Nimrud Ivories (with Other Examples of Ancient Near Eastern Ivories)* (London: British Museum, 1957) U 11, p. 226, pl. 132; M. G. Amadasi Guzzo, "Two Phoenician Inscriptions Carved in Ivory: Again the Ur Box and the Sarepta Plaque," *Or* 59 (1990) 58–66; T. C. Mitchell, "The Phoenician Inscribed Ivory Box from Ur," *PEQ* 123 (1991) 119–28.

days") between his death and his return to life. It is also interesting in revealing the intimate ritual connection between Adonis and Astarte and in suggesting the role that was played in these rituals by Astarte's female attendants and by the effigy of the God. This text, like a late text on an altar from Byblos,[85] attaches the first-person-plural pronominal suffix to the title "Lord," because in both there are two votaries: in the altar inscription, the man who dedicated it and his father who built it; in the casket inscription, ʾAmotbaʿal and Astarte.

The Greek Mystique

The use of the first-person suffix shows that one component of the Greek name *Adonis* was "My Lord," ʾadônî in Phoenician. The other component was derived from the Phoenician proclamation that the God who died was now alive: this proclamation is not preserved, but it was borrowed into the Ugaritic epic as "Victorious Baʿal is alive (ḥay), the Princely Lord of the world is (ʾiṯ)." The word "is" in Canaanite or Phoenician is yiš, although the form ʾiš, a reflex of the Ugaritic form, is also found. It occurs in Edomite (*yiš) and Ammonite (*yiš), and both forms are found in Classical Hebrew (yēš and ʾiš). If the Phoenician proclamation was "My Lord is alive, My Lord is," the second clause was ʾadônî + yiš and was pronounced, according to the general rules of contraction, ʾadônîš. Greek Adonis, consequently, was an accurate replica of the Phoenician cultic cry "My Lord is!"

Reflexes of this jubilant cry are found in Phoenician proper names "(My) Baʿal Is" (ʾšbʿl and všbʿl) and "My Lord Baʿal Is" (ʾšdnbʿl). In the other Canaanite languages, the word occurs in names composed of the name of a God, usually Baʿal, sometimes "Lord" or the name of the national God: in Moabite, in the royal name "Chemosh is" (kmsyt), if -yt is the borrowed Aramaic form; in Edomite, in the proper name "My Lord Is" (ʾdnš); in Ammonite, in the name of the king, "Baʿal Is" (bʿls); in Biblical Hebrew, in the name "Baʿal Is" (ʾšbʿl, and ʾšbl); and in Epigraphic Hebrew, possibly in the name "God Is" (ysʾl).

The existential is not used when the brothers proclaim that Joseph, the surrogate Adonis, is alive, but the boy's father does use the opposite term "is not" (ʾênennû) when he declares that Joseph is dead (mēt). Adonis, at any rate, was the Canaanite, originally Byblian, hero who died to become Lord of the Earth and whose Canaanite cultic epithet and lore were borrowed from them, or from the Phoenicians, and proudly displayed in its mystic and completely accurate transliteration.

The Greek legend of Adonis narrates his birth and death and the cycle of his infernal and terrestrial loves. His rituals unfold his untimely death, symbolized in the gardens of his delightfulness and sudden impotence, enacted in rites of mourning and seeking, realized in a vigil while his body or effigy lies in state, dramatized in the Dog Days of Summer, and lasting from the waning of the moon to the first appearance of the new moon at dawn on the third day. Ritual and legend together express the mystery of

---

85. R. Dussaud, "Inscription phénicienne de Byblos d'époque romaine," *Syria* 6 (1925) 269–73, pls. 34–35; C. R. Krahmalkov, "The Byblian Phoenician Inscription of ʿbdʾšmn: A Critical Note on Byblian Grammar," *JSS* 38 (1991) 25–32.

female sexual desire, in which a man plays a brief and ephemeral role. In this way, it may reflect the Babylonian Tammuz traditions in which the Goddess, Inanna or Ishtar, plays the main part, and Tammuz is the necessary foil; rather than the Canaanite cycle of Adonis, in which the God is the predominant figure. However, as the Ugaritic myth of Baʿal indicates by its emphasis on the role of the Goddess ʿAnat, or as the Joseph story allows in the incident of Potiphar's wife and as is witnessed by some biblical texts that allude to the Canaanite customs and later by the general exasperation of Greek men, female desire and sexuality and the stories and customs these engendered seem to be intrinsic to the indigenous Canaanite myth.

The Israel Journals

There are sporadic allusions to elements of the myth in prose and poetic texts of the Bible, but in the works of the prophet Hosea, all the elements of the myth have been transformed into a ballad of love and lust and misplaced trust. These texts are relatively late (late eighth to late sixth century B.C.E.) and exhibit the mood of their own age, but they mean to be records of earlier times and so reflect perceptions of a past that might have informed, interested or amused contemporary readers.

In the Greek legend of Adonis, Aphrodite took the boy when he was still very young, hid him in a chest, and gave the chest to Persephone for safekeeping. When Persephone saw how beautiful he was, she did not want to give him back, but Zeus decreed that each would have him for four months and that the other four months would be spent at the boy's discretion. Chance discovery and shared custody are also themes incorporated into the story of the infant Moses (Exod 2:1–10). When he was born, during the Egyptian regime that condemned all male Israelite children to death, his mother hid him at home for three months; when this was no longer possible, she put him in a reed basket and left him, watched by his sister, in the rushes by the banks of the Nile. Pharaoh's daughter found the basket, and when she saw the child she took pity on him. Thus far the myth, but the Israel version adapts the rest to human interest and to the ongoing story: so at his sister's suggestion—this turns out to be Miriam—Pharaoh's daughter gives him to his own mother to be nursed, and when he had grown, his mother returned him to the Pharaoh's daughter to be raised an Egyptian.

The rituals of Adonis also included the planting of gardens, the rapid growth and sudden desiccation of which symbolized the extravagant and ephemeral nature of desire; or represented the death of Adonis, which, in the narrative version, took place when he was hunting wild boar. There are four texts in the book of Isaiah that refer to the gardens of Adonis, to the rapid growth of the tender shoots doomed to die, to the mourning for them on the day of their death, to vigils at his tomb, and to the custom of sacrificing and eating pork in honor of this alien God (Isa 1:27–31, 17:10–11, 65:1–7, 66:17). An isolated text in Ezekiel describes the women of Jerusalem weeping for Tammuz (Ezek 8:14–15), and the latest of the biblical texts, from an edition of the book of Daniel done in the second century B.C.E., alludes to this God again as "the beloved of women." The jaundiced view of the later biblical writers was inevitable in an increasingly threatened and closed society, and it is amazing that fond memories of the God persisted to the end.

The book of Hosea[86] presents the beliefs and practices of the Kingdom of Israel as a thorough syncretism that confused the God of its ancestors with indigenous Gods, in particular with Adonis, ʾEshmun, and Melqart, the Gods of the Byblians, Tyrians, and Sidonians; and that confounded ortho-dox worship of this God with the primitive cults of the Canaanite Gods El, ʾAsherah, ʿAnat and ʿAstarte. The critique is interesting because it describes contemporary Phoenician religion in fact (but as if it were a corruption of an orthodox Jewish ideal) and because it illustrates that Israel, although it was squeezed between the ethnic and political demands of its Aramean and Judean neighbors, was an accomplished, inland, Canaanite state all of the economic and cultural sympathies of which lay with the Phoenicians.

The book is composed as a ballad in four cantos, each repeating the same basic themes, but with variations and progressions. The first portrays a land's love for Baʿal, describes her death as a failure of the crops, a fertile land become a wilderness, and then gives her new life in an erotic and productive relationship with her God. The second describes the other side of this relationship: it is about a man called *Israel* or *Ephraim,* who is enam-ored of a Goddess and who, in his blind pursuit of her love, is wounded by wild animals and enters the cycle of death on the first day, healing on the second day, and return to life at dawn on the third day. The third portrays the unproductive relations between Ephraim and Baʿal—the man, a farmer distracted by his history into becoming the heifer that must plough the land; the God, appearing in his manifestation as Bull and Calf; the prod-uct of their effort, the altars and baetyls with which the barren land was strewn. The last canto tells the stories of their dead ancestors, who in their lifetimes imitated the rites of Baʿal but did not return to life because, like Baʿal, their God and implacable enemy was Death.

The ballad, therefore, strings out the myth of Baʿal and Death in a de-veloped form that resembles its historicization in the story of Joseph and its ritualization in the legends of Adonis, and every canto is dotted with allusions to elements that are familiar from one story or the other. The bal-lad, however, is an original poetic composition, and the myth and ritual are embedded in a song that is filled out with similar allusions to biblical literature and to contemporary themes and practices. The myth is enacted in its late Canaanite or Phoenician form, without reference to the Syrian version in which Baʿal first defeats the Sea, but in an ironic and peculiarly Israelite version in which the people aspire to the role of God, and their Baʿal becomes the Death of them.

Phoenician inscriptions, Greek legend, and the reflexes of the myth in biblical texts indicate that the legend of Adonis was originally independent of the myth of Baʿal and the Sea, and that the combination of the two at Ugarit can be attributed both to local genius (specifically to the inspiration of Ilimilk) and to the synergy between the city and the Canaanite cities of

---

86. A. Levin, *Hosea and North Israelite Traditions: The Distinctive Use of Myth and Language in the Book of Hosea* (Ph.D. Thesis, University of Toronto, 2009).

the coast at this time. The charm of the myth and its celebrations was its individuality, its adaptability to popular demand, and its suitability to the appreciation by ordinary men and women of their particular life cycles. The myth of Ba῾al and the Sea, by contrast, was suffused with monarchic and nationalist sentiment. In the Ilimilk version, this is expressed in Ba῾al's sudden realization that his dramatization of this primordial cosmic victory and his subjugation of all his enemies ultimately alienated the people for whom what really counted was peace, the absence of conflict, and love flourishing in the land. In the version that migrated from Ugarit to south-central Canaan (the area of later Judah), the combined myth was transformed into the narrative of the choice of a people, the kingship of their God, their escape from death in the wilderness, and their triumphant procession to an abundant and peaceful land. Even this adaptation, however, lays bare the original suture between the two myths by juxtaposing, abruptly and without explanation, boisterous praise of God for victory over the Egyptians at the Sea and bitter complaint at the constant risk of succumbing to thirst or to the bitter waters of death.[87]

Conclusion

To judge from their relations with Ugarit, the cities of Canaan were vigorous commercial and intellectual centers in the thirteenth century. They had a cohesive culture, a consciousness of inclusive ethnic identity, a diversity of political structures, and common threads in the otherwise loose fabric of religious beliefs. They dealt individually with Ugarit, and one or the other of them—probably Byblos, where the alphabet began—was responsible for its alphabetization. With the alphabet went learning and literature, and, at least by the end of the century, Ugarit had incorporated what became the legends of Adonis into its canon. From Ugarit in turn, or from its Syrian neighbors, as early as the twelfth century in the great dispersal of peoples, the Ba῾al epic reached southern Canaan. The legends of Adonis were indigenous to the northerly people who became Israel, and the entire cycle was adopted and adapted in the part of the country that became Judah. It was a fruitful mix, reflecting the diversity of peoples who came to contribute to an always-changing Canaan.

Canaan: The Land and the People, the Townships and Territories

The thirteenth century in Canaan was a mixed blessing. The great port cities of Tyre, Sidon, and Byblos flourished, and they and the other towns along the coast had rich relations with Cyprus. For the whole land, it was a time of more intensive Egyptian tutelage when, after the battle of Qadesh in 1290 B.C.E., Egypt ceded control of Syria to the Hittites and concentrated on its Palestinian holdings. In the interior, there were many economic and social changes and a revival of simple indigenous ways. It was a century

---

87. W. H. Propp, *Water in the Wilderness: A Biblical Motif and Its Mythological Background* (HSM 40; Atlanta: Scholars Press, 1987); idem, *Exodus 1–18* (AB 2; New York: Doubleday, 1999).

in which Canaan moved from a system of city-states to regionalism and ethnic diversity.

Many Egyptians lived in various parts of the country and, besides using local Canaanite products, had luxury goods brought from home or imported from abroad.[88] They had strategically placed residences, military posts, and custom houses on the major routes and in the best farming regions.[89] They settled at Megiddo and Beth Shean in the fertile Jezreel Valley, and from there they controlled the main north–south road, the Via Maris, as well as the east–west routes from coastal sites such as Tel Nami that brought Cypriot and Mycenean perfumes and unguents via Pella, Tell es-Saʿidiyeh, and Deir ʿAlla to North Arabia in exchange for aromatics.[90] There was a large government bureau at Aphek in the Plain of Sharon, and there were Egyptian offices and a Canaanite school at Ashkelon on the southern coastal plain.[91] There were important Egyptian residences at Gezer and Lachish in the lowlands and factories and fortifications at Tell Jemmeh, Deir el-Balaḥ, Tell el-Farʿah, and Tel Seraʿ on the southern border of Canaan.[92] The quality goods, such as alabaster, ivory , and painted pottery that these agents brought from Egypt to grace their living, were soon imitated by local artists, and their Hieratic accounting system was borrowed and maintained for centuries at places like Lachish, Arad, and Tel Seraʿ.[93] Their imports from

88. B. M. Bryan, "Art, Empire and the End of the Late Bronze Age," in *The Study of the Ancient Near East in the Twenty-First Century: The William Foxwell Albright Centennial Conference* (ed. J. S. Cooper and G. M. Schwartz; Winona Lake, IN: Eisenbrauns, 1996) 33–79; C. Lilyquist, "The Use of Ivories as Interpreters of Political History," *BASOR* 310 (1998) 25–33.

89. C. R. Higginbotham, *Egyptianization and Elite Emulation in Ramesside Palestine: Governance and Accommodation on the Imperial Periphery* (Culture and History of the Ancient Near East 2; Leiden: Brill, 2000).

90. On *Megiddo*, see D. Ussishkin, "The Destruction of Megiddo at the End of the Late Bronze Age and Its Historical Significance," *TA* 22 (1995) 240–67. On *Beth Shean*, see P. E. McGovern, S. J. Fleming, and C. P. Swann, "The Late Bronze Egyptian Garrison at Beth Shan: Glass and Faience Production and Importation in the Late New Kingdom," *BASOR* 290–91 (1993) 1–27; A. Mazar, "Beth Shean in the Iron Age: Preliminary Report and Conclusions of the 1990–1991 Excavations," *IEJ* 43 (1993) 201–29; idem, "Four Thousand Years of History at Tel Beth-Shean: An Account of the Renewed Excavations," *BA* 60 (1997) 62–76. On *Tel Nami*, see M. Artzy, "Incense, Camels and Collared Rim Jars: Desert Trade Routes and Maritime Outlets in the Second Millennium," *OJA* 13 (1994) 121–47; idem, "Nami: A Second Millennium International Maritime Trading Center in the Mediterranean," in *Recent Excavations in Israel—A View to the West: Reports on Kabri, Nami, Miqne-Ekron, Dor, and Ashkelon* (ed. S. Gitin; Dubuque, IA: Kendall/Hunt, 1995) 17–40; idem, "Routes, Trade, Boats and 'Nomads of the Sea,'" *MPT*, 439–48; idem, "The Carmel Coast during the Second Part of the Late Bronze Age: A Center for Eastern Mediterranean Transshipping," *BASOR* 343 (2006) 45–64.

91. On the *Plain of Sharon*, see M. Kochavi, "Aphek," *OEANE* 1.147–51. On the *southern coastal plain*, see L. E. Stager, "Ashkelon," *NEAEHL* 1.103–12; J. Huehnergard and W. van Soldt, "A Cuneiform Lexical Text from Ashkelon with a Canaanite Column," *IEJ* 49 (1999) 184–92.

92. *NEAEHL* 1.343–47 (Deir el-Balaḥ); 2.441–44 (Tell el-Farʿah South); 2.496–506 (Gezer); 2.667–74 (Tell Jemmeh); 3.897–911 (Lachish); 4.1329–35 (Tel Seraʿ).

93. J. Weinstein, "The Collapse of the Egyptian Empire in the Southern Levant," in *The Crisis Years: The 12th Century B.C.—From beyond the Danube to the Tigris* (ed. W. A. Ward and M. Sharp Joukowsky; Dubuque, IA: Kendall/Hunt, 1992) 142–50, esp. pp. 143–44; M. Gilula, "An Inscription in Egyptian Hieratic from Lachish," *TA* 3 (1976) 107–8; O. Goldwasser, "The Lachish Hieratic Bowl Once Again," *TA* 9 (1982) 137–38; idem, "Hieratic Inscriptions from Tel Seraʿ in Southern Canaan," *TA* 11 (1984) 77–93, pls. 4–7. The early sixth-century Hebrew ostraca from Arad contain hieratic numbers and hieratic signs for commodities, and one (#34) is composed

Fig. 1.4. Ivory box from Ur with Phoenician inscription (BM WA 125028). © The Trustees of the British Museum.

Cyprus and the Aegean were shipped to Egyptian emporia at Tell Abu Ha-wam (1 Kgs 9:10–14), Shiqmona, Tel Mor, and Tell el-ʿAjjul[94] while the ports of ʿAkko, Tel Nami, Joppa, and Ashkelon, which also were connected to Cyprus and the Aegean, were Canaanite and were dedicated to agricultural exports and to the luxury requirements of the indigenous population.[95]

The thirteenth century, however, was also a time of growing ethnic aware-ness—Canaanite ethnicity being defined by its openness and inclusiveness. The local calendar was standardized by borrowing month names, as many as six of them, from the Hurrians.[96] Agriculture became popular and presti-gious as cash crops for Egyptian personnel, local consumption, and export, firing the economy. People began to move from the cities to small towns or homesteads. Housing became more uniform, woods were cleared and hill-sides were terraced, cisterns were waterproofed, and food storage facilities

completely in hieratic: cf. Y. Aharoni, *Arad Inscriptions* (Jerusalem: Israel Exploration Society, 1981).

94. J. Balensi, "Revising Tell Abu Hawam," *BASOR* 257 (1985) 65–74; E. B. French, "Tracing Exports of Mycenaean Pottery: The Manchester Contribution," in *Bronze Age Trade in the Mediter-ranean* (ed. N. H. Gale; Jonsered: Åströms, 1991) 121–25; G. Gilmour, "Mycenaean IIA and IIIB Pottery in the Levant and Cyprus," *RDAC* (1992) 113–28.

95. J. Johns, "Tell el-ʿAjjul," *OEANE* 1.38–41; M. Dothan, "Acco," *NEAEHL* 1.17–24; W. G. Dever, "ʿAkko,"*OEANE* 1.54–55; M. Artzy, "Nami: A Second Millennium International Maritime Trading Center in the Mediterranean," in *Recent Excavations in Israel: A View to the West. Reports on Kabri, Nami, Miqne-Ekron, Dor and Ashkelon* (ed. S. Gitin: Dubuque, IA: Kendall/Hunt, 1995) 17–40; C. J. Bergoffen, "Some Cypriote Pottery from Ashkelon," *Levant* 20 (1988) 161–68.

96. R. R. Stieglitz, "The Phoenician-Punic Menology," in *Boundaries of the Ancient Near East-ern World: A Tribute to Cyrus H. Gordon* (ed. M. Lubetski, C. Gottlieb, and S. Keller; JSOTSup 273; Sheffield: Sheffield Academic Press, 1998) 211–21. Some of these Hurrian month names were used at Ugarit in the thirteenth century, and all are found in the records of Alalakh in the eigh-teenth and fifteenth centuries B.C.E., when the population was predominantly Hurrian: J.-P. Vita, "Zur Menologie und zum Kalender von Alalah," *AoF* 27 (2000) 296–307. The names were more likely a legacy of the Hurrian population in Canaan than a borrowing from the Syrian calendars.

(notably jars and silos) were developed.[97] Mesopotamian law codes were studied and adapted to the needs of this new rural economy,[98] and police duties were distributed to local militias. Unlike Syria, or Ugarit in particular, where the people generally were not permitted to move from their towns and their taxable occupations, Canaanites enjoyed mobility and travel and did not have to pay property taxes to a central urban administration. There were visitors and permanent residents from Cyprus at Tel Zeror and Tel Michal, Mycenean settlers at Dan, pilgrims from overseas who visited the cult place at Tel Mevorakh, and Canaanite farmers and assorted traders and copper smiths who traveled along the trade routes to the central Jordan Valley and to the Transjordanian plateau.[99] Big cities, such as Shechem and Hazor,[100] which were not of interest to the Egyptians, were destroyed by accident or on purpose and, because they were no longer pivotal in the organization of the land or in international trade, were not rebuilt.

Gone with these large cities, especially Hazor, were foreign-language scribal schools and immemorial religious and cultural connections with Mesopotamia. Canaan, with agriculture dominating the domestic and foreign markets and monarchies crumbling, was becoming a disappointing outlet for imported luxury goods. Metalworking was in the hands of landed immigrants and of refugees from Syria and Anatolia, urbanism was being replaced by incipient tribalism, women were being absorbed into the family and away from entertainment and the arts into menial service, and internationalism was overtaken by regionalism.

---

97. J. A. Calloway, "A New Perspective on the Hill Country Settlement of Canaan in Iron Age I," in *Palestine in the Bronze and Iron Ages: Papers in Honour of Olga Tufnell* (ed. J. N. Tubb; London: Institute of Archeology, 1985) 31–49; V. Fritz, "Conquest or Settlement? The Early Iron Age in Palestine," *BA* 50 (1987) 84–100; G. London, "A Comparison of Two Contemporaneous Lifestyles of the Late Second Millennium B.C., *BASOR* 273 (1989) 37–55; E. Bloch-Smith and B. Alpert Nakhai, "A Landscape Comes to Life: The Iron Age I," *NEA* 62/2 (1999) 62–92, 101–27.

98. R. Westbrook, "Biblical and Cuneiform Law," *RB* 92 (1985) 247–64; idem, *Studies in Biblical and Cuneiform Law* (Paris: Gabalda, 1988).

99. M. Kochavi, "Tel Zeror," *IEJ* 15 (1965) 253–55; idem, "Tel Zeror," *OEANE* 5.389–90; Z. Herzog, G. Rapp Jr., and O. Negbi, eds., *Excavations at Tel Michal, Israel* (Tel Aviv: Institute of Archaeology, 1989); A. Biran, "The Collared-Rim Jars and the Settlement of the Tribe of Dan," in *Recent Excavations in Israel: Studies in Iron Age Archaeology* (ed. S. Gitin and W. G. Dever; AASOR 49; Winona Lake, IN: Eisenbrauns, 1989) 71–96. E. Stern, "Tel Mevorakh," *NEAEHL* 3.1031–35; O. Negbi, "Were There Sea Peoples in the Central Jordan Valley at the Transition from the Bronze Age to the Iron Age?" *TA* 18 (1991) 205–43; E. J. van der Steen, "Aspects of Nomadism and Settlement in the Central Jordan Valley," *PEQ* 127 (1995) 141–58; idem, "The Central East Jordan Valley in the Late Bronze and Early Iron Ages," *BASOR* 302 (1996) 51–74; idem, "Pots and Potters in the Central Jordan Valley," *ADAJ* 41 (1997) 81–93; C. J. Chang-Ho, "A Note on the Iron Age Four-Room House in Palestine," *Or* 66 (1997) 387–413; L. G. Herr, "Tell el-ʾUmayri and the Madaba Plains Region during the Late Bronze–Iron Age I Transition," *MPT* 251–64.

100. L. E. Tombs, "Shechem: Problems of the Early Israelite Era," in *Symposia Celebrating the Seventy-Fifth Anniversary of the American Schools of Oriental Research, 1900–1975* (ed. F. M. Cross; Cambridge, MA: American Schools of Oriental Research, 1979) 69–83; P. Bienkowski, "The Role of Hazor in the Late Bronze Age," *PEQ* 119 (1987) 50–61; A. Mazar, "Temples of the Middle and Late Bronze Ages and the Iron Age," in *The Architecture of Ancient Israel from the Prehistoric to the Persian Periods* (ed. A. Kempinski and R. Reich; Jerusalem: Israel Exploration Society, 1992) 161–87; Y. Yadin, "Hazor," *NEAEHL* 2.594–603; A. Ben-Tor, "The Fall of Canaanite Hazor: The 'Who' and 'When' Questions," *MPT*, 456–67.

This political and cultural parting of the Egyptian and Canaanite ways of life had begun to intensify at the end of the thirteenth century. In the last decade of the century, Pharaoh Merneptah (1212–1202 B.C.E.), in the context of his victory in Libya, describes the current situation in Canaan and the eastern regions of the empire. This concluding segment of the monumental text is composed in poetic couplets, and these are arranged in concentric order: [101]

> The princes are prostrate saying, "Peace!"
> not one among the Nine Bows raises his head.
> Tehenu is captured, Ḥatti is pacified,
> Canaan is seized by every evil.
> Ashkelon is carried off, Gezer is captured,
> Yenoʿam is made as non-existent.
> Israel is laid waste, its seed is not,
> Hurru has become a widow because of Egypt.
> All the lands together are at peace,
> everyone who was restless has been subdued.

The concentric order gives the text its own principles of interpretation. In the first couplet, it is the princes who lie prostrate, not daring to move and begging for peace. The standard portrait of the Pharaoh striding among his prostrate enemies and clubbing to death any who budged is the compelling image of their docility. The corresponding fifth couplet explains that their lands had been restless but that their allegiance was restored by force, and they are now at peace. The second couplet lists these lands. Tehenu is Libya, whose recent defeat was the occasion for this memorial inscription. Ḥatti is the Hittite Kingdom of Syria, which Merneptah's father, Ramesses II, confronted at the battle of Qadesh. The battle was a standoff, but Ḥatti is said to have been "pacified" because it did establish political boundaries between the two countries.

Canaan is the Egyptian province, and the evils that befell its territory are the subject of the lavish imagery in the fourth couplet: Canaan, because of its Hurrian heritage, is called Hurru and because of its relations with Israel is pictured as a woman; and because Israel has been ruined and has no seed to sow, it is seen as a widow without children or a barren land without produce. The hyperbole of these poetic couplets is tempered, however, by the third couplet, which has no poetic match but records what is meant in fact by the evil that seized Canaan and the desolation that swept over Hurru. Three cities are listed on a south-to-north route that might be followed by an invading Egyptian army: first is Ashkelon, which in fact was besieged

---

101. G. W. Ahlström and D. Edelman, "Merneptah's Israel," *JNES* 44 (1985) 59–61; G. W. Ahlström, "The Origin of Israel in Palestine," *SJOT* 2 (1991) 19–34; J. J. Bimson, "Merenptah's Israel and Recent Theories of Israelite Origins," *JSOT* 49 (1991) 3–29; M. G. Hasel, "*Israel* in the Merneptah Stela," *BASOR* 296 (1994) 45–61; idem, *Domination and Resistance: Egyptian Military Activity in the Southern Levant, ca. 1300–1185 B.C.* (Leiden: Brill, 1998) 194–217, 257–71; D. B. Redford, "The Ashkelon Relief at Karnak and the Israel Stela," *IEJ* 36 (1986) 188–200, pls. 22–26; L. E. Stager, "Merenptah, Israel and Sea Peoples: New Light on an Old Relief," *ErIsr* 18 (Avigad Volume; 1985) 56*–64*; F. J. Yurco, "Merenptah's Canaanite Campaign," *JARCE* 23 (1986) 189–215; B. G. Davies, *Egyptian Historical Inscriptions of the Nineteenth Dynasty* (Jonsered: Åström, 1997) 173–87; A. F. Rainey, "Israel in Merenptah's Inscription and Reliefs," *IEJ* 51 (2001) 57–75.

by Merneptah; next is Gezer, which belonged to Egypt and was an administrative center, the allegiance of which was critical; then there is Yeno'am, a town at the southern end of the Sea of Galilee and a frequent subject of Egyptian reprisals. The land of Canaan invited flights of lyric fancy, but the urban realities could be a great deal of trouble.

The balance of the parts, in short, indicates that Canaan at the end of the thirteenth century was slipping away from Egyptian control. Ashkelon once had provided Egypt with supplies but now, as in the Amarna period, apparently was aligned with Gezer in its revolt against Egypt. More than this, as the distinction between Israel and Hurri implies, the population of Canaan was being reorganized along regional and tribal lines, with (1) an agricultural economy, as the equivalence between Israel's devastation and its lack of seed suggests; and with (2) a base in small towns, supposing that Yeno'am was an Israelite town whose sack was the essence of Israel's being laid waste, and thus radically withdrawn from Egypt's however-shaky, urban-based control of the country. It was this "restlessness" that was the expression of the new, differentiated, intently self-sufficient Canaan, and the loss of the "peace" imposed by Egypt would characterize the centuries to come.

The Twelfth Century

The twelfth century in Canaan was marked by further isolation of the main coastal cities and increasing fragmentation of the inland regions. This was due to mass migration, lack of contact with Cyprus and the Greek world, the failure of the Egyptian administrative system, the proliferation of languages and religious beliefs, the lack of Classical Egyptian and Mesopotamian education, and competing social, economic, and cultural developments in neighboring countries.

The main intrusive force in Canaan was the Sea Peoples. These were not a unified group but a conglomerate of individuals or families from the western Mediterranean, the Aegean, western Anatolia, and Cyprus. They came by land, together with refugees from the collapsing kingdoms in Ḫatti and Syria; and by sea, with the travelers, traders, mercenaries, and pirates who knew the coastal waterways and the sea lanes from Cyprus to the Levant. They came in small numbers: letters from contemporary rulers of Cyprus, Ugarit, and Ḫatti mention sighting one of their fleets, which consisted of 20 ships; an attack by 7 of their ships that had a brief but strangely disruptive effect; a kidnapping by the Sikalayu, "who live on ships"; and the impossible dream of repulsing all these intruders with a fleet of 50 or even 100 ships,[102] which in fact was more than all these kingdoms together could muster. The problem, however, was not all that serious, but it was awkward or even unmanageable in Ugarit, and kingdoms like it, where townships did not enjoy mobility and where the collapse of one or more and the dispersal of their citizens could easily undermine the whole system.

The Sea Peoples came in waves, or continuously over time, and by about the mid-twelfth century were numerous enough to build five cities in the

---

102. *CAT* 2:47.

southern coastal plain; take up residence farther south in the Egyptian towns of Deir el-Balaḥ, Tel Seraʿ, Tell Jemmeh, and Tel el-Farʿah South; penetrate eastward to the lowlands at Gezer, Timnah, and Beth Shemesh; establish outposts at Tel Qasile and ʿAzor in the Plain of Sharon just north of their territory; and settle in the major ports from ʿAkko to Dor. The Egyptians maintained their control of Megiddo and Beth Shean but had left the country by the end of the century.

The Canaanites whom the Sea Peoples displaced (coastal sites such as ʾAchzib, Tel Mevorakh, Tel Michal, and Joppa were abandoned) founded new settlements such as Tel Zeror, ʿIzbet Sartah (where there is an early twelfth-century Canaanite inscription), or Aphek farther from the coast, at Taanach in the Valley of Jezreel; and in the hill country and the Lower Galilee. The northern coastal cities of Tyre, Sidon, and Byblos thrived on competition with the Sea Peoples—in importing fish, for instance, and in exporting agricultural products—and were challenged by the landward constraints of proliferating self-sufficient townships, but they found the sophisticated and urbane newcomers totally congenial.

It was a time of deep change, rather than great turmoil, and for these northern ports in particular, whose physical integrity and political institutions were not threatened, it was a chance to draw accurate maps of the Mediterranean world and to establish new long-range and short-range commercial networks. The travel, maps, and commerce are attested by the proliferation of Canaanite storage jars at Kition, Hala Sultan Tekke, and Enkomi in eastern Cyprus and at Maa-Palaekastro on the southwestern tip of the island.

The distribution of the Sea Peoples through the land reflected a common strategy and diverse origins. All the good ports south of Tyre, Sidon, and Byblos belonged to them: to the Sherden at ʿAkko; the Sikalayu at Dor; and to some elements of the Philistines, a conglomerate of Aegean and Anatolian settlers, at Ashkelon. The rest of the southern coastal plain was taken over by the Philistine confederates who settled at Gaza, Gath, and Ashdod, and specifically by the Danuna from Cilicia who took and rebuilt Ekron and established outposts at Timnah and Beth Shemesh, on the road leading to the interior through the Valley of Sorek. Other Sea Peoples occupied strategic locations on the peripheries of the Jezreel Valley and of the plains of Sharon and ʿAkko. Canaan was partitioned by this occupation of the land, and the diversity of its origins and interests led to a further segmentation of the once fairly undifferentiated Egyptian province centered on urban installations and engineered by international trade.

The Sea Peoples came to Canaan because it was a land of plenty, relatively unpopulated, traditionally open to immigrants, and on the verge of Egypt, which as Egyptian records show, was at least for some of these peoples their final destination. They did not come as conquerors, and the places that were destroyed were those that were under Egyptian control and either refused to yield territory to them or freely subverted Egyptian administration by admitting or welcoming the newcomers. Local nonbelligerents coexisted with them or followed the trend to autonomy and self-sufficiency.

Individual Sea Peoples or stragglers who had not brought their families on their migrations are portrayed on the Medinet Habu monuments, when they were driven out of the Delta that they had tried to settle and exploit, with the Syrian women they married on their overland trek or with the Canaanite women who married them when they settled in the land or with the children who were born to them while they were living in Palestine.[103]

These were clever, resilient, and adaptable people who brought with them a distinctive culture that influenced their new world and who easily blended into the Canaanite ways that typify the people from Tyre, Sidon, and Byblos. It was an urban culture, dominated by princes or kings who were ranked among their peers, characterized by large public buildings with hearths, and by domestic quarters with bathrooms.[104] They were coppersmiths, and more importantly, they knew how to work iron.[105] They had ivory workshops, the furniture inlays of which followed Egyptian decorative models, and the practical products from them, such as combs, pins, and cosmetic boxes, were traditional Canaanite.[106] They had distinctive pottery and a peculiar diet that included pork and a surfeit of beef, and they could take care of their own needs with crafts such as weaving and skills in the olive industry, but they were not particularly interested in agriculture.

They cherished the heroic ideals, such as the exaltation of Goddesses and women and, as might be extrapolated from much later biblical traditions, delighted in the glory of single combat and the virtues of demigod warriors. They adapted too quickly to their physical environment for others to imitate their material goods—no one else, for instance, made Philistine pottery—but their way of life was an inspiration, or maybe a scandal, to their neighbors. It is not possible to distinguish one Sea People culture from another in any detail, but their diverse origins and ethnic attachments eventually become apparent in their maintenance or abandonment of their heritage—religion, architecture, onomasticon, government—and of their ties to their homelands.

Sea People, particularly Philistine, territory redefined the land of Canaan. The eastern border of Canaan, which was formally at the river Jordan but which, under Egyptian administration, in fact had extended into the Jordan Valley and parts of Transjordan, was now closed at the river, isolating the Canaanites who had settled beyond it.[107] The extension had

103. D. Sweeney and A. Yasur-Landau, "Following the Path of the Sea Persons: The Women in the Medinet Habu Reliefs," *TA* 26 (1999) 116–45.

104. V. Karageorghis, "Hearths and Bathtubs in Cyprus: A 'Sea Peoples' Innovation?" *MPT*, 276–82; T. Dothan, "The Aegean and the Orient: Cultic Interactions," in *Symbiosis, Symbolism, and the Power of the Past: Canaan, Ancient Israel, and Their Neighbors from the Late Bronze Age through Roman Palaestina* (ed. W. G. Dever and S. Gitin; Winona Lake, IN: Eisenbrauns, 2003) 189–213.

105. T. Dothan, "Bronze and Iron Objects with Cultic Connotations from Philistine Temple 350 at Ekron," *IEJ* 52 (2002) 1–26.

106. D. Ben-Shlomo and T. Dothan, "Ivories from Philistia: Filling the Iron Age I Gap," *IEJ* 56 (2006) 1–38.

107. L. G. Herr, "The Settlement and Fortifiication of Tell al-ʿUmayri in Jordan during the LB/Iron I Transition," in *The Archaeology of Jordan and Beyond. Essays in Honor of James A. Sauer* (ed. L. E. Stager, J. A. Greene, and M. D. Coogan; Studies in the Archaeology and History of the

been motivated by trade (north–south from Gilead to Egypt, and east–west from Arabia to the sea) and perhaps by politics (prevention of Hittite and Syrian interference in the area), but commercial and political collapse had made it redundant.

In the twelfth century, these Transjordanian Canaanites either moved back across the river or melded with the emerging and already vigorous communities of Ammon and Moab. In the south of Canaan, in the lower part of the region designated as Hurri in the Merneptah Stele, there arose an incipient Midianite hegemony in a loose tribal syndicate that comprised Amalekites, Ishmaelites, Hagarites, and the tribes and clans that, along with Moabites, eventually would be counted among the antecedents of biblical Judah.[108] In the southern highlands, in what would become the heart of Judah, large towns clustered between Jerusalem and Hebron and thinned out toward Beersheba. The country was still ethnically Canaanite—that is, an indigenous population of mixed origins—but the people were regrouping along family, clan, and tribal lines, and allegiances were being forged that eventually would lead to nationalities and to the breakdown of Canaanite identity.

Conclusion

In the twelfth century, Tyre, Sidon, and Byblos were the only cities in Canaan (although Jerusalem may have to be included with them) to maintain their urban status, their monarchies, their territorial integrity, and their social and economic stability. They became demographically isolated and, due to the changes that took place in the rest of the land, isolated from the interior and cut off from their vast and freewheeling Canaanite heritage. The clue to their ongoing success was supplied by the Sea Peoples, and they set off on their Phoenician destiny by coveting and researching the places from which this extraordinary mismatch of peoples had come.

The Eleventh Century B.C.E.

The eleventh century was unstable and formative. There were nomads, guerrillas, and vagabonds, new groupings and alliances of peoples, new religions and the inevitable wars they inspired, a lull in creativity in a population gradually dulled by waves of refugees and immigrants and by the self-absorption that these inspired—a final fragmentation of the land of Canaan and of the deep inclusive sentiments it once inspired. The Syrian states that survived the overthrow of the Hittite Empire were governed by Neo-Hittite and Amorite rulers but were being infiltrated by upstart Arameans. Egypt was out of the picture, and Transjordan was coalescing into separate regions with self-government and diverse ties to Israel and Hurri. Canaan became limited, in effect, to the territories of the northern coastal cities—Tyre, Sidon, and Byblos—and these began to release themselves

Levant 1; Winona Lake, IN: Eisenbrauns, 2000) 167–79; L. G. Herr and D. R. Clark, "Excavating the Tribe of Reuben," *BAR* 27/2 (2001) 36–47, 64, 66.

108. G. N. Knoppers, "'Great among His Brothers,' but Who Is He? Heterogeneity in the Composition of Judah," *Journal of Hebrew Scriptures* 3 (2000) 1–2; idem, "Intermarriage, Social Complexity, and Ethnic Diversity in the Genealogy of Judah," *JBL* 120 (2001) 15–30.

from the growing inertia by turning to the Mediterranean world whence the Sea Peoples had come.

The economy of these three cities had shallow roots in their inland markets and satellite towns. Byblos maintained relations with the villages in Lebanon and Anti-Lebanon. Sidon, which was aligned with other Canaanite coastal towns such as Sarepta, kept its old connections with the cities of southern Amurru and the northern Syrian coast. Tyre had commercial establishments in the Galilee and in the plain of ʿAkko that were traditionally ascribed to the peripheral tribes of Israel, and it did business with Canaanite towns, which eventually were incorporated into Israelite territory. The three cities did not amalgamate or generally act in concert, even though mainland Tyre, not the island redoubt, belonged on and off to Sidon because, according to one classical source, after being sacked by marauding Sea Peoples on their way to Palestine, it had been resettled by Sidonians.[109]

Tyrian presence at coastal and inland sites is marked by typically "Phoenician" pottery (distinguished by its forms and decorations) usually found together with Philistine or imported Cypriot wares in otherwise indigenous contexts.[110] At ʾAchzib, eleventh-century tombs contained Cypriot pottery and local imitations of Cypriot wares, as well as typical Phoenician assemblages. The eleventh-century port of ʿAkko was managed by Sea Peoples and frequented by Tyrians and illustrates the early stages in the gradual process from Canaanite to Phoenician: in the thirteenth and early twelfth centuries, there were Canaanite pottery and metalworking shops and installations for a small-scale purple dye industry;[111] in the eleventh century, they carved pictures of their boats along the shipping lanes from ʿAkko and Tel Nami to Kition;[112] in the tenth century, at a nearby inland site, a wealthy Phoenician was buried with his Cypriot Black-on-Red pottery, locally made wares, his iron knives, and a fluted bronze bowl inscribed in eleventh-century script with the name of his father and Canaanite grandfather.[113]

At Tell Keisan, an unfortified satellite town about eight kilometers inland from the port, there was Phoenician Bichrome pottery and at least

109. H. J. Katzenstein, *The History of Tyre: From the Beginning of the Second Millennium B.C.E. until the Fall of the Neo-Babylonian Empire in 539 B.C.E.* (2nd ed.; Beer-sheva: Ben-Gurion University Press, 1997) 59–60.

110. A. Mazar, "Comments on the Nature of the Relations between Cyprus and Palestine during the 12th–11th Centuries B.C.," in *The Civilizations of the Aegean and Their Diffusion in Cyprus and the Eastern Mediterranean, 2000–600 B.C.* (ed. V. Karageorghis; Larnaca: Pierides Foundation, 1990) 94–103; idem, "The 11th Century B.C. in the Land of Israel," in *Proceedings of the International Symposium: Cyprus in the 11th Century B.C.* (ed. V. Karageorghis; Nicosia: University of Cyprus, 1994) 39–57.

111. M. Dothan, "The Significance of Some Artisans' Workshops along the Canaanite Coast," in *Society and Economy in the Eastern Mediterranean (c. 1500–1000 B.C.)* (ed. M. Heltzer and E. Lipiński; Louvain: Peeters, 1988) 295–303.

112. M. Artzy, "Mariners and Their Boats at the End of the Late Bronze Age and the Beginning of the Iron Age in the Eastern Mediterranean," *TA* 30 (2003) 231–46.

113. Y. Alexandre, "A Fluted Bronze Bowl with a Canaanite–Early Phoenician Inscription from Kefar Veradim," in *Eretz Zafon: Studies in Galilean Archaeology* (ed. Z. Gal; Jerusalem: Israel Antiquities Authority, 2002) 65–74.

one jar imported from Kouklia (Palaepaphos) in western Cyprus, as well as scarabs, scaraboids, a cylinder seal with Egyptian motifs, and seals with representations of the Tyrian Gods Ba⁽al, Reshep, and Astarte.[114] The outpost at Tel Kabri north of ⁽Akko and about five kilometers inland is also characterized by its Phoenician pottery.

In northern Galilee, the small settlements were distinguished from one another by the predominance in each of either native Galilean or intrusive Tyrian storage and transport jars.[115] At Dan, where there were installations for the smelting of bronze, there were the same types of Tyrian storage jars as well as Cypro-Phoenician Bichrome wares.[116] At Tel Hadar, on the eastern shore of the Sea of Galilee, there was a tripartite pillared store or marketplace and an adjacent granary: the local pottery indicates that it was an outlet for the Kingdom of Geshur, but the Phoenician pottery and one Euboean bowl suggest that trade was at least partly in the hands of Tyrians.[117] The Tyrians, therefore, were at home not only in the great ports but in these nondescript inland towns and marketplaces where they acquired the goods and raw materials for which they became famous. To judge from their dealings with the Kingdom of Geshur and with Galilean Israel, it appears that they preferred to do business with established political systems rather than with individual entrepreneurs or isolated markets.

The Jezreel Valley marked the southern limit of Tyrian influence. Here, and farther south, the land still belonged to Canaanites, Israelites, or Sea Peoples in the eleventh century, and the scattered Tyrian goods, almost always mixed with more numerous Cypriot wares, reflect renewed traffic from Cyprus. Megiddo was essentially Canaanite in the eleventh century, but its peaceful dealings with Philistines and Phoenicians is marked by specimens of their pottery. Beth Shean is still influenced by its Egyptian heritage, and so there are traces of Sea Peoples' material culture, but the population is basically Canaanite or specifically Israelite. The port at Tell Abu Hawam, just north of Carmel, was built and rebuilt in the eleventh century, but it remained in the hands of descendants of the Sea Peoples. Dor, south of Carmel, was a Sea People, or Siculi, settlement that around

---

114. O. Keel, "La glyptique," in *Tell Keisan: Une cité phénicienne en Galilée* (ed. J. Briend and J.-P. Humbert; Paris: Gabalda, 1980) 257–99; idem, "La glyptique de Tell Keisan (1971–1976)," in *Studien zu den Stempelsiegeln aus Palästina/Israel, Band III: Die Frühe Eisenzeit—Ein Workshop* (ed. O. Keel, M. Shuval, and C. Uehlinger; Göttingen: Vandenhoeck & Ruprecht, 1990) 163–260: #1 (pp. 165–66), #9 (190–94), #10 (194–204), #11 (204–6), #14 (210–17).

115. R. Frankel, "Upper Galilee in the Late Bronze–Iron I Transition," in *From Nomadism to Monarchy. Archaeological and Historical Aspects of Early Israel* (ed. I. Finkelstein and N. Na⁾aman; Jerusalem: Israel Exploration Society, 1994) 18–34; E. Bloch-Smith and B. Alpert Nakhai, "A Landscape Comes to Life: The Iron Age I," *NEA* 62 (1999) 62–92, 101–27, esp. pp. 78–81.

116. A. Mazar, "The 11th Century B.C. in the Land of Israel," in *Proceedings: Cyprus in the 11th Century B.C.* (ed. V. Karageorghis; Nicosia: University of Cyprus, 1994) 39–57, esp. p. 45.

117. Cf. M. Kochavi, "The Eleventh Century BCE Tripartite Pillar Building at Tel Hadar," *MPT*, 468–78; J. N. Coldstream, "The First Exchanges between Euboeans and Phoenicians: Who Took the Initiative?" *MPT*, 353–60, esp. pp. 357–59; A. Fantalkin, "Low Chronology and Greek Protogeometric and Geometric Pottery in the Southern Levant," *Levant* 33 (2001) 117–25; G. Kopcke, "1000 B.C.E.? 900 B.C.E.? A Greek Vase from Lake Galilee," in *Leaving No Stones Unturned: Essays on the Ancient Near East and Egypt in Honor of Donald P. Hansen* (ed. E. Ehrenberg; Winona Lake, IN: Eisenbrauns, 2002) 109–17.

the middle of the eleventh century renewed its contacts with Cyprus. By the end of the century, as Phoenician and Cypriot wares clearly attest, Dor was being assimilated to the coastal culture of Canaan.[118]

Inland sites such as Tel Qiri, ʿEn Hagit, and Tel Yokneʿam[119] were typical late Canaanite unfortified settlements whose shopping in Dor is revealed by traces of Phoenician and Sea Peoples wares. All the other important places farther south on the coastal plain and in the foothills were Sea Peoples or Philistine settlements (smaller sites such as those in the vicinity of Philistine Gezer kept their local Canaanite color) and had little or no trace of Phoenician and specifically Tyrian materials.[120]

Sidon's primacy and peculiarity among the cities of Canaan is recognized in later biblical texts but, although its cultural and commercial interests extended north to the former lands of the Hittites, its territory was confined to its immediate coastal environs. According to the biblical genealogical fiction (Gen 10:15–19; 1 Chr 1:15–16),[121] Canaan's children included Sidon as his firstborn, as well as Heth, the land of the Hittites. This is an odd combination, but the seemingly impossible relationship between the Canaanite city and the Indo-European land is explained in the succeeding text. First, however, Sidon and Heth are set aside, and the genealogy continues with the list of the children of Canaan, the aboriginal inhabitants of the land of Canaan: Jebusites, who are known from biblical texts to have had their capital in Jerusalem; Amorites who in earlier centuries (but more recently and most urgently after the fall of Ugarit at the beginning of the twelfth century) had drifted into Canaan—one of these was a Hittite charioteer from Ugarit who escaped the commotion in Syria and settled in Megiddo;[122] Girgashites, who are regularly included in lists

---

118. E. Stern, "New Evidence from Dor for the First Appearance of the Phoenicians along the Northern Coast of Israel," *BASOR* 279 (1990) 27–34; idem, "Phoenicians, Sikils, and Israelites in the Light of Recent Excavations at Tel Dor," in *Phoenicia and the Bible* (ed. E. Lipiński; Studia Phoenicia 11; Louvain: Peeters, 1991) 85–94; idem, "Tel Dor: A Phoenician-Israelite Trading Center," in *Recent Excavations in Israel: A View to the West* (ed. S. Gitin; Dubuque, IA: Kendall/Hunt, 1995) 81–93; idem, "The Relations between the Sea Peoples and the Phoenicians in the Twelfth and Eleventh Centuries BCE," *MPT*, 345–52. The restored Cypriot traffic has been attributed by A. Gilboa to the initiative of Sea People inhabitants of Dor who had migrated from Cyprus and who began renewing family connections in the eleventh century: "New Finds at Tel Dor and the Beginning of Cypro-Geometric Pottery Import to Palestine," *IEJ* 39 (1989) 204–18; idem, "Iron I–IIA Pottery Evolution at Dor: Regional Contexts and the Cypriot Connection," *MPT*, 413–25. Of the very little Cypriot pottery at Dor, some pieces may be specifically from Kition: cf. J. Yellin, "The Origin of Some Cypro-Geometric Pottery from Tel Dor," *IEJ* 39 (1989) 219–22.

119. S. Wolff, "An Iron Age I Site at ʿEn Hagit (Northern Ramat Menashe)," *MPT*, 449–54; *NEAEHL* 3.805–11 (Yokneʿam); 4.1228–29 (Tel Qiri).

120. On *Philistine Gezer*, see A. Shavit, "Settlement Patterns in the Ayalon Valley in the Bronze and Iron Ages," *TA* 27 (2000) 185–230. On *Tyrian materials*, a little eleventh-century Cypro-Geometric pottery has been found at ʾAchzib (a juglet in a grave), Tell Abu Hawam (several pieces), Shiqmona (two items), Tel Zeror (a juglet in a grave), Tel Qasile (four bowls), Tel Jerishe (one bowl), Tell ez-Zuwayid (one item), Tell el-Farʿah South (one item), and Tell Beit Mirsim (one item): A. Gilboa, "New Finds at Tel Dor and the Beginning of Cypro-Geometric Pottery Import to Palestine," *IEJ* 39 (1989) 204–27.

121. E. A. Speiser, *Genesis* (AB 1; New York: Doubleday, 1964) 69–70; C. Westermann, *Genesis* (BKAT 1/1; Neukirchen-Vluyn: Neukirchener Verlag, 1974) 694–99.

122. A Hittite seal made at Ugarit and found at Megiddo preserves his name and rank: C. E. Suter, "The Hittite Seal from Megiddo," *AuOr* 17–18 (1999–2000) 421–30.

of the aboriginal inhabitants of Canaan, and whose eponymous ancestor "Girgaš" (*grgš*) is often celebrated in the Phoenician onomasticon; Hivites, who raised livestock (their name, *Ḥiwwî*, is derived from the verbal root *ḥwy*, "give life, raise") and lived in tents (in Hebrew, *ḥawwot*),[123] and who derived their pseudo-ethnic status in this list from their fundamental, ubiquitous, and timeless importance to the entire population of Canaan.

Then the genealogy returns to Sidon and Heth and explains their apparently odd conjunction by listing the peoples in the former Hittite Empire and the places in the Neo-Hittite realm with which Sidon had particularly important and longstanding relations: the ʿArqites, inhabitants of the city of ʿArqa on the border between Lebanon and Syria, which is known from the fourteenth-century Amarna letters as an unwilling ally of the king of Amurru, and from written and archaeological sources of the ninth century and later as a client of Sidon and a member of the South Syrian coalition against Assyria; the Sinites, from the Kingdom of Siyannu just south of Ugarit, whose principal port at Tell Sukas was a meeting place for Phoenicians and Greeks in the ninth century and later; the Arvadites, people from the island of Arvad, who were forever in league with Sidon; the Semarites, from the city of Sumur, the capital of Amurru in the Late Bronze Age, known as Tell Kazel in the archaeological record, which eked out an existence in the twelfth and eleventh centuries but began to flourish in the ninth century, when it enjoyed renewed contacts with Sidon; and finally, the Hamathites, from Hamath on the Orontes, the principal city of the Neo-Hittite conglomerate, on which Sidonians and Byblians depended for food supplies and for access to the North Syrian and Neo-Hittite markets.[124]

The genealogy concludes with an allusion to the fact that Canaanites (that is, Sidonians and the other groups that were included in this Canaanite family) traveled or migrated to these places. It finishes as it began by mentioning Sidon, but now as the northern border of the land of

---

123. L. E. Stager, "Archaeology, Ecology, and Social History: Background Themes to the Song of Deborah," in *Congress Volume: Jerusalem 1986* (ed. J. A. Emerton; VTSup 40; Leiden: Brill, 1988) 221–34, esp. p. 225.

124. *EA* 62:13, 17, 22; 72:4; 75:26; 88:6; 100; 103:12, 36; 140:10; 239:15. The personal name *ʿrqy* "[The] ʿArqite," is engraved in alphabetic script on a fourteenth-century cylinder seal: see F. M. Cross, "The Evolution of the Proto-Canaanite Alphabet," *BASOR* 134 (1954) 15–24, esp. p. 21 n. 24.

J.-P. Thalmann, "Tell ʿArqa (Liban Nord), Campagnes I–III (1972–1974), Chantier I: Rapport préliminaire," *Syria* 55 (1978) 1–152, pls. 1–4; idem, "Les niveaux de l'âge du Bronze et de l'âge du Fer à Tell ʿArqa (Liban)," *Atti* 1, 1.217–21; idem, "Tell ʿArqa, de la conquête assyrienne à l'époque perse," *Transeu* 2 (1990) 51–57.

P. J. Riis, *Sukas I: The North-East Sanctuary and the First Settling of Greeks in Syria and Palestine* (Publications of the Carlsberg Expedition to Phoenicia 1; Copenhagen: Munksgaard, 1970); J. Lund, *Sukas VIII: The Habitation Quarters* (Publications of the Carlsberg Expedition to Phoenicia 10; Copenhagen: Munksgaard, 1986).

F. Briquel-Chatonnet, "Arwad cité phénicienne," in *Alle soglie della classicità. Il Mediterraneo tra tradizione e innovazione: Studi in onore di Sabatino Moscati* (ed. E. Acquaro; Pisa: Istituti editoriali e poligrafici internazionali, 1996) 1.63–72.

Cf. L. Badre et al., "Tel Kazel, Syria: Excavations of the AUB Museum, 1985–1987: Preliminary Reports," *Berytus* 38 (1990) 9–124.

B. Cifola, "Ashurnasirpal II's 9th Campaign: Seizing the Grain Bowl of the Phoenician Cities," *AfO* 44–45 (1997–98) 156–58.

Canaan, which extends from there southward to Gerar and Gaza, eastward
to the Dead Sea, and thence northward to Dan but certainly does not include Heth or the Hittites (Gen 10:18b–19). This genealogy was composed
by a sixth-century historian, but it is a good summary of what is known
from other sources about Sidon's relations with the cities of Syria at the beginning of the Iron Age—in some cases as early as the twelfth or eleventh
century; in others not until about the ninth century B.C.E.

Sarepta, halfway between Sidon and Tyre, was one of Sidon's more important mainland allies. In the thirteenth and early twelfth centuries, the
quantities of Mycenean wares that it accumulated distinguished it from
Tyre, just 20 kilometers to the south, which specialized in trade with Cyprus. There were no more imports in the later twelfth and eleventh centuries, but the city became a thriving industrial center producing such items
as dye, olive oil, pottery, and jewelry for the other towns in the kingdom.
Bichrome painted, burnished, and Red Slip fine wares, which eventually
were distinctively "Phoenician," were becoming progressively more popular in the local markets. By the end of the eleventh century, deprived of
creative influence from abroad, the coastal Canaanite spirit had learned
to express its genuine individuality and character. There may have been
other coastal centers that responded to Sidon's creative initiatives (Ushu
in the vicinity of Tyre is regularly associated with Sidon in earlier and later
texts)[125] and it is likely that individual Sidonian craftsmen had settled inland at Dan,[126] but it seems that Sidon in the eleventh century was content
to ply the trade routes along the coast of Syria, either directly or with a
relay at Kition in Cyprus.

Tyre's overseas interests in the eleventh century were primarily with
southwestern Cyprus and from there to the western Mediterranean. Precious goods, packaged in Bichrome or Red Slip jars and bottles, were deposited in the tombs of rich Aegean immigrants at Amathus.[127] The tombs of
warriors at Palaepaphos (Kouklia) contained Tyrian and Euboean pottery
assemblages that resembled the wares in use at this time in Tyre.[128] The Tyrians had not come to settle at these places in Cyprus but were on their way
via Crete to Sardinia and the western Mediterranean. This route is marked,
however randomly, by a Phoenician memorial inscription erected by one
of their captains at Nora in southern Sardinia, by an Iberian bronze obelus
in the tomb of one of his compatriots at Amathus, and by a Sardinian bird-
shaped askos in the tomb of a Phoenician goldsmith at Khaniale Tekke near
Knossos in Crete.[129] These overseas interests were impelled by Sea Peoples

---

125. Katzenstein, *History of Tyre*, index, s.v. "Ushu."

126. A. Kuschke, "Sidons Hinterland und der Pass von Gezin," *ZDPV* 93 (1977) 178–97,
pls. 14–17; A. Biran, *Biblical Dan* (Jerusalem: Israel Exploration Society, 1994) 125–57.

127. Cf. P. M. Bikai, "The Phoenician Pottery," in *La Necropole d'Amathonte, Tombes 113–367:
Céramiques non Chypriotes* (ed. V. Karageorghis, O. Picard, and C. Tytgat; Nicosia: Department of
Antiquities, 1987) 1–19, pls. 1–7. J. N. Coldstream, "Greek Geometric and Archaic Imports from
the Tombs of Amathus II," *RDAC* (1995) 199–214.

128. Cf. P. M. Bikai, "The Imports from the East," in *Palaepaphos-Skales: An Iron Age Cemetery
in Cyprus* (ed. V. Karageorghis: Konstanz: Universitätsverlag, 1983) 396–406.

129. On *Sardinia*, see F. M. Cross, "Phoenicians in the West: The Early Epigraphic Evidence,"
in *Studies in Sardinian Archaeology, II: Sardinia in the Mediterranean* (ed. M. S. Balmuth; Ann Arbor:
University of Michigan Press, 1986) 117–30, esp. pp. 120–23; on *Amathus*, see J. N. Coldstream,

lore and supplied by Tyrian investments in the cities and villages of coastal and mainland Canaan.

Byblos in the eleventh century is known mainly from the Egyptian report of Wenamun on his journey to Lebanon to get lumber for the ceremonial ship of Amun.[130] The journey took place early in the eleventh century (ca. 1075 B.C.E.), and the report is full of incidental information on Tyre, Sidon, and Byblos and the coastal cities of Palestine at this time. Wenamun traveled from Thebes to Tanis in the Delta, where he boarded a merchant ship of Levantine design (*mnš*),[131] whose captain was Canaanite or Philistine. It landed at Dor, a city of the Siculi Sea People and its home port, where Wenamun, because he was an Egyptian envoy traveling on one of their ships, was warmly received with gifts of bread, wine, and beef. He was due to make two other stops before the ship reached Tyre, but the gold and silver he carried to do business with these places, which are identified only by the names of their leading merchants, were stolen by one of the crew.

The ruler of Dor, whose name apparently was Canaanite, refused to take responsibility for the theft, and Wenamun after a week of waiting and much aggrieved by this obstinacy, left Dor on the Siculan ship that had brought him from Egypt. It sailed to Tyre, where it must have spent some of the four months that it took him to reach Byblos, and from there directly to his destination. Before disembarking at Byblos, Wenamun, to reimburse himself and to force the Siculi to search for the thief and return his goods, stole money belonging to the owner of the ship. The ship at last departed but, because he lacked letters of credence and was traveling in a foreign ship with a foreign crew, he was not officially welcomed and had to remain in the harbor until, in an ecstatic seizure inspired by the God Amun, one of the king's attendants revealed that the image of the God that Wenamun had brought from Egypt should be brought to the citadel from the lower city.

Wenamun leaves the image where it is and goes up to the palace himself, and the rest of the report claims to be verbatim about the haggling between him and Zakarbaʿal, the king of Byblos, with Wenamun attempting to persuade him to donate the wood for the ship of Amun, and Zakarbaʿal appealing to custom and commercial realities to insist on being paid for it. Wenamun claims that he is on official business and, technically, arrived on an Egyptian ship because, he argues, any ship that is hired by Egypt is by

---

"Status Symbols in Cyprus in the Eleventh Century BC," in *Early Society in Cyprus* (ed. E. Peltenburg; Edinburgh: Edinburgh University Press, 1989) 325–35; on a *Phoenician goldsmith at Khaniale Tekke,* see Lucia Vagnetti, "A Sardinian Askos from Crete," *British School at Athens* 84 (1989) 355–60, pl. 52.

130. J. A. Wilson, "The Journey of Wen-Amon to Phoenicia," *ANET* 25–29; H. Goedicke, *The Report of Wenamun* (Baltimore: Johns Hopkins University Press, 1975); M. Green, "*m-k-m-r* und *w-r-k-t-r* in der Wenamun-Geschichte," *ZÄS* 113 (1986) 115–19; A. Egberts, "The Chronology of *The Report of Wenamun,*" *JEA* 77 (1991) 52–67; idem, "Hard Times: The Chronology of 'The Report of Wenamun' Revised," *ZÄS* 125 (1998) 93–108; A. Scheepers, "Anthroponymes et toponymes du récit d'Ounamon," in *Phoenicia and the Bible* (ed. E. Lipiński; Studia Phoenicia 11; Louvain: Peeters, 1991) 17–83; M. Lichtheim, "The Report of Wenamun," *COS* 1.89–93; B. Sass, "Wenamun and His Levant: 1075 BC or 925 BC?" *Ägypten und Levante* 12 (2002) 247–55.

131. L. Basch, "Le navire *mnš* et autres notes de voyage en Égypte," *The Mariner's Mirror* 64 (1978) 99–123.

that fact Egyptian. But Zakarba'al asks for his letters of credence and replies that he himself has 20 ships in the port of Tanis and 50 ships in the port of Sidon, all of which do business with Egypt but none of which are by that fact Egyptian. Wenamun says that the former kings of Byblos always supplied the lumber gratis, but Zakarba'al, citing the records of these earlier transactions preserved on the papyrus scrolls in the royal archives, shows him that the Egyptian requests for wood were always accompanied by Egyptian ships laden with precious gifts. Wenamun argues that the blessing of Amun, whom Zakarba'al himself recognizes as the supreme Lord of Egypt and the original source of the literacy and learning that Egypt transmitted to Byblos, would be better than money; nevertheless, he relents and has a royal scribe summoned to write to the king of Egypt requesting payment, and by return ship receives gold and silver, fine linen, 500 rolls of papyrus, leather, ropes, lentils, and fish.

Zakarba'al then commissions 300 men with 300 oxen to cut the trees, but they have to wait until winter in order to slide them through the snow to the seashore. Wenamun finally persuades Zakarba'al that, instead of insisting on more money, it would be better to have his benefactions and the blessings of Amun recorded in a memorial stele, and to this the king gladly agrees. The report ends with Wenamun about to sail to Egypt on Byblian ships, when 11 ships of the Siculi from Dor appear in the harbor demanding his arrest. The king and the city assembly refuse and, warning him that the Siculi might try to catch him on the open seas, send Wenamun on his way. The convoy is blown off course to Alashiya in Cyprus, now a town of brigands and pirates who threaten to confiscate the cargo and kill him and the Byblian crews, until Wenamun persuades their princess that the king of Byblos would take revenge on her crews and ships, and she sends him away in peace. The report ends on this note—with Byblos as always supplying Egypt's needs and protecting its interests in the Levant.

The report, obliquely in the course of its narrative, reveals details of Byblian religion, politics, and business procedures and alludes to facets of Byblos's relations with Egypt, Palestine, and the coast of Canaan.[132] The Sea People of Dor are on good terms with Egypt and, as the name of their ruler suggests,[133] they have already begun to assimilate to the Canaanite way of life. Byblian ships, chartered in Tanis and Sidon, seem to do the bulk of Phoenician trade with Egypt: although Tyre is also mentioned, its dealings are with the remnant of the Sea Peoples in Dor. Trade is governed by formalities such as written requests for items, gifts to initiate bargaining in good faith, and an agreed price on delivery of the goods. Byblos is proud of its Egyptian cultural and religious heritage, imports papyrus from Egypt, has Egyptians at the court, scribes who can read and write Egyptian, and an Egyptian songstress to console Wenamun in his distress over the Siculan demand for his arrest. Despite these ties, the city, which excava-

---

132. J. M. Weinstein, "Egyptian Relations with the Eastern Mediterranean World at the End of the Second Millennium BCE," *MPT*, 188–96.

133. The most plausible interpretation of the name Beder is Canaanite or Phoenician *bad'il, "By-the-hand-of-'El." It is conceivable, however, that it represents *bidal, "trader," the Ugaritic equivalent of Akkadian *tamkāru*, and was a nickname given to him by his Tyrian associates.

tions confirm comprised a lower port town and an upper city, is completely independent, governed by a king and an assembly, and powerful enough to intimidate the people of Alashiya.

Although independent and relatively powerful in the early eleventh century, Byblos lost some of its prestige as the century progressed and Egyptian influence and authority continued to wane. Its joint commercial ventures with Sidon, to which the Report of Wenamun alludes, were prompted by the advantages of pooling their specialized and limited resources and facilitated by compatible market preferences and lifestyles (both were drawn to the indigenous population of Syria, and both had populist monarchic regimes), and their cooperation seems to have been fairly intensive in the early Iron Age, or perhaps even earlier. In these enterprises, Sidon may have contributed skill in bronze and steel working, and Byblos expert stone masonry, and both would have received in return raw goods such as iron, copper, ivory, and precious stones.

Their chief export, however, as in earlier centuries, and the skill for which Byblos in particular was famous was the ability to read and write. Good evidence for this is the alphabetization of the Arameans,[134] the Neo-Hittites, and eventually, the Greeks, with whom Byblians and Sidonians came in contact in North Syria and Anatolia. The earliest Aramaic inscriptions are from the ninth century, but one of these, the monumental text from Tell Fekherye, dated to about the middle of that century, is written in an eleventh-century script. This anomaly, due to deliberate archaizing (the scribe also knew both Classical Babylonian and contemporary Assyrian) is evidence that the Arameans who settled in the region in the twelfth century[135] had learned the alphabet by the eleventh century and that, like Ugaritic and Greek scribes before and after them (who knew their letters both in their archaic and in their modern form) went to schools that taught contemporary handwriting and also preserved the paradigmatic tables from which they had first learned to write and read. Sidonians were not colonizers, and Byblians when they colonized kept their language, culture, and spiritual traditions but adopted the way of life of the people among whom they settled. Thus there is usually no trace of them except what they took to their graves or what their hosts had learned from them. The Greeks learned their alphabet and their literature, the Neo-Hittites learned these

---

134. At Megiddo, a Late Bronze or early Iron (ca. 1250–1150 B.C.E.) tomb contained a ring belonging to the deceased and inscribed with his name, "ʾAdon, son of Shemaᶜ" (*ʾdn b šmᶜ*): see É. Puech, "Un anneau inscrit du Bronze Récent à Megiddo," in *Ki Baruch Hu: Ancient Near Eastern, Biblical, and Judaic Studies in Honor of Baruch A. Levine* (ed. R. Chazan, W. W. Hallo, and L. H. Schiffman; Winona Lake, IN: Eisenbrauns, 1999) 51–61. The father's name is not uncommon and is fairly widely distributed, but the son's name and the form of the word "son" (*b*, rather than *bn*) suggest his Byblian origin. This ʾAdôn could have been a scribe or tutor who moved from Byblos to teach in the local school, like *Krkr* the famous rhapsode (Hebrew *Kalkol*), who is named on three of the Megiddo ivory plaques and who, along with Heman and Dardaᶜ, was a legendary wise man of Canaan (1 Kgs 5:11).

135. H. Sader, "The 12th Century B.C. in Syria: The Problem of the Rise of the Arameans," in *The Crisis Years: The 12th Century B.C. from beyond the Danube to the Tigris* (ed. W. A. Ward and M. Sharp Joukowsky; Dubuque, IA: Kendall/Hunt, 1992) 157–63; M. R. Adamthwaite, "Ethnic Movements in the Thirteenth Century B.C. as Discernible from the Emar Texts," *AbrN* Supplement 5 (1995) 91–112.

and their language as well, but the Arameans (the pen really is mightier than the sword) took up nothing but their script and ultimately transformed and totally undermined the Assyrian Empire.

Inland Canaan in the eleventh century, apart from the Galilee which had regular social and economic relations with Tyre, was separated from the coastal cities and was being configured by immigrants, adventurers, and vagabonds. The evidence for this vibrant and unsettled time is derived from archaeological surveys and excavations, from a few inscriptions, and from biblical texts. The impression is partial and cumulative and open to conjecture, but nevertheless not without interest.

The inscriptions are personal names carved into the flange of bronze arrowheads to mark ownership of the arrow ("arrow of . . ."). There are about 50 that are inscribed and many that are plain. One is from southern Lebanon, and 5 inscribed arrowheads along with more than 20 that were not inscribed are from an isolated cache found near Bethlehem. The rest were acquired on the antiquities market and have no provenance.[136] Most can be dated by their scripts to the eleventh century, but a few are slightly earlier or later.

There are about 10 with only the names of individual men: 3 of these, with the name ʿAbdlabiʾt, "Servant of the Lioness," an epithet of the Goddess Asherah, are from near Bethlehem, and a 4th with the name ʿAbdlaʾit may contain a scribal error and be the same person or may contain an alternate epithet of this Goddess, "The Mighty One," and be from the same place. Of the other names, 1 is unique and may also be from the vicinity of Bethlehem (yšʾ); it could even be "Jesse," who was the father of 8 sons, including David, whose 3 oldest brothers joined Saul's band of heroes. One name is unusual (pʾb, "Decree of the Father"),[137] and 1 (wry), possibly Egyptian or Philistine, resembles in its unusual initial consonant the names of 2 Sea Peoples merchants (wrt and wrktr) whom Wenamun was to have visited on his way up the coast to Byblos.

There are 12 arrowheads with a name and patronymic: one of the patronymics identifies the owner as being from ʿAkko (ʿky). There is 1 with a man's name and his brother's name ("Arrow of May-Baʿal-Establish, brother of Name-of-Baʿal"). There are 14 with a name followed by a title or rank: 2 belonged to the king of Amurru, 2 belonged to officers (rb and rb ʾlp), 1 to an officer who worked for a company of merchants (rb mkrm), and 10 belonged to retainers (ʾiš, "man of") or servants (mšq, "cupbearer") of other named men. There are 4 that mention, or suggest, the warrior's place of origin or of employment: 1 was in the service of a Tyrian (ʾš špṭ ḥṣr, "the man of Shopet the Tyrian"; see fig. 1.5), and another served a man with the same name (ʾš špṭ, "the man of Shopet"), but he is not expressly called a Tyrian;

---

136. Forty-eight were listed in R. Deutsch and M. Heltzer, *Windows to the Past* (Tel Aviv–Jaffa: Archaeological Center, 1997) 9–24. Others were published subsequently by P. K. McCarter Jr., "Two Bronze Arrowheads with Archaic Alphabetic Inscriptions," *ErIsr* 26 (Cross Volume; 1999) 111–12; by P. Bordreuil and F. Briquel-Chatonnet, "Une nouvelle flèche avec inscription proto-phénicienne," *Sem* 49 (1999) 194–95; and by H. Sader, "Une pointe de flèche phénicienne inédite du Musée National de Beyrouth," *Actas* 4, 1.271–80.

137. It was considered spurious by F. M. Cross, "The Arrow of Suwar, Retainer of ʿAbday," *ErIsr* 25 (Aviram Volume; 1996) 9*–17*, esp. pp. 13*–14*.

Fig. 1.5a. Inscribed arrowhead ("The Man of Shophet, the Tyrian"), reverse (BLMJ 0868). Reproduced courtesy of the Bible Lands Museum Jerusalem. Photo by: Zeʾev Radovan.

Fig. 1.5b. Inscribed arrowhead, obverse.

1, who was the cupbearer of ʿAbday, was from Kition in Cyprus, 1 was a Sidonian, and another's name (*ʿbdny*) suggests that he was from ʿAbdon in the territory that was assigned to Asher but that actually belonged to Tyre. There are 5 arrowheads, the personal names of which allude to the origin of their owners: 1 (*ywḥnn*, "Yawḥanan") is composed of the name *Yahweh* in its North Israelite form (*yw*) and indicates that it belonged to a warrior from that region; the other 4 have names that are typical of Byblos because they are composed of *Baʿal* and *Adonis* or because they display morphology peculiar to that dialect: "son" is *b-* instead of *bn*, the final *-y* of weak roots is not elided and yields the name *bnyʾ* while the same name contracts and is pronounced *bnʾ* on an arrowhead from another place.

There are arrows belonging to fathers and their sons. Zimmaʾ and Ben ʿAnat each had two sons with inscribed arrows.[138] There is also an instance of a warrior named ʿAbday who was the leader of a larger band: he had his own inscribed arrow, was attended by a cupbearer from Kition who also had an arrow with his own name, and was accompanied by five sons who also owned inscribed arrows, and by three retainers, one of them with a Hurrian name, who were similarly outfitted.[139]

The names of these men are theophoric or hypocoristic—that is, they contain or omit the name of the man's patron God. Most of the hypocoristics contain verbal roots alluding to an activity or quality of the unnamed God ("helping, hastening to help, judging, satisfying, exalting"), but some suggest the attitudes or characteristics of the man ("servant, princely, warlike, burly, circumspect"). The majority of the theophoric names include Baʿal ("Baʿal-Remembers, Client-of-Baʿal, Name-of-Baʿal, My-God-Is-Baʿal"), but there are references to a familial God ("My-God-Is-My-Kin," "Brother"), to the Warrior Goddess Astarte, to ʿAnat ("Son of ʿAnat" [*bn*

---

138. The arrowhead with the name of one of the sons of Zimmaʾ is spurious according to Cross (ibid., 13*).

139. R. Deutsch and M. Heltzer, "ʿAbday on Eleventh-Century B.C.E. Arrowheads," *IEJ* 47 (1997) 111–12.

'*nt*]), to divinized "Kingship" (*mlk*), to transcendent Justice (*ṣdq*), and to the olden Gods El, Dagon, and Yahweh.

Some of these men were from warrior families. Many were associated, in one way or another, with Tyre, Sidon, and Byblos or with one of their towns. All were professionals and were distinguished by their rank: a king, officers, commandos (the *bn* '*nt*, "corps of 'Anat"), volunteers, subordinates, or their retainers. They were few, a select group that was identified by its insignia (inscribed arrowheads) and that was bound by membership in an elite but now defunct class of chariot warriors once renowned for its skill with the bow.[140] They cherished the heroic ideal of the brave and invincible individuals whose tactics had been rendered obsolete by the introduction of armor and of soldiers armed with javelins, spears, lances, and swords:[141] this change in weaponry and ideology is described in biblical texts referring to this interim and uncertain time in the eleventh century when brave bands of the disaffected and riffraff, who knew nothing about chariot warfare but were impelled by seemingly noble causes and certainly hopeless odds gathered with their clubs, swords, and projectiles around brave leaders. These were Phoenicians, inspired by their Canaanite past, interested in trade and the good life, sociable but not belligerent, whose arrowheads symbolized the end of the old and the beginning of a new era.

Archaeological excavations and surveys confirm the loss of northern inland Canaan to the cause of the coastal cities. The southern part of Canaan, which would become the land of Judah, was sparsely settled in the eleventh century, and the important places south of Hebron were not yet ethnically or politically distinct: Tell Beit Mirsim, southeast of Lachish, was Canaanite, but Lachish with its Egyptian connections was abandoned; Tel Masos was a center of trade; Arad was just a small unfortified settlement;[142] and Beersheba did not become a town until the tenth century. The northern part of inland Canaan, pretty well filled with irregular small settlements, was beginning to show signs of its distinctiveness (in settlement patterns, diet, pottery, and architecture) within the basic Canaanite matrix,[143] but there are no signs of prosperity, of wealth, or of intersite commerce and no trace of the minimal trade with Tyre that characterized the Galilee at this time. The south was stagnant, the north had taken itself out of the mainstream, and the Phoenician coastal cities, which were about to inaugurate a new era of international relations, would not flourish until Israel and Judah were established as chiefdoms, kingdoms, or national states.

---

140. J. P. Brown, "Archery in the Ancient World: 'Its Name Is Life, Its Work Is Death'," *BZ* 37 (1993) 26–41. There are about 30 Babylonian arrowheads from a slightly later period (ca. 1025–950 B.C.E.), most of which were inscribed with royal names, and all of which were trophies rather than ready weapons: B. Sass, "Inscribed Babylonian Arrowheads of the Turn of the Second Millennium and Their Phoenician Counterparts," *UF* 21 (1989) 349–56.

141. R. Drews, *The End of the Bronze Age: Changes in Warfare and the Catastrophe ca. 1200 BC* (Princeton: Princeton University Press, 1993).

142. I. Finkelstein, "Arabian Trade and Socio-Political Conditions in the Negev in the Twelfth–Eleventh Centuries BCE," *JNES* 47 (1988) 241–52; Y. Aharoni and M. Aharoni, "Arad," *NEAEHL* 1.75–87; D. Ussishkin, "Lachish," ibid., 3.897–911.

143. A. Zertal, "The Iron Age I Culture in the Hill-Country of Canaan: A Manassite Perspective," *MPT*, 238–50.

Conclusion

The eleventh century finally sealed the character of the Phoenician cities. They were cut off from the interior of Canaan, related at random to the
Philistine ports and confederations to the south, and encouraged to con-
sider trans-Mediterranean trade. Tyre traveled to southwest Cyprus, Crete,
and via Sardinia, to the West. Byblos, with Sidon, went to Egypt, Syria,
and Anatolia. Sidon was beginning to call at Kition in Cyprus, and individual Sidonian craftsmen and their families began to settle overseas and
in open cities such as Dan. Their literature has not survived, at least not
directly, but they brought their script, their language, and their learning
to the Arameans, the Neo-Hittites, and the Greeks, and the Greeks at least
were proud to display in their own works their great familiarity with these
congenial aristocrats of the seas.

Tyre, Sidon, and Byblos

In the tenth-century mainland, Canaan continued the process of regional and ethnic diversification. The Philistines, now recalling their common origins, formed a coalition or brotherhood of city-states. Towns of the
northern sector, which had flourished under Syrian or Egyptian hegemony,
were collected into an incipient Israelite economy. The southern regions
with the connivance of local potentates in Transjordanian Moab and Ammon were rallied under local heroes. A terrain with only topographical
distinctiveness began to be identified by its borders, and a people of a once
common stock and single aspiration was promoted by the emerging classes
among its more recent settlers into both linguistically and ethnically
separate countries. The cities and countries expressed their identity and
self-consciousness in local, distinctive pantheons and cults. International
trade, inspired and mostly controlled by the cities of the coast, depended
on regional organization and transregional cooperation and drove a wedge
between the more and less open societies. It was all a strictly Canaanite
venture, unfazed by the influence or oversight of Egypt and Mesopotamia,
unparalleled in Syria, and beset by tribal and postcolonial ambitions—a
new direction that outdid aggression and foreign interference until Canaan
was incorporated into the Assyrian Empire.

The civilization and culture of Canaan in the tenth century were shaped
by the enterprise of Tyre, Sidon, and Byblos—directly by the genius of their
people and indirectly through the way of life they fostered in the areas
under their immediate or persistent influence, and in the places brought
together in the new spirit of cooperation. The impact of these burgeoning metropolises on separate towns and townships becomes particularly
evident in the local and regional imitations or transformations of their
artistic, economic, and practical examples and in their own eagerness to
borrow from their partners or even to adopt their unique appreciation of
life in this newly expanding world.

Tyre, Sidon, Byblos: Mainland Interests

At Tyre itself, most of the ceramic imports at the end of the eleventh
century were Cypriot White Painted and Bucchero (Black Slip) wares, and

these continued with gradual abatement through the tenth and into the early ninth century.[144] Locally made pottery—sometimes (burnished) Red Slip or Bichrome—was also brought to the Tyrian stations at Joya and Khirbet Silm to the east of the city; to Qasmieh, Sarepta, Qraye, and Khalde on the coast but in the territory of Sidon north of the Litani River; southward to Tell Abu Hawam on the Bay of ʿAkko; and inland mainly to Hazor and Megiddo.[145] The open shapes (jugs, plates, bowls, cooking pots, and craters) were for ordinary use and, because they were not particularly elegant or nice, were not distributed to these places for their quality but were brought along by Tyrians for their homeliness and familiarity. The closed shapes (a few juglets and many storage or transport jars) were exported for their contents, which were probably produced in the region or further south on the mainland.

In Lower Galilee, in the plain of the Bay of ʿAkko between ʿAkko and Carmel, in the land traditionally assigned to the biblical tribe of Asher, the approximately 15 new villages that were settled in the tenth century seem to corroborate the biblical witness to the prosperity that this region enjoyed from its association with the sea,[146] specifically its involvement in the Tyrian trade network where it sold its oil, wheat, wine, and other produce to buy the tools (manufactured most likely in Cyprus) on which its agricultural ventures depended. The port at ʿAkko was not busy in the tenth century but persisted as one of the trading stations scattered along the coast, and its diminished importance is reflected in the very modest installations at Tell Keisan, ancient ʿAchshaph, which was its principal supplier.[147] Its artistic traditions, as revealed by the amulets and seals discovered at the site, are distinctive: unlike Tell Abu Hawam to the south and ʾAchzib to the north, where the Egyptianizing motifs favored by Tyrian artisans predominated, ʿAkko is distinguished by its preference for informal human and animal figures, singly or in combination, and by its relative lack of interest in religious motifs—an exception being a scaraboid depicting the Goddess Astarte on horseback.[148]

Tell Abu Hawam, across the bay from ʿAkko at the mouth of the river Kishon, with its impressive pillared storage and market facilities, was ev-

144. P. M. Bikai, *The Pottery of Tyre* (Warminster: Aris & Phillips, 1978) 57, 74.

145. S. V. Chapman, "A Catalogue of Iron Age Pottery from the Cemeteries of Khirbet Silm, Joya, Qraye and Qasmieh of South Lebanon," *Berytus* 21 (1972) 55–194; Bikai, *The Pottery of Tyre*, 20–53; C. Briese, "Früheisenzeitliche Gemalte phönizische Kannen von Fundplätzen der Levantenkuste," *HBA* 12 (1985) 7–118, esp. pp. 40–56.

146. Z. Gal, "The Lower Galilee in the Iron Age II: Analysis of Survey Material and Its Historical Interpretation," *TA* 15–16 (1988–89) 56–64; R. R. Stieglitz, "Hebrew Seafaring in the Biblical Period," *MHR* 15 (2000) 5–15.

147. M. Dothan, "ʿAkko," *NEAEHL* 1.17–23; J. Briend and J.-B. Humbert, eds., *Tell Keisan (1971–1976): Une cité phénicienne en Galilée* (Paris: Gabalda, 1980) 190–96; J.-B. Humbert, "Keisan, Tell," *NEAEHL* 3.862–67.

148. O. Keel, *Corpus der Stempelsiegel-Amulette aus Palästina/Israel von den Anfängen bis zur Perserzeit: Katalog, Band I: Von Tell Abu Farag bis ʿAtlit* (Göttingen: Vandenhoeck & Ruprecht, 1997) 530–637, ##1–297; see Tell Abu Hawam, pp. 6–8; ʾAchzib, pp. 20–76, ##1–62. The simplicity and informality of the ʿAkko designs is found on a series of blue frit seals from a Phoenician workshop at Amathus in Cyprus: see A. T. Reyes, "A Group of Cypro-Geometric Stamp Seals," *Levant* 25 (1993) 197–205.

idently very active at this time.[149] This port seems to have depended on inland supply centers, such as Khirbet Rosh Zayit,[150] ancient Cabul, on the eastern edge of the plain of ʿAkko, where there was a central administrative building as well as pillared markets and a complex of olive oil presses. In the main building, there were more than 300 storage jars of local ware, some of which contained residues of olive oil, wheat, or wine, meant for export, along with imported Cypriot Black-on-Red and White Painted, and Phoenician Bichrome, Red Slip, and Plain ware bowls, jugs, and juglets and jars destined for sale on the local market. There was a Tyrian seal with the usual Egyptian motifs that were hollowed and accented in the typically Tyrian inlay technique, along with weights of various sizes, which might be expected in a wholesale and retail outlet, and there were numerous iron implements (plows, sickles, axes, and a saw) for sale to the agricultural community. This was not a rich or impressive region, just a busy, industrious agglomeration that made money doing business with Tyre, and that comprised the 20 or so towns that, in accordance with biblical territorial claims were properly Israelite but were ceded to Tyre in the tenth century in exchange for the gold and timber it supplied to the temple in Jerusalem, and that, given their precarious economic situation, seemed to Tyre to be barely adequate payment (1 Kgs 9:10–14).

The coastal region from Carmel to the territory controlled by the Philistine city-states in the south is dotted with traces of distinctive Tyrian, Sidonian, and Byblian influence in the tenth century. The sites were trading posts catering to general needs and interests or dedicated ports and factories with specialized routes and products.

At Shiqmona, on the Carmel headland, there was a factory producing purple dye at least in the ninth and perhaps as early as the tenth century.[151] The dye does not seem to have been used on the spot and probably was shipped to Tyre for use in the textile industry.

Dor, about 30 kilometers to the south, is thought to have come under Israelite control in the tenth century, but the material evidence makes it clear that the town was a Canaanite and Sea People settlement and a regular port of call for ships from Cyprus and Sidon.[152] Tenth-century structures include

149. J. Balensi, "Revising Tell Abu Hawam," *BASOR* 257 (1985) 65–74; idem and M. D. Herrera, "Tell Abu Hawam 1983–1984: Rapport préliminaire," *RB* 92 (1985) 82–128; J. Balensi, M. D. Herrera, and M. Artzy, "Tell Abu Hawam," *NEAEHL* 1.7–14; L. G. Herr, "Tripartite Pillared Buildings and the Market Place in Iron Age Palestine," *BASOR* 272 (1988) 47–67.

150. Z. Gal, "Loom Weights or Jar Stoppers?" *IEJ* 39 (1989) 281–83; idem, "Khirbet Rosh Zayit—Biblical Cabul: A Historical-Geographical Case," *BA* 53 (1990) 88–97; idem, *Lower Galilee during the Iron Age* (trans. M. Reines Josephy; ASOR Dissertation 8; Winona Lake, IN: Eisenbrauns, 1992) 47–53; idem, "Hurbat Rosh Zayit and the Early Phoenician Pottery," *Levant* 24 (1993) 173–86; idem, "A Phoenician Bronze Seal from Hurbat Rosh Zayit," *JNES* 53 (1994) 27–31; Z. Gal and R. Frankel, "An Olive Oil Press Complex at Hurbat Ros Zayit (Ras ez-Zetun) in Lower Galilee," *ZDPV* 109 (1993) 128–40; R. Kletter, "Phoenician (?) Weights from Horvat Rosh Zayit," *ʿAtiqot* 25 (1994) 33–43.

151. N. Karmon and E. Spanier, "Remains of a Purple Dye Industry Found at Tel Shiqmona," *IEJ* 38 (1988) 184–86.

152. E. Stern, "New Evidence from Dor for the First Appearance of the Phoenicians along the Northern Coast of Israel," *BASOR* 279 (1990) 27–34; idem, "Tel Dor: A Phoenician—Israelite Trading Center," in *Recent Excavations in Israel: A View to the West* (ed. S. Gitin; Dubuque, IA: Kendall/

what may have been a small Sidonian marketplace next to the city wall—
a spacious building fronting on a paved courtyard—and some houses for
resident artisans and storekeepers and their families, built in the standard
Phoenician pier-and-rubble style (the spaces between columns of finished
stones were filled with field stones).[153] The pottery, apart from the indigenous Canaanite wares, consists of small Phoenician Bichrome containers
valued for their contents and numerous Cypriot open vessels, such as amphorae and bowls, which were appreciated more as house and table wares:
of the latter, one was made at Dor by a Cypriot potter and at least two were
imported from Kition in Cyprus.[154] Dor was an open city, as thriving ports
commonly were, and so it is not surprising that in the early eighth century
the local priest (*khn d'r*) was the son of a North Israelite woman, who gave
him the Israelite name Zechariah (*zkryw*), and a second-generation Sidonian resident, Ṣadoq, son of Mika' (*ṣdq bn mk'*),[155] who was one of the local
storekeepers or craftsmen or perhaps the priest of Dor before Ṣadoq.

About 10 kilometers south of Dor and a short distance from the coast,
at the site known as Tel Mevorakh, there was another small, tenth-century
Phoenician (or, specifically, Cypro-Phoenician) installation.[156] In the late
eleventh and early tenth century, the site consisted of a large, rectangular,
walled podium occupied by a solitary building, of which only a few ashlar
pillars remain, and of a large paved courtyard beside the podium to the
east, with some local ware and a single Phoenician jug.[157] In this association of an isolated building with a paved courtyard, Mevorakh resembles
the layout of the local marketplace at Dor, but the encircling wall and the
ashlar pillars in the building make it more imposing—an emporium, like
the common tripartite, pillared buildings where goods were collected for
sale in the adjacent open-air market. In the mid-tenth century, this building was completely dismantled and replaced by another, said to resemble
a standard four-room house, but a public building with a row of pillars,

Hunt, 1995) 81–93; A. Gilboa, "Sea Peoples and Phoenicians along the Southern Phoenician
Coast—A Reconciliation: An Interpretation of Šikila (SKL) Material Culture," *BASOR* 337 (2005)
47–78.

153. E. Stern, "Phoenicians, Sikils, and Israelites in the Light of Recent Excavations at Tel
Dor," in *Phoenicia and the Bible* (ed. E. Lipiński; Studia Phoenicia 11; Louvain: Peeters, 1991)
85–94. The massive mud-brick city wall and the gateway constructed of boulders on the outside
and of ashlar blocks on the inside and against the wall are not Phoenician but are local adaptations of Canaanite city fortifications: see I. Sharon, "Phoenician and Greek Ashlar Construction
Techniques at Tel Dor, Israel," *BASOR* 267 (1987) 21–42, esp. p. 22.

154. A. Gilboa, "Iron I–IIA Pottery Evolution at Dor: Regional Contexts and the Cypriot
Connection," *MPT*, 413–25; idem, "The Dynamics of Phoenician Bichrome Pottery: A View from
Tel Dor," *BASOR* 316 (1999) 1–22, esp. p. 12; idem and I. Sharon, "An Archaeological Contribu-
tion to the Early Iron Age Chronological Debate: Alternative Chronologies for Phoenicia and
Their Effects on the Levant, Cyprus, and Greece," *BASOR* 332 (2003) 7–80; idem, I. Sharon, and
J. Zorn, "Dor and Iron Age Chronology: Scarabs, Ceramic Sequence and 14C," *TA* 31 (2004) 32–
59; J. Yellin, "The Origin of Some Cypro-Geometric Pottery from Tel Dor," *IEJ* 39 (1989) 219–27.

155. N. Avigad, "The Priest of Dor," *IEJ* 25 (1975) 101–5, pl. 10c–d; E. Stern, *Dor, Ruler of the
Seas: Twelve Years of Excavations at the Israelite-Phoenician Harbor Town on the Carmel Coast* (Jerusalem: Israel Exploration Society, 1994) 122–29.

156. E. Stern, *Excavations at Tel Mevorakh (1973–1976), Part One: From the Iron Age to the Roman Period* (Qedem 9; Jerusalem: Hebrew University Institute of Archaeology, 1978).

157. Ibid., 66–70.

paved floors, a rear transverse room, and walls of pier-and-rubble construction, fronting on a courtyard, all within the walled enclosure.[158]

The local pottery is domestic—cooking pots, bowls, jugs, and jars—and comparable to the pottery, for instance, at Megiddo and Hazor and at Tel ʿAmal in the vicinity of Beth Shean.[159] One pot, which was inscribed with the letter *šin*, has exact parallels at Tel Qiri and at Shiqmona. There is also Phoenician Red Slip and Bichrome pottery, and a very rich assemblage of Cypriot Black-on-Red,[160] White Painted, and Bichrome wares, as well as a shaft tomb with one chamber that contained Black-on-Red jugs and some local pottery. This tenth-century site, therefore, seems to have been a trading post that was operated by Cypriots, either ethnic Greek or Phoenician, manned by local inhabitants, frequented by merchants and traders from Israel, and specializing in the exchange of luxury goods for basic agricultural products.

Another 10 kilometers south of Tel Mevorakh and about 10 kilometers from the coast was the village of Tel Zeror.[161] In the Late Bronze Age, it was a copper smelting center, where both the copper and the smiths were brought from Cyprus, but it was destroyed at the end of the thirteenth century. It was partly rebuilt in the tenth century, apparently in order to serve the farms in this part of the Plain of Sharon. Although in striking contrast to the coastal sites, it was not active in overseas trade, it was of some importance in the region, could claim its share of Cypro-Phoenician pottery, and may have sold the agricultural products it collected in the market at Tel Mevorakh.

Another site in the Plain of Sharon was Tel Michal, on the coast just north of modern Tel Aviv and ancient Tell Qasile. It was occupied in the latter part of the tenth century, having been abandoned since the end of the thirteenth, and shows some signs of settlement again in the eighth century.[162] The earlier phase of occupation is marked by a house that contained, among other things, storage jars and a silo for storing raisins, and by a big rectangular building, two rooms of which face a large courtyard. These two structures were renovated in the second phase, and three other buildings were added in adjoining parts of the mound: a large square building with a

---

158. J. D. Currid, "Rectangular Storehouse Construction during the Israelite Iron Age," *ZDPV* 108 (1992) 99–121.

159. Tel ʿAmal, occupied for most of the tenth century, specialized in weaving and dyeing: S. Levy and G. Edelstein, "Cinq années de fouilles à Tel ʿAmal (Nir David)," *RB* 79 (1972) 325–67. A jar from the latter part of the century is inscribed in Hebrew "Belonging to Nimshi" (*lnmš*), the name of Jehu's (grand)father (1 Kgs 19:16; 2 Kgs 9:2, 14, 20) and perhaps the same person: A. Lemaire, "A propos d'une inscription de Tel ʿAmal," *RB* 79 (1972) 559.

160. N. Schreiber, "A Word of Caution: Black-on-Red Pottery at Tel Mevorakh in the 'Tenth Century' B.C.," *PEQ* 133 (2001) 132–35.

161. K. Ohata, ed., *Tel Zeror. Preliminary Report of the Excavation: I. First Season, 1964; II. Second Season, 1965; III. Third Season, 1966* (Tokyo, 1966–70); E. Yannai, "A Group of Early Iron Age Lamps from the Northern Sharon Valley," *TA* 22 (1995) 279–81.

162. Z. Herzog, G. Rapp Jr., and O. Negbi, eds., *Excavations at Tel Michal, Israel* (Minneapolis: University of Minnesota Press, 1989). The stratigraphy and architecture are described by S. Moshkovitz (pp. 64–72), the wine presses by Z. Herzog (pp. 73–75), and the pottery by L. Singer-Avitz (pp. 76–87).

central platform was situated to the northeast, a single-room house with a low platform opposite the entrance was built to the east, and a complex of four houses built around a central courtyard was located in the southeast. Small objects were for personal or household use; domestic pottery such as bowls, craters, and jugs was either Phoenician Black-on-Red or Red Slip and burnished; and storage and industrial jars resembled jars found farther south at Ashdod and Arad; but there were almost no imported Cypriot wares.

At some distance from each of the two buildings that feature platforms there were winepresses, and inside and around the building with its platform against the wall opposite the entrance there were numerous goblets and chalices. The larger building is supposed to have been a sanctuary, with its central platform as the focus of open-air worship. The smaller building might also have been a cult place, but its size, layout, and apparent dedication to wine-drinking suggest that it was specifically a clubhouse where symposia were celebrated. Membership in a Phoenician symposium was limited to about 10 or 15 men, usually members of a profession, who gathered under the patronage of a particular God, and whose conversation, which ranged from amorous turns and the recitation of lyric poetry to dirges for departed members, was eased by an abundance of wine. It is possible, therefore, that Tel Michal, which was occupied for only a short time, did not have a significant relationship with its environs and was essentially a residential area for professionals, a station for merchants and traders who did business at nearby Tell Qasile, or a temporary home for foremen or skilled laborers working in the shipyards. Their common pottery, their lack of interest in things Cypriot, and their slight impact on their physical environment would be compatible with the life-style of a Byblian enclave: more interested in development than in acquisition. Whoever they were, they moved on when their work was done and took everything of interest with them.

Tell Qasile,[163] on the coast at Joppa, was the southernmost Phoenician market in tenth-century Palestine. The significant architectural features of the place include: a building on the site of the former Philistine temple with a paved floor but without any trace of cult paraphernalia; an unwalled, paved courtyard surrounding the building on three sides and covering all the earlier structures on the site, a storeroom or shed with a stone floor set in another courtyard south of the temple, which still contained some storage jars; a tripartite, pillared building with an attached house and workshop. Of the non-Philistine pottery, about half consisted of bowls, and the rest consisted of cooking pots, jugs, craters, goblets, amphorae, and storage jars which, except for the last, can be compared with wares found in northern and central Israel, although there are also Cypro-Phoenician Black-on-Red and Bichrome wares and some local imitations of Phoenician jugs. These buildings and the concomitant elimination of some of the town's

---

163. A. Mazar, *Excavations at Tell Qasile, Part One: The Philistine Sanctuary—Architecture and Cult Objects* (Qedem 12; Jerusalem: Hebrew University Institute of Archaeology, 1980); idem, *Excavations at Tell Qasile, Part Two: The Philistine Sanctuary—Various Finds, the Pottery, Conclusions, Appendices* (Qedem 20; Jerusalem: Hebrew University Institute of Archaeology, 1985).

residential areas were dictated by the new town plan and reflect Philistine interest in belonging to the emerging Phoenician commercial network. The tripartite, pillared building with attached house and workshop, in this context, is exactly what would be expected of a Phoenician, or specifically Sidonian, enclave consisting of a few craftsmen and dealers who settled in the town, married local women, raised families, and assimilated to the indigenous society: tenth- and ninth-century tombs at ʾAzor, another 10 kilometers to the south, replete with Bichrome, Black-on-Red, and Cypriot White Painted pottery would be the burials of generations of these same families of immigrants.[164]

In sum, the whole coast of Palestine from Dor to Joppa was dotted with Sidonian, Cypriot and Byblian ports, pieds-à-terre, and marketplaces. From Carmel northward, all the coastal sites, including Shiqmona and the Bay of ʿAkko with its tributaries, as well as a web of inland settlements were aligned with Tyre. South of Joppa the Philistines formed an alliance dominated by the great port cities of Ashkelon and Gaza which continued to prosper because of enduring ties to Egypt and, through alignment with Tyre, because of newly established relations with Cyprus.[165] Ashdod settled into an easy agricultural and pastoral economy, and Gath and Ekron, proud of their incipient Phoenician connections,[166] aligned themselves with Sidonian and Byblian interests.

Tyre: Overseas Ventures

The mainland cities of Phoenicia itself, especially Tyre and Sidon, expanded their already established connections with Cyprus and the Mediterranean world. Sidonians were in eastern Cyprus, Crete, Anatolia, and Greece. Byblians went with them to Cilicia. Tyre established outposts or marketplaces in western Cyprus and in southern Crete, and shared interest in Sardinia with Sidon. The three cities adopted pantheons and practices and developed cultural directions and artistic patterns that suited their outlooks and distinctive characters.

Tyrian pottery was cheap or even crude and had no commercial value.[167] At Tyre, people who could afford it imported Greek, specifically Euboean, wares, and in Cyprus they and their Cypriot or Greek hosts did the same. When Tyrian pottery shows up at these places in Cyprus in the tenth century, consequently, it is because it was valued for its contents or because Tyrians were there to use it—not just casual visitors but people who lived there and who, when they died there, took it with them to their graves. It is found in the southwest coastal area of the island, at Kouklia, ancient Palaepaphos, at Episkopi near Kourion, and at Amathus. Some of the earliest Phoenician pottery was found at Episkopi, but in small

---

164. M. Dothan, "Azor," *NEAEHL* 1.125–29.

165. S. Gitin, "Philistia in Transition: The Tenth Century BCE and Beyond," *MPT*, 162–83; J. M. Weinstein, "Egyptian Relations with the Eastern Mediterranean at the End of the Second Millennium BCE," *MPT*, 188–96.

166. T. Dothan, "An Early Phoenician Cache from Ekron," in *Ḥesed ve-Emet: Studies in Honor of Ernest S. Frerichs* (ed. J. Magness and S. Gitin; Atlanta: Scholars Press, 1998) 259–72.

167. P. M. Bikai, *The Phoenician Pottery of Cyprus* (Nicosia: A. G. Leventis Foundation, 1987) 48.

quantities and in only a few graves. At Palaepaphos, more than half the tenth-century tombs contained Tyrian pottery[168] (heavy storage jars, jars with palm tree or tree-of-life designs, Red Ware, jugs, and flasks) like the pottery found at Tyre, Tell Keisan, Tell Qasile, and some Philistine sites. At Amathus, more than one-third of the tombs contained some Tyrian pottery (1 had 13 items, 18 had 4 or more items, and the rest had between 1 and 3 items) in addition to local Cypriot and imported Greek wares.[169] Amathus, in fact, had a mix of Phoenician and Greek pottery almost exactly the same as the mix at Tyre; and the finest of the Greek wares, which were the oldest exports from Euboea, were in the Phoenician tombs.[170] These Tyrians may have come to Amathus for its iron, but they also brought with them, perhaps from Gaza and Ashkelon, Egyptian amulets and faience pendants, and at least one of them had a workshop that specialized in "Egyptian Blue" conoid seals.[171] Unlike the Sidonians who made useful goods, such as bronze bowls, or the Byblians who specialized in industrial materials, such as wood for ships, the Tyrians dealt in perfumes, dyes, specialty foodstuffs, and other nonessentials such as jewelry, antiques, and Egyptian or Egyptianizing exotica, and this is probably what they were doing in Amathus, Episkopi, and Palaepaphos at this time.[172]

Cyprus, however, was just the first stop on the Tyrian overseas routes. Kommos, a port in southern Crete, was another port-of-call for these merchants on their way to the west. The evidence consists of fragmentary late tenth-century transport jars and large jugs, such as those found in tombs at Palaepaphos, the small quantity and homogeneity of which suggest that they may have been part of one or very few shipments.[173] This in turn would mean that Kommos was not a regular destination for Tyrian ships

---

168. Idem, "The Imports from the East," in *Palaepaphos-Skales: An Iron Age Cemetery in Cyprus* (ed. V. Karageorghis; Konstanz: Universitätsverlag, 1983) 396–405; idem, "Trade Networks in the Early Iron Age: The Phoenicians at Palaepaphos," in *Western Cyprus—Connections* (ed. D. W. Rupp; Gothenburg: Åström, 1987) 125–28.

169. Idem, "The Phoenician Pottery," in *La nécropole d'Amathonte—Tombes 113–367, II: Céramiques non-Chypriotes* (ed. V. Karageorghis, O. Picard, and C. Tytgat; Nicosia: Department of Antiquities, 1987) 1–19, pls. 1–7.

170. J. N. Coldstream, "Kition and Amathus: Some Reflections on Their Westward Links during the Early Iron Age," in *Cyprus between the Orient and the Occident* (ed. V. Karageorghis; Nicosia: Department of Antiquities, 1986) 321–29; idem, "The Greek Geometric and Archaic Imports," in *La nécropole d'Amathonte—Tombes 113–367, II: Céramiques non-Chypriotes* (ed. V. Karageorghis, O. Picard, and C. Tytgat: Nicosia: Department of Antiquities, 1987) 21–31, pls. 8–17; idem, "The First Exchanges between Euboeans and Phoenicians: Who Took the Initiative?" *MPT*, 353–60; J. P. Crielaard, "The Social Organization of Euboean Trade with the Eastern Mediterranean during the 10th–8th Centuries BC," *Pharos* 1 (1993) 139–46.

171. P. Åström et al., "Iron Artefacts from Swedish Excavations in Cyprus," *Opuscula Atheniensia* 16 (1986) 27–41; P. Aupert, "Amathus during the First Iron Age," *BASOR* 308 (1997) 19–25; A. T. Reyes, "A Group of Cypro-Geometric Stamp Seals," *Levant* 25 (1993) 197–205.

172. P. Flourentzos, "The Early Geometric Tomb no. 132 from Palaepaphos," *RDAC* (1997) 205–18, pls. 25–44. The pottery in this tomb was Cypriot, but the other objects—an ivory spindle whorl, gold jewelry, bronze fibulae, iron obeloi (or, spits), and faience amulets—were products of the Tyrian market.

173. P. M. Bikai, "Phoenician Ceramics from the Greek Sanctuary," in *Kommos IV: The Greek Sanctuary, Part I* (ed. J. W. Shaw and M. C. Shaw; Princeton: Princeton University Press, 2000) 302–12.

at this time but an anchorage and base of supplies for their annual or triennial voyages to Sardinia and onward to Tarshish in southern Spain.[174] By the end of the ninth century, however, as abundant pottery and the presence of a shrine to Melqart indicate (the shrine is distinguished by a nucleus of three stone pillars fitted by plinths into a triangular base facing the entrance and standing behind an open hearth), Kommos had become a regular and reliable station on the westward sea lanes.[175]

Sidon: The Lure of the Greek World

Sidonians in the tenth century traveled—avoiding the Tyrian routes[176]— to Cyprus, Crete, Greece, and Sardinia. Unlike the Tyrians whose uniform products and settlements suggest public, royal, or civic enterprise, these Sidonians were privately financed craftsmen or small groups of entrepreneurs and businessmen who traveled and settled with their families or emigrated alone and married local women. In any case, they left little trace of themselves apart from beautiful or astonishing products, evidence of literacy and organization, and changes in the local culture from which their presence in these distant places can be deduced.

Phoenicians were not established at Kition in Cyprus before the later ninth century, when their first temple was built. But there is earlier evidence for casual Sidonian interaction with the town and with eastern Cyprus. An eleventh-century arrowhead found in the region of Sidon and inscribed "arrowhead of the Kitian, cup-bearer of ʿAbday"[177] makes it clear that there was kinship or at least commonality between the heirs of this Late Bronze Age aristocratic tradition in the two towns. There is also an early tenth-century (ca. 1000 B.C.E.) inscribed bronze bowl from the Tekke cemetery in Knossos that not only attests Sidonian presence in Crete at this time but also indicates an even earlier connection between Sidonians living in Cyprus and Crete. The bowl with its shallow hemispherical shape of Cypriot origin and its inscription that mentions two generations—it reads "cup of Shemaʿ, son of Luʾmon" (*ks . šmʿ . bn lʾmn*)—and the two burials in the tomb in which the bowl was found suggest that a Sidonian working in Cyprus and perhaps at Kition had emigrated to Knossos in Crete at the end of the eleventh century or at the beginning of the tenth, and there with his son pursued his craft.[178]

174. B. Peckham, "The Nora Inscription," *Or* 41 (1972) 457–68; F. M. Cross, "An Interpretation of the Nora Stone," *BASOR* 208 (1972) 13–19; 1 Kgs 10:22.

175. J. W. Shaw, "Phoenicians in Southern Crete," *AJA* 93 (1989) 165–83; E. D. Stockton, "Phoenician Cult Stones," *Australian Journal of Biblical Archaeology* 2–3 (1974–75) 1–27.

176. I. Strøm, "Evidence from the Sanctuaries," in *Greece between East and West: 10th–8th Centuries BC* (ed. G. Kopcke and I. Tokumaru; Mainz am Rhein: von Zabern, 1992) 40–60, pls. 5c–7; P. Bartoloni, "Le linee commerciali all'alba del primo millennio," in *I Fenici: Ieri Oggi Domani* (ed. S. Moscati; Rome: Consiglio Nazionale delle Ricerche, 1995) 245–59.

177. Ḥṣ kty mšq ʿbdy: see R. Deutsch and M. Heltzer, *Forty New Ancient West Semitic Inscriptions* (Tel Aviv–Jaffa: Archaeological Center Publications, 1994) 16–18, #4; idem, "ʿAbday on Eleventh-Century BCE Arrowheads," *IEJ* 47 (1997) 111–12.

178. J. N. Coldstream, "Greeks and Phoenicians in the Aegean," in *Phönizier im Westen* (ed. H. G. Niemeyer; Mainz am Rhein: von Zabern, 1982) 261–75; G. L. Hoffman, *Imports and Immigrants: Near Eastern Contacts with Iron Age Crete* (Ann Arbor, MI: University of Michigan Press,

Sidonians, typically, did not found colonies but settled peaceably in established and receptive communities, where they married native women and busied themselves in making unguents or other remedies,[179] in managing the extraction of raw goods (such as copper and iron in Cyprus), or in creating practical, artistic masterpieces, either for their local patrons or for export to Crete and Greece or Sidon, whence these now naturalized Cypriots had emigrated.[180] An early ninth-century funerary inscription from Cyprus may have marked the grave of just such an émigré:[181]

> [This is the grave of ʿAbdʾelonim, and in the grave where] he is lying there is nothing special. And whoever might forget the memorial offerings for this grave over this distinguished person, may these Gods obliterate that man by the hand of a citizen or by the hand of a person or at the whim of a passer-by. May marrow never be burned before him, may neither citizen nor person accord to that man a name or place memorial offerings before him.

The inscription is on a small plaque that was fitted into the entrance of the tomb. The first sentence identifies him by name—Abdelonim is reconstructed and just a guess—and alerts potential grave robbers to the futility of their labors and alludes to the list of terrible curses, canonical and known to everybody, that beset those who disturb the dead (the list is excerpted in later tomb inscriptions from Sidon and Byblos). But in the second sentence, instead of curses on the robbers, he invokes a curse on anyone who forgets to offer sacrifice in his memory. This ritual, or "peace offering" (*šlmm*), is

---

1997) 191–245, pls.140–50; M. G. Amadasi Guzzo, "Dati epigrafici e colonizzazione fenicia," *Kôkalos* 39–40 (1993–94) 221–34, esp. pp. 222–24.

179. J. N. Coldstream, "Mixed Marriages at the Frontiers of the Early Greek World," *OJA* 12 (1993) 89–107; G. Shepherd, "Fibulae and Females: Intermarriage in the Western Greek Colonies and the Evidence from the Cemeteries," in *Ancient Greeks West and East* (ed. G. N. Tsetskhladze; Leiden: Brill, 1999) 267–300; J. N. Coldstream, "Some Cypriote Traits in Cretan Pottery, c. 950–700 B.C.," in *The Relations between Cyprus and Crete, ca. 2000–500 B.C.* (ed. V. Karageorghis; Nicosia: Department of Antiquities, 1979) 257–63; idem, "Kition and Amathus: Some Reflections on their Westward Links during the Early Iron Age," in *Acts of the International Archaeological Symposium "Cyprus between the Orient and the Occident"* (ed. V. Karageorghis; Nicosia: Department of Antiquities, 1986) 321–29, esp. pp. 323–24; D. W. Jones, "Phoenician Unguent Factories in Dark Age Greece: Social Approaches to Evaluating the Archaeological Evidence," *OJA* 12 (1993) 293–303.

180. There are two Neo-Babylonian economic documents that mention "iron from Lebanon" and "iron from Yamana," the latter from Cyprus or Cilicia: see A. L. Oppenheim, "Essay on Overland Trade in the First Millennium BC," *JCS* 21 (1967) 236–54, esp. p. 241. It may have been interest in obtaining iron that led Sidonians to Cyprus, and then to North Syria and Cilicia, where supplies were abundant: see K. R. Maxwell-Hyslop, "Assyrian Sources of Iron: A Preliminary Survey of the Historical and Geographical Evidence," *Iraq* 36 (1974) 139–54. At Lefkandi, there is a tenth- or early ninth-century cremation burial of a warrior-trader, whose lavish grave gifts included (besides Phoenician Bichrome jugs and Cypriot jugs, a bronze cauldron with its parallel at Idalion in Cyprus, bronze armor (?), a bronze earring, an antique cylinder seal, and 12 stone weights) a large number of iron weapons, including a sword, a spearhead, 2 iron knives, and 25 iron arrowheads: M. R. Popham and I. S. Lemos, "A Euboean Warrior Trader," *OJA* 14 (1995) 151–58; I. J. Winter, "Homer's Phoenicians: History, Ethnography, or Literary Trope [A Perspective on Early Orientalism]," in *The Ages of Homer: A Tribute to Emily Townsend Vermeule* (ed. J. B. Carter and S. P. Morris; Austin: University of Texas Press, 1995) 247–71.

181. A. M. Honeyman, "The Phoenician Inscriptions of the Cyprus Museum," *Iraq* 6 (1939) 104–8, pls. 18–19; O. Masson and M. Sznycer, *Recherches sur les Phéniciens à Chypre* (Paris: Droz, 1972) 13–20, #1; H.-P. Müller, "Die phönizische Grabinschrift aus dem Zypern-Museum *KAI* 30 und die Formgeschichte des nordwestsemitischen Epitaphs," *ZA* 65 (1975) 104–32; É. Puech, "Remarques sur quelques inscriptions phéniciennes de Chypre," *Sem* 29 (1979) 19–43, esp. pp. 19–26.

known from its portrayal on the sarcophagus of ʾAḥirôm of Byblos and was a public fulfillment of an oath or vow.

The special interest of the curse is in its details and its implications. The dead man refers to himself as a "distinguished person" (*gibbôr*), or man of means, a warrior, for instance, who could outfit himself for battle; or a trader who could finance his operations; or a craftsman who could afford his raw materials. But now he is among the dead, and he refers to them and to himself as "these Gods" (*h[ʾln]m ʾl*), that is, the immortals, the divinized, whose divine life is sustained by sacrificial meals. The details are mainly with regard to the curse's social implications: the potential culprits are the entire local population, and this includes: "citizens" (*baʿal*); persons (*ʾdm*), that is, people who are free, not slaves, residents of the town or township; and, finally, "migrants" (*ʿbr*), people passing through, resident aliens—the ʾAḥirôm inscription from Byblos calls them "wayfarers."

The most interesting implication is that, among all these people, there was a Phoenician community who could read the man's funerary text and who understood the rituals, who would recognize his status and be glad to honor him in this way. The last sentence, therefore, explains that the curse is retaliation for the culprit's forgetfulness: because he did not make memorial offerings, none will be made for him; because he did not honor the dead, he will lose his name and reputation; because he did not recognize the divine status of the dead, no marrow (*mḥ*) will be burned for him; and what it means to be obliterated by the hand of a citizen or a person or a passerby is to be neglected by them and simply forgotten.

From their own city, or from Kition or some other enclave in Cyprus, Sidonians traveled by preference to Euboea.[182] About the turn of the millennium, two new kinds of pottery, with their prototypes in Cyprus, were introduced to Lefkandi, and throughout the tenth century the wealth and variety of Phoenician imports constantly increased in this prosperous and internationally receptive region.[183] Some of these goods may have traveled in Euboean ships, but some were the products and possessions of Sidonians who lived and worked and intermarried in Euboea and were buried with their families in the Toumba graveyard.[184]

---

182. Athenian influence was strong in Euboea at this time (see J. N. Coldstream, "Knossos and Lefkandi: The Attic Connection," in *Minotaur and Centaur: Studies in the Archaeology of Crete and Euboea Presented to Mervyn Popham* [ed. D. Evely, I. S. Lemos, and S. Sherratt; BAR Int. Series 638; Oxford: Tempus Reparatum, 1996] 133–34), and it may have been through Euboea that the Sidonians began to develop their close and enduring relations with Athens. Influence in the other direction is evident in the painting of a Euboean ship on an Attic Geometric I vase (ca. 850–825 B.C.E.): see M. Popham, "An Early Euboean Ship," *OJA* 6 (1987) 353–59.

183. V. Desborough, "The Background to Euboean Participation in Early Greek Maritime Enterprise," in *Tribute to an Antiquary: Essays Presented to Marc Fitch by Some of His Friends* (ed. F. Emmison and R. Stephens; London: Leopard's Head, 1976) 25–40; M. R. Popham, L. H. Sackett, and P. G. Themelis, *Lefkandi I—The Iron Age. Text: The Settlement, the Cemeteries* (London: Thames & Hudson, 1980) 358–62; M. Popham, "Precolonization: Early Greek Contact with the East," in *The Archaeology of Greek Colonisation: Essays Dedicated to Sir John Boardman* (ed. G. R. Tsetskhladze and F. De Angelis; Oxford: Oxford University Press, 1994) 11–34.

184. M. R. Popham, E. Touloupa, and L. H. Sackett, "Further Excavation of the Toumba Cemetery at Lefkandi, 1981," *British School of Athens* 77 (1982) 213–48; J. N. Coldstream, "The First Exchanges between Euboeans and Phoenicians: Who took the Initiative?" *MPT*, 353–60.

Among the astonishing traces of their presence and influence in these Greek lands is an engraved bowl from a particularly rich woman's burial in this cemetery: the engraving depicts three women carrying offerings to a table, another woman approaching an incense altar, and other women in procession playing musical instruments, while a Goddess, whose symbols are the tree of life flanked by animals and a disk surmounting a standing staff, stands in front of the altar. The particularly interesting aspect of this narrative scene is the fact that the Sidonian craftsman probably engraved it because it was already familiar to his patroness, or could become familiar to her, from recitals in a bilingual setting of this and other Sidonian myths.[185]

A less dramatic but not less interesting trace of shared literacy is an amphora, dating to the middle of the tenth century, from the Euboean colony in Macedonia, which has incised marks on both handles: three slashes on one but on the other three notches and, in the most conspicuous position, the Phoenician letter *kap* (*K*), which is the letter *chi* in the early Euboean alphabet.[186] The letter is exactly like the *kap* on the inscribed bowl from the Tekke tomb, was incised after firing as was the practice in Cyprus, and was written on a transport amphora from Macedonia, all of which suggests that Euboeans and Sidonians shared meaningful alphabetic symbols, maybe even whole scripts, in doing business, just as they shared the recital of literary texts at their leisure.

The evidence for Sidonians in Sardinia in the tenth century is circumstantial, derived from the local bronze figurines, which imitate, in a thoroughly Nuraghic mode, figurines in a Sidonian and North Syrian style. Because some of the local examples are dated to the late tenth century, their Phoenician models must have been available earlier. There is, coincidentally, just such a North Syrian exemplar that may have been a source of inspiration, not least because of its antiquity, for the local artists.[187] It was found in the sea off the southwestern coast of Sicily and, like later and roughly similar figurines from the ocean off southern Spain, may have been part of onboard rituals[188] or may have been thrown overboard during

185. M. Popham, "An Engraved Near Eastern Bronze Bowl from Lefkandi," *OJA* 14 (1995) 103–7; B. B. Powell, "From Picture to Myth, from Myth to Picture: Prolegomena to the Invention of Mythic Representation in Greek Art," in *New Light on a Dark Age: Exploring the Culture of Geometric Greece* (ed. S. Langdon, Columbia: University of Missouri Press, 1997) 154–93.

186. R. W. V. Catling, "A Tenth-Century Trade-Mark from Lefkandi," in *Minotaur and Centaur: Studies in the Archaeology of Crete and Euboea Presented to Mervyn Popham* (ed. D. S. Evely, I. S. Lemos, and S. Sherratt; BAR Int. Series 638; Oxford: Tempus Reparatum, 1996) 126–32; A. M. Snodgrass, "The Euboeans in Macedonia: A New Precedent for Westward Expansion," in *Apoikia. I piu antichi insediamenti greci in occidente: Funzioni e modi dell'organizzazione politica e sociale—Scritti in onore di Giorgio Buchner* (ed. B. d'Agostino and D. Ridgway; Naples: Oriental Institute, 1994) 87–93.

187. M. S. Balmuth, "Phoenician Chronology in Sardinia: Prospecting, Trade and Settlement before 900 B.C.," in *Numismatique et histoire économique phéniciennes et puniques* (Studia Phoenicia 9; ed. T. Hackens and G. Moucharte; Louvain: Université Catholique, 1992) 215–27, pls. 33–35; G. Falsone, "Sulla cronologia del bronzo fenicio di Sciacca alla luce delle nuove scoperte di Huelva e Cadice," in *Studi sulla Sicilia Occidentale in onore di Vincenzo Tusa* (Padua: Bottega d'Erasmo, 1993) 45–56.

188. G. Kapitan, "Archaeological Evidence for Rituals and Customs on Ancient Ships," in *First International Symposium on Ship Construction in Antiquity* (ed. H. E. Tzalas; Athens: Hellenic Institute for the Preservation of Nautical Tradition, 1989) 147–62.

or when setting out on a particularly dangerous or propitious voyage. They originated in Byblos, represent a God striding left with his right arm raised to wield a club, and are archaic symbols, derived from Egyptian prototypes, of the Baʿal of Byblos, the "Smiting Baʿal" (*baʿl ṣimd*), victorious over the cosmic and political adversaries of his people.[189] The evidence, in any case, is of Sardinians deriving symbols and meanings (and perhaps the myths or stories that romanced them) from Sidonians and some Byblian confreres who traveled to their island in the tenth century.

Byblos: North Syria and Anatolia

Byblos in the tenth century maintained its long-standing relations with northern Cyprus, and some Byblians traveled to North Syria and Anatolia, probably with Sidonian explorers and adventurers, but the city also concentrated on its inland and Palestinian interests. Its people were renowned for their skill in working wood, stone, and metals, and its schools were active in the dissemination of literacy. The city and people are known primarily from texts: the Bible, the *Phoenician History* by Philo of Byblos, and inscriptions from the metropolis and its dominions.

The earliest inscriptions from Byblos are from the years between the end of the eleventh and the beginning of the ninth century B.C.E.[190] One of their more interesting features is their script: it is still archaic but, in comparison with the eleventh-century scripts of the arrowheads, is formal and regularized so that the letters, which now have a normal size, shape, stance, and position on the right-to-left line, develop slowly over these more than 100 years. This script affirms a coastal Canaanite, or Phoenician, cultural self-consciousness that was shared, as bits of writing attest, by Tyre and Sidon but that was quite distinct from the burgeoning Israelite world view visible in the contemporary calendar inscription from Gezer, the letters of which lack symmetry, rotate to the left, and flaunt informality in the lengthening of their vertical lines.

Three of the earlier inscriptions from the end of the eleventh century consist of personal names, all of them unique and in one way or another quite dated: one is the name of the ancestor of the biblical tribe Manasseh (*mnš*) incised on a clay tube perhaps from a smelting furnace;[191] another, also on a clay rod and perhaps from the same mechanism, has as its theophoric element the name of the God of the Amanus Range, "Belonging to the Servant of Ḥamon" (*lʿbdḥmn*; the third on a similar clay part has the archaic divine kinship name and a patronymic, "My-Brother-Is-My-Mother, son of Bodo" (*lʾḥʾm bbd*).[192]

---

189. S. Dalley, "Near Eastern Patron Deities of Mining and Smelting in the Late Bronze and Early Iron Ages," *RDAC* (1987) 61–66, pl. 19; S. F. Bondi, "Il ruolo di Biblo nell'espansione fenicia," in *Biblo: Una città e la sua cultura* (ed. E. Acquaro et al.; Rome: Consiglio Nazionale delle Ricerche, 1994) 137–43.

190. J. C. L. Gibson, *TSSI* 3.9–24; R. Wallenfels, "Redating the Byblian Inscriptions," *JANES* 15 (1983) 79–118; M. Martin, "A Preliminary Report after Re-examination of the Byblian Inscriptions," *Or* 30 (1961) 46–78, pls. 6–15.

191. A. Lemaire, "Notes d'épigraphie nord-ouest sémitique," *Syria* 62 (1985) 31–32.

192. F. M. Cross and P. K. McCarter Jr., "Two Archaic Inscriptions on Clay Objects from Byblus," *RSF* 1 (1973) 3–8; J. Teixidor, "An Archaic Inscription from Byblos," *BASOR* 225 (1977) 70–71.

Fig. 1.6. ʾAḥirom sarcophagus. © The Directorate General of Antiquities—Beirut, Lebanon.

From about the same time, there is an extraordinary legal document inscribed on a bronze spatula, the original pseudohieroglyphic text of which had been erased to accommodate it and which records the settlement of a debt encumbering an inheritance:[193] "[Baʿal]ay paid ʿAzorbaʿal ninety shekels. I have received the silver. If you inherit, your obligations are yours, and my obligations are mine." The obvious issue was money, and this is settled first by the third-person-singular receipt, but the fundamental issue was alienation of a hereditary property, and the importance of its resolution is reflected in the use of the first-person singular and in the permanence, albeit ironically erasable, of the record.

From early in the tenth century, there is an inscription in high relief on a stone pedestal with the dedication "To the Lord and to the Lady of Byblos" (*lʾdn wlbʿlt gbl*)[194]—a unique combined reference to the God and Goddess of the city—and from the latter part of the century, there is a large jar inscribed on the shoulder with the name of the potter who fashioned it, "ʿAbdoʾ, the son of Kalbay the potter" (*ʿbdʾ bklby hy[ṣr]*). The formality and evenness of the script reflect the rootedness and well-being of the populace, but these earlier individual texts are relics of a quickly disappearing past. On the other hand, the royal inscriptions reveal the commotion, uncertainty, and instability of kingship in an evolving urban setting.

The oldest of the royal inscriptions (see fig. 1.6) is on the sarcophagus of ʾAḥirom and was composed by his son ʾIttobaʿal:

> The coffin which Ittobaʿal, son of ʾAḥirom king of Byblos, made for ʾAḥirom his father when he placed him in eternity. And should a king among kings, or

---

193. M. Martin, "A Preliminary Report after Re-Examination of the Byblian Inscriptions," *Or* 30 (1961) 46–78, pls. 6–15; idem, "A Twelfth Century Bronze Palimpsest," *RSO* 37 (1962) 175–97.

194. P. Bordreuil, "Une inscription phénicienne champlevée des environs de Byblos," *Sem* 27 (1977) 23–27, pl. 5.

a governor among governors, or a military commander come up against Byblos and uncover this coffin, may the scepter of his rule be removed, the throne of his kingship overturned, and may peace flee from Byblos. And him—may a wayfarer erase his epitaph.

The sarcophagus belonged to the king of a preceding dynasty, whose body had been removed and whose name had been erased to make room for the new text which, of course, threatens with dynastic strife and civic unrest any king or governor or military commander who might do the same to ʾAḥirom.

The sarcophagus was beautifully decorated and painted.[195] Centered on the lid are crouching lions whose heads protrude at either end in order to guard the coffin and to serve as handles. Beside them and facing each other, there are two men, similarly attired but different in appearance: one has a living upright lotus blossom in his raised right hand and a small jar in his left and may represent the king in his newly restored life; the other has a drooping lotus blossom in his left hand and raises his right hand in greeting and may be the dead king saluting his new life. One of the long sides of the sarcophagus depicts the enthroned king, a drooping lotus blossom in his left hand, before a table loaded with food and drink, behind which seven attendants process toward him with similar offerings and with gestures of mourning. The other long side shows a procession of his servants, four with baskets on their heads, one leading an animal, and three with their arms upraised in the same gesture of mourning. On the two ends of the coffin, four women beat their bared breasts or tear their hair in gestures of mourning and lamentation. The sarcophagus rests on four crouching lions, matching the lions on the lid—protective, ancient symbols of divine authority.

The motifs are mostly Egyptian, but the workmanship is Byblian, characterized by the Syrian squatness of its figures and a lack of Egyptian refinement. Also of Syrian, or more particularly, Amorite origin, but neither Egyptian nor Phoenician is the narrative theme of a banquet for the deceased, although the portrayal of the revitalized king as the true image of himself is a reflex of the Byblian myth of Adonis. ʾAḥirom clearly was a usurper, and his sarcophagus probably was pilfered and inscribed during his lifetime, perhaps early in his reign, because his son who should have succeeded him on the throne is not king and makes no claim on the throne.

The rest of the tenth-century inscriptions belong to kings of the dynasty that supplanted the line of ʾAḥirom and were written to commemorate their building and restoration of temples and dedication of statues. The first, by Yaḥîmilk, the founder of the dynasty, is inscribed on a stone that previously had been divided into registers by double horizontal lines in order to receive a pseudohieroglyphic inscription, of which traces still remain. He does not mention his father, is at pains to declare the legitimacy of his rule, and his parvenu status is confirmed by his reuse of a

195. P. Montet, *Byblos et l'Egypte: Quatre campagnes de fouilles à Gebeil (1921–1922, 1923–1924)* (Paris: Geuthner, 1928) 215–38, pls. 125–42; M. Chéhab, "Observations au sujet du sarcophage d'Ahiram," *MUSJ* 46 (1970–71) 107–17; E. Porada, "Notes on the Sarcophagus of Ahiram," *JANES* 5 (1973) 355–72.

preexisting, perhaps royal monument. It is also acknowledged implicitly in his declaration that, besides restoring the dilapidated temples of the olden Gods, whom he invokes as "Ba⁽al Šamem . . . and the Assembly of the Holy Gods of Byblos," he also introduced a new dynastic God, "Ba⁽al of Byblos," into the Assembly.[196] This God, the executive God of the city, became a permanent fixture of the Byblian pantheon and is known from later Byblian texts, eventually with the title "Almighty" (ʾaddîr). The God, though new to the formal assembly, was otherwise familiar and was invoked two centuries earlier in the salutation of a letter from the king of Byblos to the king of Ugarit.[197]

King Yaḥîmilk was succeeded by his oldest son, ʾAbîba⁽al, whose dedication to Ba⁽alat, the immemorial Goddess of the city was inscribed on the base of a statue of Shishak (ca. 945–924 B.C.E.) that he claims to have imported from Egypt, and by another son named ʾElîba⁽al, whose invocation of the Goddess was written on a statue of Osorkon I (924–889 B.C.E.). Both of the statues presumably were deposited in the temple of the Goddess, and the honor they accord these pharaohs suggests that Egypt supported the new dynasty and may have instigated the coup against ʾAḥirom that inaugurated it.[198] The last known king of the dynasty was Šiptiba⁽al, son of ʾElîba⁽al and grandson of Yaḥîmilk, whose inscription records his repairs to the foundations of the old temples that were threatening to collapse into the city's water supply. It is probably one of these kings whose seal, representing him with the symbols of eternal life, majesty, and power is set inside a frame of Egyptian, Hittite, Byblian pseudohieroglyphic, and Phoenician alphabetic signs—that is, samples of all the scripts with which an educated Byblian might boast familiarity.[199]

These inscriptions are written in a dialect peculiar to Byblos, and the occurrence of some of the same morphological traits in an early inscription from Zinjirli, in southern Anatolia just east of the Amanus Range, suggests that Byblians, from whom the locals learned the language, had arrived in this region by the tenth century.[200] The inscription is by a king, Kilamuwa, whose father, Ḥayyaʾ (Ḥayyan in the Assyrian annals), paid tribute to Shal-

---

196. C. Bonnet, "Existe-t-il un b⁽l gbl à Byblos? A propos de l'inscription de Yehimilk (KAI 4)," UF 25 (1993) 35–44.

197. CAT 2:44:8; P. Bordreuil, "Nouveaux documents phéniciens inscrits," Actas 4, 1.205–13, esp. p. 206.

198. J. M. Weinstein, "Egyptian Relations with the Eastern Mediterranean World at the End of the Second Millennium BCE," MPT, 188–96.

199. E. Gubel, "Notes sur l'iconographie royale sigillaire," Atti 2, 2.913–22; idem, "Byblos: l'art de la métropole phénicienne," in Biblo: Una città e la sua cultura (ed. E. Acquaro et al.; Rome: Consiglio Nazionale delle Ricerche, 1994) 73–96, pls. 1–9, esp. p. 80, pl. 1:4–5.

200. The Byblian dialect has morphological curiosities: (1) initial ʾalep is retained in personal names with the element ʾaḥ- "brother" (ʾḥrm, "ʾAḥirom"; later Tyrian "Ḥirom"); (2) the word "son" is b- instead of bn; (3) the 3rd-masculine-singular personal pronoun has a deictic form (hʾt) as well as a personal form (hʾ); (4) the masculine-singular demonstrative adjective "this" is zn, but z when modifying a genitive noun; (5) the 3rd-person masculine and feminine singular and the masculine-plural pronominal suffixes retain consonantal /h/, that is, are -h and -hm instead of -y and -m, or in the singular have -w instead of -y; (6) the final consonant -y is retained in third-weak roots; (7) there is a reflexive conjugation with a prefixed or infixed t; (8) the absolute infinitive with following 1st=person-singular pronoun expresses narrative past tense; (9) modality is expressed by precative l- and the imperfect, or is marked by enclitic mem.

maneser III of Assyria (858–824 B.C.E.) and who, as he says in his inscription, was himself tributary to the king of Assyria (see fig. 1.7). Although the
inscription is from the third quarter of the ninth century, the fact that it
was written in an elegant literary Phoenician but in Aramaic script, by an
Aramean scribe who was thinking in Aramaic (there is an Aramaic word and
some Aramaic orthography) and at a time when the Luwian kingdom was
being overrun by Arameans suggests that the language had been learned
much earlier and had become a part of Zinjirli's cultural heritage, to which
the king and his supporters clung for political and ethnic survival.[201]
    Kilamuwa names the kings of his dynasty and of the preceding dynasty
and refers in general to the founders of the kingdom as "those who reigned
before them." The founder of the preceding dynasty was named Gabbar,
and he was succeeded by his son, but these two were so insignificant in Kilamuwa's estimation (of both he says, "they accomplished nothing") that
the son's name was not worth mentioning; both were included because
in establishing the kingdom they also introduced new Gods into the local
pantheon. Next was the Dynasty of Kilamuwa. Its founder was his father,
Ḥayyaʾ, also a do-nothing in comparison with himself but actually well
known on the international scene, and the father of the next king, Kilamuwa's brother and predecessor Šaʾîl, who may in fact have been a man
of no importance. Finally there was Kilamuwa, another son of Ḥayyaʾ but,
as he is careful to note, not of the Aramean wife who was the mother of
Šaʾîl but of the Luwian queen named *Tml.*
    The name of the kingdom, Yaʾudiya, is Luwian, and the unnamed rulers
before the two listed dynasties may also have been Luwian. Gabbar and his
son were Arameans, but his God, "Smiting Baʿal" (*Baʿal Ṣimd*), was Phoenician, the God represented in statuary and imitated in glyptic art, the God
portrayed as conquering the Sea with clubs in the Ugaritic myth of Baʿal,
the God introduced into the Byblian pantheon by Yaḥîmilk, a God brought
to the region by Phoenician metallurgists and merchants by the tenth century. His son's God, "Baʿal of the Amanus" (*bʿl ḥmn*), whose name was included in the Ugaritic onomasticon but not in its pantheon was Lord of the
Phoenician cosmic mountain located in the territory of Zinjirli and rightfully became a mainstay of the Yaʾudi pantheon. Kilamuwa's father, Ḥayyaʾ,

---

On Zinjirli, see Gibson, *TSSI* 3.30–39; J. Tropper, *Die Inschriften von Zincirli: Neue Edition und vergleichende Grammatik des phönizischen, samʾalischen und aramäischen Textkorpus* (Münster: Ugarit-Verlag, 1993) 26–46; M. K. Hamilton, "The Past as Destiny: Historical Visions in Samʾal and Judah under Assyrian Hegemony," *HTR* 91 (1998) 215–50. The dialectal forms: the third-masculine-singular suffix on the nominative is *-h* (*bnh*, "his son"); the third-masculine-plural suffix is *-hm* (*hlpnyhm*, "those who were before them"); final *-y* is retained in third-weak roots (*ksy* [= *kussiya], "he was covered"); the reflexive form with prefixed *t-* (*ytlwn*, "they cringed"); the absolute infinitive with following first-person-singular pronoun to express narrative past tense (*wskr ʾnk,* "and I hired"). It should be noted that the third-masculine-singular suffix on accusative and genitive nouns (nouns ending in a long vowel) in this inscription is *-y,* as in later Sidonian Phoenician, and not *-w,* as in later Byblian texts.
    201. On the literary qualities of the inscription, see T. Collins, "The Kilamuwa Inscription: A Phoenician Poem," *WO* 6 (1970–71) 183–88; M. O'Connor, "The Rhetoric of the Kilamuwa In-scription," *BASOR* 226 (1977) 15–29; F. M. Fales, "Kilamuwa and the Foreign Kings: Propaganda vs. Power," *WO* 10 (1979) 6–22; A. Schade, *A Syntactic and Literary Analysis of Ancient Northwest Semitic Inscriptions* (Lewiston, NY: Edwin Mellen, 2006) 67–97.

who founded the ruling dynasty, was also an Aramean and introduced another Phoenician God, "Charioteer of ʾEl" (*rkbʾl*), called "The Lord of the Dynasty" (*bʿl bt*), into the Assembly of the Gods and became the dynastic God of the subsequent Aramean kings of Zinjirli. Kilamuwa bypassed these Aramean connections, emphasized his Phoenician intellectual heritage, and valorized his Luwian ethnicity: he associated himself with the pre-Aramaic rulers, he named his mother who was Luwian, and he described himself as the parent and benefactor of the indigenous Luwian people.

His memorial inscription is structured and literate and reveals the dimensions of Phoenician, specifically Byblian, literary influence on a traditional society. The inscription is divided into two parts by raised horizontal hatches between the lines of writing and by two vertical strokes at the end of the last line of each part. The first part deals with international affairs and the integrity of the kingdom. The second part is concerned with internal affairs and the resolution of social problems. Both parts have a similar tripartite structure and are marked by a similar repetitive cadence.

> I am Kilamuwa, the son of Ḥayyaʾ.

> Gabbar was king of Yaʾudiya and accomplished nothing;
> there was his son and he accomplished nothing.
> And there was my father, Ḥayyaʾ, and he accomplished nothing;
> and there was my brother Šaʾîl, and he accomplished nothing,
> but I, Kilamuwa, the son of Tml, what I accomplished
> even those who preceded them had not accomplished.

> My father's house was in the midst of mighty kings,
> and each one stretched out his hand to eat it,
> but I was in the hands of the kings
> like a fire devouring the beard and like a fire devouring the hand.
> And the king of the Danunians lorded it over me,
> but I hired the king of Assyria to help me,
> giving a girl for a sheep, and a boy for a garment.

> I Kilamuwa, son of Ḥayyaʾ, have sat on the throne of my father.

> Before the preceding kings, the indigenous people cringed like dogs,
> but to each I was a father, to each I was a mother, to each I was a
>   brother,
> and whoever had not seen the face of a sheep I made the owner of a
>   flock,
> and whoever had not seen the face of an ox I made the owner of a herd,
> and the owner of silver and the owner of gold,
> and whoever had not seen cotton since his youth
> was clothed in linen in my days.
> And I took the indigenous people by the hand,
> and they set their hearts on me like the heart of an orphan on its
>   mother.

> And whoever among my sons might rule in my place,
> and deface this inscription,
> may the indigenous people not respect the barbarians,
> and may the barbarians not respect the indigenous people;
> And whoever might smash this inscription,

Fig. 1.7. Kilamuwa inscription from Zinjirli. Vorderasiatisches Museum, Staatliche Museen zu Berlin, Germany, inv. no. S 6579. Reproduced by permission of the Bildarchiv Preussischer Kulturbesitz / Art Resource, NY. Photo by Gudrun Stenzel.

> may Smiting Baʻal who belongs to Gabbar smash his head,
> and may Baʻal Ḥamon who belongs to his son smash his head,
> and the Charioteer God who is Lord of the dynasty.

In the first part, after his name and title, and after listing the kings of his and of the preceding dynasty, all of whom were totally ineffectual, he states that he did something that even the earliest, and apparently notable, predynastic rulers could not succeed in doing. This, as he explains, was extricating his father's house from interference by neighboring kingdoms and especially by the Danunians of Cilicia, whose capital was at Karatepe, west of the Amanus, with the help of Assyria which supplied, in exchange for Danunian male and female slaves, food and clothing: "sheep and garments." Their interference, clearly, was not military but an arrogant disregard (*ʾdr*, "lord it over," "be high-and-mighty") for Zinjirli's borders and territorial rights, which was instigated by the Danunians and a group of "mighty" (*ʾdrm*) kings who persistently gnawed at his land, "stretched out their hand to eat it," and whom he caught red-handed. Kilamuwa's great accomplishment, in effect, was ridding his country of hunger and poverty, which were induced by this encroachment on his territory and by foraging raids, all of which ultimately could be traced to drought in the entire region—precisely the conditions that had contributed to the decline of Assyria in the tenth century.[202]

This is confirmed as the situation is reviewed in the second part of the inscription. The first section here, like the beginning of the first part, gives Kilamuwa's name and patronymic, but it adds that he is now king instead of his father. In the second section, Kilamuwa compares himself to the preceding kings in his own and the previous dynasty, but not to the earliest kings, and elaborates on his unrivaled accomplishments. His subjects who cringed before the Aramean kings are the indigenous people (*mškbm*, "those settled," or in contrast to the image of "cringing" dogs, "those lying down and sleeping"), that is, the Luwians. Kilamuwa boasts that they now have plenty of food, fine clothing, and some wealth—that is, exactly what he received from Assyria in exchange for Danunian slaves. This connection between the two sections is reinforced by repetition: in the first part there is reference to his father, his mother, and his brother; but in this part, he himself is father, mother, and brother to his people. His Luwian subjects, once treated like dogs, are acknowledged as his children, whom he takes by the hand and who love him as a fatherless child loves its mother.

The third section here corresponds to the last section of the first part, where Kilamuwa states that he extracted his country from the grasp of the neighboring kings. The problem there was infiltration by aliens who consumed the land's food. Here the aliens are identified as "Barbarians" (*bʿrrm*, "acting or speaking as wild beasts"), a separate group that Kilamuwa had integrated into the population and that, as his curse on an unworthy son makes plain, could easily be stirred up to destroy the social contract he had imposed on the land. This unsettled segment of Yaʾudiyan society was manipulated by the Danunian king and was probably the population group that was represented by his own and the preceding dynasty and from which the next dynasty arose, whose language was an archaizing Aramaic patois, or Aramaic-Phoenician creole, which to an educated Byblo-phile

---

202. J. Neumann and S. Parpola, "Climatic Change and the Eleventh–Tenth-Century Eclipse of Assyria and Babylonia," *JNES* 46 (1987) 161–81; S. W. Holloway, "Assyria and Babylonia in the Tenth Century BCE," in *The Age of Solomon: Scholarship at the Turn of the Millennium* (ed. L. K. Handy; Leiden: Brill, 1997) 202–16.

like Kilamuwa, whose monument is such an elegant literary work, would certainly have appeared "Barbarian."[203]

In such a world, the Byblians, alone or with some Sidonians, who may have still resided in the kingdom, were totally out of the social and political loops and did not merit explicit mention, but they were included among the aboriginals in the implicitly laudatory "those who preceded them." So in some fairly distant past, earlier than the Aramaization of the region and certainly earlier than its creolization, they had brought their scribes and script, religion, language, and literature[204] and their populist ideals of good government. These benefactions were not the purpose but the by-product of their passage through the region. They came as skilled craftsmen and artisans, the masons perhaps who had designed and built the original royal palaces in Ya'udiya, and in search of iron or wood (the Amanus was known as the Cypress mountain) and of the raw or semi-worked materials such as ivory or precious stones that were the basic items of their trade and the marks of a new international urban culture.[205]

The Urban Equation

The new urbanization that attracted Byblians to Anatolia and North Syria in the tenth century also drew them to Israel, Philistia, and Judah. These areas were alphabetized by the tenth century: Israel, where the alphabet was a constant of its Canaanite heritage, perhaps from time immemorial; Philistia and Judah, where literacy was a requirement of the intercity and international trade and commerce now being stirred and promoted by the Phoenicians, as everyone rushed to join in the chorus of posttribal awakening. Everywhere the alphabet and trade were cradled in a new urban culture, and everywhere urbane ideals revolved around new Gods, who were chosen precisely because they could supersede local differences and

203. P. E. Dion, *La Langue de Ya'udi* (Waterloo, Ontario: Academic Studies in Religion in Canada, 1974); Tropper, *Die Inschriften von Zincirli*; idem, "Dialektvielfalt und Sprachwandel im frühen Aramäischen: Soziolinguistische Überlegungen," in *The World of the Aramaeans, III: Studies in Language and Literature in Honour of Paul-Eugène Dion* (ed. P. M. M. Daviau, J. W.Wevers, and M. Wiegl; JSOTSup 326; Sheffield: Sheffield Academic Press, 2001) 213–22.

204. T. R. Bryce, "Anatolian Scribes in Mycenaean Greece," *Historia* 48 (1999) 257–64.

205. An inscription by the last king of the "Barbarian" dynasty (written in perfect Standard Aramaic) mentions that his predecessors used the summer and winter palaces that Kilamuwa had built (*TSSI* 2.89–92). He dismisses them as inadequate in comparison with his own, but they did survive for almost a century and must have been substantial. The palace of the dynasty preceding Kilamuwa's was destroyed by fire: see D. Ussishkin, "'Der alte Bau' in Zincirli," *BASOR* 189 (1968) 50–53.

K. R. Maxwell-Hyslop, "Assyrian Sources of Iron," *Iraq* 36 (1974) 139–54; J. D. Muhly et al., "Iron in Anatolia and the Nature of the Hittite Iron Industry," *AnSt* 35 (1985) 67–84; P. R. S. Moorey, "The Craft of the Metalsmith in the Ancient Near East: The Origins of Ironworking," in *From Gulf to Delta and Beyond* (ed. P. R. S. Moorey; Beer-Sheva 8; Beer-Sheva: Ben Gurion University of the Negev, 1995) 53–67.

W. G. Dever, "Archaeology and the 'Age of Solomon': A Case-Study in Archaeology and Historiography," in *The Age of Solomon: Scholarship at the Turn of the Millennium* (ed. L. K. Handy; Leiden: Brill, 1997) 217–51; S. Sherratt and A. Sherratt, "The Growth of the Mediterranean Economy in the Early First Millennium B.C.," *World Archaeology* 24 (1993) 361–78; S. Mazzoni, "Aramaean and Luwian New Foundations," in *Nuove fondazioni nel Vicino Oriente Antico: Realtà e Ideologia* (ed. S. Mazzoni; Pisa: Giardini, 1994) 319–39.

rural fragmentation, and whose temples, in a time of travel and curiosity, symbolized this social and economic transcendence.

At Timnah (Tel Batash) in Philistia, on the road leading from the coast to Beth Shemesh and Jerusalem, there is an inscription on a bowl found in a tenth-century context with the name of its owner or of the potter who made it, "[Be]n Ḥanan."[206] This name appears often in Hebrew, and the script has the cursive indulgence of current Hebrew writing, but the bowl and the person are Philistine and together illustrate the influence of Judean commerce and literacy on a people all too ready and eager to assimilate to their surroundings. From Gezer, in territory belonging to Israel, there is a late tenth-century inscription listing the agricultural activities appropriate to the twelve months of the year.[207] The language (the lexicon, the morphology, and the structure of the text) is strikingly similar to that of the Byblian inscriptions and was either a shared heritage or learned from these notorious educators. But the script is decisively Israelite—essentially a much more relaxed and advanced cursive; as is the idea of defining months by their characteristic activities—the months of vintage are "the two months of song"—rather than by their names. Thus it is clear that Israel had begun to distinguish itself from its Canaanite environment in an already fairly distant past.

Sometime in this historic past, Judah had borrowed the alphabet either from these Byblians or from Tyrians with whom it had normal and persistent relations. However, Judah must have borrowed and adapted it because, although the alphabet was already available in the region, it did not have enough phonemes to be entirely suited to the language of Judah. Further, this must have happened fairly early, because the Moabites got the alphabet and their script tradition from the Judeans or perhaps from their Israelite neighbors and had time to master these basics, as well as the narrative and annalistic styles in which they were used, before they wrote the monumental Mesha Stele in the mid-ninth century. A seventh-century dedicatory inscription from Ekron, by a Philistine king in honor of a Philistine Goddess, is written in Hebrew script but with the morphology, orthography, and themes of an archaic tenth-century Byblian inscription, and it may be that this place also was indebted to Byblos for its induction into the Canaanite way of life sometime in the tenth century.[208]

The Gods who were chosen were mainly familiar from an earlier clan or regional or dynastic setting, but they were new because of the political,

206. G. L. Kelm and A. Mazar, *Timnah: A Biblical City in the Sorek Valley* (Winona Lake, IN: Eisenbrauns, 1995) 111, fig. 6.4; R. Lawton, "Israelite Personal Names of Pre-Exilic Inscriptions," *Bib* 65 (1984) 330–46; F. Israel, "Note di onomastica semitica 7/1. Rassegna critico-bibliografica ed epigrafica su alcune onomastiche palestinesi: Israele e Giuda, la regione filistea," *SEL* 8 (1991) 119–37.

207. *TSSI* 1.1–4.

208. S. Gitin, T. Dothan, and J. Naveh, "A Royal Dedicatory Inscription from Ekron," *IEJ* 47 (1997) 1–16; J. Naveh, "Achish-Ikausu in the Light of the Ekron Dedication," *BASOR* 310 (1998) 35–37; R. G. Lehmann, "Studien zur Formgeschichte der ʿEqron-Inschrift des ʾKYŠ und den phönizischen Dedikationstexten aus Byblos," *UF* 31 (1999) 255–306. The king's name is ʾIkayos (ʾkyš = biblical Achish, Greek *Achaios*, "Achaean"). The Goddess is an otherwise unknown *Ptgyh*. Other inscriptions mention the Goddess Asherah who was popular in Judah at this time, but her name is written in Phoenician, not in Judean orthography (ʾšrt).

economic, and social status they acquired in an emerging nationalist environment. Byblian Baʿal, first recognized by the city in the tenth century, was the God of the Sea, specifically of the Mediterranean Sea, whose praises were sung centuries earlier in the Ugaritic epic, whose myth spread from these places to Judah, and whose liturgies were celebrated in Israel: his inauguration as head of the pantheon was celebrated by refurbishing all the ancient temples; his epithet, as it happened, was "Almighty," and he seems to have symbolized a determination by the city to reaffirm its preeminence on the Levantine coast.

Judah, as biblical and epigraphic sources reveal, was in the service of ʾEl and ʾAšerah, archetypal Canaanite Gods, but it adopted as symbol of its destiny the God Yahweh, patron of the Davidic Dynasty and the aboriginal, outlandish (proto–South Arabian), amphictyonic God of the tribes of Israel. His choice as patron of the king, city, and land was marked by the construction of a fantastic, preordained temple, by the establishment of royal cities, and by the inauguration of an era of peace and international trade.

ʾEl was also the God of ʿAmmon: his official epithet was *"The* King" (*mlkm*—the morphology is South Arabian), and he is mentioned for the first time in an early ninth-century inscription recording the dynastic oracle that assured the king of protection from all his enemies, and authorized him to build a temple.

In Moab, similarly, the choice of Kemosh as national and dynastic God is described by Mesha in the context of his victory over his Israelite enemies and in connection with a building program that included restoration of the town around the borders of the land and culminated in the building of an open-air temple for his God. The God Kemosh was not new (he was the God of Mesha's father and is known much earlier from Ugaritic and Late Bronze Age Syria), but what was new was the choice of this God as an ethnic symbol, an expression of the origins and ideals of a new national spirit.[209]

This revolution in religious structure was the concomitant of political, social, and economic change. It happened in the tenth century, when people had acquired an alphabet and script, when they noticed that their own language was a sign of their own individuality, when there was a trans-ethnic accord valorizing their diversity. The mood is perceptible, but the actual date of its happening is retrieved from mostly ninth-century or later occurrences. In Judah and Moab, their new Gods locked them into a land where borders and boundary markers and regional or traditional divisions were critical. In the Phoenician cities, by contrast, new Gods embodied their aspirations to immortality or divinity, urged them to risk and dare and wager, made life an adventure, and assured them of a constant return on their investment.

---

209. On the comparable elevation of Marduk in Babylon, see W. G. Lambert, "The Reign of Nebuchadnezzar I: A Turning Point in the History of Ancient Mesopotamian Religion," in *The Seed of Wisdom: Essays in Honour of T. J. Meek* (ed. W. S. McCullough; Toronto: University of Toronto Press, 1964) 3–23; S. Dalley, "Statues of Marduk and the Date of *Enūma eliš*," *AoF* 24 (1997) 163–71.

The God of Sidon was 'Eshmun. He is mentioned for the first time in this role, together with Melqart of Tyre, in a mid-eighth-century Assyrian text and then again with Melqart in the early seventh-century Assyrian treaty of Esarhaddon with Ba'al of Tyre.[210] His name, known from a twelfth-century Ugaritic list of offerings to the Gods,[211] from Phoenician, Punic, and Neo-Punic, from scattered occurrences, and from Latin and Greek transcriptions is derived from the root *'šm*, Ugaritic *'iṯm*. In its basic form, it denotes "guilt" or an offense against God or another. The form of his name in the Ugaritic list, however, is factitive[212] and thus connotes the removal of guilt, with "expiator" as an apt translation. His name in Phoenician is composed of the same root but with the masculine agentive afformative *-ûn*; there is also a feminine form of the name and thus a female manifestation of the divine force, 'Ašîmâ, which necessarily omits the masculine ending, but this occurs only in biblical texts as the name of a Goddess worshiped in Hamath and in Samaria and as the name of a Jewish girl buried at Kition in Cyprus in the fifth century and as the theophoric element of a personal name on a mid-eighth-century Israelite seal.[213] The epithets of the Sidonian God are composed of the element *Šd*, "daimon, genius, spirit," an immortal, personal, and familiar manifestation of the divine world,[214] and they express some special quality of his expiation: he is called, both at Ugarit and at Sidon, the "Holy Spirit" (*Šd Qdš*),[215] the spirit of sanctification, the spirit of atonement, the spirit who alleviates guilt; at Sidon, Arvad, 'Amrit, and wherever his fame spread in the Mediterranean world, he is also called the "Healing Spirit" (*Šd Rp'*), the spirit who restores to health and cures the physical and moral illnesses that lead to death. He heals the sick and takes care of the dead who await healing, is worshiped in enjoyment and in recreation, and is a transcendentally populist God totally congenial to the Sidonian mentality.

The God of Tyre was Melqart. He is known from the usual eighth- and seventh-century Assyrian sources but is mentioned first in a ninth-century inscription by the king of Arpad, who heard of him from the Tyrians who settled in Al Mina at the mouth of the Orontes and whose business took them to Carchemish and the Syrian interior. He is the God of fiery im-

---

210. E. Lipiński, *Dieux et déesses de l'univers phénicien et punique* (Studia Phoenicia 14; Louvain: Peeters, 1995) 156.

211. M. C. Astour, "Some New Divine Names from Ugarit," *JAOS* 86 (1966) 277–84; J. Wansbrough, "Antonomasia: The Case for Semitic *'TM*," in *Figurative Language in the Ancient Near East* (ed. M. Mindlin, M. J. Geller, and J. E. Wansbrough; London: School of Oriental and African Studies, 1987) 103–6.

212. The Ugaritic pronunciation *'iṯṯim* is derived from the D-stem (**'aṯṯim*), or factitive, with vowel harmony: see J. Huehnergard, *Ugaritic Vocabulary in Syllabic Transcription* (HSS 32; Atlanta: Scholars Press, 1987; rev. ed., Winona Lake, IN: Eisenbrauns, 2008) 273–75.

213. 2 Kgs 17:30; Amos 8:14; É. Puech, "Notes sur des inscriptions phéniciennes de Kition et Kato Paphos," *Sem* 39 (1990) 99–109, esp. pp. 100–103; N. Avigad, "An Unpublished Phoenician Seal," in *Hommages à André Dupont-Sommer* (ed. A. Caquot and M. Philonenko; Paris: Adrien-Maisonneuve, 1971) 3–4.

214. P. V. Mankowski, *Akkadian Loanwords in Biblical Hebrew* (HSS 47; Winona Lake, IN: Eisenbrauns, 2000) 138–40.

215. A. Caquot, "Une contribution ougaritique à la préhistoire du titre divin Shadday," in *Congress Volume: Paris 1992* (ed. J. A. Emerton; VTSup 51; Leiden: Brill, 1995) 1–12.

Fig. 1.8. Impression of seal (A.O. 3175). Photo by Pierre Bordreuil. Reproduced with permission.

molation and divinization whose paradigmatic career is represented on an eighth-century Tyrian amulet inscribed "king of the Tyrians" (see fig. 1.8) and on a fourth-century bowl depicting the stages of his personal renewal.[216] His story was told by a biblical prophet and derided by a biblical historian (Ezekiel 28, 1 Kings 18), and none of his detractors could condone the paradigm of child sacrifice or tolerate his world renown. He, as his name affirms, was "king" (*milk*) of the "city" (*qart*), the quintessentially urban God, God of the underworld, the celestial and the earthly city, the entrance to whose temple was flanked by pillars (shown in Assyrian reliefs, described by Herodotus, mentioned by the prophet, source of envy and amazement to all who viewed them) that supported the sky, held hell in place, and made room for the glorious island city. He was the God of travel and of invention, the God of adventure and discovery, whose example inspired his devotees to test death and assured them of life. He was the God of an aloof and strangely eclectic society; and everywhere they went, Tyrians brought their wildly creative works that combined the best of the old and the new and simply demanded attention.

An appreciation of this tenth-century urban revolution can be extracted from the biblical record of contemporary events in Judah and Jerusalem. The account moves easily from recollection to myth in order to include the incipient kingdom, from its origins, in the ongoing world created by Tyre (1 Kings 3–11, Ezekiel 28). The origins are legendary.

The kingdom dates from the time of Hiram, a temple builder with the commonest of Tyrian royal names but otherwise unknown, who was like a God, like Melqart specifically, in the Garden of Eden. It was created by Solomon, the Judean surrogate of the Tyrian king, portrayed as a child in a golden age, a temple builder, wise beyond belief. For both of them, Hiram and Solomon, the idyll ended abruptly in the excesses of foreign trade and commerce. The details of this ideal picture are filled out by attributing to Solomon (the initiator of the urban revolution, originator of the cult, and founder of the kingdom) achievements of subsequent kings and of contemporaries in the Tyrian network.

---

216. P. Bordreuil, *Catalogue des sceaux ouest-sémitiques inscrits* (Paris: Bibliothèque Nationale, 1986) 23–24; R. D. Barnett, "Ezekiel and Tyre," *ErIsr* 9 (Albright Volume; 1969) 6–13.

The temple was orchestrated by King Hiram of Tyre, supplied by Tyrians, constructed by Byblian masons and carpenters, adorned by a namesake Hiram of Tyre of mixed Tyrian and Israelite origin, who cast the bronze pillars at its entrance. The pillars were decorated by artists, who copied the styling of eighth-century Phoenician ivory carvers, and outfitted with ninth-century Cypriot bronze stands on wheels, antecedents of the merkabah. The temple was designed to accommodate the whole nation, an idea that gained currency in the late eighth century, when worship was centralized in Jerusalem.

The royal and ritual complex shared features of the sanctuary built by Mesha of Moab in the ninth century at Dibon, and the cities built at Hazor, Gezer, and Megiddo are like the border towns that Mesha restored as administrative and commercial centers. Solomon had no use for the horses and chariots he amassed, but they came in handy when Ahab joined the anti-Assyrian coalition in the mid-ninth century at the battle of Qarqar and were readily available at that time from his allies in Cilicia and Musri.

Foreign trade was the warp and woof of the Tyrian network to which Solomon's Judah may have aspired, but regular voyages to Tarshish did not begin until the eighth century in the reign of another Hiram. Sheba does not appear until the same time; Arabian queens are a still later phenomenon; and Judah becomes a pivot and stellar performer in the Tyrian trade network only in the seventh. Solomon's ideal Jerusalem is embellished with the accomplishments of later kings who could not be mentioned because their ideas or orthodoxy were dubious—Ahab in the ninth, Hezekiah in the eighth, Manasseh in the seventh century—but this splurge of kudos reflected the persistent belief that Tyre was at the heart of a religious revolution in the tenth century and that Jerusalem in all its grandeur must have been a part of it. The account is impressionistic and lets Tyre and Jerusalem fade in and out and illuminate each other, as a supple chronology reflects their timelessness.

Conclusion

In the tenth century, Tyre, Sidon, and Byblos began to display the civic and ethnic diversity that would continue to develop and characterize their history. Each reached out to separate parts and peoples of the mainland. Each went by distinct sea lanes to different parts of the north and west. Each displayed a different attitude and life-style, and each chose a particular God to express some link to the story of its past and some belief that let it go boldly into the future. The land was filled and becoming ever more full of new blood—immigrants from everywhere in new alliances with the natives—and the three cities distinguished themselves by blending them into their original Canaanite stock.

The Mediterranean world was wide open to them, and each had something to take and something to receive. Tyrians relied on the expertise of inland settlers and middlemen for the products and supplies that their creative touch turned into the articles of their fame. Sidon was the city of invention in metalworking and sent its craftsmen and artisans to the sources of iron, copper, gold, and silver, where they lived and worked in these and the imitative arts in exchange for rights to their resources. Byblos was the literary giant of the Levant and, with its expertise in the mysteries of wood and stone, brought writing, story, and song where it went. It was a century of new directions, and even the biblical writers who made xenophobia a cornerstone of their historiography tried to find a quiet corner of this emerging Phoenician world where their kings and their country could take root and grow and burst all bounds.

Chapter 2

The Phoenician City-States Receive and Transmit Knowledge: The Ninth Century B.C.E.

In the ninth century, Tyre, Sidon, and Byblos continued to develop their individual characteristics and became increasingly differentiated from each other and from the nations and states of inland Syria and Canaan. Syria was urbanized, Aramean and Neo-Hittite kingdoms predominated north and east of the Orontes, the coastal area was inhabited mainly by indigenous Syrians, and the coastal towns aligned themselves more closely with Sidon or Byblos to the south. In Canaan, Tyre maintained its disparate possessions in the Plain of ʿAkko, and its right to these and to the territory east of them was confirmed by Shalmaneser III's mid-century tour de force through the region. Byblos controlled the Lebanon and the Beqaʿ. Sidon was surrounded by satellite cities from Sarepta in the south to Beirut in the north.

Each of these three cities had separate and privileged relations with the urban centers of emergent nations of inland Canaan or Syria: Tyre with Judah and Jerusalem, Sidon with Israel and Samaria, Byblos with Hamath and Damascus, and each with the near and far network that was being established by its patron court. The destiny of each hung in the balance of its overseas explorations and commercial connections in Cyprus and Cilicia, in North Syria and Anatolia, in Crete and the Aegean, and in the far western Mediterranean. The ninth century, characterized by the bold self-assertion of national states, saw the beginning of a new internationalism, with all its conflicts and competitions, shifting alliances, and far-flung cooperation.

The Inland Cities in Relation to the City-States

The mainland cities are known from literary, epigraphic, and annalistic references, and from a smattering of material remains. There is some information on trade and international relations; on religion, art, and iconography; and on industry and economics; but very little on social or cultural history. The evidence provides a framework, however, that can be filled out bit by bit as each city is followed in its overland peregrinations and overseas adventures.

88

In the ninth century, a new complex of pottery forms began to appear at Tyre, at its inland satellites such as Joya and Khirbet Silm, at coastal sites such as ʾAchzib and Tell Abu Hawam on the Bay of ʿAkko, and at places such as Megiddo and Hazor in Northern Israel.[1] ʾAchzib, as the predominance of Red Slip and Black-on-Red pottery shows, was thoroughly Tyrian, but separate cemeteries and a variety of burial practices (built tombs with simple inhumations of individuals and families, cremation, and multiple burials in shaft tombs)[2] reflect the diverse origins of the population or social or economic isolation of some sectors: an early ninth-century tomb built of ashlar blocks, with a gabled roof was for a warrior who was buried with his iron weapons (a sword, dagger, knife, axe, spear, and arrows) and with drinking vessels and some imported Cypriot wares.[3]

ʿAkko's prosperity is evident in the construction of a new administrative center, and Abu Hawam's resurgence is attested by a new residential area well protected by strong dikes and retaining walls.[4] Shiqmona at the foot of Mount Carmel was proudly in the Tyrian orbit: a storage jar found there is inscribed in late ninth-century cursive script with the name of a Tyrian official (*Baʿalay*) and his rank, president of the Popular Assembly or "The Hundred" of Tyre (*rab miʾat*). The jar never reached him, however, but was destroyed by fire in storage.[5]

Sites that Tyrians frequented in the Lower Galilee (the area east of the Plain of ʿAkko and north of the Jezreel Valley) flourished in the first part of the century: a bronze seal with glass inlay from Khirbet Rosh Zayit at the eastern edge of the plain is thoroughly Egyptianizing in its motifs and design and representative of Tyrian cultural and economic dominance there and in the whole region.[6] Southeast of Carmel, at the western end of the Jezreel Valley, market towns such as Yokneʿam and Tel Qiri did business

1. P. M. Bikai, *The Pottery of Tyre* (Warminster: Aris & Phillips, 1978) 57; S. V. Chapman, "A Catalogue of Iron Age Pottery from the Cemeteries of Silm, Joya, Qraye and Qasmieh of South Lebanon," *Berytus* 21 (1972) 55–154; C. Briese, "Fruheisenzeitliche bemalte phonizische Kannen von Fundplatzen der Levantekuste," *HBA* 12 (1985) 7–118, esp. pp. 26–32.

2. M. W. Prausnitz, "Die Nekropole von Akhziv und die Entwicklung der Keramik von 10. Bis zum 7. Jahrhundert v. Chr. in Akhziv, Samaria und Ashdod," *Phönizier im Westen* (ed. H. G. Niemeyer; Mainz am Rhein: von Zabern, 1982) 31–44; M. W. Prausnitz and E. Mazar, "Achzib," *NEAEHL* 1.32–36; E. Mazar, "Phoenician Family Tombs at Achziv: A Chronological Typology (1000–400 BCE)," in *Fenicios y Territorio: Actas del II Seminario Internacional sobre Temas Fenicios, Guardamar del Segura—11 de abril de 1999* (ed. A. González Prats; Alicante: Instituto Alicantino de Cultura "Juan Gil-Albert," 2000) 189–215; M. Dayagi-Mendels, *The Akhziv Cemeteries: The Ben-Dor Excavations, 1941–1944* (Israel Antiquities Authority Reports 15; Jerusalem: Israel Antiquities Authority, 2002).

3. E. Mazar, *The Phoenician Family Tomb N. 1 at the Northern Cemetery of Achziv (10th–6th Centuries B.C.E.* (Cuadernos de Arqueología Mediterraneo 10; Barcelona: Universidad Pompeu Fabra—Laboratorio di Arqueología, 2004).

4. J. Balensi, M. D. Herrera, and M. Artzy, "Abu Hawam, Tell," *NEAEHL* 1.7–14; M. Dothan, "Acco," *NEAEHL* 1.16–23. The wall at Tell Abu Hawam was colossal and was interpreted as a fortification wall by its excavators, but it is not clear what threat was perceived or who might attack. The site was at the mouth of the river Kishon, which eventually silted up due to falling sea levels, and the construction may have been motivated by changes of this sort.

5. A. Lemaire, "Notes d'épigraphie nord-ouest sémitique: L'inscription phénicienne de Palestine no. 37 (Shiqmona)," *Sem* 30 (1980) 17–32, esp. pp. 17–19.

6. Z. Gal, "A Phoenician Bronze Seal from Hurbat Rosh Zayit," *JNES* 53 (1994) 27–31; idem, "The Lower Galilee in the Iron Age I: Analysis of Survey Material and Its Historical Interpretation,"

with the Tyrian ports and were hardly assimilated to their Israelite neighbors.[7] Tyre itself became very prosperous and traded with the Arameans, with the Hittites of Hamath and the central Syrian states, and with the kingdoms of Judah and Israel, and instead of getting involved in their wars with Assyria cooperated by paying an irregular and comparatively modest tribute.[8]

One of these occasions was in 841 B.C.E., when Shalmaneser III celebrated a successful and profitable raid against Hazael of Damascus by sweeping through this area on his way to Mount Carmel, called "The Headland of Ba'al" (*ba-'-li-ra-'-si*), where he set up his monument in the precinct of Melqart, the Ba'al of Tyre, and received tribute from "the inhabitants of Tyre and Sidon and Jehu the son of Omri," the king of Israel.[9] Tyre and Sidon (Byblos is also included sometimes) probably contributed raw resources and some finished products, but Jehu paid, besides bulk silver and gold, mostly drinking vessels that he could have obtained only on the Phoenician, specifically Sidonian market.[10]

This market was handy, at least until recently, because Ahab, his predecessor on the throne, had married Jezebel, daughter of the king of Sidon, and Samaria the capital had become a center of Phoenician crafts: its tableware was an elegant variety of Phoenician Red Slip, and it was a showcase for Sidonian ivories. The ivory inlay decorating the Samarian palace was lavish and beautiful and especially memorable for its incorporation of the portrait of Jezebel, the imperious "Woman-in-the-Window" as its most splendid symbol (see a similar example of a "woman-in-the-window," in fig. 2.1). The early kings of North Israel were all notably wealthy landowners, having made their money in olive oil and wine, and Jezebel, for all her charm and personality, sealed a coveted commercial alliance between the two countries. 'Omri, founder of the dynasty and namesake of the kingdom in contemporary Assyrian sources, charioteer, and commander of the army, could afford two talents of silver to buy Samaria as his personal property and national capital. Ahab, his son and successor, was a charioteer and a real estate tycoon. Jehu was a charioteer and the son of a textile magnate.

Jezebel had access to the royal seal but also had her own seal and did business in her own name. She is known traditionally as a strong woman and as a shrewd and unscrupulous bargainer, and her seal (see fig. 2.2) suits her reputation. It is inscribed with the Phoenician, not the Hebrew form of her name (*yzbl*, not *'yzbl*).[11] The upper register shows a winged sphinx crouching and facing an *ankh*, or symbol of life; the lower register features

TA 15–16 (1988–89) 56–64; idem, "Hurbat Rosh Zayit and the Early Phoenician Pottery," *Levant* 24 (1992) 173–82.

7. A. Ben-Tor, "Jokneam," *NEAEHL* 3.805–11; A. Faust, "Ethnic Complexity in Northern Israel during Iron Age II," *PEQ* 132 (2000) 2–27.

8. P. Garelli, "Remarques sur les rapports entre l'Assyrie et les cités phéniciennes," *Atti 1*, 1.61–66; J. Elayi, "Les cités phéniciennes entre liberté et sujetion," *Dialogues d'Histoire Ancienne* 16 (1990) 93–113.

9. *ANET* 280; *HT* 175–78; E. Lipiński, *Itineraria Phoenicia* (Studia Phoenicia 18; Leuven: Peeters, 2004) 1–15.

10. *ANET* 281.

11. N. Avigad, "The Seal of Jezebel," *IEJ* 14 (1964) 274–76, pl. 56C.

Fig. 2.1. "Woman-in-the-window" from Nimrud (BM 118159). © The Trustees of the British Museum.

a falcon with a flail on its back, standing on a bent papyrus stalk under a winged sun disk and between two crowned *uraei*, or cobras. When Ahab died, she and her family were assassinated by Jehu, acting in cahoots with Hazael of Damascus, and the bond she had forged between Israel and Sidon and their working relationship with the Arameans dissolved.

Both Jehu and Hazael were usurpers, and their synchronized coups were a critical moment in Israelite foreign affairs and in Phoenician trade relations with these inland nations. Hazael galvanized the Aramean states, created a league of "All Aram" in Syria, prompted Moab to join the alliance, and was intent on excluding Tyre, Sidon, Byblos, and their associates in Israel and Judah from this mainly military and political project.

A focus on the moment is provided by an Aramaic inscription of Hazael. The background, to which the inscription alludes, is the anti-Assyrian

Fig. 2.2. Jezebel seal (IAA 65-321). Reproduced by permission of the Israel Antiquities Authority.

alliance led by Hamath that included Israel and Damascus and the seaboard cities of Syria commercially aligned with Sidon (Sidon was not immediately involved) that had burst on the international scene first at the battle of Qarqar in 853 B.C.E. and then surfaced repeatedly under the brunt of Assyrian harassment until the coups in 841 B.C.E. Hazael extricated himself from this useless cycle, and Jehu was his witless accomplice:[12]

12. A. Biran and J. Naveh, "An Aramaic Stele Fragment from Tel Dan," *IEJ* 43 (1993) 81–98; idem, "The Tel Dan Inscription: A New Fragment," *IEJ* 45 (1995) 1–18.

[I am Hazael king of 'Aram son of . . . . . Hadad'ezer [king of 'Aram] said, ["Make a treaty with me" and . . . . . my [father] made a treaty [with him]. He went up [with him] when he made war with As[syria], and my father slept, he went to his fathers. And the king of Israel in earlier days used to enter the land of my father, but Hadad made me king, me myself, and Hadad went before me. I freed myself from the oaths on my kingdom, and I killed evil kings who harnessed a thousand chariots and a thousand horsemen: [I killed Jo]ram son of [Ahab] king of Israel, and I killed [Ahaz]iah son of [Jehoram ki]ng of the House of David, and I made [that town a ruin and I turned] their land into d[esolation] . . . . another . . . . became king of Israel . . . . [and I laid] siege to . . . .

The first line is missing, but it surely named Hazael and his father, who was not the king of Damascus but one of the district governors, called "kings," who were engaged in the wars of the king (1 Kgs 20:1).

The king at the battle of Qarqar was Hadadezer, and the war was with Assyria, and both reconstructions fit the available space: Hazael's father was killed ("slept, went to his fathers") in the battle, and this fixed Hazael's claim to be a loyal servant of king and country and justified his coup—in his own eyes, at least. It was, apparently, common knowledge that Ahab was one of the protagonists at that battle. Hazael explains that the relations between Damascus and Israel were only incidentally military and essentially commercial. Concretely, the king of Israel "used to enter, trade in the land of my father"; more specifically, trade was governed by a treaty; in more detail according to another version, the king of Damascus was defeated in battle by Ahab and was forced to make a treaty allowing Israel to establish markets in Damascus, just as Damascus until that time had been active in the bazaars of Samaria (1 Kgs 20:34). Hazael became king, in this other version, by assassinating the king, but in his own emphatic version, by the grace of God; and the first thing he did was rescind the treaty oaths weighing on his kingdom. The occasion for this was the war against Israel and Judah at Jabesh Gilead, the town Hazael claims he destroyed, and the abrogation of the oaths was signaled by murdering the kings of Israel and Judah—an exploit Hazael proudly claims as his own, although in the other version it is attributed it to the treachery of Jehu (2 Kgs 8:16–9:28).

The inscription ends in a broken context with the accession of Jehu, the next king of Israel, and with reference to a siege, which suggests that bad blood continued between them (see 2 Kgs 10:32–33, 13:22). Jehu returned to the protective shade of Assyria and to the productive trade with Tyre and Sidon that it assured. The victory stele that was erected in the monumental gateway to Dan, the economic and religious capital of the North, was smashed soon after the memory of Hazael faded, and it was reused as a block in a retaining wall.

The Aramean wars loosened Israel's grip on northern Transjordan, and Mesha of Moab (much more effectual than the vacillating Jehu) had his chance to achieve the country's independence.[13] This is dated to the reign

---

13. B. Routledge, "Learning to Love the King: Urbanism and State in Iron Age Moab," in *Urbanism in Antiquity: From Mesopotamia to Crete* (ed. W. E. Aufrecht, N. A. Mirau, and S. W. Gauley; JSOTSup 244; Sheffield: Sheffield Academic Press, 1997) 130–44; idem, "The Politics of Mesha: Segmented Identities and State Formation in Iron Age Moab," *JESHO* 43 (2000) 221–56.

of one of ʿOmri's successors and may have coincided with the defeat of Israel and Judah at Jabesh Gilead and the deaths of Joram and Ahaziah. Mesha restored and extended the borders of Moab. His capital building program was the envy of his neighbors, and he seized the initiative in overland trade. In the southern sector, he controlled access to the roads through Edom to the Red Sea. In the north, he built 100 cattle ranches[14] and three towns for his shepherds and, presumably, now sold on the open market the beef and lamb and wool that he used to surrender to Israel in tribute.

Phoenician cultural influence on Moab in the ninth century was slight and indirect, such as for instance alphabetization via Israel and Judah, and after Hazael's reorganization of Syria, Moab's economy depended mainly on trade with the Aramean federation. There are traces of Judean influence or of a shared religious heritage, in the instance of the immolation of captives and in the incident of child sacrifice recorded by Mesha. The account of his wars indicates that he was attempting to regain the cities and territories that ʿOmri and his successors had snatched when they expanded their trade routes to include the King's Highway.

One of these cities was Nebo in the northwest quadrant of Moab which, under Omride rule, had an Israelite memorial to Israelite ancestors and a Temple of Yahweh. When he captured it, Mesha killed (*hrg*) its men, women, male and female children, and pregnant women, whom he had dedicated (*ḥrm*) to ʿAštar-Kamuš. Child sacrifice, also an incident in these wars, is recorded on a black basalt stele that was found near the southern border of the land:[15]

> [I am Mešaʿ son of Ka]mušyit, king of Moab, the Di[bonite. I offered my firstborn son to ʿAštar]-Kamuš as a burnt offering because [Kamuš lov]ed him, [and I dedicated him to be his] son. And now I have made this [stele as a memorial to him].

The inscription is in three lines and is reconstructed easily from the remaining clues and from its association with the context of the wars: it begins exactly like Mesha's memorial inscription; "as a burnt offering" (*lmbʿr*) is legible and requires the cognate verb "offer" (*hʿbrty*, "I offered"); "dedication" (*ḥrm*) is a technical term used by Mesha; the first two letters of "love" ("because Kamuš loved him") are legible and do not lend themselves to any other reconstruction; "his son" is legible, the making of a memorial slab is standard and predictable, and the sacrifice of his firstborn son is noted with awe in the biblical version of Mesha's wars as the desperate tactic that finally assured him of victory over Israel (2 Kgs 3:27).

Dedication (*ḥrm*) was a profoundly primitive religious gesture: in war it involved killing (*hrg*) the victims with a weapon, usually a sword, was merciless and indiscriminate; in an act of devotion, it was an offering by fire of a chosen and intact victim, who was transformed by this awesome act from human to divine status—from child of the king to son of the God. Both

---

14. A. Dearman, ed., *Studies in the Mesha Inscription and Moab* (Archaeology and Biblical Studies 2; Atlanta: Scholars Press, 1989) 95, 98, lines 28–29: *wʾnk . mlkt[y ʿl .] mʾt . bqrn*, "And my kingdom included a hundred cattle ranches" (*bqrn*).

15. *TSSI* 1.83–84; B. Margalit, "Studies in NW Semitic Inscriptions," *UF* 26 (1994) 271–315, esp. pp. 278–80.

were common in Israel, in Israel's wars of conquest and in Israel's royal rituals, and this likely was the source of Mesha's inspiration.

Judah, as Hazael's stele says and as Mesha's memorial insinuates, was becoming involved in Israelite policy, but it lagged in international, specifically in Phoenician affairs. In the ninth century, for Judean writers, the Phoenician city-states were distinctive and interesting not because of their wealth and the products they traded but because of their Gods and their religious influence on all their contacts. The basic charm of these Gods was their humanity, how they resolved personal predicaments, how they meshed with civic and communal aspirations, how they were not kings or generals and had none of their emblems, how they were not even typically divine. But they were legendary, accessible in stories. Their transfer to Israel during the reign of Jezebel and through the reign of Jehu, when Israel otherwise might seem to have been in a commercial eddy, is evident in the stories told about them (1 Kings 17–2 Kings 13) and is a clue to the profound cultural influence that Tyre, Sidon, and Byblos actually had on their inland Israelite and Judean neighbors.

Mount Carmel was the southern border of the district of Tyre and the site of a Temple of Melqart, God of the city. It was where Jehu and the kings of Tyre and Sidon paid tribute to Shalmaneser III in 841 B.C.E. It is known as the Temple of Baʿal Lebanon in mid-eighth-century inscriptions of the Tyrian governors of Carthage in Cyprus. It is the sanctuary of Baʿal derided in a late Judean polemic against foreign Gods that, despite its pique, is well informed on the cult of the God and very jealous in claiming his attributes for the God of Israel.

There is a competition between Melqart and Yahweh on sending fire from the sky to consume a funeral pyre: this is farcical because mortal Melqart is supposed to die on the pyre in order to be awakened by summoning or shouting, as the God, but in this contest cannot summon the fire, and the shouts to rouse him are useless. The taunts that follow reveal his true attributes: the God is asleep and has to be wakened; he is on a voyage (like Heracles in Greek lore, Melqart is the God of Mediterranean travel); he is thinking of something to benefit his people, but practical wisdom and useful knowledge are precisely what characterizes Melqart. The farce continues with Yahweh's winning the competition and despite himself becoming Baʿal but not a personal God like Phoenician Melqart; instead, he is a stereotypical, generic, atmospheric, rain-giving God.

Similarly, the God of Sidon whom Ahab adopted to satisfy his treaty obligations and to please his wife was ʾEshmun, the God of Healing and Expiation, but in the story of their accession is identified with the standard black-magic Baʿal. But the identity of the God is acknowledged in the immediate sequel in anecdotes that reveal his attributes: a woman and child doomed to death by starvation are saved by a self-perpetuating source of food—this happened at Sarepta, which belonged to Sidon; a woman whose child was not healed confesses that her sin is the cause of death; a king who looks for healing in Ekron from a Philistine God finds out too late that Yahweh of Samaria, who lets him die, might have been his healer; the commander of the Aramean armies is cured of his leprosy by the lustral rites performed in honor of ʾEshmun. Yahweh mirrors the Phoenician God but not surprisingly once again lacks his human touch.

The God of Byblos was Adonis, the Baʿal who vanquished Death, the eternal youth who is the delight of women. His cult was official at the royal sanctuaries of Bethel and Dan in Israel, where he was honored as the Golden Calf, the offspring of Baʿal the Bull, the symbol of the God of Regeneration. The myth that invigorated its cult is represented on an incense stand from Taanach in the western Jezreel Valley (see fig. 2.3).[16] The stand is square and topped by a shallow bowl and consists of four registers: in the top register there is a calf cavorting under a winged sun disk and between the two pillars at the entrance to a temple; below is a tree of life flanked by ibexes and framed by lions facing forward; below this is an empty space flanked by female sphinxes; the bottom register has a full frontal naked girl with her arms raised to touch the ears of lions that stand beside her. Together they narrate Baʿal's victory over Death: he is the Calf, protected by the Sun, who in the myth was instrumental in his victory; the second register is Life, and the third is Death, the two stages in his victory; and the lowest is his sister ʿAnat, the perpetual girl, his companion on all his exploits. The God is not recognized in the account but is lumped together with the generic Baʿal, but again the confusion is sorted out in anecdotes; twice a woman's darling boy dies and is raised to life; a dead body touches the bones of a man who expects to live again (the bones in Byblian belief are the token of resurrection), and the dead body comes to life.

Dynasties and national states developed in the ninth century around strong international economies engineered, at last in their convergence, by the systems of trade and commerce being tested by Tyre, Sidon, and Byblos. Israel interfered in Moab in an effort to get involved in trade with North Africa and aligned itself with Sidon in the hope of profiting from its trade with maritime Syria. Moab evolved from a rich and productive land into a protectionist kingdom strung out along the King's Highway. Edom declared its independence, Judah labored under the dominance of Israel, Philistia was self-sustaining. The rise and interface of national states was a mixed blessing for Tyre, Sidon, and Byblos and prompted them to look to new frontiers in the cities and town of Syria, Anatolia, and throughout the Mediterranean world.

Phoenicia, Syria, and Anatolia: The Effects of National States on the City-States

The rise and establishment of national states in the ninth century created opportunities for Tyre, Sidon, and Byblos but also imposed political

---

16. R. Hestrin, "The Cult Stand from Taʿanach and Its Religious Background," in *Phoenicia and the East Mediterranean in the First Millennium b.c.* (ed. E. Lipiński; Studia Phoenicia 5; Louvain: Peeters, 1987) 61–77; idem, "The Cult Stand from Taanach: Aspects of the Iconographic Tradition of Early Iron Age Cult Objects in Palestine," in *From Nomadism to Monarchy: Archaeological and Historical Aspects of Early Israel* (ed. I. Finkelstein and N. Naʾaman; Jerusalem: Israel Exploration Society, 1994) 352–81; idem, "The Art of Palestine during the Iron Age II: Local Traditions and External Influences (10th–8th Centuries bce)," in *Images as Media: Sources for the Cultural History of the Near East and the Eastern Mediterranean (1st Millennium bce)* (ed. C. Uehlinger; Göttingen: Vandenhoeck & Ruprecht, 2000) 165–83.

Fig. 2.3. Taanach cult
stand (ASOJS 4197). Re-
produced by permission
of the Israel Antiquities
Authority.

and economic restrictions. There was private enterprise, which continued
as before and enjoyed much greater scope. There was also official or public
or palatial business, which was run according to rules in process of for-
mulation, and there were alliances and coalitions based on formal treaties
or temporary agreements. Commerce was formalized, on ancient models,
by giving gifts, writing orders, making inventories; standardizing weights,
measures, and methods of payment; and recognizing responsibilities to the

Map 3. Phoenicia and environs (produced by Christopher Brinker).

members of the corporation. But there were new problems and solutions: overland and overseas routes to be negotiated, docking and marketing rights, rates of exchange, taxes and custom duties. The cities of the Phoenician coast were faced with rivalries and competition that prompted them to adopt a common cause while maintaining their age-old individuality. Their common cause was a search for new partners and new sources of supply in familiar but less-developed regions of the mainland that were accessible by sea and on the islands of the eastern and western Mediterranean. They went to improve their international status and their own standard of living, and they went for the sake of their old and their many new clients, who were developing a taste for exotica and a growing list of staples. They went to discover a world and, with the pride engendered by centuries of successful accommodation of newcomers in their homeland, to enlighten and entertain, to share their wisdom and skills, to teach their trades, and to spread their philosophy of cooperation and their gospel of prosperity. They were empowered by their belief in Gods who, mortals like themselves, were immortalized for their lasting benefits to their people. The world they discovered was the world of genius and enterprise that they were instrumental in creating, and it thrived as long as peoples and nations could appreciate, envy, and emulate their spirit of adventure.

While Tyre had access to lands in Galilee, Sidon relied on a confederation of sister cities along the coast of Lebanon. These places provided the metropolis with skilled labor and with the supplies (such as food and ingredients for its unguents) that it needed for its domestic use and for its retail businesses in Syria and overseas. They may have been governed by Sidon, and their people may have been called Sidonians, but they did not have their own kings, usually are not mentioned in contemporary texts, and do not seem to have had any political importance beyond their relations with Sidon.[17]

The most northerly sister city was Beirut. This was a relatively important town in the fourteenth century, and the Amarna letters regularly associate it especially with Sidon and with Byblos. At this time it was fortified, but by the ninth century, when it had no king, the protective glacis was abandoned and covered with dirt and debris. Storerooms of the eighth and seventh centuries with locally made jars, and a few Cypriot and Attic transport vessels may also be indicative of Beirut's ninth-century function and connections in the Sidonian orbit.[18]

South of the city, at Khalde, there is a cemetery with 178 graves, mostly of adults but also of adolescents and children.[19] One of the graves was marked by a hewn stone inscribed with the feminine name Patatay (*ptty*), probably of Cilician origin.[20] Two of the adult graves contained scaraboid seals, one

17. D. Bonatz, "Some Considerations on the Material Culture of Coastal Syria in the Iron Age," *EVO* 16 (1993) 123–57.

18. Leila Badre, "Les découvertes archéologiques du centre-ville de Beyrouth," *CRAIBL* (1996) 87–97; idem, "Les premiers découvertes phéniciennes à Beyrouth," *Actas* 4, 3.941–61; G. Markoe, *Phoenicians* (Peoples of the Past; London: British Museum, 2000) 82.

19. R. Saidah, "Fouilles de Khaldé: Rapport préliminaire sur la première et deuxième campagnes (1961–1962)," *BMB* 19 (1966) 51–90, pls. 1–7.

20. P. Bordreuil, "Epigraphes phéniciennes sur bronze, sur pierre et sur céramique," in *Archéologie au Levant: Recueil à la mémoire de Roger Saidah* (Lyon: Maison de l'Orient, 1982) 187–92, esp. pp. 190–91, fig. 2; see P. H. J. Houwink Ten Cate, *The Luwian Population Groups of Lycia and Cilicia Aspera during the Hellenistic Period* (Leiden: Brill, 1961) 158.

with five registers of pseudohieroglyphic.[21] The second portrays two dancing figures[22] belonging to a man and a woman, respectively, both of whom
may have been merchants who used their seals (which were pierced and
could be hung about their necks) as jewelry and personal identification. A
child's grave was accoutered with a miniature painted mask, whose prototype was found in an eleventh-century context at Kition in Cyprus.[23] The
graveyard is right by the sea, and Khalde may have been a fishing village,
the small port of which would have supplied Beirut and provisioned Sidonian ships from Cyprus and Cilicia.

Sarepta, on the coast between Tyre and Sidon, was the southernmost
Sidonian partner in domestic and foreign trade in the ninth century. It is
not mentioned in the Ugaritic archives, but two inscriptions in the late
Ugaritic cuneiform alphabet, both from about the end of the thirteenth
century, have been found in the ruins of the town. The texts are written
in the Canaanite form of this script and in Phoenician rather than in Ugaritic: one is on the edge of a bowl and names the potter and the festival of
Baʿal for which he designed it ("Crater [which] Yadaʿbaʿal made for the New
Moon of Baʿal"); the other, on a jar handle, may be the name of the owner
("Adon") but could also be the epithet of Byblian Baʿal, "Adonis," and indicate that the jug was used in the rituals of this God.[24]

The biblical and archaeological evidence marks Sarepta as a Sidonian
town,[25] but the worship of Baʿal, or perhaps specifically of Byblian Baʿal,
implied by these texts may suggest that this manufacturing center, port,
and later pilgrimage destination was operated by a consortium of Byblians
and Sidonians. The town prospered in the tenth and ninth centuries, when
there were new streets and a significant use of ashlar masonry, regular contacts with Cyprus, and a flourishing pottery industry.[26]

The pottery industry, which seems to have supplied the whole Sidonian
market, was marked by new technology and by new forms, such as Red Slip
burnished bowls and Red Slip jugs with lines of black and red paint. One
of the latter, of which only a fragment is preserved, was inscribed with an
extraordinary series of cursive Phoenician letters.[27] They were painted and

---

21. W. Culican, "A Phoenician Seal from Khaldeh," *Levant* 6 (1974) 195–98, pls. 25–26.

22. Saidah, "Fouilles de Khaldé," pl. 6.53.

23. G. E. Markoe, "The Emergence of Phoenician Art," *BASOR* 279 (1990) 13–26, esp. p. 15.

24. P. Bordreuil, "L'inscription phénicienne de Sarafand en cunéiformes alphabétiques," *UF*
11 (1979) 63–67, pl. 1. É. Puech, "Nouvelle inscription en alphabet cunéiforme court à Sarepta,"
RB 96 (1989) 236–44, pl. 20.

25. 1 Kgs 17:9 ("Sarepta which [belongs] to Sidon"); R. B. Koehl, *Sarepta III: The Imported
Bronze and Iron Age Wares from Area II, X* (Beirut: Librairie Orientale, 1985).

26. W. P. Anderson, "The Kilns and Workshops of Sarepta (Sarafand, Lebanon): Remnants of
a Phoenician Ceramic Industry," *Berytus* 35 (1987) 41–66; idem, *Sarepta I: The Late Bronze and Iron
Age Strata of Area II, Y* (Beirut: Librairie Orientale, 1988); I. A. Khalifeh, *Sarepta II: The Late Bronze
and Iron Age Periods of Area II, X* (Beirut: Librairie Orientale, 1988).

27. J. Teixidor, "Selected Inscriptions," in *Sarepta: A Preliminary Report on the Iron Age* (ed.
J. B. Pritchard; Philadelphia: University of Pennsylvania Museum, 1975) 97–107, figs. 53–55, esp.
p. 101, fig. 53.1; F. M. Cross, "Early Alphabetic Scripts," in *Symposia Celebrating the Seventy-Fifth
Anniversary of the Founding of the American Schools of Oriental Research (1900–1975)* (ed. F. M.
Cross; Cambridge MA: American Schools of Oriental Research, 1979) 97–123, esp. pp. 97–98,
fig. 2. Teixidor assigned the sherd to the ninth century. Cross noted that the form and stance of
the ʾalep resemble archaic Greek *alpha*.

Fig. 2.4. Inscribed
pot sherd from
Sarepta (Penn Mu-
seum image, SAR
2460 II A-6, level
2a). © University
of Pennsylvania
Museum of Ar-
chaeology and
Anthropology.

written, as is evident from their stance and the shading of the lines, from
left to right like Greek rather than from right to left like Phoenician (see
fig. 2.4).

The first letter is only partially preserved on the left margin of the sherd,
but it is clearly a back-to-front (reversed) *yod* and is similar in stance and
shape to the earliest Greek angular-*S iota*.[28] The next letter is *ḥet*, with
slightly curved vertical lines and three more-or-less parallel horizontal
lines, a cursive prototype of the standard early Greek (*h*)*eta*. The third letter is *ʾalep*, rotated to the left 90 degrees from its usual Phoenician stance
and resembling some early rounded forms of Greek *alpha*. The last letter on
the right is a cursive *ʿayin*, drawn as an angle from the upper right down
to left, then back to the right along the horizontal, and then closed on the
right by a vertical line: it is rotated 90 degrees to the right from its Phoenician stance, resembles the less angular *omicron* of the Dipylon oenochoe,[29]
and is the prototype of this letter's rhomboid shape. What is extraordinary
about the sherd, then, is that a potter in ninth-century Sarepta decorated
a fine Sidonian jug with the Greek vowels (*iota, eta, alpha, omicron*) in their
Greek stance, but in contemporary ninth-century Phoenician forms or in
Greek forms that still resembled very closely their Phoenician archetypes.[30]

---

28. L. H. Jeffrey, *The Local Scripts of Archaic Greece* (Oxford: Clarendon, 1961) 66, pl. 1.1.

29. P. K. McCarter Jr., *The Antiquity of the Greek Alphabet and the Early Phoenician Scripts* (HSM
9; Missoula, MT: Scholars Press, 1975) pl. 4.

30. There is a graffito on a fifth-century Attic skyphos from Dor (republished in J. C. Waldbaum, "Greeks *in* the East or Greeks *and* the East? Problems in the Definition and Recognition of
Presence," *BASOR* 305 [1997] 1–17, esp. p. 9, fig. 8) that suggests that Phoenicians, or Greeks in
a Phoenician environment, retained quasi-Phoenician forms of the Greek alphabet. The letters

Just as striking as the writing of Greek vowels on a Phoenician pot is the fact that they were not written in their expected alphabetic order—which in Greek would have been *alpha, eta, iota, omicron* and in Phoenician *'alep, ḥet, yod, ʿayin*—but were written in a purely phonetic order /*i, ē, a, o*/. Because the sherd is broken, it may be that *epsilon* (Phoenician *he*) preceded these four vowels and that *upsilon* (Phoenician *waw*) followed them and that the complete sequence (*e, iē, a, o, u*) represented both the shape of the letters and the sound of the vowels as they would have been pronounced from the front of the mouth to the back and in a low-high-low mnemonic order.

At any rate, the decoration of the pot is evidence that the Greeks who were friends or partners of the Sidonians at Sarepta had borrowed the alphabet by the ninth century. It is also clear that this borrowing presupposed education, the use of mnemonic techniques, and the linguistic abilities of their Sidonian and Byblian counterparts and that there was a continuous process of transmission that was repeated even in such an unprepossessing industrial town as Sarepta. The pot may have been destined for export to Cyprus or Crete, and it may have been made and decorated by a Phoenician, Greek, or Cypriot artist, but one of its implications is that Sidonians and Greeks in the ninth century lived in cultural symbiosis.

Byblos, famous for its skill in working wood and stone, controlled the Lebanon, and it seems to have had good relations with cities of the interior. One of these was Kumidi, situated at the southern end of the Beqaʿ, the plain between the coastal range and the Anti-Lebanon.[31] The city is known from the Amarna letters and from letters of the same sort that were discovered at the site itself, one of which was sent from the king of Byblos.[32] The Late Bronze Age finds include two Phoenician inscriptions in the developed Canaanite form of the Ugaritic alphabet written, as at Sarepta, on a jar handle and on the edge of a bowl.[33] There are also contemporary Phoenician ostraca with personal names and monograms that are written in South Arabic script and from left to right.[34] Splendid ivories display Egyptian ornamental elegance, Syrian naturalness and vivacity, and Phoenician expressionism in an ensemble that prefigures the Byblian, South Syrian, style.[35]

---

look Phoenician, but the graffito must be read from left to right as a mixture of Phoenician and Greek: the Phoenician preposition *l-* written back-to-front, and the Greek personal name Ajax in the dative *aio*, indicating that the skyphos belonged "to Ajax."

31. H. Weippert, "Kumidi: Die Ergebnisse der Ausgrabungen auf dem Tell Kamid el-Loz in den Jahren 1963–1981," *ZDPV* 114 (1998) 1–38.

32. J. Huehnergard, "A Byblos Letter, Probably from Kamid el-Loz," *ZA* 86 (1996) 97–113.

33. M. Dietrich and O. Loretz, *Die Keilalphabete: Die phönizisch-kanaanäischen und altarabischen Alphabete in Ugarit* (Münster: Ugarit-Verlag, 1988) 222–31. The jar handle is inscribed "belonging to the Chief" (*lrb*), and the bowl has the letters *ymn*, probably a name derived from the ethnic designation "Ionian" (*ymn*, also written *ywn*).

34. G. Mansfeld, "Scherben mit altkanaanäischer Buchstabenschrift von Tell Kamid el-Loz," *Kamid el-Loz* (Bonn: Habelt, 1970) 29–41, pls. 3–8; W. Röllig and G. Mansfeld, "Zwei Ostraka vom Tell Kamid-el-Loz und ein neuer Aspekt für die Entstehung des kanaanäischen Alphabets," *WO* 5 (1970) 265–70.

35. R. Echt, "Fruhe phonikische Elfenbeine," in *Fruhe Phoniker im Lebanon: 20 Jahre deutsche Ausgrabungen in Kamid el-Loz* (ed. R. Hachmann; Mainz am Rhein: von Zabern, 1983) 79–91;

Kumidi is near the Litani River, had access through the valley to Syria in the north and to Palestine in the south, and evidently was on a thoroughfare linking South Arabia, Ugarit, and the cities of the coast. There are no ninth-century structural remains of the city, but the town would have continued at least as a distribution center for lumber shipped by Byblos down the east slope of the Lebanon along the Litani and Orontes into central Syria and, as an eighth-century reference to the royal palace ([*b*]*t mlk*, "[hou]se of the king") on a jar handle from Kumidi may indicate, undoubtedly maintained its close ties with the mother city.

Batrun, about 15 kilometers north of Byblos, was one of its dependencies during the Amarna age and perhaps its northern boundary but is unknown in the ninth century, except for remains of a sea wall, which may have been built to enlarge the harbor at this time.[36] Another 20 kilometers farther north lay Tripolis. Sources from the Persian period and later, taking the Hellenized name of the place literally ("Triple City"), referred to it as a city complex that was founded jointly by Tyre, Sidon, and Arvad. But it is known from a ninth-century Assyrian text of Shalmaneser III, under the name ʾAtri, as a town in the Lebanon Range at the southern border of Ḫatti, or Syria, which he visited and looted—or, in his terms, conquered—probably in 841 B.C.E. on his way home from Baʿli Raʾsi, where he had received tribute from Tyre, Sidon, and Israel.[37]

Not much is known about the place, but it would not be surprising to find that Sidon and Arvad, which were perennial associates, established an emporium in the ninth century or earlier there at the tip of Lebanon and at the very threshold of a newly assertive Syria:[38] the name is from a word with the basic meaning "explore, investigate, spy," from which is also derived a word for "merchants, traveling salesmen," and it would be appropriate if the place-name embodied these nuances. Late in the Persian period, it welcomed the conspirators organizing the Phoenician revolt, and early in the ninth century it may have been a meeting place for Sidonian and other traders traveling up and down the coast.

Sidon and Byblos did not oppose Assyria militarily and were not themselves the object of Assyrian aggression in the ninth century. The battle of Qarqar in 853 B.C.E., despite an attempt to correct the Assyrian text and include Byblos and Egypt,[39] did not directly involve Phoenicia but only the coalition consisting of Hamath, Damascus, Israel, and their allies, all of whom were in the Sidonian trade network. Associated with Israel were Que (Cilicia) and Musri (Kinet Hüyük on the Gulf of Iskenderum), which supplied Ahab with horses and 2,000 chariots. Next listed were Hamath's confederates

idem, "Les ivoires figurés de Kamid el-Loz et l'art phénicien du IIe millénaire," *Studia Phoenicia* 3 (1985) 69–83.

36. H. Frost, "The Offshore Island Harbour at Sidon and Other Phoenician Sites in the Light of New Dating Evidence," *IJNA* 2 (1973) 75–94, esp. p. 90 and fig. 16.

37. *ANET* 276–77; J. Elayi, "Tripoli (Liban) à l'époque perse," *Transeu* 2 (1990) 59–71; J. Elayi and A. G. Elayi, "La premiere monnaie de ʾTR / Tripolis (Tripoli, Liban)?" *Transeu* 5 (1992) 143–51.

38. S. Mazzoni, "Syria and the Periodization of the Iron Age: A Cross-Cultural Perspective," in *Essays on Syria in the Iron Age* (ed. G. Bunnens; ANESt [= *Abr-Nahrain*] Supplement 7; Louvain: Peeters, 2000) 31–59.

39. H. Tadmor, "Que and Musri," *IEJ* 11 (1961) 143–50.

along the coast, from south to north: ʿArqa and Arvad in Amurru; Ushnatu and Siyannu in the territory of Siyannu. The last in the list were the allies of Damascus: Arabia, which supplied 1,000 camels, and Ammon which volunteered 1,000 troops. The Phoenician cities remained untouched and profited both from the Assyrian appetite for western goods and from the common market that resulted from the alliances that were formed to promote local and national interests and resist Assyrian aggression.

Phoenicians were involved economically, individually, or indirectly with these countries and with Assyria. The king of Arvad had a Phoenician name (*Mattinbaʿl*) and was undoubtedly a Phoenician, and the Phoenician name of the king of Siyannu (*ʾAdonubaʿal*) suggests he was also ethnically Phoenician and not Syrian. Further, the Assyrian designation for the entire coalition is "the kings of the Seacoast," which is probably an allusion to the commercial ties that these countries had with one another and with the Phoenician merchants and traders of the coastal towns. Que and Musri were included for this reason (Que in particular having longstanding relations with Sidon and Byblos) so Arabia was also involved because Damascus was one of its principal markets, as was Ammon, because the main trade routes between Arabia and Damascus passed through its territory.[40]

Moreover, from the time of Ashurnasirpal II (883–859), Shalmaneser III's predecessor on the throne of Assyria, there were frequent campaigns to the west in order to gain control of its natural resources, notably iron, and to force these lands to submit and pay tribute (*madattu*) or luxury taxes (*tamartu*).[41] Tyre, Sidon, and Byblos were contributors, and their agents may have helped supply the other countries with some of the materials and products which they provided, but they themselves enjoyed a special status and seem to have been exempt from the additional taxes. To celebrate the completion of his palace at Nimrud, Ashurnasirpal invited 5,000 dignitaries from Anatolia and Syria, but he also included emissaries from Tyre and Sidon. To secure a constant flow of goods from the west, he and Shalmaneser III took towns in North Syria and turned them into Assyrian colonies and trading stations, but the Phoenician and coastal cities retained their independence. When Ashurnasirpal II marched through North Syria, he took essential resources (gold, tin, iron, cattle, sheep, and women) and products (linen garments and furniture, some of it inlaid with ivory), a portion of which may have been supplied by Phoenician craftsmen or traders. But when he went to the Mediterranean and the Lebanon, his tribute from the Phoenicians of Tyre, Sidon, Byblos, Amurru, Arvad, and other towns consisted of more-frivolous or luxury goods from the local boutiques, such as

---

40. I. Ephʿal (*The Ancient Arabs: Nomads on the Borders of the Fertile Crescent, 9th–5th Centuries B.C.* [Jerusalem: Magnes, 1984] 21, 75–76) suggested that by "Arabia" the text of Shalmaneser III meant, not North Arabia, but the Arabs of the Syrian Desert in the vicinity of the Wadi Sirhan. A major route from the Persian Gulf passed through the Syrian desert to ʿAmman, where it met the route from North Arabia to Damascus.

41. B. Cifola, "Asshurnasirpal II's 9th Campaign: Seizing the Grain Bowl of the Phoenician Cities," *AfO* 44–45 (1997–98) 156–58; H. Tadmor, "Assyria and the West: The Ninth Century and Its Aftermath," *Unity and Diversity: Essays in the History, Literature and Religion of the Ancient Near East* (ed. H. Goedicke and J. J. M. Roberts; Baltimore: Johns Hopkins University Press, 1975) 36–48.

gold, silver, tin, and copper objects, linen garments with multicolored trim, monkeys, ivory from walrus tusks, ebony, and boxwood. By the end of the century, Damascus had to pay gold (20 talents), large amounts of silver (more than 2,000 talents) and huge quantities (5,000 talents) of iron as well as linen garments with multicolored trim and furniture inlaid with ivory, most of which was imported and probably handled by Phoenician traders.

The cities of the Syrian coast that were associated with Tyre, Sidon, or Byblos in the Iron Age were cities that in the Late Bronze Age had belonged to one of the small kingdoms along the Mediterranean littoral, west of the Orontes: to Mukish (the former Alalakh, the future Patina or ʿUmqi/ ʿUnqi) in the north, to Ugarit or to Siyannu farther south, or to Amurru, an inveterate ally of Sidon, on the southern extremity of Syria. By the ninth century, at least, these countries had established relations with the Neo-Hittite principalities of inland Syria, and by the eighth some of them, nota-bly ʿUmqi, had been overrun by Arameans. They were all essentially Syrian states, with a predominantly indigenous population,[42] and the Phoenicians were content to profit from their relations with the interior or maintain quarters or marketplaces in their coastal towns or frequent their harbors as they tramped along the coast to Asia Minor and westward to the Greek Islands, and from there to the lands these people were exploring.

The principal towns and ports of Amurru were at Tell ʿArqa, Tell Kazel (ancient Sumur), ʿAmrit, and Arvad. Amurru was a confederate of Sidon and Arvad in the Amarna period and after that time had come under increasing Canaanite influence. In the mid-thirteenth century, the king of Amurru gave his daughter in marriage to the king of Ugarit, providing her with a luxurious trousseau, but the marriage ended in divorce, and the frustrated political ties did not result in improved economic relations. Amurru main-tained its independent status at least into the early Iron Age: among the ar-rowheads of this heroic time, there are two dating to the eleventh century that are inscribed in alphabetic script with the name of its Phoenician king, Zakarbaʿal (*ḥṣ zkrbʿl mlk ʾmr*, "arrow of Zakarbaʿl, king of ʾAmurru"). In the later Iron Age, perhaps as early as the tenth century but certainly by the ninth, its territory was administered by the inland Kingdom of Hamath. Its ports, under this administration or free, had Phoenician communities, agents, traders and artists, and were frequented by Phoenician ships. In the latter part of the eighth century, in recognition of Sumur's history as capital and administrative center of the country, Amurru was incorporated into the new Assyrian province of Simyra.

Tell ʿArqa, is in the foothills of the Lebanon, where the Hama gap de-bouches into the sea, halfway between Byblos and Arvad, 20 kilometers north of Tripolis and south of Tell Kazel. A fourteenth-century seal in-scribed in alphabetic script with the name "The ʿArqite" (*ʿrqy*) is the earliest evidence for Canaanites in the town.[43] In the ninth century, it was part of the coalition, led by Hamath and Damascus, that opposed Shalmaneser III

42. D. Bonatz, "Some Considerations on the Material Culture of Coastal Syria in the Iron Age," *EVO* 16 (1993) 123–57.

43. F. M. Cross, "The Evolution of the Proto-Canaanite Alphabet," *BASOR* 134 (1954) 15–24, esp. pp. 21–22.

at Qarqar in 853 B.C.E., and three more times in the next decade. It supplied
10,000 foot soldiers at Qarqar, the same number as Hamath and Israel, sur-
passed only by the 20,000 from Damascus, but unlike these three leaders
had neither cavalry nor chariotry.[44]

A ninth-century terra-cotta figurine of a woman found near the site
combines mostly Egyptian and some Syrian features in a style and tradition, the prototypes and parallels of which are all from Sidon and its dominions.[45] There is some late ninth-century Red Slip Ware, and a fragment
of a lovely Bichrome bowl, perhaps of Cypriot origin, decorated with an
ibex at the tree of life, but the eighth century is better represented in the
archaeological remains.[46] From the early part of this century, there is a
small sanctuary, constructed around a courtyard that contained an altar
and an area reserved for lustral rites, and fronted by another courtyard in
which there was a small platform with a statuette of an enthroned Goddess
adorned with astral symbols.

From the end of the century there are three Phoenician inscriptions,
written in red paint on jars that were deposited in tombs.[47] The jars identify the deceased by name and, because they are transport or storage jars,
implicitly by their profession as suppliers or traders. One of the jars has the
man's name and patronymic: "belonging to ʾAdonibaʿl, the son of ʿAnaton"
(*lʾdnbʿl / bʿntn*); the names and the apocopated writing of "son" suggest
that the deceased merchant was originally from Byblos. The second jar has
the name "Gomer" (*gmr*) and the notation *lmlk*, "belonging to the king,"
which may indicate that he worked for the royal court in Hamath. The
third name, written on a jar that was broken before being put in the grave,
is partly erased but can be read as "belonging to Ṣidqimilk" (*lṣdqmlk*), "The
God of Justice is king": if he too was a trader, the iron sword and blades
buried with him would witness to the dangers attending the profession.

Throughout the century, there is little imported pottery, and this is
mostly Black-on-Red Ware from Cyprus. This slim Cypriot connection is
still evident in a fourth-century trilingual (Phoenician, Cypriot, and Greek)
dedication from Tamassos in Cyprus by a man whose grandfather was
originally from ʿArqa: "This is the statue given and dedicated by Menahem,
son of Benhodes, son of Menahem, a son of ʿArqa (*mnḥm bn bnḥdš bn mnḥm
bn ʿrq*)." The evidence for Phoenicians, from Sidon and Byblos specifically,

---

44. H. Tadmor, "Assyria and the West: The Ninth Century and Its Aftermath," in *Unity and Diversity. Essays in the History, Literature and Religion of the Ancient Near East* (ed. H. Goedicke and J. J. M. Roberts; Baltimore: Johns Hopkins University Press, 1975) 36–48; P. E. Dion, "Syro-Palestinian Resistance to Shalmaneser III in the Light of New Documents," *ZAW* 107 (1995) 482–89; G. Galil, "Shalmaneser III in the West," *RB* 109 (2002) 40–56.

45. E. Gubel, "Notes sur un fragment de statuette phénicienne de la région d'Amurru," *Archéologie au Levant: Recueil à la mémoire de Roger Saidah* (Lyon: Maison de l'Orient, 1982) 225–31.

46. J.-P. Thalmann, "Tell ʿArqa (Liban nord). Campagnes I–III (1972–1974), chantier I: Rapport préliminaire," *Syria* 55 (1978) 1–152, pls. 1–4; idem, "Les niveaux de l'âge du Bronze et de l'âge du Fer à Tell ʿArqa (Liban)," *Atti* 1, 1.217–21; idem, "Tell ʿArqa, de la conquête assyrienne à l'époque perse," *Transeu* 2 (1990) 51–57.

47. P. Bordreuil, "Nouveaux apports de l'archéologie et de la glyptique à l'onomastique phénicienne," *Atti* 1, 3.751–55, pls. 142–43, esp. pp. 751–53, pl. 142; Thalmann, "Tell ʿArqa (Liban Nord)," 86, fig. 23.

in ʿArqa is slight, but this reflects accurately the specialized and unobtrusive role these people played in the economy of an essentially Syrian city. Tell Kazel, ancient Sumur, is just north of Tell ʿArqa, in the Plain of ʿAkkar, about four kilometers from the Mediterranean coast, on the north bank of a small river (the Nahr el-Abrash) running into the sea. It was an Egyptian administrative center, replacing Byblos, in the Amarna age, until it was overrun by the Sea Peoples in the early Iron Age. The earliest Phoenician pottery in the restored manufacturing and domestic areas dates from the tenth century. In the ninth century, the Phoenician pottery is mostly transport amphorae, although there are Red Slip and Black-on-Red jugs and juglets for imported perfumes and unguents. There are also some ninth-century Cypriot wares, but most of the ceramic assemblage continues regional styles and was made in local shops. In the early sixth century, the town was well known for its iron, and iron may have been an important commodity as early as the ninth. But the material evidence (large jars the handles of which were stamped with the floral, faunal, and geometric symbols of its merchants and traders) suggests that agriculture or viticulture was also a mainstay of the community.[48] There are other traces (an ivory plaque, some Egyptian-style amulets, pieces of a game) of the town's sophistication in the ninth century, and many of the later finds (such as eighth-century terra-cotta figurines resembling those found at ʿArqa and Sidon) show that it was Phoenicians who contributed most decisively to the culture and prosperity of the community. Apart from an owner's name on an eighth-century jar, the Phoenician inscriptions are from the late Persian or Hellenistic age.[49] Tell Kazel probably remained essentially a Syrian settlement,[50] but Phoenicians, most likely from Sidon or Arvad, introduced it to Cyprus and the Mediterranean world. Along with Tyre, Sidon, Byblos, Arvad, and other coastal towns, it paid tribute to Assyria in the ninth century, but it made the mistake of joining with Arvad and Damascus in Hamath's revolt against Sargon II of Assyria at the end of the eighth century and was crippled by the coalition's defeat at the second battle of Qarqar.[51]

It was undoubtedly the Phoenicians who persuaded the town to build a port just north of the mouth of the Nahr el-Abrash. This consisted of an L-shaped breakwater and wharf, about 120 meters south to north and

---

48. L. Badre et al., "Tell Kazel, Syria: Excavations of the AUB Museum 1985–1987. Preliminary Reports," *Berytus* 38 (1990) 9–124; L. Badre, "Recent Phoenician Discoveries at Tell Kazel," *Atti* 2, 2.627–39; E. Gubel, "The AUB Excavations at Tell Kazel, Syria: The Oriental Material from Area I," *Actes* 3, 2.118–27; L. Badre and E. Gubel, "Tell Kazel (Syria): Excavations of the AUB Museum, 1993–1998. Third Preliminary Report," *Berytus* 44 (1999–2000) 123–203; E. Capet and E. Gubel, "Tell Kazel: Six Centuries of Iron Age Occupation (c. 1200–612 B.C.)," in *Essays on Syria in the Iron Age* (ed. G. Bunnens; ANESt [= *Abr-Nahrain*] Supplement 7; Louvain: Peeters, 2000) 425–57.

49. Ibid., 457, fig. 34; H. Sader, "An Epigraphic Note on a Phoenician Inscription from Tell Kazel," *Berytus* 38 (1990) 94–97); P. Bordreuil, F. Briquel-Chatonnet, E. Gubel, "Inédits épigraphiques des fouilles anciennes et récentes à Tell Kazel," *Sem* 45 (1996) 37–47.

50. E. Gubel, "Phoenician Foundations in Archaeological Perspective," in *Nuove Fondazioni nel Vicino Oriente Antico: Realtà e ideologia* (ed. S. Mazzoni; Pisa: Giardini, 1994) 341–55.

51. R. H. Dornemann, "The Iron Age Remains at Tell Qarqur in the Orontes Valley," in *Essays on Syria in the Iron Age* (ed. G. Bunnens; ANESt [= *Abr-Nahrain*] Supplement 7; Louvain: Peeters, 2000) 459–85.

40 meters from the sea leg to land, creating a small harbor that was protected from the prevailing southwest winds. This was constructed mostly
of very large (approximately 2 × 0.5 meters) hewn limestone blocks (taken
from a quarry on the coast and just to the south of the quay), which were
laid in multiple courses, high on the windward side, lower on the leeward
side to allow loading and unloading. The northern end of the breakwater
seems to have been built of large boulders, but piles of ashlar blocks at the
eastern, landward, tip of the wharf may be the remains of a port authority
building, and there apparently was another warehouse or similar structure
near the southern end of the breakwater. South of this installation, near the
quarry, a scattering of hewn limestone blocks in the sea could be all that
remains of a southern harbor, but they may just be blocks that fell off the
rafts transporting them to the breakwater.

   Associated with the port was a small settlement, known as Tabbat al-
Hammam, with ninth-century Phoenician Red Slip wares, a few Greek
pendent semicircle cups, and a great deal of Cypriot pottery. The site was
inhabited through the Persian, Hellenistic, Roman, and Byzantine periods,
but there was nothing to indicate settlement prior to the building of the
port in the ninth century.[52] It was a typical Phoenician harbor,[53] and a
pretty clear sign that Sumur prospered in the ninth century under Phoenician auspices, probably by importing iron, and exporting grain or wine,
doing business in luxury goods with Cyprus.

   ʿAmrit, a few kilometers north of Tabbat al-Hammam, was situated on
the coast slightly south of Arvad. It was a sprawling settlement on a narrow, well-watered plain, without a port or protection for ships at anchor
(its shoreline was a deep sandy beach), lying between two streams, the
Nahr ʿAmrit on the north and the Nahr el-Qubleh to the south, and isolated from the interior by a high rugged plateau. It was founded about the
end of the seventh century, perhaps by people who had abandoned Sumur
when Nebuchadnezzar II of Babylon began campaigning in the west. Its
particular interest is that it can confirm (although from the perspective of
later times) Sumur's persistent relations with Cyprus, Sidon, and Arvad.[54]

   Its most spectacular structure is the sanctuary of ʾEshmun at the northern extremity of the town.[55] This consisted of a large rectangular pool,
about 30 × 40 meters and up to 3 meters deep, surrounded on three sides
by a broad porticoed promenade but open towards the Nahr ʿAmrit on the
north and to the stadium that eventually was built beyond it. It was wa-
tered by a perpetual spring at its southeast corner and adorned by a stone
pavilion rising above the water at its center. Associated with the lustral pool

   52. R. J. Braidwood, "Report on Two Sondages on the Coast of Syria, South of Tartous," *Syria*
21 (1940) 183–226, pls. 20–26.
   53. A. Raban, "The Heritage of Ancient Harbour Engineering in Cyprus and the Levant," in
Proceedings of the International Symposium "Cyprus and the Sea" (ed. V. Karageorghis and D. Michaelides; Nicosia: University of Cyprus, 1995) 139–88, esp. p. 154; idem, "Near Eastern Harbors:
Thirteenth–Seventh Centuries BCE," *MPT*, 428–38, esp. p. 434.
   54. N. Saliby, "ʿAmrît," in *Archéologie et histoire de la Syrie, II: La Syrie de l'époque achéménide à
l'avènement de l'Islam* (ed. J.-M. Dentzer and W. Orthmann; Saarbruck: Saarbrücker Verlag, 1989)
19–30.
   55. M. Dunand and N. Saliby, *Le temple d'Amrith dans la perée d'Aradus* (Paris: Geuthner,
1985).

and the bathing facilities, there was a large depository for broken statuary that once had stood in the sanctuary, mainly of the God Melqart, dressed as Heracles, but also of individual votaries bearing gifts. In both instances, they were modeled entirely in Cypriot style and mostly imported from Cyprus.[56] However, contemporary Phoenician inscriptions (written in a Cypriot dialect) on statues destined for the shrine were dedicated to the God ꞽEshmun of Sidon,[57] and it was undoubtedly Tyrian influence in Cyprus at this time combined with a genetic Cypriot tendency to syncretism that accounted for this God's assimilation to Melqart—just as at Kition in eastern Cyprus, there is inscriptional evidence for the worship of a God called "ꞽEshmun-Melqart."[58]

56. C. Jourdain-Annequin, *Héraclès-Melqart à Amrith: Recherches iconographiques. Contribution à l'étude d'un syncretisme* (Paris: Geuthner, 1992); idem, "Héraclès-Melqart à Amrith? Un syncrétisme gréco-phénicien à l'époque perse," *Transeu* 6 (1993) 69–86, pls. 8–12; K. Lembke, "Akkulturation in Phönizien am Beispiel der Skulpturen aus dem Quellheiligtum in Amrit," in *Sepulkral- und Votivdenkmäler östlicher Mittelmeergebiete (7. Jh. v. Chr.–1. Jh. n. Chr): Kulturbegegnungen im Spannungsfeld von Akzeptanz und Resistenz* (ed. R. Bol and D. Kreikenbom; Paderborn: Bibliopolis, 2004) 15–22, pls. 8–12.

57. P. Bordreuil, "Le dieu Echmoun dans la region d'Amrit," in *Phoenicia and Its Neighbours* (ed. E. Lipiński; Studia Phoenicia 3; Louvain: Peeters, 1985) 221–30; É. Puech, "Les inscriptions phéniciennes d'Amrit et les dieux guerisseurs du sanctuaire," *Syria* 53 (1986) 327–42. The name of the God is preserved in one inscription and reconstructed in the other. The Cypriot dialectal feature is the peculiar form of the demonstrative pronoun with prosthetic ꞽalep (ꞽz).

58. There is also a terra-cotta from the sanctuary at ꜥAmrit of an enthroned, bearded, and horned God, whose few parallels are from eastern

Fig. 2.5. Amrit Stele. Art Resource, NY; Louvre, Paris. Photo by: Erich Lessing.

At an earlier time, when the spring was the site of a more modest sanctuary, and when Sidonian culture still prevailed at Kition, the God who was venerated at this sacred source was Shadrapaʾ (*šed ropeʾ*), or "Healing Genius." This phase is represented by a large inscribed stele, known as the "ʿAmrit Stele" (see fig. 2.5) but reportedly found at the Nahr el-Abrash near Sumur, which was carved in a local variation of the North Syrian style (with a mixture of Egyptian, Neo-Hittite, Assyrian, and Syrian elements) to depict the God as a sort of ultimate Baʿal, embodying in his persona all the vivifying qualities of this Lord of the natural and cosmic order.[59] The God is represented as the Storm God with his right hand raised to strike. He stands on a lion that bestrides the mountain tops and holds in his left hand a lion cub. Above him is the winged sun disk, symbolizing order and perpetuity, and the moon rising over its crescent, a symbol of recurring cycles. None of this actually represents Shadrapaʾ or what he meant to his clients, but it does express the Syrian belief that he was not just a divinized mortal as at Sidon, but a true God. This earlier sanctuary probably had its best parallel in the Temple of ʾEshmun at Sidon where the healing waters were brought by aqueduct from the spring Yadlil, while the later monumental structure resembled and may have inspired Greek sanctuaries of Asclepios.[60] In both phases, the healing waters of the sacred spring and the recreational facilities seem to have been the rationale for the settlement at ʿAmrit, and pilgrims from Sidon, Cyprus, Arvad, and the towns along the Syrian coast were its constant source of income.

Arvad is an island slightly to the northwest of ʿAmrit. In the Amarna period, it had no king but was a community, "the people of Arvad," consistently aligned with Sidon in its resistance to Egyptian authority.[61] It is mentioned together with Sidon, along with ʿArqa and Sumur, in a few biblical texts (Gen 10:17–18, Ezek 27:8) and, according to Strabo, it was resettled by Sidonians following the invasion of the Sea Peoples.[62] Together with Sidon and Byblos, it paid tribute to Tiglath-pileser I (1114–1076 B.C.E.), and from that time on it was known to the Assyrians as an exotic place worth visiting. Among its gifts the king mentions only a crocodile and a female

Cyprus (Meniko, Chytroi, Salamis) and from Tel Michal in Israel: A. M. Bisi, "Su una terracotta di dipo cipriota da ʿAmrit," *RSF* 10 (1982) 189–96, pls. 46–49; F. Vandenabeele, "Phoenician Influence on the Cypro-Archaic Terracotta Production and Cypriot Influence Abroad," in *Acts of the International Archaeological Symposium "Cyprus between the Orient and the Occident"* (ed. V. Karageorghis; Nicosia: Department of Antiquities, 1986) 351–60, pls. 30–31, esp. pp. 353–54; H.-G. Buchholz, "Der Gott Hammon und Zeus Ammon auf Zypern," *Mitteilungen des deutschen archäologischen Instituts: Athenische Abteilung* 106 (1991) 85–128, pls. 10–21.

59. S. M. Cecchini, "La stele di Amrit: Aspetti e problemi iconografici e iconologici," *Contributi e Materiali di Archeologia Orientale* 7 (1997) 83–100.

60. H. Berve and G. Gruben, *Griechische Tempel und Heiligtumer* (Munich: Hirmer, 1961) 157–61. The Temple of Asclepios at Epidaurus, for instance, faced a plaza, and comprised the shrine of the God, an altar, and a pillared courtyard, which featured at its center an elaborate round structure (or, *tholos*) like the pavillion at ʿAmrit. Nearby were the pool where pilgrims washed, a dormitory, a stadium, and the famous theater. Asclepios, like Shadrapaʾ, was the God of Healing, and their rituals and the recreational aspects of their sanctuaries were very similar.

61. F. Briquel-Chatonnet, "Le statut politique d'Arwad au IIe millénaire," *Actas* 4, 1.129–33.

62. Idem, "Arwad, cité phénicienne," in *Alle Soglie della Classicità. Il Mediterraneo tra Tradizione e Innovazione: Studi in Onore di Sabatino Moscati* (ed. E. Acquaro; Pisa: Istituti Editoriali e Poligrafici Internazionali, 1996) 63–72, esp. p. 67.

ape. Among its pleasures he includes a boat ride to Sumur and a fishing expedition on which he harpooned a "sea horse" so intriguing to him that he carved basalt replicas of it in Ashur.[63] The town supplied 200 troops to the anti-Assyrian coalition at the battle of Qarqar in 853 B.C.E., and it is still noted as a source of mercenaries in Ezekiel's description of Tyre's dominions. At the end of the ninth century, on one of his western campaigns, Adad-nirari III set up his statue in Arvad, and it may be at this time that the Assyrians established their market or port (*kārum*) on the island, as they had earlier in the century at Aribua in ʿUmqi (875 B.C.E.) and at Til Barsip in North Syrian Bit Adini (856 B.C.E.):[64] although the earliest reference to this commercial center is from the reign of Ashurbanipal (668–633 B.C.E.),[65] there are remains of superb harbor installations on the island that may date to the earlier time.[66]

By the mid-ninth century, Arvad was an independent kingdom, ruled by a king with the good Phoenician name Mattinbaʿl ("Gift of Baʿal"), and his successors in the eighth and seventh century (whose names were the same as his or were similarly composed with the name or epithet of the God Baʿal) saw to the survival and prosperity of the island by submitting to Assyria.[67] An eighth-century monument and inscription of an Egyptian military officer probably reflects Arvad's engagement in far-flung international trade, at this time perhaps in the service of Tyre, while a sixth-century inscribed statue bore the name of a pious Egyptian who was perhaps on his way to ʿAmrit, where he hoped to install the statue as an ex voto in the sanctuary of ʾEshmun, the Healer.[68] Arvad, like Sidon, cooperated with the Assyrians and became one of their ports and eventually a formidable naval power but, unlike Sidon, it was unpretentious and easygoing and outlasted both the Assyrian and the Persian Empires.

63. Idem, "Arwad et l'empire assyrien," in *Ana šadî Labnāni lū allik. Beiträge zu alltorientalischen und mittelmeerischen Kulturen: Festschrift für Wolfgang Röllig* (ed. B. Pongratz-Leisten, H. Kühne, and P. Xella; Neukirchen-Vluyn: Neukirchener Verlag, 1997) 57–68.

64. H. Tadmor, "Assyria and the West: The Ninth Century and its Aftermath," in *Unity and Diversity: Essays in the History, Literature and Religion of the Ancient Near East* (ed. H. Goedicke and J. J. M. Roberts; Baltimore: Johns Hopkins University Press, 1975) 36–48, esp. pp. 37–38.

65. There is a text in which Ashurbanipal inquires of the Sun God whether the time is right for sending his agent to Arvad and whether this man will be well received; and another in which the king complains that the king of Arvad will not allow ships to dock at the Assyrian quay, and the assumption is that the first alludes to the impasse recorded in the second: see M. Elat, "The Monarchy and the Development of Trade in Ancient Israel," in *State and Temple Economy in the Ancient Near East, II* (ed. E. Lipiński; Louvain: Departement Orientalistiek, 1979) 527–46, esp. pp. 544–45; I. Starr, *Queries to the Sungod: Divination and Politics in Sargonid Assyria* (SAA 4; Helsinki: Helsinki University Press, 1990) 104–5.

66. H. Frost, "The Offshore Island Harbour at Sidon and Other Phoenician Sites in the Light of New Dating Evidence," *IJNA* 2 (1973) 75–94.

67. *ANET* 279, 282, 287, 291, 294, 295. Mattinbaʿal was the name of the king in the time of Tiglath-pileser III (744–727 B.C.E.) and of Esarhaddon (680–669 B.C.E.). The kings of Arvad in the time of Sennacherib (704–681 B.C.E.) and Ashurbanipal (668–633 B.C.E.) had names (ʿAbdiʾit, Yakinlaʾu) composed of the element *ʾly*, "Almighty," which was a Syrian epithet of Baʿal. When Yakinlaʾu died, his ten sons went to Nineveh, where Ashurbanipal chose one (ʿOzibaʿl) to be king of Arvad and installed the others (Abibaʿl, Adonibaʿl, Šapatbaʿl, Bodibaʿl, Baʿlasap, Baʿlhanon, Baʿlmalok, Abîmilk, Ahîmilk) as retainers at his court.

68. M. Yon and A. Caubet, "Arouad et Amrit, VIIIe–Ier siècles av. J.-C.: Documents," *Transeu* 6 (1993) 47–67, pls. 1–7.

North of the Phoenician, mainly Sidonian, towns and settlements in the
former territory of Amurru were the cities and ports of ancient Siyannu,
Ugarit's southern neighbor. These included Ushnatu on the coast near the
border with Amurru; Shuksi, presently Tell Sukas, a port on the border with
Ugarit, which also laid claim to it; and the capital Siyannu, a few kilometers
inland from this port.[69] Ushnatu and Siyannu, new among the proliferating
city kingdoms of Syria in the ninth century,[70] were allies of Hamath at the
battle of Qarqar—the former supplying 200 troops; the latter sending 30
chariots and 1,000 infantry. The name of the king of Siyannu (ʾAdonîbaʿal)
might suggest that he was a Byblian, among the many living in Hamath
and that he had been installed as king when Ushnatu joined the Hamath
confederacy.

Tell Sukas, similarly, was a sleepy little port in the ninth century, with
almost nothing Phoenician about it, the material culture of which was
dominated by imports from Hamath and inland Syria.[71] There was a small
open-air sanctuary in the port area, and a stele of the Syrian Storm God,
Egyptianizing and of Byblian inspiration, that was found a bit farther south
at Baniyas and may once have been the focus of its cult.[72] Just as ancient
Siyannu had been under the shadow of Ugarit, the principal ports and
towns of its ninth-century counterpart seem to have been satisfied clients
of Hamath.

Hamath in the ninth and eighth centuries was a refuge for adventurers
from many parts of the Near East, and among them Byblians were especially prominent. Its territory included, apart from Ushnatu and Siyannu,
the principality of Luʿash, twelfth-century Nuḫašše, the eastern neighbor
of Ugarit. In the mid-ninth century, under Urhilina (or, Irhuleni), it was
allied with Israel and the Arameans of Damascus in the anti-Assyrian coalition. Urtamis, son and successor of Urhilina, did regular business, in Baby-

69. J. Nougayrol, *Textes accadiens des archives sud* (PRU 4; Paris: Imprimerie Nationale, 1956).
Both the king of Ugarit and the king of Siyannu owned property in Shuksi (pp. 230–31), and a
vineyard of Syrian Astarte (Ishtar Hurri) in Shuksi was shared by a symposium (*mrzḥ*) in Siyannu
and by another in the Ugaritic town of Ari (p. 230): the latter is also mentioned in another
damaged text (idem, *Textes accadiens et hourrites des archives est, ouest et centrales* [PRU 3; Paris:
Imprimerie Nationale, 1955] 157). Until the early thirteenth century, when it came under direct
Hittite rule, Siyannu had been administered for the Hittites by the king of Ugarit, a situation that
undoubtedly contributed to the border disputes. Although Shuksi is not mentioned in Ugaritic
administrative texts and therefore was not a Ugaritic port and most likely belonged to Siyannu,
by the middle of the century the Hittite king could declare that it belonged to Ugarit: PRU 4,
291; W. van Soldt, "Studies in the Topography of Ugarit (2): The Borders of Ugarit," *UF* 29 (1997)
683–703, esp. pp. 696, 700, 702.

70. S. Mazzoni, "Settlement Pattern and New Urbanization in Syria at the Time of the Assyrian Conquest," in *Neo-Assyrian Geography* (ed. M. Liverani; Rome: University of Rome, 1995)
181–91.

71. M.-L. Buhl, *Sukas VII: The Near Eastern Pottery and Objects of Other Materials from the Upper
Strata* (Copenhagen: Munksgaard, 1983); J. Lund, *Sukas VIII: The Habitation Quarters* (Copen-
hagen: Munksgaard, 1986); P. J. Riis et al., *Sukas X: The Bronze and Early Iron Age Remains at the
Southern Harbour* (Copenhagen: Munksgaard, 1996); D. Bonatz, "Some Considerations of the
Material Culture of Coastal Syria in the Iron Age," *EVO* 16 (1993) 123–57.

72. M.-L. Buhl, "An Open Air Sanctuary at the Harbour of Sukas," *Actas* 4, 2.561–67; A. Abou-
Assaf, "Eine Stele des Gottes Baʿal im Museum von Ṭarṭus," *Damaszener Mitteilungen* 6 (1992)
247–52, pl. 40.

Ionian, with the king of ʿAnat on the Euphrates,[73] and either he or someone in his entourage could recite a Babylonian incantation against snake bite.[74]

The king of Hamath at the end of the ninth century was the Aramean usurper Zakkur from ʿAnat. Two of the kings who reigned in the second half of the eighth century, like Joram who reigned in the time of David in the tenth, bore the good North Israelite Hebrew names ʿAzriyau and Yaubiʾdi.[75] Most of the inscriptions from Hamath are in Aramaic but a few are in a script resembling old South Arabic.[76] Hamath, evidently, was a crossroads where foreigners and veterans of the Assyrian wars (Hittites, Arabians, Arameans, and Phoenicians or Greeks from Que) settled and became integrated in a vibrant and complex society.

Among the settlers, Byblians were the most consistently influential on the religion, art, culture, and commerce of Hamath. The Neo-Hittite building inscriptions of Urhulina are dedicated to the Goddess Baʿalat, whom other inscriptions recognize as "Queen of the Land."[77] Although Baʿalat is a title, the feminine of Baʿal, "Lord," and the equivalent of "Lady," it is also the proper name of the Goddess of Byblos. Because it is the name, transcribed as Pahalatis, and not the title or its Luwian equivalent, which was borrowed, it is certainly the Goddess of Byblos who became the queen of the Kingdom of Hamath. A text by Urhilina, protesting the neglect of her cult during the reign of his father and grandfather, makes it clear that she had been introduced into Hamath by the early ninth, but more likely in the tenth century, when every emerging kingdom in Syria and Palestine chose a new dynasty and a new God. This early impact on the religion and administration of Hamath continued throughout the ninth and into the eighth century. The worship of the Goddess is attested in the personal name "Servant of Baʿalat" (ʿbdbʿlt).

The veneration of the city God of Byblos, Adonis, is known from the name of the Overseer of the Queen's Palace, a title that occurs on building blocks and on a seal impression, "May-Adonis-Be Exalted" (ʾdnlrm skn byt mlkh). The head of the Hamath pantheon at the end of the ninth century, the God to whom the usurper Zakkur attributes his accession to the throne and his escape from the coalition that attempted to dislodge him, was Baʿalšamayim, the head of the pantheon of Byblos in the tenth century. The name of the king of Hamath in the middle of the eighth century,

---

73. S. Parpola, "A Letter from Marduk-Apla-Usur of Anah to Rudamu/Uramis, King of Hamath," in *Hama, fouilles et recherches 1931–1938, II 2: Les objets de la période dite Syro-Hittite (Âge du Fer)* (ed. P. J. Riis and M.-L. Buhl; Copenhagen: Munksgaard, 1990) 257–65.

74. J. Laessøe, "A Prayer to Ea, Shamash and Marduk from Hama," *Iraq* 18 (1956) 60–67.

75. S. Dalley, "Yahweh in Hamath in the 8th Century BC: Cuneiform Material and Historical Deductions," *VT* 40 (1990) 21–32; Z. Zevit, "Yahweh Worship and Worshippers in 8th-Century Hamath," *VT* 41 (1991) 363–66.

76. B. Otzen, "The Aramaic Inscriptions," in *Hama, fouilles et recherches 1931–1938, II 2: Les objets de la période dite Syro-Hittite (Âge du Fer)* (ed. P. J. Riis and M.-L. Buhl; Copenhagen: Munksgaard, 1990) 266–318; idem, "Petitionary Formulae in the Aramaic Inscriptions from Hama," *ZAW* 100 (1988) Supplement, 233–43; J. Borker-Klahn, "Phryger in Hama(th)?" *SMEA* 40 (1998) 279–85.

77. J. D. Hawkins, *Corpus of Hieroglyphic Luwian Inscriptions, I: Inscriptions of the Iron Age. Part 2: Text—Amuq, Aleppo, Hama, Tabal, Assur Letters, Miscellaneous, Seals, Indices* (Berlin: de Gruyter, 2000) 398–423.

before Azriyau and Yaubi'di, was Enil (*'n'l*, "El watches"), a name that is known otherwise only from Byblos.

At this time, as the weights and measures attest (there are one-shekel, two-shekel, and half-shekel weights inscribed in Phoenician script, and there is both a "shekel of Hamath" and a "royal shekel of Hamath"),[78] business was conducted in Phoenician both by individuals and by merchants of the king. The integration of these Byblians into the society of Hamath is also suggested by the ceramic assemblage, which contains some Cypriot and Greek imports but little of the contemporary Phoenician wares. Their influence (as is also clear from their work in the South Syrian school of ivory carving) was formative politically, economically, and intellectually and probably can be traced to the tenth century, when Hamath reconstituted itself through aggressive emigration out of the ruins of the Late Bronze Age Kingdom of Tunip.

The northernmost port of the old Kingdom of Ugarit was Sinaru, known in classical times as Posideion and presently by the Arabic form of that name, Ras el-Bassit. It was an extremely small settlement in the Iron Age,[79] characterized in its earliest phase by a few fragments of Greek Late Protogeometric (950–900 B.C.E.) amphoras imported from Lefkandi in Euboea;[80] in the late ninth century by some Phoenician Red Slip wares similar to those from Sarepta and Kition; and in the eighth and seventh centuries by ceramics like those from Tyre and its stations at 'Achzib and Tell Keisan.[81] The tenth- and ninth-century materials are separated in time and type from the typically Tyrian assemblages of the later centuries, and it is likely that they represent the early encounters of Euboeans and Sidonians on the Syrian coast before Al Mina (just north of Bassit at the mouth of the Orontes, and with better access to the inland markets) became the preferred place to meet.

The Ugaritic administrative texts distinguish between Sinaru (an agricultural center that supplied teams of oxen for public works and the gentry of which owned fields in the surrounding region) and the port (Akkadian *kārum*, Ugaritic *ma'ḫadu*) of Sinaru, which supplied crews for the locally owned ships and separately paid tribute to the Hittite court.[82] It may be that this distinction persisted in Phoenician times as well and that Ras el-

78. M. Heltzer, "Phoenician Trade and Phoenicians in Hamath," in *Immigration and Emigration within the Ancient Near East: Festschrift E. Lipiński* (ed. K. van Lerberghe and A. Schoors; OLA 65; Louvain: Peeters, 1995) 101–5; idem, "A New Weight from Hamath and Trade Relations with the South in the Ninth–Eighth Centuries BCE," in *The World of the Aramaeans, II: Studies in History and Archaeology in Honour of Paul-Eugène Dion* (ed. P. M. M. Daviau, J. W. Wevers, and M. Weigl; JSOTSup 325; Sheffield: Sheffield Academic Press, 2001) 133–35. The royal shekel, like the standard shekel, is inscribed "shekel of Hamath" (*šql ḥmt*) but adds the letters ŠṬ (the abbreviation for "shekel") before it and, because it resembles a schematic scarab, the royal symbol.

79. P. Courbin, "Bassit-Posidaion in the Early Iron Age," in *Greek Colonists and Native Populations* (ed. J.-P. Descoeudres; Oxford: Clarendon, 1990) 503–9; idem, *Fouilles de Bassit: Tombes du Fer* (Paris: Editions Recherche sur les Civilisations, 1993).

80. Idem, "Fragments d'amphores protogéometriques grecques à Bassit (Syrie)," *Hesperia* 62 (1993) 95–113.

81. F. Braemer, "La céramique à engobe rouge de l'âge du Fer à Bassit," *Syria* 63 (1986) 221–46.

82. W. van Soldt, "Studies in the Topography of Ugarit (1): The Spelling of the Ugaritic Toponyms," *UF* 28 (1996) 653–92, esp. pp. 680–81.

Bassit was still a port where a few ships tramping along the coast could sell some of their goods and buy provisions in the adjacent town. In this way, like Ras ibn-Hani (the port and royal residence called Ra'šu in the Ugaritic texts) across from it on the southern point of the Minet el-Baida (the Bay of Ugarit), Ras el-Bassit was able to maintain some semblance of its former bustle and some faint recollection of its place in a grander history.[83]

Al Mina, at the mouth of the Orontes, in the land of Aramean ʿUmqi (once upon a time the Kingdom of Alalakh and then the Neo-Hittite principality of Patina), comes into view toward the end of the ninth century as a hub of Greek, Phoenician, Syrian, and Aramean enterprise. It was not itself a core of creative interaction but more like a center for the transshipment of new and antique goods, situated at the intersection of land and sea routes to intellectual and artistic centers and to the sources of iron and other metals in the interior. The site did not have a natural harbor but had to rely on beachheads,[84] to which Greek sailors were accustomed, or on anchorages farther upriver, as the Tyrian explorers preferred in eighth-century Spain.

Al Mina was a modest settlement that depended on upriver sites and cities: Sabouni, about three kilometers from the sea; and Tell Tayinat, ninth-century Calneh (Assyrian *Kunulua*), east of Antioch, where the Orontes meets the ʿAmuq plain and turns southward. The site was not occupied before the ninth century, and it was only at the very end of the century, at the earliest, that a few Euboeans, perhaps from Chalcis, were living there in primitive houses of local Syrian design. Most of the pottery throughout the two-century history of the site was indigenous, but of the rest about 50 percent was Greek, imported (Euboean, Ionian, and Samian) or locally made; 30 percent was imported or imitation Cypriot; and about 20 percent was Phoenician Red Slip. The site gradually became something like a town, and by the late eighth century was conspicuous for its warehouses. In the earliest level, almost all the pottery except for some Levantine storage jars was Euboean; but in the eighth century, at first Cypriot and then Phoenician predominated. In the seventh, Corinthian and eastern Greek, especially Samian, wares were most popular. Al Mina, clearly, was a joint venture but a Euboean idea, an early invention of the Greek Orientalizing period that caught on with Greek and Phoenician Cypriots and with Syrians of Phoenician origin or cultural orientation.[85] It was not a colony, it

83. J. Lagarce, "Rapports de Ras ibn Hani avec la Phénicie et la Méditerranée orientale à l'âge du Fer," *Atti* 1, 1.223–26, pls. 56–62. Ras ibn Hani was occupied by squatters soon after it was overrun by the Sea Peoples and maintained uninterrupted relations with Cyprus until the seventh century. Beginning in the ninth century, there is some Phoenician Red Slip and Black-on-Red pottery, and Cypriot influence on local ceramic production is less pronounced.
84. J. Boardman, "Al Mina and History," *OJA* 9 (1990) 169–90, esp. p. 183.
85. J. Du Plat Taylor, "The Cypriot and Syrian Pottery from Al Mina, Syria," *Iraq* 21 (1959) 62–92; J. Boardman, "Provenance Studies of Greek Pottery of the Historic Period," in *Greek and Cypriot Pottery: A Review of Scientific Studies* (ed. R. E. Jones; Athens: British School of Archaeology, 1986) 627–747, esp. pp. 691–92; idem, "Al Mina and History," *OJA* 9 (1990) 169–90; idem, "The Excavated History of Al Mina," in *Ancient Greeks—West and East* (ed. G. R. Tsetskhladze; Mnemosyne Supplement 196; Leiden: Brill, 1999) 135–61; R. A. Kearsley, "A Pendent Semicircle Skyphos of the Geometric Period," in *Classical Art in the Nicholson Museum, Sydney* (ed. A. Cambitoglou

did not belong to any particular national or ethnic group,[86] but it was a dynamic, shared settlement in the territory of a wealthy Neo-Hittite state that at the same time was being overrun by ambitious and culturally self-conscious Arameans.[87]

The choice of Al Mina was the product of earlier contacts between Euboeans (probably from Chalcis) and Tyrians, both in southwestern Cyprus (at Kouklia, Kourion, and Amathus) and in Tyre;[88] and also of competition with Sidonians who plied the ports in southern Syria and, with their Euboean friends from Lefkandi and Eretria, did business at Ras el-Bassit and Ras ibn-Hani. The attraction of the place was the availability of the natural resources and sophisticated markets of North Syria. The river valley led to the rich, well-watered plain, for which the country ʿUmqi (= "Plain") was named, whence there was easy travel southward toward the Lebanon, northward to the Amanus and Zinjirli, northeast to Arpad in the land of Bit Agusi, to Til Barsip in the land of Bit Adini, and to Carchemish (the commercial, cultural and artistic center of North Syria).[89] The resources, natural or imported, to which ʿUmqi had access and from which it paid fabulous tribute to Assyria included gold, silver, copper, and iron; cypress and cedar; horses, cattle, and sheep. It also supplied the court with personnel, including musicians and singers, and with finished products such as purple wool, copper bowls, linen garments with multicolored trim, ivory, wood inlaid with ivory, and gold jewelry (some of which were imported, many worked by resident Phoenician craftsmen). The capital, Kunulua, was a center of Neo-Hittite culture, the wealth of which was celebrated on Shalmaneser III's gates at Balawat, the literate heritage of which was evident on ubiquitous inscribed monuments, and the eventual collapse of which astonished the civilized world.

There was a sort of artistic koine in the region, and in the ninth century a growing interest in producing, or even mass-producing smaller exportable objects.[90] Bronze, even after the ready availability of iron, continued to be very valuable, and some of the copper used in the bronze-working shops of this region must have been imported by the Cypriots whose pottery became so plentiful at Al Mina.[91] An eighth-century slate mold for rings,

and E. Robinson; Mainz: von Zabern, 1995) 17–28; idem, "Greeks Overseas in the 8th Century B.C.: Euboeans, Al Mina and Assyrian Imperialism," in *Ancient Greeks—West and East*, 109–34.

86. Waldbaum, "Greeks *in* the East or Greeks *and* the East?" 1–17.

87. T. P. Harrison, "The Evidence for Aramaean Cultural Expansion in the Amuq Plain," *Bulletin of the Canadian Society for Mesopotamian Studies* 36 (2001) 135–44; idem, "Tell Taʿyinat and the Kingdom of Unqi," in *The World of the Aramaeans, II: Studies in History and Archaeology in Honour of Paul-Eugène Dion* (ed. P. M. M. Daviau, J. W. Wevers, and M. Weigl; JSOTSup 325; Sheffield: Sheffield Academic Press, 2001) 115–32.

88. A. J. Graham, "The Historical Interpretation of Al Mina," *Dialogues d'Histoire Ancienne* 12 (1986) 51–65.

89. I. J. Winter, "Carchemish *ša kišad puratti*," *AnSt* 33 (1983) 177–97.

90. S. Mazzoni, "L'arte siro-ittita nel suo contesto archeologico," in *Contributi e materiali di archeologia orientale VII: Studi in memoria di Henri Frankfort (1897–1954)* (ed. P. Matthiae; Rome: Università degli Studi di Roma "La Sapienza," 1997) 287–327.

91. In Assyrian commerce, silver was introduced as money only at the end of the eighth century, and until then, and even afterwards, payments were made in bronze, rarely in silver, and never in gold: K. Radner, "Money in the Neo-Assyrian Empire," in *Trade and Finance in*

earrings, and pendants that was unearthed at Al Mina and that is almost
exactly like another found near Zinjirli illustrates the common traditions
of workmanship, cosmopolitan tastes, and the mass-marketing techniques
of the Tyrian traders who gathered at Al Mina.[92] A ninth-century cylinder
seal from the surface of the site is from a local boutique, where a Tyrian
artist with characteristic eclectic impulses carved an Assyrian scene of worship but highlighted it with Egyptian symbols (an *ankh*, a flail, and a papyrus flower), a Cypriot motif (a bucranium), and his own signature (a hawk
perched on the flower).[93] The Lyre Player seals,[94] of which two were found
at Al Mina, were a small collection, characterized by a lyre among the stick
figures in the engraving, produced by a North Syrian artist who created
cheap amulets by compressing Sidonian (or modified Egyptian), Assyrian,
and local styles and motifs. They were all made about the same time (ca.
740–720 B.C.E.) for a specific market (young adults), were distributed by
the Euboeans who frequented Al Mina, and have been found exclusively in
Euboean and Sidonian contexts in the eastern and western Mediterranean.
The Euboeans were surely interested in more than trinkets: the tin, iron,
and bronze would have been useful, and the ivories and inscribed monuments would have been instructive. Whatever initially attracted them,
it turned out to be the rich human resources—the intellectual, religious-
political, and artistic ferment visible in the clash of material cultures—that
most intrigued them and made the most lasting impression.

Although much of the direct and material evidence for Phoenicians and
Greeks at Al Mina is from the eighth century, there is oblique and circumstantial evidence that suggests that they were active, if not settled, in the
region by the ninth century. The archaeological data reveal that the Euboeans took the initiative in establishing a foothold at Al Mina, but the evidence of the texts argues that it was Phoenicians from Tyre who made the
earlier inroads into the now burgeoning North Syrian kingdoms.[95] There
are three sets of texts in particular that illustrate this early Tyrian influence.

There are two ninth-century (ca. 800 B.C.E.) Luwian inscriptions from
Carchemish that reflect the city's cosmopolitan status.[96] In one inscription,

Mesopotamia: Proceedings of the First MOS Symposium (ed. J. G. Dercksen; Istanbul: Nederlands
Historisch-Archaeologisch Instituut te Instanbul, 1999) 127–57.

I. J. Winter, "North Syria as a Bronze Working Centre in the Early First Millennium B.C.:
Luxury Commodities at Home and Abroad," in *Bronzeworking Centres of Western Asia c. 1000–539
B.C.* (ed. J. Curtis; London: Kegan Paul, 1988) 193–225.

92. M. Y. Treister, "North Syrian Metalworkers in Archaic Greek Settlements?" *OJA* 14 (1995)
159–78.

93. R. D. Barnett, "A Cylinder Seal from Syria," *Iraq* 6 (1939) 1–2, pl. 1.

94. J. Boardman, "The Lyre Player Group of Seals: An Encore," *Archäologischer Anzeiger* (1990)
1–17.

95. J. D. Hawkins, "The Political Geography of North Syria and South-East Anatolia in the
Neo-Assyrian Period," in *Neo-Assyrian Geography* (ed. M. Liverani; Rome: University of Rome,
1995) 87–101, pls. 1–10.

96. J. D. Hawkins, *Corpus of Hieroglyphic Luwian Inscriptions, Volume I: Inscriptions of the Iron
Age; Part 1* (Berlin: de Gruyter, 2000) 72–223; J. C. Greenfield, "Of Scribes, Scripts and Languages,"
in *Phoinikeia Grammata: Lire et écrire en Méditerranée* (ed. C. Baurain, C. Bonnet, and V. Krings;
Namur: Societé des Études Classiques, 1991) 173–85; F. Starke, "Sprachen und Schriften in Karkamis," in *Ana šadi labnāni lū allik. Beiträge zu altorientalischen und mittlemeerischen Kulturen: Festschrift für Wolfgang Röllig* (ed. B. Pongratz-Leisten, H. Kühne, and P. Xella; Neukirchen-Vluyn:

the ruler Yariris boasts that his fame has spread from Egypt to Urartu and that it is also recounted in the languages of Lydia, Phrygia, North Arabia, and Tyre. In another, he boasts that he knows 12 languages and that he can write 4 of them: Luwian, Tyrian, Assyrian, and North Arabic. In the first inscription, the geographical order and the order in which the languages are listed suggest that by "Tyrian" he meant a language that was spoken in the north in the vicinity of Carchemish. In the second, the 4 languages in fact were all known in Carchemish and its environs: Luwian is said to be "the script of the City"; South Arabic is called "Temanite" and was the language of the caravans; Tyrian is listed as his second language, because Phoenician was used among the educated Neo-Hittites at Zinjirli before the kingdom was Aramaized. It is conceivable that Greek was 1 of the 12 languages he knew, but there is clearly no doubt that Tyrians, if not their Euboean partners, were regular guests at the court of Carchemish in the ninth century and that the artists, merchants, and literati of the kingdom could read and converse in Phoenician.

There is also an Aramaic inscription of about the same date as these Luwian texts that was found near Aleppo and that was written by the king of Arpad, the country bordering ʿUmqi, on the route from Al Mina to Carchemish. It is inscribed on the base of a stele depicting the Storm God striding barefoot to the left, Syrian in demeanor with his disproportionately large head, but dressed in Phoenician (that is, refined Egyptianizing) style and carrying an archaic Syrian crescent axe over his left shoulder and an Egyptian *ankh* symbol in his right hand. The inscription identifies this figure as Melqart, the God of Tyre, and it states (in an Aramaic adaptation of the Tyrian genre) that the stele was offered in fulfillment of the vow that the king of Arpad made: "Stele that Bar Hadad, son of ʿAtarsamak, son of Hadram, king of Aram, set in place for his Lord, for Melqart, to whom he had made a vow and who heard his voice."[97] The occasion of the vow may have been some national emergency (Assyrian invasions under Adad-nirari III and his adjutant Shamshi-ilu[98] or conflict with Hamath) or some personal plight, but it is evident that Tyrians had influence at the court and that they had been resident or traveling in the land long enough to allow for the adaptation of the worship of Melqart to the age-old cult of the Syrian Storm God, Hadad. If their Euboean and Cypriot partners were also involved in these ventures, it may have been at this time and in this region that the assimilation of Melqart and Heracles, the true immortals, that eventually swept through the Mediterranean began to take shape.

Neukirchener Verlag, 1997) 381–95; S. Dalley, "Shamsi-ilu, Language and Power in the Western Assyrian Empire," in *Essays on Syria in the Iron Age* (ed. G. Bunnens; Louvain: Peeters, 2000) 79–88.

97. W. T. Pitard, "The Identity of the Bir-Hadad of the Melqart Stele," *BASOR* 272 (1988) 3–21; É. Puech, "La stèle de Bar-Hadad à Melqart et les rois d'Arpad," *RB* 99 (1992) 311–34. The idea of erecting a stele in fulfillment of a vow is Phoenician, and some of the words are reflections of Phoenician usage: "stele" (*nṣb*), "vow" (*nzr*), and the expression "hear the voice" (*šmʿ ql* in Phoenician, *šmʿ lql* in Aramaic).

98. A. R. Millard, "Adad-Nirari III, Aram and Arpad," *PEQ* 105 (1973) 161–64; idem and H. Tadmor, "Adad-Nirari III in Syria: Another Stele Fragment and the Dates of His Campaigns," *Iraq* 35 (1973) 57–64.

A third manifestation of early Tyrian presence in ʿUmqi and of their cooperation with the Euboeans at Al Mina and beyond is a pair of inscribed North Syrian horse blinkers, one of which was found in Eretria, and the other among the trophies deposited in the Heraion on Samos.[99] The two are identical, cast in bronze from ivory models, with figures in North Syrian style: three plump, round-faced, naked girls wearing necklaces and anklets and offering their breasts in their cupped hands stand on lion protomes in the upraised hands of a fourth girl, who stands below them and is similarly adorned; they all face forward in a bucolic scene that is framed by a delicate frieze with animals at play and surmounted by a winged sun whose disk is a rosette. Both are inscribed with the same text:[100] "This was given in honor of our Lord Hazaʾel by ʿUmqi in the year that our Lord crossed the River." This Hazael was the king of Damascus in the second half of the ninth century and—probably because he united Syria in the confederation of kingdoms called "All Aram," comprising "Upper Aram" and "Lower Aram"— was known both in Akkadian and in Aramaic sources as "Our Lord."[101] His crossing of the river Euphrates, modeled on the exploits of the Assyrian kings who boasted of crossing the River and of washing their weapons in the Sea, was a metaphorical expression of his great, legendary, and near-mythical renown.[102]

The blinkers may have been designed as trophies or ex votos rather than as gifts meant to be given to the king, and they were already heirlooms when they came to Eretria and were presented in the Heraion on Samos in the eighth century. They illustrate the Phoenician artistic canons—new creations that can be traced to Egyptian, Assyrian, Mycenean, and indigenous traditions—that influenced the Neo-Hittite and North Syrian artists in ʿUmqi. In their dispersal, they confirm the establishment of Greeks and Tyrians at Al Mina and inland in the ninth century. It is most likely, especially if the blinkers were designed as trophies rather than prepared as gifts, that they were kept in ʿUmqi or at Al Mina and then, before Hazael's

---

99. H. Kyrieleis and W. Röllig, "Ein altorientalischer Pferdeschmuck aus dem Heraion von Samos," *Mitteilungen des Deutschen Archäologischen Instituts, Athenische Abteilung* 103 (1988) 37–75, pls. 9–15; I. Ephʿal and J. Naveh, "Hazael's Booty Inscriptions," *IEJ* 39 (1989) 193–200; D. Parayre, "À propos d'une plaque de harnais en bronze découverte à Samos: Réflexions sur le disque solaire ailé," *RA* 83 (1989) 45–31; H. Kyrieleis, "The Relation between Samos and the Eastern Mediterannean: Some Aspects," in *Proceedings of an International Symposium: The Civilizations of the Aegean and Their Diffusion in Cyprus and the Eastern Mediterranean, 2000–600 B.C.* (ed. V. Karageorghis; Larnaka: Pierides Foundation, 1990) 129–32, pls. 29–30; D. Wicke, "Altorientalische Pferdescheuklappen," *UF* 31 (1999) 803–51.

100. The Aramaic reads: *zy ntn hdr lmrʾn ḥzʾl mn ʿmq bšnt ʿdh mrʾn nhr*. The third word is usually read *hdd*, "Hadad," and interpreted as a personal or divine name, but *reš* is distinguished from *dalet* by the greater length of its vertical.

101. F. Bron and A. Lemaire, "Les inscriptions araméenes de Hazael," *RA* 83 (1989) 35–44; A. Lemaire, "Hazael de Damas, roi d'Aram," in *Marchands, diplomates et empereurs: Études sur la civilisation mésopotamienne offertes à Paul Garelli* (ed. D. Charpin and F. Joannès; Paris: Éditions Recherche sur les Civilisations, 1991) 91–108; É. Puech, "L'ivoire inscrit d'Arslan Tash et les rois de Damas," *RB* 88 (1981) 544–62, pls. 12–13.

102. Similar renown was ascribed to King David when he defeated all the neighboring states, that is, "when he went to restore his monument at the River" (2 Sam 8:3). The ultimate origin of the ideology is the myth of the Storm God Baʿal, who established himself as king by defeating the primordial chaos called Sea and River.

mystique had faded, were taken by Euboeans or their Tyrian friends, some of them newcomers from Cyprus, to their final destinations.

The Euboean and Tyrian partnership at Al Mina did not survive the Assyrian disruption of the North Syrian synergy in the latter part of the eighth century. In the seventh century, there is mainland and East Greek pottery. In the late fifth and the early fourth centuries, lamps, seals, coins, terra-cottas, and the imported Attic pottery show that Al Mina was dependent on Sidon and Arvad and their Greek connections.[103] There are some Phoenician inscriptions on jars consisting of the names, abbreviations of names, or monograms of the exporters in these two cities and a few Aramaic inscriptions of the local producers.[104] Al Mina, until it was abandoned at the end of the fourth century, was the meeting place of Phoenicians and Greeks and in the ninth century was the purveyor of the North Syrian wisdom, with its admixture of native, Hittite, Assyrian, and Phoenician lore that helped nourish the Mediterranean world.

Symptomatic of this wisdom are the learned and artistic traditions embodied in the ivory furnishings created in ninth-century Syrian workshops. The workshops can be distinguished by the schools (the complex of design, style, technique, and repertoire) to which they belonged and by the traditions (the themes, motifs, allusions, and beliefs) that they embodied. In the ninth century, the North and South Syrian schools flourished. These can be assigned to Sidonian and Byblian émigré craftsmen, respectively, working from Phoenician paradigms and indigenous models to produce, with their students and apprentices, practical and instructive works of art that emphasized the individuality and concreteness of their subjects. They are quite distinct from the eighth- and seventh-century Phoenician school, in which archaism, formality, and idealization defined a virtuoso range of playful, entertaining and seductive artworks illustrative of Tyrian aloofness, eclecticism, otherworldliness, and urbanity.

The South Syrian school, thought to have had its center in Hamath, is characterized by a lingering fascination with Egyptian subjects and by a mixture of Egyptian and Syrian forms and techniques.[105] Ivories of this type have been found at Arslan Tash and Samaria, at Nimrud (where they would have been taken as tribute or booty), at Zinjirli, and at Til Barsip (where they were stored with ivories in a variety of styles in the house of an

---

103. J. Elayi, "Al-Mina sur l'Oronte à l'époque perse," in *Phoenicia and the East Mediterranean in the First Millennium B.C.* (ed. E. Lipiński; Studia Phoenicia 5; Louvain: Peeters, 1987) 249–66; J. Lund, "The Northern Coastline of Syria in the Persian Period: A Survey," *Transeu* 2 (1990) 13–36, esp. pp. 24–25.

104. F. Bron and A. Lemaire, "Inscriptions d'Al-Mina," *Atti* 1, 3.677–86, pls. 116–24.

105. I. J. Winter, "Is There a South Syrian Style of Ivory Carving in the Early First Millennium B.C.?" *Iraq* 43 (1981) 101–30. The style is represented especially by groups of ivories from Arslan Tash and Samaria. Partly on the basis of an ivory from Arslan Tash inscribed with the name of Haza'el, Winter suggested that the school was located at Damascus. G. Herrmann thought that the variations within the South Syrian style could be explained by postulating a number of schools in different centers: "The Nimrud Ivories, 2: A Survey of the Traditions," in *Von Uruk nach Tuttul: Eine Festschrift für Eva Strommenger. Studien und Aufsätze von Kollegen und Freunde* (ed. B. Hrouda, S. Kroll, and P. Z. Spanos; Munich: Profil, 1992) 65–79, pls. 20–34; R. D. Barnett (*A Catalogue of the Nimrud Ivories* [London: British Museum, 1957] 44–52) located the Syrian school in Hamath.

ivory merchant).[106] In Samaria, where they differ from a later Phoenician group with glass or frit inlays, they are distinguished by their themes (such as the Woman-at-the-Window), their technique (details are indicated by incised lines rather than by modeling), and their composition (such as opposed ram-headed sphinxes facing a central tree).

At Arslan Tash,[107] where some of the same features occur, the South Syrian ivories are notable for their squat figures with large heads, pudgy faces with receding forehead and chin turned to the viewer, compositions filling the entire space and pressing against the frame, and fringed clothing worn to indicate the movement of the body. There is some vague reminiscence of Egyptian motifs—the Arslan Tash ivories often represent the birth of Horus—but the figures are Syrian, and the scenes lack the refinement and attention to detail of the later Phoenician ivories. Their origin in the Byblian inspired ateliers of Hamath would be consistent with their subordination of Phoenician to local traditions and with their distribution in Israel and in Neo-Hittite centers.

The North Syrian groups of ivories originated in the tenth and ninth centuries at Tell Halaf, Zinjirli, and Carchemish where Syrian, Hittite, and Mycenean traditions converged in the programs of a Phoenician, or specifically Sidonian, school.[108] Human figures are plump, women are round-cheeked and wear their hair in ringlets, Goddesses are draped or naked but stand boldly and face forward holding flowers or lions in their outstretched hands. In one group, the haunches of animals are not carved in the round but are represented by flame-and-frond incisions.[109]

Among the popular items were pyxides, or circular boxes with vertical sides, and the scenes carved on them (procession to an enthroned figure, a hero stabbing a winged griffin, a banquet scene, a man leading a bull) were episodes from narratives or myths. Objects that could be held in the hand—such as a jug with a palmette handle, a bowl held by a swimming woman, a flask in the shape of a fish or a calf or a woman, the head of a woman, a staff decorated with female figures in the round—were designed to provoke songs or love stories. Figures were natural or individual, not stylized (a feature that was borrowed by Assyrian artists in the time of Ashurnasirpal II),[110] and scenes were realistic and conveyed movement. But

---

106. G. Bunnens, "Carved Ivories from Til Barsip," *AJA* 101 (1997) 435–50.

107. F. Thureau-Dangin et al., *Arslan Tash* (Paris: Geuthner, 1931) 89–134.

108. R. D. Barnett, *A Catalogue of the Nimrud Ivories* (London: British Museum, 1957); idem, *Ancient Ivories in the Middle East and Adjacent Countries* (Qedem 14; Jerusalem: Institute of Archaeology, Hebrew University, 1982).

109. G. Herrmann, "The Nimrud Ivories, 1: The Flame and Frond School," *Iraq* 51 (1989) 85–109, pls. 8–19.

110. I. J. Winter, "Art as Evidence for Interaction: Relations between the Assyrian Empire and North Syria," in *Mesopotamien und seine Nachbarn: Politische und kulturelle Wechselbeziehungen im alten Vorderasien vom 4. bis 1. Jahrtausend v. Chr—XXV Rencontre Assyriologique Internationale, 1978* (ed. H.-J. Nissen and J. Renger; Berlin: Reimer, 1982) 355–82; idem, "Art in Empire: The Royal Image and the Visual Dimension of Assyrian Ideology," in *Assyria 1995* (ed. S. Parpola and R. M. Whiting; Helsinki: Neo-Assyrian Text Corpus Project, 1997) 359–81; B. Nevling Porter, "Sacred Trees, Date Palms, and the Royal Persona of Asshurnasirpal II," *JNES* 52 (1993) 129–39; G. Herrmann, "The Nimrud Ivories, 3: The Assyrian Tradition," in *Assyrien im Wandel der Zeiten* (ed. H. Waetzold and H. Hauptmann; Heidelberg: Orientverlag, 1997)

the most striking features of the North Syrian schools are their differentiation over time and from center to center, the individuality of their artists and workshops, their variations within similar styles and techniques, the sense that their artistry grew out of a studied fusion of living traditions, and the effect that this deliberation had on monumental urban art.[111] The North Syrian élan is recognizable anywhere—in the ivories from the Idaean Cave, the Heraion on Samos, or from central Spain where Sidonians settled before Tyrians established colonies along the southern coast—but it is always somehow different and appropriate to its environment, the work of émigré individuals evidently assured of their heritage and appreciative of their new surroundings.[112]

Ivories in the Phoenician style, by contrast, are later, more beautiful, and more rigorously defined. Their traditions can be traced through tenth-century Tyrian workshops in Egypt to the Late Bronze Age, when indigenous Canaanite crafts were under the spell of Egyptian canons of physical beauty, but almost all of them were produced in the eighth and seventh centuries, when Tyre colonized the Mediterranean.[113] At this time they were still thoroughly dependent on Egyptian traditions for their themes, design, and symbolism.[114] They were characterized by their symmetry, grace, and proportion, by their elegant and exquisite divine, human, and animal figures, and by their delicate treatment of surfaces. They were carved as panels for furniture, thick square panels in high relief, or thin rectangular panels in shallow relief and are distinguished by their use of polychrome and glass inlay.[115]

285–90, pls. 27–32; J. M. Russell, "The Program of the Palace of Assurnasirpal II at Nimrud: Issues in the Research and Presentation of Assyrian Art," *AJA* 102 (1998) 655–715.

111. I. J. Winter, "North Syrian Ivories and Tell Halaf Reliefs: The Impact of Luxury Goods upon 'Major' Arts," in *Essays in Ancient Civilization Presented to Helene J. Kantor* (ed. A. Leonard Jr. and B. B. Williams; Studies in Ancient Israelite Oriental Civilization 47; Chicago: Oriental Institute, 1989) 321–32, pls. 62–66.

112. J. A. Sakellarakis, "The Idaean Cave Ivories," in *Ivory in Greece and the Eastern Mediterranean from the Bronze Age to the Hellenistic Period* (ed. J. L. Fitton; London: British Museum, 1992) 113–40.

P. Brize, "New Ivories from the Samian Heraion," in ibid., 163–72.

M. E. Aubet-Semmler, "Die westphönizischen Elfenbeine aus dem Gebiet des unteren Guadalquivir," *HBA* 9 (1982) 15–70; M. C. D'Angelo, "Motivi floreali e vegetali negli avori fenici de Spagna," *EVO* 6 (1983) 107–32; idem, "Aspetti iconografici degli avori fenici della peninsola iberica," *Atti* 2, 2.797–812.

I. J. Winter, "Carved Ivory Furniture Panels from Nimrud: A Coherent Subgroup of the North Syrian Style," *Metropolitan Museum Journal* 11 (1976) 25–54; G. Herrmann, *Ivories from Room SW37, Fort Shalmaneser: Commentary and Catalogue* (Ivories from Nimrud [1949–63], fascicle 4/1; London: British School of Archaeology in Iraq, 1986); idem, "Ivory Carving of First Millennium Workshops: Traditions and Diffusion," in *Images as Media: Sources for the Cultural History of the Near East and the Eastern Mediterranean (1st Millennium B.C.E.)* (ed. C. Uehlinger; Göttingen: Vandenhoeck & Ruprecht, 2000) 267–82.

113. D. Ciafaloni, "Avori fenici e pettorali egiziani," *Actes* 3, 1.260–70; S. M. Cecchini, "Avori 'fenici'?" *Actas* 4, 3.1277–85; H. Liebowitz, "Late Bronze II Ivory Work in Palestine: Evidence of a Cultural Highpoint," *BASOR* 265 (1987) 3–24.

114. R. D. Barnett, "Phoenician and Syrian Ivory Carving," *PEQ* 71 (1938–39) 4–19; D. Ciafaloni, "Tradizione e innovazione negli avori fenici, 1: Motivi egei su una placca da Nimrud," *Actas* 4, 3.971–86.

115. D. Barag, "Glass Inlays and the Classification and Dating of Ivories from the Ninth–Eighth Centuries B.C.," *AnSt* 33 (1983) 163–67; C. S. Lightfoot, "Glass in the Iron Age," in *Ana-*

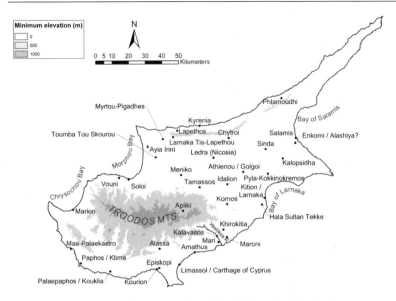

Map 4. Cyprus (produced by Christopher Brinker).

They were exported to Salamis on Cyprus, to Ialysos and Lindos on Rhodes, to the Heraion on Samos, to Mount Ida on Crete, and to Praeneste in Italy and have been found at Ramat Raḥel and Hazor in Israel and at Ashur, Nineveh, Nimrud, and Ḥarran in Assyria. They are much more uniform than the North Syrian groups and may have been produced in a few centers close to the sources of ivory (in Damascus and at Calneh in ꜥUmqi), from which they were distributed by Tyrian merchants. Their archaism and reproduction of the Late Bronze Age Egyptian mystique suited them perfectly to the interest in research into the intellectual and cultural history of the Near East that characterized the Orientalizing revolution.

The distinctiveness of the schools and traditions of ivory carving corresponds to the radical particularity of Tyre, Sidon, and Byblos within a common Canaanite heritage and agrees with their different associations and interests and with their tendency to go their separate ways. These features are evident in the distribution of their settlements along the coast of Syria, in the chronology and direction of their overseas commercial ventures, and in the transportation and temporal sequencing of their ceramics and artifacts. The ninth century marked the beginning of Phoenician expansion in the Mediterranean—to Cyprus, Greece, and the West—and the climax of their influence in the East.

tolian Iron Ages: The Proceedings of the Second Anatolian Iron Ages Colloquium Held at Izmir, 4–8 May 1987 (ed. A. Cilingiroglu and D. H. French; Oxford: Oxbow, 1991) 67–73; J. Curtis, "Glass Inlays and Nimrud Ivories," *Iraq* 61 (1999) 59–69.

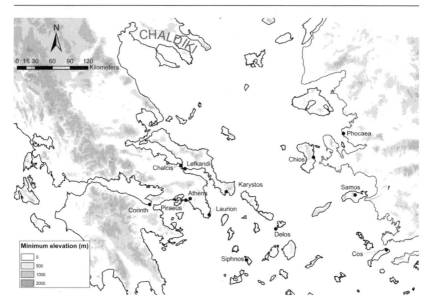

Map 5. Greece (produced by Christopher Brinker).

Cyprus and the West:
The Effects of Phoenician Travel Westward

Phoenicians began to travel to Cyprus in the eleventh century B.C.E. at the invitation of Cypriots and Greeks from Cyprus who, following their Late Bronze Age ancestors, had traveled to Canaan. They were a modest presence at first, and unconcentrated, because the island was partly a destination and partly a handy stage in journeys to North Syria, Anatolia, and the West. They came from Tyre, Sidon, and Byblos, and they landed or settled at different places along the coast, each with separate interests and objectives. Tyrians were drawn to the southwest, from Limassol to Paphos and the intervening ports. Sidonians went to the southeast, to Kition in particular, and from there to towns in the interior. Byblians, sometimes associates of the Sidonians, sailed to the north, notably to Lapethos, where they established outposts and places of business.

The Tyrians, in the employ of their city or working in syndicates, founded colonies or lived in compounds apart from the local people, traded in goods they had collected at home or along the way, and had separate graveyards for their dead. Sidonians, singly or in family associations, lived among the Cypriots and Greeks and maintained their identity through their arts and crafts, their workshops, meeting halls, and trade monopolies, and dedication to their patron Gods. From their centers and footholds in Cyprus, where they maintained varying degrees of contact with their cities of origin, these Phoenicians struck out in different directions. Some Sidonians, who were soon naturalized islanders, went to Crete and Greece and from there with their Greek friends to Italy, Sicily, and Spain. Tyrians did business with Egypt and followed trade routes that brought them to

Sardinia and North Africa. Byblians, usually in association with Sidonians, made their way to North Syria, Cilicia, and Italy.

For two centuries, Tyrian, Sidonian, and Byblian travel to Cyprus replaced the earlier movement of Cypriots to the Levantine coast and to the interior of Syria and Palestine. During this time, Cypriots and Greeks, with the Phoenicians to maintain their international network, settled into the routine of their very conservative cultural development.

Because Tyre, Sidon, and Byblos had discrete and specific relations with Cyprus, only a few interconnected places on the island were profoundly marked by their presence. Most towns and regions remained steadfastly Cypriot and Greek, and Phoenician influence is indicated by local imitations of their wares or by sporadic indulgence in the leisure and luxury they promoted. Their settlements, beginning in the ninth century, were founded to take advantage of the resources, and in some measure to tap the markets on Cyprus, but they were mainly way stations on the routes to the West and did not involve Phoenician settlement or control of the island.

At the end of the eighth century, when the Assyrians made Kition their administrative center on the island, none of the city kingdoms was Phoenician, and in the seventh century only one had a Phoenician name (Carthage, or "New City") and was governed by a Phoenician king ("Damusi"). It was not until the end of the sixth century, during the Persians Wars in particular, that Phoenicians became politically prominent on the island. Culturally (in religion, art, crafts, ceramics, life-style and burial practices) influence was mutual, and the general Phoenician affinity for Greeks from then on acquired a Cypriot tinge that became characteristic of their presence wherever they pursued their Mediterranean quest.

Kition and Southeast Cyprus

Kition was founded by Mycenean settlers from Crete and mainland Greece in the Late Bronze Age, around 1300 B.C.E. There was earlier indigenous habitation, and there are earlier tombs,[116] but there is little sign of an earlier organized settlement apart from a few ceramic finds, and a mud-brick wall on the north side of the town. When the Myceneans arrived, they added two large ashlar-and-rubble piers outside the wall and constructed an extensive temple complex inside it. These piers were connected to a street or quay and were part of a new port built below the wall on a protected lagoon at the foot of the hill on which the town was situated.[117] The temple complex comprised sanctuaries surrounded by workshops, storerooms, and residences and was dedicated to small-scale copper smelting. It was remodeled, or destroyed and rebuilt, at intervals before the beginning of the twelfth century, when the town was occupied by Greeks

---

116. V. Karageorghis, *Excavations at Kition, I: The Tombs* (Nicosia: Department of Antiquities, 1974); E. Herscher, "Kition in the Middle Bronze Age: The Tombs at Larnaca-Ayios Prodromos," *RDAC* (1988) part 1, 141–66.

117. V. Karageorghis, *Kition. Mycenaean and Phoenician Discoveries in Cyprus* (London: Thames & Hudson, 1976) 53–54, 60, 90; O. Negbi, "The Climax of Urban Development in Bronze Age Cyprus," *RDAC* (1986) 97–121, pls. 24–25.

migrating, either directly or via Anatolia, from Achaea.[118] These newcomers rebuilt the city wall with stone blocks and boulders, refurbished one of the temples using ashlar masonry,[119] and oversaw the expansion of the town that had become a haven for the recently displaced peoples fleeing the havoc of the Sea Peoples' raids on the North Syrian coast.

Most of the pottery for everyday use and special occasions was Mycenean.[120] Although some standard Cypriot pottery styles persisted,[121] others such as the more remarkable Base Ring style eventually were abandoned, and still others came to be creative amalgams of local, Aegean, and Near Eastern elements.[122] There are also Canaanite transport and storage jars inscribed with what seem to be Ugaritic, Canaanite, or Cypro-Minoan signs marking their provenance; and alabaster amphorae and jars—some made of calcite and imported from Egypt, others from Canaan made of gypsum.[123] Faience was produced locally or imported from Egypt and the Near East.[124] An enamel-coated faience rhyton (a conical ceremonial vase favored by associations of merchants for use in their symposia [*marzeaḥs*]) was decorated with a polychrome hunting scene and was the work of a local artist, originally from Sidon or Byblos, who was familiar with Aegean, Egyptian, and Levantine techniques and artistic canons.[125] Ivory masterpieces were carved locally but display Mycenean and Syrian influences.[126] All in all, the arrival in Kition of Myceneans and Achaeans, of Canaanites and refugees from Ugarit and Syria did not overwhelm the native Cypriot population or squelch the native spirit but provided the cultural stimulus that inspired them to new levels of genius.

The attraction of the site was its harbor, its access to the copper mines of Tamassos, and the availability of iron. Early on, perhaps from its foun-

---

118. V. Karageorghis and M. Demas, *Excavations at Kition, V: The Pre-Phoenician Levels. Areas I and II. Part I* (Nicosia: Department of Antiquities, 1985).

119. V. Cook, "Bronze Age Ashlar Construction in Cyprus: Theoretical Consequences," *RDAC* (1991) 93–96.

120. M. Yon and A. Caubet, *Kition-Bamboula, III: Le sondage L-N 13 (Bronze Récent et Géometrique)* (Paris: Editions Recherche sur les Civilisations, 1985).

121. M. Iacovou, "Society and Settlements in Late Cypriot III," *ESC*, 52–59; B. Kling, "Local Cypriot Features in the Ceramics of the Late Cypriot IIIA Period," *ESC*, 160–70.

122. S. Vaughan, "Base Ring Ware: A Regional Study in Cyprus," in *Provenience Studies and Bronze Age Cyprus* (ed. A. B. Knapp and J. F. Cherry; Madison, Wis.: Prehistory Press, 1994) 86–92; V. Karageorghis, "A Cypro-Mycenaean IIIC:1 Amphora from Kition," in *Greece and the Eastern Mediterranean in Ancient History and Prehistory: Studies Presented to Fritz Schachermeyer on the Occasion of His Eightieth Birthday* (ed. K. H. Kinzl; Berlin: de Gruyter, 1977) 192–98, pls. A–E; A. Caubet and E. J. Peltenburg, "Restauration d'un vase en faïence de Kition Bamboula," *RDAC* (1982) 83–85, pl. 14; M. Yon, "Note sur le 'style pastoral'," *RDAC* (1982) 109–14, pl. 19.

123. Yon and Caubet, *Kition-Bamboula III*; R. Sparks, "Egyptian Stone Vessels in Syro-Palestine during the Second Millennium B.C. and Their Impact on the Local Stone Vessel Industry," *Studies in Ancient Hebrew Semantics* (AbrN Supplement 5; Louvain: Peeters, 1995) 51–66.

124. A. Caubet and A. Kaczmarczyk, "Trade and Local Production in Late Cypriot Faience," *ESC*, 199–216; E. Peltenburg, "Appendix II: Glazed Vessels from Bronze and Iron Age Kition," in *Excavations at Kition, V: The Pre-Phoenician Levels. Areas I and II. Part II* (ed. V. Karageorghis and M. Demas; Nicosia: Department of Antiquities, 1985) 255–79.

125. E. J. Peltenburg, "Appendix I: The Glazed Vases," in *Excavations at Kition, I: The Tombs* (ed. V. Karageorghis; Nicosia: Department of Antiquities, 1974) 105–39, pls. 94–95; V. Tatton-Brown, ed., *Cyprus BC: 7000 Years of History* (London: British Museum, 1979) 44–45.

126. Karageorghis and Demas, *Excavations at Kition, V*, 329–39.

dation, and in line with its settlement by streams of displaced adventurers and entrepreneurs, Kition became a mart and a redistribution center for ships traveling the western routes. Its naturally protected inner harbor had wharves and port facilities comparable to those at Philistine Dor.[127] The winds were favorable to ships sailing along the south coast of Cyprus to the Syrian or Cilician coasts.[128] The ship that sank at Ulu Burun in Turkey on its way to Crete or Greece around 1300 B.C.E. was loaded with Cypriot copper and was using Cypriot ceramics.[129] It may have picked up the rest of its Egyptian, Syrian, and Canaanite cargo at a warehouse in Kition, where many of the same items have been found.[130]

The ship that sank 100 years later at Cape Gelidonya, just to the east of Ulu Burun, was also carrying Cypriot copper as well as scrap bronze and tools for bronze-working.[131] It has been compared to a ship from Enkomi-Alashiya docked at the Ugaritic port of Atallig, the cargo of which consisted both of raw copper and bronze and of finished products.[132] It may have been the ship of an itinerant craftsman from Kition, where there is evidence for just such recycling of scrap metal.[133]

The city's dedication to the sea is evident in the many disused stone anchors, some not from the Kition region, that were stored in the sanctuary complex or reused in the construction of floors, walls, and thresholds of the temples and workshops.[134] They were also used in the numerous graffiti of ships (like the graffiti engraved on rocks near the landing at Tel Nami and on a small altar in the port of ʿAkko)[135] that were carved into the

---

127. J. A. Gifford, "Appendix IV: Post-Bronze Age Coastal Change in the Vicinity of Kition," in ibid., 375–87; A. Raban, "The Harbor of the Sea Peoples at Dor," *BA* 50 (1987) 118–26; idem, "The Heritage of Ancient Harbour Engineering in Cyprus and the Levant," in *Proceedings of the International Symposium 'Cyprus and the Sea'* (ed. V. Karageorghis and D. Michaelides; Nicosia: University of Cyprus, 1995) 139–88; idem, "Near Eastern Harbors: Thirteenth–Seventh Centuries BCE," *MPT*, 428–38, esp. p. 429.

128. W. M. Murray, "Ancient Sailing Winds in the Eastern Mediterranean: The Case for Cyprus," in ibid., 33–43.

129. C. Pulak, "The Ulu Burun Shipwreck: An Overview," *IJNA* 27 (1998) 188–224.

130. P. T. Nicholson, C. M. Jackson, and K. M. Trott, "The Ulu Burun Glass Ingots, Cylindrical Vessels and Egyptian Glass," *JEA* 83 (1997) 143–53. C. A. Walz, *"Black Athena* and the Role of Cyprus in Near Eastern/Mycenaean Contact," in *Greeks and Barbarians: Essays on the Interactions between Greeks and Non-Greeks in Antiquity and the Consequences for Eurocentrism* (ed. J. E. Coleman and C. A. Walz; Bethesda MD: CDL, 1997) 1–27.

131. G. F. Bass, "Evidence of Trade from Bronze Age Shipwrecks," in *Bronze Age Trade in the Mediterranean* (ed. N. H. Gale; Studies in Mediterranean Archaeology 90; Jonsered: Åströms, 1991) 63–81.

132. E. Linder, "A Sea-Faring Merchant-Smith from Ugarit and the Cape Gelidonya Wreck," *IJNA* 1 (1972) 163–64; *CAT* 4:390.

133. V. Karageorghis and V. Kassianidou, "Metalworking and Recycling in Late Bronze Age Cyrus: The Evidence from Kition," *OJA* 18 (1999) 171–88; M. Artzy, "Cult and the Recycling of Metal at the End of the Late Bronze Age," in *Periplus: Festschrift für Hans-Gunter Buchholz zu seinem ächtzigsten Geburtstag am 24. Dezember 1999* (ed. P. Åström and D. Sürenhagen; Jonsered: Åströms, 2000) 27–31, pl. 1.

134. H. Frost, "Appendix I: The Kition Anchors," in *Excavations at Kition, V: The Pre-Phoenician Levels. Areas I and II. Part I* (ed. V. Karageorghis and M. Demas; Nicosia: Department of Antiquities, 1985) 281–321, pls. A–J.

135. M. Artzy, "Routes, Trade, Boats and 'Nomads of the Sea,'" *MPT*, 439–48.

altar and the columns of the temples overlooking the port at Kition.[136] The town had its own ships, captains, and crews, but it was mainly an emporium where other merchants from Cyprus or the Levantine coast could pick up the goods, either for cash or on consignment, that they traded abroad. Kition is mentioned in a few late thirteenth-century (ca. 1200 B.C.E.) and later texts. Three of these are Ugaritic administrative records and, consequently, at least laconic.[137] The other three are short but straightforward Phoenician texts. Together they suggest that Kition had Canaanite and Syrian affiliations early on and probably from the time of its foundation.

The first of the Ugaritic texts is a list of freemen, "king's men" (*bunušū milki*), who were subject to the authority of ʾAdinaʿim, a lieutenant of the court. The list is divided into two parts, each in two columns: one part on the obverse and the other on the reverse of the tablet. The heading of the first column is illegible, but the list contains 24 names, including names of well-known Ugaritic merchants and government officials, and everyone on the list probably was a resident of Ugarit: the second column on the reverse has a single entry, "twenty-five princes" (*šrm*), and undoubtedly refers to these notables—the total of course includes ʾAdinaʿim.

The heading of the second column is "men from Kition" (*bn kt*), and the list contains 23 names—most of them Hurrian, the rest Canaanite. The first column on the reverse lists the jobs assigned to them: 7 were ploughmen, 3 were gatekeepers, 1 was a constable in Ugarit, 11 were laborers in the city, and 8 were laborers on farms or in towns. Between them, these men had 21 assistants whose names were not included in the list: 2 watched the fields, and 1 watched the vineyard, and some, whose numbers are lost, made bows and arrows or built chariots. The workers were skilled, and their work was not considered menial; they were reliable and free to travel and settle where they could make a living. Their ethnic background, which made them pretty much at home in Ugarit, is an indication of the complexity of Canaanite society and a reminder that Phoenicians were a minority in Kition and everywhere on Cyprus at this time.

The second tablet from Ugarit is a list of wine rations for separate drinking parties (*mštt*) given by the king and queen of Ugarit. The queen's guests include her entourage (ʿm, "people"), the aristocratic charioteers (*maryanu*) and their squires (*znm*), and the Assyrians, who together consumed 10 jars of wine. The king's guests were officers and palace guards and "sons of the women from Kition and sons of the Egyptian men" (*bn amht kt wbn mṣrym*) who drank only 5 jars of wine. On the back of the tablet, a note appears that another 40 jars were distributed to the militia and that this brought the total consumed to 55 jars. The three parties took place at the same time.

136. L. Basch and M. Artzy, "Appendix II: Ship Graffiti at Kition," in *Excavations at Kition, V: The Pre-Phoenician Levels. Areas I and II. Part I* (ed. V. Karageorghis and M. Demas; Nicosia: Department of Antiquities, 1985) 322–36; M. Artzy, "Development of War/Fighting Boats of the Second Millennium B.C. in the Eastern Mediterranean," *RDAC* (1988) part 1, 181–86.

137. *CAT* 4:141:II, 1–23; 4:230; 4:425, 5; S. Segert, "Kition and Kittim," in *Periplus: Festschrift für Hans-Gunter Buchholz zu seinem ächtzigsten Geburtstag am 24. Dezember 1999* (ed. P. Åström and D. Sürenhagen; Jonsered: Åströms, 2000) 165–72.

The queen, attended by her women, invited military men: Assyria was negotiating with Ugarit at this time (ca. 1250–1225 B.C.E.) for access to the sea and for inclusion in its system of commercial relations,[138] and Ugarit was being pressured at the same time by the Hittites, who were preparing for war with Assyria, to remain neutral. The militia was not involved in the discussions, but their presence, drinking separately, was probably an appropriate show of strength.

The king's guests were aristocrats and important officials and two groups of foreigners. These "sons" could have been children from Kition and Egypt, but because companies and partnerships were organized as families whose heads were called "fathers" and whose associates were called "daughters," or "sons," and because women at Ugarit were almost as engaged as men in trade and commerce, as members of companies, or as individuals in their own businesses, the "sons" were probably partners in companies of Egyptians and Kitians stationed in Ugarit.

The third text is a list of properties, one of which belonged to "the sons of Kition" (*bn kt*), and this would tend to confirm that the "sons" were not children and not necessarily kin. It is known that Ugarit (the king and individual wealthy merchants) did business with Egypt, and so the presence of Egyptian trade officials in the city was expected. Kition's business with Ugarit, on the other hand, was run by women (*amht*, "maid, servant, mistress"), and this would have included such things as making or importing perfumes, jewelry, exquisite textiles, and painted pottery, and their sons would have been their retailers or overseas agents. An example of their involvement in the pottery business might be the 17 rhytons (conical ceremonial wine vessels) that were owned by the members of a Ugaritic symposium and were found abandoned near their clubhouse: one was imported from Crete, another from Cyprus; a large number were Mycenean, but some were Syrian, decorated or not, and locally made.[139] At any rate, the importance of Kitian involvement in the commercial affairs of the Ugaritic court is clear in the near parity between the queen's party for an Assyrian embassy and the king's reception for ministers from the island among his regular guests and business associates.

Phoenician texts indicate that beginning around 1200 B.C.E. some people in Kition, either Greeks or Cypriots or Canaanites, knew the Phoenician alphabet and writing conventions. Two of the texts are jar handles inscribed with "Kition" (*kt*, *Kitti*),[140] one from Tell el-ʿAjjul, once an Egyptian stronghold in the vicinity of Gaza; the other from ʿAkko. The name marked the origin of the containers and their contents, and the inscribed handles are witnesses to trade between Kition and their Sea People confreres who had settled among the Canaanites on the coast of Palestine. The third text is an eleventh-century arrowhead from the vicinity of Sidon, inscribed "Arrow of

---

138. S. Lackenbacher, "Nouveaux documents d'Ugarit," *RA* 76 (1982) 141–56.

139. M. Yon, "The Temple of the Rhytons at Ugarit," in *Ugarit, Religion and Culture: Essays Presented in Honour of Professor John C. L .Gibson* (ed. N. Wyatt, W. G. E. Watson, and J. B. Lloyd; Münster: Ugarit-Verlag, 1996) 405–22.

140. B. C. Colless, "The Proto-Alphabetic Inscriptions of Canaan," *AbrN* 29 (1991) 18–66, esp. p. 43 #13, p. 51 #21. The reading in both instances is certain, but the interpretation has been bobbled. Colless, for instance, refers to Akkadian *kutu*, Ugaritic *kt*, a pot for storing and serving liquids, but wonders why a potter would bother calling the pot a pot.

Kitay, cupbearer of ʿAbday" (*ḥṣ kty mšq ʿbdy*).[141] The particularly interesting point about this arrowhead is that a Phoenician from Kition, perhaps the child of a Sidonian settler and his Cypriot wife, identified himself by his place of origin, not by his Phoenician name and patronymic, and then found work with a Sidonian aristocrat, perhaps his father (at least four other sons of ʿAbday were archers in his employ) from the mainland.

Kition, on the evidence of its sanctuaries and locally produced Aegean-style pottery, was still an Achaean enclave in the twelfth and eleventh centuries. About the turn of the millennium, however, the temple complex and the port area were abandoned when the northern wall collapsed onto the quays below. The rest of the town was still inhabited, but mainly by Cypriots, while the Greeks and Phoenicians dispersed when business failed. In the latter part of the ninth century, the abandoned temple district was rebuilt,[142] and the port was reopened.

A small temple was built on the foundations of an earlier temple that abutted the northern city wall. Its design is unusual, but its paved floor, an offering table, an altar, and other remains indicate that it had a cultic function, and female figurines found on the floor of the Cypro-Archaic (600–450 B.C.E.) phase suggest that it was a Temple of Astarte.[143] South of this sanctuary, there were two rectangular structures with benches along one or more of their walls, which are also thought to be temples. Nearby, to the west, there was a larger building, also constructed on the ruins of a Late Bronze Age temple,[144] that is supposed to have been the first Phoenician temple at Kition. It is rectangular, with three small rooms on the west end and a large tripartite pillared hall on the east end, opening on broad courtyards to the northeast and east, and on workshops to the northwest inside the city wall. In front of the three small rooms, the remains of an ashlar and rubble-fill foundation have been reconstructed as a platform that would have been mounted by stairs on the north and south side. Similarly, in the courtyards, various pits filled with discarded ceramics and bones are

---

141. P. K. McCarter Jr., "Pieces of the Puzzle," *BAR* 22/2 (1996) 39–43, 62–63, esp. p. 40; R. Deutsch and M. Heltzer, *Windows to the Past* (Tel Aviv–Jaffa: Archaeological Center Publications, 1997) 22.

142. J. M. Webb, *Ritual Architecture, Iconography and Practice in the Late Cypriot Bronze Age* (Jonsered: Åströms, 1999) 64–84; T. Haettner Blomquist, *Gates and Gods: Cults in the City Gates of Iron Age Palestine. An Investigation of the Archaeological and Biblical Sources* (Stockholm: Almquist & Wiksell, 1999) 23–46; A. Mazar, "Temples of the Middle and Late Bronze Ages and the Iron Age," in *The Architecture of Ancient Israel from the Prehistoric to the Persian Periods: In Memory of Immanuel (Munya) Dunayevsky* (ed. A. Kempinski and R. Reich; Jerusalem: Israel Exploration Society, 1992) 161–87.

143. A. Caubet, "Les sanctuaires de Kition à l'époque de la dynastie phénicienne," in *Religio Phoenicia* (ed. C. Bonnet et al.; Studia Phoenicia 4; Namur: Société des Études Classiques, 1986) 153–68.

144. O. Negbi, "Levantine Elements in the Sacred Architecture of the Aegean at the Close of the Bronze Age," *ABSA* 83 (1988) 339–57; A. Mazar, "Comments on the Nature of the Relations between Cyprus and Palestine during the 12th–11th Centuries B.C.," in *Proceedings of an International Symposium: The Civilizations of the Aegean and Their Diffusion in Cyprus and the Eastern Mediterranean 2000–600 B.C.* (ed. V. Karageorghis, Nicosia: Pierides Foundation, 1990) 95–104, esp. p. 97; G. Gilmour, "Aegean Sanctuaries and the Levant in the Late Bronze Age," *ABSA* 88 (1993) 125–34.

understood to be *bothroi*, or receptacles for cultic waste.[145] Seventh- and
sixth-century finds of bucrania,[146] bronze male statuettes, and Bes figurines have led to the conclusion that it was a temple of a God (Melqart or
ʾEshmun naturally sprang to mind), but an early eighth-century inscription
mentioning Astarte written on a Red Slip bowl found on the floor suggested
that it was her temple.[147] The relation of this presumably religious complex
of buildings to the port or to a later temple complex about 200 meters to
the southeast and to other late shrines scattered here and there in the environs of Kition has not been investigated.

The tripartite pillared building has been identified as a temple largely on
the basis of its hypothetical reconstruction, by analogy and by conjecture.
There are temples of this sort, but the building itself was empty except for
a few religious objects and did not show any signs of liturgical activity, and
as it was rebuilt over the centuries lost every semblance of its purported religious character. The more serious difficulty with this identification, however, is that there are many tripartite pillared buildings on the Levantine
coast and in Israel that certainly are not temples but are either barracks or
stables, storehouses, or markets.[148] These all have the basic features of the
Kition building: a rectangular structure is divided into three sections, with
an open central area between pillared rooms; the floors are paved, sometimes with a different kind of pavement in the middle aisle; the building is
next to an open courtyard, close to the city gate or, as at Kition, to the port;
and the town is located on a trade route. Two of them, at Tell Abu Hawam
and Tell Qasile, are dated to the tenth century, but the others belong to the
ninth and eighth centuries.

The main difference is that at Kition the building is larger than most (except the buildings at Megiddo and Beth Shean) and that it has subdivisions
of the long rooms at one end, like storehouses at Arad and Samaria.[149] If
the Sidonians who came to Kition in the ninth century built a marketplace,

---

145. G. Nobis, "Tierreste aus dem phönizischen Kition," in *Periplus: Festschrift für Hans-
Gunter Buchholz zu seinem ächtzigsten Geburtstag am 24. Dezember 1999* (ed. P. Åström and D. Sürenhagen; Jonsered: Åströms, 2000) 121–34.

146. The use of ceremonial masks was common in Cyprus and is known in the Near East:
see. A. Caubet and J.-C. Courtois, "Masques chypriotes en terre cuite du XII s. av. J.-C.," *RDAC*
(1975) 43–49, pl. 6. Bull masks or bucrania, were typically Cypriot, and there are terra-cotta
figurines showing them being worn: V. Karageorghis, "Notes on Some Cypriote Priests Wearing Bull-Masks," *HTR* 64 (1971) 261–70; A. Hermary, "Divinités Chypriotes, II," *RDAC* (1986)
164–72, pls. 34–35, esp. pp. 164–66; S. O'Bryhim, "The *Cerastae* and Phoenician Human Sacrifice
on Cyprus," *RSF* 27 (1999) 3–20, pls. 1–3. But wearing masks gradually went out of fashion, and
masks became amulets that could be hung on a wall or pillar or around the neck: T. Monloup,
Salamine de Chypre, XII: Les figurines de terre cuite de tradition archaïque (Paris: Boccard, 1984)
99–100; M. Yon, "Instruments de culte en Mediterranée orientale," in *Acts of the International
Archaeological Symposium 'Cyprus between the Orient and the Occident'* (ed. V. Karageorghis; Nicosia:
Department of Antiquities, 1986) 265–88, esp. pp. 266–68.

147. V. Karageorghis, "Astarte at Kition," *Archäologische Studien in Kontaktzonen der antiken
Welt* (ed. R. Rolle and K. Schmidt; Göttingen: Vandenhoeck & Ruprecht, 1998) 105–8.

148. L. G. Herr, "Tripartite Pillared Buildings and the Market Place in Iron Age Palestine,"
BASOR 272 (1988) 47–67; J. D. Currid, "Rectangular Storehouse Construction during the Israelite
Iron Age," *ZDPV* 108 (1992) 99–121; M. Kochavi, "The Eleventh Century BCE Tripartite Pillared
Building at Tel Hadar," *MPT*, 468–78.

149. L. G. Herr, "Tripartite Pillared Buildings and the Market Place in Iron Age Palestine,"
BASOR 272 (1988) 47–67, esp. pp. 52–53.

they would have been restoring the town to its earlier stature as an emporium, and the other buildings and finds in the former temple complex
could be understood as related to it: the smaller temple would have been a
Cypriot sanctuary, the buildings with benches would have been the clubs,
or symposia (*marzeaḥ*), of the merchants and artisans who had settled in the
town, the religious objects would have been made or collected for sale in the
store,[150] and the more distant public buildings would have been added later
when Kition became the Assyrian administrative center of Cyprus.

It is just such a Phoenician, or specifically Sidonian, presence in Kition
that is indicated by the early ceramic remains. There is no Phoenician pottery from the tenth century. In the ninth century, there are still almost no
imported Phoenician wares, but there are a few Euboean and Attic luxury
items[151] that arrived with Greek merchants in Cyprus or with Phoenician
traders who had traveled to Greece.[152] In the late ninth and early eighth century, there continues to be surprisingly little mainland Phoenician pottery
at Kition and then only pottery of the types that would have been used in a
Phoenician household or, as in the case of miniature unguent jars, in trade.[153]

However, because at this time about one-fifth of the pottery in Cyprus
consists of local imitations of imported Phoenician ware, and because some
of this was made in Kition by Greek and Cypriot potters (Phoenician Red
Slip vases, for instance, inscribed in Cypriot syllabic with Cypriot or Greek
names) it is clear that the Sidonians who came to Kition were soon integrated into the local society.[154] Euboean and Attic wares continued to be
imported, and one rare Attic vase, made in Athens in the middle of the
eighth century, was found together with Phoenician Red Slip ware in the
tomb of a wealthy Sidonian.[155] The ceramic evidence, therefore, is more

---

150. The inscribed bowl, bucrania, statues, and figurines do not fit any pattern of worship
and are too diverse to belong to the cult of a particular God. The bull masks, in particular, are
typically Cypriot, of Aegean and not of Phoenician inspiration, and even if the bucrania mean
that the building was a temple, they also suggest that it was not a Phoenician temple.

151. J. N. Coldstream, "The Greek Geometric and Plain Archaic Imports," in *Excavations
at Kition, IV: The Non-Cypriote Pottery* (ed. V. Karageorghis; Nicosia: Department of Antiquities,
1981) 17–22.

152. Idem, "Early Greek Visitors to Cyprus and the Eastern Mediterranean," in *Cyprus and the
East Mediterranean in the Iron Age* (ed. V. Tatton-Brown; London: British Museum, 1989) 90–96;
L. Wreidt Sørenson and J. Lund, "Cypriot Finds in Greece and Greek Finds in Cyprus ca. 950–500
BC," *ESC*, 294–96.

153. P. Bikai, "The Phoenician Imports," in *Excavations at Kition, IV: The Non-Cypriote Pottery*
(ed. V. Karageorghis; Nicosia: Department of Antiquities, 1981) 23–36; J. N. Coldstream, "Early
Iron Age (Cypro-Geometric): The Rise of the Ancient Kingdoms, c. 1100–700 BC," in *Footprints in
Cyprus: An Illustrated History* (ed. D. Hunt; London: Trigraph, 1990) 47–83, esp. p. 55.

154. E. Gjerstad, *The Swedish Cyprus Expedition, vol. IV, Part 2: The Cypro-Geometric, Cypro-
Archaic and Cypro-Classical Periods* (Stockholm: Swedish Cyprus Expedition, 1948) 287; J. N.
Coldstream, "Archaeology in Cyprus 1960–1985: The Geometric and Archaic Periods," in *Archaeology in Cyprus 1960–1985* (ed. V. Karageorghis; Nicosia: Leventis Foundation, 1985) 47–59, esp.
p. 52; O. Masson, "A propos de la découverte d'une inscription chypriote syllabique à Kition en
1970," *RDAC* (1971) 49–52, pl. 21; A. Swinton, V. Izzet, and S. Aguilar Gutiérrez, "Phoenicians in
the Mediterranean: Degrees and Modes of Interaction," *Actas* 4, 4.1903–7.

155. J. N. Coldstream, "A Figured Attic Geometric Kantharos from Kition," *RDAC* (1994)
155–59, pl. 29; idem, "Pithekoussai, Cyprus and the Cesnola Painter," in *APOIKIA. I più antichi
insediamenti greci in Occidente: Funzioni e modi dell'organizzazione politica e sociale. Scritti in onore di
Giorgio Buchner* (ed. B. d'Agostino and D. Ridgway; Annali di Archeologia e Storia Antica n.s. 1;
Naples: Istituto Orientale, 1994) 77–86, esp. pp. 82–83.

consistent with a limited Sidonian commercial venture in Kition, centered around a market and some meeting places, than it is with a colony focused on a temple as large as the tripartite pillared building. These Sidonians, from the mainland city or from Sidonian settlements in northern Syria and Cilicia,[156] who came to Kition and eastern Cyprus in the tenth and ninth centuries were intent on doing business with the Greeks and left little trace of their own culture. In the ninth and eighth centuries, they were still not very numerous but now had settled right into the indigenous population and were influenced as much by this culture as they once had affected it.

Kition's longstanding Canaanite and Phoenician connections clearly distinguish it from most other places in southeastern Cyprus. Idalion, for instance, 20 kilometers northwest of Kition and an adjunct of the kingdom beginning in the fifth century, was settled toward the end of the thirteenth century, about the time of Greek immigration to Kition and, like Kition, was a fortified stronghold and cult center.[157] Unlike Kition, its inhabitants were not Achaeans but Cypriots, using coarse local wares and some finer ceramics that imitated Mycenean types.[158] The inhabitants were few and, to judge from their domestic articles (gold and silver jewelry and ivory ornaments), civilized and prosperous.[159] The town's chief industry, the probable reason it was built, and the undoubted source of its prosperity were the mining and production of iron and tempered steel.[160] Idalion was abandoned at the end of the millennium for no apparent reason but around the time that some natural catastrophe destroyed the harbor at Kition and forced the abandonment of that city. It may be, to judge from their distinctive but parallel histories, that the outlet for Idalion steel was Kition and that the loss of this marketplace put an end to Idalion's importance until it was rebuilt on a grander scale and flourished again in the seventh century.[161]

Tamassos, about 15 kilometers west of Idalion and part of the Kingdom of Kition in the fourth century, was founded about the time that Kition was abandoned, perhaps by refugees from this town. It was steadfastly Cypriot and Greek, and one of the Cypriot kingdoms mentioned by Esarhaddon in the seventh century, but it seems to have had Phoenician residents at least

156. A Red Slip jug found in a tomb at Kition and dated to the early eighth century is inscribed *Pntš*, "Belonging to Annittis," a feminine Luwian personal name: C. Bonnet, "Les étrangers dans le corpus épigraphique phénicien de Chypre," *RDAC* (1990) 141–53, esp. pp. 141–42; P. K. McCarter Jr., *The Antiquity of the Greek Alphabet and the Early Phoenician Scripts* (HSM 9; Missoula: Scholars Press, 1975) 45 and n. 41; E. Lipiński, "Notes d'épigraphie phénicienne et punique," *OLP* 14 (1983) 129–65, esp. pp. 139–41.

157. E. Gjerstad et al., *The Swedish Cyprus Expedition: Finds and Results of the Excavations in Cyprus 1927–1931. Volume II* (Stockholm: Swedish Cyprus Expedition, 1935) 460–641.

158. P. Alin, "Idalion Pottery from the Excavations of the Swedish Cyprus Expedition," *Opuscula Atheniensia* 12 (1978) 91–109.

159. L. E. Stager and A. M. Walker, *American Expedition to Idalion, Cyprus, 1973–1980* (Oriental Institute Communicatons 24; Chicago: Oriental Institute, 1989). Gjerstad et al., *The Swedish Cyprus Expedition*, 599–603.

160. P. Åström et al., "Iron Artifacts from Swedish Excavations in Cyprus," *Opuscula Atheniensia* 16 (1986) 27–41, esp. pp. 30–32; S. P. Morris, *Daidalos and the Origins of Greek Art* (Princeton: Princeton University Press, 1992) 117–36; M. Hadjicosti, "The Kingdom of Idalion in the Light of New Evidence," *BASOR* 308 (1997) 49–63.

161. P. Gaber and W. G. Dever, "Idalion, Cyprus: Conquest and Continuity," in *Preliminary Excavation Reports: Sardis, Idalion, and Tell el-Handaquq North* (ed. W. G. Dever; AASOR; New Haven, CT: American Schools of Oriental Research, 1996) 85–113.

Fig. 2.6. Kition inscribed bowl (hair offering; Kition 1435). Reproduced courtesy of the Director of the Department of Antiquities, Republic of Cyprus.

by the early eighth century and possibly from the time of its foundation. The only evidence for this is a Phoenician inscription on a Red Slip bowl found in the tripartite pillared building in Kition that can be dated, by its ceramic and paleographic typology, to the first part of the eighth century. It is almost complete and nearly unique (see fig. 2.6):[162]

1   *ml šᶜr yglb wypg[ᶜm lᶜš]trt wᶜnt*
2   *wytdr[m w]ytm lšwm*
3   *ᶜrz ʾyt bkm lšᶜ dd*
4   *ml šᶜr 100 + 20 + 9 bnd[r] tmš*
5   [   ]mṣʾ [m]šʾ hdr
6   *tm[š   ]m*

1. Tufts of hair he cut, and he offered them in supplication to Astarte and she answered him. 2. And he acquitted himself of his vow and completed their presentation: 3. "Arouse the weepers to take pleasure in the beloved." 4. Tufts of hair 129 according to the vow of Tamassos. 5. [   ] the rising of the sun, [the bearing of the] splendor. 6. Tamassos [   ]

The ritual offering of hair is known from various parts of the Near East, and its specific association with the worship of Astarte is confirmed by two late sixth-century inscriptions from Cyprus—one from Kouklia (Palaepaphos), the other from Kition.[163] What is especially interesting about this inscrip-

162. D. Dupont-Sommer, "Une inscription phénicienne archaïque récemment trouvée à Kition (Chypre)," *Mémoires de Académie des Inscriptions et Belles Lettres* 44 (1972) 275–94; *Kition 3*, #D21, pp. 149–60, pl. 17; S. Moscati, ed., *The Phoenicians* (New York: Abbeville, 1988) 99.

163. *Kition 3*, #C 1:12, pp. 103–8 = *CIS* 86 A:12, refers to "barbers who served in the liturgy" of Astarte. There is also a contemporary inscription from Kouklia recording the offering of "locks of hair" (*mḥlpt*) to Astarte of Paphos (*ᶜštrt pp*): *RPC* 81–86.

tion, therefore, is its linguistic, liturgical, and demographic evidence. Early in the eighth century, a Phoenician from Tamassos who was named after the town made a pilgrimage to Kition to pray to Astarte, the Goddess of Sidon, the Aphrodite of Paphos. It also reveals edges of the mystery permeating the liturgy: Tamassos made a vow and, because his prayer was answered, cut and offered his hair; the occasion of his vow was a critical situation, to which participants in the liturgy responded with weeping and lamentation; the resolution of the lament liturgy was the summons by Tamassos to take pleasure in the Beloved, a liturgical title of Adonis. In the light of its completion, it is evident that the lament revolved around the death of the God and that the vow anticipated his resurrection; the resurrection happened under the auspices of Astarte at the "rising of the sun" on the third day, as the narrative has it.

Linguistically, the votive text is special because of its verbal forms, notably the precative (*lš*) and the infixed-T (*wytdrm*) imperfects, which like the cult of Adonis, were unique to Byblos. It is also interesting because of its bipartite structure, which first immortalizes the stature of Tamassos before the Gods and then, like Absalom, among his peers (2 Sam 14:26). Tamassos was a copper-mining center, and it is likely that this pilgrim, a towering individual from the Byblian community there, was also in town on business. It is fitting that the bowl that brought him honor was kept as a trophy in the emporium that made his hometown prosperous.

When Kition was founded, nearby Alashiya on the Bay of Salamis was a flourishing city kingdom with strong ties to Egypt, Ḫatti, and Syria. Alashiya, often erroneously identified with the island in general rather than with a particular town in Cyprus,[164] was the ancient name of the place now called Enkomi. People from Alashiya are mentioned in the fifteenth-century Alalakh tablets. Correspondence between its king and the king of Egypt appears in the fourteenth-century Amarna letters,[165] and between the king of Byblos and the Pharaoh concerning an Egyptian envoy who had to return home via Alashiya because ships of Tyre, Sidon, and Beirut prevented him from sailing southward along the coast.[166] Alashiya imported goods directly from Egypt, but there is also a letter in the archives at Ugarit from the king of Egypt to the harbormaster in Ugarit about the purchase of ships that were being built in Alashiya.[167]

In the late thirteenth century, the king of Alashiya sent the king of Ugarit reconnaissance reports on ships of the Sea Peoples and advice on how to defend himself against their attacks, and the king of Ugarit in

164. R. S. Merrillees, *Alashia Revisited* (Cahiers de la Revue Biblique 22; Paris: Gabalda, 1987); N. Naʾaman, "The Network of Canaanite Late Bronze Kingdoms and the City of Ashdod," *UF* 29 (1997) 599–625, esp. p. 611. It is distinguished from Cyprus in Linear B texts: L. Himmelhoch, "The Use of the Ethnics *a-ra-si-jo* and *ku-pi-ri-jo* in Linear B Texts," *Minos* 25–26 (1990–91) 91–104.

165. *EA* ##33–40, pp. 104–13.

166. *EA* #114, pp. 188–90; S. Wachsmann, "Is Cyprus Ancient Alashiya? New Evidence from an Egyptian Tablet," *BA* 49 (1986) 37–40.

167. E. J. Peltenburg, "Ramesside Egypt and Cyprus," in *Acts of the International Archaeological Symposium "Cyprus between the Orient and the Occident"* (ed. V. Karageorghis; Nicosia: Department of Antiquities, 1986) 149–79; *CAT* 2:42 + 2:43; E. Lipiński, "An Ugaritic Letter to Amenophis III concerning Trade with Alashiya," *Iraq* 39 (1977) 213–17.

return addressed him deferentially as "my Father."[168] There were Ugaritic merchants at Alashiya, and Alashiyan merchants at Ugarit, one with a Hurrian name who is mentioned in a ration list, another with a Canaanite name who received a consignment of oil destined for Egypt, and another who was an agent with a major Ugaritic house involved in the horse trade between the Hittites and Egypt.[169] There is correspondence between the two cities concerning trade disputes, and scribes in Ugarit created a local version of the Cypro-Minoan syllabary in use at Alashiya.[170] There was a Cypriot quarter in Ugarit that included women from Alashiya, each accompanied by boys or girls who had come to work in the ceramic or textile industry for independent businessmen in the city.[171] Alashiya was visible from Ugarit on a clear day, and its business was principally with the Syrian mainland, while Kition, which also dealt with Ugarit, did business primarily with the west.

In both Kition and Alashiya, Mycenean and Greek influence was predominant. Unlike Kition, however, which remained fundamentally Cypriot and politically unpretentious, Alashiya was culturally Mycenean and Hurrian[172] and entwined in international politics. It was subject to Egypt early in the thirteenth century but was taken over by the Hittites in an attempt to control the Achaean (Aḫḫiyawa) raids.[173] The new administrative buildings were constructed partly of ashlar masonry, and the city was rebuilt (following a town plan like the plan at Hittite Emar on the Euphrates) in symmetrical city blocks formed by streets meeting at right angles.[174] It was captured by the Sea Peoples in the early twelfth century and was used by them for several decades as a staging area on their way to southern Canaan (there are sanctuaries with statues of Aegean Gods and with transport jars like the jars found in Philistia, but there are no storage facilities)[175] before it

---

168. J. Nougayrol et al., *Ugaritica V* (MRS 16; Paris: Imprimerie Nationale, 1968) 79–89; L. E. Stager, "The Impact of the Sea Peoples in Canaan (1185–1050 BCE)," in *The Archaeology of Society in the Holy Land* (ed. T. E. Levy; Leicester: Leicester University Press, 1995) 332–48.

169. E. Masson, "Les premiers noms sémitiques à Chypre," *Sem* 39 (1990) 41–42; *CAT* 4:149, *CAT* 4:352; D. Arnaud, "Une correspondance d'affaires entre Ougaritiens et Emariotes," in RSO 7 65–78, esp. pp. 75–76.

170. Nougayrol et al., *Ugaritica V*, 80–85; E. Masson, "La tablette chypro-minoënne 20.25 de Ras Shamra: Essai d'interprétation," *CRAIBL* (1973) 32–60.

171. *CAT* 4:102.

172. B. Kling, *Mycenaean IIIC1:b and Related Pottery in Cyprus* (Studies in Mediterranean Archaeology 87; Gothenburg: Åströms, 1989); C. Baurain, "L'écriture syllabique à Chypre," in *Phoinikeia Grammata: Lire et écrire en Mediterranée* (ed. C. Baurain, C. Bonnet, and V. Krings; Namur: Société des Études Classiques, 1991) 389–424, esp. pp. 397–406.

173. P. Dikaios, *Enkomi—Excavations 1948–1958, Volume II: Chronology, Summary and Conclusions, Catalogue, Appendices* (Mainz am Rhein: von Zabern, 1971) 509–14; A. B. Knapp, "KBO I 26: Alashiya and Hatti," *JCS* 32 (1980) 43–47.

174. G. R. H. Wright, *Ancient Building in Cyprus. Part One: Text* (Leiden: Brill, 1992) 93; O. Negbi, "The Climax of Urban Development in Bronze Age Cyprus," *RDAC* (1986) 97–121, pls. 24–25, esp. pp. 101–5; J.-C. Margueron, "Emar: A Syrian City between Anatolia, Assyria and Babylonia," in *Cultural Interaction in the Ancient Near East* (AbrN Supplement 5; Louvain: Peeters, 1996) 77–91.

175. Dikaios, *Enkomi—Excavations 1948–1958, Volume II*, 523–31; J. Gunneweg, I. Perlman, and F. Asaro, "A Canaanite Jar from Enkomi," *IEJ* 37 (1987) 168–72; A. Mazar, "A Note on Canaanite Jars from Enkomi," *IEJ* 38 (1988) 224–26; A. Killebrew, "Ceramic Typology and Technology of Late Bronze II and Iron I Assemblages from Tel Miqne–Ekron: The Transition from Canaanite to

was burned and abandoned. Alashiya disappeared with the Hittite Empire to which it belonged, and its place in world affairs was taken by Salamis.[176] But the site was still occupied by a remnant of the original indigenous population, who returned to the traditional worship of a Goddess[177] and to government by a princess and who, as the story of Wen Amon indicates, had no use for Egypt and no interest in international affairs.

Salamis was essentially a Greek city, in contact with the Near Eastern and Phoenician worlds and sometimes greedy for their products but only randomly interested in their life-styles and culture. The evidence for the foundation of the city is tombs—one at Salamis itself; others, about 40 kilometers away on the northernmost coast of the Bay of Salamis. The pottery, precious metals, and manufactured goods from the Salamis tomb, which can be dated to the mid-eleventh century, reveal a rich and varied culture of Mycenean origin but with developed Cypriot characteristics and with skills and techniques that had been borrowed from Phoenician potters and smiths.[178] The 19 tombs at Alaas on the Bay of Salamis are slightly earlier and show the same eclectic tastes but, unlike the tomb at Salamis, also include a few pieces of imported pottery.[179]

The next two centuries are blank, but the situation at Salamis in the eighth and seventh centuries, to judge from the Royal Tombs, has not really changed. An early eighth-century tomb containing a complete Attic dinner set as well as Aegean table ware and a large number of imported Phoenician dishes is unique at Salamis in its witness to trade between the Phoenician mainland, Salamis, and Greece, and its contents may be products sold by a Sidonian merchant living in Kition who traveled back and forth to these places.[180] Of the other Royal Tombs, all of which are later, one dated to the very end of the eighth century is extremely rich in Phoenician, but now specifically Tyrian, imports, including some exquisite ivory furniture.[181] Salamis, historically, lives up to its legendary founding

Philistine Culture," *MPT*, 379–405, esp. pp. 401–2; P. S. Keswani, "Models of Local Exchange in Late Bronze Age Cyprus," *BASOR* 292 (1993) 73–83, esp. p. 78.

176. M. Yon, *Salamine de Chypre, II: La tombe T. I du XIe s. av. J.-C.* (Paris: Boccard, 1971) 95–96.

177. M. Hadjicosti, "More Evidence for a Geometric and Archaic Rural Shrine of a Female Divinity at Enkomi," *RDAC* (1989) 111–20, pls. 22–23.

178. V. Karageorghis, *Salamis in Cyprus: Homeric, Hellenistic and Roman* (London: Thames & Hudson, 1969) 20–22; Yon, *Salamine de Chypre, II*.

179. Idem, *Alaas: A Protogeometric Necropolis in Cyprus* (Nicosia: Department of Antiquities, 1975). Three tombs (nos. 15, 17, and 19) each contained one small flask of Near Eastern inspiration or manufacture (p. 12, #13; p. 18, #14; p. 21, #7; p. 67).

180. J. N. Coldstream, "Early Greek Visitors to Cyprus and the Eastern Mediterranean," in *Cyprus and the East Mediterranean in the Iron Age* (ed. V. Tatton-Brown; London: British Museum, 1989) 90–96, esp. p. 93. There is only one eighth-century Phoenician inscription from Salamis (M. Sznycer, "Salamine de Chypre et les Phéniciens," *Salamine de Chypre. Histoire et Archéologie: État des recherches* [Paris: CNRS, 1980] 123–29, esp. p. 127). It is contemporary with the rich tomb, is written in cursive script on a Bichrome II sherd, and contains four letters: "ninety" (*tš'm*), or "nine" (*tš'*) plus the abbreviation (*m* = "myrrh," "marrow," "ointment" . . .) of the vessel's contents.

181. V. Karageorghis, *Salamis 5: Excavations in the Necropolis of Salamis, III* (Nicosia: Department of Antiquities, 1973) 4–122 (Tomb 79); A. Welkamp and C. H. J. de Geus, "Fit for a King? An Ivory Throne Found at Salamis, Cyprus," *Jaarbericht "Ex Oriente Lux"* 34 (1995–96) 87–99.

by Greeks returning from the Trojan War.[182] It remained resolutely Greek and, except for individuals buried in one of the Royal Tombs who took their Phoenician luxuries with them, was relatively untouched by the Tyrian or Sidonian presence on the island.

Associated with Enkomi in the copper business were two places in the interior of Cyprus: Sinda, about 15 kilometers to the west; and Athienou, 20 kilometers to the southwest of Sinda and 18 kilometers north of Kition. Sinda, like Enkomi, flourished in the thirteenth century, was destroyed toward the end of the century, rebuilt, and destroyed again in the time of the Sea Peoples' raids and subsequently occupied by squatters.[183] It was probably just a way station on the route from the copper mines of the Troodos Mountains to Alashiya, which found its prosperity in the trade that made this port famous. Athienou, ancient Golgoi, was founded in the sixteenth century but in the thirteenth and early twelfth centuries was a marketplace on the route from the copper mines to Alashiya.[184] It differed from Sinda in being a town with a much-frequented sanctuary, in having its own copper-smelting installations, and in surviving into the Iron Age when, as witnessed by an enigmatic Cypriot inscription with an exact parallel on an ostracon from Salamis, it still maintained its contacts with the east coast.[185] Both places were aligned with Enkomi, neither was Canaanite or Phoenician, and it is not until the early sixth century that there is any evidence at all (a Phoenician personal name [*šbʿl*] written on a transport jar) for contact between Golgoi and Kition.

Hala Sultan Tekke, 5 kilometers southwest of Kition, was neither an emporium like Kition nor an industrial center like Enkomi but, rather, was dedicated to the arts and crafts.[186] It was founded in the seventeenth century on a shallow lagoon opening into the Mediterranean and was abandoned in the mid-twelfth century as sea levels rose, and this channel was closed with silt.[187]

---

182. M. Yon, "Mission archéologique française de Salamine: La ville—Bilan 1964–1984," in *Archaeology in Cyprus, 1960–1985* (ed. V. Karageorghis; Nicosia: Leventis Foundation, 1985) 202–18; P. M. Bikai, "Cyprus and Phoenicia: Literary Evidence for the Early Iron Age," in *Studies in Honor of Vassos Karageorghis* (ed. G. C. Ionnides; Nicosia: Leventis Foundation, 1992) 241–48.

183. V. Karageorghis, "A Late Cypriote Hoard of Bronzes from Sinda," *RDAC* (1973) 72–82; idem, *The End of the Late Bronze Age in Cyprus* (Nicosia: Pierides Foundation, 1990) 12–13; V. Karageorghis and M. Demas, *Pyla-Kokkinokremos: A Late 13th Century B.C. Fortified Settlement in Cyprus* (Nicosia: Department of Antiquities, 1984) 30, 71; B. Kling, *Mycenaean IIIC1:b and Related Pottery in Cyprus* (Gothenburg: Åströms, 1989) 34–35.

184. T. Dothan and A. Ben-Tor, *Excavations at Athienou, Cyprus, 1971–1972* (Qedem 16; Jerusalem: Hebrew University Institute of Archaeology, 1983).

185. R. Maddin, J. D. Muhly, and T. S. Wheeler, "Metalworking," in *Excavations at Athienou, Cyprus, 1971–1972* (ed. T. Dothan and A. Ben-Tor; Qedem 16; Jerusalem: Hebrew University Institute of Archaeology, 1983) 132–38; O. Masson, "Une inscription étrange de Golgoi," *BCH* 92 (1968) 380–86.

186. P. Åström, "Hala Sultan Tekke: An International Harbour Town of the Late Cypriot Bronze Age," *Opuscula Atheniensia* 16 (1986) 7–17.

187. J. A. Gifford, "Paleogeography of Ancient Harbour Sites of the Larnaca Lowlands, Southeastern Cyprus," in *Harbour Archaeology: Proceedings of the First International Workshop on Ancient Mediterranean Harbours, Caesarea Maritima 24–28.6.83* (ed. A. Rabban; BAR International Series; Oxford: Oxbow, 1985) 45–48.

Although it had its share of Mycenean influence, most of the pottery is local and the settlement's only consistent foreign contacts were with Egypt where it obtained gold, glass, and faience.[188] Its products include a faience pendant with parallels in Ugarit and Gezer; a seal in Hittite style inscribed with local Cypro-Minoan letters, and another with the typically Cypriot depiction of a hero in combat with a griffin; a silver bowl with the name of its intended owner inscribed in the Ugaritic cuneiform alphabet but written in a rounded Cypro-Minoan hand, and a shallow, hemispherical bronze bowl with the name of its owner or artist in Cypro-Minoan syllabic signs; a mold with Cypro-Minoan signs depicting a quasi-Aegean athletic contest that was probably used to make panels for bronze four-sided stands.[189] The artisans at Hala Sultan Tekke worked in copper and bronze, silver and gold, ivory, and iron, and there is evidence for the production of dyes.[190] The people of the place lived modestly, raised their own cattle and crops, and also imported fish from Egypt.[191] The small amount of pottery from Crete, Greece, and Anatolia may suggest who visited them or where they traveled with their products and crafts. Hala Sultan Tekke was close to Kition but apparently never in competition with it, and some of its people may have moved there when the town declined.

188. V. Karageorghis, "Two Late Bronze Age Tombs from Hala Sultan Tekke," in *Hala Sultan Tekke I* (ed. P. Åström, D. M. Bailey, and V. Karageorghis; Studies in Mediterranean Archaeology 45/1; Gothenburg: Åströms, 1976) 70–89; N. Witzel, "Finds from the Area of Dromolaxia," *RDAC* (1979) 181–97, pls. 21–23.

S. L. Admiraal, "Late Bronze Age Tombs from Dromolaxia," *RDAC* (1982) 39–59, pls. 3–8; P. Åström, "Trade in the Late Cypriot Bronze Age," *ESC*, 202–8; idem, "Canaanite Jars from Hala Sultan Tekke," in *Bronze Age Trade in the Mediterranean* (ed. N. H. Gale; Studies in Mediterranean Archaeology 90; Jonsered: Åströms, 1991) 145–51.

K. O. Eriksson, "Egyptian Amphorae from Late Cypriot Contexts in Cyprus," in *Trade, Contact, and the Movement of Peoples in the Eastern Mediterranean: Studies in Honour of J. Basil Hennessy* (ed. S. Bourke and J.-P. Descoeudres; Sydney: Meditarch, 1995) 199–205.

E. Peltenburg, "The Faience Vases from Tombs 1 and 2 at Hala Sultan Tekke, 'Vizaja,'" in *Hala Sultan Tekke I* (ed. P. Åström, D. M. Bailey, and V. Karageorghis; Studies in Mediterranean Archaeology 45/1; Gothenburg: Åströms, 1976) appendix 6, pp. 104–9, pls. 54–56.

E. Peltenburg, "A Faience from Hala Sultan Tekke and Second Millennium B.C. Western Asiatic Pendants Depicting Females," in *Hala Sultan Tekke 3* (ed. P. Åström, G. Hult, and M. Strandberg Olofsson; Studies in Mediterranean Archaeology 45/3; Gothenburg: Åströms, 177) 177–200.

P. Åström and E. Masson, "Un cachet de Hala Sultan Tekke," *RDAC* (1981) 99–100.

C. D'Albiac, "The Griffin Combat Theme," in *Ivory in Greece and the Eastern Mediterranean from the Bronze Age to the Hellenistic Period* (ed. J. L. Fitton; London: British Museum, 1992) 105–12.

P. Åström and E. Masson, "A Silver Bowl with Canaanite Inscription from Hala Sultan Tekke," *RDAC* (1984) 72–76, pl. 11; M. Dietrich and O. Loretz, *Die Keilalphabete: Die phönizisch-kanaanäischen und altarabischen Alphabete in Ugarit* (Munster: Ugarit-Verlag, 1988) 206–14.

A. Kanta and M. Perna, "An Inscribed Bronze Bowl from Cyprus in the Zintilis Collection," *Kadmos* 38 (1999) 97–102.

V. Karageorghis, "A Late Bronze Age Mould from Hala Sultan Tekke," *BCH* 113 (1989) 439–45.

190. P. Åström, "A Coppersmith's Workshop at Hala Sultan Tekke," in *Periplus: Festschrift für Hans-Gunter Buchholz* (ed. P. Åström and D. Sürenhagen; Jonsered: Åströms, 2000) 33–35, pls. 2–4; idem, "Ivories from Hala Sultan Tekke, in *Ivory in Greece and the Eastern Mediterranean from the Bronze Age to the Hellenistic Period* (ed. J. L. Fitton; London: British Museum, 1992) 101–4. idem, "Hala Sultan Tekke: An International Harbour Town of the Late Cypriot Bronze Age," *Opuscula Atheniensia* 16 (1986) 7–17.

191. Idem, "Trade in the Late Cypriot Bronze Age," *ESC*, 202–8.

Just 10 kilometers northeast of Kition was Pyla-Kokkinokremos,[192] a small, short-lived settlement on a naturally defensible plateau less than a kilometer from the Bay of Larnaka. It was occupied by families belonging to an earlier wave of the Sea Peoples (the people of Aegean, Anatolian, and North Syrian origin), who arrived late in the thirteenth century and left before the end of the century. They brought with them Mycenean, late Minoan, and Anatolian wares, but they also used local pottery. They had weapons and armor but, unlike the later wave, they were not hostile, and their settlement, although it was fortified, was distinguished by the tokens of domesticity, craftsmanship, and commerce: loom weights, kitchen utensils; stone, bronze, and lead weights; a hoard of gold jewelry and raw metal, silver ingots, bits of copper ingots, bronze objects, and scrap metal—the basic homespun inventory of smiths and jewelers. It was people like these who contributed to the twelfth-century expansion of Kition, and they may have abandoned their settlement, not because it was slightly inhospitable, and not in order to move on to Philistia, but to share in the prosperity of this flourishing port.

Farther to the southwest of Kition was the site of Maroni, inhabited since the sixteenth century but known mainly from its later tombs and from an early thirteenth-century ashlar building.[193] This building featured an olive press and a metallurgical factory both of which operated together since olive oil was useful in maintaining the roasting fire needed in the smelting of copper.[194] There is the usual imported pottery at the site, but local wares and local imitations predominate. Maroni lacked a harbor and may have relied on the port at Klavassos a few kilometers to the west which, besides facilitating its commercial dealings with Enkomi would explain why Enkomi during the Amarna period imported clay for its scriptoria from this area.[195] The copper-smelting industry made Maroni a natural supplier

---

192. V. Karageorghis, "Excavations at Pyla-Kokkinokremos, 1981: First Preliminary Report," *RDAC* (1981) 135–41, pl. 45; idem, "A Late Mycenaean IIIB Chariot Crater from Cyprus," *RDAC* (1982) 77–82; idem and M. Demas, *"Pyla-Kokkinokremos: A Late 13th Century B.C. Fortified Settlement in Cyprus* (Nicosia: Department of Antiquities, 1984).

193. J. Johnson, *Maroni de Chypre* (Studies in Mediterranean Archaeology 59; Gothenburg: Åströms, 1980); G. Cadogan, 'Maroni in Cyprus, between West and East," in *Acts of the International Archaeological Symposium 'Cyprus between the Orient and the Occident* (ed. V. Karageorghis; Nicosia: Department of Antiquities, 1986) 104–13; S. W. Manning et al., *"Tsaroukkas*, Mycenaeans and Trade Project: Preliminary Report of the 1993 Season," *RDAC* (1994) 83–106, pls. 11–12; S. W. Manning and S. J. Monks, "Late Cypriot Tombs at Maroni *Tsaroukkas*, Cyprus," *ABSA* 93 (1998) 297–351, pls. 58–67.

G. Cadogan, "Maroni IV," *RDAC* (1988) part 1, 229–31; idem, "Maroni and the Monuments," *ESC*, 43–51; idem, "The Thirteenth-Century Changes in Cyprus in Their East Mediterranean Context," *MPT*, 6–16; V. Karageorghis, *The End of the Late Bronze Age in Cyprus* (Nicosia: Pierides Foundation, 1990) 5–6.

194. S. Hadjisavvas, "Olive Oil Production and Divine Protection," in *Acta Cypria 3* (ed. P. Åström; Jonsered: Åströms, 1992) 233–49; R. Maddin, J. D. Muhly, and T. S. Wheeler, "Metalworking," in *Excavations at Athienou, Cyprus, 1971–1972* (ed. T. Dothan and A. Ben-Tor; Qedem 16; Jerusalem: Hebrew University Institute of Archaeology, 1983) 132–38, esp. p. 137.

195. Y. Goren et al., "The Location of Alashiya: New Evidence from Petrographic Investigation of Alashiyan Tablets from El-Amarna and Ugarit," *AJA* 107 (2003) 233–56; P. Schuster Keswani and A. B. Knapp, "Bronze Age Boundaries and Social Exchange in North-West Cyprus," *OJA* 22 (2003) 213–23.

to Kition and Enkomi.[196] Its role as supplier, verified by the discovery in southern Sardinia of one of its transport jars,[197] helps to explain why, when the foreign markets closed down at the beginning of the twelfth century, this old settlement was abandoned.

Conclusion

Kition was the only place in southeastern Cyprus that had significant and long-standing Canaanite and Phoenician connections. It languished for centuries before it received a new start in the ninth when, as the Arameans and Assyrians threatened to take over North Syria, it became an emporium and bazaar supplying ships traveling to Cilicia, Crete, and Greece. It was not a colony. It was an emporium, an amphictyonic center for the Cypriot kingdoms, an important town when the Assyrians made it their headquarters in Cyprus. It was not a kingdom until the sixth century, when it became an instrument in the Persian Empire's struggle with Greece. It was, as later events confirmed, a Sidonian settlement in a native environment that exploited the mineral wealth of the island and the technical skills of its Greek and Cypriot population.

The Sidonians seem to have been individuals, families, or corporations rather than state-sponsored émigrés, and the bits and pieces of epigraphic material or archaeological debris that dot Kition and its environs over the next two centuries are evidence for the discreet and assimilatory presence of these shrewd and educated foreigners engaged in trade, commerce, and crafts. Among the scattered items to be counted are: early eighth-century tombs in Nicosia and at Kato Dheftera halfway between Nicosia and Tamassos; a tomb inscription from Chytroi (Kythrea), just northeast of Nicosia; two Phoenician letters on a limestone block from Khirokitia, just north of Maroni; a few names on storage jars from Kition; bronze and silver bowls, bronze horse blinkers, and inscribed vases from Idalion.[198]

---

196. S. Sherratt, "'Sea Peoples' and the Economic Structure of the Late Second Millennium in the Eastern Mediterranean," *MPT*, 292–313, esp. p. 297.

197. L. Vagnetti and F. Lo Schiavo, "Late Bronze Age Long Distance Trade in the Mediterranean: The Role of Cyprus," *ESC*, 217–43, esp. p. 221.

198. P. Flourentzos, "Four Early Iron Age Tombs from Nicosia, Old Municipality," *RDAC* (1991) 115–21. Later tombs in Nicosia contain mostly local wares, with little evidence of Phoenician influence: M. Hadjicosti, "The Late Archaic and Classical Cemetery of Agioi Omologites, Nicosia, in the Light of New Evidence," *RDAC* (1993) 173–93.

D. Christou, "Supplementary Report on the Iron Age Necropolis at Kato Dheftera," *RDAC* (1984) 174–206.

RPC, 104–7. The Chytroi tomb inscription, dated ca. 700–650 B.C.E., is fragmentary, but its formulas and its use of word dividers are like those of Sidonian inscriptions.

RPC, 102–4.

Kition 3, #D 3 and #D 12. The first is also discussed by J. Teixidor, "The Phoenician Inscriptions of the Cesnola Collection," *MMJ* 11 (1976) 55–70, esp. p. 66 #23.

G. Markoe, *Phoenician Bronze and Silver Bowls from Cyprus and the Mediterranean* (Berkeley: University of California Press, 1985) 169–72; E. Lipiński, "Le Baʿanaʾ d'Idalion," *Syria* 63 (1986) 379–82. A. M. Bisi, "Una nuova figurina inedita dell'Astarte siriana rinvenuta a Cipro," *AION* 31 (1971) 105–10, pl. 1; M. Hadjicosti, "The Kingdom of Idalion in the Light of New Evidence," *BASOR* 308 (1997) 49–63.

Kition was just an easy stage from Sidon but a giant step in Sidonian progress to the West.[199] What made Sidonians tick was cooperation with the Greeks. It was why they were in Cyprus and why they went with them from there to explore the Mediterranean. In Cilicia they were friends and accomplices of the House of Mopsos: their artistic traditions can be seen in the Neo-Hittite murals of Domuztepe and Karatepe.[200] Their pottery became common at Tarsus in the ninth century.[201] The people who had already learned their alphabet became familiar with their stories and legends and their learned Near Eastern lore.[202] Greek legend locates them in Boeotia at this time. Sporadic finds of their rich and beautiful artifacts in Euboean tombs (their own or the artifacts of their Euboean friends) show that they were there by the late tenth or early in the ninth century.[203] Some of their finest works found their way to Athens, and Crete was inundated with their magic.[204] Everywhere they went and worked, their vestiges look like individual contributions, the works of a dedicated few, the impact of limited and intense inspiration, and there is no sign anywhere of a colonizing, dominating, or conspiratorial spirit. They were, as the Cadmean legend has it, wise men from the East who came to teach and to learn.

Limassol and Southwestern Cyprus

Southwestern Cyprus was settled by Phoenicians from Tyre beginning in the eleventh century. Limassol was founded as a colony in the late ninth century and became the residence of a governor appointed by the king

199. O. Negbi, "Early Phoenician Presence in the Mediterranean Islands: A Reappraisal," *AJA* 96 (1992) 599–615.
200. I. J. Winter, "On the Problems of Karatepe: The Reliefs and Their Context," *AnSt* 29 (1979) 115–51.
201. G. M. A. Hanfmann, "The Iron Age Pottery of Tarsus," in *Excavations at Gözlü Kule, Tarsus, Volume III: Text. The Iron Age* (ed. Hetty Goldman; Princeton: Princeton University Press, 1963) 18–332.
202. M. L. West, *The East Face of Helicon: West Asiatic Elements in Greek Poetry and Myth* (Oxford: Clarendon, 1997).
203. J. N. Coldstream, "Greeks and Phoenicians in the Aegean," in *Phönizier im Westen* (ed. H. G. Niemeyer; Mainz am Rhein: von Zabern, 1982) 161–75, pls. 25–27; M. Popham, "Precolonization: Early Greek Contact with the East," in *The Archaeology of Greek Colonisation: Essays Dedicated to Sir John Boardman* (ed. G. R. Tsetskhladze and F. De Angelis; Oxford: Clarendon, 1994) 11–34; idem, "An Engraved Near Eastern Bronze Bowl from Lefkandi," *OJA* 14 (1995) 103–7; M. Popham and I. S. Lewis, "A Euboean Warrior Trader," *OJA* 14 (1995) 151–58; H. Matthäus, "Zypern und das Mittelmeergebiet: Kontakthorizonte des späten 2. und frühen 1. Jahrtausends v. Chr.," in *Archäologische Studien in Kontaktznen der antiken Welt* (ed. R. Rolle and K. Schmidt; Göttingen: Vandenhoeck & Ruprecht, 1998) 73–91.
204. E. Guralnick, "Greece and the Near East: Art and Archaeology," in *Daidalikon: Studies in Memory of Raymond V. Schroder, S.J.* (ed. R. F. Sutton Jr.; Wauconda, IL: Bolchazy-Carducci, 1989) 151–76.
J. Boardman, "The Khaniale Tekke Tombs, II," *ABSA* 62 (1967) 57–75; J. N. Coldstream, "Some Cypriote Traits in Cretan Pottery, c. 950–700 B.C.," *Acts of the International Archaeological Symposium: The Relations between Cyprus and Crete ca. 2000–500 B.C.* (Nicosia: Department of Antiquities, 1979) 257–63, pls. 44–46; idem, "Cypriaca and Cretocypriaca from the North Cemetery of Knossos," *RDAC* (1984) 122–37, pls. 23–26; idem and H. W. Catling, eds., *Knossos North Cemetery: Early Greek Tombs* (4 vols.; Athens: British School at Athens, 1996); H. Matthäus, "Die idäische Zeus-Grotte auf Kreta: Griechenland und der Vordere Orient im frühen 1. Jahrtausend v. Chr.," *ArAn* (2000–4) 517–47.

of Tyre. From there, Phoenician influence radiated through the cities and kingdoms along the south and western coasts of Cyprus in places such as Amathus, Kourion, and Palaepaphos (the original Paphos, now called Kouklia) and sometimes reached the interior. This sphere of Tyrian interest was politically, economically, and culturally distinct from the area of Sidonian monopoly centered on Kition in the southeast, and contact between the cities of these two regions was rare and deliberate. From the eleventh century onward, the Tyrian centers had distinct external relations, with Limassol as the link between Tyre and the Greek world and Palaepaphos as the home port for regular voyages to Sardinia and the western Mediterranean.

Tyrian presence in southwestern Cyprus and the establishment of Limassol as a colony are known from Phoenician inscriptions on the fragmentary remains of two bronze bowls.[205] The first inscription, preserved on six fragments of a bowl, is incomplete at the beginning and the end, but it can be reconstructed and read: "[In the . . . year of ʿAbdmilqar]t, governor of Carthage, servant of Hiram, king of the Sidonians, he gave this to Baʿal of Lebanon, his Lord, of the finest en[graved] bronze." The second inscription, on two fragments of another bowl, is more seriously damaged but can still be reconstructed and read: "[In the . . . year of ʾIlî]ṭôb, governor of Carthage, [servant of Hiram, king of the Sidonians, he gave this to Ba]ʿal of Lebanon, his Lord [. . .]." The bowls were retrieved from the antiquities market in Limassol, already broken in order to multiply their value, and were reported to be from a site north of Amathus.

Their place of origin in antiquity was Carthage, "New Town" (*qartḥadašt*), a colony named and designed as a replica of the old town, Tyre. Its colonial status merited a governor (*skn*) and a civic calendar computed according to his years of service, and required annual offerings to the God of the founding city, identified as the Baʿal of Lebanon, the Baʿal who was worshiped on Mount Carmel at Tyre's southern border, and also on the similar eminence on the northern boundary of Amathus, where the two bowls were discovered. The colony's enduring ties to the founding city are indicated by the title "servant," borne by the governors, and by naming Hiram not king of Tyre, the city, as he rightfully was but king of the people of Tyre and of the colony—specifically "king of the Sidonians," this being the ethnic equivalent of "Phoenicians" in Greek usage.

The two sets of fragments are distinct in their thickness, the quality of the metal, and their shape. The fragments of the first bowl are irregular pieces torn from the rim and edge of the bowl, while the fragments of the second bowl are straight-edged rectangular pieces cut only from the rim. The inscriptions are nearly identical in content, but they differ in their scripts. Both can be dated paleographically to about the middle of the eighth century, but the letters on the first bowl are archaic and lapidary; in contrast, the letters on the second bowl are more cursive and more developed. The bowls were offered in tribute by two successive governors of the colony, neither of whose names is completely preserved. The earlier bowl was offered by a governor whose name ended in -*t*—most likely the last

---

205. *CIS* 5; *KAI* 31; O. Masson, "La dédicace à Baʿal du Liban (*CIS* I, 5) et sa provenance probable de la région de Limassol," *Sem* 35 (1985) 33–46; M. Sznycer, "Brèves remarques sur l'inscription phénicienne de Chypre, *CIS* I, 5," *Sem* 35 (1985) 47–50, pls. 4–5a.

letter of a divine name, such as Melqart or ʿAštart, and of a personal name that began with a devotional term such as "servant-of . . ." (ʿabd), "client-of . . ." (ger), or "by-the-grace-of . . ." (bod). The name on the second bowl ends in -ṭôb, "good," a divine epithet that occurs in Amorite and Hebrew names but nowhere else in the Phoenician onomasticon.

Hiram was the king of Tyre during the reign of Tiglath-pileser III (744–727 B.C.E.), and he is included in the Assyrian annals for the years 738 and 734 B.C.E. His predecessor, included in the annals for the year 760 B.C.E., was ʾIttobaʿal, and his successors were Ṭobʾil, mentioned for the year 737 B.C.E., and Mattan, mentioned in 734 B.C.E.[206] The earlier governor of Carthage is otherwise unknown, but the later governor must be this Ṭobʾil ("Good-Is-God") of the Assyrian annals, with the constituent elements of his name ʾIlîṭôb ("My-God-Is-Good") in reverse order, as happened sometimes in adapting a personal name as a throne name. Ṭobʾil (Assyrian ṭu-ba-il), consequently, was the governor of Carthage in Cyprus before becoming king of Tyre, reigned for a short time (ca. 737–734 B.C.E.) and, to judge from his nondynastic name and from a biblical anecdote, may have been a usurper.

The anecdote appears in a sixth-century account of the Syro-Ephraimite war (737–734 B.C.E.), according to which the kings of Israel and Damascus, having failed to persuade the king of Judah to join their anti-Assyrian coalition (Israel and Damascus were on the verge of fading into history, but Judah was just beginning to assert itself in association with the Tyrian trade network and did not share their desperation), were resolved to replace him with Ṭobʾil (Hebrew ṭabʾel). There is hardly a clue in the story who this replacement might have been, except that he is presented without comment as a well-known or even paradigmatic usurper—a sort of Phoenician Quisling, Maverick, or Gerrymander whose name told the whole story.[207]

This collaborator, known as ʾIliṭob when he was governor, became king of Tyre and changed his name to Ṭobʾil during the anti-Assyrian uprising that involved Northern Israel and Damascus and pretty well all the city-states of Syria–Palestine, and now Tyre. This violated Tyre's perpetual neutrality, offended its pro-Assyrian policies and basic economic interests, and implicitly recognized an alliance of Syrian states with which it had nothing else in common. ʾIliṭob (whose regnal years coincided with those of the rebellion) was deposed, most likely by the city assembly, the Hundred, and replaced by the legitimate Mattan.

The colony of which he had been governor was operational in the mid-eighth century but was established in the last quarter of the ninth century. Classical sources know of a Carthage founded, by diverse reckonings, either in 825 or 814 B.C.E. This is usually identified as the Carthage in North Africa. However, the foundation of that colony happened exactly one century later, under the auspices of the Cypriot colony and its then-governor

206. L. D. Levine, "Menahem and Tiglath-Pileser: A New Synchronism," *BASOR* 206 (1972) 40–42; H. Tadmor, *The Inscriptions of Tiglath-Pileser III* (Jerusalem: Israel Academy of Sciences and Humanities, 1994) 106–7.

207. A. Vanel, "Tabeʾel en Is. VII 6 et le roi Tubail de Tyr," in *Studies on Prophecy* (ed. G. W. Anderson; VTSup 26; Leiden: Brill, 1974) 17–24.

Pygmalion. The likely explanation for the confusion is that it was Cypriot Carthage that was founded ca. 825 B.C.E. when, legend has it, there was a Pygmalion who was king of Tyre, and one thing or another forced his sister to travel and settle in Cyprus.

The colony is located at Limassol—until that time, unclaimed territory and in later times called Neapolis in recollection of its Tyrian name[208]— but there is little that is Phoenician and nothing that is specifically Tyrian about Limassol in the earlier record. Because it was a province and dependent on Tyre, it was not included among the seven unnamed Cypriot kingdoms that paid tribute to Sargon of Assyria at the end of the eighth century. However, the colony and its king are listed among the ten kingdoms that were subject to Assyria during the reigns of Esarhaddon and Ashurbanipal in the first half of the seventh century,[209] and it is clear that it had abandoned its colonial status by this time (that is, soon after the founding of North African Carthage) and joined the confederation of Cypriot states.

From then on, its people made do mostly with local imitations of Phoenician wares or with imports from Greece. By the end of the sixth century, tombs in the vicinity of the old town contain only local wares, as well as an Amathusian copy of a Phoenician pot.[210] A late sixth-century sanctuary in the town displayed terra-cotta figurines made according to traditional Cypriot standards and techniques. However, their best parallels, ironically, are from Carthage in North Africa and from other Tyrian colonies in Sicily and Spain.[211] Carthage in Cyprus was the earliest Tyrian colony, but it yielded the primacy to North African Carthage, perdured as a fairly nondescript kingdom, and ultimately was absorbed into its old Cypriot surroundings.

Its original colonial structure may be gathered indirectly from its satellite settlements in this part of Cyprus, especially Amathus, about 10 kilometers to the east, and Kourion, approximately the same distance to the west. At the eastern boundary of what might have been the province, at Kalavasos and Mari in the Vasilikos Valley, there are signs of Late Bronze Age development, and at a few related sites there is a residue of Phoenician presence persisting into the Cypro-Archaic period.

Fifty kilometers to the west of Kourion, in the once-powerful and influential kingdom of Palaepaphos, Phoenician influence was strong but did not survive much longer than Tyrian colonial presence. The colony at Carthage was an expression of early Tyrian interest in southwest Cyprus, and it concentrated Tyrian energies in the region from the ninth to the early seventh century, but it did not last. It gave up its productive dependence on Tyre, fell in with the Cypriot kingdoms, and was left to its own destiny.

208. E. Lipiński, "La Carthage de Chypre," in *Redt Tyrus / Sauvons Tyr: Histoire Phénicienne / Fenicische Geschiedenis* (ed. E. Gubel, E. Lipiński, and B. Servais-Soyez; Studia Phoenicia 1–2; Louvain: Peeters, 1983) 209–34.

209. Idem, "The Cypriot Vassals of Esarhaddon," in *Ah Assyria . . . : Studies in Assyrian History and Ancient Near Eastern Historiography Presented to Hayim Tadmor* (ed. M. Cogan and I. Eph'al; Scripta Hierosolymitana 33; Jerusalem: Magnes, 1991) 58–64.

210. P. Flourentzos, "The Tombs 214 and 215 from Agios Athanasios Limassol," *RDAC* (1993) 157–71, pls. 18–42.

211. V. Karageorghis, *Two Cypriote Sanctuaries of the End of the Cypro-Archaic Period* (Rome: Consiglio Nazionale delle Ricerche, 1977) 47–66 ("Part Two: Excavations of a Sanctuary at Limassol: 'Komissariato', 1953 and 1957").

Amathus and Kourion and Palaepaphos maintained their bonds of blood and cooperation but, without the political, religious, and fiscal incentives of their colonial status, drifted into independent commercial enclaves.

Amathus was an autochthonous town, settled in the eleventh century by Cypriots who had been dislocated in the upheavals caused by Mycenean and Achaean immigrants. From soon after its settlement, however, to judge from the artifacts in its tombs, it was open to deep and constant influence from Greece and Tyre.[212] It has the largest concentration of Greek Geometric wares in Cyprus, and it was clearly a port of call for Euboean merchants sailing to Tyre and for Tyrian merchants traveling to Greece.[213] Most of these imports may have been acquired by a few wealthy Cypriot families, perhaps merchants doing business with the Tyrians and Greeks,[214] because almost half of the Greek Geometric and Archaic imports were found in about 10 tombs that continued in use for over three centuries.

The heaviest concentration of Phoenician ceramics is in the earlier tombs (Cypro-Geometric I–II, 1050–850 B.C.E.), and these were probably graves of Tyrians buried abroad, because their mixed Phoenician-Euboean pottery assemblages match almost perfectly the mixed assemblages in Tyre and in the mainland Tyrian settlement at Khirbet Silm.[215] Phoenician imports continue through the ninth and eighth centuries (Cypro-Geometric III, 850–750 B.C.E.), and the repertoire was stabilized in the seventh (Cypro-Archaic I, 700–600 B.C.E.).[216] Amathus was a Cypriot town and most of its more than 500 tombs contain a preponderance of local wares.[217] Tyrians lived there apart from the local population, and by the seventh century

212. J. N. Coldstream, "Early Iron Age (Cypro-Geometric): The Rise of the Ancient Kingdoms, c. 1100–700 B.C.," in *Footprints in Cyprus: An Illustrated History* (ed. D. Hunt; London: Trigraph, 1990) 47–64.

213. Idem, "The Greek Geometric and Archaic Imports," in *La nécropole d'Amathonte. Tombes 113–367. II: Céramiques non chypriotes* (ed. V. Karageorghis and O. Picard; Nicosia: Department of Antiquities, 1987) 21–31, pls. 8–17; idem, "Greek Geometric and Archaic Imports from the Tombs of Amathus—II," *RDAC* (1995) 199–214.

Idem, "Kition and Amathus: Some Reflections on Their Westward Links during the Early Iron Age," in *Acts of the International Archaeological Symposium 'Cyprus between the Orient and the Occident'* (ed. V. Karageorghis; Nicosia: Department of Antiquities, 1986) 321–29; I. S. Lemos and H. Hatcher, "Early Greek Vases in Cyprus: Euboean and Attic," *OJA* 10 (1991) 197–208.

214. J. P. Crielaard, "The Social Organization of Euboean Trade with the Eastern Mediterranean during the 10th to 8th Centuries BC," *Pharos* 1 (1993) 139–46.

215. S. V. Chapman, "A Catalogue of Iron Age Pottery from the Cemeteries of Khirbet Silm, Joya, Qraye and Qasmieh of South Lebanon," *Berytus* 21 (1972) 55–194; W. Culican, "The Repertoire of Phoenician Pottery," in *Phönizier im Westen* (ed. H. G. Niemeyer; Madrider Beiträge 8; Mainz am Rhein: von Zabern, 1982) 45–82; J. N. Coldstream, "Cypriaca and Cretocypriaca from the North Cemetery of Knossos," *RDAC* (1984) 122–37, pls. 23–26; idem, "Early Greek Pottery in Tyre and Cyprus: Some Preliminary Comparisons," *RDAC* (1988) part 2, 35–44, pls. 10–13; idem, "The First Exchanges between Euboeans and Phoenicians: Who Took the Initiative?" *MPT*, 353–60.

216. P. M. Bikai, "The Phoenician Pottery," in *La nécropole d'Amathonte, tombes 113–367, II: Céramiques non-chypriotes* (ed. V. Karageorghis, O. Picard, and C. Tytgat; Nicosia: Leventis Foundation, 1987) 1–19; idem, *The Phoenician Pottery of Cyprus* (Nicosia: Leventis Foundation, 1987).

217. V. Karageorghis and M. Iacovou, "Amathus Tomb 521: A Cypro-Geometric I Group," *RDAC* (1990) 75–100, pls. 4–11.

there was a substantial Phoenician quarter, with a completely separate Tyrian cemetery for the cremated remains of infants.[218] Amathus had a fair port,[219] but it is possible that in earlier times it was mainly a market for goods that were brought to Limassol, or manufactured there, and then transshipped to the town. It flourished in the eighth and seventh centuries until the Assyrians made Phoenicians from Tyre their official commercial agents.[220] It may have been included among the seven Cypriot city kingdoms of Cyprus mentioned by Sargon II at the end of the eighth century, and it might be identified with one of the named Cypriot kingdoms that paid tribute to Esarhaddon in the early seventh century.[221] But in these changing times, Phoenician influence remained pervasive, and Phoenician products were abundant and conspicuous.

Phoenician pottery was plain, but it was distinctive and useful, because the type, style, or decoration of the container clearly marked the contents, and in no time at all local Cypriots copied all the forms, probably for the same reason. It became nearly impossible to distinguish between local Cypriot and Phoenician wares. The artistic traditions of the Amathus workshops (which are distinctive in Cyprus and particularly eclectic) incorporated Greek models and Phoenician themes.[222]

Tyrians imported or produced in their Amathus studios a wealth of gold and silver jewelry that inspired the local crafts, as well as silver bowls inscribed with narrative and epic scenes or with allusions to entertaining stories.[223] They brought Egyptian amulets and made creative imitations of

218. The discovery of the necropolis was reported in *BCH* 117 (1993) 752; in *AJA* 102 (1998) 313; and in V. Karageorghis, "Cyprus and the Phoenicians: Achievement and Perspectives," in *I Fenici: Ieri oggi domani* (ed. S. Moscati; Rome: Consiglio Nazionale delle Ricerche, 1995) 327–37. It dates to the Cypro-Archaic period (750–480 B.C.E.), but analysis was impeded by modern construction at the site near the beach at Amathus. It consisted of several hundred covered funerary urns containing the burned remains of infants and animals that were placed in rows and laid one on top of the other in layers.
219. There was an artificial harbor built at the end of the fourth century B.C.E.: J.-Y. Empereur, "Le port hellènistique d'Amathonte," in *Proceedings of the International Symposium 'Cyprus and the Sea'* (ed. V. Karageorghis and D. Michaelides; Nicosia: University of Cyprus, 1995) 131–37.
220. A. Hermary, "Amathonte de Chypre et les Phéniciens," *Phoenicia and the East Mediterranean in the First Millennium B.C.* (ed. E. Lipiński; Studia Phoenicia 5; Louvain: Peeters, 1980) 375–88; V. Karageorghis, "Amathus between the Greeks and the Phoenicians," *Atti* 2, 3.959–68, esp. p. 960.
221. P. Aupert, "Amathus during the First Iron Age," *BASOR* 308 (1997) 19–25, esp. p. 24; E. Lipiński, "The Cypriot Vassals of Esarhaddon," in *Ah, Assyria . . . : Studies in Assyrian History and Ancient Near Eastern Historiography Presented to Hayim Tadmor* (ed. M. Cogan and I. Eph'al; Scripta Hierosolymitana 33; Jerusalem: Magnes, 1991) 58–64.
222. C. Adelman, "A Sculpture in Relief from Amathus," *RDAC* (1971) 59–64, pl. 22; J. L. Benson, "The Amathus Workshop," *RDAC* (1982) 138–43, pls. 26–28; V. Karageorghis and J. Des Gagniers, *La céramique chypriote de style figuré: Âge du Fer (1050–500 av. J.-C.)* (Rome: Consiglio Nazionale delle Richerche, 1974) 91–93.
223. Z. Kapera, "The Amathus Gold Plaques from the Old Goluchow Collection," *RDAC* (1981) 106–14, pls. 14–15; V. Karageorghis, "Tiarae of Gold from Cyprus," in *Insight through Images: Studies in Honor of Edith Porada* (ed. M. Kelly-Buccellati; Malibu: Undena, 1986) 129–32, pl. 26; idem, *Amathonte III, Testimonia 3: L'orfèvrerie* (ed. R. Laffineur; Études Chypriotes 7; Paris: Editions Recherche sur les Civilisations, 1986) 111–24; R. Laffineur, "Bijoux et Orfèvrerie," in *La nécropole d'Amathonte—Tombes 113–367, VI: Bijoux, armes, verre, astragales et coquillages, squelettes* (ed. V. Karageorghis, O. Picard, and C. Tytgat; Études Chypriotes 14; Nicosia: Department of Antiquities, 1992) 1–32, pls. 1–9.

their styles and religious motifs,[224] and they sold antique cylinder seals and stamp seals that were cherished as heirlooms. Terra-cottas and painted bowls of local Cypriot workmanship introduced, under Tyrian inspiration, new motifs representing universal religious subjects or symbolizing the new world order that brought the Cypriot kingdoms together in the Assyrian Empire—all of them in startling contrast to the homely scenes and unsophisticated subjects familiar to their regular Cypriot clientele.[225] A couple of Phoenician inscriptions, one marking the contents of a sixth-century storage jar, the other a personal name on a fifth-century Attic bowl are the latest witnesses to Tyrian persistence in the kingdom.[226] Amathus, over the centuries, illustrates the preoccupations of the colonists and the impact of the Limassol colony on the towns in its territory.

Kourion, to the west of Limassol, was not a Tyrian colony or a Phoenician settlement but a thoroughly Greek city interested in Phoenician goods. Myceneans settled in the town in the eleventh century,[227] and as

---

J. L. Myres, "The Amathus Bowl: A Long-Lost Masterpiece of Oriental Engraving," *JHS* 53 (1933) 25–39, pls. 1–3; R. D. Barnett, "The Amathus Shield-Boss Rediscovered and the Amathus Bowl Reconsidered," *RDAC* (1977) 157–69, pls. 46–48; G. Markoe, *Phoenician Bronze and Silver Bowls from Cyprus and the Mediterranean* (Berkeley: University of California Press, 1985) nos. 4, 18, 19(?).

224. P. Aupert, "Amathonte, le Proche-Orient et l'Egypte," in *Acts of the International Archaeological Symposium 'Cyprus between the Orient and the Occident'* (ed. V. Karageorghis; Nicosia: Department of Antiquities, 1986) 369–82; A. Hermary, "Un nouveau chapiteau hathorique trouvé à Amathonte," *BCH* 109 (1985) 657–99; G. Hölbl, "Ägyptische Kunstelemente im phönikischen Kulturkreis des 1. Jahrtausends v. Chr.: Zur Methodik ihrer Verwandung," *Or* 58 (1989) 318–25, pls. 14–15; G. Clerc, "Aegyptiaca," in *La nécropole d'Amathonte: Tombes 110–385* (ed. K. Karageorghis, O. Picard, and C. Tytgat; Études Chypriotes 13; Nicosia: Department of Antiquities, 1991) 1–157; G. Markoe, "Egyptianizing Male Votive Statuary from Cyprus: A Reexamination," *Levant* 22 (1990) 111–22.

225. F. Vandenabeele, "Phoenician Influence on the Cypro-Archaic Terracotta Production and Cypriote Influence Abroad," in *Acts of the International Archaeological Symposium 'Cyprus between the Orient and the Occident'* (ed. V. Karageorghis; Nicosia: Department of Antiquities, 1986) 351–60, pls. 30–31; idem, "Has Phoenician Influence Modified Cypriot Terracotta Production?" *ESC*, 266–71; V. Karageorghis, "The Terracottas," in *La nécropole d'Amathonte: Tombes 113–367* (ed. V. Karageorghis and A. Hermary; Études Chypriotes 9; Nicosia: Department of Antiquities, 1987) 1–52, pls. 1–41; C. Beer, "Eastern Influences and Style: A Reconsideration of Some Terracottas of Cypriote Manufacture," in *Cypriote Terracottas* (ed. F. Vandenabeele and R. Laffineur; Brussels: Vrije Universiteit Brussel / Liège: Université de Liège, 1991) 77–85, pls. 16–18; S. O'Bryhim, "The Sphere-Bearing Anthropomorphic Figures of Amathus," *BASOR* 306 (1997) 39–45.

J. Karageorghis, "La vie quotidienne à Chypre d'après les terres cuites d'époque géometrique et archaïque," *Cypriote Terracottas* (ed. F. Vandenabeele and R. Laffineur; Brussels: Vrije Universiteit Brussel / Liège: Universite de Liège, 1991) 149–68, pl. 42; V. Karageorghis, *The Coroplastic Art of Ancient Cyprus* (6 vols.; Nicosia: Leventis Foundation, 1993–96); idem and J. Des Gagniers, *La céramique chypriote de style figuré: Âge du Fer (1050–500 av. J.-C.)* (Rome: Consiglio Nazionale delle Ricerche, 1974).

226. The inscription on the amphora may read *rbk lmym*, "mixture for the mayumas": M. Sznycer, "Une inscription phénicienne fragmentaire sur un tesson d'Amathonte," *BCH* 106 (1982) 243–44. The name on the base of the Attic bowl (*yknšmš*, "May the Sun Establish") is composed of common elements, but the combination is unique in Phoenician: idem, "Une inscription phénicienne d'Amathonte," *BCH* 111 (1987) 133–35.

227. O. Masson, "Les plus anciennes crémations à Chypre: Témoignagnes d'une croyance spécifique," *RDAC* (1988) part 1, pp. 321–24; D. Christou, "Kourion in the 11th Century B.C.," in *Cyprus in the 11th Century B.C.* (ed. V. Karageorghis; Nicosia: University of Cyprus, 1994) 177–87; L. Steel, "Transition from Bronze to Iron at Kourion: A Review of the Tombs from Episkopi-

late as the seventh century terra-cotta figurines still display a blend of local Cypriot and Mycenean artistic traditions. Tyrian contact with or presence in the town is indicated by a broad spectrum of goods. There are a
few imported Phoenician wares in the early tombs, a series of Phoenician
silver bowls from the eighth and the early seventh century, most of which
are inscribed with Cypro-Syllabic signs, and an early sixth-century tomb
of a Sidonian with a Phoenician and Cypro-Syllabic bilingual epitaph.[228]
There are Late Bronze Age Egyptian objects, early Iron Age stamp seals with
Egyptian themes, later representations of Nubians on painted pottery, a few
colonial Phoenician scarabs and Egyptianizing amulets of the seventh and
sixth centuries, and an Egyptianizing votive statue carved locally following traditional Cypriot tastes but inspired by Phoenician ivory carving.[229]
There are Black-on-Red perfume bottles, but they are just standard imitations of the original Phoenician style.[230]

The terra-cotta ex-votos from the Sanctuary of Apollo were locally made
or brought from Amathus or Palaepaphos, and it is only the later-seventh-
and sixth-century chariot and horse-and-rider models that reflect discor-
dant military motifs packaged by the Phoenicians.[231] Kourion's prosperity in the seventh and sixth centuries centered on the popularity of this
sanctuary, which was visited on occasion by pilgrims using Phoenician

Bamboula and Kaloriziki," *ABSA* 91 (1996) 287–300; O. Negbi, "Reflections on the Ethnicity of
Cyprus in the Eleventh Century B.C.," *MPT*, 87–93.

228. J. L. Benson, *Bamboula at Kourion: The Necropolis and the Finds, Excavated by J. F. Daniel*
(Philadelphia: University of Pennsylvania Press, 1972); idem, *The Necropolis at Kaloriziki* (Studies
in Mediterranean Archaeology 36; Gothenburg: Åströms, 1973); S. Buitron-Oliver, "Kourion: The
Evidence for the Kingdom from the 11th to the 6th Century B.C.," *BASOR* 308 (1997) 27–36.

G. Markoe, *Phoenician Bronze and Silver Bowls from Cyprus and the Mediterranean* (Berkeley:
University of California Press, 1985) 75, 175–82. The bowls are the work of at least three different artisans, whose names are inscribed on them. Another bowl is inscribed with the name of its
patron: "Of Akestor, King of Paphos."

RPC, 88–91, pl. 7:2; É. Puech, "Remarques sur quelques inscriptions phéniciennes de Chypre," *Sem* 29 (1989) 19–43, esp. pp. 39–40. The Phoenician inscription, to be dated ca. 550
B.C.E., can be read: "[This is the home] for eternity of Bikray the Si[donian. Do not disturb th]is
sar[cophagus]." There are also some inscriptions on jars that are preserved only in nineteenth-
century hand copies: O. Masson and M. Sznycer, "Kourion, 1883–1884: Inscriptions phéniciennes et objets divers," in *Studies in Honour of Vassos Karageorghis* (ed. G. C. Ioannides; Nicosia:
Leventis Foundation, 1992) 237–40.

229. I. Jacobsson, *Aegyptiaca from Late Bronze Age Cyprus* (Studies in Mediterranean Archaeology 102; Jonsered: Åströms, 1994).

E. Porada, "Glyptics," in *Bamboula at Kourion: The Necropolis and the Finds* (ed. J. L. Benson;
Philadelphia: University of Pennsylvania, 1972) 141–49.

V. Karageorghis, *Blacks in Cypriot Art*, Houston: Menil Foundation, 1988.

E. Gubel, "The Seals," in *The Sanctuary of Apollo Hylates at Kourion: Excavations in the Archaic
Precinct* (ed. D. Buitron-Oliver; Jonsered: Åströms, 1996) 163–67.

G. Markoe, "An Egyptianizing Votive Statuette from Kourion," *RDAC* (1988) part 2, 17–18,
pl. 6.

230. F. de Cree, "The Black-on-Red or Cypro-Phoenician Ware," in *Phoenicia and the Bible* (ed.
E. Lipiński; Studia Phoenicia 11; Louvain: Peeters, 1991) 95–102.

231. J. H. Young and S. H. Young, *Terracotta Figurines from Kourion in Cyprus* (Philadelphia:
The University Museum, 1955); B. C. Dietrich, "The Sanctuary of Apollo at Kourion," in *The
Sanctuary of Apollo Hylates at Kourion: Excavations in the Archaic Precinct* (ed. D. Buitron-Oliver;
Jonsered: Åströms, 1996) 17–39; N. A. Winter, "The Terracottas," in ibid., 89–137, pls. 17–33.

pottery,[232] and the town and sanctuary were indebted to the Tyrians less for their commercial involvement than for their artistic and spiritual contributions.

Although the impact of Tyrians on places like Amathus, Kourion, and (it must be deduced from their example) Limassol was early and persistent, their influence on the southern coast of Cyprus in the rest of this colonial region was almost negligible. Kalavasos, at the eastern boundary of the region about 20 kilometers northeast of Amathus on the Vasilikos River, was a literate,[233] well-organized, and wealthy indigenous Cypriot settlement in the Late Cypriot II period (ca. 1400–1200 B.C.E.), engaged in the export of copper and bronze, but it was abandoned in the twelfth century.[234]

At Mari, a few kilometers to the southwest of Kalavasos in the Vasilikos Valley, there are some Cypro-Archaic I (ca. 650 B.C.E.) remains but, apart from an imported jar and two imitation Phoenician jugs originating in Amathus, there is hardly a trace of contact with the Phoenicians.[235] At Kapsalaes, an isolated site near the town of Vavla 28 kilometers northeast of Limassol and about the same distance northwest of Kalavasos, there are remains of a sanctuary and burial ground dating from the late sixth century to Hellenistic and Roman times, but the place had no contact with the Phoenicians.[236] Similarly, at Alassa, a late Cypriot site in the interior about 15 kilometers northwest of Limassol and 10 due north of Kourion,[237] there is a late sixth-century Phoenician inscription painted on a jar that mentions the name of the grocer, the contents of the jar, and the 35th year of a king whose name is lost but undoubtedly was the king of nearby Limassol,[238] but there is no other trace of Phoenician presence. Tyrians were a dominant and creative force in colonial times, but their influence flagged in the system of kingdoms. They were concentrated at Amathus, but there was only a scattering of individuals beyond its perimeter. In exchange for raw materials (and textiles, for which there was endless demand) supplied

232. L. Ferrer Dias and J. Vaz Pinto, "Pottery from the Cella of the Temple," in *The Sanctuary of Apollo Hylates at Kourion, Cyprus* (ed. D. Soren; Tucson: University of Arizona Press, 1987) 219–31; D. Buitron-Oliver, "Pottery from the Archaic Precinct," in *The Sanctuary of Apollo Hylates at Kourion: Excavations in the Archaic Precinct* (ed. D. Buitron-Oliver; Jonsered: Åströms, 1996) 41–71.

233. E. Masson, "Premiers documents Chypro-Minöens du site Kalavassos-*Ayios Dhimitrios*," *RDAC* (1983) 131–41, pl. 18.

234. A. K. South, "Urbanism and Trade in the Vasilikos Valley in the Late Bronze Age," in *Trade, Contact and the Movement of Peoples in the Eastern Mediterranean: Studies in Honour of J. Basil Hennessy* (ed. S. Bourke and J.-P. Descoeudres; Sydney: Meditarch, 1995) 187–97, pls. 15–16; idem, "Kalavassos-*Ayios Dhimitrios* 1992–1996," *RDAC* (1997) 151–73, pls. 11–15.

235. M. Hadjicosti, "The Family Tomb of a Warrior of the Cypro-Archaic I Period at Mari," *RDAC* (1997) 252–66, pls. 49–54.

236. M. E. Morden and I. A. Todd, "Vavla-Kapsalaes: An Archaic Sanctuary Site," *Archaeologia Cypria* 3 (1994) 53–63.

237. S. Hadjisavvas, "Alassa: A New Late Cypriot Site," *RDAC* (1986) 62–67; idem, "A Late Cypriot Community at Alassa," *ESC*, 32–42; idem, "LC IIC to LC IIIA without Intruders: The Case of Alassa-*Pano Mandilaris*," in *Cypriot Ceramics: Reading the Prehistoric Record* (ed. J. A. Barlow, D. L. Bolger, and B. Kling; Philadelphia: The University Museum, 1991) 173–80; idem, "Alassa Archaeological Project 1991–1993," *RDAC* (1994) 107–17, pls. 15–21.

238. V. Karageorghis, "Chronique des fouilles et découvertes archéologiques à Chypre en 1966," *BCH* 91 (1967) 275–370, pls. 1–8, esp. p. 302, fig. 72; *RPC* 91–94, pl. 8:1.

by their Cypriot neighbors, they imported and produced the rich and satis-fying goods of sophisticated Levantine luxury.

Palaepaphos, situated at modern Kouklia, about 50 kilometers west of Amathus beyond Cape Gata, was the westernmost Tyrian settlement, in a town that had been founded by Greek immigrants in the twelfth cen-tury.[239] Tyrian imports began soon after in the early eleventh century and continued to be impressive until about the mid-ninth century but gradually abated in the Cypro-Geometric III (850–750 B.C.E.) and Cypro-Archaic I (750–600 B.C.E.) periods.[240] For instance, in Cypro-Geometric I–II (ca. 1050–850 B.C.E.), there are 27 tombs out of a total of 53 excavated that have Tyrian pottery, 5 of them with between 4 and 10 imported pieces, the rest with less than 4 items.[241] However, in the Cypro-Geometric III period (850–750 B.C.E.), there are only 3 tombs with imported Tyrian wares, and these with only 2 or 3 pieces.[242] Because not all of these tombs were assuredly Phoenician, and at least one of them was certainly a Cypriot burial,[243] the Phoenician pottery and bronzes and local imitations of them that were found in these tombs do not make Palaepaphos a final destination, a Tyrian colony, or permanent settlement but suggest that it was a stopping place for Tyrian merchants and explorers on their way to the western Mediterranean. This perception is sharpened by the fact that there were a few Greek imports, such as any settlement might acquire, but numerous traces of travel, trade, and com-merce, such as Egyptian knickknacks and heirlooms, and weights of Anato-lian, Mesopotamian, Syrian, Palestinian, and Phoenician standards.[244]

---

239. F. G. Maier and M.-L. Waartburg, "Reconstructing History from the Earth, c. 2800 B.C.–1600 A.D.: Excavating at Palaepaphos, 1966–1984," in *Archaeology in Cyprus 1960–1985* (ed. V. Karageorghis; Nicosia: Department of Antiquities, 1985) 142–72; M. E. Voyatzis, "Arcadia and Cyprus: Aspects of their Interrelationship between the Twelfth and Eighth Centuries B.C.," *RDAC* (1985) 155–63; V. Karageorghis, *The End of the Late Bronze Age in Cyprus* (Nicosia: Pierides Foun-dation, 1990) 13–16; idem, *Tombs at Palaepaphos, 1: Teratsoudhia. 2. Eliomylia* (Nicosia: Leventis Foundation, 1990).

240. P. M. Bikai, "Trade Networks in the Early Iron Age: The Phoenicians at Palaepaphos," in *Western Cyprus: Connections* (ed. D. R. Rupp; Gothenburg: Åströms, 1987) 125–28. V. Kara-georghis, "A Cypro-Archaic I Tomb at Palaepaphos-*Skales*," *RDAC* (1987) 85–95, pls. 25–32.

241. Clandestine diggings continue to produce sporadic finds, for example, a Bichrome Phoenician beer jug (950–850 B.C.E.): see D. Christou, "Chronique des fouilles et découvertes archéologiques à Chypre en 1995: Musée regional de Palaepaphos (Kouklia, Paphos)," *BCH* 120 (1996) 104–5.

242. P. M. Bikai, "The Imports from the East," in *Palaepaphos-Skales: An Iron Age Cemetery in Cyprus* (ed. V. Karageorghis; Konstanz: Universitätsverlag, 1983) 396–406; idem, *The Phoenician Pottery of Cyprus* (Nicosia: Leventis Foundation, 1987).

243. Tomb 49, the oldest and largest, contained 3 heavy Phoenician storage jars and 12 smaller fine ware Phoenician vases, but it also contained an obelos inscribed in Cypro-Syllabic with the Greek name (*Opheltas*) of the deceased: J. N. Coldstream, "Status Symbols in Cyprus in the Eleventh Century B.C.," *ESC*, 325–35; O. Negbi, "Reflections on the Ethnicity of Cyprus in the Eleventh Century BCE," *MPT*, 87–93.

244. G. Clerc, "Aegyptiaca de Palaepaphos-*Skales*," in *Palaepaphos-Skales: An Iron Age Ceme-tery in Cyprus* (ed. V. Karageorghis; Konstanz: Universitätsverlag, 1983) 375–95; idem, "Un frag-ment de vase au nom d'Ahmosis (?) à Palaepaphos-*Teratsoudhia*," in *Tombs at Palaepaphos, 1: Teratsoudhia. 2: Eliomylia* (ed. V. Karageorghis; Nicosia: Department of Antiquities, 1990) 95–103; C. Clamer, "Large Decorated Calcite-Alabaster Jar," in ibid., 104–7; J.-C. Courtois, "Aegyptiaca de Kouklia-Palaepaphos," *RDAC* (1990) 69–74; E. J. Peltenburg, "Ramesside Egypt and Cyprus," in *Acts of the International Archaeological Symposium 'Cyprus between the Orient and the Occident'*

Confirmation of Palaepaphos as a port of transit for Tyrians headed west is the discovery of a tripod in one of its early (1050–950 B.C.E.) graves that is just like a tripod found in a cave at Santadi, northwest of Nora in southern Sardinia; and (because there were sound commercial relations between Amathus and Palaepaphos) the presence in an Amathus tomb of an Atlantic obelos whose best parallel, along with tools of Iberian and Cypriot type, was found in a Nuraghic hoard at Monte Sa Idda in Sardinia.[245] Palaepaphos was a Greek Cypriot town with an impressive religious and commercial district (a tripartite pillared marketplace, courtyards, and associated foundries); with rich intellectual and artistic traditions; with tombs dating from early times to the sixth century that were endowed with quantities of fine pottery, gold jewelry, and bronze and iron implements and weapons; and at last with thousands of Cypro-Archaic (750–480 B.C.E.) and Cypro-Classical (480–325 B.C.E.) figurines from the former religious and commercial district when it revived to accommodate the popular worship of Aphrodite.[246] From the beginning, the town welcomed Tyrians and their goods, and the sharp decline in Tyrian investment in the latter part of the ninth century coincided with their discovery and exploitation of the western world.

The vicinity of Palaepaphos, like the environs of Amathus, was hardly affected by Tyrian traders, artists, and entrepreneurs, and so the major sites are practically devoid of early Phoenician artifacts. Paphos and neighboring Ktima (on the far western coast of Cyprus, about 20 and 25 kilometers northwest of Palaepaphos) used a distinctive Cypriot syllabary that can be traced at least to the eighth century[247] and were positively Greek. The items of Phoenician origin from these places include a decorated bronze bowl, dating to the mid-seventh century, which may have been imported

---

(ed. V. Karageorghis; Nicosia: Department of Antiquities, 1986) 49–79. J.-C. Courtois, "Les poids de Palaepaphos-*Skales*," in *Palaepaphos-Skales: An Iron Age Cemetery in Cyprus* (ed. V. Karageorghis; Konstanz: Universitätsverlag, 1983) 424–25; idem, "Les poids de Palaepaphos-*Teratsoudhia*: Étude méthodologique," in *Tombs at Palaepaphos, 1: Teratsoudhia. 2: Eliomylia* (ed. V. Karageorghis; Nicosia: Leventis Foundation, 1990) 123–27.

245. A. M. Bisi, "Le rôle de Chypre dans la civilisation phénicienne d'Occident: État de la question et essai de synthèse," in *Acts of the International Archaeological Symposium 'Cyprus between the Orient and the Occident'* (ed. V. Karageorghis; Nicosia: Department of Antiquities, 1986) 341–50, esp. p. 343; F. Lo Schiavo, "Cyprus and Sardinia in the Mediterranean Trade Routes toward the West," in *Proceedings of the International Symposium 'Cyprus and the Sea'* (ed. V. Karageorghis and D. Michaelides; Nicosia: University of Cyprus, 1995) 45–59, esp. p. 51.

246. J. M. Webb, *Ritual Architecture, Iconography and Practice in the Late Cypriot Bronze Age* (Jonsered: Åströms, 1999) 58–64.
Palaepaphos is the source of numerous syllabic Cypriot inscriptions: G. B. Bazemore, "The Geographic Distribution of the Cypriote Syllabic Inscriptions: Towards an Understanding of the Function of Literacy," *Acta Cypria, Part 3* (ed. P. Åström; Jonsered: Åströms, 1992) 63–96. An eleventh-century figured vase (*kalathos*) from Palaepaphos is said to mark the beginning of typically Cypriot art: Karageorghis and Des Gagniers, *La céramique chypriote de style figuré*, 5, 107.
V. Karageorghis, "Palaepaphos," in *Cyprus BC: 7000 Years of History* (ed. V. Tatton-Brown; London: British Museum, 1979) 50–52; P. Flourentzos, "The Early Geometric Tomb No. 132 from Palaepaphos," *RDAC* (1997) 205–18, pls. 26–54; V. Karageorghis and M. Iacovou, "Cypro-Geometric Material from Palaepaphos," *RDAC* (1982) 123–37; V. Karageorghis, "A Cypro-Archaic I Tomb at Palaepaphos-*Skales*," *RDAC* (1987) 85–96, pls. 25–32.

247. O. Masson, "La plus ancienne inscription paphienne," *BCH* 92 (1968) 379–80.

from North Syria,[248] and figurines and inscriptions that are connected with the cult of Aphrodite, Phoenician Astarte, in Paphos. The earliest figurine, from about the end of the eighth century, is of Astarte seated on a throne and riding side-saddle on a horse equipped with wheels: this is a wonderful crasis of the Warrior Goddess on horseback of Tyrian and Egyptian tradition, plus the wheeled horse-and-rider toys of Assyrian inspiration, and the enthroned Queen-of-Love presentation of Paphian Aphrodite.[249] The later exemplars, from Amathus, are figurines of women holding a tambourine at about shoulder height, a disk before their breasts, or a sphere at thigh height, which together represent the music, song, and dance of joyful devotion to the Goddess of Paphos.[250] Part of her cult (particularly, of her role in the annual rituals of Adonis) consisted of the offering of hair in her honor. This is described in an eighth-century Phoenician inscription from Kition, is known from late classical sources, and is recorded in a mid-fifth-century inscription from Palaepaphos that commemorates the dedication of a statue of a woman (*smlt*), of her devotee, or of Aphrodite herself; and the offering of locks of hair in the Temple of Astarte of Paphos.[251] The inscription is of interest because, with the other figurines from Amathus, it indicates that the Temple of Astarte in Paphos was frequented by Phoenician women from all over southwestern Cyprus.[252]

Paphos and Ktima began to lose interest in Phoenician products and styles sometime in the seventh century, when native Cypriot traditions were invigorated by Greek brilliance.[253] However, as late as the fifth century, there were still some Phoenicians in the town, and they prevailed upon Ba‘almilk II (ca. 425 B.C.E.), king of Kition and Idalion, to dedicate a statue on their behalf in the Temple of Astarte in Idalion.[254] However, in the end, Paphos like most of Cyprus became thoroughly Greek and, as is recorded in early fourth-century Phoenician victory inscriptions from Kition,[255] it was misled into siding with Salamis and the Athenians against the Persians and their Phoenician allies.

---

248. V. Karageorghis, "A Decorated Bronze Bowl from Armou," *RDAC* (1981) 142–45, pls. 20–22.

249. Idem, "An Enthroned Astarte on Horseback (?)," *RDAC* (1997) 195–203, pls. 23–24.

250. S. O'Bryhim, "The Sphere-Bearing Anthropomorphic Figurines of Amathus," *BASOR* 306 (1997) 39–45.

251. *RPC* 81–86. The inscription in five lines, all of them broken at the beginning and the end, can be read: . . . *smlt* '[z] . . . / . . . [*bm*]*qdš* 'z . . . / . . . [*ndrt nd*]*r wp‘lt* '[*yt*] . . . / . . . ‘*štrt pp* . . . / . . . '*p mhlpt*, ". . . this statue . . . in this sanctuary . . . she vowed and made the . . . Astarte of Paphos . . . and locks of hair."

252. A third-century Rhodian amphora from a tomb at Paphos is inscribed "For ‘Abdshahar the jeweler" (*l‘bdšhr hnsk*), who perhaps catered to the women who worshiped and made offerings to the Goddess: É. Puech, "Notes sur des inscriptions phéniciennes de Kition et Kato Paphos," *Sem* 39 (1990) 99–109, esp. pp. 108–9.

253. J. Deshayes, *La nécropole de Ktima* (Paris: Geuthner, 1963); D. Michaelides and J. Mlynarczyk, "Tombs P.M. 2520 and P.M. 2737 from the Eastern Necropolis of Nea Paphos," *RDAC* (1988) part 2, 149–70.

254. A. M. Honeyman, "The Phoenician Inscriptions of the Cyprus Museum," *Iraq* 6 (1939) 104–8, esp. p. 106, fig. 2. The inscription is badly damaged but preserves the titulary of the king and records his dedication of a statue of a man to Astarte on behalf of Paphos (*]lpp sml ‘št[rt]*).

255. *CIS* 91; M. Yon and M. Sznycer, "A Phoenician Victory Trophy at Kition," *RDAC* (1992) 157–65, pl. 51.

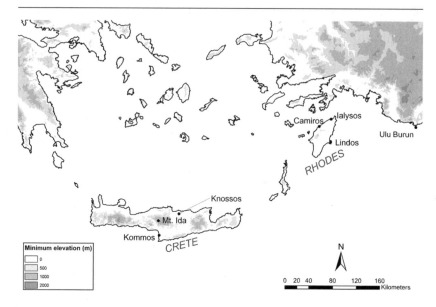

Map 6. Crete and Rhodes (produced by Christopher Brinker).

The intense contacts of Tyrians and Tyrian colonials with Amathus and
Palaepaphos between the eleventh and the late ninth or early eighth centuries and their serious abatement from the seventh century onward were
due partly to political changes in Cyprus (notably the establishment of a
confederation of kingdoms by the end of the eighth century and the ter-
mination of Limassol's colonial status) and partly to world events and a
change in Tyrian interests. For the Tyrians, almost as much as for the Sidonians, contact with Greeks was a compass and impetus. When the Greeks
stopped investing in Cyprus, and when Cyprus settled into a plodding self-
determination and the development of its indigenous culture, the Tyrians
studied the charts and traditions of the Myceneans and Greeks who had
settled in Cyprus and became more and more confident about exploring
the West.

One of the first stages in their western progress was Kommos in southern Crete. There is a small Phoenician shrine and associated with it some
ninth- and early eighth-century Phoenician pottery, mainly transport and
storage jars, the best parallels of which are from Tyre and its mainland
possessions but also a few jugs with parallels from Palaepaphos and Amathus.[256] The shrine was maintained through the ninth and into the eighth
century and was contemporaneous with the floruit of these settlements
in Cyprus. It was small, about 8 × 5 meters, with a flat roof, open to the
east, and with benches along the north and south walls and a hearth in

---

256. P. M. Bikai, "Phoenician Ceramics from the Greek Sanctuary," in *Kommos IV: The Greek
Sanctuary, Part 1* (ed. J. W. Shaw and M. C. Shaw; Princeton: Princeton University Press, 2000)
302–12; N. Kourou, "Phoenician Presence in Early Iron Age Crete Reconsidered," *Actas* 4, 3.1067–
81, esp. pp. 1067–69.

the center. In its design, it could have been a formal meeting hall such as would have been suitable for a group of merchants belonging to a *marzeaḥ* or symposium, rather than a sanctuary or a shrine established for a larger settled community.

These symposia were fraternal clubs, dedicated to a patron God, comprising a limited number of members, who contributed to the common purse and who gathered to drink wine, tell stories, and recite poetry in memory of their deceased companions. The Kommos hall, in fact, was only large enough for a few people, had jars and jugs that would have been residues of their festivities, and featured between the west wall and the hearth an aniconic representation of its patron God. The figure consisted of three short, stone pillars (the pillar in the center slightly taller than the others) set into a stone base.[257] These standing stones or baetyls, appropriately enough for a social club especially devoted to the memory of its forebears and forerunners, traditionally were memorials to the spirits of the dead and in Syrian circles were associated with the God Bethel (baetyl, *bêt-ʾel*, "Home of the God"), an ineffable spiritual presence. In the tripartite form featured in the Kommos hall, however, they are peculiar to Tyrian burial practices and are found engraved on tombstones in their colonies in Sardinia and North Africa.[258] And so it is likely that Kommos, as also suggested by the small amount of Phoenician pottery and the limited-use building, was a port of call for Tyrians who were on their way, from Tyre or from a Tyrian community in Cyprus, to Sardinia and North Africa.

Kommos, as early as the fourteenth century, had contacts with Cyprus, Syria, Egypt, and the Levant, and by the thirteenth century it was a port on the trade routes between the East and the central Mediterranean and in particular Sardinia.[259] From the late thirteenth century, Sardinia also did a brisk business with Cyprus, importing copper, bronze axes and tripod stands, smithing tools, items for personal use such as mirrors, and other products shipped in large transport jars[260]—all of this in exchange

257. J. W. Shaw, "Phoenicians in Southern Crete," *AJA* 93 (1989) 165–83; idem, "Der phönizischen Schrein in Kommos auf Kreta (ca. 800 v. Chr.)," *Archäologische Studien in Kontaktzonen der antiken Welt* (ed. R. Rolle and K. Schmidt; Göttingen: Vandenhoeck & Ruprecht, 1998) 93–104; idem, "The Phoenician Shrine, ca. 800 B.C., at Kommos in Crete," *Actas* 4, 3.1107–19.

258. A. M. Bisi, *Le stele Puniche* (Studi Semitici 27; Rome: Università di Roma, 1967) 163, pls. 49, 54.

259. L. V. Watrous, P. M. Day, and R. E. Jones, "The Sardinian Pottery from the Late Bronze Age Site of Kommos in Crete: Description, Chemical and Petrographic Analysis and Historical Context," in *Sardinian and Aegean Chronology: Towards the Resolution of Relative and Absolute Dating in the Mediterranean* (ed. M. S. Balmuth and R. H. Tykot; Studies in Sardinian Archaeology 5; Oxford: Oxbow, 1998) 337–40.

260. A. M. Bisi, "Le rôle de Chypre dans la civilisation phénicienne d'Occident: État de la question et essai de synthèse," in *Acts of the International Archaeological Symposium "Cyprus between the Orient and the Occident"* (ed. V. Karageorghis; Nicosia: Department of Antiquities, 1986) 341–50; L. Vagnetti, "Cypriot Elements beyond the Aegean in the Bronze Age," in ibid., 201–16; idem and F. Lo Schiavo, "Late Bronze Age Long Distance Trade in the Mediterranean: The Role of Cyprus," *ESC*, 217–43; V. Karageorghis, "Le commerce chypriote avec l'Occident au Bronze Recent: quelques nouvelles découvertes," *CRAIBL* (1993) 577–88; F. Lo. Schiavo, "Cyprus and Sardinia in the Mediterranean Trade Routes toward the West, in *Proceedings of the International Symposium "Cyprus and the Sea"* (ed. V. Karageorghis and D. Michaelides; Nicosia: University of Cyprus, 1995) 45–59; D. Ridgway, "Relations between Cyprus and the West in the Precolonial

Fig. 2.7. Nora Inscription.
Cagliari, Museo Archeo-
logico Nazionale 5998.

for iron, most likely, and agricultural products, pickled fish, and other
specialty foods. It is unexceptional, therefore, that by the eleventh century, when Phoenicians began to deal with the West, they should show up
in Sardinia before they ever meant to stay, and bring home some Sardinian mementos. [261]

Period," in *The Western Greeks: Classical Civilization in the Western Mediterranean* (ed. G. Publiese
Carratelli; London: Thames & Hudson, 1996) 117–20.

261. P. Bartoloni, "Protocolonizzazione fenicia in Sardegna," in *Sardinian and Aegean Chronology: Towards the Resolution of Relative and Absolute Dating in the Mediterranean* (ed. M. S. Balmuth and R. H. Tykot; Studies in Sardinian Archaeology 5; Oxford: Oxbow, 1998) 341–45.

There is a late ninth-century fragmentary inscription from Bosa in northwestern Sardinia of which only four letters are preserved.[262] This is a region that was later frequented by Sidonians, but someone on one of the first ships to land there considered the region to merit a record of the ship's exploits. This sheer sense of adventure and amazement explains why a Sidonian jeweler, who is buried in an exceedingly rich grave at Knossos in Crete, thought it entirely appropriate to take a Sardinian pitcher (an *askos*) with him when he died.[263] Another contemporary inscription (see fig. 2.7) from Nora in southern Sardinia is a carefully cadenced dedication by the captain and crew of a ship who, when caught in a storm on their way from Tarshish, found safe haven in Sardinia:[264]

btršš wgrš h'	From Tarshish, when he was driven
bšrdn šlm h'	in Sardinia, he made thank offerings,
šlm ṣb'	its crew made thank offerings,
mlktn bn šbn ngd	Malkuton, son of Subon, its captain,
lpmy	to Pumay.

The text is literary, original, and unique. It begins with a circumstantial phrase ("from Tarshish") that is resumed by a clause beginning with "and" or "when." The first two clauses are balanced, with the same parts of speech in the same word order, and the third clause is elliptical—"in Sardinia" is omitted—and parallel to the second. The last two phrases are mostly proper names: the second-last identifies the subject ("he," *hû'*) of the first two clauses, and "its captain" is anticipated by "its crew" in the third clause; the last phrase is the indirect object of the second and third clauses ("made thank offerings . . . to Pumay"). The text was inscribed on a slab of local limestone that tapers a little toward the top and was fitted with a tenon for insertion into a base so that it could be displayed. It is laconic, as if from the ship's log, and poetic; formal but with the immediacy of direct discourse, and unique among Phoenician display or dedicatory inscriptions.

The God Pumay, whose name occurs here for the first time, is known only in Cyprus and among Cypriot Phoenicians who continued to live on the island or traveled west to Carthage. The ship sailed from southwestern Cyprus to Tarsus in Cilicia, for iron perhaps, then via Crete to its destination in western Sardinia or southern Spain, when it encountered one of the legendary storms of the voyages to Tarshish. Sardinia was not a chance landfall, because the region of Nora on the Bay of Cagliari was well known to Tyrian sailors, who had visited the place as early as the eleventh century and left an inscription that, like the later steles, may have told of their troubles and recorded the name of the ship's captain.[265] Of particular interest with regard to these inscriptions is the fact that they demonstrate the literacy of the captains and crews—more than just the arithmetic and wit

---

262. *CIS* 162.

263. L. Vagnetti, "A Sardinian Askos from Crete," *ABSA* 84 (1989) 355–60, pl. 52.

264. B. Zuckerman, "The Nora Puzzle," *Maarav* 7 (1991) 269–301; A. J. Frendo, "The Particles *beth* and *waw* and the Periodic Structure of the Nora Stone Inscription," *PEQ* 128 (1996) 8–11.

265. F. M. Cross, "The Oldest Phoenician Inscription from Sardinia: The Fragmentary Stele from Nora," in *"Working with No Data": Semitic and Egyptian Studies Presented to Thomas O. Lambdin* (ed. D. M. Golomb; Winona Lake, IN: Eisenbrauns, 1987) 65–74.

expected of merchants and traders—and that they were meant for display, not for a local population unable to read them or for Phoenician colonists of whom there is no contemporary trace, but for Phoenician ships that anchored in these ports on a regular schedule of voyages to the West.[266]

Conclusion

Phoenicians from Tyre came early to southwestern Cyprus. They came with the Greeks, chiefly Euboeans (or perhaps specifically Euboeans from Chalcis) who met them at home on the mainland and in Cyprus. They sold their precious goods and bought Cypriot raw materials. Their heyday lasted through the ninth and into the early eighth century, during their colonial period and before they were absorbed into the commonality of Cypriot living. With their goods they brought education and a better way of life, a respect for antiquity and tradition, a delight in novelty, eclectic tastes in religion and art, and a sense of individuality. What they learned in Cyprus they took to the West.

Lapethos and Northern Cyprus

Byblos, in pursuing its commerce with Minoan Crete, was also in contact with Lapethos on the northern coast of Cyprus early in the second millennium.[267] There was a Byblian quarter in the town, and in the fifth and fourth centuries kings with Phoenician names appeared in a dynasty dominated by kings with Greek names. This pattern of settlement and assimilation was not unusual where Byblians went in northern Cyprus, but their interests in this part of the island were a few permanent ports of call on their routes to Crete, the Cyclades, and eventually to Italy.

The Phoenician inscriptions that are evidence for the Byblian quarter in the town are from Larnaka-tis-Lapethou, inland from Lapethos, in the Mesaoria Plain beyond the Kyrenia Range. The link between Lapethos and Italy is a sixth-century Phoenician inscription from Pyrgi that is in the dialect of Lapethos and that refers to a ritual originating in Byblos and known from the earliest of the Larnaka texts.

The earliest inscription from Larnaka, from the middle of the fourth century, records the votive offerings to Melqart in Larnaka and in the temples of Osiris and Astarte in Lapethos.[268] The offerings were made by a

---

266. There is no evidence, apart from the inscriptions, for Phoenicians at Nora or anywhere else in Sardinia before the eighth century B.C.E.: S. Moscati, P. Bartoloni, and S. F. Bondi, *La penetrazione fenicia e punica in Sardegna: Trent'anni dopo* (Atti della Accademia Nazionale dei Lincei: Classe di scienze morali, storiche e filologiche. Memorie 9/9/1, Rome, 1997); S. F. Bondi, "Riflessioni su Nora fenicia," in *Archäologische Studien in Kontaktzonen der antiken Welt* (ed. R. Rolle and K. Schmidt; Göttingen: Vandenhoeck & Ruprecht, 1998) 343–51.

267. Middle Bronze I (2000–1900 B.C.E.) Byblian daggers have been found in graves at Lapethos and in Minoan sites: K. Branigan, "Byblite Daggers in Cyprus and Crete," *AJA* 71 (1966) 123–26.

268. A. M. Honeyman, "Larnax tes Lapethou: A Third Phoenician Inscription," *Mus* 51 (1938) 285–98, pl. 6; J. C. Greenfield, *"Larnax tes Lapethou III* Revisited," in *Phoenicia and the East Mediterranean in the First Millennium B.C.* (ed. E. Lipiński; Studia Phoenicia 5; Louvain: Peeters, 1987) 391–401; M. Sznycer, "Nouvelle lecture d'un mot à la première ligne de l'inscription phénicienne de Larnaca-tis-Lapethou conservée au musée de Nicosie," *RDAC* (1988) part 2, 59–61, pl. 17.

Phoenician with a Greek name and Phoenician ancestry, Paramos, the son of Gerʿaštart, an officiant (*mqm ʾlm*) in the Temple of Melqart in Larnaka, and the prefect (*ha-ṣawwuʿ*) of Lapethos. The list starts with the most recent offering and then continues with the other offerings in chronological order. The most recent, the fifth and last, was the offering of a bronze statue of himself to Melqart in Larnaka in the sixteenth year of Praxippos, the son of Demonicus, as a memorial to himself during his lifetime and for the well-being of his offspring. The earliest offering, which is mentioned next, was a set of six silver goblets offered to Melqart in the month of Matton in the third year of Barikšamš, king of Lapethos. The next offering was a gold lamp presented to the Temple of Osiris in Lapethos in the month of Kiror in the same year. The third was a bronze statue of his father presented to the Temple of Astarte in Lapethos in the fifteenth year of Praxippos, in a month the name of which is lost. The fourth, in another month of the same year, was some gold object presented to Astarte. The inscription ends with a reference to "the Gods of Byblos who are in Lapethos."

From this inscription and from the evidence of the coins, it is possible to list the kings of the dynasty of Lapethos in the fifth and fourth centuries. In the fifth century, the kings were Demonicus I, Ṣidqimilk, Hipponicus, and Androcles: only the second had a Phoenician name, and none was mentioned in the list of offerings. In the fourth century, Barikšamš was succeeded by Demonicus II, by Praxippos I, who reigned at least 16 years, and by Praxippos II, who was deposed in 313 B.C.E. There may have been an irregularity in the succession of Demonicus II, because the inscription seems to insist on his legitimacy by referring to him as "King Demonicus, the king, king of Lapethos" (*mlk . dmwnks mlk . mlk . lpš*). No offerings were made during his reign but only in the third year of his predecessor, Barikšamš, and in the 15th and 16th years of his son Praxippos I. A particular interest of the list is that these kings, of whom only two had Phoenician names, belonged to a Phoenician family that had assimilated to the local population and taken Greek names.

The second inscription, from the end of the fourth century, is a Phoenician-Greek bilingual.[269] It marks the dedication of an altar to ʿAnat and to the Lord of Kings, Ptolemy, by a Phoenician, Baʿalšillem, son of Sasmay, who in the Greek version is called Praxidemos, the son of Sesmaos. The usual wish (*agathe tuche*) that concludes the Greek text, in turn, is rendered in Phoenician as "Good Luck" (*lmzl nʿm*). ʿAnat, the adolescent sister of the youthful Baʿal in the Ugaritic epic version of his search for power and life, is known in these later times only at Byblos and among Byblians. In this inscription, her physicality is praised, and she is called exactly that, "ʿAnat, the Power of Life" (*maʿoz ḥayyim*), while her Greek counterpart, in her pairing with Ptolemy I Soter, plays her role politically and militarily as "Athena, Deliverance, Victory" (*Athena Soteira Nikē*).

The third inscription[270] follows the pattern of the earliest in listing the last offering first and then the others in chronological order. The last was

269. *CIS* 95; *KAI* 42; G. M. Lee, "On a Phoenician Bilingual Inscription at Larnax, Lapethos," *PEQ* 101 (1969) 122.
270. *KAI* 43; cf. H. Volkmann, "Der Herrschaft der Ptolemäer in phönikischen Inschriften und sein Beitrag zur Hellenisierung von Kypros," *Historia* 5 (1956) 448–55; A. van den Branden,

made in the 11th year of the Lord of Kings, Ptolemy II, son of the Lord
of Kings, Ptolemy, which was the 33rd year of the people of Lapethos, or
275 B.C.E. It was a statue of the dedicator—"This likeness is a statue of me"
(*hsml z mš ʾnk*)*:* Yatonbaʿal, the son of Gerʿaštart, grandson of ʿAbdʿaštart,
great-grandson of Gerʿaštart, great-great-grandson of ʿAbdʾosiris, of the line
of Šallum, which he presented in the Temple of Melqart in Lapethos. He,
his father, his grandfather, and his great-grandfather all had the title *rb ʾrṣ*,
"Chief of the District [of Lapethos]"; Šallum, the progenitor of the family,
had the title *pd krml*, "Restorer of the Cultivated Land [of Lapethos]"; and
the priest in the 11th year of Ptolemy had all three titles: Priest, Chief of the
District, and Restorer of the Cultivated Land.

The earliest offering, mentioned next, was a bronze bust of his father,
Gerʿaštart, presented by Yatonbaʿal in the 4th year of Ptolemy II (281 B.C.E.).
The second, in his 5th year (280 B.C.E.), made by Yatonbaʿal when his father was still alive, consisted of altars and of sacrificial animals from his
ranch in Larnaka (*gbl šd nrnk*, "property of the plains of Larnaka"), which
were to be offered on New Moons and Full Moons in perpetuity, as in the
past, in accordance with the bronze plaques that he inscribed and nailed
to the wall, for himself and for his children, and for Ptolemy and his wife
and his household. On the same day, Yatonbaʿal made his third offering,
a burial chest (*ʾlt*) for Melqart, lined with silver, in the hope that he and
his offspring would receive honor and happiness and be remembered by
Melqart.

It is likely that Yatonbaʿal's great-great-grandfather, Gerʿaštart the son
of Šallum, was the same Gerʿaštart, the father of Paramos, who according to the first inscription was an official (*mqm ʾlm*) of the Temple of Melqart in Larnaka. It is not surprising, therefore, that when the latest offering
was made in the 33rd year of the people of Lapethos, the priest who was
appointed by Ptolemy was ʿAbdʿaštart "Chief of the District, Restorer of
the Cultivated Land" (*rb ʾrṣ pd krml*), the great-great-grandson of the first
Gerʿaštart, son of the later Gerʿaštart, and brother of Yatonbaʿal, whose
offerings are recorded in the inscription. The same family, consequently,
would have had priestly and political power in the town of Lapethos and
in its possessions in Larnaka for at least six generations, from the end of the
fifth century until the beginning of the third, during the reigns of the kings
of the Phoenician dynasty and also under the Ptolemies.

The dialect of these inscriptions is distinctive in Cyprus,[271] and the attitude and cults they describe, in conjunction with their explicit mention
of the Gods of Byblos, clearly link the Phoenician settlement at Lapethos to
Byblos. The dialectal differences are: the demonstrative pronoun is *z* (*bšt z*,
"in this year"), as at Byblos, and not *ʾz*, as elsewhere in Cyprus; the third-
masculine-singular pronominal suffix is *-w* (*wlʾštw* "and for his wife"), as
in the dialect of Byblos, and not *-y*, as usual in Cyprus and elsewhere; the
first-singular pronoun is used pleonastically in the nominative (*ytt ʾnk prm*,

"Titoli Tolemaici: 'Sa Ra,' *ṣmh ṣdq* e *anatolen dikian*," *Bibbia e Oriente* 6 (1964) 60–72; idem,
"L'inscription phénicienne de Larnax Lapethou II," *OrAnt* 3 (1964) 245–60; W. Huss, "Der 'König
der Könige' und der 'Herr der Könige'," *ZDPV* 93 (1977) 131–40; *TSSI* 3, 134–41 (#36).
    271. W. R. Lane, "The Phoenician Dialect of Larnax tes Lapethou," *BASOR* 194 (1969) 39–44.

"I gave, I, Paramos") and genitive (*hsml z mš 'nk*, "This likeness is my statue, of me"), as at Byblos; the genitive is expressed periphrastically by a relative clause instead of by the construct state or by a pronominal suffix (*l'dny*, "of my Lord," and also *l'dn 'š ly*, "of the Lord who is mine"; *qb'm šl ksp*, "cups that are of silver"); the preposition *b-* ("in, during") is written with a prosthetic *'alep* (*'b-*); the initial /L/ in "Larnaka" is written /N/; the numeral "ten" is written with *šin* (*'šrt*) instead of *samek*, and the final sibilant of the name "Ptolemy" is also transcribed as *šin* (*ptlmyš*) instead of *samek*.

The cults are concerned with life, the physical appearance of the living, and the worship of Gods who die and return to life. In the earliest inscription, Paramos offers to Melqart in Larnaka a bronze statue of himself as a memorial among the living, to Osiris in Lapethos a gold lamp, and to Astarte in Lapethos a bronze statue of his father as a memorial. Melqart, originally the God of Tyre and eventually the God of all Phoenician colonists, was the divinized king of the Terrestrial and Transcendental City, who died by fire and lived again in the flames of regeneration: Paramos held the office of "Raiser of the God" (*mqm 'lm*), who officiated at the celebration of this rite, and Yatonba'al made a silver-lined casket in which the God symbolically reposed before he was raised. Osiris, the Egyptian Adonis, was the God who died and was buried and who, mourned by Astarte, came back to life on the third day: the lamp of Osiris symbolized the continuity and regular renewal of his life, just as David's "lamp" in Jerusalem is the symbol of the perpetuity of his dynasty through his sons (1 Kgs 11:36, 15:4; 2 Kgs 8:19; Ps 132:17).

The second inscription is a dedication to 'Anat, the sister of the Ba'al who dies, and the vanquisher of the Death that overcomes him. The third inscription records gifts for the Temple of Melqart that Yatonba'al made of a statue of himself and of a bust of his father, while each was still alive, and of herds of cattle to supply the burnt offerings on the festivals of the New Moon and the Full Moon for his life and for the life of his offspring. The religious attitudes, cults, and divinities of Lapethos, like its dialect, are not typically Cypriot[272] but are vestiges obscured by Phoenician syncretism (now the liturgy of Adonis is celebrated in honor of Melqart) and by adaptation to Greek culture of a much earlier Byblian settlement in the town.

These cults of the living and dying God, especially of Adonis, are attested in other Byblian inscriptions. There is a mid-seventh-century dedicatory inscription on an ivory box (see fig. 1.4 in chap. 1 above) that alludes to the symbolic burial of the God: "This coffin [*'rn*] 'Amotba'al, daughter of Pat'isis, servant of Adonis [*'dnn*, lit., 'Our Lord'] gave as a gift to Astarte, her Mistress. May she bless her. In his days, behold, Adonis himself lay in state in it" (*bymy 'dnn [h]' bn ysd*). The ivory box is small (5 × 11 centimeters) and represents the chest or coffin (which is the usual meaning of the word *'arôn*) in which Adonis lay in state for the three days of his festival, the period referred to in the inscription as "his days."[273]

272. M. Yon and A. Caubet, "Un culte populaire de la grande déesse à Lapithos," *RDAC* (1988) part 2, pp. 1–16.

273. M. Stol, "Greek *deikterion*: The Lying-in-State of Adonis," in *Funerary Symbols and Religion* (ed. J. H. Kamstra, H. Milde, and K. Wagtendonk; Kampen: Kok, 1988) 127–28.

Astarte, as at Lapethos in the syncretistic cult of Adonis-as-Melqart, is the God's Phoenician Demeter, his lover in the land of the living, whose role in the liturgy was played by ʾAmotbaʿal, who identifies herself as the *ʾamot*, "handmaiden," "mistress," or "consort" of Adonis. The lying-in-state, as is evident from other Byblian funerary inscriptions, is the preamble to the renewal of life. The fifth-century inscription of ʾUrimilk, king of Byblos, makes a point of saying that his bones are lying in his coffin,[274] whereas a contemporary Sidonian inscription is satisfied to say that the king is lying in his coffin. The tomb inscription of his son Yahwimilk describes him lying in his coffin gathered in myrrh and bdellium, recalls his former splendor when he walked among the great clothed in purple, and invokes a curse on anyone who would dare disturb "my mouldering bones."[275]

The funerary inscription of Batnoʿam, the mother of ʿOzîbaʿal, who was king of Byblos in the fourth century, describes her lying in her coffin dressed in her royal robes and wearing a tiara and a gold mask, according to the custom among the queen mothers. A burial jar dating to the seventh century has an inscription in the Byblian dialect describing its contents as the bones of a priestess of Astarte that lay scattered until they were gathered together for her by ʾIttobaʿal, her son, or more likely her husband.[276] This concern for physical appearances in life and in death is unique to Byblos and is derived from belief in a personal regeneration, the paradigm and apotheosis of which is the cult of Adonis.

This cult, whose rituals proclaimed the death and burial of the God and expressions of Astarte's love for him, is also described in a late sixth-century Phoenician-Etruscan bilingual inscription from Pyrgi, near Rome, in Italy.[277] The Phoenician text, written on a gold sheet, is in a colonial variant of the Byblian dialect of Lapethos. The demonstrative pronoun is *ʾz*, unlike in Lapethos, but as usual in Cyprus. The preposition *b-*, "in, within," is written with a prosthetic ʾalep (*ʾb-*). The third-masculine-singular pronominal suffix is *-w* (*wbntw*).[278] The last date, the building of a sanctuary for Astarte in the month of *zibaḥšamš*, which was the immediate occasion for the inscription, is mentioned first and then the fact that Astarte in the preceding month, *kiror*, had suggested that it be built.[279] The text shifts from third-person singular in the first half to first-person singular in the second

274. *KAI* 9.
275. F. M. Cross, "A Recently Published Phoenician Inscription of the Persian Period from Byblos," *IEJ* 29 (1979) 40–44.
276. É. Puech, "Un cratère phénicien inscrit: Rites et croyances," *Transeu* 8 (1994) 47–73, pls. 6–11. The inscription reads: *qlb grtmlk kht ʿštrt ḥr ʿṣmm ʾš yrḥqn ʾtbʿ yʿnw*, "Jar for Girtmilk, priestess of Syrian Astarte. The bones that were scattered ʾIttobaʿal gathered together for her."
277. G. N. Knoppers, "'The God in His Temple': The Phoenician Text from Pyrgi as a Funerary Inscription," *JNES* 51 (1992) 105–20; P. C. Schmitz, "The Phoenician Text from the Etruscan Sanctuary at Pyrgi," *JAOS* 115 (1995) 559–75.
278. W. Röllig, "Akkadisch *tuʾum*, *diʾum*, phönizisch *tw*, aramäisch *twn*: Versuch einer Klarung," in *Alle soglie della classicità. Il Mediterraneo tra tradizione e innovazione: Studi in onore di Sabatino Moscati* (ed. E. Acquaro; 3 vols.; Pisa: Istituti Editoriale e Poligrafici, 1996) 3.1203–7.
279. R. Stieglitz, "The Phoenician-Punic Menology," in *Boundaries of the Ancient Near Eastern World: A Tribute to Cyrus H. Gordon* (ed. M. Lubetski, C. Gottlieb, and S. Keller; JSOTSup 273; Sheffield: Sheffield Academic Press, 1998) 211–21; idem, "The Phoenician-Punic Calendar," *Actas* 4, 2.691–95.

half, and this change of person is common in Byblian inscriptions. In the word *m'š*, interpreted as "dissolve, slip away," *šin* stands for etymological *samek*. The inscription reads:

> This is the shrine, for Lady Astarte, that Thefarie Velianas, king of Kaiseriya, made and offered in the month Zibaḥšamš as an offering in the house. And I built it, because Astarte was desirous of me, in the third year of my reign, in the month Kiror, on the day of the burial of the God. The years may dissolve, but of the God in my house may the years be as the stars of El.

The first section of the inscription, a nominal construction with subordinate verbal clauses, tells of the making of a cella for Astarte in an already established house, or temple, and identifies the time, the place, and the donor. The second section, consisting of a verbal clause ("And I built it . . .") modified by a subordinate verbal clause and three adverbial phrases alludes to the king as the amorous partner of the Goddess in the rituals surrounding the death, burial, and resurrection of Adonis. In other inscriptions, the lover is explicitly identified as "fiancé of Astarte" or of "Astronoe," her substitute (*mtrḥ ʿštrny*).

The last section, which is composed of a subordinate modal clause and a modal nominal construction, proclaims the king's belief in the God's perpetual rejuvenation in the liturgies of the royal temple, which reflect the eternal cycle of nature. The God dies in the heat of summer, in the month of "Sacrifice-to-the-Sun," and is buried. A month or more in advance, in the month of "Rejuvenation," his lover, Astarte, invites him to be her partner, her betrothed, and play the part of the God as he enters his new life. He is her bridegroom, and she is played by Astronoe, by a woman like ʾAmotbaʿal, who becomes Astarte for the occasion. The resurrection is not described—it never is—but is the subject of belief.

The Byblians who were at Caere and who were responsible for the composition and the carving of this inscription on gold sheets[280] and who may have been employed in the building of the Temple of Adonis and the more recent cella of Astarte seem to have been fully integrated into the local society. Their ties to Cyprus, specifically to the Byblian colony at Lapethos, seem certain on the evidence of a common dialect, literary tradition, and system of belief. The syntax of this inscription, especially its archaic modal expressions,[281] suggest that the people of Lapethos had come from Byblos

---

280. The script is elegant and written in a sure hand and must be attributed to a skilled and practiced writer, Byblian presumably, but possibly Etruscan, who could write both the Phoenician and the Etruscan versions. The gold sheets, similarly, were prepared by a Byblian goldsmith or perhaps by a local artist who had been trained by Byblian teachers: see F. Prayon, "Phöniker und Etrusker: Zur Goldlaminierung in der frühetruskischen Kunst," in *Archäologische Studien in Kontaktzonen der antiken Welt* (ed. R. Rolle and K. Schmidt; Göttingen: Vandenhoeck & Ruprecht, 1998) 329–41.

281. The first archaism is in the clause *wšnt lm'š*, "the years may dissolve / slip away," which is analyzed as the particle *lu* with the imperfect (*ym'š*), a construction known from Akkadian, Old Aramaic, Israelite Hebrew, and Punic (*CIS* 3784:1, 4937:3–4, 5510:2–3). The second archaism is the use of enclitic *mem* and especially its use in a bound form and with the definite article (*hkkbm ʾl*, "the stars of ʾEl"). The construction is known from Ugaritic and from Biblical Hebrew but is not attested in any other Phoenician text: see H. D. Hummel, "Enclitic *mem* in Early Northwest Semitic, Especially Hebrew," *JBL* 76 (1957) 85–107; J. A. Emerton, "Are There Examples of Enclitic

in the fairly distant past, that they remained aloof from the Phoenician and Cypriot mainstreams, and that some of them came to Etruria perhaps as early as Etruscan migrations from Asia Minor, or in the early eighth century with the Euboeans and the Sidonians who settled at that time in Pithekoussai.

The example of Lapethos, where minimal traces of very early Byblian presence combine with evidence from the Persian and Hellenistic periods that Byblians had been there long enough to be integrated into the local society can be applied to all of northern Cyprus. There are Late Bronze sites that the Byblians may have reached, and there are later-first-millennium locations where it is clear that they had come and already gone. The local society was indigenous or Greek, and the evidence all points to religious and industrious people who were immune to foreigners and not susceptible to change. The newcomers could adapt and adjust, but they were jealous of their traditions and generally content to leave the people as they found them.

Two of the earlier sites seem to have been workers' settlements. Apliki, south of Morphou Bay, was founded in the fourteenth century and abandoned early in the twelfth. It seems to have been a residence for workers in the copper mines and to have lasted only as long as trade in this metal was possible or profitable. [282] Toumba tou Skourou, on the eastern shore of Morphou Bay was a pottery factory. Founded in the late seventeenth century, it flourished in the sixteenth and fifteenth centuries through trade with Egypt, Crete, and the Cyclades. It still made storage and transport jars in the thirteenth century and was still in contact with Crete, but it no longer produced many of the finer wares. It was abandoned early in the troubled twelfth century when business collapsed. [283]

A third settlement, at Maa-Palaeokastro, southwest of Morphou Bay and north of Paphos, was a fortified Achaean outpost of the late thirteenth and early twelfth century. [284] Its inhabitants were related to the Sea Peoples, their dealings were mainly with North Syria, specifically Ugarit, where some of these people lived for a time, and the outpost was abandoned when they moved on to Palestine. Canaanite storage jars from the central Levant may indicate that Byblians stopped off on their way to northern Cyprus and Crete. Northwestern Cyprus, therefore, may have had early contacts with Phoenicians from Byblos, but the contacts would have been random and without lasting effect.

---

mem in the Hebrew Bible?" in *Texts, Temples, and Traditions: A Tribute to Menahem Haran* (ed. M. V. Fox et al.; Winona Lake, IN: Eisenbrauns, 1996) 321–38.

282. J. Du Plat Taylor, "A Late Bronze Age Settlement at Apliki, Cyprus," *Antiquaries Journal* 33 (1952) 133–64.

283. E. D. T. Vermeule and F. Z. Wolsky, *Toumba tou Skourou: A Bronze Age Potters' Quarter on Morphou Bay in Cyprus* (Cambridge: Harvard University Museum of Fine Arts, 1990).

284. V. Karageorghis, "Western Cyprus at the Close of the Bronze Age," in *Western Cyprus: Connections* (ed. D. W. Rupp; Gothenburg: Åströms, 1987) 115–24; V. Karageorghis and M. Demas, *Excavations at Maa-Palaeokastro 1979–1986* (3 vols.; Nicosia: Department of Antiquities, 1988).

Phlamoudhi, about 50 kilometers east of Lapethos in northeastern Cyprus, was busy in the Middle Bronze Age (ca. 1700–1400 B.C.E.) and again beginning in the sixth century B.C.E. It was a poor farming community, isolated from the rest of Cyprus and the world, and was ignored by the Byblians who were concentrated further west. The settlement at Myrtou-Pigadhes,[285] about 5 kilometers west of Larnaka-tis-Lapethou, is unexcavated except for its sanctuary. It was built in the seventeenth century, completely remodeled in the late fourteenth century under Anatolian and North Syrian auspices, and destroyed in the twelfth, along with almost everything else in the region. Unlike the other sites, it revived in the Cypro-Geometric II–III periods (ca. 950–750 B.C.E.) and at that time, as is indicated by imported Black-on-Red and Red Slip wares, came in contact with Phoenicians, most likely with the Byblians who were well established by then at Lapethos.

The later sites in northwestern Cyprus came under Greek influence, and the evidence for a significant Phoenician presence, when it was not a product of Persian intervention, is limited to the region of Lapethos. From a place called Liveras, just east of Lapethos and west of Kyrenia, there is a late sixth-century Phoenician inscription on a fragment of a Cypriot transport jar with the name of the shipper or producer, "belonging to Timaos" (*ltmy*): what is of interest is that the name is Greek, following the tendency of the Byblians who lived in Lapethos, and that this particular grower sold his produce in the region.[286] Probably from the same region and illustrating its rampant cultural symbiosis is an early sixth-century inscription on a transport jar with the name of another producer with the excellent Byblian Phoenician name ʾAdonibaʿal (*lʾdnbʿl*).[287]

Soloi, on the southern shore of Morphou Bay, was one of the kingdoms that paid tribute to the Assyrians in the seventh century: the name of its king at that time, *e-re-e-su* in Assyrian, could be either Greek *Arētos*, "Desired," or more likely Phoenician ʾArish (*ʾrš*) with the same meaning, the term that the king of Pyrgi used to describe his relationship with Astarte and a very popular masculine and feminine (*ʾršt*) Phoenician personal name.[288] Although a tomb and a sanctuary in the vicinity of Soloi evince purely Greek influence, and the later coins bear Cypro-syllabic letters, and in general there is nothing to suggest Phoenician presence in the kingdom at any time, it is just possible that this king was in fact a Byblian and that the Phoenicians at Soloi totally assimilated to the Greek way of life.[289]

---

285. J. Du Plat Taylor, *Myrtou-Pigadhes: A Late Bronze Age Sanctuary in Cyprus* (Oxford: Ashmolean Museum, 1957).

286. *RPC* 96–97, pl. 10:1. The plate was published upside down, and the text was misread accordingly.

287. *RPC* 131–32, pls. 19:2 and 20:2.

288. E. Lipiński, "The Cypriot Vassals of Esarhaddon," in *Ah, Assyria . . . : Studies in Assyrian History and Ancient Near Eastern Historiography Presented to Hayim Tadmor* (ed. M. Cogan and I. Ephʿal; Jerusalem: Magnes, 1991) 58–64, esp. pp. 60–61.

289. *ICS* 220–22; J. Des Gagniers, "Les fouilles de l'Université Laval à Soloi," in *Archaeology in Cyprus 1960–1985* (ed. V. Karageorghis; Nicosia: Department of Antiquities, 1985) 256–61; A. Hermary, "Le sarcophage d'un prince de Soloi," *RDAC* (1987) 231–33; M. C. Loulloupis, "A Rural Cult-Place in the Soloi Area," *Cyprus and the East Mediterranean in the Iron Age* (ed. V. Tatton-Brown; London: British Museum, 1989) 68–83.

Vouni, about 5 kilometers to the west of Soloi, was founded in the Persian period and is notable for its palace and its Temple of Athena.[290] Two tombs contained a storage jar, each with a Phoenician inscription: on one, the inscription, dating to about the mid-seventh century, is almost erased but seems to indicate the contents and their weight; the other is inscribed "belonging to the king" (*lmlk*), indicating that it came from the royal stores, most likely at Lapethos.[291] Other tombs contained jars with Cypro-syllabic inscriptions, and one of these describes its contents as "Phoenician," presumably wine, and notes that the jar has been sealed with wax.[292]

At Marion, farther to the southwest of Soloi and Vouni on Chrysochou Bay, there were some Cypro-Geometric I (ca. 1050–900 B.C.E.) tombs, but most of the evidence is from a sanctuary and other finds of the Cypro-Archaic I–II periods (750–480 B.C.E.).[293] There are stone sculptures inspired by Athenian and East Greek models,[294] funerary monuments imitating Greek styles, terra-cottas, when not purely local, inspired by East Greek examples, and one of them simply copying Aphrodite and Eros from the frieze of the Parthenon in Athens.[295]

It was only in the fifth century, when pro-Persian Phoenician usurpers took the throne (499–449 B.C.E.), that products were marked with the names of their Phoenician purveyors, coins were inscribed with Phoenician letters, and a Cypro-syllabic inscription records the titulary of the first Phoenician king, whose father not surprisingly had a Greek name.[296] At Ayia Irini, on the east coast of Morphou Bay, not far from Myrtou-Pigadhes and about 15 kilometers from Larnaka-tis-Lapethou, there is evidence for earlier and deeply ingrained Phoenician influence.

---

290. F. G. Maier, "Palaces of Cypriot Kings," in *Cyprus and the East Mediterranean in the Iron Age* (ed. V. Tatton-Brown; London: British Museum, 1989) 16–27; G. R. H. Wright, *Ancient Building in Cyprus* (Leiden: Brill, 1992) 127–31.

291. *RPC* 86–88.

292. *ICS* #208.

293. E. Gjerstad, *The Swedish Cyprus Expedition: Finds and Results of the Excavatiion in Cyprus, 1927–1931, Volume 1* (Stockholm: Åströms, 1935) 181–459; W. A. P. Childs, "The Iron Age Kingdom of Marion," *BASOR* 308 (1997) 37–48; J. S. Smith, "Preliminary Comments on a Rural Cypro-Archaic Sanctuary in Polis-Peristeries," *BASOR* 308 (1997) 77–98.

294. W. A. P. Childs, "The Stone Sculpture of Marion: A Preliminary Assessment," in *Cypriote Stone Sculptures* (ed. F. Vandenabeele and R. Laffineur; Brussels: Vrije Universiteit Brussel / Liège: Université de Liège, 1991) 107–16, pls. 28–30.

295. E. Raptou, "Note sur les coûtumes funéraires de Marion à l'époque classique," *RDAC* (1997) 225–37.

N. Serwint, "An Aphrodite and Eros Statuette from Ancient Marion," *RDAC* (1993) 207–17, pls. 56–59; idem, "The Terracotta Sculpture from Marion," in *Cypriote Terracottas* (ed. F. Vandenabeele and R. Laffineur; Brussels: Vrije Universiteit Brussel / Liège: Université de Liège, 1991) 213–19, pls. 52–57; idem, "A Terracota Mold Series from Marion," *Archaeologia Cypria* 3 (1994) 75–85, pls. 16–22.

296. A jar is inscribed with the name "May-the-Sun-Confirm" (*lyknšmš*). The inscription on another is partly erased (. . .]*r bn lkys*) but notes the merchant's name and the name of his father, transliterated from Greek *lukios*, "The Lycian."

RPC 79–81, pl. 1:1–2.

T. B. Mitford, "Unpublished Syllabic Inscriptions of the Cyprus Museum," *Opuscula Atheniensia* 3 (1960) 177–210, esp. pp. 184–85; *ICS* 181–83, #168, pl. 25:1–3. The king's name is Sesmaos, syllabic *sa.sa.ma.o.se*, Phoenician "Sasmay" (*ssmy*), and his father's name is Doxandros (*to.ka.sa.to.ro*).

There are some Late Cypriot (1600–1400 B.C.E.) tombs, but the town was built only in the late twelfth century, perhaps by the people who had left Myrtou-Pigadhes, and a new phase began about the turn of the millennium when the open-air sanctuary was remodeled.[297] The town flourished in the seventh and sixth centuries but was abandoned by the early fifth century.[298] The sanctuary is best known for its many terra-cotta statues that were arranged by size in semicircular rows around a central altar.[299] Most of these ex-votos represent their donor, mainly men, and some of these appear to be Phoenicians, not the typical fine-featured men pictured in Tyrian art but fleshier, more "Syrian" or "Byblian" types, and Byblian interest in self-figuration, in a person's appearance before the Gods in life and death, would have prompted them to adopt the local Cypriot custom of presenting a personal likeness in the temple.[300]

The tombs contained Phoenician Black-on-Red and Red Slip pottery that certifies either Phoenician burials or Phoenician merchandise in local burials. In one of the tombs, from the mid-seventh century, an inscription on the wall, ʿAbdoʾ, son of Kmrb (ʿbdʾ bn kmrb), identifies the deceased, who had a good Byblian name. His father's unusual name, which is homophonous with the name of the Hurrian God Kumarbi, is not Phoenician.[301] Another inscription on a small jug from the end of the seventh century identifies its contents as 140 measures of oak apples (100 + 20 + 20 ʿpṣm), an astringent used for medicinal purposes and also for making dyes and ink. They were supplied by a merchant whose identity, "Belonging to Bodʾeshmun," is hidden in its abbreviation (lbʾ). Another inscription from the fourth century painted on an amphora identifies its contents as suet (mḥ) which, according to an early inscription from Cyprus, was a sacrificial ingredient.[302] All of this suggests that Phoenicians, likely Byblians from Lapethos and its jurisdiction, had settled among the Greek immigrants and indigenous people early in the first millennium, did business with them, joined them in their worship, and were buried with them in their graveyards.

---

297. P. E. Pecorella, *Le tombe della necropoli a mare di Ayia Irini "Paleokastro"* (Rome: Consiglio Nazionale delle Ricerche, 1977); L. Quilici, *La tomba dell'età del Bronzo Tardo dall'abitato di Paleokastro presso Ayia Irini* (Rome: Consiglio Nazionale delle Ricerche / Istituto per gli Studi Micenei ed Egeo-Anatolici, 1990; P. E. Pecorella and L. Rocchetti, "The Italian Archaeological Mission at Ayia Irini," in *Archaeology in Cyprus 1960–1985* (ed. V. Karageorghis; Nicosia: Department of Antiquities, 1985) 193–94.

298. E. Gjerstad, *The Swedish Cyprus Expedition: Finds and Results of the Excavations in Cyprus 1927–1931, Volume II* (Stockholm: Swedish Cyprus Expedition, 1935) 642–824; G. R. H. Wright, *Ancient Building in Cyprus* (Leiden: Brill, 1992) 119–21.

299. G. Ikosi, "The Terracottas from Ajia Irini: Techniques and Clays," *Acta Cypria* 3 (Jonsered: Åströms, 1992) 267–309.

300. J. B. Connelly, "Standing before One's God: Votive Sculpture and the Cypriot Religious Tradition," *BA* 52 (1989) 210–16; C. Beer, "Eastern Influence and Style: A Reconsideration of Some Terracottas of Cypriote Manufacture," in *Cypriote Terracottas* (ed. F. Vandenabeele and R. Laffineur; Brussels: Vrije Universiteit Brussel / Liège: Université de Liège, 1991) 77–85, pls. 16–18, esp. pp. 80–82.

301. M. G. Amadasi Guzzo, "L'iscrizione fenicia dalla tomba N. 43," in *Le tombe dei periodi geometrico ed arcaico della necropoli a mare di Ayia Irini "Paleokastro"* (ed. L. Rochetti; Rome: Consiglio Nazionale delle Ricerche—Istituto per gli Studi Micenei ed Egeo-Anatolici, 1978) 114–16.

302. *RPC* 94–96, pl. 9.

Much of the evidence for Byblians in northern Cyprus is indirect and circumstantial and constructed from disparate bits of data. They were concentrated in Lapethos and its immediate vicinity, and their colony there can be traced back at least to the tenth century. Their easy relations with the local Greek population and the few vestiges of their commercial involvement suggest that their reason for being there was to establish an emporium for goods that they brought from home and from mainland Syria, or produced in the fertile valley of Larnaka, and to set up an import and export business with Crete and the Dodecanese. They kept away from the Tyrians in the southwest part of the island, but fairly early on they traveled with Euboeans and Sidonians to Italy and later were associated with the Sidonians in the steel industry centered on Idalion.

Conclusion

Phoenicians traveled to Cyprus in the eleventh century, and some individuals stayed and settled among the Cypriots and Greeks. By the tenth century, there were groups of Phoenician artisans and merchants in the developing urban centers; and by the ninth century, colonies, communities, or urban quarters were established in the coastal cities. These flourished into the eighth century but, beginning in the seventh, began to be reabsorbed into the staid and traditional, and now increasingly Greek kingdoms. The colony disappeared, but the settlements survived and, once aligned with the Persians, persisted until that empire fell to the Greeks.

Sidonians settled at Kition in the southeast when this port succeeded Enkomi. They did not found a colony but became increasingly numerous and influential in a Cypriot town settled by Myceneans and Sea Peoples. They formed syndicates, built warehouses, established marketplaces, and did business with ships frequenting the port. Some of them moved to Idalion and probably to Tamassos. They, along with Byblian associates, bought and worked copper, bronze, and iron. Their own ships, ships from Euboea, Egypt, Crete, and the Syrian coast, imported tin, glass, faience, amber, Canaanite commodities, ceramics, precious metals, and ivory.

They exported skilled laborers and slaves, wood, textiles, tools, weapons, and implements—an assortment of goods, not unlike the cargo of the ship wrecked at Ulu Burun, that had been brought to the port for transshipment. The Sidonians may have included some merchants on official business, but they were predominantly individual entrepreneurs who married local women, adopted local styles, and in subsequent generations produced local imitations of Phoenician pottery. It was a recognizable community, in which the king of Sidon could seek refuge from the Assyrians at the end of the eighth century, but it was more basically an international port, an open city without formal ties to the mainland city, without any political pretensions or inland possessions, unabashedly an emporium and not a kingdom.

Byblians settled in northwestern Cyprus, principally (perhaps exclusively) at Lapethos on the coast and at Larnaka in the Mesaoria Plain. Their early presence in the region can be deduced from scattered ninth-century ceramic remains, from terra-cotta representations of them worshiping in the native shrine of Ayia Irini in the seventh century, from inscriptions, and from the almost complete assimilation of the Phoenician dynasty to Greek ways by the fifth and fourth centuries. Their inscriptions from Marion, Ayia Irini, Vouni, and other unidentified places in the region, as well as their installation in the fertile Mesaoria Plain suggest that many of these Byblians were in the wholesale grocery business, supplying towns in this part of the island with local and imported goods. The inscriptions from Lapethos and from Pyrgi in Italy indicate that they were sculptors, masons, goldsmiths, and coppersmiths. Lapethos gradually settled into being a faint but still proud trace of a once vibrant port on the sea lanes to Crete and the islands and eventually to Italy and the western Mediterranean.

Tyrians went to southwest Cyprus. They were there in the eleventh century, founded a colony at Limassol in the territory of Amathus in the ninth century, from there and from home settled at Palaepaphos, from there traveled to Crete and the West in the ninth century, and founded Carthage in North Africa by the end of the eighth. Their business was supplying expensive and exotic goods to the local Cypriot bankers, merchants, and craftsmen who could afford them, in exchange for basic commodities and raw materials that they could ship home or sell to the Greeks. After the eighth century, when Tyre took over the port and government at Kition, when Limassol was absorbed into the confederacy of Cypriot kingdoms, when its colonies in the western Mediterranean began to thrive, and when Tyrians, Greeks, and Cypriots had nothing new to learn from each other, Tyre lost interest in this part of the island. It was only under the Persian Empire that Tyrians in Cyprus became belligerent and exploitive and tried to manipulate the allegiances of the kingdoms that were drawn to the Athenian side. There were Tyrian usurpers at Salamis and at Paphos, and there was the Tyrian backed Demonicus II at Lapethos, where the newly established worship of Melqart in the guise of Adonis confirms the intrusion of Tyrian ideology and the determination to control political destiny. With Tyrian interests now focused on Kition, and this town reaffirming and insisting on its Greek and Cypriot heritage, it was no time at all until Tyre's influence on Cyprus dwindled into routine and vague recollection.

Cyprus for Phoenicians was the entrance to the Mediterranean world. This was mostly a Greek world, and at first this was its principal charm, as both people competed, learned from each other, and got along. But Cypriots were different. They were natural imitators, learning easily how to produce whatever they saw and liked, quickly making the original ideas and authentic goods superfluous or redundant. For the Byblians and Sidonians, who were amenable to change and to absorption into a common culture, this was an acceptable consummation. For the Tyrians, who preferred to remain aloof and creative, redundancy was the signal to move on to new challenges. For them, Cyprus became the impetus to explore and colonize the western Mediterranean.

Chapter 3

The Phoenician Exploration of the Mediterranean World: A Result of the Pax Assyriaca in the Eighth Century B.C.E.

The eighth century began the realization of the Orientalizing revolution.[1] This was a century of change in social structures, in religious beliefs, in ethnic awareness, in political alignments, in cultural exchange. Individuals stand out and are named in literature, arts and crafts, in business, politics, and in legal and theological reforms. A commonplace Mediterranean material culture emerges, inspired by international agreements and facilitated by a move from old blood to new class consciousness, from regional to urban awareness, from small inflexible markets to overseas competition. Exploration and adventure, far horizons and fortune filled the imagination. The revolution—with people everywhere alphabetized, discovering leisure and the good life—ended in the creation of the Mediterranean world.

The two centuries, from the eighth to the sixth, of the Orientalizing revolution shadowed the two centuries, from the ninth to the seventh, of the Neo-Assyrian Empire. Assyria imposed a world order, ideological and functional,[2] and by the end of the eighth century a semblance of world peace that enabled international conversation and cooperation. North and South Syrian countries and neighbors in Neo-Hittite and northern Anatolia formed alliances that failed in their main purpose of resisting Assyrian domination but succeeded, incidentally, in establishing deep allegiances and regional self-consciousness. Transjordanians acquired national identities and became the intermediaries of North and South Arabian civilization. Palestine, including both Judah and the Philistine states, flourished in a comprehensive system of stable relationships. The cities of Phoenicia and their associates in Cyprus were tributaries of the empire, engineers of its prosperity, and their network of affiliates in the western Mediterranean added to their mystique as purveyors of the good life. Countries that re-

---

1. W. Burkert, *The Orientalizing Revolution: Near Eastern Influence on Greek Culture in the Early Archaic Age* (trans. M. E. Pinder and W. Burkert; Cambridge: Harvard University Press, 1992).

2. Peter Machinist, "Assyrians on Assyria in the First Millennium B.C.," in *Anfänge politischen Denkens in der Antike: Die nahöstlichen Kulturen und die Griechen* (ed. K. Raaflaub and E. Müller-Luckner; Munich: Oldenbourg, 1993) 77–104.

sisted the Assyrian program disappeared into the provincial system, and those that wanted to maintain their traditional isolation or independence were given more malleable leaders, prodded by governors and garrisons. The revolution, as usual, rode on the back of indigenous peoples ready for change and willing to exchange ideas, skills, and materials for the vision of a new world.

The Mainland Phoenician Cities: Sidon and the Neo-Assyrian Empire

Tyre, Sidon, Byblos, and their mainland affiliates are mentioned in Assyrian annals and official correspondence, and their history can be pieced together from scattered archaeological records. The eighth century is most notable from the combined evidence for the gradual eclipse of Sidon and the correlative, but more abrupt, establishment of a Tyrian hegemony based on its interests in the western Mediterranean.

Sidon paid tribute to Assyria early in the eighth century, in the reign of Adad-nirari III (811–782 B.C.E.) but is not included in later lists and seems to have spent the latter part of the century in conflict with Assyria and in competition with Tyre. During the reign of Tiglath-pileser III (744–726 B.C.E.), Sidon was under the authority of an imperial administrator, Qurdi-Ashur-Lamur, whose job it was to maintain order in the city and good relations with the palace. Among his officials, there was a tax collector stationed in Sidon, and he himself was in command of a contingent of the army, which he could summon, as he did when the merchants refused to pay their taxes, to put down a riot in the city.[3] In another of his letters to the king, he reported that an Ionian raiding party landed at Samsimuruna (at that time a renegade town but later, after Sidon was captured by Sennacherib and decimated by Esarhaddon, a rogue kingdom)[4] but that his troops were able to drive it off before it could ransack the place or do much damage.[5] These Ionians,[6] from the Gulf of Iskenderum and coastal Cilicia, were constant allies of Sidon, and raids like this were directed against cities and districts whose alignment with Assyria threatened to undermine Sidonian interests.

---

3. H. W. F. Saggs, "The Nimrud Letters, 1952, Part II: Relations with the West," *Iraq* 17 (1955) 126–60, Letter XII, pp. 127–30, 149–51; Letter XIII, pp. 130–31, 151.

4. N. Naʾaman, "Province System and Settlement Pattern in Southern Syria and Palestine in the Neo-Assyrian Period," in *Neo-Assyrian Geography* (ed. M. Liverani; Rome: University of Rome "La Sapienza," 1995) 103–15, esp. p. 109. Samsimuruna, under Menahem (*minuḫim*), was included among the tributary kingdoms in Sennacherib's third year (701 B.C.E.) after Sidon was subjected and Luli was deposed and replaced by ʾIttobaʿal (*ANET* 287). Under ʾAbibaʿal, who succeeded Menahem in the time of Sennacherib (A. Baer, "Un cylindre d'offrande à Sennacherib," *RA* 54 [1960] 155–58), the kingdom lasted through the reign of Esarhaddon (680–669 B.C.E.) and into the reign of Ashurbanipal (668–633 B.C.E.), when Sidon had been eliminated (*ANET* 291, 294).

5. H. W. F. Saggs, "The Nimrud Letters, 1952, Part VI: The Death of Ukinzer; and Other Letters," *Iraq* 25 (1962) 70–84, esp. pp. 76–78.

6. J. A. Brinkman, "The Akkadian Words for 'Ionia' and 'Ionian'," in *Daidalikon: Studies in Memory of Raymond V. Schoder, S.J.* (ed. R. F. Sutton Jr.; Wauconda, IL: Bolchazy-Carducci, 1989) 53–71.

During the reign of Sargon II (721–704 B.C.E.), continued Ionian attacks included raids against the kingdoms of Que and Tyre.[7] By the end of the century, Sidon (as is clear in the list of places captured by Sennacherib in 701 B.C.E.) comprised not only the capital city and a few towns in its own territory but other cities and towns that earlier in the century had belonged to Tyre or were part of the Tyrian commercial network.[8]

The capital city, called "Greater Sidon" in Sennacherib's list,[9] was divided into three districts, to judge from later royal inscriptions: the port city (*ṣîdôn yam*, or *ṣîdôn 'areṣ yam*, "Sidon-by-the-Sea") with its several harbors; the settlements on the coastal plain between the river Damur to the north and the river Qasmiyye to the south (*ṣidon šadê*, "Mainland Sidon" or "Sidon-in-the-Fields"); and the citadel comprising the palace, temple, and government areas (*ṣîdôn mošel*, "Sidon-the-Capital"). South of the capital was the suburb "Lesser Sidon," situated at Tell el-Burak, by the coast on a very fertile plain near the water sources for which the tell is named and from which aqueducts led to Sidon and Sarepta.[10]

Inland from this place was Bit Zitti, in the hills, named for its olive orchards. Farther south on the coast, near the traditional border with Tyre at the Litani River was the industrial town of Sarepta, specializing in pottery,[11] notably storage and transport amphorae, fine perfume bottles, and unguent jars made by resident Cypriot potters, as well as Red Slip bowls and jugs that begin to appear in the western Mediterranean toward the end of the eighth century. The kingdom, in effect, was small, and the places important enough to deserve mention were those on which the capital depended for human resources; for supplies such as food, oil, and water; and for the containers in which they were shipped and stored.

The other towns farther south that were in the Tyrian orbit were of interest because they were ports or provided access to routes and resources that Sidon had lost when Israel, a reliable trading partner, was captured in 722 B.C.E. and turned into the Assyrian province of Samaria. Mahalab was a large fortified Tyrian city that was south of Sarepta and in Tyrian territory

---

7. J. Elayi and A. Cavigneaux, "Sargon II et les Ioniens," *OrAnt* 18 (1979) 59–75; A. Fuchs, *Die Inschriften Sargons II aus Khorsabad* (Göttingen: Cuvillier, 1994) 290 n. 39; R. Rollinger, "The Ancient Greeks and the Impact of the Ancient Near East: Textual Evidence and Historical Perspective (ca. 750–650 BC)," in *Melammu Symposia II. Mythology and Mythologies: Methodological Approaches to Intercultural Influences* (ed. R. M. Whiting; Helsinki: Neo-Assyrian Text Corpus Project, 2001) 233–64; idem, "Homer, Anatolien und die Levante: Die Frage der Beziehungen zu den östlichen Nachbarkulturen im Spiegel der Schriftlichen Quellen," in *Der Neue Streit um Troia: Eine Bilanz* (ed. C. Ulf; Munich: Beck, 2003) 330–48.

8. J. Elayi, "Les relations entre les cités phéniciennes et l'empire assyrien sous le règne de Sennachérib," *Sem* 35 (1985) 19–26.

9. This designation is known from the Annals of Sennacherib (*ANET* 287) and from a biblical battle account and boundary list, Josh 11:8, 19:28.

10. H. Sader, "Tell el Burak: An Unidentified City of Phoenician Sidon," in *ana šadî labnāni lū allik: Beiträge zu altorientalischen und mittelmeerischen Kulturen—Festschrift für Wolfgang Röllig* (ed. B. Pongratz-Leisten, H. Kühne, and P. Xella; Neukirchen-Vluyn: Neukirchener Verlag, 1997) 363–76; J. Kamlah and H. Sader, "Deutsch-libanesische Ausgrabungen auf *Tell el-Burak*, südlich von Sidon," *ZDPV* 120 (2004) 123–40.

11. R. B. Koehl, *Sarepta III: The Imported Bronze and Iron Age Wares from Area II, X* (Beirut: Librairie Orientale, 1985) 148; W. P. Anderson, *Sarepta I: The Late Bronze and Iron Age Strata of Area II, Y* (Beirut: Université Libanaise, 1988) 418–25.

below the Litani. It was taken by Tiglath-pileser III[12] when he put down the revolt in Syria and Israel (734–732 B.C.E.) that Tyre, with uncharacteristic neglect of its commercial interests, had been foolish enough to join. It was included by a biblical geographer in the territory assigned to the tribe of Asher, together with other towns on Sennacherib's list ('Akko and 'Achzib) and two inland sites (Aphek and Rehob [Tel Kabri]) that were Tyrian settlements.[13]

The next town on the list of captured cities is Ushu, now Tell Rachidiyeh, 4 kilometers south of Tyre, situated in a fertile plain between the sea and the hills. Control of the site, noted for its woods and abundant sources of water, had been a matter of dispute between Tyre and Sidon as far back as the fourteenth century,[14] and water and other natural resources may have still been the issue in the eighth century. It was in Tyrian territory, however, and authentically if not indisputably Tyrian; and Sidonian claims left no mark in the eighth-century Tyrian human and material remains excavated at the site.[15] The dead were cremated, as was usual in Tyrian burials; the ceramic assemblage is dominated by Cypriot and Euboean wares, as was the case at Tyre; there is the usual collection of gold jewelry and scarabs of Egyptian and Tyrian manufacture; the only item that may be intrusive and attributable to Sidonian presence is an iron sword that is like one from the Kerameikos cemetery in Athens.

The third place on the list is 'Achzib, and the last is 'Akko. These were the port towns of Tel Kabri and Tell Keisan, respectively. They both had long-standing relations with Tyre, and there is nothing to suggest that Sidonian interference at the end of the eighth century was anything more than an attempt to prevent Tyre from taking complete control of trade and commerce, in Cyprus first and then in the rest of the world, on behalf of the Assyrians.

In 701 B.C.E., when Sennacherib captured Sidon and its towns, the king of Sidon was Luli, the Assyrian and Sidonian form of an originally Phoenician name *ʾIluʾili, "El is my God," which is transliterated into Greek as *Elulaios.*[16] Luli was deposed by Sennacherib, replaced by Tobaʿl, and escaped to Cyprus, probably to Kition, where, as the Assyrian text says, he

---

12. H. Tadmor, *The Inscriptions of Tiglath-Pileser III, King of Assyria* (Jerusalem: Israel Academy of Sciences and Humanities, 1994) 177, 187; N. Naʾaman, "Tiglath-Pileser III's Campaigns against Tyre and Israel (734–732 B.C.E.)," *TA* 22 (1995) 268–78.

13. Judg 1:31. This list also has two town names, 'Aḥlab and Ḥelbâ, that correspond to *Maḥalab* in the text of Tiglath-pileser III and that may be variants of the same name.

14. W. L. Moran, ed., *The Amarna Letters* (Baltimore: Johns Hopkins University Press, 1992) 235, #148: the king of Tyre needs access to Ushu for water, wood, straw, and clay but is prevented by the king of Sidon.

15. *PhByb,* 42: Philo (*PE* 1.10.10–11) relates that Tyre was settled by Hypsouranios and his brother Ousoos, traces the lineage of Sidon to the former, and attributes to Ousoos the invention of ships, which were made from the abundant woods in the area.

C. Doumet and I. Kawkabani, "Les tombes de Rachidieh: Remarques sur les contacts internationaux et le commerce phénicien au VIIIe siècle av. J.C.," *Actes* 3, 1.379–95.

16. At this time, Phoenician regularly dropped initial syllables in proper names beginning with *ʾalep*: ʾIluʾili, in which each part of the name began with *ʾalep*, was pronounced Luli; similarly, his successor's name, ʾIttobaʿl, was simplified to Tobaʿl, and 'Ahiram, the name of the king of Tyre, was pronounced Hiram. The form Elulaios was used by Josephus, *Ant.* 9.283–84.

"disappeared forever."[17] Because Kition was a native Cypriot town that, at least from the ninth century on, was frequented by Sidonian metallurgists and merchants, it should have been a congenial spot for the king to retire, although perhaps a bit less hospitable once he had abandoned his city and his people when his policies provoked the Assyrian attack. But almost a decade earlier (707 B.C.E.) when the kings of Cyprus submitted to Sargon,[18] Kition became the Assyrian administrative center of the island and was turned over to Tyre, on whose ships the Assyrian king would have relied to achieve this stunning diplomatic coup, and on whose expanding markets the Cypriot kings more than likely would have been bargaining. Consequently, according to one of the Assyrian texts recording these events, Luli fled to Cyprus on a ship out of Tyre, the city in whose affairs he had meddled and that could only have been relieved by his exile and was perhaps satisfied by his ignominious defeat.

Luli's notoriety, the crossing of Tyrian and Sidonian paths during his reign, and the final destruction of Sidon left a few other traces in the ancient literary records. An oracle concerning Tyre attributed to Isaiah the prophet is interrupted twice to deal with Sidon, these two being what the text calls the maritime kingdoms and strongholds of Canaan, and both times it is to describe events as they are recounted in Assyrian texts.[19] Corresponding to Luli's flight is the taunt addressed to the capital city, the "Virgin Daughter," Sidon: "No longer exult, oppressed Virgin Daughter Sidon. Rise up, cross over to Kition—even there you will find no rest." The second time introduces a lament recited by the Sea for Sidon, the Fortress in the Sea ("I have not travailed, and I have not given birth, and I have not brought up young men, or raised young girls"), which recalls Esarhaddon's boast that like the Flood Storm he wrecked Sidon, the fortress town in the midst of the sea, and exiled the king, his wife, and his children and carried away all his people. Luli was a bold and brilliant king, ruler of a splendid maritime kingdom, but was remembered less for his Phoenician integrity and fearless opposition to Assyria and its Tyrian sycophants than for the dismal asylum they gave him in Kition, once a Sidonian emporium but now a shoddy provincial town, an ideal place to disappear.

Tobʿal of Sidon, because he was Sennacherib's choice, was not a problem to the Assyrians. However, his successor, ʿAbdmilkot, broke his covenant with Assyria and "trusting in the Sea" threw off the humiliating yoke. Esarhaddon (680–669 B.C.E.) conquered Sidon in 677 B.C.E., wrecked it, and transported its people and the palace treasures (gold, silver, precious stones, elephant hides, ivory, ebony, boxwood, alabaster, dyed linen gar-

---

17. *ANET* 287–88.
18. N. Naʾaman, "The Conquest of Yadnana according to the Inscriptions of Sargon II," in *Historiography in the Cuneiform World* (ed. T. Abusch et al.; Bethesda, MD: CDL, 2001) 357–63.
19. Isa 23:4 can be compared with declarations of Esarhaddon (*ANET* 290–91), and 23:11–12 with the Annals of Sennacherib (*ANET* 287–88) on the capture and destruction of Sidon. These late sixth-century biblical texts make knowledge of the past the proof of prophetic prediction, just as a fifth-century text (Zech 9:1–4) gives apocalyptic vitality to the savage accomplishments of Sargon II recorded two centuries earlier: see A. Malamat, "The Historical Setting of Two Biblical Prophecies on the Nations," *IEJ* 1 (1950–51) 149–59, esp. pp. 150–51.

ments, cattle, sheep, and donkeys) to Assyria.[20] He reorganized its territory as an Assyrian province, giving Sarepta and Maʾrubbu to Tyre, and putting 16 towns, villages, and farmsteads north and east of Sidon under the direct authority of an Assyrian governor. He made a treaty with Baʿal, king of Tyre, giving him access to all the ports south of Tyre and to all the ports and towns, inland and on the coast, as far north as Byblos. Finally, he forced "the kings of Ḫatti and the seacoast," Sidon's old friends and affiliates along the Syrian and Cilician coasts, to build another port—*kāru*, the harbor district designed for merchants and traders—at a different place in Sidon and named the district "the Port of Esarhaddon."

ʿAbdmilkot's ally in this disastrous rebellion had been Sanduarri of Kundi and Sissu, and both of them were beheaded for their trouble. Neither the king nor the kingdom is known from other written sources—although Sissu, or Issos, was where Alexander defeated the Persians—but Esarhaddon does record that Sanduarri was encouraged to revolt because "he trusted in his inaccessible mountains."[21] It is likely, therefore, that his kingdom's main resource and one of the reasons Sidon found him a sturdy ally was the cedar, cypress, boxwood, oak, and pine forests of the Amanus.[22]

The kingdom's main port and capital city was at Kinet Höyük on the Gulf of Iskenderum, where in the ninth and earlier eighth centuries the imported pottery was Cypro-Cilician and Euboean; and in the latter part of the eighth century, Phoenician Red Slip and Cypriot Black-on-Red Ware with its local imitations, some still drying in the kilns.[23] Sidonians were established in Cilicia, at Karatepe among the Danunians and Luwians, and it would have been at places along the Cilician coast that they came into contact with the Ionian pirates who kept pestering the Assyrians during the reigns of Sargon and Esarhaddon. ʿAbdmilkot's alliance with Sanduarri, consequently, was a renewal of formalized relations with the region that had begun at least in the reign of Luli and that probably had been interrupted during the brief reign of Tobaʿl.

The evidence for constructive Sidonian presence in Cilicia can be eked out of a series of Phoenician inscriptions from Que written around the last quarter of the eighth century B.C.E., and from scattered references in the texts of Sargon II and Sennacherib. The story they tell is that Que, with

20. R. Borger, *Die Inschriften Asarhaddons, Königs von Assyrien* (AfO Beiheft 9; Graz: Published by the editor, 1956) Episode 5:A, II 65–III 19, pp. 48–49.
Alabaster urns were found at Ashur, and one of them was inscribed "Palace of Esarhaddon. . . . vessel of oil, large and full, which came with the rich goods of every kind from the treasure of Prince Abdmilkot, king of Sidon." Others, just like it, were found in the tombs at Almuñécar in southern Spain: see W. Culican, "Almuñécar, Assur and Phoenician Penetration of the Western Mediterranean," *Levant* 2 (1970) 28–36.
21. Borger, *Die Inschriften Asarhaddons*, Episode 6:A, III 20–38, pp. 49–50.
22. B. Watson-Treumann, "Beyond the Cedars of Lebanon: Phoenician Timber Merchants and Trees from the 'Black Mountain'," *WO* 31 (2000–2001) 75–83.
23. T. Hodos, "Kinet Höyük and Pan-Mediterranean Exchange," in *The Sea in Antiquity* (ed. G. J. Oliver et al.; BAR International Series 899; Oxford: Archaeopress, 2000) 25–38; idem, "Kinet Höyük and Al Mina: New Views on Old Relationships," in *Periplous: Papers on Classical Art and Archaeology Presented to Sir John Boardman* (ed. G. R. Tsetskhladze, A. J. N. W. Prag, and A. M. Snodgrass; London: Thames & Hudson, 2000) 145–52; N. Schreiber, *The Cypro-Phoenician Pottery of the Iron Age* (Culture and History of the Ancient Near East 13; Leiden: Brill, 2003) 278.

its own resources, and with roads and rivers that led from Mediterranean ports to the sources of silver, iron, copper, and tin in the Taurus Range was leaning toward Assyria and threatening Sidon's access to these resources; that Sidon, with the Ionians and perhaps with the kings of Cyprus tried to prevent this alliance; that eventually the kingdom of Que and the entire coastal area of Cilicia slipped away from Assyrian control, so that by the time of ʿAbdmilkot Sidon could align itself in one last desperate effort with Kundi and Sissu. In the ninth and early eighth centuries, there were good relations and an easy exchange of ideas between the communities of Luwians, Danunians, and Sidonians in this region. By the end of the eighth century, Assyria provoked a raw nationalism and belligerence that threatened to squelch the creative and entrepreneurial spirit. In this melee, however, the struggle for Sidonian independence continued.

A pivotal text in the story is the bilingual Phoenician-Luwian trophy inscription of Urik of Que.[24] The trophy is a statue of the God Baʿal standing on a chariot pulled by two oxen. The statue is limestone, more than seven feet tall, and portrays the God coiffed and robed in Assyrian style. The oxen-and-chariot base is substantial (about four feet high, six wide, and eight long) and is decorated with a city wall and three towers carved on the front of the chariot and a shield on the back of the chariot, so that the trophy as a whole represents the God's foray into battle and triumphal procession back to the capital city.[25]

The two versions of the inscription are damaged, but as far as idiom allows, they agree in most details: the Phoenician text, on the front of the chariot between the legs of the oxen, is the original; and the Luwian, distributed where space allowed on the side between the legs of an ox and on the back of the chariot is the translation. The trophy was found in an open area about 30 kilometers south of ʾAdana, 150 south of Karatepe. The absence of architectural remains at the site suggested to the excavators and editors that it had been removed from its original place of display, but it is more likely that it was set up where it was found, at the site of the victory to which it alludes, on the Cilician plain not far from the sea, where it could dominate the terrain. It was damaged in antiquity and was buried on the spot to save it from the further ravages of bad temper or time.

In some or all of this, it is comparable to a much later monument from Kition in Cyprus celebrating a victory by the king and the people of that city over Paphos and its allies (392 B.C.E.). The monument is called a "trophy" (the Greek word is transliterated *trpy* in Phoenician) and consisted of an inscribed base that was surmounted by a statue, now lost, of the God "Baʿal the Almighty" (*bʿl ʿz*), to whom the victory is attributed. It was

---

24. R. Tekoğlu et al., "La bilingue royale louvito-phénicienne de Çineköy," *CRAIBL* (2000) 961–1006.

25. R. D. Barnett, "Bringing the God into the Temple," in *Temples and High Places in Biblical Times* (ed. A. Biran; Jerusalem: Hebrew Union College, 1981) 10–20. At Karatepe, sculptures in the North and South Gateways portray processions of soldiers and musicians to an enthroned and feasting God and are preceded in the entrances to the gateways by the bilingual inscription written on tall slabs on either side of the entranceway that explains the meaning of the representations. The trophy has the God in procession on his chariot from a distant city, the soldiers symbolized by a shield, and a text to explain its significance.

erected in the harbor to celebrate a naval victory, and the inscription explicitly states ("I built it in this place, on that day") that it was erected at the time and place of the victory.[26] The Cilician trophy inscription, similarly, mentions the occasion for its dedication, alludes to victory and peace, and almost certainly refers, although in a broken context, to erecting the monument in that particular place.

The damaged text at the beginning of the inscription is restored from similar wording, almost clichés, in the Karatepe inscription, which is complete and preserved in three Phoenician exemplars. The gaps at the end of the text are filled by reconstructions that suppose the same resource and are based partly on the Luwian text, partly on the Phoenician context, and partly on the completion of broken words, the preserved letters of which allow only limited choices. The loss of Warik's ancestry is irreparable.

> (I) I am Warik, the son of . . . , of the House of Mopsos, [king of the Danunians], steward of Baʿal, who [have revived and en]larged the land of the plain [of ʾAdana, thanks] to Baʿal and thanks to the G[ods. (II) And I also produced horse [upon horse and] built camp after camp, and the king of [Assyria and] the whole house of Assyria became a father [and] a mother to me, and the Danunians and the Assyrians became one household. (III) And I built eight 8 fortresses in the east, and seven 7 in the west, and they were 15 in all, and in this place I myself Warik [have built this statue of Baʿal among all the for]tresses, and I have erected [it there, and] there I put a stop to [the contemptuous. (IV) And may Baʿal bestow] renewal, peace, victory, satisfaction [and every] delight on that king, and also on that kingdom of ʾAdana.

The first section (I, lines 1–5) identifies the king and declares his legitimacy. His name is Warik in this text, but Awarik in the Karatepe inscription, and Awarikas or Warikas in Luwian, but Urik or Urikki in Assyrian texts. His kingdom was ʾAdana, the Cilician plain (Cilicia *Pedias*), and his people were Danunians, descendants of the Greek Danaoi. He himself was a descendant of Mopsos, a hero of the Trojan War who, according to Greek legend, settled in Cilicia when the war was over and the troops dispersed. The Luwian version identifies him as an Achaean king (*hi-ya-wa-ni-sa*) and replaces the Phoenician names of the country and people with "Achaean" (*hi-ya-wa-*) and the determinative for city or land, a designation from which the name of the country, Que, in Assyrian sources (*qu-u-e*) is ultimately derived. It is this constant Greek connection that explains why Sidonians were attracted to Cilicia (Tyrians monopolized Tarsus in Cilicia *Tracheia*, "Rough" or mountainous Cilicia, Ḫilakku in Assyrian) and why there was such a persistent cultural exchange between the two peoples.

The second section (II, lines 5–10) describes his military preparations, the expansion of his cavalry and infantry, and then acknowledges the formal dependence of Que on Assyria. He chooses the language of bloodline relationships to describe the treaty between them rather than referring to its legal features, the oaths, stipulations, and curses that it contained. In the same mood, he avoids any reference to his vassal obligations—paying

---

26. M. Yon and M. Sznycer, "Une inscription phénicienne royale de Kition (Chypre)," *CRAIBL* (1991) 791–823; idem, "A Phoenician Victory Trophy at Kition," *RDAC* (1992) 157–65, pl. 51.

tribute, supplying troops—and includes them instead as local improvements in a treaty agreement among equals or, as he says, in a single household.

The third section (III, lines 10–16) offers concrete illustrations of the revitalizing and expansion of the land, describes where he stationed his infantry and cavalry, and situates the monument in the heart of the land, among the fortresses, right where it was found. The trophy is inscribed with the official written record of his treaty with Assyria and is the memorial of his victory over the contemptuous, which he attributes to Baʿal, under whose auspices he also made the treaty with Assyria. His victory, as the location of the trophy suggests, was on land and by sea, and is described in the Hassan Beyli inscription as the Assyrian defeat of the Sidonians and Ionians: they are "contemptuous" or "blasphemous" (*hnʾṣm*) because they dared attack him when he was under oath to Assyria and to Baʿal.

The last section (IV, lines 16–18) is the equivalent of the blessings and curses that usually conclude a treaty document, and Warik's prayer pretty well summarizes the flow of the inscription. "Renewal" (*kr*)[27] is an attribute of Baʿal and corresponds to the first section, where Warik announces that thanks to Baʿal and the Gods he has revivified (*yḥwt*) the land of the Plain of ʾAdana. His second wish is for "serenity" or "peace" (*štq*) and alludes to the parent-child relationship that he has established with the king of Assyria. The third prayer is for victory, symbolized in the trophy that he constructed, anticipated in his military preparations, and effected by Assyrian ruthlessness. The prayer for "satisfaction and every delight" describes the typical good life, lavishly illustrated in the Karatepe inscription, which characterized relations with Sidon until the onset of recent bitterness.

This Warik is also known from the Hassan Beyli Phoenician inscription, from the Karatepe bilingual, and from the Assyrian annals and correspondence.[28] His reign covered most of the last four decades of the eighth century B.C.E.: he paid tribute to Tiglath-pileser III in 738 B.C.E., and the Karatepe inscription from the end of the century records the accession of his son. His treaty with the Assyrians, noted in the trophy and Hassan Beyli inscriptions, is not mentioned explicitly in the Assyrian annals but is implicit in his tributary status and in other royal correspondence concerning Que and Phrygia (Muški).

Sargon II, in his seventh year (715 B.C.E.), from a base in Que, attacked Midas of Muški[29] in order to recover towns that he had taken from Que, perhaps in 722 B.C.E., when Midas along with Pisiris of Carchemish con-

27. P. Xella, "Sul nome punico ʿbdkrr," *RSF* 12 (1984) 23–30.

28. J. D. Hawkins, *Corpus of Hieroglyphic Luwian Inscriptions, Volume I: Inscriptions of the Iron Age, Part I: Introduction, Karatepe, Karkamis, Tell Ahmar, Maras, Malatya, Commagene* (Berlin: de Gruyter, 2000) 38–71, esp. pp. 38–46; H. W. F. Saggs, "The Nimrud Letters, 1952—Part IV: The Urartian Frontier," *Iraq* 20 (1958) 182–216, esp. pp. 182–207; S. Parpola, *The Correspondence of Sargon II, Part I: Letters from Assyria and the West* (SAA 1; Helsinki: Helsinki University Press, 1987) #1 (pp. 4–7), #110 (pp. 92–93), #251 (pp. 196–97); J. N. Postgate, "Assyrian Texts and Fragments," *Iraq* 35 (1973) 13–36, esp. pp. 21–34 (Nimrud Letter #39 [ND 2759]).

29. Gordion, Midas's capital, was at least partially destroyed by fire toward the end of the eighth century, but there is some disagreement on whether or not this destruction was due to Sargon's attack: see M. M. Voigt and R. C. Henrickson, "Formation of the Phrygian State: The Early Iron Age at Gordion," *AnSt* 50 (2000) 37–54.

spired against Assyria. In 710 B.C.E., Sargon wrote his son and successor, the Crown Prince Sennacherib, encouraging him to maintain good relations with Midas, who had changed his mind and indicated his willingness to enter into an alliance with Assyria by handing over 14 agents whom Urik, in violation of his treaty with Assyria, had sent to Urartu, then in revolt with Tabal against Assyria. The situation in Que remained uncertain and, as omen texts indicate, Sargon urgently inquired of the Sun God whether Tabal, Hilakku, and Kuzzurak would invade Que.[30]

Muški, under careful Assyrian watch, eventually made a treaty with Sargon, while Que was kept in line by an Assyrian governor, and Cyprus, which was known to Sargon as "the Island of the Danunians," submitted to Assyria in 707 B.C.E. and came under the same administration. In 705 B.C.E., Sargon was killed in Tabal while campaigning against the rebels, Que revolted, and as late as 696 B.C.E. Sennacherib was still engaged in western Cilicia against Tarsus;[31] and well into his reign, Esarhaddon was bedeviled by Sidon and the Ionians.

The Hassan Beyli inscription[32] was found on the western slopes of the Amanus on a pass and major route to the Cilician plains. It was inscribed on one face of a small dolerite slab, which was reused in Byzantine times as a boundary stone. The upper part of the stone is missing, but there are traces of a line of writing at the top of the preserved portion, and five more lines below it, all of which, however, are seriously damaged by the Greek boundary signs written over them. Paleographically, the inscription is earlier than the Karatepe inscription and contemporary with or slightly earlier than the trophy inscription. A coherent reading of the text makes it clear that at least one more line is missing at the top:

> (1) . . . . (2) . . . and they] wept, and the Sidonians and [Ion]ians [swore an oath (3) by Earth and] Heaven and by these Gods. And ʾIluʾili, when he waged (4) [war against] the king of Dan ‖ and against his house, and his towns, and his land, (5) the king of Assyria cr[ossed] the sea and came by land, and he brought (6) a gr[eat army] on behalf of ʾAwarik ‖ and they made a treaty in Aleppo ‖—(7) the kingdom of Assyria, and the kingdom of that king, as [one] kingdom.

The inscription backgrounds the information that is given or presumed known in Warik's trophy inscription and explains why his victory monument was erected on the open plain facing the sea: there he describes recruiting infantry and cavalry and building fortresses, thanking Baʿal and the Gods for giving respite to the Plain of ʾAdana. But here he names the enemy and attributes victory on land and sea to the king of Assyria. There the treaty is the thing and his God who sanctioned it, and the enemy is those who scoffed at it and blasphemed the God. Here the enemy makes

---

30. I. Starr, ed., *Queries to the Sun God: Divination and Politics in Sargonid Assyria* (SAA 4; Helsinki: Helsinki University Press, 1990) nos. 14–16, pp. 16–19.

31. J. D. Bing, "Tarsus: A Forgotten Colony of Lindos," *JNES* 30 (1971) 99–109; S. Dalley, "Sennacherib and Tarsus," *AnSt* 49 (1999) 73–80.

32. *KAI* no. 23; A. Lemaire, "L'inscription phénicienne de Hassan-Beyli réconsiderée," *RSF* 11 (1983) 9–19, pl. 1.

an alliance, they and their Gods are defeated, and the treaty with Assyria, although sealed first, is mentioned last.

The missing line must have named the Gods, who are referred to as "these Gods" in the third line, must have described the lamentation or propitiation ritual that culminated in weeping ("and they wept"), and must have identified ʾIluʾili (Luli), who is mentioned next without further ado. The oath they "swore" is so decisive in treaties and agreements that it becomes the word used to denote them (as ʿorkos, "oath" in Greek), and an oath by the natural elements, especially by Heaven and Earth, is standard in all treaties. The attention given to the alliance is unraveled in the following narrative, where generalities and ethnic designations give way to personal confrontation. ʾIluʾili declared war on Awarik, the king of Dan (ʾAdana, with the loss of the first syllable as in Phoenician and Assyrian)— that is, on his person and his posterity (on "his house") but not on the Plain of ʾAdana or the Danunians; the king of Assyria came by land and sea to help Awarik, not the country or the people; and the treaty was made between the Kingdom of Assyria and the Kingdom of Awarik, "that king," the vassal to whom Assyria was a father and a mother. It was a land battle, a raid perhaps by landing parties from Sidonian ships, against his towns and his territory, and the Ionians are not mentioned, although they were involved in the raid or in hindering and harassing the ships from Arvad that transported the Assyrians. The inscription ends as it began, with a treaty ("peace" [šlm]) signed at Aleppo, where there was a Temple of Hadad the Storm God, the God of Victory at sea.

ʾIluʾili and the Sidonians had no issue with the Plain of ʾAdana and the Danunians. They were, on the contrary, deeply implicated in the history, economy, and culture of the region and the people. The problem was Warik, a tiresome little war lord, who found aggrandizement in his partnership with Assyria, a plum for himself entailing no benefit whatever for his country. Luli, of course, had a full agenda of his own because Sidon's independence and prosperity were threatened by this constant and proliferating Assyrian encroachment, but more than politics and survival— something more like noblesse oblige—was involved in his alliance with the Ionians and his resistance to this outlandish pro-Assyrian dupe. Ionians were around but, as Warik emphasizes, it was a Sidonian initiative.

Sidonians were known as peaceable folk,[33] and the Luli interlude was less typical of the city's foreign relations than symptomatic of its last organized attempt to survive. The legacy of Sidon, in this region especially but also pretty well everywhere they went (preferably among Indo-European Hittites and Greeks), was the ideal of the good life, the culture of learning, wealth, ease, and artistic expression. An anecdote from a letter sent around this time by the mayor of Nineveh to the court of Sargon II at Nimrud illustrates their lack of interest in war and politics and their preference for going about their own business: "The Sidonians did not go to Calah with the crown prince, nor do they serve in the garrison of Nineveh,

---

33. The people of Laish, though they were far from ʿSidon, lived in the manner of the Sidonians, "quiet, trusting, true to their word, restrained, never troublesome" (Judg 18:7, 27–28).

but they loiter in the center of the city, each in his own lodging place."[34] It was not unusual for Sidonians to settle individually among the local residents and to pursue their arts and crafts at home. Their life-style was novel and intriguing and often imitated by individuals who could afford it, but it was puzzling and seemed lackadaisical or plain lazy to a busy urban administrator.

One of the lasting benefits of the Sidonian presence in Cilicia was the transmission of the alphabet, and with it, literacy and the makings of literature. Eighth-century Phoenician texts are the work of native bilingual scribes or of resident Sidonians, but they were meant to be recognized by local folk and read by passersby. It was one thing to do business in Phoenician, as people did, and another to display official texts that could be appreciated only with a fairly sophisticated grasp of the language. The Hassan Beyli inscription fulfilled the standard requirement that a treaty be displayed publicly in order to be acknowledged by the people it binds. The Assyrian original, the Phoenician text suggests, was in Aleppo. The copy includes the historical preamble—the narrative of Assyria's generosity toward Cilicia, which is the standard preface to a treaty—and then the record of the treaty, but there are no stipulations and no blessings or curses. People were expected to read it and "get it right," so vertical lines were included to clarify the syntax: what follows the lines is not new information and did not occur later in time but is explanatory or an appositive. The treaty, for instance, is not later in time but is the reason that the king of Assyria came to Luli's help.

Similarly, the Phoenician version of the trophy inscription distributes the elements of the treaty throughout a dedication to the God Baʿal, under whose auspices it was made, and formality yields to familiarity. It is in the first-person singular. All the emphasis is on Warik. Assyria and the Gods play subsidiary roles; the historical preamble lists Warik's benefits to the country, not Assyria's and only indirectly God's; and the formality of treaty becomes the informality of family relationships to suggest that Cilicia and Assyria are equals; victory is his, the treaty blessings are on the king, and on the land only as an afterthought. The texts, then, are literary, studied, and favored with fairly subtle argument or propaganda. They are the product of decades, perhaps centuries, of inculturation—the last pages in a history that ʾIluʾili and his generation were not ready to forget or leave to the Assyrian eraser.

The Karatepe inscription, unlike these historical and religious texts, does not refer to the treaty with Assyria but describes the remodeling of the town and its adoption of a new cult. The town is about 200 kilometers inland, on a hilltop overlooking the Ceyhan River, which wraps around the town as it meanders south to the Gulf of Iskenderum, to its west coast, opposite Kinet Höyük. It was at the junction of caravan routes and was small and compact but walled and well fortified. There were gateways on the north and south, the interior walls of which were lined with basalt orthostats, on which were carved, for the amusement

---

34. Parpola, *The Correspondence of Sargon II, Part I*, no. 153, p. 122.

Fig. 3.1. Karatepe Inscription. Photo by: Hans G. Güterbock. Reproduced with the permission of Walter Güterbock.

of individuals who entered the town, processions of people like themselves toward a merry, seated God and, for their instruction, long inscriptions in Phoenician and Luwian that named the town and its God, its builder, and why it was built.[35]

Some of the orthostats were pilfered from the ruins of Domuztepe, a ninth-century town situated on a twin hill across the river, and the rest were carved especially for the eighth-century rebuilding of Karatepe itself. The orthostats from Domuztepe are Neo-Hittite in style and execution but already exhibit a taste for Phoenician themes and motifs: a warship, for example, with a bow ram, an inward-curving stern, fore and aft platforms and railings, and bud-and-lotus garlands or interlacing volutes. The eighth-century reliefs were carved by Luwian craftsmen using Phoenician and Greek models: there are crested helmets, Bes figures, female sphinxes; the people are small and squat in North Syrian style, with Phoenician hairdos and shoes with upturned toes and ankle thongs; the chariots are Assyrian, but the lions guarding the gateways are entirely Phoenician in their fluidity and proportion. The inscriptions attest the same weave of Phoenician and Luwian culture, with some Greek admixture and a sporadic but bright Assyrian touch.

The Phoenician version of the Karatepe inscription (see fig. 3.1) is an original composition that the Luwian version adapts for the more con-

---

35. I. J. Winter, "On the Problems of Karatepe: The Reliefs and Their Context," *AnSt* 29 (1979) 115–51.

servative Hittite population of the town.[36] Its grammar and syntax[37] are professional, its literary structure is sophisticated, it coins words and uses expressions that the Luwian replaces with banalities, and it introduces a new God whom the Luwian tries to identify with the old. This new God is, or is the forerunner of, Dionysus.[38] His name is "Lord-of-the-Vineyard-and-New-Wine" (*b'l krntryš*).[39] His associates are Reshep-of-the-Goats (*ršp ṣprm*)—that is, Silenos and the Satyrs. His particular benefit to the town, once he is installed, is—beyond the pleasure, luxury, and total satisfaction already described in the text—the gift of New Wine and Satiety. He and his companions are associated, in classical sources, with Phrygia and with Midas in particular, and the career of this king is thoroughly woven into the history of Cilicia in the last quarter of the eighth century, when Karatepe was rebuilt and the new God was chosen. The Luwian version of the inscription does not have the equivalent of this God's name but persists in calling the God of Karatepe, including the God who was recently introduced into the town, "Tarhunzas," the Storm God, the Luwian Ba'al. However, it does identify Reshep-of-the-Goats as the God Runza, often represented with caprid features and, instead of listing New Wine among the benefits introduced by the new God, mentions that the Grain God and the Wine God took up residence in the town. It is clear, therefore, that this ancestral Hittite kingdom of Cilicia had become culturally Sidonian but that the Greek, that is, the Danunian or Achaean substrate continued to add to the ferment. Dionysus was a Greek God, and being celebrated in a Phoenician inscription did not mean that he was welcome in the ancient circle of Sidonian Gods.

The Sidonians were religiously conservative. When they joined forces with the Ionians, as may be gathered from the Hassan Beyli inscription, they swore an oath by Heaven and Earth. Their God was 'Eshmun (*'šmn*), "Expiator," who removed the evil or guilt causing illness and death and who consequently was also known as the "Spirit of Healing" (*šdrp'*) and the patron of the immortal dead (*rp'm*). At 'Amrit in the fifth century, his cult revolved around lustral rites, and a contemporary inscription from Sidon mentions a "Temple of 'Eshmun, the Holy Spirit, at the spring Yadlul, in the mountains" (*bt l'šmn šd qdš 'n ydll bhr*). These rites were observed at least from the eighth century onward, when the Assyrian administrator Qurdi-Ashur-Lamur had to intervene when his tax-collector, in a fit of pique over Sidonian reluctance to pay their taxes, cut the aqueduct bringing water

---

36. M. Weippert, "Elemente phönikischer und kilikischer Religion in den Inschriften vom Karatepe," in *XVII. Deutscher Orientalistentag vom 21. bis 27. Juli 1968 in Würzburg* (ed. W. Voigt; ZDMG Supplement 1; Wiesbaden: Franz Steiner, 1979) 191–217; M. G. Amadasi Guzzo and A. Archi, "La bilingue fenicio-ittita geroglifica di Karatepe," *VO* 3 (1980) 85–102; K. L. Younger Jr., "The Phoenician Inscription of Azatiwada: An Integrated Reading," *JSS* 43 (1998) 11–47.

37. A. Schade, *A Syntactic and Literary Analysis of Ancient Northwest Semitic Inscriptions* (Lewiston, NY: Edwin Mellen, 2006) 15–65.

38. W. Burkert, *Greek Religion* (trans. J. Raffan; Cambridge: Harvard University Press, 1985) 161–67; T. Gantz, *Early Greek Myth: A Guide to Literary and Artistic Sources* (Baltimore: Johns Hopkins University Press, 1993) 112–19, 135–39.

39. A. J. Frendo, "Phoenician Wine Could Be Divine," *Actas* 4, 2.607–11.

from the mountain to the temple in Sidon.[40] ʾEshmun was a civic God, the God of Sidon and its citizens: his worship was peculiar to the city and was translated to other towns only by particular syncretisms, as in the cult of ʾEshmun-Melqart in Kition or by the later tendency to rationalize, simplify, and universalize pantheons.

The Goddess of Sidon was Astarte. She was worshiped in Sidon as "the Queen" enthroned in her temple, "The Mighty Heavens" (*šmm ʾdrm*), and by Sidonians at Kition in Cyprus, where the ritual offering of hair in honor of her beauty and mourning for her lover were remembered by later Greek writers as characteristic of her cult.[41] She is pictured on a clay plaque of unknown provenance, and on many similar plaques from Sidon and Egypt (the quintessential woman, inviting awe, provoking adoration, and exciting love), as young, curly haired, full breasted, with a round belly and prominent navel, her arms by her side, standing in the facade of a temple, whose columns rest on couchant lions and whose capitals are crowned with a head of Egyptian Bes.[42] In late sixth-century Kition, she is the "Holy Queen" (*mlkt qdšt*), and her feast day includes a procession to her temple led by dancers and musicians and a festive meal with meat and cakes. The cakes were in her image—curly haired, naked, womanly, her arms extended in a gesture of welcome and protection—sweetened and baked in the coals, but they were more nourishing than physically flattering.[43] In Jerusalem at this time, her feast was a family affair in honor of the Queen of Heaven, celebrated by children and men, officiated by women, and scandalous to the jaded officers of a no-longer very playful God.[44]

Although Astarte's cult was centered on Sidon, she herself was universal and celestial. An eighth-century dedication on a bronze bowl identifies her in her astral manifestation with Egyptian Isis, "For ʿAštar-ʾIsis" (*lʿštrʾsy*).[45] As the Goddess of the former Egyptian province of Canaan, she was known as "Hurrian Astarte" (*ʿštrt ḥr*) or "Ashti" (*ʿšty*), the Egyptianized form of her name, and was frequently represented armed and on horseback.[46] An

---

40. H. W. F. Saggs, "The Nimrud Letters, 1952—Part II: Relations with the West," *Iraq* 17 (1955) 126–60, no. 13, esp. pp. 130–31, 151.

41. H. W. Attridge and R. A. Oden, *The Syrian Goddess (De Dea Syria)* (Texts and Translation 9; Missoula, MT: Scholars Press, 1976).

42. W. A. Ward, "The Goddess within the Facade of a Shrine: A Phoenician Clay Plaque of the 8th Century B.C.," *RSF* 24 (1996) 7–19.

43. B. Peckham, "Notes on a Fifth-Century Phoenician Inscription from Kition, Cyprus (CIS 86)," *Or* 37 (1968) 304–24; V. Karageorghis and L. E. Stager, "Another Mould for Cakes from Cyprus, A: The Mould and Its Interpretation; B: In the Queen's Image," *RSF* 28 (2000) 3–11, pls. 1–2.

44. Jer 7:18 ("the children gather wood, their fathers light fires, the women knead dough to make cakes for the Queen of Heaven"); 44:17 ("we will burn incense to the Queen of Heaven and pour out libations to her, as we used to . . . , for then we had plenty to eat and had a good life and saw no evil").

45. R. Deutsch and M. Heltzer, *New Epigraphic Evidence from the Biblical Period* (Tel Aviv–Jaffa: Archaeological Center Publication, 1995) 40–42.

46. J. Leclant, "Astarté à cheval d'après les représentations égyptiennes," *Syria* 37 (1960) 1–67; R. du Mesnil du Buisson, "Astart cavalière et armée dans le mythe de la planète Venus," *MUSJ* 45 (1969) 523–38, pl. 1; R. Stadelmann, *Syrisch-Palästinensische Gottheiten in Ägypten* (Leiden: Brill, 1967) 99–101; M. Weippert, "Über den asiatischen Hintergrund der Göttin 'Asiti'," *Or* 44 (1975) 12–21; J. M. Blázquez, "Astarte, Señora de los caballos en la Hispania preromana," *RSF* 25 (1997) 79–95, pls. 11–15.

eighth-century Ammonite seal from Sidon recording a vow made to her is an unusual witness to the fame that this particular cult of hers enjoyed: "[Vow of X, son] of Abinadab, which he vowed to Ashti in Sidon—may she bless him" (*ndr 'bndb š ndr l'št bṣdn tbrkh*).[47] In effect it is an amulet, written in Ammonite but on the pattern of Phoenician dedications.

There is an eighth-century statue from Seville in Spain (see fig. 3.2) that, like the clay plaque, portrays her as the Goddess of Love, curly haired, full breasted, with round belly and prominent navel. But it is also like the Queen of Heaven, seated on a throne, her right hand raised and beckoning. The statue was dedicated to her by two brothers, the second or third generation of Sidonian settlers in Spain, and is a striking witness to the vitality of this devotion to the metropolitan Goddess, Hurrian Astarte.[48] Her cult was also official as well as familial, and a later funerary inscription in the Byblian dialect identifies

---

47. *WSS* #876, pp. 328–29; P. Bordreuil, *Catalogue des sceaux ouest-sémitiques inscrits* (Paris: Bibliothèque Nationale, 1986) #80, pp. 70–71; W. E. Aufrecht, *A Corpus of Ammonite Inscriptions* (Lewiston, NY: Edwin Mellen, 1989) #56, pp. 145–48; U. Hübner, *Die Ammoniter: Untersuchungen zur Geschichte, Kultur und Religion eines transjordanischen Volkes im 1. Jahrtausend v.Chr.* (Wiesbaden: Harrassowitz, 1992) #12, pp. 51–52.

48. M. G. Amadasi Guzzo, "Astarte in Trono," in *Studies in the Archaeology and History of Ancient Israel in Honour of Moshe Dothan* (ed. M. Heltzer, A. Segal, and D. Kaufman; Haifa: Haifa University Press, 1993) 163–80; C. Bonnet and P. Xella, "L'identité d'Astarte-ḥr," in *Alle soglie della classicità: Il Mediterraneo tra tradizione e innovazione. Studi in onore di Sabatino Moscati, Volume Primo: Storia e Cultura* (ed. E. Acquaro; Pisa: Poligrafici, 1996) 29–46.

Fig. 3.2. Astarte statue from Seville. Reproduced with permission of Museo Arqueológico Provinciál, Siviglia.

the deceased as "priestess of Hurrian Astarte."[49] Worship of ʾEshmun and Astarte was characteristic of Sidonians and, although people took them wherever they went and often were named after them, they remained Gods of the mainland city and of the native Sidonian landscape.

At Sarepta there is some evidence for the worship of Astarte by an association (*mrzḥ*) of merchants.[50] This is a small building, about 20 feet long by 8 feet wide, built of well-hewn sandstone blocks, with a paved floor oriented east–west, across the street from the pottery factories. There are benches along the walls, a table against the west wall made of ashlar blocks faced with gypsum and provided with an oblong basin and drain, and in front of it a socket in the floor into which a wooden pillar or a statue with socle would have been fitted. There were twelve lamps nestled in front of the table and many other small objects on it or near the statue base: an ivory head of the "woman-at-the-window" type, beads, gaming pieces, masks, figurines of women playing a drum or holding a bird or pregnant and seated, a few figurines of men, and Egyptian-style faience amulets. The building was still in use in the seventh century, when Sarepta belonged to Tyre, and most of these objects are typical Tyrian bric-a-brac, but there is also inscriptional evidence that Sidonians originally established the association: a dedication on an ivory plaque of a statue to the Goddess, "This statue Shallum, son of Mapʿol, son of ʿUzzî, made for Tannit ʿAštarte." The statue was presented by a merchant from Cyprus, as his dialect indicates, and his inscription identifies Astarte of the original Sidonian club with Tannit, who came with the Tyrians who took over the commercial and industrial site.

Enduring Sidonian influence at Sarepta is indicated by a dedication to Shadrapa (*šdrpʾ*), the Genius of Healing, and Sidonian commercial interest in the town is marked by the early eighth-century ostracon on which the Greek vowels /i, e, a, o/ were written, from left-to-right like Greek but using contemporary Phoenician forms of the letters *yod*, *ḥet*, *ʾalep*, and *ʿayin*,[51] by some aspiring bilingual merchant eager to improve his business connections with the Greeks of Cyprus or Greece. The building was large enough to seat between 10 and 20 people, the table with basin and drain were suitable for ablutions or for libations of wine. In the socket in front of it, a statue or emblem of Astarte, patroness of the association, would have been placed, and the entire complex would have been perfectly suited for the meetings of the merchants, traders, and artisans who belonged to this particular club.

The clubs, or symposia, and their activities are described in contemporary texts and works of art. The most graphic is a lush scene on a bronze

49. É. Puech, "Un cratère phénicien inscrit: Rites et croyances," *Transeu* 8 (1994) 47–73, pls. 6–11.

50. J. B. Pritchard, *Recovering Sarepta, a Phoenician City* (Princeton: Princeton University Press, 1978) 131–48; idem, *Sarepta IV: The Objects from Area II, X* (Beirut: Université Libanaise, 1988) 31–71.

51. F. M. Cross, "Early Alphabetic Scripts," in *Symposia* (ed. F. M. Cross; Cambridge, MA: American Schools of Oriental Research, 1979) 97–123, esp. pp. 97–98, 113, fig. 2.

Fig. 3.3. Bronze bowl from Salamis, Cyprus (BM Catalogue of Bronzes no. 186).
© The Trustees of the British Museum.

bowl from Salamis in Cyprus (see fig. 3.3).[52] At the top, a woman sits on a
throne nursing a child and facing a man who reclines on a couch, beside
which there is a footstool or bench: she reaches toward him with lotus
flowers in her left hand, and he reciprocates with a bouquet of budding
branches in his left hand. Behind him a servant approaches them carrying a jug of wine from a stand on which there is a crater with another jug
suspended in mid-air above it. To the right of this scene, a man reclines
on a couch, like the couch on which the man reclined at the top, and
points to the man and woman while conversing with a naked girl who sits
astride him and entertains him with lyre and song. To their right and also
gesturing toward the man and woman, a man sits on a chair and drinks. A
lotus flower separates him from another man, who in his left arm carries

52. G. Markoe, *Phoenician Bronze and Silver Bowls from Cyprus and the Mediterranean* (Berkeley:
University of California Press, 1985) #Cy5, pp. 174–75; V. Karageorghis, "*Erotica* from Salamis,"
RSF 21 (Supplement; 1993) 7–13, pl. 1.

a naked girl clinging to him, and with his right hand points to the man and woman. To their right, and directly opposite the man and woman, another naked couple reclines on another identical couch. To the right of this couple, two men carry a large jar of wine, slung on a pole between them, toward the crater and the suspended wine jug. Behind these men, there is a lotus flower, and beyond it and facing the other way, there is a procession toward the man and woman consisting of a woman carrying a jug in her right hand and a drinking bowl in her left, a woman playing the tambourine, a man playing the flute, a woman playing a lyre and, at the head of the procession, a woman dancing. All the men and women wear Egyptian wigs or are clothed in Egyptian-style garments, and the action unfolds around a central medallion that depicts Pharaoh and his attendant facing his God and smiting captives. The scene, clearly, has a symbolic or narrative as well as a literal meaning.

The bowl itself (on which it is portrayed) is just like the bowls from which the members of the club drink wine, and the scene is first a literal rendering of a *marzeaḥ*. The narrative or symbolic meaning is commemoration of the dead, who are represented by the enthroned woman and reclining man, towards whom all the participants direct their attention and who alone among the members do not drink or sing or make love or play music but just contemplate each other and offer each other symbols of their rebirth. The club has just enough members—seven men, seven women, and three attendants—to fill the hall at Sarepta, and every feature of the scene is characteristic of the *marzeaḥ*.

The best (but jaundiced) description of a *marzeaḥ* can be extracted from a contemporary biblical text that criticizes all aspects of the institution as practiced in Israel in the eighth century.[53] It is an association of wealthy merchants, independent but well connected to the royal court, who make their money selling agricultural products, wheat and corn especially. It comprises about 10 members presided over by a steward or symposiarch whose title is "beloved friend," and one of his special functions is concern for the dead. It owns an expensive house furnished with couches and benches inlaid with ivory and meets regularly—on a "day" filled with anticipation—in session or in solemn assembly, under the patronage of its God. Its meetings are luxurious feasts at which the members wash and anoint themselves with fine perfumed oil, listen to songs composed for the occasion and sung to the music of the lyre, drink wine mixed in craters from large bowls, grieve for members of the club who have died as they would for an only child, exhort one another to confidence in their expected rebirth, and dally with the invited girls to celebrate life and express their hope in this regeneration.

Elements of this description are corroborated by other texts and artifacts. For instance, the Samaria ivories, whose themes are love, death and

---

53. Cf. J. Rilett Wood, *Amos in Song and Book Culture* (JSOTSup 337; London: Sheffield Academic Press, 2002) 23–46. Specific references to the *marzeah* are distributed throughout the text of Amos (2:6–8; 3:12–15; 4:1–5; 5:1–6, 11–12, 21–23; 6:1–7, 8–11; 8:4–6, 9–10), but it is the club, its membership, and their practices that are its constant theme and the source of its dramatic cohesion.

rebirth, were carved by Phoenician artists for this kind of furniture.[54] And the Samaria ostraca, a large group of receipts from eighth-century Israel, deal exclusively with shipments of wine and fine oil.[55] Other indications in the text, notably fear and loathing of the merchants who had a great deal of money, little respect for tradition, and no scruples, provide insight into a new international social class that included men and women with increasing power and influence.

The evidence for specifically Sidonian trade and commerce is anecdotal. A bronze weight in the shape of a calf's head is inscribed "Royal Standard— Shekel of Sidon" (*Š Ṭ šql ṣdn*).[56] It was found in Crete and indicates that there was a common as well as a royal standard, implies that Sidon was doing business with the island in the eighth century, and adds specificity to the numerous imports in Crete that otherwise can be traced only indiscriminately either to Phoenicia or to Cyprus.[57] A mid-eighth-century transport amphora found in Kition is inscribed with the names of three members of the syndicate who shipped it and is countersigned in a different hand with its contents ("oil" [*šmn*]) and the name of the recipient.[58] An early eighth-century Red Slip juglet from Kition is inscribed with the name of the dealer, the Cilician woman Annittis (*ʾntš*).[59] Another woman from Cilicia whose seal was inscribed with her title, "Steward" (*hbrkt*), like four other seals from Cilicia belonging to "stewards" (*hbrk*), supplied the provisions for a public or private residence or commercial club.[60] Her rank is suggested by the seal of a woman from Zinjirli, not far from where the Cilician steward worked, on which a seated woman, who is identified as "Ahotmilk, wife of Yišaʿ," is served by another woman, who approaches her holding a wine jug in her left hand and offering her a drinking bowl with her right.[61]

At Tell Kazel, ancient Sumur, there are imported Cypriot ceramics, Black-on-Red juglets, Sarepta amphorae, and Sidonian Red Slip jugs, as well as evidence of a prosperous mid-eighth-century terra-cotta workshop that was most likely operated by a guild of professional women. The workshop has a paved floor, plenty of food stored in amphorae, a massive dump of purified

---

54. E. Ferris Beach, "The Samaria Ivories, *Marzeaḥ*, and Biblical Text," *BA* 56 (1993) 94–104.

55. *TSSI* 1.5–15.

56. F. Bron and A. Lemaire, "Poids inscrits phénico-araméens du viiie siècle av. J.-C.," *Atti* 1, 3.763–70, pl. 145. The weight is 6.5 grams. Another weight in the shape of a lion, also from Sidon and inscribed "Royal Standard—five" (*Š Ṭ ḥmš*), weighs 20.9 grams and is evidently not according to the Sidonian standard. In "Royal Standard," the letter Š stands for "shekel," and the letter Ṭ is a stylized scarab and a royal symbol.

57. G. L. Hoffman (*Imports and Immigrants: Near Eastern Contacts with Iron Age Crete* [Ann Arbor: University of Michigan Press, 1997] 19–108) lists approximately 29 imports from Egypt, 2 from Syria–Palestine, 14 from the Levant, 65 (especially ceramics) from Cyprus, 48 from Phoenicia, and 20 (especially ivories) from North Syria.

58. *Kition* 3, #D3, pp. 131–32, pl. 20:1.

59. C. Bonnet, "Les étrangers dans le corpus épigraphique phénicien de Chypre," *RDAC* (1990) 141–53, esp. pp. 141–42.

60. *WSS* ##717–21, pp. 266–67; A. Lemaire, "Essai sur cinq sceaux phéniciens," *Sem* 27 (1977) 29–40; E. Lipiński, "Notes d'épigraphie phénicienne et punique," *OLP* 14 (1983) 129–65, esp. pp. 133–39; *IFPCO* 125–26; M. G. Amadasi Guzzo, "Le iscrizioni puniche," in *Missione Archeologica Italiana a Malta: Rapporto preliminare della Campagna 1970* (Rome: Consiglio Nazionale delle Ricerche, 1973) 87–94, esp. no. 14, p. 94.

61. *WSS* #1102, p. 417.

river clay and heaps of gravel. It produced large and small terra-cottas, painted and unpainted, of nude women holding their breasts; of women playing the tambourine or carrying a pet; of seated pregnant women, some wearing a necklace and pendant with the solar disk and inverted crescent moon of celestial Astarte, not unlike terra-cottas being produced in Sidonian workshops at Tell ʿArqa, and Tabbat al-Hammam.[62]

A tomb on the outskirts of Sidon contained four urn burials of members of the family of ʿAqam, whose name is written on one of them, and among their grave goods was a Greek pyxis from Argos (a jewelry box for the mother) operated earlier than the tomb itself and probably a memento of his travels to Greece.[63] Similar urns from Lebanon or Cyprus, also inscribed, contained the remains of a man named Selem (*ṣlm*) in veneration of the deified Sun Disk, and of a woman called Akbarot (*ʿkbrt*, "Mouse"),[64] both of whom most likely belonged to the new class of merchants and traders. This inclusion of women in commerce and in public life, a preference for dealing with Greeks in Cyprus or Greece, and a passion for traveling abroad were characteristics of Sidonian society that became particularly noticeable in the eighth century.

Sidonian influence on Israel persisted until the kingdom was incorporated into the Assyrian provincial system after the destruction of Samaria in 722 B.C.E. Samaria Ware, an elegant version of standard Phoenician Red Slip, graced the tables of the wealthy, as ivory adorned their meeting places. Israel's business community included travelers (*ʾanšê tārîm*), those who were engaged in foreign trade; merchants (*rokelîm*), those who controlled the domestic market; and retail dealers (*soḥarîm*), those who had shops or peddled goods.[65] In the very early eighth century, there were Israelite traders working with Judeans and Philistines at Kuntillet ʿAjrud on the incense route to ʿAqaba and Arabia.[66] There are seals of Israelite merchants and traders, some of them women, and at Hazor and Samaria containers inscribed in Phoenician with the names of Sidonian traders who shipped their goods to these places.[67] They were distrusted because they were cosmopolitan—in more traditional terms, because they were rich and unscrupulous and oppressed the poor—and shared religious and cultural values with their rascally "Canaanite" partners.

62. M. Yon and A. Caubet, "Appendix II: Les céramiques importées de l'Ouest," pp. 98–104 in L. Badre et al., "Tell Kazel, Syria: Excavations of the AUB Museum 1985–1987," *Berytus* 38 (1990) 9–124.

63. R. Saidah, "Une tombe de l'âge du Fer à Tambourit (Région de Sidon)," *Berytus* 25 (1977) 135–46; P. Courbin, "Une pyxis géometrique argienne (?) au Liban," *Berytus* 25 (1977) 147–57; P. Bordreuil, "Epigraphe d'amphore phénicienne du 9e siècle," *Berytus* 25 (1977) 159–61.

64. M. Heltzer, "Phoenician Epigraphic Miscellanea," *AO* 16 (1998) 77–84, esp. pp. 78–79, figs. 4–9; S. Dalley, "The God Ṣalmu and the Winged Disk," *Iraq* 48 (1986) 85–101.

65. M. Elat, "The Monarchy and the Development of Trade in Ancient Israel," in *State and Temple Economy in the Ancient Near East, II* (ed. E. Lipiński; Louvain: Department Orientalistiek, 1979) 527–46.

66. E. Ayalon, "The Iron Age II Pottery Assemblage from Horvat Teiman (Kuntillet ʿAjrud)," *TA* 22 (1995) 141–205; W. Zwickel, "Überlegungen zur wirtschaftlichen und historischen Funktion von Kuntillet ʿAǧrud," *ZDPV* 116 (2000) 139–42.

67. B. Delavault and A. Lemaire, "Les inscriptions phéniciennes de Palestine," *RSF* 7 (1979) 1–39, pls. 1–14, esp. pp. 7–12, 21–22.

There is a curious omission in the Sidonian cultural repertoire: the theory and practice of treaty agreements. There were business agreements, there were oaths and alliances (with the Ionians, for instance, and perhaps at Ionian instigation), and Warik could pattern his Phoenician inscriptions after Assyrian treaty texts, but the words and the ideas of covenant are missing. This is all the more curious because everyone else in the Near East (Arameans, Israelites, Luwians, Assyrians, and their allies) organized their international affairs according to this formality. The Greeks too, who relied on the Phoenicians for so much of their cultural development, borrowed this institution, not from the Sidonians with whom they worked so closely in Cilicia, but from Assyria through their Neo-Hittite neighbors in Asia Minor.[68] An inscription from Arslan Tash in North Syria emphasizes this cultural divide between Sidon and other Near Eastern nations.[69] It is written on clay in an Aramaic script, but it follows Hebrew orthographic practice, and its language looks Phoenician but is more particularly North Israelite. It is distinguished as Israelite rather than Phoenician by its biblical form and content. It is a *mĕzûzâ* or doorpost amulet invoking the Sinai covenant against night demons, even though the beliefs it expresses do not conform to biblical orthodoxy. The covenant is under the auspices of the God Ashur and the Assembly of Gods and Goddesses, and the hex is invoked in the name of Horon and his wives. The lack of covenant institutions or ideology is consistent with the Sidonian character: individualism and willingness to assimilate to new environments; a people centered on a city whose political, religious, civic, and commercial functions are clearly defined; a country with a representative government whose monarch is "the king of the Sidonians" and not king of Sidon; a city whose identity is expressed in its artistic and religious tradition.

Conclusion

In the eighth century, Sidonian commercial designs were thwarted by increasing Assyrian aggression. Their centuries-old presence in Cilicia and their involvement in the lumber and metal business were threatened by the aspirations and alliances of the emerging nations and by the Assyrian mentality of world domination. Gradually the Syrian port towns, Arvad most grievously, were torn from their partnerships with Sidon and put to work as the naval arm of Assyria. Tyre, whose Cypriot, Palestinian, Egyptian, and overseas connections were developing into a priceless commercial network, became the Assyrian client of choice. By mid-century, Sidonian enterprise in the West was beginning to crumble; by the end of the century, Sidon itself was teetering into oblivion; and by the early seventh century, it was swallowed by the empire. There were still individuals, families, and companies traveling and working abroad, but the impulse away from

---

68. M. Weinfeld, "Covenant Terminology in the Ancient Near East and Its Influence on the West," *JAOS* 93 (1973) 190–99; idem, "The Common Heritage of Covenantal Traditions in the Ancient World," in *I Trattati nel Mondo Antico: Forma, Ideologia, Funzione* (ed. L. Canfora, M. Liverani, and C. Zaccagnini; Rome: "L'Erma" di Bretschneider, 1990) 175–91.

69. F. M. Cross and R. J. Saley, "Phoenician Incantations on a Plaque of the Seventh Century B.C. from Arslan Tash in Upper Syria," *BASOR* 197 (1970) 42–49, fig. 1.

home wavered, and adventurers and discoverers were replaced by refugees and migrants.

The Mainland Phoenician Cities: Tyre and the Neo-Assyrian Empire

Tyre took advantage of Assyrian self-interest, the short-sightedness of Syrian states bent on national identity, and the gradual decline of Sidon to establish itself as the arbiter of fashion in the Mediterranean world. By mid-century, the Syrian chiefdoms, through a system of alliances, affirmed their Aramean identity as "All Aram," consisting of the states in "Upper and Lower Aram," and together defied the Assyrian Empire.[70] South Syrian coastal states indulged in prestigious Phoenician Red Slip wares but were steadfast in their agricultural and homespun traditions.[71] Arvad, on which Sidon had always relied, became an Assyrian port,[72] the "Harbor of the King," and the base from which it attacked Sidonian interests in Anatolia and Cyprus. Hamath maintained its unique identity until it became an Assyrian province in 720 B.C.E., but the Neo-Hittite regime in ʿUmqi was gone, and Tyre, whose enterprise at Al Mina depended on it, was impelled to establish an alternative network.[73] In Cyprus, similarly, the city of Carthage was a ninth-century Tyrian foundation, but in the surge of nationalist spirit it was absorbed into the system of Cypriot kingdoms by the end of the eighth or in the early seventh century. As Sidon tumbled through its spiral of destruction, Tyre retrieved the pieces (at Kition for instance) and, relying on Assyrian organization and native shrewdness, went west and reworked its interests into a worldwide network.

Tyre and Tiglath-pileser III

Tyre paid tribute to Assyria in the ninth century but, for the first part of the eighth century, when Assyria was ineffectual in the west, was free to manage its own affairs. Then in the reign of Tiglath-pileser III (744–726 B.C.E.), after decisive battles with the Syrian states and successful campaigns against the Philistine cities, Assyria reorganized the Levant into a northern province of Calneh (738 B.C.E.), with its capital at Kullanu, the former capi-

---

70. S. Grosby, "*ʾrm klh* and the Worship of Hadad: A Nation of Aram?" *Aram* 7 (1995) 337–52; S. Mazzoni, "Syria and the Periodization of the Iron Age: A Cross-Cultural Perspective," *ANESt* Supplement 7 (2000) 31–59; E. Lipiński, *The Aramaeans: Their Ancient History, Culture, Religion* (Louvain: Peeters, 2000); D. Talshir, "The Relativity of Geographic Terms: A Re-Investigation of the Problem of Upper and Lower Aram," *JSS* 48 (2003) 259–85; S. Ponchia, *L'Assiria e gli stati transeufratici nella prima metà dell'VIII sec. a.C.* (Padua: Sargon, 1991).

71. D. Bonatz, "Some Considerations on the Material Culture of Coastal Syria in the Iron Age," *EVO* 16 (1993) 123–57; S. Mazzoni, "Pots, People and Cultural Borders in Syria," in *Landscapes, Territories, Frontiers and Horizons in the Ancient Near East, II: Geography and Cultural Landscapes* (ed. L. Milano; Padua: Sargon, 2000) 139–52.

72. M. Elat, "Phoenician Overland Trade within the Mesopotamian Empires," in *Ah, Assyria . . . : Studies in Assyrian History and Ancient Near Eastern Historiography Presented to Hayim Tadmor* (ed. M. Cogan and I. Ephʿal; Scripta Hierosolymitana 33; Jerusalem: Magnes, 1991) 21–35, esp. p. 27.

73. N. Naʾaman, "Lebo-Hamath, Ṣubat-Hamat, and the Northern Boundary of the Land of Canaan," *UF* 31 (1999) 417–41; R. Lebrun, "Aspects de la présence louvite en Syrie au VIIIe siècle av. J.-C.," *Transeu* 6 (1993) 13–25.

tal of ʿUmqi; a central province of Sumur, with its capital at Simirra (738 B.C.E.); and a southern province that was centered on Dor (732 B.C.E.). The cities of Phoenicia, located between Sumur and Dor, were not included in this provincial system but were tributaries of the empire, maintaining their independence and some autonomy under the supervision of an Assyrian administrator.

Hiram of Tyre reigned until 738 B.C.E. The king's name is mentioned by the governor of Carthage in Cyprus in his dedication of a bronze bowl to the Baʿal of Lebanon. Because the script of this dedication is fairly archaic and would fit better before rather than after mid-century,[74] it is likely that Hiram's reign was fairly long and, as Tyre's contributions to Assyria attest, very prosperous. In this year, when ʿUmqi became a province and the North Syrian coastal kingdoms paid tribute, Hiram was also included among these distant tributaries[75] because of his involvement in the Tyrian-Euboean joint venture at Al Mina, the landing called *Riʾši Ṣuri*, "headland of Tyre" or "Cape Tyre," by Tiglath-pileser III and designated by him an "emporium" (*bit kāri*) on the seashore, a "royal store-house," a gateway to the boxwood mountains of the Amanus Range.[76]

Later in this last year of his reign, Hiram was accused of conspiracy with Rezin, the king of Damascus, and both were forced to submit and make reparations.[77] He was succeeded by Mittin (737–735 B.C.E.), predictably pro-Assyrian, who was deposed by Ṭobʾil, Hiram's lieutenant and a former governor of Carthage in Cyprus, but was reinstated when the Syro-Ephraimite rebellion (734–732 B.C.E.) was crushed and Ṭobʾil was disgraced. Tyre came under the scrutiny of an Assyrian administrator, the "Chief Eunuch," and Mittin had to pay an enormous indemnity—150 talents, or about 10 tons of gold),[78] but the city had gotten rebellion out of its system and could settle back into its favored-Assyrian-client status for decades to come.

During the reign of Tiglath-pileser III, when these kings ruled,[79] Assyria gradually took control of all the trade networks in which Tyre had an interest, and the maneuvers of the other kings of the region were designed to alleviate, stall, or prevent this outcome. At stake were the taxes that Assyria imposed on goods in transit. At issue were the land routes and the Mediterranean ports and the kings and countries that controlled them: the north–south routes along the coast and on the King's Highway in Transjordan; the east–west routes from Transjordan and Arabia to Tyre and to Gaza.

Damascus and Tyre were intermediate destinations on the King's Highway, so Hiram and Rezin were natural partners, especially because Rezin,

---

74. J. B. Peckham, *The Development of the Late Phoenician Scripts* (HSS 20; Cambridge: Harvard University Press, 1968) chap. 4, pl. 7:1.

75. B. Oded, "The Phoenician Cities and the Assyrian Empire in the Time of Tiglath-Pileser III," *ZDPV* 90 (1974) 38–49, esp. p. 42.

76. H. Tadmor, *The Inscriptions of Tiglath-Pileser III, King of Assyria* (Jerusalem: Israel Academy of Sciences and Humanities, 1994) 104–5 (Iran Stele IIB:12–13), 136–43 (Summary Inscription 4), 144–49 (Summary Inscription 5).

77. Ibid., 186–89 (Summary Inscription 9, lines 5–8).

78. Ibid.,106–7, 170–71.

79. Ibid., 265–68; N. Naʾaman, "Rezin of Damascus and the Land of Gilead," *ZDPV* 11 (1995) 105–17; idem, "Tiglath-Pileser III's Campaigns against Tyre and Israel (734–732 B.C.E.)," *TA* 22 (1995) 268–78.

who was probably a usurper, had control of Gilead in northern Transjordan, which was a critical link on this route.[80] The King's Highway led from Arabia to the Euphrates, so Samsi, queen of the Arabs, was necessarily a coconspirator.[81] With Africa and Arabia in mind, Rezin secured the port and marketing facilities at Elat on the Red Sea. Furthermore, the road from Transjordan to Tyre passed through Israel, and it is not surprising that it (also ruled by a usurper from Gilead) was part of the anti-Assyrian intrigue, or that Tell Keisan, the Tyrian town in the Plain of ʿAkko where the road ended, was put under direct Assyrian administration.[82]

Tyre was engaged in overland and maritime trade with the Philistine cities and with Egypt, which Assyria was anxious to monitor, and which it effectively controlled by imposing taxes on Tyre,[83] exacting tribute from the more northerly cities, and transforming Gaza, with its traditional close ties to Egypt, into an Assyrian emporium (*bit kāri*). Judah could not be forced to join the resistance; Edom could not be drawn into the conflict; Moab aligned itself with Judah and was harassed by Kedar, an important tribe in the Arab confederacy; and Ammon, a stable but developing country, joined Moab, Edom, and Judah in paying tribute.[84] Tiglath-pileser put an end to the confusion in a series of campaigns—the first against Philistia (734 B.C.E.), the next two against Damascus (733–732 B.C.E.)—in which Philistia became a protectorate and Damascus, the instigator, was destroyed. There was no change in the system of taxation, and the difference now was that Assyria, under the agency of Tyre, took charge of an unwieldy trade network, the common cause of which had given it greater cohesion.

The Assyrian records and the tribute and gift lists associated with these years provide an insight into trade and commerce in eighth-century Tyre and a preliminary inventory of the goods and services that were exchanged. In conjunction with the archaeological record, there is some information available on business practices, prices, and the use of money. Formerly anonymous merchants and traders are named, the structure of craftsmen guilds takes shape, a monied business class emerges, and individuals realize the clichés of fortune and fame. The networks of international trade interlace, and commercial contracts and state treaties replace traditional allegiances—with varying but frank effects on nationalism, ethnicity, culture,

---

80. W. T. Pitard, *Ancient Damascus: A Historical Study of the Syrian City–State from Earliest Times until Its Fall to the Assyrians in 732 B.C.E.* (Winona Lake, IN: Eisenbrauns, 1987) 179–89; P. E. Dion, *Les Araméens à l'âge du Fer: Histoire politique et structures sociales* (Études Bibliques 34; Paris: Lecoffre, 1997) 211–15.

81. I. Ephʿal, *The Ancient Arabs: Nomads on the Borders of the Fertile Crescent, 9th–5th Centuries B.C.* (Jerusalem: Magnes, 1984) 25–37, 83–86.

82. H. W. F. Saggs, "The Nimrud Letters 1952—Part II: Relations with the West," *Iraq* 17 (1955) 126–60, Letter XII, esp. pp. 127–30, 150; Tadmor, *The Inscriptions of Tiglath-Pileser III*, 176–77, line 8; pp. 186–87, line 1.

83. Saggs, "The Nimrud Letters 1952—Part II," 127–30, 149–51.

84. N. Naʾaman, "Forced Participation in Alliances in the Course of the Assyrian Campaigns to the West," *Ah, Assyria . . . : Studies in Assyrian History and Ancient Near Eastern Historiography Presented to Hayim Tadmor* (ed. M. Cogan and I. Ephʿal; Scripta Hierosolymitana 33; Jerusalem: Magnes, 1991) 80–98, esp. pp. 91–94; Saggs, "The Nimrud Letters, 1952—Part II," 131–33, 152 (Letter XIV).

and politics. Tyre became the major player on the Levantine mainland and, with its increasing overseas connections, a hub in the Mediterranean world.

Tyre and North and South Arabia

Samsi, queen of the Arabs, joined her trading partners Tyre, Damascus, and Samaria in their protest against the system of Assyrian oversight and taxation. She had sworn allegiance to Tiglath-pileser III in 734 B.C.E. but soon after was persuaded to join the rebellion.[85] She was defeated, her caravans were despoiled, and she was forced to flee into the Syrian Desert, but she soon changed her mind again and submitted to Assyria. The loot seized from her by the Assyrians included 20,000 sheep, the array of prosperous nomads; 30,000 camels, the pledge of successful desert trade,[86] with their loads of 5,000 bags of spices of all kinds; as well as more than 1,000 people to train and care for the animals and work the spices into perfumes or aromatics. These spices came from North and South Arabia along the King's Highway, east of the Jordan, the route that Samsi traveled, and eventually reached Assyria; or went by trunk roads and connecting highways through Beersheba to Gaza in the south of Palestine; or to Tyre on the north coast; or to Damascus in the fertile land west of the Syrian Desert.

The texts that narrate the submission of Samsi also mention some remoter Arab tribes, more or less beyond Assyria's purview, that paid their dues to the empire but were not conquered. Among these were Tema (or, Taymāʾ) and Sheba (or, Sabāʾ), and the gifts they sent included gold and silver besides the usual camels and spices.[87] Tema's involvement in the trade network is known from a boast by the ruler of Carchemish, sometime around 800 B.C.E., that he could write four languages, including Tyrian and Temanite.[88] Both Tema and Sheba are also mentioned in a mid-eighth-century text (dated 775–750 B.C.E.) as the place of origin of shipments destined for Assyria.[89] In this text, the governor of Suhu and Mari on the Euphrates records that a caravan from Tema and Sheba arrived unannounced at his town, Hindanu, and that he therefore attacked and looted it,[90] taking 200 camels and 100 of their drivers. Among the goods he mentions are dyed wool of various kinds, alabaster, and iron but unexpectedly neither

85. I. Ephʿal, *The Ancient Arabs: Nomads on the Borders of the Fertile Crescent, 9th–5th Centuries B.C.* (Jerusalem: Magnes, 1984) 33–36, 83–87.

86. J. Retso, "The Domestication of the Camel and the Establishment of the Frankincense Road from South Arabia," *Orientalia Suecana* 40 (1991) 187–219; M. Elat, "Die wirtschaftlichen Beziehungen der Assyrer mit den Arabern," in *Festschrift für Rykle Borger zu seinem 65. Geburtstag am 24. Mai 1994* (ed. S. M. Maul; Groningen: Styx, 1998) 39–57.

87. Ephʿal, *The Ancient Arabs*, 36, 87–92; 1 Kgs 10:2.

88. A. Livingstone, "New Light on the Ancient Town of Taimaʾ," in *Studia Aramaica: New Sources and Approaches* (ed. M. J. Geller, J. C. Greenfield, and M. P. Weitzman; Oxford: Clarendon, 1995) 133–43; F. Starke, "Sprachen und Schriften in Karkamis," in *Ana šadi Labnāni lū allik. Beiträge zu altorientalischen und mittelmeerischen Kulturen: Festschrift für Wolfgang Röllig* (ed. B. Pongratz-Leisten, H. Kühne, and P. Xella; Neukirchen-Vluyn: Neukirchener Verlag, 1997) 381–95.

89. A. Cavigneaux and B. K. Ismail, "Die Statthalter von Suhu und Mari im 8. Jh. v. Chr. anhand neuer Texte aus den irakischen Grabungen im Staugebiet des Qadisija-Damms," *BaghM* 21 (1990) 321–456, esp. pp. 346–47, 351, 357.

90. M. Maraqten, "Dangerous Trade Routes: On the Plundering of Caravans in the Pre-Islamic Near East," *Aram* 8 (1996) 213–36, esp. pp. 227–29.

incense nor spices. The goods the caravan did bring, obviously, were not from South Arabia but were products that were acquired along the way in exchange for the gold (and maybe silver) and the fragrances that it carried. The alabaster was from Egypt or Gaza; dyes are what made Tyre famous; and iron, which was always plentiful in Hindanu,[91] could have been picked up in Damascus.

Damascus was notable even in the ninth century for the huge amounts of iron that it could afford to pay the Assyrians.[92] In the time of Sargon II (721–704 B.C.E.), its territory was traversed by Arab nomads and caravans, usually peaceably and regularly working for the Assyrians but sometimes belligerently, as when Ammili'ti, son of Amiri, with 300 camels raided the Assyrian caravan, transferring booty from Damascus to Assyria.[93] One of the towns in the territory of Damascus is mentioned by the Assyrian governor as having been transformed into a marketplace or "merchant town," selling iron, copper, and grapes. The governor himself was suspected of selling iron to the Arabs, but he replied that it was local businessmen who had been selling iron to them and that he, although he dealt in iron, sold only copper to the Arabs.[94] The iron, to judge from mid-sixth-century texts,[95] would have come from Lebanon (*Labnānu*)—that is, either from otherwise unknown deposits there or from Tyrians who imported it from Cyprus; and from Ionia (*Yamana*)—that is, from the Cilician mines first fully exploited by the Tyrians in Tarsus. Temanites and Sabaeans, accordingly, on their way to the Euphrates and farther east,[96] would have had easy access to iron, either from government stores or from private entrepreneurs such as these Syrian Arabs and their suppliers. They did not join the tax revolt in the later years of Tiglath-pileser III or attract much attention simply because, although they paid the regular perquisites and gave the usual gifts to the Assyrian government, they were not included in its system of taxation.

Tyre, Judah, and the Philistine Cities

Judah and the three Transjordanian kingdoms (Moab, Edom, and Ammon) also belonged to a different system, which Tyre was able to turn to its advantage when first Damascus and then Israel were defeated, and the grand alliance failed. This system included Egypt and the Philistine cities, and it was for this reason that Tiglath-pileser III first went against Gaza and

91. S. W. Cole, *Nippur IV: The Early Neo-Babylonian Governor's Archive from Nippur* (OIP 114; Chicago: Oriental Institute, 1996) 113–15.

92. S. Mazzoni, "Gli stati siro-ittiti e "l'età oscura": Fattori geo-economici di uno sviluppo culturale," *EVO* 4 (1981) 311–41.

93. M. Elat, "Die wirtschaftlichen Beziehungen der Assyrer mit den Arabern," in *Festschrift für Rykle Borger zu seinem 65. Geburtstag am 24. Mai 1994* (ed. S. M. Maul; Groningen: Styx, 1998) 39–57; Parpola, *The Correspondence of Sargon II, Part 1*, 136–37 (#175); also 135–36 (##173–74), 139–40 (##177–78).

94. Ibid., 140–41 (#179).

95. A. L. Oppenheim, "Essay on Overland Trade in the First Millennium B.C.," *JCS* 21 (1967) 236–54. The documents, dated 551 and 550 B.C.E., are inventories of goods shipped to Babylon from some unspecified place in the Levant.

96. H. Lassen, V. F. Buchwald, and W. W. Müller, "A Bronze Sword from Luristan with a Proto-Arabic Inscription," *AfO* 35 (1988) 136–53. The sword, dated ca. 800 B.C.E., is inscribed on the hilt *lhp hn'*, "Belonging to Hafi—Good Luck."

why its king, Hanun, who instinctively fled to Egypt, could be persuaded to return and govern the city after it became clear that Assyria was not interested in harming him or his dominion but was just determined to take advantage of Gaza's market potential.

Jerusalem, beginning in the reign of Tiglath-pileser III and down to the turn of the century, gradually transformed itself from a dynastic freehold and temple town into a national capital, in such a splendid burst of intellectual fervor, social reorganization, and cultural revolution that the reign of Hezekiah (715–687 B.C.E.) became the paradigm of the legendary reign of Solomon—each with its Hiram of Tyre, its magnificent temple where the whole nation could congregate, its queen of Sheba, its travels to Tarshish and to the Red Sea, its wealth, wisdom, and literary production.[97]

When the Philistine cities paid tribute to Assyria or withheld it, as Ashdod did in the time of Hezekiah, so did Judah. But when any one of them threatened to ruin the system—as Ashkelon, Ekron, and Gaza did later in his reign by seeking independence in a separate peace with Assyria, Hezekiah intervened to keep the confederation working. Although some of the towns in the Gaza region were pillaged or wrecked during Tiglath-pileser's campaign, it was at this time that Judah's southern market terminal at Beersheba began to thrive.[98] This town was built for business and planned around the public square and warehouses at the city gate. Although it was small, it could rely on other settlements in the vicinity that were established at the same time, where the routes from Arabia and Africa and Edom passed on to Tell Jemmeh,[99] the staging area for caravans to Egypt, or on farther to Gaza and then to the more northerly Philistine cities and eventually to Jerusalem.

---

97. P. J. King, "The Eighth, the Greatest of Centuries?" *JBL* 108 (1989) 3–15; B. Halpern, "Sybil, or the Two Nations? Archaism, Kinship, Alienation, and the Elite Redefinition of Traditional Culture in Judah in the 8th–7th Centuries B.C.E.," in *The Study of the Ancient Near East in the Twenty-First Century: The William Foxwell Albright Centennial Conference* (ed. J. S. Cooper and G. M. Schwartz; Winona Lake, IN: Eisenbrauns, 1996) 291–338. There are four South Arabic inscriptions on potsherds, two of them found in Stratum 10 (ca. 586 B.C.E.), that indicate that South Arabian merchants were in town and that Judean merchants knew their language and script and did business with them. The pots are Judean wares and were inscribed after firing in a technique that is characteristically Judean. One inscription is a South Arabic personal name, and the others are monograms: see Y. Shiloh, "South Arabian Inscriptions from the City of David, Jerusalem," *PEQ* 119 (1987) 9–18; M. Hofner, "Remarks on Potsherds with Incised Arabian Letters," in *Excavations at the City of David, 1978–1985 Directed by Yigal Shiloh, Volume VI: Inscriptions* (ed. D. T. Ariel; Qedem 14; Jerusalem: Hebrew University Institute of Archaeology, 2000) 26–28.

At least one trader from Northern Israel traveled to Spain and left his signet ring at Cádiz: it is an oval stone in a gold setting, inscribed in eighth-century Hebrew script with his name and patronymic, "Belonging to Naʿimʾel, son of Paʾarat (*lnʿmʾl // pʾrt*); in the upper register, there is a drawing of him facing forward, flanked by facing birds, and in the lowest register a winged sun disk: *IFPCO* 137–39; *WSS* 128–29 (#267).

98. J. A. Blakely and J. W. Hardin, "Southwestern Judah in the Late Eighth Century B.C.E.," *BASOR* 326 (2002) 11–64, esp. pp. 24–30. L. Singer-Avitz, "Beersheba: A Gateway Community in Southern Arabian Long-Distance Trade in the Eighth Century B.C.E.," *TA* 26 (1999) 3–75.

99. P. Wapnish, "Camel Caravans and Camel Pastoralists at Tell Jemmeh," *JANES* 13 (1981) 101–12; I. Finkelstein, *Living on the Fringe: The Archaeology and History of the Negev, Sinai, and Neighbouring Regions in the Bronze and Iron Ages* (Monographs in Mediterranean Archaeology 6; Sheffield: Sheffield Academic Press, 1995) 139–53.

The Philistine cities were culturally Phoenician but materially Judean by the end of the eighth century. A Philistine inscription from this time found at Tell Qasile near Joppa is a receipt for "thirty shekels of gold from Ophir for the Temple of Horon" (*zhb . ʾpr . lbyt . ḥrn Š 30*): the alphabet is Phoenician; the orthography and the script are Philistine; the cult of the God Horon was introduced into the region by Judeans; and gold from Ophir in the Sudan is among the exotic imports that biblical texts ascribe to Hiram of Tyre and Solomon.[100] But there is also a Hebrew ostracon from the same place in which a man of Judah named ʾAḥîyāhû is credited with a shipment of 1100 measures of oil to the royal stores.[101]

At Tel Batash, biblical Timnah, the pottery is Philistine, but there are a fair number of Judean royal (*lmlk*, "For the King") storage jars, one of them inscribed with the name and patronymic (*lṣpn ʾbymʿs*, "Sapan, [son of] Abimaʿas") of the Judean supplier. There were also three clay molds— one in Phoenician style, for casting statuettes of the Judean Goddess Asherah (*ʾšrt*).[102] In nearby Beth Shemesh, a distribution center for olive oil, a unique and startling monkey-faced horse was found among its numerous terra-cotta figurines that must surely have been a cartoon of the exotic imports from far away Tarshish, which have also been ascribed to the legendary joint ventures of Solomon and Hiram of Tyre.[103]

Inscriptions from Ekron and a few inscribed jars also illustrate this cultural and material complexity of the Philistine cities. Most of the pottery is Philistine, but a Phoenician decanter of uncertain provenance is inscribed in Phoenician script with the Judean name Natanbaʿal (*lntnbʿl*)[104] (the Phoenician spelling would have been Yatanbaʿal). Handles from two jars are inscribed "for the king at Hebron" (*lmlk ḥbrn*),[105] indicating that they were destined for the royal Judean storehouses in that town. In the seventh century, the name Asherah (*ʾšrt*) is incised on storage jars[106] destined for the cult of the Goddess in Jerusalem—where to the chagrin of many, her

---

100. A. Lemaire, "Phénicien et Philistien: Paléographie et dialectologie," *Actas* 4, 1.243–49. The number 30 is indicated by three parallel horizontal lines, instead of by the symbols for 20 + 10, as in Phoenician. Diphthongs are not contracted in unaccented syllables (*byt*) but are contracted in accented syllables (*ḥrn* <*ḥwrn).

Horon was still the God of this area (Jamnia) in the third century B.C.E.: see H. W. Haussig, ed., *Götter und Mythen im Vorderen Orient* (Stuttgart: Klett, 1965) 289. Horon is invoked in the Israelite inscription from Arslan Tash and is known from a personal name (*ʿAbdḥawron*) and from a few geographical names (Horonayim, Mount Hawran).

1 Kgs 9:28, 10:11. The gold was considered especially pure (Isa 13:12; Job 22:24, 28:16) and fit for a king (1 Kgs 22:49) or a queen (Ps 45:10). On the possible locations of Ophir, see E. Lipiński, "L'or d'Ophir," in *Numismatique et histoire économique phéniciennes et puniques* (ed. T. Hackens and G. Moucharte; Studia Phoenicia 9; Louvain-la-Neuve: Université Catholique de Louvain—Séminaire de Numismatique Marcel Hoc, 1992) 205–14.

101. J. Naveh, "Writing and Scripts in Seventh-Century B.C.E. Philistia: The New Evidence from Tell Jemmeh," *IEJ* 35 (1985) 8–21, pls. 1–3, esp. p. 16, fig. 4:1.

102. A. Mazar and G. L. Kelm, "Batash, Tel (Timnah)," *NEAEHL* 1.152–57.

103. 1 Kgs 10:22; S. Bunimovitz and Z. Lederman, "Beth-Shemesh," *NEAEHL* 1.249–53; R. Kletter, "A Monkey Figurine from Tel Beth Shemesh," *OJA* 21 (2002) 147–52.

104. R. Deutsch and M. Heltzer, *New Epigraphic Evidence from the Biblical Period* (Tel Aviv–Jaffa: Archaeological Center, 1995) 39–40.

105. T. Dothan and S. Gitin, "Miqne, Tel (Ekron)," *NEAEHL* 3.1051–59.

106. S. Gitin, "Seventh Century B.C.E. Cultic Elements at Ekron," in *Biblical Archaeology Today, 1990* (ed. A. Biran and J. Aviram; Jerusalem: Israel Exploration Society, 1993) 248–58.

worship was enshrined—but her name is spelled in Phoenician (with final -*t*) and not in Judean (with final -*h*).

By contrast, an ostracon marks the pieces of an ivory harp with which it was found as having been made "for Ba'al and for Padi,"[107] that is, for the king of Ekron and for Ba'al, the God of Byblos. An eighth-century royal inscription from the temple in Ekron also illustrates this cosmopolitan outlook: "The House 'Akayush, son of Padi, son of Yissod, son of 'Ada, son of Ya'ir, the prince of Ekron, built for his mistress *Pithogayah*. May she bless him and keep him and prolong his days, and may she bless his land."[108] Its language is Phoenician, specifically the dialect of Byblos.[109] The four earlier kings in the dynasty had Phoenician names, but the name of the current king is Greek ('*kys* = Greek *Achaios* = "Achaean").[110] A Greek Goddess[111] was the patroness of the city. The kings of Ashkelon, Ashdod,[112] and Gaza, similarly, usually had Phoenician names, although a pretender to the throne of Ashkelon appointed by Sennacherib naturally enough had an Assyrian name (Sharruludari). The people of Ashdod rejected the king imposed on them by Sargon and chose one of their own, "the Ionian," as their king, although they wrote and pronounced his name as Phoenician *Yamani*.[113] Ashkelon and Ashdod continued to worship their Aegean Gods and, like the Gods of Samsi, queen of the Arabs, the Assyrians coveted them and even carved pictures of them being carried into exile.[114]

The ordinary, everyday pottery of these cities was Philistine; their nicer dishes were Phoenician. Along with Gaza, they maintained ties with Egypt, but their overland trade was controlled by Assyria and regulated by an Arab "Gatekeeper" whom Tiglath-pileser installed in Gaza.[115] The Philistine cities and Judah, in short, were swept up into the new internationalism, but

107. S. Gitin and M. Cogan, "A New Type of Dedicatory Inscription from Ekron," *IEJ* 49 (1999) 193–202.

108. T. Dothan and J. Naveh, "A Royal Dedicatory Inscription from Ekron," *IEJ* 47 (1997) 1–16.

109. Among the dialectal features are: the omission of the relative pronoun ("house he built"); the third-masculine-singular pronominal suffix in -*h* ("his Mistress, bless him, keep him, his days, his land"); feminine nouns are formed with vowelless -*t* ('*dth*, "his mistress"); the blessing "prolong the days"; the inclusion of the land ("may she bless his land") as a distinct object of blessing.

110. J. Naveh, "Achish-Ikausu in the Light of the Ekron Dedication," *BASOR* 310 (1998) 35–37.

111. C. Schäfer-Lichtenberger, "The Goddess of Ekron and the Religious-Cultural Background of the Philistines," *IEJ* 50 (2000) 82–91.

112. M. Dothan, "Ashdod," and L. E. Stager, "Ashkelon," in *NEAEHL* 1.93–103 and 103–12, respectively.

113. R. Rollinger, "The Ancient Greeks and the Impact of the Ancient Near East: Textual Evidence and Historical Perspective (ca. 750–650 BC)," in *Melammu Symposia II. Mythology and Mythologies: Methodological Approaches to Intercultural Influences* (ed. R. M. Whiting; Helsinki: Neo-Assyrian Text Corpus Project, 2001) 233–64, esp. pp. 245–53.

114. R. D. Barnett, "Lachish, Ashkelon and the Camel: A Discussion of Its Use in Southern Palestine," in *Palestine in the Bronze and Iron Ages: Papers in Honour of Olga Tufnell* (ed. J. N. Tubb; London: Institute of Archaeology, 1985) 15–30.

115. I. Eph'al, *The Ancient Arabs: Nomads on the Borders of the Fertile Crescent, 9th–5th Centuries B.C.* (Jerusalem: Magnes, 1984) 24–36, 93; M. Elat, "Die wirtschaftlichen Beziehungen der Assyrer mit den Arabern," in *Festschrift für Rykle Borger zu seinem 65. Geburtstag am 24. Mai 1994* (ed. S. M. Maul; Groningen: Styx, 1998) 39–57, esp. pp. 48–49.

they remained a separate commercial network that in the eighth century was infiltrated by Phoenicians and, with Assyrian collusion, manipulated to Tyre's advantage.

Tyre, Judah, and Transjordan

Judah's position in this network is known from Assyrian and biblical texts. Judah was not involved in the revolt against Assyria but, on the contrary, protested its loyalty by sending gifts of gold and silver to Tiglath-pileser III. However, toward the end of the century Hezekiah, relying on popular uprisings in Ekron and Ashkelon, tried to cripple Assyria's interests in the network and monopolize trade with Egypt. He failed, was invaded by Sennacherib, and Judah lost much of its territory to Ashdod, Gaza, and the restored regime in Ekron.[116] Assyria clearly was interested in keeping the network intact and functional and did not press the invasion against Jerusalem. In fact, when Hezekiah paid tribute (this included no specifically Judean products but only items that were available in the network, such as gold, silver, and precious stones, cosmetics, couches inlaid with ivory, elephant hides, wood, women, and male and female musicians), good relations were restored and confirmed, as they were under Tiglath-pileser III and Sargon II, by marriage.[117]

Further details on this network depend on biblical descriptions of foreign relations in the time of Solomon and on the supposition that these anecdotal records (1 Kings 9–10) were elaborated from recollections of late eighth-century Judah. There is the same cast of characters, including Hiram of Tyre, the queen of Sheba, and traders and merchants and kings of Arabia. There are the same goods and services, including gold and silver, precious stones and wood, ivory furniture, women, musicians, camels, and exotic animals. There are the same partners, such as Tarshish, Tyre, Sidon, Egypt, Moab, Edom, and Ammon. There is the same cultural milieu, symbolized for the tenth century by the utterances of Solomon and realized in the eighth century by the emergent literary traditions that eventually coalesced in the Bible—traditions drawing on the Greek, Syrian, Mesopotamian, and Transjordanian classics of the time—literature articulating the Canaanite, Amorite, and Hittite heritage of Israel and Judah. Judah was pivotal in the network, tried to dominate it, and wound up monopolizing the transit trade on which Tyre depended.

When Jerusalem was taken by the Babylonians early in the sixth century, Tyre was quoted as saying: "The Gate to the nations is broken; it is my

---

116. *ANET* 287–88; N. Na'aman, "Forced Participation in Alliances in the Course of the Assyrian Campaigns to the West," in *Ah, Assyria . . . : Studies in Assyrian History and Ancient Near Eastern Historiography Presented to Hayim Tadmor* (ed. M. Cogan and I. Eph'al; Scripta Hierosolymitana 33; Jerusalem: Magnes, 1991) 80–98, esp. pp. 94–97.

117. A tomb in the Northwest Palace at Nimrud contained fabulously rich grave goods and the remains of women. Two of them have West Semitic names, one of which is probably Judean, and have been identified as "Yaba, queen of Tiglath-pileser, king of Assyria," and "Atalya, queen of Sargon, king of Assyria." The other women buried in the tomb were probably Hezekiah's daughters, and one of them may have been Naqiya, the wife of Sennacherib; see S. Dalley, "Yaba, Atalya and the Foreign Policy of Late Assyrian Kings," *State Archives of Assyria Bulletin* 12 (1998) 83–98.

turn, I will get my fill from her desolation." These nations, as the context of the saying suggests, included the Philistines, Moab, Edom, and Ammon, the people on Judah's periphery who thought they would profit from its decimation.[118] In the eighth century, however, the countries of Transjordan were just beginning to play their part in international trade. They all paid tribute to Assyria, and their kings are mentioned by name, but their contributions seem to have been quite ordinary items such as "garments of their lands" or "commodities of their countries," not the "purple wool," "linen and multicolored" garments, and "costly articles, produce of land and sea" that were provided by places like Tyre, Byblos, and Gaza.[119]

Edom had an outlet on the Red Sea at Tell el-Kheleifeh servicing trade from South Arabia and Africa, via Beersheba to the Mediterranean Coast. The pottery remains are Edomite, Judean, Cypro-Phoenician, Egyptian, Philistine, and East Greek,[120] but there is no evidence for Edomite products of any commercial value. At Abu al-Kharaz in Gilead, which had Cypriot connections in the Late Bronze Age, there is an early eighth-century carved bone handle, like an ivory handle from Nimrud and another from Hazor,[121] which suggests that there was a Gileadite artistic tradition, inspired by Phoenician canons, but it is local and singular and not indicative of any active share in the market.

Ammon achieved national status in the ninth century, and in the early eighth was distinguished by a unified religion celebrated in the cult of El, by an established royal dynasty and educated public administration, and by capitol building projects. At the end of the eighth century, tradesmen and craftsmen (individuals or entire families) were deported to Nimrud by the Assyrians, but there is little direct evidence for their contribution to the productivity or economy of their own country, except that one man among them, without lineage, is identified as a fuller.[122]

A glimpse of Transjordanian contributions to international trade is available from Tell al-Mudayna in Moab, however. This town is on a secondary road parallel to the King's Highway and about 20 kilometers southeast of Madeba, on the eastern border of the Jordanian Plateau, the jurisdiction of which, according to the Mesha Inscription and biblical texts, was disputed by Israel, Moab, and Ammon. The excavations have revealed the city wall, a multichambered gate, a temple, and a commercial or industrial building,

---

118. Tyre's reaction (Ezek 26:2) is preceded (Ezekiel 25) by a description of what was said and done by these other nations. The rest of Ezekiel 26–28 is taken up with Tyre's trade network.

119. Cf. Tadmor, *The Inscriptions of Tiglath-Pileser III, King of Assyria*, 171.

120. P. Bienkowski and E. van der Steen, "Tribes, Trade, and Towns: A New Framework for the Late Iron Age in Southern Jordan and the Negev," *BASOR* 323 (2001) 21–47.

121. P. M. Fischer, "Cypriot Finds at Tell Abu al-Kharaz, Transjordan," in *Acta Cypria, Part 2* (ed. P. Åström; Jonsered: Åströms, 1992) 84–89; idem and G. Herrmann, "A Carved Bone Object from Tell Abu al-Kharaz in Jordan: A Palestinian Workshop for Bone and Ivory?" *Levant* 27 (1995) 145–63; P. Beck, "The Art of Palestine during the Iron Age II: Local Traditions and External Influences (10th–8th Centuries B.C.E.)," in *Images as Media: Sources for the Cultural History of the Near East and the Eastern Mediterranean (1st Millennium B.C.E.)* (ed. C. Uehlinger; Göttingen: Vandenhoeck & Ruprecht, 2000) 165–83.

122. U. Hübner, *Die Ammoniter: Untersuchungen zur Geschichte, Kultur und Religion eines transjordanischen Volkes im 1. Jahrtausend v. Chr.* (Wiesbaden: Harrassowitz, 1992) 15–129.

all dated to the early eighth century.[123] The building had two stories, including domestic space above and work areas on the first floor, and may be identified as part of a textile factory that produced fabrics known as "garments of the land." Three weights found in the building were for measuring ingredients used in the factory or for other commodities, such as the incense used in the upstairs living quarters or in the adjacent temple. Seals found in or near the gate and scattered elsewhere on the site are distinguished by groups of round holes that could have represented, when impressed, stars or constellations. Bullae with marks of the string that attached them to papyri probably came with shipments or purchase orders received in the temple, the factory, or in some other business in the town.

The temple is especially notable for its incense stands, one of which was inscribed on its pedestal: "Incense altar that ʾElishamaʿ made to embellish the Temple of ʾAwt" (*mqṭr ʾš ʿš ʾlšmʿ lysp bt ʾwt*).[124] The script could be Moabite, but the language is Ammonite.[125] The Goddess ʾwt is unknown, but if her name, as its etymology suggests, signifies "Sign" or "Portent," she could have been the embodiment of the celestial elements, and she might be the Goddess represented in a statue found near ʿAmman.[126] It has neither arms nor hands. The torso is without depth and flattened, but her shoulders have shape, and her breasts are beautifully sculpted so that attention is drawn to the lunar disk centered below them and to the crescent moon whose tips, in lieu of her hands, support them. The symbolism, clearly, is the thing, and the name ʾAwt is fitting for the Goddess, who had the features of Venus, the Queen of Heaven (Astarte among the Phoenicians), and who was, it might be imagined, the patroness of desert travel.

Tell al-Mudayna, consequently, can be seen as a trading town where textiles, probably woolens, were woven and where ʾElishamaʿ, a wealthy Ammonite merchant, could commemorate his reliance on the Goddess by dedicating an incense altar in her temple. The town may have had only regional economic significance, but it belonged to one of the limited networks that did business with the incense merchants from Arabia (the dyed wool stolen from them in Hindanu could have come from just such a place) and furnished part of the regular tribute that Moab had to pay to Assyria. In at least these ways, the networks underwrote the system of international trade that Tyre engineered.

---

123. P. M. M. Daviau and M. Steiner, "A Moabite Sanctuary at Khirbat al-Mudayna," *BASOR* 320 (2000) 1–21; R. Chadwick, "Iron Age Gate Architecture in Jordan and Syria," *Bulletin of the Canadian Society for Mesopotamian Studies* 36 (2001) 125–34; P. M. M. Daviau and P. E. Dion, "Economy-Related Finds from Khirbat al-Mudayna (Wadi ath-Thamad, Jordan)," *BASOR* 328 (2002) 31–48.

124. P. E. Dion and P. M. M. Daviau, "An Inscribed Incense Altar of Iron Age II at Hirbet el-Mudeyine (Jordan)," *ZDPV* 116 (2000) 1–13; A. F. Rainey, "The New Inscription from Khirbet el-Mudeiyineh," *IEJ* 52 (2002) 81–86.

125. The relative pronoun ʾš is Ammonite but not Moabite; the spelling ʿš, "he made," without the final vowel-letter is Ammonite, not Moabite; diphthongs [ay] and [aw] contract to [ê] and [ô] and are not written in Moabite, but in Ammonite, as in this inscription, [ay] contracts (*bt* = *bêt* < **bayt*) but [aw] does not (*ʾwt* = *ʾawt*). The name ʾElshamaʿ is good Ammonite but is not attested in Moabite.

126. Abdel-Jalil ʿAmr, "A Nude Female Statue with Astral Emblems," *PEQ* 117 (1985) 104–11.

Tyre at the Turn of the Eighth Century

Tyre, after Tiglath-pileser III, began to redefine itself as the creative center of its world. It was able to monopolize overland and overseas trade, to invent money, and to revolutionize how business was done. Its products and distinctive pottery began to show up everywhere, the challenge of new frontiers became the features of its Gods and stuff of its legends, and its urban instincts characterized the Tyrians wherever they went. The Tyrian people produced works of art, collected and sold heirlooms and luxuries, and set the standards for refinement and good taste. But they were essentially business people, importers, exporters and retailers of food, drink and clothing—some of it basic, some exotic, purveyors of pleasure and the good life. They continued to rely on the resources of the mainland networks and of their own establishments around the Plain of ʿAkko, but the West was their new focus, and the Mediterranean was becoming their world.

The Plain of ʿAkko

The coastal towns south of Mount Carmel facing the Plain of Sharon were not exploited systematically by Tyre until the seventh century and perhaps not legitimately until its exclusive rights to these ports was confirmed by Esarhaddon. North of Carmel, all the ports and the inland towns that served them had always belonged to Tyre, and from them its influence radiated along the main arteries of the Jezreel and Jordan valleys to cities such as Megiddo and Hazor[127] and to smaller towns and villages that belonged to Israel.

ʾAchzib, north of the Bay of ʿAkko, is known from its cemeteries and artifacts and from a few texts. The texts are seventh-century tombstone inscriptions written in an extremely unskilled Phoenician script on oblong sandstone monuments:[128] of the six deceased, only one followed the custom of recording his father's name; one identified himself by his profession ("the smith") and by his devotion to Tannit, whose symbol is prominent on the stone; another, called "Fats" or "Fatso" (*tbry*), identified himself by describing his appearance and including a drawing of his burly face; one included the abbreviation of his name (*tb*) and above it his monogram (a *T* in a rectangular frame); one had an unusual name (*zkrmlk*; the elements are common, but their combination is unique); and one (*ʿmskr*, "Remembrance Is My Kin") was the first to be named after the God of historical memory, who became popular in the waning years of the western colonies. These tombstones were from the southern cemetery, but there were three other graveyards, all in use from about the ninth century to the seventh,[129]

127. N. Holmes Kantzios, "Phoenicians in Palestine: Another Side of the Homeland," *Actas* 4, 3.1061–66.

128. G. R. Driver, "Seals and Tombstones," *ADAJ* 2 (1953) 62–65, pl. 8:6–8; F. M. Cross Jr., "Phoenician Tomb Stelae from Akhziv," in *The Akhziv Cemeteries: The Ben-Dor Excavations, 1941–1944* (ed. M. Dayagi-Mendels; Jerusalem: Israel Antiquities Authority, 2002) 169–73.

129. M. W. Prausnitz, "Israelite and Sidonian Burial Rites at Akhziv," *Proceedings of the Fifth World Congress of Jewish Studies 1969*, vol. 1: *Ancient Near East, Bible, Archaeology, First Temple Period* (Jerusalem: World Union of Jewish Studies, 1971) 85–89; idem, "Achzib," *NEAEHL* 1.32–35; P. Smith, L. Horwitz, and J. Zias, "Human Remains from the Iron Age Cemeteries at Akhziv, Part 1: The Built Tomb from the Southern Cemetery," *RSF* 18 (1990) 137–50, pls. 12–15.

where the earlier Phoenician tombs are distinguished by their Red Slip, Black-on-Red, and Cypriot wares.[130]

Among the terra-cottas is a model shrine, trimmed in red paint, which symbolizes Astarte on its façade as the lunar disk and in its cella as an empty throne with the Sibitti, or Pleiades, filling its backrest. But the throne is modeled abstractly (there are eight Sibitti for symmetry's sake), as plain horizontal and vertical curved surfaces, to represent the evening sky meeting the horizon.[131] The stamp seals and amulets[132] are often Egyptianizing, as might be expected in a Tyrian town. They are poorly executed, however, and lack the usual Tyrian refinement, although they do have its typical balance and symmetry: a male and female dancer, for instance, each with one hand raised and clasping the other's raised hand, dance pleasingly around a stylized tree of life.[133] A caprid facing left is balanced by the forelegs and head of another caprid facing right, but it is forced by the lack of space to share the same body.[134]

There are miniature masks of women, of men (one of them grotesque), and of a bull, but the terra-cotta figurines are all of women. They include the stylized seated pregnant woman that is typical of most Tyrian sites; domestic scenes of a woman kneading dough, bathing, or holding a child; dance scenes with women in full-length flowing robes playing the flute or tambourine; and informal representations of a woman standing naked or caressing a lover.[135] ʾAchzib, as these bits of evidence suggest, was a populous town, drifting in the mainstream of Tyrian culture and commerce but independent, self-sufficient, very low-keyed, and undistinguished by any peculiar genius or exclusive product—a port community awash in the transit trade.

Tel Kabri, biblical Rehob, just southeast of ʾAchzib, north of the Bay of ʿAkko, was a few kilometers inland on a wadi route to the interior. Its Bronze Age splendor was gone and forgotten, and it was a nondescript walled town with a watchtower, which may have been a military post or relay station. It was destroyed by the Assyrians in the eighth century and was lightly settled in the seventh by Tyrian troops, perhaps, and East Greek mercenaries.[136] ʿAkko, on the northern tip of the bay, was the port for Tell

---

130. M. W. Prausnitz, "A Phoenician Krater from Akhziv," *OrAnt* 5 (1966) 177–88; W. Culican, "Some Phoenician Masks and Other Terracottas," *Berytus* 24 (1975–76) 47–87, esp. p. 58 n. 22.

131. Idem, "A Terracotta Shrine from Achzib," *ZDPV* 92 (1976) 47–53; repr. *Opera Selecta: From Tyre to Tartessos* (Gothenburg: Åströms, 1986) 481–93; M. Dayagi-Mendels, ed., *The Akhziv Cemeteries: The Ben-Dor Excavations, 1941–1944* (Jerusalem: Israel Antiquities Authority, 2002) 160–62.

132. O. Keel, *Corpus der Stempelsiegel-Amulette aus Palästina/Israel* (Göttingen: Vandenhoeck & Ruprecht, 1997) 20–77, nos. 1–162.

133. Ibid., no. 160, p. 74.

134. Ibid., no. 85, p. 57.

135. R. Kletter, *The Judean Pillar-Figurines and the Achaeology of Asherah* (BAR International Series 636; Oxford: Tempus Reparatum, 1996) 280–85; Dayagi-Mendels, ed., *The Akhziv Cemeteries*, 145–60.

136. E. Stern, *Archaeology of the Land of the Bible, Volume II: The Assyrian, Babylonian, and Persian Periods (732–332 BCE)* (New York: Doubleday, 2001) 58–101; W. D. Niemeier, "Greek Mercenaries at Tel Kabri and Other Sites in the Levant," *TA* 29 (2002) 328–31.

Keisan, and locally made transport jars sometimes were stamped with the design of a ship, a merchantman with high curved bow and stern, one bank of oars, and a mast anchored by cables and surmounted by a crow's nest.[137] By the end of the eighth century, it was producing distinctive pottery (featuring spiral or zigzag lines combined with droplets, eyes, or flower buds) that was mainly for local consumption and was unparalleled except at ʾAchzib and Tell Keisan.[138] South of Keisan, on the fringes of the Jezreel Valley, there were Phoenician villages at Yokneʿam and Tel Qiri that were probably supply depots for agricultural produce but that were leveled when nearby Megiddo became the capital of an Assyrian province.[139]

Tell Keisan, as reported in the Amarna letters, was a Canaanite town aligned with ʿAkko, both of them governed by princes with Hurrian names, and both of them faithful vassals of Egypt in its struggle with the insurgent Ḫapiru.[140] Its Canaanite name, Akshapa, is preserved in biblical texts as Akshap (*ʾkšp*), but its Phoenician name, **Kašpôn* (from the same root but with deletion of the initial *ʾalep* and the addition of the afformative *-ôn*), is known from Assyrian *kaspuna*. The town became the Assyrian administrative center of the ʿAkko region toward the end of the eighth century, and Assyrian influence began to color an otherwise distinctive Canaanite-and-Egyptian cultural matrix. The eighth-century architectural remains are from domestic and artisanal sectors with large houses and courtyards, paved squares, ovens, and workshops.[141]

The pottery is basically Phoenician, although Assyrian wares become progressively more prominent in the seventh century. Among the distinctive Phoenician types are transport jars with pointed bases, small handles, and low necks designed to be sealed, similar to jars found in Tyre, Megiddo, and Hazor, as well as in Cyprus, Spain, and Carthage.[142] Jars of this type were mass-produced according to strict specifications, because they were made to be packed tightly, secured by ropes through their handles, in the holds of ships, like the ship on the stamped jar handle from ʿAkko and like the two ships loaded with hundreds of these jars that sank off Ashkelon.[143] Commercial connections with Cyprus are still evident in the large, seventh-century loop-handled jars that were made at Kalopsidha, an

---

137. D. Conrad, "Stempelabdruck eines Schiffes vom Tell el-Fuhhar (Tel ʿAkko)," in *Periplus: Festschrift für Hans-Gunter Buchholz* (ed. P. Åström and D. Sürenhagen; Studies in Mediterranean Archaeology 127; Jonsered: Åströms, 2000) 37–41, pl. 5.
138. Idem, "The Akko Ware: A New Type of Phoenician Pottery with Incised Decoration," in *Studies in the Archaeology and History of Ancient Israel in Honour of Moshe Dothan* (ed. M. Heltzer, A. Segal, and D. Kaufman; Haifa: Haifa University Press, 1993) 127–42.
139. A. Ben-Tor and Y. Portugali, eds., *Tel Qiri: A Village in the Jezreel Valley* (Qedem 24; Jerusalem: Hebrew University, Institute of Archaeology, 1987); A. Ben-Tor, "Jokneam," *NEAEHL* 3.805–11.
140. *EA* ##366–67, pp. 364–65.
141. J. Briend and J.-B. Humbert, ed., *Tell Keisan (1971–1976): Une cité phénicienne en Galilée* (Orbis Biblicus et Orientalis: Series Archaeologica 1; Fribourg: Editions Universitaires / Göttingen: Vandenhoeck & Ruprecht, 1980) 131–56, 157–79.
142. J.-B. Humbert, "Keisan, Tell," *NEAEHL* 3.862–67.
143. R. D. Ballard et al., "Iron Age Shipwrecks in Deep Water off Ashkelon, Israel," *AJA* 106 (2002) 151–68.

inland site equidistant from the Bay of Salamis and the Bay of Larnaka,[144] and imported to Keisan from Kition or Salamis.

The intersection of local Phoenician, Assyrian, and Egyptian traditions can be seen in the personal seals.[145] The authentic Egyptian seals are heirlooms from the Middle Bronze Age, and Phoenician seals copy their motifs or their hieroglyphic signs; seals of Assyrian inspiration have symbols of Nabu, Marduk, or the Moon God[146] (there are parallels to the representation of the Moon God in seals from nearby Shiqmona on the tip of Cape Carmel and from Mount Nebo in distant Moab),[147] and one seal depicts the scene from the *Epic of Gilgamesh*, in which Gilgamesh and Enkidu kill Humbaba in the Cedar Forest.

But the linear, angular, and schematic style of the seals, their preference for symbolic and mythic animals and for representations of Astarte in the constellation of lunar disk, crescent moon, and stars are totally distinctive of the Tell Keisan workshops. The terra-cottas are exclusively of women, as at ʾAchzib, but Tell Keisan has no scenes from daily life, no figures of the seated pregnant woman, shuns realism for the ritualism of women playing a drum (there is one like it from Shiqmona), and for impressionistic studies of women's facial features (a few like them found their way to Shiqmona, Tel Kabri, Megiddo, and Beth Shean).[148]

Tell Keisan and the other towns of the ʿAkko region suggest a pattern of Tyrian settlement in which an administrative and commercial center situated slightly inland, like Keisan, and a nearby port town, such as ʿAkko (from which the ships that foundered off Ashkelon may have sailed) were dependent on the production and storage facilities of farm towns, such as Qiri and Yokneʿam, and on the protection of outposts, such as Kabri, scattered in the interior—every one of them with its specialization and all of them radiating from the island capital. The pattern, in the case of Tyre, included the island capital as the port city, mainland Ushu as the administrative and commercial center, Mahalab to the north as its protective outpost, and places such as Silm and Joya a few kilometers inland as satellite towns.[149] The pattern allowed or promoted distinctive cultural developments, commercial relations, and industrial or agricultural produc-

---

144. J. Gunneweg and I. Perlman, "The Origin of the 'Loop-Handled Jars' from Tell Keisan," *RB* 98 (1991) 591–99.

145. O. Keel, "La glyptique de Tell Keisan (1971–1976)," in *Studien zu den Stempelsiegeln aus Palästina/Israel, III: Die frühe Eisenzeit. Ein Workshop* (ed. O. Keel, M. Shuval, and C. Uehlinger; Göttingen: Vandenhoeck & Ruprecht, 1990) 163–258. Repr. from O. Keel, "La glyptique," in *Tell Keisan (1971–1976): Une cité phénicienne en Galilée* (ed. J. Briend and J.-B. Humbert; Göttingen: Vandenhoeck & Ruprecht, 1980) 257–99.

146. A. Spycket, "Le culte du dieu-lune à Tell Keisan," *RB* 80 (1973) 384–95, pl. 7; idem, "Nouveaux documents pour illustrer le culte du dieu-lune," *RB* 81 (1974) 258–59, pl. 15.

147. S. Saller, "Iron Age Tombs at Nebo, Jordan," *Liber Annuus* 16 (1965–66) 165–298, esp. pp. 225–31. The pottery associated with the seal was Phoenician, and the lyre represented on the seal is consistent with a Phoenician milieu: cf. B. Lawergren, "Distinctions among Canaanite, Philistine and Israelite Lyres, and Their Global Lyrical Contexts," *BASOR* 309 (1998) 41–68, esp. pp. 53–54.

148. Kletter, *The Judean Pillar-Figurines and the Archaeology of Asherah*, 280–85.

149. S. Vibert Chapman, "A Catalogue of Iron Age Pottery from the Cemeteries of Khirbet Silm, Joya, Qraye and Qasmieh of South Lebanon," *Berytus* 21 (1972) 55–154.

tion in each satellite system but was based on a sense of Tyrian identity, the characteristics of which were independence, imitation, and eclecticism.

Independence was expressed in the establishment of separate settlements, often walled, defined by occupation or profession. Imitation, in arts and crafts for instance, resided in a genius nourished by communal recollection and individual daring. Eclecticism, as in literature and religion, was the spiritual analogue of trade and commerce, the sense that value was comparable, that thoughts and deeds like things could be exchanged. These traits could have extraordinary effects, such as colonization and the creation of a Mediterranean world or, as exemplified by Tell Keisan and the ʿAkko region, just be the stuff of satisfaction in a productive life.

Cilicia and Cyprus

In the time of Tiglath-pileser III, Tyre and Sidon were under the authority of the same Assyrian administrator. One of the region's products was timber from the Lebanon which, because it was cut and milled for the shipyards, Tyre was prevented from selling to the Philistine cities or to Egypt,[150] and Tyre simply acquiesced. Sidon, by contrast, was unruly and aggressive and, to resist Assyria, encroached on Tyrian territory. By the time of Sargon II (721–704 B.C.E.), the Assyrian vendetta against Sidon and its favoritism for Tyre, combined with Tyre's shrewd but bewildering reliance on Assyria to protect and promote its growing monopoly led to direct military intervention in their affairs.

For Sargon's seventh year (715–714 B.C.E.), the Assyrian annals record that "the Ionians since the distant past had killed inhabitants of the city of Tyre and of the land of Que and had interrupted their trade" and that Sargon sailed against them with ships from the land of Ḫatti and "caught them like fish in the midst of the sea and so restored peace to the land of Que and to the city of Tyre."[151] Que's perspective on the situation is revealed in the inscriptions on Urikki's trophy and boundary monuments and differs in omitting Tyre's involvement, the issue of trade, and how exactly Sargon gained his victory. The "ships of the land of Ḫatti" were the ships from the towns on the Syrian coast, excluding the Tyrian and Euboean station at Al Mina, that were conspicuous in their allegiance to Sidon and that now formed the Assyrian fleet anchored at Arvad. The inhabitants of Tyre were not the inhabitants living on the island redoubt, which was impervious to piracy, but Tyrians, citizens of Tyre, living at Tarsus in Cilicia, for instance, and working at their Al Mina trading station.

Trade, similarly, was not between Tyre and Que but between each of these separately and Assyria, and its interruption by Ionian pirates (sailing along the Cilician coast and operating from ports in Cyprus) provided Sargon with a motive and an urgent excuse to intervene. What is remarkable about this is: first, Tyre's inability or unwillingness to defend itself or its commercial interests—the pirates were persistent and elusive, harassing ships from "the distant past" and lurking "in the midst of the sea" but

150. Saggs, "The Nimrud Letters, 1952—Part II," Letter XII, pp. 127–30, 149–51.

151. A. Fuchs, *Die Inschriften Sargons II. aus Khorsabad* (Göttingen: Cuvillier, 1994) 109, 319–20; see also pp. 34, 290, 290 n. 39, 440.

reportedly were no match for the ships from Ḫatti; and second, Assyria's dependence on Phoenician trade (controlled forever by Sidon in Cilicia, and by Tyre from any of its satellite sources), through the gateway of the Orontes to the Euphrates.

Tyre is mentioned in the Assyrian sources, Sidon in the Phoenician, and the impression these give is that Sidon was the more belligerent, if only because it was the more threatened and the more resentful of foreign interference. However, neither (for all Tyre and Sidon's cultural and commercial zing) was a serious political or naval power. This impression is reinforced by the account of a second Assyrian intervention in Tyrian affairs about seven years later during the reign of Sargon (707 B.C.E.). The text,[152] known from several exemplars, including an inscribed stele found at Kition where Sargon claims to have displayed it, is about the submission of Cyprus to Assyrian rule and the establishment of a Tyrian protectorate on the island.

The island is called just that, the *island* (*ia-a'*), under the jurisdiction of the land of Adnana, the land of the Danunians. It is visualized as the very distant abode of seven kings, a seven-day journey into the middle of the western sea, although anyone who sailed there, Sargon's representatives among them, knew it could be reached in about a day from the Cilician or Tyrian coast. Its impossible distance, almost off the map, explains why previous kings of Assyria had not heard of this exotic place and certainly had not subjected it. The ignorance, moreover, was mutual and near universal, except that someone in Cyprus had heard of Assyria and the Tyrian governor (*šilṭa ṣuraya*) of Carthage (appointed by the city and well acquainted with mainland affairs) and had submitted and brought tribute to Sargon. To return the favor and to establish the governor's credit among the seven kings, Sargon sent an officer and the royal guard to Cyprus. It was a diplomatic coup, but at this show of strength and at the mere report of Sargon's splendid success in the west, the kings were awestruck and sent their tribute—gold, silver, locally made ebony, and boxwood furniture—to the king in Babylon.

What is extraordinary is the ease and lightheartedness of it all. The seven kings of Cyprus, soon to be ten, became part of the Assyrian nexus. The province of Carthage was included among them and its governor, for his part in the intrigue, was promoted to royalty. Kition, where the amphictyony met under Sidonian auspices, became the capital of an Assyrian province, home to a Tyrian governor, and administrative center for the island's resources. There was no battle, the island was taken by storytelling and a sail-past, and the tribute it paid was just the first installment in a fruitful trade agreement. Tyrian ships were involved, but it was one ship, at best a flotilla, not a fleet; the Persian guard was on parade, dazzling, and looking grand. The capitulation was a success and the very exemplar of Tyrian expediency and acquiescence.

---

152. *ANET* 284; A. Fuchs, *Die Inschriften Sargons II. aus Khorsabad*, 175–77, 337, 393–98; N. Naʾaman, "Sargon II and the Rebellion of the Cypriote Kings against Shilta of Tyre," *Or* 67 (1998) 239–47; idem, "The Conquest of Yadnana according to the Inscriptions of Sargon II," in *Proceedings of the XLVe Rencontre Assyriologique Internationale*, vol. 1: *Historiography in the Cuneiform World* (ed. I. T. Abusch et al.; Bethesda MD: CDL, 2001) 357–63.

Tyrian cultural influence in Cyprus declined as its political and economic clout increased and as the city's focus shifted to North African Carthage and the western Mediterranean. Although it was predominant, it was not exclusive, and Byblians and Sidonians, especially in the eastern part of the island, were a notable presence so that no kingdom was exempt from the Phoenician pioneering spirit. The proof of their presence was the development of an effective and influential Cypriot culture that could absorb their heritage as it hastened to define its Hellenic destiny.[153]

From Chytroi (Kythrea), about 15 kilometers northeast of Nicosia and 10 from the north coast, there is a Phoenician funerary inscription, dated to the end of the eighth or the early seventh century, and the assumption must be that the dead man was from an open and bilingual society and expected the locals or some Phoenician traveler to read it and invoke his blessed memory.[154] Near Ledra, now Nicosia, there are tombs from approximately the mid-eighth century, in which a few Phoenician wares and their imitations are mixed with mostly Cypriot burial gifts.[155] The royal tombs at Salamis could be fabulously wealthy, filled with ivory furniture made by Tyrian craftsmen and with works of art imported by Tyrian merchants or produced locally by Phoenician-trained Cypriot artists. However, the ideology and meaning of the tombs was totally Greek, inspired by Homer and by reminiscences of the heroic age: kings buried with their horses, their ceremonial chariots, bridles, harnesses, armor, and ornaments along with their royal robes, their prized gold, silver and bronze possessions, their knickknacks, and their best Phoenician and Greek dinnerware.[156]

A new city was founded at Idalion in the ninth or early eighth century to handle copper and iron coming from the Troodos mines to the port at Kition[157] and was settled by Cypriots, by Sidonians from the port, and by Byblians who worked in the mines or with the finished or with imported metals. They made the gilded silver paterae, the bronze horse blinkers inscribed with the Byblian name Ba'ana', and the bronze lance tip inscribed with the name of the Byblian Goddess 'Anat, all of which were found in an early fourth-century cache.[158] They had some Phoenician Red Slip Ware, but most of the pottery was Cypriot, and the many gold, silver, glass, and

---

153. H. Matthäus, "Zypern und das Mittelmeergebiet: Kontakthorizonte des späten 2. und frühen 1. Jahrtausends v. Chr.," in *Archäologische Studien in Kontaktzonen der antiken Welt* (ed. R. Rolle and K. Schmdt; Göttingen: Vandenhoeck & Ruprecht, 1998) 73–91.

154. *RPC* 104–7.

155. P. Flourentzos, "Four Early Iron Tombs from Nicosia, Old Municipality," *RDAC* (1981) 115–28.

156. V. Karageorghis, *Excavations in the Necropolis of Salamis I, Text* (Salamis 3; Nicosia: Department of Antiquities, 1967) 6–24, pls. 2–18, 108–16; pp. 74–89, pls. 65–85, 136–43; idem, *Excavations in the Necropolis of Salamis III, Text* (Salamis 5; Nicosia: Department of Antiquities, 1973) 4–122; J. H. Crouwel, "Chariots in Iron Age Cyprus," *RDAC* (1987) 101–18; D. W. Rupp, "The 'Royal Tombs' at Salamis (Cyprus): Ideological Messages of Power and Authority," *Journal of Mediterranean Archaeology* 1 (1988) 111–39; S. Welkamp and C. H. J. de Geus, "Fit for a King? An Ivory Throne Found at Salamis, Cyprus," *Jaarbericht "Ex Oriente Lux"* 34 (1995–96) 87–99.

157. P. Gaber, "The History of Idalion: A History of Interaction," in *Visitors, Immigrants, and Invaders in Cyprus* (ed. P. W. Wallace; Albany: State University of New York at Albany, Institute of Cypriot Studies, 1995) 32–39.

158. G. Markoe, *Phoenician Bronze and Silver Bowls from Cyprus and the Mediterranean* (Berkeley: University of California Press, 1985) 169–88; *RPC* 110, pl. 10:2; 112, pl. 13:2.

faience works, as well as quantities of bronze and iron weapons and jewelry indicate that it was a mining, factory, and artisan town with a skilled work force and a few influential Phoenician traders and craftsmen.[159] Tamassos in the eighth century is the origin of a dedication in the temple at Kition by a Phoenician whose family was sufficiently assimilated to name him *Tamassos* but who, himself was still sufficiently ethnic to make the dedication in Phoenician on a Red Slip bowl.[160]

At Amathus, Greek pottery imports are concentrated in a few tombs that were used for generations, and some of the deceased had been associates of the Amathus "Workshop," which was distinguished by its use of Attic Geometric designs to decorate local and Phoenician pottery.[161] A rich but otherwise typical Cypriot tomb assemblage included a very large display of local wares, a small selection of Euboean and Attic ceramics, and a few Phoenician perfume jars.[162] Phoenician pottery was buried in many graves, among which Tyrian tombs are identified by their Phoenician wares, with a selection of Cypriot and Greek pottery and a spattering of Egyptian relics; and terra-cottas, locally made but displaying mainland Phoenician themes.[163]

Nora, if its territory was situated in the Vasilikos Valley, was a thoroughly traditional Cypriot kingdom. Soloi, on the northwest coast on the Bay of Morphou, may have had a Phoenician king or a Cypriot king with a Phoenician name, in the seventh century. Paphos included a Tyrian quarter and along with Kourion was a nucleus from which Phoenician influence radiated into the interior. Both were starting places for travel farther west (to Chalcis in Euboea, for instance, and then Italy, North Africa, and Sardinia), and the graves reflect the rich and eclectic tastes of the merchants and bankers who organized the expeditions.[164] In short, what made the Phoenicians so influential in Cyprus and what made the biggest impression

---

159. P. Alin, "Idalion Pottery from the Excavations of the Swedish Cyprus Expedition," *Opuscula Atheniensia* 12 (1978) 91–109; E. Gjerstad, *The Swedish Cyprus Expedition* (4 vols.; Stockholm: Swedish Cyprus Expedition, 1935) 2.460–641.

160. *Kition* 3, 149–60, #D21.

161. J. N. Coldstream, "Greek Geometric and Archaic Imports from the Tombs of Amathus—II," *RDAC* (1995) 199–212, pls. 16–19; J. L. Benson, "The Amathus Workshop," *RDAC* (1982) 138–43, pls. 36–38.

162. C. Tytgat, "La tombe NW 194 de la nécropole nord d'Amathonte," *RDAC* (1995) 137–85, pls. 11–13; J. N. Coldstream, "Amathus Tomb NW 194: The Greek Pottery Imports," *RDAC* (1995) 187–98, pls. 14–15.

163. P. M. Bikai, *The Phoenician Pottery of Cyprus* (Nicosia: Leventis Foundation, 1987); idem, "The Phoenician Pottery," in *La nécropole d'Amathonte, tombes 113–367, II: Céramiques non-Chypriotes* (ed. V. Karageoroghis, O. Picard, and C. Tytgat; Études Chypriotes 8; Nicosia: Department of Antiquities, 1987) 1–19, pls. 1–7; G. Clerc, "Aegyptiaca," in *La nécropole d'Amathonte—Tombes 110–385* (ed. V. Karageorghis, O. Picard, and C. Tytgat; Études Chypriotes 13; Nicosia: Department of Anjtiquities, 1991) 1–157; V. Karageorghis, "Amathus between the Greeks and the Phoenicians," *Atti* 2, 3.959–68.

164. M. E. Morden, "The Function of Foreign Imports in Cypriot Early Iron Age Assemblages," in *Visitors, Immigrants, and Invaders in Cyprus* (ed. P. W. Wallace; Albany: State University of New York at Albany, Institute of Cypriot Studies, 1995) 40–50. Among the personal belongings in a late eighth-century tomb at Kourion was a monumental Euboean krater featuring a tree-of-life, which was the favorite motif of a potter working in Chalcis: D. Buitron-Oliver, "Kourion: The Evidence for the Kingdom from the 11th to the 6th Century B.C.," *BASOR* 308 (1997) 27–36, esp. pp. 29–30.

on them was the profound and vigorous native culture they encountered and the island's constantly renewed engagement with the Greek world (witnessed in the eighth century, for instance, by imported pottery and its exquisite imitations),[165] to which it really belonged.

Kition, although not included among the kingdoms, continued under the Tyrians and Persians as the religious center of the Cypriot amphictyonic league. At Kathari, in the northern part of the town, a Late Cypriot cultic ruin was found that was rebuilt in the ninth century, destroyed by fire at the end of that century, and rebuilt in the eighth as part of a greater commercial and temple complex. At about the same time, a temple was built at Bamboula in the eastern sector of the site, near the harbor. Beginning in the seventh century, three more intramural and three extramural temples were constructed.[166]

This flurry of construction marked the inauguration of Kition as the administrative center of Cyprus, and the new buildings comprised headquarters as well as temples for the Cypriot, Greek, and Phoenician population of the island.[167] The Bamboula edifice, for instance, featured statuettes of women with uplifted arms, a Cypriot cultic gesture, and its pottery, apart from some authentic and imitation seventh-century Phoenician Red Slip (Samaria) ware, was Cypriot.[168] Most of the pottery of Kition in the ninth and eighth centuries is also Cypriot, and despite the increase in Phoenician pottery from the second half of the eighth century through the seventh, Cypriot pottery continued to predominate.[169] Kition, like its name, was always Cypriot. Sidonians, when they settled there, tended to assimilate and, as everywhere, blended into the populace.[170] Tyrians liked to keep their distance, and as they took over Kition in the seventh century, it was typical of them to build an encompassing town wall and separate temples for sojourners and for the rest of the population. Phoenician inscriptions become common beginning in the seventh century, and it is symptomatic of the town's societal mix that prized Phoenician Red Slip pottery was engraved with the names of its Cypriot and Greek patrons.[171] Kition was

---

165. J. N. Coldstream, "Geometric Skyphoi in Cyprus," *RDAC* (1979) 255–369, pls. 29–31; A. Demetriou, "The Impact of the Late Geometric Style of Attica on the Free Field Style of Cyprus," in *Periplus: Festschrift fur Hans-Gunther Buchholz zu seinem ächtzigsten Geburtstag am 24. Dezember 1999* (ed. P. Åström and D. Sürenhagen; Jonsered: Åströms, 2000) 43–50, pl. 6.

166. A. Caubet, "Les sanctuaires de Kition à l'époque de la dynastie phénicienne," in *Religio Phoenicia* (ed. C. Bonnet, E. Lipiński, and P. Marchetti; Studia Phoenicia 4; Namur: Société des Études Classiques, 1986) 153–58.

167. V. Karageorghis, "Fouilles de Kition-Bamboula," *BCH* 102 (1978) 916–20; idem, "Astarte at Kition," in *Archäologische Studien in Kontaktzonen der antiken Welt* (ed. R. Rolle, K. Schmidt, and R. F. Docter; Göttingen: Vandenhoeck & Ruprecht, 1998) 105–8.

168. Idem, "Fouilles de Kition-Bamboula," *BCH* 105 (1981) 993–96; 106 (1982) 722–27; D. Christou, "Kition-Bamboula," *BCH* 118 (1994) 672–77.

169. M. Yon and A. Caubet, *Kition-Bamboula III: Le sondage L-N 13 (Bronze Récent et Géometrique)* (Paris: Editions Recherche sur les Civilisations, 1985); S. Hadjisavvas, "Recent Phoenician Discoveries on the Island of Cyprus," *Actas* 4, 3.1023–33; Bikai, *The Phoenician Pottery of Cyprus*.

170. A. Swinton, V. Izzet, and S. Aguilar Gutiérrez, "Phoenicians in the Mediterranean: Degrees and Modes of Interaction," *Actas* 4, 4.1903–7.

171. O. Masson ("A propos de la découverte d'une inscription chypriote-syllabique à Kition en 1970," *RDAC* [1971] 49–52, pl. 21) discusses three inscriptions: an imported Phoenician Red

Fig. 3.4. Bowl with decoration of religious ritual; Cypriot, eighth century B.C.E.; bronze, H. 1⁹⁄₁₆ in. (4 cm), diameter 5¼ in. (13.3 cm) (MMA 74.51.5700). © The Metropolitan Museum of Art.

where the Cypriot kingdoms congregated, a religious center, a market, and the natural place for Sargon to erect the stele proclaiming their subjection to Assyria.

Phoenicians, wherever they went, were purveyors of the good life, of which money-mindedness was an engine and artistic creation and leisure an expression. In Cyprus, examples of their ingenuity include some of the basics such as pottery and party wares that came to define a life-style mediating luxury and the pleasures of simplicity. But elegant and precious drinking bowls crafted around this time can also tell the story of this cosmopolitan society.

One of the tombs at Kition, which was pretty well filled with Phoenician Red Slip wares, also contained an imported Attic Geometric drinking bowl,

---

Slip pitcher with five Cypro-Syllabic signs (*mo-ne-m-si-ta*) on its shoulder, another jug with seven signs (*te-ro-pa-no-to-ta-ko*), and a Red Slip juglet with the Greek name *Thales* in syllabic script.

Fig. 3.5. Royal Egyptian victory and mythological scenes, ca. 675 B.C.E. Found at Idalion (Louvre, Paris, A.O. 20134). Reproduced by permission of the Réunion des Musées Nationaux / Art Resource, NY. Photo by: Herve Lewandowski.

dated to the mid-eighth century (760–750 B.C.E.).[172] This bowl brings back to Cyprus a Phoenician motif (the Tree-of-Life flanked by rampant goats, repeated on the opposite side of the bowl as the Tree flanked by Attic birds) that its artist learned from an expatriate Phoenician, perhaps a Sidonian from Kition, who had settled in Greece. At Idalion, around this time, just such a Sidonian artist made a bronze bowl (see fig. 3.4) adorned with a ritual scene portraying a Goddess entertained by three female musicians who stand behind her playing the flute, lyre, and tambourine and by a female singer and six girls who dance in front of her.[173]

This narrative simplicity contrasts with the decoration on later silver bowls (ca. 710–675 B.C.E.) from the same place. One of these combines

172. J. N. Coldstream, "A Figured Attic Geometric Kantharos from Kition," *RDAC* (1994) 155–59, pl. 29.
173. *PBSB* #Cy3, 171–72, 246–47.

Assyrian symbolism with witty Phoenician commentary. The symbolism starts with a rosette medallion, a cipher for eminence; continues in the inner or lower register with repeated portrayals of a four-winged Assyrian genius killing a lion; and ends in the outer register with a procession of cavalry, infantry, and bowmen led by the king dressed in Assyrian style and riding in a chariot. The commentary, to identify itself, begins by inserting Phoenician palmettes into the inner register; then balances the Assyrian genius against a long-haired boy in a short kilt who kills an Assyrian griffin; and continues in the outer register by stopping the deadly procession with the ridiculous image of a small crooked man leading a camel to the shade of an oak tree.[174]

Another of these bowls has a more stylized and subtle polemic. In the medallion, there is an Egyptian king striding right, holding a mace in his raised right hand, and threatening suppliant captives, whom he holds with his left (see fig. 3.5). This much is standard or stereotypical. A bearded attendant with a corpse draped over his right shoulder—the image of Heracles with the lion-skin shawl—stands behind him holding a spear and a fan. Perched above him, a winged sun disk and a Horus falcon survey the scene. The inner register portrays human-headed and falcon-headed sphinxes trampling a prostrate enemy, and the outer register alternates between a man in Egyptian garb wielding a sword against a lion or griffin and a Phoenician hero in a lion skin or carrying a lion over his shoulder fighting them, Heracles style, with his bare hands.[175] An anti-Assyrian polemic is clear in the designs on both these bowls, but the mock Egyptianizing style of the second and its inclusion of Heracles turn it into a Cypro-Phoenician spoof on Tyrian intrigue in the Assyrian subjection of Cyprus.

Bowls from Tyrian enclaves in the western part of the island display eclectic designs that were influenced by the tastes of their Cypriot patrons and by the current political situation. A bowl from Amathus, dated to about the end of the eighth century, combines Egyptian motifs with Assyrian propaganda.[176] A central rosette is surrounded by sphinxes wearing sun-disk-and-uraeus crowns; the inner register shows two Assyrians picking flowers from a stylized tree, with Harpocrates and Isis to one side of them and Nephthys and Horus to the other; the outer register portrays the siege of a walled city by an Assyrian army and the destruction of its outlying orchards—a source of pride and a subject of boasting by Assyrian kings.[177] At Kourion the earlier bowls, from about the third quarter of the eighth century, have Egyptian motifs and rustic Cypriot themes, such as birds swimming and deer cavorting through papyrus plants, or horses and their

174. Ibid., #Cy1, 169–70, 242–43.

175. Ibid., #Cy2, 170–71, 244–45; J. Boardman, "Heracles' Monsters: Indigenous or Oriental?" in *Le bestiaire d'Héraclès: IIIe Rencontre héracléenne* (ed. C. Bonnet, C. Jourdain-Annequin, and V. Pirenne-Delforge; *Kernos* Supplément 7; Liège: Centre Internationale d'Étude de la Religion Grecque Antique, 1998) 27–35, esp. p. 30.

176. *PBSB* #Cy4, 172–74, 248–49.

177. S. W. Cole, "The Destruction of Orchards in Assyrian Warfare," in *Assyria 1995: Proceedings of the 10th Anniversary Symposium of the Neo-Assyrian Text Corpus Project, Helsinki, September 7–11, 1995* (ed. S. Parpola and R. M. Whiting; Helsinki: Neo-Assyrian Text Corpus Project, 1997) 29–40.

foals and cows and their calves standing in a papyrus thicket.[178] Toward the end of the century, however, narrative or descriptive scenes are combined with a clutter of Egyptian and Assyrian motifs, because the bowls were designed by technically gifted but increasingly eclectic and culturally vapid Tyrian artists to suit the fancy of the Cypriot kings with whose names they are engraved.[179]

Around this time, Tyrians had lost interest in Cyprus. Black-on-Red pottery, a product of Cypriot style and Tyrian artistry and popular (especially the small perfume bottles) from about the end of the tenth century on wherever Tyrian and Cypriot merchants traveled on the mainland, dropped out of favor.[180] Euboean Late Geometric pottery became plentiful both at Tyre and at Amathus.[181] In Tyre a whole new pottery complex (including a less cumbersome storage jar) was designed and found its way to the towns in its territory, its trading station at Al Mina, its former colony at Amathus, and its ports in the western Mediterranean.[182] On Cos and Rhodes, Black-on-Red neck-ridge flasks for perfumes or unguents that were popular in the Middle Geometric period (850–750 B.C.E.) were replaced in the latter part of the eighth century on Cos by local Greek imitations,[183] and on Rhodes by Red Slip or Bichrome mushroom-lipped juglets,[184] which were made by Tyrian expatriates from the mainland or Cyprus and exported with their contents to Italy and Sicily.[185] It was at this time too that Tyrians made

---

178. *PBSB* ##Cy9, Cy10, and Cy12, 179, 180–81, 260–61, 263.

179. A similar artistic fatigue is apparent in contemporary Phoenician ivories: see S. Frankenstein, "The Phoenicians in the Far West: A Function of Neo-Assyrian Imperialism," in *Power and Propaganda: A Symposium on Ancient Empires* (ed. M. T. Larsen; Mesopotamia 7; Copenhagen: Akademisk Förlag, 1979) 263–94, esp. p. 277. *PBSB* ##Cy6, Cy7, Cy8, Cy14, 175–79, 182, 252–59.

180. N. Schreiber, *The Cypro-Phoenician Pottery of the Iron Age* (Culture and History of the Ancient Near East, 13; Leiden: Brill, 2003).

181. J. N. Coldstream, "Early Greek Pottery in Tyre and Cyprus: Some Preliminary Comparisons," *RDAC* (1988) part 2, pp. 35–44, pls. 10–13.

182. P. M. Bikai, *The Pottery of Tyre* (Warminster: Aris & Phillips, 1978); idem, "The Late Phoenician Pottery Complex and Chronology," *BASOR* 229 (1978) 47–56; S. Vibert Chapman, "A Catalogue of Iron Age Pottery from the Cemeteries of Khirbet Silm, Joya, Qraye, and Qasmieh of South Lebanon," *Berytus* 21 (1972) 55–194; A. Sagona, "Levantine Storage Jars of the 13th to 4th Century B.C.," *Opuscula Atheniensia* 14 (1982) 73–110; C. Briese, "Früheisenzeitliche bemalte phönizische Kannen von Fundplätzen der Levanteküste," *HBA* 12 (1985) 7–118, esp. pp. 30–37; J. D. Muhly, "Phoenicia and the Phoenicians," in *Biblical Archaeology Today* (ed. A. Biran; Jerusalem: Israel Exploration Society, 1985) 177–91.

183. J. N. Coldstream, "Greeks and Phoenicians in the Aegean," in *Phönizier im Westen* (ed. H. G. Niemeyer; Mainz am Rhein: von Zabern, 1982) 261–75.

184. C. Doumet-Serhal, "La cruche à 'arête sur le col': Un fossile directeur de l'expansion phénicienne en Méditerranée aux 9ème et 8ème siècles avant J.-C.," *Berytus* 41 (1993–94) 99–136; D. W. Jones, "Phoenician Unguent Factories in Dark Age Greece: Social Approaches to Evaluating the Archaeological Evidence," *OJA* 12 (1993) 293–303.

185. J. N. Coldstream, "The Phoenicians at Ialysos," *Bulletin of the Institute of Classical Studies* 16 (1969) 1–7, pls. 1–3; A. M. Bisi, "Ateliers phéniciens dans le monde égéen," *Studia Phoenicia* 5 (1987) 225–37; L. Wriedt Sørensen, "Traveling Pottery Connections between Cyprus, the Levant, and the Greek World in the Iron Age," in *Res Maritimae: Cyprus and the Eastern Mediterranean from Prehistory to Late Antiquity* (ed. S. Swiny, R. L. Hohlfelder, and H. Wylde Swiny; American Schools of Oriental Research Archaeological Reports 4; Atlanta: Scholars Press, 1997) 285–99; A. Peserico, "Il ruolo di Rodi e dell'area egea nell'espansione fenicio verso Occidente: La documentazione ceramica," in *Patavina Orientalia Selecta* (ed. E. Rova; Padua: Sargon, 2000) 139–64; N. Schreiber,

Fig. 3.6a. Assyrian relief, depicting Tyre (BM Or. Dr. IV, 8). © The Trustees of the British Museum.

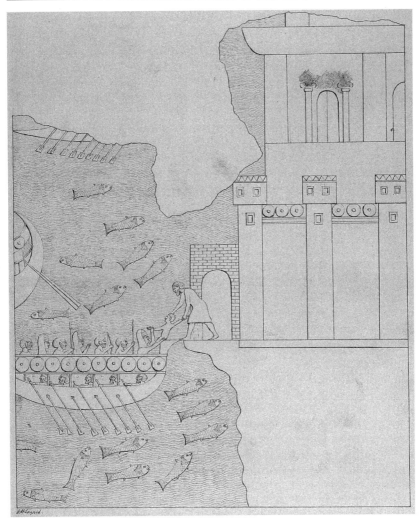

Fig. 3.6b. Assyrian relief, depicting Tyre (BM Or. Dr. IV, 8). © The Trustees of the British Museum.

their way to the Heraion on Samos and to the Athena Lindia on Rhodes[186] and to Corinth, where the city endorsed some of their cults and religious

---

The Cypro-Phoenician Pottery of the Iron Age (Culture and History of the Ancient Near East 13; Leiden: Brill, 2003) 286–306.

    186. I. Strøm, "Evidence from the Sanctuaries," in *Greece between East and West: 10th–8th Centuries* BC (ed. G. Kopcke and I. Tokumaru; Mainz am Rhein: von Zabern, 1992) 46–60, pls. 5c–7; E. Guralnick, "East to West: Near Eastern Artifacts from Greek Sites," in *La circulation des biens, des personnes et des idées dans le Proche-Orient ancien: Actes de la 38e Rencontre Assyriologique Internationale, Paris, 8–10 juillet 1991* (ed. D. Charpin and F. Joannès; Paris: Editions Recherche sur les Civilisations, 1992) 327–40; L. Schofield, "The Influence of Eastern Religions on the Iconography of Ivory and Bone Objects in the Kameiros Well," in *Ivory in Greece and the Eastern*

Fig. 3.7. Impression of seal with couchant lion (REH-042). Reproduced by permission of the Hecht Museum, Haifa.

customs and where the potters of Early proto-Corinthian wares were impressed by their pictorial repertory. Tyrian colonists sailing to Sicily may also have borrowed the Corinthian names *Thapsos* ("Lush Land") and *Syracuse* ("Vineland").[187] The Cypriot experience was not forgotten, but Cyprus was not the right inspiration for the new world.

The Island Capital: Tyre as a City

The city of Tyre in the eighth century is known from Assyrian pictorial representations (see fig. 3.6a–b), from biblical descriptions, and from a few chance finds. Aspects of its religious, economic, and social life can be reconstructed from Phoenician and other Northwest Semitic inscriptions and seals, by analogy with the Assyrian system of international trade on which Tyre was dependent, and in relation to countries such as Judah, Philistia, and Egypt, with which the city was in constant contact. Its artistic heritage is immediately evident in its ivories, and its literary traditions can be surmised from copies or parodies of them in biblical and later literature.

The city completely outclassed its physical setting. It was built on a rocky island (whence its name, Tyre [*ṣur*, "Rock"]) that was about 700 meters wide and 1,000 in length, lying less than a kilometer from shore, with a natural port at its north end and an artificial harbor on the south side.[188] In the time of Shalmaneser III (859 b.c.e.), the city, seen from the mainland shore, was represented as walled, protected by high corner towers, with a

Mediterranean from the Bronze Age to the Hellenistic Period (ed. J. L. Fitton; London: British Museum, 1992) 173–84.

187. S. P. Morris and J. K. Papadoulos, "Phoenicians and the Corinthian Pottery Industry," in *Archäologische Studien in Kontaktzonen der Antiken Welt* (ed. R. Rolle and K. Schmidt; Göttingen: Vandenhoeck & Ruprecht, 1998) 251–63; G. Markoe, "The Emergence of Orientalizing in Greek Art: Some Observations on the Interchange between Greeks and Phoenicians in the Eighth and Seventh Centuries b.c.," *BASOR* 301 (1996) 47–67.

188. H. J. Katzenstein, *The History of Tyre, from the Beginning of the Second Millennium b.c.e. until the Fall of the Neo-Babylonian Empire in 538 b.c.e.* (Jerusalem: Schocken Institute for Jewish Research, 1973) 9–15.

rocky shore from which shallow rowboats with high bows and sterns and manned by a helmsman and one rower transported tribute to the Assyrian king.[189] In the time of Sennacherib (701 B.C.E.), the high wall had crenellated towers at regular intervals, and behind it the city rose in multistoried buildings, among which one of the most prominent was the Temple of Melqart, distinguished by the pillars that flanked its entrance. The city in the palace reliefs is seen from the seaward side, and Luli, king of Sidon, is shown standing on the dock helping his son into a ship, where his wife and her two attendants, along with a bowman, two spearmen, and the helmsman are waiting to flee to Cyprus. The ship has a round bow and stern, two banks of five oars, and is hung with shields. The harbor is filled with others like it, and each is accompanied by a warship carrying troops and passengers, and equipped with a ram, a square superstructure above the bow, a furled sail, two banks of eight oars, and a high curved stern, while around them the sea is filled with fish and with marine life of many kinds.[190] Tyre had other types of ships that were not pictured on this occasion—broad sturdy work boats for carrying and tugging logs from the Lebanon, and merchantmen capable of carrying 400 or more large jars of wine piled in two or three tiers—but the impression of the city derived from these reliefs is confirmed and elaborated by the written sources.[191] It was "a great city" and majestically isolated from its mainland possessions, situated on a bare rock, behind whose walls and turrets the pillars of the Temple of Melqart issued defiance (Ezekiel 26). But, more than a city, it was a ship, its captain was a God, its people were merchants, the whole world contributed to its fabulous wealth, and the Mediterranean world belonged to it (Ezekiel 27–28).

The Cemetery at Tyre

On the mainland shore, approximately where Shalmaneser III stood and viewed the city, there is an eighth-century cemetery that provides a homelier glimpse of Tyre as it reached its apogee and stood on the verge of colonizing the West.[192] The cemetery, which was clandestinely excavated and thus despoiled, may have contained as many as 200 burials, each consisting of funerary urns, personal possessions, votive offerings, and tombstones. There was a similarly situated cemetery at Amathus in Cyprus, and the burial practices and paraphernalia have parallels in North African Carthage and at other western sites. The graves, perhaps of relatives of people who traveled west, are some indication of who these people were, how they lived, and what they believed.

---

189. R. D. Barnett, *Assyrian Palace Reliefs and Their Influence on the Sculptures of Babylonia and Persia* (London: Batchworth, 1960) nos. 157–60.

190. S. Parpola and K. Watanabe, *Neo-Assyrian Treaties and Loyalty Oaths* (SAA 2; Helsinki: Helsinki University Press, 1988) figs. 8–9.

191. A. Millard, "The Phoenicians at Sea," in *The Sea in Antiquity* (ed. G. J. Oliver et al.; BAR International Series 899; Oxford: Archeopress, 2000) 75–79. R. D. Ballard et al., "Iron Age Shipwrecks in Deep Water off Ashkelon, Israel," *AJA* 106 (2002) 151–68. These ships are estimated to have been about 7 meters wide and 14 meters long.

192. H. Seeden, "A *Tophet* in Tyre?" *Berytus* 39 (1991) 39–87; M. E. Aubet Semmler, "Une nécrpole récemment découverte à Tyr," in *Liban: L'Autre Rive* (Paris: Flammarion, 1998).

All the burials were cremations. The cinerary urns, containing bone and ash, were locally made or imported from Cyprus. They were medium sized—between 14 and 18 inches tall, 8–11 inches in diameter at the neck, and 12–15 inches at the widest part of the body—with handles from the rim to the body. They were more or less carefully made, but all were decorated with painted horizontal bands and thin lines in shades of red and black, and some had series of concentric circles between the bands around the neck and upper body. Urns like them are from mainland sites or from Carthage in North Africa.[193] Associated with them in the burials were trefoil-lipped (perfect for pouring) Red Slip wine jugs and Red Slip or Bichrome (Red-and-Black) perfume and ointment jars with a mushroom lip made for pouring into the hand and dabbing or anointing. Parallels to these are from the mainland, from Cyprus, and from Spain.[194] These ceramics are ordinary but attractive enough, residues of a plain comfortable life that the dead, immortalized by their funeral fires, might continue to use on their blessed journey to some island similar to their own or to some distant shore.

The personal possessions were mostly amulets, beads, and pendants of various kinds that had once been worn on necklaces: the amulets included a bronze scorpion, and a forearm and clenched fist with the thumb squeezed between the first and second fingers; the beads were bronze, green soapstone, or blue frit; the pendants were pyramidal and lozenge shaped.[195] An unusual offering was a small wooden box containing four terra-cotta figurines (a horse-and-rider, a bearded man, an altar, and a model shrine) that were possibly a child's toys or examples of a potter's art. There were also some amulets that had been imported from Egypt, either heirlooms, or contemporary works by Tyrians living in Egypt.[196] One is a scarab, once mounted on a finger ring, that was decorated with cobras and lotus blossoms flanking concentric circles like the circles on the funerary urns. Other scarabs have the throne names of Thutmosis III or Ramesses II, or Egyptian Gods and symbols, or cryptographic signs. There is one scarab, with parallels from Rhodes and Ibiza, on which a bearded Phoenician man wearing the crown of Egypt and seated on a couch holds the Egyptian symbol of life. These trinkets and amulets are mementos of simple lives and, especially in the case of the scarabs, tokens of an enduring life. But it is interesting that their symbols are not indigenous but are borrowed, archaic or archaicizing, and not quite assimilated into the local plain taste.

The tombstones were often adorned with some motif and sometimes inscribed with the name of the deceased.[197] They are irregular in shape, size, and finish. They are between two and three feet tall, half a foot to more

193. Seeden, "A *Tophet* in Tyre?" 53–62.
194. Ibid., 62–75.
195. Ibid., 76–82.
196. W. A. Ward, "The Scarabs, Scaraboid and Amulet-Plaque from Tyrian Cinerary Urns," *Berytus* 39 (1991) 89–99.
197. H. Sader, "Phoenician Stelae from Tyre," *Berytus* 39 (1991) 101–26; idem, "Phoenician Stelae from Tyre (Continued)," *SEL* 9 (1992) 53–79; M. G. Amadasi Guzzo, "Osservazioni sulle stele iscritte di Tiro," *RSF* 21 (1993) 157–63; P. Bartoloni, "Considerazioni sul "tofet" a Tiro," *RSF* 21 (1993) 153–56; G. Garbini, "Iscrizioni funerarie da Tiro," *RSF* Supplement 21 (1993) 3–6; S. Moscati, "Non e un tofet a Tiro," *RSF* 21 (1993) 147–51.

than a foot in width, and between four and eight inches thick. They are usually smooth on the front and sides, but the back and foot are unfinished, and one was just a reused stone anchor on which was incised a schematic boat with a mast and a rounded bow and stern. Of the tombstones with no names, one is squat and almost square, smooth at the top but rough below, and has in the smooth section the face of a woman, heart shaped, with hollow eyes and a wry smile, which all together look like the mason's rendering of a theatrical or religious mask emerging from the stone.[198] Another, more-rectangular stone presents a male torso in the shape of a monolithic shrine or baetyl, which was, as Philo of Byblos explained, a stone endowed with life.[199] The architrave, represented by two horizontal lines at the top of the monument, corresponds to his shoulders; the uncarved edges of the monument are his arms; the slightly curved vertical lines of the baetyl follow the shape of his body from chest to waist; the physical life of the stone is indicated by including his navel, a small hole at the appropriate place in the stone, and his genitals, hanging incongruously below the baetyl. The third anonymous stele is carved with a lotus bud amulet, like the lozenge pendants found in the graveyard, which hangs on a necklace carved around the top of the stone, as if the stone itself represented the deceased.

Of the inscribed monuments, one has an inverted crescent moon over a lunar disk, the symbol of the Goddess Tannit, and a very common motif on Carthaginian tombstones. Above the moon in the curved top of the stele, there are also four vertical lines that resemble eyebrows and thus make the crescent and disk look like an eye—something like the Eye-of-Horus amulet that was found among the grave goods. Another has a round sun disk, but on another with the crescent and disk, the disk is more oval and shaped like an eye. There is another stele with an Egyptian *ankh* or symbol of life carved on the back, and there are two others with baetyls carved into their face. One is just an empty rectangular space; the other is drawn as a carved stone planted in the ground, which is indicated by a horizontal line, and inscribed below ground with a Cypro-Syllabic sign (-*wo*-). All the motifs are obviously symbolic, even the woman's face is not representative of her but is an allusion. And all the symbols are of life as it was and as it was expected to continue. Some, like the *ankh* or the Eye are borrowed from Egyptian lore, and some, like the baetyls, are common in Syria and Canaan, but there is a tendency, most evident in the male torso as shrine, to give the symbols a particularity or a personal turn. Although the ideas and beliefs they express are profound—life in the utterly ineffable—the representations are crude, and there is no trace of the wonderfully delicate, Egyptian inspired feeling that characterizes Tyrian (that is, typically "Phoenician") artistic works. The tombstones, in fact, seem to reflect the collaboration of unskilled or inexperienced masons who could copy a text but did not know

---

198. There is a similar stele at Knossos in Crete, but the face is featureless and, instead of the stone being a representation of the woman, the woman appears to be the stone: N. Kourou and E. Grammatikaki, "An Anthropomorphic Cippus from Knossos, Crete," in *Archäologische Studien in Kontaktzonen der antiken Welt* (ed. R. Rolle and K. Schmidt; Göttingen: Vandenhoeck & Ruprecht, 1998) 237–49.

199. H. W. Attridge and R. A. Oden Jr., *Philo of Byblos: The Phoenician History* (CBQ Monograph 9; Washington, DC: Catholic Biblical Association, 1981) 53 (#1.10:23).

how to write, and slightly better educated next of kin with unsophisticated tastes.

The inscriptions are written sloppily. They are placed at the top of the steles but without regard for the available room. Letters are not written along a baseline or hung from a top line but tend to drift downward and sometimes have a wrong or reversed stance, as if they had been inscribed by a seal maker. They are often of disproportionate sizes or must be scrambled to fit into the available space. Like the designs and motifs, they seem to be the work of the masons, not of trained scribes, and they look childish or uneducated.

The inscriptions usually give just the name of the deceased, but once there is a personal name and patronymic, once the personal name is omitted and only the patronymic is given ("son of Tannit'ala'"), once the woman's husband is mentioned ("wife of 'Elîm"), and once the text says that the stele was erected on behalf of a woman ("For 'Amotišmon"). The names are mostly theophoric (that is, they contain the name and/or epithet of a God or Goddess), but the stele with the Cypro-Syllabic sign was inscribed with the old nontheophoric name Girgush (*grgš*). The Gods are Melqart (*milqart'abî*, "Melqart-Is-My-Father"), Ba'al (*li-ba'lay*, "Belonging-to-Ba'al"), 'Eshmun ('*amotišmon*, "Maid of 'Eshmun"), and Hamon (*gaddihamon*, "My-Good-Luck-Is-Hamon"). The Goddesses are Astarte (*'aštartla'at*, "Astarte-Is-Victorious"), Asherah in the guise of the lioness (*labi'ay*, "Belonging-to-the-Lioness"), Isis (*'abd*['is], "Servant-of-Isis"), and Tannit (*tannit'ala'*, "Tannit-Is-Exalted"; *tannitšaba'a*, "Tannit-Has-Given-Satisfaction").

The choice of divine names is instructive but not surprising: Melqart was the God of Tyre; Ba'al, the God of the Weather; 'Eshmun, the God of Health; and Hamon, the God of the Amanus, who as Ba'al Hamon, the God of the Ecliptic, became the patron of the Carthaginian constitution; Asherah was the source of life; Astarte, the confederate of Ba'al who shared his epithet "Victorious"; Isis, the Mother; Tannit appears in fifth-century Carthage as the refulgence of Hamon. The woman Tannitšaba'a, "Tannit-Has-Given-Satisfaction," who is identified as the "wife of the God" (*'išt 'elîm*), may have been the partner of the cultic official whose titles were the "Raiser of the God" (*mqm 'lm*) and "Husband of 'Astronoe" (*mtrh 'štrny*), who participated in the dramatic rites of Melqart; that is, she would have played the part of Astronoe, wife-for-the-day of the official who played the part of the God.[200]

Similarly, 'Amotišmon, "Maid of 'Eshmun," because it is preceded by the preposition "for," may not have been her name but an indication of her cultic rank. Apart from these two women and the man Girgush, and perhaps the child buried with its terra-cotta toys, the graveyard does not betray the secrets of the dead but does reveal the expectations of the families who named them and the piety of those who buried them.

---

200. E. Lipiński, "La fête de l'ensevelissement et de la resurrection de Melqart," in *Actes de la XVIIe Rencontre Assyriologique Internationale: Bruxelles, 30 juin–4 juillet 1969* (ed. A. Finet; Ham-sur-Heure: Comité Belge de Recherches en Mésopotamie, 1970) 30–58.

Traders, Trade, and Trade Mechanisms

Tyrian trade and commerce can be glimpsed by analogy with Assyrian practices, which are better documented, and from artifacts and inscriptions. The trademarks of the merchants, the stamp seals that begin to appear in the eighth century and abound in the seventh, can be traced from country to country where Tyrians did business. They had weights and measures, and money, and they made a name for themselves: for example, Urik in Cilicia, Shamshi-ilu in Syria,[201] Tob'il in Tyre, and Luli in Sidon. Traders who were once known by their place of origin are now identified by their names, and enterprising artists and businessmen who traveled the world inscribed their instruments and artifacts with their names or devices. These must supply the sights and sounds of bold and ambitious men and women, bustling market places, busy wharves, the va et vient of ships of many flags filling the waters of Tyre.

Trade had its conditions and consequences. The basic condition was literacy, because trade, placing orders, and giving receipts required the ability to read and write and count, and because traders, when not on their own or working for companies, also acted as couriers or ambassadors for their town or the palace. With trade went wealth; with literacy went literature; with travel, bilingualism; and with prosperity imitation. Thus Assyrian themes made their way into Greek art,[202] the literary heritage of Assyria filtered into Judah and became the textbooks of the biblical authors,[203] foreigners learned Phoenician,[204] and ease and recreation in exotic places became a part of the ideal life.[205] Merchants, the distributors of imported or domestic goods, and traders, those engaged in imports and exports, belonged to clubs or fraternities under the auspices of patron Gods. As in their Mycenean and Greek embodiments,[206] their meetings were the occasions for the

201. S. Dalley, "Shamshi-ilu, Language and Power in the Western Assyrian Empire," in *Essays on Syria in the Iron Age* (ed. G. Bunnens; ANESt 7; Louvain: Peeters, 2000) 79–88.

202. B. B. Powell, "From Picture to Myth, from Myth to Picture: Prolegomena to the Invention of Mythic Representation in Greek Art," in *New Light on a Dark Age: Exploring the Culture of Geometric Greece* (ed. S. Langdon; Columbia: University of Missouri Press, 1997) 154–93.

203. B. Peckham, *History and Prophecy: The Development of Late Judean Literary Traditions* (New York: Doubleday, 1993) 79–88.

204. The learning process is evident from the mistakes that were made. An abecedary on a limestone tablet is written boustrophedon, the first line correctly from right to left, the second line from left to right and with one letter (*lamed*) upside down: A. Lemaire, "Fragment d'un alphabet ouest-sémitique du viiie siècle av. J.-C.," *Sem* 28 (1978) 7–10, pl. 1. On the reverse of an ivory plaque from Nimrud depicting a sphinx, its position in the piece of furniture for which it was made (*b'ht*, "in the first [row]") is written first in Aramaic where the T (*taw*) is back-to-front; and again below it in Phoenician, where the *'alep* and the *taw* are back-to-front and the *ḥet* is upside down: A. Lemaire, "Note sur quelques inscriptions sur ivoire provenant de Nimrud," *Sem* 26 (1976) 65–69, pls. 6–9, pp. 65–66, pl. 6; J. and D. Oates, *Nimrud: An Assyrian Imperial City Revealed* (London: British School of Archaeology in Iraq, 2001) 218, fig. 130. This type of mistake suggests that the letters were being copied from tables of script that had been made for artists inscribing seals, where names are inscribed in negative in order to show up positively when stamped.

205. A. K. Thomason, "Representations of the North Syrian Landscape in Neo-Assyrian Art," *BASOR* 323 (2001) 63–96.

206. S. P. Morris, "A Tale of Two Cities: The Miniature Frescoes from Thera and the Origins of Greek Poetry," *AJA* 93 (1989) 511–35; J. B. Carter, "Ancestor Cult and the Occasion of Homeric Performance," in *The Ages of Homer: A Tribute to Emily Townsend Vermeule* (ed. J. B. Carter and S. P. Morris; Austin: University of Texas Press, 1995) 285–312.

composition and recitation of epic and lyric poetry. Trade in the eighth century was not just a business but a whole new way of life.

In the ninth century, copper and bronze were used as currency. In the eighth, bronze was no longer used, and copper became the preferred metal. But silver was introduced as currency early in the century and, by the seventh century, it replaced copper as the standard,[207] a development that may reflect a change in prices, which were not regulated and fluctuated wildly. It may also reflect a change in the range of commodities that were being bought and sold because, depending on the standard (royal, local, import—each either "heavy" or "light"), 1 silver shekel was the equivalent of 1 copper mina or 60 copper shekels. This preference for silver required and in turn was precipitated by its availability and not surprisingly the main sources of silver were precisely those places where Tyrians and Sidonians were entrenched and busy, and in which the Assyrians now developed a keen interest: the Laurion mines in Attica, mines in Cilicia, in Etruria, and in southern Spain.[208]

Phoenician interest in these silver mines can be detected by mapping the places where hoards of silver have been discovered.[209] These hoards consisted of scrap or unworked silver that resembles a silversmith's supply of raw material. The scrap material included broken or discarded jewelry, and the unworked silver had been shaped into rolls or ingots, often in measured sections, ready to be cut into pieces and weighed. The earlier hoards, from the tenth, eleventh, or twelfth century B.C.E. are from towns in Israel (Megiddo, Beth Shean, Gezer) or Judah (Arad, Eshtemoa) that lay along trade routes traveled by Tyrians, or in Phoenician (Dor, Tell Keisan) or Philistine towns (Ashkelon).

There are ninth-century hoards at Tyrian ʿAkko and at ʿEn Hofez, between Dor and Tell Keisan; eighth-century hoards from the Tyrian settlement at Amathus in Cyprus and from the Sidonian enclaves at Zinjirli in North Syria, Knossos in Crete, and Eretria; and seventh-century hoards from Ekron that can be traced to the mines at Laurion, Siphnos, and Chalkidiki in Greece. Some of the earlier hoards may have belonged to jewelers, but the later were the petty cash of more or less wealthy Phoenician traders and craftsmen who are described in a biblical text as "Canaanite folk, weighers of silver" who, as their silver, "have been cut into pieces."[210]

These merchants and traders, as is clear not only from the distribution of the silver hoards but also from the weights they used and from stray bits of epigraphic evidence, were Tyrian, Sidonian, and Byblian. An inscription

207. F. M. Fales, "An Overview of Prices in Neo-Assyrian Sources," in *Économie antique: Prix et formation des prix dans les économies antiques* (ed. J. Andreau, P. Briant, and R. Descat; Toulouse: Musée archéologique départemental de Saint-Bernard-de Comminges, 1997) 291–312; K. Radner, "Money in the Neo-Assyrian Empire," in *Trade and Finance in Ancient Mesopotamia* (ed. J. G. Dercksen; Leiden: Nederlands Historisch-Archaeologisch Instituut te Istanbul, 1999) 127–57.

208. Ibid., 129; G. E. Markoe, "In Pursuit of Silver: Phoenicians in Central Italy," *HBA* 19–20 (1992–93) 11–31; D. W. J. Gill, "Silver Anchors and Cargoes of Oil: Some Observations on Phoenician Trade in the Western Mediterranean," *PBSR* 56 (1988) 1–12.

209. C. M. Thompson, "Sealed Silver in Iron Age Cisjordan and the "Invention" of Coinage," *OJA* 22 (2003) 67–107.

210. Zeph 1:11: "All the Canaanite folk are gone: cut in pieces are all the weighers of silver" (*kî nidmah kol ʿam kenaʿan // nikretû kol neṭîlê kesep*).

from Tel Zeror, about 10 kilometers southeast of Dor, was incised on the base of a bowl and identifies its owner or vendor as "Baʿlʾilî, the merchant" (*bʿlʾl hmk*[*r*]):[211] the name, in the form ʾIlîbaʿl, is known only at Byblos. One of its components (the noun *ʾl*, "God") seems to be found exclusively in Byblian names, and Baʿal (*baʿl*) is the name of the tutelary God of Byblos. Another inscription, on the shoulder of a transport jar from Tell Jemmeh, just southeast of Gaza, reads, "Belonging to Bim-Melek" (*lbmlk*), written in the dialect of Byblos, where the [n] of the word "son" (*bin*) is assimilated to the following consonant and is not written. Earlier in the eighth century, there were Byblian merchants who passed through the caravanserai at Kuntillet ʿAjrud on the fringe of the Sinai and wrote an invocation on the plaster wall of the entranceway: "When El arises may the mountains melt! Blessed be Baʿal on the day of battle! May El cause devastation on the day of battle."[212]

Byblian traders in Hamath used weights corresponding to the common or royal standard of that city but inscribed in Byblian script: "Shekel of Hamath" (*šql ḥmt*), "two Shekels of Hamath" (*šqly ḥmt*), and "Royal Shekel of Hamath" (*Š* + *T šql ḥmt*).[213] Similarly, Sidonian merchants used weights in the royal or common standard of their city. A royal weight, in the shape of the head of a calf, weighing 6½ grams is inscribed "Royal Shekel of Sidon" (*Š* + *T šql ṣdn*), and another in the shape of a lion and weighing almost 21 grams is inscribed "five Royal Shekels" (*Š* + *T ḥmšt*). Of weights in the common Sidonian standard, one is a tortoise weighing almost 12 grams and inscribed in Aramaic, the official language of the Assyrian Empire, "Shekel of Sidon—for the tithe" (*šql ṣydn ʿšrtn*).[214]

The weights are usually made of bronze. In the eighth century, they are relatively rare, regularly animal shaped, and inscribed with the name of the city, their standard, or their weight written in full. In the seventh century, when they become common, they are generally square and inscribed with a one-letter abbreviation, presumably of their weight, standard or city. One found at Nimrud but perhaps from Tyre is a lion weighing 250 grams and inscribed by an unskilled writer, "Royal—100" (*lmlk* + symbol).[215] Two others from Tyre are also lions but weigh only 4 grams. The weights from ʿAkko are square: weights weighing 21 grams or some multiple of it are inscribed with ʿayin, while those weighing 16 grams are inscribed with the letter *ḥet*. The weights from Amathus are square. Three from Ashkelon are animal shaped. A tortoise weighing 2½ grams is inscribed "fourth part of a shekel" (*plg rbʿt šql*). However, the rest are square and are inscribed with

---

211. R. Delavault and A. Lemaire, "Les inscriptions phéniciennes de Palestine," *RSF* 7 (1979) 1–37, esp. p. 20, #42, pl. 11.

212. *AHI* 82 #8:023. The final imprecation uses a construction (*lšm* = *lu* + *yšm*) that is peculiar to the Byblian dialect.

213. F. Bron and A. Lemaire, "Poids inscrits phénico-araméens du VIIIe siècle av. J.-C.," *Atti* 1, 3.763–70, esp. pp, 763–65, pl. 145; M. Heltzer, "Phoenician Trade and Phoenicians in Hamath," in *Immigration and Emigration within the Ancient Near East: Festschrift E. Lipiński* (ed. K. van Lerberghe and A. Schoors; Louvain: Peeters, 1995) 101–5.

214. J. Elayi and A. G. Elayi, *Recherches sur les poids phéniciens* (Transeu Supplement 5; Paris: Gabalda, 1997) 46–48, 156–59, 369, fig. 1:2, 3, 5, pls. 1:2, 3, and 2:5.

215. Ibid., 46, 155–56, fig. 1:1, pl. 1:1. Its Tyrian provenance is suggested by its use of "to the king" (*lmlk*) instead of the royal symbol used by Byblian and Sidonian traders.

a Phoenician letter: those inscribed with ʿayin weighing roughly 21 grams or some multiple of it, and those inscribed with ḥet weighing 16 grams. Although merchants and traders gradually shed their anonymity and are known by their names in the eighth and seventh centuries, Phoenician weights (unlike seventh-century Judean weights, which conformed scrupulously to a national standard)[216] still belonged to cities and conformed, more or less honestly, to their urban standards.

Tyrian craftsmen, such as goldsmiths, silversmiths, ivory carvers, or the masons who did the gravestones in the mainland necropolis, belonged to guilds and worked in shops, so their individual genius was masked by the style, technique, and traditions of a school. In Assyria, their training would have set them apart, and they would have belonged to formal associations that kept legal, financial, and administrative records, worked under the auspices of a religious institution, and trained apprentices. A goldsmith guild in Ashur was located in a separate part of the temple that also housed the scriptorium.[217]

In Tyre, all of these groups, or just the wealthier or more prestigious would have joined clubs (marzeaḥs) that had similar interests in money, education, and religious tradition. Tyrian merchants and traders worked for the city, and business was centered on the ports, where there were customs offices, warehouses, and stores (in Assyrian terms, these were the kāru and the bit kāri), and the city officials, along with the officials at the Tyrian ports of ʿAkko and ʾAchzib would have reported to the chief Assyrian administrator at Kaspuna.

The traders, those who traveled to acquire goods in exchange for their wares or for money, were financed by the king, the city government, the company to which they belonged or, because many of them were extremely wealthy, by bankers or individuals who owned their own business, lent money, or distributed goods on consignment.[218] Sargon II borrowed money from traders to finance the rebuilding of Dur Šarruken, and one of them complained that the king still owed him almost 35,000 silver shekels.[219] Companies of traders, by analogy with the Late Bronze institution at Ugarit or with contemporary practice in Babylonia,[220] would have been organized as families, consisting of partners who by written agreement were "brothers" working under the direction of a "father" and responsible for one another's welfare (a trader, for instance, who was enslaved for bankruptcy would be ransomed by his brothers) and operating according to strict codes

216. R. Kletter, "The Inscribed Weights of the Kingdom of Judah," TA 18 (1991) 121–63. These weights also differed from the Phoenician in being dome-shaped, made of limestone, and inscribed with their precise value.
217. K. Radner, Ein neuassyrisches Privatarchiv der Tempelgoldschmiede von Assur (Saarbruck: Saarbrücker Verlag, 1999).
218. M. Elat, "Der tamkāru im neuassyrischen Reich," JESHO 30 (1987) 233–54; K. Deller, "Tamkāru-Kredite in neuassyrischer Zeit," JESHO 30 (1987) 1–29; K. Radner, "Traders in the Neo-Assyrian Period," in Trade and Finance in Ancient Mesopotamia (ed. J. G. Dercksen; Leiden: Nederlands Historisch-Archaeologisch Instituut te Istanbul, 1999) 101–26.
219. S. Parpola, The Correspondence of Sargon II, Part I: Letters from Assyria and the West (SAA 1; Helsinki: Helsinki University Press, 1987).
220. S. W. Cole, Nippur IV: The Early Neo-Babylonian Governor's Archive from Nippur (OIP 114; Chicago: Oriental Institute, 1996).

of respect and politeness. Placing an order was expressing a "desire," and filling an order was satisfying a "need" or wish. Merchants, unlike traders, did not travel but bought and sold the goods that were produced in the city and in its satellite towns or imported into the country by Tyrian traders or acquired in a market at home or in a foreign port where Tyrians had colonial interests. Assyria became rich by taxing these imports, and Tyre became famous by assembling goods from around the world in its markets.[221]

Seals

These artisans, merchants, traders, bankers, and administrators were the proud owners of the stamp seals that began to proliferate in the eighth century and became almost commonplace in the seventh. They were marked with the personal names and sometimes the family names of important individuals, and regularly with the designs that explained their names or professions, reflected their partnership in associations, or expressed their new class consciousness. A seal, usually worn on a necklace, and in the eighth century rarely in a ring, was an ornament or maybe an amulet, and in some cases may have had symbolic rather than practical significance. But when they were used, it was to seal documents, most of which were perishable like papyrus and did not survive, such as letters, decrees, inventories, orders, and receipts. The seals are dated and can be distinguished as Phoenician, Aramean, Assyrian, Judean, or Transjordanian, by their scripts and names and by their designs.

Assyrian traders were installed in the capital ports and markets of Syria and Palestine. In Gaza, which controlled trade between the Assyrian provinces and Egypt, both Tiglath-pileser III and Sargon II appointed the local Arab sheikh to oversee Assyrian and Egyptian commerce in the city.[222] In Jerusalem, according to a tirade against Nineveh written after the empire had collapsed, Assyria "increased its traders more than the stars of heaven, more than the locust that spreads its wings and flies away" so that its "royal representatives were like grasshoppers, its officials like clouds of locusts" (Nah 3:15–17). In the provinces, as at home, and despite the inference of anonymity that might be drawn from this tirade, traders' names were their credentials, so transaction records would name the buyer and the seller, and ignorance of a trader's name deserved notice.[223]

Of the Assyrian traders known by name from contemporary documents, only about half are native Assyrians, and the rest are natives of the countries where Assyria did business: Phoenicians, Arameans, Arabs, Judeans, Egyptians, and Anatolians.[224] The official languages of the empire were

---

221. M. Elat, "Phoenician Overland Trade within the Mesopotamian Empires," in *Ah, Assyria . . . : Studies in Assyrian History and Ancient Near Eastern Historiography Presented to Hayim Tadmor* (ed. M. Cogan and I. Eph'al; Jerusalem: Magnes, 1991) 21–35; idem, "Die wirtschaftlichen Beziehungen der Assyrer mit den Arabern," in *Festschrift für Rykle Borger zu seinem 65. Geburtstag am 24. Mai 1994* (ed. S. M. Maul; Groningen: Styx, 1998) 39–57.

222. Ibid., 48–49.

223. Idem, "Der *Tamkāru* im neuassyrischen Reich," *JESHO* 30 (1987) 233–54, esp. p. 240.

224. For lists of their names, see M. Elat, "Die wirtschaftlichen Beziehungen der Assyrer mit den Arabern," in *Festschrift für Rykle Borger zu seinem 65. Geburtstag am 24. Mai 1994* (ed. S. M. Maul; Groningen: Styx, 1998) 39–57, esp. pp. 52–57; and K. Radner, "Traders in the Neo-Assyrian

Assyrian and Aramaic, and the seals of these traders reveal the convergence of Assyrian tradition and of West Semitic (specifically Aramean) innovation by the end of the eighth century: stamp seals are used together with cylinder seals on the same document, or cylinder seals with typical Assyrian scenes are signed in Aramaic with the name of their Aramean owners, or cylinder seals have Aramean scenes and names, or stamp seals with Aramean names or writing now sport Assyrian motifs.[225] Assyrian commerce, in effect, reflected the cosmopolitan constitution and international yearning of the empire.

Tyrian commercial interests attracted its entrepreneurs to Egypt and Assyria and to all the adjacent lands before the financial boom of the late eighth and the seventh centuries led them to establish permanent stations (sources of supply at first and later centers of local distribution) in the western Mediterranean. In Assyria, where there were never any Phoenician settlements, there were individuals from the Mediterranean coast who had become accredited agents in places like Nineveh and Nimrud. Most of these are known from seventh-century texts,[226] but there is a little bit of evidence for their involvement in the eighth century.

There is a deed of conveyance from Nineveh dated 709 B.C.E. and stamped with the owner's seal, in which Dagan Milki, perhaps from Tyre or from one of the Philistine cities, sells three slaves, including a Philistine and a Byblian to a local Assyrian dealer and has as witnesses an Israelite (*Paqaḥ*) and a Judean (*Nadbiyāhû*) official, an Assyrian scribe and three other Assyrians without rank, a Tyrian scribe (*ʾAḥiram*), and the Sidonian scribe (*Tabnî*) who wrote the tablet.[227]

In Egypt and Libya—where there were a few Phoenician enclaves (in the Delta, at Memphis, south of Memphis at Heracleopolis, and in Cyrenaica) to which Tyre shipped wine and where Tyrians drew on Egyptian letters and artistic traditions and from which they exported Egyptian heirlooms and exotica—the evidence for the Phoenicians' presence is mostly material and mute.[228] A particularly eloquent exception is a writing board,[229] also

Period," in *Trade and Finance in Ancient Mesopotamia* (ed. J. G. Dercksen; Leiden: Nederlands Historisch Archaeologisch Instituut te Instanbul, 1999) 101–26.

225. M. Trokay, "Interconnections in Glyptic during the Neo-Assyrian Period," *AbrN* 33 (1995) 96–112.

226. K. Radner, ed., *The Prosopography of the Neo-Assyrian Empire, Volumes 1/I and 1/II* (Helsinki: Neo-Assyrian Text Corpus Project, 2000–2001) passim.

227. E. Lipiński, "Phoenicians in Anatolia and Assyria, 9th–6th Centuries B.C.," *OLP* 16 (1985) 81–90.

228. E. Gubel, "Phoenician Foundations in Archeological Perspective," in *Nouve Fundazioni nel Vicino Oriente Antico: Realtà e Ideologia* (ed. S. Mazzoni; Pisa: Giardini, 1994) 341–55; J. Padró, "Découverte de céramiques phéniciennes à Héracléopolis Magna (Egypte)," *Atti 2*, 3.1103–8; J. Boardman, "Settlement for Trade and Land in North Africa: Problems of Identity," in *The Archaeology of Greek Colonisation: Essays Dedicated to Sir John Boardman* (ed. G. R. Tsetskhladze and F. De Angelis; Oxford: Oxbow, 1994) 137–49; Ballard et al., "Iron Age Shipwrecks in Deep Water off Ashkelon, Israel," 151–68; E. Gubel, "Das libyerzeitliche Agypten und die Anfänge der phönizischen Ikonographie," in *Agypten und der östliche Mittelmeerraum im 1. Jahrtausend v. Chr.* (ed. M. Görg and G. Hölbl; Wiesbaden: Harrassowitz, 2000) 69–100; G. Hölbl, "Die Problematik der spätzeitlichen Aegyptiaca im östlichen Mittelmeerraum," ibid., 119–61, pls. 1–9; G. E. Markoe, "The Emergence of Phoenician Art," *BASOR* 279 (1990) 13–26.

229. K.-T. Zauzich and W. Röllig, "Eine ägyptische Schreibpalette in phönizischer Umgestaltung," *Or* 59 (1990) 320–32, pl. 12.

an heirloom, which bears witness to Phoenician commercial involvement in one of these centers. The reverse has a hieratic inscription, dated by its script to about the fourteenth century B.C.E., which inventoried grain supplies for the unidentified city during a twelve-day period. On the obverse, the figure of a young man was carved and painted. The circular letter ʿayin was repeated eight times on the right side to represent the hieratic symbol for "day" on the reverse, and a Phoenician inscription was added to identify the young man who was the new owner of the palette. The inscription, written across the top, down the left side, and up the middle, reads:[230] "Life and prosperity! Writing board of ʿAyyil, collector of taxes" (*ḥy wṭb ʾrz ʿyl msʿ hpʾ*). In this way, the writing board shares with seals their amuletic character and their desire to identify the individual not only by name and occupation but by some physical or symbolic likeness, in this case as the "young man" drawn on the obverse, which is the meaning of his name, and as the keeper of records, day-books, or inventories such as the inventory written on the reverse. A particularly interesting fact about the palette is that it seems to be from the town where ʿAyyil worked six centuries later in a Tyrian port or marketplace collecting taxes from his fellow bankers, traders, and pedlars on behalf of the Egyptian administration.

Among the eighth-century seals that can or might be attributed to Tyre or to a Tyrian,[231] the most surprising is a seal that is inscribed in the middle and lower registers and is read "Belonging to the king of the Tyrians" (*lmlk / ṣrm*; see fig. 1.8).[232] The top register shows a pillar surmounted by a blazing fire, with altars or offering tables on either side of it, a crescent moon above the left and a star above the right table, and a winged sun disk surmounting the narrative complex. The scene represents the apotheosis of Melqart—his divinization in the fire, his ascension into the cosmic order, his cultic presence among his people—so that the picture and the legend match perfectly. The seal is an amulet, and may never have been used as identification. It is particularly interesting because Melqart, whose name means "King of the City" and who is known from other texts as Lord of the City, is called "King of the Tyrians," king of the people of Tyre, whose divinization presaged and provoked their destiny. Much later, in the fifth century, these symbols disappear and Melqart is presented as a man and with the human features of Heracles: two seals of an individual, who was perhaps a mercenary, are inscribed with his initials (ʿayin–nun, the first and last letters of a name such as ʿAbdḥamon) and with pictures of him. On one he is a naked, very muscular hoplite leaning forward and holding a sword

---

230. The word "tablet" (*ʾrz*) is lit., "cedar, cedar panel." The word "young man" used as a personal name is found in Biblical Hebrew but does not occur in Phoenician. The title "collector," lit., "remover" of taxes has cognates in Biblical Hebrew and in Akkadian (*nasāḥu*, "deduct, subtract," said of taxes). The word "taxes" (*pʾ*) is known in Phoenician as the designation of a small coin and in Arabic (root *pʾy* [*fiʾa*]) as "tax, price."

231. A seal that was published without a photograph and is usually read "Seal of the Tyrian" (*ḥtm š ṣry*) is not Phoenician and should be read *ḥtm mṣry*, "Seal of Musri": A. Lemaire, "L'écriture phénicienne en Cilicie et la diffusion des écritures alphabétiques," in *Phoinikeia Grammata: Lire et Écrire en Mediterranée* (ed. C. Baurain, C. Bonnet, and V. Krings; Namur: Société des Études Classiques, 1991) 133–46, esp. pp. 135–36.

232. P. Bordreuil, "Charges et fonctions en Syrie–Palestine d'après quelques sceaux ouest-sémitiques du second et du premier millénaire," *CRAIBL* (1986) 290–308, figs 1–9, esp. pp. 298–305, figs 3–8; *CSOSI* 23–24, #7.

and shield; on the other, he is the naked and almighty Heracles slaying the Nemean lion.[233]

In the eighth century, however, seal designs are generally adaptations of Egyptian motifs that, like the Melqart seal, tend to match the person named with his characteristic features. A seal inscribed "Protector" (*mʿzr*), an epithet of Baʿal in Tyrian dynastic names, features a four-winged scarab, a royal symbol of perpetuity. Another seal is inscribed "Exalted" (*dly*) and has this scarab holding the sun disk between its legs as a token of exaltation and perpetual renewal.[234] Less subtle is the seal inscribed "Likeness of Horus" (*mntḥr*): in the top register, two birds face each other, and in the middle register, two human-headed sphinxes face each other. Both together express the notion of "image." In the bottom register, there is a falcon, the usual representation of Horus, with its wings spread.[235]

There is only one eighth-century seal that is set in a ring and it may never have been used except as jewelry: it is a scarab inscribed with the name "Servant-of-the-King" (*ʿbdmlk*) and pictures an Assyrian-type griffin rising on its haunches before a stylized Egyptian lotus blossom.[236] The stone is carnelian and the bezel gold, and it would have been a nice piece of jewelry, but the name is written in reverse image. The mistake would have been a constant embarrassment to the owner if it was ever used in transactions. There are also two seals of a man named "Young Lion" (*lkpr*), one displaying a winged aegis with the head and feet of a lion; the other featuring a vigorous four-winged youth wearing the Egyptian double crown and holding a lotus blossom in each hand.[237]

Similarly, a man whose name means something like "Buddy" (*lzyʾ*, from the root *zwy*, "draw together") had a seal, in the upper register of which two birds face each other and in the lowest register of which a bull's head is flanked by the seven stars of the Sibitti, the seven benevolent demons of Assyrian lore who are grammatically and mythically one.[238] There are other seals in which the standard motifs are humanized to represent the person named. For instance, a man whose name is "My-Brother-Is-King" (*lḥmlk*) is pictured as a sun disk with a head and arms like a man flying.[239] Others are abstract; for instance, a man called "Suppliant" (*lḥnʾ*) has a seal whose dominant feature is stylized arms lifted in supplication.[240] Others have a complete narrative scene; for instance, the seal of "By-the-Power-of-Baʿal" (*lbdbʿl*) represents a couchant lion, seen from above, attacked from either side by a man, the owner of the seal, with a spear (see fig. 3.7).[241]

---

233. Ibid., 40 ##33–34.

234. Ibid., 25–26 ##10–11.

235. Ibid., 26–27 #12.

236. R. Deutsch and M. Heltzer, *Windows to the Past* (Tel Aviv–Jaffa: Archaeological Center, 1997) 61–62.

237. *CSOSI* 35 #24; *WSS* 410–11 ##1086–87.

238. *CSOSI* 27 #13.

239. *WSS* #159. The personification of the sun disk is known from Assyrian art, and Ezekiel's cherubim had wings as well as human faces and hands (Ezekiel 1 and 10).

240. *WSS* 409–10 #1083.

241. N. Avigad, "Some Decorated West Semitic Seals," *IEJ* 35 (1985) 1–7, pl. 1, esp. pp. 1–3, pl. 1a; *WSS* 270–71 #726.

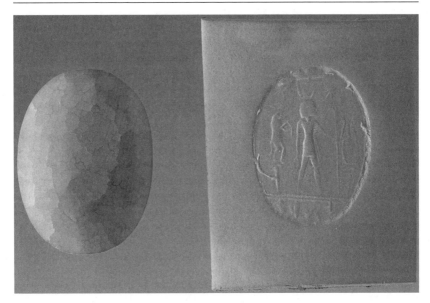

Fig. 3.8. Seal and impression with man and baboon (A.O. 10882). Reproduced by permission of the Louvre Museum, Paris.

What is particularly noticeable about these Tyrian seals is that they express the individuality and the personality of their owners. They do this by adapting stylized features borrowed from an Egyptian repertory, along with a splattering of Assyrian icons, in a creative and religious but common or sometimes comical attempt to bring traditional forms into touch with the realities of the new world. There are not many of these seals, none of the men or women is identified as working for the king or for another individual or as belonging to a consortium, and it may be supposed that the owners of the seals were in charge of the ventures under their names.

There is one group of seals flaunting the same iconography that, because some belonged to named kings, may all be seals of kings or court officials or merchants commissioned by the court. The essential design is a man dressed in Egyptian garb, sometimes wearing the Egyptian crown; striding right, sometimes left, holding a scepter in his far hand, left or right, depending on which way he walks; and raising his near hand, either right or left, in salutation.[242] The seals are Phoenician, Israelite, Judean, Philistine, Ammonite, Moabite, and Aramaic from the eighth and early seventh century, and provenance rather than date seems to account for the slight stylistic variations. The seals are formal or stereotypical and generally were not designed to suggest the character, personality, or attributes of their owners.

242. P. Bordreuil, "Inscriptions sigillaires ouest-sémitiques III: Sceaux de dignitaires et de rois syro-palestiniens du VIIIe et du VIIe siècle avant J.-C.," *Syria* 62 (1985) 21–29; E. Gubel, "Le sceau de Menahem et l'iconographie royale sigillaire," *Sem* 38 (1990) 167–70, pl. 26; idem, "The Iconography of Inscribed Phoenician Glyptic," in *Studies in the Iconography of Northwest Semitic Inscribed Seals* (ed. B. Sass and C. Uehlinger; Göttingen: Vandenhoeck & Ruprecht, 1993) 101–29.

A Phoenician seal inscribed "friend" (*l-rgm*) adds to the usual scene a monkey sitting on a lotus pedestal behind the man and a crescent moon and lunar disk—symbols of the Gods Ḥamon and Tannit—just above his head. Another, belonging to a man whose name, "Calf" (*l-ʿglʾ*), refers to a manifestation of Baʿal, varies the scene by seating monkeys on floral pedestals behind and in front of the man and by placing a winged sun disk above his head. A third seal, inscribed with the name "Precious" (*l-mksp*), has a bird on a lotus pedestal behind him and the Egyptian *ankh*, or sign for life, in front of him.[243]

Another from the end of the Assyrian period and inscribed with the name "Uzzo" (*l-ʿzʾ*) abandons the Egyptian stylization and portrays the man with four wings and dressed in Assyrian fashion.[244] The scaraboid seal of Menahem (*lmnḥm*),[245] the king of Samsimuruna in the time of Sennacherib, has the striding figure on the top side of the seal and four registers on the under side: falcons facing a cobra, worshipers facing a four-winged man, a lion pursuing a caprid, and his name followed by an *ankh*. A seal belonging to "God-Heard" (*l-šmʿ*), possibly a Sidonian, has eight-pointed stars above the man, a horned uraeus in front of him, and behind him a papyrus reed surmounted by a bird on an empty cartouche.[246] A seal, perhaps from Kition, is quite similar but much busier: the man holds a tall lotus scepter in his left hand and an *ankh* sign in his right hand by his side. The scepter is surmounted by an eight-pointed star; the man is preceded by an empty cartouche resting on a reed and surmounted by the feathers of *maat* and is followed by the baboon of Thoth standing on a reed pedestal under a crescent moon (see fig. 3.8).[247]

Two North Israelite seals, both belonging to palace officials in the reign of the last king and similar enough to be from the same workshop in Samaria, show the men in Israelite dress but add nothing to the plain stylized portrait of the pharaonic striding figure.[248] This adherence to the Phoenician model is also evident in another North Israelite example with the name "ʾAbiḥalil" and on a bone plaque from Dor.[249] However, two seals also belonging to North Israelite royal officials have variants on the standard design. One is inscribed "splendid" (*lprʿ*) and shows the man striding right, wearing a tunic and mantle, holding a staff in his left hand, with his right hand by his side instead of being raised in salutation. The other is inscribed "Peqah" (*pqḥ*), the name of the general who murdered the king of Israel and usurped the throne in the time of Tiglath-pileser III, and has the man

243. *WSS* 415 #1099; 414 #1096; 412 #1090.

244. *CSOSI* 38–39 #30; *WSS* 422 #1114.

245. B. Buchanan and P. R. S. Moorey, *Catalogue of Ancient Near Eastern Seals in the Ashmolean Museum*, vol. 3: *The Iron Age Stamp Seals (c. 1200–350 B.C.)* (Oxford: Clarendon, 1988) 44 #291, pl. 10; E. Gubel, "Le sceau de Menahem et l'iconographie royale sigillaire," *Sem* 38 (1990) 161–70, pl. 26.

246. *CSOSI* 32–33 #21.

247. Ibid., 34–35 #23; *WSS* 276 #741. The writing of the man's name (*yšdʾ*), where etymological *samek* (*ysdʾ*) is replaced by *šin*, belongs to the dialect of Kition.

248. A. Lemaire, "Name of Israel's Last King Surfaces in a Private Collection," *BAR* 21 (1995) 49–52 (*lʿbdy ʿbd hwšʿ*); *WSS* #146 (*ḥbly*).

249. *WSS* 409 #1081; E. Gubel, "Nouveaux documents pour l'étude de la civilisation phénicienne," *Actas* 4, 3.1005–18, esp. p. 1007.

walking left, wigged, wearing a tunic and mantle, his left hand by his side, and his right hand poised to hurl a javelin.[250] The Judean seals belong to "servants" of the reigning monarch. The seal of "Shebaniah, the servant of ʿUzziah" (*šbnyw ʿbd ʿzyw*), shows him wigged and wearing a long robe, standing beneath a winged sun disk. The seal of "Ushnaʾ, the servant of ʾAhaz" (*l-ʾšnʾ ʿbd ʾḥz*), has him holding a scepter in his left hand and an Egyptian symbol of life, the *ankh*, in his right hand, which hangs by his side.[251] An Aramaic seal of "The-Divine-Kinsman-Is-His-Father" (*l-ʾḥʾbh*) has the unadorned standard design,[252] as does the North Syrian seal of "The Karizite" (*lkrzy*).[253] The seal of "My-Father-Is-Baʿal" (*l-ʾbybʿl*), the king of Samsimuruna, adds behind the striding man a bird perched on a papyrus stalk.[254] The latter addition is also found on the Ammonite seal of "His-Name-Is-Father" (*šmʾb*), but the seal of "God Heard" (*l-šmʿ*) adds in the same position an obelisk with pseudo-Egyptian signs.[255] Of the Moabite seals with the striding-man design, all belong to the early seventh century, and all have significant variants that, following the pattern of the Tyrian seals, adjust the standard scene toward a description of the individual who owned the seal.[256] On the seal of "He Saves" (*l-ḥṣl*), the striding man is dressed in Assyrian garb and has an Assyrian hair style; on the seal of "Servant of Horon" (*lʿbdḥwrn*), the man stands before an offering table on which there is a chalice and a pile of flat loaves of bread; and on the seal of "The Egyptian" (*lmṣry*), who was the king of Moab in the mid-seventh century, the man is portrayed as an Egyptian, wearing a Hathor crown composed of a sun disk with horns and is preceded and followed by the Egyptian symbol of life (*ankh*). On the seal of Hanun (*l-ḥnn*), king of Gaza, the man's sceptre has an *ankh* finial, and he is surrounded by the lunar disk, a crescent moon, and a star, a complex of elements borrowed from the Tyrian repertory. The basic design of these seals was introduced in Tyre and from there spread to the countries, or the cities and the individuals that belonged to the Tyrian network. They were popular—almost a craze—in the latter part of the eighth century, when this network was established, and lasted well into the seventh century in peripheral stations.

Sidonian craftsmen and traders, individually or with their business partners or families, tended to take up permanent residence in foreign lands, and their seals, because they reflect their origins, beliefs, or professions, lack the homogeneity of the Tyrian group. There is a deed of sale, for instance, in which Milkyaton, the son of ʿAbdʾilšoqed, sells his property in the village of Mazanu in the district of Nimrud to his compatriot Giraya.[257] The deed was stamped three times with Milkyaton's seal and was witnessed by four Assyrian residents of the town and by two other Phoenicians, Šedʾilšoqed

250. Bordreuil, "Inscriptions sigillaires ouest-sémitiques, III," 26–28.
251. Ibid., 22–23.
252. *WSS* 417–18 #1103.
253. *CSOSI* 27–28 #14.
254. Bordreuil, "Inscriptions sigillaires ouest-sémitiques, III," 24–25.
255. *CAI* 28–29 #12 (*l-šmʿ*); 83–84 #35 (*šmʾb*).
256. *WSS* 377–78 #1022; 383–84 #1041; 413 #1093.
257. E. Lipiński, "Acte de vente immobilière de Milkyaton, fils d'Abd-el-Shoqed (668 av. J.-C.)," *Sem* 39 (1990) 23–27.

Fig. 3.9. Impression of seal with man in fringed robe (BLMJ Seal 1804). Reproduced courtesy of the Bible Lands Museum Jerusalem.

and Ḥaluṣ. Milkyaton may have been a second-generation Sidonian in the town, the property having been acquired by his father. The seal, similarly, may have been inherited from his father, because it is not engraved with Milkyaton's name but with a hovering eagle, an image that would suit his father's name, "Servant (ʿabd) of the-God-Who-Watches" (ʾil šoqed), better than his own. The other two Phoenicians were members of the Sidonian community in Mazanu, and Milkyaton's situation was like that of individuals explicitly identified as Sidonians who were associated with one, two, or three compatriots in Nineveh, and in a small town in the region of Bit Adini in North Syria.[258]

The personal names of these Sidonians are unusual, or peculiar to Sidon, and this feature and a certain disregard for or mishandling of Egyptian motifs seem to be characteristic of Sidonian seals in general. One of the earliest of these belongs to "Yadullo'" (*lydlʾ*), a rare form of an uncommon verb and the root name of the sacred spring of ʾEshmun in Sidon, whose seal portrays a schematic, stick-figure, crested griffin facing a stylized three-branched tree.[259] Another, perhaps from ʿAmrit, pictures a winged sun disk flanked by full moons above a sloop with a high papyrus-tipped prow and stern in which the tackle and crew are replaced by the letters (*ḥb*), which may be the name Ḥabî, otherwise unknown except as the name of a North Syrian demonic power.[260]

A third seal, belonging to "Servant-of-the-Terrible" (*ʿbdʾym*), a divine epithet known from another Syrian seal, frames the name between a schematic sun disk and double lines, fits a two-winged scarab into the register below, and fills the top register with falcons facing deformed *ankh* signs.[261] Two other seals are notable for their personal names derived from names of the Gods of Sidon. The first, carved in Assyrian style, belonged to "May-Ṣid-Prolong-Life" (*l-ṣdyrk*), whose name contains the name of the eponymous ancestor of Sidon and the Phoenicians, who is represented on the seal as a bearded man wearing a beret, standing on a lion, and surrounded by symbols of enduring life (a crescent moon, an *ankh*, an eight-pointed star, and a miniature tree-of-life).[262] The other belonged to someone whose name "The-Genius-Is Exalted" (*l-šdrmn*) contains the epithet of ʾEshmun, God of Sidon, often known as the Genius (*šed*) of Holiness and Healing. He is represented on the seal as a man in a long fringed robe, holding a miniature tree-of-life in his left hand and a scale weight in his right, and flanked by papyrus staffs that support empty cartouches surmounted by the feathers of *maat*, the material basis of world order—all of this beneath a winged sun disk (see fig. 3.9).[263] Sidonian seals, like the Tyrian, are relatively rare and individualized; but unlike the Tyrian, which tend to picture the physical characteristics of their owners, they are prosopopoetic, embodying the personal or spiritual characteristics of the seal owners rather than their physical likeness.

Seals, as amulets, jewelry, or playthings—like the Lyre Player seals[264]—or as useful legal and commercial instruments were also status symbols that

---

258. R. Zadok, "Phoenicians, Philistines, and Moabites in Mesopotamia," *BASOR* 230 (1978) 57–65, esp. p. 57.

259. *CSOSI* 20–21 #3; *WSS* 378 #1023.

260. *CSOSI* 25 #9; *WSS* 274 #737; P. Xella, "Haby," in *Dictionary of Deities and Demons in the Bible* (ed. K. van der Toorn, B. Becking and P. W. van der Horst; Leiden: Brill, 1999) 377.

261. Deutsch and Heltzer, *Windows to the Past*, 62 (*br ʾymh*, "Son-of-the-Terrible").

CSOSI 29 #16. There is a another uninscribed seal that is sufficiently similar to be by the same jeweler: E. Gubel, "Notes iconographiques à propos de trois sceaux phéniciens inédits," *Contributi e Materiali di Archeologia Orientale* 4 (1992) 167–86, esp. pp. 168–69.

262. N. Avigad, "Notes on Some Inscribed Syro-Phoenician Seals," *BASOR* 189 (1968) 44–49, esp. pp. 47–49; *WSS* 414–15 #1098.

263. Ibid., 416 #1101.

264. J. Boardman, "The Lyre Player Group of Seals: An Encore," *ArAn* (1990) 1–17.

identified their owners by name and emblem or profession. A basalt touch-stone, on whose flat tip there is a seal of the Assyrian Moon God (a lunar crescent raised on a tripod above the full moon and stars) is inscribed on one side with the name of the smith or merchant who used it, "Hamon Declares" (*pʿrḥmn*), the attribute of the Assyrian Moon God being discern-ment, and his Phoenician equivalent *Ḥamon*.[265] Similarly, a series of seals from Cilicia, whose authenticity is not entirely above suspicion, identifies four men and one woman as "stewards" (*hbrk, hbrkt*) of the God Baʿal or of some unidentified person but is devoid of symbolism or representation.[266] There is another seal of a woman from the same region, which identifies her, "Ahotmilk, wife of Yissaʿ" (*l-ʾḥtmlk ʾšt yšʿ*), as a priestess. The Goddess she adores is depicted wearing a long dress and a cap with streamers, sitting on a throne, and receiving a drinking bowl from a woman, who ostensibly is Ahotmilk, who stands in front of her wearing a long dress and apron.[267]

Another in South Syrian style belonged to "Daughter-of-Ashima" (*bt'šm*), her professional name as priestess of Ashima, Goddess of Samaria and female counterpart of ʾEshmun. Just as the priestess is identified by her devotion, so the Goddess is portrayed physically on the seal as a four-winged genie with a Hathor crown (a sun disk set within horns) wearing an Assyrian cloak and striding right between Egyptian *ankh* signs.[268] A seal that belonged to a Byblian royal official has his name and rank, "ʿAzzam[ilk], Servant of ʿAzorbaʿal" (*lʿzm ʿbd ʿzrbʿl*), above a human-headed sphinx in Egyptian headdress, an *ankh*, and a stylized lotus blossom.[269] The seal of another Byblian, "Adonis-Regards-Favorably" (*ʾdnšʿ*), pictures him kneeling on one knee above a two-winged scarab, his hands raised palm-forward in supplication, and adds jocularity and mimicry to the scene by placing a lion cub (instead of Harpocrates) in front of himself in almost the same position, but sitting instead of kneeling, above a lotus blossom.[270]

There are others whose design approximates the attribute or character-istics of their owners. A seal inscribed with the name "Competitor" (*ḥrṣ*) has as its emblem a cock fight.[271] Seals with a recumbent sphinx reflect the attentiveness of men named "Servant" (*ʿbdʾ*) or "Client of the God Milk" (*lgrmlk*).[272] A seal of "Servant-of-Baʿal" (*ʿbdbʿl*), where the God is represented by the sun disk, has a crescent and a full moon, and service is suggested by cobras in attendance on a falcon, the sign of Horus, God of Heaven and counterpart of Baʿal.[273] All of these seals distinguished their owners, who wore them as professionals—craftsmen, priestesses, court officials, mer-

---

265. *CSOSI* 21–22 #4. P. Bordreuil, "Contrôleurs, peseurs et faussaires: trois épigraphies phé-niciennes énigmatiques," in *Numismatique et histoire économique phéniciennes et puniques* (ed. T. Hackens and G. Moucharte; Studia Phoenicia 9; Louvain: Université Catholique, 1992) 13–20.

266. A. Lemaire, "Essai sur cinq sceaux phéniciens," *Sem* 27 (1977) 29–40.

267. *WSS* 416 #1102.

268. Ibid., 265–66 #715.

269. *CSOSI* 22–23 #6; *WSS* 264–65 #713.

270. *CSOSI* 22 #5; *WSS* 409 #1082.

271. W. E. Aufrecht, "A Phoenician Seal," in *Solving Riddles and Untying Knots: Biblical, Epi-graphic, and Semitic Studies in Honor of Jonas C. Greenfield* (ed. Z. Zevit, S. Gitin, and M. Sokoloff; Winona Lake, IN: Eisenbrauns, 1995) 385–87.

272. *WSS* 414 #1095; 273 #734.

273. *CSOSI* 24–25 #8; *WSS* 277 #743.

chants, trade associates in a company doing business with Egypt—and as creative and idiosyncratic people who were the instigators and organizers of travel and settlement in the western Mediterranean.

The other eighth-century seals belonged to the men and women who were swept up into the expanding Phoenician and Palestinian network. They are in Aramaic, the signets of Assyrians or officials from the Syrian kingdoms of Israel, Judah, and Transjordan. They have ethnic and national characteristics, although some bear emblems that defy boundaries of this sort and attempt to express the individuality of their owners in a sophisticated cosmopolitan medium. Like the Phoenician seals, they are relatively rare in the eighth century but abound in the seventh and are a reflection of the social, economic, and political changes in these daring and exciting times.

There is one group of seals that is Aramean in inspiration and might have belonged to associates or partners from the coalition of Syrian states. It is distinguished by its representation of a roaring lion, either couchant or passant, dominating and usually filling the field. It appears alone on three seals but is generally accompanied by the name of the owner.[274] There are about 20 seals altogether, and they cluster around the middle of the eighth century, although there is one Phoenician copy from the fifth century. Three of the seals are North Israelite, the most famous being the seal of Shemaᶜ the servant of Jeroboam, king of Israel. The others are of individuals without rank or title. The Ammonite examples differ in adding to the field either a bird, a favorite Ammonite icon, or a winged scarab, and they are also distinguished by personal names, the theophoric element of which is the name "God" (*ʾEl*).[275] The majority are plain Aramaic seals, belonging to otherwise unknown men, and they differ markedly from the standard, more-personalized Aramaic seals. All of these lion seals, consequently, seem to have belonged to members of the same syndicate, which was operating around mid-century, during the reign of Jeroboam of Israel (786–746 B.C.E.), when the west was free of Assyrian interference, and Israel cooperated with Ammon and the Aramean states to reaffirm its cultural and economic presence in the area formerly under the domination of Damascus (2 Kgs 14:25, 28; Amos 6:14).

Standard Aramaic seals belonging to agents of the Assyrian kings, members and officers of the Syrian courts, temple personnel, or individuals from various Aramean kingdoms were customized for their owners from a small repertory of Egyptian, Assyrian, and local motifs.[276] The seal of Bar Rakib, son of Panammu, king of Zinjirli, is adorned with a winged sun disk and with a yoke, symbol of Rakibʾel, patron of the dynasty.[277] Royal retainers at Zinjirli in the reign of Barṣur, the father of Panammu (ca. 750 B.C.E.),[278] and at Arpad in the reigns of ʾAbiram and his son ᶜAtarsamak (ca. 775 and

---

274. A. Lemaire, "Trois sceaux inédits avec lion rugissant," *Sem* 39 (1990) 13–21, pl. 2. *CSOSI* 77 ##87–88).

275. *CAI* 15–16 #6, 17–18 #7, 190–91 #72.

276. *CSOSI* 57–107 ##60–140; *WSS* 280–319 ##750–856.

277. Ibid., 280–81 #750.

278. R. Deutsch and M. Heltzer, *New Epigraphic Evidence from the Biblical Period* (Tel Aviv–Jaffa: Archaeological Center, 1995) 75–76.

750 B.C.E.), and a eunuch in the service of Sargon of Assyria[279] had seals
with their name and rank but without any design or adornment. The seals
of temple personnel, however, may have a symbol of the God (for instance,
the seal of the servant of Hadad is adorned with a four-winged scarab)[280] or
feature the cult of the God (such as the seal of Barak, servant of the Morning and Evening Star ['tršmn], which depicts the lavish Syrian service of this
astral God and Goddess).[281]

Agents of the Assyrian government, or of Aramean states under Assyrian administration, imitate Assyrian fashion, while those dealing with
Phoenicians have seals in an Egyptian or Syrian style. Thus, a man called
"The-Morning-Star-Is-My-Help" (l'tr'zr) had a seal featuring a star flanked
by Egyptian ankhs rising above a four-winged scarab.[282] The seal of a man
called "The-Sun-Is-God" (lssr'l) was filled with a winged sun disk.[283] The
seal of "My-Brother-Is-a-Rock" ('ḥṣr) portrays a muscular man in Assyrian
garb kneeling on one knee and holding the winged sun disk, Atlas-style,
above his head.[284] And the seal of a Syrian merchant is distinguished by a
Horus falcon wearing the Egyptian double crown, standing on a papyrus
plant in a boat with a duck-headed prow and stern.[285]

Besides these seals of stalwart and successful men, there are also two
belonging to professional and entrepreneurial women. One, featuring a
winged sun disk, belonged to "Sister, the daughter of Nasri" (l'ḥt brt nṣry),
whose name suggests that she was a business associate in some company
organized as usual along family lines.[286] The other belonged to "My-Lord-
Is-Exalted" (lmr'ly), a reference perhaps to Adonis redivivus, of whom she
was a devotee, and she herself is pictured on the seal, wearing a skirt and
blouse, her hair in ringlets, her arms raised to display lotus blossoms held
in each hand.[287] Seals were prestigious, and their owners evidently were
given to display, but they were primarily symbols of a new transnational
aristocratic class, a commercial, religious, and political elite flourishing under the Assyrian imperial system.

Ammonite seals, like seals of Phoenicians and Arameans, are rare from
the eighth century and belonged to an exclusive group of politicians, craftsmen, and merchants.[288] Five are aniconic, two belong to the striding-man
group, and three to the roaring-lion series, and five feature birds and/or a
man with his hands raised in supplication. There is also a seal belonging to
"By-the-Power-of-El" (lbyd'l), who was the servant of Pudu'el ('bd pd'l), the

---

279. WSS 281–82 #752, 282 #753, 283 #755.
280. Ibid., 311 #832.
281. CSOSI 75–76 #85.
282. WSS 313 #837.
283. CSOSI 78–79 #91. The element ssr is an epithet of the Sun God Shamash.
284. WSS 286 #763.
285. Ibid., 309 #827.
286. Ibid., 283 #756.
287. CSOSI 79 #92.
288. CAI; U. Hübner, Die Ammoniter: Untersuchung zur Geschichte, Kultur und Religion eines
transordanischen Volkes im 1. Jahrtausend v. Chr. (Wiesbaden: Harrassowitz, 1992) 45–130. There
are about 20 eighth-century seals (CAI [= Hübner]: ##4 [78], 6 [128], 7 [26], 8 [79], 12 [140], 13
[65], 20 [83], 27 [114], 32 [42], 35 [145], 45 [137], 60 [3], 72 [126], 96 [45], 97 [122], 103 [61],
119 [53], 120 [119], 121 [124], 128 [148]) and 20 sixth-century seals, but at least 95 from the
seventh century.

king of Ammon in the third year of Sennacherib (701 B.C.E.), with a bull on the flat side and, on the curved side, a monkey sitting on a plant, eating fruit.[289] Another has the name "In-the-Hands-of-El, son of El-Offers" (*lbd'l bn ndb'l*) on the flat side, but on the curved side has the same name and, most likely as a rude pun on it, the drawing of a naked girl offering her breasts cupped in her hands.[290]

The seal of Elnatan has a four-winged scarab, and the seal of Yišʿaʾ has a winged sun disk and two stars.[291] The most elaborate is the seal of Ezra (*l-ʿzrʾ*), which features a man with his hands raised in supplication, like a whole series of seals, but adds to the scene a picture of the God to whom he prays and a scattering of astral symbols.[292] Of the aniconic seals, one belonged to Nasarʾel the goldsmith, one belonged to Elaʾ the daughter of Omer (*lʾlʾ bt ʾmr*), two belonged to sons of the same man, one belonged to the son of a man whose own personal seal represents him as a suppliant, and one, which may be later than the eighth century, is inscribed in Ammonite script with a Judean name.[293]

All these seals belonged to professionals: one to a craftsman; one to a royal official; the roaring lion and striding-man groups to men involved in international trade; the aniconic series to associates in family businesses; the suppliant group perhaps to priests or temple administrators; another to a bumptious merchant such as Bodʾel, whose seal would make sense and be acceptable to like-minded Ammonites; and others to sophisticated men such as Elnatan, the iconography of whose seal might identify him as a royal agent, or such as Yišʿaʾ, whose seal displays icons identifying him as engaged in Moabite traffic.

Moabite seals, of which about 30 can be dated to the eighth century, belonged to court officials or to members of various organizations.[294] The officials include three scribes (*spr*), the court historian (*hmzkr*), and a "son of the king," whose seals are either aniconic or feature simply a star and a crescent moon.[295] Another group related to these adds a sun disk, dots that represent the sky, a cultic stand or schematic tree-of-life or, just as a filler, one or more birds, to the star and crescent motif.[296] A third group, one of which belonged to a scribe, features the stand or tree along with the star and crescent but adds one worshiper facing it or two worshipers flanking it.[297]

---

289. *CAI* 30–33 #13.

290. Ibid., 263–64 #103.

291. Ibid., 77–78 #32, 49–50 #20.

292. Ibid., 251–52, #97.

293. Ibid., 65–66 #27. Ibid., 295 #121. Ibid., 114–15 #45 (*Išbʾl bn ʾlyšʿ*) and #120, pp. 293–94 (*lʿzʾ bn ʾlyšʿ*). Ibid., 292 #119 (*lʾlšmʿ bn ʾlʿz*); compare 249–50 #96 (*lʾlʿz bn mnḥm*). Ibid., 11–12 #4 (*lḥnnyh b[n] nwryh*).

294. *WSS* 372–98, 407; S. Timm, "Das ikonographische Repertoire der moabitischen Siegel und seine Entwicklung: Vom Maximalismus zum Minimalismus," in *Studies in the Iconography of Northwest Semitic Inscribed Seals* (ed. B. Sass and C. Uehlinger; Göttingen: Vandenhoeck & Ruprecht, 1993) 161–93.

295. *WSS* 372–74 ##1006, 1008–11.

296. Ibid., 375 #1013, 377 #1021, 378 #1024, 381 #1033, 381–382 #1035, 383 ##1–39.

297. Ibid., 373 #1007, 375 #1014, 375–76 #1016, 376 #1018, 379 #1026, 382 #1037, 384 #1042.

Another small group, which may be of Assyrian inspiration, has the winged sun disk—once in an angular and schematic form, once with the disk in human form.[298] The fifth and sixth groups feature fantastic figures: in four cases a griffin, alone or with some other symbol;[299] and in three instances a four-winged young man or woman outfitted in Egyptian style.[300] In the first group, the personal names are mostly composed with the divine element "Chemosh," the name of the national God of Moab. This would have been fitting for members of the royal court, although the "son of the king" (either an official or the child of a favorite wife) has the Judean name Manasseh. This national consciousness is less evident in the names of members of the second, fourth, and fifth groups, where only about half incorporate Chemosh, and it is entirely absent in the names of the men in the third and sixth groups. The group distinctions, plausible but plainly conjectural, suggest specialization among the men (and the woman outfitted in Egyptian style) according to craft or profession or, if they all belonged to the merchant class, developed skills in handling different commodities or expertise in the various languages required for foreign trade.

Seals from the Northern Kingdom of Israel disappear after the fall of Samaria in 722 B.C.E. Before that time, there are just a few in the roaring-lion or striding-man groups or (belonging to individuals) decorated with regional variants of the ubiquitous Phoenician or pseudo-Egyptian iconography.[301] They are rarely aniconic and are sometimes incised in Assyrian style.[302] Judean seals, like the seals of other countries, are rare in the eighth century but very common during the seventh and into the sixth century, when they far outnumber the seals from other areas.[303] Many in the eighth and seventh centuries belonged to kings, princes, royal and cultic officials, and regional administrators. They reflect the complete reorganization and centralization of the kingdom after Judah had come under Assyrian control.[304]

---

298. Ibid., 381 #1032, 379 #1025.

299. Ibid., 377 #1020, 382 #1036; Deutsch and Heltzer, *Windows to the Past*, 59–61.

300. *WSS* 374 #1012; 376 ##1017, 1019; 378 #1023.

301. D. Parayre, "A propos des sceaux ouest-sémitiques: Le rôle de l'iconographie dans l'attribution d'un sceau à une aire culturelle et à un atelier," in *Studies in the Iconography of Northwest Semitic Inscribed Seals* (ed. B. Sass and C. Uehlinger; Göttingen: Vandenhoeck & Ruprecht, 1993) 27–51, esp. pp. 34–35.

302. R. Deutsch and A. Lemaire (*Biblical Period Personal Seals in the Shlomo Mossaieff Collection* (Tel Aviv–Jaffa: Archaeological Center, 2000) list 21 Israelite seals (pp. 1–27) and 71 Judean seals (pp. 28–98).

303. *CSOSI* 45–55, ##40–59; *WSS* 49–166 ##1–399; the bullae (pp. 167–241) all belong to the seventh and sixth centuries.

304. G. Barkay and A. G. Vaughn, "New Readings of Hezekiah Official Seal Impressions," *BASOR* 304 (1996) 29–54; F. M. Cross, "The Seal of Miqneyaw, Servant of Yahweh," in *Ancient Seals and the Bible* (ed. L. Gorelick and E. Williams-Forte; Malibu, CA: Undena, 1983) 55–63, pls. 9–10; idem, "King Hezekiah's Seal," *BAR* 25 (1999) 42–45, 60; idem, "A Bulla of Hezekiah, King of Judah," in *Realia Dei: Essays in Archaeology and Biblical Interpretation in Honor or Edward F. Campbell Jr. at His Retirement* (ed. P. H. Williams Jr. and T. Hiebert; Atlanta: Scholars Press, 1999) 62–66; N. S. Fox, *In the Service of the King: Officialdom in Ancient Israel and Judah* (Cincinnati: Hebrew Union College, 1999) 216–35 (*lmlk* stamps); R. Hestrin, "Hebrew Seals of Officials," in *Ancient Seals and the Bible* (ed. L. Gorelick and E. Williams-Forte; Malibu: Undena, 1983) 50–54; A. R. Millard, "Owners and Users of Hebrew Seals," *ErIsr* 26 (Cross Volume; 1999) 129*–33*.

In the eighth century, these and seals of individuals featured Assyrian or pro-forma Egyptian motifs as well as specifically Judean designs comprising animals and birds, sailing ships, or enthroned divine figures, or even a bearded divine figure sitting enthroned in a boat and flanked by incense burners. Their owners, regularly men but occasionally women had names composed of some form of the divine name Yahweh, the God of Jerusalem—the form -*yaw* in the earlier names, as in Northern Israel, but the form -*yahû* after the religious reformation toward the end of the century. However, other names, hypocoristic or composed with the divine name El, were also popular and acceptable.

In the seventh century, in line with the reformation, there was an impulse toward simplicity and uniformity noticeable in such diverse areas as weights and measures, the mechanical production of terra-cotta figurines of the Goddess now reduced to folk status,[305] and the standardization of the literary language. The result was that seals became either aniconic or were limited to symbolic, geometric, or architectural designs, and almost all their owners bore orthodox religious names. In a system of this sort, it is likely that the seals belonged to individuals working for the government in a hierarchy dominated by the temple and palace or responsible for organizing internal production, overseeing transportation, and handling imports and exports—people fluent in Phoenician, Assyrian, Aramaic, and the dialects of Transjordan. Judah at this time was a "gate to the nations," importing from North and South Arabia and the countries east of the Jordan products for its own use and for transshipment to the ports of Tyre. Its exports were agricultural. Its merchants and traders belonged to a leisured class whose symposia provided entertainment and promoted the production of literary works that became the backbone of the Bible. The system worked well, and Tyre, which felt none of its constraints, could count on it.

The seals can be distinguished by their script and iconography according to the nationality of their owners. Because they were, besides being ornaments and amulets, the signatures of their owners, they are also generally and specifically distinctive in their portrayal of their personalities. The least forthcoming in this respect are the Judean seals, which generally are obscured by the pall of orthodoxy, and the most revealing are the seals of the Phoenicians, whose individualities are highlighted. To whom the seals belonged is indicated by their names, and who these people were and to what associations they belonged is indicated sometimes by their titles or by the seal designs they shared with other members of a group. The Tyrians and Sidonians, and the Byblians insofar as their seals can be isolated seem to have been independent rather than agents of the state, although Tyrians are distinguished within this group by their civic pride and by the urban instincts that are apparent in their founding of a "New City," or Carthage, to mark the stages of their westward travels. At the other extreme, Judean seal owners seem to have belonged to a strict hierarchy of officialdom. In

305. J. B. Burns, "Female Pillar Figurines of the Iron Age: A Study in Text and Artifact," *Andrews University Seminary Studies* 36 (1998) 23–49; R. Kletter, "Pots and Polities: Material Remains of Late Iron Age Judah in Relation to Its Political Borders," *BASOR* 314 (1999) 19–54.

between there was a mixture of public and private operators, and throughout there were groups or cliques with international associations.

Conclusion

As the eighth century progressed, Assyria became the main catalyst in
the development of nations and of international cooperation, and in the
concomitant emergence of individuals, intent on furthering communal interests and promoting their own. Syrian states banded together against Assyria and went missing. Phoenician, Palestinian, and Transjordanian city-
states and kingdoms joined each other in the Assyrian cause and entered
into great prosperity. A Cypriot confederacy flourished while it could count
on Sidon's cooperation but disintegrated after its amphictyonic capital at
Kition was desecrated by the Assyrians, and the balance of power shifted
to Tyre and the individual kingdoms in western Cyprus, with which it had
longstanding relations.

The Western Mediterranean

Phoenician travels to the western Mediterranean began in the early Iron
Age but acquired momentum and deliberation from Greek example beginning in the early eighth century.[306] They were undertaken separately by the
individual cities.[307] They were taken in association with good friends for
particular social, economic, and political reasons.[308] They followed different routes, to known destinations, and with varying results for themselves
and the people they met.[309] They differed from earlier ventures in their

---

306. S. Moscati, "Precolonizzazione Grece e precolonizzazione fenicia," *RSF* 11 (1983) 1–7;
G. Kopcke, "What Role for Phoenicians?" in *Greece between East and West: 10th–8th Centuries* BC
(ed. G. Kopcke and I. Tokumaru; Mainz: von Zabern, 1992) 103–13.

307. P. Bartoloni, "Aspetti precoloniali della colonizzazione fenicia in Occidente," *RSF* 18
(1990) 157–67; P. Bernardini, "I *Phoinikes* verso Occidente: Una riflessione," *RSF* 28 (2000) 13–
33. A more common opinion is that travel, settlement, or colonization was initiated by Tyre
alone, or that "Phoenicians" meant "Tyrians": S. Moscati, *Tra Tiro e Cadice: Temi e problemi degli
studi fenici* (Studia Punica 5; Rome: Università degli Studi di Roma, 1989); I. J. Winter, "Homer's
Phoenicians: History, Ethnography, or Literary Trope? [A Perspective on Early Orientalism]," in
The Ages of Homer: A Tribute to Emily Townsend Vermeule (ed. J. B. Carter and S. P. Morris; Austin:
University of Texas Press, 1995) 247–71.

308. S. Frankenstein, "The Phoenicians in the Far West: A Function of Neo-Assyrian Imperi-
alism," in *Power and Propaganda: A Symposium on Ancient Empires* (ed. M. T. Larsen; Copenhagen:
Akademisk Förlag, 1979) 263–93; W. Culican, "Phoenicia and Phoenician Colonization," in *The
Cambridge Ancient History*, vol. 3/2: *The Assyrian and Babylonian Empires and Other States of the
Near East from the Eighth to the Sixth Centuries* B.C. (2nd ed.; Cambridge: Cambridge University
Press, 1991) 461–546; S. F. Bondì, "Le commerce, les échanges, l'économie," in *La civilisation
phénicienne et punique: Manuel de recherche* (ed. V. Krings; Leiden: Brill, 1995) 268–81.

309. I. Strøm, "Evidence from the Sanctuaries," in *Greece between East and West: 10th–8th
Centuries* BC (ed. G. Kopcke and I. Tokumaru; Mainz: von Zabern, 1992) 46–60; S. Sherratt and
A. Sherratt, "The Growth of the Mediterranean Economy in the Early First Millennium* BC,"
World Archaeology 24 (1993) 361–78; P. Bartoloni, "Le linee commerciali all'alba del primo millennio," in *I Fenici: Ieri oggi domani* (ed. S. Moscati; Rome: Consiglio Nazionale delle Ricerche,
1995) 245–59.
C. R. Whittaker, "The Western Phoenicians: Colonisation and Assimilation," *Proceedings of
the Cambridge Philological Society* 200 [n.s. 2] (1974) 58–79; A. Swinton, V. Izzet, and S. Aguilar Gutiérrez, "Phoenicians in the Mediterranean: Degrees and Modes of Interaction," *Actas* 4,
4.1631–44.

regularity and persistence and in their enduring results, as the traditional East, after long acquaintance and a profitable mutuality, finally discovered itself in a world dominated by Europe and Africa.[310]

Traces of Byblian explorers and settlers traveling from the town itself or from one of its outposts among the Philistines are evident in Italy and Sicily. Sidonians, from their capital and from various places along the Syrian and Cilician coasts and Crete, went with Eretrians to Italy, Tharros in Sardinia, southwestern Spain, and Carthage in North Africa. Tyrians, from the city or from ports on the Bay of ʿAkko, from western Cyprus, from Al Mina, Rhodes, and Tarsus went with Chalcidians and Corinthians to Italy, to Sulcis and Nora in Sardinia, to southeastern Spain, to Malta, and to Utica and Carthage in North Africa.

The kinds of footholds or settlements that they established in these places in the eighth century suggest differing purposes for their travels. Except in Malta, they only went where there were good harbors and to places situated at convenient or strategic intervals on routes from and back to home. Even in Malta, they chose spots with ready land or water access to the people, the products, and the resources of the interior. In some places, they were looking for metals,[311] in others for supplies, in others for exotic plants, foods, or animals. In exchange, they brought samples of their luxuries and textiles; their alphabet; and artistry and skills in metallurgy, shipbuilding and sailing, weaving and dyeing, and the products they picked up along the way. In the eighth century, they were not very numerous. They were as much regular visitors or transients as settlers, interested mainly in finding things for the people at home or farther along in their travels. But they were impressed by the local culture, and their outposts, settlements, and colonies reflected their determination to shape this new world in the image of the old.

Malta

Malta lies less than 100 kilometers south of Sicily and about 300 north of Libya. Its situation just off the main westward and eastward shipping lanes can help explain its spotty and idiosyncratic adaptation of Phoenician and Greek cultural influences and material trends between the eighth and the sixth centuries, before the island was exploited by Carthage. The expectation, based on possible traces of early contacts, that eastern mainland Phoenicians were an important presence on Malta in the eighth century fades into the realization that the island was inhabited by an indigenous population and by a few Phoenicians who had come from prior settlements in the eastern, or Greek, and in the western, or Punic, Mediterranean.

---

310. A. M. Bisi, "Modalità e aspetti degli scambi fra oriente e occidente fenicio in età precoloniale," in *Momenti precoloniale nel Mediterraneo antico* (ed. E. Acquaro et al.; Rome: Consiglio Nazionale delle Ricerche, 1988) 205–26.

311. J. D. Muhly, "Copper, Tin, Silver and Iron: The Search for Metallic Ores as an Incentive for Foreign Expansion," *MPT*, 314–29; G. Markoe, "In Pursuit of Metal: Phoenicians and Greeks in Italy," in *Greece between East and West: 10th–8th Centuries BC* (ed. G. Kopcke and I. Tokumaru; Mainz am Rhein: von Zabern, 1992) 61–84, pls. 8–21; idem, "In Pursuit of Silver: Phoenicians in Central Italy," *HBA* 19–20 (1992–93) 11–31.

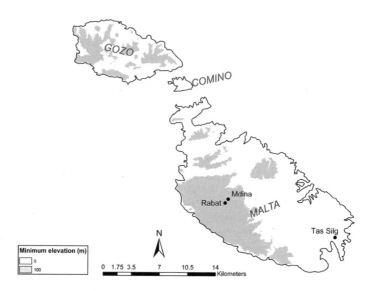

Map 7. Malta (produced by Christopher Brinker).

The ceramic evidence for Phoenician presence in Malta prior to the seventh century[312] is mainly indirect. There are no architectural remains, and the pottery was found in tombs, many of which were reused over the centuries, the typological sequence of which can be established but the absolute chronology of which is conjectural. There are some Greek, mainly proto-Corinthian wares and some recognizably Phoenician pieces distinguished by their shapes, fabrics, and finishes. More important than these are the wares in early burials, some supposedly a]s early as the ninth century, which were locally made but are manifestly degradations of original Phoenician imports. From these it may be deduced that, before there was Phoenician settlement on the island, there was a period of productive contact between the indigenous population and these people on their travels from the eastern Mediterranean.[313]

Equally compelling evidence, requiring similar extrapolation, consists of two Phoenician inscriptions from the Rabat/Mdina area in the west-central part of the island, exactly where most of these early tombs were located. These are memorials on small unadorned stone slabs found together buried deep underground, by chance and without archaeological context,[314] which can be dated paleographically to about the turn of the

312. P. Vidal González, *La Isla de Malta en Época Fenicia y Punica* (BAR International Series 653; Oxford: Tempus Reparatum, 1996); idem and E. Groenewoud, "El primer habitat fenicia de la isla de Malta," *Actas* 4, 3.1429–42.

313. Claudia Sagona, *The Archaeology of Punic Malta* (ANESt Supplement 9; Louvain: Peeters, 2002) 29–39.

314. *CIS* 1, 123 bis; *IFPCO* 19–23 ##4–5, pl. 2, fig. 2; C. Sagona, *The Archaeology of Punic Malta* (ANESt Supplement 9; Louvain: Peeters, 2002) 275–76, fig. 338:7.

century (700 B.C.E.).[315] The script is a mixture of cursive and formal forms, and the writing, like the writing on the tombstones from the graveyard at Tyre, is unprofessional (lines are crooked, letters are disproportional and sometimes poorly spaced or even unfinished) and probably not done by a scribe but by the mason who carved the stones.

The steles, according to the inscriptions, were put in place (perhaps the place where they were found) to commemorate a ritual in honor of Baʿal Ḥamon. Neither the God nor the ritual is mentioned again in inscriptions from Malta,[316] but both are found in later inscriptions at Sicily and Sardinia and at Carthage where, along with his female hypostasis Tannit, he presided over civic ceremonies. The memorials are also unique in mentioning only the names of the votaries without their patronymics. This may indicate that they were transients or recent arrivals, who had no family on the island by which they could identify themselves or acquaintances who would recognize them by their lineage. The omission contrasts, for instance, with a similar but slightly later stele from Sulcis in Sardinia that has the man's name and patronymic as well as the name of his grandfather and thus places him in the third generation of one of the families who founded the colony in the latter part of the eighth century.[317]

The ritual, involving a vow, immolation (*molek*) of a child, and deposition of a stele in fulfillment of the vow solemnized the "release" or "departure" (*molek* is from *hlk*, "to go, travel"), the apotheosis or canonization, of the victim in the flames of the sacrificial fire.[318] The implications are that the men who dedicated the steles were relative newcomers, who arrived in Malta from somewhere else in the western Mediterranean, had children by the wives they brought or by Maltese women they married, offered two of them in sacrifice to a God who is known only in Tyrian settlements or colonies. They lived in a community of which they were founding members and which comprised at least a literate mason and someone who could read the dedications but which was sufficiently self-contained and established to warrant this solemn public ritual.

The evidence from the tombs is similarly sketchy across the island. There are fewer than 800 tombs, with about 1,000 burials in first-millennium B.C.E. Malta.[319] Of these, less than 30 tombs have been dated to the eighth

---

315. *TSSI* 3.72–77 ##21–22; M. Gras, P. Rouillard, and J. Teixidor, "The Phoenicians and Death," *Berytus* 39 (1991) 127–76, esp. pp. 160–61; P. K. McCarter Jr., *The Antiquity of the Greek Alphabet and the Early Phoenician Scripts* (HSM 9; Missoula, MT: Scholars Press, 1975) 49–50, 132–33.

316. An exception is a Neo-Punic graffito "To Baʿalḥamon and Tannit" (*lbʿlḥmn wtnt*) on a lintel from the temple at Tas Silg: G. Garbini, "Le iscrizioni puniche," in *Missione Archeologica Italiana a Malta: Rapporto preliminare della Campagna 1964* (Rome: Centro di Studi Semitici, 1965) 79–87, esp. pp. 79–80.

317. *IFPCO* 97–99 #17, pl. 33.

318. J. Hoftijzer and K. Jongeling, *Dictionary of the Northwest Semitic Inscriptions* (Leiden: Brill, 1995) s.v. *mlk* (p. 5); H.-P. Müller, "Hebraisch *molek* und punisch *ml[ʾ]k[t]*," in *Michael: Historical, Epigraphical and Biblical Studies in Honor of Prof. Michael Heltzer* (ed. Y. Avishur and R. Deutsch; Tel Aviv–Jaffa: Archaeological Center, 1999) 243–53. The Biblical Hebrew equivalent of Phoenician *hlk/molek* is *ʿabar/*maʿbar*, "pass, passage," a word that is also used of the manifestation or epiphany of God (e.g., Exod 33:19–23, 34:6; Isa 28:18–19; Amos 5:17, 7:8).

319. G. A. Said-Zammit, *Population, Land Use and Settlement on Punic Malta: A Contextual Analysis of the Burial Evidence* (BAR International Series 682; Oxford: Archaeopress, 1997); idem,

and seventh centuries, and fewer than 10, almost all in the Rabat/Mdina area, belong to the earliest phase of Phoenician settlement, in the second half of the eighth century.[320] Over the millennium, only between 10 and 15 percent of the tombs had deposits of jewelry or semiprecious collectibles, and in the earliest settlement there were only 2 conspicuous burials.

One of these, the tomb of a woman and her husband, was in fact almost lavish. She was buried with her bracelets, four silver and one bronze, wearing a silver ring; and he, lying beside her on her left, was wearing three silver rings and a bronze bracelet. Half the grave was filled with grave goods, belonging separately to each of them, which included lamps, cooking pots, Maltese adaptations of Phoenician mushroom-lipped unguent jars, locally made cups along with a Rhodian and a proto-Corinthian cup, a trefoil-lipped wine jug, and three amphorae, one of them imported from the Levant.[321]

If this couple was typical, the early settlers may have married Maltese (in this case, it may have been the woman who was Phoenician) and lived, perhaps in a separate part of town, among the native population. The burial itself, however, is not typical, because other eighth-century tombs and the graves that were marked with the sacrificial steles contained cremations, and the difference in contemporary burial practice, which certainly reflects different beliefs, may also have been indicative of different ethnic or at least different geographical origins. The evidence from the tombs, however, is representative of a population consisting of just a few families and, while this seems to be symptomatic of the social structure of early Phoenician settlements in Malta, it is not the whole story.

What is most characteristic of ancient Malta is its lack of homogeneity, which is surprising for a very small island where nothing is very far from everything else, but perhaps it was a function of being one of three islands—Malta, Comino, Gozo—in an off-center archipelago. There does not seem to have been any central government. People gravitated to Rabat/Mdina, which was situated near the western coast on the highest hill in Malta. It must have been a sort of capital, because about 40 percent of the graves are located there, but the diversity of its population is signaled by its extraordinary number of separate cemeteries.

A mid-third-century B.C.E. building inscription from Gozo records the names of the mayor, the magistrate, the building inspector, and the priest who officiated at its dedication but makes it clear that these officials had their authority from the "People of Gozo" (ʿm gwl), the assembly of all

---

"The Phoenician Tombs of the Maltese Islands," *Actas* 4, 3.1365–75; Sagona, *The Archaeology of Punic Malta*.

320. Sagona (ibid., 39, 49) lists 16 tombs belonging to the Archaic, or Orientalizing, Phase (1000–750 B.C.E.) and 12 that belong to the Established Phase I (750–600 B.C.E.). Said-Zammit (*Population, Land Use and Settlement on Punic Malta*, 26–29) says that 6 dated tombs belong to Phase I (720–600 B.C.E.) and, according to statistical probability, that 21 of the 517 undated tombs can be assigned to the same period.

321. Sagona (*The Archaeology of Punic Malta*, 205, 808–12 #105, figs. 22–26) dated the tomb to Early Phase I (750–600 B.C.E.) or specifically to the second half of the eighth century. It was dated to the mid-seventh century by M. Gras, P. Rouillard, and J. Teixidor, "The Phoenicians and Death," *Berytus* 39 (1991) 127–76, esp. p. 145.

its citizens.[322] But apart from the omnium-gatherum at Rabat/Mdina, the inhabitants lived either in tiny communities distributed where land-use directed all over the islands or, to judge from later Punic times, on latifundia or large estates comprising dwellings, processing and storage buildings, and cemeteries.[323] This dispersal and diversity is reflected in an absence of tradition, either material or cultural, among the Phoenicians living on the islands. In most general terms, Malta was not colonized by the Phoenicians who kept coming to visit or to stay, there were no permanent links (political, religious, or economic) with any of the mainland Levantine cities, and their presence had no deep or lasting effect on the thinking, beliefs, business, or standard of living of the native Maltese.

Malta, in fact, despite signs of immigrant life, does not seem to have been "Phoenician" in any standard or stereotypical form.[324] The perfume and unguent jars, trademarks of Phoenician joie de vivre, which came from Tyre and Rhodes to every important place in Italy and Sicily, are missing in Malta.[325] When identification is possible, Tyre or one of its mainland or Cypriot ports seems to be the place of origin of the imports or immigrants, but the things themselves and the people associated with them seem to be either intrusive and without historical effect, or integral but merely an embellishment of the dominant local culture. Four small oil bottles that were picked up by farmers in the Rabat/Mdina area are imports (there are some like them in Sicily and Spain), and a Cypriot-style jug has its best parallels in Tyre, ʾAchzib, and Tell Keisan, but there the story ends.[326]

Duplicate second-century bilinguals written by two brothers are, in their Phoenician version, dedications to "Melqart, the Lord of Tyre" (*lmlqrt bʿl ṣr*) but, in their Greek version, dedications to Melqart by "Tyrians"—each version indicating in its own way that neither the God nor the people really belonged in Malta.[327] A bronze amulet in Egyptian style containing an incantation written on papyrus and featuring a drawing of the Goddess Isis is unique among Phoenician artifacts and inscriptions.[328] Its Egyptianizing and eclectic impulse is typical of the Tyrian spirit, but it has no religious context among the Phoenicians or indigenous people on Malta.

---

322. *IFPCO* 23–25 #6; M. Heltzer, "The Inscription *CIS I*, 132 from Gozo and the Political Structure of the Island in the Punic Period," *JMS* 3 (1993) 198–204.

323. A. Ciasca, "Insediamenti e cultura dei Fenici a Malta," in *Phönizier im Westen* (ed. H. G. Niemeyer; Madrider Beiträge 8; Mainz am Rhein: von Zabern, 1982) 133–54. Said-Zammit, *Population, Land Use and Settlement on Punic Malta*, 2.

324. S. Moscati, "Some Reflections on Malta in the Phoenician World," *JMS* 3 (1993) 286–90; A. Ciasca, "Malte," in *La civilisation phénicienne et punique: Manuel de Recherche* (ed. V. Krings; Leiden: Brill, 1995) 698–711.

325. A. Peserico, "Il ruolo di Rodi e dell'area egea nell'espansione fenicia verso Occidente: La documentazione ceramica," in *Patavina Orientalia Selecta* (ed. E. Rova; History of the Ancient Near East: Monograph 4; Padua: Sargon, 2000) 139–64.

326. E. M. C. Groenewoud and P. Vidal González, "Malta, a Phoenician Port of Trade?" *Actas* 4, 1.369–78.

327. *IFPCO* 15–17 ##1 bis, pl. 1.

328. T. C. Gouder and B. Rocco, "Un talismano bronzeo da Malta contenente un nastro di papiro con iscrizione fenicia," *Studi Magrebini* 7 (1975) 1–18, pls. 1–4; H.-P. Müller, "Ein phönizischer Totenpapyrus aus Malta," *JSS* 46 (2001) 251–65.

The island was famous for its linen; Diodorus said that it was remarkably sheer and soft.[329] The vats in which the flax was cured or where the finished product was dyed have been found all over Malta and Gozo.[330] This industry flourished from the Bronze Age to the Roman period, and various kinds of dyes were used. When Tyrians first started coming to the islands, they became involved in the business and contributed to it their process of making the purple dye for which they were famous. Not surprisingly, one of the earliest of these textile installations is at Mtarfa in Rabat/Mdina, and the manufacture of purple dye from the murex has left traces near the harbor on the southeast coast, in the vicinity of the temple precinct at nearby Tas Silg.[331] This Phoenician temple, a remodeling of a prehistoric shrine,[332] belonged to Astarte, the Goddess of Tyre and of all its colonies, except Carthage, where she was assimilated to and then replaced by Tannit. Her worship, attested by later dedications and inscribed jars in the temple and by a few inscriptions from various parts of the island, may be the only traditional and consistently maintained feature of Phoenician settlement on the island.[333] But these and the textile business she was expected to oversee were rooted in Maltese experience.

Phoenician settlement on Malta also differs from the usual pattern. The good harbors are on the east and southeast coasts, but apart from the southeastern port and its adjacent dye works and the nearby Temple of Astarte, the Phoenicians settled inland. Rabat/Mdina was about 15 kilometers away and less than 5 kilometers from the west coast, but the cliffs there made it inaccessible from the sea. They would pass through good farmlands on the way, and the valleys of the Rabat region were particularly fertile. Their settlement pattern indicates that they stopped in Malta to acquire its agricultural products (foodstuffs probably for their journey), linen for their sails, and the fine linen clothing made according to their tastes and specifications, which they planned to sell on their trips home or farther west.

329. Diod. 5.12.1–4.

330. Claudia Sagona, "Silo or Vat? Observations on the Ancient Textile Industry in Malta and Early Phoenician Interests in the Island," *OJA* 18 (1999) 23–60.

331. Ibid., 23–25, 35.

332. A. Ciasca, "Some Considerations regarding the Sacrificial Precincts at Tas-Silg," *JMS* 3 (1993) 225–44; C. Malone, "God or Goddess: The Temple Art of Ancient Malta," in *Ancient Goddesses: The Myths and the Evidence* (ed. L. Goodison and C. Morris; London: British Museum, 1998) 148–63, 213–14.

333. M. G. Amadasi Guzzo, "Divinità fenicie a Tas-Silg, Malta: I dati epigrafici," *JMS* 3 (1993) 205–14; idem, "Quelques tessons inscrits du sanctuaire d'Astarté à Tas Silg," *Actas* 4, 1.181–96. In late Punic times, Tannit, as a surrogate of Astarte, was imported from Carthage, and her name (*tnt, ltnt*) and some odd abbreviations of it (*lt, t, tn, tt*) are found on pottery fragments in the temple: see A. J. Frendo, "What Do the Letters TT at Tas-Silg, Malta, Mean?" in *Alle soglie della classicità: Il Mediterraneo tra tradizione e innovazione. Studi in onore di Sabatino Moscati* (ed. E. Acquaro; Pisa: Poligrafici, 1996) 3.1127–33.

IFPCO 23–25 #6; 27–28 #9; 30–31 #15; 38–39 #31; A. J. Frendo, "A New Punic Inscription from Zejtun (Malta) and the Goddess Anat-Astarte," *PEQ* 131 (1999) 24–35. The Punic inscriptions discovered by the Italian mission to Malta (Missione Archeologia Italiana a Malta) were presented in its annual reports (*Rapporto preliminare della Campagna*, 1963–70) published in Rome by the Centro di Studi Semitici (1964–68, 1970, 1972, 1973). The finds in the first four seasons (1963–66) were presented by G. Garbini (1964, 83–96; 1965, 79–87; 1966, 53–67; 1967, 43–45); those from the fifth season (1967) by B. Pugliesse (1968, 47–48); and those from the last three seasons (1968–70) by M. G. Amadasi Guzzo (1970, 67–75; 1972, 121–27; 1973, 87–94).

The Phoenician settlers did some of the work; they or their partners probably made the globular-based beakers that were popular on the island and became fashionable in Sicily, Sardinia, and North Africa.[334] But the clustering of their tombs, and so presumably of their dwellings, suggests that they were merchants and traders who organized and managed the textile industry and, because they had an interest in the production of flax, perhaps they also oversaw the production of a whole range of marketable agricultural goods. These things were perishable; they were bought to be sold in some other country. The deals were made with native Maltese who did not live in a monied economy, and many of the settlers moved on, taking their things with them, and were replaced by business associates who also stayed for just a short time. The whole Phoenician settlement process left few traces, apart from some tombs, imported wares, and a bit of jewelry.

Conclusion

Phoenician settlers in Malta were few, transient, and Tyrian. They were not from the city itself but from some of its mainland possessions, and they came not directly from home but from prior settlements in the west. The steady stream that began in the latter part of the eighth century was preceded by explorers who estimated the island's commercial possibilities, its resources, and its usefulness as a port of call, beginning at least by early in the century. Those who stayed awhile were merchants and traders, some or perhaps many of them women who were attracted by the textile industry, or hangerson whose business it was to keep the ships supplied and their crews satisfied. Most who came, moved on or back to where they came from, but some were overtaken by disease and death, and others actually planned to stay until they died. Transience was a part of corporate life in Malta, agents and associates in firms taking turns there and at the other stations where their companies did business. When they left, they took their belongings—the things that, if they had been left behind, would have left Malta looking almost as Phoenician as, structurally, it had become. But as it was, according to Diodorus, Malta provided them with linen and artisans skilled in every craft, and safe harbors; while they, these seafaring merchants, left nothing on the island except the prosperous life-style and the increasing renown of the native Maltese.[335]

Italy

In the early eighth century, Phoenicians began regular travel to Italy on voyages that also took them to Sardinia and Spain, or to Sicily and Malta, and then via North Africa back to their homeland ports. They went with Euboeans and later Corinthians; and when any of them stayed in Italy, they resided individually or settled in communal enclaves with these Greek colonials or among the native Etruscans, Latins, and Campanians. They came for the iron, silver, and human resources, not to establish settlements

---

334. W. Culican, "The Repertoire of Phoenician Pottery," in *Phönizier im Westen* (ed. H. G. Niemeyer; Madrider Beiträge 8; Mainz am Rhein: von Zabern, 1982) 45–82, esp. pp. 72–73.
335. Diod. 5.12.3.

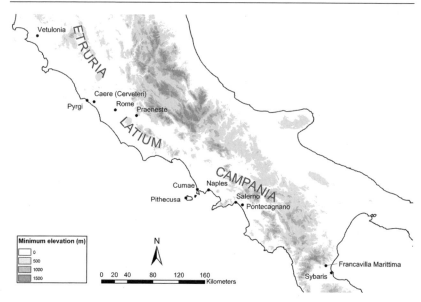

Map 8. Italy (produced by Christopher Brinker).

or build colonies. The relics of their regular and systematic presence include the luxurious goods they imported but mainly their impact on local artistic traditions. Among these traders and explorers were representatives of the three mainland capital cities: Sidonians in Etruria and at Pithecusa, Byblians in Latium (with an easy va-et-vient between them), and Tyrians at Cumae and in Campania. They were persistent throughout the eighth century, following the lead of their Greek sponsors but, gradually yielding to energetic Italian initiatives, their focus shifted to Sicily, Sardinia, Spain, and North Africa in the seventh.

This distribution of Phoenician interests and investments in Italy is reflected in the few eighth-century Phoenician inscriptions from central and southern Italy. There is an owner's name, "Belonging to ʾElîmilk" (]l-ʾlm[lk), on an early proto-Corinthian cup from a woman's grave at Pithecusa on the island of Ischia, where it was found with a wine jug and three bronze fibulae in a cremation burial dated to the last decade of the eighth century.[336] From the same graveyard but about a generation earlier, there is an imported Greek amphora inscribed after firing with the personal name "Twister"(kpln) which, when it was used later for an infant burial, was also decorated with Greek letters and with symbols designed to remove it from the world of trade and commerce to which its owner, the father of the

---

336. P. K. McCarter Jr., "A Phoenician Graffito from Pithekoussai," *AJA* 79 (1975) 140–41; G. Buchner, "Testimonianze epigrafiche semitiche dell-VIII secolo a.C. a Pithekoussai," *Parola del Passato* 33 (1978) 130–42, esp. pp. 137–40; G. Buchner and D. Ridgway, *Pithekoussai I: Tombe 1–723 scavato dal 1952 al 1961* (Rome: Bretschneider, 1993) 288–90, Tomb 232, Tavola 95, pl. 140:95.

Fig. 3.10. Silver Bowl from Praeneste (61565). Reproduced by permission of the Museo Archeologico di Villa Giulia, Rome.

child, belonged.[337] The infant was buried with its bronze ring, a carved bone pendant of a double-axe, as well as a steatite scarab imported from Egypt.

From Praeneste, southeast of Rome, in a tomb filled with imports from various parts of the Near East,[338] there is a late eighth-century silver bowl inscribed with the name of the smith, "ʾEshmun-Has-Determined, son of Astarte's Man" (ʾšmnyʿd bn ʿštʾ). The man's name, composed of the divine element ʾEshmun, and his patronymic, with its peculiar spelling of "Astarte," are Sidonian. Another bowl (see fig. 3.10) from the same tomb describes the symbolic destiny of the king, arbiter of life, vanquisher of death. The medallion features the king in his smiting pose striding over

---

337. Ibid., Tomb 575, pp. 569–70, Tavole 204, 224, pl. 196. See G. Garbini, "Un'iscrizione aramaica a Ischia," *Parola del Passato* 33 (1978) 143–50.

338. F. Canciani and F.-W. von Hase, *La tomba Bernardini di Palestrina* (Rome: Consiglio Nazionale delle Ricerche, 1979).

captives; the central frieze displays horses prancing in the open fields; and the outer frieze tells the story of the king riding to the hunt in his chariot, feasting at a table beneath a winged sun disk, attacked suddenly by a fabulous ape who lives in a cave, rescued by the Sun who carries him to the sky, then pursuing and killing the ape, and finally returning in triumph to his walled and turreted city.[339]

From Pontecagnano in Campania,[340] near Salerno, there is another Phoenician silver bowl, signed by the smith "Buddy, son of My-Brother-Is-King" (blṣ' bn ḥmlk). His name is unique, but his patronymic is Carthaginian, and the Egyptianizing motifs on the bowl are typical of Tyrian workmanship.[341] From Francavilla Marittima, near Sybaris on the south coast of Italy, there is a seal from the mid-eighth-century tomb of a young girl that is inscribed with her father's name, "Ransomed" (lpdy).[342] The name is known in North Syria and Philistia and later in Carthage; the seal belongs to the North Syrian Lyre Player group, and two others like it from the same workshop were found in Etruscan graves.[343] There is another grave in the same place of a woman, perhaps the girl's mother, who was buried with her jewelry (bronze and silver rings, fibulae, scarabs, and an amber necklace) and with a Phoenician amphora and a Geometric Corinthian jewelry box and juglet.[344]

Of unknown provenance and from the very end of the eighth century is a gold ring inscribed with an oared ship riding the waves and with the invocation "May you, O Raʿ, make Tibsol shine" (tzk lrʿ 'yt tbšl).[345] The design suggests that the owner was a seafaring merchant or captain of a ship, and the invocation of the Egyptian Sun God would suit the eclectic spirit of an eighth-century Tyrian.

---

339. C. Hopkins, "Astrological Interpretations of Some Phoenician Bowls," JNES 24 (1965) 28–36, pls. 17–19; G. Hölbl, Beziehungen Ägyptischen Kultur zu Altitalien (Leiden: Brill, 1979) 296–320.

340. B. d'Agostino, "Relations between Campania, Southern Etruria, and the Aegean in the Eighth Century BC," in Greek Colonists and Native Populations: Proceedings of the First Australian Congress of Classical Archaeology, 1985 (ed. J.-P. Descoeudres; Oxford: Clarendon, 1990) 73–85.

341. B. d'Agostino and G. Garbini, "La patera orientalizzante da Pontecagnano riesaminata," Studi Etruschi 45 (1977) 51–62, pls. 7–8; M. Heltzer, "A Recently Discovered Phoenician Inscription and the Problem of the Guilds of Metal-Casters," Atti 1, 1.119–23; J. Teixidor, "L'epigraphe araméenne de la coupe en argent de Pontecagnano," Syria 67 (1990) 491–93, fig. 10; M. G. Amadasi Guzzo, "Varia Phoenicia," RSF 20 (1992) 96–104, esp. pp. 98–99.

342. G. Garbini, "Scarabeo con iscrizione aramaica dalla necropoli di Macchiabate," Parola del Passato 33 (1978) 424–26; M. G. Amadasi Guzzo, "Note Epigrafiche," VO 2 (1979) 1–8, pl. 1, esp. pp. 3–8; idem, "Fenici o Aramei in Occidente nell'VIII sec. a.C.?" Phoenicia and the East Mediterranean in the First Millennium B.C. (ed. E. Lipiński; Louvain: Peeters, 1987) 35–47, esp. p. 36.

343. J. Boardman, "The Lyre Player Group of Seals: An Encore," ArAn (1990) 1–17, esp. pp. 6–7, figs. 10–11. Boardman doubts that the seal is inscribed and interprets all the lines read as letters as part of the stick-figure representation of a lion attacking a man who has his hands raised and knees bent in a vain attempt to defend himself.

344. P. Zancani Montuoro, "Francavilla Marittima: Necropoli e ceramico a Macchiabate, zona T. (Temparella)," Atti e Memorie della Societa Magna Grecia 21–23 (1980–82) 7–64, esp. pp. 29–40, pls. 11–16.

345. G. Garbini, "Un'iscrizione fenicia su un anello d'oro," RSF 17 (1989) 41–53, pl. 6. The name Tibsol (tbšl) is unique and, because the common Semitic root meaning "to cook" is inappropriate, it may be a Cypriot dialectal spelling of tbšr, from the root bšr, "to bring good news," so the name would mean "May you [the God or Goddess] bring good news."

Finally, there is an inscription that seems to illustrate a program of literacy initiated by Phoenicians who traveled to central Italy. It was scratched on the surface of a small globular flask, belongs to the very early eighth century, and seems to be three of the short Greek vowels separated by two vertical-line word-dividers [*e* | *o* | *i*].[346] The vertical dividers are unusual in Greek: the Nestor cup from Pithecusa uses two dots as punctuation marks;[347] and in Phoenician they are unique between letters. The letters are primitive: the [*e*] with its vertical line above and below the horizontals; the [*o*] oval, open, and tilted to the right; the [*i*] in a cursive Phoenician or back-to-front Greek form, looking in fact like an awkward Greek [*n*]. The inscribed jar is from Latium, northeast of Rome, and it does seem that someone, a Greek, Latin, or Etruscan, had just learned what was most distinctive about the Greek and Phoenician alphabets and was proud to write it on a prized possession.

All these inscriptions are symptomatic of Phoenician dealings with Italy. Like the Francavilla Marittima seal, they are found at sites that Phoenicians frequented in their travels but never meant to settle. They are by Tyrians as at Pontecagnano, or by Sidonians as at Praeneste, or by Byblians as at Francavilla Marittima. They were found in indigenous contexts: in burials of the women who married Phoenicians; or of the children they bore; or in the graves of patrons of the Phoenician arts; or buried with the customers of the Greek, Phoenician, and Etruscan ships sailing up and down the coast.

The paradigm of Phoenician presence in Italy is Pithecusa on the Island of Ischia in the Bay of Naples. This was a Euboean colony, founded early in the eighth century, at least by 775 B.C.E., in a concentrated and combined effort by Eretrians and Chalcidians (unlike their separate ventures in the east) after an indeterminate period of exploration and casual contact.[348] They came to do business with the Italians, especially the Etruscans, who

---

346. A. M. Bietti Sestieri, *The Iron Age Community of Osteria dell'Osa: A Study of Socio-Political Development in Central Tyrrhenian Italy* (Cambridge: Cambridge University Press, 1992) 184, fig. 8:9; D. Ridgway, "Phoenicians and Greeks in the West: A View from Pithekoussai," in *The Archaeology of Greek Colonisation: Essays Dedicated to Sir John Boardman* (ed. G. R. Tsetskhladze and F. De Angelis; Oxford: Oxford University Press, 1994) 35–46, esp. pp. 42–43.

347. G. Buchner and D. Ridgway, *Pithekoussai I. La Necropoli: Tombe 1–723 scavate dal 1952 al 1961* (Rome: Bretschneider, 1993) 215–23, Tomb #168, p. 219, tavola 73, pls. 126–28.

348. J. N. Coldstream, "Prospectors and Pioneers: Pithekoussai, Kyme and Central Italy," in *The Archaeology of Greek Colonisation: Essays Dedicated to Sir John Boardman* (ed. G. R. Tsetskhladze and F. De Angelis; Oxford: Oxford University Press, 1994) 47–59; B. d'Agostino, "Euboean Colonisation in the Gulf of Naples," in *Ancient Greeks West and East* (ed. G. R. Tsetskhladze; Leiden: Brill, 1999) 207–27.

A. M. Snodgrass, "The Euboeans in Macedonia: A New Precedent for Westward Expansion," in *Apoikia. I più antichi insediamenti greci in Occidente: Funzioni e modi dell'organizzazione politica e sociale. Scritti in onore di Giorgio Buchner* (ed. B. d'Agostino and D. Ridgway; Naples: Istituto Universitario Orientale, 1994) 87–93.

D. Ridgway, "The Foundation of Pithekoussai," in *Nouvelle Contribution à l'étude de la société et de la colonisation eubéennes* (Naples: Institut Francais, 1981) 45–56, figs. 1–3; A. J. Graham, "Pre-Colonial Contacts: Questions and Problems," in *Greek Colonists and Native Populations* (ed. J.-P. Descoeudres; Oxford: Clarendon, 1990) 45–60.

owned the natural resources and controlled the waterways.[349] They came
regularly and, as their cemeteries attest, in droves,[350] and they were accompanied by some of their longstanding Phoenician partners, by Sidonians
who knew the Eretrians at Lefkandi, and by Tyrians who met Chalcidians
at Al Mina. The Sidonians came directly from home or via Cyprus, Cilicia,
or Crete. The Tyrians, similarly, traveled from the mainland, from Carthage
and its satellites in Cyprus, from Rhodes, or from Egypt and Crete. Cooperation among the Euboeans ended at the time of the Lelantine war,
and around 735 B.C.E. the Eretrians left Pithecusa to found Cumae a few
kilometers away on the mainland.[351] The colony dwindled as the Romans
and Etruscans flourished, as the Chalcidians lost interest in the island and
founded colonies in southern Italy and Sicily, and as the Phoenicians began
to concentrate on Sardinia, North African Carthage, and Spain.

   Some Phoenicians were buried at Pithecusa, and many of the Greek and
Italian burials contained more or less exotic Phoenician products, but it
was a thoroughly Greek and Euboean cemetery: adults were cremated and
their ashes covered with stone cairns, children were laid in the ground, and
babies were buried in amphorae or storage jars.[352] Among the less exotic
products contributed by Phoenicians were everyday pottery items, such
as transport amphorae in which babies were buried or small closed jugs of
various shapes and decorations designed for perfume and unguents. Some
of them were perhaps meant specifically for funerary rites; most of them
were imports from Phoenician centers on Crete or Rhodes.[353] Among the
more exotic grave deposits were seals, either scarabs or scaraboids[354] or seals
of the Lyre Player group. All of these, or at least the more flamboyant,
typify the burials of the husbands, wives, and children of the founding
Phoenician families.[355]

   The scaraboids—with the shape but without the design of scarabs—were
made of white or yellow faience and manufactured in Egypt. The steatite

349. M. G. Amadasi Guzzo, "Mondes étrusque et italique," in *La Civilisation Phénicienne et Punique: Manuel de Recherche* (ed. V. Krings; Leiden: Brill, 1995) 663–73; J. Klein, "A Greek Metal-working Quarter: Eighth Century Excavations on Ischia," *Expedition* 14 (1972) 34–39.
   350. R. Osborne, "Pots, Trade and the Archaic Greek Economy," *Antiquity* 70 (1996) 31–44.
   351. J. P. Crielaard, "How the West Was Won: Euboeans vs. Phoenicians," *HBA* 19–20 (1992–93) 235–60.
   352. J. N. Coldstream, "Prospectors and Pioneers: Pithekoussai, Kyme and Central Italy," in *The Archaeology of Greek Colonisation: Essays Dedicated to Sir John Boardman* (ed. G. R. Tsetskhladze and F. De Angelis; Oxford: Oxford University Press, 1994) 47–59, esp. p. 52.
   353. A. Peserico, *Le brocche "a fungo" fenicie nel Mediterraneo: Tipologia e cronologia* (Rome: Consiglio Nazionale delle Ricerche, 1996); idem, "Il ruolo di Rodi e dell'area egea nell'espansione fenicia verso Occidente: La documentazione ceramica," in *Patavina Orientalia Selecta* (ed. E. Rova; History of the Ancient Near East Monograph 4; Padua: Sargon, 2000) 139–64, esp. pp. 146–50.
   354. F. De Salvia, "Appendix 2: I reperti di tipo egiziano," in G. Buchner and D. Ridgway, *Pithekoussai I. La necropoli: Tombe 1–723 scavate dal 1952 al 1961* (Accademia Nazionale dei Lincei: Monumenti Antichi 4; Rome: Bretschneider, 1993) 761–811.
   355. Buchner and Ridgway, *Pithekoussai I*. These tombs represent about two-thirds of the total number of graves that have been excavated which, in turn, cover only a small part of a very large cemetery: J. Boardman, "Orientalia and Orientals on Ischia," in *Apoikia. I più antichi insediamenti greci in Occidente: Funzioni e modi dell'organizzazione politica e sociale. Scritti in onore di Giorgio Buchner* (ed. B. d'Agostino and D. Ridgway; Naples: Istituto Universitario Orientale, 1994) 95–100.

scarabs were made by Phoenician artists in Egypt and featured the names, written in hieroglyphics, of Egyptian Gods and Goddesses, or the names of pharaohs of the Late Bronze Age. Some of the faience scarabs were also pseudo-Egyptian, archaizing and made in Egypt, but others were produced on the Phoenician mainland or on Rhodes. Both kinds were apotropaic and worn as jewelry, and some of them were hung on necklaces with gold, bronze or, more often, silver pendants. The steatite scarabs are dated to the second half of the eighth century, with more in the third quarter than in the fourth; the scaraboids are evenly distributed in the third and fourth quarters, and all the faience scarabs belong to the last quarter of the eighth century. Most of the scarabs were buried with boys and girls, very few with women, and next to none with men.

The grave goods associated with them were sometimes plain but usually ranged from generous to lavish. A baby girl, for instance, was buried with the two bronze fibulae that fastened her clothing and with a faience scarab imported from Egypt.[356] A twelve-year-old girl was buried with an imported Late Geometric Corinthian bowl and a locally made wine jug, but was also adorned with a silver bracelet and two bronze bracelets, a silver necklace, two silver fibulae, three silver clasps, four silver rings, a steatite and a faience scarab, and two Lyre Player seals.[357] A ten-year-old boy and a two-year-old girl were buried together in a grave that contained Pithecusan and Calabrian pottery, imported Early proto-Corinthian wares, Phoenician globular jugs imported from Rhodes, an iron pin, bronze fibulae and rings, and a faience scarab of Pharaoh Bocchoris.[358] The cairn covering a woman's cremated remains concealed local and imported wares, including four Phoenician globular jugs from Rhodes, silver and bronze jewelry, and a steatite scarab.[359] The grave of an eighteen-year-old man also had local and imported wares, a bronze ring, and a faience scarab in a silver setting.[360] The Egyptian, Rhodian, and Corinthian connections illustrated by these scarabs and by the grave goods associated with them suggest that some at least of these burials were of Phoenicians from Tyre and its dependencies.

The Lyre Player seals[361] originated in a North Syrian workshop. They are neither Egyptian nor Egyptianizing and cannot be classified as Tyrian but come from a region in which Sidonians had a stake and spread through the Greek world (Cilicia, Cyprus, the Aegean, Attica, and Italy) where Sidonians were at home. They are distinguished by their outline drawings and stick figures and by their inclusion of a Lyre Player as the signature of the artist who devised them. They all date to the short period between 750 and 725 B.C.E., when his workshop was busy and were popular among a

---

356. Buchner and Ridgway, *Pithekoussai I*, Tomb #706, pp. 677–78.

357. Ibid., Tomb #591, pp. 578–81.

358. Ibid., Tomb #325, pp. 378–82, pl. 157; D. Ridgway, "The Rehabilitation of Bocchoris: Notes and Queries from Italy," *JEA* 85 (1999) 143–52.

359. Buchner and Ridgway, *Pithekoussai I*, Tomb #166, pp. 208–11; A. Peserico, *Le brocche "a fungo" fenicie nel Mediterraneo: Tipologia e cronologia* (Rome: Consiglio Nazionale delle Ricerche, 1996) 62, 86–88.

360. Buchner and Ridgway, *Pithekoussai I*, tomb #472, pp. 474–76.

361. J. Boardman, "The Lyre Player Group of Seals: An Encore," *ArAn* (1990) 1–17.

young, adventuresome set who traveled to the West, especially to Italy, at this time.

They were not serious works of art but more like baubles or play things or personal identification badges. Thus, some of them are quite worn from fingering, but many are pristine, and most likely none was ever used as a seal. At Pithecusa[362] they were buried with children, mainly young boys, and usually in simple burials, except the Lyre Player seals that were found in graves of girls or women or in tombs that also contained steatite scarabs. Three baby boys and one man were buried with only their seal, but the graves of another man and of some older boys also contained some imported pottery, a piece of worked or unworked iron, an ivory pendant, or a second seal, either of the Lyre Player group or of a usable kind. A young woman was buried with a seal, with bronze and silver fibulae, and with the gold and silver clasps that adorned her robe. Girls whose graves contained Lyre Player and steatite seals were buried with all their jewelry and with the pottery, imported and locally made, that identified their social standing. The Lyre Player seals, in short, belonged to young people who took them to their graves or, more often, put them in the graves of their children. They were not as rich or as established as the owners of scarab seals and may have been crewmen, potters, fishermen—in general, the nonprofessional people who made life work for the rest of the Phoenician (or specifically, Sidonian) community.

The Phoenician pioneers who came to Italy included men and women who, if they meant to stay in the West, married into the local or Greek community, or established settlements of their own.[363] The latter conforms to the Tyrian pattern and is suggested by small sites along the coast of Ischia that have not been explored but that seem not to have been part of the Pithecusan dynamic. The former is verified by mixed grave goods, by Greek vowels in a Phoenician hand, by Phoenician men's names (*'Elîmilk* and *Kiplōn*) in the tombs of a local woman and of a Greek infant, and by analogy with the Euboean community with whom the Sidonians were confederate, where intermarriage is attested by the Italian fibulae worn by women buried in Greek graves.[364] The more detailed structure of Phoenician, Greek, and Italian relationships can be gathered from the kinds and

---

362. Buchner and Ridgway, *Pithekoussai I*, 739–40. They were found in Late Geometric I (750–725 B.C.E.) tombs: ##223, 420 (two), 433, 436, 519, 549 (four), 571, 574 (two), 591 (two), 592 (two), 595, 605, 634, 644, 647, 662 (two), 675, 688; in LG I–II tombs (ca. 725 B.C.E.): ##371, 478, 524, 701; and in LG II (725–700 B.C.E.) tombs: 284 (two), 329, 455, 557, 631, 684. Including the unpublished examples, there are more than 100 Lyre Player seals from Pithecusa: see G. Buchner, "Die Beziehungen zwischen der euböischen Kolonie Pithekoussai auf der Insel Ischia und dem nordwestsemitischen Mittelmeerraum in der zweiten Hälfte des 8. Jhs. v. Chr.," in *Phönizier im Westen* (ed. H. G. Niemeyer; Madrider Beiträge 8; Mainz am Rhein: von Zabern, 1982) 277–306.

363. J. Boardman, "Aspects of 'Colonization'," *BASOR* 322 (2001) 33–42.

364. J. N. Coldstream, "Mixed Marriages at the Frontiers of the Early Greek World," *OJA* 12 (1993) 89–107; T. Hodos, "Intermarriage in the Western Greek Colonies," *OJA* 18 (1999) 61–78; G. Shepherd, "Fibulae and Females: Intermarriage in the Western Greek Colonies and the Evidence from the Cemeteries," in *Ancient Greeks West and East* (ed. G. R. Tsetskhladze; Leiden: Brill, 1999) 267–300.

distribution of their material and cultural goods and from the technical and artistic traditions that they shared.

The Phoenicians came for iron and silver for which they paid with gold; with products from their suppliers at home and along the way, most of them perishable; and with the things they produced on the spot. They brought customs, such as symposia (*marzeaḥ*), and the chalices, carafes, and cauldrons associated with them, which their Etruscan and Italian hosts would adopt and imitate in their local wares.[365] They brought their Goddesses, Astarte the naked Goddess and the image of feminine beauty, and ʿAnat, the ideal of life and youthful passion. With them came the technologies (molds and metalworking) that allowed the Etruscans and Campanians to produce endless terra-cotta and metal copies of them.[366] They came with ceramic bottles and juglets that were distinctive and attractive and appreciated for the precious oils, ointments, and perfumes they contained. They reproduced them when they arrived and taught the local potters to imitate them and native specialists to emulate their contents.[367]

They introduced Etruscan artists to the techniques of gold lamination, granulation, and filigree and showed them how to make silver settings and swivels, and looped, and twisted-wire silver attachments for pendants.[368] They introduced Italians—Etruscans, Latins, Campanians—to sophisticated and luxurious living. They taught them how to transfer features from other media to ceramics: volutes from architecture, interlacing patterns from textiles, calligraphy from writing instruments, narrative scenes and symbolic motifs from metalwork.[369]

Individuals could enjoy imports, precious or semiprecious, for their own sakes or because they relieved the tedium of too-familiar things such as glass, faience, alabaster, and amber or curiosities such as tridacna shells or ostrich eggs.[370] The rich could indulge in really serious affectations—horses

365. L. W. Sørensen, "Traveling Pottery Connections between Cyprus, the Levant, and the Greek World in the Iron Age," in *Res Maritimae: Cyprus and the Eastern Mediterranean from Prehistory to Late Antiquity* (ed. S. Swiny, R. L. Hohlfelder, and H. W. Swiny; American Schools of Oriental Research Archaeological Reports 4; Atlanta: Scholars Press, 1997) 285–99, esp. p. 295.

366. R. M. Ammerman, "The Naked Standing Goddess: A Group of Archaic Terracotta Figurines from Paestum," *AJA* 95 (1991) 203–30; H. Damgaard Andersen, "The Origin of Potnia Theron in Central Italy," in *Interactions in the Iron Age: Phoenicians, Greeks and the Indigenous Peoples of the Western Mediterranean* (ed. H. G. Niemeyer; Hamburger Beiträge zur Archäologie 19–20; Mainz am Rhein: von Zabern, 1996) 73–113.

367. M. N. Sodo, "Un *alabastron* etrusco-fenicio da Cerveteri," *RSF* 27 (1999) 37–42, pl. 4.

368. F. Prayon, "Phöniker und Etrusker: Zur Goldlaminierung in der frühetruskischen Kunst," in *Archäologische Studien in Kontaktzonen der Antiken Welt* (ed. R. Rolle and K. Schmidt; Göttingen: Vandenhoeck & Ruprecht, 1998) 329–41; W. Culican, "Phoenician Jewellery in New York and Copenhagen," *Berytus* 22 (1973) 31–47, pls. 1–5, esp. p. 41; F. De Salvia, "Un aspetto di *Mischkultur* ellenico-semitica a Pithekoussai (Ischia): I pendagli metallici del tipo a falce," *Atti* 1, 1.89–95, pls. 7–10; G. Markoe, "In Pursuit of Metal: Phoenicians and Greeks in Italy," in *Greece between East and West: 10th–8th Centuries BC* (ed. G. Kopcke and I. Tokumaru; Mainz am Rhein: von Zabern, 1992) 61–84, pls. 8–21, esp. pp. 61–63.

369. A. Rathje, "Oriental Imports in Etruria in the Eighth and Seventh Centuries B.C.: Their Origins and Implications," in *Italy before the Romans: The Iron Age, Orientalizing and Etruscan Periods* (ed. D. Ridgway and F. R. Ridgway; London: Academic, 1979) 145–83.

370. J. Boardman, "The Lyre Player Group of Seals: An Encore," *ArAn* (1990) 1–17, esp. pp. 2–6; M. G. Amadasi Guzzo, "Mondes étrusque et italique," in *La civilisation phénicienne et punique: Manuel de recherche* (ed. V. Krings; Leiden: Brill, 1995) 663–73.

and chariots, ivory furniture imported by Tyrians or Sidonians or made locally by Etruscan shops from imported tusks, elaborate bronze, silver, and gilt bowls; and the pomp, pornography, and amazing myths and legends they portrayed.[371]

The earliest of these Phoenicians, as at Pithecusa, were Sidonians and Byblians—those whose artistic and cultural traditions are generally described as "North Syrian."[372] They were followed within a generation or two by the typical "Phoenicians," the people from Tyre who are characterized by their specialization in archaic and archaizing Egyptian traditions, objets d'art and curios.[373] There are traces of their commerce and evidence for their presence in Etruria and Campania, where Euboean influence was predominant, and in Latium where it was not,[374] but their real heritage was the simple enjoyment by the local population of their relaxed, inclusive, and usually brilliant way of life.

Pithecusa (and Phoenician Italy more generally) in the latter part of the eighth century was a stage between the mainland cities and the Phoenician foundations in Sardinia and Africa. In the third quarter of the century, there are a very few items, such as drinking bowls and wine jugs, that were imported from Pithecusa to Carthage. But it is not until the last quarter of the century that Carthaginian wares, in about the same numbers, begin to show up at Pithecusa and that transport amphorae, in greater numbers, from places in Etruria where the Phoenicians of Pithecusa were involved are found in Carthage.[375] At Sulcis in southwestern Sardinia, also late in the century, there is some Phoenician pottery from Pithecusa and Etruria, but in the northwest, at Sant'Imbenia near Alghero, the imports from Italy,

---

371. M. E. Aubet, *Los marfiles orientalizantes de Praeneste* (Publicaciones Eventuales 19; Barcelona: University of Barcelona, Institute of Archaeology and Prehistory, 1971); A. Rathje, "Oriental Imports in Etruria in the Eighth and Seventh Centuries B.C.: Their Origins and Implications," in *Italy before the Romans: The Iron Age, Orientalizing and Etruscan Periods* (ed. D. Ridgway and F. R. Ridgway; London: Academic Press, 1979) 145–83.

372. I. Strøm, "Relations between Etruria and Campania around 700 BC," in *Greek Colonists and Native Populations: Proceedings of the First Australian Congress of Classical Archaeology, 1985* (ed. J.-P. Descoeudres; Oxford: Clarendon, 1990) 87–97; M. G. Amadasi Guzzo, "Mondes étrusque et italique," in *La civilisation phénicienne et punique: Manuel de recherché* (ed. V. Krings; Leiden: Brill, 1995) 663–73, esp. p. 665.

373. G. Hölbl, *Beziehungen der ägyptischen Kultur zu Altitalien, I: Texte; II: Katalog* (Leiden: Brill, 1979); M. Cristofani, "Gli Etruschi e i Fenici nel Mediterraneo," in *Atti* 2, 1.67–75.

374. M. Botto, "Anfore fenicie dai contesti indigeni del *Latium Vetus* nel periodo orientalizzante," *RSF* 21 (1993) Supplement, 16–27, pls. 2–3; idem, "Il commercio fenicio fra Sardegna e costa tirrenica nella fase precoloniale: Considerazioni sulla patera di bronzo della tomba 132 di Castel di Decima," in *Actes* 3, 1.193–202; A. M. Bietti Sestieri, *The Iron Age Community of Osteria dell'Osa: A Study of Socio-Political Development in Central Tyrrhenian Italy* (Cambridge: Cambridge University Press, 1992) 46–49, 230–39.

375. R. F. Docter and H. G. Niemeyer, "Pithekoussai: The Carthaginian Connection. On the Archaeological Evidence of Euboeo-Phoenician Partnership in the 8th and 7th Centuries B.C.," in *Apoikia. I più antichi insediamenti greci in Occidente: Funzioni et modi dell'organizzazione politica e sociale. Scritti in onore di Giorgio Buchner* (ed. B. d'Agostino and D. Ridgway; Naples: Istituto Universitario Orientale, 1994) 101–15; D. Ridgway, "The Carthaginian Connection: A View from San Montano," in *Archäologische Studien in Kontaktzonen der Antiken Welt* (ed. R. Rolle and K. Schmidt; Göttingen: Vandenhoeck & Ruprecht, 1998) 301–18; P. Barnardini, "Tiro, Carthagine e Pitecusa: Alcune riflessioni," *Actas* 4, 3.1255–61; A. Bonazzi and F. Durando, "Analisi archeometriche su tipi anforici fenici occidentali arcaici da Pithekoussai, Cartagine e Ibiza," *Actas* 4, 3.1263–68.

again in minimal amounts, begin earlier in the century and are Euboean and Sidonian.[376]

Very little of the pottery in Sardinia is commercial, such as transport amphorae, and the personal items are what an individual might require on a regular basis or use on the special occasions when merchants met for a drink. The earlier relations between Carthage and Phoenician Italy, similarly, are consistent with travel back and forth by individual merchant ships on an irregular basis, but by the end of the eighth century they became more frequent and systematic, organized perhaps by shipping companies or colonies. In short, Carthage and Sardinia began to assume independent importance, not in connection with Phoenician involvement in Italy but toward the end of the eighth century, when the Phoenicians started disengaging themselves from the flourishing Etruscan and Italian states in favor of these less-developed regions.

Conclusion

The Phoenicians who went to Italy were not an undifferentiated lot but individuals, crews, and companies from Tyre, Sidon, and Byblos, either directly or via their emporia and possessions in the eastern Mediterranean. There is the evidence of analogy that, as Tyrians cooperated with Chalcidians at Al Mina and with Corinthians in Greece, so they joined them at Pithecusa. Sidonians, inveterate companions of the Eretrians at Lefkandi and in Chalkidiki, traveled with them to Ischia and Etruria. And Byblians, who are certainly present in Caere at the end of the sixth century and who regularly attended the Sidonians as their literary, architectural and naval specialists, settled with them among the Greeks and Italians. There is the specific evidence of inscriptions, of Egyptian and Egyptianizing scarabs, of the Lyre Player seals, of the Phoenician pottery from Rhodes, of ivories belonging both to the North Syrian and to the Phoenician styles, and of gold, silver, and bronze bowls by master craftsmen from diverse artistic traditions—evidence that the Phoenicians in Italy were citizens of these three mainland cities. There is also the evidence of the colonies and settlements to which, separately, as in Sardinia, Sicily, and Spain, or jointly, as in North African Carthage, all three cities contributed.

Carthage

The nag about Carthage is that it was supposed to have been founded toward the end of the ninth century (825 and 814 B.C.E. are traditional dates) by Phoenicians from Cyprus, and there are some tantalizing Phoenician texts that might be interpreted in this sense, but no amount of tug on the archaeological evidence can stretch it back that early. There is nothing implausible about an earlier foundation. Phoenicians had already sailed into the Atlantic. But the evidence of the texts and the material corroboration

---

376. D. Ridgway, "Phoenicians and Greeks in the West: A View from Pithekoussai," in *The Archaeology of Greek Colonisation: Essays Dedicated to Sir John Boardman* (ed. G. R. Tsetskhladze and F. De Angelis; Oxford: Oxbow, 1994) 35–46; P. Bartoloni, "A proposito di commerci arcaici," *Actas* 4, 1.299–303.

put the foundation of Carthage about 100 years later than classical calculations allowed.

What is clear is that the founding of the colony at Carthage was not a random or chance affair. Phoenicians knew these western waters, sailed them with their Greek associates, reconnoitered the coasts and currents, looked for good harbors with conspicuous landmarks and easy access to the interior, searched out hospitable sites or uninhabited shores, and settled in a few choice locations. The ship from western Cyprus that survived a storm at sea and found safe haven at Nora knew that it had landed in Sardinia because it was on the map, and it was not the first of the Tarshish ships to drop anchor there. The sailors left on display a monument to their gratitude for the ships that followed, because they would not be the last, and the ship sailed home likely as not along the coast of Africa, not just to anchor at Utica or Carthage, but because those were chartered waters and there they found the prevailing winds.[377] That was 100 years before, in the era of explorers. It would have been impossible for a Cypriot or any other Phoenician ship just to chance on Carthage in the eighth century and completely uncharacteristic of the Phoenicians just to stumble on the idea of claiming it as a colony.

An inscription on a gold pendant from one of the oldest tombs in Carthage, generally dated to about the end of the eighth century (ca. 700 b.c.e.), is the earliest written evidence for the founding of the colony, at Carthage:[378] "For Astarte! For Pygmalion! Yada'milk, son of Padiya, an armed soldier whom Pygmalion armed" (*l'štrt lpgmlyn yd'mlk bn pdy ḥlṣ 'š ḥlṣ pgmlyn*). The pendant is about an inch in diameter with a folded loop at the top so that it could be hung from a necklace. The text is staccato and perfectly suited to its meaning. It starts with a battle cry invoking his Goddess and his commander: balance and repetition is the essence of these whoops, as in "For 'Anat! For 'Anat" inscribed on a lance head from Idalion; or "For Yahweh! For Gideon!" to the sound of a trumpet. The medallion was this soldier's dog tag and its invocation of Astarte (the Aphrodite of Paphos) and of Pygmalion (whose Greco-Phoenician name commemorates the Cypriot Dwarf God Bes)[379] identifies him as a Phoenician from western Cyprus.

His name is unique, but his patronymic is common and, like the battle cry, the statement is unadorned and simply names the man. The last part, marked by a repeated "armed," identifies him as a member of a military unit with a mission—called and equipped by the commander. The mission, as the circumstances of the find indicate, was to establish the colony

377. F. M.Cross, "An Interpretation of the Nora Stone," *BASOR* 208 (1972) 13–19; M. G. Amadasi Guzzo and P. G. Guzzo, "Di Nora, di Eracle gaditano e della più antica navigazione fenicia," in *Los Fenicios en la Peninsula Iberica, II: Epigrafía y Lengua. Glíptica y Numismática. Expansión e Interacción* (ed. G. del Olmo Lete; Sabadell [Barcelona]: AUSA, 1986) 59–71.

378. C. R. Krahmalkov, "The Foundation of Carthage, 814 b.c.: The Douïmès Pendant Inscription," *JSS* 26 (1981) 177–91. See also J. Ferron, "Le médaillon de Carthage," *Cahiers de Byrsa* 8 (1958–59) 45–56, pl. 1; idem, "Les problèmes du médaillon de Carthage," *Mus* 81 (1968) 255–61.

379. V. Wilson, "The Iconography of Bes with Particular Reference to the Cypriot Evidence," *Levant* 7 (1975) 77–103; H.-P. Müller, "Pygmaion, Pygmalion und Pumaijaton: Aus der Geschichte einer mythischen Gestalt," *Or* 57 (1988) 192–205.

at Carthage. Because the inscription is dated paleographically to the latter part of the eighth century (ca. 725 B.C.E.) and the tomb to around the end of the century, Yadaʿmilk would have been in his prime when he was commissioned and sent from Cyprus and about 50 years old when he died. This military component of the founding party was a token of its official status and a sign of the deliberation involved in the colonization. It would also account for the purported designation of the oldest quarter of Carthage as the "Byrsa" or "fort." Additionally, it tends to confirm (because it indicates that the settlement was to be exclusive of marauders and trespassers—the sea lanes were familiar, and there were Euboean settlers nearby)[380] that it was originally a Tyrian foundation.

The late eighth-century foundation of Carthage in Cyprus is corroborated by two other inscriptions, in themselves circumstantial and flimsy evidence but cumulative in conjunction with Yadaʿmilk's inscribed pendant. One of the inscriptions is a fourth-century dedication from Olbia in northeastern Sardinia by a man whose name is lost but who identifies himself as a Carthaginian (*bʿm qrthdšt*, "of the citizens of Carthage") and who lists his Carthaginian ancestors to the 15th generation.[381] Allowing about 25 years per generation and dating the inscription paleographically to about 350 B.C.E., we can calculate that his earliest named ancestor lived in Carthage around 725 B.C.E., and, like Yadaʿmilk, would have been a member of the founding generation.

The other inscription is a funerary monument from Carthage[382] that records the erection of a stele celebrating the sacrifice of a girl to the God Baʿal Ḥamon: "Stele of the ritual passage of a female citizen that was made by Bodsay, son of Milqartgad, for Baʿlhamon, the Lord." The stele is carved to represent a three-pillared shrine, a "Bethel" (*baetyl*) or House of God like the one in the Tyrian compound at Kommos in Crete, and many like it have been found at Tyrian Sulcis in Sardinia. The ritual was a foundation sacrifice like the sacrifices commemorated on the steles from Malta. The script places the inscription at about the same time as the gold pendant inscription or slightly later. It seems that the stele, which commemorates a public ceremony, was erected to record the offering of the sacrifice that accompanied the official founding of the city, the man's father being among the first settlers, he himself among the earliest citizens, and the victim one of the youngest children born in the new colony.[383] These two inscriptions together with the gold pendant reach back through time and the generalities of travel and colonization to the proud and daring individuals who pioneered the civilization of North Africa and the western Mediterranean.

380. J. Boardman, "Early Euboean Settlements in the Carthage Area," *OJA* 25 (2006) 195–200.

381. *IFPCO* 113–15 #34, pl. 42; idem, "Iscrizioni fenicie e puniche in Italia," *Bolletino d'Arte* 71 (1986) 103–18, 86–87 #22. The inscription records the dedication of a mausoleum to Baʿal Ḥamon (*lʾdn[y lbʿl ḥmn] ʾdn*), the patron God of mortuary rituals in Carthage.

382. *CIS* 5684. The inscription in four lines reads: *nṣb mlkt bʿl / ʾš pʿl bdsy / bn mlqrtgd lb / ʿlḥmn ʾdn*. The feminine form of the sacrificial term, *mlkt*, shows that the victim was a girl.

383. 1 Kgs 16:34; F. M. Cross, "A Phoenician Inscription from Idalion: Some Old and New Texts Relating to Child Sacrifice," in *Scripture and Other Artifacts: Essays on the Bible and Archaeology in Honor of Philip J. King* (ed. M. D. Coogan, J. C. Exum, and L. E. Stager; Louisville: Westminster John Knox, 1994) 94–107.

Carthage was situated on a peninsula jutting into a large and perfectly protected bay, with anchorages on either side—natural harbors at the outermost tip of the peninsula. Eventually, a harbor and dry dock were built in the lower city at the foot of the citadel hill.[384] There are architectural remains, pottery from the eighth century, and evidence, not surprisingly, for early settlement on the Byrsa hill and along the outermost coast near the harbors. The settlement was planned, not haphazard, and the buildings (the earlier houses built of mud brick; the seventh-century houses in the pier-and-rubble style) were laid out along an orthogonal grid.[385] An early pottery cache, not associated with any of these buildings and sometimes thought to be a foundation deposit, was laid on bedrock at the foot of a crevice. It was all locally made by a Phoenician potter copying Greek, or Pithecusan, originals and consisted of some items for personal use, such as a lamp and two drinking bowls; and others intended for trade, such as a bird-shaped vase, an amphora, a dipper, a sprinkler, and some juglets.[386] The pottery associated with the buildings consisted of transport amphorae made on Pithecusa and in Etruria, some fine wares of Euboean, Italian, and Etruscan make, and some amphorae and jugs from Sardinia.[387] Finds of Phoenician pottery from here and there on the site demonstrate close connections between Carthage and towns such as Tell Keisan on the eastern mainland and with Tyre itself.[388] Most of this pottery is domestic tableware, and much of it is of a style and finish that belongs to about the mid-eighth century in Tyre. Some of it was found with ceramics from Euboea and Pithecusa, and some of it is comparable to wares from the earliest levels at sites in southern Spain. There is no pottery suggesting that the site was already inhabited by an indigenous people, and it seems clear that Carthage was founded by Tyre and by Tyrians from Carthage in Cyprus around

384. W. Huss, *Geschichte der Karthager* (Munich: Beck, 1985) 44–51.

385. H. G. Niemeyer, "The Early Phoenician City-States on the Mediterranean: Archaeological Elements for Their Description," in *A Comparative Study of Thirty City-State Cultures: An Investigation Conducted by the Copenhagen Polis Centre* (ed. M. H. Hansen; Copenhagen: Reitzels, 2000) 89–115, esp. p. 107.

386. W. Culican, "Aspects of Phoenician Settlement in the West Mediteranean," *AbrN* 1 (1959–60) 36–55, esp. pp. 40, 47–48 (repr. *Opera Selecta: From Tyre to Tartessos* (Gothenburg: Åströms, 1986) 629–48, esp. pp. 633, 640–41); C. Briese, "Die Chapelle Cintas: Das Grundungsdepot Karthagos oder eine Bestattung der Grundergeneration?" in *Archäologische Studien in Kontaktzonen der Antiken Welt* (ed. R. Rolle and K. Schmidt; Göttingen: Vandenhoeck & Ruprecht, 1998) 419–51, pls. 35–37; idem, "Complies with Cypriot Pottery Standard: Adaptation of Phoenician Models and Vice Versa," *Actas* 4, 3.963–69.

387. R. F. Docter et al., "Early Central Italian Transport Amphorae from Carthage: Preliminary Results," *RSF* 25 (1997) 15–58, pls. 1–8; M. Kollund, "Sardinian Pottery from Carthage," in *Sardinian and Aegean Chronology: Towards the Resolution of Relative and Absolute Dating in the Mediteranean* (ed. M. S. Balmuth and R. H. Tykot; Studies in Sardinian Archaeology V; Oxford: Oxbow, 1998) 355–58; R. F. Docter, "Carthage and the Tyrrhenian in the 8th and 7th Centuries B.C.: Central Italian Transport Amphorae and Fine Wares Found under the Decumanus Maximus," *Actas* 4, 1.329–38.

388. M. Vegas, "La ceramica fenicia del siglo VIII en Cartago," *Actas* 4, 3.1237–46; M. Botto, "Indagini archeometriche sulla ceramica fenicia e punica del Mediterraneo centro-occidentale," *RSF* 29 (2001) 159–81, esp. pp. 160–64.

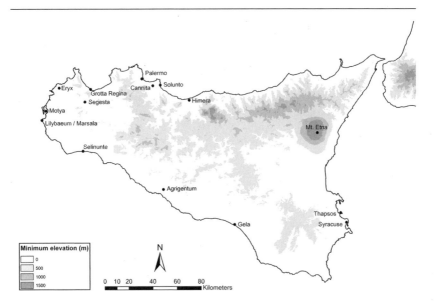

Map 9. Sicily (produced by Christopher Brinker).

725 B.C.E.[389] Its earliest relations were with the Phoenicians and Greeks at Pithecusa and in central Italy.

Conclusion

Carthage differed from Italy and Malta, places that were frequented by Phoenicians, in being a destination rather than a place to visit, work, or do business; and an authentic colony, an independent town with political, religious, and economic ties to its founding city. Its founders were from western Cyprus, Tyre, mainland towns such as Tell Keisan in the Tyrian orbit, and from North Syria and Cilicia, where Sidonian and Byblian interests were once predominant. They came after years of prospecting in the West revealed a new world in the making that was independent and self-sufficient, not just a source of wonders and resources to people back home. They came when their ancestral homes were being swamped by Aramean inertia and Assyrian politics, paralyzed by a lackadaisical Cypriot amphictyony, stymied by Judean organization and Transjordanian ambition. They settled in Carthage, almost an island, like Tyre, with rocky headlands, great harbors, and nearby ports and fortresses. It was on the edge of a rich and diverse interior, where they could establish a capital for their satellites in Europe without interference or competition from an indigenous population and as a counterbalance to increasing Greek interests in Egypt and Africa.

---

389. H. G. Niemeyer, "A la recherche de la Carthage archaïque: Premiers résultats des fouilles de l'Université de Hambourg en 1986 et 1987," *Historie et Archéologie de l'Afrique du Nord*, vol. 1: *Carthage et son Territoire dans l'Antiquité* (Paris: Comité des Travaux Historiques et Scientifiques, 1990) 45–52.

Like Tyre, the town was open and eclectic. But, unlike Tyre, it was a Tripolis, a haven for Byblian craftsmen, Sidonian refugees, and Tyrian emigrés from Italy. It was a remarkable, fast-growing town that could count on suppliers in Sicily and Malta, enjoy manufactured goods from Sardinia, fresh produce from southern Spain, and pickled fish from outlandish Atlantic ports. It began abruptly toward the end of the eighth century, flourished along with its mother city from the seventh to the mid-sixth, and then replaced it, becoming the capital city of Phoenicia—the stunning, belligerent metropolis of the Western world.

Sicily

Phoenicians landed in western Sicily at the very end of the eighth or early in the seventh century B.C.E., soon after Carthage was founded. They were not related to the people who founded Carthage—not from the same place or not from the same economic and social class. But they were from the mainland, apparently, and were probably skilled workers and technicians who came to provide services and supplies to individuals who were traveling to the new colony. They lived in isolation from the other western colonials during the seventh century, when their maintenance of the colony was essential, but they were absorbed into the Carthaginian orb beginning in the sixth century, when their location acquired strategic importance.

Motya, where they first arrived, is an island in a shallow lagoon on the western tip of Sicily, near Marsala.[390] It would have been known to Phoenician ships from Malta or Sardinia—a statue of their God was thrown into the sea off Selinunte just to the southeast[391]—and could have provided safe anchorage for ships on their way from Italy to Carthage, 160 kilometers away. The island was farmland and woodland, without any other resources, and was inhabited by indigenous Elimians when the Phoenicians arrived.[392] The Carthaginians built a wall around it and, as the lagoon silted up, a road to the main island.[393] However, before this time, the Phoenicians raised the crops and cattle they needed and acquired wine and oil and other necessities from the native communities. Motya is very small, flat, not much above sea level, accessible from all sides, protected by barrier reefs to the west, and reached through narrow passages to the north and

390. B. S. J. Isserlin et al., "Motya, 1955: Report of the 1955 Trial Excavations at Motya near Marsala (Sicily) undertaken by the Oxford University Archaeological Expedition to Motya," *PBSR* 26 (1958) 1–29, pls. 1–4; idem, "The Oxford University Archaeological Expedition's Trial Excavations at the Phoenician Site of Motya near Marsala (Sicily), Summer 1955," *Atti del settimo congresso internazionale di Archeologia Classica* (Rome: "L'Erma" di Bretschneider, 1961) 2.41–43; idem, "Motya: Urban Features," *PhWest*, 113–31; B. S. J. Isserlin and J. Du Plat Taylor, *Motya—A Phoenician and Carthaginian City in Sicily, I: Field Work and Excavation* (Leiden: Brill, 1974).

391. G. Falsone, "Sulla cronologia del Bronzo fenicio di Sciacca alla luce delle nuove scoperte di Huelva e Cadice," *Studi sulla Sicilia Occidentale in onore di Vicenzo Tusa* (Padua: Bottega d'Erasmo, 1993) 45–56, pls. 13–18.

392. S. F. Bondì, "Fenici e indigeni in Sicilia agl'inizi dell'età coloniale," in *Donum Natalicum: Studi presentati a Claudio Saporetti in occasione del suo 60. compleanno* (ed. P. Negri Scafa and P. Gentili; Rome: Borgia, 2000) 37–43.

393. Idem, "Nuove acquisizioni storiche e archeologiche sulla Sicilia fenicia e punica," *Actas* 4, 1.83–89.

south. Its topography and its lack of any other attraction or of any facilities except a dry dock on the southeast, which is of indeterminate date but was rebuilt with hewn stones when the Carthaginians arrived in the sixth century, suggest that it was chosen from the beginning as a shipyard, where vessels under any flag were outfitted and repaired.

Traces of construction have been preserved, and there seems to have been a residential quarter more or less in the middle of the island; an industrial sector on the northwest, where the city gate was located when the wall was built, with cemeteries next to it on the western shore; and a commercial district to the southeast in the vicinity of the dry dock.[394] The late eighth century is represented by one building in the residential quarter, by silos cut into the rock, a well, a few Phoenician amphorae and mushroom-lipped jugs, and some proto-Corinthian pottery.[395] However, there are no burials from this time, and the installation did not develop into anything like a town until well into the seventh century. The earliest phases, in fact—Stratum VII (700–650 B.C.E.) and Stratum VI (650–600 B.C.E.)—are poorly represented in every respect, and it is not until the sixth century, when Motya came under Carthaginian control, that there is much evidence for communal organization.

The identity of the original settlers, who presumably were shipwrights, sailmakers, and the like, can be surmised from the material remains in the later strata when the people still maintained their distinctiveness in the predominantly Carthaginian cultural environment. These remains are associated with burial practices and include the burials themselves, the tombstones, the onomasticon, and the level of literacy illustrated in the inscriptions.[396]

There were no tombstones in the century of the first two strata; the deceased were just cremated and buried in urns in unmarked graves. Steles begin to appear in Stratum V (600–550 B.C.E.), and they are omnipresent in Stratum IV (550–500 B.C.E.) and Stratum III (500–450 B.C.E.). The earliest are plain, rectangular stone slabs set into the ground and then rectangular slabs with plinths to hold them upright. Next in this sequence are square stones with an empty square frame outlined or hollowed in the center, and then rectangular steles with one or more baetyls (that is, narrow rectangular steles) carved into their face.

394. M. L. Fama, *Mozia: Gli scavi nella "Zona A" dell'abitato* (Bari: Edipuglia, 2002) 21–23.

395. Ibid., 41, 109–10; A. Peserico, *Le brocche "a fungo" fenicie nel Mediterraneo: Tipologia e cronologia* (Rome: Consiglio Nazionale delle Ricerche, 1996) 59–62, 83–86; A. Ciasca, "Mozia: Sguardo d'insieme sul tophet," *VO* 8 (1992) 113–55, esp. p. 117; G. Falsone, "Sicile," in *La civilisation phénicienne et punique: Manuel de Recherche* (ed. V. Krings; Leiden: Brill, 1995) 674–97.

396. A. Ciasca et al., "Saggio preliminare sugli incinerati del tofet di Mozia," *VO* 10 (1996) 317–46.

S. Moscati and M. L. Uberti, *Scavi a Mozia—Le stele. I: Testo, II: Illustrazioni* (Rome: Consiglio Nazionale delle Ricerche, 1981); G. Falsone, "An Ovoid Betyl from the Tophet at Motya and the Phoenician Tradition of Round Cultic Stones," *JMS* 3 (1993) 245–85; V. Tusa, "Il santuario fenicio-punico di Mozia, detto di 'Cappiddazzu,'" *Actas* 4, 3.1397–1417.

M. G. Amadasi Guzzo, *Scavi a Mozia: Le iscrizioni* (Rome: Consiglio Nazionale delle Ricerche, 1986); idem, "La documentazione epigrafica dal *Tofet* di Mozia e il problema del sacrificio *molk*," in *Religio Phoenicia* (ed. C. Bonnet, E. Lipiński, and P. Marchetti; Studia Phoenicia 4; Namur: Société des Etudes Classiques, 1986) 189–207.

The aniconism of this sequence is not unique, but the persistence of the baetyls, found in the ninth-century *marzeaḥ* compound at Kommos and on the earliest stele from Carthage, is striking. The later sequence is decorated with symbolic or realistic human figures. There is the picture of a woman, fully clothed, proffering her breasts in her hands as images of the naked Goddess used to do; or of a woman holding a tympanum, like mainland terra-cotta figurines, or of a woman with one arm at her waist and the other raised in greeting, a standard male gesture. There are representations of men, as on a set of eighth-century mainland seals, striding to the right, Egyptian fashion, with one hand raised in greeting, but also of men with both arms hanging or outstretched by their side. The most striking feature of both sequences is their archaism—that is, their maintenance of symbols, sometimes from other media, which were misrepresented and apparently no longer understood.

This simplicity and archaism is also evident in the script. Only 40 of the more than 1,200 steles are inscribed. Two of them, which were meant to be inscribed, have only the red painted letters that were written to guide the engravers. These people seem to have been illiterate, able to follow the dotted lines or to copy letters from a table or scripts, but not able to write. Their writing, consequently, is ugly, sloppy, irregular, and sometimes wrong: the same letter may have different shapes and stances every time it occurs in the same inscription; there are letters of widely different sizes in the same text and letters whose components are completely disproportionate. The letters, some of which seem to be borrowed from the script of Byblos, look older than they are and do not change much over more than a century.

The inscriptions are short and follow a few simple patterns. Some false beginnings indicate switching from one pattern to another, but two of them stop mid-sentence for lack of space on the stone, and apparently neither the mason nor the patron noticed their meaninglessness. There are also some mistakes that suggest the compositor had a Cypriot, specifically a Kition or Lapethos, pronunciation: [l] for [n] in the word "son" [*bl* for *bn*]; [*šin*] for [*samek*] in the word for "statue" [*šml* for *sml*]; [*k*] for [*q*] in the word "just" used as a name [*ṣdk* for *ṣdq*]. All in all, it seems that people at Motya generally did not read or write and that those who could were not educated but mostly copied from old lessons or tables of scripts. They had a residue of the culture of the first settlers and the scraps of knowledge left by the ships that visited their port, reminiscences and rote, but no living tradition.

This impression of a community out of the mainstream of Phoenician and Punic culture and almost frozen in time is reinforced by the evidence of the burials. All of the deceased with tombstones and inscriptions were males. Most of their names were composed with the usual divine elements, among which *Baʿal* or one of his epithets predominates, but none includes the name of a Goddess, in particular Astarte, the most common element in Carthaginian personal names. All of these inscriptions date to the sixth century and later, and therefore the dedications are to Baʿal Ḥamon, the municipal God of Carthage, but his consort Tannit, almost always included in the Carthaginian dedications, is not mentioned even in the latest texts.[397]

The dedications are called "gifts" (*mtnt*) or fulfillment of a vow (*ndr*), or they are the stele itself (*nṣb*) or memorials of the sacrifice of a female infant (*mlkt* or *mlkt b'l*), as they are at Carthage. About two-thirds of the burial urns that were marked by uninscribed steles contained animal remains (sheep, goats, birds, and fish, but no cattle or pigs), and only about one-quarter contained the remains of neonatal or infant immolations, almost exactly the opposite of the percentages at Carthage.[398] Motya, then, as the cumulative evidence insists, was not in the Punic cultural loop. Besides, as the burial evidence suggests, it was anything but populous or prosperous, and its fixation on tradition left it isolated and strangely stagnant.

The peculiarity of the people of Motya can be traced to their places of origin and to their purpose in traveling to this isolated spot in the west. They were unlike the Tyrians and Cypriots in Carthage. There were no artists and craftsmen among them as there were among the Byblians, Sidonians, and Tyrians who lived and did business in Italy with their partners and comrades from Greece. The island had no natural resources to attract them, as Malta enticed other Phoenicians with its linen and dyes and the renown of its textile industry. Motya was in a protected harbor, in a neutral zone, far from the Greeks who had occupied eastern Sicily, unaligned with the colony at Carthage and outside its dominion, at the center of all the sea-lanes opening up to the Phoenician establishments in North Africa, Sardinia, and Spain. Its people may have come from many places where shipping provided a living—Byblos, Sidon, Arvad, or the ports frequented by Sidonians along the Syrian coast, from Sidonian Kition and Byblian Lapethos in Cyprus, or the Tyrian ports at 'Akko and 'Achzib—and where naval skills rather than civic attachments were their passports to the new world that had opened up with the founding of Carthage.

They differed from the folks at home and from the traders, merchants, entrepreneurs, and adventurers who traveled west, by becoming a single-class community of skilled laborers and sailors (nothing at Motya suggests a social or civic hierarchy) who married Sicilian women and gradually forgot all but the basics of their former Phoenician way of life. When Carthage took charge, its officers did not think for a moment about settling in Motya with this peculiar people or the riffraff they attracted but went to Solunto or Palermo, although some of its sailors and shipwrights, like those who introduced the island to the ritual of child sacrifice,[399] stayed and joined the workforce. Unlike Carthage, Motya was not a colony; it did not have a government or maintain ties with its cities of origin. It was just a new home for people who took advantage of the recent founding of Carthage to find interesting work in the west.

---

397. G. Falsone, "Il simbolo di Tanit a Mozia e nella Sicilia punica," *RSF* 6 (1978) 137–51, pls. 29–30.

398. A. Ciasca et al., "Saggio preliminare sugli incinerati del tofet di Mozia," *VO* 10 (1996) 317–46.

399. Amadasi Guzzo, *Scavi a Mozia: Le iscrizioni*, ##24, 25, 31.

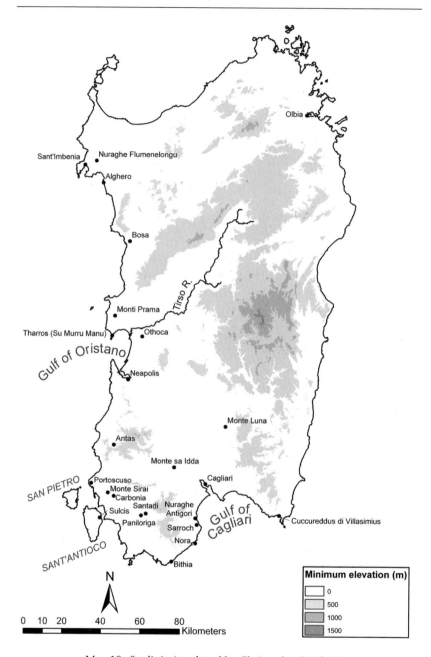

Map 10. Sardinia (produced by Christopher Brinker).

Sardinia

Phoenicians were familiar with Sardinia as a primary destination for centuries before they began to stop there on their way to Spain or to establish naval bases, supply stations, and markets for an inchoate Carthaginian metropolis. In the eighth century, some Sidonians from Italy visited the northwest sector of the island, and others from their mainland capital along with Byblians built the harbor at Tharros in the west-central sector. The few vestiges of their enterprise differ in almost all respects from the material evidence for Tyrian interests in Sulcis, in the southwest, and in perimeter outposts that they established throughout this area. Some of these Tyrians came from Italy, and some belonged to the wave of people from the mainland city and from Cyprus who founded Carthage. However, they did not become seriously involved in Sardinia until they lost interest in Italy and took up the Carthaginian cause. The Phoenicians who stayed in Sardinia tried to match the industry of the indigenous people, and their towns became the artistic centers of the Western world that revolved around Carthage.[400]

The Sardinians, heirs of the Nuraghic civilization, especially the people in the southern half of the island, had been influenced by Mycenean and Cypriot metallurgy in the fourteenth century, began making local imitations in the thirteenth, and continued to enjoy Cypriot cooperation from the twelfth century to the end of the millennium.[401] In the eleventh and tenth centuries, there were imports from Spain (bronze weapons, farm implements, and personal items) both at inland sites and at Alghero on the northwest coast. There were also imports on the south coast at Bithia and Sarroch but not on the southwest coast, where Tyrians later settled.[402]

In the ninth and early eighth centuries, at inland sites but again notably in the northwest part of the island, the Nuraghic population was engaged in an exchange of ideas and goods (weapons, implements, domestic and personal items) with Etruria, in particular with Vetulonia.[403] By the later eighth century, Sardinia was absorbed by regionalism, with groups of settlements coming under something like a central authority, their competitive spirit marked by new defensive systems. Homesteads or individual settlements were reorganized to include workshops and marketplaces. Most had imports; some may have profited from the Etruscan slave trade.

---

400. B. Peckham, "The Phoenician Foundation of Cities and Towns in Sardinia," in *Sardinia in the Mediterranean: A Footprint in the Sea. Studies in Sardinian Archaeology Presented to Miriam S. Balmuth* (ed. R. H. Tykot and T. K. Andrews; Monographs in Mediterranean Archaeology 3; Sheffield: Sheffield Academic Press, 1992) 410–18; idem, "Phoenicians in Sardinia: Tyrians or Sidonians?" in *Sardinian and Aegean Chronology: Toward the Resolution of Relative and Absolute Dating in the Mediterranean* (ed. M. S. Balmuth and R. H. Tykot; Studies in Sardinian Archaeology 5; Oxford: Oxbow, 1998) 347–54.

401. F. Lo Schiavo, "La Sardegna prima dell'insediamento dei Fenici," *BSHRDN*, 28–31.

402. Idem, R. D'Oriano, and E. De Miro, "Le tappe intermedie: Sardegna e Sicilia," *La Magna Grecia e il lantano Occidente: Atti del Ventinovesimo Convegno di Studi sulla Magna Grecia, Taranto, 6–11 Ottobre 1989* (Tarentum: Istituto per la Storia e l'Archeologia della Magna Grecia, 1990) 99–213, esp. pp. 100–133.

403. M. Gras, *Trafics tyrrhéniens archaïques* (Rome: École Francaise de Rome, 1985) 113–59; C. Tronchetti, "La Sardegna e gli Etruschi," *Mediterranean Archaeology* 1 (1988) 66–82; M. Kollund, "Sea and Sardinia," *HBA* 19–20 (1992–93) 201–14.

Their own merchants and traders began to acquire distinct social status, some of the women fancied stylish fashions and Italian fibulae, and they all cooperated in bringing to the Phoenicians who plied their coastal waters the metal products and the agricultural and pastoral goods that were assembled from the inland villages.[404] Thus, the Phoenicians came to charted lands, where they encountered an experienced and sophisticated people, and their arrival coincided with a surge of economic, cultural, and social developments.

The earliest evidence for Phoenician interest in Sardinia is from the region of Alghero in the northwest corner of the island. From a bronze hoard at Nuraghe Flumenelongu in this vicinity, there is a bronze statuette of the striding and smiting Ba'al, a favorite icon of eighth- and seventh-century Phoenician bronze; and silver bowls from Cyprus and Italy, the typological ancestry of which can be traced to second-millennium Syria and more specifically to Byblos.[405] The Sardinian smith in whose hoard it was found obtained it either from a Phoenician trader who wandered by at some earlier time or, if it was an heirloom, from a Byblian or Sidonian who visited nearby Sant'Imbenia, probably on the way to Spain, sometime in the eighth century.[406] This Sant'Imbenia was a Nuraghic village, situated in good farm country, with easy access both eastward to rich mineral resources (silver, iron, copper, and lead) and westward to the sea.[407]

One grave contained an early Phoenician amphora (Type A, 750–650 B.C.E.), another an amphora of a later type (Type B, 650–600 B.C.E.),[408] and others had Nuraghic imitations of these Phoenician originals. Phoenician ceramics (Red Slip, Samaria ware, Sidonian oil bottles) were found together with Etruscan and Euboean wares, some of which (a Euboean chevron drinking bowl [*skyphos*], for instance) are typical of the mid-eighth century.[409] All of this suggests that Phoenicians, a few at any one time, began stopping at ancient Alghero around the middle of the eighth century and continued to do so until about the mid-seventh century.

This is also the conclusion to be drawn from the evidence of the Phoenician inscriptions, both of them incomplete, from Sant'Imbenia.[410] One of them, written on a cup, can be completed as the personal name "Abî'ezer" or "Abî'azîz" (']b'z[r or ']b'z[z) and is from the early eighth century. The

---

404. Regarding Etruscan slave trade, see D. Nash Briggs, "Metals, Salt, and Slaves: Economic Links between Gaul and Italy from the Eighth to the Late Sixth Centuries BC," *OJA* 22 (2003) 243–59; regarding Italian fibulae, see F. Lọ Schiavo, "Le fibule della Sardegna," *Studi Etruschi* 46 (1978) 25–46; see also G. S. Webster, *A Prehistory of Sardinia 2300–500 BC* (Monographs in Mediterranean Archaeology 5; Sheffield: Sheffield Academic Press, 1996) 153–94.

405. A. M. Bisi, "La diffusion du 'Smiting God' Syro-Palestinien dans le milieu phénicien d'Occident," *Karthago* 19 (1980) 5–14, pls. 1–9.

406. F. Barreca, *La civiltà fenicio-punica in Sardegna* (Sardegna Archeologica: Studi e Monumenti 3; Sassari: Delfino, 1986) 15–17; S. F. Bondi, "Recenti studi e nuove prospettive sulla Sardegna fenicia e punica," *Actes* 3, 1.165–74.

407. S. Bafico et al., "Fenici e indigeni a Sant'Imbenia (Alghero)," *BSHRDN*, 44–53.

408. S. Bafico, R. D'Oriano, and F. Lo Schiavo, "Il villaggio nuragico di S. Imbenia ad Alghero (SS): Nota preliminare,"*Actes* 3, 1.87–98; P. Bartoloni, "Anfore fenicie e ceramiche etrusche in Sardegna," in *Il commercio etrusco arcaico: Atti dell' Incontro di Studio, 5–7 dicembre 1983* (Rome: Consiglio Nazionale delle Ricercher, 1985) 103–18.

409. Bafico et al., "Fenici e indigeni a Sant'Imbenia (Alghero).

410. Ibid., 52–53.

other was incised on the shoulder of a jar, can be dated to the end of the century, and consists of a man's name and patronymic "ʿAbdʿazîz, son of ʿAbdbaʿal" (*ʿb]dʿzz bn [ʿb]dbʿl*). The date of the earlier inscription, which hangs on tiny threads of ceramic and paleographical evidence, is also supported by an inscribed sandstone fragmentary stele from Bosa, on the coast about 25 kilometers south of Alghero and 50 north of Tharros, the reading of which is certain (]*bm ʾn*[), although its meaning is unclear.[411] Its script makes it a younger contemporary of the Nora inscription and thus datable to about the end of the ninth century or the early èighth and, whether or not it was part of a similar dedicatory stele, indicates that Phoenicians stopped long enough to write their names and scraps of their history and expected others to pass by and read it. It is clear, therefore, that Phoenicians were coming steadily to the northwest coast of Sardinia at least by the mid-eighth century, in the wake of the Etruscans. Furthermore, although some of them may have stayed for a while, it was a stop on a longer voyage—to Spain along the sea lanes charted by Sardinians and Iberians before them or just to Tharros, farther south—and not a final destination.

Tharros was a destination, probably for Sidonians and Byblians, as Phoenicians ventured south along the western coast of Sardinia later in the eighth century.[412] It was situated on a narrow headland jutting southward into the Gulf of Oristano and was paired with a mainland settlement at Othoca, near the mouth of the river Tirso, which flows from the northeast into the gulf, and it had unhindered access to the valley of the Campidano to the southeast. There are practically no architectural remains from the eighth century, and the characteristics of the place must be assessed from its artistic productions and its ceramic inventory and then reconstructed from the evidence of later times.

The oldest habitations are supposed to have been at Othoca and the site of Su Murru Manu. Othoca was situated on a lagoon set into the gulf coast halfway between the rivers that flow into it:[413] its setting, therefore, on an inlet in a gulf that was itself protected from the open water by the Tharros promontory, was not unlike that of Motya, an island in a lagoon protected from the open water by an encircling barrier reef. There is slight evidence for something like a residential area on an elevation on the south shore of the lagoon, but the date is in doubt, and the nearby cemetery was not operational until the end of the seventh century. It is the general layout that is perhaps the best argument for an early date. A mainland settlement near the mouth of a river (in this instance, of two rivers) with a port town on an adjacent island (or in this case, on the outlying promontory) exactly suits the Phoenician ideal of a settlement, at home or abroad.

Tharros originally would have been the port area at Su Murru Manu at the northeast end of the peninsula, on the site of a Nuraghic village and not far from the Nuraghic sanctuary at Monti Prama, and where the later

---

411. *CIS* 162; *IFPCO* 99 #18, fig. 14.
412. M. Botto, "I commerci fenici e la Sardegna nella fase precoloniale," *EVO* 9 (1986) 125–49, esp. p. 135.
413. S. Moscati, P. Bartoloni, and S. F. Bondi, *La penetrazione fenicia e punica in Sardegna: Trent'anni dopo* (ANLM 9/9, fasc. 1; Rome,1997) 35, 57, 59.

breakwater was built.[414] There is nothing, however, to suggest that it was properly a town at the end of the eighth century—planned and diversified, a complex of commercial, industrial, residential, religious, political, and military environs[415]—rather than, as the ceramic evidence might suggest, a single-district settlement. The town was built in the seventh century and extended from this area all along the promontory to the south.[416] Its two cemeteries, one south of the town and the other near the settlement to the north, mark the development of Tharros from its original site to the impressive walled city it became in the seventh century and later, as it was taken up into the bustle of the Carthaginian empire.

The eighth-century material remains include pottery, jewelry, bronze utensils, and carved burial steles. The pottery[417] is Red Slip or Grey ware, both of them eastern Phoenician, the latter also common in eighth-century Italy and in southern Spain: the plates have narrow rims and can be dated to the second half of the eighth century; Red Slip jugs belong typologically to the end of the century; the bowls have parallels in early seventh-century Spain and Carthage.

The jewelry is the product of Tharros workshops, and its inspiration is mostly North Syrian and Cypriot.[418] It is mainly from the seventh and sixth centuries,[419] but some pieces are from the end of the eighth. A necklace of large crystal beads in a tomb that also contained a Nuraghic bronze model of a quiver has an exact parallel in an eighth-century royal tomb at Salamis in Cyprus.[420] There are gold earrings with pendants in the shape of a basket or lantern or orb-in-a-cage, which have parallels at Sarepta as well as in Cyprus and Syria, and which were distributed to most of the major sites in the West. Other earrings with filigree were a Tharros specialty, having no parallels in the East, that found their way later to Cádiz and Carthage.[421] A green jasper gem shows the God Ba'al, patron of Sidon and Byblos, armed with a bow and an axe.[422]

A seal inscribed in a late eighth-century script with the Egyptian personal name "Horus-Is-Great" ('ḥr) depicts a recumbent sphinx, done in a pudgy Syrian style, wearing an Egyptian crown, and facing a uraeus, while the honorific floats out of an empty cartouche resting on the back of the sphinx.[423] The only eighth-century bronzes, such things as torches, incense

414. Ibid., 57–61. E. Linder, "The Maritime Installation of Tharros (Sardinia): A Recent Discovery," *RSF* 15 (1987) 47–55.

415. G. Tore and A. Stiglitz, "Interazioni territoriali tra Fenici e Indigeni in Sardegna. Urbanizzazione e territorio: Spazio rurale e spazio urbano," *Actas* 4, 4.1909–18.

416. E. Acquaro, "Tharrica 1988–1991," *Actes* 3, 1.16–19.

417. T. C. Mitchell, "The Pottery," *Tharros*, 50–58.

418. S. Moscati and M. L. Uberti, *Testimonianze fenicio-puniche a Oristano* (ANLM 8/31, fasc. 1; Rome, 1988) 6–22, pls. 1–26; S. Moscati, *I gioelli di Tharros: Origini, caratteri, confronti* (Rome: Consiglio Nazionale delle Ricerche, 1988).

419. G. Pisano, "Jewelry," *Tharros*, 78–95.

420. *Tharros* 39.

421. W. Culican, "Phoenician Jewellery in New York and Copenhagen," *Berytus* 22 (1973) 31–47, pls. 1–4.

422. Idem, "Ba'al on an Ibiza Gem," *RSF* 4 (1976) 57–68, pls. 1–2, esp. pp. 57–58; repr. *Opera Selecta: From Tyre to Tartessus* (Gothenburg: Åströms, 1986) 467–80, pls. 8–9, esp. pp. 467–68.

423. *WSS* 277 #745.

burners, and tripods, are from Othoca.[424] The steles all postdate the eighth century, but they resemble contemporary steles from Sidon and ʿAmrit. Many feature geometric or symbolic designs (baetyls, crescent moons, lozenges, and bottles), but the steles with human portraits reflect the Sidonian propensity for a prosopopoetic rather than totally realistic representation of the person whose grave they mark.[425] Also later than the eighth century are square limestone blocks finished to look like four-legged wooden stools. The representational transfer from one medium to another (from custom-built wooden furniture to monumental public architecture) is characteristic of North Syrian and Sidonian craftsmen, and the blocks themselves resemble backless thrones from Tell Halaf in North Syria.[426] Tharros was originally a Sidonian establishment and, except for its native Nuraghi neighbors, peculiar for a people who generally preferred to settle in an already inhabited and administered locality (as on Pithecusa with the Euboeans, for instance); and it differs from other such places in its total lack of Greek influence, at least until the sixth century, when Corinthian and Attic ceramics came to Sardinia from Carthage.[427]

These material remains reflect a modest Phoenician (Sidonian and Byblian in particular) presence in the Gulf of Oristano toward the end of the eighth century. The pottery, bronzes, and masonry were for the use of the residents who, as some mixed grave gifts suggest, were on good terms with the local Nuraghic people. The main occupation of the residents at this time was making jewelry: the repertory eventually included earrings, hair-rings, finger-rings, bracelets, necklaces, pendants, and amulet cases. The jewelry was mostly of gold and silver, and there was also some bronze, but no iron. The silver could be purchased locally, but the gold had to be imported, and both probably were brought from Spain. The markets for the jewelry were in Sardinia, North Africa, Spain, Malta, and later in Sicily, but in the early years some of it was sent back to the boutiques in the East, custom-made to suit Assyrian, Cypriot, and Greek tastes. As the markets expanded, Tharros became a town, the port was built where the breakwater is located, and the population diversified and grew in cooperation and competition with Sulcis to the south.

Sulcis is situated on an island at the southwest corner of Sardinia. It is connected to the mainland by an isthmus, which was originally a series of islets joined by the Phoenicians to form a causeway. There is a narrow harbor north of the isthmus in fairly shallow water, and south of it a broad harbor in deep water and rivers, along which the Phoenicians would have

---

424. Moscati and Uberti, *Testimonianze fenicio-puniche a Oristano*, 6–22, pls. 1–26.

425. S. Moscati and M. L. Uberti, *Scavi al Tofet di Tharros, I: Monumenti Lapidei* (Rome: Consiglio Nazionale delle Ricerche, 1985) 71–73; S. Moscati, "Découvertes phéniciennes à Tharros," *CRAIBL* (1987) 483–503.

426. Idem, *Due statue di Tell Halaf e i troni fenici* (ANLR 8/41, fasc. 3–4; Rome, 1986) 53–56, pls. 1–3.

427. C. Tronchetti, "Problematica della Sardegna," in *Les céramiques de la Grèce de l'Est et leur diffusion en Occident* (Paris: Centre Nationale la Recherche Scientifique, 1978) 140–41; G. Tore, "Nota sulle importazioni in Sardegna in età arcaica," in ibid., 142–46, pls. 73–74; M. L. Uberti, "Ceramica Greco-Orientale da Tharros nel Museo Nazionale Archeologico di Cagliari," *OrAnt* 20 (1981) 295–304, pls. 26–33.

had access into the interior. The town began at the port and spread westward to the low Monte de Cresia and the Fortino hills that rise slightly
inland. There were two cemeteries, one at the north and the other at the
south extremity of the town, and a ritual burial ground or *Tophet* further
north and, eventually, outside the town wall.[428]

Associated with Sulcis, as with Tyre and other Tyrian possessions, were
outlying towns, ports, and fortifications—among them Portoscuso, Monte
Sirai, Paniloriga, and Bithia, forming a strategic or sustaining mainland
arc around Sulcis, bending inland from the west coast and down to the
south coast.[429] The Phoenician character and chronology of Portoscuso,
15 kilometers up the coast from Sulcis, can be gathered from its cemetery
at nearby San Giorgio: here 11 cremation burials with Phoenician burial
amphorae, a Red Slip bowl, an early Red Slip trefoil-lipped jug, jewelry,
and iron weapons were found that can be dated by comparison with similar finds at Sant'Imbenia and at Morro de Mezquitilla and Doña Blanca in
southern Spain to around the middle of the eighth century.[430] Inland, 6 kilometers southeast of Portoscuso and 15 northeast of Sulcis is Monte Sirai,
a burg on a small plateau overlooking the routes to and along the coast. It
was built on the site of a recently abandoned Nuraghic village and became
a large and well-planned residential settlement, but it had no industrial or
artisanal areas and no public buildings. It seems to have been home to the
farmers who worked the surrounding land and a service center for overland
trade and commerce centered on Sulcis and Portoscuso.[431] It may have been
founded before the end of the eighth century, but there is no compelling
ceramic evidence that it was.[432] It is just as likely that it was the first in the
series of perimeter towns that included Paniloriga and Bithia, which were
built to support the development of Sulcis in the seventh century. Bithia
on the south coast of Sardinia was built around 675 B.C.E. for the same
reasons.[433] It had a small harbor, was situated at the mouth of a stream
that gave it ready access to the interior, and was located at the western
extremity of the Gulf of Cagliari, in easy sailing distance of Nora, Cagliari,
Cuccureddus (Villasimius), and the native settlements on the gulf.[434] Of

---

428. E. Acquaro, "Sardinia," in *The Phoenicians* (ed. S. Moscati; New York: Abbeville, 1988)
210–25, esp. pp. 214–18.

429. Moscati, Bartoloni, Bondi, *La Penetrazione fenicia e punica in Sardegna. Trent'anni dopo,*
51–56.

430. P. Bernardini, "La necropoli fenicia di San Giorgio di Portoscuso," *BSHRDN,* 55–57.

431. P. Bartoloni, "L'insediamento di Monte Sirai nel quadro della Sardegna fenicia e punica," *Actes* 3, 1.99–108; idem, "Monte Sirai," *BSHRDN,* 85–89.

432. A. Peserico, "La ceramica fenicia: Le forme aperte," *RSF* 22 (1994) 117–44; G. Balzano,
Ceramica fenicia di Monte Sirai: Le forme aperte del vano C33 (RSF Supplement 27; Rome: Consiglio
Nazionale delle Ricerche, 1999).

433. P. Bartoloni, "La ceramica fenicia di Bithia: Tipologia e diffusione areale," *Atti* 1, 2.491–
500; idem, "L'insediamento fenicio-punico di Bitia," *BSHRDN,* 81–83.

434. S. F. Bondì, "Riflessioni su Nora fenicia," *ASKaW,* 343–51; M. Botto, "Nora e il suo
territorio: Resoconto preliminare del'attiività di ricognizione degli anni 1992–1995," *Actas* 4,
3.1269–76.

The earliest Phoenician material from Cagliari is an amulet representing the God who pro-
tects against snake bite and is inscribed ʿbr | lḥ, "Pass on, Poison." The inscription can be dated to
about 600 B.C.E.: M. L. Uberti, "Dati di epigrafia fenicio-punica in Sardegna," *Atti* 1, 3.797–804,
pls. 156–57, pp. 802–3, pl. 156:2.

Paniloriga,[435] 20 kilometers inland and halfway to Monte Sirai, nothing remains except a graveyard that began to be used toward the end of the seventh century, but it must have belonged to the system of perimeter towns, involved in particular with Bithia in the commercial affairs of Sulcis.

Sulcis itself, according to the ceramic evidence, was founded sometime around 725 B.C.E. There are mushroom-lipped jugs from this time and later, and tableware with parallels in Italy and Carthage.[436] There are also transport amphorae and burial urns from this time, including a Late Geometric (725–700 B.C.E.) Euboean cinerary urn from Pithecusa.[437] The pottery assemblage, in one limited area of the site, contained open forms (that is, bowls, cups, plates) from the eighth century but mostly from the early seventh; and closed forms (that is, jugs and amphorae) from the mid-eighth century but again mostly (75 percent) from the early seventh century.[438] Sulcis, therefore, would have been founded later than Portoscuso, having been reconnoitered from there; but rose in a more advantageous, secure, and spacious place, in a studied and more deliberate act of colonization, and for clear political reasons.

A date around this time (rather than earlier in the century) for Sulcis is also suggested by the epigraphic evidence. The oldest inscription, from the earliest stratum of the graveyard, also cannot be dated much earlier than the turn of the century (ca. 700 B.C.E.). It is punched into a piece of gold leaf that once covered a metal or wooden ex voto and, although only partly preserved, the formulas are familiar and the inscription can be reconstructed with some probability and read: "[This is a gold sheath for] Baʿal, which ʾAbi don[ated] because [he heard his cry] and [blessed him]."[439] The next oldest inscription is on a seal and consists of a personal name and patronymic, "Belonging to Gerʾeshmun, the son of Himilk" (*lgrʾšmn bn ḥmlk*).[440] The design of the seal is an elaborate Egyptianizing ritual scene involving Horus, Isis, Sekhmet, and Khons under the aegis of the winged sun disk, and it is just exquisite and tantalizing enough to suggest its Tyrian origin. These inscriptions agree then with everything else from the site, that the foundation of Sulcis, which marked the climax of Tyrian involvement in southwest Sardinia, was completed later rather than earlier in the eighth century.

E. Acquaro, "Italia: Sardegna," *Insediamenti fenici e punici nel Mediterranea occidentale* (Rome: Libreria dello Stato, 1993) 103–26.

435. Moscati, Bartoloni, Bondì, *La penetrazione fenicia e punica in Sardegna*, 55.

436. A. Peserico, *Le Brocche "a fungo" fenicie nel Mediterraneo: Tipologia e cronologia* (Rome: Consiglio Nazionale delle Ricerche, 1996) 66–67, 92–96; idem, "Phonizisches Tafelgeschirr und regionale Keramik-Produktion im westlichen Mittelmeerraum," *ASKaW*, 375–87.

437. P. Bartoloni, *Orizzonti commerciali sulcitani tra l'VIII e il VII sec. A. C.* (ANLR 8/8, fasc. 1; Rome, 1986) 219–26; P. Bernardini, "Un insediamento fenicio a Sulci nella seconda metà dell'VIII sec. A.C.," *Atti* 2, 2.663–73.

P. Bartoloni, "Urne cinerarie arcaiche a Sulcis," *RSF* 16 (1998) 165–79.

438. Idem, "S. Antioco: Area del Cronicario (Campagne di scavo 1983–86): I recipienti chiusi d'uso domestico e commerciale," *RSF* 18 (1990) 37–79, pls. 5–6; P. Bernardini, "S. Antioco: Area del Cronicario (Campagne di scavo 1983–86)," *RSF* 18 (1990) 81–89.

439. IFPCO 121 #38, pl. 46. The text, in four lines, read something like: (1) [*psl ḥrṣ z l*] (2) *bʿl* ʾš *yt*[*n*] (3) ʾ*b k*[*šmʿ ql*] (4) *w*[*brk*].

440. WSS 273, #733.

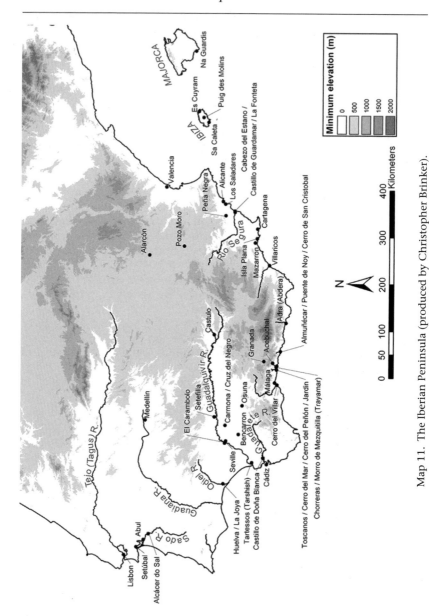

Map 11. The Iberian Peninsula (produced by Christopher Brinker).

The Tyrian affiliation of Sulcis, most evident in the perimeter stations that it established, is also clear from its close ties, from the beginning, with Carthage, North Africa, and Egypt. It differs from Tharros not only in these connections but in its artistic choices[441] and in its Euboean (later its Greek)

441. S. Moscati, "Centri artigianali fenici in Italia," *RSF* 1 (1973) 37–52, pls. 12–31, esp. pp. 46–48.

differential, because some who settled in Sulcis probably came from Pithecusa. The perimeter towns all differed from one another and from Sulcis: landlubbing and lackluster Monte Sirai, for instance, had almost nothing in common with the cosmopolitan attitudes of Bithia and none of the inventiveness and creativity of the island city; and Antas, a later foundation just outside the perimeter, had no strategic importance but was conceived as a pilgrimage center and was soon very popular with both Tyrians from Sulcis and Sidonians from Tharros.

The peculiarity of Sulcis, therefore, was determined not only by the genesis and ties of its people but also by their particular goals and directions. Like Tharros, Sulcis had close relations with the indigenous Nuraghi, but these people differed from region to region, and the newcomers in Tharros mixed with them, while the men of Sulcis kept them at bay. Like Tharros, Sulcis was on the way to Spain, but to different places in Spain, for different reasons, with other associates and different attitudes when they landed. Sulcis was founded after Carthage, and for Carthage, probably by the same groups of people who went to Carthage, while Tharros maintained direct relations with its mainland cities of origin as long as it could.

Spain

Phoenicians arrived in Spain decades before they began exploiting Sardinia. They settled by the rivers that debouched into the Atlantic west of Gibraltar and into the Mediterranean east of Gibraltar.[442] To the west they landed at the mouth of the Riotinto and moved inland along the valley of the Guadalquivir to the region of Seville, perhaps along the Guadiana to Medellín. To the east, they did not leave the coastal areas but clustered around river mouths where indigenous Tartessians came to meet them: a cluster of sites around Málaga at the river Guadalhorce; another a few kilometers east centered around Toscanos on the Rio de Vélez; and 6 kilometers farther east, a cluster around Morro de Mezquitilla at the river Algarrobo. They persisted in this pattern as they moved farther east and northward in the seventh century, to Villaricos at the mouth of the Almanzora, on to Alicante where there is a Phoenician inscription from mid-century, and then to Valencia, when their ships (such as a ship discovered at Mazarron north of Villaricos) began to stop regularly at Ibiza along the way.[443]

---

442. M. E. Aubet Semmler, "Zur Problematik des orientalisierenden Horizontes auf der Iberischen Halbinsel," *PhWest*, 309–35; M. Pellicer Catalán, "Distribución y función de los asentamientos fenicios en Iberia," *Actes* 3, 1.109–22.

443. J. Sanmartín Ascaso, "Inscripciones fenicio-púnicas del sureste hispanico (I)," *AuOr* 4 (1986) 89–103; repr. *FPI*, 1.89–103. A. González Prats, A. García Menárguez, E. Ruiz Segura, "La Fonteta: A Phoenician City in the Far West," *Bierling*, 113–25; A. González Prats, "La Fonteta. El asentamiento fenicio de la desembocadura del Río Segura (Guardamar, Alicante, España). Resultados de las excavationes de 1996–1997," *RSF* 26 (1998) 191–228; A. J. Sánchez Pérez and R. C. Alonso de la Cruz, "La ciudad fenicia de Herna (Guardamar del Segura, Alicante)," *RSF* 27 (1999) 127–31. J. Elayi, A. González Prats, E. Ruiz Segura, "Une lampe avec inscription phénicienne de La Fonteta (Guardamar, Alicante)," *RSF* 26 (1998) 229–42, pls. 10–14. The name "Melqart-has-Gratified" (*mlqrtysp*) is written on the bottom of a lamp, the type of which is common in the eighth and seventh centuries but the actual archaeological context of which is 670–640/630 B.C.E. I. Grau Mira, "Settlement Dynamics and Social Organization in Eastern Iberia during the Iron Age (Eighth–Second Centuries BC)," *OJA* 22 (2003) 261–79; I. Negueruela

From west of Gibraltar, they traveled north into Portugal,[444] and from the places east of Gibraltar, they sailed to North Africa and along the coast of Morocco to the fishing grounds off the Canary Islands. They did not come to colonize, and at first they stayed only as long as it was convenient or necessary on any voyage before sailing back to their ports of origin in the eastern Mediterranean. Gradually in the Atlantic regions, they began to settle among the native Tartessian communities, while on the Mediterranean coast they started to build permanent settlements with economic, social, and political ties to Carthage. Unlike the Nuraghic Sardinians who, enjoying the stability of their traditions and a satisfactory way of life, dealt with the Phoenicians as equals, the Tartessians were in flux, displaced by Celtic migrations, in the throes of economic and social change, and became deeply affected by the ideas of these clever and enterprising Phoenicians.

The Phoenicians who came to Spain were from different places.[445] Sidonians, most likely, and perhaps Byblians with them, came to the Atlantic regions. Tyrians, who according to a common opinion were the sole or chief protagonists of colonization or commercial expansion in Spain,[446] probably monopolized only the Mediterranean coastal sites. The Sidonians might have been joined by friends from Kition or from ports along the coast of Syria or Cilicia, although the terrible pressure that Assyria put upon the mainland city and its emporium in Cyprus may have driven many of their more skilled and enterprising citizens to take advantage of the opportunities opening up in the West.

The Tyrians, similarly, could have counted on compatriots from their mainland ports and possessions to fill the quota of the dozen or more sites clustered in their area of interest. The difference between these sites, as between those west of Gibraltar—or, the reason that they settled in many small places right next to each other rather than in one comprehensive location—can be explained in part by the diverse geographical origin of the ships and passengers that voyaged to Spain.[447] In part it can be explained by the sociability, prosperity, and cultural sophistication of the Tartessians with whom they came in contact, in part by the rugged and inhospitable coastline that discouraged settlement beyond the alluvial plains where

---

et al., "Seventh-Century Phoenician Vessel Discovered at Playa de la Isla, Mazarron, Spain," *IJNA* 24 (1995) 189–97; C. Gómez Bellard, "Die Phönizier auf Ibiza," *MM* 34 (1993) 83–107, pl. 12.

444. Phoenician traffic with or settlement among the Celts and others of the Tagus and Sado river valleys did not begin before 700 B.C.E.: see I. Gamer-Wallert, "Der neue Skarabäus aus Alcácer do Sal," *MM* 23 (1982) 96–100, pl. 27; F. Mayet, M. C. Tavares da Silva, Y. Makaroun, "L'établissement phénicien d'Abul (Portugal)," *CRAIBL* (1994) 171–88; M. Pellicer Catalán, "La colonización fenicia en Portugal y la orientalización del Occidente de la Peninsula Iberica," *ASKaW*, 531–38; A. M. Arruda, *Los Fenicios en Portugal: Fenicios y mundo indígena en el centro y sur de Portugal (siglos VIII–VI a.C.)* (Cuadernos de Arquelolgía Mediterránea 5–6; Barcelona: Universidad Pompeu Fabra and Laboratorio de Arqueología, 2002).

445. M. Pellicer Catalán, "Distribución y función de los asentamientos fenicios en Iberia," *Actes* 3, 2.298–310.

446. M. E. Aubet, "El comercio fenicio en Occidente: balance y perspectivas," in *I Fenici: Ieri oggi domain* (ed. S. Moscati; Rome: Consiglio Nazionale delle Ricerche, 1995) 227–43, esp. p. 231; G. Maass-Lindemann, "Cerámica fenicia en la Metrópolis y en las colonias fenicias del s. VIII según la forma de platos," *Actas* 4, 4.1595–1600.

447. M. Pellicer Catalán, "Distribución y función de los asentamientos fenicios en Iberia," *Actes* 3, 2.298–310.

they landed.[448] In part the difference was due to specialization at the various sites: fishing at one, an iron foundry at another, pottery kilns or textile factories or facilities for jewelers or ship outfitters at others. In part it was the organization of each around a particular private consortium or royal franchise, and in part it was the social and civic complexity that required parceling and physical distribution of functions—industrial, residential, commercial, naval, military, administrative, and religious.[449] This diversity and specificity cannot be illustrated at every turn, but it is a regular nuance or discrete detail in the more general historical picture.

The Atlantic Region

The main Phoenician sites in the Atlantic region of Spain were at Huelva on the Riotinto, at Cádiz in the estuary of the Guadalete just east of the Guadalquivir, and in a complex of native towns—El Carambolo, Setefilla, Cruz del Negro, Carmona, Acebuchal, Bencarron, and Osuna—in the vicinity of Seville in the valley of the Guadalquivir. Huelva was situated on a conglomeration of hills at the confluence of the river Odiel and the Riotinto, not far from the coast. It was a native village, but Phoenician presence is indicated by architectural (parts of a pillar and rubble wall) and ceramic remains.[450] Cádiz, presently a safe harbor protected by an arm stretching along the coast into the bay of Guadalete, was originally a group of three islands at the mouth of the river: a small island that may have been a residential area; a long island separated from it by the narrow channel of La Caleta, and running northwest to southeast along the coast which, apart from the cemetery at its western tip, may have been the location of the industrial and commercial complex; and another, more or less at right angles to it and almost connecting it to the mainland, which might have belonged to the port authority.[451]

A bit upstream from Cádiz, on an eminence on the west bank of the Guadalete, was the small mainland site now known as Castillo de Doña Blanca.[452] It satisfied the Phoenician demand, illustrated in the settlements at Tharros and Sulcis, for paired onshore and offshore establishments, and their early presence at this site and on the islands is attested by ceramic, epigraphic, and artistic evidence. Like Cádiz and Doña Blanca, the towns and villages near Seville (mostly within a 5-kilometer radius) where there is

448. M. E. Aubet Semmler, "Zur Problematik des orientalisierenden Horizontes auf der Iberischen Halbinsel," in *PhWest*, 309–35, esp. p. 312.

449. C. R. Whittaker, "The Western Phoenicians: Colonisation and Assimilation," *Proceedings of the Cambridge Philological Society* 20 (1974) 58–79; M. E. Aubet Semmler, "Los Fenicios en España: Estado de la cuestión y perspectivas," *AuOr* 3 (1985) 9–38, pls. 1–9; B. Treumann-Watkins, "Phoenicians in Spain," *BA* 55 (1992) 29–35; M. Almagro-Gorbea, "La 'Precolonización fenicia' en la Península Ibérica," *Actas* 4, 2.711–21.

450. D. Ruiz Mata, "The Beginnings of the Phoenician Presence in Southwestern Andalusia," *Bierling*, 263–98, esp. pp. 266–74.

451. J. L. Escacena, "Gadir," *FPI*, 1.39–58; M. L. Lavado et al., "El asentamiento antiguo de Cádiz a través de las últimas excavaciones arqueológicas," *Actas* 4, 2.869–79; A. Muñoz Vicente and L. Perdigones Moreno, "Estado actual de la arqueología fenicio-púnica en la ciudad de Cadiz," in ibid., 881–91; F. Ponce, "Sobre la ubicación del Cádiz fenicio," in ibid., 905–14; O. Vallespín Gómez, "La Caleta: Puerto antiguo de Cádiz," in ibid., 915–21.

452. D. Ruiz Mata, "The Ancient Phoenicians of the 8th and 7th Centuries B.C. in the Bay of Cadiz: State of Research," *Bierling*, 160–98.

evidence for Phoenicians were not founded by them and were not colonies but, rather, places where they took up residence among the native population, did business with them, and taught them how to write, work ivory, and turn pottery on the wheel. These Sidonian centers at Huelva, Cádiz, and Seville were interconnected and, although they may not have been colonies, seem at least to represent a partnership intent on infiltrating and exploiting this truly golden triangle in the prosperous valleys of southern Spain for the benefit of the mainland city and its émigrés.

Huelva was a station for processing silver mined by Tartessians in the Riotinto region or brought down from Seville and then transshipped to Cádiz.[453] From Cádiz it was exported to silversmiths at Pithecusa and Tharros and home to the mainland craft shops and to the markets, where unworked silver was on the verge of replacing bronze as the currency of the Assyrian Empire. There may also have been bronze workshops using copper and tin from the interior, and two bronze statuettes of the Smiting God (striding with a club in his raised right hand) found at Huelva may have been fashioned by its craftsmen.[454] There is Phoenician Red Slip Ware at the site, and ceramic typology (the relative dates of dinner plates is judged by the increasing width of their rims) suggests a date for the installation around the middle of the eighth century B.C.E.[455] An earlier date might be suggested by an Attic Middle Geometric (800–750 B.C.E.) pyxis, but the other Greek ceramics (Euboean and Corinthian perhaps from Pithecusa) belonging to the second half of the century would leave it fairly isolated.[456]

Three Phoenician inscriptions from Huelva are dated to the seventh and sixth centuries, but a fourth incised after firing on a large Red Slip container must be dated around the middle of the eighth century or even earlier:[457] the inscription is broken, and the second and third lines are difficult to decipher, but the first line may have marked the contents of the jar, "Honey" (*d*]*bš*), and the name, Orîmilk (*ʾrm*[*lk*), of the merchant or producer who sold it. Huelva, on this evidence, had been established as a Phoenician industrial site at least by the mid-eighth century, and its inhabitants were already providing for themselves or dealing with the natives for the metals (silver, bronze, and maybe iron)[458] and the produce they needed.

Cádiz has an eighth-century North Israelite seal in a gold setting inscribed "Belonging to The-Lovely-One-Is-My-God" (*lnʿmʾl*)[459]—"Lovely" be-

---

453. Cf. J. D. Muhly, "Copper, Tin, Silver and Iron: The Search for Metallic Ores as an Incentive for Foreign Expansion," *MPT*, 314–29; M. Pellicer Catalán, "Huelva tartesia y fenicia," *RSF* 24 (1996) 119–40; Ruiz Mata, "The Beginnings of the Phoenician Presence in Southwestern Andalusia," *Bierling*, 266–74.

454. I. Gamer-Wallert, "Zwei Statuetten syro-ägyptischer Gottheiten von der 'Barra de Huelva,'" *MM* 23 (1982) 46–61, pls. 11–24.

455. J. Fernández Jurado, "Die Phönizier in Huelva," *MM* 26 (1985) 49–60; P. Rufete Tomico, "Die phönizische Rote Ware aus Huelva," *MM* 30 (1989) 118–34.

456. P. Cabrera, "El comercio de productos griegos de época geometrica en el sur de la península ibérica: Nuevos elementos," *Actes* 3, 1.222–29, esp. pp. 222–23.

457. F. González de Canales, L. Serrano, J. P. Garrido, "Nuevas inscripciones fenicias en Tarteso: Su contexto histórico," *Actas* 4, 1.227–38.

458. M. E. Aubet Semmler, "The Phoenician Impact on Tartessos: Spheres of Interaction," *Bierling*, 225–40.

459. A. Lemaire, "Le sceau *lnʿmʾl* de Cadiz," *Syria* 62 (1985) 38–41.

ing an epithet of Adonis. There is also an early eighth-century (800–775 B.C.E.) Phoenician inscription on local pottery from Doña Blanca with the archaic personal name "Lion" (*'rw*).[460] At the extreme eastern end of the ancient town, at the site of a later temple identified by classical sources, five statuettes of the striding God were recovered from the ocean.[461] He is not in a smiting stance as in the two examples from Huelva, where he may represent the patron God of the forge and of ore-carrying ships, but his arms are either raised in front of him or are carried by his side; he wears a conical pseudo-Egyptian crown and an Egyptian loin cloth, but his features, especially his beard and almost wry smile, are Phoenician. His feet were fitted with tenons to be inserted into a wooden support for display and worship, and it may be that the God they represent is Baʿal, not in his brazen aspect, but as the source of agricultural fertility and natural bounty. This would have been appropriate enough for Cádiz, which was renowned for its forests, rich soil, and bountiful harvests, for its smiths and reliable gold resources, its saltworks, and for the fish it caught in its own waters and down around Lixus on the north coast of Morocco,[462] both for local consumption and for export to the east.

Cádiz was Phoenician in the eighth century, as scattered ceramic evidence from the port and its mainland environs attests.[463] The original inhabitants persisted in their way of life, living better perhaps for doing business with the Phoenicians but not inclined to mimic the newcomers.[464] It was a natural commercial center,[465] known earlier to Cypriots and Mycenaeans, established by Iberians who discovered Italy and Sardinia on their own, and finally by Phoenicians, importing from and exporting to the eastern Mediterranean, prospering from the territorial network that the Sidonians and their friends had established in the golden triangle west of Gibraltar.

460. J.-L. Cunchillos, "Las inscripciones fenicias del Tell de Doña Blanca (III): TDB 89001 y 89003," *AuOr* 8 (1990) 175–81, #TDB 89001, esp. pp. 175–79.

461. L. Perdigones Moreno, "Hallazgos recientes entorno al santuario de Melkart en la isla de Sancti Petri (Cádiz)," *Atti* 4, 3.1119–32.

462. C. R. Whittaker, "The Western Phoenicians: Colonisation and Assimilation," *Proceedings of the Cambridge Philological Society* 20 (1974) 58–79, esp. p. 62; A. Perea Caveda, "Phoenician Gold in the Western Mediterranean: Cádiz, Tharros and Carthage," in *Encounters and Transformations: The Archaeology of Iberia in Transition* (ed. M. S. Balmuth, A. Gilman, and L. Prados-Torreira; Monographs in Mediterranean Archaeology 7; Sheffield: Sheffield Academic Press, 1997) 135–40; J. I. Vallejo Sánchez et al., "Factorías de salazones en la Bahía Gaditana: Economia y organización espacial," in *XXIV Congreso Nacional de Arqueología: Cartagena 1997* (Murcia: Instituto de Patrimonio Historico, 1999) 107–14. The pottery from Lixus is comparable with that from Castillo de Doña Blanca and from El Carambolo and Cruz del Negro near Seville: see G. Maass-Lindemann, "Die phönikische Keramik von Lixus im Vergleich mit südandalusischer Keramik," *MM* 31 (1990) 186–93.

463. O. Vallespín Gómez, "La Caleta: Puerto antiguo de Cádiz," *Actas* 4, 2.915–21; G. Maass-Lindemann, "Vasos fenicios de los siglos VIII–VI en España: So procedencia y posición dentro del mundo fenicio occidental," *FPI*, 1.227–47; R. González, F. Barrionuevo, L. Aguilar, "Presencia fenicia en el territorio tartésico de los esteros del Guadalquivir," *Actas* 4, 2.785–94.

464. P. Bueno Serrano, "Tartesios y Fenicios: Protagonistas de un acercamiento entre culturas," in *XXIV Congreso Nacional de Arqueología: Cartagena 1997* (Murcia: Instituto de Patrimonio Histórico, 1999) 45–55; M. E. Aubet Semmler, "Some Questions Regarding the Tartessian Orientalizing Period," *Bierling*, 199–224.

465. G. Bunnens, "Le rôle de Gadès dans l'implantation phénicienne en Espagne," *FPI*, 2.187–92; M. E. Aubet, "Cádiz y el comercio atlántico," *Actas* 4, 1.31–41.

Castillo de Doña Blanca was also an Iberian settlement when the Phoenicians moved in and joined them early in the eighth century.[466] Most of the pottery is local, dating to the ninth and eighth centuries.[467] The Phoenician pottery is predominantly Red Slip, but some is Bichrome or Polychrome. There are plates with narrow rims (but those from the seventh century have wider rims), trefoil-lipped wine jugs, mushroom-lipped unguent jugs, amphorae of a type belonging to the first half of the eighth century, Samaria wares, and lamps—that is, an assortment of domestic and kitchen pottery vessels. There are traces of a wall, a building with a plastered floor, and the remains of two burial tumuli.[468] The first was for native burials, quite large (about 20 meters in diameter and almost 2 meters deep) with a cremation hearth in the center dug out of the rock, which was surrounded by ashes collected into local ceramic containers or into holes in the rock and covered with clay, the whole complex being in use throughout the eighth century. In the other nearby tumulus, there were cremations of well-to-do Phoenicians surrounded by a variety of gifts including incense burners, bottles, alabaster perfume jars, gold, silver and glass jewelry, and hand-painted cups—the remains of two or three generations of merchant families.

Castillo de Doña Blanca, in short, seems to have been a mainland residential area for the Phoenicians who controlled the operations in the port town of Cádiz. It was established early in the eighth century, like the town, and continued into the seventh. It illustrates quite dramatically the coexistence and the cooperation between the Sidonians, as these Phoenicians should probably be identified, and the cadre of Iberian notables who welcomed them.

The apex of the grand Phoenician triangle seated at Huelva and Cádiz was Seville and its environs. Their presence is immediately evident in their material remains, and their influence is clear in the self-transcendence of an already advanced culture and civilization. Beginning in the early eighth century, Sidonians and Byblians came looking for gold, lead, silver, tin, and iron, all of which were abundant in this area.[469] They brought literacy, learning, insight, styles, skills, and techniques to a people that was ethnically diverse, centrally organized, and commercially independent.[470] In

466. D. Ruiz Mata, "Castillo de Doña Blanca (Puerto de Santa Maria, Prov. Cádiz): Stratigraphische Untersuchung einer orientalisierenden Ansiedlung," MM 27 (1986) 87–115, pl. 15c; idem, "Las cerámicas fenicias del Castillo de Doña Blanca (Puerto de Santa Maria, Cádiz)," FPI, 1.241–63; idem, "The Ancient Phoenicians of the 8th and 7th Centuries B.C. in the Bay of Cádiz: State of Research," Bierling, 160–98.
467. J. L. López Castro, "Carthage and Mediterranean Trade in the Far West (800–200 B.C.)," Rivista di Studi Punici 1 (2000) 123–44, esp. pp. 125–31.
468. I. Córdoba Alonso and D. Ruiz Mata, "Sobre la construcción de la estructura tumular del Túmulo 1 de Las Cumbres (Castillo de Doña Blanca)," Actas 4, 2.759–70.
469. J. M. Blázquez, "El influjo de la cultura semita (fenicios y cartagineses) en la formación de la cultura ibérica," FPI, 2.163–78; idem, "Panorama general del desarollo histórico de la cultura tartésica desde finales de la edad del bronce, s. VIII a.C, hasta los origenes de la culturals turdetana e ibérica: Los influjos fenicios," RSF 19 (1991) 33–48.
470. U. Morgenroth, "Southern Iberia and the Mediterranean Trade Routes," OJA 18 (1999) 395–401; J. R. Alvarez-Sanchis, "The Iron Age in Western Spain (800 BC–AD 50): An Overview," OJA 19 (2000) 65–89.

ceramics, there was Red Slip and Grey Ware to be imitated, and the pottery wheel and paint to make it possible.[471] In the way of life-style, there was new clothing, seen in the fibulae and buckles they adopted; a cuisine that included wine, oil, vinegar, and pickled fish; and lamps to light their homes. In gold jewelry, there was granulation, and in toiletries there were ivory combs.

In religious beliefs, there was the Goddess Astarte and Ba'al, the God of land, sea, and sky and the stories told about them. And in religious practice, there were amulets featuring the Craftsman God Bes, mythical beasts such as the Griffin, and symbols such as the Tree-of-Life; or there was anointing, incense, and libations for their funeral rites. The Phoenicians brought with them what they had learned in Cilicia about mining and smelting, writing to unite a cultured and articulate people, and the chance to belong to a cosmopolitan Mediterranean world.

There is a mid-eighth-century Phoenician inscription from El Carambolo, just south of Seville (see fig. 3.2 above).[472] The earliest pottery from this site is local and handmade, but Red Slip and wheel-made wares—bowls, urns, wine jugs, and a high percentage of transport amphorae—appear in the eighth century.[473] The inscription is written on the base of a statuette of Astarte seated on a throne:

> This throne they made, Ba'alyaton, the son of Do'mmilk, and 'Abdba'al, the son of Do'mmilk, the son of Yaš'ul, for Hurrian Astarte, Our Lady, because she heard the sound of their words.

The inscription has some interesting features. Perhaps because the Goddess raises her right hand in benediction, it omits the final prayer for blessing. It shares with the Cypriot dialect of Phoenician the pronunciation of the demonstrative pronoun—"this ('z) throne"—with a prosthetic *'alep*. Then, the statuette is dedicated to "Hurrian Astarte," the Goddess of Syria, mentioned in twelfth-century ritual texts from Ugarit, whose cult and priesthood are also known from seventh-century Byblos.

Again, like inscriptions from Byblos, the inscription switches person, referring in the third-person plural to the two brothers who dedicated the statuette, but in the first-person plural to "Our Lady, Hurrian Astarte"; the switch in this instance mimics the beginning of their prayer—they invoked her name, asked her favor, and she heard their words. Their father's name is rare and is used mainly by Sidonians, and the grandfather's name

---

471. J. I. Vallejo Sánchez, "Las cerámicas grises orientlizantes con decoración bruñida y las decoraciones indígenas," in *XXIV Congreso Nacional de Arqueología: Cartagena, 1997* (Murcia: Instituto de Patrimonio Histórico, 1999) 85–93; C. Mata Parreño, "La influencias del mundo fenicio-púnico en los origines y desarrollo de la cultura ibérica," *Actes* 3, 2.225–44.

472. J. M. Solá-Solé, "Nueva Inscripcion Fenicia de Espana," *RSO* 41 (1966) 97–108, pls. 1–2; F. M. Cross, "The Old Phoenician Inscription from Spain Dedicated to Hurrian Astarte," *HTR* 64 (1971) 189–95; M. G. Amadasi Guzzo, "Astarte in Trono," in *Studies in the Archaeology and History of Ancient Israel in Honour of Moshe Dothan* (ed. M. Heltzer, A. Segal, and D. Kaufman; Haifa: Haifa University Press, 1993) 163–80; C. Bonnet and P. Xella, "L'identité d'Astarté-ḥr," in *Alle soglie della classicità. Il Mediterraneo tra tradizione e innovazione: Studi in onore di Sabatino Moscati*, vol. 1: *Storia e Culture* (ed. E. Acquaro; 3 vols.; Pisa: Istituti Editoriali e Poligrafici, 1996) 29–46.

473. Ruiz Mata, "The Beginnings of the Phoenician Presence in Southwestern Andalusia," *Bierling*, 294.

is archaic in its use of an imperfect verbal form instead of the more familiar perfect or participial (Sa'ul) form. The bronze statuette was made locally,[474] by the brothers or by one of their community, and is the precursor of a long Spanish tradition of enthroned Goddesses,[475] most of which have been found in funerary rather than in ritual contexts.

The brothers belonged to the third generation of a Sidonian or Byblian family with Cypriot connections that may have emigrated, for instance, from Kition in Cyprus in the grandfather's day and settled in Spain early in the eighth century. From the likes of them and their compatriots and from their Greek associates, the indigenous people of southern Spain learned their letters and eventually devised a syllabary, a blend of consonantal and vocalic signs,[476] with which to express an identity enriched by contact with these men and women from the East. Unlike other ethnic groups, they did not learn the alphabet (the sounds in a significant and memorable order) but, as in their other borrowings, they were pleased to approximate what they saw without clinging to its meaning.

The Spanish ivories are good illustrations of this deliberate trifling with tradition.[477] They are mostly from Setefilla, Cruz del Negro, Acebuchal, Bencarron, and a few other places in the radius of Carmona, and mainly from the seventh century B.C.E. Later examples are found at La Joya, the necropolis of Huelva, and at Medellín on the river Guadiana. None is from a coastal settlement. They are all from cemeteries, all for cosmetic use, and all presumably from the graves of Phoenician or native women. All of them have prototypes in the North Syrian, Sidonian ivories of the ninth and eighth century, and their rendering of these original designs resembles and may have been influenced by the simplification and stylization on the bronze and silver bowls from Cyprus and Etruria. They are all from a few workshops, the creation of a handful of craftsmen, all of whom may have been the descendants, in the third or fourth generation, of the original Sidonian settlers and their Phoenician or native wives. These émigrés were likely to have been among the artisans and traders who lived in Carmona beginning about the mid-eighth century,[478] when it was still a native village and when Phoenician products (Red Slip plates, Grey Ware cups, Red-and-Black painted jars) were conspicuous, and into the seventh, when there is nothing left of them except their influence on the material culture (the use of the pottery wheel, pillar-and-field-stone walls, and the ivories in the nearby necropolises).

474. W. Röllig, in his "Contribución de la inscripciones fenicio-púnicas al estudio de la protohistoria de España" (*AuOr* 4 [1986] 51–58, esp. p. 53) is unsure of the provenance, date, and significance of the statuette.

475. M. C. Marín Ceballos and R. Corzo Sánchez, "Escultura femenina entronizada de la Necrópolis de Cádiz," *Atti* 2, 3.1025–38.

476. J. de Hoz, "Escritura fenicia y escrituras hispánicas: Algunos aspectos de su relación," *FPI*, 2.73–84; idem, "The Phoenician Origin of the Early Hispanic Scripts," in *Phoinikeia Grammata: Lire et écrire en Méditerranée* (ed. C. Baurain, C. Bonnet, and V. Krings; Namur: Société des Études Classiques, 1991) 669–82.

477. M. E. Aubet Semmler, "Die westphönizischen Elfenbeine aus dem Gebiet des unteren Guadalquivir," *HBA* 9 (1982) 15–70.

478. M. Belén et al., "Presencia e influencia fenicia en Carmona (Sevilla)," *Actas* 4, 4.1747–61.

These ivories imitate the motifs, themes, and techniques of Phoenician originals[479]—but of originals that were not themselves ivories but were sketchbook models of decorative items that could be incorporated indiscriminately into carved metal bowls or into ivory designs. They are copies, therefore, made to suit local tastes rather than contribute to a living artistic tradition. The original compositions are resolved into their components and rearranged, without regard for their narrative or symbolic appeal, to fit into right-angled frames. There are figures and pictures, but they are incised and not shaped and, although they are interesting or attractive or amusing, there is no action, no idea, no persuasiveness.

An ivory comb from Cruz del Negro[480] depicts a lion attacking a stag, a poignant and moving scene in its original representations but here more a parody of emotion. The lion does not attack but just stands behind the deer, its legs braced as if to back away, its ribs showing in wavy lines but without any sign of musculature. A bird sits on its back to fill the empty space above. The stag is lying down, a startled look in its eye but no sign of resistance. A lotus blossom appears in the empty space above, the flame-and-frond design used to represent its haunches reduced to zigzag lines like the contemporary saw-toothed letter *šin*. The animal itself was drawn by someone who had seen a picture but apparently never seen a stag, because it looks in this rendition like a giant rabbit.

From Acebuchal[481] there is a large comb representing antithetic recumbent gazelles facing and nuzzling a central schematic palmette while the space above them is filled with long-stemmed lotus blossoms. The palmette, a conceit derived from the decoration of Phoenician (particularly Cypriot) metal jars and bowls,[482] is substituted for the Tree-of-Life, and the gazelles, who should be raised on their hind legs taking life and sustenance from it, observe it with studied disinterest. All this is far from the floruit of Phoenician art, but it does illustrate what more than a century of assimilation to Tartessian mores, the orderly tastes of wealthy women, an esthetic uncluttered by myth and legend, children with some training but not much finesse and more interested in selling their works than in preserving the tradition could do to an original and benevolent artistic inspiration.

The Mediterranean Region

Along the Mediterranean coast east of Gibraltar, the Phoenicians, Tyrians, and their kin it may be supposed chose two main sites to settle in the eighth century. The earlier, from around mid-century, was at Morro de Mezquitilla, due south of Granada, on the east bank of the river Algarrobo, set on the seaside of a narrow alluvial plain that stretches from the hills behind to the Mediterranean. Associated with it was Trayamar on the west bank of the river, Chorreras about a kilometer to the east; a few kilometers

---

479. Aubet Semmler, "Die westphönizischen Elfenbeine aus dem Gebiet des unteren Guadalquivir."
480. Ibid., 23, fig. 2b.
481. Ibid., 32, fig. 6b.
482. B. B. Shefton, "The Paradise Flower, a 'Court Style' Phoenician Ornament: Its History in Cyprus and the Central and Western Mediterranean," in *Cyprus and the East Mediterranean in the Iron Age* (ed. V. Tatton-Brown; London: British Museum, 1989) 97–117.

still farther east were Almuñécar and the necropolises of Cerro de San Cristobal and Puente de Noy at the river Seco and Abdera at the river Adra.

The later site, from the end of the eighth century, was at Toscanos on the Rio de Vélez and the associated sites and cemeteries of Alarcón, Jardín, Cerro del Mar, and Cerro del Peñón, also on the river. Migration westward along the coast continued late in the century and then into the seventh, with subsidiary settlements at Cerro del Villar and Málaga on the Guadalhorce. All this was separate from the Sidonian and Byblian zone west of Gibraltar, involved a different strategy, and had very distinctive consequences.[483]

Morro de Mezquitilla was a steel town.[484] The iron was mined and smelted elsewhere, but the foundries, forges, and workshops were here on the coast. Slag, bits and pieces of iron sheets, bars, and wire, as well as iron jewelry and accessories (fibulae, pendants, and rings), implements and tools (punches, blades, hooks, nails, rivets, fish hooks, and needles for making and repairing nets) along with raw copper, lead, and bronze were dropped and left scattered all over the site.[485] There were high-heat ovens and blast pipes. Charcoal could be produced from the nearby woods, and ships waited in the harbor to transport ingots, unfinished materials, and finished products to markets in the East and to ports along the way.

C14 and ceramic dating converge on the mid-eighth century at the latest for the beginning of the operation.[486] The width of plate rims, which is diagnostic in these southern settlements, is smallest in the first phase of Morro de Mezquitilla and then follows the usual progression into the seventh century.[487] Fine tableware, mushroom-lipped jugs, and amphorae match mid-eighth-century examples from Tyre, Sarepta, Al Mina, and Ras el-Bassit.[488] There are some personal items, such as an amulet with the name Amon-Re᷄ in cryptographic hieroglyphic signs dropped by one of the original settlers,[489] and there is some sign of rudimentary living quarters in the first phase of the settlement.

However, the earliest buildings were the factories and storage facilities, and Morro de Mezquitilla seems to have been designed as an exclusively industrial complex, while the residential areas were constructed away from the toxic fumes at nearby Chorreras and in the more salubrious settings of Almuñécar and Abdera farther east. The cemetery at Trayamar across the

---

483. Compare M. E. Aubet Semmler, "Phoenician Trade in the West: Balance and Perspective," *Bierling*, 97–112.

484. H. Schubart, "Morro de Mezquitilla: Vorbericht über die Grabungskampagne 1982 auf dem Siedlungshügel an der Algarrobo-Mündung," *MM* 24 (1983) 104–31; idem, "El Asentamiento Fenicio del s. VIII a.C. en el Morro de Mezquitilla (Algarrobo, Málaga)," *FPI*, 1.59–83; idem, "Phönizische Eisenschmiede auf dem Morro de Mezquitilla," *ASKaW*, 545–57.

485. K. Mansel, "Los hallazgos de metal procedentes del horizonte fenicio mas antiguo B1 del Morro de Mezquitilla (Algarrobo, Málaga)," *Actas* 4, 4.1601–4.

486. Ibid., 1601; G. Maass-Lindemann, "Die Zeitbestimmung der frühen phönikischen Kolonien des 8 Jhs. v. Chr. in Spanien," *ASKaW*, 539–44.

487. J. A. Barceló et al., "Analisis estadístico de la variabilidad de los platos fenicios en el sur de la Península Ibérica," *Actas* 4, 4.1459–66.

488. G. Maass-Lindemann, "Orientalische Importe vom Morro de Mezquitilla," *MM* 31 (1990) 169–77; idem, "La primera fase de la colonización fenicia en España según los hallazgos del Morro de Mezquitilla," in *Los Fenicios en Málaga* (ed. M. E. Aubet; Málaga: University of Málaga Press, 1997) 47–60.

489. I. Gamer-Wallert, "Ein Amuns-Kryptogramm vom Morro de Mezquitilla," *MM* 24 (1983) 145–48, pl. 11.

river was exclusive, perhaps designed for government officials or factory administrators, the tombs at Almuñécar were made for the merchants or for the captains who transported and sold the iron, and the other necropolises would have been for a motley crew of native and other laborers. Chorreras was a short-lived community (ca. 750–700 B.C.E.) that did not survive the eighth century.[490] The houses are stone and well built, with plenty of room between them, and laid out along wide streets. Plate rims match the narrowness of the plate rims at Morro de Mezquitilla. The wares are all culinary (related to food production, storage, and consumption) and domestic (amphorae and jars, Red Slip jugs, polychrome pithoi, Grey Ware bowls, juglets for lotions or perfumes, oil bottles, lamps with one or two nozzles, and fibulae). When the place was abandoned near the end of the eighth century, the people may have moved back to Morro de Mezquitilla (the full extent of this settlement has not been determined), but it is more likely that they, or those who survived the calamity or weathered the change that made them leave, went east to Almuñécar or Abdera.

There are a few eighth-century (ca. 725 B.C.E.) tombs just up the hill east of Chorreras, and five impressive built tombs from the mid-seventh century and later at Trayamar.[491] Three of these tombs were damaged by recent construction in the area, but one (Tomb 1) is well preserved, and another (Tomb 4) is intact. Neither is early enough to have belonged to original settlers or their families, but both were family tombs and belonged to people who had done very well in the business. Tomb 1 was built of beautifully finished hewn stone, with a stone roof and a perfectly fitted stone floor, and the spacious entrance was approached by a steeply sloped path, or dromos. The chamber was large, about four by three meters, and contained two burials, one slightly later than the other, and an array of grave goods: amphorae, mushroom-lipped and trefoil jugs, incense burners, and jewelry.[492]

Tomb 4 was of the same type but more beautiful and spacious. It held five burials, three earlier cremations of Tyrian settlers from the East, and two later inhumations of their native-born offspring[493] and an almost excessive number of grave goods. Among these was a magnificent gold pendant, slightly more than an inch (2.5 centimeters) in diameter, which is Tyrian and Egyptianizing in its workmanship (especially its lavish use of filigree) and design: a winged sun disk hovering above a full and a crescent moon that shines down on a baetyl guarded on either side by a uraeus, over which flutters the Horus falcon—the whole representing the transitions from death to life, from a terrestrial to a celestial existence.[494] The tombs

---

490. M. E. Aubet Semmler, "Aspectos de la colonización fenicia en Andalucía durante el siglo VIII a.C.," *Atti* 1, 3.815–24; G. Maass-Lindemann, "Chorreras 1980," *MM* 24 (1983) 76–103.

491. M. E. Aubet Semmler, "Nueva necrópolis fenicia de incineración en Lagos (Málaga)," *Actes* 3, 1.20–40; H. G. Niemeyer and H. Scharbert, *Trayamar: Die phönizischen Kammergräber und die Niederlassung an der Algarrobo-Mundung* (Mainz: von Zabern, 1975).

492. Ibid., 60–77, pls. 12–14, 29–39, 48–50.

493. G. Lindemann, "Phoenikische Grabformen des 7./6. Jahrhunderts v. Chr. im westlichen Mittelmeerraum," *MM* 15 (1974) 122–35; P. Gasull, "El sistema ritual fenicio: Inhumación e incineración," *MM* 34 (1993) 71–82; M. L. Ramos Sainz, "Los ritos de incineración e inhumación en las necrópolis hispanas (ss. VIII–II a.C.)," *Actas* 4, 4.1693–97.

494. H. G. Niemeyer, "The Trayamar Medallion Reconsidered," in *Oriental Studies Presented to Benedikt S. J. Isserlin* (ed. R. Y. Ebeid and M. J. L. Young; Leeds University Oriental Society: Near Eastern Researches 2; Leiden: Brill, 1980) 108–13. The medallion is the frontispiece and pl. 54a–b

themselves are late (later than Toscanos and Almuñécar), and their construction resembles that of contemporary tombs at Utica and Carthage.[495] It may be that the families buried in them came from North Africa in order to supervise the foundries, which by this time were producing iron mainly for export to Carthage.

Almuñécar, although sometimes thought to have been founded before the mid-eighth century,[496] is later than Chorreras, earlier than Trayamar. It once lay on a headland between the Rio Verde to the east and the Rio Seco to the west, beyond which was an early cemetery at a site called Laurita at Cerro de San Cristobal and a later cemetery just north of it at a place called Puente de Noy. The earliest Greek pottery, including an imitation proto-Corinthian pitcher made in Pithecusa dates to the last quarter of the eighth century.[497]

The earliest Phoenician settlement is known mainly from its tombs.[498] There were 20 tombs, but only 8 of them could be salvaged.[499] Each burial was in a cinerary urn, and the urn most often was associated with trefoil-lipped and mushroom-lipped jugs, all of them imported from mainland Phoenicia. The urns were of alabaster, had the inscriptions and cartouches of ninth-century or 22nd Dynasty pharaohs, and were like similar heirlooms that Esarhaddon looted when he destroyed Sidon in 677 B.C.E.

It is not unlikely that they were brought to Almuñécar with the Tyrian traders who, to take advantage of the operations at Morro de Mezquitilla, came to settle there around 725 B.C.E., well before this part of Spain was drawn into the Carthaginian orbit. A burial urn from this phase (ca. 650 B.C.E.) is also made of alabaster, but it is not an Egyptian heirloom and is inscribed in black paint with the name and the patronymic, both of them Carthaginian, of the deceased, "Burial of Magon, son of Hannibal" (*qbr mgn bn ḥ[nbʻl]*).[500] Their living conditions at Almuñécar, and their dealings with the local peoples, can be surmised from the more modest settlement at nearby Abdera, where there is some local handmade pottery and the usual Phoenician Red Slip, Polychrome, and Grey Ware.[501]

The topographical context of all these sites that radiated from Morro de Mezquitilla, at river mouths, on alluvial plains, in easy communication with the local inhabitants on whom all their work and livelihood depended, suggests that the Phoenicians had established good relations with

---

in H. G. Niemeyer and H. Scharbert, *Trayamar: Die phönizischen Kammengräber und die Niederlassung an der Algarrobo-Mündung* (Madrider Beiträge 4; Mainz: von Zabern, 1975).

495. Ibid., 112–22.

496. F. Molina Fajardo and A. Bannour, "Almuñécar a la luz de los nuevos hallazgos fenicios," *Actas* 4, 4.1645–63.

497. P. Cabrera, "El comercio de productos griegos de epoca geometrica en el sur de la penín-sula ibérica: Nuevos elementos," *Actes* 3, 1.222–29.

498. J. Maluquer de Motes, "Descubrimiento de la necrópolis de la antigua ciudad de Sexi en Almuñécar (Granada)," *Zephyrus* 14 (1963) 57–61, pls. 1–4.

499. W. Culican, "Almuñécar, Assur and Phoenician Penetration of the Western Mediter-ranean," *Levant* 2 (1970) 28–36.

500. M. J. Fuentes Estañol, "Corpus de las insripciones fenicias de España," *AuOr* 4 (1986) 5–30, esp. pp. 9–10, #06.01 = idem, *Corpus de las Inscripciones Fenicias de España* (Barcelona: published by the author, 1986).

501. A. Suárez et al., "Abdera: Una Colonia Fenicia en el Sureste de la Península Ibérica," *MM* 30 (1989) 135–50.

their neighbors and had worked out a policy of cooperation.[502] A visible clue to the modes of cooperation might be the inscriptions—graffiti on jars, all of which are fragmentary.[503] There are 14 of them, about half of which can be dated to the later eighth century, and what is interesting about them is that they are mostly badly written. Some are just plain wrong, with letters back-to-front, upside down, or in the wrong stance, as if inscribed by people who were not familiar with Phoenician or were used to writing from left to right. These, of course, could be Phoenicians, except that there are two inscriptions written by Phoenicians—a jar marked "honey" (*d*]*bš*), another with the personal name "Ada" (*ʾ*]*dʾ*)—that are alright. It seems just as likely, then, that the inscriptions are by local people who sold supplies to the settlers or who had joined the work force and were learning how to write Phoenician. This, at any rate, would be the level of cooperation that might be expected and that ultimately produced the hybrid Spanish scripts.

Toscanos is situated in the alluvial plain on the west bank of the Rio de Vélez and, before the river basin silted up, was situated on the coast. Just north of it but south of the hills rising in the near distance were the cemeteries at Alarcón and Jardín, and across the river but still in the plain was the cemetery at Cerro del Mar.[504] Toscanos was an emporium, in a farming district, enjoying the riches brought from the interior[505] and the abundance of the sea. It had warehouses and pottery barns, a good harbor and, at least later, an artificial port.[506] Ships like the one that sank off Mazarron, just west of Cartagena, or ships under Greek flags stopped to pick up pottery, produce, textiles, dyes, dried and pickled fish, amber and precious metals, bric-a-brac, and exotic animals from the Atlantic coast of Morocco—whatever the market would bear.[507]

Toscanos was founded abruptly and decisively (there is suddenly a large established population) toward the end of the eighth century, in conjunction with the community at Cerro del Villar on the Guadalhorce near Málaga, which kept it supplied with all these things, especially pottery,

---

502. C. Blasco, M. Luz Sánchez, and J. Calle, "Algunos aspectos de la relaciones entre el mundo orientalizante y los indígenas de la submeseta sur," *Actas* 4, 4.1763–70.

503. W. Röllig, "Phönizische Gefässinschriften vom Morro de Mezquitilla," *MM* 24 (1983) 132–44, pl. 10.

504. H. G. Niemeyer and H. Schubart, *Toscanos: Die altpunische Faktorei an der Mündung des Río de Vélez, I: Grabungskampagne 1964* (Madrider Forschungen 6; Berlin: de Gruyter, 1969).

505. T. Chapa Brunet, "Models of Interaction between Punic Colonies and Native Iberians: The Funerary Evidence," in *Encounters and Transformations: The Archaeology of Iberia in Transition* (ed. M. S. Balmuth, A. Gilman, and L. Prados-Torreira; Monographs in Mediterranean Archaeology 7; Sheffield: Sheffield Academic Press, 1997) 141–50.

506. C. R. Whittaker, "The Western Phoenicians: Colonisation and Assimilation," *Proceedings of the Cambridge Philological Society* 20 (1974) 58–79, esp. pp. 58–61, 71; M. E. Aubet Semmler, "Notes on the Economy of the Phoenician Settlements in Southern Spain," *Bierling*, 79–95; O. Arteaga and H. D. Schulz, "El puerto fenicio de Toscanos: Investigación geoarqueológica en la costa de la Axarquia (Vélez-Málaga—1983/84)," in *Los Fenicios en Málaga* (ed. M. E. Aubet; Málaga: University of Málaga Press, 1997) 87–154.

507. I. Negueruela et al., "Seventh-Century BC Phoenician Vessel Discovered at Playa de la Isla, Mazarron, Spain," *IJNA* 24 (1995) 189–97; P. Rouillard, "Phéniciens et Grecs à Toscanos: Note sur quelques vases d'inspiration gréco-géometrique de Toscanos (1967)," *MM* 31 (1990) 178–85; M. E. Aubet, "El comercio fenicio en Occidente: Balance y perpsectivas," in *I Fenici: Ieri oggi domani* (ed. S. Moscati; Rome: Consiglio Nazionale delle Ricerche, 1995) 227–43.

transport jars in particular.[508] Málaga also supplied Cerro del Villar wood, wheat, barley, oil, and wine, and the meat, fruit, and legumes, which its residents and those at Toscanos enjoyed. It flourished, along with Toscanos, in cooperation with the local population, all through the seventh century (there is a Phoenician inscription from the end of the century),[509] when continued expansion led to the founding of nearby Málaga, and as long as it remained independent of Carthage.

The urgency and motivation for the development of Toscanos and Cerro del Villar was the recent foundation of Carthage in North Africa. This was the only legitimate *de jure* Tyrian colony—planned, permanent, organized, governed locally on behalf of the mother city—apart from Carthage in Cyprus. The other Tyrian settlements in the West, either originally or eventually, whether started by the city, by corporations, or by individuals were designed to service it. The emporium at Toscanos became one of its main sources of supply.

Conclusion

These settlements in Spain illustrate some of the more interesting or intriguing features of Phoenician worldwide strategy. They chose their destinations, they followed already discovered routes, they established relays between nearer and more distant outposts, they made arrangements with the local people where they planned to stay, they maintained networks, they did not interfere with each other, and they kept contact with their home ports. They reached Spain first, from Italy and bypassing Sardinia, following the routes already charted by Iberians and Sardinians, and then stopped permanently in Sardinia, at Tharros or at Sulcis.

The first to reach Spain, the Sidonians and Byblians, went to the farthest Atlantic ports, and those who came later, the Tyrians, stayed inside the straits. From the Atlantic they shipped goods back home, and from the Mediterranean they went home via Carthage. In Spain the Sidonians set up a network of communities living and working with the indigenous peoples in the area bounded by Cádiz, Huelva, and Seville. The Tyrians, who were ever more aloof, stayed in coastal communities and did official business

---

508. M. E. Aubet Semmler, "Notas sobre las colonias del sur de España y su funcion en el marco territorial: El ejemplo del Cerro del Villar (Málaga)," *Atti* 2, 2.617–26; idem, "Die phönizische Niederlassung vom Cerro del Villar (Guadalhorce, Málaga): Die Ausgrabungen von 1986–1989," *MM* 32 (1991) 29–51, pls. 9–22; idem, "A Phoenician Market-Place in Southern Spain," in *Ana šadî labnāni lū allik: Beiträge zu altorientalischen und mittelmeerischen Kulturen. Festschrift für Wolfgang Röllig* (ed. B. Pongratz-Leisten, H. Kühne, and P. Xella; Neukirchen-Vluyn: Neukirchener Verlag, 1997) 11–22.

M. E. Aubet et al., *Cerro del Villar—I: El asentamiento fenicio en la desembocadura del río Guadalhorce y su interacción con el hinterland* (Málaga: Junta de Andalucia, 1999).

509. J. Gran Aymerich and J. R. Anderica, "Populations autochtones et allogènes sur le littoral méditerranéen andalou: De Málaga à Vélez-Málaga et Frigiliana (VIIIe–VIe s. av. J.-C.)," *Actas* 4, 4.1811–14.

J. Teixidor, "La inscripción fenicia de Guadalhorce," *AuOr* 8 (1990) 263–64. The inscription, written in an expert cursive hand on the shoulder of an amphora is the name of the supplier "ʾEshmunyaʿad, son of ʿAbdʾeshmun" (ʾšmny]ʿd bn ʿbdʾš[mn). Compare M. Sznycer, "L'inscription phénicienne du Guadalhorce," in *Málaga phénicienne et punique: Recherches franco-espagnols, 1981–1988* (ed. J. Gran-Aymerich; Paris: Éditions Recherche sur les Civilisations, 1991) 144–46, pl. 6.

with the people of the interior who, except for the few who joined their communities, kept their distance. Spain was as close as Sidonians came to colonization. For Tyrians, it was an outpost at the edge of the world and, increasingly, of a world entirely centered on Carthage.

Conclusion:
The Phoenicians in the Mediterranean

The eighth century was an age of discovery and bold change. In Judah, it was a model for the Solomonic age, a source of pride and wonderment. In Syria, it marked the emergence of the Aramean states and of a system of alliances that stretched to the Black Sea and embraced the Kasku (Katku among the Arameans), which resulted in the supranational unity of "All Aram." In Assyria, it was the beginning of an empire that ruled the known world. In Greece, it was the generation after Homer, the end of heroic aspiration, the age of colonization. In Anatolia, it marked the emergence of alphabetized and linguistically diverse peoples. In Palestine and Transjordan, city-states and nations joined the Phoenician trade network. In Cyprus, the kingdoms aligned at the amphictyonic center at Kition became estranged when the port was taken from Sidon by the Assyrians and ceded to Tyre, and Tyre had to think about establishing another foothold in the West.

In Phoenicia, Sidon gradually lost its precedence, and Tyre flourished under the auspices of Assyria. It was the age of individual entrepreneurs, of a new class of merchants and traders, of silver and money and a monied class, of governments having to protect public interests. It was the century of travel and of permanent settlement in distant places. Most amazingly of all, it was the century when Tyre, having thought about it and planned it, finally inaugurated a colony at Carthage, the "New City" in North Africa that would become, like the old mainland city, the hub of an array of satellite towns and the center of a new European world, a world about which the Assyrians knew absolutely nothing.

Phoenicians went west, individually, and intermittently, beginning in the tenth century. It was in the eighth that they went regularly and in convoys and began to stay, not just stop, where they landed. Italy was first, because the Euboeans and then Corinthians were there and because the Etruscans, with their eastern and quasi-Greek heritage were such sophisticated and congenial hosts. Spain was next and then Sardinia on the voyages to and from the Atlantic. Carthage was the big decision, and after it was made, Malta and Sicily fell into place.

The Phoenicians went on business to keep their mainland cities happy, to satisfy the intensive markets they had created in all the lands back home. Then they went because it was a good place to live, and they were welcome because they brought fine things from many different places and were not belligerent. They learned easily and taught what they already knew. Finally, they went because the East was getting to be too small and divided, too exclusive and precarious, too dangerous, and not sufficiently profitable. At last, it was just a place where they lived until they were Africanized and Europeanized and enrolled in another cycle of national awakening.

Chapter 4

The World of Tyre in the
Seventh Century B.C.E.

The seventh century in mainland and diaspora Phoenicia was a fine time of synthesis, syncretism, and consolidation. A major impulse was the inspiration of Assyrian hegemony and the sense of living in a unified world under a supreme, transnational God. Tyre acquired control of the eastern Mediterranean and slowly relinquished its interests in the western Mediterranean basin to the settlements there, which enjoyed increasing independence in the Carthaginian nexus. Greeks were established as their suppliers and connoisseurs. Sidon and Byblos learned to survive in the thrall of a worldwide Tyrian economy and, rattling along in their once cooperative systems, were more or less satisfied with managing a few assets in Palestine and overseas. Native peoples, who had been caught up in the whirl of Phoenician invention, began to assert themselves. Cities, countries, and patronal states became distinctive by working together in the international concert. Everything the world had learned from the Phoenicians took shape in new and appreciative social and cultural constellations. The seventh century turned out to be the epicenter of the Orientalizing revolution.

Tyre and Its Worldwide Economy

Tyre, with the connivance of Egypt and Assyria, and by profiting from their conflicting self-interests, weathered all the storms of the seventh century and was regarded on the mainland and abroad as the seal of wisdom, wealth, and good taste. It had the cooperation of many and very little competition and came to monopolize international trade. Sidon was crushed in 677 B.C.E., when it tried to free itself from constant Assyrian interference in its trade and commerce. Its king was beheaded; Esarhaddon (680–669 B.C.E.) imposed an embargo on the city and built a new port, named after himself, which took over its ancient trade networks. Esarhaddon then made a treaty with Baᶜal, king of Tyre, giving him the ports and inland routes that until then had belonged to Sidon and Byblos. In 674, Esarhaddon invaded Egypt but was defeated, and Tyre took advantage of this failure to "put his trust in his friend," Pharaoh Taharqa (690–664 B.C.E.), who had campaigned in Judah and visited the Levantine coast about ten years earlier.[1] Tyre stopped paying regular tribute to Assyria.[2]

---

1. D. B. Redford, "Taharqa in Western Asia and Libya," ErIsr 24 (Malamat Volume; 1993) 188*–91*.

2. ANET 292.

However, Esarhaddon forced Tyre to submit and went on to attack Egypt again in 671 B.C.E., successfully this time, but Tyre, persisting in its good relations with Egypt, once more refused to pay tribute to Assyria. Esarhaddon prepared another invasion but died on his way to Egypt, and Tyre was free until forced to submit when Ashurbanipal (668–627 B.C.E.) launched another successful campaign against Egypt in 666 B.C.E. In 664 B.C.E., after still another Assyrian invasion, Psammetichus I succeeded Taharqa. For the rest of the century, but especially after the decline of Assyria late in Ashurbanipal's reign, Tyre and the southern Levant increasingly aligned themselves with Egypt, and some towns such as Ushu, on the mainland opposite Tyre, and ʿAkko, a Tyrian port farther south, openly revolted against Assyria. Tyre, in effect, remained fairly unscathed and grew more prosperous as these mighty neighbors battled for its friendship and loyalty.

Tyre's treaty with Assyria[3] had more benefits than constraints, and its text reveals some interesting features of the city's social, religious, political, and economic structure in the seventh century. The treaty was made with Esarhaddon by the king of Tyre, Baʿal, and by the people of Tyre. The people were represented by a council of elders. The king was subject to the authority of an Assyrian royal deputy, three of whose prerogatives are listed: he assisted at the deliberations of the council; as ambassador, he was the first to receive and read the letters sent from the Assyrian king to Baʿal; and he had to be present when Baʿal did business or talked with the captain of any foreign ships docked in Tyre.

The merchant ships of Tyre belonged either to the king or to the people, but their captains and crews were not necessarily from the city itself: one of the treaty stipulations was that the cargo of a Tyrian ship wrecked off the Philistine or the Assyrian coast, by that fact became the property of the king of Assyria; however, the persons on board the ship were to be returned to their own country. The Philistine coast may have extended south from Joppa or may have included only the area from Ashdod south to Ashkelon and Gaza. The Assyrian coast included, presumably, all the Phoenician ports north of Philistia and north of Tyre. This presumption is based on other stipulations that gave Baʿal access to ports south and north of Tyre, ports that the treaty describes as belonging to Esarhaddon.

To the south, Baʿal acquired the right to trade in ʿAkko, in Dor south of the Tyrian border at Mount Carmel, and as far as Philistine territory, so perhaps in Joppa. Because all of these were immemorial friends and allies of Tyre, they were now assigned by the treaty to its official jurisdiction. To the north, where thanks to Esarhaddon Tyrian territory included Sarepta, his rights extended past Sidon, now known as the Port of Esarhaddon, as far as Byblos and all the towns in the Lebanon. Along with access to these ports, Baʿal and the people of Tyre also received the overland trade routes that led to them, but because these were in Assyrian territory (Dor was in the province of Dor, ʿAkko probably in the province of Megiddo, Sidon and Byblos perhaps in the province of Sidon), they had to pay the usual taxes and tolls.

---

3. S. Parpola and K. Watanabe, *Neo-Assyrian Treaties and Loyalty Oaths* (SAA 2; Helsinki: Helsinki University Press, 1988) #5, pp. 24–27; N. Naʾaman, "Esarhaddon's Treaty with Baʿal and Assyrian Provinces along the Phoenician Coast," *RSF* 22 (1994) 3–8.

The treaty is under the auspices of Assyrian, Syrian, and Phoenician Gods[4] and is protected by a series of nasty curses. The purpose of these, of course, is to uphold the law—the mutual oath and the legal obligations— and in this sense, they are consistent with the treaty's concern for justice and fairness, in the case of shipwrecked sailors, for instance, who are not to be harmed, or of hired merchant marines to whom no injustice shall be done. On the Assyrian side, only Goddesses are invoked: Mullissu, wife of Ashur, the Great God, and patroness of Nineveh, the capital; Ishtar of Arbela, mother, the source of mercy, forgiveness, and inspiration; Gula, the great healer; the seven sisters (*Sebetti*) of the Pleiades. The Syrian Gods are Bethel and ʿAnat-Bethel, the male and female principals of immortal Memory, symbolized by stone baetyls or steles at home in Syria and North Israel.[5] They are not unknown as symbols at Tyre but are not attested at Sidon and are familiar simply as ʿAnat at Byblian sites in Cyprus.[6] On the Phoenician side of the treaty oath sworn by Baʿal of Tyre, there are Gods of seafaring, the metropolitan Gods of Tyre and Sidon, and the Goddess Astarte.

The first of the seafaring Gods is the Storm God *Baʿal Šamem*, "The Lord of Heaven," the God of the sky, of thunder and lightning, who presided over the Byblian pantheon in the tenth century B.C.E., who, along with El (the God of the Earth) and the Sun (the God of the Underworld), administered the curses at eighth-century Karatepe, and who in the archaizing mood of later days became the object of popular devotion in the colonies.[7] The second is *Baʿal Malage*, otherwise unattested, whose name makes him "Lord of the High Seas," of the open seas, or what the biblical text with reference to Tyre's overseas voyages calls "the heart of the seas."[8]

---

4. G. Bunnens, "Aspects religieux de l'expansion phénicienne," *RelPh*, 119–25; H. J. Katzenstein, "Some Reflections on the Phoenician Deities Mentioned in the Treaty between Esarhaddon King of Assyria and Baʿal King of Tyre," *Atti* 2, 1.373–77.

5. K. van der Toorn, "Worshipping Stones: On the Deification of Cult Symbols," *JNSL* 23 (1997) 1–14; E. D. Stockton, "Phoenician Cult Stones," *Australian Journal of Biblical Archaeology* 2/3 (1974–75) 1–27; K. van der Toorn, "Anat-Yahu, Some Other Deities, and the Jews of Elephantine," *Numen* 39 (1992) 80–101. The foundation legend of Bethel in Israel was incorporated into the Jacob cycle (Genesis 28–35). According to the treaty, the curse of Bethel and ʿAnat-Bethel is to be devoured by a lion (Parpola and Watanabe, *Neo-Assyrian Treaties and Loyalty Oaths*, 27), and this is corroborated by biblical legend and prophecy (1 Kings 13, Hos 13:7).

6. P. Naster, "*Ambrosiai Petrai* dans les textes et sur les monnaies de Tyr," *RelPh*, 361–70. A fifth-century inscription from Idalion in Cyprus (*CIS* 95; *RES* 453) records the dedication of a parapet to ʿAnat by the king of Kition and Idalion. A fifth-century bronze lance from Idalion (*RES* 1210; *RPC* 110–11, pl. 10:2) is inscribed "For ʿAnat / for ʿAnat" (*lʿnt / lʿnt*). A Greek-Phoenician bilingual from Lapethos in northern Cyprus mimics that battle cry in its dedication of an altar to ʿAnat and to Ptolemy I Soter (*CIS* 95; *KAI* 42).

7. E. Lipiński, *Dieux et Déesses de l'Univers Phénicien et Punique* (Studia Phoenicia 14; Louvain: Peeters, 1995) 84–86; *PoB*, 41 #7; A. R. W. Green, *The Storm-God in the Ancient Near East* (Biblical and Judaic Studies from the University of California, San Diego 8; Winona Lake, IN: Eisenbrauns, 2003); H. Niehr, *Baʿalšamem: Studien zu Herkunft, Geschichte und Rezeptionsgeschichte eines phönizischen Gottes* (OLA 123; Louvain: Peeters 2003). The God is special to Byblos and is mentioned in inscriptions from Byblos (*KAI* 4), Karatepe (*KAI* 26), Ekron (*KAI* 266), Umm el-ʿAmed (*CIS* 7), Kition (*RES* 1519B), Cagliari (*CIS* 139), and Carthage (*CIS* 379, 3778).

8. See Arabic **ljj*, a root unattested in Phoenician but known in Syriac and Hebrew in the word *log* or *luga*ʾ, "liquid measure," and in the Arabic words "depths of the sea" (*lujj* and *lujja*),

The third God is *Ba'al Sapon*, "Lord of Mount Saphon," the dwelling place of the Gods in North Syria where the Orontes flows into the sea, and a beacon and safe haven for ships. He is mentioned along with *Ba'al Hamon*, "Lord of the Amanus," on a mid-sixth-century amulet from Tyre and in a contemporary Phoenician letter sent to Saqqara from a merchant at the Tyrian outpost at Daphne, just east of the Egyptian Delta.[9] The curses for noncompliance with the treaty that are associated with these Gods correspond exactly to their meteorological and maritime attributes:[10] "May they raise an evil wind against your ships"—this is Ba'al Šamem; "may they undo your moorings and tear out your mooring pole"—these are the doings of Ba'al Saphon; "may a strong wave sink you in the sea, and a violent tide rise against you"—this means Ba'al Malage.

The metropolitan Gods include only Melqart of Tyre and 'Eshmun of Sidon but not the God of Byblos, which was identified earlier in the treaty as one of the cities belonging to Esarhaddon. Because Tyre had taken control of Sidonian territory, and because its king, Ba'al, governed with the consent of the people represented by their elders, the basic curses invoking these Gods are destruction of the land and deportation of the people. The king, curiously, is exempt. Because Tyre was famous as the purveyor of the good life, particularly as the merchant of purple and crimson robes, destruction of the land includes in particular lack of food and clothing and of oil for their anointing. Deportation is mentioned twice and turns out later in the story of Tyre to be a favorite Assyrian form of intimidation.

Although the treaty was not especially onerous (it was, on the contrary, overly generous), Ba'al of Tyre was encouraged by his friendship with Taharqa of Egypt to disregard it, and Assyria, predictably (and in the name of the Gods), always retaliated. There is not much evidence for a belligerent Tyre. Walled cities and fortified outposts at home and abroad are more symptomatic of its aloofness. However, the treaty's invocation of Astarte, the Goddess of Love and War (she is often portrayed in Egyptian lore naked, astride a charger) makes it clear that siding with Egypt entailed, from the Assyrian perspective, readiness for battle as much as, from the Tyrian point of view, luxurious living, commercial savvy, and a raw determination to bolster a traditional and now-burgeoning market. Astarte is called upon to break Tyre's bow in the heat of battle, to make the people crouch at the feet of their enemy (which corresponds to the standard portrait of the pharaoh smiting a defenseless prisoner who cringes at his feet), and, of course, to divide their precious goods among their enemies.

Something like these and the other curses in fact happened to Tyre in Assyrian times but not nearly so dramatically. When Ba'al rebelled (which meant not paying taxes and tribute) during the reign of Esarhaddon, he was forced, by a siege depriving the city of food and water, to pay his debts, to give dowries to his daughters, whom the king deported to Nineveh, and

---

"fathomless" (*lujji*), and with other nuances ("clamor," "relentlessness") that might be associated with the deeps.

9. *KAI* 50; P. Bordreuil, "Attestations inédites de Melqart, Ba'al Hamon et Ba'al Saphon à Tyr," *RelPh*, 77–86.

10. Parpola and Watanabe, *Neo-Assyrian Treaties and Loyalty Oaths*, 27.

to let the Assyrians reorganize his land and take control of some of his towns.[11]

It was essentially the same story when Baʿal rebelled again in the reign of Ashurbanipal: a siege, involving siege works, road closures, and a naval blockade forced him to submit and surrender his daughter and his son to deportation.[12] This fulfilled the curses, but it was just standard procedure, and Assyria was not really interested in doing damage to Tyre or its foreign relations.

Much the same befell Egypt when Esarhaddon defeated Taharqa, Tyre's mainstay in Africa: he deported the queen and her attendants, and the heir to the throne, as well as gold, silver, and linen, but he spent more time reorganizing the country, installing kings and governors, harbor-masters, and administrators who would promote trade and good relations with Assyria.[13] Ashurbanipal was even more lenient with Baʿal of Tyre, restoring his son and heir, Yaḥimilk, who was expected to cooperate with Assyria but who was too inexperienced because he "had not yet crossed the sea" to Cyprus or the far western colonies.[14]

The treaty, by referring to the rights of the king, of the people, who were represented by a council of elders, and of the merchant marines recognized that trade and commerce were in the hands of the court and a civic corporation and of the individuals or syndicates whom they hired to outfit and man their ships.[15] Although being allowed to do business in all the ports from Philistia to Syria also gave them access to the roads that led to these ports and along the coast, nothing more is said about these roads and who traveled them, or about overland trade or who managed it or how it worked. Similarly, although the treaty concentrates on shipping and ports, it is silent about where the ships came from and where they went, with whom they did business in the mainland ports, and what commodities were traded. But there are other texts, in the annals of Esarhaddon and Ashurbanipal, that together with some biblical texts help in sketching a rough map of Tyre's seventh-century world.

Esarhaddon and Ashurbanipal are proud to list among their subjects and tributaries kings of the mainland, the seashore, and the islands.[16] There are 22 of them, listed in a fixed order, and apparently taken from a master list that kept track of any changes in government. The list always begins with Baʿal of Tyre, but Sidon, because it had become an Assyrian province and had no king, is not mentioned. Second, and aligned with Tyre is Manasseh

---

11. *ANET* 291, 292.

12. Ibid., 295–96.

13. Ibid., 293.

14. Ibid., 296.

15. Such a syndicate, or association of business people, is mentioned in a mark on a Cypriot amphora found at Tell Rachidiyeh, on the coast facing Tyre. The inscription, which can be dated to the mid-seventh century, reads "House of the Association" (*bt ḥbr*), referring to the jar's destination. See *Liban: L'Autre Rive—Exposition présentée à l'Institut du monde arabe du 27 octobre au 2 Mai 1999* (Paris: Flammarion, 1998) 125.

S. F. Bondì, "Note sull'economia fenicia—I: Impresa privata e ruolo dello stato," *EVO* 1 (1978) 139–49.

16. *ANET* 291, 294; J. Elayi, "Les cités phéniciennes et l'empire assyrien à l'époque d'Assurbanipal," *RA* 77 (1983) 45–58.

of Judah, who was specially favored by Assyria and had supplied laborers to help build the port of Esarhaddon in Sidon and the arsenal palace in Nineveh. He would also provide troops for Ashurbanipal's Egyptian campaign, and his sisters were at the royal court in Nineveh.[17] The next two are the kings of Edom and Moab, included in this position because of their relations—not least in overland trade—with Judah. Next, and possibly as the guardians of the ports where some of this trade debouched, are the king of Gaza, Sillibel, and the king of Ashkelon, Mitinti—the former with an Assyrian name, the latter with a good Phoenician name. The seventh and eighth are the kings of Ekron, with the Greek name Ikausu, and of Byblos, with the name Milkʾasap, which is common among kings of this city: they are linked in the list as they seem to have been in cultural and commercial reality, and Ekron follows naturally on the preceding Philistine cities.

Next are the kings of Arvad and Samsimuruna: Arvad was the port in Northern Syria that supplied the Assyrians with a navy and, together with Samsimuruna, was once a Sidonian confederate. The last two kings of the mainland are from Ammon in Transjordan and from Ashdod on the coast, which were in the network of kings but remained independent of each other and of the whole group. The rest of the 22 are the 10 kings of Cyprus, most or all of whom have Greek names and ruled in kingdoms scattered all over the island, mainly on the coast but also inland. The map of the Tyrian world, from the perspective of Assyria, included only countries and kings that were under Assyrian dominion, and only those that cooperated and were active in the system of international trade.

The same map, from a Judean perspective, is filled out with the names of places on long-distance overseas and overland trade routes, so that the world of Tyre seems much bigger and somehow boundless. This map was drawn late in the sixth century and inserted into an earlier, but still sixth-century portrayal of Tyre as a ceremonial bark whose captain, the king of Tyre, naturally saw himself as the God for whom the bark was constructed.[18] It was the seventh-century world and, like the network of kings

---

17. M. Cogan and H. Tadmor, *II Kings: A New Translation with Introduction and Commentary* (AB 11; New York: Doubleday, 1988) 265; S. Dalley, "Yabâ, Atalyâ, and the Foreign Policy of Late Assyrian Kings," *State Archives of Assyria Bulletin* 12/2 (1998) 83–98, esp. p. 93; R. Achenbach, "Jabâ und Atalja—zwei jüdische Königstöchter am assyrischen Königshof? Zu einer These von Stephanie Dalley," *BN* 113 (2002) 29–38.

18. M. Liverani, "The Trade Network of Tyre according to Ezek. 27," in *Ah, Assyria . . . : Studies in Assyrian History and Ancient Near Eastern Historiography Presented to Hayim Tadmor* (ed. M. Cogan and I. Ephʿal; Scripta Hierosolymitana 33; Jerusalem: Magnes, 1991) 65–79; M. A. Corral, *Ezekiel's Oracles against Tyre: Historical Realities and Motivations* (Biblica et Orientalia 46; Rome: Pontifical Biblical Institute, 2002). The map is in Ezek 27:12–25a. It resembles and draws on a seventh-century genealogical presentation of the map of the world in Gen 10:1–7, 20, 21a, 22–23, 31–32, which was filled out, in the rest of this chapter, by a sixth-century writer interested in ethnography.

R. D. Barnett, "Ezekiel and Tyre," *ErIsr* 9 (Albright Volume; 1969) 6–13, pl. 4. The building of the ship is described in Ezek 27:3b–9a + 11bβ, its sinking in Ezek 27:25b–26, and lamentation for its loss in Ezek 27:28–32. The captain of the ship, the God who sailed in it, is described in Ezek 28:1–10. The writer who inserted the map of the Tyrian trade world edited these portrayals in order to turn the ceremonial bark into a heavily laden merchantman (Ezek 27:9b–10, 11aβ, 27, 33–36) and its captain into the fabulously rich and vainglorious king of Tyre (Ezek 28:11–26).

in the western confederacy, it was the creation of Assyrian political, economic, and cultural policies, made possible by Tyrian ingenuity and ambition.

The list of places on the map begins with Tarshish and ends with voyages of the ships of Tarshish. At the beginning, Tarshish is Tarsus in Cilicia, supplying Tyre with silver, iron, tin, and lead in exchange for its expensive wares. At the end, the ships of Tarshish distribute Tyre's merchandise on voyages to the western Mediterranean where the same products were available. In between, there are four groups of five countries that did business with Tyre. The first includes Ionia, Cappadocia (*Tubal* in Hebrew, *Tabal* in Assyrian texts), Phrygia, Armenia (or *Bet Togarmah*), and Rhodes and the islands, where Tyre traded in slaves, bronze vessels, horses, war horses and mules, ivory tusks, and ebony.

In the second group, Syria dealt in emeralds, coral, agate, purple, embroidered work, and linen. Judah and the "land of Israel" (not called the "Kingdom of Israel" because it was now an Assyrian province) had wheat, oats, honey, and oil for sale; Damascus had wine of Helbon and white wool; and Cilicia (named "Dan," as in the Hassan Beyli inscription) and a country called "Outer Ionia" (*yawan meʾuzal*) had wrought iron, calamus, and cassia.

The third group includes places in North and South Arabia and their merchandise: saddlecloths from Dedan; lambs, rams, and goats from North Arabia and Qedar; spices, precious stones, and gold from Sheba and Raʿamah. The fourth group comprises cities in Assyria—Haran, Canneh, Eden, Ashur, and Chilmad—where there was a brisk business in clothing and carpets. The map leaves out the coastal cities (these are mentioned in the description of the building and sinking of the good ship Tyre) and moves counterclockwise from north to west to south, and back to Assyria in the east, where the power lay. By listing specific goods in particular places, it gives Tyre economic control of the known world in the eastern Mediterranean and, from the perspective of a seafaring empire, in the lands adjacent to it. It gives a significant nod in the direction of Tarshish in the western Mediterranean, and the clear implication is that Tyre inhabited a much larger world.

The story of the ship of Tyre into which this map was inserted describes its construction, the reaction of the Mediterranean world to its foundering, and the tragic fate of its captain, who went down with his ship.[19] The story is told in poetic form, beginning with a hymn of praise, then turning into a lamentation, and ending with a complaint and a critical aside. It expresses in the awe and admiration of the poet the fundamental and amazing influence that Tyre had on a world largely of its own creation.

The poem begins with Tyre's declaration "I am perfectly beautiful," on which the poet then elaborates by attributing her beauty as she rides at anchor to the artistry and devotion of those who built her: "Your hull was laid in the heart of the seas, your builders made you perfectly beautiful." This praise, which suits Tyre as the ceremonial ship, and Tyre as the famously

---

19. Ezek 27:3b–9a + 11bβ; 27:25b–26, 28–32; 28:1–10. The rest of Ezekiel 27–28 is by the editor, who inserted the map of the world and adjusted the original context to suit it.

beautiful island city, naturally leads into the names of the builders and a detailed list of the precious materials they used. Her planks were of fir from Mount Hermon, her mast was a cedar of Lebanon, her oars were of oak from Mount Bashan (all three of these mountains were habitations of the Gods), and her deck was made of ivory inlaid in pine from the coast of Kition in Cyprus. Her sail and ensign were embroidered linen from Egypt, and her awning was blue and purple fabric from Elisha in Cyprus.

With the ship built and outfitted, the poet turns to her company and crew, all of whom were from prestigious Phoenician cities: her rowers were from Sidon and Arvad, her pilots were from Tyre itself, and old salts and skilled men from Byblos were the shipwrights who kept her trim. And so the poem lauds Tyre as a wondrous monument to Phoenician, Cypriot Greek, and Egyptian cooperation, and the prelude ends by repeating in awe, "These are the ones who made you perfectly beautiful."

The lamentation, alluding to the sixth-century collapse of foreign trade when relations among the 12-member kingdoms of the western confederacy were disrupted by Babylonian invasions under Nebuchadnezzar[20]— Judah was captured, Transjordan subjected, Syria harassed, Philistia destroyed, Tyre besieged for more than a decade, distant Egypt left to its own devices—begins with the sinking of the ship and records the reaction of the Mediterranean world. The ship was beautiful at anchor, magnificent in the open seas, but when it sailed into the high seas it foundered in a mighty east wind. At the shouts of her crew and the roar of the waves, all the other ports, the rowers, sailors, and pilots abandoned their ships, spread the awful news and, staying on dry land, performed mourning rituals (crying bitterly, pouring dust on their heads, rolling in ashes, shaving their beards), and raised the lament, "Who was ever like Tyre, now dumbfounded in the midst of the sea." The sinking of Tyre was a tragedy that immobilized the whole Mediterranean world, just as her brilliance had been its impetus to greatness.

In the next part of the poem, the sinking of Tyre is blamed on its captain. The apology maintains the exuberance and admiration that characterized the description of the ship, the ceremonial bark, by comparing the captain to Melqart, the God of Tyre, whose insight, ingenuity, and bold adventures constantly benefited his people, a mortal who achieved divine status by dying (Ezek 28:1–10). The criticism, however, is attributed to Yahweh, the God of Judah, and this sense of wonderment is creased by the bitterness of parti pris. The apology begins, as does the story of the bark, with a bold announcement: the captain declares, "I am a God (*'El*), I sit on the throne of God (*'Elohim*) in the heart of the sea." The criticism begins with Yahweh's retort, "But you are a man (*'Adam*) and not a God (*'El*), although you think your mind is like the mind of God (*'Elohim*)."

The poem elaborates on this retort by comparing the captain to Daniel, proverbially wise, interpreter of dreams, and revealer of divine secrets but still a man, and the argument becomes more ironic by drifting from the captain's divine pretensions to the mundane and mercantile realities of Tyre's greatness: "By your wisdom and understanding, you became wealthy,

---

20. *HistTyre* 295–347.

you amassed silver and gold in your treasuries. By your great wisdom, by your trade, you became very rich, grandiose in your wealth."

But then the argument, because it can only ridicule but not disprove the belief that Melqart, the captain, is a God, turns into a petty *ad hominem*: because the captain's divine pretensions are based, the argument goes, on the wealth he gained through trade, he can be deflated simply by bringing against him "aliens and the most terrible of nations, who will draw their swords against the beauty of your wisdom and will defile your splendour." The captain's wisdom, in the drift of the argument, is as beautiful as his ship and founders with it when it sinks, but the storm turns out to be the Babylonians, and he dies by their sword.

Thus the argument ends when death by the sword (unlike death by immolation that assured Melqart's, the captain's, divinization and divine status) proves that he is just a man: "Will you say, 'I am God (*'Elohim*)' in the presence of your murderers—although you are a man (*'Adam*) and not a God (*'El*)—in the hands of those who wound you? At the hands of strangers, you will die the death of the uncircumcised." The criticism that crept into this valedictory for Tyre was attributed to Yahweh, the God of Jerusalem, and was meant to magnify him, but first it reveals Judah's total intricacy in the world of Tyre and its jealousy of an incomparable sister city and its disappointment at not being on board the ship, or at least among those on shore who lament her.

The poem relieves this disappointment by ending with a lamentation for the king of Tyre. He is Ba'al, namesake of Melqart, who is the Ba'al ("Lord") of Tyre and, as an inscribed seal reveals, the "king of the Tyrians."[21] According to the poem, the king was in fact the seal, symbol of merchants and traders, in the signet ring worn by God in the Garden of Eden (Ezek 28:11–19). The ring is pure gold. The stone, cleverly wrought and beautiful, stands out in a list of nine precious stones, all of them found in Cyprus, all of them actually used in signet rings. The king is in the Garden of Eden, protected by a cherub, that magnificent four-winged mythical creature so often engraved on seals and, as pictured on the inscribed seal, walks on stones of fire on the mountain of God. But pride in his wisdom, beauty, and vast trade was his downfall, and he was thrown out of the garden of God into the world. There the fire that emanated from him and that was intended to divinize him merely incinerated him and left him as dust on the earth.

And so the lamentation comes back to the claim that the king of Tyre really is a God, and agrees with it, and is filled with sorrow at his mortality. The lamentation, as the whole poem, is intrigued by the heroic role that Melqart played in Tyre's commercial and colonial exploits (the image of the labors of Heracles, whom the colonials in the sixth century identified with their God) and by the glory of Tyre, in which Judah and the rest of the known world was pleased to share in the seventh century.

---

21. P. Bordreuil, "Charges et fonctions en Syrie–Palestine d'après quelques sceaux ouest-sémitiques du second et du premier millénaire," *CRAIBL* (1986) 290–308, figs. 1–9, esp. pp. 298–305, figs. 3–8; idem, *CSOSI* 23–24 #7.

This representation of Tyre, as long as it enjoyed the favor of the Assyrians and before it was absorbed into a dwindling Neo-Babylonian Empire, is confirmed by all the historical evidence. It was a brilliant, independent city, and in the system of political and commercial alliances imposed or encouraged by Assyria thrived among a coalition of city-states and nations that, under the same impulses, also achieved distinction and self-definition.

Mainland Phoenicia in "Cooperation with Assyria"

The seventh century was an organized and energetic time throughout the Levant. Judah was associated closely with Tyre. The Philistine cities had diverse foreign relations. The coastal Phoenician towns were dependencies of Tyre, Sidon, or Byblos or of each other. Transjordan, via Judean or Tyrian intermediaries, had commercial and cultural relations with Tyre or one of the Philistine conglomerates. Egypt during the reign of Psammetichus I (664–610 B.C.E.) was in and out of Palestine but an accomplice of Assyria and a constant presence. For the latter part of the seventh century, in his last decades, and during the reign of Necho (610–594 B.C.E.), Egypt became the dominant foreign power in the region. The century ended in the discombobulation of Babylonian interference and disregard.

Sidon was situated on a promontory. On its south side, there was a bay that formed a natural protected harbor. North of the promontory, partly protected by a reef and a small island, there were two ports: the more westerly and seaward incorporated the reef into its system of breakwaters; the more landward was enclosed by the north–south pier of the western port and by the east–west jetty at its northern tip. One of these, or the whole complex was called "The Port of Esarhaddon," which he built, or rebuilt, after he destroyed Sidon "like the Flood," tore down its walls, murdered ʿAbdmilkot, its king whom he had captured at sea (undoubtedly with ships from the Assyrian port at Arvad), and ransacked the city in 677 B.C.E.

Sidon and its territory, excepting Sarepta to the south, which was ceded to Tyre, but including 16 named towns to the north of the city,[22] became an Assyrian province. The city still functioned, despite the rhetoric of its total destruction, but it was entirely owned and operated by the Assyrians, with an Assyrian governor and without a king or royal family. ʿAbdmilkot's wives, children, and palace personnel were deported to Ashur. Sidon remained the premier trade center in the Levant but under new management. It trafficked in expensive goods and artistic expertise: Esarhaddon's loot (he apparently was not interested in staples) included gold, silver, precious stones, linen garments, and garments with multicolored trim, elephant hides, ivory, ebony, boxwood, alabaster jars filled with the finest oil, rich goods of every kind.[23] Sidon survived this Assyrian regime, restored its

---

22. E. Lipiński, "Le royaume de Sidon au VIIe siècle av. J.-C.," *ErIsr* 24 (Malamat Volume; 1993) 158*–63*.

23. *ANET* 291; W. Culican, "Almuñécar, Assur and Phoenician Penetration of the Western Mediterranean," *Levant* 2 (1970) 28–36; repr. *Opera Selecta: From Tyre to Tartessos* (Gothenburg: Åströms, 1986) 673–84.

monarchy when the empire failed, and soon overtook Tyre by the favor of the Babylonians[24] and Persians.

There are a few Phoenician inscriptions from seventh-century Sidon, from places where its people settled, or from countries that had come under its influence. Inscriptions from Sidon include an Ammonite seal that, besides the name of its owner, mentions the fact that it was offered in fulfilment of a vow to Astarte (*l'št*) in Sidon:[25] the offering formula is Phoenician, but the script and language are Ammonite, and the ex-voto was probably left in her temple by some trader from Transjordan who regularly did business with the Phoenicians. A tombstone from Sidon inscribed with the name ʾAbihûʾ, the son of Murroʾ (*ʾbhʾ bn mrʾ*), suggests by its script and by the name of the man's father that he—his own name would be good Hebrew and is not found in Phoenician—was from Cyprus, perhaps specifically from Kition.

Similarly, an ostracon found in a Sidonian tomb has a name that is found in Cyprus, although it is also good Hebrew as well as common Phoenician, and it identifies him as an Ionian merchant (*mnḥm šḥr ywn*).[26] A deed of sale from Nineveh is stamped with the seal of "ʿAbdisilli, the Sidonian": he may have been a deportee when Sidon was taken over by the Assyrians or, more likely (because it was probably "business as usual" when Assyria assumed the management of Sidon's affairs), a Sidonian merchant who had taken up residence in the Assyrian capital.[27]

From Kythrea in north-central Cyprus, in a totally Cypriot context, there is a clay sarcophagus inscribed in Phoenician with a curse, like the curses on later Sidonian coffins, against anyone who might disturb the eternal rest of this settler from the distant coasts.[28] From Cilicia there is a Phoenician seal of a Hittite jailor inscribed with his name and profession ("Belonging to Muwatillis, the jailor" [*lmwtlš ḥrpd*]),[29] and a late seventh-

24. M. Elat, "Phoenician Overland Trade within the Mesopotamian Empires," in *Ah, Assyria . . . : Studies in Assyrian History and Ancient Near Eastern Historiography Presented to Hayim Tadmor* (ed. M. Cogan and I. Ephʿal; Scripta Hierosolymitana 33; Jerusalem: Magnes, 1991) 21–35, esp. pp. 29–31.

25. *WSS* 328–29 #876.

26. J. Teixidor, "Deux inscriptions phéniciennes de Sidon," *Archéologie au Levant: Recueil à la mémoire de Roger Saidah* (Lyon: Maison de l'Orient, 1982) 233–36.

27. J. N. Postgate, "More 'Assyrian Deeds and Documents,'" *Iraq* 32 (1970) 125–64, pls. 18–32, #9, esp. pp. 142–43, pls. 23, 31c. The name is written in Akkadian (*ab-di-si-l[u] lú ṣi-du-na-a-a*) at the beginning of the deed. The theophoric element (*si-[l]u*) occurs as *Sillis* in Greek transliterations of Phoenician names of men from Sidon, Tyre, Kition, and Ashkelon: O. Masson, "Recherches sur les Phéniciens dans le monde hellénistique," *BCH* 93 (1969) 679–700, esp. pp. 679–87. It is probably the name of the Goddess *Sala*, or *salas*, "Daughter," known from Old Babylonian and Hurrian texts: W. G. Lambert, "Old Testament Mythology in Its Ancient Near Eastern Context," in *Congress Volume: Jerusalem 1986* (ed. J. A. Emerton; VTSup 40; Leiden: Brill, 1988) 124–43, esp. pp. 136–37. She is known from the Ugaritic-Akkadian proper name *Ili-sala*, and her name occurs in the bilingual from Tell Fekherye as *Sala* in the Assyrian version and as *Swl* in the unvocalized Aramaic version.

28. *RPC* 104–8, pl. 8:2.

29. *WSS* 265 #714; Lachish Letter 4:5–9 (J. C. L. Gibson, *Textbook of Syrian Semitic Inscriptions, I: Hebrew and Moabite Inscriptions* [Oxford: Clarendon, 1971] 41–43) in a report to headquarters notes: "Concerning the jail [*ʿl dbr byt ḥrpd*], there is no one there. As to Samakyahu, Shemayahu took him and brought him to the city. And I your servant am not sending the witness there today but I will send him when morning comes around." The root *rpd* is not found otherwise in

century boundary stone inscribed in Phoenician with the complicated history of the transfer of a particular parcel of land and its chattels.[30] These inscriptions reflect both the eclipse of Sidon in the seventh century and its enduring ties to places, especially in Cilicia and Cyprus, where its citizens had boldly gone in earlier times.

Byblos is mentioned in Esarhaddon's treaty with Ba'al of Tyre, together with the Lebanon and cities in the mountains, as the northernmost part of Assyria territory on the seacoast. Ba'al is given access to its towns, villages, and ports of trade but must pay the usual taxes to Assyria. Byblos, despite this, remained an independent kingdom, and the privileges accorded to Tyre do not imply any territorial, commercial, or political control of its land. It was part of the western coalition, listed with Philistine Ekron, and two kings bearing the traditional Byblian throne names 'Urumilk and Milk'asap ruled from the time of Sennacherib to about the mid-seventh century.[31]

Additionally, men and women whose Phoenician names might suggest that they came from Byblos had good jobs in the empire: a man named 'Aḥubast, mentioned occasionally as a witness in legal documents from 696–663 B.C.E. held the office of "Head Doorman";[32] the woman named 'Amat'aštart was superintendent (*šakintu*) of the palace at Nimrud, and her daughter Ṣubetu, whose name means "Gazelle" or "Pretty" in Phoenician, married another Phoenician, a Byblian, whose name was Milkiram ben 'Abdazûz, perhaps the Milkiram who was the eponym of the year 656/655 B.C.E.[33]

There was another woman from Byblos who officiated at the rites of Adonis celebrated by Byblian expatriates in Ur. Her name is 'Amotba'al bat Pat'isis, "Servant-of-Ba'al daughter of Gift-of-Isis," and she was in fact the servant of Adonis. She carried a small ivory box, or miniature coffin, in which, as its inscription affirms, Adonis lay during the three days of his festival. The box was found along with other ivory toilette articles (combs, a mirror, a kohl pot and stick, a pyxis, and a jar in the form of a crouching sphinx, all of which would have been suitable for a woman of her rank) in

---

Phoenician. In Biblical Hebrew it can mean "support," and in Old South Arabic it has the meaning "support, revetment, retaining wall."

30. P. G. Mosca and J. Russell, "A Phoenician Inscription from Čebel Ireš Daği in Rough Cilicia," *Epigraphica Anatolica* 9 (1987) 1–28, pls. 1–4; A. Lemaire, "Une inscription phénicienne découverte récemment et le mariage de Ruth la Moabite," *ErIsr* 20 (1989) 124*–29*; G. A. Long and D. Pardee, "Who Exiled Whom? Another Interpretation of the Phoenician Inscription from Čebel Ireš Daği," *AuOr* 7 (1989) 207–14.

31. *ANET* 287, 291, 294.

32. E. Lipiński, "Les Phéniciens à Ninive au temps des Sargonides: Ahoubasti, portier en chef," *Atti* 1, 1.125–34. The preservation of the initial *'alep* in his name is a feature of the Byblian dialect.

33. Idem, "Phéniciens en Assyrie: L'éponyme Milkiram et la surintendante Amat-Ashtart," *Atti* 2, 1.151–54. The eponym lent his name to the year. Short accented [a] usually becomes [o] at this time in Phoenician, but this change seems not to have taken place in the dialect of Byblos in verbs used in proper names, for example, Milk'asap and Milkiram: see W. R. Garr, *Dialect Geography of Syria–Palestine, 1000–586 B.C.E.* (Philadelphia: University of Pennsylvania Press, 1985; repr. Winona Lake, IN: Eisenbrauns, 2004) 33–35.

a room in the Temple of the Moon God Nana and his consort Ningal,[34] appropriately enough since the Festival of Adonis was linked to the phases of the new and waning moon. Another woman who was a priestess of Astarte is memorialized by a funerary urn that contains her bones (the bones of the dead were the pledge of their resurrection) gathered for her by her companion, ʾIttobaʿal.[35]

These named people are joined by the unnamed masons and craftsmen who went overseas and were buried at Caere in Italy, where their descendants more than a century later built a sanctuary for Astarte;[36] and by the merchants and traders who stayed in Byblos and whose inscribed and decorated seals reveal their names and aspirations.[37] One of these is Paṭʾisi, "Gift of Isis," who sees himself as a mythical griffin confronting a uraeus, and another is Milkiram who surrounds his name with Egyptian symbols of life and regeneration.[38] Byblos was fairly inconspicuous in the seventh-century bustle, but it was nevertheless a respected and very productive member of the international community.

Tyrian and Sidonian presence on the Syrian coast north of Byblos and its territory had been vital in the ninth and eighth centuries but dwindled in the seventh when Tyre went west, Sidon folded, and local Phoenician regimes, with Greek and Cypriot connivance, catered to the Assyrians. Al Mina in the eighth century was a Tyrian and Chalcidian station frequented by Cypriots, but in the seventh century, in keeping with the changes reflected in the new town plan, its dealing were mainly with Samos and Rhodes,[39] and it was the port of the Assyrian province of Kunulua to which it belonged.

Arvad, the island kingdom and traditional Sidonian confederate, provided a port and a navy to the Assyrians, and in the reigns of Esarhaddon and Ashurbanipal is listed, in tandem with Samsimuruna, in the western coalition. A new king, Yakinlu, who came to the throne late in the reign of Esarhaddon, was uncooperative. He confiscated the taxes and tolls due to the Assyrian port authority, prevented ships from docking there, killed the captain and looted the goods of any that did, and was generally unreceptive to Assyrian envoys. He was brought into line by Ashurbanipal, who imposed tribute on Arvad in addition to its naval commitment. When Yakinlu died, Ashurbanipal appointed one of his sons, ʿAzibaʿl, as Yakinlu's successor and kept the other nine in Nineveh as hostages.[40]

34. M. G. Amadasi Guzzo, "Two Phoenician Inscriptions Carved in Ivory: Again the Ur Box and the Sarepta Plaque," *Or* 59 (1990) 58–66; idem, "Varia Phoenicia," *RSF* 20 (1992) 95–104, esp. pp. 95–97; G. Garbini, "L'ancella del signore," *RSF* 18 (1990) 207–8; T. C. Mitchell, "The Phoenician Inscribed Ivory Box from Ur," *PEQ* 123 (1991) 119–28; P. Xella, "L'identità di *ʾdn* nell'iscrizione sulla scatola di Ur," *RSF* 20 (1992) 83–91.
35. É. Puech, "Un cratère phénicien inscrit: Rites et croyances," *Transeu* 8 (1994) 47–73, pls. 6–11.
36. M. A. Rizzo, "Alcune importazioni fenicie da Cerveteri," *Atti* 2, 3.1169–81.
37. Among the Byblian seals may be included *WSS* 264–65 #713, 270 #724, and 273 #735.
38. *WSS* 278 #747, 412 #1091.
39. J. Boardman, "The Excavated History of Al Mina," in *Ancient Greeks East and West* (ed. G. R. Tsetskhladze; Leiden: Brill, 1999) 135–61, esp. pp. 159–60.
40. F. Briquel-Chatonnet, "Arwad et l'empire assyrien," in *Ana šadî Labnāni lū allik. Beiträge zu altorientalischen und mittelmeerischen Kulturen: Festschrift für Wolfgang Röllig* (ed. B. Pongratz-

Arvad was in the province of Simirra, the capital of which, Sumur, at Tell Kazel, retained its distinctive Syrian and Phoenician mix, continued to do business with Cyprus, and perhaps developed closer ties with Byblos immediately to the south. These places, then, were involved in a peculiar dynamic. Arvad was part of the western alliance because it had the navy that Assyria needed. The other two were not directly part of this coalition but belonged with Arvad in a collateral network that was immediately subject to Assyria and gave it access to the Greek Mediterranean world.

The towns in Tyrian territory along the coast north of Mount Carmel maintained their distinctive provincial Phoenician character throughout the seventh century. South of Carmel, the towns and ports belonged to Tyre or Sidon, and south of these was the territory of the Philistines where Tyre and Byblos shared commercial and cultural hegemony.

The most northerly town in Tyrian territory was Sarepta, which had belonged to Sidon but was ceded to Tyre by Esarhaddon. There are ceramic imports from Cyprus in the earlier seventh century—miniature perfume bottles that combine Phoenician fashion (black lines on polished Red Slip) and form (mushroom-lip or neck-ridge juglets) with Cypriot technique (multiple brush- and compass-drawn concentric circles)—and from Rhodes in the latter part of the century.[41] The most distinctive Tyrian item is an inscribed ivory plaque found in a symposium (*mrzḥ*) club house (*bt ḥbr*) and dedicated to Tannit-ʿAstarte, a melding of Goddesses—Tannit of the Tyrians who now occupied the site and Astarte of the earlier Sidonian community—and a dual divinity of the sort especially popular among Cypriot Phoenicians.[42] There was an occupational gap at Sarepta at the end of the seventh century,[43] when Tyre began to feel the weight of the Babylonian Empire, and a cultural break is visible when life begins again in the sixth.

The Tyrian sites in western Galilee continued to prosper under Assyrian tutelage. ʾAchzib, 25 kilometers south of Tyre is known mainly from its three cemeteries. These seem to have been occupied by people of different origins, ethnicity, beliefs, and occupations, among them naval personnel and workers in the shipyards. There was a mortuary chapel associated with the northern cemetery, where child sacrifice was memorialized.[44] In the eastern cemetery, there were shaft tombs with benches on three walls, inhumation was the norm, pottery deposits included water jugs and storage

Leisten, H. Kühne, and P. Xella; Neukirchen-Vluyn: Neukirchener Verlag, 1997) 57–68, esp. pp. 64–65.

　41. R. B. Koehl, *Sarepta III: The Imported Bronze and Iron Age Wares from Area II, X* (Beirut: Librairie Orientale, 1986) 148.

　42. J. B. Pritchard, *Recovering Sarepta, a Phoenician City: Excavations at Sarafand, Lebanon, 1969–1974, by the University Museum of the University of Pennsylvania* (Princeton: Princeton University Press, 1978) 104–8, fig. 103; idem, "The Tanit Inscription from Sarepta," *PhWest*, 83–92, pl. 9; M. G. Amadasi Guzzo, "Two Phoenician Inscriptions Carved in Ivory: Again the Ur Box and the Sarepta Plaque," *Or* 59 (1990) 58–66; idem, "*Tanit-ʿštrt* e *Milk-ʿštrt*: ipotesi," *Or* 60 (1991) 82–91; P. Bordreuil, "Tanit du Liban (Nouveaux documents religieux phéniciens, III)," in *Phoenicia and the East Mediterranean in the First Millennium B.C.* (ed. E. Lipiński; Studia Phoenicia 5; Louvain: Peeters, 1987) 79–85, esp. pp. 81–82.

　43. W. P. Anderson, *Sarepta I: The Late Bronze and Iron Age Strata of Area II, Y* (Beirut: Lebanon University, 1988) 421.

　44. M. W. Prausnitz and E. Mazar, "Achzib," *NEAEHL* 1.32–36.

Fig. 4.1. Seal from ʿAkko, picturing a man with an ibex (IAA 73-216). Reproduced by permission of the Israel Antiquities Authority.

jars, most of the small finds were women's jewelry, and the tombs may have been prepared for potters and weavers as well as musicians and escorts from the busy harbor.

In the southern cemetery, there were built tombs and shaft tombs and, until the late seventh century when the practice stopped, cremation was as common as inhumation.[45] There are seven tombstones from this grave-yard, roughly finished and undecorated, and inscribed in an unprofessional scrawl with the name of the dead men:[46] most of them without parentage, one a blacksmith (*ḥnsk*), the rest stevedores or otherwise employed in the port. Among the terra-cottas, there were grotesque masks and amulets that ships from the town brought to Carthage.[47] Beautiful figurines of a seated pregnant woman are most characteristic of ʾAchzib, however, and in the

---

45. M. W. Prausnitz, "A Phoenician Krater from Akhziv," *OrAnt* 5 (1966) 177–88; idem, "Die Nekropolen von Akhziv und die Entwicklung der Keramik vom 10. bis zum 7. Jahrhundert v. Chr. in Akhziv, Samaria und Ashdod," *PhWest*, 31–44; P. Smith, L. Horwitz, and J. Zias, "Human Remains from the Iron Age Cemeteries at Akhziv, Part I: The Built Tomb from the Southern Cemetery," *RSF* 18 (1990) 137–50, pls. 12–15; M. Dayagi-Mendels, *The Akhziv Cemeteries: The Ben-Dor Excavations, 1941–1944* (Israel Antiquities Authority Reports 15; Jerusalem: Israel Antiquities Authority, 2002).

46. G. R. Driver, "Seals and Tombstones," *ADAJ* 2 (1953) 62–65, pl. 8:6–8; R. Hestrin, *Inscriptions Reveal: Documents from the Time of the Bible, the Mishna and the Talmud* (Jerusalem: Israel Museum, 1972) 144–45 ##142–43; B. Delavault and A. Lemaire, "Les inscriptions phéniciennes de Palestine," *RSF* 7 (1979) 1–39, pls. 1–15, #2–5, esp. pp. 3–4, pls. 1–3; F. M. Cross Jr., "Phoenician Tomb Stelae from Akhziv," in M. Dayagi-Mendels, *The Akhziv Cemeteries: The Ben-Dor Excavations, 1941–1944* (Israel Antiquities Authority Reports 15; Jerusalem: Israel Antiquities Authority, 2002) 169–73.

47. W. Culican, "Phoenician Demons," *JNES* 35 (1976) 21–24, fig. 1; E. Stern, "Phoenician Masks and Pendants," *PEQ* 108 (1976) 109–18, pls. 9–11.

sixth century traveled with these people to Cyprus and Carthage and the towns in Syria and Palestine frequented by their ships.[48]
ʿAkko, 15 kilometers south of ʾAchzib, came under Sidonian control for a time during the reigns of Luli and his successors but was returned to Tyrian management by Esarhaddon. One notable seventh-century relic from the site is a seal (see fig. 4.1) showing a man, preceded by an ibex, greeting a God dressed in Egyptian fashion who sits enthroned in front of a smoking incense stand, while behind him an attendant lifts a scepter, and a monkey raises its forepaws in adoration.[49] To this scene, which is drawn in the negative so as to be impressed positively, a positive text was added as a commentary, changing the magical seal into an amulet. Above the scene the owner inscribed his name, now lost, introduced by "This belongs to . . ."; and written vertically between the God and the incense stand is the name ʾElnaʿ ("Before El, Tremble!" *ʾl nʿ*), which occurs as a geographical name and may have been the owner's hometown.[50]
    Tel Kabri, between ʾAchzib and ʿAkko, was a Tyrian military outpost. In the seventh century, it was fortified by a casemate wall, and its pottery, which included east Greek wares, comprised transport and storage jars and dinner dishes suitable for the garrison and, probably, for its detachment of Greek or Cypro-Phoenician mercenaries.[51]
    There was similar pottery at Tell Keisan, as well as Assyrian pottery and a complete assemblage of coastal Phoenician wares like the wares at ʿAkko and ʾAchzib and, later in the century, pottery from Cyprus, Ionia, and Rhodes. But the place is noted especially for its basket-handled amphorae from Cyprus.[52] Tell Keisan, ancient ʿAchshaph or Kaspuna, was the Assyrian headquarters in this region between Tyre and Carmel and a distribution center for Phoenician goods, including textiles made locally and overseas. One of these products is the small unguent jar that made its way to Tell es-Saʿidiyeh, halfway between the Sea of Galilee and the Dead Sea in Transjordan, which is emblazoned with a doggerel Phoenician advertisement incised under its handle: *kul yušman / ʾiš laḥḥa biyya*, "All will be scented / who smear themselves with me."[53] Some of these places were destroyed in the Babylonian invasions at the end of the century, but all of them had thrived through their association with Tyre and with Assyrian incentives and encouragement.

---

48. W. Culican, "Dea Tyria Gravida," *Australian Journal of Biblical Archaeology* 1 (1969) 35–50; repr. *Opera Selecta: From Tyre to Tartessus* (Gothenburg: Åströms, 1986) 265–80.
    49. *WSS* 266–67 #716.
    50. There is a place in the vicinity of ʿAkko and ʾAchzib called Neʿiʿel (Josh 19:27), with the elements *ʾl* and *nʿ* in the opposite order.
    51. A. Kempinski and W. D. Niemeier, "Kabri, 1992," *IEJ* 43 (1993) 181–84.
    52. J. Briend and J.-B. Humbert, *Tell Keisan (1971–1976): Une cité phénicienne en Galilée* (Paris: Gabalda, 1980) 131–56; J.-B. Humbert, "Récents travaux à Tell Keisan (1979–1980)," *RB* 88 (1981) 373–98, pls. 8–10; J.-F. Salles, "À propos du niveau 4 de Tell Keisan," *Levant* 17 (1985) 203–4; J. Gunneweg and I. Perlman, "The Origin of 'Loop-Handle Jars' from Tell Keisan," *RB* 98 (1991) 591–99; J.-B. Humbert, "Keisan, Tell," *NEAEHL* 3.862–67.
    53. A. Lemaire, "Une inscription phénicienne de Tell es-Saʿidiyeh," *RSF* 10 (1982) 11–12, pl. 6. A vertical line separates the main clause from the following subordinate relative clause—a syntactical signal otherwise known only in Moabite—and suggests a poetic cadence for the text.

The coastal territory between Mount Carmel and Joppa had been parceled out to Sidon and Byblos, but they abandoned places such as Tel Mevorakh and Tel Michal sometime between the tenth and the sixth centuries, and Sidon lost Dor to Tyre in the early seventh century. Dor was the capital of the Assyrian province named after it and a strategic port for trade between Cyprus and the coastal plains.[54]

The most interesting find from the seventh-century city is a scapula with a fragmentary boat scene and a Cypriot Syllabic inscription.[55] On the left, a ship pulls away from the dock: three rowers wearing Egyptian-style caps look out to sea and the captain, standing in the stern, looks back to shore, his left hand to his forehead in a gesture of supplication; the stern is decorated with a duck's head facing forward, and a railing on which a tarpaulin could be hung stretches from there to the bow. On the shore, a woman who wears a veil and a long embroidered robe stands in a doorway and looks out to sea at the departing ship, with a libation bowl in her raised right hand and her left arm extended in entreaty. Behind her, to the right of this scene and facing away from it, a priest wearing an Egyptian wig raises his left hand in veneration of an Assyrian-style Tree-of-Life that stands in a portable shrine, under an awning draped over a rope-and-pole device. On the reverse, an inscription identifies the man, perhaps a captain like the one portrayed, who dedicated the scapula, perhaps in a temple pavilion like the one depicted in the scene. Of special interest are the personal grief and trepidation that preceded a voyage, the public rituals performed when setting out on an overseas voyage, and the eclectic styles (Egyptian, Assyrian, Cypriot, and Phoenician), typical of the Tyrian mentality and most likely representative of the mixed population and culture of the port city at this time.

Six and one-half kilometers north of Dor and 8 kilometers south of Mount Carmel was the port of ʿAtlit. It belonged to Sidon in the Persian period, and the harbor may have been used by Sidonians in the late eighth or early seventh century, but it seems likely that the port was built, and the town with it, when this whole stretch of coastline was ceded to Tyre. ʿAtlit is a promontory jutting half a kilometer northward into the Sea. South of the promontory is the natural harbor of ʿAtlit Bay, and northeast of it is the artificial harbor.[56] This consisted of perpendicularly aligned moles, on the north side extending from the promontory and on the east reaching out from the shore, built of large and tightly fitted ashlar blocks. Quays similarly built joined them at right angles along the promontory and along the shore, and towers at intervals and at the end of the moles served as warehouses and stores.[57]

---

54. E. Stern, *Archaeology of the Land of the Bible, II: The Assyrian, Babylonian, and Persian Periods, 732–332 BCE* (New York: Doubleday, 2001) 50–101.

55. Idem, "A Phoenician-Cypriote Votive Scapula from Tel Dor: A Maritime Scene," *IEJ* 44 (1994) 1–12.

56. G. Markoe, *Phoenicians* (London: British Museum, 2000) 69–70.

57. A. Raban, "The Heritage of Ancient Harbour Engineering in Cyprus and the Levant," in *Cyprus and the Sea* (ed. V. Karageorghis and D. Michaelides; Nicosia: University of Cyprus, 1995) 139–88, esp. pp. 154–58; idem, "Near Eastern Harbors: Thirteenth–Seventh Centuries BCE,"

The earliest burials are cremations, but the later, when ʿAtlit belonged to Sidon, were inhumations in rock-cut shaft tombs.[58] The earliest graves were of adults and of children whose bodies had been burned and buried in the sand. The pottery associated with them was local, coarse, and domestic (bowls, jugs, cooking pots, lamps and the like) or elegant Red Slip and Black-on-Red wares, or White Painted pottery from Cyprus decorated with zigzags and encircling bands. The seals and amulets from the time of Tyrian occupation, mostly from the sixth century, often depict Melqart in his Greek guise as Heracles,[59] and small finds have some of their better parallels in Sardinia.[60] Two large, bustling ports situated so close to each other as were Dor and ʿAtlit are signs of Tyre's prosperity in the seventh century. But their proximity may also suggest that the ports were specialized, with Dor, for instance, importing from Cyprus, ʿAtlit exporting to the western Mediterranean, and both of them counting on the various inland markets of Judah, Transjordan, and Philistia.

The Mainland Affiliates of the Phoenicians: The Western Coalition of the Assyrian Empire

The mainland countries in the western coalition were integral to the political, cultural, and commercial network centered on Tyre. They were more or less Phoenician in the seventh century, and their organization and interests reflect the dynamic of the Tyrian enterprise and are carried along in the vector of the Assyrian Empire. What is not known directly about Tyre, Sidon, and Byblos can be surmised and reconstructed on the analogy of their inland neighbors.

Judah

Judah was a faithful, treaty-bound vassal of Assyria in the seventh century, ruled by kings of the Davidic Dynasty in uninterrupted succession. In 701 B.C.E., Hezekiah, through interference in Philistine affairs, lost 46 towns and their territories to Ashdod, Ekron, and Gaza[61] and was left "like a bird in a cage" in Jerusalem. This city, which he had made the religious center of the nation, became the economic and cultural hub of a trim city-state in the half-century reign of his son and successor, Manasseh.[62] At the end

---

MPT, 428–38; idem, "Conceptual Technology of Phoenician Harbours in the Levant," *Actas* 4, 3.1095–1106.

58. C. N. Johns, "Excavations at Atlit (1930–1931): The Southeastern Cemetery," *QDAP* 2 (1933) 41–104, pls. 14–37; idem, "Excavations at Pilgrims' Castle, ʿAtlit (1933): Cremated Burials of Phoenician Origin," *QDAP* 6 (1937) 121–52; C. N. Johns, A. Raban, and E. Linder, "ʿAtlit," *NEAEHL* 1.112–20.

59. O. Keel, *Corpus der Stempelsiegel-Amulette aus Palästina/Israel: Katalog, Band I* (Göttingen: Vandenhoeck & Ruprecht, 1997) 758–77, ##1–26.

60. G. Hölbl, *Ägyptisches Kulturgut im phönikischen und punischen Sardinien* (Leiden: Brill, 1986) 39–42.

61. Some of these towns, such as Beth Shemesh, were simply abandoned in the seventh century, while their Philistine neighbors, in this case Timnah (Tel Batash), flourished: see S. Bunimovitz and Z. Lederman, "The Final Destruction of Beth Shemesh and the *Pax Assyriaca* in the Judean Shephelah," *TA* 30 (2003) 3–26.

62. A. F. Rainey, "Manasseh, King of Judah, in the Whirlpool of the Seventh Century B.C.E.," in *kinattūtu ša dārâti: Raphael Kutscher Memorial Volume* (ed. A. F. Rainey; Tel Aviv: Tel Aviv University Press, 1993) 147–64; I. Finkelstein, "The Archaeology of the Days of Manasseh," in *Scripture*

of the century, when Assyria was losing its grip, his grandson Josiah reorganized the kingdom on a retrograde tribal model and squandered the goodwill of nations through exclusive religious reform and by misguided meddling in world affairs.[63] In 586 B.C.E., Jerusalem was captured and sacked by the Babylonians, and a century of prosperity and splendid achievement crumbled in its hands.

An indicator of the power and centralized organization of this hereditary kingdom is the large number and general uniformity of its personal seals.[64] There are many seals of government officials: there are seals of named kings, and of "The King"; seals of his family—"Daughter (*bt*) of the King" and "Son (*bn*) of the King"; seals of the palace manager, the one "who is in charge of the household" (*'šr 'l hbyt*) and of retainers simply called "servant" (*'bd*) of the king (see, for example, fig. 4.2); there are seals of officers (*šr*), of the mayor of Jerusalem (*šr h'r*), of the prison warden (*š'r hmsgr*), and of the man in charge of public works (*'šr 'l hms*); seals of scribes (*hspr*) and priests (*hkhn*), who may or may not have been independent of the palace. Some seals include a regnal year and the name of a man or a town and probably had to with records of tithes or taxes. Some seals belonging to women have only their name; others also identify them as the wife or the daughter of some named man.

There are hundreds of men's seals, at least ten times as many as there are in neighboring countries, and most of them have just the man's name and patronymic, separated by a double line, but without any representation or design. When they are iconic and locally inspired, they usually represent plants such as pomegranates and floral patterns, animals (a horse, a dog, a roaring lion, an ibex running, a grazing doe), a fish, or a bird. Others have linear or geometric designs or astronomical features—a winged sun, a crescent moon, sometimes in association with an altar, or a star. Human figures are rare and most often generic, although there is a seal with girls dancing around a palm tree, another with a chain of dancing girls, one with the portrait of a winged and naked Goddess, and one with a winged God facing another winged creature.

The iconography of other seals is inspired by Egyptian motifs, directly via Judah's traditional Egyptian connections, or indirectly through familiarity with the Phoenician repertory: scarabs, an *ankh* sign, a uraeus, Horus seated on a lotus, a lotus blossom, or the eye of Horus. All of these seals

---

and Other Artifacts: Essays on the Bible and Archaeology in Honor of Philip J. King (ed. M. D. Coogan, J. C. Exum, and L. E. Stager; Louisville: Westminster John Knox, 1994) 169–84.

63. N. Naʾaman, "The Kingdom of Judah under Josiah," *TA* 18 (1991) 3–71.

64. N. Avigad and B. Sass, *Corpus of West Semitic Stamp Seals* (Jerusalem: Israel Academy of Sciences and Humanities, 1997) 49–263, ##1–711; R. Deutsch, *Messages from the Past: Hebrew Bullae from the Time of Isaiah through the Destruction of the First Temple. Shlomo Moussaieff Collection and an Up to Date Corpus* (Tel Aviv–Jaffa: Archaeological Center, 1999); R. Deutsch and A. Lemaire, *Biblical Period Personal Seals in the Shlomo Moussaieff Collection* (Tel Aviv–Jaffa: Archaeological Center, 2000); N. Avigad, M. Heltzer, and A. Lemaire, *West Semitic Seals: Eighth–Sixth Centuries BCE* (The Reuben and Edith Hecht Museum Collection B; Haifa: University of Haifa Press, 2000); R. Deutsch, *Biblical Period Hebrew Bullae: The Josef Chaim Kaufman Collection* (Tel Aviv–Jaffa: Archaeological Center, 2003); idem, "A Hoard of Fifty Hebrew Clay Bullae from the Time of Hezekiah," in *Shlomo: Studies in Epigraphy, Iconography, History and Archaeology in Honor of Shlomo Moussaieff* (ed. R. Deutsch; Tel Aviv–Jaffa: Archaeological Center, 2003) 45–98.

were used on papyrus documents (of the numerous bullae, many have marks of the string that bound the papyrus on their reverse), and they belonged—as orders, receipts, reports, or directives—to artisans, merchants, traders, and administrators. Their large number suggests that their owners were not working in a competitive market but were members of a monopoly that operated through a hierarchically arranged local, regional, and national network. Their aniconism, which was sponsored by the court and the religious institutions interested in promoting the exclusive worship of the once dynastic and now political, national, and transcendent God, suggests that the plain seals with a name and patronymic may have been the signets of public servants, while those with pictures or designs belonged to independent entrepreneurs and secular business people who had more personal, traditional, or international tastes.

The seals are an indicator of widespread literacy in seventh-century Judah. This followed an educational policy, the focus of which was political and religious, and which is also manifested in occasional texts (letters, lists, and the like) and in an abundant and sophisticated literature. The occasional texts are inscriptions from Jerusalem, the intellectual capital of Judah, and from settlements on the periphery of the kingdom, where soldiers, merchants, and farmers resided; the literature is in the many biblical texts that were composed, in Jerusalem, in these exciting and vibrant times. The smaller sites provide a glimpse into Judean society and economy and into the ordinary links in the chain of international relations. Jerusalem is the prime analogate for the spiritual revival that accompanied the universal political, social, and economic upswing in the seventh century, mainly motivated by Assyria, but which is less palpable in the countries of the Tyrian alliance the archives and literatures of which were never published and have not survived.

From a small and short-lived site near Yabneh Yam, 15 kilometers south of Joppa and less than half a kilometer from the coast, there is an ostracon with a letter from a Judean farmhand to the commandant of his community protesting the injustice that has been done to him.[65] The letter is written in a good practiced hand and the case, based on laws codified in the Bible,[66] is presented in a logical, literary, and persuasive factum. The plaintiff was working in the grain harvest, and on a particular day, the eve of the Sabbath, was accused of not completing the tasks assigned to him—reaping, stooking, and storing—specifically of not storing the grain in the barn.[67] The letter is in Hebrew, the foreman, who was in charge of

---

65. J. Naveh, "A Hebrew Letter from the Seventh Century B.C.," *IEJ* 10 (1960) 129–39, pl. 17; idem, "Some Notes on the Reading of the Meṣad Ḥashavyahu Letter," *IEJ* 14 (1964) 158–59; S. B. Parker, *Stories in Scripture and Inscriptions: Comparative Studies in Northwest Semitic Inscriptions and the Hebrew Bible* (Oxford: Oxford University Press, 1997) 13–35.

66. The earlier form of the law is in Exod 22:25–26, in the context of laws dealing with the disadvantaged, and was included in the seventh-century code. The version in Deut 24:10–15, which belongs to the sixth-century revision of the code, rephrases the law and puts it in the context of a just economy.

67. The emphasis throughout the factum is on storing (*'sm*) the grain, the last job of a harvester: "Your servant was a harvester, your servant had stored on the estate, and your servant harvested, and stooked, and stored as usual before the Sabbath. Just when your servant had stooked the harvest and stored as usual, along came Hoshaʿyahu son of Shubay and took the

Fig. 4.2. Judean titled seal, picturing a rooster (IAA 32.2525). Reproduced by permission of the Israel Antiquities Authority. Photo by: Miki Koren.

public works (*šr ḥms*), had a Judean name, and the commandant (*šr*) was a Judean government official who was expected to know and observe the law of Judah.

However, Yabneh Yam is in Philistine territory (there is a Philistine inscription from nearby ʿAzor), and the pottery assemblage, which is indigenous coastal, contains enough east Greek wares (Ionian cups, Rhodian wine jugs, Samian cooking pots and transport amphorae) to suggest that

garment of your servant. Just as I had finished my harvesting that particular day, he took the garment of your servant. And all my brothers have testified on my behalf, those harvesting with me in the heat of the sun, my brothers have testified that I am innocent in the matter of the storing (*mʾ[s]m*)."

the site billeted Greek mercenaries or Greco-Phoenicians from Kition.[68] There was similar pottery in all the Philistine and Phoenician coastal towns and settlements, in both Syria and Palestine, and there were Greek garrisons at Tel Kabri and Tell Keisan, but there was no Greek pottery and there were no Greek troops in Judah.[69] This site near Yabneh Yam, therefore, illustrates how Judah could cooperate with the Philistines; how its local economy, which in this case, and generally, was under the control of the central government, was based in agriculture; and how Judah's involvement in the Tyrian trade network could simply consist of supplying migrant labor and food to its neighbors.

The southern part of Judah flourished in the seventh century, partly because this region made up for the territory that Judah had lost to Philistia in the west, and partly, or perhaps mainly, because of booming trade with Edom and Arabia. The outpost at Ḥorvat ʿUza, 30 kilometers east of Beersheba, has yielded ostraca that illustrate how a small trading center in the Negeb worked. There is a Hebrew ostracon, written in an untrained hand, that has the names and the patronymics of three men from three different towns in the Negeb who worked for ʾAḥiqam, son of Menaḥḥem: they could have been soldiers and he their captain, or he might have been involved in overland trade with Edom, and they would have been his business associates.[70]

---

68. J. Naveh, "Writing and Scripts in Seventh-Century B.C.E. Philistia: The New Evidence from Tell Jemmeh," *IEJ* 35 (1985) 8–21, pls. 1–3, esp. p. 18, fig. 4:2; A. Fantalkin, "Meẓad Ḥashavyahu: Its Material Culture and Historical Background," *TA* 28 (2001) 3–167; R. Wenning, "Nachrichten über Griechen in Palästina in der Eisenzeit," in *Proceedings of the First International Congress on the Hellenic Diaspora from Antiquity to Modern Times, Volume I: From Antiquity to 1453* (ed. J. M. Fossey; Amsterdam: Gieben, 1991) 207–19; J. C. Waldbaum and J. Magness, "The Chronology of Early Greek Pottery: New Evidence from Seventh-Century B.C. Destruction Levels in Israel," *AJA* 101 (1997) 23–40.

69. A.-M. Collombier, "Céramique grecque et échanges en Mediterrr(née orientale: Chypre et la côte syro-phénicienne (fin VIIIe–fin IVe av. J.-C.)," in *Phoenicia and the East Mediterranean in the First Millennium B.C.* (ed. E. Lipiński; Studia Phoenicia 5; Louvain: Peeters, 1987) 239–48; G. Lehmann, "Trends in the Local Pottery Development of the Late Iron Age and Persian Period in Syria and Lebanon, ca. 700 to 300 B.C.," *BASOR* 311 (1998) 7–37.

W. D. Niemeier, "Archaic Greeks in the Orient: Textual and Archaeological Evidence," *BASOR* 322 (2001) 11–32.

See P. E. Dion, "Les *ktym* de Tel Arad: Grecs ou Phéniciens?" *RB* 99 (1992) 70–97. The letters *qš* on two bowls at Arad (Y. Aharoni, *Arad Inscriptions* [Jerusalem: Israel Exploration Society, 1981 115–17 ##102–3) are the name of the Edomite God Qaws written by a Phoenician from Kition, where the diphthong [*aw*] was pronounced [*ô*] and, like any vowel, was not written, and where *samek* (*s*) was pronounced *šin* (*š*), whence the writing *qš* and the pronunciation Qôš.The syncretism and eclecticism involved in this invocation of an Edomite God by Phoenicians were considered enrichments and were typical of the religious mentality in Kition. On the bowls, see F. M. Cross, "Two Offering Dishes with Phoenician Inscriptions from the Sanctuary of ʿArad," *BASOR* 235 (1979) 75–77; N. Naʾaman, "The Abandonment of Cult Places in the Kingdoms of Israel and Judah as Acts of Cult Reform," *UF* 34 (2002) 585–602, esp. pp. 597–98.

70. I. Beit-Arieh, "The Ostracon of Aḥiqam from Ḥorvat ʿUza," *TA* 13 (1986) 40–45, pl. 2. The first word, reconstructed as [ʿ]*lm*, is a label from the root ʿ*ly*, "to go up," which sometimes has a military connotation, or from the root ʿ*ll*, "to act," and so identifies the three men as his "escort" or "agents."

There is also an ostracon written in Edomite with instructions from the cult center at Ḥorvat Qitmit, 10 kilometers to the southwest:[71] "Says Lamelek: Say to Bilbil, 'Are you well? I invoke blessings on you by Qaws. And now: Provide the meal which is in the keeping of ʾAḥiʾimmî and offer up ʿAzaʾel on the altar, today, lest the meal become rancid.'" The format of the instructions resembles that of contemporary Hebrew letters from nearby Arad, with the expected substitution of the Edomite God Qaws for Yahweh of Judah in the salutation. The instructions are also comparable to the prescriptions for the ritual of the Scapegoat ʿAzaʾzel, except that the Edomite custom includes an offering of meal and the sacrifice of a goat ("The Goat-of-El"), whereas the biblical rite requires two goats, one of which was to be offered in sacrifice in Jerusalem, while the other is to be kept alive and sent out into the wilderness—where Ḥorvat ʿUza was located—to ʿAzaʾzel (Lev 16:7–10).

A third ostracon, quite fragmentary, has the remains of a prophetic text, written in literary Hebrew, apparently in poetic form, by a skilled scribe.[72] The prophecy, which may have originated in Jerusalem, calls for conversion and, of course, because the genre requires it, threatens judgment for noncompliance. Ḥorvat ʿUza, clearly, was a community where Edomites and Judeans convened and worked cooperatively, most likely in local and long-distance trade, and probably under the central authority in Jerusalem.

Tell ʿIra, halfway between Ḥorvat ʿUza and Beersheba, has Edomite pottery, large transport jars made in the vicinity of Jerusalem and many with potters' marks, as well as standard and unusual clay figurines made locally, and some Hebrew inscriptions.[73] One of these, like the first from Ḥorvat ʿUza, is a list of three men, with names or nicknames, but without patronymics, who are described as "the bodyguard of Berekiah," presumably armed men who traveled with him and protected him from brigands, the usual bane of merchants and traders.[74] Another is a fragmentary letter containing a report ("Your servant . . . has written to report . . ."), another a receipt, and others are personal or place-names written on jars to indicate their origin or their destination.[75]

71. Idem, and B. Cresson, "An Edomite Ostracon from Horvat ʿUza," *TA* 12 (1985) 96–101; H. Misgav, "Two Notes on the Ostraca from Horvat ʿUza," *IEJ* 40 (1990) 215–17. I. Beit-Arieh, "New Data on the Relationship between Judah and Edom toward the End of the Iron Age," in *Recent Excavations in Israel: Studies in Iron Age Archaeology* (ed. S. Gitin and W. G. Dever; AASOR 49; Winona Lake, IN: Eisenbrauns, 1989) 125–31.

72. Idem, "A Literary Ostracon from Horvat ʿUza," *TA* 20 (1993) 55–65; F. M. Cross, "An Ostracon in Literary Hebrew from Ḥorvat ʿUza," in *The Archaeology of Jordan and Beyond: Essays in Honor of James A. Sauer* (ed. L. E. Stager, J. A. Greene, M. D. Coogan; Studies in the Archaeology and History of the Levant 1; Winona Lake, IN: Eisenbrauns, 2000) 111–13; repr. idem, *Leaves from an Epigrapher's Notebook: Collected Papers in Hebrew and West Semitic Palaeography and Epigraphy* (HSS 51; Winona Lake, IN: Eisenbrauns, 2003) 135–37.

73. I. Beit-Arieh, ed., *Tel ʿIra: A Stronghold in the Biblical Negev* (Tel Aviv: Institute of Archaeology, 1999).

74. Idem, "A First Temple Period Census Document," *PEQ* 115 (1983) 105–8. One of the three had a normal sentence-name, "Yahweh-Requites," but the others were called "Baldy" (*gbḥ*) and "Heavy" (*mwqr*).

75. Idem, ed., *Tel ʿIra*, 405–11.

These places in the Negeb were not on the main roads but presumably were part of the overland trade network, regulated by Jerusalem, that connected Beersheba to the coast and to Edom and Arabia. Their administrators, not surprisingly, liked to keep lists and had subordinates who filed reports. One of their scribes was trained in a local country school, but their people were literate, religious, and susceptible to persuasion by a sophisticated, and instructive, missive from the city. In an integrated and centralized system such as Judah's, these rural settlements were the foundation of the new society and economy.

A perception of how Jerusalem functioned at the heart of this system is available in the literature it fostered. Some of it was prophecy, such as the noncanonical letter to Ḥorvat ʿUza, and some of it was history and law. Its most interesting aspect, its most illuminating feature in an increasingly international society, was its borrowings from the literatures of the world. Seventh-century Jerusalem, at least in this sense, was the paradigm of the intellectual revolution fostered by Assyria and made possible by the Phoenician construction of a common world.[76]

Babylonian and Assyrian literature influenced the expression of Judah's basic beliefs. The story of creation in the first chapter of Genesis draws on the ancient and canonical Babylonian version, in which Marduk was the protagonist in overcoming chaos, and it is moved by more recent or contemporary astronomical theories that demystified the planets and promoted the worship of a supreme God.[77] The same myth, the *Enūma elish*, supplies the materials for the description of the exodus as a journey that took the people from Egypt, brought them through the sea on dry ground, and culminated in the construction of a tabernacle and temple for their God. The story of creation in the second chapter of Genesis begins like the *Enūma elish* (in both, the beginning is signaled by the phrase "on the day"), but it continues with the themes of humanity and marriage unraveled in *Atrahasis,* and of self-transcendence developed in *Gilgamesh*: the setting for the story is the Garden of Eden, which is modeled on the gardens of Paradise built by Assyrian and Judean kings,[78] and is situated surreally in Jerusalem and between the Tigris and the Euphrates. The life-spans of the antediluvians were calculated with the help of Babylonian mathematics,[79] and the flood story follows in every detail the version in *Gilgamesh*.

The depth of Assyrian influence on Judeans' thinking, beliefs, and practices is most striking in the borrowing of the Assyrian treaty format (the instrument of stable and enduring relations among nations) to express their

76. B. Peckham, *History and Prophecy: The Development of Late Judean Literary Traditions* (New York: Doubleday, 1993).

77. B. Halpern, "Late Israelite Astronomies and the Early Greeks," in *Symbiosis, Symbolism, and the Power of the Past: Canaan, Ancient Israel, and Their Neighbors from the Late Bronze Age through Roman Palaestina* (ed. W. G. Dever and S. Gitin; Winona Lake, IN: Eisenbrauns, 2003) 323–52.

78. L. E. Stager, "Jerusalem and the Garden of Eden," *ErIsr* 26 (F. M. Cross Volume; 1999) 183*–94*; E. Cook, "Near Eastern Sources for the Palace of Alkinoos," *AJA* 108 (2004) 43–77.

79. D. W. Young, "On the Application of Numbers from Babylonian Mathematics to Biblical Life Spans and Epochs," *ZAW* 100 (1988) 331–61; idem, "The Influence of Babylonian Algebra on Longevity among the Antediluvians," *ZAW* 102 (1990) 321–35.

covenant relationship with their God.[80] It was an unprecedented, unparalleled, and astonishing move (to contemporary critics it was their "covenant with death"), leading to centralization and the consequent political, economic, and social reform that allowed the country to slip into the western alliance and the Tyrian network. It reveals the impact of the empire, but it also indicates very clearly that the people of Judah and Jerusalem thought of their treaty with Assyria as a real blessing, in no sense a constraint, but a divinely inspired liberation.[81]

The cities of Phoenicia were most evidently influential in the arts and crafts and commerce, but they also contributed to the literary renaissance in Judah. This may have been indirectly through the people of North Israel with whom the Phoenicians, quondam Canaanites, were affiliated or directly by regular contact with Phoenicians in Jerusalem or in the coastal regions where Tyrians, especially, had settled. An obvious instance is the biblical story of Joseph (the eponym of the northern tribes), which is modeled on and actually refers to the legends of Adonis, the God of Byblos, whose story was told and whose rites were practiced in Samaria.

Less obvious but just as startling is an allusion in the preface to the flood story in Genesis to a Greek tradition on the causes of the Trojan War.[82] In this preface and in the Hesiodic tradition to which it alludes, the motive for the catastrophe, the flood or the war, was that the Gods had taken beautiful women as their wives and had produced a heroic race of demigods who threatened God's, or Zeus's, divine prerogative. The preface is just an allusion to this alternative tradition, which is not developed (a device that this particular writer regularly uses) but that would have been familiar to readers of the story. This alternative interpretation might have been learned from the world travelers who reached coastal Phoenicia and Philistia, or it could have been brought to Jerusalem by Tyrians who went regularly to central Greece, but the literati of Judah and Jerusalem were obviously receptive and delighted.

A third instance is similar. It is the incorporation of a Phoenician world view, which also has resonances in Hesiod and the Greek cosmologists, into the early chapters of Genesis by a sixth-century Judean writer filling out the seventh-century story of the origin of the world. This view was compiled by Philo of Byblos[83] around 100 C.E. from the ancient legends and lore of

80. S. Parpola, "Assyria's Expansion in the 8th and 7th Centuries and Its Long-Term Repercussions in the West," in *Symbiosis, Symbolism, and the Power of the Past: Canaan, Ancient Israel, and Their Neighbors from the Late Bronze Age through Roman Palaestina* (ed. W. G. Dever and S. Gitin; Winona Lake, IN: Eisenbrauns, 2003) 99–111.

81. Isa 28:15. The covenant with Yahweh is called a "treaty" (Deut 5:2–3) or an "oath" (Deut 29:11) or a "blessing" (2 Kgs 18:31), and their treaty with Assyria is described in the exact terms of their covenant with God (2 Kgs 18:31–32).

82. R. S. Hendel, "Of Demigods and the Deluge: Toward an Interpretation of Genesis 6:1–4," *JBL* 106 (1987) 13–26.

83. H. W. Attridge and R. A. Oden Jr., *Philo of Byblos*, The Phoenician History: *Introduction, Critical Text, Translation, Notes* (CBQ Monograph 9; Washington, DC: Catholic Biblical Association, 1981); J. Ebach, *Weltentstehung und Kulturentwicklung bei Philo von Byblos: Ein Beitrag zur Überlieferung der biblischen Urgeschichte im Rahmen des altorientalischen und antiken Schöpfungsglaubens* (Beiträge zur Wissenschaft vom Alten und Neuen Testament 108; Stuttgart: Kohlhammer, 1979).

Tyre, Sidon, and Byblos and was presented from four different perspectives. The first is cosmological and, like the beginning of Genesis, explains the creation of the world, animals, and plants in the same sequence and using the same or equivalent terms, with some differences in interpretation. In the Phoenician version, for instance, there were "Observers of the Heavens" who worshiped the sun, the moon, the stars, and the great constellations, but in the biblical version these astronomical elements are denuded of their divinity and incorporated into the workings of the cosmic clock.

The second perspective is cosmogonical and goes over the same material to describe the inhabited world: the wind and darkness of the first telling, for instance, acquire names, the first man is born, and he discovers nourishment from trees—all this in the Genesis sequence but in a factual, non-narrative account. The third is ethnographic and recounts, with allusion to Tyre and Sidon, the origins of civilization, and this also has parallels in Genesis asides on the origin of clothing, strife, agriculture, pastoralism, urbanism, metalworking, music, wine, worship, and the like.

The last perspective is theological and traces the origin and succession of the Gods, beginning with the Gods of Byblos, and even this shows up in Genesis with random references to the epithets of the olden Gods. Judeans, as these examples suggest, went eagerly into the seventh century, rewriting their history to show how they belonged to the modern world and how the world belonged to them, driving the timid among them to warn them not to abandon their traditional ways.

Judah exemplifies the impact of seventh-century changes on small countries caught up in the organization and enthusiasm of a successful imperial system. These included everything from large-scale reorganization to details of a written code and a legal system accessible to all, from foreign trade to local commerce, from farming to schooling. It differed from the other countries in the network by keeping records of these changes, some critical and some approving, and by writing histories that traced its cultural development. There was a great deal more to the seventh century than politics and economics, and Judah is a window to what this was and what it meant.

Transjordan

The Transjordanian states, Moab, Edom, and Ammon, were tributaries of Assyria in the seventh century. They were, each in its own way, aligned with Judah and Philistia in the Tyrian network and were important intermediaries in the Arabian transit trade with Nineveh. Assyrian influence, especially the dent of Assyrian aggression, was more acute in northerly Ammon,[84] and Judean enterprise and commercial organization were predominant in the more southerly Moab and Edom. The involvement of these states in the Tyrian network is emblematic of the swirl and excitement among native peoples and established nations created by the enthusiasm that pervaded the new world discovered by the Phoenicians.

---

84. C.-M. Bennett, "Neo-Assyrian Influence in Transjordan," in *Studies in the History and Archaeology of Jordan, I* (ed. A. Hadidi; Amman: Department of Antiquities, 1982) 181–87.

Edom

Edom occupied the land from the southern tip of the Dead Sea to the
Gulf of ʿAqaba, and from the Wadi Araba, the continuation of the Jordan
Valley, to the desert fringe about 100 kilometers to the east. In the seventh
century, as an Assyrian protectorate, Edom expanded (there were, for instance, many new agricultural communities) and flourished.[85] The Wadi
Feinan copper mines, in the northwestern part of the country, achieved
their maximum output, and huge slag heaps indicate that thousands of
tons of metal were produced for export.[86] There were new towns, and the
more important were established along the major north–south trade route,
the King's Highway, leading to the Red Sea and Arabia: Bozrah (Tell el-
Buseirah), capital of Edom, Tawilan, Petra (Umm el-Biyara), and ʿAqaba
(Tell el-Kheleifeh). The Wadi Feinan is due east of the Beersheba valley in
Judah, where Edomite merchants and traders took up residence, and many
other Edomite towns, settlements, and outposts were scattered along these
southern Judean roads leading to Philistia.[87] Edom's business, apart from
agricultural products and copper, was managing the toll roads from South
Arabia, through the Negeb of southern Judah, to the coastal cities of Philistia, possibly to Gaza, perhaps (as in the eighth century) to Ashdod and
Ekron.[88]

Edomite pottery has been found at numerous sites in the Negeb, along
the routes followed by individual traders who were working for themselves,
in syndicates, or in the service of the royal court. The everyday wares are
little different from the local wares of these southern regions, but the decorated wares, which imitate Assyrian pottery and metalwork and Phoenician
painted and burnished wares, are typically Edomite and become increasingly popular as the seventh century progresses.[89] ʿAqaba, the gateway for

85. E. A. Knauf, "The Cultral Impact of Secondary State Formation: The Cases of the Edomites
and the Moabites," in *Early Edom and Moab: The Beginning of the Iron Age in Southern Jordan* (ed.
P. Bienkowski; Sheffield Archaeological Monographs 7; Sheffield: Collis, 1992) 47–54.

86. E. A. Knauf and C. J. Lenzen, "Edomite Copper Industry," in *Studies in the History and
Archaeology of Jordan, III* (ed. A. Hadidi; London: Routledge & Kegan Paul, 1987) 83–88; P. Bien-
kowski, "The Origins and Development of Edom," in *Nuove fondazioni nel Vicino Oriente antico:
Realtà e ideologia* (ed. S. Mazzoni; Pisa: Giardini, 1994) 253–68.

87. J. R. Bartlett, "Edomites and Idumaeans," *PEQ* 131 (1999) 102–14.

88. L. Singer-Avitz, "Beersheba: A Gateway Community in Southern Arabia Long-Distance
Trade in the Eighth Century B.C.E.," *TA* 26 (1999) 3–74, esp. p. 58.

In an Assyrian letter from about 715 B.C.E. that lists the ambassadors who brought tribute to
Nimrud, a first group includes ambassadors from Egypt, Gaza, Judah, Moab, and Ammon who
arrived on the twelfth of the month; and a second group that arrived later includes the emissaries
from Edom, Ashdod, and Ekron: see H. W. F. Saggs, "The Nimrud Letters, 1952, Part II: Relations
with the West," *Iraq* 17 (1955) 126–60, Letter 16, pp. 134–35; M. Weippert, "The Relations of
the States East of the Jordan with the Mesopotamian Powers during the First Millennium BC," in
Studies in the History and Archaeology of Jordan, III (ed. A. Hadidi; London: Routledge & Kegan Paul,
1987) 97–105, esp. p. 100; A. R. Millard, "Assyrian Involvement in Edom," in *Early Edom and
Moab: The Beginning of the Iron Age in Southern Jordan* (ed. P. Bienkowski; Sheffield Archaeological
Monographs 7; Sheffield: Collis, 1992) 35–39.

89. P. J. Parr, "Edom and the Hejaz," in ibid., 41–46; S. Hart, "Area D at Buseirah and Edomite
Chronology," in *Trade, Contact, and the Movement of Peoples in the Eastern Mediterranean: Studies
in Honour of J. Basil Hennessy* (ed. S. Bourke and J.-P. Descoeudres; Mediterranean Archaeology
Supplement 3; Sydney: Meditarch, 1995) 241–64.

Arabian trade—in gold, precious stones, camels, spices, and fragrances—had wares of both kinds as well as Judean, Midianite, Greek, Arabian and Egyptian pottery. Beersheba, at the other end of the trade routes, had mostly Judean wares but with a mixture of coastal, Edomite, and Egyptian pottery types.[90] An ostracon from Arad, in the territory of Judah but within the same trade network, contains a list of merchants' names, including a Judean, an Edomite, and two Phoenicians called Eshmnʾadonay, a syncretistic name and a favorite at Kition in Cyprus.[91] Two of the sites, ʿEn Haseva, near the western border of Edom, and Ḥorvat Qitmit, just inside the eastern border of Judah, featured wayside shrines where travelers could offer incense and libations and dedicate cylindrical stands to which (with the assistance of resident potters) animal, human, or divine figurines were custom fitted. Both places are Edomite, with Edomite dedications and forms of worship, but the buildings and the ceramic offerings display Phoenician and perhaps specifically Cypriot Phoenician influence.[92]

Edomite merchants figure in a number of personal seals and in an inscription concerning a private club or *marzeaḥ*. Two of the seals, one unearthed in Babylon, the other found at Petra, belonged to Qausgabri, the king of Edom during the reign of Esarhaddon (680–669 B.C.E.) and in the first year of Ashurbanipal (668 B.C.E.). Both have three registers, with the king's name and title displayed in the upper and lower, while the central register is filled with a crescent and full moon and linear designs on the Babylon seal, and with a winged and kilted sphinx striding to the right on the Petra seal.[93] From Bozrah, the capital of Edom, there is a seal of "Mulkbaʿal, servant of the king." The name and title are written in three registers, and above these in the top register are what appear to be three standing stone shrines or baetyls.[94] A seal impression with the legend "Belonging to Qausʿanali, servant of the king" was found at ʿAqaba (Tell el-Kheleifeh), and there are many others like it on the handles of jars, jugs, and craters.[95] This Qausʿanali had done well because, without his title, he was mentioned in a Hebrew letter from Arad[96] as the recipient of food rations, such as were distributed regularly to the Phoenician merchants from Kition, the Kittiyyim, who traveled along these trade routes through Judah and Edom to the Red Sea and Arabia.

---

90. P. Bienkowski and E. van der Steen, "Tribes, Trade, and Towns: A New Framework for the Late Iron Age in Southern Jordan and the Negev," *BASOR* 323 (2001) 21–47, esp. pp. 23–26.

91. Y. Aharoni, *Arad Inscriptions* (Jerusalem: Israel Exploration Society, 1981) 52 #26; G. I. Davies, *Ancient Hebrew Inscriptions: Corpus and Concordance* (Cambridge: Cambridge University Press, 1991) #2:026.

92. I. Finkelstein, "Ḥorvat Qitmit and the Southern Trade in the Late Iron Age," *ZDPV* 108 (1992) 156–70; P. Beck, "Transjordanian and Levantine Elements in the Iconography of Qitmit," in *Biblical Archaeology Today, 1990* (ed. A. Biran; Jerusalem: Israel Exploration Society, 1993) 231–36; idem, "Horvat Qitmit Revisited via ʿEn Hazeva," *TA* 23 (1996) 102–14; I. Beit-Arieh, ed., *Ḥorvat Qitmit: An Edomite Shrine in the Biblical Negev* (Tel Aviv: Tel Aviv University Press, 1995).

93. *WSS* 387–88 ##1048–49.

94. Ibid., 388 #1050.

95. Ibid., 389–90 #1051.

96. Aharoni, *Arad Inscriptions*, 26 #12: "Take one jar of oil and two measures of flour and give them to Qausʿanali right away."

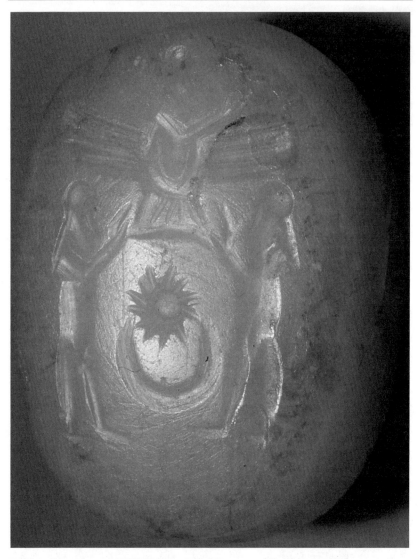

Fig. 4.3. Edomite seal (BM 136202). © The Trustees of the British Museum.

From Jerusalem there is a seal of an Edomite businesswoman, inscribed on one side with her name, "Munaḥḥamit, wife of Padamilk" and on the other with an elaborate ritual scene: two men flanking a crescent moon into which a radiant star descends raise both their hands to a winged anthropomorphic sun disk depicted as bearded, wearing a round hat and a short skirt, striding to the left, with his right arm raised in salutation and his left holding a scepter (see fig. 4.3).[97]

97. *WSS* 391–92 #1053.

From ʿAqaba, again, there is a seal of Yotam, whose design consists of a ram walking left toward a bird; and from Aroer in the Judean Negeb, a seal of Qausʾ that features a couchant griffin and an Egyptian *ankh* symbol; of unknown provenance is the seal of "Qausʾimmi, [son of] Laʿadʾil," on which the names are written above and below a ritual scene, and the seal of "Qausʾadonay" which presents a God, bearded, wearing a crown and a long plain robe, and enthroned on a bull, who is greeted by two worshipers who wear belted and pleated robes.[98] All of the seals are individualized by their iconography and personalized by names, or names and titles, or names and patronymics, or in the case of the woman from Jerusalem, her name and the name of her patron. She may have been involved in a syndicate or a family business, the other individuals in private enterprise, the servants of the king in public trade and commerce, with the king himself probably in a purely executive role.

The *marzeaḥ* inscription, dated to about the mid-seventh century B.C.E. or a little later, is in a cursive hand on a sealed papyrus roll.[99] The text is elegantly written, in two lines, with divider dots between words:

1 *kh . ʾmrw . ʾlhn . lgrʾ . lk . hmrzḥ . whrḥyn . wh*
2 *byt . wyš°ᵃ . rḥq . mhm . wmlkʾ . hvlš*

Thus says God to Geraʾ: "Yours is the marzeaḥ, and the millstones, and the house, and Yišaʿaʾ is excluded from them. And Malkoʾ is the depositary."

Inquiry had been made to the patron God of the *marzeaḥ*, or symposium, or confraternity, as to which of the two contestants, Geraʾ or Yišaʿaʾ, should be its leader. God chose Geraʾ, giving him control of the *marzeaḥ*, possession of the house where their meetings took place, and of the millstones which were at the heart of the joint enterprise, and dismissed his rival. God's response, delivered orally through a prophet, was a legally binding decision on the litigants and on the members of the guild and was entrusted in writing to a depositary—literally, to "The Third," someone who was not involved in the dispute. The papyrus was sealed with his seal, and the bulla reads, in three registers separated by double horizontal lines. "—— || Belonging to Malkoʾ || the Kitian." The seal is Transjordanian: Cypriot seals, for instance, generally are free field, are not divided into registers, and do not have double horizontal lines. The top register is missing in a break in the bulla, but it contained Malkoʾ's device, something simple, such as celestial symbols, to suit the general layout of the seal. The second and third registers were for his name and place of origin: there are four letters on each line, and so the last letter of his name (an ʾalep) was written in the third register with the name of his hometown, "the Kitian."

The papyrus is of unknown provenance, and it is not entirely certain that it is Edomite rather than Moabite, but what is particularly interesting

98. Ibid., 392–94, ##1054–57.

99. P. Bordreuil and D. Pardee, "Le papyrus du marzeaḥ," *Sem* 38 (1990) 49–68, pls. 7–10; F. M. Cross, "A Papyrus Recording a Divine Legal Decision and the Root *rḥq* in Biblical and Near Eastern Legal Usage," *Leaves from an Epigrapher's Notebook*, 63–69.

is (1) that the disputants have Phoenician names,[100] and (2) that the depository, who also has a Phoenician name, is identified as coming from Kition in Cyprus, and (3) that the legal proceedings are recorded, not in Phoenician, but in a Transjordanian language and script. A *marzeaḥ* was a club for merchants, traders, or entrepreneurs in some specialization who met under the auspices of a patron God to drink and play and remember the departed of their corporation. In this particular instance, perhaps in general, the symposiarch's authority was established by a decree of the patron God and extended to ownership or at least control of the club's assets. The members of this particular club apparently were millers and probably included, besides Phoenicians from Kition, representatives of the other nationalities and ethnic groups who traveled along these roads from Arabia and ʿAqaba to Jerusalem or the Philistine coast.

In the early sixth century, when Judah was broken by the Babylonians, the Edomites rushed in to pick up the pieces, grabbing territory, commandeering trade routes, forging ties with Tyre. But in the seventh century, they were just avid competitors with the Judeans, Phoenicians (specifically Tyrians and their associates from Kition in Cyprus), Philistines, Moabites, and Arabs who were stationed there or traveled the trade routes. The Phoenicians had been active in the region for ages (they were at Kuntillet ʿAjrud in the very early eighth century, and an artist at Beersheba much later in that century or in the early seventh copied their coroplastic art),[101] but the Edomites were upstarts and, in the opinion of later Judean writers, bumpkins and boors. They were, nevertheless, country cousins to the Judeans, shrewd and ambitious, and an essential factor in the worldwide web of trade relations.

Moab

Moab is the country east of the Dead Sea and north of Edom. Along with Edom, and included right after Tyre and Judah, it was part of the Assyrian western confederacy, but neither country appears on the Judean map of the world dominated by Phoenician commerce. There are some Phoenician imports, notably of cosmetics palettes for women, but in the seventh century Moab is known mainly from the personal seals of some of its more successful entrepreneurs.[102]

---

100. All three names occur in Phoenician, but the names *ysʿ* and *mlkʾ* also appear on seventh-century Moabite seals: see *WSS* 379–80 #1028; F. Yisrael, "Note di onomastica semitica 7/2: Rassegna critico-bibliografica ed epigrafica su alcune onomastiche palestinesi: La Transgiordania," *SEL* 9 (1992) 95–114, esp. p. 108.

101. R. Kletter and Z. Herzog, "An Iron Age Hermaphrodite Centaur from Tel Beer Sheba, Israel," *BASOR* 331 (2003) 27–38.

102. H. O. Thompson, "Iron Age Cosmetic Palettes," *ADAJ* 16 (1971) 61–70, figs. 1–8; D. Barag, "Phoenician Stone Vessels from the Eighth–Seventh Centuries BCE," *ErIsr* 18 (Avigad Volume; 1985) 72*–73* [English summary], 215–32 [Hebrew]; D. Homès-Fredericq, "A Cosmetic Palette from Lehun, Jordan," in *Trade, Contact and the Movement of Peoples in the Eastern Mediterranean: Studies in Honour of J. Basil Hennessy* (ed. S. Bourke and J.-P. Descoeudres; Mediterranean Archaeology Supplement 3; Sydney: Meditarch, 1995) 265–70, pl. 17:2.

WSS 372–86 ##1006–47; R. Deutsch and A. Lemaire, *Biblical Period Personal Seals in the Shlomo Moussaieff Collection* (Tel Aviv–Jaffa: Archaeological Center, 2000) 193–208 ##186–201.

There are approximately 54 of these seals that can be dated to the seventh century. Four belonged to scribes (*hspr*), one to the court historian (*hmzkr*), and one to "Manasseh, son of the king," the heir apparent to the throne of Judah. His Moabite seal features a star and a crescent moon, but the same legend occurs on his Judean seal, where these symbols are replaced by a winged sun disk shaped like a scarab.[103] Three of the earlier seals are aniconic, one inserts a row of birds, an Ammonite device, into the usual astral repertoire, and another is unique in depicting a galloping horse. The rest of the seals fall into three groups.

The typically Moabite group consists of about 24 seals adorned with a star and crescent moon: these together may represent the composite divinity ʿAthtar-Kemosh known from the Mesha Stele, because ʿAthtar is the morning star and Kemosh, because he was worshiped only at open-air sanctuaries or high places, seems to have been a Celestial God. On some of these seals, the crescent rests on a horizontal line representing the horizon; on others, the star and crescent are balanced by a winged sun disk or aligned with an *ankh* sign or very schematic, sceptre-like Tree-of-Life. Only a few of the owners have names composed with the divine name Kemosh (see, e.g., fig. 4.4), and the rest are hypocoristic nominal or verbal names.

A second group incorporates some Assyrian motifs. Two of these seals portray a pair of worshipers facing a star that twinkles before their eyes while a crescent moon rises above their heads; another like them features stick-figure men worshiping a central crescent enclosing a twinkling star; and another has the central star but lacks the crescent. On three others, men in long robes face a central altar, above which hovers a winged sun disk or a crescent moon or a star set within a crescent moon. There is also a seal on which worshipers address a blazing sun (a sun with rays) and a crescent moon, while a winged sun disk with a blazing sun above it hovers over them. On one seal the central object of worship is an Assyrian-style Tree-of-Life, above which hover a winged sun disk and the crescent moon. Another pictures a single worshiper flanked by stylized trees; and another, the script of which is Moabite but the layout of which is Ammonite (the name is written vertically behind the figure and not in a horizontal register) features a single worshiper in Assyrian dress and sporting an Assyrian beard and hairdo, who holds an *ankh* staff in his right hand and raises his right hand in adoration. None of their names are composed with the divine element Kemosh, but one is Phoenician in origin (*lbʿl*), one is Arabic (*ʿbdwhbn*), and the rest are Moabite kinship (*ʾb*, "Father," or *ʾḥ*, "Brother") or hypocoristic nominal names.

The third group of seals, adorned with fantastic men, beasts, or divine beings, reflects a more cosmopolitan taste. Five represent griffins and fill the open field with a stylized *ankh* sign or a Tree or Plant-of-Life. One portrays a four-winged man wearing an Egyptian kilt and crown and holding a Plant-of-Life in either hand. Another shows winged sphinxes facing a plant, and below them and the name is a winged sun disk. Another features an anthropomorphic winged sun disk with the disk as a man raising his

---

103. *WSS* 372–73 #1006; Deutsch and Lemaire, *Biblical Period Personal Seals in the Shlomo Moussaieff Collection*, 194 #187; *WSS* #16.

Fig. 4.4. Impression of Moabite seal
with inscription, star, and crescent
(BLMJ 1848). Reproduced courtesy of
the Bible Lands Museum Jerusalem.

arms in greeting or adoration. In the top register of another seal, there is
a four-winged female with an Egyptian double crown who holds a branch
in either hand, while a winged sun disk holds sway in the bottom register.
Two of the names are composed with the divine element Kemosh and are
clearly Moabite, as are other kinship or hypocoristic nominal names, but
one of the seals depicting a griffin belonged to a man with an Ammonite
name (*'mr'l*), and the seal with the four-winged man belonged to someone
with an Edomite or Philistine name (*b'lntn*).

These Moabite seals are a narrow but bright entry into the political, social, religious, and economic life of the country in the seventh century
B.C.E. There was some public or government intervention, either administrative or commercial, witnessed by the seals of scribes and members of the
court. In a special case, Manasseh of Judah, son of Hezekiah, king of Judah,
in the line of David, whose Moabite lineage the Bible admits or flaunts,
apparently held dual citizenship, or a Moabite laissez passer, when he was
crown prince: the privilege presumably was not executive but commercial
and illustrates the deep and enduring, if sometimes strained, relations between Judah and Moab.

The star-and-crescent seals, like the earlier aniconic seals, are representative of seventh-century universalism, which promoted trans-tribal Gods
toward transcendent, symbolic, or abstract status. Subgroups in this class of
seals belonged to members of the same syndicate or guild or were made in
the same workshop, but all most likely reflect the theology of a newly flourishing union of tribes. The quasi-Assyrian seals (the formal dress, the pose,
the gesture, the prominence of the sun disk) are an indication of the influence of the empire on the people who were involved in the international
schemes of trade and tribute. The cosmopolitan group of seals is a trace of
Phoenician and worldly realism, straddling the line between conventional
and secular aspiration. Moabite society, or at least its commercial echelons,

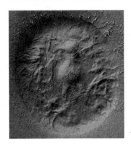

Fig. 4.5. Impression of Ammonite seal with bird and inscription (private collection). Reproduced courtesy of the owner.

was individual and personal and apt to fit into the worldwide enterprise engineered by the Phoenicians of Tyre and its mainland affiliates.

Ammon

The Ammonites lived north of Moab, south of Gilead, east of the Jordan, in towns and settlements radiating from the city of ʿAmman,[104] which was situated at the junction of the North Arabian route through the Wadi Sirhan and the South Arabian route that proceeded northward along the King's Highway from the Gulf of ʿAqaba. The country is mentioned in Assyrian tribute lists and from these, from Ammonite seals and inscriptions, and from an assortment of biblical texts, it is possible to compose a complete king list from the mid-eighth century to the end of the seventh century B.C.E.[105] Apart from this peek into Ammon's political history—its cultural, economic, and religious history in the seventh century—as the history of Moab, is reconstructed from a few artifacts and inscriptions.

There are more than 200 Ammonite personal seals, mostly from the seventh (and only a few from the sixth) century.[106] There are seals of kings, officials, and professionals and seals of women who were their daughters or wives. Their names suggest their ethnicity, and the totality of their names reveals their virtual or actual pantheon. Their iconography is Ammonite or colored by Syrian, Assyrian, and Phoenician themes and motifs. The seals can be grouped by the names and possible filiations, or by particular devices and designs. In the absence of evidence on Ammon's role in the

104. B. MacDonald, "Ammonite Territory and Sites," in *Ancient Ammon* (ed. B. MacDonald and R. W. Younker; Leiden: Brill, 1999) 30–56.

105. U. Hübner, "Das ikonographische Repertoire der ammonitischen Siegel und seine Entwicklung," in *Studies in the Iconography of Northwest Semitic Inscribed Seals* (ed. B. Sass and C. Uehlinger; Göttingen: Vandenhoeck & Ruprecht, 1993) 131–57, 187–98.

106. *WSS* 320–71 ##857–1005; 409–24 ##1081–1119; *BPPS* 157–92 ##150–92; W. E. Aufrecht, "Ammonite Texts and Language," in *Ancient Ammon* (ed. B. MacDonald and R. W. Younker; Leiden: Brill, 1999) 163–88; R. Deutsch and M. Heltzer, *New Epigraphic Evidence from the Biblical Period* (Tel Aviv–Jaffa: Archaeological Center, 1995) 69–71; A. Levin, "A Newly Discovered Ammonite Seal," *IEJ* 46 (1996) 243–47; R. Deutsch and M. Heltzer, *Windows to the Past* (Tel Aviv–Jaffa: Archaeological Center, 1997) 56–58; R. Deutsch, "A Royal Ammonite Seal Impression," in *Michael: Historical, Epigraphical and Biblical Studies in Honor of Prof. Michael Heltzer* (ed. Y. Avishur and R. Deutsch; Tel Aviv–Jaffa: Archaeological Center, 1999) 121–25; R. W. Younker, "An Ammonite Seal from Tall Jalul, Jordan: The Seal of ʾAynadab Son of Zedekʾil," *ErIsr* 26 (F. M. Cross Volume; 1999) 221*–24*; M. Heltzer, "An Ammonite Seal with a Monkey," in *Assyriologica et Semitica: Festschrift für Joachim Oelsner anlässlich seines 65. Geburtages am 18. Februar 1997* (ed. J. Marzahn and H. Neumann; Munster: Ugarit-Verlag, 2000) 107–9.

political and commercial network of the western alliance, the seals preview some of the particular relations and individual connections of these men and women that locate them, however tentatively, on the map of the seventh century B.C.E.

Women's seals identify their owners as the "daughter" (*bt*) or "servant" (*'mt*)—meaning a woman with an official status, either marital or professional, in relation to a named man. The seal of "'Abiḥay, daughter of Yinaḥḥim" is organized in three registers separated by double-line dividers, the most common glyptic design. It features her name in the upper register, a winged sun disk in the central register, and her father's name in the lowest register.[107] Her father, Yinaḥḥim, had his own seal, with his name spread over the upper and lower registers and a charging bull emblazoned in the very prominent, middle register. Her brothers Menaḥḥem, Elishaʿ, and 'Amar'el also had their personal seals, and it is clear that the whole family, excepting the mother, who did not have a seal, was professional and may have worked in the same business.[108]

There are seals of two women, 'Elshagub and Ḥatʿuzzat, who are daughters of 'Elishamaʿ.[109] Each seal has a different design: 'Elshagub's is in three registers, with her name and patronymic in the upper and lower, and the middle register occupied by two seated monkeys flanking a plant; Ḥatʿuzzat's has the second-most popular design, oval with a central figure, in this case a bird, and with the name and patronymic written around the edge (see fig. 4.5). Their names are also interesting: 'Elshagub, "The God 'El is Exalted," is a typical Ammonite name composed with the divine name 'El, the national God of Ammon,[110] whose sobriquet was "The King" (**milkom*); the name Ḥatʿuzzat, "Sister of al-ʿUzzah," is composed of the Phoenician prefix "sister," written as in Phoenician without initial *'alep* (*ḥt* instead of *'ḥt*), and the Arabic theophoric element,[111] al-ʿUzzah (ʿUzzat in Ammonite) being the Great Goddess of North Arabia, and so it is representative of the fairly cosmopolitan and outward-looking spirit of seventh-century Ammon, which was caught up in the international mood of the traffic traveling its roads.

Several women among the almost 20 with personal seals who do not have kinship ("father," "sister") names, have North or South Arabic names (*ltmyrš, ʿl, ʿlyh,ʿnmwt, ḥmdn*). However, most of the names of the husbands

---

107. *WSS* 325 #867.

108. Ibid., 347 #935, 334 #894 (Elishaʿ), 342 #919 ('Amar'il), 350 #944 (Menaḥḥem). There is also a seal of Yinaḥḥim, son of Bana'il (347–48 #936), who presumably is a different person, and of his brother 'Amara', son of Bana'il (342 #918).

109. *WSS* 326–27 #871; A. Levin, "A Newly Discovered Ammonite Seal," *IEJ* 46 (1996) 243–47.

110. P. M. M. Daviau and P. E. Dion, "El, the God of the Ammonites? The Atef-Crowned Head from Tell Jawa, Jordan," *ZDPV* 110 (1994) 158–67; W. E. Aufrecht, "The Religion of the Ammonites," in *Ancient Ammon* (ed. B. MacDonald and R. W. Younker; Leiden: Brill, 1999) 152–62. The affix *-m* in the epithet *mlkm* is like the determinative on masculine-singular nouns in old South Arabic.

111. F. Israel, "Note ammonite—1: Gli arabismi nella documentazione onomastica ammonita," *SEL* 6 (1989) 91–96; K. P. Jackson, "Ammonite Personal Names in the Context of the West Semitic Onomasticon," in *The Word of the Lord Shall Go Forth: Essays in Honor of David Noel Freedman in Celebration of His Sixtieth Birthday* (ed. C. L. Meyers and M. O'Connor; Winona Lake, IN: Eisenbrauns, 1983) 507–21.

(of women called "servant") and fathers (of women called "daughter") are good, old-fashioned Ammonite. Thus, it seems that Ammon was especially intricate with the Arabs, who were alternately renegades and the allies and boutique suppliers of the Assyrians. [112]

Professionals, merchants, and administrators with seals include scribes (*hspr*), a goldsmith (*hṣrp*), a doctor (*hrpʾ*), a standard-bearer (*hnss*) (his device is a four-winged scarab, suggestive of royal authority, flanked by standards), [113] and Mattanʾil, who was "Manager of the Royal Estates" (*mtnʾl šr nhl*) and whose seal belongs to the Running-Charging-Bull class. [114] There is a seal of Puduil who was king of the Ammonites in the time of Sennacherib (701 B.C.E.) and Esarhaddon (675 B.C.E.), that is carved in Phoenician style—a design footnoted in a lower register by a name: the upper register pictures a striding Egyptian-style sphinx and takes up most of the seal; as often in Phoenician but uniquely in Ammonite, the possessive "belonging to . . ." (*l-*) before his name is omitted, as is his rank "king" (*hmlk*), [115] and he seems to have enjoyed the fuss and sophistication conferred by his civilian status. There is also a seal of his foreign minister, "Biyadʾil, servant of Puduʾil" (*bydʾl ʿbd pdʾl*), whose iconography aligns it with two distinct classes of Ammonite seals: on the front or stamp side, there is a Running-Bull framed by a single oval line, and on the top there is a monkey sitting on a papyrus flower (see fig. 4.6), eating fruit, a playful turn on the Phoenician portrayal of Harpocrates seated on a lotus blossom with his finger to his lips. [116]

The seal of another Ammonite king, "Barakʾil, the King" (*lbrkʾl hmlk* ||), who came to the throne after Puduʾil, is aniconic but it includes, as do some other seals, two vertical lines to mark the end of the text. [117] The seal of his chamberlain (*nʿr*) is also aniconic, but his name (*btš*) is Arabic, and the design of the seal is unusual in having a large dot in the lines separating the two registers. [118] There is also a seal of ʿAbdaʾ, who was the chamberlain (*nʿr*) of ʾIlram, a private individual of some rank or means. [119]

ʿAmminadab, who was king about the mid-seventh century during the reign of Ashurbanipal, had two ministers with seals: ʾAdonînûr (*ʾdnnr*), whose seal is aniconic; and ʾAdonîpilleṭ, whose seal shows a bird-headed and lion-footed winged figure dressed in Assyrian style standing beneath a crescent moon and a star. [120] Baʿalyišaʿ, who was king of Ammon toward the end of the seventh century, had a seal like the seal of Puduʾil—its device is a sphinx—but the seal itself is totally Ammonite, in three registers with the design in the middle, and with a sphinx that lacks the grace and litheness

---

112. I. Ephʿal, *The Ancient Arabs: Nomads on the Borders of the Fertile Crescent, 9th–5th Centuries B.C.* (Jerusalem: Magnes, 1984) 112–42; R. Byrne, "Early Assyrian Contacts with Arabs and the Impact on Levantine Vassal Tribute," *BASOR* 331 (2003) 11–25.

113. *WSS* 324 #865.

114. Ibid., 352 #952.

115. Ibid., 357 #965.

116. Ibid., 321 #857.

117. Deutsch, "A Royal Ammonite Seal Impression."

118. *WSS* 324 #863.

119. Ibid., 324 #864.

120. *WSS* 321 #858 (ʾAdonipilleṭ), 322 #859 (ʾAdonînûr).

Fig. 4.6. Impression of
Ammonite seal (two-
sided, one side shown)
with monkey and in-
scription (Paris, BN, CM,
De Clercq Collection
2512).

of the Phoenician original. [121] His minister (ʿbd) was Milkomʾûr, and his seal
also is entirely in the Ammonite glyptic tradition: his name and title are
in the top and bottom register, and in the middle register there is a four-
winged scarab flanked by standards, [122] like the seal of the standard-bearer,
a symbol of royal authority.

Among the seals of scribes, there is one belonging to a man with an Arabic name (ḥty) who was the personal scribe of ʾAdonʾab (ʾdnʾb): [123] his Ammonite handwriting is atrocious, and he may have been responsible mainly
for the company's Arabic correspondence. There are also 15 or more seals
inscribed with abecedaries instead of proper names, [124] which may have
belonged to scribes or teachers or seal-makers. [125] The abecedaries contain
the first 4, 5, 8, 10, or 11 letters of the alphabet and might be indicative

---

121. R. Deutsch, "Seal of Baʿalis Surfaces: Ammonite King Plotted Murder of Judahite Governor," *BAR* 25 (1999) 46–49, 66. Although the king's name on the seal is written *bʿlyšʿ*, he is
usually identified with the sixth-century king of Ammon, Baʿalîs (written *bʿlys*), mentioned in Jer
40:14. This does not explain the loss of the final *ʿayin* of *bʿlyšʿ* (meaning "Baʿal-has-saved"), and it
misses the meaning and derivation of *bʿyls*, "Baʿal-Exists," from *bʿl* + *ys* < *yt̠*: see G. A. Rendsburg,
"The Ammonite Phoneme /T̠/," *BASOR* 269 (1988) 73–77.

122. *WSS* 322 #860.

123. Ibid., 323–24 #862.

124. Ibid., 366–71 ##992–1005; *BPPS* 189 ##183–84.

125. A. R. Millard, "ʾbgd . . . : Magic Spell or Educational Exercise?" *ErIsr* 18 (Avigad Volume;
1985) 39*–42*.

of the patterns of rhyme or rhythm used in learning the 22 letters. Two of
the abecedaries are preceded by the genitive preposition *l-*, "belonging to,"
which usually precedes the name of the seal's owner. More than half are
aniconic, with the letters in one register, or in two registers separated by a
double line, and their owners would have been identified by the choice of
letters and their handwriting. The 6 or so that have some design have a bird
facing a papyrus plant or a worshiper facing the plant, or facing the plant
with a bird above it. Their uniformity suggests that they were the work of
apprentices in a writers' guild and may have served as their personal seals
until they made a name for themselves.

The existence of these sorts of guilds or corporations or family businesses, or the stratification of society that promoted several members of
the same family into public or professional service is suggested by the various possible groupings of seals by genealogy or iconography. ʾIlram, for instance, whose chamberlain (*nʿr*) had his own seal, may be the ʾIlram whose
son (*bn*) Hiṣṣilʾil also had a personal seal.[126] There is also a seal of ʾIlram,
one of three sons of ʾEliʿezer, who may be the same man.[127] There are seals
of three sons of ʾElishaʿ, of two of his grandsons and one of his great-
grandsons.[128] And there is a seal of ʾElishaʿ, the son of Yinaḥḥim, possibly
the same man,[129] whose sister ʾAbiḥay and brothers ʾAmarʾil and Menaḥem
also owned seals. Finally there are seals of two sons of Menaḥḥem.[130] There
are at least four generations, if these people are all related, and it is evident
that the whole family was successful and may be supposed that each was
educated and trained; it is even possible that they all worked for the same
company or family business.

Similarly, Biyadʾil, who was foreign minister in the reign of Puduʾil, had
two sons with seals who may have followed him into public service.[131]
There are similar instances of transgenerational notoriety—a seal-bearing
father who is succeeded by one or two sons with seals—in families with
more modest profiles.

The iconography of the seals,[132] on the other hand, can suggest groupings of seal owners, not all of whom were members of the same family.
The seals that portray Harpocrates, the child Horus, as a monkey seated
on a lotus or papyrus blossom belonged to Biyadʾil, minister of the king;
to one of his sons; to ʾElishaʿ, the son of Yinaḥḥim; to a son of ʾAmarʾil; to
one of the sons of ʾEliʿezer; and to three other, unaffiliated persons.[133] The
running-charging-bull seal series comprises two variants: three registers,
with the bull portrayed in the center and the name of the owner in the
upper and lower registers; and two registers, with the bull either at the top

126. *WSS* 324 #864 (= *BPPS* 157 #150) is the seal of the chamberlain, and *BPPS* 177 #170 is
the seal of the son.
127. *BPPS* ##165, 174, 181.
128. *WSS* ##960, 975, 979. Ibid., ##951, 969, 986.
129. *BPPS* 165 #158.
130. *WSS* 334 #893, 337–38 #905.
131. Ibid., 340 #914, 346 #931.
132. Hübner, "Das ikonographische Repertoire der ammonitischen Siegel und seine Entwicklung," 130–60.
133. *WSS* ##857, 894, 914, 933, 949, 951, 972; Heltzer, "An Ammonite Seal with a Monkey."

or at the bottom. Each is a little different from the others, neither series
seems to be by the same gem-cutter or from the same workshop, and only
two belonged to individuals with titles or whose families are known. Both
of these are in the three-register series: one belonging to Mattan'il, who was
the manager of the king's estates; the other to Shuʿal, the son of 'Elishaʿ.[134]
But the common image does suggest some shared ideology or employment.

The other iconographic series include genuine Ammonite images (a central standing bird surrounded by the owner's name and patronymic, like
the seal belonging to the woman Ḥatʿuzzat) and some that seem to toy
with borrowed icons (a central ram's head with flanking birds, a variant
with a bull's head in the middle); human figures, some with Assyrian features, done in a quasi-Phoenician style: a worshiper with arms outstretched
and hands raised; a naked girl as a sort of signature on the seal of a woman,
or a clothed girl just for the fun of it; a striding man with a staff in his left
hand and his right arm by his side; a bearded and winged bull man; and
a man in an Egyptian kilt stabbing a standing lion.[135] The most striking
feature of all these seals is their individuality, the differences in style, the
nuances in portraying the same motif, so that even members of the same
family or corporation defined themselves by truth-to-tell personal seals.

These series, founded on filiation or iconography, are local Ammonite
creations that draw on Syrian, Assyrian, and Phoenician artistic traditions,
or in the case of aniconic seals, on the worldwide tendency at this time,
fostered by the Assyrian Empire, toward an exclusive, transcendental, and
abstract conception of God. The divine name occurring most frequently on
seals is 'El—the epithet Milkom, which biblical texts identify as the name
of the God of Ammon, is very rare—but the other theophoric elements
reflect an awareness of a vibrant international pantheon comprising Ammonite tribal kinship divinities and the Gods of Syria, Assyria, Arabia, and
Phoenicia.

The same kind of openness to foreign influence, tempered by an insistence on adaptation and personal appropriation, is evident in Ammonite art and architecture and in a rare literary composition. A group of
double-faced caryatids, for instance, that were part of a balustrade imitate
the North Syrian ivories representing a Woman-at-the-Window but remove
the woman from the window in order to incorporate her into the architecture.[136] There are statues of men and women[137] that display local style
(right arm hanging by the side, left folded across the breast and holding

---

134. *WSS*. Three registers: ##881, 928, 943, 952, 971, 979, 985, 991. Two registers: ##896,
908, 937, 942, 948.

135. *Ammonite images*: ibid., ##887, 892, 906, 927, 963, 977; Levin, "A Newly Discovered
Ammonite Seal."

Borrowed icons: WSS ##886, 890, 895, 920, 931, 967, 988.

Human figures: ibid., ##902, 907, 911, 921, 934, 937, 950, 965, 968, 970, 976.

136. F. Zayadine, "Recent Excavations on the Citadel of Amman: A Preliminary Report,"
ADAJ 18 (1973) 17–35, pls. 12–26, esp. pp. 33–35, pls. 21–23; K. Prag, "Decorative Architecture
in Ammon, Moab and Judah," *Levant* 19 (1987) 121–27; Abdel-Jalil ʿAmr, "Four Unique Double-
Faced Female Heads from the Amman Citadel," *PEQ* 120 (1988) 55–63.

137. M. M. Ibrahim, "Two Ammonite Statuettes from Khirbet el-Hajjar," *ADAJ* 16 (1971)
91–97, pls. 1–3; A. Abou-Assaf, "Untersuchungen zur ammonitischen Rundbildkunst," *UF* 12

a bouquet) as well as imitations of Egyptian, Assyrian, or Syrian features (headdress, hair style and clothing). Each presents the face of some individual whose piety it memorializes, and one is actually identified by an inscription on the pedestal as the grandson of Šanipu, the king of Ammon in the time of Tiglath-pileser III.[138]

Ammonite literary aspirations and this penchant toward individuality and even personality are revealed in an inscription on a small bronze bottle from the end of the seventh century:[139]

> Composition of ʿAmminadab, king of the ʿAmmonites, son of HissilʾIl, king of the ʿAmmonites, son of ʿAmminadab, king of the ʿAmmonites: "Vineyard, and wine press, and conduit, and vat, may they bring pleasure and happiness, for many days and for years to come."

The sentiments are pretty well universal, but the ditty has its peculiar cadence, its repetitions, its assonance and alliteration, and was probably composed for recital at a party (or, *marzeaḥ*) for the king and his cronies in international trade.

Ammon was originally a small, ethnically uniform, and stable kingdom: it is identified in Assyrian texts as "the House of Ammon," and in its own texts its people are known as "the Children of Ammon." This was still the case in the seventh century, but by this time it belonged to the international community created and operated by Assyria and managed by Tyre. There are a few Phoenician imports, trinkets and luxuries among them,[140] and there is evidence for partnership with the Philistines and for cultural interchange with Syria and Assyria, but mostly it is a matter of personal seals witnessing to Ammonite engagement in world trade. There may have been syndicates and corporations, and it may be supposed that kings were significant players, but there is a strong argument for private enterprise, individuals working in their own businesses, or families, living in compounds or multiroom houses,[141] with generations of experience. North and South Arabia were among their suppliers, and their customers included all who needed exotic tribute to send to Assyria, but Ammon's trademark and strength was the independence and gumption of its people.

(1980) 7–102, pls. 1–17; Abdel-Jalil ʿAmr, "Four Ammonite Sculptures from Jordan," *ZDPV* 106 (1990) 114–18, pls. 7–8.

138. *CAI* 106–9; Hübner, 23–26.

139. H. O. Thompson and F. Zayadine, "The Tel Siran Inscription," *BASOR* 212 (1973) 5–11; H.-P. Müller, "Kohelet und Aminadab," in *"Jedes Ding hat seine Zeit . . .": Studien zur israelitischen und altorientalischen Weisheit. Diethelm Michel zum 65. Geburtstag* (ed. A. A. Diesel et al.; Berlin: de Gruyter, 1986) 149–65; I. Kottsieper, "Zur Inschrift auf der Flasche vom Tell Siran und ihrem historischen Hintergrund," *UF* 34 (2002) 353–62.

140. D. S. Reese and C. Sease, "Some Previously Unpublished Engraved Tridacna Shells," *JNES* 52 (1993) 109–28; idem, "Additional Unpublished Engraved *Tridacna* and *Andara* Shells," *JNES* 63 (2004) 29–41; H. O. Thompson, "Iron Age Cosmetic Palettes," *ADAJ* 16 (1971) 61–70, figs. 1–8.

141. P. M. M. Daviau, "Domestic Architecture in Iron Age Ammon: Building Materials, Construction Techniques, and Room Arrangement," in *Ancient Ammon* (ed. B. MacDonald and R. W. Younker; Leiden: Brill, 1999) 113–36.

Philistia

The main Philistine cities were Ashdod, Ashkelon, and Gaza on the coast and Ekron, about 20 kilometers inland from Ashdod, Gath having disappeared from history after its capture by Damascus in the ninth century. These and their satellite towns, many of which had political and commercial relations with Judah, had assimilated to the Phoenician way of life and prospered in the seventh century. All are included in the Assyrian lists of tributary states during the reigns of Esarhaddon (680–669 B.C.E.) and Ashurbanipal (668–627 B.C.E.), where Gaza is mentioned along with Ashkelon, Ekron with Byblos, and Ashdod with Ammon.

The Phoenicianization of Philistia is most obvious in its adoption of the onomasticon and language of the various Phoenician cities.[142] The Kingdom of Gaza was the gateway to Egypt and Arabia. Gaza city was an Assyrian custom house, jealously guarded by them from Egyptian interference.[143] An outpost at Tell er-Ruqeish, on the coast, 20 kilometers south of the city was fortified, and its storehouses with Phoenician, Cypriot, Greek, and Egyptian pottery provide evidence of brisk trade.[144] Another outpost at Tell Jemmeh, just a few kilometers east of Ruqeish and southeast of Gaza, was a station for camel caravans[145] traveling through the Sinai to Egypt or through the Negeb of Judah to Edom and the Red Sea. There are Philistine inscriptions from this place written in a beautiful flowing hand but in a hybrid Hebrew-Phoenician script.[146] Most of the names are Phoenician (the rest being presumably Philistine), and patronymics of men are usually marked, as if they were Greek gentilics, by a suffixed letter *šin* (*ʾdnš*, "son of ʾAdon"; *ppš*, "son of the Paphian"), or in one instance (as in the dialect of Byblos, where "son" is written *b-* instead of *bn*) by a prefixed letter *b-* (*bmlk*, "son of Malk"). Patronymics of women, or possibly their matronymics, are marked by the feminine suffix *-yh* (*qsryh*, "daughter of Qsr, or "son of the woman Qsr").

There are also Philistine inscriptions from Tel Seraʿ, about 20 kilometers farther east of Tell Jemmeh, that are written in a similar but not identical, hybrid script and in which the names are Phoenician and South Arabian.[147] The Philistines of the Kingdom of Gaza, in short, borrowed Phoenician as their lingua franca and wrote it in a script that they learned first from the

---

142. J. Naveh, "Writing and Scripts in Seventh-Century B.C.E. Philistia: The New Evidence from Tell Jemmeh," *IEJ* 35 (1985) 8–21, pls. 2–3; A. Lemaire, "Phénicien et Philistien: Paléographie et dialectologie," *Actas* 4, 1.243–49.

143. I. Finkelstein, "Ḥorvat Qiṭmit and the Southern Trade in the Late Iron Age," *ZDPV* 108 (1992) 156–70; A. Spalinger, "Ashurbanipal and Egypt: A Source Study," *JAOS* 94 (1974) 316–28.

144. E. Oren et al., "A Phoenician Emporium on the Border of Egypt," *Qadmoniot* 19 (1986) 83–91 [Hebrew].

145. P. Wapnish, "Camel Caravans and Camel Pastoralists at Tell Jemmeh," *JANES* 13 (1981) 101–21.

146. J. Naveh, "Writing and Scripts in Seventh-Century B.C.E. Philistia: The New Evidence from Tell Jemmeh," *IEJ* 35 (1985) 8–21, pls. 2–3, esp. pp. 11–15, pls. 2b, 3; A. Kempinski, "Some Philistine Names from the Kingdom of Gaza," *IEJ* 37 (1987) 20–24.

147. F. M. Cross, "Inscriptions from Tel Seraʿ," in *Leaves from an Epigrapher's Notebook: Collected Papers in Hebrew and West Semitic Palaeography and Epigraphy* (HSS 51; Winona Lake, IN: Eisenbrauns, 2003) 155–63.

Phoenicians, with whom they did business, and later modified by studying under the Judeans, with whom they had age-old diplomatic ties.

Ashkelon was the chief port of Philistia and the terminal of land routes from Gaza, Ekron, Timnah, Gezer, and Ashdod. Although traditionally aligned with Egypt, it was forced to submit to Assyria and became a reluctant staging area in Esarhaddon's campaigns against its patron.[148] It was not incorporated into the Assyrian provincial system but as a vassal remained independent in the empire, where its loyalty was always in doubt. Prior to setting up this camp, Esarhaddon inquired of the Sun God whether Ashkelon, relying on troops from Egypt (and two other states whose names are lost), would interfere with his preparations.[149] Ashkelon, however, was not geared for war and was more concerned about its place in the Mediterranean trade network than about its position in the empire.[150]

Ashkelon, built on the coast, with walls and towers was an international port. In the heart of town (only very partially excavated) was a marketplace with a winery, warehouses, shops, administrative buildings, and a customs house.[151] Most of the pottery is coastal Philistine, but there is also imported Phoenician Red Slip, with its local imitations, and Phoenician storage jars and fine ceramics, as well as central and southern Judean pottery, Ionian drinking cups, East Greek Wild Goat wine jugs, and Cypriot, Corinthian, Chian, and Samian wares. Ashkelon's Egyptian connections, or perhaps even the existence of an Egyptian enclave in the town are evident from weights and from a variety of ritual and religious items: a bronze offering table, a statuette of Osiris, amulets and Bes figurines, situlae with representations of Min, and an array of bronze statuettes of Egyptian Gods. In later times, Ashkelon was famous for its wine,[152] and this may have been one of its principal exports in the seventh century.

Ashkelon also used Phoenician as its official language and wrote in a hybrid Phoenician-Judean-Philistine script. There is a seal of ʿAbdʾilʾib, the son of Shibʿat, who was the servant of Mitinti (*mtt* on the seal, *Mitinti* in the Assyrian annals), the son of Sidqaʾ.[153] Mitinti, mayor of Ashkelon (he is not named king on the seal) paid tribute to Esarhaddon in 677 B.C.E. and to Ashurbanipal in 667 B.C.E. The final [t] in his name, as in the name Shibat, distinguishes it from standard Phoenician and, as in North Arabic, is a

148. L. E. Stager, "Ashkelon," *NEAEHL* 1.103–12; D. M. Master, "Trade and Politics: Ashkelon's Balancing Act in the Seventh Century B.C.E.," *BASOR* 330 (2003) 47–64.

149. I. Starr, ed., *Queries to the Sun God: Divination and Politics in Sargonid Assyria* (Helsinki: Helsinki University Press, 1990) 94–97.

150. M. Elat, "The Economic Relations of the Neo-Assyrian Empire with Egypt," *JAOS* 98 (1978) 20–34.

151. L. E. Stager, "Ashkelon and the Archaeology of Destruction: Kislev 604 BCE," *ErIsr* 25 (Aviram Volume; 1996) 61*–74*; idem, "The Fury of Babylon: Ashkelon and the Archaeology of Destruction," *BAR* 22/1 (1996) 56–69, 76–77; D. M. Master, "Trade and Politics: Ashkelon's Balancing Act in the Seventh Century B.C.E.," *BASOR* 330 (2003) 47–64.

152. B. L. Johnson and L. E. Stager, "Ashkelon: Wine Emporium of the Holy Land," in *Recent Excavations in Israel: A View to the West* (ed. S. Gitin; Dubuque, IA: Kendall/Hunt, 1995) 95–109.

153. J. Naveh, "Writing and Scripts in Seventh-Century B.C.E. Philistia: The New Evidence from Tell Jemmeh," *IEJ* 35 (1985) 8–21, pls. 2–3, esp. pp. 9, 18, pl. 2a; O. Keel, *Corpus der Stempelsiegel-Amulette aus Palästina/Israel* (Göttingen: Vandenhoeck & Ruprecht, 1997) 688–89; *WSS* 399–400 #1066.

final morpheme of Philistine masculine names. His father's name, in root and structure, is good Phoenician, while the name of the owner of the seal, ʿAbdʾilʾib, "Servant-of-the-God-of-the-Fathers," is truly archaic, harking back to the Sea Peoples' earliest contact with Canaan—its theophoric element is not found anywhere else in Phoenician but is known from Ugaritic pantheon lists.

There is another seal in Philistine script belonging to ʾAḥaʾ, and a seal belonging to a Judean woman called "Abigail, wife of ʿAšyahū" (ʾbgyl ʾšt ʿšyhw), and this diversity is completely consistent with the international status of the city.[154] An ostracon recording the sale of a cereal crop[155] illustrates the almost creole quality of the local language, in which the script is hybrid, the orthography is Hebrew, the morphology is dialectal Phoenician, and the lexicon and onomasticon are common to both languages (the syntax is obscured by the fragmentary condition of the ostracon).

Ashdod, like Ashkelon, reveals a mixture of Philistine, Phoenician, and Hebrew elements in the seventh century. There is a great deal of Phoenician Red Slip pottery, mostly transport jars, which is an argument for trade between Ashdod and Tyre and its Palestinian possessions north and south of Mount Carmel. Excavations on the site uncovered a potters' quarter (a street, courtyards, and houses used as workshops) and some brief inscriptions written in Judean Hebrew. One reads, "the potter" (phr) and would have contained his name, which is now lost; others designate weights and measures; and another is "Royal Measure" (lmlk) and is inscribed on a jar handle. Like Ashkelon, the city was coveted by Egypt (its position in the western alliance and in the Tyrian trade nexus was a good reason), and it may have been captured by Psammetichus I in the third quarter of the seventh century.[156]

Sites on or near the coast but north of the Sorek Valley have connections or affinities with the Philistine cities without belonging to the same system of city-states. Tel Qasile, near Joppa, left no seventh-century architectural remains, but its unusual pottery assemblage may reflect its trade network.[157] There are bowls of various types that resemble comparable items in Philistine (Timnah), Phoenician (ʾAchzib, Tell Keisan), and southern Judean (Beersheba) sites; cooking pots like those at Hazor in Northern Israel and at Ashdod; storage jars with parallels at Ashdod and Tell Keisan; and jugs that can be compared to others from Philistia, central Judah, and the Tyrian towns at Tell Keisan and Yokneʿam. Tel Qasile, therefore, was not isolated from Philistia and Judah but differs from the Philistine cities

---

154. Keel, *Corpus der Stempelsiegel-Amulette aus Palästina/Israel*, 690–91 and 688–89.

155. F. M. Cross, "A Philistine Ostracon from Ashkelon," *BAR* 22/1 (1996) 64–65; repr. in idem, *Leaves from an Epigrapher's Notebook: Collected Papers in Hebrew and West Semitic Palaeography and Epigraphy* (HSS 51; Winona Lake, IN: Eisenbrauns, 2003) 164–65.

156. M. Dothan, "Ashdod," *NEAEHL* 1.93–102; *WSS* 399 #1065 (*lmlk* is inscribed above the drawing of a soldier leading a naked captive). According to Herodotus (2.157) Psammetichus I besieged Ashdod for 29 years before capturing it, and the seal may reflect this implausible and tiresome situation.

157. A. Mazar, *Excavations at Tell Qasile, Part One: The Philistine Sanctuary: Architecture and Cult Objects* (Jerusalem: Hebrew University—Institute of Archaeology, 1983) 113–14; idem, *Excavations at Tell Qasile, Part Two: The Philistine Sanctuary: Various Finds, the Pottery, Conclusions, Appendixes* (Jerusalem: Hebrew University—Institute of Archaeology, 1985) 109–10.

in its decided outreach to the places in the Plain of ʿAkko and the Jezreel Valley that were under Tyrian jurisdiction.

By contrast, ʿAzor, which lay just 10 kilometers southeast of Tell Qasile, had predominantly Cypriot connections from the Late Bronze Age through the ninth century. The same may hold true for the seventh century (a scaraboid adorned with a prancing horse would be consistent with Cypriot tastes), and the only serious connection with the Philistine cities south of the Sorek is an inscription on a transport jar identifying the producer of its contents as Shulmay (*šlmy*), a good Phoenician name but written in a fine Philistine hand,[158] although obviously this could indicate dealings with a Philistine merchant south of the border without implying Philistine involvement at the site. The Sorek Valley, then, is the border between the Philistine cities where Phoenician and Judean cultural and commercial influences melded, and the sites south of Mount Carmel where Phoenician and Cypriot influences predominated.

The most important Philistine city of the interior was Ekron, about 20 kilometers due east of Ashdod.[159] The city was graced with a large temple, designed in part according to Assyrian palace models[160] (a large courtyard, a reception hall with a throne room, a long sanctuary with two rows of pillars, a raised stone dais opposite the entrance), the storerooms of which were filled with gold, silver, bronze, and ivory objects (including a golden uraeus from an Egyptian crown), and all the necessary ceramic utensils.[161] The city flourished in the seventh century, starting during the Assyrian regime but accelerating in the second half of the century under Egyptian tutelage,[162] when the lower town outside the walls filled with migrant workers. The sources of this prosperity were a strong textile industry (attested by hundreds of loom weights) and a remarkably successful oil and perfume industry (attested by more than 100 oil presses and by numerous

---

158. J. Perrot, A. Ben-Tor, and M. Dothan, "ʿAzor," *NEAEHL* 1.125–29; Naveh, "Writing and Scripts in Seventh-Century B.C.E. Philistia," 18, fig. 4:2.

159. S. Gitin, "Tel Miqne–Ekron: A Type-Site for the Inner Coastal Plain in the Iron Age II Period," in *Recent Excavations in Israel: Studies in Iron Age Archaeology* (ed. S. Gitin and W. G. Dever; AASOR 49; Winona Lake, IN: Eisenbrauns, 1989) 15–58; idem, "The Neo-Assyrian Empire and Its Western Periphery: The Levant, with a Focus on Philistine Ekron," in *Assyria 1995* (ed. S. Parpola and R. M. Whiting; Helsinki: Neo-Assyrian Text Corpus Project, 1997) 77–103.

160. S. Gitin, "Israelite and Philistine Cult and the Archaeological Record in Iron Age II: The 'Smoking Gun' Phenomenon," in *Symbiosis, Symbolism, and the Power of the Past: Canaan, Ancient Israel, and Their Neighbors from the Late Bronze Age through Roman Palaestina* (ed. W. G. Dever and S. Gitin; Winona Lake, IN: Eisenbrauns, 2003) 279–95; S. W. Holloway, *Assur Is King! Assur Is King! Religion in the Exercise of Power in the Neo-Assyrian Empire* (Culture and History of the Ancient Near East 10; Leiden: Brill, 2002) 203–11.

161. S. Gitin, "Philistia in Transition: The Tenth Century B.C.E. and Beyond," *MPT*, 162–83.

162. Idem, "Tel Miqne–Ekron in the 7th Century B.C.E.: The Impact of Economic Innovation and Foreign Cultural Influences on a Neo-Assyrian Vassal City-State," in *Recent Excavations in Israel: A View to the West* (ed. S. Gitin; Dubuque, IA: Kendall/Hunt, 1995) 61–79, pls. 1–4; idem, "Neo-Assyrian and Egyptian Hegemony over Ekron in the Seventh Century B.C.E.: A Response to Lawrence E. Stager," *ErIsr* 27 (Hayim and Miriam Tadmor Volume; 2003) 55*–61*; N. Naʾaman, "Ekron under the Assyrian and Egyptian Empires," *BASOR* 332 (2003) 81–91; L. E. Stager, "Ashkelon and the Archaeology of Destruction: Kislev 604 BCE," *ErIsr* 25 (Aviram Volume; 1996) 61*–74*, pp. 70*–71*.

commercial incense burners).[163] Another measure of Ekron's prosperity can be seen in the numerous hoards of silver (ingots, broken pieces, and discarded jewelry) found in the temple complex and in some wealthy homes in the heart of the city.[164]

The silver in these hoards was probably used as money and, along with its industries, the incense-importing business, some luxury items, and the records of merchants at Nineveh, it is a clue to Ekron's involvement in trade and commerce. The olive presses, it has been estimated, could produce about 1,000 tons, or 48,000 large transport jars, of oil per year;[165] and a large amount of the finished product must have found its way into the trade network either for local consumption or for export to the western Mediterranean. The textile industry, similarly, was too vigorous to have been producing goods destined for sale in Ekron alone. There is also evidence for direct trade with Tyre (the silver jewelry in the hoards represents international tastes but was Phoenician in its inspiration, and engraved tridacna shells found at Ekron were a Phoenician specialty) and for merchants from Ekron doing business in Assyria.[166] Like trade with North and South Arabia, for which the only tangible evidence is a group of incense stands, most of the evidence for Ekron's involvement in the Phoenician trade network is indirect and partial.

Ekron, along with its sister city Timnah,[167] illustrates the characteristic Philistine melding of Judean and Phoenician cultural influences. There is

163. The stands, usually called "altars," were for burning incense and other fragrances used in the production of perfume. They were found in the industrial (oil and textile) areas and in domestic contexts in the wealthy residential areas but not in the temple or in ritual or liturgical contexts: see S. Gitin, "Incense Altars from Ekron, Israel and Judah: Context and Typology," *ErIsr* 20 (Yadin Volume; 1989) 52*–67*; idem, "New Incense Altars from Ekron: Context, Typology and Function," *ErIsr* 23 (Biran Volume; 1992) 43*–49*.

164. A. Golani, "Three Silver Jewelry Hoards from Tel Miqne–Ekron," *Actas* 4, 3.987–99; A. Golani and B. Sass, "Three Seventh-Century B.C.E. Hoards of Silver Jewelry from Tel Miqne–Ekron," *BASOR* 311 (1998) 57–81; R. Kletter, "Iron Age Hoards of Precious Metals in Palestine: An 'Underground Economy'?" *Levant* 35 (2003) 139–52; C. M. Thompson, "Sealed Silver in Iron Age Cisjordan and the 'Invention' of Coinage," *OJA* 22 (2003) 67–107.

165. S. Gitin, "The Neo-Assyrian Empire and Its Western Periphery: The Levant, with a Focus on Philistine Ekron," in *Assyria 1995* (ed. S. Parpola and R. M. Whiting; Helsinki: Neo-Assyrian Text Corpus Project, 1997) 77–103, esp. p. 87.

166. *Silver:* Golani and Sass, "Three Seventh-Century B.C.E. Hoards of Silver Jewelry from Tel Miqne–Ekron."
Tridacna: B. Brandl, "Two Engraved Tridacna Shells from Tel Miqne–Ekron," *BASOR* 323 (2001) 49–62. The shells are from the Indian Ocean, their workmanship is Phoenician, and their distribution—in Palestine (Ekron, Tell el-Farʿah South, Arad), Transjordan (ʿAmman, Buseirah), Babylonia (Susa, Warka, Babylon), Assyria (Ashur, Nimrud), and in the Heraion on Samos—is indicative of Phoenician commercial persistence.
Ekron doing business in Assyria: E. Lipiński, "Deux marchands de blé phéniciens à Ninive," *RSF* 3 (1975) 1–6. The tablet is dated 660 B.C.E., in the eponym of Girsapon, whose Phoenician name would be normal for a man from Ekron. The men selling grain have names known at Ekron (Padi, also the name of a king of Ekron) or betraying the Byblian influence (Adoniḥay, "Adonis-is-Alive") typical of Ekron. The grain is weighed according to the Judean standard, and this mixture of Judean and Phoenician elements is usual in Philistia, at Ekron in particular. The buyers and witnesses are Aramean.

167. A. Mazar and G. L. Kelm, "Batash, Tel (Timnah)," *NEAEHL* 1.152–57; A. Mazar, "The Northern Shephelah in the Iron Age: Some Issues in Biblical History and Archaeology," in *Scripture and Other Artifacts: Essays on the Bible and Archaeology in Honor of Philip J. King* (ed. M. D.

an inscription, for instance, incised on a seventh-century storage jar that reads "for Ba'al and for Padi" (*lb'l | wlpdy |*), with the names set off by vertical dividers. Both are good Phoenician, and therefore Philistine, personal names, but Ba'al is also a God and the name of the contemporary king of Tyre. If the reference were to the kings of Ekron and Tyre, the inscription's storage-jar context would suggest a commercial relationship between them, while the omission of their royal titles would brand it as extraordinarily informal and personal. But if the reference is to God and the king, the use of the word-dividers and the repetition of the preposition "for" give it a ring, make it a saying or a motto or a rallying cry—exactly like the invocation of the king and the Goddess on the Pygmalion pendant from Carthage—and simultaneously satisfy the Assyrian ideal of revering "God and King."[168] Ba'al, however, was the God of Byblos—the major cities had their individual Ba'al or "Lord," but the Ba'al of historical record was the God of the ancient city where his story was remembered and retold.

These cultural and specifically religious connections with Byblos are also attested in the inscription that was composed for the dedication of the dynastic temple in Ekron.[169] Its format, with the text written between horizontal lines, its morphology (third-singular personal suffixes in *-h*), its lexicon, and its explicit concern for the land (the king invokes blessings on himself and on the land [*'ereṣ*] of Ekron) have good and unique parallels in Byblian inscriptions of the tenth to fifth centuries B.C.E. The cultural mix at Ekron is also evident in the contents of the inscription. The king (*šr*, "prince," "mayor") is 'Akayus, Ikausu in Assyrian, Achish in the Hebrew Bible, Achaios or Anchises in Greek,[170] the son of Padi, king of Ekron. The temple was dedicated to a Goddess whose name (*ptgyh*) evokes Mycenean memories but does not have a Phoenician equivalent, although there are other inscriptions, incised on storage jars in the temple, that feature Asherah, the Goddess worshiped in contemporary Jerusalem (*'ašerâ*), invoked in a Phoenician spelling (*'šrt*) of her name.[171]

The overall impression is that Ekron was an early convert to the Phoenician, perhaps specifically Byblian way of life in which it was alphabetized and acculturated, that it entered easily into the Tyrian trade network late in the eighth century, and that it flourished in the seventh century in a

Coogan, J. C. Exum, and L. E. Stager; Louisville, KY: Westminster John Knox, 1994) 247–67; G. L. Kelm and A. Mazar, *Timnah: A Biblical City in the Sorek Valley* (Winona Lake, IN: Eisenbrauns, 1995).

168. S. Gitin and M. Cogan, "A New Type of Dedicatory Inscription from Ekron," *IEJ* 49 (1999) 193–202. The injunction is also reflected in Isa 8:19 and Hos 10:3.

169. T. Dothan and J. Naveh, "A Royal Dedicatory Inscription form Ekron," *IEJ* 47 (1997) 1–16; R. G. Lehmann, "Studien zur Formgeschichte der 'Eqron-Inschrift des *'kyš* und den phönizischen Dedikationstexten aus Byblos," *UF* 31 (1999) 255–306; V. Sasson, "The Inscription of Achish, Governor of Eqron, and Philistine Dialect, Cult and Culture," *UF* 29 (1997) 627–39.

170. J. Naveh, "Achish: Ikausu in the Light of the Ekron Dedication," *BASOR* 310 (1998) 35–37; R. Byrne, "Philistine Semitics and Dynastic History at Ekron," *UF* 34 (2002) 1–23.

171. A. Demsky, "The Name of the Goddess of Ekron: A New Reading," *JANES* 25 (1997) 1–5; C. Schäfer-Lichtenberger, "The Goddess of Ekron and the Religious-Cultural Background of the Philistines," *IEJ* 50 (2000) 82–91; S. Gitin, "Seventh-Century B.C.E. Cultic Elements at Ekron," in *Biblical Archaeology Today, 1990* (ed. A. Biran and J. Aviram; Jerusalem: Israel Exploration Society, 1993) 248–58.

creative symbiosis with Judah, at first under Assyrian auspices, and in the end under the aegis of Egypt. At the end of the century, it was this Egyptian connection that was its undoing, when ʾAdon, the king of Ekron with an orthodox Byblian Phoenician name, appealed in vain to the pharaoh to honor the pact between them and save him from Nebuchadnezzar of Babylon.[172]

Philistia, the territory and city-states south of the Sorek Valley and north of the Wadi el-Arish, was an independent region stimulated and bedeviled by the tug of war between Assyria and Egypt. It was the outlet for overland trade with Egypt and Arabia and a gateway for people and products from Cyprus and the Aegean. Its connections with Phoenicia were both traditional and recently updated (borrowings of scripts and dialects; participation in the new monetary policy; import of interesting, exotic, and expensive doodads), and its position as intermediary between Judah and Phoenicia in the global trade network is evident in its catering to the demands and tastes of its former antagonist. The Judean perspective on this old and new Philistia is revealed in the story of Samson, which was spun out of the legends of Heracles (the same type of divine origin, a liking for strong women, similar trials and tribulations, final immolation) and in which the gruff Judean becomes the admirable, irrepressible, malleable, and immortal Greek (Judges 13–16).[173] Its own culture was radically Palestinian, and its ability to assimilate to these dominant ethnicities marks it as typical of the new world order.

Tyre in the Western Mediterranean

Tyre turned much more resolutely to the western Mediterranean in the seventh century. The colony at Carthage in North Africa was becoming the hub of a new Phoenician world. There was not much room for development in the east. Judah and Transjordan were stable and assertive and became independent and demanding in the network of nations. Assyrian patronage started to wear thin, and its constant tussle with Egypt and interference in Tyre's relations with this old and constant partner was becoming less and less profitable to the island metropolis. Going west was not just a matter of "business as usual." The battering of Sidon and the marginalizing of Byblos had benefited Tyre, but the rivalry of these cities was essential to Phoenician identity. It was a matter of development and survival.

172. B. Porten and A. Yardeni, *Textbook of Aramaic Documents from Ancient Egypt, 1: Letters* (Jerusalem: Hebrew University, 1986) 6, #A1.1. The letter invokes a blessing on Pharaoh by the Gods of heaven and earth and by Baʿal Shamayim, the head ("Great God") of the pantheon of Ekron, who were probably guarantors of the treaty that Ekron had made with Egypt.

173. See T. Gantz, *Early Greek Myth: A Guide to Literary and Artistic Sources* (Baltimore: Johns Hopkins University Press, 1993) 374–466. By the sixth century, when this story of Samson was written, Heracles had been assimilated to Melqart, the God of Tyre—both were travelers, benefactors of their people, immortal heroes; but the writer of the story, who also knew the Phoenician legends of Melqart (1 Kings 18), turned Heracles into a legendary hero of Dan, the tribe of Israel (whose hereditary land the Philistines had usurped), with affinities to the Greeks of Cilicia and Cyprus.

Cyprus

Cyprus began the seventh century under Assyrian hegemony. This diminished Sidon's role, fragmented the Cypriot amphictyony once centered at Kition, and promoted Tyre as agent of the empire, but it did not give Assyria direct military, commercial, or cultural control. Cyprus left the seventh century a congeries of independent city-states in regional configurations and alliances that left it open to Attic and Egyptian influences. The Phoenicians were a little bit everywhere on the island, but their interests, as usual, were leading them away to ever-more-specific destinations farther West. And now the Cypriots went with them.

The ten Cypriot kingdoms that paid tribute to Esarhaddon and Ashurbanipal in the first half of the seventh century (in 673 and 664 B.C.E.) were governed by Greek Cypriot rulers, except Carthage in the southwest, whose king had a Phoenician name.[174] Other places that are of some importance in the archaeological record are not listed and either were included in the territory of another kingdom, as Amathus was in the Kingdom of Carthage, or Lapethos and Ayia Irini in the northern kingdom of Chytroi; or were Assyrian protectorates, like Kition, which in the eighth century had become the Assyrian capital of Cyprus. The kingdoms are listed by region, and their order suggests the boundaries of each region: the eastern region comprised the kingdoms of Idalion, Chytroi, and Salamis, and this order describes a triangle from the southeast to the north and then to the east; the western region formed another triangle with the Kingdom of Paphos in the south, Soloi in the north, and Kourion on the southern coast; the central region consisted of Tamassos, Carthage, Ledra, and Nora, and the order of their listing staggers the inland kingdoms of Tamassos and Ledra against the coastal kingdoms of Carthage and Nora. These regions were topographical and may have corresponded to economic and administrative realities, but they seem to reflect Assyrian familiarity with a map of the island rather than any concrete or cultural involvement in the affairs of the kingdoms or the lives of the people.

The war between Chalcis and Eretria put an end to Euboean overseas interests, especially to Euboean pottery exports to Cyprus, and most of the imported pottery in seventh-century Cyprus was East Greek and Corinthian. Places such as Amathus and Salamis where Tyre had an investment imported the most, while Kition, which had been a Sidonian settlement until it was taken over in the Assyrian reorganization of the island, imported very little.[175] Phoenician pottery characteristic of the seventh

---

174. A. T. Reyes, *Archaic Cyprus: A Study of the Textual and Archaeological Evidence* (Oxford: Clarendon, 1994) 49–68.

175. J. N. Coldstream, "The Greek Geometric and Plain Archaic Imports," in *Excavations at Kition, IV: The Non-Cypriote Pottery* (ed. V. Kaarageorghis; Nicosia: Department of Antiquities, 1981) 17–22; idem, "The Greek Geometric and Archaic Imports," in *La Nécropole d'Amathonte, Tombes 113–367, II: Céramiques non-Chypriotes* (ed. V. Karageorghis, O. Picard, and C. Tytgat; Nicosia: Department of Antiquities, 1987) 21–31; A.-M. Collombier, "Céramiques grecque et échanges en Méditerranée orientale: Chypre et la côte syro-phénicienne (fin VIIIe–fin IVe siècles av. J.-C.," in *Phoenicia and the East Mediterranean in the First Millennium B.C.* (ed. V. Karageorghis; Studia Phoenicia 5; Louvain: Peeters, 1987) 239–48; L. Wriedt Sørensen, "Traveling Pottery Connections between Cyprus, the Levant, and the Greek World in the Iron Age," in *Res Maritimae:*

century (including wide-rimmed mushroom-lipped and trefoil-lipped jugs) is found at Limassol, Kition, and Idalion and in larger quantities at Amathus and Salamis.[176] Some of the more popular wares such as the trefoil-lipped jugs and a small handle-less bowl that were produced on the island from metal prototypes show up in Italy in the seventh century, where they were copied either in ceramic or in silver.[177]

Local Cypriot pottery included figurative wares in the Free Field style (the figures are not set into geometric frames but are painted on the open surface of the vessel) that emerged toward the end of the eighth century, partly under Attic influence, and that reveals some of the interests, occupations, and aspirations of the artists and their patrons.[178] There are few maritime scenes but many military and rustic scenes: chariots, horses and riders, archers and armed warriors, birds and animals, and people with flowers or holding or leading an animal. Cyprus, according to the pottery record, was mainly native Cypriot in the seventh century, but there was still an established Greek population, and Phoenicians (Byblians in the north, Tyrians along the southern coast, and a remnant of the Sidonians at Kition and Idalion) were a distinct minority.

The terra-cotta industry catered to the Cypriot market,[179] where it was used mostly in ex-votos but also in toys, mementos, and tomb gifts. Phoenician influence could affect details, such as the rendering of the nose or ears, but also extended to the introduction of new themes into the Cypriot repertory.[180] At Kourion, statuettes of bulls and of male votaries in long robes were popular,[181] but the preferred offerings were statuettes of women and men: women with their arms raised and men on horseback. Phoenician influence is perceptible in the partial or complete nakedness of some of the women, in the larger size of many terra-cottas, and in the addition of saddle cloths (such as were used by Assyrian cavalry) to the horse's accoutrements.[182] At Amathus, where most of the terra-cottas are

Cyprus and the Eastern Mediterranean from Prehistory to Late Antiquity (ed. S. Swiny, R. L. Hohlfelder, and H. Wylde Swiny; Atlanta: Scholars Press, 1997) 285–99.

176. P. M. Bikai, *The Phoenician Pottery of Cyprus* (Nicosia: A. G. Leventis Foundation, 1987) 56–58. Amathus produced the most representative assemblage of seventh-century Phoenician pottery: idem, "The Phoenician Pottery," in *La Nécropole d'Amathonte, Tombes 113–367, II: Céramiques non-Chypriotes* (ed. V. Karageorghis, O. Picard, and C. Tytgat; Nicosia: Department of Antiquities, 1987) 1–19, pls. 1–7.

177. A. Rathje and L. Wriedt Sørensen, "Ceramic Interconnections in the Mediterranean," *Actas* 4, 4.1875–83.

178. A. Demetriou, "The Impact of the Late Geometric Style of Attica on the Free Field Style of Cyprus," in *Periplus: Festschrift für Hans-Günter Buchholz* (ed. P. Åström and D. Sürenhagen; Jonsered: Åströms, 2000) 43–50, pls. 6–15; V. Karageorghis and J. Des Gagniers, *La Céramique chypriote de Style Figuré: Âge du Fer (1050–500 av. J.-C.)—Texte* (Rome: Consiglio Nazionale delle Ricerche / Istituto per gli Studi Micenei ed Egeo-Anatolici, 1974).

179. G. Markoe, *Phoenicians* (London: British Mueum, 2000) 158–60.

180. C. Beer, "Eastern Influences and Style? A Reconsideration of Some Terracottas of Cypriote Manufacture," in *Cypriote Terracottas* (ed. F. Vandenabeele and R. Laffineur; Brussels: Vrije Universiteit Brussel / Liège: Université de Liège, 1991) 77–85, pls. 16–18. V. Karageorghis, *The Coroplastic Art of Ancient Cyprus* (6 vols.; Nicosia: A. G. Leventis Foundation, 1993–96).

181. J. H. Young and S. H. Young, *Terra-cotta Figurines from Kourion in Cyprus* (Philadelphia: University of Pennsylvania Press, 1955) 218–19.

182. V. Karageorghis, "Three Iron Age Wall-Brackets from Cyprus," *RSF* 3 (1975) 161–67, pls. 35–37. The oldest of the brackets, possibly from Kourion but of unknown provenance,

later, Phoenician tastes in the seventh century are evident in the choice of subjects and in the modification of Cypriot originals.[183] There are scenes of women who stand at a table and make bread, as at eighth-century ʾAchzib, and statuettes of women holding or playing tambourines, as at Shiqmona and Tyre. There are also the usual representations of naked women proffering their breasts, as well as a version of the woman with arms raised, whose robe, in Phoenician fashion, falls open to reveal her pudenda and painted breasts.

At Kition, where the earlier terra-cottas were exclusively Cypriot, there is a similar interest in portraying the sexuality and nurturing instincts of women, as well as everyday domestic scenes, and the popular Tyrian theme of the seated and pensive pregnant woman.[184] In general, Phoenician influence on the production and export of terra-cottas did not antedate the seventh century and, though marked, was modest.[185] It was a woman's work (domestic scenes, a feminine perspective, and toys for the children were most popular among the Phoenicians),[186] and its limited impact probably reflects women's status in a mercantile society.

The bronze and silver drinking bowls that have been found at Idalion, Tamassos, Salamis, Amathus, and Kourion were made by Phoenician or Cypriot craftsmen, most likely for Cypriot clients and according to their specifications.[187] The decoration of the bowls features Egyptianizing themes

features a nude girl standing beneath two carefully carved bull heads. It contrasts with the second which, in better Cypriot taste, represents two fully clothed women facing each other under a bull's head. The third bracket portrays a man armed with a sword who carries an axe in his right hand and a bow in his left.

Idem, *The Coroplastic Art of Ancient Cyprus*, vol. 3: *The Cypro-Archaic Period: Large and Medium Size Sculpture* (Nicosia: A. G. Leventis Foundation, 1993) 6, 36, 86.

J. H. Crouwel and V. Tatton-Brown, "Ridden Horses in Iron Age Cyprus," *RDAC* (1988) Part 2, 77–85, pls. 24–26; N. A. Winter, "The Terracottas," in *The Sanctuary of Apollo Hylates at Kourion: Excavations in the Archaic Precinct* (ed. D. Buitron-Oliver; Jonsered: Åströms, 1996) 89–144, pls. 17–33.

183. V. Karageorghis, "The Terracottas," in *La nécropole d'Amathonte, tombes 113–367, III: 1. The Terracottas; 2. Statuettes, Sarcophages et stèles décorées* (ed. V. Karageorghis, O. Picard, and C. Tytgat; Nicosia: Department of Antiquities, 1987) 1–52, pls. 1–41.

184. F. Vandenabeele, "The Terracottas of the Cypro-Geometric Period," in *Cypriote Terracottas* (ed. F. Vandenabeele and R. Laffineur; Brussels: Vrije Universiteit / Liège: Université de Liège, 1991) 57–68; idem, "Phoenician Influence on the Cypro-Archaic Terracotta Production and Cypriot Influence Abroad," in *Acts of the International Archaeological Symposium "Cyprus between the Orient and the Occident"* (ed. V. Karageorghis; Nicosia: Department of Antiquities, 1986) 351–60, pls. 30–31.

185. Idem, "Has Phoenician Influence Modified Cypriot Terracotta Production?" *ESC*, 266–71; A. M. Bisi, "Le rayonnement des terres cuites chypriotes au Levant aux premiers siècles de l'âge du Fer," *ESC*, 256–65; H. Kyrieleis, "New Cypriot Finds from the Heraion of Samos," in *Cyprus and the East Mediterranean in the Iron Age* (ed. V. Tatton-Brown; London: British Museum, 1989) 52–67.

186. J. Karageorghis, "La vie quotidienne à Chypre d'après les terres cuites d'époque géometrique et archaïque," in *Cypriote Terracottas* (ed. F. Vandenabeele and R. Laffineur; Brussels: Vrije Universiteit Brussel / Liège: Université de Liège, 1991) 149–69, pl. 42.

187. *PBSB*. The bowls belonging to Period III (710–675 B.C.E.) are Cy 1 and Cy 2 from Idalion, Cy 4 from Amathus, Cy 6–8, 12, 14 from Kourion, Cy 15 from Tamassos, and Cy 17 of unknown provenance. The bowls from Period IV (675–625 B.C.E.) are Cy 5 and 20 from Salamis, Cy 11 from Kourion, Cy 18 from Amathus, Cy 21 from Palaepaphos, and Cy 13, 16, 19, 22, of unknown provenance. Cy 8 from Kourion (pp. 177–79, 256–59) was made for Akestor, the king of Paphos,

typical of Tyrian artistic traditions but mixes them with current Assyrian motifs and embellishes them with Phoenician narrative friezes and some stunning Cypriot designs. The central medallion portrays a striding pharaoh with his right hand raised to club a squatting suppliant prisoner, or replaces this with a four-winged Assyrian genius stabbing a lion, or with an Assyrian rosette or, on a bowl from Tamassos that undoubtedly was engraved for a Cypriot client, with a beautiful prancing horse.

The inner register can continue the contest thematic of the medallion or present naturalistic or symbolic pastoral scenes: horses grazing, animals and trees, or a file of couchant sphinxes or griffins flanking a stylized tree. The outer register usually is more imaginative: an afternoon in the country for the king of a walled city, or the siege of a city; a king riding in a chariot followed by his retinue; a feast with music and good food or a *marzeaḥ* with much drinking and lewd behavior; or a series of religious and mythological vignettes in Egyptian or Egyptian and Assyrian style. The bowls, designed to feast the eyes when lifted to the lips, illustrate the depth of Phoenician interaction with indigenous craftsmanship and artistic traditions, and the impact that the Assyrian Empire and contemporary events could have on the archaizing canons of their schools.

The effect of Phoenician intervention in the island's economy is evident from the seventh- and sixth-century proliferation of personal stamp seals.[188] The earliest of the seals are Phoenician, from western Cyprus, but the production of Cypriot seals that they encouraged was established by the second half of the seventh century. The Phoenician seals and most of the local seals are anepigraphic, and this is peculiar to Cyprus. Their design, because of this lack of personal name and patronymic, is free form and without line-dividers or registers, except for a residual and nonfunctional exergue on a few seals. The devices of the Phoenician series contain familiar motifs,[189] but, except for the earliest, their layout, form, and workmanship betray generations of assimilation to Cypriot standards and tastes. The earlier tend to preserve the refined Egyptianizing features of their subjects (for instance, seals from Kition and Kourion representing Isis nursing Horus).[190] However, the later are satisfied with rough sketches and careless composition (for example, seals with a striding man holding a scepter are cartoons in comparison with the earlier models from Kition and Idalion).[191]

There are regional and local differences. Ayia Irini, for instance, which is usually aligned with Amathus and Kourion is also distinguished from them by the preservation of its Byblian heritage and its artistic ties to North Syria. Together with their very large number (there are more than 300 from Ayia Irini alone), these seals from inland and coastal sites are indirect evidence for a brisk and diversified Phoenician market in seventh-century Cyprus.

---

by Timocrates, as its Cypro-Syllabic inscription attests. Cy 6 from Kourion (pp. 175–76, 252–53) is inscribed "Kyprothales" in Cypro-Syllabic script, the name of the artisan or the client.

188. A. T. Reyes, *The Stamp-Seals of Ancient Cyprus* (Oxford: Oxford University School of Archaeology, 2001).

189. Ibid., 85–124.

190. Ibid., 126 #293 (Kition) and #294 (Kourion).

191. Ibid., 99–101 #179 (Idalion), ##180–81 (Kition), ##184–93 (provenance unknown).

Direct evidence for Phoenician activity in Cyprus at this time is supplied by the very few inscriptions and some random archaeological finds. From the temple precinct at Kition, there are two bronze statuettes of striding men, similar to the striding men shown on seals, wearing an Egyptian crown and kilt: one with both arms by his side; the other with his right hand raised in benediction.[192] There is also some Phoenician Red Slip pottery from Kition, and three pieces in particular (a fragment and two mushroom-lipped juglets)[193] are inscribed in Eteo-Cypriot Syllabic script with the names of their owners. On the outskirts of town is a tomb in whose antechamber there was a burial of cremated remains and in whose chamber a woman and child were buried with imported Red Slip and White Painted wares, as well as with some local Cypriot wares and eight local imitations of Phoenician Red Slip bowls.[194]

From Pyla, about 10 kilometers northeast of Kition, there is a quasi-pyramidal limestone cippus inscribed in Phoenician, "what ʾEshmunhilles the sculptor made for his Lord, for Reshep his tutelary spirit."[195] There is a hole on the top of the stele into which the socle of a statuette or a bust, the likeness of himself or of his God, could have been slipped.

Idalion, one of the cities mentioned by the Assyrian kings, was under Cypriot rule in the seventh century, but there are two inscriptions that indicate at least some Phoenician presence in the latter part of the century. A large geometric pedestal bowl, Cypriot in inspiration, was decorated in black paint with the name of its Phoenician owner: the name is "Pygmon" (*pgmn*), formed from the Greek root (*pgm-*) of the name "Pygmalion" by adding the Phoenician agentive *-ôn* instead of the Phoenician adjective *-aliôn*.[196] A pair of bronze horse blinkers from the city is inscribed "Baʿana's Horse" (*phl bʿnʾ*): each portrays a papyrus brake and a griffin with its raised left foot resting on a lotus blossom;[197] the personal name Baʿanaʾ, borne by a later king of Sidon, originally was derived from the name of a warrior class called "The Sons of ʿAnat," the ever-adolescent Warrior Goddess who continued to be worshiped at Byblos and in the Byblian colony of Lapethos in Cyprus.

---

192. V. Karageorghis, "Kition," in *Cyprus BC: 7000 Years of History* (ed. V. Tatton-Brown; London: British Museum, 1979) 83–86, esp. p. 85 ##260–61.

193. O. Masson, "À propos de la découverte d'une inscription chypriote syllabique à Kition en 1970," *RDAC* (1971) 49–52, pl. 21.

194. S. Hadjisavvas, "Recent Phoenician Discoveries on the Island of Cyprus," *Actas* 4, 3.1023–33.

195. *RES* 1214; P. Lacau, "Une inscription phénicienne de Chypre," *Bulletin de l'Institut Français d'Archéologie Orientale* 2 (1902) 207–11, fig. 1; A. Caquot and O. Masson, "Deux inscriptions phéniciennes de Chypre," *Syria* 45 (1968) 295–320, esp. pp. 295–302. The word translated "sculptor" (*hqlʿ*) could also mean "slinger," from a homophonous root, and allude to the missiles that were the attributes of Reshep and that made this God the Semitic equivalent of Apollo, with whom he is identified at Idalion.

196. *RPC* 112–13, pl. 14:2; J. Teixidor, "The Phoenician Inscriptions of the Cesnola Collection," *MMJ* 11 (1976) 55–70, esp. p. 68, #27; É. Puech, "Remarques sur quelques inscriptions phéniciennes de Chypre," *Sem* 29 (1979) 19–43, esp. pp. 28–29.

197. *RES* 1209A–B; *RPC* 108–10, pl. 12; Puech, "Remarques sur quelques inscriptions phéniciennes de Chypre," 30–31; E. Lipiński, "Le Baʿanaʾ d'Idalion," *Syria* 63 (1986) 379–82; P. Bordreuil and E. Gubel, "Bulletin d'antiquités archéologiques du Levant inédites ou méconnues," *Syria* 63 (1986) 417–35, esp. p. 421, fig. 5A–B.

There is Phoenician pottery in a Cypriot tomb at Kornos near Idalion, and there are Cypriot ostraca and graffiti and a Phoenician inscription on a transport amphora from Golgoi, about 12 kilometers east of Idalion.[198] There is a mortuary inscription of Sidonian type from Chytroi,[199] one of the Cypriot kingdoms tributary to Assyria, about 25 kilometers north of Idalion and 10 kilometers from the northern coast of Cyprus. On the south coast, in the Vasilikos Valley, a tomb at Maroni showed Red Slip and Black-on-Red pottery and featured heirloom Phoenician ("Samaria Ware") table settings.[200] The tomb of a young Cypriot warrior, buried with his wife and their child, at nearby Mari contained just one imported Phoenician jug and a variety of imitations of Phoenician wares.[201] From Amathus, a Phoenician center, there is only one Phoenician inscription and this on a locally made Cypriot amphora.[202]

From Ayia Irini on the west coast, which probably belonged to the Byblian Kingdom of Lapethos, there is a small Cypriot jug inscribed after firing with the name of the merchant, the identification of its contents, a dye or ink, and probably the amount: "140 gallnuts" (*'ṣm*).[203] The impression created by these scattered artifacts and inscriptions is that the Phoenicians had come and gone, that they were a modest presence among Cypriots and Greeks, that their greatest impact on Cyprus had been in the preceding centuries, and that what counted in the seventh century was the survival of their ideals, ambition, performance, and productivity in the lifestyle and emulation of their Cypriot hosts.

Phoenicians from Cyprus radiated through the western Mediterranean. There was some traffic between Cyprus and the Greek emporium at Naucratis in the Egyptian Delta[204] and, as the steatite scarabs attest, from there to Italy. There are Cypriot terra-cotta votive figurines on Rhodes, Chios, Delos, and at the Heraion on Samos.[205] On Rhodes, at Ialysos, Camiros, and Exochi, there were faithful copies of Cypro-Phoenician Black-on-Red

---

198. P. Flourentzos, "Two Tombs from the Late Cypro-Archaic Necropolis of Kornos," *RDAC* (1987) 141–47, pls. 44–49. The tombs barely antedate the end of the seventh century, and only one of them (Tomb 5, pp. 141–44) contained a bit of Phoenician Red Slip, Black-on-Red, and Black Slip pottery.

O. Masson, "Kypriaka," *BCH* 92 (1968) part 2, 375–409, pls. 21–22, esp. pp. 380–86; idem, "Chypriotes et Phéniciens à Golgoi de Chypre," *Sem* 39 (1990) 43–46, pls. 43–44.

RPC 113–14, pl. 14:3–4; Puech, "Remarques sur quelques inscriptions phéniciennes de Chypre," 27. The inscription is "Shubba'al" (*šb'l*), the personal name of the merchant whose products were contained in the jar and who may or may not have been a resident of Golgoi.

199. *RPC* 104–7, pl. 8:2.

200. A. Christodoulou, "A Cypro-Archaic I Tomb-Group from Maroni," *RDAC* (1972) 156–60.

201. M. Hadjicosti, "The Family Tomb of a Warrior of the Cypro-Archaic I Period at Mari," *RDAC* (1997) 251–66, pls. 49–54.

202. M. Sznycer, "Une nouvelle inscription phénicienne d'Amathonte (Chypre)," *Sem* 49 (1999) 195–97.

203. *RPC* 94–95, pl. 9:1.

204. W. M. Davis, "Ancient Naukratis and the Cypriotes in Egypt," *Göttinger Miszellen* 35 (1979) 13–23; idem, "The Cypriotes at Naucratis," *Göttinger Miszellen* 41 (1980) 7–19.

205. J. Boardman, *Excavations in Chios 1952–1955: Greek Emporio* (London: British School of Archaeology at Athens / Thames & Hudson, 1967) 193; G. Schmidt, *Kyprische Bildwerke aus dem Heraion von Samos* (Samos VII) (Bonn: Habelt, 1968); H. Kyrieleis, "New Cypriot Finds from the Heraion of Samos," in *Cyprus and the East Mediterranean in the Iron Age* (ed. V. Tatton-Brown; London: British Museum, 1989) 52–67; L. Wriedt Sørensen, "Cypriote Terracottas from Lindos in the

perfume and unguent jars and wine jugs and of Red Slip mushroom-lipped jugs made by Phoenicians or Greeks for local use and export to Italy, Spain, and the western Mediterranean.[206] There was also a Rhodian school of ivory carving that produced Orientalizing works and faience workshops that could copy Egyptianizing pieces imported by Tyrians from Cyprus or Al Mina.[207]

The treasury of the Heraion on Samos became the repository of votive offerings from around the world, including ivories such as these and Cypriot pottery and limestone statuettes.[208] Some of it was brought by Phoenicians from Cyprus, some perhaps the reward of Samian piracy, much of it the gift to the sanctuary of pilgrims who had collected bric-a-brac, art, and exotica—notably from Assyria and Babylonia—that were sold on the Phoenician market.[209] Other Greek sanctuaries began to treasure Near Eastern artifacts[210] and became the customers of these Phoenicians from Cyprus and of their confreres from Tyre and its mainland possessions. With the collectables, they brought literature and culture[211] (words, treaty forms, astronomy, luxury) and participation in the economic surge overtaking the Mediterranean world. A few places lagged and were left out of the race.[212]

The Phoenician effect on Cyprus was centuries old in the seventh century and can only be sorted out of its native Greek and Cypriot adaptations.

Light of New Discoveries," in *Cypriote Terracottas* (ed. F. Vandenabeele and R. Laffineur; Brussels: Vrije Universiteit / Liège: Université de Liège, 1991) 225–40, pls. 64–69.

206. J. N. Coldstream, "The Phoenicians of Ialysos," *Bulletin of the Institute of Classical Studies of the University of London* 16 (1969) 1–8, pls. 1–3; A. Peserico, *Le brocche "a fungo" fenicie nel Mediterraneo: Tipologia e cronologia* (Rome: Consiglio Nazionale delle Ricerche, 1996) 114; idem, "Il ruolo di Rodi e dell'area egea nell'espansione fenicia verso Occidente: La documentazione ceramica," in *Patavina Orientalia Selecta* (ed. E. Rova; Padua: Sargon, 2000) 139–64; W. Culican, "Almuñécar, Assur and Phoenician Penetration of the Western Mediterranean," *Levant* 2 (1970) 28–36, pls. 25–27; repr. in idem, *Opera Selecta: From Tyre to Tartessos* (Gothenburg: Åströms, 1986) 673–84.

207. L. Schofield, "The Influence of Eastern Religions on the Iconography of Ivory and Bone Objects in the Kameiros Well," in *Ivory in Greece and the Eastern Mediterranean from the Bronze Age to the Hellenistic Period* (ed. J. L. Fitton; London: British Museum, 1992) 173–84.

208. G. Shipley, *A History of Samos, 800–188 BC* (Oxford: Clarendon, 1987) 42–46; I. Strøm, "Evidence from the Sanctuaries," in *Greece between East and West: 10th–8th Centuries BC* (ed. G. Kopcke and I. Tokumaru; Mainz: von Zabern, 1992) 46–60, pls. 5e–7; H. Kyrieleis, "The Heraion at Samos," in *Greek Sanctuaries: New Approaches* (ed. N. Marinatos and R. Hägg; London: Routledge, 1993) 125–53.

209. A. Jackson, "Sea-Raiding in Archaic Greece with Special Attention to Samos," *The Sea in Antiquity* (ed. G. J. Oliver et al.; BAR International Series 899; Oxford: Hedges, 2000) 133–49; J. Curtis, "Mesopotamian Bronzes from Greek Sites: The Workshops of Origin," *Iraq* 56 (1994) 1–25.

210. E. Guralnick, "Greece and the Near East: Art and Archaeology," in *Daidalikon: Studies in Memory of Raymond V. Schoder, S.J.* (ed. R. F. Sutton Jr.; Wauconda, IL: Bolchazy-Carducci, 1989) 151–76; idem, "East to West: Near Eastern Artifacts from Greek Sites," in *La circulation des biens, des personnes et des idées dans le Proche-Orient Ancien* (ed. D. Charpin and F. Joannès; Paris: Éditions Recherche sur les Civilisations, 1992) 327–40; idem, "A Group of Near Eastern Bronzes from Olympia," *AJA* 108 (2004) 187–222.

211. S. Dalley and A. T. Reyes, "Mesopotamian Contact and Influence in the Greek World: 1. To the Persian Conquest," in *The Legacy of Mesopotamia* (ed. S. Dalley; Oxford: Oxford University Press, 1998) 85–106.

212. H. W. Catling, "New Light on Knossos in the 8th and 7th Centruries B.C.," *Annuario della Scuola Archeologia di Atene* 61 (1983) 31–43.

The Phoenicians themselves had adjusted to Cyprus. There seems to have been little recent immigration from the mainland cities and towns. The islanders were self-sufficient, and imports were rare, mainlanders visited but did not stay, and the island was settling down into its Cypriot and Greek self. The Phoenicians on Cyprus, perhaps assimilated Cypriots too, joined the westward race.

Carthage

Carthage was founded by settlers from Cyprus toward the end of the eighth century B.C.E.[213] It was a colony, like Carthage in Cyprus, deliberately constituted in the name of Tyre and intended as the center of a new Phoenician venture in the western Mediterranean. It was an open city, settled by residents of the island, by people from the mainland city and its Palestinian possessions, and by the individual merchants, craftsmen, laborers, and adventurers who traveled to Italy, Sicily, Sardinia, or Spain. It began as a compound on the Byrsa hill, with houses and workshops in the fields below, and harbor facilities and warehouses in the natural port just to the south of them. By the end of the seventh century, it had become a planned and multipurpose town, with the residential streets, which now crept over the adjoining Juno hill, following the contour of the hills and the downtown streets laid out on an orthogonal grid.

The oldest parts of the settlement can be recognized in a few scattered remains of walls, workshops, and tombs.[214] In one sector of the hill settlement there was early pottery (a lamp and a proto-Corinthian rounded jug [aryballos]) associated with a foundation strong enough to support a multistoried house.[215] The hilltop compound was walled. Houses at the foot of the hill had stone foundations, brick walls, and beaten-earth floors. In the workshop area near the shore, where the floors were also of beaten earth, there were traces of an iron foundry (blast pipes, slag, deeply burned earth), a murex or purple dye industry; and pottery ovens with pieces of heavy amphorae, storage jars, cooking pots, lamps, jugs, and plates.[216] The earliest infant burials are in the Tannit precinct just west of the port: the cremated remains were gathered in urns, red burnished with black linear decoration, laid on bedrock, covered with little stone cairns, and sometimes accompanied by a figurine or a vase. This phase of the cemetery was sealed by a layer of yellow clay and was succeeded by a totally different burial configuration: plain urns buried in the clay and covered by tombstones. The earliest adult burials were interments on the slopes of the Byrsa hill,[217] and the earliest

---

213. C. Baurain, "Le rôle de Chypre dans la fondation de Carthage," *Carthago*, 15–27.

214. D. B. Harden, *The Phoenicians* (Ancient Peoples and Places 26; New York: Praeger, 1962) 66–75; S. Lancel, "Les fouilles de la mission archéologique française à Carthage et le problème de Byrsa," *Carthago*, 61–89; R. Rakob, "La Carthage archaïque," *HAAN*, 31–43; H. G. Niemeyer, "A la recherche de la Carthage archaïque: Premiers résultats des fouilles de l'Université de Hambourg en 1986 et 1987," ibid., 45–52.

215. Lancel, "Les fouilles de la mission archéologique française à Carthage et le problème de Byrsa."

216. Rakob, "La Carthage archaïque."

217. Harden, *The Phoenicians*, 30–35.

built tombs are like tombs at Amathus in Cyprus.[218] New settlers kept arriving throughout the seventh century (there was good farmland in the interior, west of the maritime city), and the city hit its stride in the sixth century.

Among the earlier pottery, there is an abundance of Red Slip and a sample of Euboean, Corinthian, and Pithecusan wares, but pottery imports of the early seventh century were gradually replaced by locally made wares.[219] There are many transport amphorae from the Phoenician mainland and from Spain in the first half of the century, suggesting that Carthage at first depended on these places for its supplies of food, wine, and oil.[220] The pottery found in a cache, sometimes said to be a foundation deposit of the new colony, consisted of amphorae, juglets, and perfume bottles with Cypro-Geometric, proto-Corinthian, Italian, and Greek antecedents and could have been imported from Amathus in Cyprus, where a similar crasis of ceramic traditions had occurred.[221] Earlier seventh-century pottery from houses in the center of the city was mainly from central Italy and included fine wares from Etruria, Latium, Campania, and Pithecusa and handmade Italo-Phoenician transport amphorae from Pithecusa and Cerveteri.[222] The colony was the clearinghouse for ships sailing back to the eastern mainland and at first counted on them as a source of supply. However, things began to change around the mid-seventh century and, when Carthage had established good relations with neighboring North African countries,[223] it soon became self-sufficient and the core of a western Mediterranean Phoenicia that would revel in the wonderments of its Eastern origins.

The built tombs were influenced by Cyprian standards.[224] The earliest was the tomb in which Yada'milk, the leader of the Cypriot contingent, was buried with his wife. The Pygmalion medallion was emblematic of his illustrious career, and their tomb is a mark of their prestige in the early Carthaginian community.[225] It was large, built of hewn and finished blocks, the walls plastered inside as if waiting for painted designs, the ceiling paneled. His body was laid on a pallet to the left of the entrance, and he wore

218. A. M. Bisi, "Chypre et les premiers temps de Carthage," *Carthago*, 29–41, esp. pp. 34–35.

219. C. Picard, "Les navigations de Carthage vers l'Ouest: Carthage et le pays de Tarsis aux VIIIe–VIe siècles," *PhWest*, 167–73; A. Peserico, *Die offenen Formen der Red Slip Ware aus Karthago: Untersuchungen zur phönizischen Keramik im westlichen Mittelmeerraum* (Hamburger Werkstattreihe zur Archäologie 5; Munster: LIT Verlag, 2002).

220. M. Botto, "Indagini archeometriche sulla ceramica fenicia e punica del Mediteraneo centro-occidentale," *RSF* 29 (2001) 159–81, esp. p. 172.

221. C. Briese, "Die *Chapelle Cintas*: Das Gründungsdepot Karthagos oder eine Bestattung der Gründergeneration?" *ASKaW*, 419–52, pls. 35–37.

222. R. F. Docter, "Carthage and the Tyrrhenian in the 8th and 7th Centuries B.C.: Central Italian Transport Amphorae and Fine Wares Found under the Decumanus Maximus," *Actas* 4, 1.329–38.

223. M. Fantar, "L'impact de la présence phénicienne et la fondation de Carthage en Mediterranée occidentale," *Carthago*, 3–14; Y. B. Tsirkin, "The Economy of Carthage," ibid., 125–35.

224. Bisi, "Chypre et les premiers temps de Carthage."

225. M. Gras, P. Rouillard, and J. Teixidor, "The Phoenicians and Death," *Berytus* 39 (1991) 127–76, esp. pp. 141–45; M. Gras and P. Duboeuf, "L'architecture de la tombe de Yada'milk à Carthage: Essai de Restitution," in *Da Pyrgi a Mozia: Studi sull'archeologia nel Mediterranea in Memoria di Antonia Ciasca* (ed. M. G. Amadasi Guzzo, M. Liverani, and P. Matthiae; Vicino Oriente: Quaderno 3/1; Rome: Università degli Studi di Roma, "La Sapienza," 2002) 253–66.

a bronze bracelet and a gold ring. His wife was placed on the ground to his left, with a large silver bowl at her head and a wine jug and a lamp in a niche within reach, and a Phoenician urn, broken deliberately, lay between them. The pottery they shared included a Phoenician amphora and urn, a proto-Corinthian drinking bowl, a trefoil-lipped wine jug, and cooking pots. His jewelry contained, besides his gold pendant, an ivory scarab inlaid with gold and set in a silver ring. Her ornaments featured a gold necklace, a gold jewelry box, and a gold amulet case. Yada'milk describes himself as a soldier who was commissioned by Pygmalion, but he seems to have been the commandant of the new colony.

The colonials kept arriving on the ships that supplied them and, consequently, came from Tyre, its Palestinian possessions, from Cyprus, and from the communities that had already been established in the West. Their diversity is represented in their arts and crafts. Their graves have yielded female masks like those from 'Achzib; shallow pedestal bowls like bowls at towns near Tyre and Sidon; perfume bottles, called "Sidonian," the parallels of which are from Sidon and Sarepta; as well as terra-cottas of a lone figure in a boat crossing to the afterlife, or of groups of figures in an open-air sanctuary similar to the homely designs from Cyprus.[226]

The seventh-century gold and silver jewelry (medallions, pendants, rings, earrings) is plain, with west Mediterranean parallels; or has the Egyptianizing motifs favored by Tyrian artists; or features the Sign of Tannit, which was adopted as the colonial symbol.[227] But two small ivory figurines from graves in the oldest cemeteries[228] depict a woman with pudgy features and a receding chin, wearing an Egyptian wig that reveals her large Hathor or cow-like ears, fully clothed but cupping perfectly delineated breasts, and with a stylish collar necklace like others found in contemporary Carthaginian graves. The style (her physical features, the mixture of motifs, the melding of Syrian modesty and Phoenician brass) is North Syrian or Anatolian, but the figurines were obviously made locally by an émigré artist, assuredly from Sidon, and trained in this Syrian tradition.

The foundation myth of Carthage[229] was transmitted in Greek sources and gave the bold and exciting facts romantic truth and epic reality. Elissa was the sister of Pygmalion, king of Tyre, and the daughter of Mittin or, as a variant has it, of Ba'al. In either case, she was a princess, the daughter of a king—of Mittin, who is mentioned as king in the Assyrian annals for the year 734 B.C.E.; or of Ba'al, who was king around the turn of the century and into the reign of Esarhaddon. Her brother Pygmalion is invoked in the victory shout recorded on Yada'amilk's medallion as the founder of

226. A. M. Bisi, "Les sources syro-palestiniennes et chypriotes de l'art punique (à propos de quelques objets de Carthage)," *Antiquités Africaines* 14 (1979) 17–35.

227. B. Quillard, *Bijoux Carthaginois, I: Les Colliers; II: Porte-Amulettes, Sceaux-Pendentifs, Pendants, Bouiles, Anneaux et Bagues (d'après les collections du Musée National du Bardo et du Musée National de Carthage)* (Louvain-la-Neuve: Institut Supérieur d'Archéologie et d'Histoire de l'Art, 1987); C. Picard, "L'essor de Carthage aux VIIe et VIe siècles," *Carthago*, 43–50.

228. A. M. Bisi, "Une figurine phénicienne trouvée a Carthage et quelques monuments apparentés," *Mélanges de Carthage: Offerts à Charles Saumagne, Louis Poinssot, Maurice Pinard* (Cahiers de Byrsa 10; Paris: Geuthner, 1964–65) 43–53, pls. 1–5.

229. C. Baurain, "Le rôle d'Chypre dans la Fondation de Carthage," *Carthago*, 15–27, esp. pp. 18–22.

Carthage and was a hero to his men, but he was a wicked king according to the legend and a lustful scoundrel who murdered his sister's husband, Zakarbaʿal. Elissa escaped to Cyprus—Elissa (*Alashiya*) was the name of Enkomi, and then Salamis and, among the Greeks, of the whole island—and from there, she and her maiden friends sailed to Carthage. It is the same story that is told and retold, about the men who planned the colony, about the women who captured its romance, and about the silent earth that cried out for recognition.

Sardinia

Phoenicians in seventh-century Sardinia had irregular relations with the eastern mainland and concentrated on consolidating and developing the network of western settlements. They were established on the island, and the native Nuraghi population, whose way of life had changed from the moment of their settlement, continued to benefit from their industry and outreach. They came to Sardinia for its resources, and they stayed to maintain this vital link between Europe and North African Carthage.

Until about the mid-seventh century, there was a uniform Eastern–Western Mediterranean ceramic tradition.[230] From that time, very few forms traveled from East to West, and the Western settlements in Sardinia and elsewhere produced their own domestic, ritual, and commercial wares. Red Slip lost its international status, the nearly ubiquitous mushroom-lipped jug developed into a peculiarly Western form,[231] and there was ceramic variety from place to place.[232] In Sardinia, even between places in the same region, uniformity was not to be expected, because each town went with the tastes of its settlers from the East and its contacts in the West.

In the ninth and eighth centuries, relations with Etruria were evident mainly in Nuraghic settlements from central to northern Sardinia.[233] In the seventh century, southern Sardinia became involved in trade and cultural exchanges with Etruria, and this is evident first in the interior, where it is witnessed primarily by expensive imported items, and later in the Phoenician inland sites and coastal areas, where it is visible in plainer goods, such as amphorae, jugs, and drinking bowls meant for symposia.[234] The imports themselves (the silver, bronze, bone, and ceramic materials) were Orientalizing, the work of assimilated Phoenicians living in Etruria or of Etruscans trained in the Phoenician boutiques.[235]

---

230. P. Bartoloni, "Apunti sulla ceramica fenicia tra Oriente e occidente dall'VIII al VI sec. a.C.," *Transeu* 12 (1996) 85–95.

231. A. Peserico, *Le brocche "a fungo" fenicie nel Mediterraneo: Tipologia e cronologia* (Rome: Consiglio Nazionale delle Ricerche, 1996) 161.

232. A. Ciasca, "Note sul repertorio ceramico fenicio di Occidente," *Dialoghi di Archeologia* 5/2 (1987) 7–12.

233. See, for instance, F. Lo Schiavo, "Le fibule della Sardegna," *Studi Etruschi* 46 (1978) 25–46.

234. P. Bartoloni, "Anfore fenicie e ceramiche etrusche in Sardegna," in *Il commercio etrusco arcaico: Atti dell'Incontro di Studio, 5–7 dicembre 1983* (ed. M. Cristofani et al.; Rome: Consiglio Nazionale delle Ricerche, 1985) 103–18; C. Tronchetti, "La Sardegna e gli Etruschi," *Mediterranean Archaeology* 1 (1988) 66–82.

235. M. Gras, *Trafics tyrrhéniens archaïques* (Bibliothèques des Écoles Françaises d'Athènes et de Rome 258; Rome: École Française de Rome, 1985) 135–44.

The Sardinian exports to Etruria included native Nuraghic bronze weapons and tools, household goods such as bronze cauldrons and lamps and decorated ceramic pitchers.[236] Modeled on small bronze, ivory, or ceramic originals but influenced by Greek representational ideas were large or even life-size ceramic statues by acculturated Phoenician craftsmen or their Sardinian apprentices.[237] By the seventh century, the Phoenicians had settled in to the Sardinian rhythm, and their Nuraghi hosts were accustomed to their social and economic demands. Their exports, such as Sardinian amphorae in Latium, and imports were handled by Phoenician traders,[238] and this continuing Italian nexus is consistent with pioneering ninth-century Nuraghic contacts and with the eighth-century origins of Phoenician settlements in Sardinia.

Tharros was a mixed community of Sardinian elite and Phoenician (specifically, Sidonian) professionals.[239] In the seventh century, it was spread out along the Tharros peninsula in the Gulf of Oristano, where the residences, stores and workshops, public buildings, and graveyards were located; at Othoca on the opposing coast, which gave residents access to the adjacent farmlands; and at Monti Prama on the mainland just north of the peninsula at the edge of the vast Sinis plain, a sanctuary town where the Phoenicians met and did business with the native aristocracy.[240] Although there are few architectural remains on the peninsula (a large fifth-century ashlar building built on the site of an earlier structure), its topography, especially its transformation of the surrounding area (the Sardinians abandoned their separate fortified nuraghe to live in open villages with streets, public squares, and drainage systems), suggests that Tharros in the seventh century was becoming an expansive and vibrant urban center.[241]

Some small finds from Tharros offer clues on the mentality, origins, and connections of the Phoenician settlers. There is an ivory cosmetic spoon in the shape of a naked swimming girl holding a deep receptacle in her outstretched hands.[242] The item is commonplace, and the girl usually is presented as a lithe and dainty Egyptian maiden, but in this example she is squat, chubby, and Syrian or Anatolian in appearance—that is, hardly "Phoenician" at all, but rather, Sidonian. Similarly, a pendant in the shape of a naked girl holding her breasts and a ceramic bust of a woman feature the

236. M. Køllund, "Sea and Sardinia," *HBA* 19/20 (1992–1993) 201–14.

237. L. Bonfante, "The Etruscan Connection," in *Studies in Sardinian Archaeology, II: Sardinia in the Mediterranean* (ed. M. S. Balmuth; Ann Arbor: University of Michigan Press, 1986) 73–83.

238. M. Botto, "Anfore fenicie dai contesti indigeni del *Latium Vetus* nel periodo orientalizzante," *RSF* 21 (1993) Supplement, 16–27, pls. 2–3; E. Acquaro, "Los Fenicios y Púnicos en Cerdeña," *Actas* 4, 1.71–81.

239. P. Bernardini, "Fenomeni di interazione tra Fenici e indigeni in Sardegna," in *Fenicios e Indígenas en el Mediterráneo y Occidenti: Modelos e Interacción* (ed. D. Ruiz Mata; Cádiz: University of Cádiz, 1998) 39–98, esp. p. 48.

240. *PFPS* 57–61.

241. E. Acquaro, "Tharrica 1988–1991," *Actes* 3, 1.16–19; P. van Dommelen, "Some Reflections on Urbanization in a Colonial Context: West Central Sardinia in the 7th to 5th Centuries B.C.," in *Urbanization in the Mediterranean in the 9th to 6th Centuries B.C.* (ed. H. Damgaard Andersen et al.; Copenhagen: University of Copenhagen—Museum Tusculanum, 1998) 243–78.

242. L. Vagnetti, "La 'nuotatrice' di Tharros," *RSF* 21 (1993) 29–33.

full-bodied Oriental type of Sidonian art.[243] Three bronzes—a lamp holder, an incense stand, a tripod cauldron-base—were imports from Cyprus, and the last was an heirloom, cast most likely in the eleventh century;[244] these three reveal another facet of this Sidonian heritage.

Finally, there is an incense-offering or libation ensemble[245] that gives a local twist to the triple-baetyl monuments of Tyrian origin. The base and the three uprights were carved in one piece of limestone. The center upright has a steep-sloped roof structure jutting above the others and below this roof an inverted crescent draped over a full moon. The lateral uprights look like crenellated towers, and their top surface is scooped out to receive the incense or libation. The Tharros ensemble, all in all, transforms the symbolism of the traditional funerary monument into the current realities of urban life. The central, roofed structure represents the temple, and the lateral towers represent the wall of the city, which as implied by their ritual function is the city of God. The representation is unique, but it seems to summarize the memories and aspirations of the founding generation from Sidon and its possessions as it joined in the planning of a new Western Phoenicia.

Much of what is known about ancient Tharros is gathered from the contents of its tombs. Cremation, with one exception, was reserved for babies who died at or soon after birth.[246] It was accompanied by the offering of a lamb or kid, and the burial urns contained the ashes of both the animal and the child as well as of the wood (olive, lentisk shrub, or small oak), and in a few of the urns there was also a seashell.

The inhumations are notable for the vast amounts of expensive jewelry and trinkets they contained.[247] The gold was from Spain, the silver from Spain or the Iglesiente region of southern Sardinia, the smiths were from the East, the techniques were traditional, and the work was local.[248] The jewelry consisted mainly of finger rings, earrings, necklaces, bracelets, and pendants. The trinkets, or amulets, some of them imported, featured Egyptian Gods such as Bes, Horus, and Harpocrates and a whole array of Phoenician specialities: there is the God Ba'al, the naked adolescent girl, the bust of a woman; there are body parts, including an eye, a hand and arm, a heart, feet and legs, and phalli; there are also plants (pineapples, lotus and papyrus flowers) and many animals (monkeys, dolphins, dogs, and cats) and symbols (acorns, altars, obelisks, axes, and writing tablets). Tharros, however, specialized in gold jewelry, which it exported throughout the

243. S. Moscati, "Centri artigianali fenici in Italia," *RSF* 1 (1973) 37–52, pls. 12–31, esp. pp. 50–51, pls. 29b, 31b.

244. Idem and M. L. Uberti, *Testimonianze fenicio-puniche a Oristano* (ANLM 8/31, fasc. 1; Rome: Accademia nazionale dei Lincei, 1988) 6–61, pls. 1–26, esp. pp. 43–52.

245. Moscati, "Centri artigianali fenici I Italia," 49, pl. 29a.

246. F. G. Fedele, "Tharros: Anthropology of the *Tophet* and Paleoecology of a Punic Town," *Atti* 1, 3.637–50.

247. R. D. Barnett and C. Mendelson, *Tharros: A Catalogue of Material in the British Museum from Phoenician and Other Tombs at Tharros, Sardinia* (London: British Museum, 1987).

248. S. Moscati, *I Gioielli di Tharros: Origini, Caratteri, Confronti* (Rome: Consiglio Nazionale delle Ricerche, 1988).

Punic world, especially to Carthage, where most but not all of its styles are represented.[249]

Sulcis, with its satellite towns in the Iglesiente region of southern Sardinia, was distinct in its origins, constitution, and management from the Phoenician center at Tharros. It was a Tyrian settlement with close ties to Pithecusa,[250] founded as an outpost and supply depot for Carthage. It had not been a Nuraghic settlement before the Phoenicians arrived and, although there may have been intermarriage with the natives, Sulcis remained aloof from its surroundings, as was usual in Tyrian towns, and relations with the Sardinians were relegated to its outlying stations, notably at Monte Sirai.[251] It maintained its original ties to Cyprus and mainland Phoenicia into the seventh century, but its most consistent and productive links were with Carthage and with Greek sites in Italy.

There are architectural remains at Sulcis, but the pottery is more revealing of the makeup of the population. Houses were built on both sides of the streets, constructed of brick with stone foundations and consisted of small square rooms, floors of tufa or beaten earth, and a courtyard with a well or cistern.[252] The pottery, much of it from the cremation burials, was Euboean and Corinthian,[253] Pithecusan, Etruscan, Phoenician, and Carthaginian. Some of the Phoenician wares, a bowl, for instance, and a set of cups, are imitations of Greek originals.[254]

A few of the wares from both early and late in the seventh century are adaptations of Sardinian forms.[255] Others are reproductions of Eastern mainland models. About 40 percent of this standard Phoenician pottery consists of transport amphorae, storage jars, and domestic containers.[256] The rest includes household wares[257] (carinated and tripod bowls, deep rounded cups, plates with narrow rims, and one-wick lamps) as well as the signature mushroom-lipped jugs, the earlier of which were imported from

---

249. R. D. Barnett, "Phoenician and Punic Arts and Handicrafts: Some Reflections and Notes," *Atti* 1, 1.19–26, pls. 1–6, esp. pp. 22–23. S. Moscati, "Découvertes phéniciennes à Tharros," *CRAIBL* (1987) 483–503, esp. p. 483.

250. P. Bartoloni, "Le relazioni tra Cartagine e la Sardegna nei secoli VII e VI a.C.," *EVO* 10 (1987) 79–86, esp. p. 80; *PFPS* 50–56.

251. S. Moscati, *Fenici e Greci in Sardegna* (ANLR 3/40, fasc. 7–12; Rome, 1985) 265–71; P. Bernardini, "Fenomeni di interazione tra Fenici e indigeni in Sardegna," in *Fenicios e Indígenas en el Mediterráneo y Occidente: Modelos e Interacción* (ed. D. Ruiz Mata; Cádiz: University of Cádiz, 1998) 39–98, esp. p. 47.

252. C. Tronchetti, "Sardaigne," *CPPMR*, 712–42, esp. p. 721.

253. P. Bernardini, "Lo scavo nell'area del Cronicario di S. Antioco e le origini della presenza fenicia a Sulci," *Riti funerari e di olocausto nella Sardegna fenicia e punica: Atti dell'incontro di studio Sant'Antioco, 3–4 ottobre, 1986* (Cagliari: Edizioni della torre, 1990) 135–49.

254. Idem, "Un insediamento fenicio a Sulci nella seconda metà dell'VIII sec. a.C.," *Atti* 2, 2.663–73, esp. pp. 668–69.

255. P. Bartoloni, "Urne cinerarie arcaiche a Sulcis," *RSF* 16 (1988) 165–79; idem, "Riti funerari fenici e punici nel Sulcis," *Riti funerari e di olocausto nella Sardegna fenicia e punica: Atti dell'incontro di studio Sant'Antioco, 3–4 ottobre, 1986* (Cagliari: Edizioni della torre, 1990) 67–81, esp. p. 75; idem, "Ceramica fenicia tra Oriente e Occidente," *Atti* 2, 2.641–53, esp. pp. 648, 651.

256. Idem, *Orizzonti commerciali sulcitani tra l'VIII e il VII sec. a.C.* (ANLR 8/41, fasc. 7–12; Rome, 1987) 219–26, esp. pp. 221–24; idem, "S. Antioco: Area del Cronicario (campagne di scavo 1983–1986): I recipiente chiusi d'uso domestico e commerciale," *RSF* 18 (1990) 37–79, pls. 5–6.

257. P. Bernardini, "S. Antioco: Area del Cronicario (campagne di scavo 1983–1986): La ceramica fenicia—forme aperte," *RSF* 18 (1990) 81–98.

the East and probably traveled with the settlers. The later, up to about the mid-seventh century, were locally made.[258] There are also shallow drinking bowls (the form was adapted from the Greek skyphos, but the ceramic finish and the painted decoration are Phoenician), which were popular everywhere in the Punic Mediterranean, but the best parallels of which are found at Toscanos in southern Spain, Motya in Sicily, and at Carthage.[259] There were local variations: Red Slip at Sulcis is dark and framed by black lines, but at Tharros it is light and edged with colored bands. But in general, Sulcis, Carthage, and Spain followed the same ceramic trends and even exchanged their wares.[260]

The graveyard on the north side of town is interesting, not only for the typology of the urns in which the cremated remains were buried and for the large number of Egyptian amulets and knickknacks included in the burials, but especially for its tombstones.[261] Among the early steles is one, the iconography of which is adapted from the representation of kings, court officials, and merchant bankers on eighth- and early seventh-century seals from Tyre and other countries in the Tyrian trade network:[262] a man wearing a long robe belted at the waist strides to the right, with a floral staff (or a lance) in his left hand and his right hand raised in blessing. The difference is in the details and the context that remove him from simply human stature to being the divinized mortal who was Melqart, and this in a distinctively Sardinian, perhaps specifically Sulcian, mode.

He is set into an aedicule; columns support the architrave in which a crescent is draped over a full moon. He stands on a pedestal, and so in effect is an effigy of the God in his temple. But his facial features are not Egyptianizing or refined as in the Eastern exemplars, and he wears a Syrian cap—a sort of mitre with a broad pendant band rolled upward at the nape of his neck. The stele is unique at Sulcis, and the divine status of its figure (also represented on a seal from Cyprus)[263] is suggested as well by the fact that the next-earliest steles (none of them antedating the sixth century by much) are aniconic or abstract, while steles with representations of women or men, done under Greek influence, follow only in the latter part of that

258. A. Peserico, *Le broche "a fungo" fenicie nel Mediterraneo: Tipologia e cronologia* (Rome: Consiglio Nazionale delle Ricerche, 1996) 66, 92, 135, 225–26.

259. C. Briese and R. Docter, "Der phönizische Skyphos: Adaption einer griechischen Trinkschale," *MM* 33 (1992) 25–69.

260. A. Peserico, "Phönizisches Tafelgeschirr und regionale Keramik-Produktion im westlichen Mittelmeerraum," *ASKaW*, 375–87.

261. G. Hölbl, *Ägyptisches Kulturgut im phönikischen und punischen Sardinien I–II* (Leiden: Brill, 1986) 54–58 and passim. There are fewer of these Egyptian or Egyptianizing items at Sulcis than there are at Tharros. Some are seventh century, but the majority are later and so register the influence of Carthage and North Africa in southern Sardinia.

S. Moscati, *Stele sulcitane con animale passante* (ANLR 8/36, fasc. 1–2; Rome, 1982) 3–8, pls. 1–13; idem, *Le stele di Sulcis: Caratteri e confronti* (Rome: Consiglio Nazionale delle Ricereche, 1986); idem and S. F. Bondì, *Italia Punica* (Milan: Rusconi, 1986) 240–62; M. L. Uberti, "La collezione punica Don Armeni (Sulcis)," *OrAnt* 10 (1971) 277–312, pls. 39–47. The majority of steles postdate the seventh century, and steles with an animal passant (usually a lamb or sheep) date to the third and second centuries B.C.E.

262. G. Pesce, "Due opere di arte fenicia in Sardegna," *OrAnt* 2 (1963) 247–56, pls. 41–45, esp. pp. 247–53, pls. 41–42.

263. E. Acquaro, "Appunti su una stele da Sulcis," *OrAnt* 8 (1969) 69–72, pl. 1.

century. As in the ceramic repertory, stele styles varied from place to place. Thus, Sulcis steles differed from steles at Tharros or from Carthage, with which otherwise Sulcis was closely related, and even from the steles at its own establishment at Monte Sirai.

There are three seventh-century inscriptions from Sulcis. The latest, from about the middle of the century, is the legend "belonging to Gerʾeshmun, son of Ḥimilk" on a stamp seal.²⁶⁴ The seal has a winged sun disk above a ritual scene featuring the child Harpocrates facing an animal-headed goddess and seated on a lotus-flower pedestal flanked and held by Horus, who wears the double crown of Egypt, and by Isis, who is adorned with a horned-disk headdress—with both of them identified by hieroglyphic signs. The name is Phoenician or Punic, the surname is more typically western Mediterranean, and the iconography is in the Egyptianizing Tyrian tradition.

The earlier inscription, from the beginning of the century, was hammered into a piece of gold plating,²⁶⁵ which was designed to cover the finial of a scepter, like the scepter carried by Melqart on the Sulcis stele, or on seals by eastern notables who assumed the grand striding-smiting pose. The man's name (ʾAbî), the antiquity of the finial, and its dedication to Baʿal make it likely that it was made and dedicated in the East and arrived in Sardinia with its owner.

There is a third inscribed object from Sulcis that is of similar interest.²⁶⁶ It is a silver cup, made in the seventh century for a symposium, from a southern Etruscan workshop. It was kept as an heirloom, restored, and inscribed in the third century B.C.E. Its inscription reads:

> To the Lord, to Baʿal ʾAddir. May he bless [ybrk]. Skyphos [skt] weighing 59 shekels, which the artisans restored in the time of the aldermen [rabbîm] Magon and ʿAzormilk, in the year of the magistrates [špṭm] in Sulcis [slky], ʾAddirbaʿal and Milkyaton, and in the time of the chief priest Bodʿaštart, son of ʾAriš, son of Ḥimilkot.

The prayer for "blessing" without specifying a particular object, the omission of the donor's or craftsman's name, and the inclusion of a full slate of eponymous officeholders, indicate that the cup was designed from the beginning, and not just from its third-century refurbishment, as public property. It is a Phoenician adaptation of a Greek original (it has handles and a foot, as Greeks insisted). If the dedication is original or authentic, it may have been made in a Byblian workshop—Baʿal ʾAddîr is the manifestation of this God peculiar to Byblos—or as a foundation gift from the Byblian community in Etruria to the people of Sulcis.

The close connection between Sulcis (along with its outposts in the Iglesiente region of southwestern Sardinia) and Carthage led to direct control by the Punic capital and eventually to less-than-benign neglect. Monte Sirai, where there were residences (with beaten-earth and tufa pavements,

---

264. *WSS* 273 #733; S. Moscati, *L'arte della Sardegna punica* (Milan: Jaca Book, 1986) pl. 71; idem, ed., *The Phoenicians* (New York; Abbeville, 1988) 528.

265. F. Barreca, "Nuove iscrizioni fenicie da Sulcis," *OrAnt* 4 (1965) 53–57, pls. 1–2, esp. pp. 55–57, pl. 2.

266. P. Bartoloni and G. Garbini, "Una coppa d'argento con iscrizione punica da Sulcis," *RSF* 27 (1999) 79–91, pl. 5.

as at Sulcis itself) and some public buildings in the seventh century, had a
Phoenician and Sardinian population of around 300.[267] The pottery (about
40 pieces from 3 of the rooms) relates the earliest phase to Tyre and Tell Keisan, and the later seventh-century and early sixth-century phase to Sulcis,
to Bithia in the Iglesiente, and to Cuccureddus di Villasimius on the Gulf
of Cagliari.[268]

The seventh-century burials at Monte Sirai, as throughout Sardinia at
this time, were cremations, with the urns simply buried in the ground or
placed in a stone-lined grave.[269] Of unknown provenance, but probably
from the Iglesiente region, is a terra-cotta statuette of a naked woman lying
on her back and in labor pains, her vagina open to give birth, her mouth
twisted, gasping for breath.[270] It is a strange mixture of artistic sensitivity
and technical naïveté but a good example of the vigorous indigenous traditions that mellowed the Phoenician élan and that resisted and outlasted
their dominant presence.

Sardinia was a principal player in the Phoenician policy of westward
expansion. Each site, Tharros and Sulcis most clearly, was different, marked
by the distinctiveness of the town or district in eastern Phoenicia that had
contributed most to its establishment.[271] Each belonged to a specific network: Sulcis, for instance, to the Iglesiente and to the Toscanos-Carthage
nexus; and Tharros, with its Nuraghic base in central Sardinia, to a circuit
that included Atlantic Spain, the Gulf of Cagliari, and Motya in Sicily. In
the seventh century, the Phoenicians were so well established that their
presence was no longer conspicuous. From the start, Carthage was the focus of all these Sardinian foundations, and by the sixth century, the tide
turned and Carthage began to dominate the politics, religion, and material
culture of the island.[272]

Spain

Phoenicians in Spain in the seventh century were still distinguished by
their habitat and their native context, those on the Atlantic coast less being influenced by Greeks and more engaged in the aboriginal communities,
those on the Mediterranean being regularly in contact first with Samians
and then with Phocaeans,[273] while remaining as aloof as possible from the

267. P. Bartoloni, "L'insediamento di Monte Sirai nel quadro della Sardegna fenicia e punica," *Actes* 3, 1.99–108; C. Perra, "Monte Sirai: Gli scavi nell'abitato 1996–1998," *RSF* 29 (2001)
121–30.

268. A. Peserico, "La ceramica fenicia: Le forme aperte," *RSF* 22 (1994) 117–44. On Bitia, see
S. Moscati and S. F. Bondì, *Italia Punica* (Milan: Rusconi, 1986) 226–39. On Villasimius, see L. A.
Marras, "I Fenici nel golfo di Cagliari: Cuccureddus di Villasimius," *Atti* 2, 3.1039–48.

269. P. Bartoloni, "Contributo alla cronologia delle necropolis fenicie e puniche di Sardegna," *RSF* 9 (1981) Supplement, 13–29, figs. 1–3. See also M. Botto, "Nora e il suo territorio:
Resoconto preliminare dell'attività di recognizione degli anni 1992–1995," *Actas* 4, 3.1269–76.

270. Pesce, "Due opera di arte fenicia in Sardegna," 253–56, pls. 43–45.

271. Bartoloni, "Le relazioni tra Cartagine e la Sardegna nei secoli VII e VI a.C.," 80.

272. See, for example C. Del Vais, "Nota preliminare sulla tipologia dei vasi "à chardon" da
Tharros," *RSF* 22 (1994) 237–41.

273. J. Maluquer de Motes, "La dualidad commercial fenicia y griega en Occidente," *FPI*,
2.203–10; U. Morgenroth, "Southern Iberia and the Mediterranean Trade-Routes," *OJA* 18 (1999)
395–400.

native communities. It was a century everywhere of population growth and hunkering down,[274] not just working, doing business, making money, but making a good life in new surroundings and providing necessities and delicacies for fellow colonials and the folks back home.

On the Atlantic side, in Tartessos as it is called, the native Spaniards were smart and sophisticated, while on the Mediterranean coast and the adjacent inland regions they were more rustic, but all were invigorated by the Phoenician presence and contributed accordingly to the prosperity of the settlers.[275] The Greeks brought their culture—notably their alphabetic script—and the Phoenicians brought a whole new way of life:[276] changes in agriculture (donkeys) and eating habits (figs and fish), in pottery making (the wheel), mining (better furnaces, cupellation), clothing (fibulae, belt buckles), housing and town planning, religion (incense, burial customs), and social organization (banquets, founding of an aristocracy). Spain was the new frontier and constant throb of the Western Phoenician world.[277]

In the valley of the Guadalquivir, from the region of Seville as far as Castulo in the northwest, there were many more places where Phoenicians settled down and numerous native sites that, as the Phoenician pottery from the residential areas and the graveyards clearly indicates, profited from their contact with the colonials.[278] There was acculturation on both sides: the traders and artisans were no longer foreigners; the Spaniards did business with them, as the Phoenician amphorae suggest, and became accustomed to their ways, as Phoenician tripod mortars, unguent bottles and plates, locally made Red Slip and Black-on-Red bowls, and handmade imitations of their wares[279] attest. At Cruz del Negro, just east of Seville, there was a cemetery with Phoenician Red Slip wares, ivory grave gifts, and cremation urns unceremoniously buried in the ground alongside inhumations and the tumuli of the local aristocrats.[280]

At Carmona, just to the south, there were buildings constructed either in the pillar-and-rubble style or with stone foundations and adobe walls. One of them, from the late seventh century, had a floor of beaten earth painted bright red and contained three amphorae with painted decorations that were inspired by scenes on the ivories from this Phoenician enclave.[281] At Montemolín, farther west, there was a similar housing complex, built

274. C. R. Whittaker, "The Western Phoenicians: Colonisation and Assimilation," *Proceedings of the Cambridge Philological Society* 20 (1974) 58–79; C. G. Wagner and J. Alvar, "Fenicios en Occidente: La colonización agrícola," *RSF* 17 (1989) 61–102.

275. M. E. Aubet Semmler, "The Phoenician Impact on Tartessos: Spheres of Interaction," *Bierling*, 225–40.

276. M. Almagro-Gorbea, "El mundo orientalizante en la Península Ibérica," *Atti* 2, 2.573–99.

277. H. Schubart, "Phönizische Niederlassungen an der ibrischen Südküste," *PhWest*, 207–34.

278. F. Ben Abed, "Les Phéniciens dans la péninsule ibérique: Une nouvelle lecture des données archéologiques," *Actes* 3, 1.109–22; R. González, F. Barrionuevo, and L. Aguilar, "Presencia fenicia en el territorio tartésico de los esteros del Gualdalquivir," *Actas* 4, 2.785–94.

279. J. M. Martín Ruiz, "Ceramicas a mano en los yacimientos fenicios de Andalucía," *Actas* 4, 4.1625–30.

280. M. E. Aubet Semmler, "Zur Problematik des orientalisierenden Horizontes auf der iberischen Halbinsel," *PhWest*, 309–35; C. G. Wagner and J. Alvar, "Fenicios en Occidente: La colonización agrícola," *RSF* 17 (1989) 61–102, esp. pp. 92–93.

281. M. Belén et al., "Presencia e influencia fenicia en Carmona (Sevilla)," *Actas* 4, 4.1747–61.

in the Phoenician stone-and-adobe style. One of these buildings also had a stamped red floor, with pottery of various forms and one amphora decorated in the same way, but the presence of animal bones—beef, pig, sheep, and goat—suggests that it was an abattoir or even a ritual slaughterhouse, from which fresh or salted meat was shipped to the neighboring towns.[282] The Phoenicians, as these details illustrate, may have come at first to exploit the vast resources of the region, but they assimilated and settled in and were essential to the development of the local economy.

Iron and bronze razors, bronze lamp standards (alternatively identified as incense stands), and bronze statuettes are further evidence of the presence of Phoenician workshops in the region of Seville. The standards, featuring three coronets of down-curling petals of papyrus blossoms, have their prototypes in ivory, faience, and clay examples found on Cyprus and in Northern Israel and were made in various Spanish workshops: they have been found near Seville and at Castulo, in a rich Phoenician tomb at La Joya near Huelva and in the district of Málaga.[283] The razors, in the same way, come from El Carambolo, Setefilla, Cruz del Negro, and Acebuchal in the periphery of Seville, and from La Joya near Huelva and Las Cumbres in the vicinity of Cádiz, but they are a typically seventh-century Phoenician product and are very common throughout southern Spain.[284] The bronze figures[285] are large statuettes or life-size statues made in Spain (three found their way to the Heraion in Samos) by Phoenician artists and their Spanish apprentices. Two or three in a Syro-Phoenician style are from Seville, one a version of the striding man who holds a scepter in his left hand and raises his right in greeting, the other an adaptation of this pose, in which the left hand held a shield and the right was raised to hold a javelin.[286] These poses are typical, but the facial features are individual and seem to represent a living subject, perhaps a well-known figure, or the patron who commissioned this particular statue.

The earliest Greek pottery in Spain is a lone Middle Geometric II (800–760 B.C.E.) crater from Huelva,[287] brought by one of the pioneering Sidonian settlers, and it antedates by 50 to 100 years the regular influx of Attic (SOS) oil jars from Pithecusa imported—these too probably by Phoenicians rather than Greeks—to the Mediterranean coast of southern Spain. At Huelva there is little Greek pottery before the end of the seventh century. In the eighth and early seventh century, indigenous Tartessian pottery predominated, but it dropped from 80 to 60 percent and by the end of the century to 25 percent of the total, as it was gradually displaced by the

282. F. Chaves et al., "El complejo sacrificial de Montemolín," *Actas* 4, 2.573–81.

283. W. Culican, "Phoenician Incense Stands," in *Oriental Studies Presented to Benedikt S. J. Isserlin* (ed. R. Y. Ebeid and M. J. L. Young; Leiden: Brill, 1980) 85–101, pls. 1–4; F. J. Jiménez Ávila, "Timiaterios 'chipriotas' de bronce: Centros de producción occidentales," *Actas* 4, 4.1581–94.

284. J. Mancebo Dávalos, "Análisis de los objetos metálicos en el período orientalizante y su conexión con el mundo fenicio: Los cuchillos afalcatados," *Actas* 4, 4.1825–34.

285. M. Almagro Basch, "Über einen Typus iberischer Bronze-Exvotos orientalisichen Ursprungs," *MM* 20 (11979) 133–83, pls. 13–26.

286. Ibid., 136–40, pls. 13–14a; 140–42, pl. 16a–b.

287. B. B. Shefton, "Greeks and Greek Imports in the South of the Iberian Peninsula: The Archaeological Evidence," *PhWest*, 337–70, esp. p. 342.

wares used in the expanding Phoenician community.[288] Their pottery was distinctive, lacking some forms popular at other sites, producing different styles of common ceramic types, such as bowls and jugs, and not following the normal development of pottery forms—notably the gradual but insistent widening of the rims of plates.[289] This combined with other diagnostic features may be an indication of a change in diet among the Phoenicians in Spain that was resisted at Huelva.[290] The Greek pottery was ordinary but nicer than the Phoenician and, in the days before it could be had from Samian and Phocaean peddlers, came back to Huelva with Phoenician merchants on their return voyages from Italy or Sardinia.[291]

The Phoenicians who came to Huelva for its metals (gold, silver, iron, tin, and copper) met a vigorous and advanced native population with developed traditions and ready to learn.[292] What is known about the Phoenicians at Huelva is gathered mostly, although not exclusively, from reflections of them among these indigenous Tartessians. In the ninth and eighth centuries, these people erected burial steles on which were engraved figures of warriors and their weapons, along with pictures of mirrors, combs, fibulae, and the musical instruments they had received from the Phoenicians in trade.[293]

In the seventh century, the cemetery at La Joya,[294] just northeast of the town, has aristocratic burials, both cremations and inhumations, accompanied by traditional gifts such as horses, chariots, bridles, braziers, swords, and shields but also by Phoenician ivories, gold jewelry, alabaster, amber, decorated ostrich eggs, incense burners, and mirrors. One man was buried with his sword and with an iron knife of Cypriot manufacture and at his feet an urn with the cremated remains of his Phoenician wife. In an adjacent but separate section of the cemetery, amid the ashes of on-the-spot cremations or of some ritual involving incense, bodies were buried in a contracted or quasi-fetal position. There were few grave goods. One of the dead was a woman with bad teeth, whose robe was fastened with a Phoenician fibula; all were adults and very likely household slaves, either captured by the Tartessians or bought from Phoenicians who had picked them up along the way.

---

288. M. Pellicer Catalán, "Huelva Tartesia y Fenicia," *RSF* 24 (1996) 119–40.

289. P. Rufete Tomico, "Die phönizische Roteware aus Huelva," *MM* 30 (1989) 118–34.

290. J. A. Barceló et al., "Análisis estadístico de la variabilidad de los platos fenicios en el sur de la península ibérica," *Actas* 4, 4.1459–66. The change in diet may have included various fish dishes: in contemporary Judah, fish was a growing part of the national diet and had to be included in a revision of the dietary laws (Deut 14:9–10).

291. P. Cabrera, "Greek Trade in Iberia: The Extent of Interaction," *OJA* 17 (1998) 191–206.

292. M. E. Aubet Semmler, "Some Questions Regarding the Tartessian Orientalizing Period," *Bierling*, 199–224, esp. pp. 206–10.

293. E. Galán Domingo, "Las estelas del Suroeste entre el Atlántico y el Mediterraneo," *Actas* 4, 4.1789–97; A. J. Domínguez, "New Perspectives on the Greek Presence in the Iberian Peninsula," in *The Hellenic Diaspora, from Antiquity to Modern Times, Volume I: From Antiquity to 1453* (ed. J. M. Forsey; Amsterdam: Gieben, 1991) 109–61, esp. pp. 112–13.

294. J. P. Garrido et al., "Sobre las inhumaciones de la necrópolis orientalizante de la Joya, Huelva: Problematica y perspectivas," *Actas* 4, 4.1805–10.

Before the Phoenicians arrived, the people of Huelva and its environs and the silver miners in the valley of the lower Guadalquivir[295] made pottery by hand and lived in round or oval houses made of perishable materials. But by the seventh century, they were using the wheel and had begun to build rectangular houses in the Phoenician stone-and-adobe style, with paved floors and sometimes with benches against the walls.[296] In addition to these oblique reflections, there is also direct evidence for Phoenician presence, as in two seventh-century bronze statuettes of the striding hero[297] that still maintain some of the original Egyptian characteristics of the form (an Atef crown or the crown of Upper Egypt) but display Syrian facial features. These Phoenicians, who probably were of Sidonian extraction but certainly were not from the places that sent settlers to the Mediterranean coast of Spain, were glad to live among the indigenous people (although some of them kept their distance), and they flourished and assimilated, as they did at Huelva, in direct proportion to the cultural and material resources of their hosts.

Cádiz was very prosperous in the seventh century, trading in wine, oil, grain, precious metals, salt, skins, and slaves.[298] There are no architectural remains from this period, but there is some pottery and plenty of jewelry, similar in quality and design to the jewelry found at Carthage and at Tharros in Sardinia.[299] Each of these three towns had its own gold workshops and produced a great deal the same sort of jewelry, but each also had its specialities and fashions, with Cádiz fixed between the relative austerity of the Carthaginian shops and the ostentation of Tharros.[300] There are earlier pieces (the signet ring inscribed *ln'm'l* and a statuette of Ptah, whose face is overlaid in gold) that may be imports, but most of the jewelry was created in the seventh and sixth centuries, with gold from the Sierra Morena and Estremadura supplied by Tartessian miners and middlemen. There were earrings of many distinctive types, finger rings, medallions, and pendants, most or all of them made for the local market (silver and silver jewelry, by contrast, was shipped to Eastern markets)[301] and for a wealthy male and female clientele.

The population at Doña Blanca increased in the seventh century and was progressively more Phoenician, with stone-and-adobe or pillar-and-rubble

---

295. D. Ruiz Mata, "El Poblado metalúrgico de época tartésica de San Bartolomé (Almonte, Huelva)," *MM* 22 (1981) 150–70.

296. M. Belén, "Importaciones fenicias en Andalucia Occidental," *FPI*, 2.263–78.

297. I. Gamer-Wallert, "Zwei Statuetten syro-ägyptischer Gottheiten von der 'Barra de Huelva,'" *MM* 23 (1982) 46–61, pls. 1–25.

298. M. E. Aubet Semmler, "Phoenician Trade in the West: Balance and Perspectives," *Bierling*, 97–112.

299. J. L. Escacena, "Gadir," *FPI*, 1.39–52, pls. 1–14. M. L. Lavado et al., "El Asentamiento Antiguo de Cádiz a través de las últimas excavaciones arqueológicas," *Actas* 4, 2.869–79. C. Carballo Torres, "Objetos de adornos personales fenicios en materials no metálicos," *Actas* 4, 4.1467–73.

300. A. Perea Caveda, "Phoenician Gold in the Western Mediterranean: Cádiz, Tharros and Carthage," in *Encounters and Transformations: The Archaeology of Iberia in Transition* (ed. M. S. Balmuth, A. Gilman, and L. Prados-Torreira; Monographs in Mediterranean Archaeology 7; Sheffield: Sheffield Academic Press, 1997) 135–40.

301. Ruiz Mata, "El poblado metalúrgica de época Tartéssica de San Bartolomé (Almonte, Huelva)."

houses and wheel-made pottery. [302] The town specialized in silver mined in the interior but refined and worked on the spot and then exported to Sardinia, Carthage, and the markets in mainland Phoenicia. The pottery included domestic items, such as Red Slip cups, Grey Ware shallow bowls, and two-wick lamps; and commercial articles including amphorae and large-capacity pots with double handles that were decorated with bands of red marked off by narrow black lines or with concentric circles in red or black. [303] Unlike Huelva, where the rim width of plates is not chronologically significant, Cádiz followed the standard west-Phoenician pattern of increasingly wider rims. [304]

Amphorae like those at Doña Blanca were also found in indigenous communities in the interior, and their contents probably represented partial payment for the silver and other goods and services that they supplied to the Phoenician merchants on the coast. The names of some of these people are preserved on an amphora and on ostraca (fragments of Red Slip or Grey Ware bowls or plates) that may have accompanied the shipments: the amphora was inscribed with the gentilic designation "from ʿAkko" (ʿky), referring to the merchant who sold the goods and not to the product; [305] an ostracon from about the middle of the seventh century consists of the first four letters of the alphabet (ʾbgd), the first two written with a ligature, like a monogram; [306] a fragment of a Red Slip bowl is inscribed in early seventh-century script with a name that is only partially preserved; and a fragment of a Red Slip plate, similarly, has only the beginning of the name in a slightly later script. [307] The fact that these were ostraca rather than usable dishes identified by the name of their owners or potters is clear from another seventh-century fragment inscribed with a personal name and a number, "belonging to ʾEshmun, 100" (lʾšmn + symbol for 100), "one hundred shekels." [308] This fellow could have been a supplier or silver smith, for instance, and the shekels would have his share of a shipment of raw silver or payment for silver jewelry that was being exported to the mainland or to one of the colonies.

Some of the silver at Doña Blanca and some of the salt and fish at Cádiz came from Phoenician establishments in Portugal. All of these were situated on rivers (the Tagus, Sado, and Arade), and all but one were indigenous

---

302. Idem, "The Beginnings of the Phoenician Presence in Southwestern Andalusia—with Findings from the Excavations at Cabezo de San Pedro (Huelva), San Bartolomé (Almonte, Huelva), Castillo de Doña Blanca (Puerto de Santa María, Cádiz) and El Carambolo (Camas, Sevilla)," *Bierling*, 263–98, esp. pp. 274–86.

303. Idem, "Las cerámicas fenícias del Castillo de Doña Blanca (Puerto de Santa María, Cádiz)," *FPI*, 1.241–63.

304. Idem, "The Ancient Phoenicians of the 8th and 7th Centuries B.C. in the Bay of Cádiz: State of the Research," *Bierling*, 155–98, esp. pp. 184–90.

305. J.-L. Cunchillos, "Las inscripciones Fenicias del Tell de Doña Blanca (IV)," *Sefarad* 52 (1992) 75–83, esp. pp. 81–83.

306. Idem, "Las inscripciones Fenicias del Tell de Doña Blanca (II)," *Sefarad* 51 (1991) 13–22.

307. Idem, "Las inscripciones Fenicias del Tell de Doña Blanca (IV)," 75–78 (ʾb[y]) and pp. 78–80 (yḥ[mlk]).

308. Idem, "Inscripciones Fenicias del Tell de Doña Blanca (V)," *Sefarad* 53 (1993) 17–24; J. Naveh, "The Phoenician Hundred-Sign," *RSF* 19 (1991) 139–44.

settlements with small Phoenician enclaves.[309] The exception is Abul, about 40 kilometers from Lisbon, on the Sado halfway between Setúbal and Alcácer do Sal.[310] Like all the sites, it began to be frequented by Phoenicians sometime in the first half of the seventh century, but unlike them, it was built by Phoenicians for their own use, at a distance from the two nearest native towns. It was in the center of a region famous for its salt marshes, and because it seems to have consisted mainly of storerooms and warehouses, it may have been intended for the production and marketing of this commodity.

The other sites are marked as familiar with the Phoenicians by pieces of their pottery or, as at Rocha Branca at the mouth of the Arade, by the presence of the bones of donkeys, an animal introduced into Spain by them, or as at Alcácer do Sal, by a Phoenician seal.[311] The seal is a takeoff on the traditional scene of caprids flanking the Tree-of-Life and shows monkeys on either side of a date palm with their hands raised in veneration of the fruit. The affiliation of these sites is unknown, although the isolation of Abul would be typical of a Tyrian settlement, but their number and duplication suggest that they were the outposts of more than one of the established centers on the Atlantic coast of Spain.

Málaga and its work station at Cerro del Villar at the mouth of the Rio Guadalhorce were the most westerly of the settlements on the Mediterranean coast of Spain. Málaga was a Punic colony, founded by Carthage in the second half of the seventh century, in fertile farmland, and at some distance from the Phoenician foundations at Toscanos and Morro de Mezquitilla.[312] It maintained good relations with the local native farming communities, and is distinguished from them by its pottery[313] (some household wares but mostly transport and storage amphorae) and by a few specialty items. One is a cylinder seal, an heirloom like similar seals found at Carthage, depicting the Goddess Asherah, naked, holding flowers in each hand, with her lion at her feet, attended by two worshipers—one

---

309. M. Pellicer Catalán, "La colonización fenicia en Portugal y la orientalización de la Península Ibérica," *ASKaW*, 531–38; A. M. Arruda, *Los Fenicios en Portugal: Fenicios y mundo indígena en el centro y sur de Portugal (siglos VIII–VI a.C.)* (Cuadernos de Arqueología Mediterránea 5–6, 1999–2000; Barcelona: Universidad Pompeu Fabra—Laboratorio de Arqueología, 2002); J. L. Cardoso, "Fení008 e Indígenas em Rocha Branca, Abul, Alcácer do Sal, Almaraz e Santarém: Estudio comparado dos mamíferos," *Actas* 4, 1.319–27.

310. F. Mayet, C. Tavares, and Y. Makaroun, "L'établissement phénicien d'Abul (Portugal)," *CRAIBL* (1994) 171–88.

311. Cardoso, "Feníctos e Indígenas em Rocha Branca, Abul, Alcácer do Sal, Almaraz e Santarém: Estudio Comparado dos Mamíferos"; A. M. Cavaleiro Paixão, "Ein neues Grab mit Skarabäus in der eisenzeitlichen Nekropole Olival do Senhor dos Mártires," *MM* 22 (1981) 229–35, pl. 16; I. Gamer-Wallert, "Der neue Skarabäus aus Alcácer do Sal," *MM* 23 (1982) 96–100, pl. 27.

312. C. G. Wagner and J. Alvar, "Fenicios en Occidente: La Colonización Agrícola," *RSF* 17 (1989) 61–102; J.-P. Morel, "Quelques remarques sur l'économie phénico-punique dans ses aspects agraires," *Actas* 4, 1.411–23.

313. A. Recio Ruiz, "Vestigios materiales cerámicas de ascendencia fenicio-púnica en la provincia de Málaga," *MM* 34 (1993) 127–41; J. Gran Aymerich, ed., *Málaga phénicienne et punique: Recherches franco-espagnoles 1981–1988* (Paris: Editions Recherche sur les Civilisations, 1991).

human, the other wearing an animal mask.[314] Another is a carved ivory plaque made as a furniture ornament in a Carthaginian workshop, showing worshipers standing in the entrance to a temple, facing each other and together holding a central staff-of-life with a lotus blossom finial, while above the lintel a winged sun disk is attended by flanking uraei.[315] Málaga, from the Punic word for "Royal City" (*mlk-t*), was founded to take advantage of the abundance of agricultural products in the region.

The work station at Cerro del Villar[316] is 7 kilometers west of Málaga, on an island at the mouth of the river Guadalhorce. It owned farms on the west bank of the river that supplied some of its needs,[317] and it either raised by itself or bought from the local farmers the wheat and barley, cattle, sheep, and goats that were produced in the surrounding rich alluvial plain. The houses were built in the pillar-and-rubble or stone-and-adobe style on paved (cobblestone or stamped earth) streets and consisted of between four and six rooms around a central courtyard.

There is pottery for local domestic use and evidence of fishing (hooks and weights) and dyeing (murex shells), but the main business was the pottery barn that turned out large transport and storage jars for the produce it supplied to Carthage, especially, and to Toscanos. It was a busy site (there is pottery from Cerveteri, Athens, Corinth, and Samos, as well as Carthage) but for a short time, and it was abandoned early in the sixth century when the river silted, and the island (today a hillock in the plain) was flooded.

Toscanos,[318] on the river Vélez, was a walled and densely populated town in the seventh century. Its involvement in the export business is attested by the new warehouse that was built at this time and by the very high percentage of transport amphorae in the pottery assemblage.[319] The town was well planned, with the houses facing onto streets, the residential areas separated from the factories and storerooms, and specialized operations such as the forge located at the edge of town. There were horses and donkeys, oxen and beef cattle, sheep and goats, a few dogs, as well as pigs and chickens—

314. A. Blanco, "Notas de arqueología Andaluza," *Zephyrus* 11 (1960) 151–63, pls. 1–6, esp. pp. 151–53.

315. J.-M. J. Gran Aymerich, "La scène figurée sur l'ivoire de Malaga et l'imagerie phénicienne," *Sem* 38 (1990) 145–53; idem, "Málaga, fenicia y punica," *FPI*, 1.127–47, esp. p. 141, fig. 4.1.

316. M. E. Aubet Semmler, "Die phönizische Niederlassung vom Cerro del Villar (Guadalhorce, Málaga): Die Ausgrabungen von 1986–1989," *MM* 31 (1990) 29–51, pls. 9–22; idem, "Notas sobre las colonias del sur de España y su función en el marco territorial: El ejemplo del Cerro del Villar (Málaga)," *Atti* 2, 2.617–26; idem, "A Phoenician Market Place in Southern Spain," in *Ana šadî labnāni lū allik. Beiträge zu altorientalischen und mittelmeerischen Kulturen: Festschrift für Wolfgang Röllig* (ed. B. Pongratz-Leisten, H. Kühne, and P. Xella; Neukirchen-Vluyn: Neukirchener Verlag, 1997) 11–22.

317. Idem, "Die phönizische Niederlassung vom Cerro del Villar (Guadalhorce, Málaga): Die Ausgrabungen von 1986–1989."

318. H. G. Niemeyer, "Orient im Okzident: Die Phöniker in Spanien. Ergebnisse der Gradungen in der archäologischen Zone von Torre del Mar (Málaga)," *MDOG* 104 (1972) 5–44; idem, "El Yacimento Fenicio de Toscanos: Urbanistica y función," *AuOr* 3 (1985) 109–26.

319. M. E. Aubet Semmler, "Los Fenicios en España: Estado de la Cuestión y Perspectivas," *AuOr* 3 (1985) 9–30, pls. 1–9, esp. pp. 20–21; Pellicer Catalán, "Huelva Tartesia y Fenicia," 125.

everything needed for food, transport, haulage, and protection in an area with access to iron but especially renowned for its farmland.[320] There is Greek pottery, some of which may have arrived in Phoenician ships sailing from Italy or Sicily.[321] There are also, as there were at Carthage, locally made Phoenician imitations of Greek drinking bowls.[322] And it is just as likely that Greeks—individuals such as Kolaios from Samos at first, and later Phocaeans from Massalia—were trading with Phoenicians at Toscanos and with the indigenous people in southern Spain by the mid-seventh century, who were becoming, at least in their symposia, fashionably Hellenized.[323]

Toscanos was started by individuals or groups from mainland Phoenicia, as indicated by some of the stonework done by a master mason from the East, but developed in the seventh century with an influx of laborers and professionals from the Western colonies, in particular from Carthage.[324] It was a mixed community, a base probably for some Greek merchants, who came to do business but not to settle,[325] had a wide range of investments including the station at Abul in Portugal, and became a mainstay of Carthaginian expansion.

The Phoenicians at Morro de Mezquitilla and affiliated sites east of Toscanos had become accustomed to the rhythms of life and death in southern Spain. There was some new construction at Mezquitilla, following a new town plan and using better adapted building techniques.[326] There were richly endowed cremation burials at Trayamar, across the river Algarrobo to the west, and at Almuñécar, farther to the east.[327] In both cemeteries, there

---

320. M. E. Aubet Semmler, "Notes on the Economy of the Phoenician Settlements in Southern Spain," *Bierling* 79–95, esp. p. 90.

321. B. B. Shefton, "Greeks and Greek Imports in the South of the Iberian Peninsula: The Archaeological Evidence," *PhWest*, 337–70, esp. pp. 338–39.

322. P. Rouillard, "Phéniciens et Grecs à Toscanos: Note sur quelques vases d'inspiration gréco-géométrique de Toscanos (1967)," *MM* 31 (1990) 178–85, pls. 20–21; C. Briese and R. Docter, "Der phönizische Skyphos: Adaption einer griechischen Trinkschale," *MM* 33 (1992) 25–69, esp. pp. 25, 38.

323. Shefton, "Greeks and Greek Imports in the South of the Iberian Peninsula: The Archaeological Evidence," 345–50; J. Boardman, "Copies of Pottery: By and for Whom?" in *Greek Identity in the Western Mediterranean: Papers in Honour of Brian Shefton* (ed. K. Lomas; Mnemosyne Supplement 86; Leiden: Brill, 2004) 149–62.

324. Niemeyer, "Orient im Okzident: Die Phöniker in Spanien," 13–20, 29–35. R. F. Docter, "Karthagische Amphoren aus Toscanos," *MM* 35 (1994) 123–39.

325. T. Júdice Gamito, "Greeks and Phoenicians in Southwest Iberia—Who Were the First? Aspects of Archaeological and Epigraphic Evidence," in *The Hellenic Diaspora—from Antiquity to Modern Times, I: From Antiquity to 1453* (ed. J. M. Fossey; Amsterdam: Gieben, 1991) 81–108; J. de Hoz, "The Greek Man in the Iberian Street: Non-Colonial Greek Identity in Spain and Southern France," in *Greek Identity in the Western Mediterranean: Papers in Honour of Brian Shefton* (ed. K. Lomas; Mnemosyne Supplement 86; Leiden: Brill, 2004) 411–27.

326. D. Marzoli, "Anforas púnicas de Morro de Mezquitilla (Málaga)," *Actas* 4, 4.1631–44, pp. 1631–32.

327. M. L. Ramos Sainz, "Los ritos de incineración e inhumación en las necrópolis hispanas (ss. VIII–II a.C.)," *Actas* 4, 4.1693–96.

W. Culican, "Almuñécar, Assur and Phoenician Penetration of the Western Mediterranean," *Levant* 2 (1970) 28–36, pls. 25–27; repr. in idem, *Opera Selecta: From Tyre to Tartessos* (Gothenburg: Åströms, 1986) 673–84; M. Pellicer Catalán, "Sexi fenicia y púnica," *FPI*, 1.85–107; F. Molina Fajardo, "Almuñécar a la luz de los nuevos hallazgos fenicios," ibid., 193–226; idem and A. Bannour, "Almuñécar a la luz de los nuevos hallazgos fenicios," *Actas* 4, 4.1645–63.

were shaft tombs cut into the rock leading to burial niches or chambers, with Egyptian or Egyptianizing alabaster urns for the ashes, Red Slip ceramic grave goods, sometimes amulets or decorated ostrich eggs, and silver or gold imported jewelry.[328]

At Abdera there were pottery works, and the boats that sank just off the coast farther east at Mazarron were carrying pottery that may have come from its ovens.[329] The boats were small, could navigate the rivers on which all the Phoenician settlements on this coast of Spain were situated, and stayed fairly close to shore as they traveled from one place to another.[330] The faunal remains indicate that the crew had been eating goat, rabbit, and chicken that they picked up along the way. The pottery included domestic wares, some with Red Slip, as well as urns, and transport and storage jars for commercial use. It was boats like these that kept all the sites in the domain of Morro de Mezquitilla in touch.

In the seventh century, Phoenicians from this southern region, perhaps in cooperation with confreres from Carthage, began exploring the east coast of Spain. They are especially prominent in the vicinity of Alicante, but there are traces of them in the region of Valencia, and as far north as the mouth of the Ebro. By mid-century, these places were overtaken in importance by Ibiza, a Carthaginian foundation, and by the end of the century, this Phoenician and Punic northward movement along the east coast of Spain was arrested by the founding of Massalia and Emporion by the Greeks.

In the Alicante region, there are numerous small sites in the valley of the Rio Segura and its tributaries that had commercial and cultural relations with the Phoenicians.[331] The earliest is La Fonteta, with offshoots at Cabezo del Estano and Castillo de Guardamar, at the mouth of the river, and at Los Saladares and Peña Negra just slightly inland.[332] It occupied between six and eight hectares and seems to have been settled early in the century. There are houses with stone foundations and adobe walls, and evidence for metallurgical installations—furnaces, iron and copper slag, molds, vent

---

328. H. G. Niemeyer, "The Trayamar Medallion Reconsidered," in *Oriental Studies Presented to Benedikt S. J. Isserlin* (ed. R. Y. Edied and M. J. L. Young; Leiden: Brill, 1980) 108–13; M. Blech, "Goldschmuck aus Almuñécar," *MM* 27 (1986) 151–67, pl. 19.

329. A. Suárez et al., "Abdera: Una colonia fenicia en el Sureste de la Península Ibérica," *MM* 30 (1989) 135–50, pls. 11–12; I. Negueruela et al., "Seventh-Century BC Phoenician Vessel Discovered at Playa de la Isla, Mazarron, Spain," *IJNA* 24 (1995) 189–97; idem, "Descubrimiento de dos barcos fenicios en Mazarrón (Murcia), *Actas* 4, 4.1671–79; N. Easterbrook, C. More, and R. Penfold, eds., *Master Seafarers: The Phoenicians and the Greeks* (London: Periplus, 2003) 40–49.

330. M. Barthélemy, "El comercio fluvial fenicio en la península ibérica," *Actas* 4, 1.291–97.

331. A. González Prats and A. García Menárguez, "El conjunto fenicio de la desembocadura del río Segura (Guardamar del Segura, Alicante)," *Actas* 4, 4.1527–37. A. M. Poveda Navarro, "Penetración cultural fenicia en el territorio indígena del valle septentrional del Vinalopó (Alicante)," ibid., 1863–74.

332. A. González Prats, "La Fonteta—El asentamiento fenicio de la desembocadura del Río Seguar (Guardamar, Alicante, España): Resultados de la excavaciones de 1996–1997," *RSF* 26 (1998) 191–228, pls. 2–9; idem, A. García Menárguez and E. Ruiz Segura, "La Fonteta: A Phoenician City in the Far West," *Bierling*, 113–25; A. J. Sánchez Pérez and R. C. Alonso de la Cruz, "La ciudad fenicia de Herna (Guardamar del Segura, Alicante)," *RSF* 27 (1999) 127–31; A. González Prats, "Las importaciones y la presencia fenicias en la Sierra de Crevillente (Alicante)," *FPI*, 2.279–302.

pipes, and ashes. At the end of the century, a defensive wall and a moat were built.

The pottery comprised Phoenician amphorae and tableware, including a great variety of plates (Red Slip, Grey Ware, monochrome, and bichrome) and mushroom-lipped wine jugs, and indigenous wares. There is also a Red Slip lamp, dating to about 675 B.C.E., which is inscribed on the base with the name of its owner, Melqartyosep (*mlqrtysp*).[333] At the end of the century, there were imported Greek wares, such as Ionian cups, Rhodian cups; Corinthian, Chian, and Samian amphorae; and East Greek aryballoi.

At Peña Negra, which seems to have been a crafts center, there were Red Slip amphorae with Phoenician potters' marks, and household wares, as well as silver and gold necklace beads, and bronze fibulae, pendants, and jugs. Near these places, in the Bajo de la Campana, and presumably destined for them, there was a seventh-century shipwreck of a vessel that was transporting lead and tin ingots, as well as African elephant tusks inscribed with Phoenician letters.[334] La Fonteta, it seems, was originally or soon became a joint enterprise of Phoenicians and Carthaginians—the defensive system would suit the Carthaginian mentality at the end of the century. Their presence at a large number of sites in the region made a clear and lasting impression[335] and immediately attracted neighboring Phocaeans to join in their venture.

Phoenician presence farther north was less intense. In the region of Valencia, the evidence consists of seventh- and sixth-century amphorae found along the coast and in the interior.[336] Just south of the river Ebro, there was a site consisting of a few isolated houses and other buildings with Phoenician pottery and some Greek but no local wares: it looks like a farming village that supplied field crops and meat to the Phoenician merchants who visited the area.[337] Phoenician amphorae were found at several other sites on the lower Ebro, and between the Ebro and Greek Emporion.[338] The most interesting of these is on a point that juts into the river. It consists of four irregularly shaped, quadrangular rooms and one semicircular room abutting them. In this room, there were about 100 Phoenician transport amphorae, one of them of an Ibiza type, as well as bronze and iron objects. The site was occupied by indigenous people who supplied grain to the Phoenicians in their own containers, which had been stored in this

---

333. J. Elayi, A. González Prats, and E. Ruiz Segura, "Une lampe avec inscription phénicienne de La Fonteta (Guardamar, Alicante)," *RSF* 26 (1998) 229–42, pls. 10–14.

334. Aubet Semmler, "Phoenician Trade in the West: Balance and Perspectives," 106.

335. M. Almagro-Gorbea, "Pozo Moro y el influjo fenicio en el periodo orientalizante de la Península Ibérica," *RSF* 10 (1982) 231–72, pls. 50–56; J. M. Blázquez, "La colonización fenicia en la alta Andalucia (Oretania), s. VIII–VI a.C.," *RSF* 14 (1986) 53–80, pls. 1–4; W. Trillmich, "Early Iberian Sculpture and 'Phocaean Colonization,'" in *Greek Colonists and Native Populations: Proceedings of the First Australian Congress of Classical Archaeology held in Honour of Emeritus Professor A. D. Trendall, Sydney, 9–14 July 1985* (ed. J.-P. Descoeudres; Oxford: Clarendon, 1990) 607–11.

336. A. Ribera and A. Fernández, "Las ánforas del mundo fenicio-púnco en el País Valenciano," *Actas* 4, 4.1699–1711.

337. D. Asensio et al., "Las cerámicas fenicias y de tipo fenicio del yacimiento del Barranc de Gàfolo (Ginestar, Ribera d'Ebre, Tarragona)," *Actas* 4, 4.1733–45.

338. O. Arteaga, J. Padró, and E. Sanmartí, "La expansion fenicia por las costas de Cataluña y del Languedoc," *FPI*, 2.303–14.

semicircular room or granary, in exchange for bronze and iron implements. It was operational for about 25 years and was destroyed by fire at the end of the seventh century.[339] This entire area, from Valencia to the Ebro, it seems, was a source of food supplies for the people working in the Alicante region and living on Ibiza.

Ibiza, according to Diodorus (5.16), was founded 160 years after the foundation of Carthage. This seems about right, because it puts the settlement of Ibiza around 665 B.C.E., following the classical calculations, or around 565 B.C.E., following the archaeological schedule and, although most of the remains support the sixth-century date, it is clear that Carthaginians were living on and making productive use of the island in the seventh century.

There is a site known as Sa Caleta near the town and harbor at the southeast tip of the island where there was a settlement in the second half of the seventh century. It covers about four hectares (ca. ten acres) and consists of an agglomeration of rectangular buildings separated by laneways, with some Red Slip pottery, the best parallels of which are at Cerro del Villar near Málaga, and with bits of lead and silver from the Argentera mines in the eastern part of the island.[340] This complex included residences (the domestic pottery consists of Red Slip plates and bowls, lamps, polychrome funerary urns, storage jars, and various forms of Grey Ware), workshops, and storage areas, but these became redundant and the site was abandoned when the town of Ibiza was established. Sa Caleta occupied a promontory exposed to the winds, and this was essential to the pine-tar industry that began there and the successful management of which encouraged Carthage to establish a permanent colony nearby on the island.

The town of Ibiza had an excellent harbor, partly enclosed by an island, as good town planning prescribed. There are few traces of the town, but there is some evidence for an early sanctuary on the harbor island.[341] More general settlement, though sparse, is marked by the relatively large percentage of bronze arrowheads that can be dated typologically to this time.[342] The oldest terra-cotta and ivory figurines illustrate a variety of styles and imply that the first settlers came from many different places.[343] They came from Cyprus, for instance, and Sicily, either directly or via Carthage, and

---

339. M. Mascort, J. Sanmartí, and J. Santacana, "Aldovesta: Les bases d'un modèle commercial dans le cadre de l'expansion phénicienne au nord-est de la péninsule ibérique," *Atti 2*, 3.1073–79.

340. C. Gómez Bellard, "Die Phönizier auf Ibiza," *MM* 34 (1993) 83–107; idem, "Baléares," *CPPMR*, 762–75.

341. M. P. San Nicolás Pedraz, "Interpretación de los sanctuaries fenicios y púnicos de Ibiza," *Actas 4*, 2.675–89.

342. J. Elayi and A. Planas Palau, *Les pointes de flèches en bronze d'Ibiza dans le cadre de la colonisation phénico-punique* (Transeuphratène Supplement 2; Paris: Gabalda, 1995). There are 139 arrowheads belonging to 31 different types. Types I, VIII, and XVI belong to the seventh century: there are 32 of type VIII.

343. A. M. Bisi, "Sull'iconografia di due terrecotte puniche di Ibiza," *Studi Magrebini* 7 (1975) 19–36, pl. 1; idem, "Iconografie fenicio-cipriote nella coroplastica punica (a proposito di alcune terrecotte di Ibiza)," *Studi Magribini* 8 (1976) 25–38, pls. 1–4; idem, "La coroplastica fenicia d'Occidente (con particolare riguardo a quella ibicena)," *FPI*, 1.285–94; M. C. D'Angelo, "Artigianato eburneo da Ibiza: Las sfinge," *Actas 4*, 4.1511–17.

the later colonists, as the mixed archaeological message indicates,[344] were also of diverse origins.

An inscription from the town supplies a little perspective to these scattered finds.[345] It is on a small, rectangular bone plaque and records the dedication of a gate, to which it was affixed by a hole in each of its corners, by ʾEshmunʾabî (*ʾšmnʾb*), who traces his ancestry to the seventh generation. The inscription is dated paleographically to around the middle of the seventh century. The dedication is to ʾEshmunmelqart, the syncretic God of Sidon and Tyre whose cult is known only from Kition in Cyprus.

The man's name and the names of his forbears are an assortment from the Sidonian onomasticon, and the seven generations, amounting to about 180 years, fix the origin of the family in late ninth-century Kition. The inscription shows that there were émigrés in the town of Ibiza in the mid-seventh century and that at least one of them came from Kition, where his was one of the founding families, after it fell under Tyrian control, and that the various segments of the new society brought their civic or ancestral Gods with them.

The island sometimes is thought to have been a port of call on a longer and much more promising voyage, but its proximity to the coast of Spain (Alicante is just a day's sail and is visible on a clear day) make this redundant. But if the island was a destination, then its attraction for the settlers and colonists surely was the forests for which it was renowned: Ibiza's Phoenician name is "Balsam-Island" (*ʾy bsm*), and the Greeks, according to Diodorus (5.16), gave it the epithet "Abounding-in-Pine-Trees" (*Pituoussai*). And so it was settled and then colonized by skilled workers from various places in the eastern and western Mediterranean, under the auspices of Carthage, who prepared the timbers and pine caulking used in building boats such as those that sank at Mazarron (made of pine and partially caulked inside and out with pine tar) or who made balm and pharmaceuticals from the pine and balsam resin.

The Phoenicians who came to Spain in the eighth century had become part of the cultural landscape in the seventh. They adopted Iberian ways; the Tartessians, Spanish, and later the Portuguese followed Oriental fashions. The newcomers in the seventh century were associated with the vital, even if at first modest expansion of Carthage, and their energies were directed to the acquisition of garden, agricultural, and forest products as much as to the usual exploitation of Iberian mineral resources. The swing from the far western to the eastern coast of Spain coincided with this new emphasis on the Punic capital and the diminishing importance, in the perception of the colonials, of their places of origin in mainland Phoenicia. The Atlantic region of southern Spain, where the Sidonians had been the predominant foreign presence, was routinely Tartessian. The Phoenicians

344. C. Gómez Bellard, "L'île d'Ibiza dans le commerce en Méditerranée occidentale à l'époque archaïque: Quelques données nouvelles," in *Numismatique et histoire économique phéniciennes et puniques* (ed. T. Hackens and G. Moucharte; Studia Phoenicia 9; Louvain: Université Catholique de Louvain, 1992) 299–309; B. Costa and J. H. Fernández, "El establecimiento de los fenicios en Ibiza: Algunas cuestiones actualmente en debate," *Actas* 4, 1.91–101.

345. M. G. Amadasi Guzzo and P. Xella, "Eshmun-Melqart in una nuova iscrizione fenicia di Ibiza," *SEL* 22 (2005) 47–57.

of the Mediterranean region sent probes into Portugal, the Carthaginians went down the Atlantic coast of Africa, and together they made the development of the east coast of Spain their joint venture.

Conclusion

In the seventh century, Tyre presided over a vast network of economically alert, culturally attuned, and politically energized national states. The design was Tyrian (the infusion of lust for the good life, ambition, and hard work), and the engineering was Assyrian—cooperation, forced if not voluntary, as an ideal, and the possibility of progressing beyond the confines of tradition to a kind of self-transcendence in the empire. Pretty well everybody was part of the system or was crushed by it or just fell by the wayside.

In the eastern Mediterranean homeland, there was a confederation of Assyrian tributary states that was the basis of an intricate economic network. Tyre controlled the seaboard region from the Byblian frontier to Joppa, had access to the port towns, and built a new harbor south of Carmel at ʿAtlit. South of Joppa to the Egyptian border was Philistine territory, dominated by the port at Ashkelon and the industrial center at Ekron. Beyond Philistia was Judah, a now completely centralized economy, and to the east of this vibrant and creative nation were the Transjordanian states, each with its peculiar affiliations: Ammon with the city-states of Syria, Moab with North Arabia, and Edom with South Arabia and Egypt. Across the sea in Cyprus, the native kingdoms had been shaped by their relations with the Phoenicians, maintained cultural and economic ties with them, and encouraged them in their longstanding Hellenic bent. These native Cypriots and their Cypriot-Phoenician confreres went on to the coast of Syria, to Rhodes, and to places such as Samos, which would send explorers with them to the far western Mediterranean.

In the West, Carthage was establishing itself as the pivot of another Phoenician network. The town was growing, populated by immigrants from the homeland and from places previously settled in the colonial West, nurtured by established settlements in Italy, Sicily, Malta, Sardinia, and Spain and, toward the end of the century, supported by its own colonies in Spain, at Ibiza and Málaga, and in northwestern Sicily. In all these places, the novelty of the Phoenicians dissolved in the seventh century, the settlers assimilated, and the indigenous peoples learned to express their native differentiation in the habits and skills and aspirations they had once borrowed from these foreigners. Carthage was a Tyrian colony; but as a town, the inhabitants assumed an ethnic identity and became the "Phoenicians" familiar to the Greeks and then the Romans.

Chapter 5

The Sixth-Century Phoenician World Becomes a Differentiated Semitic and European World

The sixth century was a time of retrenchment for the cities in mainland Phoenicia and of consolidation for the colonies and settlements in the West. The Phoenician world, in the East and in the West, became militarized in response to senseless Neo-Babylonian assaults, aggressive Persian organization, and renewed Egyptian ambition. Greeks took over the bold enterprising approach to business and politics that had been characteristic of the Phoenicians, and what remained of the Mediterranean world the Phoenicians had created was ceded to their Punic counterparts.

Tyre between the Babylonians and the Egyptians

Tyre diminished in importance in the sixth century and did not regain its stature until the last quarter of the century, when it became one of the principal architects of the Persian navy. It lost control of the continental commercial network when Judah, the hinge on which trade with Transjordan and Arabia swung, was captured. It was not important to the Babylonians and was harassed by them throughout the first half of the century. It was alternately wooed and threatened by the Egyptians and because of them lost its mainland possessions and its commercial and cultural dominance in Cyprus, where most of its attention gradually focused on its enclave in Kition. It maintained its political, religious, and demographic bonds with its colony in Carthage, but it was no longer influential in its other possessions in the West, which now gravitated to this developing North African hub.

From the beginning of the sixth century, Tyre and its associates in Judah were caught up in the competition between the Neo-Babylonian Empire under Nebuchadnezzar II (604–561 B.C.E.) and the XXVIth Dynasty of Egypt under Necho (609–594 B.C.E.), Apries (588–568 B.C.E.), and Amasis (568–526 B.C.E.)—Psammetichus II (594–588 B.C.E.) having no trace. Necho intervened in Judean affairs first by killing Josiah, in a prelude to the battle of Carchemish in 605 B.C.E., then deposing his legitimate heir, Jehoahaz, who was taken hostage to Egypt, and finally installing another son,

369

Jehoiakim, as his vassal and tributary in Jerusalem (2 Kgs 23:28–37). But
Egypt had little authority in Judah, and Jehoiakim with his son Jehoiakin
and then his successor, Zedekiah, became subject to Nebuchadnezzar. Both
Jehoiakim and Zedekiah, relying on Tyre and Sidon and their partners
in Transjordan and expecting the intervention of Egypt, rebelled against
Babylon (2 Kings 24, Jer 27:1–7). But Egypt had been neutralized,[1] and
Jerusalem was besieged and slipped unnoticed into exile the first time (597
B.C.E.); then was captured, destroyed, humiliated and exiled in the end
(586 B.C.E.). Tyre, in effect, was left alone (Sidon does not enter into the
picture until later) to bear the brunt of Babylonian determination.

Tyre was besieged by the Babylonians in 585 B.C.E., early in the reign
of ʾIttobaʿal, and remained under siege until the end of his reign in 572
B.C.E.[2] The siege, despite its ludicrous length, was unsuccessful.[3] There was
no naval blockade of the island city, and the landward embargo, manned
by small contingents from Uruk and Sippar,[4] interfered with its business
and its reputation but did not threaten its physical survival. Some people,
probably from its mainland farming communities rather than from the city
itself, were captured and deported to Babylonia, to a town (also a farming
community) situated between Uruk and Nippur and named "Tyre" (ṣur[r]u)
after them. These exiles are mentioned in Babylonian texts dating to the
decade (573–563) following the siege of ʿTyre, but the place is not mentioned after the 42nd year of Nebuchadnezzar (563 B.C.E.), which suggests
that the exiles went back home when Nebuchadnezzar died and the situation in Tyre began to return to normal.[5]

After the siege, following the reign of ʾIttobaʿal, Tyre was ruled by a compromise king, the Babylonian appointee Baʿal (572–562 B.C.E.), by magistrates appointed by the city assembly (562–556 B.C.E.), by an illegitimate
aspirant to the throne (555 B.C.E.), and by two kings in the line of ʾIttobaʿal
who were summoned from among the exiles in Babylon (554–530 B.C.E.).[6]
During the reign of Baʿal, encouraged by Babylon's failure to take Tyre, the
Egyptians began again to interfere in Phoenician (both Tyrian and Sidonian) affairs. Apries (588–568 B.C.E.) paraded to Sidon by land and, learning from Nebuchadnezzar's mistake, launched a naval blockade against Tyre
with ships built on Cyprus (presumably by Greek, not Phoenician Cypriots)

1. Nebuchadnezzar attacked Egypt in 601 B.C.E. and, although it was a standoff, Egypt did
not interfere in Judean affairs until later in the sixth century: see D. J. Wiseman, *Chronicles of
Chaldaean Kings (626–556 B.C.) in the British Museum* (London: British Museum, 1956) 29–31.

2. *HistTyre* 322–29.

3. Ezek 29:17–20; H.-P. Müller, "Phonizien und Juda in exilisch-nachexilischer Zeit," *WO* 6
(1971) 189–204, esp. pp. 192–93.

4. I. Ephʿal, "Nebuchadnezzar the Warrior: Remarks on His Military Achievements," *IEJ* 53
(2003) 178–91, esp. pp. 183, 185–87.

5. E. Unger, "Nebuchadnezar II. und sein *šandabakku* (Oberkommisar) in Tyrus," *ZAW* 44
(1926) 314–17; idem, *Babylon: Die Heilige Stadt nach der Beschreibung der Babylonier* (Berlin: de
Gruyter, 1931) 282–94 #26; F. Joannès, "La location de Ṣurru à l'époque néo-babylonienne," *Sem* 32 (1982) 35–43; idem, "Trois textes de Ṣurru à l'époque néo-babylonienne," *RA* 81 (1987)
147–58, esp. p. 149; S. Zawadzki, "Nebuchadnezzar and Tyre in the Light of New Texts from the
Ebabbar Archives in Sippar," *ErIsr* 27 (Hayim and Miriam Tadmor Volume; 2003) 276*–81*.

6. *HistTyre* 327–29.

and manned by Greek mercenaries,[7] recruited most likely from the motley crew at Naucratis. Amasis (568–526 B.C.E.), who is said to have "conquered" Cyprus,[8] formalized Egyptian relations with the island kingdoms and could count on them as allies when he challenged Babylon's hold on the southern Levant.[9] In the reign of Baʿal, in short, Tyre belonged nominally to Babylon (in 564 and 563, Babylonian troops were sent to Tyre to restring the puppet king),[10] but it became increasingly subject to Egyptian control, or at least more and more involved in the widening Egyptian orbit.

Following Baʿal's reign, after the death of Nebuchadnezzar and during the reigns of his three successors (561–556 B.C.E.), in the absence of legitimate heirs in the line of ʾIttobaʿal, Tyre was ruled by judges. When Nabonidus (556–539 B.C.E.) came to the throne, the Tyrians summoned members of the royal family from Babylon and again came under monarchic rule during the reigns of Mahirbaʿal (554–550 B.C.E.) and of Hiram (550–530 B.C.E.). Tyre and Sidon acquiesced to Persian rule (starting in 539 B.C.E.) and, during the reign of Cambyses (530–522 B.C.E.), they became the mainstay of the Persian fleet that masterminded the invasion of Egypt.[11]

Judean writers in their own laconic and allusive manner kept track of Tyrian history, particularly its involvement with Egypt and Babylon, in the sixth century. The early years of Egyptian and Babylonian competition enter into biblical chronology: the defeat of Necho at the battle of Carchemish (605 B.C.E.) is recorded in the Babylonian Chronicle, as is a later but unsuccessful Babylonian campaign against Egypt (601 B.C.E.), and both are used to fix the dates of two successive oracles about Egypt in the book of Jeremiah (46:2, 13). A jaundiced view of the close economic ties between Tyre and Judah pictures the island city rejoicing over the siege and fall of Jerusalem; because "the gateway to the nations is broken, it has swung open to me" (Ezek 26:2), but a more critical perspective blames the fall of Jerusalem on its association with this mercantile people, these "Canaanites, weighers of silver" (Zeph 1:11). The campaign of Apries against Tyre, Sidon, and Cyprus is remembered in a biblical text as his attempt to lift the second siege of Jerusalem (Jer 37:7, 11; 44:30).[12]

There was war between Amasis and Nebuchadnezzar (564 B.C.E.), when Tyre counted on Egyptian support to shrug off its compromise king and Babylon rushed troops to Tyre to get Baʿal back on his feet. The war is not recounted, but it is rehearsed in an oracle (Jer 46:20–21) that describes Nebuchadnezzar as a gadfly alighting on a lovely heifer—adapting the image of

---

7. Herodotus 2.161; Diod. 1.68.1; A. T. Reyes, *Archaic Cyprus: A Study of the Textual and Archaeological Evidence* (Oxford: Clarendon, 1994) 72–73.

8. Herodotus 2.182; Reyes, *Archaic Cyprus*, 72–78.

9. Ibid., 75–76.

10. Zawadzki, "Nebuchadnezzar and Tyre in the Light of New Texts from the Ebabbar Archives in Sippar," 279*.

11. H. T. Wallinga, "The Ancient Persian Navy and Its Predecessors," in *Achaemenid History, I: Sources, Structures and Synthesis* (ed. H. Sancisi-Weerdenburg; Leiden: Nederlands Instituut voor Het Abije Oosten, 1987) 47–77.

12. Zedekiah's reliance on Egypt at this time is immortalized in the parable of the eagle and the cedar of Lebanon (Ezek 17:1–18).

Zeus pursuing Io[13]—and alludes to Amasis's settlement of Greek and Cypriot merchants and mercenaries at Naucratis. The effects of the 13-year siege on Tyre's prestige and its ability to function well in the international trading community are expressed hyperbolically in a lament over the downfall of the island kingdom by the whole Mediterranean world (Ezek 26:17–18): "How you have perished, founded from the seas, renowned city, who was powerful on the Sea. . . . Now the coastlands are terrified on the day of your downfall, and the islands in the Sea are astounded at your extinction."

A more elaborate oracular reminiscence weaves together Tyre's Cypriot connections, its Mediterranean trade, its overseas settlements, its wheat deals with Egypt, and its competition with Sidon into a lamentation over the siege and fall of the illustrious city "whose merchants were princes, whose traders were honored throughout the world" (Isa 23:1–7, 10–12).[14] The siege of Tyre may have been Nebuchadnezzar's attempt to disrupt Egyptian foreign policy, but according to these Judean writers, it marked the beginning of the end of Tyre's total dominance of the Mediterranean markets and, in effect, the ruin of the city.

It was not quite the end of its mercantile interests, however, or of its reputation. The biblical book of Jonah, written around this time, is a spoof on Jerusalem orthodoxy, but it knows about Tyre in its heyday: that you could catch the boat for Tarshish at Joppa, that Tarshish is at the ends of the earth, beyond the reach of the God who made the Sea and dry Land, and that the sailors who dared the voyage would seek safe passage by tossing images of the Storm God into the raging Sea (Jonah 1:1–16, Ps 107:23–32).[15]

More concretely, there is inscriptional evidence for Minaean, ancient South Arabian, trade with Tyre and Sidon, but the reference is only to doing business, and no commodities are specified.[16] But there are two Babylonian tablets, from the 5th and 6th years of Nabonidus (551 and 550 B.C.E.), that list the products shipped by Tyrian traders and accepted on consignment in Uruk: copper, lapis lazuli, iron, cloth, alum, dye, honey, wine, spices, and resin.[17] These records indicate, at least, that the Tyrian trade network was still operational: the copper was from Cyprus, the iron from Lebanon and Ionia, the cloth and dye were, and, according to Ezekiel, the honey used to come from Israel, the wine from Damascus, and the spices from South Arabia. But the tablets may also suggest that the Tyrians deported to Surru, in the vicinity of Uruk, had spent less time in farming than in cultivating the commercial interests of their Babylonian hosts who, now

---

13. M. L. West, *The East Face of Helicon: West Asiatic Elements in Greek Poetry and Myth* (Oxford: Clarendon, 1997) 445–46.

14. This poem, dating soon after 539 B.C.E., was interpreted in Isa 23:8–9, 13–18, which was written later in the century.

15. G. Kapitan, "Archaeological Evidence for Rituals and Customs on Ancient Ships," in *Proceedings of the First International Symposium on Ship Construction in Antiquity* (ed. H. E. Tzalas; Piraeus: Hellenic Instiitute for the Preservation of Nautical Tradition, 1989) 147–62; A. J. Brody, *"Each Man Cried Out to His God": The Specialized Religion of Canaanite and Phoenician Seafarers* (HSM 58; Atlanta: Scholars Press, 1998).

16. C. Robin, "Première mention de Tyr chez les Minéens d'Arabie du Sud," *Sem* 39 (1990) 135–47, pl. 5.

17. A. L. Oppenheim, "Essay on Overland Trade in the First Millennium B.C.," *JCS* 21 (1967) 236–54.

that Nabonidus had withdrawn and left the Levant alone, were glad to do business with them.

A seal and bullae (purportedly from Tyre, its territory, or its spheres of influence) illustrate the city's pride, unpredictable creativity, and enduring, constantly renewable indebtedness to Egyptian artistic and religious traditions. A green jasper scarab seal has a winged sun disk hovering over an enthroned and crowned, falcon-headed Goddess who holds a flower in her left hand and raises her right hand in greeting to the ibis-headed God Thoth before her:[18] scattered in the empty spaces in the design are the letters of the name "Client-of-Astarte" (*gr'štrt*), undoubtedly the man who, as Thoth, stands before Astarte in one of her Egyptian guises to receive her blessing.

Two of the bullae[19] represent purely Egyptian themes: the child Horus kneeling on a lotus blossom, crowned with the sun disk, his left hand to his mouth; a seated Goddess, crowned with horns and sun disk, seated, nursing her child. Two others, impressed from signet rings, represent Melqart, the God of the city, seated on a sphinx-armrest throne, a sceptre in his left hand, his right hand raised in benediction. In both designs, his throne is placed under a winged sun disk, and he receives the incense offering of his people; in one design, where a crescent moon accompanies the sun disk, he is represented in his celestial temple, but in the other he is seated in a canopied, possibly movable shrine. The fifth bulla presents two beautiful, lithe horses turned neck-to-haunch: it is without any religious affiliation but is a witness to the haughty, independent, and ever-creative Tyrian artistic spirit.

Sidon and the Dynasty of ʾEshmunʿazor

Sidon began to revive when the Assyrians were defeated and their port at Kar Esarhaddon came under Sidonian authority. In the early years of the sixth century, Sidon was in conversation with Tyre and Judah but, unlike them, did not provoke the Babylonians to attack or lay siege. Along with Tyre and Cyprus, it attracted the attention of Egypt under Apries, who is said to have attacked it, and under Amasis, whose offerings[20] along with a few Cypriot terra-cottas and limestone statues were dedicated in its Temple of ʾEshmun. Sidon came into its own at the end of the century when it worked for the Persians and during the fifth century when it was increasingly aligned with the Greeks.

From the advent of the Persian Empire, Sidon was ruled by the Dynasty of ʾEshmunʿazor. The founder of the dynasty is otherwise unknown, and there is no sign of his accomplishments and no record of his burial. His name is unique in Phoenician. It is mentioned only in the inscriptions of

---

18. *WSS* 273 #735.

19. E. Gubel, "Cinq bulles inédites des archives tyriennes de l'époque achéménide," *Sem* 47 (1997) 53–64.

20. A bronze jug and a sistrum with the cartouche of Amasis were discovered in Sidon and are presumed to have been ex-votos brought or sent to the Temple of ʾEshmun: see M. Dunand, "Note sur quelques objets provenant de Saïda," *Syria* 7 (1926) 123–27, pl. 32; W. Culican, "Quelques aperçus sur les ateliers phéniciens," *Syria* 45 (1968) 275–93, pls. 19–22, esp. p. 279, pl. 19:1–3.

his successors and occurs only rarely, perhaps with reference to him, in the Punic onomasticon. He was a priest of Astarte and not indebted to a royal line. His dynastic chapel dedicated to ʾEshmun and Astarte, where the Amasis offerings and the Cypriot ex-votos were presented, left no architectural trace. His reign coincided with that of Cyrus, with the early years of Cambyses, and with the last years of Amasis. Taking into account the relative and adjustable chronologies of his children and his successors, his reign covered the years 539–525 B.C.E.

The earliest inscription, at the foot of an Egyptian anthropoid sarcophagus, is of his son and successor, Tabnît. This name too is unique, both in Phoenician and in Punic. But the word occurs as a common noun in Biblical Hebrew, meaning "plan, image, or design," used with reference to holy things in expressions such as "images of the Gods," "plan of the temple," or "design of an altar." The name *Tabnît*, then, means something like "Configuration" of the Goddess Astarte, which was potentially pretentious but eminently appropriate for a king who was, like his father, "priest of Astarte."

He was embalmed and buried in a sarcophagus that was being prepared for an Egyptian general (the lid was beautifully finished, but one exterior side of the coffin was only roughly hewn) and that was looted and shipped from Egypt after Cambyses' Egyptian campaign (522 B.C.E.) or during the reign of Darius I (521–486 B.C.E.; fig. 5.1b). With the anthropoid sarcophagi for his wife and for his son and successor, both unfinished and stolen at the same time from the same workshop in Giza or Saqqara, it remained on display in Sidon until he died and until his tomb was prepared for it.[21]

These sarcophagi became the model for late sixth-century terra-cotta anthropoid sarcophagi at Arvad and for the early fifth-century Greek marble sarcophagi at Sidon. They began a fad that lasted a little more than 100 years among royalty in Sidon and among wealthy merchants in Tyre, Beirut, Tripolis, Arvad, and Egypt and that traveled with them to Cyprus, Sicily, Spain, and Malta.[22] Tabnît's tomb was the first in the royal necropolis, adjoining but apart from the chamber tombs that were dug deeper but off the same central entrance shaft, and that were prepared for members of the dynasty. Examination of his embalmed remains indicates that Tabnît died when he was about 50 years old, and so, according to the likely but adjustable schedule, he was born about mid-century (550 B.C.E.), before his father (who was 25 when he was born) had acquired the throne, and he reigned during the last quarter of the sixth century.

His tomb was simple and contained only insignia of his royal office: a plain gold headband, a gold armband, a gold necklace, gold and coral

21. K. Lembke, *Phönizische anthropoide Sarkophage* (Damaszener Forschungen 10; Mainz am Rhein: von Zabern, 2001) 6–8, 26–42; H. Richter, "Katalog der Fundgruppen," in *Die phönizischen anthropoiden Sarkophage, Teil 1: Fundgruppen und Bestattungskontexte* (ed. S. Frede; Mainz am Rhein: von Zabern, 2000) 65–153, pls. 1–144, esp. pp. 65–69, 72–74, pls. 1–4, 11–12; S. Grallert, "Die ägyptischen Sarkophage aus der Nekropole von Sidon," in *Die phönizischen anthropoiden Sarkophage, Teil 2: Tradition – Rezeption – Wandel* (ed. S. Frede; Mainz am Rhein: von Zabern, 2002) 191–215, pls. 52–88.
22. K. Lembke, "Die phönizischen anthropoiden Sarkophage aus den Nekropolen der Insel Arados," *Damaszener Mitteilungen* 10 (1998) 97–130.

beads from another necklace, a silver wristband, and a bronze mirror.[23] His inscription[24] tells the same plain story and is totally taken up with his sarcophagus (see fig. 5.1a), as if acquiring it were his main accomplishment. It is undated, without context in his life, isolated from world affairs, and his kingship pales in the light of his priestly office:

> I, Tabnît, priest of Astarte, king of the Sidonians, son of ʾEshmunʿazor, priest of Astarte, king of the Sidonians, am resting in this coffin. Whoever you are, anyone, who might come upon this coffin, do not open its cover, and do not disturb me, because there is nothing with me of silver, and nothing with me of gold, and nothing of any value, except me myself resting in this coffin. Do not open its cover, and do not disturb me, for such a thing is an abomination to Astarte. And if you should open its cover and disturb me, may you not have seed under the sun or resting place with the Rephaim.

He gives priority to his and his father's priesthood of Astarte and to the good pleasure of Astarte as the ultimate ennobling motivation. The penalty for disturbing his rest is lack of rest among the noble dead who are undergoing healing, and lack of progeny among the living, which was precisely the problem that plagued his reign.

Succession was always a problem, but it was especially acute in this extremely tight-knit dynasty. The first king, ʾEshmunʿazor I, had three children: a son Tabnît, a daughter ʾImmîʿaštart ("My Mother-Is-Astarte"), and a younger son, Anush (ʾAnîš). Tabnît married his sister, and they had a son, ʾEshmunʿazor, who died before reaching majority and was succeeded by his cousin, Bodʿaštart, the son of Anush, who in turn was succeeded by his son Yatonmilk. The children of the second generation had unique, unusual, or eccentric names, but the children and grandchildren of the collateral line had common, nondynastic names. Anush, the brother of Tabnît, is a name known only from a late sixth-century inscription from Motya in western Sicily[25] and as the name of the father of the king of Sidon who was with the fleet at the battle of Salamis[26]—Tetramnēstos, son of Anusos. Anush, biblical Enosh, was born after Tabnît and died before ʾEshmunʿazor and before he could be king. Bodʿaštart, his son, that is, Tetramnēstos, was king of Sidon in 480 B.C.E. and acceded to the throne after ʾEshmunʿazor II, who reigned 14 years and died ca. 486 B.C.E.

ʾImmîʿaštart, born around 548 B.C.E., was a priestess of Astarte, and her name reflects this special vocation. She lived after the death of her son, was buried in another of the unfinished Egyptian anthropoid sarcophagi that Tabnît had provided for his family and that was placed in the first chamber of the family underground vault. Her husband, Tabnît, died around 500 B.C.E., her younger brother, Anush, around 490 B.C.E., and she outlived both of them. Her sarcophagus—lined with a sycamore pallet on which she

23. P. Schafer, "Grabbeigaben und Beifunde," in *Die phönizischen anthropoiden Sarkophage, Teil 2: Tradition, Rezeption, Wandel* (ed. S. Frede; Mainz am Rhein: von Zabern, 2002) 129–82, pls. 37–50, esp. pp. 130–31, pl. 37a.

24. *KAI* 13; C. Peri, "A proposito dell'iscrizione di Tabnit," *RSF* 24 (1996) 67–72.

25. M. G. Amadasi Guzzo, *Scavi a Mozia: Le Iscrizioni* (Rome: Consiglio Nazionale delle Ricerche, 1986) 40 #37.

26. Herodotus 7.98; T. Kelly, "Herodotus and the Chronology of the Kings of Sidon," *BASOR* 268 (1987) 39–56.

Fig. 5.1a. Tabnît inscription on base of sarcophagus (King of Sidon). © Istanbul Archaeological Museum.

was laid to rest wearing a gold diadem, a gold ring on her left hand, and many bangles on both arms—is undecorated and uninscribed.

ʾEshmunʿazor, son of Tabnît and ʾImmîʿaštart, was buried in the third Egyptian anthropoid sarcophagus, not in the family vault, the chambers of which had not been dug, but in a shallow covered grave in a fairly distant necropolis. His inscription[27] was written in six and a half lines at the head of the sarcophagus but, when the upper surface of the cover had been scraped to receive it, was written again in a significantly expanded version on the lid below the collar and face of the Egyptian figure. His version is written in the first-person singular as a quotation of his lament over a brief and miserable existence. The second version, written by his mother, is mostly in the first-person plural and recounts the building projects and political accomplishments of her co-regency. His birth was inauspicious, his death, always imminent but unprepared, was sudden, and his separate burial reflects his exclusion and marginality during his lifetime.

> In the month Bul, in the fourteenth (14th) year of the reign of ʾEshmunʿazor, king of the Sidonians, son of King Tabnît, king of the Sidonians, King

27. *KAI* 14.

Fig. 5.1b. Sarcophagus (King of Sidon). © Istanbul Archaeological Museum.

ʾEshmunʿazor, king of the Sidonians, said: "I have been cut off, before my time, the child of libations (*bn msk*) during the days of rogation (*ymm ʾzrm*), an orphan, son of a widow, and I am lying in this coffin in this grave in the mortuary chapel which I built."

He was born out of season as an answer to prayer (his parents were both priests of Astarte) after his father died. The rest of his lament is devoted to curses on anyone who would disturb his resting place, or even think ("speak") about it, and the curses are pretty much that they will endure pain and shame like his own: lack of resting place, being cut off by a mighty king, failure to produce offspring. The dynasty, so far, had run a disastrous course.

The revised version, like all revisions of literary texts, begins by repeating key parts of the original, in this case the same words in opposite sentence order; to mark changes to the original, in this case the change to the mother as speaker—she could not record her achievements on her own sarcophagus, where there was plenty of room, but as coregent she could slip in a word or two on her son's coffin. She begins her text with his lament ("I have been cut off before my time . . . , an orphan, son of a widow"), prefacing it with "because I am pitiful," which clearly is her sentiment. Then she gives his genealogy, which was first in his lament, but she extends it to include the founder of the dynasty and herself ("and my mother is ʾImmîʿaštart, priestess of Astarte, our Mistress, the Queen, daughter of King ʾEshmunʿazor, king of the Sidonians"). With this she ends the words of her son and begins speaking in the first-person plural about her co-regency.

The first thing "we" did was build a temple for Astarte in the port city and install her on a throne symbolizing the mighty heavens. Then "we built" a temple for ʾEshmun in the mountain by the stream Yadlul and enthroned him in the mighty heavens (the lofty terrace on which it was founded still stands).[28] Finally, "it was we who built" a temple for the Baʿal of Sidon and Astarte-Name-of-Baʿal. The revision ends by repeating the curses from the king's lamentation, but just before this it adds another sentence: "And moreover the Lord of Kings *gave us* Dor and Joppa, the mighty wheat lands which are in the Plain of Sharon, in return for the heavy tribute *which I paid*, and we added them to the territory of the land to belong to the Sidonians for ever." This territory, the Assyrian province of Dor, from time immemorial was administered by Tyre, and its transfer[29] with its taxes and tolls to Sidon implies a free and more generous contribution to the Persian war effort than Tyre was prepared or willing to make. The tribute could have been money (not coinage, which the Phoenician cities had not started minting), but it was money spent on the ships, captains, and crews, for which Sidon was renowned. There may have been one particular campaign

28. L. Ganzmann, H. van der Meijden, and R. A. Stucky, "Das Eschmunheiligtum von Sidon: Die Funde der türkischen Ausgrabungen von 1901–1903 im Archäologischen Museum in Istanbul," *Istanbuler Mitteilungen* 37 (1987) 81–130, pls. 25–38; R. A. Stucky, "Das Heiligtum des Ešmun bei Sidon in vorhellenistischer Zeit," *ZDPV* 118 (2002) 66–86.
29. P. Briant, "Dons de terres et de villes: L'Asie Mineure dans le contexte achéménide," *Revue des Études Anciennes* 87 (1985) 53–72.

or naval battle that prompted the recompense,[30] but it is just as likely that the Lord of Kings was rewarding the new, unabashedly pro-Persian policy introduced by the Queen Mother (*"which I paid"*). And it was this for which the next king began to pay the price.

The next king was Bod῾aštart, son of Anush, nephew of Tabnît and ʾImmîʿaštart, older cousin of the unfortunate ʾEshmunʿazor. He was born ca. 520 B.C.E., when his father was 25, ascended the throne when he himself was about 35, and reigned about 485–465 B.C.E., with his son Yatonmilk, born the same year as ʾEshmunʿazor, as co-regent from 470 B.C.E. and as king from 465 to 450 B.C.E. He was with the fleet at Salamis, where the Phoenicians made such a surprisingly poor showing, and when he and his son died, the Sidonians were ready for a change of dynasty with a pro-Athenian policy.

Bodʿaštart, being of a collateral nonpriestly line, set out to legitimize himself by imitating and outdoing the dynasty's religious fervor. At the beginning of his reign he erected an extraordinary monument to Astarte:[31]

> It was in the month Mopaʿ, in the year of the becoming king, of King Bodʿaštart, king of the Sidonians, that Bodʿaštart, king of the Sidonians, built the triumphant emblem of the land for his Goddess, for Astarte.

The inscription is on the limestone base that supported the divine emblem. It was erected at the beginning of his reign, to legitimate it, and he insists on the fact that he has become king of the Sidonians. The emblem, an emblem of the land, described as "exultant" or "triumphant" (ʿlz), commemorated the land's jubilation when he became king, and triumphed over rivals or potential usurpers who arose after the sudden death of ʾEshmunʿazor, when the Queen Mother was still co-regent.

A few years afterward, before the battle of Salamis, when he was still sole ruler, and later when his son Yatonmilk was co-regent, Bodʿaštart wrote other inscriptions to celebrate his construction of the Temple of ʾEshmun.[32] The inscriptions are peculiar: they exist in multiple copies; they are written on the inside faces of blocks that were added to buttress the retaining wall of the temple terrace built by ʾImmîʿaštart; they are idiosyncratic in their construction and composition. His solo dedications, of which there are more than a dozen exact copies, establish his legitimacy as king of the Sidonians, as king of the city of Sidon and all its boroughs, and as builder of the Temple of ʾEshmun:

> King Bodʿaštart, king of the Sidonians, grandson of King ʾEshmunʿazor, king of the Sidonians, in Sidon-by-the Sea, Sidon-of-Heaven-on-High, Sidon-of-the-Industrial-Land (*ršpm*), Sidon-the-Capital which he built, and of Sidon-in-the-Fields, built this house to his God, to ʾEshmun the Holy Spirit (*šd qdš*).

---

30. T. Kelly, "Herodotus and the Chronology of the Kings of Sidon," *BASOR* 268 (1987) 39–56.

31. *CIS* 4; C. Bonnet, "Phénicien *šrn* = accadien *šurinnu*? À propos de l'inscription de Bodashtart *CIS* I, 4," *Or* 64 (1995) 214–22.

32. *KAI* 15, 16; C. Bonnet and P. Xella, "Les inscriptions phéniciennes de Bodashtart roi de Sidon," in *Da Pyrgi a Mozia: Studi sull'archeologia nel mediterraneo in memoria di Antonia Ciasca* (ed. M. G. Amadasi Guzzo, M. Liverani, and P. Matthiae; Vicino Oriente, Quaderno 3/1; Rome: Università degli Studi di Roma, "La Sapienzà," 2002) 93–104, pls. 1–3.

Sidon-the-Capital is downtown Sidon, where the palace was located. Sidon-by-the-Sea is the port. Sidon-of-Heaven-on-High is the city on the hill where the ʾEshmun Temple was located, called "Mighty Heavens" in the ʾEshmunʿazor inscription. Sidon-in-the-Fields was the suburb outside the walls and pavement and beyond the residential areas. Industrial Sidon, literally, "The-Land-of-Burnings, of Smoke" was the factory area, the area of the shipyards and foundries, where weapons were made and battering rams for ships, the location of the pottery barns and the murex factories. The epithet of the God, bedevilled by the script, which did not always distinguish nicely between / d / and / r /—thus, "Holy Prince" (*šr* instead of *šd*) is a standard reading—is illustrated by a contemporary seal[33] inscribed "Client of the Benevolent Spirit" (*lgršd*), which portrays the spirit (*šed*) seated on a cherub throne, wearing a miter, holding a staff with flower finial in his right hand, and raising his left hand in benediction.

The second set of inscriptions omits this description of the city and inserts between the king's name and his ancestry the name of his son: "King Bodʿaštart, and his legitimate son (*wbn ṣdq*) Yatonmilk, king of the Sidonians, grandson of King ʾEshmunʿazor, king of the Sidonians, built this house for his God, for ʾEshmun, the Holy Spirit." His legitimacy was his right of succession to the throne, but he is included only in the later inscriptions (there was endless tinkering with the retaining wall) because his father was well, and he was too young when the first refurbishment was finished, before the battle of Salamis (born around 500 B.C.E., co-regent from about 475 B.C.E., king ca. 465–450 B.C.E.).

Sidon was not anxious to experiment with another theocratic regime when it came time to replace the priestly dynasty of ʾEshmunʿazor. The Phoenicians, welcoming winners and not looking for trouble, aligned themselves with Persia, but the new dynasty in Sidon was too enthusiastic. Tabnît went on Cambyses' Egyptian campaign, imitated the mad king in desecrating Egyptian tombs,[34] and stole coffins, just enough for his own priestly family, from Egyptian workshops—not much of a life's work. But from then to the end of the Persian period, anthropoid sarcophagi, done by Greeks, were all the rage for those who could afford them. His wife, ʾImmîʿaštart, during her co-regency, made war a business, and her reward was receipt of the province of Dor and some ascendancy over Tyre.

She could not have succeeded without her son, ʾEshmunʿazor, a particularly challenged boy, as dynastic figurehead, but she was smart enough to make the best of things. Bodʿaštart saved the inbreeding of the dynasty, struggled for legitimacy, clung to customs, creeds, and foreign policy but went down swinging at the battle of Salamis, when Sidon's fame in naval matters keeled over. His son was a decent and reliable sort who, naturally, made no mark. Father and son were buried in Greek marble anthropoid sarcophagi, de rigueur for royalty since Tabnît, in chambers dug off the main entrance shaft of the dynastic vault, next to ʾImmîʿaštart.

War was a business, and Sidon regained its prestige among the Phoenician cities doing business with the Persian navy. The Egyptians toyed with

---

33. *CSOSI* 36 #26; *WSS* 274 #736.
34. Herodotus 3.37.

it earlier in the century, but Sidon was independent and took advantage of the Babylonian squeeze on Tyre to stay on course with its Syrian, Cypriot, and overseas partners. Money was becoming the new economy, and Sidon came into it in Cilicia, Greece, and Persia in the sixth century. When it began minting its own coins, it naturally chose for their designs a ship under sail, the warrior king of Persia, and the three-tiered platform of the Temple of ʾEshmun.[35]

Byblos and Religious Conservation

Byblos in the sixth century was still the silent partner, cast in the shadow of Tyre, Sidon, and Arvad, supplying the architects, masons, and shipbuilders that kept life going and the good life accessible. Its kings, or city council, built a temple precinct toward the end of the century, high on a platform of carefully hewn stones, and it may have been experts from Byblos who designed the platform Temple of ʾEshmun in Sidon and who supervised the construction of the supporting wall of the temple in Jerusalem.[36] It was émigrés from Byblos or from its colony at Lapethos in Cyprus who, as the language of its dedication attests, built the precinct of Astarte at Pyrgi in Italy. The silence is broken only by texts such as these, written at home by its kings and by some of its citizens who, like the masons at Pyrgi, were making their fortunes abroad.

A characteristic of Byblos is its religious conservatism. The earliest of the sixth-century inscriptions is on an ostrich egg,[37] a luxury item of choice especially in the sixth century, particularly in the western Mediterranean.[38] The inscription was written in red paint on an egg decorated in black designs: "ʿAbdbaʿal vowed it and made it for Baʿal of Byblos. May he bless him" (*ndr wpʿl ʿbdbʿl lbʿl gbl. lybrk*). The precative particle (*l-*, "may he") is used exclusively in Byblian and in western Mediterranean inscriptions written by expatriate Byblians: inscriptions in other dialects omit the particle, and the optative is marked simply by the verb's initial position. The inscription makes it clear that ʿAbdbaʿal prayed, vowed that he would make an offering to Baʿal if his prayer was answered, and when it was answered did what he had vowed. The special interest of the decorated and inscribed egg is the persistence of Byblians in their devotion to Baʿal: the God is known from a tenth-century building inscription from Byblos, and this devotee remained faithful to his God and went to the trouble of sending

---

35. J. W. Betlyon, *The Coinage and Mints of Phoenicia: The Pre-Alexandrine Period* (HSM 26; Chico, CA: Scholars Press, 1982) 3–4, pl. 1:1–2.

36. M. Dunand, "La défense du front méditerranéen de l'empire achéménide," in *The Role of the Phoenicians in the Interaction of Mediterranean Civilizations* (ed. W. A. Ward; Beirut: American University, 1968) 43–51; idem, "Byblos, Sidon, Jerusalem: Monuments apparentés des temps achéménides (résumé)," in *Congress Volume: Rome, 1968* (VTSup 17; Leiden: Brill, 1969) 64–70, pls. 1–2.

37. P. Bordreuil, "Nouveaux documents phéniciens inscrits," *Actas* 4, 1.205–13, esp. pp. 205–6.

38. G. Pisano, "Beni di lusso nel mondo punico: Le uova di struzzo—II," in *Da Pyrgi a Mozia: Studi sull'archeologia nel Mediterraneo in memoria di Antonia Ciasca* (ed. M. G. Amadasi Guzzo, M. Liverani, and P. Matthiae; Vicino Oriente—Quaderno 3/2; Rome: Universita degli Studi di Roma, "La Sapienza," 2002) 391–401.

his offering back home by one of the ships on its regular voyage, or perhaps brought it back to Byblos himself.

There is another dedicatory inscription hammered into a fine strip of silver that was rolled and inserted into a bronze sheath. It belongs on paleographical grounds to the second half of the sixth century[39] and, like the ostrich egg shell, it records the fulfillment of a vow in Byblos by an expatriate or colonial Byblian. It quotes the vow, describes its fulfillment at a particular time, and treats these elements and the precious metal on which they were inscribed as having the timeless characteristics of an amulet:

lrbt l‘štrt	To the Mistress, to Astarte
rbt gbl nd‘r	the Mistress of Byblos, the vow
‘bdk rkb’š	of your servant Rakkob’is
bn ‘bd‘štrt	son of ‘Abd‘astart,
hgbly ’š ndr	a Byblian, who vowed
’t ndr’ z ’š	this vow of his which
kn ’nḥn bt wss	was: "We, the house, and the horses
ltbrk wtḥlṣ’	may you bless, and may you preserve him,
’t ‘bdk wbny’	your servant, and his sons
w’štw wbt ’by’	and his wife, and this house of his fathers
zn wl’t’sp	and may you accept
hmtn z ytn’t	this dedication." I dedicated
mzbḥ ‘sr ybnm	an altar, ten rams
wšnm ’lp w‘sr	and two oxen and
wšnm ‘zm	twelve goats
wksp ‘srm	and twenty-four
w’rb‘ lšptb‘l	shekels for Siptiba‘al,
mlk gbl hnṣr	king of Byblos, the Guarantor.
wkn rb khnm bt	The Chief Priest of the temple
’lm ‘štrt	of the Goddess Astarte was
bdb‘l hkhn	Bodba‘al the Holy
hqdš	Priest.

The inscription is by a Byblian, mentions the king of Byblos who founded the dynasty that ruled in the fifth century, and is dated by the year of the eponymous priest of Astarte. The language contains Byblian idioms (the precative *l*-) and dialectal forms (the pronominal suffix -*w*), mixed with phonological features of the dialect of Kition (the interchange of *samek* and *šin* in the proper name Rakkob’iš, "Charioteer of Isis," of *šin* and *samek* in the number "ten," and of *lamed* and *nun* in the word for "rams" [*ybnm* instead of *yblm*]). Most surprisingly, it is written in the orthography of the Western provinces where, under the glare of Greek, consonants could stand for vowels: ‘*ayin* (*nd‘r*) is pronounced /ā/ (*nadār*), and final ’*alep* (*ndr’*) is pronounced /ō/ (*nidrō*). The inscription, therefore, to unravel its patois, records the fulfillment of a vow made by a Byblian world traveler, raised in Cyprus, traveling on business in the Punic West, but everywhere a Byblian.

---

39. A. Lemaire, "Amulette phénicienne giblite en argent," in *Shlomo: Studies in Epigraphy, Iconography and Archaeology in Honor of Shlomo Moussaieff* (ed. R. Deutsch; Tel Aviv–Jaffa: Archaeological Center, 2003) 155–74.

The silver amulet was kept in a bronze case that was worn on a necklace and that functioned as a constant prayer to Astarte for blessing and security. She is called the "Mistress" (*rbt*) of Byblos, not to be confused with the founding Goddess, whose name was the "Lady" (*ba'alat*) of Byblos,[40] and she had a temple, priesthood, and sacrificial cult in the city, as she did in just about every Phoenician community beginning in the sixth century. The man's name makes him a devotee of Egyptian Isis, who became increasingly popular at this time, a mystical representation of the more sensual Byblian Astarte. The blessing he sought on "us, the house and the horses," or on "your servant and his sons and his wives and this house of his fathers" resembles the blessings invoked on Pharaoh in the fourteenth-century B.C.E. Amarna letters from Cyprus: "may your prosperity, and the prosperity of your household, your sons, your wives, your horses, your chariots, your country, be very great."[41] Cyprus where he was raised was horse country, Byblos where he was born was a real stickler for tradition, and the Punic Mediterranean where he had settled was beginning to imitate the Greek custom of writing vowels.

The king mentioned on the amulet, Šiptiba'al, is the third bearing this name in the succession of Byblian kings. He is named as "Guarantor" (*ḥnṣr*) of the vow (the 24 shekels were to pay for the altar and the sacrificial animals that Rakkob'iš vowed), and this arrangement illustrates how a personal prayer arose from the matrix of a civic cult. He is mentioned in the genealogy of the epitaph of his son 'Urumilk, also a recurring Byblian dynastic name, whose inscription envisages him buried in a palace among the magnates (**rabbim*) in the realm of the dead, and who invokes as his patrons Ba'al of Heaven, Almighty Ba'al, and All the Holy Gods of Byblos.[42] If 'Urumilk's son reigned after him, his name is not preserved, and he was without issue. The next king, a grandson of 'Urumilk but in a collateral line, son of a scion who also did not rule, was Yaḥwîmilk, also a typical Byblian royal name.

If Šiptiba'al was a contemporary of 'Eshmun'azor I of Sidon (539–525 B.C.E.), his men would have been among the shipwrights and interpreters who worked for Cambyses. His son, 'Urumilk, therefore, would have been a contemporary of Tabnît of Sidon (525–500 B.C.E.), both still supplying ships and skilled labor to the Persian navy. If there was a son of 'Urumilk who reigned, he was a contemporary of 'Eshmun'azor II (500–486 B.C.E.) and, like this unfortunate king of Sidon, he reigned just a short time and died without an heir.

---

40. Astarte is also called "Mistress" (*rbt*) in an inscription on a green jasper scarab ("To the Goddess, to Astarte, Mistress of Byblos, you who granted favour to this people") and P. Bordreuil, who published it ("Astarte, la Dame de Byblos," *CRAIBL* [1998] 1153–64), proposed that she was therefore the "Lady" (*ba'alat*) of Byblos. But the titles are distinct, and the latter is a proper name. The scarab was an amulet, and its inscription has the abrupt change of person (from third to second) that characterizes the text of the silver amulet (from third to first: "his vow . . ." / "I dedicated").

41. *EA* 105–12 ##33–39.

42. É. Puech, "Remarques sur quelques inscriptions Phéniciennes de Byblos," *RSF* 9 (1981) 153–68, esp. pp. 153–58; W. Röllig, "Eine phönizische Inschrift aus Byblos," *Neue Ephemeris für semitische Epigraphik* (Wiesbaden: Harrassowitz, 1974) 1–15.

The last known king of this line is Yaḥwîmilk, grandson of ʾUrumilk, and son of Yiḥḥarbaʿal, who did not reign: his name is also traditional in the Byblian king list, and he was the contemporary of Bodʿaštart of Sidon (485–465 B.C.E.) and his son Yatonmilk (465–450 B.C.E.). His funerary inscription[43] is badly broken, but it mentions his service to the Lord of Kings, the King of the Medes and Persians, his distant travels in the company of the Magnates, his acquisition of the wealth of the sea, and his engagement in the wars of the Persian kings. His epitaph is a window on the revival of the Phoenician coastal cities in the latter sixth and early fifth centuries, and this partly arbitrary juxtaposition of the royal lines of Sidon and Byblos illustrates the perils that war and rapine created for them.

The fact that there are few inscribed sixth-century seals from Byblos suggests, not so much that commerce was in the hands of the city rather than of individuals (the owner of the silver amulet was engaged in foreign trade, a captain in the navy or of his own ship, but in any case a regular in the Byblian *va et vient*), as that business was transacted in money—not coinage, of which there is none at Byblos until late in the fifth century[44]—but in precious metals such as silver. Two of these seals manifest the impact of Greek style and iconography that will also be evident in the earliest coinage. One of them is plain, decorated only with four stars and inscribed with an epithet of Apollo, "Archer." Apollo was a favorite of Phoenicians in Cyprus, where he stood for Reshep, the Semitic God of the arrows of plague and pestilence, and the seal may be another indication of the connections between Kition and Byblos. The seal, however, is particularly interesting because of its inscription, in which the Greek epithet (*ekbolos*) is simply transliterated into Phoenician letters (*hkbls*).[45]

Another is a seal representing Hermes (see fig. 5.2).[46] The God wears a short Greek mantle and headdress, carries a shepherd's crook in his left hand, and guides a sheep with his right. In front of him is the name "Baʿal," with the first two letters in Phoenician script (*bʿ*) and the last letter in Greek, *lambda* instead of *lamed*. The first of these seals is ellipsoidal and pierced lengthwise, and the second is set in a metal frame, and it is possible that they too were meant to be worn as amulets rather than used in business transactions. Their reflection of Greek culture must be indicative of real changes taking place in Byblos and in Phoenicia at this time.

The Gods of Byblos in the sixth century, on the contrary, were all but unaffected by contemporary influences and had remained unchanged over the centuries. The resident Gods, the owners of the city, its Lord and Lady, were those whose personal attributes had become their proper names, the Baʿal and Baʿalat of Byblos. This Baʿal had been introduced to the city in the tenth century as the God of the Yeḥîmilk Dynasty—which included him and his sons ʾAbîbaʿal and ʾElîbaʿal and his grandson Šiptibʿal (before

---

43. J. Starcky, "Une inscription phénicienne de Byblos," *MUSJ* 45 (1969) 259–73, pl. 1; F. M. Cross, "A Recently Published Phoenician Inscription of the Persian Period from Byblos," *IEJ* 29 (1979) 40–44.

44. *CMP* 111–13.

45. *CSOSI* 41 #36.

46. Ibid., 42 #37.

Fig. 5.2. Seal and impression with Hermes and inscription (mixture of Greek and Phoenician; Paris, BN, CM, Henri Seyrig Collection 1973.1.489).

the record runs out)—and by the sixth century had acquired the epithet "Almighty" (*ʾaddîr*). The Baʿalat of Byblos, by contrast, belonged, together with Adonis, to an earlier generation of the Gods and is known from the Amarna age through the tenth century and up to the latest times. She was the signature Goddess of the city, who attracted the singular devotion of kings and who was recognized as "My Lady" by Yaḥwîmilk, the last of the kings in the dynasty of Šiptibaʿal.

During the reign of this sixth-century Šiptibaʿal, the popular favorite was Astarte, Goddess of Love and War. She belonged to the generation of the Gods that included Baʿal and was especially attractive not only for her attributes but also for her involvement in the lives of the people. A scarab[47] dedicated to her, and dated to the end of the century, has the design of a personal stamp seal but clearly, from the content of the dedication, was an amulet. Its inscription reveals the immediacy of her presence in Byblian affairs: "To the Goddess, to Astarte the Mistress of Byblos, who you yourself acted graciously toward this people" (*lʾlm lʿštrt rbt gbl ʾš pʿlt ʾt nʿm lʿm zʾ*). Her charm was not just her munificence but her actual presence and her approachableness, so that her devotees, such as the owner of this amulet or Rakkobʾiš, owner of the silver amulet, switch easily from a public or third-person proclamation of her dignity to an intimate, second-person appreciation of her favorable interventions.

ʾUrumilk, the son of this Šiptibaʿal, and king of Byblos around the turn of the century, invoked in his curses anyone who might violate his tomb besides Almighty Baʿal and Baʿalat who governed the city, the head of the divine assembly, Baʿalšamem, and "all the Holy Gods of Byblos." These are known from the tenth-century inscription of Yaḥîmilk, and their inclusion in this sixth-century inscription in the same order illustrates the weight of tradition in Byblian religion.

Baʿalšamem[48] was the serene God of the Sky and of all celestial phenomena, of sunlight and darkness, of starlight and clouds, of storms and winds, and so the natural God of seafarers. He is included among the great Gods invoked in Esarhaddon's treaty with Baʿal of Tyre and is the subject of a dedication five centuries later at Umm el-ʿAmed, an all-Phoenicia pilgrimage center south of Tyre. But he is peculiar to the Byblian pantheon and is found exclusively in the places where Byblians traveled or settled: in Cilicia at Karatepe and Hassan Beyli, where they taught their script and language; at Kition in Cyprus, where the old folk maintained the archaic cult; in Sardinia, according to a third-century inscription by a fifth-generation resident of the Isle of Hawks near Cagliari; and at Carthage in North Africa. In Cilicia and Carthage, he was one God among several who were invoked, but at Byblos he presided over the Assembly of the Gods and these, "all the Holy Gods of Byblos," were the specialists overseeing times and seasons and every human need.

---

47. Bordreuil, "Astarté, la Dame de Byblos."

48. H. Niehr, *Baʿalšamem: Studien zu Herkunft, Geschichte und Rezeptionsgeschichte eines phönizischen Gottes* (Studia Phoenicia 17; Louvain: Peeters, 2003).

The Southern Mainland between Phoenicia and Arabia

The southern mainland, which includes the coastal cities, the cities of the coastal plains, and the cities and countries along the established inland routes to North and South Arabia, was left in a passive and largely maintenance predicament by the involvement of Tyre, Sidon, and Byblos in the military and commercial affairs of the Persian Empire. The Transjordanian kingdoms maintained relations with the Arabian nations. Judah, the newly minted province of Yehud, was a shadow of its former political and commercial self, but it was a robust heartland of intellectual and literary activity that was driven largely by reflection on its earlier complete involvement in the glorious Tyrian network. The coastal cities and towns maintained some syndicated relations with their relatives in the west, but were mostly sidekicks and suppliers of the newly formed and now much diminished consortium of Tyre, Sidon, and Byblos.

Judah Writes about Its History and Its Future

Judah is paradigmatic in reconstructing the mood of sixth-century Phoenicia. It was alone in its consciousness, in its ability to produce histories and commentaries on the recent past, and in its desire to imagine the impending future. But the past was dotted with Phoenician ruins, and the future included the aspirations of the entire region where Judah was presently biding its time. Tyre, Sidon, and Byblos, although they did not leave histories or prophecies or administrative records to prove it, lived through the whirl of the sixth century by trying to absorb their past and create the same sort of myth or illusion of restoration.

The Babylonians captured Jerusalem (586 B.C.E.), broke down the walls of the city, looted and burned the temple, demolished the palace and the homes of the wealthy, and then deported the leaders and all the skilled workmen they could use, leaving only the otherwise useless to till the land (2 Kgs 24:4–16, 25:8–12). Rural areas around Jerusalem fell back into the age-old rhythms and, although trade and commerce were in tatters and the machinery of centralized and unforgiving uniformity was broken, urban life persisted in its habits and routines, the most important of which was its educational system. In this system, generations of the late eighth and early seventh centuries produced a wonderful and varied literature, and now this was what the postwar generation continued to teach, as the circumstances required, by reading and rewriting it and by writing commentaries on it, either in the margins or interlinearly, or sometimes in whole new works.[49] All the predestruction texts were studied, and all were mined for their contemporary meaning, and screeds and manifestos or gossip and hearsay made the laborious and often tedious work of the schools available to an increasingly jaundiced public.

---

49. B. Peckham, *History and Prophecy: The Development of Late Judean Literary Traditions* (New York: Doubleday, 1993).

The earliest of these school texts and the most influential was a historical work completed around 550 B.C.E., after about 35 years of reflection on the history of Israel up to the fall of Jerusalem. The people who studied, wrote, and taught this history (now contained in the biblical books from Genesis to Kings) were the grandchildren and heirs of the generation that had composed the Judean classics (ca. 700–650 B.C.E.) that the history incorporated, and they naturally were inclined to accept it as true. Their sixth-century teachers added explanation and commentary but also introduced them to logical argument and to the notion of fate, and together they produced a didactic History with precepts and paradigms that were easy to learn and remember.

The most basic idea was that Jerusalem was destroyed because it was beset by a history of sin, and that the city was doomed, but those who survived could be restored by observing the law that was found in the text they were studying. This sin, essentially the worship of Gods other than their own, was not congenital to Israel but was absorbed from the foreign nations with whom their ancestors had associated. In this web of evil influences, Tyre, Sidon, and Byblos were prominent because they worshiped Baʿal, the "Other God" par excellence in the History's estimation and under his auspices became the fabled center of a network of nations in a glorious Mediterranean world. This bold reappraisal and shifting of blame obviously did nothing to restore almost two marvelous centuries of cooperation between Judah and its neighbors and slammed the door to anything like international cooperation.

Many schools were influenced by the simple and uncompromising catechism that the History advocated, and so individual works such as Jeremiah were rethought, became cramped with its jargon, and ended up as vehicles of this isolationist doctrine. There were other schools and individual authors, however, for whom the catechism and dogma were relative nonsense. The line of reflection that produced the book of Joel rejected its logic and its notion of fate and anchored itself in common sense: bad things happen; the burning of the temple by the Babylonians was a natural catastrophe, unique, limited, and involving no general principles, comparable to a plague of locusts, which is easily solved when the locusts depart or die and new growth begins.

The book of Jonah dismisses the doctrine by showing that history is not inevitable, that the past does not just roll on inexorably, that God is not totally preoccupied with Judah as the History supposed. Its horizon is the Mediterranean world created by Tyre, Sidon, and Byblos. At Joppa Jonah boards a Phoenician ship bound for Tarshish in the far West; the sailors are pious and pray, each to his own God, during the storm, and they expect Jonah to do the same; Jonah professes adherence to Baʿalšamem, the God of seafarers, but he does not pray; and enacting the ritual in which a statue of God is tossed into the sea to ensure a safe voyage, they throw Jonah into the sea and the storm abates; he gets a ride in a whale, the big fish that makes the Sea magical, and that impressed the Assyrian kings (Jonah, after all, is on his way to the Assyrian capital at Nineveh) as far back as the early eleventh century B.C.E. In the story, the Phoenicians, far from being a threat to the beliefs and practices of the Judean prophet, are an inspiration he struggles to ignore, just as he ignores his mission to Nineveh.

The book of Isaiah belonged to a school that was active after the publication of the History. The original was published early in the seventh century and predicted the fall of Jerusalem. The sixth-century school preserved it and, now that the prophecy had come true, pondered its contemporary implications. In this rethinking, there are two distinct and consistent perspectives (one inclusive, the other exclusive), which can be traced to two different scholars and teachers: the earlier wrote in the reign of Cyrus (539–530 B.C.E.) and the later in the years preceding the reign of Darius I (522–486 B.C.E.), and so both were contemporaries of ʾEshmunʿazor I of Sidon and of Šiptibaʿal of Byblos.

About Tyre and Sidon, both scholars were fairly irenic (Isa 23:1–7, 10–12; 23:8–10, 13–18). Tyre is associated with Tarshish and the coastal settlements that it founded long ago in the far West, with Cyprus where its ships found anchorage, and with Egypt where it was engaged in the grain trade, and its ruin naturally causes consternation and elicits lamentation in all these places. Sidon, like Tyre, is identified as a city of merchants, prospering so much from Tyre's long-distance maritime trade that it can be called "Daughter of Tarshish." Unlike Tyre, however, and to its shame, it did not found settlements or colonies abroad, and even Cyprus, where Sidon had commercial and religious status, was lost at the end of the eighth century when Luli, king of Sidon, fled to Kition in Cyprus, only to find that it was no longer well disposed to him or his city.

The later writer compares Tyre to a harlot plying her trade but even on this indelicate point holds his tongue because, by returning to her harlotry, her foreign trade (as will happen, he is sure, in the proverbial 70 years), Tyre will again become Jerusalem's main supplier. There is nothing, then, in either of these writers that is critical of Tyre and nothing to suggest that the religion of Tyre and Sidon, or specifically worship of Baʿal, was what led Judah astray. Tyre is the subject of admiration and perhaps of a little jealousy. Sidon is not as bold but is an easy second. These are the sentiments of Judean historians in complete sympathy with the two competitor cities as they prepared to enter fully into the promise of the Persian Empire.

This admiration for Tyre, and for Egypt, its main resource in the sixth century, is explored fully in the book of Ezekiel (Ezekiel 26–28 [Tyre], 29–32 [Egypt]). In this book, the siege of Jerusalem is announced, and the fall of the city is reported (Ezek 24:2, 33:21), but the actual siege and capture of the city, its death, is recounted of Tyre, and its languishing in death is told of Egypt, and only its restoration, its return from the dead, is reported of its people, but not of the city itself.[50] Tyre the ship, its captain a God in the Garden of Eden, sailing the seas, and collecting the wealth of nations is the very image of what Judah and Jerusalem aspired to become. Pharaoh, a cedar of Lebanon in the Garden of Eden, a young lion among the nations, the dragon in the Sea, will descend into Sheol, the realm of Death, to join the Assyrian and Elamite kings, the princes of Cilicia and Anatolia, and the

---

50. Ezek 26:1–14 (siege and capture of Tyre); chaps. 31–32 (Egypt's sojourn in the realm of the dead); chaps. 34, 36–37 (Israel—restoration and return to life).

kings of the Sidonians, all of them better off than the dead bodies of Israel that lie unburied on the ground, bones awaiting resurrection.

It is obvious from the conjunction and the sequence of the descriptions that Tyre and Egypt in the sixth century were recognized as being in a special relationship that would endure beyond death, as the beliefs of the metropolis and of the land of the pharaohs prescribed. This totally positive attitude to Tyre and Egypt is embedded in the book that Ezekiel wrote in Babylonia. When it came under the scrutiny and sober reflection of the priestly school in Jerusalem, some learned marginal notes were added, and a sense of outrage led to the inclusion of critical and condemnatory notes that completely dispelled the sense of awe and admiration in the original. As punishment for its presumption, Tyre will disappear and be forgotten; as punishment for its sins—wealth and pride—the captain will be expelled from the Garden of Eden and left lying on the ground. Egypt, similarly, a big fish in the Nile, will be hauled up onto the banks of the river to rot or, in political terms, will be drained by Nebuchadnezzar and will never again be a mighty kingdom. In the original book of Ezekiel, Jerusalem aspired to be like these wonderful places, but in the rethought school version, they were sources of evil—mainly in their very successful pursuit of wealth—and inimitable, which of course was a reflection of how much Judah and Jerusalem in the sixth century were out of the commercial loop.

In the sixth century, Judah was trying to pull itself together. The royal family was in exile;[51] local government was in the hands, first of Babylonian administrators and their Judean appointees, later of representatives of the Persian court; and when the time came, there was no consensus concerning the restoration of the monarchy. Temple service was suspended, but there were attempts to collect and compose libretti or Psalms for recitation at regular religious gatherings in the various quarters of the city, and there were talk and a wave of rumors about a possible theocratic government.[52]

With the Edict of Cyrus, some people began to filter back, but there were disputes about who should be welcomed back—everyone, everyone from Israel and Judah, only Judah, or just the chastened—and about the relative merits of those who had gone into exile and those who had stayed and taken the initiative in urban reconstruction. Change and upheaval vibrated through the social order. Edom, in the seventh century a competitor for the routes and markets in the south of Judah, had sided with the Babylonians and, with their victory, began to gnaw at the borders of Judah, taking land that eventually was incorporated into Idumea, and leaving the once-wonderful Judah to eke out a future as the tiny province of Yehud. It certainly was not "business as usual." Public sentiment, to judge from the screeds composed at this time, opposed any engagement, even if it were possible, in international trade and commerce. For awhile, therefore, Judah

---

51. E. F. Weidner, "Jojachin, Konig von Juda, in babylonischen Keilschrifttexten," in *Mélanges Syriens offerts à monsieur René Dussaud* (2 vols.; Paris: Geuthner, 1939) 2.923–35, pls. 1–5.

52. C. L. Meyers and E. M. Meyers, "Jerusalem and Zion after the Exile: The Evidence of First Zechariah," in *"Šaʿarei Talmon": Studies in the Bible, Qumran, and the Ancient Near East Presented to Shemaryahu Talmon* (ed. M. Fishbane and E. Tov; Winona Lake, IN: Eisenbrauns, 1992) 121–35.

was engrossed in reflection on its astonishing history and in plotting its future, and pretty well disappeared from the world scene.

Coastal Palestine Is Phoenician

South of Tyre and as far as Gaza, the significant material and epigraphic remains in the sixth century are Phoenician. There are few sites, compared with the number of sites in the seventh century, and none of them abounds in information or evidence. What there is, however, suggests that this area that Tyre, especially, but also Sidon and Byblos dominated in the seventh century was left mainly to itself, until Darius I (522–486 B.C.E.) transferred the stretch from Dor to Joppa and the adjacent Plain of Sharon from Tyrian jurisdiction to Sidonian control.

ʾAchzib remained a Phoenician town, but its relations were with coastal towns to the north or south or with settlements in the western Mediterranean rather than with Tyre, to which it always belonged. There are family tombs [53] dated between the seventh and fourth centuries B.C.E. and comparable with tombs at Sidon in the fifth century and in the vicinity of Sarepta in the sixth and fifth centuries that consisted of a single chamber with benches along its four walls and niches in three walls, entered through an opening from a vertical shaft. There are a few sixth-century tombstones inscribed in a kind of scribble with the name of the deceased head of the family. [54] Sloppy writing was acceptable on steles of these common folk (it is characteristic of the eighth-century tombstones from Tyre), but it is interesting that the deceased at ʾAchzib thought of the tombstone as their everlasting property (they are all inscribed "belonging to . . ."), just as kings thought of their sarcophagi and burial places as their home for all eternity.

There are some early masks (eighth and seventh centuries) from ʾAchzib, and these, or others like them, were prototypes that influenced production in the western Mediterranean, [55] but the sixth-century masks and busts (or, protomai) are equally at home along the coastal strip (see fig. 5.3). [56] The masks were for display, were not meant to be worn, and are exclusively of men: one is grotesque, supposedly dramatic or apotropaic; one is personalized and seems to represent someone who might have posed for it; and the third is a satyr mask with Greek features.

This last mask has drab, fragmentary parallels in the fifth century down south at Tel Sippor, about 16 kilometers inland from Ashkelon, [57] but it has an excellent parallel in the design on a scarab seal, of unknown provenance, but perhaps from ʾAchzib. [58] A naked, reclining, partially stupefied

---

53. E. Mazar, "Phoenician Family Tombs at Achziv: A Chronological Typology (1000–400 BCE)," in *Fenicios y Territorio: Actas del II Seminario Internacional sobre Temas Fenicios, Guadamar del Segura, 9–11 de abril de 1999* (ed. A. González Prats; Alicante: Instituto Alicantino de Cultura, 2000) 189–225.

54. B. Delavault and A. Lemaire, "Les inscriptions phéniciennes de Palestine," *RSF* 7 (1979) 1–37, pls. 1–14, esp. pp. 3–5, pls. 2–3.

55. W. Culican, "Some Phoenician Masks and Other Terracottas," *Berytus* 24 (1975–76) 47–87, esp. pp. 55–64.

56. Cf. E. Stern, "Phoenician Masks and Pedants," *PEQ* 108 (1976) 109–18, pls. 9–11.

57. Ora Negbi, *A Deposit of Terracottas and Statuettes from Tel Sippor* (ʿAtiqot 6; Jerusalem: Department of Antiquities, 1966) ##78, 79, 84, pp. 18–19.

58. *CSOSI* 38 #29.

satyr, whose face resembles the masks props himself on his right elbow and lifts a very large, prominent beaker to his lips in his left hand. In the field in front of him are four letters (*'bk'*) that do not make sense in Phoenician but do make sense as the transliteration of a Greek word preceded by the definite article (Phoenician *'ayin* is the vowel *omicron* in Greek)—such as *bikos* = "Oh! beaker," or *bakxos* = "Oh! Bacchus." Either would suit the genius and wit of this port city, to which nothing Greek was entirely alien.

The masks of women are protomai, that is, busts representing their faces and part of their neck, and the two types reflect the dominant cultural influences on the town and region.[59] The first, earlier type is Egyptianizing and illustrates the continuing impact of Tyrian tradition: the woman wears an Egyptian wig and has the stunned or expectant look of the "Woman-at-the-Window" watching for her lover, whom she fears is dead. The later type is Greek and illustrates 'Achzib's freedom from Tyrian tradition and entry into the Greek world, so the woman is veiled and smiling. The earlier masks, from the early sixth century, were found as burial goods, and the later masks, from the second half of the sixth century, were from sanctuaries and their debris pits, with a large number from a deposit of this sort at Tel Sippor.[60] These protomai may have represented goddesses or attitudes of reverence toward them by individual women or sororities.[61] The 'Achzib masks at times are beautifully executed. Those at Tel Sippor, in some aniconic fit, were all deliberately smashed.

The pendants[62] were made of glass in various combinations of colors (blue and white or yellow and black) and represent male heads, bearded or grotesque, that resemble the masks. At 'Achzib, as at 'Atlit, they were deposited in tombs. At Tel Michal, near Tel Aviv, they were left in tombs or in the temple. At 'Umm el-'Amed, a sanctuary just south of Tyre, they were found of course as offerings in the temple; but at Beersheba in the far south, they were also preserved in a temple debris pit. There are some, in Tyrian ports such as Tell Abu Hawam, near Carmel, and Al Mina, where the Orontes debouches into the sea, that were kept at home. These pendants, obviously, were treasured possessions that men wore and with which they were buried or that they dedicated in sanctuaries as personal mementos.

South of 'Achzib, and 5 kilometers north of 'Akko, near an Israeli settlement called Shave Ziyyon, a shipwreck strewed its cargo along a kilometer of seabed.[63] It was a merchantman, because the cargo included transport amphorae and other pottery, and its most interesting merchandise was a consignment of terra-cotta figurines. These represent women, standing wearing a tunic and sometimes a shawl, with their left arm across their breast, and raising their right hand in salutation. They stand between 13 and 40 centimeters tall, including their rectangular bases, and two of them have applied to their base the sign of Tannît (the symbol of "Woman" represented by a triangle surmounted by a horizontal bar and a round feature-

59. Stern, "Phoenician Masks and Pendants," 114–16.
60. Negbi, *A Deposit of Terracottas and Statuettes from Tel Sippor*, 14–15, ##43–52.
61. Ibid., 3–4.
62. Stern, "Phoenician Masks and Pendants," 117.
63. E. Linder, "A Cargo of Phoenicio-Punic Figurines," *Archaeology* 26 (1973) 182–87.

Fig. 5.3. Mask from ʾAchzib (IDAM). Reproduced by permission of the Israel Antiquities Authority. Photo by: Miki Koren.

less face centered on the apex of the triangle), a Goddess known from Tyre who became the metropolitan Goddess of Carthage at the end of the sixth century. The scatter of the cargo indicates that the ship was inbound, to Shave Ziyyon, which conceals an ancient site; to ʿAkko, from which it was blown off course; or (more likely) to ʾAchzib, which the high seas prevented it from reaching. A shipment like this from Carthage (or more likely from one of the other western colonies, since there are no terra-cottas like them from the North African metropolis)[64] illuminates the independent role of a city such as ʾAchzib in the Mediterranean network established by Tyre, Sidon, and Byblos.

64. W. Culican, "A Votive Model from the Sea," *PEQ* 108 (1976) 119–23, pls. 12–14; repr. in idem, *Opera Selecta: From Tyre to Tartessos* (Gothenberg: Åströms, 1986) 437–41, pls. 12–14, esp. p. 437.

From the same cargo, perhaps, comes a terra-cotta model of an outdoor religious ceremony.[65] It represents an almost-square, walled courtyard, onto which one or more houses might face, with an entrance quite a way to one side. In the right corner by the entrance stands a figure of the pregnant Goddess—a figurine commonly found independently of a cultic context— and opposite her in the far left corner there is a figure of a priest with short hair and a full beard who has a cloth band over his left shoulder and raises his right hand in blessing. Several figures are missing, but there are four women in the middle of the courtyard, wearing veils, with their hair done in Greek fashion, who sit around an oven with a beehive-shaped dome and five openings—one below for inserting the fuel and four in the dome itself for placing food on the fire. The scene has been explained with reference to biblical texts (Jer 7:18; 44:15–19, 25) that describe women, with the connivance of their husbands and the help of their children, performing a familial ritual that consists of gathering wood, making a fire, and baking cakes for the Queen of Heaven.[66] A contemporary Phoenician text from Cyprus describes the same ritual as a public ceremony in the Temple of Astarte, presided over by three male officiants.[67] Elements of the model, such as the figure of the priest, have parallels in Carthage, but the depiction of ordinary everyday scenes, including kneading and baking bread, is a favorite theme in Cyprus, and it is likely that the ship that foundered off Shave Ziyyon had stopped in Cyprus, or even that the cargo that it carried was partly Cypriot and partly transshipped from the West.[68]

Inland from ʾAchzib, on a plateau at the top of a mountain from which there is a good view of Lower Galilee from the Golan Heights to the Mediterranean, there is a fort-like complex consisting of a watchtower, guardrooms, and a walled enclosure in which there are two other buildings.[69] The larger of these consisted of a hall and an anteroom. The floor of the hall was covered with paving stones, the roof was supported by pillars, and there were benches along three walls, a table or altar with steps in one corner, and an altar or podium against the facing, benchless wall. The benches were littered with juglets and bottles, and the hall was the repository for a green slate on which pictures of Isis, Osiris, and Horus were incised and also for a bronze statuette of Osiris and four votive bronzes: (1) a bronze situla—a teardrop-shaped ritual vessel with upright handles; (2) a small

---

65. Ibid.

66. Ibid.; V. Karageorghis and L. E. Stager, "Another Mould for Cakes from Cyprus: A. The Mould and Its Interpretation; B. In the Queen's Image," *RSF* 28 (2000) 3–5, 6–11, pls. 1–2; M. Weinfeld, "The Worship of Molech and of the Queen of Heaven and Its Background," *UF* 4 (1972) 133–54, esp. p. 150.

67. B. Peckham, "Notes on a Fifth-Century Phoenician Inscription from Kition, Cyprus (CIS 86)," *Or* 37 (1968) 304–24; J. P. Healey, "The Kition Tariffs and the Phoenician Cursive Series," *BASOR* 216 (1974) 53–60.

68. Culican, "A Votive Model from the Sea," 120; J. Karageorghis, "La vie quotidienne à chypre d'après les terres cuites d'époque géométrique et archaïque," in *Cypriote Terracottas* (ed. F. Vandenabeele and R. Laffineur; Brussels: Vrije Universiteit Brussels / Liège: Université de Liège, 1991) 149–69, pl. 42.

69. R. Frankel and R. Ventura, "The Miṣpe Yamim Bronzes," *BASOR* 311 (1998) 39–55, esp. p. 39; J. Kamlah, "Zwei nordpalästinische 'Heiligtümer' der persischen Zeit und ihre epigraphischen Funde," *ZDPV* 115 (1999) 163–90, esp. pp. 164–66.

Apis bull; (3) a weight in the shape of a recumbent ram; (4) and a cavorting lion cub, so lifelike that it must have been done by someone who had seen cubs playing. The predominant motifs, clearly, are Egyptian, and the engraved situla is the parade piece. The space above the top register, just below the rim, was left blank for an Egyptian invocation but was filled out with a Phoenician inscription. The top register shows the journey of the solar bark, towed by four jackals, and observed by four baboons. The second register is an offering scene in which a worshiper presents libations, a lotus flower, food, and drink to a row of Egyptian Gods and Goddesses. The third register has the procession of the souls of the dead, three kneeling human figures with jackal heads, and three kneeling figures with falcon heads.

Local flavor is supplied by the Phoenician inscription and, surprisingly in the Galilee region which from time immemorial was Tyrian, it was written in Byblian script and according to Byblian scribal conventions. The inscription reads: "Belonging to ʿAkbar, son of Bodʾeshmun: I had it made for Astarte because she heard my voice" (*lʿkbw . bn . bd . ʾšmn . ʾpʿl . lʿštrt . kšmʿ . ql*).[70] The typical Byblian stylistic feature is the shift in person from reportage ("belonging to ʿAkbar") to first-person testimony ("I had it made").

The purely Egyptian, not Egyptianizing, motifs of the bronzes combined with the Byblian Phoenician literary overlay are most easily understood if the bronzes were part of the loot collected by mercenaries returning from the late sixth-century Persian campaigns against Egypt. The hall where they were found was their barracks or mess hall and naturally enough has some of the features of a mercantile clubhouse. The whole complex of watchtower, guardrooms, and walled enclosure was built under Persian reorganization of the country in preparation for these invasions. Byblians were not soldiers, but they were famous for their creative skills, and their main contribution to these preparations was their ability to speak, read, and write Egyptian. The contingent assigned to this outpost could have been shipwrights or metalworkers, but it is just as likely that they were translators and interpreters.

ʿAkko, a great port and an important administrative center in the early Persian period, prospered in the sixth century.[71] It was one of the harbors in which the Phoenician fleet, comprising Tyrian, Sidonian, and Arvadian ships assembled before the invasions of Egypt under Cambyses and Darius I. The Persian offices were housed in a large building constructed of hewn stone with seven large rooms around a central courtyard.[72] Nearby was another building, constructed in the Phoenician pier-and-rubble fashion, that was in use throughout the Persian period, and one of its disposal

---

70. M. Weippert, "Eine phönizische Inscrift aus Galiläa," *ZDPV* 115 (1999) 191–200; A. Lemaire, "Epigraphie et Religion en Palestine à l'époque achéménide," *Transeu* 22 (2001) 97–113, esp. pp. 98–99.

71. M. Dothan, "Tel Acco," *NEAEHL* 1.17–24.

72. E. Stern, "The Phoenician Architectural Elements in Palestine during the Late Iron Age and the Persian Period," in *The Architecture of Ancient Israel from the Prehistoric to the Persian Periods* (ed. A. Kempinski and R. Reich; Jerusalem: Israel Exploration Society, 1992) 302–9.

pits contained terra-cotta figurines and a fifth-century Phoenician ostracon that identified it, or perhaps just its four-pillared room, as a sanctuary.[73]

In another area were storerooms that were built and stocked in preparation for the Egyptian campaigns, and in all these buildings Attic pottery abounded.[74] Nearby, in the cemetery found at Lohamei HaGeta²ot,[75] there were several sixth-century graves that are more typical of the local Phoenician population. One was the grave of an infant buried in an amphora. Another was a grave marked by a line of small stones that contained two bronze bracelets and a green jasper seal.[76] The seal is Egyptianizing and depicts Isis nursing Harpocrates. She is enthroned beneath a full moon cradled in the crescent moon, wears a crown with horns and the sun disk, holds Harpocrates on her lap, and is worshiped by a falcon-headed man, who stands before them with hands raised in adoration. There is a seal like it from ʿAtlit, and both are what might be expected in a region and a town that traditionally belonged to Tyre.

Inland from ʿAkko, at the eastern edge of the plain, Tell Keisan continued to be an important market town in the sixth century.[77] A new, very large building complex facing onto a street or square was constructed on the debris of an earlier structure that had been leveled to make room for it.[78] There were local and Galilean wares, trefoil-lipped jugs with Cypriot-style decorations, Cypriot basket-handled amphorae (exclusive to Tell Keisan, strangely, with none at ʿAkko, where they were unloaded), and Greek wares, including Attic and East Greek, as well as Rhodian and Corinthian. The amphorae were from Kalopsidha, 20 kilometers southeast of Salamis in Cyprus, and had Phoenician letters (abbreviations of the suppliers' names or indications of contents) incised on their handles or letters and symbols painted on the body of the jars.[79]

The Keisan traders who bought these goods, unlike most other traders in other places, still used personal seals.[80] One of these is a cylinder seal, already archaizing, done in the old-fashioned stick-figure style and representing what may be a hunting scene taken from an Assyrian

73. Dothan, "Tel Acco," 22.

74. J. Briend, "L'occupation de la Galilée occidentale à l'époque perse," *Transeu* 2 (1990) 109–23, esp. pp. 112–13; B. B. Shefton, "Reflections on the Presence of Attic Pottery at the Eastern End of the Mediterranean during the Persian Period," *Transeu* 19 (2000) 75–82.

75. M. Peleg, "Persian, Hellenistic and Roman Burials at Lohamei HaGeta²ot," *ʿAtiqot* 20 (1991) 131–52.

76. B. Brandl, "A Phoenician Scarab from Lohamei HaGeta²ot," *ʿAtiqot* 20 (1991) 153–55.

77. E. A. Bettles, *Phoenician Amphora Production and Distribution in the Southern Levant: A Multi-Disciplinary Investigation into Carinated-Shoulder Amphorae of the Persian Period (539–332 BC)* (BAR International Series 1183; Oxford: Archaeopress, 2003) 89–90.

78. E. Nodet, "Le niveau 3 (periode perse)," in *Tell Keisan (1971–1976): Une cité phénicienne en Galilée* (ed. J. Briend and J.-B. Humbert; Paris: Gabalda / Göttingen: Vandenhoeck & Ruprecht, 1980) 117–29; J.-B. Humbert, "Keisan, Tell," *NEAEHL* 3.862–67.

79. É. Puech, "Inscriptions, Incisions et Poids," in *Tell Keisan (1971–1976): Une cité phénicienne en Galilée* (ed. J. Briend and J.-B. Humbert; Paris: Gabalda / Göttingen: Vandenhoeck & Ruprecht, 1980) 301–10, pls. 91–96, 137.

80. O. Keel, "La glyptique de Tell Keisan (1971–1976)," in ibid., 257–99, pls. 88–90; repr. in idem, M. Shuval, and C. Uehlinger, *Studien zu den Stempelsiegeln aus Palästina/Israel, Band III: Die frühe Eisenzeit: Ein Workshop* (Göttingen: Vandenhoeck & Ruprecht, 1990) 163–260, pls. 6–10.

repertoire.[81] Another is a scarab stamp seal with the cartouche, slightly de-based, of Psammetichus II (594–588 B.C.E.), which the engraver modeled on the perennially more popular cartouche of Thutmosis III.[82] A winged sphinx with gross features, or at least without the elegance typical of Tyrian glyptic, was probably made locally, as was a seal with a straight-legged gazelle nibbling on a stylized plant.[83]

An interesting mixture of styles is presented on a late sixth-century scaraboid. The basic scene draws on the traditional representation of a king bearding a lion with his right hand and preparing to stab it with his left. The update portrays the king in Persian fashion with a long beard, his hair tied in a bun on his neck, and wearing a Persian bonnet (*kidaris*) or turban. The Phoenician touch (derived from the Egyptian) has the king naked to the waist and wearing a kilt or loincloth.[84] Tell Keisan, in short, was a provincial market town for the Galilee, with its own particular suppliers, among whom those in eastern Cyprus were conspicuous. It was an artisan center under influences old and new, operating independently in a nominal Tyrian sphere, and like all the eastern Phoenicians, ripe for change and clamoring for things Greek.

Tell Abu Hawam, at the mouth of the river Qishon at the northern foot of Mount Carmel was inconspicuous in the sixth century and comes to historical focus only at the end of the century, or in the early fifth, in a couple of private stamp seals.[85] One of these, depicting a bull attacked from the front and back by lions is fairly traditional and has a good parallel at Tharros in Sardinia; the other, with naked men dancing, is peculiar to the region and perhaps inspired by the ritual performances at the Temple of Melqart on the mountain. South of Carmel, the Phoenician, chiefly Tyrian, towns and settlements, now deprived of their Judean and Philistine support, were in disarray in the sixth century. The lull lasted until Persia curtailed Tyrian control of the coastal region and, in the reign of ʾEshmunʿazor (500–486 B.C.E.), gave Sidon a chance to exploit the Plain of Sharon.

ʿAtlit, just south of Mount Carmel, still reflected its Tyrian connections in the Egyptianizing or specifically Tyrian iconography of its personal stamp seals:[86] images of Heracles predominate, and one seal features a nude male dancer, but others portray Bes as Lord of Animals, the Sun God Reʿ, Isis nursing Horus, or the Horus falcon. Dor, a little farther south, had a residential area neatly laid out in orthogonal blocks, as recommended by Greek town planning, but all the houses were still built in the standard

---

81. Keel (1980) 258 #2, pl. 88:2 = idem (1990) 167–68 #2, pl. 6:2.

82. Idem (1980) 270–71 #12, pl. 88:12 = idem (1990) 207–8 #12, pl. 7:12.

83. Idem (1980) 271 #13, pl. 88:13, and 277 #20, pl. 89:20 = idem (1990) 208–10 #13, pl. 7:13, and 230–31 #20, pl. 8:20.

84. Idem (1980) 277–78 #21, pl. 89:21 = idem (1990) 231–32 #21, pl. 8:21.

85. J. Balensi, I. Dunaux, and G. Finkielszteyn, "Le niveau perse à Tell Abu Hawam: Résultats récents et signification dans le contexte régional côtier," *Transeu* 2 (1990) 125–36; O. Keel, *Corpus der Stempelsiegel-Amulette aus Palästina/Israel: Von den Anfängen bis zur Perserzeit. Katalog, Band 1: Von Tell Abu Farag bis ʿAtlit* (Göttingen: Vandenhoeck & Ruprecht, 1997) ##2, 19.

86. M. G. Klingbeil, "Syro-Palestinian Stamp Seals from the Persian Period: The Iconographic Evidence," *JNSL* 18 (1992) 95–124, esp. pp. 98–99.

Tyrian pier-and-rubble style.[87] Tel Mevorakh, on the Nahal Tanninim near
the northern boundary of the Plain of Sharon was a granary town in the
fifth century, when it was under Sidonian jurisdiction, and perhaps also in
the sixth, when Tyre still managed the region for the Persians and collected
its tithes and taxes.[88]

A group of inscribed bronze ex-votos from ʾElyakin, an inland site between Mevorakh and Tel Michal and 20 kilometers south of Dor,[89] also
illustrates the enduring impact of Tyre on the Plain of Sharon even in the
fifth century. Only one of the inscriptions is in Phoenician, commemorating an offering from three men to "our Lord," and the other six are
in Aramaic, and each commemorates the gift from an individual "for the
life of his soul."[90] All are dedications to the God ʿAstarim (ʿštrm), and one
Aramaic offering specifies that he is the God of the Sharon (lʿštrm zy dšrnʾ).
The God ʿAštar is known chiefly from Ugaritic ritual and mythic texts and
from South Arabian inscriptions.[91] His name occurs once in a Phoenician
personal name ʿAštarḥannoʾ (ʿštrḥnʾ)[92] and, in its cultic form ʿštrm, in the
personal name of a ninth-century king of Tyre (*Astharymos*).[93] The cultic
form, with a final -m, is the South Arabian (Sabaean) pronunciation, which
was simply transliterated into Aramaic, where -m does not belong, and
Phoenician, where it is ambiguous. There is some architectural evidence
for a sanctuary at ʾElyakin,[94] and these ex-votos are residues of South Arabian commercial relations that flourished in the seventh century and were
maintained, with surprising vigor, into the fifth.

At Tel Michal,[95] or Makmish, the Phoenician settlement at the end of
the sixth century (Stratum XI, 525–490 B.C.E.) was characterized by grain
storage silos, ovens, and domestic pottery (such as jugs, juglets, decanters,
lamps, mortars, and cooking pots) and by basket-handled storage jars from
Cyprus, as at Tell Keisan, all restricted to one small part of the site.

The cemetery at this time had three kinds of burials: in simple graves,
in stone-line graves and, for infants, burial in large jars. The grave goods

---

87. E. Stern, "The Dor Province in the Persian Period in the Light of the Recent Excavations
at Dor," *Transeu* 2 (1990) 147–55.

88. Idem, *Excavations at Tel Mevorakh (1973–1976), Part One: From the Iron Age to the Roman
Period* (Qedem 9; Jerusalem: Hebrew University—Institute of Archaeology, 1978) 79. N. Schreiber,
"A Word of Caution: Black-on-Red Pottery at Tel Mevorakh in the 'Tenth Century' B.C.," *PEQ* 133
(2001) 132–35; P. Briant, "Dons de terres et de villes: l'Asie Mineure dans le contexte achéménide," *Revue des Études Anciennes* 87 (1985) 53–72.

89. J. Kamlah, "Zwei nordpalästinische 'Heiligtumer' der persischen Zeit und ihre epigraphischen Funde," *ZDPV* 115 (1999) 163–90.

90. R. Deutsch and M. Heltzer, *Forty New Ancient West Semitic Inscriptions* (Tel Aviv–Jaffa:
Archaeological Center 1994) 69–89; M. Heltzer, "On Possible Traces of Archaic Mimation in
Phoenician," *Actas* 4, 1.239–41.

91. I. Kottsieper, "ʿštrm: Eine südarabische Gottheit in der Scharonebene," *ZAW* 113 (2001)
245–50; A. Jamme, "Le panthéon sud-arabe préislamique d'après les sources épigraphiques," *Mus*
60 (1947) 57–147, esp. pp. 85–97.

92. Kottsieper, "ʿštrm: Eine sudarabische Gottheit in der Scharonebene," 245.

93. Josephus, *Ag. Ap.* 1.117–26.

94. Kamlah, "Zwei nordpalästinische 'Heiligtümer' der persischen Zeit und ihre epigraphischen Funde," 170–72.

95. Z. Herzog, G. Rapp Jr., and O. Negbi, eds., *Excavations at Tel Michal, Israel* (Tel Aviv: Institute of Archaeology / Minneapolis: University of Minnesota, 1989).

were personal possessions such as jewelry, or sometimes weapons, and very rarely included pottery vessels or supplies for life in the beyond.[96] ʾArshap, about 4 kilometers south of Tel Michal, was settled in the same period but, unlike Tel Michal which was Tyrian, seems to have been one of the farming communities established when Sidon acquired jurisdiction over the Plain of Sharon.[97]

The port of Joppa, which was ceded to Sidon at this time, features a large warehouse built in the fifth century to replace an earlier structure that had fallen into disrepair.[98] A burial near the port from this earlier phase contained a juglet with a late sixth-century Phoenician inscription (*kd ḥrms*) identifying it as a juglet (*kd*) belonging to a man, either Greek or Phoenician, presumably Sidonian, with the Greek name Hermes.[99]

South of the Plain of Sharon, at Tel Sippor, about 10 kilometers inland from Ashkelon, in a pit associated with an adjacent sanctuary, a large number of terra-cotta figurines and stone statuettes were found that date between the late sixth and the mid-fourth centuries B.C.E.[100] About half of the terra-cottas were "Rhodian," that is, made with Rhodian clay, or from real or imitation Rhodian molds, or by artisans from Rhodes. These included representations of mothers with children, of robed girls, and of clothed or naked boys, of pygmies, satyrs, and festal scenes.

The other terra-cottas were by local artists using clay from the coastal area to make "Persian Riders" and Greek-style kourai (robed girls) and kouroi (naked boys), or clay from the Judean foothills to fashion bearded men, horse-and-rider outfits, pregnant women, and naked girls. The settlement, clearly, maintained the earlier attachment of this originally Philistine region to Judah and to the Phoenicians and, with its Rhodian relations, probably was Tyrian—apparently an outpost overseeing the movement of goods from the interior and South Arabia, and also along the coast from Gaza and Tell Jemmeh and the Arabs of northern Sinai.[101]

The big change in southern mainland Phoenicia in the sixth century, apart from the influx of Greek merchants and Greek goods, was the glaring lack of enthusiasm and creativity. Tyre maintained cultural dominance, but the more important cities and towns north of Mount Carmel went their

---

96. Lily Singer-Avitz, "Local Pottery of the Persian Period (Strata XI–VI)," in *Excavations at Tel Michal, Israel* (ed. Z. Herzog, G. Rapp Jr., and O. Negbi; Tel Aviv: Institute of Archaeology / Minneapolis: University of Minnesota Press, 1989) 115–64, esp. pp. 116–19, 137–38.

97. I. Roll and O. Tal, eds., *Apollonia–Arsuf: Final Report of the Excavations, Volume I: The Persian and Hellenistic Periods* (Tel Aviv: Institute of Archaeology, 1999) 208; O. Tal, "Some Notes on the Settlement Patterns of the Persian Period Southern Sharon Plain in Light of Recent Excavations at Apollonia–Arsuf," *Transeu* 19 (2000) 115–25, esp. p. 117.

98. J. Kaplan and H. Ritter-Kaplan, "Jaffa," *NEAEHL* 2.655–59.

99. R. Avner and E. Eshel, "A Juglet with a Phoenician Inscription from a Recent Excavation in Jaffa, Israel," *Transeu* 12 (1996) 59–64, pl. 1.

100. O. Negbi, *A Deposit of Terracottas and Statuettes from Tel Sippor* (ʿAtiqot 6; Jerusalem: Department of Antiquities, 1966); idem, "A Contribution of Minerology and Palaeontology to an Archaeological Study of Terracottas," *IEJ* 14 (1964) 187–89, pls. 42–43.

101. N. Naʾaman, "The Boundary System and Political Status of Gaza under the Assyrian Empire," *ZDPV* 120 (2004) 55–72, esp. p. 60. On Tell Jemmeh, see E. Stern, *Material Culture of the Land of the Bible in the Persian Period, 538–332 B.C.* (Jerusalem: Israel Exploration Society / Warminster: Aris & Phillips, 1982) 22–25.

own way. Sidon was rejuvenated in the last third of the sixth century under the enterprising dynasty of ʾEshmunʿazor, but the fulfillment of its grand vision was achieved only in the fifth, when it managed to balance adhesion to the Persian Empire with its delight in all things Greek. Byblos was a diligent partner, busy in innovative religious architecture and in overseas trade. The towns and settlements south of Carmel, even when they had to pay tolls and taxes to Sidon, were steadfastly Tyrian in their material culture. The difference was that nothing much new was happening, and the sheer routine was stifling the old and great Phoenician spirit.

Transjordan Is Diminished

The Transjordanian states were embroiled with Babylon in the early sixth century, with the Persians later in the century, with the North Arabian tribes and the Kingdom of Qedar between times, and became severely distanced from what remained of the Tyrian international network. Ammon maintained some normalcy throughout the century. Moab disappeared into the conquerors' provincial systems. Edom, encouraged at first by the Babylonians, annexed the southern part of Judah but then was absorbed into the Qedarite realm. Babylon, under Nabonidus (556–539 B.C.E.), redirected trade with South Arabia. The Transjordanian peoples, once their kingdoms and political integrity were gone did not have either the incentive or the energy to retain, let alone restore any semblance of their former transnational interests.

Ammon, under the last king of the dynasty that had guided it through most of the seventh century, had become a noted wine producer. This king, Amminadab, wrote a text to memorialize his contribution to the industry.[102] It is written on a very small bronze bottle in a balanced, cadenced, and rhythmic style, for which the king himself unabashedly takes credit, and he throbs with pride and palpable delight in his vineyards, winepresses, and the details of their construction. Later in the sixth century, there is evidence for at least one installation of this sort[103] (the wine cellars, seals, and seal impressions of the wine merchants), and his seems not to have been an idle boast. A corroboration of sorts of the industry and an instant illustration of the king's meaning is a bronze *phiale* or drinking bowl, inscribed with the name of the merchant and symposiast ("belonging to ʾElišomer, son of ʾEliʿozer"), who was able to enjoy the king's benevolence with his friends.[104]

102. H. O. Thompson and F. Zayadine, "The Tel Siran Inscription," *BASOR* 212 (1973) 5–11; idem, "The Ammonite Inscription from Tell Siran," *Berytus* 22 (1973) 115–40; F. M. Cross, "Notes on the Ammonite Inscription from Tell Siran," *BASOR* 212 (1973) 12–15; repr. in idem, *Leaves from an Epigrapher's Notebook: Collected Papers in Hebrew and West Semitic Palaeography and Epigraphy* (HSS 51; Winona Lake, IN: Eisenbrauns, 2003) 100–2; C. Krahmalkov, "An Ammonite Lyric Poem," *BASOR* 223 (1976) 55–57; W. H. Shea, "The Sīrān Inscription: Amminadab's Drinking Song," *PEQ* 110 (1978) 107–12; I. Kottsieper, "Zur Inschrift auf der Flasche vom Tell Sīrān und ihrem historischen Hintergrund," *UF* 34 (2002) 353–62.

103. O. Lipschits, "Ammon in Transition from Vassal Kingdom to Babylonian Province," *BASOR* 335 (2004) 37–52, esp. p. 38.

104. U. Hübner, *Die Ammoniter: Untersuchungen zur Geschichte, Kultur und Religion eines transjordanischen Volkes im 1. Jahrtausend v. Chr.* (Wiesbaden: Harrassowitz, 1992) 30–31.

The normalcy that Ammon seems to have maintained is evident in its literary, or at least literate productions and in its persistence in business as usual.[105] From Heshbon (Tell Hisban) in the first half of the sixth century, there are economic documents[106] (a list of disbursements to the king and to five of his cronies and consignments of goods and services) written in Ammonite, and from the second half of the century similar lists, now written in Aramaic, the official language of the Persian Empire. From Tell el-Mazar, where there is the same language distribution, the early dossier contains a letter with a witty mix of business and pleasure from the merchant Palṭi to his partner ʿAbdʾil on establishing a line of credit.[107] Seals of merchants and traders such as these two have the designs that were used in the seventh century, but they are all from the earlier years of the century and, consequently, are less numerous.[108]

The seals of women feature lotus blossoms or buds.[109] The seals of men feature real or imaginary animals, such as bulls, rams, or winged sphinxes.[110] They may have symbols, such as a four-winged scarab flanked by floral standards, a star, or a suppliant framed by a crescent moon and a star.[111] Or they are aniconic.[112] Among the last, there is a seal of Palṭi, son of Tam, who conceivably is the merchant who received a line of credit from his partner.

The Kingdom of Moab, along with the Kingdom of Ammon, was dismantled by Nebuchadnezzar in 582 B.C.E.[113] Edomites, as many biblical writers agree, were complicit with the Babylonians in the siege and capture of Jerusalem and, as one of these prophetic sources protested (Amos 1:9–12), bought some of the Judean captives who had fallen into the Tyrian slave trade. The overland trade routes from the Gulf of ʿAqaba to Gaza were paralyzed by the intrusion of the Qedarite Kingdom, and Edomites who had found work as middle men and mercenaries, looked to settle down in the once urban and prosperous land of Judah. It was Qedarite Arabs who guided Cambyses through the desert on his Egyptian campaign, the Qedarites who managed the trade routes to the sea,[114] and movement along the coastal roads to the settlements in the Plain of Sharon and beyond, and it

---

105. A. Lemaire, "Les transformations politiques et culturelles de la Transjordanie au VIe siècle av. J.-C.," *Transeu* 8 (1994) 9–27, esp. pp. 16–18.

106. F. M. Cross, "Ammonite Ostraca from Tell Hisban," *Leaves from an Epigrapher's Notebook*, 70–102.

107. K. Yassine and J. Teixidor, "Ammonite and Aramaic Inscriptions from Tell el-Mazar in Jordan," *BASOR* 264 (1986) 45–49, #3, esp. pp. 47–48. Palṭi refers to ʿAbdʾil as his "brother," the term generally used for blood relatives and for business partners. He asks for a favor (money probably, but the word is lost) and offers to give an I.O.U. (šʿrt), which he recognizes might be distasteful (šʿrrt), as his pledge. The pun, in such dire straits, reveals imagination and perhaps even a literary bent.

108. There are about 150 Ammonite seals, and around 25 might be dated to the early sixth century: see A. Lemaire, "Les transformations politiques et culturelles de la Transjordanie au VIe siècle av. J.-C.," *Transeu* 8 (1994) 9–27, esp. pp. 17–18.

109. *WSS* ##868, 869, 872.

110. Ibid., ##908, 931, 940.

111. Ibid., ##860, 883, 910.

112. Ibid., ##941, 966, 969.

113. I. Ephʿal, *The Ancient Arabs: Nomads on the Borders of the Fertile Crescent, 9th–5th Centuries B.C.* (Jerusalem: Magnes, 1984) 178.

114. Ibid., 195.

undoubtedly was these people who brought with them the cult of ʿAštarim to the shrine at ʾElyakin.

The diminution of Phoenician influence on the mainland south of the capital cities in Lebanon was matched by the total disintegration of the tightly engineered political and commercial network that flourished in the seventh century, when every city and state on either side of the Jordan longed for the good life and was proud to be an eager participant. The Babylonians, missing the point of cooperation, meant to take over all of it themselves, and the Persians further disheartened these peoples by urging them to recoup and reassert their past, while leaving them, except for imposts and micromanaged supervision, to their own devices and now questionable traditions. The sixth century spun from expectation to despair and spiraled downward into drab determination. The East was just old countries; the future was in the newfangled West.

The Syrian Coast: Influenced by Cyprus, Greece, Egypt, and Persia

The cities and ports on the Syrian coast, north of Byblos and Beirut, were mainly in the Arvadian, and therefore Sidonian, orbit. The exception was Al Mina, an emporium that Tyre had established in the eighth century to anchor its Aegean trade and that served the city well right through the seventh century.

Al Mina, called "The Headland" by its founders and "the Tyrian Headland" by the Assyrians, was abandoned, or at least nonoperational, from quite early in the sixth century until about the last quarter of the century.[115] This gap corresponds to the years of the siege of Tyre and the following time of wavering between monarchic (even dynastic) and republican rule in the city, dithering during the reign of Nabonidus (556–539 B.C.E.), and the uncertainty attending the transition to Persian rule. The old emplacements at Al Mina were leveled, and the new warehouses, stores, and workshops were organized on a different plan.[116] There was more Greek (specifically, Attic) pottery, as was the norm at all coastal sites, but the buildings and their contents were Phoenician or Syrian.[117] The site more or less abruptly lost its Tyrian cachet. In the fifth century, its coinage was from Arvad or Sidon.[118] And by the fourth century, burials were in clay coffins in the basement of

---

115. N. Naʾaman, "Raʾshu, Reʾsi-ṣuri, and the Ancient Names of Ras Ibn Hani," *BASOR* 334 (2004) 33–39; J. Boardman, "The Excavated History of Al Mina," in *Ancient Greeks West and East* (ed. G. R. Tsetskhladze; Leiden: Brill, 1999) 135–61, esp. pp. 139–40.

116. J. Y. Perreault, "Les *emporia* grecs au Levant: Mythe ou réalité?" in *L'Emporion* (ed. A. Bresson and P. Rouillard; Paris: Boccard, 1993) 59–83, figs. 1–13, esp. p. 66; M. E. Aubet, "Arquitectura colonial e intercambio," in *Fenicios y Territorio: Actas del II Seminario Internacional sobre Temas Fenicios, Guardamar del Segura, 9–11 de abril de 1999* (ed. A. González Prats; Alicante: Instituto Alicantino de Cultura, 2000) 13–45, esp. pp. 29–31.

117. J. Elayi, "Al Mina sur l'Oronte à l'époque perse," in *Phoenicia and the East Mediterranean in the First Millennium B.C.* (ed. E. Lipiński; Studia Phoenicia 5; Louvain: Peeters, 1987) 249–66, esp. pp. 257–60.

118. J. Lund, "The Northern Coastline of Syria in the Persian Period: A Survey of the Archaeological Evidence," *Transeu* 2 (1990) 13–36, esp. pp. 24–25.

houses in accordance with local Syrian customs.[119] It may be, in fact, that
Al Mina at the end of the sixth century was among the independent ports
and religious places of coastal Syria that relied on the system of services
established by Arvad.

Ras el-Bassit, 25 kilometers south of Al Mina, was a small port with
modest needs and making modest contributions to passing Phoenicians,
Cypriots, and Greeks.[120] There were some sixth-century buildings[121] and
a cemetery that had been in use since the eighth century. This consisted
of 49 tombs, containing about 61 burials that followed Syrian, not Phoenician, customs: they were incinerations, the bones and ashes gathered in
urns placed in a small hole in the ground and covered with another pot,
with rare and simple grave offerings.[122] In the eighth and seventh centuries, about half of the ceramics were Phoenician, but in the late seventh
and early sixth century, Cypriot and Syrian wares began to predominate.[123]

In the sixth century, especially in the later years (after 510 B.C.E.), there
was an abundance of Attic pottery.[124] From the end of the century, there is
a lone Athenian tetradrachm.[125] Also from the end of the century, there is
a Phoenician inscription: it is the name of the merchant or the producer
(*lgrbʿl*, "Belonging to Gerbaʿal") written on a basket-handled amphora from
Cyprus, which was found in a house together with a drinking bowl, a black
glazed Attic cup, and some Black Figured Ware.[126] It has been suggested,
because there were so few burials, especially adult burials, that there were
not more than 12 people living at Bassit at any one time. It was a transient
community, many of whom died and were buried elsewhere,[127] staying in
Bassit to eke out a living supplying Cypriot, Greek, and Phoenician ships in
exchange for what they wanted, then sailing with them to some rumored
better place.

Tell Sukas, about halfway between Bassit and Arvad, was a predominantly Greek settlement in the sixth century.[128] The cemetery consisted of
inhumations and burial pyres, presumably of the Greek dead, and cremations with burial of the ashes in jars, most likely of the Phoenician dead: the
burial urns were Cypriot, and the pottery associated with the Greek burials

119. Elayi, "Al Mina sur l'Oronte à l'époque perse," 260.

120. P. Courbin, *Fouilles de Bassit: Tombes du Fer* (Paris: Editions Recherche sur les Civilisations, 1993) 117.

121. Lund, "The Northern Coastline of Syria in the Persian Period," 23.

122. Courbin, *Fouilles de Bassit*, 115–17.

123. Ibid., 7, 47–68.

124. J. Y. Perreault, "Céramique et échanges: Les importations attiques au proche-orient du
VIe au milieu du Ve siècle avant J.-C. Les données archéologiques," *BCH* 110 (1986) 145–75, esp.
pp. 149–50, 153.

125. G. Le Rider, "L'atelier de Posideion et les monnaies de la fouille de Bassit en Syrie," *BCH*
110 (1986) 393–408, esp. p. 394; J. Lund, "The Northern Coastline of Syria in the Persian Period:
A Survey of the Archaeological Evidence," *Transeu* 2 (1990) 13–36, esp. p. 23.

126. P. Bordreuil, "Epigraphes phéniciennes sur bronze, sur pierre et sur céramique," in *Archéologie au Levant: Recueil à la mémoire de Roger Saidah* (Lyon: Maison de l'Orient, 1982) 187–92,
esp. pp. 191–92.

127. Courbin, *Fouilles de Bassit*, 100.

128. P. J. Riis, *Sūkās VI: The Graeco-Phoenician Cemetery and Sanctuary at the Southern Harbour*
(Publications of the Carlsberg Expedition to Phoenicia 7; Copenhagen: Munksgaard, 1979) 9–32.

was East Greek in the seventh and sixth centuries and Attic in the sixth.[129] Control of the site was disputed, apparently, and it was destroyed early in the century and again about mid-century, then razed and abandoned early in the fifth century, around the time of the battle of Salamis and the defeat of the Greeks in Cyprus.[130] More than 100 years later, Sukas was resettled from Arvad, and Phoenicians and Greeks lived in relative harmony.

Arvad is an island city with good harbors and with extensive property on the mainland, including the sanctuary site at ʿAmrit and, in the sixth century, Tell Kazel (or Sumur).[131] An inscription from the Temple of Seti I at Abydos, written by a mercenary from Arvad in the service of Psammetichus II (594–588 B.C.E.), reads: "I am ʿAbdoʾ, son of Kanish, from Arvad. I have seen all the sights of the temple."[132] A personal seal from the environs of the city[133] belonging to Gerʿashtart (*grʿštrt*) and dating to the early sixth century reflects the standard Phoenician, or Egyptianizing, school: a griffin-headed Goddess is enthroned beneath a winged sun disk, holding a lotus blossom in her left hand and raising her right hand in blessing of an ibis-headed man, representing Thoth, who stands in front of her and who is balanced artistically by a mummiform figure, representing Ptah, who stands behind her.

Another seal from later in the century but from the same place,[134] by contrast, reflects a Syrian and specifically an Arvadian, perspective: a large human-headed fish, his hand raised in salutation, swims to the left beneath a five-pointed star and a sun disk that rides in a crescent moon. The early coins from Arvad share some of the same motifs; the seal owner's name is abbreviated (*bet* + *ʿayin*) and is meant to be deciphered from the iconography as *Bodʿaštart*, "By the hand of Astarte," the first part of the name being signaled by the incongruous hand, the second part by the star, the symbol of Astarte; the rest of the picture, the fish gliding in water, the sun disk riding in a boat-shaped crescent moon, identifies the seal bearer as the captain of a ship or an overseas trader engaged in the maritime adventures of Arvad.

A third seal, from the end of the sixth or early fifth century B.C.E. and said to be from ʿAmrit, is a fresh rendering of eastern and western Mediterranean traditions (see fig. 5.4).[135] Its owner's name was Barosh (*brš*)[136] meaning "Cypress" or "the man from the Amanus, the Cypress mountain." The scene is composite. In the standard Phoenician mood, a man strid-

129. Ibid., 10–32.

130. Lund, "The Northern Coastline of Syria in the Persian Period," 17.

131. J. Elayi, "Les sites phéniciens de Syrie au Fer III / Perse: Bilan et perspectives de recherche," in *Essays on Syria in the Iron Age* (ed. G. Bunnens; ANESt Supplement 7; Louvain: Peeters, 2000) 327–48, esp. pp. 333–38; H. Sader, "Le territoire des villes phéniciennes: Reliefs accidentés, modèles unifiés," in *Fenicios y Territorio: Actas del II Seminario sobre Temas Fenicios, Guardamar del Segura, 9–11 de abril de 1999* (ed. A. González Prats; Alicante: Instituto Alicantino de Cultura," 2000) 227–61, esp. pp. 232–35.

132. *RES* 604.

133. *CSOSI* 35–36 #25.

134. Ibid., 37–38 #28.

135. Ibid., 39 #31; *WSS* 278–79 #749.

136. The name *brš* was written on the seal as it should appear on the impression, and so the name is back-to-front on the impression, as are all the individual letters except /b/.

Fig. 5.4. Seal and impression with smiting god and wolf (Paris, BN, CM, De Clercq Collection 2506).

ing, left foot forward, in the smiting-pharaoh or Smiting-God position, and wearing the Egyptian double crown holds a club in his raised right hand. In a different mood, however, his long robe is not Egyptian, and he is poised to strike not a human captive but a she-wolf leaping at him to protect her young, whom he restrains by holding her by the ears with his left hand. Her young, in another surprise accommodation, are not wolf cubs but four young boys who stand beneath her, their legs apart for balance, to suck her full and prominent teats. Above her are the usual symbols of rank and authority, the hovering winged sun disk, a crescent moon, and a bright multirayed twinkling star. This combination of moods and bold adaptation of motifs seems to exceed the natural ability of the engraver (who did not write his patron's name correctly) and ordinary artistic inspiration and was inspired by myths and legends that its owner had learned.

The Smiting God is Syrian and represents the defeat of the Sea in primordial time. The she-wolf and her nurselings are from the Roman foundation myth. The conflict between invasive and indigenous cultures is a reflection of the mood in sixth-century Italy, when east Phoenician inspiration yielded to Carthaginian determination. It might be, then, that the seal belonged to a man from Arvad, who had lived abroad and adapted to his Latin or Etruscan environment, and who understood how the two stories intersected and refreshed each other.

This mix of Egyptian inclinations, imported motifs, and local tastes is verified and supplemented in the anthropoid sarcophagi found in graveyards on the coastal plain between Antarados, opposite the island, and ʿAmrit, about 6 kilometers to the south.[137] There are three kinds, terracotta, basalt, and marble, and each kind consists of various subtypes distinguished by workshop or date. The oldest are the six terra-cotta sarcophagi, five of which were found in the same family tomb,[138] all but one of which belonged to women.

All were modeled, in their form and in some particular features, on the Egyptian anthropoid sarcophagi that Tabnît of Sidon acquired sometime after 525 B.C.E., but the workmanship and the artistic impulses were Cypriot, Greek, and local.[139] The two earliest (ca. 510–490 B.C.E.) were inspired by the style of Cypriot terra-cotta figurines—they wear earrings and do their hair in ringlets—but also have local Phoenician features. Two others belonging to women can be dated to the early fifth century (ca. 490–470 B.C.E.), and Greek influence—for example, pursed lips imitating the "archaic smile"—is evident. The last two (ca. 470–450 B.C.E.) belong to a woman who is quite Greek and to a man whose headdress and pectorals are adaptations of those on the Egyptian anthropoid sarcophagi at Sidon. The five basalt sarcophagi (480/70–460/50 B.C.E.) overlap in time with these last two, and by preserving the Egyptian mood and the local flair while taking on some Greek features, were meant as a studied alternative to the Greek marble sarcophagi being introduced at the same time. They

137. K. Lembke, "Die phönizischen anthropoiden Sarkophage aus den Nekropolen der Insel Arados," *DM* 10 (1998) 97–129, pls. 24–35, esp. p. 97; S. Frede, *Die phönizischen anthropoiden Sarkophage, Teil I: Fundgruppen und Bestattungskontexte* (Mainz am Rhein: von Zabern, 2000) 107–25 ##II.1–II.29.

138. Lembke, "Die phönizischen anthropoiden Sarkophage aus den Nekropolen der Insel Arados," 99–106; J. Elayi and M. R. Haykal, *Nouvelles découvertes sur les usages funéraires des Phéniciens d'Arwad* (Transeu Supplement 4; Paris: Gabalda, 1996) 87–117.

139. Lembke, "Die phönizischen anthropoiden Sarkophage aus den Nekropolen der Insel Arados," 101–16.

could not compete, of course, and the project was soon abandoned, while the Greek marble sarcophagi remained popular until the third quarter of the fourth century.

Three of the basalt sarcophagi were carved for women, and two were designed for men. The women's hairstyles and eyes are Greek, but their ears are large and protruding, as on Egyptian anthropoid sarcophagi. The men wear turbans and, in hands that emerge incongruously from the plain coffin lid, hold an Egyptian *was* sceptre that, in its original setting, was reserved for high-ranking functionaries. These five people may have been related, either by blood or by business ties, and are representative of the local Phoenician gentry that had deep roots in Arvad. The family buried in the terra-cotta sarcophagi had its ties with Cyprus, perhaps its origin there, where there was a strong Egyptian presence in the sixth century, and demonstrates a similar but differently directed social conservatism. This "family" too may have comprised individuals involved in the same industry, such as textiles, or in a trading company specializing in imports from Cyprus. At any rate, these two groups illustrate some of the complexity of native Arvadian society before Athens became the arbiter of gentility and good taste.

Sidonian contact with Arvad, evident in its anthropoid sarcophagi that were modeled on the original Egyptian sarcophagi that its people had seen and sketched in Sidon, is also evident in the cult and rituals at ʿAmrit, 5 kilometers south of Arvad and its mainland emplacement at Antarados. This was the central sanctuary of the Arvad amphictyony, which comprised at this time the towns of the Syrian coastal region[140] from Bassit in the north to Tell Kazel and Tell ʿArqa in the south, and it was a pilgrimage site for the Phoenicians of southeastern Cyprus. The rituals were lustral, centered on the Maʿabed and consisting of physical and moral cleansing in the healing waters of this porticoed pool. The God of the sanctuary was ʾEshmun,[141] the God of Sidon, the Expiator, who was invoked in the inscriptions that are associated with it either by his name or by his title Shadrapaʾ (*šdrpʾ*), "Healing Genius."

The earliest of these inscriptions, written on what is commonly known as the ʿAmrit Stele, is from Sumur, Tell Kazel, near the coast but a bit farther south.[142] The inscription reads:[143] "This is the stele which Pilles, son of ʿAbday, gave to his lord, to Šadrapaʾ, because he listened to the sound of his words." The inscription is written in standard Phoenician, except that the demonstrative "this" has the dialectal form (ʾz) of Cypriot Phoenician.

---

140. Lund, "The Northern Coastline of Syria in the Persian Period," 29–30.

141. P. Bordreuil, "Le dieu Echmoun dans la région d'Amrit," in *Phoenicia and Its Neighbours* (ed. E. Lipiński; Studia Phoenicia 3; Louvain: Peeters, 1985) 221–30, esp. pp. 228–30.

142. M. Yon and A. Caubet, "Arouad et Amrit, VIIIe–Ier siècles av. J.-C. Documents," *Transeu* 6 (1993) 47–67, pls. 1–7, esp. pp. 58–60; S. M. Cecchini, "La stele di Amrit: Aspetti e problemi iconografici e iconologici," in *Studi in Memoria di Henri Frankfort (1897–1954): Presentati dalla scuola romana di Archeologia Orientale* (ed. P. Matthiae; Contributi e Materiali di Archeologia Orientale 7; Rome: Università degli Studi di Roma, "La Sapienza," 1997) 83–100, esp. pp. 83–84.

143. É. Puech, "Les inscriptions phéniciennes d'Amrit et les dieux guérisseurs du sanctuaire," *Syria* 53 (1986) 327–42, esp. pp. 335–39.

The design on the stele[144] is an archaizing blend of genres (such as the "Smiting God" and the "Master of Animals") and artistic traditions (including Syrian, Neo-Hittite, Egyptianizing Phoenician, Cypriot, Assyrian, and Babylonian) and, besides reflecting Tell Kazel's checkered cultural career, is a fairly learned attempt to picture Shadrapaʾ, of whom this is the first and only Phoenician impression, as a God.

The God, clothed in Egyptian fashion and wearing an Egyptian crown, is pictured striding to the right, his left arm extended before him, his right arm raised in the smiting gesture. He stands on a lion, his left foot on its head, his right on its arched and forwardly curved tail, and holds a lion cub by its hind feet in his left hand. The lion, like him, strides to the right on the tops of twin wooded mountains. Above the God's head is a crescent moon cupping a full moon, and above it, fitted umbrella-like into the curved top of the stele, is a winged sun disk. He obviously is a God, filling all the space between earth and sky, riding on a lion, age-old symbol of divinity, above the mountains, where cosmic Gods traditionally reside, and in charge of terrestrial affairs, symbolized by dominion over the animals but, in the case of this God, by control of a live and squirming cub that arches upward trying to bite his hand. He looks like almost any Syro-Phoenician God—for instance, Baʿal, Melqart, or Reshep—but this is the only picture of the God, and the text identifies him as the Lord Shadrapaʾ.

Two other inscriptions from ʿAmrit, one dating to the sixth century and one to the fifth, are dedications to the God ʾEshmun. The later is written on the leg of a statue that came from Cyprus or was made by a Cypriot Phoenician:[145] "This (ʾz) is the statue that ʿAbdʾeshmun gave to his lord, to ʾEshmun, because he pitied him and heard his voice." The demonstrative, again, is Cypriot, and the limestone statue, like other sixth- and fifth-century examples,[146] represented the donor and allowed him to be present in the sanctuary as long as the limestone lasted.

The earlier, slightly damaged inscription was inscribed on a building block:[147] "This (ʾz) is the [. . .] which ʾEshmun[ʾadon the] Arvadite, and his brothers, sons of ʾAdonbaʿal, grandsons of Bodmilqart, made for their Lord, for ʾEshmun, because he heard the sound of their words. May he bless them." What is particularly interesting about this text are the personal names. The name of the brother from Arvad combines the name of ʾEshmun, the God of ʿAmrit, and his title, so that the full name means "ʾEshmun is Lord." The father's name, ʾAdonbaʿal, means "Adonis is Baʿal." Together, the names in the three generations include the name of Baʿal, God of natural elements, and the names of the Gods of Tyre, Sidon, and Byblos (that is, Melqart, ʾEshmun, Adonis) and, separately and in sequence, suggest that the process of syncretism, the assimilation to each other of

---

144. Cecchini, "La stele di Amrit: Aspetti e problemi iconografici e iconologici."

145. P. Bordreuil, "Le dieu Echmoun dans la région d'Amrit," in *Phoenicia and Its Neighbours* (ed. E. Lipiński; Studia Phoenicia 3; Louvain: Peeters, 1985) 221–30, esp. pp. 225–28; É. Puech, "Les inscriptions phéniciennes d'Amrit et les dieux guérisseurs du sanctuaire," *Syria* 53 (1986) 327–42, esp. pp. 332–35.

146. Yon and Caubet, "Arouad et Amrit, VIIIe–Ier siècles av. J.-C. Documents," 57–58.

147. Bordreuil, "Le dieu Echmoun dans la région d'Amrit," 221–25; Puech, "Les inscriptions phéniciennes d'Amrit et les dieux guérisseurs du sanctuaire," 327–31.

the premier Gods, that began in Cyprus, had crossed over with Cypriot pilgrims to the sanctuary at ʿAmrit.

The intrusion of Cypriot art and ideas into the region of Arvad is suggested by a terra-cotta statuette of an enthroned God found in the necropolis at ʿAmrit.[148] The statuette was carelessly molded, as if from memory and by an artist inexperienced in the genre, and represents Baʿal Ammon, a God imported into Cyprus from Libya during the sixth century, when Egyptianizing tastes on the island were most pronounced. The enthroned God is a typical Phoenician conceit, but this God wearing ram's horns, envisaged as a ram and seated on a throne the arms of which are in the shape of rams is a North African creation. Terra-cotta statuettes of this Baʿal have been found at Meniko, Chytroi, and Salamis in Cyprus, and at Tel Michal (Makmish) on the coast south of Mount Carmel, but limestone statues of the God have been found in all the important ancient Phoenician sites in Cyprus.[149] The statuette from ʿAmrit might have been made in the Arvad region but probably was brought to Arvad by the Cypriot Phoenician who eventually died there and was buried in this graveyard just north of ʿAmrit.

At ʿAmrit there are also numerous limestone statues of Melqart, some from the late sixth but most from the fifth century B.C.E. The limestone is Cypriot,[150] and the statues were ex-votos that accompanied the pilgrims or were shipped separately to ʿAmrit. Eventually, when they were worn out, or to make room for others, they were discarded in refuse pits. Of the statues that can be identified, some represented the individual worshipers, and some were statues of Melqart in his guise as Heracles, a syncretism that became popular in Cyprus in the late sixth century:[151] the hero, in Phoenician fashion wears a belted Egyptian kilt and strides, left foot forward, with his right arm raised in the Smiting-God position, his left by his side; as Heracles, he wears a lion-skin on his back (vanquishing the Nemean lion was the first of his exploits and the paradigm for the whole series), its head worn as a hat, its front paws tied around his neck and hanging over his chest. This Greco-Phoenician syncretism is matched by another at ʿAmrit, according to which Cypriot Phoenicians, whose worship of Melqart indicates that they were Tyrians, identified their God with ʾEshmun, the God of Sidon worshiped in Arvad, and ʿAmrit—the two of them together becoming the unique God ʾEshmun-Melqart known at Kition in the fourth century. Practice usually anticipates articulate belief, and shipping statues

---

148. A. M. Bisi, "Su una terracotta di tipo cipriota da ʿAmrit," *RSF* 10 (1982) 189–96, pls. 46–49.

149. V. Karageorghis, *Two Cypriot Sanctuaries of the End of the Cypro-Archaic Period* (Rome: Consiglio Nazionale delle Ricerche, 1977) 17–66, figs. 1–3, pls. 1–6, esp. pp. 35–36, 45; F. Vandenabeele, "Phoenician Influence on the Cypro-Archaic Terracotta Production and Cypriot Influence Abroad," in *Acts of the International Archaeological Symposium "Cyprus between the Orient and the Occident"* (ed. V. Karageorghis; Nicosia: Department of Antiquities, 1986) 351–60, pls. 30–31, esp. pp. 353–54. H.-G. Buchholz, "Der Gott Hammon und Zeus Ammon auf Zypern," *Mitteilungen des deutschen archaologischen Instituts: Athenische Abteilung* 106 (1991) 85–128, pls. 10–21. V. Karageorghis, *Two Cypriot Sanctuaries*, 45. Ibid., 35.

150. C. Jourdain-Annequin, "Héraclès-Melqart à Amrith? Un syncrétisme Gréco-phénicien à l'époque perse," *Transeu* 6 (1993) 69–86, pls. 8–12, esp. p. 72.

151. Idem, *Héraclès-Melqart à Amrith: Recherches iconographiques—Contribution à l'étude d'un syncretisme* (Paris: Geuthner, 1992) 33, 36.

of Melqart to a pilgrimage shrine of ʾEshmun was a first step toward allow-ing, eventually, that they were one and the same God.

The Syrian coast in the sixth century was dotted with small Phoenician habitations that supplied Arvad with food and agricultural produce and with men and matériel for its grand navy. The city presided over a socially and ethnically mixed population, both on the island and on the adja-cent mainland, and was responsible for maintaining the amphictyonic, or loosely federal shrine at ʿAmrit that, in the sixth century, assumed the role that once belonged to Sidonian Kition among the Cypriot kingdoms. Along with its age-old ties to Sidon, it had increasingly important connec-tions with eastern Cyprus and, assuming that the seal of Barosh, the Ama-nus man, reveals familiarity with the culture of central Italy, maintained relations through such talented craftsmen, travelers, and traders with the Phoenician colonies and its own enclaves in the West. Its navy was among the best in the Persian fleet, and the Persian Empire was the new network in which Arvad thrived.

Cyprus: Cypriot Culture Begins to Come into Its Own

In the sixth century, the Phoenicians in most cities and kingdoms on the island were slowly vanishing into the Cypriot and increasingly Greek woodwork. There were some places—Kition, for example, and Lapethos—where Phoenicians were predominant, but island politics was in the hands of the indigenous and ever-resilient kingdoms,[152] and Phoenicians busied themselves with developments in the far West. This decline of Phoenician interest in Cyprus coincided with the Babylonian siege of Tyre (585–572 B.C.E.) and its aftermath, and with Egyptian interference in the regular traf-fic between Tyre and the island under Apries (588–568 B.C.E.) and Amasis (568–526 B.C.E.).[153] The international situation improved when Phoenicia and Cyprus were absorbed into the Persian Empire, and it returned to nor-mal when Egypt was defeated by Cambyses (522 B.C.E.) and became on the international scene mainly a boutique of exotic trinkets and beliefs. The Empire, as the Egyptians, had little effect on Cyprus,[154] but the island's Phoenician heritage is still perceptible in indigenous adaptations of their cultural and commercial élan, and a continuing Phoenician presence be-comes evident in new styles and trends introduced onto the island from their replenished imperial resources.

Southwestern Cyprus

At Amathus in southwestern Cyprus, there are architectural, artistic, and ceramic remains of the sixth-century Phoenician community. Next to a

---

152. A.-M. Collombier, "Organisation du territoire et pouvoirs locaux dans l'île de Chypre à l'époque perse," *Transeu* 4 (1991) 21–43.

153. *Cyprus* 108–10.

154. G. E. Markoe, "Egyptianizing Male Votive Statuary from Cyprus: A Reexamination," *Le-vant* 22 (1990) 111–22; *Cyprus* 112–13; T. Petit, "Presence et influence perses à Chypre," in *Achae-menid History, VI: Asia Minor and Egypt—Old Cultures in a New Empire* (ed. H. Sancisi-Weerdenburg and A. Kuhrt; Leiden: Nederlands Instituut voor het Nabije Oosten, 1991) 161–78.

well-constructed public building that was dated to the fifth century and dubbed "The Palace," there was a sturdy warehouse with a few adjacent workshops.[155] The warehouse was roofed in thick Red Slip tiles. Some sectors contained storage jars, amphorae of local manufacture, or Attic Black Figure Ware. In another area, there were limestone columns with "Hathor" capitals—that is, with the head of the Goddess Hathor in place of the proto-Ionic capital, the volutes of which her out-rolled hair resembled. The workshops had scale weights and jewelry, bronze slag, and a kiln or terracotta and stone figurines (of the latter, one unfinished and others with Cypriot syllabic signs), and they had access via a system of conduits to a nearby source of water. The storehouse apparently belonged to a syndicate with Phoenician, Greek, and Cypriot affiliations that worked mainly in stone and clay and produced building or personal and devotional materials for the local community.

The personal or devotional material, imported from Egypt or made locally in various ateliers, consisted of scarab seals, amulets, and terra-cottas that were deposited with their owners in tombs. The terra-cottas[156] represent standard Phoenician themes or images of a Cypriot or Cypro-Phoenician way of life. A few are earlier or later, but most belong to the seventh and sixth centuries. There are women, standing or sitting, standing and playing a tambourine, standing and carrying an offering, or holding a child in their left arm and lifting their right hand to their mouths, standing naked and proffering their breasts, or in Greek style standing fully and elegantly clothed and holding a flower. There are men holding tambourines, or some sort of disk, against their chest and men riding horses, both very popular sights in sixth-century Cyprus. There are scenes of daily life (making bread or taking a bath) and models of familiar and useful things (bells, boats, baskets, tables, incense stands, shrines with pillared doorways and celestial symbols of Astarte above their empty entrance). Birds and animals abound: bulls, lions, horses, dogs, sheep and goats, and a monkey with a finger to its lips, Harpocrates style, as often depicted on Egyptianizing seals.

The seals and amulets reflect the resurgence of Egypt's prestige earlier in the century and the end-of-century affirmation of Tyrian trade supremacy under the Persian Empire.[157] There are scarabs with Negroid heads, some imported from Naucratis, and others made from molds found at Amathus,[158] with parallels at ʿAkko and at Camiros on Rhodes. There are scarabs and scaraboids with Egyptian or Egyptianizing designs on their stamp side: hieroglyphic signs, cartouches of long-dead pharaohs, pharaoh smiting

---

155. Idem, "Amathonte de Chypre: Bilan de deux campagnes de fouilles (1988 et 1989) au 'palais' d'époque archaïque et classique," *Transeu* 4 (1991) 9–20, pls. 1–17.

156. V. Karageorghis, "The Terracottas," in *La nécropole d'Amathonte, Tombes 113–367, III: i. The Terracottas; ii. Statuettes, sarcophages et stèles decorées* (ed. V. Karageorghis, O. Picard, and C. Tytgat; Études Chypriotes 9; Nicosia: Department of Antiquities, 1987) 1–52, pls. 1–41.

157. G. Clerc, "Aegyptiaca," in *La nécropole d'Amathonte, tombes 110–385, Volume V* (ed. V. Karageorghis, O. Picard, and C. Tytgat; Études Chypriotes 13; Nicosia: Department of Antiquities, 1989) 1–156; P. Aupert, "Amathonte, le Proche Orient et l'Égypte," in *Acts of the International Archaeological Symposium "Cyprus between the Orient and the Occident," Nicosia 8–14 September, 1985* (ed. V. Karageorghis; Nicosia: Department of Antiquities, 1986) 369–82, pls. 35–38.

158. Clerc, "Aegyptiaca," 19–21.

a cowering enemy, images of the Gods, worship scenes, men at play or at prayer, monkeys, and domestic animals. The amulets are statuettes of the Gods, notably Bes, Harpocrates (the child Horus), Hathor, and Ptah, or symbols of power, of which the most popular was the Eye-of-Horus.[159] The Phoenicians of Amathus, clearly, had regular commercial and cultural contact with Egypt, and they and their compatriots were under its antiquarian spell.

The ceramics are mostly local and mostly Cypriot, but there are some imported Phoenician and Attic wares. A portion of the local pottery may have been buried with acclimatized Phoenicians, and a similar amount of the imported Phoenician ceramics may have belonged to members of the Cypriot community. Phoenician pottery comes from a little more than ⅓ of the tombs (97 out of 254) and generally constitutes a small percentage of the ceramic assemblage in any particular tomb: about half of these tombs had only 1 item, a quarter had 2 or 3 items, and the rest contained 4 or more pieces—and this in tombs the number of pottery goods of which might range from about 50 to 200.[160]

The imports are mostly drinking vessels and perfume and unguent jars, but there are some storage jars and a bit of tableware. Attic pottery[161] becomes more common, of course, in the fifth century, but there is some in sixth-century tombs—in one instance, in a tomb that also contained Phoenician imports. Some of the pottery, such as Ionian cups, is common, but there are a few painted wares with narrative scenes in two of the tombs.[162] In one tomb, there is a wine jug depicting a battle scene and another with Apollo playing the lyre and standing between his mother, Leto, and his sister Artemis. In the other, where there were numerous Ionian cups, there is also a cup decorated with the image of Pegasus, which may have been brought from Marion in northwestern Cyprus, where there are five others like it. The pottery of Amathus, in short, was made locally, except for a few Phoenician pieces prized for their contents and some Greek tablewares, such as Ionian cups, that were in vogue around the Mediterranean or designer wares by well-known artists and portraying cherished epic and mythical themes.

Sixth-century Phoenician art from Amathus is mostly representative of religious beliefs and practices. A favorite is Pygmalion, the grotesque pygmy God, the Cypriot Phoenician adaptation of Egyptian Bes, the God of music and dance, guardian of sleep, dispenser of male sexual power, and

---

159. Ibid., 51–143.

160. P. M. Bikai, "The Phoenician Pottery," in *La nécropole d'Amathonte, Tombes 113–367, II: Céramiques non-Chypriotes* (ed. V. Karageorghis, O. Picard, and C. Tytgat; Nicosia: Department of Antiquities, 1987) 1–19, pls. 1–8; C. Tytgat, *Les nécropoles sud-ouest et sud-est d'Amathonte, 1: Les tombes 110–385* (Études Chypriotes 11; Nicosia: Department of Antiquities, 1989). Tomb #130, with burials from the mid-eighth to the late fifth centuries contained 92 pottery items, of which only 4 were imported Phoenician. Tomb #137, from about the mid-sixth century, also had 4 Phoenician imports but out of a total of 60. Tomb #159, also from the mid-sixth century, had only 1 Phoenician pot out of a total of 161.

161. M. Robertson, "The Attic Pottery," in *La nécropole d'Amathonte, Tombes 113–367, II: Céramiques non-Cypriotes* (ed. V. Karageorghis, O. Picard, and C. Tytgat; Nicosia: Department of Antiquities, 1987) 32–43, pls. 18–25.

162. Ibid., Tomb #184 (pp. 33–35) and Tomb #344 (pp. 36–37).

protector of women in childbirth. There is a terra-cotta mask, too small to be worn, showing his horns and pointed ears, his terribly wrinkled face, his wide mouth, thin lips and bared teeth.[163] A carved limestone block[164] presents one of the many variant representations of Pygmalion. The God is grotesque, as usual, with horns and pointed ears and a tail, a head that is too large, no neck, and his tongue protruding obscenely, but he is massive and modeled on Humbaba, the denizen of the Lebanon who was undone by Gilgamesh and Enkidu and, in their protocols, by all the Neo-Assyrian kings. Another favorite is bull masks.[165] These are either terra-cotta miniatures or actual bulls' heads hollowed and carved to be worn in some religious ritual. Neither is found at Amathus, but there are terra-cotta figurines from the site depicting men wearing just such masks, as there are from Ayia Irini and Kourion farther west and from Golgoi in central Cyprus. The masks, miniatures, and figurines acquired their religious significance in the post-Mycenean era from association with Phoenician Baʿal, the God of weather and storms at Sea, but they seem to have been peculiar to the Cypriot population of the island.

Amathus remained indebted to its Phoenician heritage: it was the principal city of the Kingdom of Carthage and the only city on Cyprus that did not join Salamis in the revolt against Persia in the early fifth century B.C.E.[166] It became less important, however, as Phoenician, or specifically Tyrian, power became concentrated in Kition, an emporium and a central sanctuary town, at first, then a kingdom under the auspices of the Persian Empire. The original Carthage in Cyprus would be remembered as the founder of North African Carthage.

The other cities and towns in western Cyprus are like Amathus demographically. This is true, apparently, even of Limassol, Phoenician Carthage. In the late sixth century, two tombs from Limassol contained exclusively Cypriot grave goods.[167] However, there is also some evidence from this time that the city was still the busy capital of a kingdom. This is a Phoenician inscription from Alassa, a site in the Kingdom of Carthage, 15 kilometers northwest of Limassol and about 20 northwest of Amathus. It was written in ink in three lines, the ends of which are lost, on the shoulder of a Cypriot jar found in a pillaged tomb. It begins with a regnal formula: "In the thirty-sixth year of King [ ]." The second line ("In this mixture there is perfume [ ]") describes the contents of the jar. The last line names the manufacturer ("Milkirom, son of Milk[baʿal]").[168] The regnal date suggests that the perfumed oil in this jar, and presumably in others like it, was due to be shipped to the royal stores in Limassol but instead was deposited

163. V. Karageorghis, "Notes on Some Terracotta Masks from Amathus Now in the British Museum," *RSF* 18 (1990) 3–15, pls. 1–3, esp. pp. 3–6. pl. 1:1.

164. C. Adelman, "A Sculpture in Relief from Amathus," *RDAC* (1971) 59–64, pl. 22.

165. V. Karageorghis, "Notes on Some Cypriote Priests Wearing Bull-Masks," *HTR* 64 (1971) 261–70; S. O'Bryhim, "The *Cerastae* and Phoenician Human Sacrifice on Cyprus," *RSF* 27 (1999) 3–20, pls.1–3.

166. Herodotus 5.104.

167. P. Flourentzos, "The Tombs 214 and 215 from Agios Athanasios Limassol," *RDAC* (1993) 157–71, pls. 18–42.

168. *RPC* 91–94, pl. 8:1.

with Milkirom when he died unexpectedly. The length of the king's reign further suggests that the kingdom, comprising Cypriots as well as Phoenicians, was at peace, and commerce in luxury goods indicates at least relative prosperity.

Kourion, about 20 kilometers due west of Limassol, shows traces of the Phoenicians in the sixth century but was especially renowned for its sanctuary of Apollo Hylates. His cult, as indicated by the lavish votive offerings, flourished in the seventh and sixth centuries. Terra-cottas abound,[169] mostly depicting male votaries either in attitudes of worship (with their arms raised, for instance, or carrying a sacrificial animal or wearing a mask) or in their professional roles in the infantry or cavalry, although horses, horse-and-riders, and chariots do not appear in any number before the fifth century. There are also terra-cotta animals, among them bulls and deer, and the entire repertory is repeated in gold, silver, and bronze statuary.[170]

Among the votive offerings there are also Phoenician-style seals, three from the early seventh century, and one from the early sixth, all of them probably locally made.[171] Their designs are traditional Levantine, such as antithetic figures facing a central Tree-of-Life; or Egyptianizing, either pseudo-hieroglyphs or Isis nursing the child Horus; or a Cypriot mixture of both, as on a cubical seal with geometric shapes on one side, a falcon-headed sphinx on another, a spearman wearing a crested helmet, and a galloping horse on the third and fourth, and a rosette on the base.

There is a similar mix in the miniature, sixth-century, limestone statuettes of men:[172] one wears an Egyptian wig, another wears a Cypriot conical hat, and the third is a young man who wears his hair long and fastened by a wreath or crown in Greek fashion. Phoenician influence is also evident in another statuette that follows the traditional Egyptian artistic canons. The man is trim, well-proportioned, properly coiffed (in order to portray a local inhabitant), his eyes and ears are large, his right arm is by his side, and his left is bent across his chest, but both fists are clenched.[173]

From Kourion, but not from the sanctuary of Apollo, there is some further evidence of Phoenicians' adaptation to their Cypriot and eventually Greek environment. A painted jug from Kandou just north of Kourion[174] gives a local take on a cultic procession to the Phoenician Goddess: two women stand and face a central Tree-of-Life, the one on the left holding a lotus flower in her left hand and a jug in her right, the one on the right holding the flower in her right hand and a small sacrificial animal in her

---

169. N. A. Winter, "The Terracottas," in *The Sanctuary of Apollo Hylates at Kourion: Excavations in the Archaic Precinct* (ed. D. Buitron-Oliver; Jonsered: Åströms, 1996) 89–137, figs. 70–75, pls. 17–33.

170. A. Oliver Jr., "The Metalwork," in ibid., 151–62, pls. 47–67.

171. E. Gubel, "The Seals," in ibid., 163–67, fig. 80, pl. 68.

172. A. Hermary, "Les sculptures en pierre," in ibid., 139–49, pls. 34–46, esp. pp. 140–41, pls. 34–35.

173. G. Markoe, "An Egyptianizing Votive Statuette from Kourion," *RDAC* (1988) part 2, 17–18, pl. 5.

174. V. Karageorghis, "Kypriaka X," *RDAC* (1987) 97–100, pls. 33–35, esp. pp. 99–100, pls. 34, 35:2.

left; it leaves out many of the details that are known from texts and from other representations but is correct in seeing it as a woman's ritual.

There is also a bilingual Phoenician-Cypriot inscription on a tombstone from Kourion[175] that was carved to resemble a window in a house, with a balustrade, and resembling in detail the earlier Phoenician ivories depicting the Woman-at-the-Window, the woman or Goddess mourning her lost lover. The Cypriot inscription is illegible, but the Phoenician version, appropriately enough, reads: "House of Eternity for Bikri the Sidonian is this coffin" (*bt*] *ʿlm lbkry ḥṣ[dny ḥl]t z[ʾ*). The stone was found separately, but there is another like it that was part of a built tomb at Kourion, and both may have been constructed for Sidonians, like Bikri, who brought their skills to Cyprus and settled among the local inhabitants. Although Kourion was Cypriot in the sixth century, Phoenician influence lingered, and the Phoenicians were well remembered.

Palaepaphos, presently Kouklia, was home to the cult of Aphrodite, Phoenician Astarte. The cult of Aphrodite is said to have included ritual bathing, anointing with perfumed oil, incense offerings, processions, and prostitution.[176] The cult of Astarte may have had a similar assortment of rituals, but it also specialized in offerings of hair—a man's hair according to an eighth-century text from Kition; a woman's hair according to Lucian's *Syrian Goddess* and, most likely, according to a fragmentary late sixth-century Phoenician inscription from Palaepaphos itself:[177]

] *smlt ʾ[z*	] This statue of a woman [
bm]qdš ʾz[	] in this sanctuary [
]*r wpʿlt ʾ[yt*	]and I made the [
l]ʿštrt pp [	for] Astarte of Paphos[
] *ʾp mḥlpt* [	] Moreover, locks of hair[178] [

There are many statues of men in the sanctuary of Aphrodite, some clothed or coiffed in Egyptian style, and there are steles in the form of miniature shrines, or *naiskoi*, some of them with a woman or the Goddess in the niche,[179] but there are no sculptures of women. It is interesting, therefore, that this inscription, which mentions the dedication of a statue of a woman—the word "statue" is masculine (*sml*) when depicting a male, and feminine (*smlt*) when it represents a woman—was not found in the sanctuary of Aphrodite but in the ruins of a Byzantine church into which it had

---

175. *RPC* 89–91, pl. 7:1–2; E. Lipiński, *Itineraria Phoenicia* (Studia Phoenicia 18; Louvain: Peeters, 2004) 55–56.

176. P. H. Young, "The Cypriot Aphrodite Cult: Paphos, Rantidi, and Saint Barnabas," *JNES* 64 (2005) 23–44, esp. p. 27.

177. *Kition* 3.149–60 #D21; H. W. Attridge and R. A. Oden, trans., *The Syrian Goddess (De Dea Syria) Attributed to Lucian* (Texts and Translations 9; Missoula, MT: Scholars Press, 1976) #6, pp. 13–14; *RPC* 81–86, pl. 1:3.

178. The word *mḥlpt*, "locks of hair," occurs only here in Phoenician, but twice in Biblical Hebrew (Judg 16:13, 19), where Samson surrenders his hair to Delilah, his own personal Aphrodite.

179. V. Wilson, "The Kouklia Sanctuary," *RDAC* (1974) 139–46, pl. 21, esp. pp. 140–43; F. G. Maier, "History from the Earth: The Kingdom of Paphos in the Achaemenid Period," *Transeu* 12 (1996) 121–37, pls. 11–20, esp. pp. 127–28.

been incorporated,[180] and which, as often happened, may have been built on the site of a sanctuary (*mqdš*) of Astarte, quite separate and at some distance from the Temple of Aphrodite.

The sanctuary of Astarte of Paphos was the most conspicuous sign of the presence of Phoenicians in the city, who probably lived in a separate quarter around it where, as Tyrians usually preferred, they could keep apart from the indigenous Cypriot population with whom otherwise they continued to have very close cultural and commercial connections. But it is also these Tyrians who were responsible for the Egyptian and Egyptianizing features of the Cypriot sculptures, some of which witness to a brisk trade with Naucratis, for the idea of erecting votive steles in a temple, for the image of the Striding and Smiting God represented on some of them, for the *naiskoi* that were modeled on the Woman-at-the-Window and featured the Goddess in the central niche, for the numerous incense altars, and for the ashlar-block construction of some of the public buildings. Palaepaphos had a good harbor[181] and was pivotal for the Phoenicians, Tyrians, and colonists, on their voyages to the colonies, but it was a Cypriot city that would soon abandon old Levantine for new Greek ways.

Sites in north and northwest Cyprus, with the exception of Lapethos, manifest a similar predominance of Cypriot culture, with only traces or reminiscences of Phoenician presence. Marion,[182] about 35 kilometers overland to the north of Palaepaphos, is notable for the large number of terra-cottas found in its open-air sanctuary and on a nearby plateau. There are some Phoenician names, but they are written in Cypriot script, and the pottery is marked, if at all, by Cypro-Syllabic signs.[183] Egyptian faience objects are perhaps the result of Phoenician trade, but they are very scarce, and peculiarly Phoenician articles such as incense stands, mushroom-lipped juglets, and statuettes of naked women are extremely rare.[184] The terra-cottas[185] portray Cypriot themes: some horses and riders, or men wearing tall pointed caps or helmets perhaps inspired by Assyrian military garb, a few women fully clothed, and many women praying with upraised arms.

Ayia Irini, similarly, is characterized by its thousands of terra-cottas, life-size and smaller, but these mostly portray soldiers belonging, to judge from their distinctive types of weapons and armament, to different branches of

---

180. *RPC* 81.

181. R. L. Hohlfelder, "Ancient Paphos beneath the Sea: A Survey of the Submerged Structures," in *Proceedings of the International Symposium "Cyprus and the Sea"* (ed. V. Karageorghis and D. Micaelides; Nicosia: Department of Antiquities, 1995) 191–208.

182. W. A. P. Childs, "The Iron Age Kingdom of Marion," *BASOR* 308 (1997) 37–48.

183. T. B. Mitford, "Unpublished Syllabic Inscriptions of the Cyprus Museum," *Opuscula Atheniensia* 3 (1960) 177–210, esp. pp. 184–85. J. S. Smith, "Preliminary Comments on a Rural Cypro-Archaic Sanctuary in Polis-Peristeries," *BASOR* 308 (1997) 77–98, esp. pp. 80–81.

184. Childs, "The Iron Age Kingdom of Marion," 40; Smith, "Preliminary Comments on a Rural Cypro-Archaic Sanctuary in Polis-Peristeries," 80, fig. 3.

185. N. Serwint, "The Terracotta Sculpture from Marion," in *Cypriote Terracottas* (ed F. Vandenabeele and R. Laffineur; Brussels: Vrije Universiteit Brussel / Liège: Université de Liège, 1991) 213–19, pls. 52–57; idem, "The Terracotta Sculpture from Ancient Marion: Recent Discoveries," in *Acta Cypria: Acts of an International Congress on Cypriote Archaeology held in Göteborg on 22–24 August 1991—Part 3* (ed. P. Åström; Jonsered: Åström, 1992) 382–426.

the military.[186] From Liveras, just west of Lapethos on the north coast of Cyprus, there is a late sixth-century Phoenician inscription on a sherd from a transport amphora, originating perhaps in Lapethos, that reads "belonging to Timay" (*ltmy*), a simple transliteration of the Cypriot Greek name *Timaios*.[187] Lapethos itself was a Cypro-Phoenician town, the kings of which had Greek or Phoenician names, and the terra-cottas of which (all portrayals of women in ritual settings) are from different ateliers working with Phoenician or Cypriot styles and techniques on Phoenician, Egyptianizing, or local Cypro-Phoenician subjects.[188]

Southeastern Cyprus

Southeastern Cyprus maintained its specifically Phoenician character throughout the sixth century. Kition, because of being a Sidonian trading post and an amphictyonic center for the Cypriot kingdoms, was dominated by settlers and administrators from the Tyrian mainland in the sixth century. The kingdoms of Idalion and Tamassos, the aristocracy of which included traders and craftsmen from Sidon and Byblos, were independent until absorbed into the Kingdom of Kition in the fifth and fourth centuries. Salamis, apart from a few Phoenician adventurers, was a Cypriot and Greek establishment. Scattered evidence from other towns, such as Golgoi, Ledra, and Arsos, suggests a regular *va et vient* between these Phoenician enclaves and their neighbors.

Tamassos, in the center of Cyprus, about 20 kilometers west of Idalion and southwest of Ledra and 40 kilometers northwest of Kition, was at the heart of the copper-mining region.[189] It was walled and fortified in the sixth century and graced by intramural and extramural temples and their associated metal (copper, tin, and gold) and glass workshops.[190] The royal tombs were built of hewn stones and roofed with inclined stone slabs resting against each other at their summit but, although located underground at the end of a steep passageway, they were constructed to resemble the wood-finished palaces of the kings. The entrance had proto-Aeolic capitals, the side walls had false doors, there were false windows above the real doors, and below these windows was a frieze featuring "Tree-of-Life" ornamentation, and the roof slabs were carved to look like logs. Their eclectic style (the false wood finish was Anatolian, the false doors were Egyptian, and the capitals and ornamentation were Phoenician) betrays the cultural mix of

---

186. J. Breton Connelly, "Standing before One's God: Votive Sculpture and the Cypriot Religious Tradition," *BA* (December 1989) 210–15, 218.

187. *RPC* 96–97. The inscription was published upside down (pl. 10:1) and read backwards and could not be deciphered. Right-side up, the reading is obvious.

188. Lipiński, *Itineraria Phoenicia*, 81–87; M. Yon and A. Caubet, "Un culte populaire de la grande déesse à Lapithos," *RDAC* (1988) 1–16, pls. 1–4.

189. G. R. H. Wright, *Ancient Building in Cyprus, Part One: Text* (Leiden: Brill, 1992) 121–27, esp. p. 121; U. Zwicker, "Kupfer aus Tamassos," in *Periplus: Festschrift für Hans-Günther Buchholz zu seinem achtzigsten Geburtstag am 24. Dezember 1999* (ed. P. Åström and D. Sürenhagen; Jonsered: Åströms, 2000) 195–99, pl. 59, esp. p. 195.

190. H.-G. Buchholz, "Der Beitrag der Ausgrabungen von Tamassos zur antiken Baugeschichte Zyperns," in *Archaeology in Cyprus 1960–1985* (ed. V. Karageorghis; Nicosia: A. G. Leventis Foundation, 1985) 238–55, esp. pp. 241–43; Wright, *Ancient Building in Cyprus, Part One: Text*, 123.

the kingdom and the finesse of the royal house,[191] which are also illustrated in the fabulous and varied contents of the tombs.

Phoenician influence is witnessed directly in characteristic artifacts and indirectly in the goods that they imported and distributed through their network of dealerships. An inscription on an amphora with the personal name "Adonimilk" (*l'dnmlk*) suggests that the proprietor of the pot, whose provenance is unknown, and producer of its contents hailed originally from Byblos.[192] Similarly, two bronze statuettes from the third quarter of the sixth century[193] are Cypriot adaptations of traditional Phoenician iconography: one is of a man striding, his left foot forward, his left arm by his side, his right arm bent with the palm of his hand turned upward and toward his face; the other is like it except that it is smaller, and the right arm is bent across his chest. Near the exterior wall of one of the royal tombs, and presumably part of the original construction, there were two sets of life-size guardian statues, a pair of sphinxes, and two pairs of lions, whose Egyptian style tells the continuing story of Phoenician involvement in Cyprus's international relations in the sixth century.[194] Details of the story also appear in the small articles buried with the dead in the same necropolis:[195] imported alabaster, faience amulets, a shield of Cypriot type with Egyptian ornamentation consisting of two rows of lotus blossoms enclosing a row of Hathor busts, a faience cylinder for kohl eye makeup, a Greek Black Figure drinking cup, and a Rhodian scaraboid in a Cypriot gold setting. The Phoenicians, clearly, had become part of the history of Tamassos in the sixth century.   .

Idalion too was a Cypriot city. Phoenicians had fitted into the metropolitan fabric and by the sixth century had become leaders in the business and religious community, but they were a distinct minority blended into an indigenous culture. There are three Cypro-Syllabic inscriptions and three Phoenician inscriptions that provide some perspective on this situation.

The most interesting of the Cypriot inscriptions is on a bronze plaque recording the compensation paid to the doctors who tended the wounded during the siege of the city by Kition and the Persians.[196] The plaque was placed in the Temple of "Athena of Idalion"; the compensation was paid by "the king and the city"; everyone mentioned is Cypriot and a proud nationalist (the eponym, Philokypros, the son of Onasagoras, to whose term the siege is dated; the king, Stasikypros, a newcomer to the throne; and the doctors, Onasilos and his brothers, the sons of Onasikypros); the compensation to the family is a choice of money (one talent of silver) or tax-free property from the royal holdings, and in addition, Onasilos receives money calculated according to the Idalion standard. There are in fact coins of this king that feature a sphinx, or the head of Aphrodite, on the obverse and a lotus flower on the reverse, the Aphrodite option being an innova-

191. Buchholz, "Der Beitrag der Ausgrabungen von Tamassos zur antiken Baugeschichte Zyperns," 243; Wright, *Ancient Building in Cyprus, Part One: Text*, 125–26.
192. *RPC* 131–32, pl. 20:2.
193. O. Masson, "Deux statuettes de bronze de Tamassos," *BCH* 92 (1968) Part 2, 402–9.
194. E. Hirscher, "Archaeology in Cyprus," *AJA* 102 (1998) 330–31.
195. H.-G. Buchholz, "Ägyptisierendes aus Tamassos," *RDAC* (1993) 195–206, pls. 54–55.
196. *ICS* 234–35 #217.

tion, whereas the sphinx and the lotus had been introduced earlier in the sixth century and continued until Idalion was absorbed by Kition in the mid-fifth century.[197] The plaque, taken by itself, suggests that Idalion was uniquely and resolutely Cypriot, and it offers interesting insights into the society, government, and religion of the city, but the Egyptianizing motifs of the coinage reveal significant Phoenician participation in its trade and commerce.

Another Cypro-Syllabic inscription, on an indeterminate bronze object, probably a scepter, mace, or handle, also mentions "Athena who is in Idalion" and is a dedication by a king whose abbreviated name is also found on a pre-Stasikypros coin series.[198] The third sixth-century Cypriot inscription is on a silver libation ladle, which reads: "Ammus dedicated [it] to the Goddess of Golgoi."[199] The Goddess is Aphrodite, and relations with Golgoi in the near vicinity of Idalion are not surprising. The etymology of the suppliant's name is uncertain, but the probabilities are Phoenician: from the root ꜥ*m*, "kinsman, folk," for instance, with a Greek-Cypriot ending; or a hypocoristic name (emphasizing its verbal force by deleting its divine component) from ꜥ*ms*, "carry, sustain,"[200] or from ꜥ*mṣ*, "be strong, prevail."

The few Phoenician inscriptions associated with Idalion reinforce the impression that this segment of the population specialized in trade and commerce. There is the name "Return, O Baꜥal" (*šbꜥl*), painted in black letters on a Phoenician transport amphora found at Golgoi.[201] Its provenance helps confirm the connection between Idalion and this town, which may in fact have belonged to the kingdom.[202] Another transport amphora, found at Idalion, has the personal name "Kalbon" (*klbn*), derived from the root meaning "dog," a word regularly used to imply submission to a potentate or a God: the name is followed by the letter ʾ*alep*, which is written again below the name and is an abbreviation for the contents of the jar (ʾ*kl*, "food, cereal, game") or their quality (ʾ*addir*, "special") or perhaps just their origin (ʾ*dyl*, "Idalion").[203] The third inscription is painted on the wall of a funerary urn and seems to be a personal name, perhaps "Maꜥîk," comparable to the name "Maꜥôk" borne by the father of Achish, the Philistine king of Gath (1 Sam 27:2), and so either Anatolian or Greek.[204]

The last inscription is a name painted in a cursive script on the underside of a Cypriot Bichrome footed bowl.[205] Ceramic typology ("Bichrome IV") has suggested a date for the bowl in the seventh century, but the script looks later than this and would fit easily in the early sixth century. The

---

197. Ibid., 250–52 #227.

198. Ibid., 245 #218; 251 #227.

199. Ibid., 245–46 #219.

200. The personal name ꜥ*ms* ("Amos") occurs in the sixth century on a large, two-handled container from Kition (*Kition* 3.140–41 #D13, pl. 19:2).

201. *RPC* 113–14, pl. 14:3–4.

202. Lipiński, *Itineraria Phoenicia*, 59–60.

203. The letter ʾ*alep* is also written on a sixth-century transport amphora from Kition: É. Puech, "Remarques sur quelques inscriptions phéniciennes de Chypre," *Sem* 29 (1979) 19–43, esp. pp. 36–37.

204. *RPC* 111–12, pl. 13:1.

205. Ibid., 112–13, pl. 14:1–2.

name has been read in a variety of ways but seems to be "Pugmon" (*pgmn*), a form of the name "Pygmalion" (= *pgm* + *alion*), in which the root *pgm*, as in "Pygmy," is modified by the Phoenician agentive ending *-on*. The root name, of course, and its familiar form are Greek, but Phoenicians knew exactly how to rewrite it as Phoenician and how to find an appropriate etymology for the name that they, and perhaps the Greeks with them, gave to the Egyptian God Bes, who dominated the iconography and religion of Phoenician Cyprus in the seventh and sixth centuries.

The pro-Persian siege of Idalion directed by the Phoenicians of Tyrian origin in Kition could not cope with the huge fortifications that were built toward the end of the sixth century,[206] and so the siege was abandoned. These fortifications enclosed the royal acropolis, as well as the temples of the Gods and Goddesses (Apollo and Adonis, Athena and Astarte).[207] These can be appreciated mainly through the hundreds of statues and statuettes, some made in local workshops and some brought from other towns, and other offerings, dedicated to them. One votive offering of an Astarte figurine (the Goddess is naked and offers her breasts) is Phoenician, specifically "Syrian" or Sidonian.[208] It is almost anomalous—there are very few other terra-cotta Goddesses in the same chubby and softly rounded style—in an otherwise thoroughly Cypriot environment.

The Cypriot terra-cottas may have begun earlier but abound in the sixth century, represent a variety of subjects in a mixed population, and are the products of numerous distinct workshops.[209] Many of the figures are of men, horsemen, or chariots, but women have their place: women carrying a child or water carriers with an amphora on their heads. Early sixth-century examples feature model sanctuaries, female musicians, or women bearing offerings, giving birth, or seated with a child.[210] Idalion was at the crossroads leading to Kition in the south and to Salamis in the east and became prosperous as the clearinghouse in the copper industry centered on Tamassos.[211] It resisted the siege but belonged to Kition by the mid-fifth century and became the basis of economic growth and the source of respectability of this upstart kingdom.[212]

---

206. P. Gaber, "The History of Idalion: A History of Interaction," in *Visitors, Immigrants and Invaders in Cyprus* (ed. P. W. Wallace; Albany: State University of New York—Institute of Cypriot Studies, 1995) 32–39, esp. p. 33.

207. Ibid., 38; O. Masson, "Le sanctuaire d'Apollon à Idalion (fouilles 1868–1869)," *BCH* 92 (1968) part 2, 386–402; R. Senff, *Das Apollonheiligtum und Statuenausstattung eines zyprischen Heiligtums* (Studies in Mediterranean Archaeology 94; Jonsered: Åströms, 1993).

208. A. M. Bisi, "Una nuova figurina inedita dell'Astarte Siriana rinvenuta a Cipro," *AION* 31 (1971) 105–10, pl. I.

209. P. Gaber-Saletan, *Regional Styles in Cypriote Sculpture: The Sculpture from Idalion* (New York: Garland, 1986); A. Caubet, "The Terracotta Workshops of Idalion during the Cypro-Archaic Period," in *Acta Cypria: Acts of an International Congress on Cypriote Archaeology held in Göteborg on 22–24 August 1991, Part 3* (ed. P. Åström; Jonsered: Åströms, 1992) 128–51.

210. Ibid., 131–32.

211. Gaber, "The History of Idalion: A History of Interaction," 32–33.

212. A. Hermary, "Le statut de Kition avant le Ve s. av. J.-C.," in *Alle soglie della Classicità: Il Mediterraneo tra tradizione e innovazione. Studi in onore di Sabatino Moscati*, vol. 1: *Storia e Cultura* (ed. E. Acquaro; Pisa: Istituti Editoriali e Poligrafici Internazionali, 1996) 223–29.

Kition was not among the federation of Cypriot kingdoms, and even in the sixth century it was not under monarchic rule.[213] There was, however, civic organization and clear religious identity. Because the dominant group seems to have come from Tyre or the Tyrian mainland, the town may have been under a system of magistrates like that at Tyre in mid-century. But because Kition had always been independent, and because its population also included many Cypriots and Greeks, it was not a colony administered by a governor appointed by Tyre. On the contrary, its quasi-republican form of government encouraged private enterprise, and early in the century Tyrian merchants and mercenaries from Kition were circulating in the region of Arad in southern Judah.[214] One of them, "Malko᾿ the Kitian" (*mlk᾿ kt[y]*), appears in a legal decision determining ownership of the property and presidency of a *marzeaḥ*, or club of merchants, in this area.[215] Kition's religious identity is characterized by its Tyrian eclecticism. The Tyrians at Arad, for instance, were glad enough to worship the Edomite God Qos, not least because Edomites and Kitians had economic and military interests in the region.[216] Similarly, there was a temple at the western edge of Kition near the port that was refurbished toward the end of the sixth century,[217] and which two inscriptions identify as the Temple of Astarte, but the site is bursting with Hathor figurines and with steles topped by the bust of Hathor supporting a small shrine,[218] which implies that Astarte could be pictured in Kition, among the sophisticated at least, in the guise of Hathor who, like Astarte, was venerated as "the Queen of Heaven."

Although there are statuettes of Melqart and of Ptah and Bes, most of the sixth-century figurines and terra-cottas represent women.[219] Unlike the citizens of Idalion, Amathus, or Salamis, the people of Kition did not appreciate terra-cottas representing scenes of daily life, dogs and cats, or boats, warriors, horses, and chariots. Their artistic inspiration is mainland but not specifically Tyrian—that is, not sophisticated or Egyptianizing but, like the sixth-century painted pottery,[220] local, clumsy, and common. The women express maternal instincts or religious sentiment. There are many terra-cottas of pregnant women, the type known as Dea Tyria Gravida, but

---

213. Ibid.

214. M. Heltzer, "Kition according to the Biblical Prophets and Hebrew Ostraca from Arad," *RDAC* (1988) part 1, 167–72; P.-E. Dion, "Les *ktym* de Tel Arad: Grecs ou Phéniciens?" *RB* 99 (1992) 70–97.

215. P. Bordreuil and D. Pardee, "Le papyrus du marzeah," *Sem* 38 (1990) 49–68; idem, "Epigraphie moabitique: Nouvel examen du 'papyrus du marzeah,'" *Sem* 50 (2000) 224–26.

216. F. M. Cross, "Two Offering Dishes with Phoenician Inscriptions from the Sanctuary of ʿArad," *BASOR* 235 (1979) 75–78. The dishes are inscribed *qš* which is the Kitian spelling of *qs*, the name of the national God of Edom.

217. M. Yon, "Mission archéologique française de Kition-Bamboula 1976–1984," in *Archaeology in Cyprus, 1960–1985* (ed. V. Karageorghis; Nicosia: A. G. Leventis Foundation, 1985) 219–26, esp. p. 221.

218. A. Caubet and M. Pic, "Un culte hathorique à Kition-Bamboula," *Archéologie au Levant: Recueil à la Mémoire de Roger Saidah* (Lyon: Maison de l'Orient, 1982) 237–49.

219. S. Sophocleous, *Atlas des Représentations Chypro-Archaïques des Divinités* (Gothenberg: Åströms, 1985) 28–56; M. Yon and A. Caubet, "Ateliers de figurines à Kition," in *Cyprus and the East Mediterranean in the Iron Age* (ed. V. Tatton-Brown; London: British Museum, 1989) 28–43.

220. V. Karageorghis and J. des Gagniers, *La céramique chypriote de style figuré: Âge du Fer (1050–500 av. J.C.)—Texte* (Rome: Consiglio Nazionale delle Ricerche, 1974) 104–6.

unlike the mainland examples the woman lacks mystical gravity and sometimes is not only pregnant but carries a baby in her arms. There are statuettes of women and children and women with their hands on their breasts
(the gesture is the thing; their breasts are not depicted) and women who are
completely naked. Musicians, who would have performed at the festivals,
wear long robes and hold a tambourine, while other women carry offerings such as a bowl, a loaf of bread, or a cake, a bird or a small animal or,
as in a procession, a lamp on their heads. The terra-cottas do not antedate
the sixth century and probably were made by and for people who fled the
turmoil clattering through the mainland settlements around the time of
the siege of Tyre.

There are Phoenician inscriptions from Kition that identify personal belongings or are the residue of commerce, some that may reflect contact
with North African Carthage, and an ostracon inscribed on both sides that
records offerings to the Gods and payments to various personnel and incidentally describes rituals in the temple. Two fragmentary inscriptions contain personal names that are known in Egypt and Carthage but are very
unusual in the East,[221] and another is part of a vow formula that is familiar
from the Western colonies.[222] The inscriptions written on personal effects
are personal names: on a bowl, on an alabaster jar, and on a fragment
of a marble monument.[223] The commercial items are transport amphorae
inscribed with the name of the merchant, or with his name and an indication of the contents of the jar.[224] There are ostraca with lists of names and
patronymics, or names and occupations, and one ostracon with a personal
name and place of origin, "ʿAbdsakkun from ʿAkko."[225] These inscriptions
open a small window onto life in Phoenician Kition and its relations with
mainland towns, with Egypt, and especially with Carthage.

The Kition tariffs list expenses, in varying small amounts, for the months
ʾEtanim in the fall and Paʿulot in the early spring, around 525 B.C.E.[226] They

---

221. One reads "belonging to Magon son of G[. . . .]" (*lmgn bn g*[ ]): M. Heltzer, "A New Fragment of a Phoenician Tomb-Inscription from Mnemata (Larnaca-Kition)," *RDAC* (1989) 93–94.
The name *Mgn* is very common in Carthage, beginning in the sixth century, and from there
found its way back to the East. The other inscription has the personal name "[ʿAbd]paʿam" ([ʿbd]
pʿm) followed by an *ankh* sign: J.-F. Salles, *Kition-Bamboula II: Les égouts de la ville classique* (Paris:
Éditions Recherches sur les Civilisations, 1983) 104–6 #374. The divine name Paʿam, a transliteration of Greek *Pygm-*, occurs in the sixth century at Abu Simbel in Egypt and later in Carthage.

222. *RPC* 118, pl. 16:2.

223. *Kition* 3.167–68 #D34, pl. 23:5 (*lmlqrtmpls*); 133–34 #D5, pl. 20:3 (*klsy* . . .); 87–88 #B39
(*lʾhlbʿl*).

224. *Name of merchant: Kition* 3.139–40 #D12, pl. 19:1 ([*ly*]*tnbʿl*); 140–41 #D13, pl. 19:2
(*lʿms*); 162 #D25 pl. 22:2 (*ʾhlm*[*lk*]); 166 #D32, pl. 21:1, 3 (*mqnbʿl*); *RPC* 117–18, pl. 16:1 (*lʾbs*).

Merchant's name plus contents of jar: Kition 3.135–36 #D7, pl. 20:4 (*bʿly zyt*, "Baʿalay—Olives");
141–42 #D14 (*ḥ* | ʾ | *ṣdqʾ*, "Red Wine | Vintner's Choice | Ṣidqô": see É. Puech, "Remarques sur
quelques inscriptions phéniciennes de Chypre," *Sem* 29 (1979) 19–43, esp. pp. 36–37.

225. *Kition* 3.164–65 #D30, pl. 23:1; 148–49 #D20, pl. 18:5; 145–46 #D17, pl. 18:4 ([ʿbd]*skn*
ʿky).

226. B. Peckham, "Notes on a Fifth-Century Phoenician Inscription from Kition (CIS 86),"
Or 37 (1968) 304–24, pls. 49–50; *RPC* 21–68, pls. 4–5; J. P. Healey, "The Kition Tariffs and the
Phoenician Cursive Series," *BASOR* 216 (1974) 53–60; *Kition* 3.103–26 #C1; L. Manfredi, "Monete
e valori ponderali fenici a Kition," *RSO* 61 (1987) 81–87; R. R. Stieglitz, "The Phoenician-Punic
Menology," in *Boundaries of the Ancient Near Eastern World: A Tribute to Cyrus H. Gordon* (ed.
M. Lubetski, C. Gottlieb, and S. Keller; JSOTSup 273; Sheffield: Sheffield Academic Press, 1998)
211–21; idem, "The Phoenician-Punic Calendar," *Actas* 4, 2.691–95.

are written on either side of a 5″ × 7″ alabaster tablet, length-wise on one side and width-wise on the other. Each month begins with offerings to the God of the New Moon, continues with donations made to specified or named people who participated in the Festival of Astarte in the fall and in the Festival of the Waters in the spring,[227] and ends with payments to the permanent staff of the temple.

The Festival of Astarte

1. Expenses of the month ʾEtanim.
2. On the New Moon of the month ʾEtanim
3. for the God of the New Moon—2 *qpʾ*.
4. . . /// |
5. For the builders who built the house of Astarte of Kition—2 *qr*.
6. For the 20 marshals and persons who stood watch along the route—[ ]
7. For the singers from the city, attendants of the Holy Queen on this day [ ] *qpʾ*.
8. For the 2 boys—2 *qpʾ*.
9. For the 2 butchers—2 *qr*.
10. For the 2 bakers who baked a basket of cakes for the Queen
11. together with Parmen—3 *qr*.
12. For the 3 boys—3 *qpʾ*.
13. For the barbers who worked at the service—2 *qpʾ*.
14. For the 20 artisans who made the braziers of Adonis in the house of Mukol—[ ].
15. For ʿAbdʾeshmun, chief scribe, supervisor on this day—3 *qr* and 3 *qpʾ*.
16. For the dogs and puppies—2 *qr* and 2 *pʾ*.
17. [For . . . .] appointed on this day—2 *qr*.
18. [. . . . . .]

The entry on donations to the God of the New Moon is separated from the rest of the list of expenses by four lines, three oblique and one vertical. The Festival of Astarte of Kition that follows this entry included a procession, organized and directed by men and accompanied by male singers, to her house. This house, built for the occasion and associated with the Temple of Mukol, was a portable tabernacle or pavilion rather than a permanent structure, and it was carried in the procession before being erected in the courtyard of Mukol's Temple. The ritual included the preparation of sacrifice by two butchers and their assistants and the baking of cakes for her, the Queen of Heaven, by two bakers and their assistants and by a Greek cook called Parmen and his sous-chef. There were barbers present at the service, and the ritual also included offerings of hair in her honor. The numerous incense stands (it took 20 workmen to get them ready) suggest that burning of incense to Adonis, her lover, was an important part of the celebration. The remaining entries do not pertain to the festival but to the general upkeep of the temple: the chief scribe oversaw, among others, the junior scribe who wrote this tariff; the dogs and puppies were part of the healing ceremonies performed in the temple precinct in the

---

227. M. Yon, "Le maître de l'eau à Kition," *Archéologie au Levant: Recueilà la mémoire de Roger Saidah* (Lyon: Maison de l'Orient, 1982) 251–63; R. M. Good, "The Carthaginian *mayumas*," *SEL* 3 (1986) 99–113.

name of the God ʾEshmun; the person mentioned in the second-to-last line had some specific administrative function, and the last line may have mentioned another official.

Elements of this celebration (the baking of cakes with her image—naked, arms outstretched, legs akimbo—the offering of incense, the involvement of men in her rituals) are known from biblical texts describing public processions in Jerusalem and family festivities in her honor in the capital and other cities of Judah. In Kition, her festival was celebrated publicly in the Temple of Mukol, an archaic Canaanite God kept alive among the Greeks and retrieved from them at this late date by the Greco-Phoenicians of Kition. The water ritual, Phoenician *mym*, is known in Greek as *hydrophoria*, "Transport of Water," and this meaning was borrowed into the Punic of North African Carthage, where the Greek was simply translated and the festival was called *Mayyuʿmas* (*myʿms*), "Water-Is-Carried." [228] The Phoenician word, perhaps pronounced *mayyum, is derived from the root "waters" and may mean something like "Watering," but it does not include the notion of carrying. The Kition ritual was conducted by a "Lord (*baʿal*) of the Waters," whose title alludes to the God Baʿal, who was acknowledged as the Lord of the Storm and of the Sea, and who in fact may be the "God" who is mentioned (*ʾlm*) as the patron of the ritual. The Waters were, or flowed, around this God, as in a trench or channel, and a representative from Carthage, ʿAbdʾabastis, was part of the ceremony, while another participant called Adam, in his role as the representative of primordial man, had a special place beside the Waters. The ritual took place in the Temple of Mukol (Apollo among the Phoenicians) and of "the Sun" (š[*mš*]), with whom Mukol could be identified. There was incense, taken care of by the temple personnel, sacrifice of the animals that were supplied by shepherds under the supervision of ʿAplakad and by those under the supervision of another man whose name is lost, song by a maiden, and music played by twenty-two maidens with timbrels or tambourines, like the musicians represented among the terra-cottas.

The ritual reflects the enactment and abatement of the primordial Flood as told in the story of Deucalion, son of Prometheus. [229] The Flood, caused by incessant torrential rain, was designed by the Gods to eradicate the evil race who first populated the world, and the only survivors were the people and living things who sailed safely in the ark built by Deucalion, where the whole world found peace. The memorial of this salvation is the Festival of the Waters, which was celebrated in the temple built over the great chasm (great in the telling, small in the cultic details) caused by the Flood. The essence of the ritual consisted in pouring water from the sea into this crevice, commemorating at once the resurgence of the Flood and the disappearance of the waters. Deucalion, following the pattern of the worldwide Flood, offered sacrifice in thanksgiving for deliverance, and this custom persisted at Kition.

---

228. Ibid. The Carthaginian name of the festival is derived from *may, "water," plus *yuʿmas, "is carried," which is the passive of the causative stem of the root ʿms (p. 101).

229. H. W. Attridge and R. A. Oden, trans., *The Syrian Goddess (De Dea Syria) Attributed to Lucian* (Texts and Translations 9; Missoula, MT: Scholars Press, 1976) 19–21 ##12–13.

The Festival of the Waters

1. Statute of rewards.
2. On the New Moon of the month of Paʿulot
3. for the God of the New Moon—2 *qpʾ*.
4. For the Baʿal of the Waters encircling the God [   ].
5. For the temple personnel who were by the braziers of Mukol and Sh[amash].
6. For ʿAbdʾabastis the Carthaginian [   ].
7. For ʾAdam who took his place by the waters [   ] *qpʾ*.
8. For the shepherds who were under ʿAplakad—2 *qr*; who were under the [   ].
9. For the Maiden, and for the 22 maidens at the sacrifice [   ].
10. For the dogs and the puppies—3 *qr* and 3 *pʾ*.
11. For the 3 assistants—3 *qpʾ*.
12. [For the 2 . . . .]—2 *qpʾ*.

The disbursements to the participants in the Festival of the Waters are enclosed by normal monthly expenditures for the God of the New Moon, and for the puppies and dogs and their trainers. The festival itself in antiquity was associated with recitations and revelry, a feature of the Kition ritual, and the *Mayyuʿmas* was often connected with the *outré* partying of the *marzeaḥ*. If the record does reflect the convening of a club of this sort, the festival was appropriate to a company trading on the high seas, whose patron God was Baʿal, the God of the Weather, and whose company included ʿAbdʾabastis as its Carthaginian representative.

Kition was the Phoenician center of central and southeastern Cyprus. Cypriot and Greek elements were competitive, but they were not as prominent or independent as they became in the fourth century when, out of ethnic pride or because no ethnic group could understand the others, all the public inscriptions were trilingual. The Phoenician settlers emigrated from Tyre or its mainland holdings around the time of the siege of the city (or because of the intrusion of the Persians—one too many empires in less than a century), and their acquisitiveness and natural bent for adventure soon prompted them to infiltrate the kingdoms of Tamassos and Idalion. Bits and pieces of text and material put Kition in direct contact with Egypt and North African Carthage, as well as with southern Judah and Edom, and this foreign trade and the island wars invigorated Kition through the sixth and the fifth centuries.

The Western Mediterranean Becomes Increasingly Carthaginian

Phoenicians in Italy, Sicily, Sardinia, and Spain came increasingly under the the authority of Carthage in the sixth century, under the influence of the Western Greeks, and under the management of the indigenous peoples. Emigrants or refugees from the homelands kept arriving, and there were imports from Egypt and the East, but the spirit of the times, the ideas, attitudes, and aspirations were generated in the established world of the West. The thrill of discovery took shape in alliances and political organization, and adventure dwindled down to regional travel, military maneuvres, and naval battles. The fascination of the orientalizing revolution was dissolving into self-interest and routine.

Sicily

Sicily in the sixth century was mostly Greek—people who had settled first along the coast and now moved inland among the traditionally and culturally diverse Sicilians[230]—but the far west and northwest of the island belonged to the Phoenicians. This territorial division was sometimes disputed, and the friction was an easy excuse for Carthage, in the person of a loyal and ambitious general, to intervene on behalf of the peaceable settlers and in its own imperial interests.[231] The Phoenician towns, partly because of these North African incursions, but mainly because of normal political and demographic pressures, were easily drawn into the Carthaginian orbit.[232]

Palermo, on the north coast of Sicily, was settled in the seventh century, as some tombs might suggest, but the town was established in the early sixth.[233] It is situated on a promontory near the river Eleuthero and had easy access to the fertile farmland in the interior,[234] the settlers having come, most likely, to raise sheep, goats, and cattle and to grow food for themselves and for the growing population of Carthage. Their grave goods suggest,[235] and inscriptions from nearby Grotta Regina attest[236] that they were fourth- or fifth-generation Sidonians from Tharros in Sardinia, and it is not surprising, consequently, that they fit right in with the native population and with Greeks when they arrived. The town expanded in the sixth century, about the time that Solunto,[237] across the bay to the east, was settled by Carthaginians and by colonials from Sulcis in Sardinia.

The inscriptions from the Grotta Regina are later than the sixth century. They are graffiti incised and painted on the walls of the grotto by pilgrims, from Palermo perhaps and the other Phoenician towns in the northwest, and many of them are short blessings or curses. The blessings often invoke the genius Shadrapaʾ, the hypostasis of ʾEshmun, God of the Sidonians, and

---

230. D. Asheri, "Carthaginians and Greeks," in *The Cambridge Ancient History*, vol. 4: *Persia, Greece and the Western Mediterranean c. 525–479 B.C.* (ed. J. Boardman et al.; 2nd ed.; Cambridge: Cambridge University Press, 1988) 739–80; I. Morris, "Mediterraneanization," *MHR* 18 (2003) 30–55.

231. G. Falsone, "Sicile," *CPPMR*, 674–97; S. F. Bondì, "Nuove acquisizioni storiche e archeologiche sulla Sicilia fenicia e punica," *Actas* 4, 1.83–89.

232. M. H. Fantar, "Présence de la Sicile en Afrique Punique," *Kôkalos* 39–40 (1993–94) 211–20.

233. V. Tusa, "La presenza fenicio-punica in Sicilia," *PhWest*, 95–112, esp. pp. 99–100.

234. A. Spanò Giammellaro, "I Fenici in Sicilia: Modalità insediamentali e rapporti con l'entroterra: Problematiche e prospettive di ricerca," in *Fenicios y Territorio: Actas del II Seminario Internacional sobre Temas Fenicias, Guardamar del Segura, 9–11 de abril de 1999* (ed. A. González Prats; Alicante: Instituto Alicantino de Cultura, 2000) 295–335, esp. pp. 307–10.

235. W. Culican, "West Phoenician Luxury Items: Some Critical Notes," *HBA* 12 (1985) 119–45.

236. G. Coacci Polselli, M. G. Amadasi Guzzo, and V. Tusa, *Grotta Regina—II: Le iscrizioni puniche* (Rome: Consiglio Nazionale delle Ricerche, 1979); G. Pisano and A. Travaglini, *Le iscrizioni fenicie e puniche dipinte* (Studia Punica 13; Rome: Università degli Studi di Roma, "Tor Vergata," 2003) 135–53 ##Si 1–Si 65.

237. C. Greco, "La necropolis punica di Solnto," *Actas* 4, 3.1319–35.

suggest that at least some of the pilgrims were originally from this city, or from Sidonian ʿAmrit on the Syrian coast.

The grave goods are both Phoenician and Greek, and the Phoenician items are jewelry and amulets, the best parallels of which are from Tharros or from Carthage and other western sites where Carthaginians traveled. A gold earring in the shape of a crux ansata, for instance, is matched by similar earrings at Carthage and Ibiza. A silver ring with a double band from another tomb is matched by a dozen like it from tombs at Tharros. Similarly, there are silver bracelets, rings, and earrings with granulated gold droppers that have parallels at Tharros. There are also headbands or diadems that are the most characteristic of all Tharros jewelry. A child's burial dating to the end of the century contained 17 Egyptianizing amulets that have individual parallels at other Punic sites[238] but as a group are most like the finds at Tharros. Palermo, it would be simplest to suppose, was settled by families from Tharros who came to Sicily to develop the farmland, sold their produce to Carthage, and turned the land into large prosperous estates.

Motya, a small island at the far western tip of Sicily, did very well in the sixth century.[239] An open-air courtyard was added to the sanctuary,[240] and north of it a small industrial complex for making pottery, bricks, and purple dye was constructed.[241] A road was built across the lagoon to the necropolis at Birgi on the mainland, incidentally providing easier access to the new town at Eryx to the north. The dry dock was improved and, in the latter part of the century, a crude brick wall with evenly spaced towers was built around the island and the burnt-offering precinct, now inside the wall, was enlarged.[242] It was not so much a prosperous time as a progressively more busy time. The population increased; some of the newcomers were used to fancier clothing and developed the dye works, and there was a demand for housing and cheap domestic wares. The shipyard built, repaired, and outfitted warships for the Carthaginian navy and ships to transport local agricultural produce. The wall reflected the mood of the

238. C. A. Di Stefano, "Un corredo funerario tardo-arcaico dalla necropolis punica di Palermo," in *Da Pyrgi a Mozia: Studi sull'archeologia del Mediterraneo in Memoria di Antonia Ciasca* (ed. M. G. Amadasi Guzzo, M. Liverani, and P. Matthiae; Vicino Oriente—Quaderno 3/1; Rome: Università degli Studi di Roma, "La Sapienza," 2002) 189–99, pls. 1–2.

239. S. Moscati, "Il VI secolo a Mozia," *RSF* 22 (1994) 173–78.

240. V. Tusa, "Il santuario fenicio-punico di Mozia, ditto di 'Cappiddazzu,'" *Actas* 4, 3.1397–1417.

241. A. Spanò Giammellaro, "Strutture in mattoni crudi nelle aree 'industriali' di Mozia," in *Da Pyrgi a Mozia: Studi sull'archeologia del Mediterraneo in Memoria di Antonia Ciasca* (ed. M. G. Amadasi Guzzo, M. Liverani, and P. Matthiae; Vicino Oriente—Quaderno 3/2; Rome: Università degli Studi di Roma, "La Sapienza," 2002) 545–53, pls. 1–13; D. S. Reese, "Whale Bones and Shell Purple-Dye at Motya (Western Sicily, Italy)," *OJA* 24 (2005) 107–14.

242. A. Ciasca, "Mozia in Sicilia: Un esempio di cinta urbana in area coloniale fenicia," *Lixus* (Rome: École Française de Rome, 1992) 79–84; idem, "Il sistema fortificato di Mozia (Sicilia), *Actas* 3, 1.271–78; idem, "Techniche murarie e fortificazioni puniche in Sicilia," in *Fenicios y Territorio: Actas del II Seminario sobre Temas Fenicios, Guardamar del Segura, 9–11 de abril de 1999* (ed. A. González Prats; Alicante: Instituto Alicantino de Cultura, 2000) 57–70; M G. Amadasi Guzzo, "La documentazione epigrafica dal *tofet* di Mozia e il problema del sacrifiicio *molk*," in *Religio Phoenicia* (ed. C. Bonnet, E. Lipiński, and P. Marchetti; Studia Phoenicia 4; Namur: Société des Études Classiques, 1986) 189–207; A. Ciasca, "Mozia: Squardo d'insieme sul *Tofet*," *VO* 8 (1992) 113–55.

time, and rebuilding it every few years did something to assuage the fear that crept through an often-troubled century.

The pottery workshops operated under the auspices of household spirits who were represented by female *protomai* or busts, and the firing, often defective, was done in the furnaces in the industrial area.[243] The domestic pottery was ordinary, consisting of pots, pans, plates, cups, and jugs, but the workshops also produced the urns and amphorae that were used for burials in the sacrificial precinct. The sacrifices and burials were of babies up to six months of age or of immature lambs and goats, or both, but there was a variety of sacrificial offerings, including birds, fish, cattle, pigs, and deer,[244] all of them made by the men, not the women, and the fathers of the infants. The grave goods were chosen from the domestic pottery or from among the things the person wore, or occasionally were terra-cotta masks or protomai.[245] But, as in adult burials, even when these included jewelry, they were poor or unremarkable.[246] The grave stones, similarly, were unpretentious and showed people as they were or as they comported themselves in the sacrificial rites, or portrayed them in the chosen symbols of their spiritual regeneration.

Sicily was not a showcase of Phoenician wit and sophistication. The people lived in farming communities or trading stations or in shipyards and were characterized by dedication to hard work, skilled labor, satisfaction with life, and nonchalance in the face of a meaningful death. They got along with the native people and were unfazed by belligerent Greeks. They were thoroughly Western Phoenicians, proud to be included in an expanding Carthaginian Empire.

Sardinia

Sardinia, at least the towns and outposts in the south, particularly those that had Etruscan connections, came under the direct governance of Carthage in the time of Malkoʾ and the Magonids in the latter half of the sixth century.[247] Tharros maintained some independence and prestige, but Sulcis and its inland dependencies, such as Monte Sirai, became a Carthaginian province, were important mainly as the source of agricultural and mineral products, and declined. Nora and Bithia on the south coast began to thrive, and Cagliari became the administrative center or capital of the southern district. There were some Carthaginian settlements, such as Olbia in the northeast and Neapolis on the south shore of the Gulf of Oristano, opposite Tharros, and some of the farms north and west of Cagliari hired

243. C. Beer, "Two Female Terracotta Protomai from Motya, Area K (Campaign of 1991)," *Actas* 4, 3.1249–54; M. P. Toti, "Alcune considerazioni sulla produzione vascolare di officine dell'isola de Mozia (II)," in *Da Pyrgi a Mozia: Studi sull'archeologia del Mediterraneo in memoria di Antonia Ciasca* (ed. M. G. Amadasi Guzzo, M. Liverani, and P. Matthiae; Vicino Oriente—Quaderno 3/2; Rome: Università degli Studi di Roma, "La Sapienza," 2002) 555–65.

244. A. Ciasca et al., "Saggio preliminare sugli incinerati del Tofet di Mozia," *VO* 10 (1996) 317–46.

245. A. Ciasca and M. P. Toti, *Scavi a Mozia: Le terrecotte figurate* (Collezione di Studi Fenici 33; Rome: Consiglio Nazionale delle Ricerche, 1994).

246. V. Tusa, "La Sicilia fenicio-punica: Stato attuale delle ricerche e degli studi e prospettive per il futuro," *Atti* 1, 1.187–97, pls. 37–47, esp. pp. 189–90.

247. *PFPS* 63–97.

share-croppers from North Africa.[248] Sardinia was diverse and brilliant in its original Phoenician phases, but it was being organized into a functional and fortified imperial property[249] and began to slide slowly into a homogeneous and uniformly drab Carthaginian state.

Tharros, where there are no sixth-century architectural remains, is marked by the wealth of jewelry and imported luxury items left as grave goods.[250] Amulets are mostly Egyptianizing and imported from Carthage, although some indicate cultural relations with Greece, Sicily, Etruria, and Spain.[251] Green jasper seals, of which there are hundreds, some carved in Greek style, were made from the precious stone mined just southeast of Tharros and were a popular export to Carthage.[252] An Egyptianizing subset of these seals (three are green jasper, one cornelian, and one steatite) draws on old, Eastern, Phoenician tradition and portrays a kneeling, falcon-headed man with his arms outstretched in a gesture of adoration.[253] A rude, Hellenizing, but probably local adaptation of this figure is a terracotta plaque with a romping ithyphallic Silenus, left hand raised, and right hand on his hip as he kneels and whirls in his dance.[254]

Greek influence is also evident in designer ceramics, specifically Rhodian unguent bottles imported to Tharros from Naucratis via Cagliari, and in pots, or *askoi*, in the shape of animals and birds, which were particularly popular in the seventh century but were still appreciated in the sixth and later.[255] It appears that Tharros was still rich but slightly isolated in the sixth century. Cagliari and the south of the island were easily accessible by road through the Campidano Plain, and this town may have been the source of Etruscan, Greek, and Egyptian goods as long as they lasted. Sulcis was a forlorn competitor now dragooned into the Carthaginian swirl. Neapolis, the "New City" or Sardinian "Carthage" opposite Tharros on the Gulf of Oristano, was built by Carthage to control its exports, and the grand old town had to depend on its old friends in southern Spain and on their new neighbors on the east coast to remain competitive.

Sulcis, unlike Tharros where there are no sixth-century Phoenician inscriptions, has left a single inscribed signet ring[256] depicting a ritual scene: under a winged sun disk, but slightly above the other figures, Harpocrates,

---

248. S. F. Bondì, "Recenti studi e nuove prospettive sulla Sardegna fenicia e punica," *Actes 3*, 1.165–74, esp. p. 168.

249. P. Bartoloni, "Il controllo del territorio nella Sardegna fenicia e punica," in *Fenicios y Territorio: Actas del II Seminario Internacional sobre Temas Fenicias, Guardamar del Segura, 9–11 de abril de 1999* (ed. A. González Prats; Alicante: Instituto Alicantino de Cultura, 2000) 47–56.

250. *Tharros* 41.

251. Ibid., 108–17.

252. S. Moscati and A. M. Costa, "L'origine degli scarabei in diaspro," *RSF* 10 (1982) 203–10.

253. G. Savio, "Sigilli punici di Sardegna," *AION* 59 (1999) 386–92, pl. 1.

254. L. I. Manfredi, "Terracotte puniche di Sardegna," *AION* 49 (1989) 1–7, pls. 1–2, esp. pp. 4–7, pl. 2b.

255. M. L. Uberti, "Ceramica Greco-orientale da Tharros nel Museo Nazionale Archeologico di Cagliari," *OrAnt* 20 (1981) 295–304, pls. 26–33; M. Medde, "*Askoi* zoomorfi dalla Sardegna," *Rivista di Studi Punici* 1 (2000) 157–87.

256. *WSS* 273 #733. There is an eighth-century Phoenician seal from Tharros inscribed ʿḥr (*WSS* 277 #745). The text is a transcription of the Egyptian title "Horus is Great": Y. Muchiki, *Egyptian Proper Names and Loanwords in North-West Semitic* (SBLDS 173; Atlanta: Society for Biblical Literature, 1999) 31–32.

the child Horus, sits on a lotus flower, facing an animal-headed Goddess in a long robe; to the left of the standard supporting the lotus flower is falcon-headed Horus wearing the double crown of Egypt, and behind him is Sekhmet, the source of sickness and death; to the right of the standard, opposite Sekhmet, stands Isis, the mother of Harpocrates and embodiment of the royal throne, wearing the horned-disk crown. This ritual scene is an indulgent, mystical interpretation of the Phoenician names that appear below it in a separate register, "Ger'eshmun, son of Himilk" (*gr'šmn bn ḥmlk*), because the son's name, "Client-of-'Eshmun," evokes 'Eshmun, the God of Healing, and his father's name means "The Divine King Is My Kinsman." Both names are otherwise unknown at Sulcis but are well established in the Carthaginian onomasticon, and the ritual scene is isolated in the iconographic evidence from Sulcis.

The owner of the ring , it seems clear, was not from Sulcis but was probably from Carthage—the Carthaginian tax collector, trade representative, or ambassador to the city and the southern province. His likeness, in fact, may be preserved in a statue from Sulcis,[257] of which only the head remains, which portrays an elegant young man with a straight nose, thin lips slightly parted in a smile, a small painted beard, oval eyes accentuated by mascara, his hair in tight curls tufted by a head band. There is nothing quite like it in the Punic repertory, and if it is not his true likeness, his Egyptian demeanor suggests that it may be a picture of the young man as the ideal sixth-century Carthaginian.

There are hundreds of tombstones from Sulcis dating between the sixth and the second century B.C.E.—some of the earlier with Egyptian precursors, the later sometimes copying Carthaginian developments.[258] Many of the steles have niches or aedicules that, borrowing an Egyptian idea, represent the eternal dwelling, the *bêt'ôlam*, of the deceased, in which they are depicted realistically, ideally, or symbolically. Men stand and face out or are shown in profile: a popular model has a man striding, his right arm by his side, his left arm with clenched fist across his bare chest, wearing a short Egyptian-style kilt.[259] Women also liked this model and were shown wearing a long robe with a stole over their left shoulder held by their left hand, while their right arm hung by their side and held an *ankh* or symbol of life. But they also appreciated the more traditional image in which they held a tambourine or a bouquet of lotus flowers and papyrus stalks to their breast.

There were also abstract or symbolic representations in which the niche is empty or filled by a baetyl or house of God (*bêt 'el*) or, especially in later examples, by a lamb or another animal *passant*, the animal of their burial sacrifice represented alive. The tombstones were found alongside cremation burials in cinerary urns, but those with niches or aedicules allude to the eternal dwelling of the inhumed dead, who actually rested in bicameral

---

257. Manfredi, "Terracotte puniche di Sardegna," 2–4, pls. 1, 2a.

258. S. Moscati, "Centri artigianali fenici in Italia," *RSF* 1 (1973) 37–52, pls. 12–31, esp. pp. 46–48; idem, *Sardegna Punica* (Milan: Rusconi, 1986) 240–62, pls. 34–39; idem, *Le Stele di Sulcis: Caratteri e Confronti* (Rome: Consiglio Nazionale delle Ricerche, 1986) 88–90.

259. G. Falsone, "Da Nimrud a Mozia: Un tipo statuario di stele fenicio egittizzante," *UF* 21 (1989) 153–93, esp. pp. 170–72.

hypogaea, or underground two-room houses that were reached by a vertical shaft or through a stepped corridor. All things Egyptian, apparently, were pleasing to the stylish sixth-century Phoenicians of Carthage and Sulcis.

In the Sulcis region in southwestern Sardinia, there are a few coastal hamlets and numerous inland settlements between them and the Gulf of Cagliari. These were situated on roadways and waterways and have been identified as forts,[260] somehow connected with Carthaginian invasions under Malko' and the Magonids or with their attempt to militarize the region against some (unidentifiable) enemy. But they probably reflect the political and economic reorganization of its territories, this perhaps being the real contribution of these envoys from Carthage, when Sulcis began to cater exclusively to Carthaginian interests.

At Monte Sirai, the main administrative building was presumed to have been destroyed in one of these raids,[261] but in fact it seems that it was just torn down and rebuilt to handle a provincial and increasingly centralized agricultural program. Other effects of these closer ties between Monte Sirai and the North African capital include: home improvements; a change in burial practices, with inhumation replacing cremation; and iconography, in which a woman can be portrayed on a tombstone with the symbolism of the Carthaginian Goddess Tannit—her head a featureless orb, her body an inverted pyramid, her arms bent to support her breasts but resembling a horizontal bar between her head and her body—the whole woman in effect represented as the stylized and easy-to-scribble "Sign of Tannit."[262]

Towns and commercial outposts around the Gulf of Cagliari were caught up in Carthaginian politics. Cucureddus di Villasimius, a trading post at the mouth of the Rio Foxi on the eastern shore of the gulf, burned and was abandoned. Its destruction has been blamed on Carthage, but this is unlikely because its easy access to the interior along this river and its commercial ties with Tharros would have given it strategic importance in the Carthaginian province.[263] Cucureddus was also a trade link between southern Sardinia and Etruria,[264] a venture that Carthage promoted but a business that the Phocaeans envied. It was undoubtedly Phocaean pirates

260. M. Gharbi, "La forteresse punique et son territoire: Réflexion sur la présence punique en Sardaigne et en Tunisie," *Actes* 3, 2.71–82; F. Barreca, "The Phoenician and Punic Civilization in Sardinia," in *Studies in Sardinian Archaeology, II: Sardinia in the Mediterranean* (ed. M. Balmuth; Ann Arbor: University of Michigan Press, 1986) 145–70, esp. pp. 154–55.

261. P. Bartoloni, "Le relazioni tra Cartagine e la Sardegna nei secoli VII e VI a.C.," *EVO* 10 (1987) 79–86, esp. p. 82.

262. C. Perra, "Monte Sirai: Gli scavi nell'abitato 1996–1998," *RSF* 29 (2001) 121–30, pls. 3–6; P. Bartoloni, "Scavi nelle necropoli di Monte Sirai," *Da Pyrgi a Mozia: Studi sull'Archeologic nel Mediterraneo in Memoria di Antonia Ciasca* (ed. M. G. Amadasi Guzzo, M. Liverani, and P. Matthiae; Vicino Oriente—Quaderno 3/1; Rome: Università degli Studi di Roma, "La Sapienza," 2002) 69–77; Moscati, "Centri artigianali fenici in Italia," pls. 12–31, pls. 13a, 13b, and 26b.

263. Bartoloni, "Le relazioni tra Cartagine e la Sardegna nei secoli VII e VI a.C.," 82; L. A. Marras,"Su alcuni ritrovamenti fenici nel Golfo di Cagliari," *RSF* 11 (1983) 159–65, pl. 30; idem, "I Fenici nel Golfo di Cagliari: Cucureddus di Villasimius," *Atti* 2, 3.1039–48.

264. L. Marras, P. Bartoloni, and S. Moscati, *Cucureddus* (ANLR 8/42, fasc. 7–12; Rome: Accademia Nazionale dei Lincei, 1987) 225–48, pls. 1–3.

that destroyed the station, thereby provoking retaliation by Carthage and the Etruscans at the battle of Alalia in 538 B.C.E.[265]

These Phocaeans may also have been responsible for the attack on Cagliari. This town, called Karalay (*krly*) in Phoenician and Punic, was founded at the beginning of the sixth century, at the same time as Cuccureddus. Its population was from Sulcis with some admixture of immigrants from Carthage. One of them wòre an amulet with an engraving of a horse, the traditional emblem of the God who protects against snake bite, which is inscribed appropriately enough "Pass on, Poison" ('*br* | *lḥ*).[266] The Phocaean attack took place around mid-century, and with the sack of Cuccureddus, it was one of the events that persuaded Carthage, whose Sardinian headquarters were at Cagliari, to keep the pirates out of Sardinian waters.

Nora and Bithia, west of the gulf on the south coast of Sardinia were Phoenician and native Nuraghic and held no special interest for Carthage. Nora remained essentially a port of call,[267] as it had been for centuries, for convoys sailing to western Sardinia and to Spain. The pottery includes numerous transport amphorae as well as Etruscan and some Attic wares[268] and is what might be expected in a mixed community whose main source of employment was provided by the supply depot. The amphorae, for instance, were not associated with a factory or with farmsteads[269] and were used for preserving and transporting salt fish. Graves were plain cists—that is, cavities lined with stones—and as was usual in Sardinia in the latter part of the sixth century inhumation replaced incineration.[270]

Bithia was perhaps even more inconspicuous than Nora in the sixth century.[271] It observed the same burial practices, but among the grave goods there were also iron weapons: swords, daggers, javelins, and lances. There was some Attic pottery and a fair number of Etruscan drinking vessels and perfume bottles,[272] and traditional Phoenician mushroom-lipped jugs for perfumes and unguents remained popular until the end of the century. Bithia receded into obscurity in the fifth century, but in the mid-fourth it became a Carthaginian military outpost.[273] Nora and Bithia, all in all,

---

265. *PFPS* 78.

266. M. L. Uberti, "Dati di epigrafia fenicio-punica in Sardegna," *Atti* 1, 3.797–804, pls. 156–57, esp. pp. 802–3, pl. 156:2.

267. S. Finocchi, "La laguna e l'antico porto di Nora: nuovi dati a confronto," *RSF* 27 (1999) 167–92; idem, "Considerazioni sugli aspetti produttivi di Nora e del suo territorio in epoca fenicia e punica," *RSF* 30 (2002) 147–86.

268. C. Tronchetti, "La presenza della ceramica attica arcaica nella Sardegna fenicio-punica," *Atti* 1, 2.501–7, pl. 89.

269. M. Botto, "Nora e il suo territorio: Resoconto preliminare dell'attività di ricognizione degli anni 1992–1995," *Actas* 4, 3.1269–76.

270. S. Moscati, *Italia Punica* (Milan: Rusconi, 1986) 208–25, esp. p. 216.

271. F. Barreca, "Nuove scoperte sulla colonizzazione fenicio-punica in Sardegna," *PhWest*, 181–84, pls. 19–21; P. Bartoloni, "La ceramica fenicia di Bithia: Tipologia e diffusione areale," *Atti* 1, 2.491–500; Moscati, *Italia Punica*, 226–39.

272. Tronchetti, "La presenza delle ceramica attica arcaica nella Sardegna fenicio-punica," *Atti* 1, 2.501–7, pl. 89; idem, "La Sardegna e gli Etruschi," *Mediterranean Archaeology* 1 (1988) 66–82.

273. F. Barreca, "Le fortificazioni fenicio-puniche in Sardegna," in *Atti del I Convegno Italiano sul Vicino Oriente Antico, Roma, 22–24 Aprile, 1976* (Rome: Consiglio Nazionale delle Cicerche, 1978) 115–28.

were quaint villages, the inhabitants of which were probably descendants of early Western settlers. Some tombstones at Nora have recessed or nestled frames, a typically Cypriot design also found at Carthage, adapted from ivories portraying the Woman-at-the-Window,[274] and it is not unlikely that Nora like Carthage maintained its traditional ties with Cyprus. Bithia, as the Etruscan and Greek pottery (specifically, the cups and jugs meant for a symposium) suggests, was linked commercially to Caere,[275] and it may have been established by expatriate Phoenicians from there or from other towns in southern Etruria.

Pyrgi, the port of Caere,[276] was home to a Cypriot Phoenician enclave that came from the Byblian town of Lapethos on the north coast of that island. Phoenicians from Sidon and Tyre had a lasting impact on central Italy in the eighth and seventh centuries, but the Tyrians moved on to Sardinia and the Sidonians settled among the Italians and became indistinguishable from their neighbors. What was left was their cultural heritage witnessed, for instance, in beliefs and in representations of the Goddess.[277] The temple at Pyrgi, built by Etruscans about the mid-sixth century and then enlarged and dedicated by them and by Cypriot Byblians toward the end of the century was dedicated to Astarte. These two building phases bracket the Etruscan and Carthaginian defeat of the Phocaeans at the battle of Alalia,[278] and although the Phoenician phase may have been inspired by this victory, the temple dedications make no explicit mention of it. But Astarte of Pyrgi is presented as the consort of the Etruscan king in a ritual that takes place in the Month-of-Renewal (*krr*) and that involves the burial of the God and, without mentioning his return, the expectation of his eternal life.[279] The God is Byblian Adonis (although the liturgy to which the dedications refer assimilates him to Melqart of Tyre, as do the later Phoenician texts from Lapethos) in whose revivification a Sacred Marriage—that is, the espousal by the Goddess of a human representative of the God—is an essential feature. Implicitly, then, the building of the sanctuary of Astarte at Pyrgi was presented as a joint venture of the Etruscan king, who is mentioned by name, and of the Carthaginians, for whom Melqart was emblematic of their colonization by Tyre, and for whom the cycle of his death and revival

---

274. S. F. Bondì, "Un tipo di inquadramento architettonico fenicio," in ibid., 147–55, pls. 7–12.

275. P. Bartoloni, "Anfore fenicie e ceramiche etrusche in Sardegna," *Il Commercio Etrusco Arcaico: Atti dell'Incontro di Studio, 5–7 dicembre 1983* (Quaderni del Centro di Studio per l'Archeologia Etrusco-Italica 9; Rome: Consiglio Nazionale delle Ricerche, 1985) 103–18; S. Moscati, *Fenici e Greci in Sardegna* (ANLR 8/40, fasc. 7–12; Rome: Accademia Nazionale dei Lincei, 1986) 265–71, esp. pp. 267, 270; C. Tronchetti, "La Sardegna e gli Etruschi," *Mediterranean Archaeology* 1 (1988) 66–82, esp. pp. 71–75.

276. F. R. Serra Ridgway, "Etruscans, Greeks, Carthaginians: The Sanctuary at Pyrgi," in *Greek Colonists and Native Populations* (ed. J.-P. Descoeudres; Oxford: Clarendon, 1990) 511–30.

277. R. Miller Ammerman, "The Naked Standing Goddess: A Group of Archaic Figurines from Paestum," *AJA* 95 (1991) 203–30; H. Damgaard Andersen, "The Origin of Potnia Theron in Central Italy," *HBA* 19/20 (1992–93) 73–113.

278. F. Prayon, "Historische Daten zur Geschichte von Caere und Pyrgi," in *Die Göttin von Pyrgi: Archäologische, linguistische und religions-geschichtliche Aspekte* (ed. A. M. Modona and F. Prayon; Florence: Olschki, 1981) 39–53.

279. P. Xella, "Sul nome punico *ʿbdkrr*," *RSF* 12 (1984) 23–30.

was the symbol of their victory over the Phocaeans and the renewal of trade and good relations with Etruria.

Phoenician Sardinia was definitively in the Carthaginian orbit in the seventh century, but in the sixth century it was incorporated into a Carthaginian administrative district. Tharros was an exception, but apparently it was shadowed by the foundation of another "Carthage" just across the Gulf of Oristano. Carthage was becoming increasingly bellicose, and its envoys to Sardinia were among the military elite, and their business in the southern province could easily be perceived as an invasion. The material evidence, however, suggests that it was a deliberate and systematic reorganization of the economy and politics of Sulcis and its territories and of the towns radiating from Cagliari on the south coast that did brisk business with the Etruscans of Caere. Interference by the Phocaeans was meant to break this connection but brought Carthage and Etruria together and eventually led to the treaty with Rome that made Sardinia a North African preserve.

Egypt

Egypt was the prime source of Phoenician culture from time immemorial, and in the sixth century, as it probably had been forever, it was a constant destination of traders and adventurers from the eastern mainland. There are traces of them in inscriptions and other artifacts from the Delta to Sudan, and their travels can be tracked in the Egyptian products that came back with them to Syria, Palestine, and Cyprus. However, they had competition from the Greek consortiums that were established at Naucratis at the end of the seventh century in the Delta and that were the chief distributors of Egyptian goods in Carthage and the Western colonies.

Egyptian items arrived in almost all the Phoenician coastal towns of Syria and Palestine,[280] most of them presumably with Phoenician merchants returning home, some possibly with ambassadors from Egypt. They sometimes have political overtones and regularly have religious significance. At Byblos there are statues of the Gods, a statue of a priest holding an image of Osiris, a New Year's gourd, a vase, amulets, and a blue frit figurine of a man. At Tyre there is a dedication to Neith, the Saite Goddess of war. In Sidon there is a sistrum inscribed with the name of Amasis (569–526 B.C.E.) that was presented in the temple as a votive offering, as in the early fourth century there are two altars with the name of Achoris (392–380 B.C.E.). There are bronze figurines at Ashkelon, a bronze mirror and scarabs at ʿAtlit, and scarabs at Tell Kazel, ʿAkko, ʾAchzib, ʿAmrit, and Tell Sukas. There is a statue of a priest of Osiris at Arvad, a blue faience scarab at Ras el-Bassit, and New Year's gourds at Sukas and Tell ʿArqa,. The items are jewelry or knickknacks that illustrate contemporary interest in Egyptian exotica or offerings that illustrate either traditional ties to Egypt, as at Byblos, or the eclecticism and religious syncretism of the sixth-century Phoenicians.

---

280. J. Elayi, "La place de l'Égypte dans la recherche sur les Phéniciens," *Transeu* 9 (1995) 11–24, esp. pp. 12–16.

It was in this century that Phoenician personal names increasingly incorporated as their theophoric element the names of Egyptian Gods,[281] and that Egyptian Gods such as Bes, a guardian deity, Isis, and Harpocrates, the child Horus, became especially popular and that curiosity about Egyptian religion and religious texts influenced the production of Phoenician votive art.[282] There is, for instance, a scarab from Tharros that reproduces an image from the Book of the Dead showing the bark of the dead being held aloft above the head of the deceased. Similarly, there is a gold finger ring from Carthage, dated early in the sixth century, that shows Ba'al enthroned, his right hand holding a scepter, his left raised in benediction: this much is standard Phoenician iconography, but in this instance the throne and the reigning God are placed into the papyrus boat that transports the dead to their life beyond the horizon. Or, again, the Warrior Goddess is transformed into the Goddess of Love by being crowned with the tiara of Isis, where the sun disk is enclosed in horns, or the mystery of life and death is represented by the child Harpocrates protected by Isis and a winged Goddess. There are many similar votive pieces and thousands of scarabs and amulets the number and popularity of which suggest that they were mass produced (which they may have been), but it is apparent that at least some of these artists worked for purchasers who knew that what they had in hand reflected perennially shared beliefs.

Phoenicians from Arvad and Sidon, perhaps from the other cities as well, supplied the ships that accompanied Cambyses' overland invasion of Egypt (525 B.C.E.),[283] and the ships from Sidon sailed home with the anthropoid sarcophagi that the Persian king looted from the graveyards and workshops at Saqqara and gave them as a gift for their services. At Tell el-Mashkuta in the western Delta, there are Phoenician inscriptions on amphorae, some imported from Thasos but most from mainland Phoenicia,[284] which usually name the producer of the jars' contents, the trader who shipped them, or the merchant who sold them in Egypt. This was a lively market (other fragmentary amphorae are inscribed in Greek, Demotic, or Aramaic) situated at the head of the Wadi Tumilat through which, when it was still a waterway, a canal to the Red Sea was dug during the reigns of Necho II (610–594 B.C.E.) and Darius I (522–486 B.C.E.).[285] Along this canal, perhaps, traveled the Phoenician ships that Necho II dispatched, on their circumnavigation of Africa. The ships that eventually composed the Red Sea fleet also used it when (among other ventures) they were sent to supply the Egyptian and Persian forts at Dorginarti in Lower Nubia and to transport the merchants

---

281. Ibid., 17–18.

282. G. Hölbl, "Ägyptische Kunstelemente im phönikischen Kulturkreis des 1. Jahrtausends v. Chr.: Zur Methodik ihrer Verwendung," *Or* 58 (1989) 318–25.

283. H. J. Katzenstein, "Gaza in the Persian Period," *Transeu* 1 (1989) 67–86, esp. pp. 71–72.

284. R. T. Lutz, "Phoenician Inscriptions from Tell el-Mashkuta," in *The World of the Aramaeans, III: Studies in Language and Literature in Honour of Paul-Eugène Dion* (ed. P. M. M. Daviau, J. W. Wevers, and M. Weigl; JSOTSup 326; Sheffield: Sheffield Academic Press, 2001) 190–212.

285. A. Lemaire, "Les Phéniciens et le commerce entre la Mer Rouge et la Mer Mediterranée," in *Phoenicia and the East Mediterranean in the First Millennium B.C.* (ed. E. Lipiński; Studia Phoenicia 5; Louvain: Peeters, 1987) 49–60, esp. pp. 59–60; C. A. Redmount, "The Wadi Tumilat and the 'Canal of the Pharaohs,'" *JNES* 54 (1995) 127–35.

who sold jewelry, scarabs, amulets, and antiques to the court at Meroe and Napata in the Sudan.[286]

Phoenicians, in fact, went pretty well everywhere in Egypt and are documented by their wares and occasionally by their written records.[287] Perhaps from Memphis, but of unknown provenance is an ornamented and inscribed *situla*—a small vase shaped like a woman's breast, associated with the Goddess Isis, and designed to contain a liquid to be sprinkled in a ceremony in honor of the dead.[288] The decorative scene shows the deceased standing before Isis, Nephthys, Neith, and Selket, Goddesses who protect the dead from all evil. The inscription reads, "May Isis grant favour and life to ʿAbdptah son of ʿAbdo" (*ʾsy ttn ḥn wḥym lʿbdpth bn ʿbdʾ*).

A similar prayer for life is found on the base of a sixth-century statue of Harpocrates of Egyptian origin,[289] maybe from Memphis ("May Harpocrates grant life to ʿAmos son of ʾEshmunyaton son of ʿAzormilk"). The exact prayer for favor and life is found in a much later inscription from Memphis, "May [Isis, Astarte and my Gods] bless me and my sons . . . and their mother, and grant them favour and life in the eyes of the Gods and the children of Adam."[290]

The name ʿAbdptah and the theophoric element "Ptah" are also found in an inscription from Abu Simbel: "Bless ʿAbdptah (*ʿbdpth*), son of Yagurʾeshmun, to his lord Amasis"; the wish is endorsed by two men, perhaps his sons, one called Ptahay (*ptḥy*), a name meaning "The One of Ptah," the other ʿAbdʾis (*ʿbdʾs*), "Servant of Isis."[291] Other inscriptions from the same place are graffiti that record the names of three Phoenician mercenaries who went with Amasis on his Nubian campaign (591 B.C.E.):[292] two of the men have Phoenician names, although one of these is known only from Abu Simbel and Abydos, but the third acquired the nickname "the Nubian" (*kšy*), and they all say simply "who went on the campaign to Kush with Amasis" (*ʾš ʾl šd kš dl ḥms*). In the fifth century at Abydos, there are graffiti of Phoenician pilgrims from various places, including Memphis and Kition, who came to the Temple of Osiris, and ostraca at Elephantine that mention Phoenician merchants or mercenaries, many of them now

286. L. A. Heidorn, "The Saite and Persian Period Forts at Dorginarti," in *Egypt and Africa: Nubia from Prehistory to Islam* (ed. W. V. Davies; London: British Museum, 1991) 205–19; A. Lohwasser, "Eine phönizische Bronzeschale aus dem Sudan," *Ägypten und Levante* 12 (2002) 221–34.

287. E. Bresciani, "Fenici in Egitto," *EVO* 10 (1987) 69–78; G. Scandone and P. Xella, "Egypte," *CPPMR*, 632–39.

288. P. K. McCarter Jr., "An Inscribed Phoenician Funerary *Situla* in the Art Museum of Princeton University," *BASOR* 290–91 (1993) 115–20; M. G. Amadasi Guzzo, "Su tre iscrizioni fenicie dall'Egitto: Formule augurali e cronologia," in *Alle soglie della Classicità: Il Mediterraneo tra tradizione e innovazione—Studi in onore di Sabatino Moscati* (ed. E. Acquaro; 3 vols. Pisa: Istituti Editoriali e Poligrafici Internazionali, 1996) 3.1047–61.

289. *TSSI* 3.141–44 #38. The inscription ends with the signature of the man who carved the statue and wrote the inscription: "The inscriber was Ninbaʿal the sculptor" (*whq nnbʿl bnʾ*).

290. *KAI* 48.

291. *CIS* 111.

292. Ibid., 112, 113; C. R. Krahmalkov, *Phoenician-Punic Dictionary* (Studia Phoenicia 15; Louvain: Peeters, 2000) s.v. *šd* (pp. 457–58).

with Egyptian names, and jar fragments from Thebes on which most of the names are Egyptian or a mixture of Egyptian and Phoenician.[293]

From Saqqara, near Memphis, there are many ostraca of the fifth century and later that contain the names of Phoenicians (including a man from Tyre who was barber to the king [*glb mlk*]) and fragments of some of their business records.[294] There is also a papyrus dated to the mid-sixth century[295] that contains a letter to ʾArišat from her sister Bassaʾ: they may have been siblings, but the letter makes it clear that "sister" meant that they were business associates in the same company or "house." ʾArišat is a Phoenician name ("Désirée") and she was living in Saqqara in a quarter called Par-ʿArot (*prʿrt*) or had traveled there on business. Bassaʾ is an Egyptian name, and she was living in Tahpanhes (Greek Daphnae) in the eastern Delta. The two places were government centers and home to East Greek mercenaries, Phoenician mercenaries and traders, and Jewish settlers (Jer 2:16, 44:1, 46:14).[296]

The introduction to the letter, as usual, mentions the addressee and includes the name of the sender and the salutation, and supposes that the letter will be read aloud by the messenger or a scribe:

> To ʾArišat, the daughter of ʾEshmunyaton.
> Say to my sister ʾArišat:
> "Your sister Bassaʾ says:
> 'I hope you are well: I too am well.
> I have blessed you by Baʿal Ṣapon and all the Gods of Tahpanhes:
> "May they keep you well."'"

Baʿal Ṣapon is the titular God of Daphnae and in one biblical text is an alternative name of the town itself (Exod 14:1). The salutation is composed of quotations within quotations, the last being the blessing on ʾArišat that was the subject of Bassaʾs invocation of the Gods.

The body of the letter acknowledges payment of a debt, gives instructions on how to handle the remaining moneys, and asks for the receipts:

> I have received the money you sent me
> and you are quit today of the 3¼ shekels.
> And Ha[wat] I will send up to you at Parʿarot,
> and you should furnish Tapnay with all the money I have in your keeping,
> and supply Yaʾa[t] with credit among the important people of the city.
> So that I might know about these things for certain,
> send me the letters of remittance by someone in your house.

293. M. Lidzbarski, *Phönizische und aramäische Krugausschriften aus Elephantine* (Berlin, 1912); G. Pisano and A. Travaglini, *Le iscrizioni fenicie e puniche dipinte* (Studia Punica 13; Rome: Università degli Studi di Roma, "Tor Vergata," 2003) 80–106.

294. J. B. Segal, *Aramaic Texts from North Saqqarah (with Some Fragments in Phoenician)* (London: Egyptian Exploration Society, 1983) 139–45, pls. 35–38.

295. *KAI* 50; D. Pardee et al., *Handbook of Ancient Hebrew Letters* (Sources for Biblical Study 15; Chico, CA: Scholars Press, 1982) 165–68; J. C. Greenfield, "Notes on the Phoenician Letter from Saqqara," *Or* 53 (1984) 242–44.

296. T. F. R. G. Braun, "The Greeks in Egypt," in *The Cambridge Ancient History*, vol. 3/3: *The Expansion of the Greek World, Eighth to Sixth Century B.C.* (ed. J. Boardman and N. G. L. Hammond; 2nd ed.; Cambridge: Cambridge University Press, 1982) 32–56, esp. pp. 43–47.

At the beginning Bassaʾ sends ʾArišat a receipt for the money she sent, and at the end she asks ʾArišat to send her confirmation in writing that she has followed all the instructions she received: Bassaʾ seems to be the head of the company, or overseer of its business in Tahpanhes, and ʾArišat was responsible for the Memphis operations ("your house"). The middle section of the letter is about other members of the house, and although two of the names are broken it is likely that all of them were women. Hawat is assigned, literally, "sent upstream" (ʿly) to Memphis. Tapnay, who is also in Memphis, or works out of the town, receives money to invest or to buy goods for use in the house or for resale.

Yaʾat, if she is engaged in commerce, will not buy the things she sells but will receive them on consignment and is expected to make a profit for her backers and therefore needs a good credit (btḥ, "trustworthiness") rating; but it is also possible that she is not engaged in buying and selling and that her trustworthiness just makes her a reliable member of the financial establishment. Women's business is usually supposed to have been in the textile industry (or in ceramics), and this is possibly what Bassaʾ and ʾArišat and their sisters did; however, because the company can count on the financial backing of the city officials (rbrb ʿr, "the lords of the city"), and because the letter is all about money and not about products, it may be that it was a company of bankers that financed Delta merchants and traders in their business ventures. Daphnae was a multicultural town, and the corporation, besides its Phoenician connections, may also have done business in Demotic and Greek.

Phoenicians were almost omnipresent in Egypt (individually, in syndicates, and sometimes settled), and it is striking that Naucratis was Greek and free of Phoenician commercial and cultural influence.[297] The town was situated on the most westerly branch of the Nile and as far upriver as a large ship could sail. It was settled by Milesians toward the end of the seventh century in the reign of Psammetichus I (664–610 b.c.e.) and was developed by them and East Greeks from Phocaea, Chios, Samos, and Rhodes during the reign of Amasis (569–526 b.c.e.), when Naucratis acquired the trade monopoly in the western Delta.[298] Its commercial dealings, on which the Egyptians levied taxes in silver, in gold, and in kind,[299] were mainly with the home ports of its settlers. It was also in the scarab business and its several factories where these were mass-produced exported frit, faience, and steatite scarabs mainly to Carthage and central Italy but also to Spain and

---

297. J. Padró, "Découverte de céramiques phéniciennes à Héracléopolis Magna (Egypte)," *Atti* 2, 3.1103–8. The site is ca. 100 kilometers south of Memphis. In the ninth- and eighth-century strata, in buildings associated with the royal graveyard, and in a residential quarters, there were Phoenician amphorae and Cypriot wine jugs.

J. Boardman, "Settlement for Trade and Land in North Africa: Problems of Identity," in *The Archaeology of Greek Colonisation: Essays Dedicated to Sir John Boardman* (ed. G. R. Tsetskhladze and F. De Angelis; Oxford: Oxbow, 1994) 137–49.

298. Braun, "The Greeks in Egypt," 37–43; C. Ampolo and E. Bresciani, "Psammetico re d'Egitto e il mercenario Pedon," *EVO* 11 (1988) 237–53.

299. M. Clauss, "Ein aussergewöhnliches Zwillingspaar: Zwei Stelen des Pharao Nektanebos 1. (380–362 v. Chr.) lösen nun das Rätsel einer im Meer verschwundenen Stadt Ägyptens," *Antike Welt* 37/3 (2006) 51–55.

Sardinia.[300] These are all sixth-century products, and their distribution indicates the extent of Greek influence, however shallow, on the Punic world.

Phoenicia was deeply involved with Egypt from time immemorial. Its relations with Egypt of the Twenty-Sixth Dynasty (664–525 B.C.E.), on the other hand, and during the sixth century in particular, were mostly superficial and sporadic. Religion was taken seriously, religious literature was studied, and Egyptian Gods, or at least their names and iconography, were adopted. The most engaged of the Phoenicians were from Cyprus and Tyre, but later written records show that Byblos and Sidon also maintained their Egyptian connection in the sixth century. The big difference at this time was that whatever they did and wherever they went in Egypt they encountered Greeks involved in similar ventures: merchants, mercenaries, sailors, shipbuilders, pilgrims, and imitators of ancient Egyptian artifacts. This Greek connection and the direct competition diminished the contribution of the Tyrian cohorts and changed what lately had been a Phoenician Mediterranean into a differentiated Semitic and European world.

Malta

Malta, unlike most of the western Mediterranean sites, was free of Greek merchants and travelers, but like most was a potential market for eccentric religious notions and material bric-a-brac from Egypt. It was a stop for ships sailing west from Italy and Sicily and for eastbound ships from North Africa, and the Temple of Astarte at Tas Silg on the southeast coast was a famous and worthwhile place to visit. The sixth century at Phoenician sites was generally a time of consolidation, but on Malta it was marked particularly by self-satisfaction and isolation.

There are very few tombs from this period, less than 20, apparently, although estimates vary, but half of them contained pretty, expensive, though not exceptional items (gold, silver, copper, and tin jewelry, as well as ivory, faience, and glass)[301] that may have been kept for generations in the families of the women who operated the textile businesses. Local wares are practical, such as transport and storage jars; or domestic, such as plates and bowls; or cosmetic, such as perfume bottles; or convivial, such as wine jugs and drinking bowls.[302] Greek wares are more common at Tas Silg, where visitors abounded, than in the grave contexts of the permanent residents in the vicinity of Rabat on the west coast of the island and are mainly Laconian or Attic Black Figure drinking vessels: jugs, kraters, and chalices.[303] They were brought by traders or by ships' passengers who

300. A. Feghali Gorton, *Egyptian and Egyptianizing Scarabs: A Typology of Steatite, Faience and Paste Scarabs from Punic and Other Mediterranean Sites* (Oxford: Institute of Archaeology, 1996) 141, 177–80.

301. G. A. Said-Zammit, *Population, Land Use and Settlement on Punic Malta: A Contextual Analysis of the Burial Evidence* (BAR International Series 682; Oxford: Archaeopress, 1997) 22–23; C. Sagona, *The Archaeology of Punic Malta* (ANESt Supplement 9; Louvain: Peeters, 2002) 54, 283.

302. Idem, *Punic Antiquities of Malta (and other Ancient Artefacts Held in Ecclesiastic and Private Collections)* (ANESt Supplement 10; Louvain: Peeters, 2003) 16–20, 78–93.

303. G. Semeraro, "Osservazioni sui materiali arcaici di importazione greca dall'arcipelago maltese," in *Da Pyrgi a Mozia: Studi sull'archeologia nel Mediterraneo in Memoria di Antonia Ciasca* (ed. M. G. Amadasi Guzzo, M. Liverani, and P. Matthiae; Vicino Oriente: Quaderno 3/2; Rome: Università degli Studi di Roma, "La Sapienza," 2002) 489–520, pls. 1–12.

stopped to worship at the shrine of Astarte and were of no interest to the inhabitants of the island except perhaps the established Phoenician merchants or the traders and recent arrivals, who imported them.

One of these traders or émigrés was buried in a tomb marked by a small pillar carved from local limestone. The tomb was discovered by chance and was damaged by the construction that uncovered it, and it contained only a large transport amphora, one handle of which was stamped with a seal, perhaps his own, but now illegible, and a bronze amulet case.[304] The case is octagonal, its cap topped with the Horus falcon, and it held an inscribed magical papyrus. The right side of the papyrus is filled with a drawing of Isis, mother of Horus and guide to life beyond death: she is clothed in a long, fringed tunic tied with a knotted belt, wears a head scarf the flaps of which fall on her shoulders, carries an *ankh* in her right hand by her side and a scepter in her left hand, and is identified as Isis by the hieroglyph "throne" (*ȝs.t*) that rests on her head.

The inscription has five lines: the first two are complete; the ends of the next three lines to the left of Isis are preserved, and it is likely that their beginnings are complete because the text makes sense as it is preserved and because, if there were more text, it would have begun asymmetrically to the right of Isis and her staff. The inscription[305] is a blessing on the bearer and a curse on whoever might oppose him:

šḥq ʿz lb ṣrkm	Laugh, strong of heart, at your adversary!
lʿg dkk wḥ ʾyb	Deride, distress, cast adrift the enemy!
sl bs ʿl ʿn	Make light of him, shame him, on the sweet waters!
ʾp ṭ lym sg tl	Confuse him, on the seas enclose him, mock him!

The five lines of script seem to resolve into four lines of poetry. The first two lines set the amulet-bearer apart from his competitors as bold and courageous: the imperatives could be plural but are probably singular, although "your" in "your adversary" is plural. There is parallelism between "mock" and "laugh at" and between "adversary" and "enemy," a nice balance between the four words of each line, and contrast between the one who is strong of heart and those who are distressed and cast adrift. The second set of lines is composed mostly of staccato imperatives and compares the plight of the enemy on the rivers (on the sweet waters, literally, "on the springs" [ʿl ʿn]) and on the high seas (*lym*), and it balances "shame" and "confusion" and "making light of" and "mocking." The extra word "enclose" on the last line that has no parallel in the third matches the extra word "cast adrift" on the second line that has no parallel in the first.

The papyrus, therefore, can be read as a seafaring trader's spell against his competitors (the plural "your" in the first line would refer to him and his company) when they are at sea and when they enter the estuaries to do business with the people of the interior. He is addressed and encouraged by

304. T. C. Gouder and B. Rocco, "Un talismano bronzeo da Malta contenente un nastro di papiro con iscrizione fenicia," *Studi Magrebini* 7 (1975) 1–18, pls. 1–4.

305. Ibid., 8–18, pls. 1–2; T. C. Gouder, "Some Amulets from Phoenician Malta," *Heritage* 1 (1979) 311–15, esp. p. 314; H.-P. Müller, "Phönizischer Totenpapyrus aus Malta," *JSS* 46 (2001) 252–65; R. Ben Guiza, "À propos des décans égyptiens et de leur réception dans le monde phénicien et punique," *Transeu* 29 (2005) 49–81, pls. 1–4.

Isis or by one or more of the canonical Gods of enchantment. The amulet has its best parallels at Carthage and at Tharros in Sardinia, and the trader may have traveled or emigrated from one of these places. But the spell was composed specifically for him, perhaps from a sort of magical logbook, and it has a humorous sea shanty edge, although its casing and design are Egyptian and they evoke the more serious matter of life and death. He died and was buried with members of the Phoenician community at Rabat, with whom he did business and among whom perhaps he had settled.

Carthage

Carthage in the sixth century was intricately involved in the affairs of Italy, Sicily, and Sardinia, founded outposts and colonies in North Africa and along the Atlantic coast, and depended on the old and new settlements (Phoenician, Punic, and Greek) in Spain. It also maintained its cultural and political ties with Cyprus and Tyre but extricated itself, or at least kept itself at arm's length, from the lugubrious and imperialistic military affairs that engulfed the old country.

The city was larger than any other in the Phoenician West in the sixth century. In the early part of the century, tombs on the slope of the Byrsa citadel contained local wares along with Corinthian and Ionian cups, Attic Black Figure vases, pottery from Campania, Grey Ware from Ampurias and amphorae from Marseilles.[306] Throughout the century, gold jewelry in styles known from Egypt, Cyprus, and the mainland Phoenician cities was unexceptionable among grave deposits.[307] In the latter part of the seventh century, grave goods began to be standardized, and in the earlier sixth century, the repertory was fixed,[308] with six items becoming *de rigueur*: a two-wick lamp and its saucer, one round-mouth wine jug and another with a trilobate mouth, and two jars with handles. Traditional Red Slip wares disappear, and novelties such as razors and Egyptianizing female protome masks are introduced. In the second half of the century these masks become Hellenized, and terra-cotta figurines, Greek or from Greek molds, become popular.

Also in the sixth century, mostly in infant burials, terra-cotta figures of men or women at prayer (men with a raised hand or women with folded arms, lamenting their children) are common.[309] They are modeled on Cypriot prototypes, notably from Ayia Irini and Kourion, and the earliest bell-shaped types are typical of burials on the citadel and at Salammbo and in places where Carthaginians traveled or settled at this time: in Malta and at Motya; in Sardinia at Nora, Bithia, Monte Sirai, and Carbonia; on Ibiza at Isla Plana; and at Puig des Molins.

---

306. M. Fantar, "L'archéologie punique en Tunisie 1991–1995," *Actas* 4, 1.63–70.

307. A. Perea Caveda, "Phoenician Gold in the Western Mediterranean: Cádiz, Tharros and Carthage," in *Encounters and Transformations: The Archaeology of Iberia in Transition* (ed. M. S. Balmuth, A. Gilman, and L. Prados-Torreira; Monographs in Mediterranean Archaeology 7; Sheffield: Sheffield Academic Press, 1997) 135–40, esp. pp. 135–36.

308. H. Bénichou-Safar, *Les tombes puniques de Carthage: Topographie, structures, inscriptions et rites funéraires* (Paris: Éditions du Centre National de la Recherche Scientifique, 1982) 291–304.

309. J. Ferron and M. E. Aubet, *Orants de Carthage, Volumes I–II* (Collection Cahiers de Byrsa 1; Paris: Geuthner, 1974) 37–44, 61–154.

Burials were cremations or inhumations, and among the latter many
still wore, as a precaution in the grave, the scarab and scaraboid amulets
that had protected them during their lifetime.[310] There are 13 scarabs from
9 seventh-century tombs, but there are more than 200 from an unspecified
number of sixth-century tombs. A very few of these were made for a Greek
clientele; some were Phoenician; others Punic; some were early or late
Egyptian, either authentic or copies; others were Egyptianizing and made
for a Punic market; and almost half were from the Naucratis factory. The
same distribution, but in smaller numbers, is found in Sardinia, but Ibiza
with still fewer has none of the Greek, Egyptianizing, or Naucratis models.
The scarabs buried in Carthage in the Dermech and Douïmès cemeteries
reveal some similarities to scarabs in the same style from Cyprus, Al Mina,
and Rhodes. On the evidence of the tombs, therefore, Carthage in the sixth
century maintained its original and privileged relations with Tyre and Cyprus, was caught up in the Egyptianizing craze they promoted, became a
good customer of the Greek factories at Naucratis, and was developing its
political and cultural contacts with Phoenicians, Greeks, and indigenous
peoples in Italy, Sicily, Sardinia, and Spain.

About mid-century, around the time that Tyre had restored the monarchy and was trying to reassert itself in the Levant, Carthage was drawn
inexorably into regional and international affairs in the Phoenician West.
The city was becoming populous and rich,[311] and increasingly dependent
for its supplies of raw and manufactured goods on the network of cities in
the West. Relations with Etruria, especially with Caere, date back almost
to the time of the foundation of the city. In the seventh century and in
the first half of the sixth, these relations are indicated by an exchange of
ceramic goods—with Etruscan Bucchero in Carthage, for instance, and Carthaginian amphorae in southern Etruria.[312]

At the same time, Carthage was on good terms and, directly or through
its establishments in Spain, did business with the Phocaeans who had
founded Marseilles (Massalia) and Ampurias (Emporion). But the system
collapsed early in the second half of the century, when the Phocaeans built
Alalia in southern Corsica and, in an effort to test the markets in Latium,
tried to keep the Carthaginians out of Italian waters by interfering with
their staging ports in southern Sardinia. The sea battle at Caere between the
Phocaeans and the Carthaginians and their Etruscan allies was inconclu-
sive, but it disrupted the commercial relations between these old friends,

310. P. Gasull, "El sistema ritual fenicio: Inhumacion e incineracion," *MM* 34 (1993) 71–82;
A. Feghali Gorton, *Egyptian and Egyptianizing Scarabs: A Typology of Steatite, Faience and Paste
Scarabs from Punic and Other Mediterranean Sites* (Oxford: Institute of Archaeology, 1996) 139–48
(Carthage), 151 (Ibiza), 155–57 (Sardinia).
311. C. Picard, "L'essor de Carthage au VIIe et VIe siècles," in *Cartago* (ed. E. Lipiński; Studia
Phoenicia 6; Louvain: Peeters, 1988) 43–50.
312. J.-P. Thuillier, "Nouvelles découvertes de Bucchero à Carthage," in *Il commercio etrusco
arcaico: Atti dell'incontro di studio, 5–7 dicembre 1983* (ed. M. Cristofani et al.; Rome: Consiglio
Nazionale delle Ricerche, 1985) 155–63; Y. B. Tsirkin, "The Economy of Carthage," in *Cartago*
(ed. E. Lipiński; Studia Phoenicia 6; Louvain: Peeters, 1988) 125–35; J.-P. Morel, "Nouvelles données sur le commerce de Carthage punique entre le VIIe siècle et le IIe siècle avant J.-C.," *HAAN*,
67–100.

created lasting bad blood, and ushered in a series of military confrontations with the Sicilian Greeks.

Before this diplomatic and naval fiasco, Carthage, under the tutelage of a patriotic general and an aristocratic family, had been more successful in protecting its interests and avoiding war. Malko' (*mlk'*), apparently, made his reputation in Africa building a navy and securing the borders of Carthage before trying, with less success, to organize Sicily and Sardinia as separate administrative districts.[313] Sicily did not take much persuasion because the three towns of Motya, Palermo, and Solunto were already its shipyard and its food terminals, and cooperated readily with each other. The new policy aggravated the Greeks, however, and eventually led to the miscalculation and debacle at Himera. From Sicily, because Palermo was a Tharros foundation, it was a short step to Sardinia.

Perhaps because Malko' began with Tharros, which was determined to control its own territorial destiny, the administrative change was thwarted, and Malko' was summoned back to Carthage, where he became the butt of gossip and the stuff of legend.[314] However, the reorganization that he planned occurred under the sons of Magon, Hasdrubal (*'izriba'al*), and Hamilcar (*ḥimilkat*), and at the end of the sixth century the treaty with Rome confirmed Carthage's control of the sea lanes in southern and western Sardinia and its preferential status as a trading partner in all the local ports.[315]

This Magon (*mgn*) succeeded Malko' as the commander of Carthage.[316] The tomb of one of his children, probably his firstborn, was marked by a stele inscribed:[317]

nṣb mlk bʿl	Memorial stele of a male infant
'š ytn mgn bn ḥn'	which Magon son of Ḥanno'
lbʿl ḥmn	gave to Baʿal Hamon

The script fits well in the mid-sixth-century sequence, and the stele is one of the earliest types of funerary monuments from Carthage.[318] It is shaped like a throne, and its backrest is carved to resemble three standing stones, or *baetyls*—the middle one larger and taller than the others, like the cult object in the early Phoenician building at Kommos in Crete or like tombstones at Sulcis in Sardinia.

---

313. Cf. R. Rebuffat, "Le pentécontores d'Hannon," *Karthago* 23 (1995) 20–30; W. Huss, *Geschichte der Karthager* (Munich: Beck, 1985) 59–64.

314. V. Krings, *Carthage et les Grecs c. 580–480 av. J.-C.: Textes et Histoire* (Studies in the History and Culture of the Ancient Near East, 13; Leiden: Brill, 1998) 33–91; idem, "Quelques considérations sur l' "empire de Carthage": À propos de Malchus," *Atti* 4, 1.167–72; P. Bernardini, "La battaglia del Mare Sardo: Una rilettura," *RSF* 29 (2001) 135–68.

315. H. Bengston, *Die Verträge der griechisch-römischen Welt von 700 bis 338 v.Chr* (Die Staatsverträge des Altertums 2; Munich: Beck, 1962) 16–20.

316. K. Geus, *Prosopographie der literarisch bezeugten Karthager* (Studia Phoenicia 13; Louvain: Peeters, 1994) 173–75.

317. *CIS* 5685, pl. 99.

318. J. B. Peckham, *The Development of the Late Phoenician Scripts* (Cambridge: Harvard University Press, 1968) 129.

Another almost identical but earlier, likely seventh-century stele from Carthage records the offering of a female infant (*nṣb mlkt bʿl*).[319] A slightly later sixth-century tombstone with a similar inscription from the children's cemetery at Salammbo[320] lists five generations and records an infant sacrifice by a descendant of one of the original Carthaginian settlers: "Gerʿaštart, son of Kalboʾ, son of ʾAris, son of Šabuaʿ, son of ʿAbdsakkun." Child sacrifice in early Malta and Carthage marked the foundation and solemn consecration of the settlement or city and in these later instances seems to have signified the dedication of a whole family to its civic duty. The baetyl, similarly, symbolized the family's lineage, particularly its ancestral worship. The offering of Magon's child, consequently, was a religious and political act establishing his family in the public life of Carthage.

This Magon was the father of Hannoʾ, grandfather of Hasdrubal and Hamilcar, and great-grandfather of another Hannoʾ, the son of Hamilcar. It was an altogether illustrious family. The first Hannoʾ may have been the Carthaginian suffete who founded Lixus in Morocco, explored the Atlantic coast of Africa, and generally contributed to the development of Carthaginian foreign trade.[321] Magon himself initiated the policy of replacing the militia with professional troops and mercenaries, thus freeing the citizenry for more productive commercial careers.[322] His son Hannoʾ, who married a Sicilian and who may have been the mayor of Solunto, was the Carthaginian commander at the battle of Himera.[323] Hasdrubal and Hamilcar were responsible for the reorganization of southern Sardinia.[324] Hannoʾ, the son of Hamilcar, was active in city politics in the fifth century, but in his lifetime the illustrious family lost its leadership role.[325] Magon's sacrifice of his child to the God of Carthage, Baʿal Hamon, certainly did succeed in establishing his lineage throughout the sixth century and into the fifth.

Carthage was independent in the sixth century and the capital of an expanding empire, but it still maintained its colonial bonds with Cyprus and mainland Phoenicia. These had been bonds of blood and origin, but they persisted as religious and cultural ties and became formalized in diplomatic relations sealed by treaty.[326] The city was represented at the Festival of the Waters in Kition toward the end of the century by its ambassador ʿAbdʾabast the Carthaginian. The fleets from Tyre, Sidon, Byblos, and Arvad

---

319. *CIS* 5684, pl. 98.

320. J. Ferron, "Inscription punique archaïque à Carthage," in *Mélanges de Carthage offerts à Charles Saumagne, Louis Poinssot, Maurice Pinard* (Cahiers de Byrsa 10; Paris: Geuthner, 1964–65) 55–64, pl. 1.

321. *Lixus: Actes du colloque organisé par l'Institut des sciences, de l'archéologie, et du patrimoine de Rabat avec le concours de l'École française de Rome, Larache, 8–11 novembre 1989* (Rome: École Francaise de Rome, 1992); G. Maass-Lindemann, "Die phönikische Keramik von Lixus im Vergleich mit sudandalusischer Keramik," *MM* 31 (1990) 186–93; P. Rouillard, "Maroc," *CPPMR*, 776–85; K. Geus, *Prosopographie der literarisch bezeugten Karthager* (Studia Phoenicia 13; Louvain: Peeters, 1994) 96 (Hannoʾ [1]), 98–105 (Hannoʾ [3]).

322. Ibid., 173–75.

323. Ibid., 97.

324. Ibid., 36–40, 130.

325. Ibid., 105.

326. A. Ferjaoui, *Recherches sur les relations entre l'Orient phénicien et Carthage* (Orbis Biblicus et Orientalis 124; Göttingen: Vandenhoeck & Ruprecht, 1993) 56–59.

that had gone with Cambyses to Egypt refused to proceed against Carthage because they were bound to it by solemn oaths.[327] Carthage had economic agreements with Tyre, and it was treated independently by the Persian Empire under Darius I and Xerxes. In the West, it made treaties with Etruria and Rome, established its agencies in Sicily and Sardinia, and founded colonies in North Africa and Spain. Its foundation had been a deliberate and concerted effort by the Eastern mainland cities, and its development into a metropolis was the achievement they had in mind.

Spain

The sixth century in Spain belonged to the indigenous peoples. They had learned from the enterprising Phoenicians who came from the East, had worked with them when they became Europeanized and Africanized, and could deal with the Greeks when they took advantage of the established Phoenician and Punic networks in southern and southeastern Spain. The Atlantic regions still had traces of the Phoenicians who settled among them, but the Mediterranean towns and ports were totally taken up into the Carthaginian ethos and gradually became indistinguishable from the Iberian entrepreneurs and peasants who increasingly supplied the goods and services on which the metropolis depended. Not many came from the East anymore, imports were few and mostly were transshipped from sites in the West, old world ceramic tastes were disappearing,[328] Spain was its own country and fast becoming Punic, the Carthaginian Mediterranean was the new world, and in the details of life and death all the changes are apparent.

West of Gibraltar, at the mouths and along the courses of the rivers Guadiana, Odiel, Guadalquivir, and Guadalete, where the Sidonians once were culturally dynamic, there is still a subtle and restrained Phoenician presence in the sixth century. There is evidence for continued settlement, recent imports from the eastern mainland, and trade in Greek pottery, but the predominant presence is Iberian.

At Cádiz there is a sixth-century Phoenician graveyard with a score of in situ cremation burials, several of young people, most of them simple or even devoid of grave goods, but two of them with gold jewelry from a local shop—altogether a cemetery that is representative of the settlement's mix of more and less prosperous citizens.[329] At the nearby mainland site of Doña Blanca, by contrast, there is some miniscule evidence for continuing imports from the eastern mainland. From early in the century or perhaps

---

327. J. Elayi, "The Relations between Tyre and Carthage during the Persian Period," *JANES* 13 (1981) 15–29.

328. U. Morgenroth, "Southern Iberia and the Mediterranean Trade Routes," *OJA* 18 (1999) 395–401; G. Maass-Lindemann, "Vasos fenicios de los siglos VIII–VI en España: Su procedencia y posición dentro del mundo fenicio occidental," *FPI*, 1.227–39, pls. 1–8; A. Peserico, *Le brocche "a fungo" fenicie nel Meditrraneo: Tipologia e cronologia* (Rome: Consiglio Nazionale delle Ricerche, 1996) 101.

329. L. Perdigones Moreno, A. Muñoz Vicente, G. Pisano, *La Necrópolis Fenicio-Punica de Cádiz, Siglos VI–IV a.deC.* (Studia Punica 7; Rome: Università degli Studi di Roma, Dipartimento di Storia, 1990) 11–31; A. Perea Caveda, "Phoenician Gold in the Western Mediterranean: Cádiz, Tharros and Carthage," in *Encounters and Transformations: The Archaeology of Iberia in Transition* (ed. M. S. Balmuth, A. Gilman, and L. Prados-Torreira; Monographs in Mediterranean Archaeology 7; Sheffield: Sheffield Academic Press, 1997) 135–40.

the end of the seventh, there is a fragment of an amphora inscribed "from ʿAkko" (*ʿky*).[330] This specific type of amphora is of Eastern manufacture and is most common in eighth-century Lebanon and Israel, although it persists into the seventh and sixth at Sidon and at Al Mina and Ras el-Bassit along the North Syrian coast.[331]

Also from the earlier sixth or seventh century is a fragment of a Red Slip bowl incised after firing with the notation "for ʾEshmun—100" (*lʾšmn* + symbol).[332] These 100 shekels may have belonged to or been destined for the sanctuary just west of Cádiz on the east side of the estuary of the Guadalquivir, an unassuming, almost domestic adobe structure consisting of one small room and an open paved courtyard[333] and resembling a *marzeaḥ* or merchant clubhouse under the auspices of ʾEshmun rather than a place of communal or public worship. Cádiz depended on such societies of shopkeepers, traveling merchants and overseas traders for its prosperity and for its daily bread. Salt was an important industry.[334] Inland indigenous sites, such as Trebujena in the Gadalquivir basin or Pancorvo[335] on the Guadalete (distinguished by the Phoenician amphorae in which they transported their goods or by the Phoenician arrowheads that they used in the hunt) sold their agricultural produce and the game they bagged to Cádiz.

There is some Greek pottery at Cádiz and Doña Blanca in the sixth century, but Huelva became a showcase for East Greek wares in the early part of the century and for Attic Black Figure pottery later in the century.[336] There were transport amphorae from Chios, Samos, and Miletus, for instance, but dinner dishes and drinking vessels, especially Ionian cups, were very popular.[337] Although Samians, including Kolaios of Samos, were the first Greeks to take advantage of the Iberian network created by the Phoenicians, it seems that the pottery business was a monopoly of Phocaeans operating out of Massalia and Emporion (some of the East Greek wares in Huelva may have originated in these places)[338] and that it flourished only as long as

330. J.-L. Cunchillos, "Las inscripciones fenicias del Tell de Doña Blanca (IV)," *Sefarad* 52 (1992) 75–83, esp. pp. 81–83.

331. A. G. Sagona, "Levantine Storage Jars of the 13th to 4th Century B.C.," *Opuscula Atheniensia* 14 (1982) 73–110, esp. pp. 75–78, 92–95 (Type 2).

332. J.-L. Cunchillos, "Inscripciones fenicias del Tell de Doña Blanca (V)," *Sefarad* 53 (1993) 17–24; J. Naveh, "The Phoenician Hundred-Sign," *RSF* 19 (1991) 139–44.

333. W. E. Mierse, "The Architecture of the Lost Temple of Hercules Gaditanus and Its Levantine Associations," *AJA* 108 (2004) 545–76, esp. pp. 562–63.

334. P. Fernández Uriel, "La industria de la sal," *Actas* 4, 1.345–51.

335. M. L. Lavado Florido, "El comercio a través del Guadalquivir en época antigua: El yacimiento de la Monjas (Trebujena-Cádiz,)" *Actas* 4, 1.385–93; J. Mancebo Dávalos and E. Ferrer Albelda, "Approximación a la problemática de las puntas de flecha en el periodo orientalizante: El yacimiento de Pancorvo (Montellano, Sevilla)," *Zephyrus* 41–42 (1988–89) 315–30.

336. A. J. Domínguez and C. Sánchez, *Greek Pottery from the Iberian Peninsula: Archaic and Classical Periods* (Leiden: Brill, 2001) 5–19.

337. P. Rouillard, *Les Grecs et la Péninsule ibérique du VIIIe au IVe siècle avant Jésus-Christ* (Paris: Boccard, 1991) 110, table 3.

338. A. J. Domínguez, "New Perspectives on the Greek Presence in the Iberian Peninsula," in *The Hellenic Diaspora from Antiquity to Modern Times*, vol. 1: *From Antiquity to 1453 A.D.* (ed. J. M. Fossey and J. Morin; Amsterdam: Gieben, 1991) 109–61, esp. pp. 109–16.

J. Maluquer de Motes, "La dualidad commercial fenicia y griega en Occidente," *FPI*, 2.203–10; P. Cabrera, "Greek Trade in Iberia: The Extent of Interaction," *OJA* 17 (1998) 191–206.

M. Kerschner, "Phokäische Thalassokratie oder Phantom-Phokäer? Die frühgriechischen Keramikfunde im Süden der iberischen Halbinsel aus der agäischen Perspektive," in *Greek Identity*

they maintained peaceable relations with Carthage, for whom the flow of goods and services from Iberia was critical in the sixth century. Phoenician presence, as evidenced by innovative pottery assemblages, continued to be strong in the Huelva region.[339] And it perdured, as witnessed by traditional burial practices, even in indigenous settlements.[340] It may not have been exclusively from the Phoenicians, however, but from the Phocaeans as well that southwestern Iberia learned its letters—not the alphabet (the consonants in a fixed and memorable order) that they or the Phoenicians could have taught them—but random signs from available alphabets that they borrowed to compose a syllabary for religious and commercial use.[341] After the battle of Alalia, East Greek imports in southern Spain stopped, and the Attic wares that replaced them arrived with merchants, sailors, and settlers on Carthaginian ships.

Inland along the Guadalquivir, there is some sixth-century Greek pottery at El Carambola, Carmona, and Seville,[342] but the noteworthy sites are characterized instead by inherited Phoenician artifacts and the continuation of deep-rooted Orientalizing tastes. There are bronze incense stands or candelabras of Cypriot artistic inspiration, and curved knives, usually of iron, whose handles are finished in wood, bone, or ivory that are found in burial or ritual contexts[343] and that seem to have traveled inland from Cádiz and Huelva. An abattoir at Montemolín was built according to Phoenician specifications (rectangular rather than round, with stone foundations and adobe walls) and contained local handmade and Phoenician wheel-made pottery. And apparently, because it was too big to cater only to local needs, it belonged to the Phoenician meat-distribution network.[344]

At Cancho Roano, on a tributary of the Guadiana that debouched at Medellín, there was a similar large building.[345] It housed a thriving textile industry,[346] was central to a small, self-sufficient, indigenous community

in the Western Mediterranean: Papers in Honour of Brian Shefton (ed. K. Lomas; Leiden: Brill, 2004) 115–48, esp. pp. 123–25.

339. P. Rufete Tomico, "Die phönizische Rote Ware aus Huelva," *MM* 30 (1989) 118–34.

340. At Onoba in the district of Huelva, the Orientalized native aristocrats were buried with their chariots, harnesses, and their shields and also with mirrors, ivories, ostrich eggs, and amber ornaments: Domínguez, "New Perspectives on the Greek Presence in the Iberian Peninsula," 117–18.

341. T. Júdice Gamito, "Greeks and Phoenicians in South West Iberia—Who Were the First? Aspects of Archaeological and Epigraphic Evidence," in *The Hellenic Diaspora from Antiquity to Modern Times*, vol. 1: *From Antiquity to 1453 A.D* (ed. J. M. Fossey and J. Morin; Amsterdam: Gieben, 1991) 81–108; J. Rodríguez Ramos, "El origen de la escritura sudlusitano-tartessia y la formación de alfabetos a partir de alefatos," *RSF* 30 (2002) 187–221.

342. A. J. Domínguez and C. Sánchez, *Greek Pottery from the Iberian Peninsula: Archaic and Classical Periods* (Leiden: Brill, 2001) 19–22.

343. F. J. Jiménez Ávila, "Timiaterios 'Chipriotas' de bronce: Centros de producción occidentales," *Actas* 4, 4.1581–94; J. Mancebo Dávalos, "Análisis de los objetos metálicos en el período orientalizante y su conéxion con el mundo fenicio: Los cuchillos afalcatados," in ibid., 1825–34.

344. F. Chaves et al., "El complejo sacrificial de Montemolín," *Actas* 4, 2.573–81.

345. V. M. Guerrero, "El palacio-santuario de Cancho Roano (Badajoz) y la comercialización de ánforas fenicias indígenas," *RSF* 19 (1991) 49–82, pls. 4–7; S. Celestino Pérez, "Cancho Roano: Un centro comercial de caracter politico-religioso e influencia oriental," *RSF* 20 (1992) 19–46, pls. 2–6.

346. J. Gran Aymerich, "Le détroit de Gibraltar et sa projection régionale: Les données géo-stratégiques de l'expansion phénicienne à la lumière des fouilles de Malaga et des recherches en cours," in *Lixus: Actes du colloque organisé par l'Institut des sciences de l'archéologie et du*

that had its own wheel-made domestic pottery but could also boast of curved iron knives and expensive gold and silver jewelry. There was Attic Red Figure Ware later in the fifth century, but for now Cancho Roano was typical of the inland places that cherished their Phoenician memories decades after they had come into their own.

The Phoenician and Punic towns on the Mediterranean coast of Spain seem to have been narrowly focused on Carthaginian interests in the sixth century. Cerro del Villar[347] at the mouth of the Guadalhorce and at the entrance to a fertile plain supplied Carthage with agricultural products. It had a large pottery barn specializing in transport amphorae, and like all coastal sites it trafficked in East Greek wares.[348] It was abandoned early in the sixth century, when its people moved to Málaga, but was resettled in the fifth century by Carthaginians.

Málaga was closely tied to metropolitan Carthage, continuing in Cerro del Villar's role as supplier of agricultural products and as a large and central Punic town in its own right. It imported ivories from Carthage and received pottery, including transport amphorae, drinking vessels, and decorated wares from Attica, Corinth, Chios, Samos, and Lesbos.[349]

Toscanos was an emporium and overseas trade center until the close of the seventh century, but in the sixth, along with its satellite towns, turned almost exclusively to food production and began to rely on a network of indigenous farm communities.[350] The satellites west of the Rio Vélez, from Peñon to Alarcón, were set off from the countryside by a perimeter wall.[351] But the town's full integration into Iberian society is indicated by the handmade pottery found alongside Phoenician wheel-made wares and, especially at Alarcón, by the use of local Grey Ware in turning Phoenician

patrimoine de Rabat avec le concours de l'École Française de Rome, Larache, 8–11 novembre 1989 (Rome: École Française de Rome, 1992) 59–69, esp. pp. 63–67.

347. M. E. Aubet Semmler, "Notas sobre las colonias del sur de España y su función en el marco territorial: El ejemplo del Cerro del Villar (Málaga)," *Atti* 2, 2.617–26; idem, "Die phönizische Niederlassung von Cerro del Villar (Guadalhorche, Málaga)," *MM* 32 (1991) 29–51, pls. 9–22; idem, "Nuevos datos arqueológicos sobre las colonias fenicias de la Bahía de Málaga," in *Lixus: Actes du colloque organse par l'Institut des Sciences de l'Archéologie et du Patrimoine de Rabat avec le concours de l'École Francaise de Rome, Larache, 8–11 novembre 1989* (Rome: École Française de Rome, 1992) 71–78; M. E. Aubet et al., *Cerro del Villar—I: El Asentamiento Fenicio en la desembocadura del Río Guadalhorce y su interacción con el hinterland* (Seville: Junta de Andalucía—Consejeria de Cultura, 1999).

348. Domínguez and Sánchez, *Greek Pottery from the Iberian Peninsula*, 22–25.

349. J. Gran Aymerich, "La scène figurée sur l'ivoire de Malaga et l'imagerie phénicienne," *Sem* 38 (1990) 145–53; idem, "Le détroit de Gibraltar et sa projection régionale," 63; Domínguez and Sánchez, *Greek Pottery from the Iberian Peninsula*, 25–29.

350. M. E. Aubet, "Arquitectura colonial e intercambio," in *Fenicios y Territorio: Actas del II Seminario Internacional sobre Temas Fenicios, Guadamar del Segura, 9–11 de abril de 1999* (ed. A. González Prats; Alicante: Instituto Alicantino de Cultura, 2000) 13–45; A. Delgado Hervás, A. Fernández Cantos, and A. Ruiz Martínez, "Las transformaciones del s. VI en Andalucía: Una visión desde las relaciones entre fenicios e indígenas," *Actas* 4, 4.1781–87.

351. H. Schubart, "Alarcón: El yacimiento fenicio y las fortifcaciones en la cima de Toscanos," in *Fenicios y Territorio: Actas del II Seminario Internacional sobre Temas Fenicios, Guardamar del Segura, 9–11 de Abril de 1999* (ed. A. González Prats; Alicante: Instituto Alicantino de Cultura, 2000) 263–94.

pottery forms.[352] Toscanos was not as wealthy or exclusive as it had been up to the end of the seventh century, but its apparent decline in the sixth was actually a sign of complete involvement in producing perishables instead of collectibles in order to supply food for the growing population of the Punic empire.

Morro de Mezquitilla went through a similar crisis, or critical change in priorities, during the sixth century: at Frigiliana, for instance, 4 kilometers inland, there was an Iberian farming community that worked for the town and was sufficiently assimilated to the Phoenician way of life that it cremated its dead and buried their ashes in imitation Punic urns.[353]

Adra, or Abdera, was overshadowed by the Carthaginian station at Villaricos, which was established, apparently, to monitor relations between the metropolis and the settlements along the eastern seaboard of Spain.[354] In the region of Alicante, the port of La Fonteta[355] at the mouth of the Rio Segura was busy in the seventh century; was clumsily fortified in the early sixth century, perhaps against the Phocaeans at Emporion; and by mid-century, lost its commercial advantage. Nearby Peña Negra was a Spanish settlement with a Phoenician community that did business with the many villages in the Vinalopo Valley.[356] There are amphorae with monograms and personal names, and there is a locally made Red Slip plate with the name Bod'eshmun (*bd'šmn*), of the potter.[357] Like La Fonteta, it dwindled and lost its importance around the middle of the century.

352. J. M. Martín Ruiz, "Cerámicas a mano en los yacimientos fenicios de Andalucía," *Actas* 4, 4.1625–30; G. Maass-Lindemann, "El yacimiento fenicio del Alarcón y la cuestión de la cerámica gris," in *Fenicios y Territorio: Actas del II Seminario Internacional sobre Temas Fenicios, Guardamar del Segura, 9–11 de Abril de 1999* (ed. A. González Prats; Alicante: Instituto Alicantino de Cultura, 2000) 151–68.

353. D. Marzoli, "Anforas púnicas de Morro de Mezquitilla (Málaga)," *Actas* 4, 4.1631–44, esp. p. 1637; E. García Alfonso, "La colonización arcaica y el mundo indígena de la Andalucía mediterránea y su traspaís: Una propuesta de análisis," in ibid., 1799–1804, esp. p. 1802; J. Gran Aymerich and J. R. Anderica, "Populations autochtones et allogènes sur le litoral méditerranéen andalou: De Málaga à Vélez-Málaga et Frigiliana (VIII–Vie s. av. J.-C.)," in ibid., 1811–14, esp. p. 1813.

354. A. Suárez et al., "Abdera: Una colonia fenicia en el Sureste de la Península Ibérica," *MM* 30 (1989) 135–50; C. G. Wagner, "The Carthaginians in Ancient Spain: From Administrative Trade to Territorial Annexation," in *Punic Wars* (ed. H. Davijver and E. Lipiński; Studia Phoenicia 10; Louvain: Peeters, 1989) 145–56; M. Belén Deamos, "Religious Aspects of Phoenician-Punic Colonization in the Iberian Peninsula: The Stelae from Villaricos, Almería," in *Encounters and Transformations: The Archaeology of Iberia in Transition* (ed. M. S. Balmuth, A. Gilman, and L. Prados-Torreira; Monographs in Mediterranean Archaeology 7; Sheffield: Sheffield Academic Press, 1997) 121–33.

355. A. González Prats, "La Fonteta: El asentamiento fenicio de la desembocadura del río Segura (Guardamar, Alicante, España): Resultados de las excavaciones de 1996–1997," *RSF* 26 (1998) 191–228, pls. 2–9; A. J. Sánchez Pérez and R. C. Alonso de la Cruz, "La ciudad fenicia de Herna (Guardamar del Segura, Alicante)," *RSF* 27 (1999) 127–31; A. González Prats and A. García Menárguez, "El conjunto fenicio de la desembocadura del río Segura (Guardamar del Segura, Alicante)," *Actas* 4, 4.1527–37; A. González Prats, A. García Menárguez, and E. Ruiz Segura, "La Fonteta: A Phoenician City in the Far West," *Bierling*, 113–25.

356. A. M. Poveda Navarro, "Penetración cultural fenicia en el territorio indígena del valle septentrional del Vinalopó (Alicante)," *Actas* 4, 4.1863–74; I. Grau Mira, "Settlement Dynamics and Social Organization in Eastern Iberia during the Iron Age (Eighth–Second Centuries BC)," *OJA* 22 (2003) 261–79.

357. A. González Prats, "Las importaciones y la presencia fenicias en la Sierra de Crevillente

At Pozo Moro in the region of Valencia, a funerary monument depicts infant sacrifice as practiced in the Punic community. An enthroned God wearing a bull mask sits at a table. He grasps in his left hand the legs of a sacrificial pig lying on it, and raises in his right hand a bowl containing the body of an infant. A priest wearing a bull mask approaches from the right to offer him a second bowl, and another priest, also wearing a bull mask, raises a knife to kill another infant in a third bowl.[358] It is obscenely graphic and probably represents the separate stages in a single ritual in which a baby is sacrificed or, conceivably, in which a piglet is sacrificed in its place.

The evidence for activities in the native communities in the region is less dramatic. They regularly stored and shipped their goods in authentic or imitation Punic amphorae,[359] and there are recurrent signs of earlier Phoenician presence and continuing Phoenician influence at stations along the coast[360] and at several places in the Ebro Valley.[361] But, as everywhere on the eastern seaboard of Spain, Phoenician presence waned, and their influence faded through the sixth century as Iberian culture became progressively more sophisticated and assertive.

Ibiza was a Carthaginian island. In the sixth century, it had managerial status over the Punic markets in the regions of Alicante and Valencia,[362] and as these regions were abandoned or absorbed into the native syndicates, it probably continued to broker their commercial relations and oversee their contribution to the imperial network. Ibiza itself worked efficiently with the Punic province in Sardinia and northwestern Sicily[363] but was linked especially closely, both politically and culturally, with the North African metropolis. The population was concentrated in the port city and had not spread across the island as it did eventually in the fifth and fourth centuries.[364] Burial practices followed recent Carthaginian customs, with inhumation instead of cremation, at first in simple rock graves and later in elaborate hypogaea[365] but differed in the paucity of grave goods. There were

(Alicante)," *FPI*, 2.279–302, esp. p. 294; L. A. Ruiz Cabrero, "Comercio de ánforas, escritura y presencia fenicia en la península ibérica," *SEL* 19 (2002) 89–120.

358. S. O'Bryhim, "The *Cerastae* and Phoenician Human Sacrifice on Cyprus," *RSF* 27 (1999) 3–20, pls. 1–3, esp. pp. 12–13, pl. 3.

359. C. Mata Parreño, "Las influencias del mundo fenicio-punico en los origenes y desarrollo de la cultura iberica," *Actes* 3, 2.225–44; A. Ribera and A. Fernández, "Las ánforas del mundo fenicio-punico en el país valenciano," *Actas* 4, 4.1699–1709.

360. O. Arteaga, J. Podró, and E. Sanmartí, "La expansión fenicia por las costas de Cataluna y del Languedoc," *FPI*, 2.303–14.

361. M. Mascort, J. Sanmartí, and J. Santacana, "Aldovesta: Les bases d'un modèle commercial dans le cadre de l'expansion phénicienne au nord-est de la péninsule ibérique," *Atti* 2, 3.1073–79; D. Asensio et al., "Las ceramicas fenicias y de tipo fenicio del yacimiento del Barranc de Gafols (Ginestar, Ribera d'Ebre, Tarragona)," *Actas* 4, 4.1733–45.

362. A. Ribera and A. Fernández, "Las ánforas del mundo fenicio-púnico en el País Valenciano," *Actas* 4, 4.1699–1711, esp. p. 1711.

363. C. Gómez Bellard, "La fondation phénicienne d'Ibiza et son développement aux VIIe et VIe s. av. J.-C.," *Atti* 2, 1.109–12; idem, "Die Phönizier auf Ibiza," *MM* 34 (1993) 83–107, pl. 12, esp. pp. 103, 106.

364. C. Gómez Bellard, "Asentamientos rurales en la Ibiza punica," *FPI*, 1.177–92; J. H. Fernández and B. Costa, "La investigación Phenicio-púnica en Ibiza a principios de los años noventa," *Actas* 4, 4.1519–26, esp. pp. 1522–23.

365. J. H. Fernández, "Necrópolis del Puig des Molins (Ibiza): Nuevas perspectives," *FPI*, 1.149–75; B. Costa Ribas, J. H. Fernández Gómez, and C. Gómez Bellard, "Ibiza fenicia: La pri-

only a few expensive burial offerings: an ivory sphinx, ostrich-egg cups, masks and vases, and a silver scarab.[366] These may suggest that social and economic disparity was emerging between the descendants of the original settlers and the newly arrived and increasingly ugly entrepreneurs.[367] One of the former, in a late sixth-century inscription carved into a bronze plaque in the grotto at Es Cuyram, records the fulfillment of a vow made to the Carthaginian God 'Arshup-Melqart (*'ršpmlqrt*) and identifies himself as belonging to the fourth generation of the family in Ibiza.[368]

Conclusion

The sixth century witnessed the definitive separation of the Phoenician East from the Punic West. Tyre, Sidon, Arvad, and Byblos saw their future in the Persian Empire, and their mainland possessions were dedicated to its imperial goals, while belligerence became the business that trade and commerce had been. Carthage received the people—the citizens and the refugees who fled from these cities and towns and filtered out of the Cypriot kingdoms—and became the Western metropolis. In the seventh century, Tyre had financial control of an amazing network of nations, and in the sixth Carthage presided over a conglomerate of regions and provinces that had all been converted to a Phoenician idealism and way of life; and now were learning to articulate their original differences. The Orientalizing revolution in which the great cities of the East had distinguished and defined themselves yielded to an African and European reformation in which Carthage and the Punic West discovered a plainer, more material regeneration.

mera fase de la colonización de la isla (siglos VII y VI a.C.)," *Atti* 2, 2.759–95; B. Costa and J. H. Fernández, "La secuencia cronológica de la necropolis del Puig des Molins (Eivissa): Las fases fenicio-punicas," *Actes* 3, 1.295–310.

366. W. A. Ward, "A Silver Scarab from Ibiza," *RSF* 20 (1992) 67–82, pl. 7; M. C. D'Angelo, "Artigianato eburneo da Ibiza: Las sfinge," *Actas* 4, 4.1511–17; G. Pisano, "Beni di Lusso nel Mondo Punico: Le Uova di Struzzo," in *Da Pyrgi a Mozia: Studi sull'archeologia nel Mediterraneo in Memoria di Antonia Ciasca* (ed. M. G. Amadasi Guzzo, M. Liverani, and P. Matthiae; Vicino Oriente—Quaderno 3/2; Rome: Università degli Studi di Roma, "La Sapienza," 2002) 391–401.

367. R. Gurrea and J. Ramón, "Excavaciones arqueologicas en la acropolis de Eivissa (calle de Santa Maria): El horizonte arcaico," *Actas* 4, 4.1555–79.

368. J. M. Solá-Solé, "Inscripciones fenicias de la peninsula iberica," *Sefarad* 15 (1955) 41–53, #2, esp. pp. 45–46; M. J. Estanyol i Fuentes, *Corpus de la inscripciones fenicias, punicas y neopunicas de España* (Barcelona: Pub. by the author, 1986) #07.15, pp. 25–26; J. Ferron, "Las inscripciones votivas de la plaqueta de 'Es Cuyram' (Ibiza)," *Trabajos de Prehistoria* n.s. 26 (1969) 295–304, pl. 1.

Chapter 6

The Carthaginian World of the Fifth and Fourth Centuries B.C.E.: Between the Persians and the Greeks

In the fifth and fourth centuries, the Mediterranean world that the Phoenicians had created for themselves began to harden. Travel and adventure melded into immigration. The urge to explore dwindled into the search for jobs. Coinage regulated the exciting probabilities of trade and commerce and gradually replaced the conversation of merchants and the interchange of exotic goods, good stories, and great ideas with the distribution of mass-produced and mundane commodities. Money was spent on building huge fleets, hiring mercenaries, and turning pleasant latifundia into forts. War became a way of life, people were driven into defining their ethnicities, and an unclear future, the stuff of apocalyptic vision, led to archaizing and reinventing the past.

The Persian Empire molded these two centuries, determined their priorities, and framed their major events, but it had strangely little effect on Phoenician life and culture.[1] There are Persian objects or affectations—the latest fashions show up in sculptures; the Great King's portrait is hammered into Sidonian coins—but there is no Persian élan. The international network of commerce and culture that the Phoenician cities had promoted was organized to death in a satrapal and provincial system. Countries, regions, and city-states were autonomous but increasingly self-enclosed and separated in a system of surveillance and suspicion. The Greeks, early inspiration for and immemorial associates of the Phoenicians, took up the cultural slack, and their spirit breathed new life into these proud cities, ever the soul of the Mediterranean world into which they now receded.

Byblos: The Šiptiba'al Dynasty Continues

The Persians promoted divisions and factionalism among the subject peoples to ensure the security of the Empire. This was a seemingly benign program consisting of positive steps such as encouraging national pride and the restoration of religious forms and institutions. This is most explicit in the instance of ancient Judah, much diminished as newly minted Yehud, and totally isolated in the imperial scheme, where there are records

---

1. J. Elayi, "La domination perse sur les cités phéniciennes," *Atti* 2, 1.77–85.

452

of rebuilding the temple, reinstituting the liturgy, and canonizing the law along with the narrative of its origins. This fragmentation is also attested in the case of Byblos, whose story in the fifth and fourth centuries revolved around its monumental temple and the kings who rebuilt it in the late sixth, upgraded it in the early fifth, and refurbished it in the mid-fifth century.[2]

Coinage was introduced in the seventh century in Lydia under Gyges and Croesus and soon after was adopted in Greece, but it did not become meaningful as money until the Persian period.[3] Byblos may have been the earliest of the mainland Phoenician cities to mint coins, but this did not happen before the mid-fifth century,[4] and the earlier kings are known only from the inscriptional evidence. From the mid-fifth century on through the fourth, by contrast, the kings of Byblos are known particularly from the iconography and legends of their coins.

About the mid-fifth century, King Yaḥwîmilk[5] of Byblos built an out-door chapel for the Mistress (*ba'alat*) of the city and described his work in a stele that was set into one of its walls. On the stele, under the canopy of a winged sun disk, the Goddess sits on her throne, dressed in a long robe and wearing the horned-globe crown of Isis, holding her scepter in her left hand and raising her right hand to bless the king who stands before her, wearing a Persian bonnet with neck-flap and a Persian coat over his embroidered tunic, with his right hand raised to salute her and his left extended to offer her a cup of wine. The text of the stele, below this scene, begins by acknowledging that she made him king in answer to his prayers. He had, after all, just chanced upon the throne because he was a grandson of ʾUrumilk, the second king in the dynasty founded by Šiptibaʿal, but he was in a collateral line because his father, Yiḥḥarbaʿal, had not reigned.[6] The text continues with a description of the chapel and the stele that adorned it.[7]

---

2. Idem, "Studies in Phoenician Geography during the Persian Period," *JNES* 41 (1982) 83–110, esp. p. 92.

3. D. Kagan, "The Dates of the Earliest Coins," *AJA* 86 (1982) 343–60; K. Radner, "Zu den früheste lydischen Münzprägungen aus der Sicht Assyriens," in *Brüchenland Anatolien? Ursachen, Extensität und Modi des Kuturaustausches zwischen Anatolien und seinen Nachbarn* (ed. H. Blum et al.; Tübingen: Attempto, 2002) 45–57; A. Lemaire, "La circulation monétaire phénicienne en Palestine à l'époque perse," *Actes* 3, 2.192–202.

4. J. Elayi, "Le phénomène monétaire dans les cites phéniciennes à l'époque perse," in *Numismatique et histoire économique phéniciennes et puniques* (ed. T. Hackens and G. Moucharte; Studia Phoenicia 9; Louvain-la-Neuve: Université Catholique de Louvain, 1992) 21–31, pl. 6, esp. pp. 22–23; J. W. Betlyon, *CMP*, 111–35; idem, "Canaanite Myth and the Early Coinage of the Phoenician City-States," in *Ancient Economy in Mythology: East and West* (ed. M. Silver; Savage, MD: Rowman and Littlefield, 1991) 135–61.

5. The name is composed of *milk*, "king," the divine personification of Kingship, and a modal form of the verb "to live" (*ḥwy*). In the basic (G) stem, it would mean "may Milk live" and might be pronounced *Yaḥwimilk. In the factitive (D) stem, it could mean "may Milk renew life" and might be pronounced *Yaḥawwimilk. In the causative (Y) stem, the meaning would be "may Milk give life," and it might be pronounced *Yiḥwimilk. Regarding the stele, see *CIS* 1.1; *TSSI* 3.93–99.

6. É. Puech, "Remarques sur quelques inscriptions phéniciennes de Byblos," *RSF* 9 (1981) 153–68, esp. pp. 158–62.

7. P. Xella, "Pantheon e culto a Biblo: Aspetti e problemi," in *Biblo: Una città e la sua cultura* (ed. E. Acquaro et al.; Rome: Consiglio Nazionale delle Richerche, 1994) 195–214, esp. pp. 206–8.

The main features of this chapel, archaeological traces of which are left in the temple precinct of Byblos, were a bronze altar in the center of a courtyard, which was surrounded by a portico, and the text lingers on the description of its pillars, capitals, and roof. The altar is gone, but its square pediment remains and some of the piazza and a few of the pillars. The embellishment consisted of covering the scene of divine worship with gold leaf, and the inscription singles out for admiration the gold on the winged sun disk and the gold adorning the two figures, whose design otherwise was only roughly incised in the stone.

The scene, without this embellishment, is represented on a small, 4″ × 6″ terra-cotta plaque[8] with a plain back and with two holes at the top that would allow it to be hung on a cord or chain as an amulet. The scene is set in a chapel in a paved plaza represented by a platform, with a portico represented by two columns, capitals, and a roof. The entrance is surmounted by an oblong entablature that is entirely filled by a winged sun disk and supports two addorsed lions. The roof is flat and consists of beams covered by a fringed canopy. This porticoed chapel is substantial and done in high relief. The ritual scene, by contrast, is simply scratched or incised in the clay between the pillars and under the sun disk. As on the stele, the Goddess sits on an armless throne, holding her scepter in her left hand, and raising her right hand to bless the king, who stands before her to offer her a cup. The Goddess is dressed in an ankle-length plain robe, with a necklace, and wears a soft hat without the double crown of Egypt; she is twice the size of the king and almost fills the chapel; her grandeur, kindness, and accessibility are the attributes the simple incised drawing portrays.[9] The king is dressed and assumes the same attitude as on the stele of Yaḥwîmilk. The plaque, clearly, was meant as a copy of the ritual scene depicted on the stele to commemorate the revelation of the Goddess in her temple at the accession of Yaḥwîmilk to the throne of Byblos.

The stele, its words and the picture, were not incidental but were integral to the fulfillment of his vow, and Yaḥwîmilk returns to it at the end of his inscription in his admonition to any king or mortal who would contemplate changing the text or enlarging the chapel. They must take care of the altar, the gold leaf design, and the portico, but above all they must show respect for the stele, its inscription (summarized by citing its first words, "I am Yaḥwîmilk, king of Byblos"), its base, and the foundation deposit (its "secret place") beneath it. This was the "work" (*mlʾkt*) of his reign, it was what gave him legitimacy and "favor in the eyes of the Gods, and in the eyes of the people of this land, and favour with the land itself." He ends with the warning that any disrespect for him or for the Goddess and her chapel would make the anticipated royal or merely mortal culprit offensive, literally "putrid," before all the Gods of Byblos.

---

8. E. Gubel, "Une nouvelle représentation du culte de la Baʿalat Gebal?" in *Religio Phoenicia* (ed. C. Bonnet, E. Lipiński, and P. Marchetti; Studia Phoenicia 4; Namur: Société des Études Classiques, 1986) 263–76.

9. G. Mussies, "Identification and Self-Identification of Gods in Classical and Hellenistic Times," in *Knowledge of God in the Graeco-Roman World* (ed. R. van den Broek, T. Baarda, and J. Mansfield; Leiden: Brill, 1988) 1–18.

It is probable that the earliest coins from Byblos were issued during the reign of Yaḥwîmilk.[10] These are on the Attic standard for the larger denominations and on the Phoenician standard for the smaller but resemble Attic coins, and iconographically are unlike all the subsequent series.[11] The obverse has a crouching sphinx wearing the double crown of Egypt, while the reverse has a decorative rendition of a lotus plant and blossom, and both sides are spare, with no attempt to fill the empty spaces. The coins, therefore, present an amalgam of Attic, Egyptian, and traditional Phoenician iconographic traditions that reflect the king's prayer on his stele that his Mistress might bless him, give him life, and extend the years of his reign over Byblos.

The name of the king who reigned before Yaḥwîmilk is lost in the lacuna at the beginning of his funerary inscription.[12] This was incised on the body of a white marble sarcophagus, written between ruled lines like old Byblian royal inscriptions. The marble is broken on all sides except the top, so the first line of the text is preserved and, although its beginning is lost and some letters are missing at the end, it can be reconstructed from earlier and later inscriptions and from several lines of conjecture. The second line has a few original expressions, but the blanks can be filled in with the required clichés of royal funerary texts. These reconstructions highlight the bits of preserved text by setting them in a readable context:

> 1. [I, ʿOzîbaʿl, king of Byblos, son of ʾUrumilk, king of Byblos, am lying in this resting place], I alone. And here I am resting in this coffin, wrapped in bdellium and myrrh. 2. [And you, any king or any mortal, if you seek anything in it, or if you seek to open] the cover of this coffin or to disturb my decaying bones, seek him out Almighty God, and on every road. . . .]

The Phoenician text in each line is the same length. The theophoric element in the names of the kings of sixth- and fifth-century Byblos usually alternates between *milk* (king) and *baʿal* (lord): the brother of this conjectured ʿOzîbaʿal, the younger son of ʾUrumilk and father of Yaḥwîmilk, was named Yiḥḥarbaʿal.

His coffin was classic Byblian, with nothing of Egyptian anthropoid or sculpted Greek pretension, but marble as fashion prescribed. He was partially embalmed, and his basic concern, which he shared with all Byblians, was the preservation of his bones. The first line emphasizes "I"—his name, his solitude in the grave, his appearance in death. The second line emphasizes the "you" of the potential grave robber and contrasts his seeking for treasure with his being sought relentlessly by the Almighty throughout the world. It ends, in Byblian literary style, by shifting to the second person of direct address to the dynastic God, "the Almighty" (*haʾaddîr*).

---

10. É. Puech, "Les premières émissions byblites et les rois de Byblos à la fin du Ve siècle avant J.-C.," *Atti* 2, 1.287–98, esp. p. 295.

11. *CMP* 111–13.

12. J. Starcky, "Une inscription phénicienne de Byblos," *MUSJ* 45 (1969) 259–73; F. M. Cross, "A Recently Published Phoenician Inscription of the Persian Period from Byblos," *IEJ* 29 (1979) 40–44; W. Röllig, "Eine neue phönizische Inschrift aus Byblos," *Neue Ephemeris für semitische Epigraphik* (Wiesbaden: Harrassowitz, 1974) 2.1–15; I. Schiffmann, "Studien zur Interpretation der neuen phönizischen Inschrift aus Byblos (*Byblos* 13)," *RSF* 4 (1976) 171–77.

Adventure and business, travel on land and sea and beyond the grave are the topics of the remaining, badly broken five lines. He went on distant overland journeys with the King of the Medes and Persians, the Lord of Kings, and with the Great Kings (*rbm*) and brought home the booty he acquired and the gifts he received for the storehouses in Byblos. He speaks of the wealth of the sea (*hwn ym*) and of making war with "them," likely the Greeks, not improbably at Salamis: a Byblian contingent is not included by name among the protagonists in any of the Greek wars, but the king seems proud of his inclusion even a minor role with great kings such as Bodʿaštart of Sidon, Mattin of Tyre, and Mahirbaʿal of Arvad. Most of his inscription has been about his world travels (and pursuit of the vandals), and he concludes by talking about his death, about his journey to meet his fathers, and reflecting on how strange, how utterly foreign (*zar*) this journey appears. His speech ends as it began by saying that he is lying alone in his resting place, and he lets silence descend upon him with the gold mask (*ṣmd*) laid on his face.[13]

The Almighty (*hʾdr*) whom this king invoked was the God of this particular dynasty. "Mighty" (*ʾdr*) is a favorite word in the scribal lexicon of Byblos, but the epithet belongs specifically to Baʿal, the civic God of Byblos, who is mentioned with this title, "Almighty Baʿal" (*bʿl ʾdr*), in the inscription of ʾUrumilk,[14] the father of ʿOzibaʿal. Both of these are funerary inscriptions, and in both the God is summoned to deal with a violator of the tomb because, as on funerary monuments at third- and second-century Constantine in the realm of Carthage,[15] and as the God who is manifested in the mortal Adonis, he is the familiar of death and of enduring life. In the inscription of ʿOzibaʿal, he is invoked as "the Almighty," without the title "Baʿal," and there is no mention of any other God. But in the inscription of ʾUrumilk, he is paired with "the Mistress" (*baʿalat*), and together, as God and Goddess of the city, they are included between "the Lord of Heaven" and "all the Holy Gods of Byblos"—that is, the head of the pantheon and the assembly over which he presides.

ʾUrumilk's inscription is rich in its details of his death and burial and their ritual implications and curiously silent about affairs of government or submission to the great king. Some of the details are repeated in his son's inscription: death is a journey to his ancestors, the tomb is his resting place, he is alone there, he does not want to be disturbed or to have anyone buried next to him. Peculiar to his text is the religious or ritual aspect of his burial. The coffin in which he is buried has been placed in a grave, and this is his home among the Great Ones. The coffin contains his bones, the mortal tokens of his eventual resurrection. His home, consequently, is not in an ordinary burial ground but is in a sanctuary (*maqôm*), fit for a God, where his waiting imitates the triduum of Adonis, his "Almighty Baʿal." His

---

13. J. Curtis, "Gold Face-Masks in the Ancient Near East," in *The Archaeology of Death in the Ancient Near East* (ed. S. Campbell and A. Green; Oxbow Monograph 51; Oxford: Oxbow, 1995) 226–31.

14. *KAI* 9; M. Dunand, *Fouilles de Byblos 1* (Paris: Geuthner, 1939) 31–32, #1143a, b, c; Puech, "Remarques sur quelques inscriptions phéniciennes de Byblos," 153–58.

15. A. Berthier and R. Charlier, *Le sanctuaire punique d'El-Hofra à Constantine*, vol. 1: *Texte* (Paris: Arts et Métiers Graphiques, 1955) 14–22, #4–19.

death, burial, and eternal rest are ritual and exclusive affairs: the ancestors are his "fathers," the former kings; his home is not among common people but among the important people of the past; in defense of his immortality, he appeals to his dynastic God, to the Goddess of the city, and to the entire assembly of the Gods of Byblos.

The political situation during his reign, to which he does not refer, is suggested by a cuneiform text from Babylon.[16] The text is dated to the 23rd of the month Ululu of some year (the text is damaged) in the reign of Darius I (522–486 B.C.E.) and lists the tithe sent by the Babylonian governor of Byblos to the God Shamash in Sippar. The tithe consisted of 12 shekels of silver, a mina and 50 shekels of red purple wool, a mina and 24 shekels of blue purple wool, 2 jars of wine, and 1 cedar beam. The tithe was personal, but the amounts are not staggering (a mina is 60 shekels), and the items are not unusual, because temples needed money and wine and, not surprisingly, because the coastal cities were famous for their wood and purple dyes. The real curiosity of the text is that there was a governor, a Persian administrator, in Byblos (whether this was original Persian policy or an innovation in the latter part of the reign of Darius depends in part on the missing date) and that this does not seem to have impinged very much or at all on the autonomy of the king or the city.

From the time of ʾUrumilk's predecessor, Šiptibaʿal, there are dedications to the Gods of Byblos; one to Baʿal, painted on a decorated ostrich egg; and two to Astarte, the Lady of Byblos, one on the silver amulet of a colonial sea captain and one on the scarab acknowledging her benefits to the people. From his own reign, perhaps, there is further evidence of her popularity and from later times continued witness to her and to Baʿal's privileged place in the devotion of the people.

A fifth-century lead disk found in the sea near Byblos features a scene that a local silversmith might have used to design and advertise drinking cups from his shop.[17] The center of the model shows papyrus stalks radiating from a central boss to encircling lines. The outer frieze pictures Astarte on horseback, her right arm drawn back and poised to hurl a javelin, hunting an antelope that runs behind a lion pursuing a second antelope, and these behind another lion chasing an ibex. The theme is an adaptation of the traditional representation of Astarte as the Goddess of War to the Assyrian and then Persian ideals of the royal hunt in a park, or Paradise. There is another lead prototype very much like it in motif and workmanship that was found at Memphis[18] where, as a dedication to Astarte attests, there was a Byblian enclave until at least the late second century:[19]

---

16. M. Dandamayev, "A Governor of Byblos in Sippar," in *Immigration and Emigration within the Ancient Near East: Festschrift E. Lipiński* (ed. K. van Lerberghe and A. Schoors; Louvain: Peeters, 1995) 29–31.

17. E. Gubel and S. Cauet, "Un nouveau type de coupe phénicienne," *Syria* 64 (1987) 193–204, esp. p. 202.

18. Ibid., 200.

19. *KAI* 48. A fragment of a stele or offering table found by chance at Byblos has the cartouche of Pharaoh Shishak and in the open spaces around it, added independently, a Phoenician inscription that has been restored to read (*RES* 505): "What Abibaʿal, interpreter of the Byblian community in Egypt, dedicated to Baʿalat of Byblos, for the life of the Byblians."

1. The dedication which I offered—I, Paʿalʿastart, son of ʿAbdmilkot, son of Banobaʿal, son of ʿAbdmilkot, son of Banobaʿal, 2. son of ʿAbdmilkot, because they protected me, me myself—to my Lady, to the Almighty Isis, the Goddess Astarte, and the Gods who 3. are my Gods. May they bless me and my sons ʿAbdʾosiris and Banobaʿal and ʿAbdšamš and Paʿalʿastart, and their 4. mother Hannaʿaštart, and give them favour in the sight of the Gods and of the children of Adam.

There are Byblian dialectal features—the relative pronoun, the pleonastic use of the first-person pronoun, the epithet "Almighty" (ʾdrt)—but what is most startling is the explicit syncretism whereby Astarte, who herself had become synonymous with "the Goddess," is assimilated to Isis, the Goddess *tout court*, the Almighty.

Inscriptions from fourth-century Byblos are rare, but two of them mention Astarte. The later, from the middle of the century, is on the edge of a marble plate dedicated to her in thanksgiving and in the hope of her continuing attention:[20] "For my Lady, for Astarte. May she bless me." The earlier is on the outside of the backrest of an empty throne[21] and represents the intermediate stage in the syncretism that was complete by the time of the Memphis stele. The Phoenician text reads, "for Baʿalat of Byblos" (lbʿlt gbl). Above it in Greek, there is the interpretation, "Astarte, the Great Goddess" (*astarte thea megiste*). This omits the dedication ("for . . ."), and would be an exact translation of "Astarte, Almighty Goddess" (ʿštrt ʾlm ʾdrt), like "the Almighty Goddess Isis" (lʾlm ʾdrt ʾs) on the Memphis stele. It is not a translation of the Phoenician text on the throne, but it does express the growing belief, among the Phoenicians, in One God and One Goddess, each with many possible manifestations and increasingly, as in the case of the empty throne, without any particular physical representation.

These theological trends did not obscure the distinction and separate identity of the Gods and Goddesses, and at Byblos in particular the cult of the Mistress (baʿalat) of the city continued and is attested through the fourth century. There are remains of a very small limestone statue inscribed with the name "Mistress of Byblos" (bʿlt gbl) that is contemporary with the empty throne.[22] She is seated, like the Goddess on the terra-cotta plaque, on an armless and backless throne, clothed in a long belted robe, but the insignias of her divinity, such as her scepter and gesture of benediction, are omitted, while her naturalness is emphasized by accentuating the soft contours of her body and her hands demurely folded in her lap. She looks like one of her votaries, any unexceptional woman citizen (bʿlt) of Byblos, completely different from but entirely analogous to her majestic presence before Yaḥwîmilk, the king of Byblos.

The dynasty inaugurated by Šiptibaʿal III, the king mentioned in the inscription on the silver amulet of the colonial sea captain, included his son ʾUrumilk, his grandsons ʿOzibaʿal and Yiḥḥarbaʿal, and his great-grandson

---

20. P. Bordreuil, "Astarté, la Dame de Byblos," *CRAIBL* (1998) 1153–64, esp. pp. 1153–54.
21. Ibid., 1156–57.
22. E. Gubel and P. Bordreuil, "Statuette fragmentaire portant le nom de la Baalat Gubal," *Sem* 35 (1985) 5–11, pls. 1–2.

Yaḥwîmilk. The second coin series from Byblos[23] is similar to the first and, like it, also differs from the following series: the obverse has a seated, human-headed and winged sphinx wearing the double crown of Egypt with a uraeus on the front; the reverse has a falcon, the symbol of Horus, wearing the double crown of Egypt and carrying a scepter and flail, symbols of Osiris, with the spaces filled by a lotus blossom. Three Phoenician letters (ʿ, g, k—the abbreviation of the denomination of the coin and the initials of the king's name, *germilk*,[24] "Client of the King") are followed by his title, "king of Byblos" (*mlk gbl*). This king was the son of Yaḥwîmilk, otherwise unrecorded and unknown, and the last king of the dynasty.

There are two transitional coin series that use some of the Egyptianizing iconography enjoyed by Yaḥwîmilk and his son but anticipate the seafaring iconography on the coins of the following kings.[25] One series has a sphinx on the obverse and a galley on the reverse. Another has the galley on the obverse and a vulture on the reverse:[26] the ship, equipped with a battering ram, transports three marines wearing Greek armor and rides the waves over a winged sea horse; the vulture stands over the body of a ram. These coins were issued by the first kings of a new dynasty, and their iconography is clearly indicative of a new belligerence stalking Byblos.

The names of the following kings and the order of their reigns[27] are known from their coins, from the mention of the second in his mother's funerary inscription, and from references to the last in the time of Alexander the Great. ʾElpaʿol's coins[28] are like the coins of the preceding king, except that death is represented by a lion standing over the body of a bull, the sea is pictured as undulating lines, his nationality is symbolized by a murex shell (the source of red and purple dye, which the Greeks called "Phoenician," *phoenix*), and his name and title are written on the reverse: "ʾElpaʿol, king of Byblos." The next king, ʿOzibaʿal, whose coins are similar to these,[29] was a son of the high priest of the Goddess of Byblos. His mother's funerary inscription,[30] in fine print on a plain marble coffin, tries to make the best of his precarious claim to the throne by describing herself as a real lady, lying in state, dressed in a bright robe, a tiara on her head, and a gold mask on her mouth,[31] "just like the queen mothers who were before me." The last two kings of Byblos used the same coins,[32] and chose throne

---

23. Puech, "Les premières émissions byblites et les rois de Byblos à la fin du Ve siècle avant J.-C."

24. Ibid., 292–96.

25. Ibid., 290–92.

26. *CMP* 113–16.

27. J. Elayi and A. G. Elayi, "L'ordre de succession des derniers rois de Byblos," *Syria* 70 (1993) 109–15.

28. *CMP* 116–17.

29. Ibid., 118–20.

30. *KAI* 11; P. Swiggers, "The Phoenician Inscription of Batnuʿam," *Orientalia Lovaniensia Periodica* 11 (1980) 11–16; J. Azize, "The Genre of the Bitnoam Inscription," *ANESt* 42 (2005) 318–33.

31. N. Theodossiev, "The Dead with Golden Faces: Dasaretian, Palagonian, Mygdonian and Boeotian Funeral Masks," *OJA* 17 (1998) 345–67; idem, "The Dead with Golden Faces, II: Other Evidence and Connections," *OJA* 19 (2000) 175–210.

32. *CMP* 120–21.

Fig. 6.1. Byblian coin of ʿAyyinʾel (ANS 1953.117.2). Reproduced courtesy of the American Numismatic Society.

names that might be heartening in these troubling times: ʾAddirmilk, invoking the "Almighty" source of kingship, and ʿAyyinʾel, "God Sees," appealing to a God beyond political borders (see fig. 6.1). Before Byblos surrendered to Alexander the Great, a clue to the common expectation that normalcy would prevail (and the time it took before Byblos did surrender) is the many hoards of coins of the last three kings that were buried and long forgotten.[33]

About 100 years later, a touch of normalcy is indicated by the dedication of incense altars in the temple precinct of Byblos:[34] "These two incense altars I made, I ʿAbdʾeshmun, son of ʾIsaʿoʾ the builder, for Adonis and for the statue of Baʿal. May they bless him and give him life." A contemporary inscription from Cagliari in Sardinia[35] is perhaps by another Byblian, because it records the dedication of two incense altars to the Lord of Heaven, the president of the Byblian pantheon. The pleonastic pronoun in the inscription from Byblos (". . . I made, I . . .") is typical of the local dialect. The man's father was an architect, and this deserves mention because he designed the altars. The dedication to Baʿal and Adonis is unusual, but not surprising, because they are the same person, mortal and transcendent, understood as the darling youth doomed to die, and as the God who will overcome death. This belief was immemorial and enduring among Byblians and is reflected in another, late fifth-century inscription from Cagliari repeated in beautiful

    33. P. Naster, "Trésors de monnaies de Byblos du IVe s. av. J.-C. trouvés à Byblos," in *Numismatique et histoire économique phéniciennes et puniques* (ed. T. Hackens and G. Moucharte; Studia Phoenicia 9; Louvain-la-Neuve: Université Catholique de Louvain, 1992) 41–49, pl. 10; J. Elayi and A. G. Elayi, "Nouveau trésor de monnaies de Byblos (1992)," *Revue Belge de Numismatique* 139 (1993) 17–30, pls. 1–5.

    34. C. R. Krahmalkov, "The Byblian Phoenician Inscription of ʿbdʾšmn: A Critical Note on Byblian Grammar," *JSS* 38 (1993) 25–32.

    35. *IFPCO* 101–2 #23.

cursive script on the waist of two identical funerary urns: "Rise up, you my wife, to live among the Most High" (*ʿrm ʾt ʾšt lḥwt bʿlnm*).[36]

Byblos was always special. It was not known for its exploits but for fidelity to its tradition. It did not have a great deal of territory, its coins did not circulate beyond its borders, and it was famous not for its wealth but for its expertise. It invented the alphabet, brought it and a companion literature to the world, taught people its language, and shared with them its religion. It had its own archaic dialect: it used a prefixed *l-* (*l-ybrkn*) or a suffixed *-m*[37] (*ʿr-m*) to express the optative ("may he bless me," "may you rise up, my wife"); it used the first-person-singular personal pronoun pleonastically, in the nominative ("I did it, I myself"), genitive ("my name, of me"), dative ("I made for me, for myself"), and accusative ("because they kept me, me myself"); it distinguished cases, and with the genitive used distinct forms of the demonstrative pronoun and of the object-marker; it had its own relative pronoun, demonstratives, and third-person pronominal suffixes; it could tolerate abrupt changes of person in a narrative text; and expressed a sequence of first-person action in a past narrative by the infinitive + the first-person-singular pronoun. Byblos in the fifth and fourth centuries entertained a Persian-appointed Babylonian governor (he was glad to lavish its luxuries on his temple in Sippar) but was autonomous and secure in its old routines.

The sequence of kings during the fifth and fourth centuries in Byblos, if assigned relative dates on an arbitrary sliding scale, finds an anchor in the story of the other cities and eventually situates Byblos in the stream of world affairs:

Šipṭibaʿal		520
ʾUrumilk		500
ʿOzîbaʿal		480
Yaḥwîmilk	1st coin series	460
. . . .	2nd coin series	440
. . . .	3rd coin series	420
. . . .	4th coin series	400
ʾElpaʿol	5th coin series	380
ʿOzîbaʿal	6th coin series	370
ʾAddîrmilk	7th coin series	360
ʿAyyinʾel	8th coin series	350

ʿOzîbaʿal mentions making money and going to war for the Persians and alludes to fighting with them against the Greeks. The first two coin series are Egyptianizing in their iconography, but the next two less so, and then Egyptian influence is missing, and local, or ethnic Phoenician iconography sets in after Egypt extracted itself from the Empire in 404 B.C.E. ʾElpaʿol was replaced by ʿOzîbaʿal II, a relative of the king with credentials from his priestly family. The Phoenician revolt led by Sidon in 351 B.C.E. would

---

36. Ibid., 115–16 #35, pl. 43.

37. Enclitic *mem* generally is not recognized in Phoenician, and its use in Biblical Hebrew is disputed: see J. A. Emerton, "Are There Examples of Enclitic *mem* in the Hebrew Bible?" in *Texts, Temples, and Traditions: A Tribute to Menahem Haran* (ed. M. V. Fox et al.; Winona Lake, IN: Eisenbrauns, 1996) 321–38.

account for ʾAddirmilk's brief reign (few of his coins were in circulation) and for the accession of ʿAyyinʾel. The founder of the dynasty was a contemporary of Tabnît of Sidon, and his successor, ʾUrumilk, was king of Byblos during the reign of ʾEshmunʿazor and the co-regency of ʾImmîʿaštart, when the kings of Tyre were ʾIttobaʿal, Hirom, and Mattin. The calendar gives a sort of rationality to the sequence and eventually to the role of Byblos and its sister cities in Mediterranean affairs.

Tyre and Vicinity on the Island: From a Monarchy to a Republic

Tyre in the fifth and fourth centuries missed the impetus it had received earlier from the inland nations.[38] Judah was a Persian province, a fraction of its former territory, absorbed in its reconstruction, conservative and xenophobic. The Transjordanian nations were drawn into the Nabatean vortex or, like Edom, now Idumea, were inconspicuous confederates of the Empire. The Arabs who managed Gaza and Sinai for the Assyrians acquired free and independent control of it. The creative network had dissipated, and Tyre could rely only on its ports and towns in the coastal strip north of Mount Carmel, or on its former dependencies south of Carmel in the Plain of Sharon, now administered by Sidon.

From coins and inscriptions and classical sources, many of the kings of Tyre are known. In the fifth century, they fought in the Persian navy, digging the Nile canal for Darius I, and a canal across the Mount Athos peninsula for Xerxes' invasion of Europe,[39] but otherwise were satisfied with managing their mainland possessions, supervising their colonies in Cyprus, and maintaining their trading stations in the Aegean. In the fourth century, there was the turmoil of repeated rebellion in the Persian Empire, social unrest,[40] and interference by a council of elders and an assembly of citizens and its elected president.[41] Still the monarchy perdured into the early third century, when Tyre evolved naturally into a republic and, beginning in 275/274 B.C.E., adopted the calendar of "the people of Tyre."

An inscription on a votive ship dating to the late sixth century helps to establish the chronology of the kings in that century and in the early fifth.[42] The text was incised from stern to stem along the plimsoll line of a marble warship, but only the prow of the ship and the end of the inscription are preserved. The inscription reads: ". . . he bles]sed Tyre, and saved the Sidonians from thick clouds, and did not leave King ʾIttobaʿal, son of

---

38. A. Lemaire, "Populations et territoires de la Palestine à l'époque perse," *Transeu* 3 (1990) 31–74.

39. B. S. J. Isserlin, "The Canal of Xerxes: Facts and Problems," *ABSA* 86 (1991) 83–91, pl. 4; idem, "The Canal of Xerxes and the Phoenicians," *Actas* 4, 1.815–18.

40. J. Elayi, "La révolte des esclaves de Tyr relate par Justin," *BaghM* 12 (1981) 139–50.

41. F. Verkinderen, "Les cités phéniciens dans l'empire d'Alexandre le Grand," in *Phoenicia and the East Mediterranean in the First Millennium B.C.* (ed. E. Lipiński; Studia Phoenicia 5; Louvain: Peeters, 1987) 287–308.

42. A. Lemaire, "Inscription royale phénicienne sur bateau votif," in *Teshûrôt LaAvishur: Studies in the Bible and the Ancient Near East, in Hebrew and Semitic Languages. Festschrift Presented to Prof. Yitzhak Avishur on the Occasion of His 65th Birthday* (ed. M. Heltzer and M. Malul; Tel Aviv–Jaffa: Archaeological Center, 2004) 117*–29*.

the King, Ḥîrôm King of Tyre, in dread."[43] The unusual phrasing at the end of the text indicates that Ḥîrôm was king and that his son ʾIttobaʿal was co-regent or officially crown prince and this, combined with the information from classical sources, suggests the following king list:[44]

ʾIttobaʿal III	590
Baʿal	575
Baʿalyatar	560
Mahirbaʿal	556–552
Ḥîrôm III	552–532
ʾIttobaʿal IV	532–512
Ḥîrôm IV	512–490
Mattin III	490–470

The model ship, on this reading, was dedicated by ʾIttobaʿal IV while his father Ḥîrôm III, was still king, that is, around 532 B.C.E. His grandson, Mattin III, son of Ḥîrôm IV, was commander of the Tyrian fleet at the battle of Salamis in 480 B.C.E.

The missing half of the inscription probably mentioned the ship, the vow the king made when it was threatened by impenetrable clouds, the name of the God to whom the vow was made, and the dedication of the ship when the prayer was answered. A typical reconstruction with all these elements and about the same length as the second half of the inscription would be:

> [This is the ship that ʾIttobaʿal, king of Tyre, the captain, vowed and dedicated to his Lord, to Melqart of Tyre, because he bles]sed Tyre and saved the Sidonians from thick clouds and did not leave King ʾIttobaʿal, son of the king, Ḥîrôm, king of Tyre, in dread.

This version indicates that the ship is the symbol of Tyre, that the king is its captain, and that the people of Tyre, ethnically Sidonians, are its crew. But it also suggests that thick clouds were not just meteorological facts but symbols of the constant dread of being lost at sea. The votive ship in this way represents the enduring prayer of the king for his city and, interestingly enough, reflects the description of Tyre and prediction of its destiny in a more or less contemporary lament over the city.

The votive ship is marble, but there are drill holes for adding a rudder and a wooden superstructure; similarly, in the lament, Tyre is a ship, beautifully constructed and outfitted.[45] As the prayer on the votive ship, the lament calls the king of Tyre its "captain" (*nagîd*), and goes on to associate him with the God Melqart—the prayer on the ship acknowledging him as client of the God, the lament making him the God's embodiment (Ezek 28:1–19). In the inscription, the threat to Tyre, the occasion of the vow, and the reason for the dedication of the ship was a storm at sea, and similarly the lament is occasioned by a huge storm in which the ship Tyre risks sinking into the heart of the sea (Ezek 27:25–36; also 26:15–21). The encompassing connection between the two, of course, is that both

---

43. Ibid., 121*.
44. Ibid., 124*, 127*–28*.
45. Ibid., 118*–19*; Ezek 27:1–9.

are laments, typical and paradigmatic and suited to any particular occasion—one recording the terrified cries of the storm-tossed, the other the
fulfillment of their vow when their cries are heard. Although different in
genre and sensibility, the ship and the poem tell the same fabulous story.

There are gaps in the king list that are partially remedied by the sequence of coins, but the coinage is more helpful in suggesting the spirit of
the city in these critical centuries. The earliest coins, from about the last
three decades of the fifth century,[46] are on the Phoenician standard and are
marked as either "half-shekel" or "one-thirtieth" of a mina—that is, two
shekels. The obverse shows a dolphin riding the waves and below them
a murex, the symbol of Phoenician ethnicity; the reverse portrays an owl
with crook and flail, instead of a vulture, and thus conflates contemporary
Attic and archaic Egyptian motifs.

Around the turn of the century, the coinage becomes more explicitly
ethnic, with the obverse representing a bearded God, presumably Melqart,
with bow and arrow, riding a winged seahorse above the waves, where a
dolphin plays.[47] The reverse keeps the owl, crook, and flail but adds the
initials of the king, from which his name might be surmised, and in the
last four series of coins his regnal year. The initials *M* or *MB* on the third
series could be the abbreviation for *Mattinba'al*; *Z* on the fourth series, with
regnal years up to 13, could be the initial for *Zakarba'al*. About the middle
of the century, the mints shifted to the Attic standard, in recognition of the
dominant economy. The last king, 'Azzamilk,[48] whose name was abbreviated 'ayin, reigned 39 years and issued coins from 348 b.c.e. to the capture
of the city in 332 b.c.e.; and again from 327 to 308 b.c.e., Tyrian coins appear from the first 17 years of his reign; but in his last years, coins appear
with the image of Alexander.[49] Ethnicity and archaism, evidently, had been
a deliberate counterbalance to predictable and complete absorption into
the Greek world.

In its heyday, Tyre's international trade depended, not only on the network of nations, but on the material contributions of towns in its dominions. But in the fifth and especially in the fourth century, the equivalent
of produce and manufactured goods was money; and taxation, as bits of
evidence reveal, became to the Tyrian economy what its navy and merchant marine and shipping companies and intrepid captains were to foreign trade. There are three seals dated to the 12th, 14th, and 16th years of
the reign of 'Azzamilk (his name is abbreviated 'ayin or 'ayin + zayin) that
were used to stamp receipts of taxes from individual towns. The taxes were
called "tithes" ('šr) and represent tolls on transit trade that were collected

46. *CMP* 39–76, esp. pp. 39–44. Colin M. Kraay and P. R. S. Moorey had proposed ca. 445
b.c.e. as the date of the earliest issue: "Two Fifth-Century Hoards from the Near East," *Revue
Numismatique* 10 (1968) 181–235, pls. 19–28, esp. p. 191.

47. *CMP* 44–59.

48. A. Lemaire, "Le royaume de Tyr dans la seconde moitié du IVe siècle av. J.-C.," *Atti 2*,
1.131–50.

49. Idem, "Le monnayage de Tyr et celui dit d'Akko dans la deuxième moitié du IVe siécle
av. J.-C.," *Revue Numismatique* 18 (1976) 11–24; F. Verkinderen, "Les cités phéniciennes dans
l'empire d'Alexandre le Grand," in *Phoenicia and the East Mediterranean in the First Millennium b.c.*
(ed. E. Lipiński; Studia Phoenicia 5; Louvaian: Peeters, 1987) 287–308, esp. pp. 299–300, 303.

from Sarepta in 336 B.C.E., from Bêt Zêt in 334 B.C.E. and from ꜥAchshaph (Tell Keisan) in 332 B.C.E. The first two towns lay along the coast and had belonged to Sidon before being ceded to Tyre in the seventh century, and the third controlled travel from the interior to the port of ꜥAkko.

A fourth seal[50] differs in substituting for the town name the destination of the tax "for the palace" (*lbt*) and in using a different date formula, substituting for the abbreviation of ꜥAzzamilk's name the letter *bêt* and the numeral 1. This formula also occurs on Tyrian coins from the mid-fourth century that have been attributed to Mazday, satrap of Cilicia and administrator during the Phoenician revolt (351/350 B.C.E.)[51] until ꜥAzzamilk became, or was appointed, king. The three city seals indicate that taxes affected key places on main routes and were collected every second year. The fourth seal, however, allows for annual taxes imposed on individuals, indicates that they predate ꜥAzzamilk, shows that they were approved by and perhaps specific to the Persian administration, and suggests that coinage began when the system of taxation was introduced.

There are other texts that support an annual income tax, which was not imposed on towns but on individuals or corporations or on latifundia and which was payable not to the city or king but to a district administrator. These include a bulla, a group of tesserae that declare exemption from taxes, and what possibly are sealings by the tax collector.[52] Exemption is expressed by participial forms of the root *ḥnn*, meaning "be gracious, show favor," with an adverb (*tmt*) that means "completely." The participles are masculine singular (*ḥn*), feminine singular or plural (*ḥnt*), and masculine plural (*ḥnm*) and modify some unexpressed subject—that is, the individual or group that "has been shown complete favor" and exempted from the taxes. There are two masculine-singular tesserae that display, besides this declaration, the sign of Tannît above the text and a dolphin below it. The feminine tesserae also display the sign of Tannît—a stylized Tree-of-Life in the geometric shape of a woman—and one of them is dated to the 11th year of ꜥAzzamilk of Tyre.

The bulla has the masculine-plural form and also provides exemption for one year, explicitly—the year is 271/270 B.C.E., "the fourth of the people of Tyre"—but it places the sign of Tannît at the end. The administrative sealing, of which there are nine exemplars, is from a government office building in Kedesh in Upper Galilee. It too has the sign of Tannît in its top register, and below in two lines of text identifies the official as the "superintendent of the territory," literally, "the one who is over the land"

---

50. All four seals were published by J. C. Greenfield, "A Group of Phoenician City Seals," *IEJ* 35 (1985) 129–34.

51. *CMP* 55–56.

52. P. Bordreuil, "Nouvelles inscriptions phéniciennes de la côte de Phénicie," in *Actes 3*, 1.187–92, esp. pp. 190–92; idem, "Bulles et poids de Tyr," in *Alle soglie della classicità. Il Mediterraneo tra tradizione e innovazione: Studi in honore di Sabatino Moscati*, vol. 1: *Storia e Culture* (ed. E. Acquaro; Pisa: Istituti Editoriali e Poligrafici, 1996) 47–58; M. G. Amadasi Guzzo, "Hypothèse sur quatre 'tessères' phéniciennes inscrites," in *Michael: Historical, Epigraphical and Biblical Studies in Honor of Prof. Michael Heltzer* (ed. Y. Avishur and R. Deutsch; Tel Aviv–Jaffa: Archaeological Center, 1999) 39–43; D. T. Ariel and J. Naveh, "Selected Inscribed Sealings from Kedesh in the Upper Galilee," *BASOR* 329 (2003) 61–80, #1, esp. pp. 62–64, fig. 1.

(ʾš ʿl ʾrṣ). Two other sealings from the same office,[53] dated according to the era of the "people of Tyre" to 165 and 164 B.C.E., mention particular groups in the civic assembly who belong to "families" (šphm)—that is, to companies or corporations or businesses, who paid taxes in those years but who, if they were relieved of this obligation, would be exempted using the masculine-plural form. This annual tax, then, was regional, levied on individuals or groups, and is known chiefly from exemptions to it. It was under the jurisdiction of a regional administrator, "the one who is over the land." It was symptomatic of a more general system of taxation that seems to have begun in the Persian period, and coinage was integral.

The sign of Tannît on these documents is curious. The Goddess herself is known from personal names in early seventh-century Tyre and as the patroness of a symposium in later seventh-century Tyrian Sarepta, but she does not seem to have had in the city the official status that she acquired in Carthage and its dominions. Rather, the sign in late Tyre looks like a flag, a badge, or a sort of trademark (analogous to manufacturers' or merchants' marks on pottery vessels) that marked Tyrian identity, as the murex shell became the symbol of Phoenician, "Sidonian," ethnicity. Marked by this symbol, the tax exemptions, like the taxes themselves, were also tokens of a territory and a community. The sign of Tannît reveals a popular, material, and territorial consciousness (something expressed just as well but spontaneously in the shared use of pottery of a standard type or of a particular origin and distribution)[54] that allowed people living outside the city on the Tyrian mainland to resist complete absorption into Greek culture and to identify themselves as Tyrians.

The sign of Tannît was probably reintroduced into Tyre by travelers and official emissaries from Carthage. One of these travelers came to Tyre in the later fourth century, but he died during his visit, and it was important at the time that his stele record both his genealogy and, however oddly, his Carthaginian origin: "Tombstone of Yaʿmos, the son of Giroʾ, son of ʿAbdmilqart, son of ʿAbdoʾ, son of Carthage."[55] Another third-century visitor seems to have been on official business, or at least made it known that he had an official-sounding name and belonged to the sixth generation of a family of officers:[56] "This tombstone belongs to Judge, the son of Hannibal, son of Milqarthilles, son of ʿAzorbaʿal the Judge, son of Ḥannoʾ the General, son of ʾAdonibaʿal the General."

---

53. Ibid., 64–70 #2, figs. 2, 3.

54. A. M. Berlin ("From Monarchy to Markets: The Phoenicians in Hellenistic Palestine," *BASOR* 306[1997] 75–88) describes the distribution of the various forms of a particular type of pottery in the late second century B.C.E. and suggests (p. 85) that, at least in the Hula Valley settlements, it was a material expression of their identity. The pottery is Tyrian (p. 77), and the Sidonian community at Marisa did not find it congenial (p. 85).

Elizabeth A. Bettles, *Phoenician Amphora Production and Distribution in the Southern Levant: A Multi-disciplinary Investigation into Carinated-Shoulder Amphorae of the Persian Period (539–332 BC)* (BAR International Series 1183; Oxford: Archaeopress, 2003).

55. P. Bordreuil and A. Ferjaoui, "À propos des 'Fils de Tyre' et des 'Fils de Carthage,'" in *Carthago* (ed. E. Lipiński; Studia Phoenicia 6; Louvain: Peeters, 1988) 137–42.

56. H. Sader, "Nouvelle inscription punique découverte au Liban," *Sem* 41–42 (1991–92) 107–16.

Every year, Carthage sent its representatives to Tyre to celebrate the Festival of Melqart,[57] and there is an inscription that can be dated sometime between the first and second Punic Wars, that is ca. 250 B.C.E., that records what one of these embassies contributed to preparations for the festivities.[58] The inscription is on the front of a small marble casket, which would have alerted pilgrims entering the temple that the fountain to their left was noteworthy for its capacity and cost and exceptional because it was made for Melqart of Tyre in fulfillment of a vow by the Carthaginian delegation:

> (1) [For my Lord, for Melqa]rt. On the left of the entrance hall was made this fountain (2) [. . . .] by the standard of Tyre, and for 1070 [heavy] shekels in the coinage of Tyre, (3) according to the vow made by your servant ʾAdonibaʿal the Judge, son of ʿOzimilk, (4) son of [. . . . .] the Judge, son of Bodmilqart the Judge, son of Doʿmmilk. (5) [And ʾAdonibaʿal] the Judge, son of ʿOzimilk, made half of this fountain (6) [and Judge, the General, son of Bodmilqar]t gave the other half of this fountain (7) [　　　　　　　　　　un-der the] auspices of Judge, son of Bodmilqart (8) [　　　　　　] entrance [　　　　　　] son of (9) [　　　　　　son of] Bodbaʿal.

The delegation comprised the two named men[59] and the complement of the ship or flotilla that was dispatched to Tyre. Their Carthaginian origin is indicated by the titles of their officers ("Judge" and "General" are western Mediterranean ranks), and they acknowledge that they are visitors by noting that what they did conformed to Tyrian measurements and was paid for with Tyrian coinage, whose shekels differed from the Carthaginian in weight.

The inscription begins with the making of the fountain, expressed passively as "this fountain was made," in fulfillment of a vow: it was ʾAdonibaʿal, the judge, whose vow it fulfilled, who made (pʿl) it, or made half of it, and it was the other delegate, the general and judge, the son of Bodmilqart, who contributed (ytn) the other half. ʾAdonibaʿal was one of the two judges appointed each year in Carthage, and he traces his genealogy through five aristocratic generations to include family members who were judges before him. His associate, similarly, was one of the two generals who were appointed for limited terms in Carthage. This delegation representing the government of Carthage, therefore, included its civic and military leaders (they may have taken office at the time of this annual pilgrimage to Tyre), who took part in the celebrations by their worthy presence and through their substantial donations to the temple.

The dedication "for My Lord, for Melqart" at the beginning of the inscription is balanced by the later reference to "your servant." The title "Lord," "Baʿal" (bʿl), or "My Lord" (bʿly), belongs to Melqart as the "Lord" of Tyre. Two identical, bilingual, second-century inscriptions, purportedly

57. J. Elayi, "The Relations between Tyre and Carthage during the Persian Period," *JANES* 13 (1981) 15–29, esp. p. 17.

58. *RES* 1204; *NSI* 8; J. Teixidor, "Les functions de *rab* et de suffète en Phénicie," *Sem* 29 (1979) 9–17, pl. 1. The beginning of the first 6 lines is damaged, but the first can be restored ([*lbʿly lmlq*]*rt*): with this restoration, the line has 32 letters, and the next 5 lines can be reconstructed to the same length. The last 3 lines are mostly lost.

59. Ibid., 11–12.

from Malta but probably from Tyre[60] record offerings by two brothers "to our Master (*'dnn*), to Melqart, Lord (*b'l*) of Tyre." The inscriptions are on marble bases that support small, tapered, acanthus-leaf columns and, although these are not original,[61] the brothers' offerings may have been similarly aniconic.

There is also a second-century seal from Kedesh in the Galilee with "Lord of Tyre" (*b'l ṣr*) in the lower register and in the upper register a rectangular shrine or naiskos, too small for a representation of the God, but an adequate frame for an aniconic baetyl of Melqart.[62] A later second-century inscription on a marble plaque[63] is damaged but is sufficiently repetitive to allow a reasonable reconstruction:

1. [This is the plaque that 'Abd]nergal [vowed], son of
2. [Rašpyi]šib, son of 'Abdnergal, son of
3. [Rašpyi]šib from the district of 'Ashtarot, under
4. [the feet of] my [Lo]rd Melqart in the shrine
5. [of my Lord for] ever. May he bless me.

The district of 'Aštarot is located south of Tyre around Umm el-'Amed where there was a temple to the God Milk-of-'Aštarot: this inscription has numerous turns that resemble the idiom of inscriptions from that place.[64] The plaque, then, could have been set up in the Temple of Melqart at Tyre but, because the "shrine" (*'šr*) mentioned in the text is usually a chapel or niche in the temple of another God, the plaque (*lûḥ*) might have been placed as a sign beneath this niche (literally, "under the feet of"), which contained an aniconic baetyl of "my Lord (*b'ly*) Melqart" in the Temple of Milk-of-'Aštarot, or Milk'astart, at Umm el-'Amed.

Melqart was exclusively the God of Tyre, worshiped by Tyrians as the God of that city and not of any other place. Sling-stones from the early fourth century with the slogan "Melqart has prevailed" (*mlqrt nṣḥ*) were Tyrian weapons.[65] A prophet who wore an amulet proclaiming "Ba'alyaton, man of God, who is bound to Melqart"[66] lived in Tyre in the late fifth century or drew his inspiration from its God. And so, just south of the city, at Umm el-'Amed, other Gods were worshiped, and Melqart simply was not God.

Umm el-'Amed is 19 kilometers south of Tyre near the coast on the way to 'Achzib and 'Akko.[67] It is situated on a high plateau, off the main road,

60. *CIS* 122 bis; *KAI* 47; M. G. Amadasi Guzzo and M. P. Rossignani, "Le iscrizioni bilingui e gli *Aguiei* di Malta," in *Da Pyrgi a Mozia: Studi sull'archeologia del Mediterraneo in memoria di Antonia Ciasca* (ed. M. G. Amadasi Guzzo, M. Liverani, and P. Matthiae; Vicino Oriente—Quaderno 3/1; Rome: Università degli Studi di Roma, "La Sapienza," 2003) 5–28, pls. 1–3.

61. Ibid., 6–18.

62. Ariel and Naveh, "Selected Inscribed Sealings from Kedesh in the Upper Galilee," 71–72, fig. 5.

63. Bordreuil, "Nouvelles inscriptions phéniciennes de la côte de Phénicie," 187–90.

64. Ibid.

65. Idem, "Nouveaux documents phéniciens inscrits," *Actas* 4, 1.205–15, esp. pp. 206–7, figs. 6–8.

66. Idem, "Attestations inédites de Melqart, Baal Hamon et Baal Saphon à Tyr," in *Religio Phoenicia* (ed. C. Bonnet, E. Lipiński, and P. Marchetti; Studia Phoenicia 4; Namur: Société des Études Classiques, 1986) 77–86, esp. pp. 77–82; *WSS* 268 #719.

67. M. Dunand and R. Duru, *Oumm el-'Amed: Une ville de l'époque hellénistique aux échelles de Tyr, Volumes 1–2* (Paris: Maisonneuve, 1962).

with places to anchor or beach a boat but no harbor, and it seems to have been chosen for its relative inaccessibility.[68] Its pottery, apart from Rhodian wine jars,[69] is Phoenician "Semi-Fine" ware, including jars for wine and oil, which were made in Tyre and distributed to the Tyrian settlements in the Galilee, at Tell Keisan, and at coastal sites from ʿAkko to Dor.[70] Monumental old-style temples and public buildings dominate the site and are segregated from the residential and industrial sectors that served them.[71] It is a rural religious site, self-sufficient, Tyrian but neither urban nor Hellenized,[72] a sort of retreat for the ancient Gods and traditional worship, a pilgrimage center for travelers along the coast.

Both temples were built on high podiums in large paved and porticoed courtyards and flanked by rooms and buildings associated with the cult. The larger was dedicated to Milkʿastart,[73] and the smaller to Baʿalšamem. The God Milkʿastart was the Canaanite antecedent of Tyrian Melqart, mentioned in twelfth-century texts from Ugarit as the king (*milk*) of departed and deified kings, whose eternal dwelling was at ʿAštarot, named for the Goddess Astarte, and so the divine source of their expected regeneration.

The God went West with Tyrian travelers and is also known from a few late Punic and Neo-Punic texts but was retrieved from tradition after centuries of anticipation by the founders of Umm el-ʿAmed sometime in the early third century B.C.E. These aristocratic folk left portraits in stone of their rituals and of themselves as they wished to be remembered: a procession of thurifers, men (some with their attendants) and women elegantly dressed,[74] steles with their names and sometimes their titles—priest (*khn*) of Milkʿastart, rabbi (*rbn*), Chief Doorkeeper (*rb šʿrm*). The doorkeeper set up a stele for his father, who was also Chief Doorkeeper. A man dedicated a stele to the memory of his daughter, another to the memory of his father and mother. There are memorials in fulfillment of vows by pilgrims or passersby, and there are others by people who identify themselves as residents of the town, known then as Hammon. One of these citizens offered Milkʿastart, the God of Hammon, two gold bowls. A group, identified as "Gods, Messengers of Milkʿastart and his Servants, Citizens of Hammon," built a portico for Astarte in the chapel of the God of Hammon, Milkʿastart, in the 26th year of Ptolemy III, the 53rd year of the people of Tyre (221 B.C.E.).[75]

This group, at the end of its dedicatory inscription, claims to have built all the additions to the other, smaller temple. One of these additions was a

---

68. Ibid., 88, 90.

69. J. D. Grainger, *Hellenistic Phoenicia* (Oxford: Clarendon, 1991) 70.

70. A. M. Berlin, "From Monarchy to Markets: The Phoenicians in Hellenistic Palestine," *BASOR* 306 (1997) 75–88, esp. pp. 77, 78, 82, 84.

71. N. C. Vella, "Defining Phoenician Religious Space: Oumm el-ʿAmed Reconsidered," *ANESt* 37 (2000) 27–55, esp. pp. 31–34.

72. Grainger, *Hellenistic Phoenicia*, 82.

73. E. Lipiński, *Dieux et Déesses de l'Univers Phénicien et Punique* (Studia Phoenicia 14; Louvain: Peeters, 1995) 269–74.

74. A. Maes, "Le costume phénicien des stèles d'Umm el-ʿAmed," in *Phoenicia and the Bible* (ed. E. Lipiński; Studia Phoenicia 11; Louvain: Peeters, 1991) 208–30.

75. *TSSI* 3.118–21 #31; Dunand and Duru, *Oumm el-ʿAmed*, 1.181–96.

chapel built between the temple and the portico.[76] It has a wide entrance
between pillars that support a lintel decorated with a winged sun disk and
uraei that hover over a crescent enveloping a full moon. Opposite the entrance, at the far wall, there is a high stone podium reached by five steps,
and around it were found figurines and scattered pieces of a throne with
sphinx armrests that had been placed on the podium. The throne cannot
be rebuilt, but there is one just like it, of approximately the same date,
and also on a stone base, from a site just a few kilometers north of Umm
el-ʿAmed.[77] The throne is empty and has sphinx armrests. There are drawings of two people on the backrest, and on the front of the seat there is a
crescent moon flanked by lotus blossoms, while the front of the base is
inscribed: "(1) To my Lady, to Astarte, who is within this guardian-spirit
throne (2) of mine, of me ʿAbdʾabastis, son of Bodbaʿal." The Goddess is
not depicted but, the text says, is believed to be present on her throne. She
herself is represented by the full and crescent moon, and her benevolence,
normally indicated by her right hand raised in greeting or benediction,
is symbolized by the guardian spirits, the cherubim or sphinxes, who are
the armrests between which she is enthroned (ʾš bgw hšd z). The chapel
attached to the smaller temple at Umm el-ʿAmed, presumably, would also
have been dedicated to Astarte enthroned on the cherubim.

Among the texts from Umm el-ʿAmed, there are vows to the old Gods
El and Osiris, which may indicate that they were accommodated in the
smaller temple,[78] but the temple itself was dedicated to Baʿalšamem. This
is indicated by an inscription, dated to the 143rd year of the people of
Tyre (132 B.C.E.), which records that ʿAbdʾelim from Beirut, in fulfillment
of a vow to Baʿalšamem, deliberately and freely and with his own money
rebuilt the entrance and doors of the temple.[79] Although Astarte had her
own sanctuary at Kharayeb, north of Tyre,[80] here at Umm el-ʿAmed in both
temples, as at Pyrgi near Rome in Italy, her shrine was in the precinct of
another God.

At Umm el-ʿAmed there was a small permanent community that took
care of the temples, presided over the rituals, and supplied their own and
liturgical needs. There were olive presses and so presumably olive orchards
on the plateau. There were nearby tombs for the burial of their dead,
whether citizens or pilgrims, and their tombstones and memorials were
carved by resident masons or by one of the monument makers from Tyre.[81]
The local government probably was mandated by the governor of Tyre (the
office is known from the inscribed coffin of a fourth-century governor of

76. Vella, "Defining Phoenician Religious Space," 34–43.

77. *RES* 800, 918; P. Swiggers, "Le trône d'Astarté: Une inscription tyrienne du second siècle av. J.-C.," in *Redt Tyrus / Sauvons Tyr: Histoire Phénicienne / Fenicische Geschiedenis* (ed. E. Gubel, E. Lipiński, and B. Servais-Soyez; Studia Phoenicia 1–2; Louvain: Peeters, 1983) 125–32; J. R. Davila and B. Zuckerman, "The Throne of ʿAshtart Inscription," *BASOR* 289 (1993) 67–80.

78. *RES* 504a, 504b; Dunand and Duru, *Oumm el-ʿAmed*, 188–89 ##7–8.

79. *CIS* 7; Dunand and Duru, *Oumm el-ʿAmed*, 181–84 #1.

80. Grainger, *Hellenistic Phoenicia*, 77.

81. Sterling Dow, "A Family of Sculptors from Tyre," *Hesperia* 10 (1941) 351–60. The family was in business from the early second to the late first century B.C.E. Their names were Greek, they worked on Rhodes, and two members of the family received Rhodian citizenship.

Tyre, who died and was buried in Kition on Cyprus)[82] and comprised citizens who were considered divinely appointed "Gods" (*'elim*) and "messengers" (*mal'akim*) of Milk'astart and his servants (*'abadêyû*).

The pilgrims were individuals, perhaps on their way elsewhere or representatives sent to this shrine by organizations or governments: there is a mid-fourth-century bilingual inscription, for instance, that mentions that sailors from Tyre were deputed by 'Abd'astart, the king of Sidon, to bring statues of the Gods of Tyre and Sidon to the sanctuary of Apollo on Delos.[83] The community of Umm el-'Amed was founded after the siege and capture of Tyre (332 B.C.E.) and did not survive by much the fall of Carthage (146 B.C.E.), and it is likely that the establishment of these old-fashioned or archaic cults at Umm el-'Amed reflected current Tyrian and Carthaginian concerns about their vanishing ethnicity.

The Tyrian Mainland: In the Path of Persians, Greeks, and Egyptians

The earlier decades of the fifth century involved the Tyrian navy in Persia's wars with Greece, the second half of the century kept it on the alert against Egypt, the first part of the fourth century implicated it in Cypriot schemes and revolts against Persia, and the end of the century put it at the disposal of Alexander and his successors. The navy was a good source of revenue, and there were other ships and shipping companies that could handle trade and commerce down the coast to Egypt or across to Cyprus and the Aegean and manage Tyre's steadily diminishing business with the western Mediterranean cities. Relations with its inland dominions were affected by its failure to maintain jurisdiction over the Plain of Sharon, by the lack of new or developing markets, and by the dullness and cultural blank that was imposed on Tyre's creative imagination by war, provisioning of mercenaries, and unworthy alliances.

This imagination, which made Tyre forever famous, is still symbolized in the early fifth century by one particularly practical and personal work of art. This is a small bronze amulet (square like a scapular, with a tang for suspension from a necklace, and engraved on both sides) that purportedly was found at a site near Tyre. On the front of the amulet, the child Horus sits naked on a lotus flower, his knees bent and pulled up toward him, a flail in his right hand at his shoulder, his left elbow resting on his knee as he holds his left index finger to his lips. This much is fairly standard, and the thorough Egyptianizing marks it as typically Tyrian. But in front of the child, there is a very large uraeus, or cobra, that raises itself up on three pairs of feet, and looks like a scorpion on alert. On the back of the amulet, there is a drawing of Isis protecting the child Horus who sits on her lap, and above them this prayer in two lines is addressed to the Goddess:

---

82. *RPC* 69–78, pl. 6.

83. J. Elayi, "L'inscription bilingue de Délos *CIS* 114," *BaghM* 19 (1988) 549–55. The texts are on the edge of a marble base and refer to the images it supported. The Greek version reads: "Consecrated sailors from Tyre dedicated images of Tyre and Sidon to Apollo." The Phoenician text is damaged but mentions 'Abd'astart, king of Sidon, who was a contemporary of 'Azzamilk, king of Tyre.

"Destroy! Protect!" (*šmd / nṣr*).[84] The iconography is traditional, except for the scorpion, and the text is quick to interpret its special religious symbolism on a magical piece of occasional and creative art.

ʾAchzib, situated on the coast between the mouths of two small streams, was noted in the fourth-century description of the Phoenician coast by Pseudo-Scylax,[85] but the only tangible evidence for its occupation at that time is a single transport jar with the name of the producer or the shipper inscribed on its shoulder.[86] The site flourished until the sixth century and was remarkable for its rich burials, but it declined in the fifth century, from which the significant remains are a few terra-cotta figurines (a stately woman holding a dove in her arms, a man turning a pottery wheel, the head of a horse whinnying, a mask of a grimacing figure), a government building, and storehouses or workshops along a street at nearby Nahariya.[87]

ʿAkko, just to the south of ʾAchzib and across the bay from the Mount Carmel settlements at Tell Abu Hawam and Shiqmona, was still a busy port in the fifth and fourth centuries. It was predominantly Tyrian in the fifth century (a graffito[88] from the Temple of Osiris at Abydos was scribbled by "PaʿalʾAbastis . . . the Tyrian, a resident of ʿAkko, from Memphis in Egypt"), but it became progressively Hellenized in the fourth, when there was a Greek quarter in the town. From the mid-fifth century there is a seal impression of a merchant that preserves marks of the papyrus and of the thread that tied the document (probably meant for an associate in the business) and that displays the usual Egyptianizing preferences of Tyrians.[89] The top register retains only the first letter (*Z*) of his name; the middle register has his father's name (*Baʿlyasop*); the bottom register is filled by his trademark, an *ankh* ("life") sign flanked by uraei.

From earlier in the fifth century, there is a seven-line ostracon that was found discarded with terra-cotta figurines of men and women, broken statues, and part of a throne with a seated Goddess. These were in a small pillared building, next to an imposing courtyard complex containing mainly Attic imports, which the ostracon identifies as the chapel (*ʾšrt*) of a Goddess:[90]

> By order. Let the craftsmen give a large
> crater to Shalit who oversees the chapel, ten
> cups, and twenty-five engraved cups, and seventy

84. H. Sader, "Deux épigraphes phéniciennes inédites," *Syria* 67 (1990) 315–22, esp. pp. 318–22.

85. C. Müller, *Geographi Graeci Minores* (Paris: Didot et Socii, 1882) 1.78–79 #104; E. Lipiński, *Itineraria Phoenicia* (Studia Phoenicia 18; Louvain: Peeters, 2004) 302–3.

86. B. Delavault and A. Lemaire, "Les inscriptions phéniciennes de Palestine," *RSF* 7 (1979) 1–39, pls. 1–14, esp. p. 5 #6, pl. 3 ([*l*]*ʾdnmlk*).

87. M. Dayagi-Mendels, *The Akhziv Cemeteries: The Ben-Dor Excavations, 1941–1944* (Jerusalem: Israel Antiquities Authority, 2002) 148 #5, 151 #12, 153–54 #16, 158–59 #23; J. Briend, "L'occupation de la Galilée occidentale à l'époque perse," *Transeu* 2 (1990) 109–23, esp. pp. 110–11.

88. *KAI* 49 #34.

89. N. Avigad, "Seals and Sealings," *IEJ* 14 (1964) 190–94, pl. 44, esp. p. 194, pl. 44D.

90. M. Dothan, "Tel Acco," *NEAEHL* 1.17–22; J. Briend, "L'occupation de la Galilée occidentale à l'époque perse," *Transeu* 2 (1990) 109–23, esp. pp. 112–14; M. Dothan, "A Phoenician Inscription from ʿAkko," *IEJ* 35 (1985) 81–94, pl. 13.

large goblets, and sixty plates
and sixty water jugs, and
fifty-seven large fluted glasses,
and thirty small deep bowls.

The inscription has one Persian loanword ("order") and two words simply transcribed from the Greek ("goblets, plates"), but it is especially interesting for the information that it has on the local community. The ostracon is an order for metal and ceramic wares to be made for the chapel, whose president is Shalit: the word "chapel" is feminine, indicating that it was devoted to a particular Goddess. The order is given to the craftsmen, literally, "the children of the craftsman," members of the guilds of potters and smiths who, as usual, are organized and described as families. The first item ordered is a large crater (*'gn kbd*) in which water and wine is mixed, and with it drinking cups: 10 are plain cups (*glnm*), 25 are inlaid or engraved (*mml'm*), and presumably each kind is for a different occasion or for a distinct group of worshipers or guests.

Next is an order for 70 big goblets (*pkšt 'drt*), 60 plates (*lpm*), and 60 water jugs (*lg mm*). The list ends with an order for 57 items that are *mypḥt*, "blown" or "hammered," so of glass or metal, maybe fluted bowls or glasses, and 30 small, deep copper bowls (*dqrt ṣʿrt*). The official placing the order was an individual or, as at Carthage, the committee that oversaw religious institutions in the city. The craftsmen worked with a variety of materials, metals, ceramic, and perhaps glass. The organization for which the order was placed was the community associated with the shrine of a Goddess—Astarte, if the enthroned Goddess belonged to the chapel—consisting of about 30 members, presided over by a man whose name was not Phoenician.

An assemblage of East Greek pottery from a separate area in the western sector of ʿAkko has suggested the presence there of a Greek colony, specifically of a colony of Greek merchants during the first half of the fourth century.[91] It consists mostly of plain domestic wares, with some fancier Black Glazed drinking bowls, and a few Attic Red Figured craters for festive or cultic occasions. They came from Ionia, southern Anatolia, or Cyprus, and some of them were cherished possessions, broken and mended in antiquity. Traces of this community persist through the late third into the mid-second century.

The third-century evidence is a ceramic fragment from the same area of ʿAkko on which are painted scenes of single combat on ships.[92] Above the scenes is an alternating series of wreaths and what appears to be a thrashing of wings of a large bird. In the scenes below, there is a sequence of men standing in ships that have battering rams but are stripped of their sails and oars. The men are dressed in short tunics, seem to be bare-chested, and fight with swords and shields. The ships belong to the Ptolemaic navy, the

---

91. Idem, "An Attic Red-Figured Krater from Tell ʿAkko," *IEJ* 29 (1979) 148–51, esp. p. 151; A. Raban, "A Group of Imported 'East Greek' Pottery from Locus 46 at Area F on Tel Akko," in *Studies in the Archaeology and History of Ancient Israel in Honour of Moshe Dothan* (ed. M. Heltzer, A. Segal, and D. Kaufman; Haifa: Haifa University Press, 1993) 73–98.

92. A. Raban, "A Nautical Scene from ʿAkko," *IEJ* 42 (1992) 194–98.

fighting men look like contemporary Greeks, and the story told through the sequence of duels, or of the same duel repeated, is borrowed from Homer's battle among the ships, in particular the duel between Hector and Ajax,[93] during which the appearance of an eagle in flight is recognized as a good omen for the Achaeans.

The second-century evidence is a Greek inscription:[94]

> To Hadad and Atargatis,
> the Gods who listen to prayer,
> Diodotos, the son of Neoptolemos,
> for himself and for Philista
> his wife, and his
> children [dedicated] this altar
> in fulfilment of a vow.

The husband's name could be the Greek translation of Phoenician *baʿalyaton*, "Baʿal has given," and his wife's name might be a transcription of Phoenician *Pilist*, "Watched-Over," but the father's name is Greek and, once again, taken from the *Iliad*.[95] The Gods, on the other hand, are not Greek but Aramaic and at home in Syria. The inscription, however, in its formal details, is like standard Phoenician memorials. It begins, like Phoenician texts, with the dedication and, like contemporary Carthaginian texts, with a dedication to a God and Goddess ("To the Lord, to Baʿal Ḥamon, and to Tannît, Presence-of-Baʿal . . ."). It acknowledges that these Gods have heard the prayer of their suppliant—not a critique of uncaring Greek Gods but a confession that concludes the corresponding Phoenician texts. It names the suppliant and provides his patronymic, it mentions his wife and children (this is unusual only in putting her first), and it records that the offering was made in fulfillment of a vow, a characteristic of all Phoenician memorials. The inscription suggests, therefore, that this Greek family was originally from Syria, settled in the ʿAkko region, joined the Greek community, and adopted local Phoenician customs and religious expressions.

The Phoenician community in the region at this same time still considered itself Tyrian and, like Tyre, had commercial relations with Carthage in North Africa. There are six jar handles, five from ʿAkko itself, and one from Tel Kabri just to the north,[96] with the same kind of seal impression—all dated according to the era of Tyre or the people of Tyre. Two from the 18th year have "Year 18" (= 257 B.C.E.) followed by the name of the dealer, and below the writing is the picture of a club, the symbol of Heracles of Tyre. Two omit the dealers' names and spell out the year ("seventy-first year of the people of Tyre" = 204 B.C.E.), and one of these omits the club. Two others, one from the 118th year (157 B.C.E.), the other from the 119th (156 B.C.E.), have the personal name of the dealer and use numbers for the year,

---

93. *Iliad* 13.788–837; Raban, "A Nautical Scene from ʿAkko," 195–96.

94. M. Avi-Yonah, "Syrian Gods at Ptolemais Accho," *IEJ* 9 (1959) 1–12.

95. Ibid., 4.

96. A. Kempinski and J. Naveh, "A Phoenician Seal Impression on a Jar Handle from Tel Kabri," *TA* 18 (1991) 244–47; J. Naveh, "Excavation of the Courthouse Site at ʿAkko: Phoenician Seal Impressions," *ʿAtiqot* 31 (1997) 115–19.

but one adds "Ty[re]" at the end, after the number. Both begin with the word "Tyrian" (*ṣrt*ʾ), which may have been something like a brand name. These people with seals were merchants, perhaps wine merchants, and the similarity of their seals suggests that they belonged to the same company, which was in business for a little more than 100 years.

The evidence for continuing trade with Carthage is slight and is also a seal,[97] now on the base of an amphora, not on its handle, the emblem of which is the sign of Tannît. The seal can be dated to the second century, just before the fall of Carthage, and hundreds of years later than the shipment of terra-cotta figurines from a shipwreck near Shave Ziyyon between ʿAkko and ʾAchzib, which were also marked with the sign of Tannît.[98]

Tell Keisan, ancient ʿAchshaph or Kaspuna, was purveyor to the port at ʿAkko and a collection and distribution center for the settlements and farmsteads scattered across the plains from ʿAkko to Megiddo.[99] In the later phase of the Persian-period occupation of the town,[100] there are vestiges of two buildings: in one, a residence with four rooms, there was a figurine of a seated monkey that might have amused a child, a knife blade and an arrowhead for the hunter, a jar handle from the storeroom, and a loom weight for the workplace; in the other, there were three large rooms with pillars supporting the roof.

From the earlier phase, there are the wide walls of what may have been a warehouse, the ground plan of a large administrative center with courtyard, and some foundations in what seems to have been a residential district. There are a few sherds inscribed with single letters, a sherd with three letters that can be completed as the personal name Kalboʾ, and a fragment of a transport amphora with the symbol *T*,[101] indicating that it was destined for the royal stores in Tyre. The pottery was locally made, or Cypriot or, in the case of cups and drinking bowls, imported from Attica.[102] From this earlier phase, as well, there is a green jasper seal[103] whose device displays Tyrian manipulation of Persian themes. Under a crescent moon, a king holds a winged bull by the horns with his left hand and is prepared to stab it with the dagger in his right hand. The king is bearded, has his hair in a chignon *à la perse*, and wears a Persian five-pointed crown. But instead of the long, full-sleeved robe worn by the Great Kings, he wears a loin cloth and is bare chested. The crescent moon is the emblem of Tell Keisan. His clothing is Egyptianizing and makes him an authentic Tyrian. The seal is pierced to be worn on a necklace like an amulet, and these local

97. M. Dothan, "A Sign of Tanit from Tel ʿAkko," *IEJ* 24 (1974) 44–49, pl. 9A.

98. E. Linder, "A Cargo of Phoenicio-Punic Figurines," *Archaeology* 26 (1973) 182–87.

99. Briend, "L'occupation de la Galilée occidentale à l'époque perse," 115–17.

100. E. Nodet, "Le niveau 3 (période perse)," in *Tell Keisan (1971–1976): Une cité phénicienne en Galilée* (ed. J. Briend and J.-B. Humbert; Paris: Gabalda, 1980) 117–29.

101. É. Puech, "Inscriptions, Incisions et Poids," in ibid., 301–10, pls. 90–96, esp. p. 304, ##11, 12, 15.

102. B. Shefton, "Some Special Features of Attic Import on Phoenician Sites in Israel," *Actas* 4, 3.1121–33.

103. O. Keel, "La glyptique," in *Tell Keisan (1971–1976): Une cité phénicienne en Galilée* (ed. J. Briend and J.-B. Humbert; Paris: Gabalda, 1980) 257–99, pls. 89–91, esp. pp. 277–78, pl. 89:21.

and Tyrian subversions of a Persian glyptic commonplace reveal a certain independence and nonchalance under Persian rule.

Tyre's southern border was at Mount Carmel. There are inscriptions of various dates found by chance on the mountain and in excavations at Shiqmona at the foot of the mountain on its seaward side.[104] These include a fragment of a late third-century building inscription with the names of the builders, of the scribe who composed the text, and of the mason who inscribed it on the stone.[105] The inscriptions from Shiqmona were painted on wine jars and consist of the name of the vintner, the kind of wine, the year, the royal symbol (*Ṭ*), and the name of the town of origin.[106] The vintner, apparently, was not an individual but a company called "Mattin and Sons" (*bn mtn*). The name of the town, which is the ancient name of Shiqmona, was Gat Karmel, an ally of Gezer and an annoyance to Jerusalem mentioned in the Amarna letters. The wine was sweet (*ḥmr*), the date of the vintage was the 25th year of King ʿAzzamilk (324/323 B.C.E.), and the royal symbol indicated that the wine was destined for his table in Tyre.

The Southern Coastal Plain Is Hellenized

In the fifth and fourth centuries, the towns, ports, and anchorages south of Carmel were controlled either by Tyre or by Sidon. Earlier all this territory had belonged to Tyre, but the sweep from Dor to Joppa was acquired by Sidon in the fifth century, during the reign of ʾEshmunʿazor II and his mother, ʾImmîʿaštart, in return for their contribution to the Persian war effort, and many new agricultural centers were established.[107] North of Dor and south of Joppa was monopolized by Tyre, but both Tyre and Sidon from their separate jurisdictions continued to do business, but on a minor scale, with former markets in the interior.

Judah and Jerusalem were once major partners with Tyre in the great network of nations, and intermediaries in trade with Edom and Arabia. In the fifth century, Judah was a Persian province, but by the end of the century or early in the fourth, its southern district was incorporated into the province of Idumea.[108] Trade was reduced and was parleyed by Tyrians or by their Arabian or Idumean associates. In the mid-fifth century, there was a Tyrian quarter in Jerusalem, and they imported fish and all sorts of merchandise (Neh 13:16).[109] However, the excitement was gone; it was fish mongering and grocery shopping, not foreign trade; there was no pride,

---

104. *IPP* 13–18 ##24–38, pls. 6–11.

105. *IPP* 13–14 #24, pl. 6.

106. F. M. Cross, "Jar Inscriptions from Shiqmona," *IEJ* 18 (1968) 226–33, pl. 25; *IPP* 15–16 ##25–27, pls. 7–8.

107. E. Stern, *Material Culture of the Land of the Bible in the Persian Period, 538–332 B.C.* (Warminster: Aris & Phillips, 1982) 16–20; J. Elayi, *Économie des cités phéniciennes sous l'Empire Perse* (Annali, Istituto Universitario Orientale di Napoli Supplement 62; Naples: Istituto Universitario Orientale, 1990) 33–39.

108. A. Lemaire, "Populations et territoires de la Palestine à l'époque perse," *Transeu* 3 (1990) 31–74, esp. pp. 31–54; idem, "Épigraphie et religion en Palestine à l'époque achéménide," *Transeu* 22 (2001) 97–113.

109. D. Edelman, "Tyrian Trade in Yehud under Artaxerses I: Real or Fictional? Independent or Crown Endorsed?" in *Judah and the Judeans in the Persian Period* (ed. O. Lipschits and M. Oeming; Winona Lake, IN: Eisenbrauns, 2006) 207–46.

no sense of adventure or of belonging to a worldwide consortium; and the only reason it was reported in the biblical text was because doing business on the Sabbath violated a Jerusalem bylaw.

At the end of the century, an ostracon from Elat on the Gulf of ʿAqaba[110] records the names of men involved in overland trade from Gaza, or perhaps Ashkelon, or maybe even Ashdod. The list suggests that they worked together for the same company, presumably Tyrian, but the names indicate that some of the men were from Carthage or the Punic West.[111] This overland trade also brought Tyrian merchants to Idumea.

Among the hundreds of Aramaic administrative documents from Khirbet el-Qom, biblical Maqqedah, halfway between Hebron and Lachish and a little southeast of the Idumean capital at Marisa, there is one Phoenician document in cursive script on a sherd from a transport jar:[112] "In the thirty-fifth year of the king. Shebugram of Mattin and Sons. Boday of ʿ[. . . .] and Sons." All the Aramaic documents can be dated between 362 and 312 B.C.E., and all have to do with agriculture, farming, and payment (in silver at times but usually in produce or products) of tithes, taxes, or debts. The Aramaic texts were dated according to the reigns of Persian and Hellenistic era kings, but the lone Phoenician ostracon was dated according to the reign of ʿAzzamilk, king of Tyre, whose 35th year was ca 314/313 B.C.E.: the shipment it accompanied, therefore, was 10 years later than the shipment of Shiqmona sweet wine. The second and third lines of the inscription are proper names identifying individual merchants. One is Carthaginian; the other is Phoenician; in two separate companies, one of which was the Shiqmona vintner, "Mattin-and-Sons," mentioned 10 years earlier.

These Tyrian wine merchants were stationed in the coastal cities, which were not necessarily in their commercial jurisdiction, and were particularly active during the reign of ʿAzzamilk. Ashkelon, famous for its wine, was reckoned a Tyrian port.[113] Ashdod was not, but there is an Aramaic dedication that shows that at least one Phoenician merchant was familiar with the place.[114] Gaza, similarly, was predominantly Arab, but Tyrian merchants lived in the city, at the junction of roads from South Arabia and Egypt, and one of the Phoenician inscriptions, on a wine jar, dates the vintage to the 4th year of ʿAzzamilk of Tyre.[115] Trade with Judah and Jerusalem, evidently, was symptomatic of much broader Tyrian interests in the interior.

---

110. J. Naveh, "The Scripts of Two Ostraca from Elath," *BASOR* 183 (1966) 27–30, esp. pp. 27–28 #2070; *IPP* 28–29 #56, pl. 14.

111. Two of the three names on the reverse of the ostracon are known only from Carthage. Of the five names on the obverse side, Shallumlahayy (*šlmlḥy*), with the precative form peculiar to the Byblian dialect, is also found in Punic texts.

112. A. Lemaire, *Nouvelles inscriptions araméenes d'Idumée au Musée d'Israël* (Transeu Supplement 3; Paris: Gabalda, 1996) #203, pp. 121–23, pl. 47.

113. E. Lipiński, *Itineraria Phoenicia* (Studia Phoenicia 18; Louvain: Peeters, 2004) 331–35.

114. F. M. Cross, "An Ostracon from Nebi Yunus," *IEJ* 14 (1964) 185–86, pl. 41H.

115. L. Mildenberg, "Gaza Mint Authorities in Persian Time: Preliminary Studies of the Local Coinage in the Fifth Persian Satrapy. Part 4," *Transeu* 2 (1990) 137–46, pls. 4–7, esp. pp. 139–42; I. Skupinska-Lovset, "A Phoenician Face Vase?" *PEQ* 106 (1974) 157–58, pl. 30; J. Naveh, "Unpublished Phoenician Inscriptions from Palestine," *IEJ* 37 (1987) 25–30, pls. 1–2, esp. pp. 28–30, pl. 2A, B.

Inland from Ashkelon, at the site called Tel Sippor, there are traces of Tyrian presence in the fourth century. These are stone and terra-cotta statuettes found in a disposal pit, thought to be the depository or favissa of a sanctuary, although nothing of the sanctuary remains.[116] The stone statuettes are of soft white limestone imported from Cyprus. The terra-cottas were locally made or imported from Cyprus and Rhodes. The locally made are typically Tyrian in their eclecticism and represent standard themes such as clothed pregnant women, naked girls, bearded men, horses, or horse-and-rider. The imported statuettes were mainly of Greek inspiration, representing a mother-and-child, or kourai (young, clothed girls), kouroi (young naked boys), pygmies, or satyrs. Together these terra-cottas display a range of practical concerns and religious sentiment:[117] horses were handy, horse-and-rider was a Persian icon, naked girls were leisured reminders of Astarte, mother-and-child represented Demeter and Kore, and satyrs spelled revelry. Tel Sippor, 17 kilometers due east of Ashkelon was a way station for travelers to the interior, evidently including both men and women, and a stop for merchants such as individuals on their way to Jerusalem and Maqqedah.

'Atlit, on the coast south of Mount Carmel, continued as a Tyrian port in the fifth and fourth centuries but is known mainly from its graveyards. In the preceding centuries, all the dead, including infants, teenagers, and adults, were cremated: the bodies were laid on brushwood in the sand and were buried on the spot.[118] In the fifth and fourth centuries, as at Carthage and elsewhere in the West, burials were in chambers carved in the rock and reached through a vertical shaft.[119] The burials were at least partly standardized: each shaft was closed by a covering stone; above and below the stone, and at the head and feet of the bodies, there were Phoenician amphorae in fixed numbers.

Among the grave goods, there were scarabs and amulets, mostly Egyptian or Egyptianizing but some with Greek subjects, and personal belongings to identify the deceased: a young girl was buried with coins, an anklet, bronze bracelets, and silver earrings; a man took his weapons with him (an iron javelin and bronze arrowheads) but also wore an iron finger ring and carried two green jasper scarabs representing Heracles in his belligerent moods—thrashing the lion, carrying his bow and his club, and advancing in a running-kneeling position; a woman was dressed in a robe arranged with fibulae, carried a kohl stick, and wore earrings, a ring, a bracelet, and a necklace with silver, crystal, carnelian, coral, ivory, and glass beads. Not many tombs were searched, but the hundred or so burials in tombs that were give the impression of a well-off, proud, and independent people.

Dor was a port, industrial center, emporium, and later a haven for Hellenized Sidonians who set out to make money under the capital's new

---

116. O. Negbi, *A Deposit of Terracottas and Statuettes from Tel Ṣippor* ('Atiqot 6; Jerusalem: Department of Antiquities, 1966) 1–7.

117. Ibid., 4.

118. C. N. Johns, "Excavations at Pilgrims' Castle, 'Atlit (1933): Cremated Burials of Phoenician Origin," *QDAP* 6 (1936–38) 121–52, pls. 35–39.

119. Idem, "Excavations at 'Atlit (1930–1): The South-Eastern Cemetery," *QDAP* 2 (1933) 41–104, pls. 14–37.

agrarian policy. Town planning set apart administrative, religious, and residential sectors. Houses were built in blocks along streets with an orthogonal layout.[120] The outside walls of public buildings were constructed of ashlar blocks.[121] The outside walls of houses and the inside and dividing walls of both houses and public buildings were built in the standard pier-and-rubble design.[122] There were stores and shops against the city wall facing a street parallel to it, an impressive public building in the center of town, a large warehouse on the street leading to the port, and a public square at the city gate.[123] There were purple dye factories by the sea north and south of town; there were bronze and iron works and a glass factory at the southern harbor; spindle whorls and loom weights are all that remain of the textile industry; statuettes and figurines were imported and made locally.[124] Dor was a provincial capital in Assyrian times, and it was practically the capital of the Plain of Sharon when Darius I transferred its tariffs and taxes and natural resources to the jurisdiction of Sidon.

The Hellenization of the population is evident in their keen taste for Greek and, especially, Attic pottery. Up until the end of the sixth century, good Phoenician dishes sufficed; but abruptly, and probably because of the influx of Sidonians and as a result of the changed Sidonian economy, first East Greek wares and then the entire range of Attic pottery became a must.[125] The earliest Attic imports are Black Figure cups and drinking bowls by the Haimon painter and his school: the figures include Athena, Heracles, Triton, and Apollo, and the scenes are of Dionysus at ease, satyrs chasing maenads, and revellers lolling amid the grape vines.[126] The Red Figure wares from about the middle of the fifth century include cups, drinking bowls, and craters that portray Aphrodite and Eros, Leda and the swan, a siren, and similar episodes from epic and legend, and feature lush scenes such as satyrs preparing for a symposium.[127] Black Glaze pottery, mainly cups and drinking bowls, began to be imported in the fifth century but were especially popular in the fourth, when tableware predominated.[128] The Greeks loved garum, a fish sauce, and plates with a space reserved for dipping fish into it were favorites[129] among individuals with a stomach for

---

120. E. Stern, "The Dor Province in the Persian Period in the Light of the Recent Excavations at Dor," *Transeu* 2 (1990) 147–55.

121. I. Sharon, "Phoenician and Greek Ashlar Construction Techniques at Tel Dor, Israel," *BASOR* 267 (1987) 21–42.

122. Stern, "The Dor Province in the Persian Period in the Light of the Recent Excavations at Dor," 151; idem, "Between Persia and Greece: Trade, Administration and Warfare in the Persian and Hellenistic Periods (539–63 BCE)," in *The Archaeology of Society in the Holy Land* (ed. T. E. Levy; London: Leicester University Press, 1995) 432–44, esp. p. 439.

123. Idem, "The Dor Province in the Persian Period in the Light of the Recent Excavations at Dor," 151; idem, "Between Persia and Greece: Trade, Administration and Warfare in the Persian and Hellenistic Periods (539–63 BCE)," 438.

124. Idem, "The Persistence of Phoenician Culture," *BAR* 19/3 (1993) 39–49, esp. pp. 47, 49; A. Stewart and S. R. Martin, "Attic Imported Pottery at Tel Dor, Israel: An Overview," *BASOR* 337 (2005) 79–94, esp. p. 79.

125. Stern, "The Persistence of Phoenician Culture," 44, 46.

126. Stewart and Martin, "Attic Imported Pottery at Tel Dor, Israel: An Overview," 82–83.

127. Ibid., 84.

128. Ibid., 85–86.

129. Ibid., 86.

this luxury made locally or imported from Spain. Everyone liked wine, but drinking out of fancy Greek cups and bowls and making a party, a *marzeaḥ*, of it was a pastime of the sophisticated merchant class, their suppliers, and their clients. Nothing Persian, except perhaps a horse-and-rider toy, really pleased, but once Athens prevailed, everything Greek became the rage.

Toys and playthings in the shape of figurines and statuettes[130] easily melded into art or expressions of cultural identity, religious beliefs, and human realities. A terra-cotta naked woman cupping her breasts in her hands expresses hope and desire and the ideals embodied in the Goddess Astarte. A seated man wrapped in a cloak, wearing a round flat hat, and stroking his beard is not just any Hellenized thinker but is known by his hat as Hermes, the God of Trade and mischief. A woman, smiling broadly, sitting with her legs apart, beckoning, and a woman in a veil and long belted robe are different ideas of charm. A warrior wears a Greek helmet. A naked boy, sitting with his left leg folded under him and his right bent behind him, resting on his left hand, his head bald and too big, his belly slightly distended is a symbol—a "Temple Boy"—of dedication to the Gods in life and in death. The figurines and statuettes are Phoenician, the way Phoenicians at Dor thought of themselves and their Gods in a Greek world.

Inscriptions reveal the same blend. There are Greek graffiti on local pottery.[131] An Attic drinking bowl was incised after firing with the letters *LAIU*, written from left to right, the first letter in Phoenician script, the next three in Attic script but written with a Phoenician cursive flourish.[132] The Phoenician preposition *L-* denotes ownership (for example, *lzbl* means that the vase on which it is written belongs to Zebul),[133] but the three vowels are the name Ajax (*Aias*, in the oblique case following the preposition), the hero battling among the ships on the ʿAkko ostracon. The Phoenician inscriptions from Dor are of various genres and are representative of daily routine in the port city. There is a fragment of a ceramic vessel with the owner's name and vocation, "Milknoʿam, servant of ʾEshmun."[134] There are inventories listing the number of jars in a shipment or the number of jars distributed to named individuals, but neither list specifies its contents.[135] A receipt, badly damaged but reconstructed with some probability, seems to indicate that there were Tyrians and Sidonians living in Dor.[136] A letter to

130. E. Stern, "A Favissa of a Phoenician Sanctuary at Tel Dor," *JJS* 33 (1982) 35–54; idem, "The Beginning of the Greek Settlement in Palestine in the Light of the Excavations at Tel Dor," in *Recent Excavations in Israel: Studies in Iron Age Archaeology* (ed. S. Gitin and W. G. Dever; AASOR 49; Winona Lake, IN: Eisenbrauns, 1989) 107–24; idem, "Phoenician Finds from Tel Dor, Israel," *RSF* 19 (1991) 97–105, pls. 9–16.

131. Stewart and Martin, "Attic Imported Pottery at Tel Dor, Israel: An Overview," 79.

132. J. C. Waldbaum, "Greeks *in* the East or Greeks *and* the East? Problems in the Definition and Recognition of Presence," *BASOR* 305 (1997) 1–17, esp. p. 9, fig. 8.

133. *IPP* 18–19 #39, pl. 11.

134. Naveh, "Unpublished Phoenician Inscriptions from Palestine," 26, pl. 1:E.

135. Idem, "Phoenician Ostraca from Tel Dor," in *Solving Riddles and Untying Knots: Biblical, Epigraphic, and Semitic Studies in Honor of Jonas C. Greenfield* (ed. Z. Zevit, S. Gitin, and M. Sokoloff; Winona Lake, IN: Eisenbrauns, 1995) 459–64, esp. pp. 462–64.

136. Ibid., 461–62.

an official assures him that a particular man, whose name is lost, will give him good advice.[137]

A shipwreck[138] a few kilometers south of Dor gives some idea of the activity in the town. The ship was 13½ meters long, displacing 23 tons, and was headed to port when it sank. It came from Karystos on the southern tip of Euboea, where it may have been built,[139] and it was loaded with blue schist from that region, with lead from the Laurion mines in Attica, and with 13 tons of rock from Kourion in southwestern Cyprus. The pottery on board was mainly from Cyprus, where it had unloaded about half its cargo before picking up the rocks: there were various types of transport jars, including Basket-Handle jars similar to those found at Tell Keisan; there was a crew of four or five, and the mugs, bowls, and cooking pot they used were like those at Amathus, Limassol, and Kition in southern Cyprus; these ceramic materials date the wreck to the end of the fifth century B.C.E.

There were Greek woodworking tools stored separately or lying here and there in the ship and wooden pegs like the pegs used in the construction of the ship, and so at least one of the men on board was a carpenter or shipwright. It seems clear that the ship was transporting building supplies for a specific construction project in Dor: the rock could be finished by Phoenician or Greek masons in the town, the blue schist was decorative and could be turned into wall tiles, and the wood the carpenter needed was available or stored locally. It might have been a public project or commissioned by an administrator or entrepreneur, but in either case expense does not seem to have been an issue. It is most interesting, of course, that there was a Euboean ship at Dor and that the port did business with Cyprus and Greece.

Between Dor and Joppa, there were numerous sites, all established soon after Sidon began to administer the territory, many of them destroyed or abandoned after the mid-fourth-century Phoenician revolt led by Sidon.[140] Tel Mevorakh,[141] 10 kilometers south of Dor, was a latifundium, or agricultural estate, with a large central building for grain storage. Most of the pottery was local and domestic, but as everywhere, there were also many Greek (mainly Attic) imports. South of Tel Mevorakh was Apollonia/Arsup, and just south of this was Tel Michal.

Although Arsup[142] was a farming community, its people shared the same liking for things Greek as their urban compatriots. A small marble plaque, for instance, decorated with the scene of a funeral meal is so thoroughly

---

137. Ibid., 459–60.

138. E. Linder and Y. Kahanov, *The Ma'agan Mikhael Ship: The Recovery of a 2400-Year-Old Merchantman: Final Report* (2 vols.; Jerusalem: Israel Exploration Society / Haifa: University of Haifa, 2003–4). Ma'agan Mikhael is a kibbutz 35 kilometers south of Haifa.

139. R. R. Stieglitz, "Classical Greek Measures and the Builder's Instruments from the Ma'agan Mikhael Shipwreck," *AJA* 110 (2006) 195–203.

140. J. Elayi, "Studies in Phoenician Geography during the Persian Period," 96–101; O. Tal, "Some Notes on the Settlement Patterns of the Persian Period Southern Sharon Plain in Light of Recent Excavations at Apollonia-Arsuf," *Transeu* 19 (2000) 115–25.

141. E. Stern, *Excavations at Tel Mevorakh (1973–1976), Part One: From the Iron Age to the Roman Period* (Qedem 9; Jerusalem: Hebrew University—Institute of Archaeology, 1978) 26–45, 76–85.

142. I. Roll and O. Tal, eds., *Apollonia-Arsuf: Final Report of the Excavations*, vol. 1: *The Persian and Hellenistic Periods* (Tel Aviv: University of Tel Aviv—Institute of Archaeology, 1999).

Greek that it could have belonged to an immigrant family.[143] However, because the scene also reflects the mood of a symposium, and because the plaque has a tenon allowing it to be easily displayed, it probably belonged to a local *marzeaḥ* that commissioned it in Athens; an Attic bowl inscribed with the name ʿAbdʾeshmun, similarly, reflects the business interests of the Sidonian merchant who purchased it.

Four kilometers south of Arsup and 13 north of Joppa is Tel Michal.[144] At this site, there were a few buildings, some workshops, and the usual Attic pottery, but the local pottery is domestic, and the town seems to have been built for laborers and not to have been very prosperous. Most of the burials, for example, contained no grave goods, and those that did had nothing special: a bronze bracelet, bronze earrings, an iron javelin tip, and only one silver ring. Tel Michal, like a cluster of small towns to the south and east,[145] seems to have been mainly a supplier to the city of Joppa. Joppa was a major port[146] and, early in the Persian period, was where Sidonians and Tyrians offloaded building materials for the temple in Jerusalem.

A few kilometers south of Joppa, on the way to Nebi Yunus, there was a small settlement and supplier of the port where a transport jar inscribed with the producer's name was found.[147] At Nebi Yunus itself, there are two interesting inscriptions. One inscription is a late fourth-century ostracon recording that a Phoenician named Baʿalṣid made a donation of a number (now lost) of shekels.[148] The inscription is Aramaic, the man's name suggests he was a Sidonian, and the donation implies that Nebi Yunus, once the shrine of the prophet Jonah, was even at this time a well-known and much-frequented place of worship.

The other is a late third-century inscription on an offering table dedicated to ʾEshmun, the God of Sidon, and presumably also the God of Nebi Yunus, in fulfillment of a vow.[149] The dedication was made by an officer called ʿAbdoʾ and his troops called "the ranks of the men of ʿAbdoʾ" (*hʿrkt ʾš ʿbdʾ*). Their names are listed, and they are assigned to six squads of four men; the squads are separated syntactically by the use or omission of the conjunction *waw*. The first squad includes ʿAbdoʾ's brother, two other men, and a son of ʿAbdʾeshmun. The second squad includes two brothers, a man with name and patronymic, and another son of ʿAbdʾeshmun. The third squad again has two brothers, a son of ʿAbdoʾ the commanding officer, and a third son of ʿAbdʾeshmun. The fourth squad includes two men, one with

---

143. M. Fischer and O. Tal, "A Fourth-Century Attic Marble *Totenmahlrelief* at Apollonia-Arsuf," *IEJ* 53 (2003) 49–60.

144. Z. Herzog, G. Rapp Jr., and O. Negbi, eds., *Excavations at Tel Michal, Israel* (Minneapolis: University of Minnesota / Tel Aviv: University of Tel Aviv—Nadler Institute of Arhaeology, 1989).

145. J. Sapin, "Recherches sur les resources et les functions économiques du secteur de Ono à l'époque perse," *Transeu* 4 (1991) 51–62.

146. J. Kaplan and H. Ritter-Kaplan, "Jaffa," *NEAEHL* 2.655–59.

147. Y. Shapira, "An Ancient Cave at Bat Yam," *IEJ* 16 (1966) 8–10, pls. 2–3; B. Peckham, "An Inscribed Jar from Bat Yam," *IEJ* 16 (1966) 11–17, pl. 4A, B.

148. F. M. Cross, "An Ostracon from Nebi Yunus," *IEJ* 14 (1964) 185–86, pl. 41H.

149. B. Delavault and A. Lemaire, "Une stèle 'molk' de Palestine dédiée à Eshmoun? *RES* 367 reconsidéré," *RB* 83 (1976) 569–83, pl. 44; C. Picard, "Le monument de Nebi-Yunus," *RB* 83 (1976) 584–89; *IPP* 24–26 #48; A. Gianto, "Some Notes on the Mulk Inscription from Nebi Yunus (*RES* 367)," *Bib* 68 (1987) 397–401.

and one without patronymic, and a third man and his son. The fifth squad has a man and his son and two more sons of ʿAbdʾeshmun. The last squad has two brothers, the son of one of the brothers in the third squad, and a man with no patronymic.

The troops were not stationed at Nebi Yunus but went there on pilgrimage to fulfill a vow they made. Four-man squads, soldiers, bodyguards, or work-gangs seem to have been the basic unit. They belonged to a few families: the platoon drew on no more than 14, and 19 of its 25 members were from just 8 different families. The families may not have been from the same place, but they were probably from the same region and could have lived in Joppa, a few kilometers to the north, in Jamnia, a bit to the south, where there was still an important Sidonian community in the second century,[150] or in Marisa, the capital of Idumea, to the east. But they made their vows to ʾEshmun, the God of Sidon, and they were probably descendants of the Sidonians who took advantage of Persian foreign policy to settle several centuries earlier in the Plain of Sharon.

Sidon: What We Know from Art, Religion, and Coins

The story of Sidon in the fifth and fourth centuries revolves around its kings, their writings, wars, and rebellions, their coinage, their Athenian connections, and their burials. They belonged to three dynasties—ʾEshmunʿazor, Baʿalšillem, and Straton or ʿAbdʿaštart—whose succession marked the city's transition from traditional to Hellenic ideals. Their mentality, and perhaps the mentality of their people is revealed in their art and religious beliefs. Their chronology is relative, and in centuries defined by much more interesting developments, it is relatively unimportant.

The earliest dynasty acquired the rights to the products and income of the Plain of Sharon, and this change from Tyrian to Sidonian jurisdiction is seen in the archaeological record no earlier than the fifth century. The founder of the dynasty located the dynastic chapel on a hillside overlooking the littoral, bounded on the north by a pleasant stream, and chose the site mainly because of its proximity to the mountain spring Yadlil, which supplied its lustral rites.[151] This king involved his house completely in the affairs of the Persian Empire and so assured its turbulence and eventual demise. His son Tabnît inaugurated an aggressive foreign policy, and this was developed by his daughter when she was regent to include the raw competition with Tyre that ultimately won her the Plain of Sharon. They were buried in a royal necropolis they devised for themselves, in elaborate sarcophagi the exotic beauty of which, instead of being on permanent ostentatious display, was muffled in dank underground caverns. Their son was incompetent, although in his reign the building of a truly impressive

150. B. Isaac, "A Seleucid Inscription from Jamnia-on-the-Sea: Antiochus V Eupator and the Sidonians," *IEJ* 41 (1991) 132–44.

151. R. A. Stucky, "Il santuario di Eshmun a Sidone e gli inizi dell'Ellenizzazione in Fenicia," *Scienze dell'antichità: Storia, archeologia, antropologia* 5 (1991) 461–82; idem, "Das Heiligtum des Ešmun bei Sidon in vorhellenistischer Zeit," *ZDPV* 118 (2002) 66–86; E. M. C. Groenewoud, "Use of Water in Phoenician Sanctuaries," *ANESt* 38 (2001) 139–59.

dynastic temple was begun, and when he died the dynasty survived for a time in a collateral line.

Bod'aštart, son of Tabnît's younger brother Anusos, cousin of the ill-fated 'Eshmun'azor, and grandson of the founder of the dynasty, became king when he was in his prime. The circumstances of his cousin's death, the unprecedented power amassed by the Queen Mother, 'Immi'aštart, and his exclusion from the priestly family made him excessively concerned with the legitimacy of his line. He prepared for this at the very beginning of his reign by building a monument, dedicated to Astarte, to commemorate his glorious accession.[152] Throughout his reign, he sought to embellish the dynastic shrine of 'Eshmun, on whose patronage his legitimacy depended, and in the later building phases included his son Yatonmilk as his crown prince, co-regent, and legitimate heir.[153] During his reign, the Sidonian fleet outdid the Phoenician and was the mainstay of the Persian navy, and this removed any lingering doubt about his legitimacy in the popular imagination.

It was during his reign and his son's co-regency that Sidonian craftsmen began to produce Greek-style sarcophagi modeled on the three Egyptian anthropoid sarcophagi in which his predecessors in the dynasty were buried.[154] The absolute date of these marble imitations depends on the dates assigned to the kings, but their relative chronology can be computed according to their typological development and with reference to the sequence of the burial chambers in which they were placed.[155] The earliest[156] have been assigned to Bod'aštart and his wife. They are still anthropoid: head and shoulders are defined, whereas in later examples the face is simply applied to the top of the sarcophagus; arms seem to rest tight beside the body; and knees, legs, and feet are clearly indicated; while in later examples, although the interior of the sarcophagus may be anthropoid, the body shape of the exterior consists mainly of a tapering from head to foot. They are also still quite Egyptian in appearance (he, for instance, has large protruding ears and wears the Egyptian goatee), and the most obvious Greek touches are their facial features and hairdo (she, for instance, has round cheeks with tight curls around her face and long ringlets over her breast).[157]

152. *CIS* 4; Corinne Bonnet, "Phénicien *šrn* = accadien *šurinnu?* À propos de l'inscription de Bodashtart *CIS* I, 4," *Or* 64 (1995) 214–22.

153. C. Bonnet and P. Xella, "Les inscriptions phéniciennes de Bod'aštart roi de Sidon," in *Da Pyrgi a Mozia: Studi sull'archeologia del Mediterraneo in memoria di Antonia Ciasca* (ed. M. G. Amadasi Guzzo, M. Liverani, and P. Matthiae; *Vicino Oriente*—Quaderno 3/1; Rome: Università degli Studi di Roma, "La Sapienza," 2002) 93–104, pls. 1–3; P. Xella and J. A. Zamora López, "L'inscription phénicienne de Bodashtart *in situ* à Bustān eš-Šeḫ (Sidon) et son apport à l'histoire du sanctuaire," *ZDPV* 121 (2005) 119–29.

154. S. Frede, ed., *Die Phönizischen Anthropoiden Sarkophage, Teil 1: Fundgruppen und Bestattungskontexte; Teil 2: Tradition-Rezeption-Wandel* (Mainz am Rhein: von Zabern, 2000–2002).

155. H. Richter, "Katalog der Fundgruppen," in ibid., *Teil 1: Fundgruppen und Bestattungskontexte*, 65–153, pls. 1–144, esp. pp. 65–107, pls. 1–71; S. Frede, "Die phönizischen Städte und ihre Nekropolen," in ibid., 5–63, esp. pp. 8–27; A. Nunn, "Nekropolen und Gräber in Phönizien, Syrien und Jordanien zur Achämenidenzeit," *UF* 32 (2000) 389–463, esp. pp. 444–50.

156. Richter, "Katalog der Fundgruppen," ##I. 1. 3 and I. 1. 4, pp. 69–72, pls. 5–10.

157. N. Meissner, "Tradition und Rezeption: Griechischer Einfluss auf die phönizische Steinplastik des 5. und 4. Jhs. v. Chr.," in *Die Phönizischen Anthropoiden Sarkophage, Teil 2: Tradition-*

The burial chambers were dug in the rock on the four sides of an access shaft. The earliest burial chamber, on the east side, contained the anthropoid sarcophagus of ʾImmiʿaštart. Across the shaft on the west side lay the sarcophagus assigned to Bodʿaštart, beside him on the north side the sarcophagus attributed to his wife, and across from her in the south chamber the sarcophagus of their son Yatonmilk. Over the next century, chambers were added, and these and the first four chambers, which were designated originally for single burials, were filled with the sarcophagi of the successive royal families.

From the eleventh year of Xerxes (475 B.C.E.), in the reign of Bodʿaštart and during the co-regency of Yatonmilk, there are records in Aramaic of the duty paid by ships at the port of Thonis in the Egyptian Delta.[158] The records are dated between March and December (the weather in January and February was unseasonable)[159] and to the day of arrival and departure. The ships were classified as large or small and identified as Ionian, from Phaselis on the coast of Lycia, or Sidonian, from a port called *kzry*, or *kzdy* on the coast of Palestine. The typical cargo of the Sidonian ships included wine (of Xerxes' 10th or 11th year), cedar boards or beams, iron, bronze, tin, empty jars, and old or new oars, but some ships carried wool or oil, and one transported clay from Samos.

These ships were charged 10 percent duty on their cargo, which was completely inventoried, and the captain and crew were charged a smaller percentage in cash or in kind. For example, a small ship with 800 jars of wine of year 11, 510 kilograms of clay, 170 kilograms of wood, and 300 new oars paid 10 percent of this cargo into the king's warehouse, and the captain and crew were charged another 88 jars of wine. The rest of the cargo went on to Memphis or to Naucratis (in whose foundation Phaselis had participated), where the ship loaded cargo for the journey home—usually natron, on which it was taxed, and some other commodity. Inbound and outbound Ionian ships carried some of the same cargo—including Sidonian wine—but had to pay cash in addition to duty on their cargo and the crew's personal taxes.[160]

All ships were identified by the name of their captains (a captain of a Sidonian ship has a Greek name), and they had to pay equivalent duty, the usual tithe, and taxes in their home ports. The Sidonian ships sailed from a port in Palestine because the bulk of their cargo consisted of wine, oil, or wool from the Plain of Sharon, while the rest, notably the wood

---

Rezeption-Wandel (ed. S. Frede; Mainz am Rhein: von Zabern, 2002) 109–28, pls. 33–36, esp. pp. 110–11.

158. B. Porten and A. Yardeni, *Textbook of Aramaic Documents from Ancient Egypt*, vol. 3: *Literature, Accounts, Lists* (Jerusalem: Hebrew University, 1993) #C3.7, pp. 82–193; P. Briant and R. Descat, "Un registre douanier de la satrapie d'Egypte à l'époque achéménide (*TAD* C3.7)," in *Le commerce en Égypte ancienne* (ed. N. Grimal and B. Menu; Cairo: Institut Français d'Archéologie Orientale, 1998) 59–104; idem, "Le commerce en Méditerranée orientale au Ve siècle av. J.-C. à travers le registre douanier d'Eléphantine (*TADAE* C3.7)," *Transeu* 19 (2000) 175–76.

159. O. Tammuz, "*Mare Clausum*? Sailing Seasons in the Mediterranean in Early Antiquity," *MHR* 20 (2005) 145–62.

160. A. Yardeni, "Maritime Trade and Royal Accountancy in an Erased Customs Account from 475 B.C.E. on the Aḥiqar Scroll from Elepantine," *BASOR* 293 (1994) 67–78.

Fig. 6.2. Half-shekel coin of Sidon (ANS 1977.158.736). Reproduced courtesy of the American Numismatic Society.

and metals, was transshipped from Sidon or some other northern port. This indicates that Sidon, its kings, bankers, and merchants really did profit from the territorial concession to the Dynasty of ʾEshmunʿazor.

The following kings are known from their coinage and a few texts, but their story is subsumed in the history of Greece and Persia recounted in classical sources. Coinage began in Sidon, as in the other mainland Phoenician cities, about the middle of the fifth century.[161] The earliest series has a ship with furled sail on the front.[162] On the back, depending on the value of the coin, there is an archer represented full-length or only down to his knees, a battlement, or an eye.[163] The second series has on the front a ship with a partly furled sail riding on two lines of waves, and on the back an archer as on the first series or kneeling on one knee (see fig. 6.2), or a chariot drawn by a team of prancing horses, with the king of Persia and his driver.[164] Both these series and the kings who issued them are assigned traditionally to the third quarter of the fifth century, a time of relative peace in Sidon, on which, as a consequence, the classical sources are silent.

The second of these might be the king who was buried in the Greek monumental coffin, placed in the earliest chamber that was added next to the chamber containing the anthropoid sarcophagus of ʾImmiʿaštart, the mother of ʾEshmunʿazor. This magnificent marble monument is dated to about 430–420 B.C.E. and is attributed to a Greek sculptor from the Ionian school.[165] The scene at the head of the coffin is a funerary banquet at which the Persian

161. CMP 3–38; J. Elayi and A. G. Elayi, *Le monnayage de la cité phénicienne de Sidon à l'époque perse (Ve–IVe s. av. J.-C.)*, vol. 1: *Texte*; vol. 2: *Abbréviations, bibliographie, index, figures et planches* (Transeu Supplement 11; Paris: Gabalda, 2004).

162. J. Elayi and A. G. Elayi, "The First Coinage of Sidon with a Galley Bearing the So-Called Triangular Sail," *American Journal of Numismatics* 2nd series 3–4 (1991–92) 1–9, pls. 1–2.

163. CMP 3–4; Elayi and Elayi, *Le monnayage de la cité phénicienne de Sidon*, 1.387–89, 617–25.

164. CMP 4–6; Elayi and Elayi, *Le monnayage de la cité phénicienne de Sidon*, 1.389–91, 625–27. Elayi and Elayi, "La scène du char sur les monnaies de Sidon d'époque perse," *Transeu* 27 (2004) 89–108, pl. 1.

165. I. Kleeman, *Der Satrapen-Sarkophag aus Sidon* (Berlin: Mann, 1958); J. Borchhardt, "Die Dependenz des Königs von Sidon vom persischen Grosskönig," in *Beiträge zur Altertumskunde Kleinasiens: Festschrift für Kurt Bittel*, vol. 1: *Text* (ed. R. M. Boehmer and H. Hauptmann; Mainz am Rhein: von Zabern, 1983) 105–20, pls. 22–24.

king[166] reclines, his wife sits at his feet, and an attendant serves him, while another waits behind him. On the corresponding short side at the foot of the coffin, his four bodyguards whisper, grope for words, and attempt to console each other. The scenes on the long sides, by contrast, celebrate the king's life. On the left, from foot to head, the king descends from his throne to mount his horse. On the opposite side, from head to foot, the king and his entourage hunt in the royal garden or paradise. In the guise of the Great King, it appears, the Sidonian king who was buried in this coffin could combine sycophantic submission to Persia and wholehearted appreciation of Greek art.

The coins in the third series[167] have abbreviations of the names of the kings and have been assigned to a dynasty mentioned in a dedicatory inscription that was found in the precinct of ʾEshmun in Sidon:[168]

Fig. 6.3. Sidonian coin of Baʿalšillem I (ANS 1997.9.197). Reproduced courtesy of the American Numismatic Society.

This is the statue which was offered by Baʿalšillem, son of king Baʿanaʾ king of the Sidonians, son of king ʿAbdʾamon king of the Sidonians, son of king Baʿalšillem king of the Sidonians, to his Lord, to ʾEshmun, at the spring Yiddal. May he bless him.

The inscription is on the base of a white marble statue of a "Temple Boy"[169]—a male child, naked except for a garment draped over his legs, lounging and leaning on both arms, with a bird in his right hand, and a chubby child's body with a mature and slightly too-large, bald head—which was found

---

166. Ibid.," 108, 117. Borchhardt proposed that the scene represented Artaxerxes I (464–423 B.C.E.) and his wife, Damaspia. He also argued that the coffin was made for the Sidonian king Baʿana, known from the next coin series.

167. Elayi and Elayi, *Le monnayage de la cité phénicienne de Sidon*, 1.391–400, 627–35: this series includes the coins of three kings and combines the issues that J. W. Betlyon (*CMP* 6–9) distributes separately over the three reigns.

168. M. Dunand, "Nouvelles inscriptions phéniciennes du temple d'Echmoun à Bostan ech-Cheikh, près Sidon," *BMB* 18 (1965) 105–9, pls. 1–2; E. T. Mullen Jr., "A New Royal Sidonian Inscription," *BASOR* 216 (1974) 25–30; M. O'Connor, "The Grammar of Getting Blessed in Tyrian-Sidonian Phoenician," *RSF* 5 (1977) 5–11, esp. pp. 5–6.

169. C. Beer, *Temple-Boys: A Study of Cypriote Votive Sculpture, Part 2: Functional Analysis* (Stockholm: University of Stockholm, 1993) 90–92.

with ten others like it in a channel leading from the spring to the temple. Three of these also have brief dedications to ʾEshmun, and a fourth is dedicated to Astarte and ʾEshmun.[170] The purpose of these dedications may have been to fulfill a vow made during the time of incubation and petition for a child, because ʾEshmunʿazor was the answer to prayer.

These particular statues are perhaps from Cyprus, where they are most common, especially in the Idalion region,[171] and it is not improbable that the royal family itself was from Cyprus. The name Baʿanaʾ is known from Idalion. The other names are composed with the divine element Baʿal instead of with ʾEshmun or Astarte, as was the custom at this time in Sidon, and the royal family could have been émigrés from Idalion earlier in the fifth century, when that city became part of the Kingdom of Kition, a Tyrian emirate.

The obverse of the coins of the first three kings features a ship and beneath it two addorsed lions: the ship has a line of shields hung along the bulwark and a battering ram and is being rowed past a walled city that has, depending on the value and size of the coin, between two and five towers (see fig. 6.3). The reverse has either the standard and politically correct chariot scene, or the king of Persia, in a more mythological mood, slaying a lion that stands before him on its hind legs. The belligerence expressed in these scenes may correspond to the mood of the time or may be just a reflection of the royal family's chequered history.

The fourth series covers the reign of the last king in this dynasty and the reigns of the rest of the kings of Sidon up to Alexander the Great. The series is distinguished by the design of the front of the coins.[172] On all denominations, it is a war ship, with a battering ram and a stern post (aphlaston) for the captain's colors, with oars but without a mast or sails, riding the waves on the high seas, out of sight of the battlemented city. The coins of Baʿalšillem II add his initial *B* above the ship (see fig. 6.4), but the rest have the kings' initials on the reverse.

The back of the larger denominations portrays a bearded figure, his right hand raised in salutation, riding in a chariot drawn by prancing horses (two on the coins of Baʿalšillem, three on the rest), while the king of Sidon, carrying his scepter, runs behind it, because loyal kings used to boast of being allowed to run beside the wheel of their lord. The scene is ceremonial, and the bearded figure is the king of Persia, but hardly Baʿal, the God of the Sidonians.[173] The back of the smaller denominations might portray an archer, holding a bow in his left hand and a spear in his right; or, on the $\frac{1}{16}$-shekels, show a man, an ideal or mythic man, or realistically the king of Persia, or perhaps the king of Sidon, holding an attacking, upright lion by its mane with his left hand, and stabbing it with his right. This coin series, all in all, celebrates Sidon's naval prowess, ostensibly in the proud service of the king of Persia, but otherwise draws on the themes of the earlier series.

---

170. J. Elayi, *Sidon, cité autonome de l'Empire Perse* (Paris: Idéaphane, 1990) 45–46.
171. Beer, *Temple-Boys: A Study of Cypriote Votive Sculpture, Part 2: Functional Analysis*, 53–58.
172. Elayi and Elayi, *Le monnayage de la cité phénicienne de Sidon*, 1.400–435; *CMP* 11–21.
173. *CMP* 11–21; Elayi and Elayi, *Le monnayage de la cité phénicienne de Sidon*, 1.90 and passim.

Ba'alšillem II[174] reigned 36 years, according to his coins, and so his reign coincided with the reign of Artaxerxes II (404–359 B.C.E.) and was nearly as long. Apart from the fact that he and his ships fought in the Persian navy, he has left no mark in the history of Sidon. The next king, 'Abd'astart I,[175] whose name is abbreviated '*B* on his coins, reigned 14 years. He is sometimes thought to have been the son of Ba'alšillem II, the child represented by the "Temple Boy" of his inscription, but he probably inaugurated a new dynasty and certainly initiated a new foreign policy. Early in his reign, and late in the reign of Artaxerxes II, he was publicly recognized as a "Friend" (*proxenos*) of Athens.[176] In the decree in his favor, he is called Straton, a clipped form of his Phoenician name and pleasingly Greek, and he and his descendants are awarded this treaty of friendship (*proxenia*) for having facilitated an Athenian embassy's access to the Persian king. The decree also provides for continued diplomatic relations between Straton and the Athenian assembly and gives special privileges to the Sidonian merchants living in Athens.[177]

It was probably in connection with this treaty that Straton joined the Revolt of the Satraps, already in progress,[178] and fudged his loyalty to Persia. This happened in 359 B.C.E., most likely—the slightly confused time of the accession of Artaxerxes III (359–338 B.C.E.) and of the aborted Syrian campaign of Pharaoh Tachos who, when he was deposed by his son Nectanebo II, took refuge in Sidon.[179] Straton had a reputation for luxurious living and a liking for Greek entertainment[180] and apparently was unfazed when, in the last years of his reign following the Revolt, Mazday, prefect of Cilicia and of all the Western provinces, took over the administration of Sidon.

The presence of Sidonian merchants in Athens and some idea of their privileged status is indicated by a Phoenician-Greek bilingual inscription dated later in the fourth century from the port at Piraeus:[181]

> On the 4th day of the *marzeah* in the 14th year of the people
> of Sidon, it was decided by the Sidonians in assembly: to crown
> Shamaba'al, son of Magon, who is president of the corporation
> in charge of the house of the God and of the buildings in the
> courtyard of the house of the God with a gold crown of twenty

174. Ibid., I.90–181, 400–410, 635–50; vol. 2, pls. 15–33, ##460–1234.

175. Ibid., 1.181–230, 410–19, 650–67; vol. 2, pls. 34–45, ##1235–1519.

176. M. N. Tod, *A Selection of Greek Historical Inscriptions, II: From 403 to 323 B.C.* (Oxford: Clarendon, 1948) 116–19 #139; Elayi and Elayi, *Le monnayage de la cite phénicienne de Sidon*, 1.651–55.

177. R. P. Austin, "Athens and the Satraps' Revolt," *JHS* 64 (1944) 98–100.

178. Ibid., 98.

179. R. A. Moysey, "Observations on the Numismatic Evidence Relating to the Great Satrapal Revolt of 362–1 B.C.," *Revue des Études Anciennes* 91 (1989) 107–39; Elayi and Elayi, *Le monnayage de la cite phénicienne de Sidon*, 1.656–57.

180. F. Millar, "The Phoenician Cities: A Case-Study of Hellenisation," *Proceedings of the Cambridge Philological Society* 209 (n.s. 29) (1983) 55–71, esp. p. 68.

181. *KAI* 60; J. Teixidor, "L'assemblée législative en Phénicie d'après les inscriptions," *Syria* 57 (1980) 453–64; W. Ameling, "*KOINON TON SIDONION*," *Zeitschrift für Papyrologie und Epigraphik* 81 (1990) 189–99; M.-F. Baslez and F. Briquel-Chatonnet, "Un exemple d'intégration phénicienne au mond grec: Les Sidoniens au Pirée à la fin du IVe siècle," *Atti* 2, 1.229–40.

drachmas sterling because he tended the courtyard and did all
the public service assigned to him: that the men who preside
on our behalf over the house of the God should write this decision
on a carved stele and set it up in the portico of the house of the
God for all to see; that the corporation be guarantors of this
stele, that they provide twenty drachmas sterling of the money
of the God, the Baʿal of Sidon, so that the Sidonians will know
that the corporation knows how to reward men who have done
public service for the corporation.

The *marzeaḥ* was an annual festival celebrated by a small group, or corporation, of merchants under the patronage of a particular God, in this case,
of Baʿal, the God of Sidon. The group had a president and its own house
(this one porticoed and set in a courtyard with other buildings) and its
own finances (here considered to be the house, courtyard, and money of
the patron God).

The Sidonians of the inscription are the people of Sidon, merchants and
others, living in Athens who did not belong to the corporation headed
by Shamabaʿal but were an organized community that met in assembly,
made decisions, and issued decrees. This community honored the leader
of the *marzeaḥ* with a gold crown, for which it paid 20 drachmas. It also
appointed a committee to supervise this and, presumably, any other corporation—"those who preside on our behalf over the house of the God"—and
the corporation had to repay it for the monument and the inscription that
they displayed in the *marzeaḥ* meetinghouse.

The interesting part of the inscription, apart from this perspective on
civic and religious organization, is that it is written in a Greek idiom (the
Phoenician word order is strained) and was written by someone who at
least thought in Greek and may have done a first draft in Greek.[182] The
honors, crown and monument, are typically Greek. The Greek version consists of two lines added at the end of the Phoenician text and is no more
than a label highlighting the financial cooperation of the Assembly and the
marzeaḥ: "Assembly of the Sidonians: Diopeithēs the Sidonian." The president's name, *Šamaʿbaʿal*, in the Phoenician text could mean "Baʿal-Hears,"
but his Greek name, *Diopeithēs*, "Persuaded-by-God," suggests that it was
understood as "Hears-Baʿal."

The era of Sidon, based on the date of the Greek parallels to the decree,
began in the fourth century, probably when the city surrendered to Alexander the Great (333 B.C.E.), and so its 14th year would be 320/319 B.C.E.[183]
Interestingly enough, no mention is made of the king of Sidon, whom
Alexander appointed at that time, and it is fairly clear that the Sidonian
merchant community in the port of Athens, still Sidonian citizens, had

---

182. G. A. Cooke, *A Text-Book of North-Semitic Inscriptions: Moabite, Hebrew, Phoenician,
Aramaic, Nabataean, Palmyrene, Jewish* (Oxford: Clarendon 1903) 94–99 #34; M.-F. Baslez and
F. Briquel-Chatonnet, "De l'oral à l'écrit: Le bilinguisme des Phéniciens en Grèce," in *Phoinikeia
Grammata: Lire et Écrire en Méditerranée* (ed. C. Baurain, C. Bonnet, and V. Krings; Namur: Société
des Études Classiques, 1991) 371–86.
183. Baslez and Briquel-Chatonnet, "Un exemple d'intégration phénicienne au mond grec:
Les Sidoniens au Pirée à la fin due IVe siècle."

been there at least since the reign of Straton I and had become completely Hellenized and democratized.

The Hellenized *marzeah* and the city assembly are both known from mainland Sidonian inscriptions. The first is an inscribed drinking bowl that can be dated to about the mid-fourth century, perhaps to the reign of Straton I, in fact of unknown provenance but perhaps from Sidon.[184] The text is Phoenician, but the idiom (the offering speaks in the first person and refers to itself as special) is Greek:[185] "We two bowls are a pleasing gift for the *marzeah* of Shamash." The patron God of this *marzeah* was Shamash, the Sun, and its annual festival may have been celebrated in the month called "Sacrifice to the Sun."[186] The Sun's patronage is especially appropriate because he was the overseer of the living and the dead, and the *marzeah* featured wine and song in memory of former members of the club.

The second inscription, on a marble obelisk from Sidon, records the offering by a city official:[187]

> The offering which Abdmiskar, temporary president of the Assembly, assistant president [of the city], son of Ba'alsaloh, gave to his Lord, to Shulman. May he bless him.

Sidon, like Carthage, according to this text, was administered by two "presidents" or "chiefs" (*rab*). The city, like the Sidonian community in Athens, was governed by an Assembly, and the vice-president was also leader of the Assembly. Because the Assembly was permanent and the administrators were not, Abdmiskar was temporary president of the city Assembly. The Assembly gave the city stability in the succession of kings, and when Straton I joined the Revolt of the Satraps, the Persian envoy Mazday took control of Sidon as president of the Assembly.

There are two monuments that may also be associated with Straton's reign. At the foot of the colossal podium on which the Temple of 'Eshmun was built, there is a group of smaller structures.[188] One of these was an open building with steps, like an orchestra or theatre, and associated with it was a decorated marble rostrum.[189] The rostrum is set on a high, hewn-stone base. It is rectangular, open at the back for easy access, and decorated with two rows of reliefs. The upper relief on the front depicts the assembly of the Gods: Zeus is enthroned and raises his right hand in salutation while the Gods stand in front of him and behind him; before him stands Athena, next to her Apollo playing the lyre, and next to him three more Goddesses and Eros; behind him stand Hera, Amphitrite, and Poseidon. The relief

---

184. N. Avigad and J. C. Greenfield, "A Bronze *phialē* with a Phoenician Dedicatory Inscription," *IEJ* 32 (1982) 118–28, pl. 12A.

185. M. G. Amadasi Guzzo, "Under Western Eyes," *SEL* 4 (1987) 121–27.

186. Avigad and Greenfield, "A Bronze *phialē* with a Phoenician Dedicatory Inscription," 126–28.

187. *RES* 930; J. Teixidor, "Les fonctions de *rab* et de suffète en Phénicie," *Sem* 29 (1979) 9–17, pl. 1, esp. pp. 14–16.

188. M. Dunand, "L'iconographie d'Echmoun dans son temple sidonien," *Atti* 1, 2.515–19, esp. p. 515.

189. R. A. Stucky, *Tribune d'Echmoun: Ein griechischer Reliefzyklus des 4. Jahrhunderts v. Chr. in Sidon* (Beiheft zur Halbjahresschrift "Antike Kunst"; Basel: Vereinigung der Freunde antiker Kunst, 1984).

continues on both sides with more Goddesses, and the scene ends with a racing quadriga and a priestess on the back edge in attendance on the Gods. The lower relief features women playing the flute and lyre, surrounded by dancing maenads and cavorting satyrs. The rostrum and theatre are thought to have been commissioned by Straton I,[190] and they clearly evoke the lush life and the delight in Greek entertainment for which he was famous.

The other monument is the Greek sarcophagus in which it is possible that he was buried. Known as the "Lycian" sarcophagus, because of its shape and decoration and its probable origin in an atelier at Xanthos, the capital of Lycia, it is considered to be of Greek (or possibly of especially skilled Phoenician) workmanship.[191] It was added to the burial chamber which contained the sarcophagus of Yatonmilk; is dated stylistically to about 400 or, more exactly, 390–385 B.C.E., and is usually assigned to one of the kings in the preceding dynasty, Baʿanaʾ or Baʿalšillem II, who reigned around that time.[192] It has a ridged cover, as high as the coffin itself, with lion protomes at either end of each long side for lifting the cover: the gable at one end features addorsed female sphinxes, their lovely bodies seen in profile but their heads facing out, and on the end of the coffin below it, two centaurs face each other in mortal combat; the gable at the other end features fierce, winged griffins facing each other, and below them on the end of the coffin, two centaurs attacking a warrior, who collapses beneath them and raises his shield to protect himself.

The long sides of the coffin, which together with one adjacent short side, are by different master sculptors in the same school,[193] depict a lion hunt from quadrigas, an acceptable Near Eastern motif, and a wild-boar hunt on horseback, which is more typically Greek. The sarcophagus is very large and clearly was meant for display—it would be perfectly at home in the fabulous necropolis at Xanthos—not to be hidden in an underground vault. It probably was not prepared for any Sidonian king, and Straton I, if eventually he was buried in it, acquired it at the time of the Revolt of the Satraps, which involved all of Lycia's neighbors.

The king who followed Straton I is known from Greek sources as Tennēs, a transliteration of the divine name Tinnit. From the abbreviation (Tʿ) on his coins, we know that this is the shortened form of a name composed of the divine name and an epithet that began or ended with the letter ʿayin, such as "Tinnit-Is-Exalted" (tinnitʿalaʾ) or "Tinnit-Has-Satisfied" (tinnitšbaʿa)—names attested on earlier tombstones at Tyre; or, but less

190. Idem, "Il santuario di Eshmun a Sidone e gli inizi dell'ellenizzazione in Fenicia," *Scienze dell'antichità* 5 (1991) 461–82, esp. p. 463.

191. J. Elayi, "Les sarcophages phéniciens d'époque perse," *Iranica Antiqua* 23 (1988) 275–322, esp. pp. 304–12. M.-T. Langer-Karrenbrock, *Der Lykische Sarkophag aus der Königsnekropole von Sidon* (Charybdis 3; Münster: LIT, 2000) 188. J. Ferron, "Contacts et échanges culturels attestés par les sept sarcophages à scènes en relief phéniciens sculptés entre le début du VIe et la fin du IVe siècle av. J.-C.," *Transeu* 12 (1996) 41–57.

192. Langer-Karrenbrock, *Der Lykische Sarkophag*, 163–64; B. Schmidt-Dounas, *Der Lykische Sarkophag aus Sidon* (Istanbuler Mitteilungen 30; Tübingen: Wasmuth, 1985) 117; L. Mildenberg, "Baana: Preliminary Studies of the Local Coinage in the Fifth Persian Satrapy: Part 2," *ErIsr* 19 (Avi Yonah Volume; 1987) 28*–35*.

193. Schmidt-Dounas, *Der Lykische Sarkophag*, 99–100; Langer-Karrenbrock, *Der Lykische Sarkophag*, 204.

likely, "Tinnit-Is-Astarte" (*tinnit'aštart*)—attested at Sarepta. His coins have the standard obverse and reverse of this series and are dated on the obverse to his 1st–5th years.[194] His reign (ca. 351–347 B.C.E.) was notable for the revolt that he led against Persia when Artaxerxes III (358–338 B.C.E.) was king.[195]

The sources for this revolt are the stories in Diodorus Siculus, ostraca from Sidon that may be pertinent to preparations for it in Sidon, and the archaeological evidence for its suppression. According to Diodorus,[196] the revolt was carefully planned and, although it included Tyre and Arvad, began in Sidon itself when the people, fed up with the whimsical demands of the Persian administration, killed some of the Persian officials, destroyed their paradise, and burned their horse barns. Tennēs asked for troops from Egypt, where the Persian campaign of 351 B.C.E. had just ended in disaster, and received 4,000 mercenaries under Mentor of Rhodes to bolster the Sidonian militia. Tennēs could also count on help from the united cities of Cyprus, notably from Salamis, where the rebels deposed the pro-Persian king Evagoras II,[197] a crafty, ambitious maverick whom Artaxerxes III in turn sent to suppress the revolt on the island and later appointed regent of Sidon.

The army sent against Sidon was under the joint command of the satrap of Syria and of Mazday of Cilicia, who had already intervened in Sidonian affairs in the time of Straton I. Tennēs tried to avoid battle, first by giving 100 members of the city Assembly as hostages to the Great King, but they were executed; and then by trying to negotiate the surrender of the city, and he too was executed for his trouble. The Sidonians had tried to strengthen its defenses, but Mentor betrayed the city, and when the townspeople saw Persian troops on the walls with the mercenaries who had joined them, they destroyed their ships, and many of them died defending the city.

An implicit corroboration of the revolt and its unsuccessful conclusion is found in the archaeological evidence. From Sidon itself, there are a few fragmentary sculptures and terra-cottas unearthed in the Temple of ʾEshmun,[198] which might have been damaged in the battle, although any fourth-century date for the statuary would be possible. In the Plain of Sharon, Sidon's sites that were downsized or diminished in importance about the middle of the fourth century[199] may have been neglected when their people fled to the city to help in preparations for the confrontation with Persia, or because Sidon was much too busy with the politics of the revolt or too preoccupied with collecting their tolls and taxes to pay attention to

---

194. Elayi and Elayi, *Le monnayage de la cité phénicienne de Sidon à l'époque perse*, 1.230–43 (##1520–1626) 419–21; vol. 2, pls. 46–48.

195. L. Mildenberg, "Artaxerxes III Ochus (358–338 B.C.): A Note on the Maligned King," *ZDPV* 115 (1999) 201–27.

196. Diod. 16.40.3–16.46.6; H. Klengel, "Aufstände im vorhellenistischen Syrien: Versuch einer historischen Berwertung," *ErIsr* 24 (Malamat Volume; 1993) 130*–37*.

197. *Cyprus* 143 n. 3, 146–47.

198. L. Ganzmann, H. van der Meijden, R. A. Stucky, "Das Eschmunheiligtum von Sidon: Die Funde der türkischen Ausgrabungen von 1901 bis 1903 im Archäologischen Museum in Istanbul," *Istanbuler Mitteilungen* 37 (1987) 81–130, pls. 25–38, esp. pp. 102–17, pls. 32–36.

199. D. Barag, "The Effects of the Tennes Rebellion on Palestine," *BASOR* 183 (1966) 6–12.

their economic development. Finally, ostraca from the Temple of ᵓEshmun, if they do not have to do with temple service, may be related to the recruiting or training of the militia or to the supervision of gangs working on the city's defenses.

The ostraca[200] were found in a pottery dump at the foot of the temple podium. The longest has 16 lines with two names plus patronymics per line, and a horizontal stroke between the 8th and 9th lines, suggesting that the group of 32 men was divided into two gangs, if such they were, of 16. The others, when they are not too damaged to tell, have 4 or 8 lines, with one name plus patronymic per line and might indicate that the groups could be divided further into work crews or military squads with an even number of men. These would have been members of the Sidonian militia, mentioned by Diodorus, or some of the volunteers who dug ditches to slow the advance of Persian chariotry to the city wall.

The next coin series[201] is distinguished by the initials ʿayin-ʿayin on the back, and years 1–4 on the front, and it has been assigned to Evagoras II of Cyprus, who was appointed regent and took over the government of Sidon after Tennēs was executed. The initials undoubtedly stand for ʿAbdʿastart, the name of the next legitimate king in the dynasty, whom the upstart Evagoras supplanted for 4 years.[202] According to Diodorus, he was so incompetent that he had to escape to Cyprus, presumably to Salamis, where the new regime put him to death.[203] The legitimate heir, ʿAbdʿastart II, issued coins with the initials ʿayin-beth and reigned 10 years before the advent of Alexander in 333 B.C.E. It was this king, known as Straton II, who was buried in the Weeping Women sarcophagus,[204] a beautiful marble monument that represents a Greek temple, the columns of which frame 18 individual, perhaps legendary, women mourning the deceased king.

Apart from the rostrum and theater at the foot of the ᵓEshmun podium, which were commissioned by Straton I, there are two other buildings[205] that may have been added to the temple precinct in the reign of his grandson, Straton II. The smaller is a square pool enclosed by high ashlar walls. On the west side, there is a wide opening or entrance way, opposite it on the east side an empty throne resting on a high pediment, and above it high on the rear wall a frieze the panels of which are separated by dividers or frames. The first panel is missing; the second panel pictures a young hunter on horseback, led by his dog, pursuing a stag; the third panel con-

200. A. Vanel, "Six 'ostraca' phénicienne trouvés au temple d'Echmoun près de Saïda," *BMB* 20 (1967) 45–95, pls. 1–4; idem, "Le septième ostracon phénicien trouvé au temple d'Echmoun, près de Saïda," *MUSJ* 45 (1969) 345–64; J. W. Betlyon, "Notes on the Phoenician Ostraca from near Sidon," *BMB* 26 (1973) 31–34.

201. Elayi and Elayi, *Le monnayage de la cité phénicienne de Sidon à l'époque perse*, 1.243–66 (##1627–1787) 421–24; vol. 2, pls. 48–53.

202. *CMP* 18–20.

203. Diod. 16.46.2; *Cyprus* 147 n. 3.

204. J. Elayi, "Les sarcophages phéniciens d'époque perse," 312–17.

205. R. A. Stucky, "Die 'piscine du trône d'Astarté,' und das 'bâtiment aux frises d'enfants: Zwei frühhellenistische Bauten im Eschmunheiligtum bei Sidon und ihre Friese," in *Sepulkral- und Votivdenkmäler östlicher Mittelmeergebiete (7. Jh. v. Chr.–1 Jhr. n. Chr.): Kulturbegegnungen im Spannungsfeld von Akzeptanz und Resistenz* (ed. R. Bol and D. Kreikenbom; Akten des Internationalen Symposiums Mainz 01–03. 11. 2001; Mainz: Bibliopolis, 2004) 7–13, pls. 5–7.

tinues the hunt, but the dog is gone, the horseman is followed by another hunter on foot, and the stag is mortally wounded; the fourth panel, instead of being separated by a divider, is surrounded by a narrow frame and shows a very tall man, with his son, hailing the arrival of the hunter, and behind them and facing away from them, a servant feeding the dog. The first panel was probably like it, with a similar frame, and these or other people waving farewell as the young man left for the hunt.

The second building is adjacent to the first on the north and consists of many rooms around a central square that has stairs on the east leading to a lower terrace. The main entrance to the building is on the west, and to the left of this entrance another relief is carved in the monumental wall. The panels are surrounded by narrow frames, like the end panels at the pool, and divided into two registers. In the upper register, the first panel has a woman standing in front of a tree offering a duck or goose to a corpulent man while a dog tries to jump up on him for attention; in the second panel, a young man riding a stag looks back to bid farewell to a woman; in the third panel, a naked boy offers a duck or goose to a woman who reaches out to take it, while between them a smaller boy (naked, crouching, like a "Temple Boy") with the same dog stretches up his hands to get it first. In the lower register, the first panel shows the woman turning back to feed the duck or goose, and above it a water jug hangs mid-air; the second panel shows the young man riding an antelope, preceded by a youthful herald and by a young boy with a beribboned palm branch, and between the ribbons, something round, over his left shoulder.

The iconography of the reliefs is an amalgam of current and archaic symbols. The empty throne, like that at Tyre, is generally associated with the worship of Astarte, and the young hunter in the tableaux is usually identified as ʾEshmun. This would indicate that the smaller building was a shrine to the dynastic Gods. It would also explain the pool, because the cult of ʾEshmun revolved around healing lustral waters; and perhaps the dog too because, besides being associated with the hunt, dogs were natural companions in the healing process. However, the hunter was not ʾEshmun, who is never revealed in this role, but the immortal *Ṣid*, "Hunter, Provider,"[206] the eponymous God of Sidon, who was retrieved at this time as the ancestor of all Phoenicians and who was recognized at Antas in Sardinia in the mid-fourth century and later as "Sid, Splendid in his Paternity."

He had a brother, according to legend, who might be identified with the hunter following on foot, and it would suit the story line if the people in the last panel were imagined as the ideal Phoenicians. The archaizing religious imagination apparent in this relief would be part of Straton II's family tradition, evident in his father's choice of the divine name Tinnit (derived by vowel harmony from an original *Tannit, an epithet of Asherah, the Goddess of the Sea and Mother of all people), which was otiose until the Carthaginians reinvented the Goddess as their imperial patroness.

---

206. H. W. Attridge and R. A. Oden Jr., *Philo of Byblos: The Phoenician History* (CBQ Monograph 9; Washington, DC: Catholic Biblical Association, 1981) 43–44 n. 64; M. Dunand, "L'iconographie d'Echmoun dans son temple sidonien," *Atti* 1, 2.515–19, esp. p. 516.

Fig. 6.4. Sidonian coin of Ba'alšillem II (ANS 1944.100.71301). Reproduced courtesy of the American Numismatic Society.

The relief at the entrance to the larger building has also been interpreted as portraying incidents or themes from an ʾEshmun ritual cycle, and this might in fact help explain some elements of the relief, such as the dog and the "Temple Boy," but it leaves most of them blank.[207] A more comprehensive interpretation understands the relief as a procession to the Temple of ʾEshmun that imitates the Attic fall festival in honor of Apollo (the *puanopsia*), which includes a young boy carrying a palm branch, festooned with ribbons and a dangling round cake: for the Attic festival, the boy's parents must still be alive, and they may be represented in the upper register of the relief.[208] This festival was familiar enough to imitate from its celebration in the Temple of Apollo on Delos, his birthplace, where it was witnessed by the embassy that Straton II, who commissioned the frieze, sent to dedicate to Apollo emblems of the Gods of Tyre and Sidon.[209]

Mazday was in charge of the Fifth Satrapy (which included Cilicia, all the lands west of the Euphrates, and Cyprus) under Artaxerxes III and was appointed governor of Babylon by Alexander the Great.[210] His Sidonian coins belong to the fourth series, are dated according to the regnal years of the Persian king,[211] and must be intercalated during the reigns of the Sidonian monarchs, when he acted as regent or co-regent.

207. Ibid.

208. Stucky, "Die 'piscine du trône d'astarté,' und das 'batiment aux frises d'enfants,'" 12.

209. *CIS* 114. The Phoenician text reads: "[In year . . . of] the reign of king 'Abda[shtart], king [of the Sidonians]. . . ."

210. P. Bordreuil, "La fin de la carrière du satrape Mazday d'après une monnaie araméenne," *CRAIBL* (1998) 219–29.

211. Elayi and Elayi, *Le monnayage de la cité phénicienne de Sidon à l'époque perse*, 1.291–323 (##1924–2149) 426–29; vol. 2, pls. 60–68. Elayi and Elayi ("Le monnayage sidonien de Mazay," *Transeu* 27 [2004] 155–62, pls. 2–3, esp. p. 157) proposed that the dates on Madzay's coins cor-

His coins dated to years 1–6 (358/7–352 B.C.E.) correspond to the last 6 years of the reign of Straton I, after the Revolt of the Satraps, when he was first appointed to oversee the king's business. The coins dated to years 9–11 (years 7–8 are missing) fit with the last 3 years of Tennēs, after his revolt and before his execution. Years 13 and 15 are missing, but year 14 would correspond to the 4th year of Evagoras II, when his incompetence had become too embarrassing. The last years of his regency, years 16–21, correspond to the last years of Artaxerxes and the first 6 years of Straton II, which would suggest that this was an uneasy or uncertain time in Sidon. Mazday governed with the power of a satrap appointed by the Persian king, but his local authority probably derived from his ability to work amicably with the Assembly of Sidonians, who seem to have monitored the constitutional behavior of kings.

Straton II was deposed by Alexander, and Abdalonymos, probably from the same royal family, was appointed king in his place. The king is known from the story of his appointment told by Diodorus and from a Phoenician-Greek bilingual that records a dedication by his son on the island of Cos.[212] The Greek version is succinct and seems to be a summary and interpretation of the Phoenician: "To Aphrodite, Diotimos, son of Abdalonumos, king of Sidon, made a dedication for the sailors." The Phoenician is in the first-person singular, says what was made, and explains how it was financed:

> To my Lady, to Astarte. I made this stairway to the sea,
> I [. . . .], son of King ʿAbdʾalonim, king of the Sidonians,
> for the life of a[ll the sailors] who [. . . .], from all the taxes
> that I levied on the [. . . .]

Diotimos's Phoenician name,[213] if the Greek was a translation, may have been something like ʿAbdbaʿal, or the same as his father's. His inscription suggests that he was the harbor master in Cos, with the authority to collect the usual toll on all ships, or on all Phoenician ships, entering and leaving the harbor. His father died at the battle of Gaza (312 B.C.E.), fighting for Demetrius against Ptolemy I and is thought to have been buried in the magnificent Alexander Sarcophagus[214] that was placed in the chamber that was dug next to the one containing the sarcophagi of Yatonmilk and Straton I in the royal necropolis of Sidon.

Philocles, son of Apollodoros, was the successor of Abdalonymos and the last king of Sidon.[215] He was, as his name and patronymic reveal,

---

responded to his own years as satrap. L. Mildenberg ("Gaza Mint Authorities in Persian Time: Preliminary Studies of the Local Coinage in the Fifth Persian Satrapy. Part 4," *Transeu* 2 [1990] 137–46, esp. p. 138) pointed out that Mazday did not issue coins as satrap but as regent of Sidon, that the coins are Sidonian, that he put his name where the kings put their initials, that he did not include his Persian title.

212. Diod. 17.47.1–6. M. Sznycer, "Retour à Cos: Nouvel examen de la partie phénicienne de la bilingue gréco-phénicienne," *Sem* 49 (1999) 103–16.

213. F. Briquel-Chatonnet, "Quelques remarques sur l'onomastique des Phéniciens d'après les inscriptions grecques," *Actes* 3, 1.203–10.

214. Sznycer, "Retour à Cos: Nouvel examen de la partie phénicienne de la bilingue gréco-phénicienne," 114–16.

215. J. Seibert, "Philokles, Sohn des Apollodoros, König der Sidonier," *Historia* 19 (1970) 337–51; H. Hauben, "Philocles, King of the Sidonians and General of the Ptolemies," in *Phoenicia*

completely Hellenized: he donated money for the rebuilding of Thebes, made repeated offerings to the worship of Apollo and Artemis on Delos, funded a festival there named after himself, and in turn was accorded religious honors as Liberator of the Aegean Islands at another festival in his honor on Delos. He was a Ptolemaic appointee, spent his career building the Ptolemaic Empire, and received his honorary title "King of Sidon" as a Ptolemaic administrator and naval strategist. His career was emblematic of the contemporary craze among Sidonians, Tyrians, and Byblians to adopt Greek fashions, move to Greek ports,[216] embrace Greek religion, and just be Greek.

In Athens and the Piraeus, there are Phoenician inscriptions and Phoenician-Greek bilinguals of Sidonians, of Tyrians from Kition in Cyprus, of a Carthaginian, and of Irene, a citizen of Byzantium.[217] In the fourth century, during the reigns of Straton I, Tennēs, and Straton II, Sidonian artists who carved signet rings for rich Jews in Samaria reproduced some Persian, but mostly Greek, themes:[218] Greek Gods and heroes; graceful boys, nude or clothed, looking nonchalant; a dancing maenad; Eros; a satyr and a nymph rolling dice. In the early third century, when Philocles was endowing the Artemision and the shrine of Apollo on Delos, Iomilkos (the Greek equivalent of Phoenician *Yḥmlk* "Yaḥwîmilk") from the Byblian colony of Lapethos in Cyprus was making offerings of gold crowns in the same temples.[219]

In 276 B.C.E., Heracleides the Phoenician (*phoinikos*) sold metal for a statue to the Temple of Apollo on Delos, and in 269 B.C.E., the Tyrian ivory merchant Heracleides, son of Basileukos, sold it two hippopotamus tusks.[220] At Demetrias in Thessaly in the third century, there are numerous Greek epitaphs by Phoenician men and women from Arvad, Ashkelon, Kition, Tyre, and especially Sidon who had settled in that thriving cosmopolitan town.[221] Their names are etymologically Greek or translations, transliterations, or approximations to a Phoenician original. At Delos in the late second century, a Tyrian merchant stopped to dedicate a statue to Asklepios

---

and the East Mediterranean in the First Millennium B.C. (ed. E. Lipiński; Studia Phoenicia 5; Louvain: Peeters, 1987) 413–27.

216. M.-F. Baslez, "Le rôle et la place des Phéniciens dans la vie économique des ports de l'Égée," in ibid., 267–85.

217. *Sidonians*: CIS 115 = KAI 54, CIS 116 = KAI 53 (Athens, bilinguals); CIS 119 = KAI 59 (Piraeus, Phoenician). *Tyrians from Kition*: CIS 117 = KAI 55; RES 388. *A Carthaginian*: CIS 118 = KAI 58. *Irene*: CIS 120 = KAI 56.

218. M. J. Winn Leith, *Wadi Daliyeh I: The Wadi Daliyeh Seal Impressions* (Discoveries in the Judaean Desert 24; Oxford: Clarendon, 1997); F. M. Cross, "Personal Names in the Samaria Papyri," *BASOR* 344 (2006) 75–90.

219. O. Masson, "Le 'roi' carthaginois Iômilkos dans des inscriptions de Délos," *Sem* 29 (1979) 53–57; M.-F. Baslez, "Carthaginiois dans les inscriptions de Délos: Problèmes d'identification," *Actas* 4, 1.197–203.

220. Idem, "Un marchand d'ivoire à Délos en 269," in *Numismatique et histoire économique Phéniciennes et Puniques* (Studia Phoenicia 9; ed. T. Hackens and G. Moucharte; Louvain: Université Catholique de Louvain, 1992) 311–20.

221. O. Masson, "Recherches sur les Phéniciens dans le monde hellénistique," *BCH* 93 (1969) 679–798, esp. pp. 687–98; F. Vattioni, "I Fenici in Tessalia," *AION* 42 (1982) 71–81.

in fulfillment of a vow made to ʾEshmun,[222] and by the end of the century, Tyrian families that had become wealthy doing business on the island built funerary monuments, often inscribed in Greek and always in thoroughly Greek style:[223] their Tyrian ethnicity being apparent only in their business acumen and in their insistence on being buried in a separate sector of the necropolis.

The Northern Coastal Towns:
Common Sense and Syrian Influence

The towns along the coast north of Byblos did not suffer this Hellenization but, if anything, progressively adapted to Syrian culture. They often indulged themselves with nice Greek tableware, but this was just a sign of the times around the Mediterranean and did not conflict with a generally simpler life-style. They differed from the big cities, most likely, because they were not particularly or ostentatiously rich and were not burdened with the same intellectual, artistic, and religious heritage.

This difference is noticeable even at Sarepta, lying about halfway between Tyre and Sidon, north of the Litani River. It belonged to Sidon and then to Tyre and had links with Cyprus, but it was an industrial town important to them mainly for its pottery and for the taxes it paid, and their cultural influence on it was minimal. The ceramic remains from the fifth and fourth centuries include fragments of storage jars and crudely made figurines.[224] A few inscriptions on these fragments indicate a certain level of literacy:[225] a fifth-century fragment has the personal name *Suḥ*, otherwise known only from a contemporary biblical text as the name of a man from the territory of Asher, roughly the Plain of ʿAkko; a fourth-century name scratched on the bottom of a bowl is badly written, and one of the letters in the name is written back-to-front; another fourth-century text is a scribal exercise consisting of the alphabet and the beginning of a form-letter; another on a sherd from a decorated storage jar is a dedication to the Gods Shadrapaʾ and Sh[alom]. Sarepta's Cypriot link is maintained, and the renown of this Sidonian God of Healing (Shadrapaʾ ["Healing Genius"], and Shalom ["Health"] are epithets of the God ʾEshmun) is confirmed by a fourth-century Cypriot-Greek bilingual dedication to his Greek equivalent, Asklepios, by a man named Timon, son of Timon.[226] Sarepta had its peculiarities and its specializations but, like the other towns along the northern coast it was quite ordinary and predictable.

222. M.-F. Baslez and F. Briquel-Chatonnet, "L'inscription gréco-phénicienne de l'Asklepion de Délos," *Sem* 38 (1990) 27–37, pl. 3.

223. M.-T. Le Dinahet-Couilloud, "Une famille de notables tyriens à Délos," *BCH* 121 (1997) 617–66.

224. W. P. Anderson, *Sarepta I: The Late Bronze and Iron Age Strata of Area II, Y* (Beirut: Université Libanaise, 1988) 420–23; J. B. Pritchard, *Sarepta IV: The Objects from Area II, X* (Beirut: Université Libanaise, 1988) 31–71.

225. Idem, *Recovering Sarepta, a Phoenician City* (Princeton: Princeton University Press, 1978) 97–102, ##95–98.

226. O. Masson, "Pèlerins Cypriotes en Phénicie (Sarepta et Sidon)," *Sem* 32 (1982) 46–49; Pritchard, *Sarepta IV*, 26–27.

The same applies to Kumidi (Kamid el-Loz) in the Litani Valley, about 50 kilometers southeast of Beirut, at the junction of main north–south and east–west roads. It was important in the Late Bronze Age but in the fifth–fourth century is conspicuous only for its burials.[227] The graveyard is dated by its scattered Attic pottery, seals, and coins to the 80 years between the mid-fifth and the early fourth century. There were about 90 burials divided equally between men, women, and children. The dead were placed in the ground, most often not in coffins, sometimes on their side in a fetal position, but usually in a prone position. Women died in their thirties, men in their forties, and few children died in infancy. There were very plain grave goods, food and drink mostly, and the dead were buried with only their identifiers, the things they wore or used: children wore earrings and ring-amulets on their fingers; women had rings on their right hands, tied their robes with fibulae, wore seals and scarabs as amulets, and sometimes were laid to rest with their needles or spindle whorls or with eye shadow and beauty oils beside them; many, following Greek custom, had a coin in their mouth to pay Charon to ferry them across the river Styx to Hades.[228] It was a simple society, classless and ethnically integral, in touch with the world but not much affected by it.

Beirut was under the jurisdiction of Sidon,[229] as it had been at least since Assyrian times. It had a protected harbor, and the fifth- and fourth-century port, of which only one quay is visible, was built of large ashlar blocks—its top level mortared and provided with mooring pillars.[230] The adjacent area was residential and artisanal.[231] The domestic dishes included some Attic tableware (late Black Figure cups, Red Figure craters and cups, and Black Glazed cups, mugs, plates, and bowls), but most of the pottery was ordinary and locally made pieces such as lamps, plates, bowls, basins, cooking pots, cups, jugs, and storage jars. Some of the late fourth-century items were inscribed with Phoenician names or monograms or with Greek or Phoenician letters, but one fragment had a drawing of a ship with sail, rudder, and anchor. The workshops are represented by scales, weights, and coins and produced such things as terra-cotta figurines, bone handles, pipes and pins, bronze needles, nails, glass ornaments, and bronze jewelry and utensils—mostly or exclusively meant for the local market. The little that remains of Persian period Beirut suggests that it enjoyed a modest renewal, perhaps as a dockyard for the Sidonian navy and merchant marine, without becoming too involved in the cultural trends of the mother city.

---

227. H. Weippert, "Kumidi: Die Ergebnisse der Ausgrabungen auf dem *Tell Kāmid el-Lōz* in den Jahren 1963 bis 1981," *ZDPV* 114 (1998) 1–38.

228. E. Lipiński, "Phoenician Cult Expressions in the Persian Period," in *Symbiosis, Symbolism, and the Power of the Past: Canaan, Ancient Israel, and Their Neighbors from the Late Bronze Age through Roman Palaestina* (ed. W. G. Dever and S. Gitin; Winona Lake, IN: Eisenbrauns, 2003) 297–308, esp. p. 299.

229. J. Elayi and H. Sayegh, eds., *Un quartier du port phénicien de Beyrouth au Fer III / Perse: Archéologie et histoire* (Supplement 7; Paris: Gabalda, 2000).

230. H. Sayegh and J. Elayi, "Rapport préliminaire sur le port de Beyrouth au Fer III / Perse (Bey 039)," *Transeu* 19 (2000) 65–74, pls. 3–4.

231. J. Elayi and H. Sayegh, eds., *Un quartier du port phénicien de Beyrouth au Fer III / Perse: Les objets* (Supplement 6; Paris: Gabalda, 1998).

Tripolis, just about halfway between Byblos and Arvad, captured the ancient imagination as the town with three boroughs, cofounded by Tyre, Sidon, and Arvad.[232] Nothing remains of the place except a late fourth-century silver coin,[233] which tends to confirm the ancient legend. The coin was struck on the Attic standard, as were coins of Tyre in the later fourth century. The front features a ship sailing to the right, with a large eye on its prow, and with shields hung from the railing, much as on coins from Arvad, but with oars, as on coins from Sidon, and an aphlaston or stern post, as on coins of Sidon and Arvad. Below the ship, there is an eight-pointed star and a bow—the latter perhaps being an allusion to the archer who appears on coins of Tyre and Sidon. On the back, there is a lion passant to the right, a common Phoenician motif, and above it the name of the city, *'tr*, and a symbol. The name is from the root *twr*, which means "to explore, to go about," and can be applied to merchants who travel on business. This designation of the place as a merchant or market town is what underlies the Greek name, except that the Phoenician root, without the initial *'alep*, which was added to make it the place-name *'Atri*, was interpreted etiologically as Tripolis, the triple-borough town. Tripolis, besides potentially giving the founding cities equal commercial access to the Syrian interior, was neutral ground where their representatives could meet in council and discuss strategy, as they did in fact, according to Diodorus,[234] when Tennēs proposed to them the Phoenician Revolt. This is, coincidentally, exactly the time that the coin was struck, and its singularity may be a relic of their plan, quickly abandoned, to mint a common Phoenician coinage.

Tell ʿArqa, north of Tripolis in the territory controlled by Arvad, was once a town that could supply 2,000 troops to the anti-Assyrian confederacy but was now a small and insignificant rural site.[235] Tell Kazel, ancient Ṣumur, and once the capital of the whole area, was now a farming town that shipped agricultural products to Arvad and its satellite towns. There is some Greek pottery, there are Cypriot jars that might have contained supplies for the pilgrims on their way to ʿAmrit, and a jar stamped "the servants of ʾEshmun" was likely destined for officiants at that sanctuary.[236] The main structure in the fifth–fourth century was a warehouse with numerous storage bins several meters in diameter and a separate area for keeping transport jars that were designed to be stowed and secured in ships.[237]

---

232. J. Elayi, "Tripoli (Liban) à l'époque perse," *Transeu* 2 (1990) 59–71.

233. The coin is described and placed in its tri-borough iconographic and political context by J. Elayi, "La première monnaie de *'tr* / Tripolis (Tripoli, Liban)?" *Transeu* 5 (1992) 143–51, pl. 1.

234. Diod. 16.41.1–3.

235. J.-P. Thalmann, "Tell ʿArqa, de la conquête assyrienne à l'époque perse," *Transeu* 2 (1990) 51–57, pl. 3.

236. J. Elayi, "Les importations grecques à Tell Kazel (Simyra) à l'époque perse," *Annales Archéologiques de Syrie* 36–37 (1986–87) 130–35; E. Gubel, "Tell Kazel (Ṣumur/Simyra) à l'époque perse: Résultats préliminaires des trois premières campagnes de fouilles de l'Université Américaine de Beyrouth (1985–1987)," *Transeu* 2 (1990) 37–49, pl. 2, esp. p. 44; P. Bordreuil, F. Briquel-Chatonnet, and E. Gubel, "Inédits épigraphiques des fouilles anciennes et récentes à Tell Kazel," *Sem* 45 (1996) 37–47, esp. pp. 41–44.

237. L. Badre et al., "Tell Kazel, Syria: Excavations of the AUB Museum, 1985–1987—Preliminary Reports," *Berytus* 38 (1990) 9–124, esp. pp. 41–46.

The dominant influences in both places were Syrian and rural, not urban and cosmopolitan as in the southern Phoenician cities.

Arvad, a small island about 2 kilometers from the Syrian shore, now controlled the territory that once belonged to the kingdoms of ʿUmqi, Ugarit, Siyannu, and Amurru. It had extensive mainland possessions and, as it had been the enforcer of the Assyrian navy, became with Sidon, Tyre, and Cilicia the mainstay of the Persian fleet.[238] Its coins, which did not circulate beyond its territory, used the Persian standard and gave prominence to its marine identity.[239] The front of the earliest coins pictures a man with a full beard and braided hair, stripped to the waist, his lower body a fish with fins and tail, holding a fish by the tail in each hand; the later coins show just his head, crowned with a laurel wreath. The back of all the coins shows a ship, with an eye on the prow, an aphlaston on the stern, and shields hung along the bulwark, but without oars, and beneath it one or two fish or, in the first half of the fourth century, a winged sea horse, as on contemporary Tyrian coins. On the front or the back of all series except the earliest, there is the abbreviation (*Mʾ*) of "King of Arvad," and in the later series, this is followed by the first letter in the name of the king. The bearded figure might be a God, either the God of Arvad[240] or a retrieval of the God of the Sea Peoples whom the Philistines called Dagon, but is just as likely a mythic presentation of the king of Arvad, the apotheosis of the island city.

Arvad differed from its southern congeners in being a Syrian city, traditional and not fazed by Hellenic fads.[241] Its terra-cottas might represent current or popular subjects, but they did not look like the terra-cottas crafted in Cyprus or Phoenicia.[242] Its monumental tombs are unique to the region, and its built tombs with peaked or flat roofs and barely enough room for the coffin are eccentric.[243] A man with a Greek name set up a marble plaque as a memorial, and on it he inscribed in the local Phoenician patois: "Hermayos—what he dedicated for the repose of the concubine of his."[244]

A seal, perhaps from the region, has a typical worship scene but gives it a local twist: a tall stick-figure Goddess stands under a winged sun disk holding a tambourine, while a much shorter man, a king holding a small scepter with a ram's head, reaches up to her in amazement.[245] Arvad's port

238. Elayi, "Studies in Phoenician Geography during the Persian Period," 86–91; idem, "Les sites phéniciens de Syrie au Fer III / Perse: Bilan et perspectives de recherche," *ANESt Supplement* 7 (2000) 327–48, esp. pp. 332–35; H. Sader, "Le territoire des villes phéniciennes: Reliefs accidentés, modèles unifiés," in *Fenicios y Territorio: Actas del II Seminario Internacional sobre Temas Fenicios, Guardamar del Segura, 9–11 Abril de 1999* (ed. A. González Prats; Alicante: Instituto Alicantino de Cultura, 2000) 227–62, esp. pp. 232–35; Lipiński, *Itineraria Phoenicia*, 279–83.

239. J. Elayi and A. G. Elayi, *Trésors de monnaies phéniciennes et circulation monétaire (Ve–IVe siècles avant J.-C.)* (Supplement 1; Paris: Gabalda, 1993) 361; *CMP* 77–110.

240. J. Elayi and A. G. Elayi, "La divinité marine des monnaies préalexandrines d'Arwad," *Transeu* 21 (2001) 133–48, pls. 2–3.

241. J. Elayi and A. G. Elayi, "Quelques particularités de la culture matérielle d'Arwad au Fer III / Perse," *Transeu* 18 (1999) 9–27, pls. 1–6.

242. J. Elayi, "Deux 'ateliers' de coroplastes nord-phéniciens et nord-syriens sous l'Empire Perse," *Iranica Antiqua* 26 (1991) 181–216, pls. 1–9.

243. Idem and M. R. Haykal, *Nouvelles découvertes sur les usages funéraires des Phéniciens d'Arwad* (Paris: Gabalda, 1996) 49–78, pls. 1–39.

244. J. Teixidor, "L'inscription phénicienne de Tartous (*RES* 56)," *Syria* 56 (1979) 145–51.

245. S. M. Cecchini, "Il re e la dea con il disco su un sigillo a stampo di Tell Afis," in *Da Pyrgi*

at Al Mina at the mouth of the Orontes gave it access to the Syrian interior and was home to Phoenicians, Greeks, and Arameans who inscribed their initials on Attic Black Glazed wares.[246] There is nothing at Arvad or in its territories of the polish and excitement of its sister cities—just old-fashioned hard work and good sense.

Cyprus and Its Small Kingdoms

Phoenician Cyprus in the fifth and fourth centuries consisted of a few kingdoms in the southeast and northwest of the island.[247] They are known from inscriptions, coinage, architecture, and other artifacts, from their occasional dealings with the Greek kingdoms, and from classical sources. The kingdoms were city-states, each with its capitol, suburbs, and adjacent territory, independent of one another but not antagonistic unless moved by Athens or Persia,[248] and capable of acting in concert, unanimously or not, as the political, economic, or military situation required. All together yielded to Persian authority, all but Amathus joined the Ionian Revolt, all except those with Phoenician kings refused to get involved in the wars against Greece, but even the Greek kingdoms supported Sidon, Tyre, and Arvad in the Phoenician anti-Persian uprising under Tennēs. There are vestiges of once-pervasive Phoenician influence in most of the kingdoms, but only a few of the well-established coastal kingdoms maintained their original Phoenician character.[249] All of the kingdoms, Greek and Phoenician, were dissolved by Ptolemy I at the end of the fourth century.

Kition, formerly the administrative and amphictyonic center of Cyprus, came under Tyrian jurisdiction in the sixth century, when Cyprus became part of the Persian Empire, and emerged as a separate kingdom in the early fifth century. The first king, known from inscriptions and coins, was Baʿalmilk (ca. 479–449 B.C.E.).[250] There were none of his coins in the Larnaka Hoard,[251] buried around 480 B.C.E., but there was a coin (the obverse with a lion turning to look back, and the reverse smooth) that generally is assigned to Kition, and coins of an earlier series have been cataloged.[252] These coins may have been issued by the governors appointed by Tyre to

---

a Mozia: Studi sull'Archeologia nel Mediterraneo in Memoria di Antonia Ciasca (ed. M. G. Amadasi Guzzo, M. Liverani, and P. Matthiae; Vicino Oriente—Quaderno 3/1; Rome: Università degli Studi di Roma, "La Sapienza," 2002) 153–61, pls. 1–2.

246. F. Bron and A. Lemaire, "Inscriptions d'Al-Mina," *Atti* 1, 3.677–86, pls. 116–24; J. Elayi, "Al-Mina sur l'Oronte à l'époque perse," in *Phoenicia and the East Mediteranean in the First Millennium B.C.* (ed. E. Lipiński; Studia Phoenicia 5; Louvain: Peeters, 1987) 249–66.

247. A.-M. Collombier, "Organisation du territoire et pouvoirs locaux dans l'île de Chypre à l'époque perse," *Transeu* 4 (1991) 21–43.

248. Diod. 16.42.4; M. Yon, "Chypre entre la Grèce et les Perses: La conscience grecque de Chypre entre 530 et 330 a.C.," *Ktema* 6 (1981) 49–56; F. G. Meier, "Factoids in Ancient History: The Case of Fifth-Century Cyprus," *JHS* 105 (1985) 32–39.

249. A.-M. Collombier, "Le développement des villes maritimes de Chypre à l'époque des royaumes autonomes (VIIIe–IVe s. av. J.-C.)," *Transeu* 19 (2000) 173–74; J. Seibert, "Zur Bevölkerungsstruktur Zyperns," *Ancient Society* 7 (1976) 1–28.

250. *Cyprus* 114.

251. A. Destrooper-Georgiades, "Le trésor de Larnaca (IGCH 1272) ré-examiné," *RDAC* (1984) 140–61.

252. Lipiński, *Itineraria Phoenicia*, 88–89.

administer the territory. The hoard, which contained at least 700 coins, was dispersed, and fewer than 500 were recovered. The coins were all dated to the early fifth century, were all in circulation long enough to become very worn, and altogether are an index of Kition's commercial relations with other kingdoms: 39 from Idalion, almost 100 from Lapethos, 53 from Salamis, and nearly 300 from Paphos.

Another hoard from Jordan, in the Hauran near the Syrian border, and dated to around 445 B.C.E.,[253] contained 5 coins of Baʿalmilk: the obverse has Heracles wearing a lion skin, with a club in his right hand, and a bow in his left; the reverse has a lion, below it a ram's head, and above it the king's name. There were no coins of his son in this hoard, but there was one coin from Tyre and a few from Idalion, Lapethos, Salamis, and Paphos. The hoard also contained bits of silver, silver jewelry, and silver coins from Athens and Sicily, Macedonia, Thrace, Ionia, Caria, Lycia, and other places—all of it perhaps a jeweler's store of scrap metal.[254]

During Baʿalmilk's reign, Greece and Persia struggled for control of Cyprus.[255] Cimon of Athens attacked Kition, Kourion, and Salamis, where a pro-Persian Phoenician usurper (perhaps from Kition) had become king, but Cimon died in the doing, and it turned out to be just part of the mid-century routine without any political, military, or economic consequences. This attack is not mentioned by Baʿalmilk, although victory in battle is recorded twice by a later king, and the only inscription that might be attributed to his reign is a temple tariff, written in red paint on a tablet that was perforated at the top so that it could be hung on a wall:[256] "For ʿAbdʾelim son of Ḥimilk and the 4 workers—140 *K*; for Menaḥem son of Baʿalšamaʿ son of Ḥimilk—20 *K* 100 *QR*, and the 22 workers." We do not know to which coins the symbols *K* and *QR* refer,[257] what work was being done in the temple, if it was the family of Ḥimilk to which the supervisors belonged, or whether it was the work they did that deserved to receive public recognition. It is curious, at any rate, as we attempt to understand the kingdom's mentality, that most inscriptions from Kition have a religious or practical purpose and, while local issues are acknowledged implicitly, politics, foreign relations, and world affairs (the usual stuff of Greek narrative history) are ignored.

Baʿalmilk's son and successor, ʿOzîbaʿal, is known from coins and from references to him in later inscriptions. There are six hoards, from around 425 B.C.E. and later, that contain some of his coins. A hoard from Syria has two of his coins, both resembling the coins of his father: the obverse shows Heracles wielding a club, and the reverse has a lion attacking a stag.[258] There were also two coins from Salamis, many from Sidon, and one from Tyre, as well as Greek coins from all around the Mediterranean, but there

253. C. M. Kraay and P. R. S. Moorey, "Two Fifth Century Hoards from the Near East," *Revue Numismatique* 10 (1968) 181–235, pls. 19–28, esp. pp. 181–210, pls. 19–23.

254. Ibid., 228–31.

255. *Cyprus* 121–26; J. Pouilloux, "L'époque classique à Chypre," *Journal des Savants* (1989/2) 147–61.

256. *CIS* 87; *Kition* 3.126–28 #C3, pl. 15:2.

257. L. I. Manfredi, "Monete e valori ponderali fenici a Kition," *RSO* 61 (1987) 81–87.

258. Kraay and Moorey, "Two Fifth Century Hoards from the Near East," 210–22, pls. 24–27.

were none from Idalion, Lapethos, and Paphos. Both the Larnaka and the Jordanian hoards did have coins from Idalion (the obverse with a sphinx and Cypriot syllabic signs, the reverse with just an incuse empty square), but in the reign of ʿOzîbaʿal, who is identified in inscriptions from the reign of his successor as "king of Kition and Idalion," Idalion was no longer an independent kingdom.

Two inscriptions from Idalion mention ʿOzîbaʿal's successor, Baʿalmilk II, who was king of Kition from the last quarter of the fifth century into the first decade of the fourth. The longer and better preserved is inscribed in one line on a block of white marble:[259]

> [In the month] Marpaim in the third (3rd) year of his reign Baʿalmilk, king of Kition and Idalion, son of King ʿOzîbaʿal, king of Kition and Idalion, son of King Baʿalmilk, king of Kition, gave [and dedicated] this parapet in honour of ʿOzîbaʿal, king of Kition and Idalion, son of King Baʿalmilk, king of Kition, to his Lady, to ʿAnat, because she heard [his voice. May she bless him.]

Baʿalmilk not only acknowledges (by noting that his grandfather was king only of Kition) that it was his father who took Idalion but honors ʿOzîbaʿal for doing it and legitimizes him as king of Idalion by making an offering in his name to ʿAnat, the Goddess of Idalion: the coup gave Kition legitimacy among the ancient kingdoms but obviously was not popular among the Cypriots and Sidonians in the capital. Besides building this parapet, Baʿalmilk II undertook other renovations in the temple, as he had in Kition, built an administrative center, and introduced a new system of accounting.[260] His use of pious persuasion in establishing good relations with old allies is also indicated by the second, fragmentary inscription,[261] which repeats his genealogy and goes on to record that he dedicated a statue of Astarte in the Temple of Aphrodite (her Greek equivalent) at Paphos.

There are other inscriptions that do not name Baʿalmilk but can be assigned to his reign. All are short, some are fragmentary, and a few are of interest.[262] An elegant marble stele is inscribed with the four generations of what might have been a founding family of the kingdom; the bottom of an Attic Black Glazed bowl was scratched with the name of the vendor (Baʿalyaton) and the notation that it was sold to the king's store ("for the king" plus the royal symbol Ṭ); a tall limestone stele is decorated with a big chicken and signed "Šamuʾ, daughter of ʿOzîbaʿal the engraver," but the chicken is weird, the design is ugly, and there is a mistake in the signature—not really a very good advertisement; the body of a Bichrome red bowl is inscribed with the name of its owner, "Melqartmaggin," which incorporates the name of the patron God of the city, and a Plain White

---

259. *RES* 453; P. Berger, "Mémoire sur deux nouvelles inscriptions phéniciennes de l'île de Chypre," *CRAIBL* (1887) 1–30, pls. 1–2, esp. pp. 15–30; A. M. Honeyman, "The Phoenician Inscriptions of the Cyprus Museum," *Iraq* 6 (1939) 104–8, pls. 18–19, esp. pp. 104–5, fig. 1, pl. 18.

260. L. E. Stager and A. M. Walker, *American Expedition to Idalion, Cyprus, 1973–1980* (Oriental Institute Comunications 24; Chicago: Oriental Institute, 1989) 12, pls. 6–7; M. Yon, "Sur l'administration de Kition à l'époque classique," *ESC* 363–75, esp. p. 367; M. Hadjicosti, "The Administrative Centre of the Phoenician Domination at Idalion," *Actas* 4, 3.1019–21.

261. Honeyman, "The Phoenician Inscriptions of the Cyprus Museum," 106, fig. 2.

262. *Kition* 3.90–91 #B41, pl. 13:12; 174 #D40, pl. 23:4; 91–93 #B42 pl. 16:1; 167–68 #D34, pl. 23:5; 169–70 #D36, pl. 22:3, 5.

Cypriot jug has the name of the God 'Eshmunmelqart, a hybrid created after Tyrian Kition took over Sidonian Idalion.

The most interesting inscriptions, however, are the inscriptions on imported white marble tombstones that indicate that Judeans had settled in Kition in the sixth century, perhaps before the advent of the Persians and before the city and territory became Tyrian.[263] One is the tombstone of a man with a Phoenician name whose father, grandfather, and great-grandfather, a scribe, had Jewish names and who probably was Jewish himself. Another is a 2-meter-tall stele dedicated by a man with the Phoenician name Ba'alrôm to his mother and father. His father and grandfather have Phoenician names, but his great-grandfather's name was Levi; his mother's name was 'Ašîmarabbatiya, "Ashima Is My Mistress," which incorporates the name of the Goddess of Samaria (Amos 8:14), whose ancestors had Phoenician names, her great-grandfather with the typically Cypriot Phoenician name Pumay. Kition was multicultural (Greek, Cypriot, and Phoenician), and it is not surprising that Judean businessmen who had met merchants from Kition in their own land would want to settle in the town.

Salamis, under Evagoras I, a pan-Hellene and an honorary citizen of Athens, tried to persuade Kition to join the Greek cause.[264] Ba'almilk II (and his dynasty) disappeared in the fray, and Milkyaton, a usurper perhaps or just more decidedly pro-Persian, became king. The first thing he did was defeat Evagoras, and he recorded his stunning victory on a monument erected at Kition, where the victory occurred, and at Idalion, where protocol demanded it.

The Idalion text is engraved in two lines on a marble statue base:[265] "This is the statue that Milkyaton, king of Kition and Idalion, son of Ba'alrom, gave to his God, to Rešepmukol. I defeated my enemies and their allies who came out to do battle." The statue is missing, but it represented either the king, or more likely, Reshepmukol, the God of Idalion: in his second year, Milkyaton offered a hammered gold bowl to "Reshepmukol in Idalion."[266] This God is identified in Idalion with Apollo Amyclae: the dedication of a statue to Reshepmukol by the prince Ba'alrôm, Milkyaton's nephew, is accompanied by a trilingual inscription in which the Phoenician name of the God is rendered Apollo *Amuklaios* in the Greek and Cypriot versions.[267] The author of another dedication takes the next logical step by transcribing the Greek epithet into Phoenician and offering his statue to "Reshep Amukol (*hmkl*) who is in Idalion."[268] The identification of the Gods was

---

263. S. Hadjisavvas, A. Dupont-Sommer, and H. Lozachmeur, "Cinq stèles funéraires découvertes sur le site d'Ayios Georghios, à Larnaca-Kition, en 1979," *RDAC* (1984) 101–16, pls. 19–21; M. Heltzer, "Epigraphic Evidence concerning a Jewish Settlement in Kition (Larnaca, Cyprus) in the Achaemenid Period (IVth cent. BCE)," *AuOr* 7 (1989) 189–206.

264. *Cyprus* 125–43.

265. *CIS* 91; F. Bron, "Sur l'inscription phénicienne de Chypre *CIS* I, 91," *RSF* 8 (1980) 181–83, pl. 45; P. G. Mosca, "Once Again *CIS* I, 91," *RSF* 10 (1982) 177–85.

266. *CIS* 90; *KAI* 38.

267. *CIS* 89.

268. A. Caquot and O. Masson, "Deux inscriptions phéniciennes de Chypre," *Syria* 45 (1968) 295–321, esp. pp. 302–21.

easy enough at least because both Reshep and Apollo carried a bow and pestilential arrows, and their epithets were homophonous. The identification reflects popular belief and practice in fourth-century Kition and Idalion, but it also has a significant historical and theological pedigree.[269] The God Mukol was worshiped at fifteenth-century Beth Shean in Israel, he had a temple in sixth-century Kition, and his name occurs as the theophoric element in personal names in inscriptions that can be dated paleographically to late in the reign of Ba'almilk II.[270] His name, from a Semitic root meaning "be capable, successful, strong," is the source of the Spartan name Amyclae and of the epithet *Amuklaios* of the local Apollo: his statue there is said to have resembled a bronze pillar with some human features,[271] and according to the sixth-century tariffs from Kition, there was a carved pillar in the Temple of Mukol, a carved pillar with its own cult attendants. The Reshepmukol of Idalion, therefore, is a syncretism, inaugurated in the reign of Milkyaton, of Mukol of Kition and Reshep of Idalion, whom the Greeks and Cypriots of Idalion worshiped, quite correctly, as Apollo Amyklaios. This syncretism, like that of 'Eshmun and Melqart (who became the God 'Eshmunmelqart with his particular cult in Kition),[272] was proposed early in the reign of Milkyaton, perhaps by the king himself, to create a religious and cultural bond between the two cities—one Cypriot and Sidonian; the other Cypriot, Greek, and Tyrian—whose rickety relationship might otherwise dissolve into open antagonism.

The Kition monument[273] records the same victory but from a different perspective and includes more detail:

> This is the trophy which Milkyaton, king of Kition and Idalion, son of Ba'alrom, and all the people of Kition dedicated to their Lord, to Mighty Ba'al, when our enemies and their allies, the Paphians, had gone out to do battle with us, on the tenth day of the month Ziyyub in year 1 of his reign over Kition and Idalion, and when the army of the men of Kition went out to do battle with them. In this place on that day I built it, when Mighty Ba'al gave might to me and to all the people of Kition, and I was victorious over all our enemies and their allies, the Paphians, and I dedicated, I and all the people of Kition, this trophy to Mighty Ba'al my Lord because he heard their voice. May he bless them.

---

269. W. Burkert, "Rešep-Figuren, Apollon von Amyklai und die 'Erfindung' des Opfers auf Cypern," *Grazer Beiträge* 4 (1975) 51–79; E. Lipiński, "Reshep Amyklos," in *Phoenicia and the East Mediterranean in the First Millennium B.C.* (ed. E. Lipiński; Studia Phoenicia 5; Louvain: Peeters, 1987) 87–99.

270. *CIS* 86A, 14; 86B, 5. *Kition* 3.41–42 #A28, pl. 7:4); 143–44 #D15, pl. 18:1.

271. Burkert, "Rešep-Figuren, Apollon von Amyklai und die 'Erfindung' des Opfers auf Cypern," 71–75.

272. *Kition* 3.19–20 #A5, pl. 3:1, 3; 25 #A10, pl. 4:4; 25–29 ##A11–15, pl. 5:1–5; 36 #A25, pl. 7:2); P. Xella, "'Divinités doubles' dans le monde phénico-punique," *Sem* 39 (1990) 167–75, esp. p. 173; Lipiński, *Dieux et déesses de l'univers phénicien et punique*, 289–92.

273. M. Yon and M. Sznycer, "Une inscription phénicienne royale de Kition (Chypre)," *CRAIBL* (1991) 791–823; idem, "A Phoenician Trophy Inscription," *RDAC* (1992) 157–65, pl. 51; idem, "'J'ai emporté la victoire sur tous nos ennemis . . .': Brèves remarques sur le verb *nṣḥ*," *Sem* 41–42 (1991–92) 89–100; P. Xella, "Le dieu *b'l 'z* dans une nouvelle inscription phénicienne de Kition (Chypre)," *SEL* 10 (1993) 61–69.

The inscription has an insistent democratic bias: it is the men of Kition who fought, it is to the king and the people that God gave the victory, it is the king and all the people ("I and all the people") who dedicated the trophy; it is not Evagoras, the king of Salamis, and his ally, the king of Paphos, who are identified as the enemy, but it is the Salaminians and the Paphians who are "our enemies and their allies." This tone is emphasized by using the first person: the first paragraph begins and ends in the third person, but the invasion is expressed in terms of "our" and "us"; the second paragraph records the victory and the dedication of the trophy in the first-person singular and plural but at the end shifts to the third person to give the king and the people one voice and one wish. This democratic bias is new for Kition but typical of Idalion (the doctors who offered their services at the time of the siege of Idalion by the Medes and Kitians were rewarded by "the king and the city"),[274] and it could be due to the populist attitude of the Sidonians who lived there, or could be credited to Athenian influence.[275]

In either case, it was another bold attempt by Milkyaton to maintain good relations among the ethnic groups and between the dual capitals of his kingdom. The trophy—the Greek word is just transliterated (*trpy*)—was set up where the victory occurred and, by a surreal temporal feat, on the same day, just as the memorial of Urikki's victory was set up on the very spot in the Cilician plain. Like this memorial, the Kition monument, of which only the base survived, probably was a statue of Mighty Ba‘al, the titular God of Kition who was introduced by the founding dynasty:[276] all those kings chose names to honor him, and the second, the founder's first-born, was the God's namesake, "My-Might-Is-Ba‘al" ('Ozîba‘al).

There are other inscriptions from the reign of Milkyaton but no more by the king himself. A fragmentary inscription records the offering of a marble bowl in his 4th year to a god whose name is lost.[277] In his 18th year, a man with the Phoenician name ‘Abdsasm, son of Šama‘a’is ("Servant-of-Sasm, son of Isis-Listens") dedicated a statue inscribed in Phoenician and Cypriot to "Apollo of Cyprus" (*alasiotas*), which the Phoenician transcribes as Reshep-’Alahiyotas.[278] A trilingual from Tamassos in Milkyaton's 30th year records the dedication of a statue to the same God, but in this dialect his epithet "the Cypriot" is *Eleita* in Greek, approximately *Ieleita* in Cypriot, and *Alayiyita* in Phoenician.[279]

The political and religious diversity that characterized the divided kingdom was matched by ethnic complexity and social stratification. An

274. *ICS* 235–44.

275. *Cyprus* 115.

276. *Kition* 3.170–71 #D37, pl. 16:3. A very fragmentary inscription (]lb‘l kty h[) was thought to contain a reference to Ba‘al of Kition, but it is the personal name (to be completed either ’lb‘l or ’hlb‘l) of a man from Kition followed by his profession ("the . . .").

277. *Kition* 3.20–21 #A6, pl. 3:2, 4; J. Teixidor, "The Phoenician Inscriptions of the Cesnola Collection," *MMJ* 11 (1976) 55–70, esp. pp. 56–57 #1.

278. *RES* 1213.

279. Ibid., 1212; *ICS* 224–26 #215.

inscription dated to the king's 3rd and 6th years gives some idea of the popular attempt to reduce the friction:[280]

> On the 16th day of the month Paʿulot in the third year of the reign of King Milkyaton [king of Kition and] Idalion, son of Baʿalrôm . This is the statue which Reshepyaton, son of ʾIzratîbaʿal, the interpreter of Cretan, gave and dedicated and [inscribed] to his Lord, to Melqart . ʾAdonîšamš, son of Reshepyaton, the interpreter of Cretan, placed and arranged this platform and the steps of the platform and the railings . And ʿAbdpumay, and ʿAbdmelqart, the two sons of ʾAdonîšamš, the son of Reshepyaton, the interpreter of Cretan arranged the [. . . .] in the sixth year of King Milkyaton, king of Kition and Idalion, because Melqart heard his voice. May he bless him.

The inscription is divided by dots into three significant sections or paragraphs: the first highlights the 3rd year of the reign of Milkyaton; the second is parenthetical and notes that Reshepyaton had dedicated a statue to Melqart; the next, with reference to the first, records that in the 3rd year of Milkyaton his son placed the statue on a platform with steps and a railing; the last mentions the embellishments that were added by two of his grandsons—their names are separated from each other by a dot to give them prominence as the authors of the inscription—in the 6th year of Milkyaton, and it ends by alluding to the occasion for all these renovations and with a prayer for the king.

The family of Reshepyaton is known from two other inscriptions:[281] one is fragmentary but preserves the name "[Reshep]yaton, the interpreter of Cretan"; the other is the dedication of a stele by ʾEshmunʾadonî, son of ʿAbdmelqart, son of Reshepyaton, who as always is identified as "the interpreter of Cretan." The statue that this Reshepyaton had offered, dedicated, and inscribed was probably of Melqart in his manifestation as Heracles: in examples from Kition,[282] the God is young, wears a kilt and his lion-skin stole, strides with his left foot forward, and raises his right arm in a menacing, warlike gesture. It was removed from its original setting to the marble base on which this inscription is written and which is fitted with a socket to receive it. The restored offering was installed by his son in a more auspicious setting, embellished even further by two of his grandsons.

His son was born in the fifth century, because his sons were old enough in the 6th year of Milkyaton (ca. 386 B.C.E.) to commission work in the temple. Reshepyaton himself, therefore, lived around the middle of the fifth century, and his father, ʾIzratîbaʿal, was alive at the beginning of that century. The family, by this calculation, would have been one of the founding families of the Kingdom of Kition and, as their devotion to Melqart indicates, emigrated directly from Tyre. Reshepyaton was famous at least in his own family as "the interpreter of Cretan," the man who deciphered and understood Cypro-Syllabic texts and, if it was still a spoken language, the

---

280. *CIS* 88; *Kition* 3.178–84 #F1; C. Bonnet, "'L'interprète des Crétois' (phén. *mlṣ* [*h*]*krsym*): De Mari aux Phéniciens en passant par Ougarit," *SMEA* 36 (1995) 113–23.

281. *Kition* 3.23–25 #A9, pl. 4:5); 88–90 #B40, pl. 12:2 = *CIS* 44.

282. M. Yon, "À propos de l'Héraklès de Chypre," in *Iconographie Classique et Identités Régionales* (ed. L. Kahil, C. Augé, and P. Linant de Bellefonds; BCH Supplement 14; Paris: École Française d'Athènes / Athens: Boccard, 1986) 287–97, esp. pp. 288–89.

Cypriot dialect spoken in Kition. It was an accomplishment ("interpreter of Cretan" was not an office, and no one else received the title), and it enabled the recently established Kingdom of Kition to accommodate the indigenous people by encouraging bilingualism or even trilingualism among the Phoenician population.

The last two clauses in the inscription mimic the ending of Milkyaton's trophy inscription, in which victory is an answer to prayer, and therefore it is not unlikely that the occasion for embellishing and rededicating the statue was also the defeat of Evagoras of Salamis. The main difference is that Milkyaton attributed the victory to Mighty Ba‘al, the God of Kition, who heard the prayer of the people, while the immigrant family gave glory to Melqart, the God of Tyre, for hearing the prayer of the king. Milkyaton, besides, dedicated the trophy on the exact day and at the very spot of the victory, but the family, making assurance doubly sure, waited three or six years until the Peace of Antalcidas (ca. 386 B.C.E.) ended the hostilities, put a final stop to Athenian and Salaminian intrigue, and left control of Kition and all Cyprus to the Persians.[283]

Milkyaton's chronology, populism, and appeal to Mighty Ba‘al are probably conceits he used to authenticate his kingship: Mighty Ba‘al was introduced to Kition by the Ba‘almilk Dynasty, and appeal to the God could make Ba‘almilk's usurpation, if it was that, look like a smooth transition; defeat of the city's enemies at an exact time and place at the very beginning of his reign could prove its legitimacy; inclusion of the people in his exploits and his hope for the future could relax their resentment. The determination and skill that Milkyaton showed in this use of propaganda are matched by his civic improvements, including a new sewer and drainage system, and his careful preparations for the war with Salamis, in particular the construction of dry docks for his warships.[284]

These dry docks are north of the temple courtyard and separated from it by a fairly narrow walkway. There are certainly 6 and possibly as many as 10 sheds running 30 meters south to north, each 6 meters wide with inclined slipways just wide enough for the keel and with a low wall and pillars on either side of each to provide leverage and to support a tiled roof. They are like the dry docks in fifth-century Piraeus and could service long, narrow, light, and fast triremes similar to the triremes in the Athenian navy. It was in this area that his trophy was set up, and Milkyaton could have attributed his naval victory over the Salaminians and Paphians not only to the God of Kition and the bravery of its people but to his personal foresight in building the naval yards and to the superior skill of his craftsmen in repairing and outfitting its war ships.

283. G. Shrimpton, "Persian Strategy against Egypt and the Date for the Battle of Citium," *Phoenix* 45 (1991) 1–20.

284. O. Callot, "Les Hangars du Port de Kition (Ve–IVe s. av. J.C.)," in *Res Maritimae: Cyprus and the Eastern Mediterranean from Prehistory to Late Antiquity* (ed. S. Swiny, R. L. Hohlfelder, and H. Wylde Swiny; ASOR Archaeological Reports 4; Atlanta: Scholars Press, 1997) 71–81; M. Yon, "Les hangars du port chypro-phénicien de Kition: Campagnes 1996–1998 (Mission Française de Kition-Bamboula)," *Syria* 77 (2000) 95–116.

Evagoras I of Salamis was a distinguished adversary,[285] and his defeat brought Milkyaton instant fame. He was from a long line of kings that could trace its genealogy to a hero of the Trojan War. He reigned almost 40 years, made alliances with Athens and Egypt, was a friend of Isocrates and the subject of one of his orations. His goal was supremacy in Cyprus, and he consistently worried the Persians and their Phoenician allies (his privateers patrolled the Cilician coast and, incredibly, threatened Tyre and other mainland cities) until they finally suppressed his ambitions.[286] His political convictions were not shared by everyone, but the pro-Persian factions in Salamis seem to have comprised mainly Phoenicians or men with Phoenician names. His own grandfather, who commanded the Cypriot wing of the Persian navy at the Battle of Salamis in 480 B.C.E. was Gorgos, grandson of Siromos,[287] and both these names could be just Cypriot pronunciations of Phoenician names (*grgš* and *ḥîrôm*) given to them by their mothers. There was also, apparently, a Phoenician usurper in mid-fifth-century Salamis,[288] and Evagoras himself succeeded to the throne only by ousting the Phoenician usurper Abdemon (ʿAbdḥamôn), who had been promoted by Baʿalmilk II of Kition. Evagoras obviously came by his antipathies honestly, but Milkyaton was his ideological and aggressive match and ultimately was more successful.

Idalion probably contributed to Kition's aggrandizement in the reign of Milkyaton, but it seems to have been neglected.[289] It was an administrative and industrial center, with archives, warehouses filled with rows of storage jars, oil and wine presses, and factories for its bronze and iron works.[290] It was also a religious center with many temples and offerings by Phoenicians, Greeks, and Cypriots. There are Cypriot sculptures together with Phoenician "Temple Boy" dedications in the sanctuary of Aphrodite.[291] There is a lance tip inscribed with the battle cry "for ʿAnat | for ʿAnat" in the Temple of Athena.[292] And there are votive bronzes, Cypriot statues of worshipers,

---

285. *Cyprus* 125–43; M. Yon, "Chypre entre la Grèce et les Perses: La conscience grecque de Chypre entre 530 et 330 a.C.," *Ktema* 6 (1981) 49–56.

286. S. Ruzicka, "Glos, son of Tamos, and the End of the Cypriot War," *Historia* 48 (1999) 23–43.

287. *Cyprus* 115 n. 5.

288. O. Masson, "Les inscriptions syllabiques et alphabétiques de Cellarka," in *Excavations in the Necropolis of Salamis II: Texte* (ed. V. Karageorghis; Nicosia: Department of Antiquities, 1970) 269–78. The entrance of Tomb 33A was inscribed in Cypro-Syllabic with the name and patronymic of the deceased: he was Phoenician (ʿAbdbaʿal (*aputupalo* in Cypriot), and his father was Lycian (pp. 269–73).

289. P. Gaber and W. G. Dever, "Idalion, Cyprus: Conquest and Continuity," in *Preliminary Excavation Reports: Sardis, Idalion, and Tell el-Handaquq North* (ed. W. G. Dever; AASOR 53; Cambridge, MA: American Schools of Oriental Research, 1996) 85–113.

290. M. Hadjicosti, "The Kingdom of Idalion in the Light of New Evidence," *BASOR* 308 (1997) 49–63; idem, "The Administrative Centre of the Phoenician Domination at Idalion"; E. Herscher, "Archaeology in Cyprus: Dhali Abeleri and Moutti tou Arvili (Ancient Idalion)," *AJA* 102 (1998) 332–34.

291. C. Beer, *Temple-Boys: A Study of Cypriote Votive Sculpture, Part 2: Functional Analysis* (Stockholm: Stockholm University Press, 1993) 53–55; P. Flourentzos, "A Group of Sculptures from Idalion," in *Periplus: Festschrift für Hans-Günter Buchholz zu seinem achtzigsten Geburtstag am 24. Dezember 1999* (ed. P. Åström and D. Sürenhagen; Studies in Mediterranean Archaeology 127; Jonsered: Åströms, 2000) 59–62, pls. 19–22.

292. *RPC* 110–11, pl. 10:2.

and Phoenician dedications, most of them by kings and citizens of Kition, to Reshepmukol in the Temple of Apollo.[293] It is perhaps symbolic of the city's dwindled importance that two of its four gates, according to a late fourth-century Greek ostracon, led elsewhere, to Kition and to Tamassos, which Kition then controlled.[294]

Pumayyaton (362–312 B.C.E.), the son and successor of Milkyaton, was the last king of Kition.[295] Before the middle of the century, he bought the Kingdom of Tamassos for 50 talents from its king, Pasikypros, who had wasted his money in lavish living and now could retire to Amathus. A broken inscription from the Temple of ʾEshmun in Sidon records an offering by a king whose name is lost, but because it also mentions Tamassos it has been attributed to Pumayyaton.[296] The inscription can be dated to about the same time as his purchase of Tamassos, and it may be a sign of his involvement in the Phoenician Revolt led by Tennēs of Sidon, perhaps by helping to finance it: his coinage is gold on the Persian standard (there are some silver coins on the Rhodian standard),[297] and a large issue in his 30th year (333/32 B.C.E.) would coincide, similarly, with Alexander's siege of Tyre[298] when, perhaps, he helped finance Tyre's resistance or the escape of the Tyrian children to Carthage.

His involvement in the Phoenician Revolt may also be indicated by the discovery at Idalion of numerous coins of Evagoras II of Salamis, who was sent to settle the aftermath of the revolt on Cyprus.[299] Pumayyaton's behavior during the siege of Tyre (333 B.C.E.) exasperated Alexander, and after it but before his 34th year (328 B.C.E.), he was forced to surrender Tamassos to Nicocreon of Salamis. Finally, along with the Phoenician kings of Lapethos and Kerynia in northern Cyprus and the king of Marion in the west, he made the sorry mistake of supporting Antigonus in the struggle for succession and was put to death by Ptolemy.

There are many Phoenician inscriptions dated to his reign, either explicitly or paleographically, but there are none written by the king. Some record offerings made in the temples, but most are tombstones or grave markers. There were many graveyards, all outside the city. Tombs were dug in the rock, one or two chambers in a row, often with one or more coffins

293. O. Masson, "Le sanctuaire d'Apollon à Idalion (Fouilles 1868–1869)," *BCH* 92 (1968) 386–402; R. Senff, *Das Apollonheiligtum von Idalion: Architektur und Statuenausstattung eines Zyprischen Heiligtums* (Studies in Mediterranean Archaeology 94; Jonsered: Åströms, 1993) 15.

294. F. M. Cross, "An Ostracon in Greek Bearing the Names of the Gates of Idalion," *Leaves from an Epigrapher's Notebook: Collected Papers in Hebrew and West Semitic Paleography and Epigraphy* (HSS 51; Winona Lake, IN: Eisenbrauns, 2003) 278–81; O. Masson, "Les fouilles américaines à Idalion (1971–1980) et leurs résultats épigraphiques," *Kadmos* 31 (1992) 113–23, pls. 1–4, esp. pp. 116–19.

295. *Cyprus* 150–59.

296. *RES* 824.

297. A. Destrooper-Georgiades, "Presentation of New Material and Work in Progress on Cypriote Classical Numismatics," in *Acta Cypria: Acts of an International Congress on Cypriote Archaeology held in Göteborg on 22–24 August 1991* (ed. P. Åström; Jonsered: Åströms, 1992) part 2, 54–66.

298. *Cyprus* 151.

299. L. E. Stager and A. M. Walker, *American Expedition to Idalion, Cyprus, 1973–1980* (Oriental Institute Communications 24; Chicago: Oriental Institute of the University of Chicago, 1989) 447–56, pls. 1–2.

in each, although some chambers were empty. The entrance, which was closed with a stone slab, was approached along a sloped walkway (*dromos*) where the tombstone was placed. There are four anthropoid sarcophagi, each for the burial of the woman whose face adorns its lid, but none of them is inscribed.[300] Usually burials were in plain, rectangular, stone coffins that were lined with cedar, pine, or cypress.[301] In the graveyard that included tombs of some Judean émigrés, burial offerings typically consisted of containers of food and drink for the journey to the realm of the dead.[302]

The tombstones are fairly elaborate marble inscribed steles (*mṣbt*) that a deceased man prepared for himself, or for himself and his wife, or for his father.[303] An epitaph begins, "I am ʿAbdosiris, son of ʿAbdsasm, son of Hor," and goes on to say that he dedicated the stele during his lifetime to mark the place of his eternal rest, and for his wife, who died before him. A man named Menahem dedicated a tombstone to his father, who was a rhapsode (*mšl*) and son of a rhapsode, and ʿAbdʾeshmun erected "a stele among the living" for his father, who was a night watchman (*šmr ll*) in Kition. A man named Arish dedicated a stele to his father (called "the Persian") and to his mother, over their eternal resting place. Arish was Chief Broker, as was his father and the four generations that preceded him, and his mother belonged to a family that could trace its ancestry to Ezra, "the chief inspector of wells."[304] The men who set up the tombstones had standard Phoenician names, but some of the men whom they commemorated had Greek names that were transliterated into Phoenician characters: "Menexenos [*mlgsns*], the vintner," "Archetos" (*ʾrktʾ*). One had a name (*tršy*) derived from a word for "wine" that was the Phoenician equivalent of Dionysus. These steles, it seems clear, marked the tombs of men and women who were somehow prominent or who belonged to old or even the founding families in Kition.

The grave markers are not identified as steles (*mṣbt*) and are inscribed with the name, and sometimes patronymic, of the deceased.[305] Five marked the graves of women: one was the wife of Milkyaton, the chief mason; one was the daughter of Yatonbaʿal; two name their mothers and grandmothers; one, whose marble gravestone is now the lintel in the central archway entrance of a church, was the daughter of a Carthaginian and the wife of a man from Kition who traced his lineage to the fifth generation. There is a tombstone of a man who was indentured to an accountant whose name and whose father's name were Carthaginian. There was a blacksmith named Haggai who lists the generations back to his great-great-grandfather. An exceptional grave marker has a portrait of the deceased in profile, with Greek curls and features, bare chested, his right hand raised in salutation, his left grasping the stole thrown over his left shoulder, his Phoenician name inscribed above his head.[306]

300. M. Yon, "Les sarcophages 'sidoniens' de Kition," *Sem* 39 (1990) 177–86, pl. 6.

301. Idem, "Développements récents sur la ville phénicienne de Kition," 1295.

302. Idem and O. Callot, "Nouvelles découvertes dans la nécropole ouest de Kition (Aghios Giorghios, époque classique)," *RDAC* (1987) 149–70, pls. 50–54.

303. *Kition* 3.48–60 ##B1–8.

304. Ibid., 3.96–100 #B45, pl. 16:4.

305. Ibid., 3.60–78 ##9–31.

306. *RPC* 121–23, pl. 17:1.

All these can be dated to the reign of Pumayyaton, but there are other inscribed tombstones from the early third century.[307] Most are plain like the fourth-century stones, but one is a bilingual epitaph marking the eternal "home" of Murnos, the Lycian, a maker of goblets. Another describes the plain stone coffin as a "box" (*tb*). And another is the elegant marble tombstone of Kalbo', who was a sixth-generation citizen of Kition.

The dedicatory texts that are dated to the reign of Pumayyaton were inscribed on steles, statue bases, and an altar. A damaged marble stele lacks the date, but it may belong to the early years of Pumayyaton's reign, before he bought Tamassos, because he is mentioned as king only of Kition and Idalion.[308] It records the offering and dedication of two pedestals in the Temple of 'Eshmunmelqart, the God whom Milkyaton introduced into Kition to please the faithful of the combined Kingdom of Kition and Idalion. An inscribed altar dated to Pumayyaton's 21st year, when he was also king of Tamassos, records the offering of the altar and of the two lions that flanked it to the God "Reshep-of-the-Arrows" by his priest Bodo'.[309] The God is unique to Kition and probably was a local manifestation of Apollo, who was worshiped at Idalion as Reshepmukol. A fragmentary inscription on a marble base records the dedication of a statue in Pumayyaton's 34th year and indicates that he was no longer king of Tamassos.[310] In his 37th year, Ya'isha, the daughter of Šama'a' and the wife of Ba'alyaton, who was a slave in the Temple of Astarte, dedicated a bronze statue of herself to her Lady Astarte.[311] In his 42nd year, the chief scribe, in fulfillment of his vow, dedicated a statue of his son (perhaps a Temple Boy statuette) to the God 'Eshmun: the scribe was the son of "the Cilician" (*klky*), and his son was given the same name. There are no dedicatory inscriptions from Pumayyaton's last eight years, and the monarchy ended when he died.

The republican era of Kition began in 311 B.C.E. after Pumayyaton's death and is mentioned in a late fourth-century inscription from Kition and in a third-century inscription from Idalion. The Kition inscription[312] records an offering to "the Mother of Supplications" ('*m h'zrt*). It is damaged, and the endings of its three lines need to be reconstructed: the ending of the last line is the formulaic "because she heard [his voice. May she bless him]," and the reconstruction is certain; the second line names the donor, his father, and his grandfather and, because it is the family of Bodo' who was the priest of "Reshep-of-the-Arrows" in Pumayyaton's 21st year (341 B.C.E.), the end of the line is easily filled out with the names of his earlier ancestors in that inscription; the first line has the date of the offering to the day, month, and the second year, and the ending would have had the specification of the year and identification of the offering. Paleographically, it belongs at the end of the fourth century, and the reconstruction "second year [of the people of Kition, this statue]" gives the line the same

307. *Kition* 3.78–87 ##B32–38; 93–95 #B43, pl. 12:2; 100–101 #B46, pl. 14:2.
308. Ibid., 3.15–18 #A3, pl. 2:2.
309. *CIS* 10; *KAI* 32; *Kition* 3.14–15 #A2, pl. 2:1.
310. Ibid., 3.42–44 #A29, pl. 8:1–2.
311. Ibid., 3.11–13 #A1, pl. 1:1.
312. *CIS* 13; *Kition* 3.38–41 #A27, pl. 7:3.

length as the second. The donor is ʿAbdosiris, the son of Bodoʾ, who was a priest in 341 B.C.E., and in the second year of the people of Kition (309 B.C.E.) he would have been old enough to have a son for whom he could pray and offer a statue (a Temple Boy statue perhaps) to the Mother of Supplications.

The inscription from Idalion[313] is dated to "the thirty-first year of the Lord of Kings Ptolemy, son of Ptolemy the Lord of Kings, which is the fifty-seventh year of the men of Kition," or 255 B.C.E. The Kition inscription does not have any synchronism because Ptolemy I Soter (305–285 B.C.E.) was not yet king. The Idalion text records the offering to Reshepmukol by Batshillem (in fulfillment of a vow that her brother made before he died) of statues of his three sons. The dating follows the Kition calendar, but Batshillem adds a local touch by synchronizing the second year of the people of Kition with the year when the canephora of Arsinoe—the wife of Ptolemy II Philadelphus, who with her husband was the object of worship—was ʾAmotosiris of Idalion.

Phoenician Cyprus did not undergo the Hellenizing transformation embraced by the mainland cities in the fifth and fourth centuries because it was already embedded in Greek and Cypriot culture. Kition was a bilingual or trilingual town, and it had no trouble adopting Greek Gods into its pantheon, but it was basically Tyrian and jealous of its ethnic distinctiveness. Lapethos was ruled by a Phoenician dynasty whose kings enjoyed Greek names, whose coins displayed their Gods ʿAnat and Melqart in the guise of Athena and Heracles, and whose people were bilingual, but it remained Phoenician in its dialect and cultic traditions. Amathus was indigenous Cypriot, but its Phoenician minority was politically influential and culturally conservative. Nevertheless, it was a Greek island in a Greek world, and the Phoenicians, even the Tyrians who were averse to assimilating, were notoriously accommodating.

Egypt Is Influenced by the Greeks and Cypriots

In the fifth and fourth centuries, Phoenician merchants, mercenaries, and pilgrims still traveled to Egypt, and there were Phoenician enclaves at places such as Memphis and Elephantine, but the Phoenicians no longer inspired a significant cultural dynamic. It was Greeks and Cypriots, especially at Naucratis in the sixth century and into the fifth, who were most influential and, in this time of archaizing and reinventing the past, it was the Egyptian mystique that counted.

Among the pilgrims to Abydos, according to an Aramaic papyrus dated to 417 B.C.E., there were two brothers from Sidon: "On the third day of the month Kislev . . . of the seventh year of Darius the King, ʿAbdbaʿal of Sidon . . . came with his brother ʿAzorbaʿal to Abydos in Egypt before Osiris, the Great God."[314] Graffiti on pillars of the early thirteenth-century Temple of Osiris in the same place mark the visits of pilgrims and the curious from

---

313. *CIS* 93; *KAI* 40.
314. J. Teixidor, "Un nouveau papyrus araméen du règne de Darius II," *Syria* 41 (1964) 285–90; J. Naveh, "Old Aramaic Inscriptions," *AION* 16 (1966) 19–36, esp. pp. 30–31.

Tyre or the places where they lived or were stationed in Egypt or from Cyprus. Sometimes they wrote just their names, but usually they wrote "I am"
with their name and patronymic and sometimes their profession or town
of origin. One was from Kition, another was indentured to a Phoenician in
Memphis, and another was a Tyrian who came from ʿAkko and was living
in Memphis after he had been released from his indenture to a Phoenician
from Memphis.

Bodo the mercenary (*mqrd*) has no hometown and does not reveal his
genealogy. A few men (there were no women among the visitors to the
temple, or at least among the "graffitists") identify themselves as apprentices, and there were a variety of jobs or careers for which they might have
been preparing: one man is an aspiring green grocer (*mlḥm*), one is a date
grower (*tmr*); there are a drummer (*mtpp*), a plasterer (*kps*), a perfumer (*rqḥ*),
and an interpreter (*mlṣ*). The Phoenicians from Cyprus, perhaps more specifically from Lapethos, do not explicitly identify this as their place of origin, but they are detected by their dialect, which substitutes /L/ for /N/ in
the personal pronoun "I" (*ʾlk* for *ʾnk*), in the word "son" (*bl* for *bn*), and the
spelling of their names (e.g., *mtl* for *mtn*).

The Phoenicians at Elephantine, an island near Aswan garrisoned by
Jewish soldiers, were merchants securing the trade routes with Nubia for
the Persian Empire. The remains of their enterprise are 53 legible ostraca[315]
with their names and a few notations. Thirteen of the men have names
without patronymics, and of these most names are Phoenician but one is
Egyptian. When the patronymic is given, either both names are Phoenician
or both names are Egyptian; or the son's name is Egyptian but his father's
name is Phoenician; or the son's name is Phoenician and the father's name
is Egyptian. Some of the Phoenician traders at Elephantine may have been
relative newcomers in Egypt or perhaps were simply in transit, but others
belonged to families who had lived in Egypt for several generations and
were becoming Egyptianized.

Among the notations on the ostraca, the most common is the expression "for the king" (*lmlk*) followed by the royal symbol (*T*) indicating that
the shipment was to be sent to the Persian administrator in Egypt or eventually to the king. One ostracon has only "the Cretans" (*hkrsym*), which
suggests that there was a Cypriot corporation or trading company at Elephantine and that the jars with this mark belonged to or were destined
for them. The ostraca usually do not indicate the contents of the jars or
shipments, but there is one ostracon with "for the king" and the royal
symbol that refers to products of the gardens (*gnt*): a slightly later and badly
damaged letter,[316] a wholesale grocery list, sent to the manager of an estate
that had its own traders and shipped its goods overland and by river indicates that these products might have included white and red onions, beans,
green and ripe olives, figs, almonds, cumin, or sesame—all to be shipped
in sealed containers.

---

315. M. Lidzbarski, *Phönizische und aramäische Krugauschriften aus Elephantine* (Berlin, 1912).
316. *KAI* 51; N. Aimé-Giron, "Adversaria semitica: Papyrus phénicien," *Bulletin de l'Institut
Français d'Archéologie Orientale* 38 (1939) 1–18.

An Aramaic letter from Elephantine[317] deals with a financial problem faced by a club or corporation (*marzeah*) of merchants and traders. The fact that it is in Aramaic might suggest that its members were brokers representing the Jewish community, but all the personal names are just as likely Phoenician, and the language of the letter, besides being the lingua franca of the Empire, reflects cooperation between the merchants and the dominant Jewish community. The letter has an address but no greeting and is fairly abrupt:

> To Haggay. I talked to Ashyon about the marzeah money. This is what he said to me, to Itto: "Well, I will give it to Haggay or Yigdol." Speak to him and get him to give it to the two of you.

Haggay seems to have been president of this particular corporation, and Yigdol may have been the president of another. Itto, then, was probably the supervisor of temple cults and of religious organizations such as these, an office known from Carthaginian records and from the *marzeah* memorial at Piraeus. Ashyon, as analogy with the Piraeus memorial suggests, was the secretary and treasurer of the Phoenician community. Corporations had money but, as the letter indicates, also expected at least occasional contributions from the community. The letter is business-like, money is the issue, the negotiations involved were congenial to merchants; the hierarchy of civic, religious, and commercial organization that the letter reveals is surely what made things work.

The ostracon does not name the patron gods of the several clubs, but they might very well have been Egyptian, or the Egyptian equivalent of a Phoenician God. A statue of Harpocrates, the child Horus, is inscribed in Egyptian and Phoenician.[318] It is a bronze statuette of the child, standing naked, his left foot forward, and his left arm by his side, his right arm bent, and his right index finger to his lips. The Phoenician text, which can be dated paleographically to the early fifth century, reads: "May Harpocrates give life to Amos, the son of ʾEshmunyaton, son of ʾAzormilk," and at the end in half-size script adds, to remind the curious that writing was an art, "And Ninbaʿal its sculptor inscribed it." The Egyptian text has the same prayer for life, but Amos and his father are identified by their Egyptian names. Another dedication to the God Harpocrates, this one dated to the end of the fourth century, begins almost the same way ("May Harpocrates give life to his servant, to ʿAbdʾeshmun . . .") and ends with the name of man who made it ("Its maker is Salah son of [—]"). But it lists five generations before ʿAbdʾeshmun, the first two his father and grandfather with Phoenician names, but the three earlier generations with Egyptian names.[319]

---

317. M. Lidzbarski, *Ephemeris für Semitische Epigraphik: Dritter Band, 1909–1915* (Giessen: Alfred Töpelmann, 1915) 119–21; B. Porten, *Archives from Elephantine: The Life of an Ancient Jewish Military Colony* (Berkeley: University of California Press, 1968) 179–86; B. Becking, "Temple, *marzeah*, and Power at Elephantine," *Transeu* 29 (2005) 37–47.

318. *RES* 2; J. Ferron, "La statuette d'Harpocrate du British Museum," *RSF* 2 (1974) 77–95, pls. 22–27.

319. *KAI* 52; Y. Muchiki, *Egyptian Proper Names and Loanwords in North-West Semitic* (SBLDS 173; Atlanta: Society of Biblical Literature, 1999) 23, 35, 39.

From the fifth century, there is an inscribed stone statue of Isis, seated on a high-backed throne, holding the child Horus on her knee.[320] The inscription reads: "Girsapon, son of Ezra, son of Shallikot, whom she bore to my Lady, to Astarte." The text and statue implicitly identify Isis, whose likeness it is, and Astarte, whose name she bears. The inscription is unusual in naming Girsapon's father and his mother, but it is totally ingenuous in declaring his mother the embodiment of the Goddess and himself the child of Astarte. This identification of Isis and Astarte is explicit in the inscription on the base of a statue of Horus from Memphis that presents the statue to "the Goddess, Almighty Isis, the Goddess Astarte."[321] The merchants of Elephantine, except perhaps the Cypriots, were quasi-Egyptian in their individual and family lives, as were these devotees of Isis, but in their corporate lives they were probably too alert to the international order and too ethnically aware to adopt Egyptian patron Gods.

Cypriots at home on Cyprus borrowed, via the Greeks of Cyrene and Naucratis, the Egyptian cult of the Ram-Headed God known as Zeus Ammon, and it became a fetish from the sixth century onward everywhere on the island where Cypriots were dominant, but not in the Greek or Phoenician cities.[322] At Naucratis in the Egyptian Delta, Cypriot artists and craftsmen specialized in stone statuary done in Egyptian style or with Egyptian motifs, and sculptures from their workshops were exported to Cyprus and coastal sites in Syria and Palestine.[323] It became the fashion, for instance, to have columns with Hathor capitals, and to sculpt stylishly effete Egyptian men, striding, wigged, an oval face, narrow chest, and flabby belly, arms by their side or bent across their chest, wearing a broad collar, bracelets on their upper arms, and short kilt with a front vent.[324] These Cypriots maintained their indigenous characteristics, remained distinct from the Greeks and Phoenicians, and for all their appreciation of the Egyptian mystique had enough sturdy common sense not to succumb to it but remain faithful to their own culture and traditions.

Malta Remains Traditional

The Phoenician communities on Malta were equally aloof to the mainstream African ethos. There were ripples from the Carthaginian Empire that affected religion and politics (inhumation replacing cremation, tight civic organization), but in the fifth and fourth centuries Phoenicians on Malta clung to their east Mediterranean heritage. They were farmers mostly

---

320. *RES* 535.

321. Ibid., 1.235; *KAI* 48.

322. E. Lipiński, "Zeus-Ammon et Baʿal-Ḥammon," *RelPh* 307–32; H.-G. Buchholz, "Der Gott Hammon und Zeus Ammon auf Zypern," *Mitteilungen des Deutschen Archäologischen Instituts: Athenische Abteilung* 106 (1991) 85–128, pls. 10–21.

323. A. Möller, *Naucratis: Trade in Archaic Greece* (Oxford: Oxford University Press, 2000) 161–63; U. Höckmann and D. Kreikenbom, eds., *Naukratis: Die Beziehungen zu Ostgriechenland, Ägypten und Zypern in archäischer Zeit. Akten der Table Ronde in Mainz, 25.–27. November 1999* (Möhnsee: Bibliopolis, 2001); A. Hermary, "Naucratis et la sculpture égyptisante à Chypre," *Naukratis* (2001) 27–38, pls. 1–2; S. Fourrier, "Naucratis, Chypre et la Grèce de l'Est: Le commerce des sculptures 'chypro-ioniennes'," *Naukratis* (2001) 39–54, pls. 3–4.

324. Hermary, "Naucratis et la sculpture égyptisante à Chypre," 27–33.

and, though they may have continued to export their linen products, trade and the accumulation of wealth were not important. The population grew, and, on the east coast where this growth was especially strong, this may have been due to immigration from Sicily and Sardinia.

More than 1,000 tombs have been located on Malta,[325] most of them from the third century and from the period of Roman occupation, and only around 100 from the fifth and fourth centuries. All are chamber tombs, single, double, or triple, reached by a shaft that may have steps or rungs cut into the rock, facilitating access to the chamber entrances.[326] The deceased were laid on the ground, on a wooden bed, on a broad stone bier at the back of the chamber, or in five cases were buried in terra-cotta coffins: sometimes older tombs were reused, and it was only at the beginning in the third century that cremation again became an acceptable practice. There were few grave goods, mostly pottery, all chosen from a standardized repertory, few trinkets and almost nothing of exceptional quality. Sometimes the tombs were clustered, but often they were isolated, and by preference dug into gentle slopes.[327] There were no gravestones, no epitaphs, no inscribed objects and, except for 5 tombs with faces, fetishes, or symbols chiseled in the wall,[328] all the burials were severely anonymous.

This uniform simplicity is also evident in the types of pottery and the kinds of trinkets.[329] There was one basic ware: thick walled with a pale pink or yellow slip, badly fired, and therefore often with surface blisters. A similar ware, wheel made and with fine or coarse clay, was most common at the southeast sanctuary at Tas Silg. A third kind of ware at the end of the fourth century was reserved for cinerary urns. The pottery types in tombs of this period were limited: most graves contained one or two amphorae and a jug or two with a trefoil mouth, but urns were rare, and unguent bottles appeared only late in the fourth century, there were small bowls, larger drinking bowls, plates, stemmed cups, and lamps, all quite plain but, toward the end of the fourth century, decorated with thin red horizontal lines. Only a small percentage of the total number of tombs had ornaments, or jewelry, or toys.

There was a gold amulet case containing a sheet of gold inscribed with hieroglyphs, and in the debris of the centuries 3 gold rings, 2 earrings, 5 beads, and 1 gold pendant. There were about 60 pieces of bronze jewelry and accessories, and around 30 pieces of silver, some glass beads, and 1 iron bracelet. There were some rustic terra-cotta figurines (of roosters, horses, rabbits, one of a pig with a rider), but they did not feature in the burials

325. G. A. Said-Zammit, *Population, Land Use and Settlement on Punic Malta: A Contextual Analysis of the Burial Evidence* (BAR International Series 682; Oxford: Archaeopress, 1997) 7–12.

326. C. Sagona, *The Archaeology of Punic Malta* (ANESt Supplement 9; Louvain: Peeters, 2002) 237–60.

327. G. A. Said-Zammit, "The Phoenician Tombs of the Maltese Islands," *Actas* 4, 3.1365–75, esp. p. 1367.

328. P. Vidal González, *La Isla de Malta en Época fenicia y púnica* (BAR International Series 653; Oxford: Tempus Reparatum, 1996) 32.

329. Sagona, *The Archaeology of Punic Malta*, 79–81, 88, 101, 125–26, 154–56, 174–75, 198, 210, 217–18, 228–29, fig. 344, 281–91; Said-Zammit, *Population, Land Use and Settlement on Punic Malta*, 19–22.

and sometimes were dropped or discarded in the tomb shaft. There was a hoard of fourth-century Sicilian coins from Mqabba, but local coinage did not begin before Malta became a Roman province in 218 B.C.E., and there were no coins in the tombs.[330] It appears from these remains that, apart from the potters, the stone masons who dug the tombs, and the women who produced fine linen, there were no artists or craftsmen on Malta—no one who worked in silver or gold or ivory and apparently no one who was interested in importing the products of these workshops. The few nice, unusual, or expensive items in the tombs seem to have come with people who immigrated to Malta in the seventh and sixth centuries or with later sailors, pilgrims, visitors, or migrant workers who stayed awhile on the island.

The simplest of the terra-cotta sarcophagi is a rectangular box designed to look like the wooden chests used in some burials.[331] It is red clay and about 5½′ long × 2⅓′ wide and deep, and it rests on four legs of about the same height. The sides and ends resemble three wood panels, with the central panel slightly inset, and the lid is another panel of the same size. The top consists of three oblong slabs fitted into the lid, with four holes drilled into the slab at the head of the coffin, perhaps for libations but probably just finger holes for ease of placement. Of the anthropoid clay sarcophagi, only one is actually preserved, another is available only in a drawing, and the other two are missing.[332] The preserved sarcophagus contained the skeleton of a woman and an iron finger ring. The coffin itself has no straight edges or flat surfaces but suggests, without illustrating, the contours of her entire body. The lid is shallow and represents her as she was at death, wrapped in a shroud with only her face and her toes uncovered. Her face is quite broad, her lips are full, her chin is square and slightly juts, her nose is proportional, her nostrils flare, her ears are prominent as in the Egyptian originals, and her eyes are shut. She was small (the coffin is only about five feet long from head to toe), sturdy, and important enough to have a coffin made for her that mimicked her shape and bore the imprint of her death mask.

The first settlers in Malta were literate Phoenicians, and their earliest inscriptions marked foundation sacrifices by two leaders of the expedition. There is almost nothing from the fifth and fourth centuries, but in Roman times, in the third and second centuries, there is some rudimentary evidence of literacy and learning.[333] An early fourth-century text written in large ornamental letters on a lintel reads "Gate of ʿAbdilaʾay" (*šʿr ʿbdlʾy*)[334] and perhaps marked the entrance to the town quarter or to a sector of the temple precinct that housed this particular guild, which was known by

330. G. K. Jenkins, "The Mqabba (Malta) Hoard of Punic Bronze Coins," *RSF* 11 (1983) 19–36, pls. 2–20; L. I. Manfredi, "Tipi monetali a Malta e Biblo," *RSO* 70 (1996) 289–301; L. Sole, "Iconografie religiose fenicie nelle emissioni di *Melite* (Malta)," *Transeu* 29 (205) 171–87, pls. 5–7.

331. Sagona, *The Archaeology of Punic Malta*, 262, 820 #122, pls. 30:2, 31:1.

332. Ibid., 262–63, 818–19 #117, 819–20 ##119 and 121, pls. 29:15–17, 30:1, 3; H. Richter, "Katalog der Fundgruppen," in *Die Phönizische Anthropoiden Sarkophage, Teil 1: Fundgruppen und Bestattungskontete* (ed. S. Frede; Mainz am Rhein: von Zabern, 2000) 65–153, esp. pp. 142–44, pls. 128–29.

333. *IFPCO* 15–52, ##1–19, pls. 1–13.

334. Ibid., 26–27 #8, fig. 1.

its ancestral name. A mid-third-century inscription on a stone block set into the wall of a tomb is the one exception to the universal absence of epitaphs:[335]

> Room in the house of eternity. Tomb h[ewn]
> for Naqiya at her own expense. Month of
> Marpa'im in the year of Hannibal,
> son of Bodmilk.

The epitaph is unusual: it is pithy and staccato, omits Naqiya's ancestry and Hannibal's title, but it shows that years were dated by eponym, implies that tombs generally were dug at public or family expense, and thinks of them as rooms in the mansion of eternity. Naqiya was independent (she is neither "wife" nor "daughter"), wealthy enough to pay for her tomb, may have been a merchant or overseas trader, and her exceptional epitaph might suggest that she was not Maltese.

The remaining inscriptions are associated with sanctuaries and worship. The latest, from around the end of the third century, is beautifully inscribed on a small, square marble plaque to commemorate the renovation of sanctuaries and altars by the assembly of Gawl (ʿm gwl).[336] The endings of the first seven lines are lost, but repetition and the use of papponomy facilitate their reconstruction:

> The assembly of Gawl made and restored [these] three [altars and the] sanctuary of the temple of Ṣid-is-Baʿal and the sanctuary of [the temple of 'Eshmun and the] sanctuary of the temple of Astarte and the sanctuary [of the temple of Milkastarte] in the time of the Rab Arish, in charge of the militia, son of Joel, [son of ʿAbd'eshmun the] judge, son of Zybqum, son of ʿAbd'eshmun, son of Joel, [son of Arish]. The sacrificer was Baʿalshillek, son of Ḥanno, son of ʿAbd'eshmun [son of Ḥanno, son of] Billo, son of Killam, son of Jazer. The inspector of the quarry was Joel, [the representative of] the assembly of Gawl.

Gawl is the island of Gozo in the Maltese archipelago, a little northwest of the main island of Malta. The four temples, or "houses," probably formed the boundaries of a precinct in which the three altars were installed. The sanctuaries (mqdš) were spaces in these houses frequented by the devotees of these Gods and so requiring maintenance.

The names of two of the Gods are missing, but because Astarte and Ṣid are easily Punic, or western Mediterranean, it may be that the other two were the homeland Gods of Sidon and Tyre: the name of the God Milkʿastarte (mlkʿštrt) was inscribed on the edge of a small offering bowl at Tas Silg in a fine late fourth-century script,[337] maybe Carthaginian, but not at all typical of the other writing. The stonework was done by the squads, or ranks (ʿrkt), under Arish and was supervised by Joel, a representative of the assembly or "people." The date of the repairs is established by the tenure of Arish, a sixth-generation inhabitant of Malta, as commander (Rab),

---

335. Ibid., 17–19 #2, pl. 2.

336. *CIS* 132; *KAI* 62; *IFPCO*, 23–25 #6, pl. 2; M. Heltzer, "The Inscription *CIS, I,* 132 from Gozo and the Political Structure of the Island in the Punic Period," *JMS* 3 (1993) 198–204.

337. M. G. Amadasi Guzzo, "Le iscrizioni puniche," in *Missione Archeologica Italiana a Malta: Rapporto preliminare della Campagna 1970* (Rome: Consiglio Nazionale delle Ricerche, 1973) 87–94, pls. 57–62, esp. pp. 92–94, pl. 62:5–6.

and the antiquity of the settlement, perhaps of the temple complex as well, is also insinuated by the genealogy of his younger colleague, the sacrificial priest Baʿalshillek, who was an eighth-generation Maltese. The provenance of the inscription is unknown, and it is possible that it refers to renovations of the temple precinct at Tas Silg, rather than an unidentified site on Gozo, by the people of that island.

Tas Silg, in the southeast of Malta, is situated on a promontory overlooking the island's main harbor. It was the site of an ancient shrine of the Goddess who in Punic times was worshiped as Astarte.[338] The late Punic and Neo-Punic inscriptions associated with her shrine were incised on locally made ceramic vessels that the pilgrims offered to her or that contained the food offerings shared by her worshipers.[339] They usually consist of one or two letters or illiterate signs, but one reads "belonging to the priest," one has "belonging to the sanctuary," and two others, one of them on the rim of a cooking pot,[340] have "for Astarte."

According to two other inscriptions, the offering represents the fulfillment of a vow: on a limestone block, there is the laconic "Apis offered what he vowed. Blessed be he to the Lady, to Astarte."[341] On a very small bone plaque, there is another offering—in fulfillment of a vow "to the Lady, to Astarte"—of the basin to which the plaque was affixed.[342] Travelers, pilgrims, merchant sailors, and the just plain curious were lured by the ancient megalithic ruins at Tas Silg and drawn by devotion to Astarte, who at this time was uniquely the Goddess. Their offerings were simple, their literary skills generally limited, their interest in the occult expressed in the abbreviations of their names and the name of the Goddess, and in the signs and scratches they made on the poor containers for their gifts.

The bilingual inscriptions,[343] the actual provenance of which is unknown, would have been conspicuous at the Tas Silg sanctuary. The inscribed pottery is very plain, but the bilinguals are duplicated on bases that now support marble columns that taper upward from a basic acanthus leaf design. The Greek version might have been intelligible to the officiants, but it would have been appropriately mysterious to most of the visitors at the sanctuary. The dedication to Melqart would have been out of place in the sanctuary of Astarte, but perhaps not in the temple complex mentioned in the Gozo inscription. The Phoenician text reads:

> To our Lord, to Melqart, the Baʿal of Tyre, what your servants ʿAbdosiris and his brother Osirisšamor, the two sons of Osirisšamor, the son of ʿAbdosiris, vowed because he heard their voice. May he bless them.

338. Idem, "Divinità fenicie a Tas-Silg, Malta: I Dati Epigrafici," *JMS* 3 (1993) 205–14; A. Ciasca, "Some Considerations Regarding the Sacrificial Precincts at Tas-Silg," *JMS* 3 (1993) 225–44.

339. *IFPCO* 28–51; M. G. Amadasi Guzzo, "Quelques tessons inscrits du sanctuaire d'Astarte à Tas Silg," *Actas* 4, 1.181–96.

340. A. J. Frendo, "A New Punic Inscription from Zejtun (Malta) and the Goddess Anat-Astarte," *PEQ* 131 (1999) 24–35.

341. *IFPCO* 27–28 #9, pl. 4.

342. Ibid., 38–39 #31, pl. 9.

343. *CIS* 122 bis; *KAI* 47; *IFPCO* 15–17 #1, pl. 1.

The Greek version gives the Greek names of the father and his sons ("Dionysus and Sarapion, sons of Sarapion"), and the Greek name of the God, but it omits the vow, the fact that it was heard, and the concluding prayer; instead of saying that the God is Lord of Tyre, it says that it is the boys who are from Tyre; it reveres Melqart as "Heracles the Leader" (*archēgetēs*), the hero and benefactor of his people, the initiator and leader of colonizing expeditions throughout the Mediterranean. If the monuments were brought from Tyre, or more specifically from Umm el-ʿAmed,[344] by these pilgrim brothers (their transport could be more recent) and, if they were meant to adorn the precinct at Tas Silg, they would be witnesses to the far-flung renown of the sanctuary and to the enduring connection between Punic Malta and the eastern mainland cities that first colonized it.

Malta was an island, an archipelago, to itself. It was not Hellenized and did not care for Greek things: the bilinguals are oddities; in all the tombs, there were only 16 sherds of Greek pottery, and at Tas Silg in the fifth and fourth centuries, where more might have been brought by pilgrims, there were fewer than 50.[345] There are no signs of foreign trade or interest in fancy or exotic products. The island was not aggravated by the militarism that plagued Carthage, Sicily, and Sardinia throughout these centuries. There was no money, except what Naqiya spent and the hoard of bronze Sicilian coins that perhaps belonged to her. Malta was marked by satisfaction with its traditional way of life, shunned Carthaginian cultural advances, and at last slipped quietly and intact into the Roman Empire.

Sicily Is Carthaginian

In the fifth and fourth centuries, Sicily was under the thumb of Carthage. Its residents were a mixed breed, settled from abroad, resettled from Sardinia, mingled with the natives, and invaded from North Africa. Its story is absorbed into the history of Carthage, but its own particularity is suggested by its paltry material remains.

Its earliest Punic vestiges are two anthropoid marble sarcophagi from tombs at Cannita, which is situated slightly inland between Palermo and Solunto. The earlier is completely lifelike:[346] the coffin reveals the woman's rounded shape and tapers from her broad shoulders to her toes. The lid is a portrait of her clothed in a full-length, pleated robe, her right hand by her side, her left clasping a small alabaster bottle; her head is large, her cheekbones are high, her eyes are small and heavily lidded, her lips are full and her chin square; she wears sandals and her feet rest on a high plinth.

---

344. M. G. Amadasi Guzzo and M. Pia Rossignani, "Le iscrizioni bilingui e gli *AGUIEI* di Malta," in *Da Pyrgi a Mozia: Studi sull'archeologia del Mediterraneo in memoria di Antonia Ciasca* (ed. M. G. Amadasi Guzzo, M. Liverani, and P. Matthiae; Vicino Oriente—Quaderno 3/1; Rome: Università degli Studi di Roma, "La Sapienza," 2002) 5–28, pls. 1–3.

345. G. Semeraro, "Osservasioni sui materiali arcaici di importazione greca dall'arcipelago Maltese," in *Da Pyrgi a Mozia: Studi sull'archeologia del Mediterraneo in memoria di Antonia Ciasca* (ed. M. G. Amadasi Guzzo, M. Liverni, and P. Matthiae; Vicino Oriente—Quaderno 3/2; Rome: Università degli Studi di Roma, "La Sapienza," 2002) 489–531.

346. H. Richter, "Katalog der Fundgruppen," in *Die Phönizischen Anthropoide Sarkophage, Teil 1: Fundgruppen und Bestattungskontexte* (ed. S. Frede; Mainz am Rhein: von Zabern, 2000) 66–153, esp. pp. 145–46, pls. 132–33.

The coffin also contained an ivory amulet, some unidentified metal, and a polished black pot.

The later sarcophagus[347] reveals some of the woman's contours by bulges in her heavy upper body and at her knees, and it suggests that she is robed, by showing her bare feet resting on a plinth. Both her arms are by her side, but they are disproportionately thin, and she wears armlets high on her upper arms, just below her deltoids. Her face is oval, her eyes are large, her nose is straight, her lips are full and slightly parted, and her chin is small and round. Her hair is combed back and tied and falls in ringlets on her breast. Both sarcophagi were done in the Greek style favored by Phoenicians in the early fifth century and were carved for wives of first- or second-generation settlers from Tharros who made their money managing large estates that shipped their produce to Carthage.

There are almost no inscriptions that can be dated to the fifth or fourth centuries, and only a few from the third and these generally late in the century. Most of the burial steles at Motya in the sixth century were not inscribed,[348] but in these later centuries there were not any steles and, because burial rites had changed, graves usually were unmarked. When the traditional rites were followed, however, the fact that a vow had been made was acknowledged on an inscribed gravestone. Twice the acknowledgment was made to the God Ba'al Ḥamon by two members of the same family.[349] Twice it was made to Ba'al.[350] Twice the dedication makes it clear that erecting a burial stele was all that had been vowed.[351] And once, by contrast, there is a gravestone with just the name and the occupation of the deceased ("Tomb of Mithra, the potter") without any mention of a vow made to any God.[352] From Lilybaeum (Marsala) just south of Motya, there is a stele from early in the third century with a vow to Ba'al Ḥamon, as was usual in the area.[353] However, another from the end of the third century follows the Carthaginian custom of including Tannit before Ba'al Ḥamon.[354]

From the same date, at Eryx to the north of Motya, there is an inscribed marble plaque commemorating an offering to Astarte of Eryx[355] that follows the pattern of similar dedications from Carthage. It begins with a description of the offering and its location, then the name and genealogy of the man who made the offering, the acknowledgement that his voice had been heard, a concluding prayer for blessing, and finally, the date according to the eponym of the judge presiding that year. Sicily was occupied by Carthage and drained of its resources, and it is not surprising that there are so few vestiges of Carthaginian influence.

---

347. Ibid., 144–45, pls. 130–31.
348. M. G. Amadasi Guzzo, "La documentazione epigrafica dal *Tofet* di Mozia e il problema del sacrificio *Molk*," *RelPh* 189–207, esp. pp. 192–93.
349. *IFPCO* 63–64 #13, pl. 17; 68 #18, pl. 20.
350. Ibid., 64–65 #14, pl. 17; 66–67 #16, pl. 18.
351. Ibid.,64–65 #14, pl. 17; 67 #17, pl. 19.
352. Ibid., 55–56 #3, pl. 14.
353. Ibid., 57–58 #5, pl. 15.
354. Ibid., 56–57 #4, pl. 14.
355. Ibid., 53–55 #1, fig. 6.

Sardinia between Carthage and Rome

Sardinia became progressively more Carthaginian in the fifth and fourth centuries.[356] Treaties with Rome gave Carthage exclusive trading rights with the island. North African settlers filled the urban and rural spaces left by the lack of emigration from the cities of the East, which were too engaged in the Persian Empire and its wars and too preoccupied by the Greek world. Sardinia developed a Carthaginian frame of mind. It was this and not any obvious need that provoked country towns to fortify themselves.[357] It was imperial fiscal policy that forced them to adopt coinage. It seemed reasonable to these towns to follow the example of Carthage and revamp their political system, introducing a popular assembly with a president[358] who was in charge of external affairs, and a secretary who oversaw internal affairs, such as public works and security. Sardinian resistance to Africanization, when it appeared, was expressed mainly in discrete cultural and religious archaisms and lingering attachments to the people's Phoenician origins.

Olbia in the northeast corner of Sardinia was a Punic town, established by the North African metropolis in mild defiance of Rome, as a symbol of its authority on the island. This Carthaginian connection is made explicit in a late fourth-century funerary inscription found in a small tomb built against the city wall.[359] It begins: "To my Lord, to Baʿal Ḥamon, the Lord, the room which was vowed by ʿAbdtiyon, a man of the people of Carthage." It goes on to list his ancestry to the fourteenth generation and, at 25 or 30 years to a generation, this would place him in one of the founding families of Carthage. The dedication of a "room" implies that he expected to live forever in the mansion of Eternity, and this explains his gratitude to the great God who "heard his voice many times." In the same period at Olbia, there was a building on a single-stratum site with numerous local storage jars and transport jars from Tharros on the west coast. One of the Tharros jars had a ceramic seal preserving its contents, and these corroborate the other evidence that the building was a fish market selling fresh mullet and imported pickled fish.[360] It would be a satisfying but incredible coincidence, although not entirely impossible, if the store belonged to the man from Carthage who made enough money from it before it burned to the ground to build himself a tomb.

---

356. *PFPS* 63–97.

357. F. Barreca, "Le fortificazioni fenicio-puniche in Sardegna," in *Atti del 1 Convegno Italiano sul Vicino Oriente Antico, Roma, 22–24 Aprile 1976* (Rome: Consiglio Nazionale delle Ricerche, 1978) 115–28; M. Gharbi, "La forteresse punique et son territoire: Réflexion sur la présence punique en Sardaigne et en Tunisie," *Actes* 3, 2.71–82.

358. L. I. Manfredi, "I suffeti e l'assemblea del popolo in Sardegna," *RSF* 25 (1997) 3–14.

359. *RES* 1216; *KAI* 68; *IFPCO* 113–15 #34, pl. 42; E. Lipiński, "Carthaginois en Sardaigne à l'époque de la première guerre punique," in *Punic Wars* (ed. H. Devijver and E. Lipiński; Studia Phoenicia 10; Louvain: Peeters, 1989) 67–73, esp. pp. 70–73; G. Chiera, "Osservazioni su un testo punico da Olbia," *RSF* 11 (1983) 177–81.

360. P. Cavaliere, "Anfore puniche utilizzate come contenitori di pesce: Un esempio olbiese," *MEFRA* 112 (2000) 67–72; F. Delusso and B. Wilkens, "Le conserve di pesce: Alcuni dati da contesti italiani," *MEFRA* 112 (2000) 53–65.

Cagliari was the capital of the southern sector of Sardinia under the Carthaginian regime,[361] an important port and a staging area for convoys to Ibiza and Spain. There are traces of a city wall built in the fourth century, probably because of the perceived threat from Rome, which was later resolved when Roman merchants and colonizers were excluded from Sardinia by the terms of its second treaty with Carthage (348 B.C.E.).[362] There were two sanctuaries in the town (one of them with a portico) and two cemeteries. The tombs were mostly rock-cut chambers reached by a vertical shaft and containing single burials. There were a few painted tombs, and typical grave goods included jewelry, statuettes, and amulets, some made of green jasper from Tharros. There are similar tombs with comparable burial gifts at Monte Luna,[363] a Punic settlement probably founded by Cagliari and about 30 kilometers inland to the north. This was a prosperous agricultural and industrial site, with imported wares from Carthage and Italy and with coins from Sicily and other places in Sardinia.

There are six inscriptions that illustrate some aspects of the religious, political, and social life of this Punic community. The earliest, from the end of the fifth century, was found in one of the Cagliari tombs.[364] It was done in cursive script, in red paint, and repeated on two identical funerary urns: "Awaken, you, my wife, to life among the Most High." The imperative is augmented by an enclitic *mem*, unique to the dialect of Byblos, and the sentiments reflect belief in bodily resurrection in a divine world, also unique to Byblos. Another inscription from a mid-fourth-century funerary context reads "ʾEshmun has heard." It was written on a terra-cotta hand placed in the tomb, and praises ʾEshmun, the patron God of the Sidonians, for having healed her hand.[365]

From the end of the century, there is an inscription on the front of an elaborately sculpted base recording the offering of two funeral steles and two incense burners that once were inserted into the base.[366] The offerings were dedicated "to the Lord, to Baʿalšamem on the Isle of Hawks" (the island of San Pietro just west of Sulcis in southwestern Sardinia) to fulfill a vow made by Baʿalḥannoʾ, an indentured servant of Bodmelqart, and the fifth generation of one of the founding families of Cagliari: both the Cagliari family and the settlers on the Isle of Hawks probably came from Carthage, where the cult of Baʿalshamem was first established in the West. Continuing this trend of worshiping the Gods of other places, probably the places from which these people or their ancestors came to Cagliari, there is a third-century inscription that records the dedication of a bronze altar to Astarte of Eryx in Sicily.[367]

---

361. S. Moscati, *Italia Punica* (Milan: Rusconi, 1986) 187–201, pls. 24–27.

362. H. Bengston, *Die Verträge der griechisch-römischen Welt von 700 bis 338 v. Chr.* (Die Staatsverträge des Altertums 2; Munich: Beck, 1962) 306–9 #326.

363. A. M. Costa, "La necropoli punica di Monte Luna: Tipologia tombale," *RSF* 11 (1983) 21–38, pls. 2–3; Moscati, *Italia Punica*, 202–7, pl. 28.

364. *IFPCO* 115–16 #4, pl. 43.

365. M. L. Uberti, "Dati di epigrafia fenicio-punica in Sardegna," *Atti* 1, 3.797–804, pls. 156–57, esp. pp. 801–2, pl. 156:3.

366. *CIS* 139; *KAI* 64; *IFPCO* 101–2 #23, pl. 35.

367. Ibid., 99–100 #20, pl. 34.

There are two other dedicatory inscriptions that also provide a perspective on the political and social order in the district of Cagliari in late Punic and Roman times. From Cagliari itself, there is a small, sculpted marble block dating to the mid-third century with 11 lines of detail on the building of a sanctuary.[368] The sanctuary was built of hewn stone by "all the people (*'am*) of Cagliari (*krl*) great and small." The date is fixed by giving the names of the judge (*špṭ*) and of the secretary (*rb*) of the city assembly (*'am*), the names of the six men who were put in charge of the work, and the name of the chief priest that year. The inscription ends with the name of the man who inscribed it in the marble, his profession (a builder), his civic status (a freedman [*'îš ṣîdôn*]), and the wish, "May he live!" From Santuaici in the district of Gerrei just north of Cagliari, there is a mid-second-century trilingual (Latin, Greek, and Punic) on the base of a bronze altar, fragments of which were found with it.[369] The altar was dedicated to "'Eshmun, the Provider of Respite and Relief" (*m'rḥ*) in the Punic version, Aescolopius Merre in the Latin, and Asklepios Merre in the Greek, and the Punic version adds that the altar weighed 100 pounds. It was dedicated by a man with the Latin name Cleon (Greek Kleôn), transcribed into Punic as Akleyon (*'klyn*), who was an associate in the society of salt workers, because 'Eshmun heard his prayer and healed him. The inscription is earlier than the Third Punic War, when Carthage was destroyed and its political system collapsed, and so the inscription is dated to the year when Himilkot and 'Abd'eshmun, the sons of Ḥimilk, were presidents of the Assembly. Recollections such as these are a small part of the story of Cagliari, anecdotes in the loosely tuned chronicle of Sardinia that fit nicely into the tighter matrix of the history of Carthage.

South of the capital on the Gulf of Cagliari, there was a small Punic settlement and exurb of Nora on the site of the abandoned Nuraghe Antigori, where some domestic pottery of the fifth and fourth centuries has been recovered.[370] Nora, 15 kilometers to the south of it and about 30 kilometers south of Cagliari, was ideally situated on a cape providing easy defense, a good harbor, and safe anchorages.[371] Earlier it had been a port of call for ships sailing to the Atlantic, but in the fifth and fourth centuries it was a depot that specialized in shipping food (fruit, cereals, meat, and fish), building materials, and metals to Carthage.[372] Apart from submerged quays and remnants of a road running along the isthmus, two sanctuaries, a children's graveyard, and burial steles are just about all that remains of this once busy town.[373] Five of the steles adorned with sculpted baetyls were inscribed "vow of" (*ndr*) with the name, and twice with the patronymic of the man (all the names are masculine) who made the vow, a vow that obviously consisted of promising to erect the stele if his prayer was

---

368. Ibid., 116–20 #36, pl. 44.

369. *CIS* 143; *KAI* 66; *IFPCO* 91–93 #9, pl. 30.

370. P. Bartoloni, "Ceramica fenicia e punica dal Nuraghe Antigori," *RSF* 11 (1983) 167–75.

371. S. Finocchi, "La laguna e l'antico porto di Nora: Nuovi dati a confronto," *RSF* 27 (1999) 167–92.

372. Idem, "Considerazioni sugli aspetti produttivi di Nora e del suo territorio in epoca fenicia e punica," *RSF* 30 (2002) 147–86.

373. Moscati, *Italia Punica*, 208–25.

heard.[374] A large Black Glazed pot with a dedication to Tannit incised on its rim[375] may have belonged to a Carthaginian, because the Goddess was not worshiped in Sardinia. Nora was completely rebuilt by the Romans who took over the island in 238 B.C.E.

Bithia (Neo-Punic *bytʿn* = **Bîtân*), another 15 kilometers farther south, was founded in the seventh century, but in the Punic period there is a gap between the early fifth century and the end of the fourth, and the town seems to have just lingered on into Roman times.[376] There was a Temple of Bes, the grotesque dwarf God who is mentioned in inscriptions from Cyprus and in an old inscription from Nora under the name Pumay, and associated with it were a large number of terra-cotta statuettes.[377] These were made by potters and thus resemble jars, amphorae, or bells to which any pertinent bodily part was clumsily attached. The potters were not interested in form or sensitive to appearance but in their own unskilled way tried to express some particular idea.

Bes, at least at Bithia, was a God of physical well-being, and the terracottas always express some physical pain, lack, or deformity. Faces are tortured, gaping, pockmarked, stunned, or in agony. When arms and hands are attached, they gesture toward the head, eyes, ears, throat, chest, or genitals, and all of this is done crudely but still with an astonishing primitive charm. The town, to judge from these statuettes, was dedicated to making pottery, mainly storage and transport amphorae, to be sold to other towns, and its Temple of Bes was a last resort for the very sick and wounded from all around. Under Roman rule, the temple received a new, very large statue of the God.[378] In the late second or the early third century C.E., as recorded in a Neo-Punic memorial inscription,[379] cisterns, aqueducts, and altars were added by "all the people (*ʿam*) of Bithia," who worked on them and paid for them with their own money, all of them with Latin names, in the year that one president of the Assembly was "Bobaʿal, the Roman" (*ha-roʾmî*).

Sulcis on the southwest corner of Sardinia is distinguished in the fifth century and later by its artifacts, notably its tombstones, sculptures, terracottas and inscriptions.[380] The tombstones[381] illustrate cultural dependence on Carthage in both design and development, but the repertoire as a whole is unique to Sulcis. There are plain blocks, some with an L-shaped base to keep them in place, but the majority represent an aedicule, a niche or room between columns, containing a symbol or a portrait of the person. The aedicule is sometimes plain, with rectangular pillars and without entablature, and at times very elaborate, with Doric columns and decorated friezes. The

---

374. *RES* 1217–21; *IFPCO* 104–7 ##26–30, pls. 37–40.

375. *RES* 1222; *IFPCO* 104 #25, pl. 37.

376. Moscati, *Italia Punica*, 226–39.

377. G. Pesce, *Le Statuette Puniche di Bithia* (Rome: Università di Roma—Centro di Studi Semitici, 1965).

378. P. Agus, "Il Bes di Bitia," *RSF* 11 (1983) 41–47, pls. 6–8.

379. *IFPCO* 133–36 #8, pl. 55.

380. Moscati, *Italia Punica*, 240–62.

381. Idem, *Le Stele di Sulcis: Caratteri e Confronti* (Rome: Consiglio Nazionale delle Ricerche, 1986).

simplest is an aedicule containing a single baetyl, a living stone, a contrary sign that life persists in death.

The personalized steles most often profile a man in the Striding-God pose, with one arm raised, the other holding a sceptre or lance. There are also pictures of women facing the world, clothed in long robes, holding a child to their breast, symbol of regeneration; or a tambourine, as if they were participating in a joyful ritual; or holding an *ankh*, the symbol of life, in their lowered right hand. [382] The cultic steles are smaller and later and show a ram, a sacrificial animal, alive and walking, a conception unique to Sulcis. [383] All the tombstones, in their own way, give death a tinge of expectation or immortality.

There is generally nothing special about the Sulcis terra-cottas, but there are some figurines and sculptures that step out of the common Punic mold. An example is a white marble tombstone with an aedicule, resembling a temple and featuring a statue of a woman, and below the aedicule the dedication: "Vow of your servant Milkyaton the Judge, son of Mahirbaʿal the Judge." [384] The woman stands with her weight on her left leg and her right leg bent slightly backward. She is clothed in a full-length, pleated robe, holds a bowl of fruit in her left hand, and lifts her right hand to sweep her shawl away from her face. She stands between Ionic columns with Doric capitals, and a panther lies in the entablature above her head. The woman is identified as Demeter or Persephone, but in this funerary context, she probably represents Milkyaton's wife in the storied transition from death to life.

There is another sculpture on the small marble base of a bronze statuette that was offered in honor of a mother, who is also a grandmother, in fulfillment of a vow by her son and grandson. [385] The base resembles the aedicula on tombstones and on three sides has figures framed by columns, all of them Punic personages carved in Greek style. On the front, beneath the dedicatory inscription, Heracles sits naked and nonchalant on a lion skin draped over a four-legged stool, conversing with the woman standing in front of him. He is a bit flabby, and she a bit stocky, and with her right hand raised to her head and her left stroking her belly, seems to be pregnant. On the left side, behind Heracles, a similarly robust woman seated on a stool in a full, pleated robe and wearing a veil motions with her right hand toward the couple on the front panel and offers them the dove she holds in her outstretched left hand. On the right side, behind the woman with Heracles, a stout, bearded man sits on a stool, naked to the waist but wearing a long robe that falls in pleats down to his bare feet, and with a similar motion offers the couple on the front panel three stalks of corn. The Greek styling seems to conceal a thoroughly Sardinian scenario: the couple on the front

---

382. S. Moscati and P. Bartoloni, "Reperti Punici Figurati della Collezione Dessy: Catalogo di Piero Bartoloni," *RANL* 42 (1987) 197–223, pls. 1–15, esp. pp. 200–201, pl. 1.

383. S. Moscati, "Stele sulcitane con animale passante," *RANL* 8/36, fasc. 1–2 (1981) 1–8, pls. 1–13.

384. *CIS* 176; S. M. Cecchini and M. G. Amadasi Guzzo, "La stele *C.I.S.*, I, 176," *HAAN*, 101–11, pl. 1.

385. G. Pesce, *Sardegna Punica* (Cagliari: Sarda Fratelli Fossataro, 1960) 85, pls. 74a–c; *IFPCO* 120–21 #37, pl. 45.

panel, in the guise of Deianeira and Heracles, is the mother/grandmother confronting her death and metamorphosis; the woman on the left, in the garb of Aphrodite, is Astarte, the Goddess of Love, physicality, and life; the man in the right panel is the God Ṣid, the eponymous God of the Phoenicians, whose cult was established at Antas, a short distance north of Sulcis, and whose proffered cornstalks symbolize regeneration and growth.

Other inscriptions offer incidental insight into the workings of the town. A tomb inscription, slightly damaged but easily reconstructed, records the vow and dedication of one of the presidents of the city Assembly:[386] "[To the Lord, to Baʿal ʾAddir, the vow of Girʾeshmu]n, the judge, son of Q[artyaton], son of Girʾeshmun, son of [Padi, because] he heard the sound of his words. May he bless him." The city Assembly system seems to have been imposed by Carthage on all its holdings, and it is not surprising that the name of the judge's father includes as its theophoric element the name of the deified city of Carthage (*qart* = "City"), because Tyre's tutelary God was Melqart, "King of the City," including its terrestrial, infernal, and celestial manifestations.

The God Baʿal ʾAddir, whose name is reconstructed here, is mentioned in three other inscriptions from Sulcis. It occurs on the front of a lead disk, which was engraved like a coin with a border of dots, or like a stamp seal, because the name is written back-to-front, from left to right, and would be legible (and not just decipherable) only if impressed in clay.[387]

Another occurrence is on a seventh-century silver bowl, from an Etruscan workshop, which was repaired in the mid-third century and inscribed:[388]

> To the Lord, to Baʿal ʾAddir. May he bestow blessings.
> A libation bowl whose weight is 59 [shekels] which the accountants restored
> at the time of the commanders Magon and ʿAzormilk,
> in the year of the judges of Sulcis ʾAddîrbaʿal and Milkyaton,
> and at the time of the chief priest Bodʿaštart son of ʾAriš *

The heirloom was an Ionian drinking bowl of a kind used at symposia, and it had been kept about 400 years before it was restored, as the paleography of the script indicates, in the middle of the third century. The "accountants" (*mḥšbm*) worked for the town treasury and could dispense public funds to restore what had become a prized antique; in Sicily, these officials could issue coinage stamped with their title. The "commanders" (*rabbîm*, often abbreviated with a capital *R*) were officers, deputies, or secretaries of the town council who were appointed for a fixed "time" (*ʿt*) or term in order to recruit police and militia and oversee public works. The "judges" (*šptm*) or magistrates were appointed for one year to preside over the council, interpret and enforce laws, and defend the city's domestic and foreign interests. The chief priest probably represented the ministers of all the temples on the city council. The asterisk reproduces some similar decorative mark at the end of the Punic text.

---

386. Uberti, "Dati di epigrafia fenicio-punica in Sardegna," 800–801, pl. 156:4.
387. *IFPCO* 123–24 #41, pl. 48.
388. P. Bartoloni and G. Garbini, "Una coppa d'argento con iscrizione punica da Sulcis," *RSF* 27 (1999) 79–91, pl. 5.

The third mention of the God Baʿal ʾAddir is in a contemporary text on a marble base that once supported an offering made in fulfillment of a vow by a man who gives his genealogy to the fifth generation.[389] The God is known in fifth-century Byblos, and his cult at Sulcis may have migrated from there, from Carthaginian North Africa, or specifically from Constantine, where it was popular and where there was a regular *va-et-vient* with Sulcis.

Also intrusive from North Africa, and again probably not by a Carthaginian, is a tombstone inscribed with a late second-century dedication to Tannit:[390] it is not at home in Sardinia or Sulcis, where there was no cult of the Goddess, and it is non-Carthaginian and odd in being dedicated to her alone without her consort Baʿal Ḥamon. But there is a first-century B.C.E. Latin–Neo-Punic bilingual on a limestone statue base that records the building of a sanctuary for "the Lady, for ʾElat."[391] It is possible that this ʾElat, which means "Goddess," is the proper name of Asherah, as it was in Late Bronze Ugarit, for instance, of whom "Tannit" was just the hypostasized epithet: the theological reflection implied by this line of research is sophisticated but totally consistent with the archaism, ethnicity, and attempt at simplification that characterize the last centuries of the Empire. It was certainly much too recherché for the Roman reader, and the Latin omits the entire phrase. The inscription notes that the sanctuary was built "ex senatus consulto," as the Latin has it, and "according to the good pleasure of the select of Sulcis," in Neo-Punic, where "the select, body of the select, selectmen" (*ʾarîšā*ʾ) replaces the more populist Punic institution of "the Assembly of the people" (*ʿam*).

The remaining Neo-Punic (later than the destruction of Carthage in 146 B.C.E.) inscriptions from Sulcis are of incidental social interest. There is a marble base inscribed with the name, profession, and genealogy of the man whose statue was on it, "Rapiʾus, the steward, son of Ṣadoq."[392] As steward (*hbrk*, *ʾabarak*), of a temple, a government establishment, or a wealthy family, it was his job to provide their basic needs (including food, drink, and clothing) and all the good things that made life easy; his name is Latin, or perhaps just a Latinized form of the Punic name Rapiʾ, but his father's is standard West Semitic.

A marble plaque commemorates the statue for Felix Ceresius that was erected by Pullius Agbor, the commandant, son of Macarius, "for his glory and the glory of his people."[393] It may be supposed, because Pullius was a military man, that Felix was a superior officer and that "his people" (*lʾmm*) were the troops. Pullius adds, almost as an afterthought, that he also made the base (Neo-Punic *bʿṣṣ* = *basis*) on which the statue of the officer and his army stood.

The last of the Sulcis Neo-Punic inscriptions is written on a memorial stone that was erected in memory of "ʿAbdmelqart, son of ʿAbdmelqart, son

---

389. Ibid., 84 n. 29.
390. Uberti, "Dati di epigrafia fenicio-punica in Sardegna," 798, pl. 157:2.
391. *IFPCO* 129–31 #5, pl. 53.
392. Ibid., 125–26 #1, pl. 50.
393. Ibid., 126–29 #2, pl. 51.

of ʿAbdmelqart." This is an extraordinary use of the same name by three generations. It was erected by his three sons, "along with their sister, she is Naʿima)," the pretty one (*hnʿmʾ hyʾ*).[394]

Sulcis made the transitions from a Sardinian metropolis to a Carthaginian regional center and finally to a Roman town with noticeable ease and aplomb. It had administrators galore in the fifth and fourth centuries and later, and functioned nicely in the Empire. It had distinctive perspectives on death and could visualize its ancestors associating with the Gods. Its concern for restoring a cherished antique reflects a general trend at this time toward archaizing and an attempt to revitalize the past. The smooth transitions masked a steady decline.

Monte Sirai, an outpost and dependency of Sulcis, fell into a more precipitous decline in the Punic period after Cagliari became the capital of the Carthaginian province of Sardinia. It lost its military importance, was reduced to an agricultural center, and acquired increasingly indigenous status. Funeral steles copy the Sulcis repertoire, but as if from a sketchbook, without any feeling for the human form and with little understanding of their meaning.[395] None of them was inscribed. The tombs were rock-cut chambers, usually with single burials, that were reached by a sloped walkway (*dromos*). Grave goods generally were very modest, although there was one tomb with an extravagant array of gifts.[396]

The once-proud fort was remodeled as a sanctuary. The statue of its Goddess is massive and is said to have the remains of North Syrian, Anatolian, and Etruscan artistic traditions, as interpreted in this third-century native retreat.[397] The Goddess's body is essentially a baetyl, an oblong block tapering toward the top, with little or no representation of her bodily parts: her arms are barely distinguishable from her torso, the right arm bent toward her nonexistent breasts, her left stretching across her body to her undefined genitals; she plunks down, has no legs. Her head is large and slightly grotesque: her hair is in corn rows at the top and hangs in a single ringlet by each ear; her ears, a semicircle enclosing a circle, are large; her eyebrows fill her forehead and curve down to follow the line of her nose; her pug nose sits above full smiling lips and a square chin; her eyes are incised lines, and her face is full and flat; the whole head rests on a very thick neck on top of the baetyl body. The sanctuary had known better times, even quite recently, as is indicated by an inscribed bronze plaque dating to the fourth century that records the dedication of an altar to Baʿal by a fourth-generation resident of the town and mentions the name of the very skilled, literate engraver who did such splendid work.[398]

---

394. Ibid., 131–32 #6, pl. 54.

395. S. F. Bondì, *Le stele de Monte Sirai* (Rome: Consiglio Nazionale delle Ricerche, 1972); Moscati, *Italia Punica*, 263–82, pls. 41–46.

396. M. G. Amadasi and I. Brancoli, "La Necropoli," in *Monte Sirai, II: Rapporto preliminare delle Missione archeologica dell'Università di Roma e della Soprintendenza alle Antichità di Cagliari* (ed. S. Moscati and G. Pesce; Rome: Università di Roma—Istituto di Studi del Vicino Oriente, 1965) 95–121.

397. Moscati, *Italia Punica*, 270–71; S. M. Cecchini, "La statua dell'acropoli di Monte Sirai," *Atti 2*, 2.683–89.

398. G. Garbini, "L'iscrizione punica," in *Monte Sirai, II: Rapporto preliminare delle Missione*

Antas is another 20 kilometers north of Monte Sirai on the way to Tharros.[399] It was a pilgrimage center, founded by Cagliari and Sulcis, that was opened in the fifth century and lasted into late Roman times. The temple, situated in a small plain nestled among steep hills, was a rectangle about 30' × 60', with its large entrance hall and smaller cella separated by a natural rock formation that occupied most of the middle room. The temple was dedicated to "Ṣîd, Mighty-in-His-Paternity," the legendary God of Hunting and Fishing (ṣyd), the eponymous God of Sidon.[400] His earlier presence in the Punic pantheon is recognized in a scattering of personal names that include his name as their theophoric element. But the revival of his cult at this time corresponds to a renewal of ethnic sensibilities among the Phoenicians of the western Mediterranean who began to redefine themselves as "Sidonians," descendants of this eastern Mediterranean ancestor, in order to counterbalance their accelerating absorption into a non-Phoenician (indigenous and Greek, or Roman) world.

There are small finds, such as terra-cottas, arrowheads, coins, and amulets that may have been personal effects just dropped and abandoned, but there are also about 30 Punic and Neo-Punic inscriptions dedicated to the God Ṣid.[401] Two (one from the later fourth, the other from the mid-third century) were by representatives of the Assembly of Cagliari, and one (also from the mid-third century) by a representative of the Assembly of Sulcis whose father and grandfather had been judges. But most of the inscriptions record vows or the fulfillment of vows by individuals because the God answered their prayers. One inscription quotes the prayer ("She made a vow to Father Ṣid: 'May he establish progeny for Hatlat.' Listen to her prayer"), and one says explicitly that the vow was brought to a successful conclusion.[402]

The dedications are sometimes on the bases of statues long lost, which are described as a statue, bronze statue, gold-plated stone statue, statue of the God Horon, or statue of the God Shadrapa'. There are also some inscriptions that record particular renovations in the temple, and among these might be included an inscription on a bronze plaque with a dedication to Melqart:[403] "To the Lord, to Melqart, on behalf of the Tyrians, from the mightiest to the least of them, when they erected [a gold-plated statue] to him, and confirmed a firstborn child as his precious possession" (*wšt bkr*

---

archeologica dell'Università di Roma e della Soprintendenza alle Antichità di Cagliari (ed. S. Moscati and G. Pesce; Rome: Università di Roma—Istituto di Studi del Vicino Oriente, 1965) 79–92, pls. 34–35.

399. E. Acquaro, ed., *Ricerche Puniche ad Antas: Rapporto preliminare della Missione archeologica dell'Università de Roma e della Soprintendenza alle Antichità di Cagliari* (Studi Semitici 30; Rome: Università di Roma—Istituto di Studi del Vicino Oriente, 1969); Moscati, *Italia Punica*, 283–88.

400. *PhByb* 42–45; G. Garbini, *La religione dei Fenici in Occidente* (Studi Semitici n.s. 12; Rome: Università degli Studi "La Sapienza," 1994) 23–29.

401. M. Fantar, "Les inscriptions," in *Ricerche Puniche ad Antas* (Studi Semitici 30; Rome: Istituto di Studi del Vicino Oriente, 1969) 47–93 ##1–20, pls. 23–38; Uberti, "Dati di epigrafia fenicio-punica in Sardegna," 797, pl. 156:1; G. Garbini, "Nuove epigrafi fenicie da Antas," *RSF* 25 (1997) 59–67 ##22–25, pls. 9–10; idem, "Nuove iscrizioni da Antas," *Rivista di Studi Punici* 1 (2000) 115–22 ##26–30.

402. Idem, "Nuove iscrizioni da Antas," 119–20 #29, 120–21 #30.

403. Idem, "Nuove epigrafi fenicie da Antas," 65–67, pl. 10:2.

ysg[*l*]). It is clear that Melqart, the God of Tyre and an older God from the East, was special to the ethnicity of Tyrians in the West (as was Ṣid to those who were proud to be Phoenicians) and that his ancient rituals, revived here in the mid-third century, included the occasional offering of a first-born child.

The inscriptions refer to Ṣid either by his full title ("Splendid-in-His-Paternity"), or as "Splendid" or once as "Father," but it was the Punic version of the full title (*ṣîd 'addîr biʾabîyû*) that the Romans used, combining transliteration with metathesis and translation in their rendition of his name, *Sardus Pater* which, of course, instantly reduced the "Father of the Phoenicians" to a Sardinian totem.

Tharros on the central west coast of Sardinia was thoroughly aligned with North African Carthage in the Punic period and was monitored by the Sardinian Carthage that was founded by the metropolis just across from it on the Gulf of Oristano. An inscription on a beautiful framed, marble plaque may illustrate this fact.[404] It begins like the bronze plaque from Antas, "To the Lord, to the Holy God, Melqart, on behalf of the Tyrians." It is contemporary with the Antas dedication and like it captures the nostalgia that began to sweep over the western Phoenicians at this time. The first part describes the construction of a portico, its pillars, roof, and entrances of hewn stone and plaster. The next part lists the names of the commander (*rab*) who oversaw the project, of the mason, the builders, the carpenter, and the plasterer. The commander was a former judge, or president of the Assembly, and the sixth generation of a family of judges. The inscription ends with the date according to the eponym of the current judge in Tharros, and according to the eponym of the judges in Carthage and, though the plaque is damaged at this point, probably according to the eponym of the commanders and the high priest in Carthage. This Carthage likely is in North Africa, although it might be the "Neapolis" across the Gulf of Oristano, but in either case it indicates the Sardinian town's tight relations with the metropolis.

There are remains of a fourth-century building project at the northern end of the Tharros peninsula in the area of the children's graveyard, but most of what is known about the Punic town is gathered from its burial practices.[405] Tombs contained pottery, jewelry, knickknacks, amulets, coins, and souvenirs. The bodies of adults were placed on their backs, on the bare earth or perhaps on a wooden bier, males with their weapons, females with their jewelry, all with food, drink, and lamps for the journey, and with a Sicilian or Carthaginian coin to pay the boatman to Sheol.[406] Babies were cremated on pyres laid on the bare ground and made of grass, shrubs, and small tree branches, and their ashes were gathered in urns, sometimes

404. *IFPCO* 109–12, pl. 41; Lipiński, "Carthaginois en Sardaigne à l'époque de la première guerre punique," 67–70.

405. *Building project remains*: M. T. Francisi, "Tharros: Documenti grafici per la restituzione di edifiici nell'area del *tofet*," *Actas* 4, 3.1309–17. *Burial practices*: *Tharros* 38–48.

406. Ibid., 46.

along with the ashes of a lamb or kid, and with some token of affection such as a seashell or even a pebble.[407]

The pottery was Punic or Greek. The Punic wares were containers and dishes, unguent jars and lamps, but nothing of much interest except a few liquid containers (*askoi*) in the shape of a duck, a dove, or a chicken.[408] The Greek wares were mostly Attic or local imitations made especially for the burials, Black or Grey or with Red figures and designs, and included cups, plates, bowls, wine jugs, and goblets.[409] The jewelry consisted of various types of gold, silver, and bronze earrings, or hair bands, finger rings, bracelets, and necklaces. The knickknacks included terra-cotta figurines inspired by the Sicilian Greek, and later Carthaginian, cult of Kore-Persephone, local green jasper scarabs, pieces of ivory or bone, and razors, some of them decorated with a symbol of a God or a scene from a myth or legend. Amulets were Egyptianizing and depicted familiar Gods such as Ptah, Bes, Isis, Horus, Harpocrates; or they were plain Punic and represented human body parts (arm, hand, feet, legs, eye, heart) or birds, fish, or animals; or things like acorns, axes, obelisks, or writing tablets. The steles[410] are like those in Carthage and at Nora but unlike the Sulcis steles. There is a tendency to aniconism, and representations, when they occur, can be very schematic or wanting in finesse. There is one representation that pictures a sanctuary with a central stairway leading to a baetyl enthroned between two incense stands. Human figures are rare, and abstractions such as baetyls, lozenges, or bottles abound.

A few of these steles are inscribed with the name and sometimes the profession of the deceased.[411] One stele has just an abbreviation (the first and last letters) of the personal name Hannibal. One refers to the gravestone (*mnṣbt*) as belonging to the dead man, and two refer to the grave (*qbr*) as personal property: one of these, inscribed on a stele topped by an Egyptian double crown, has "Tomb built by Jezebel, the wife of ʿAzorbaʿal, the son of Miqim." There is an early fourth-century tombstone of a scribe, another of a vintner, and a memorial inscribed on a silver plaque that prays, "Protect ʿAbdoʾ, the son of Šimšay, the son of Mattin, the architect." A similar invocation is inscribed on a silver strip above a scene depicting a procession of the Gods: "Protect and keep and bless ʾUšay." The texts are few, mostly from the fourth century, and the silence of the majority of tombstones is probably symptomatic of the increasing anonymity of the town itself.

It is evident from the meager remains of once-vibrant settlements in Sardinia that Carthage just drained its provinces. Sulcis may have been resilient in the face of death, but there are no signs of a joie de vivre. Tharros kept making the jewelry for which it was famous, but it was more expensive than beautiful, and the Phoenician wonderment was gone. Sardinia

---

407. F. G. Fedele, "Tharros: Anthropology of the *Tophet* and Paleoecology of a Punic Town," *Atti* 1, 3.637–50.

408. M. Medde, "*Askoi* zoomorfi dalla Sardegna," *Rivista di Studi Punici* 1 (2000) 157–87.

409. *Tharros* 50–65.

410. Moscati, *Italia Punica*, 289–318, pls. 50–55, esp. pp. 303–4; idem, "Découvertes phéniciennes à Tharros," *CRAIBL* (1987) 483–503, esp. pp. 487–88; G. Tore, "Le stele puniche del tophet di Tharros (Sardegna): Nota preliminare," *AION* 35 (1975) 127–32, pls. 1–2.

411. *IFPCO* 88–90 ##5–7, pl. 29; 93–97 ##12–16, pls. 31–32; 103 #24, pl. 36); 108 #31, pl. 39.

became a reliable source of food for the Empire, but Carthage contributed nothing to its cultural or intellectual well-being, and the island was ripe when the Romans came to swallow it.

Spain: Indigenous Commerce and Food Production

Spain in the fifth and fourth centuries was defined by its increasingly important indigenous population. There was deep and enduring Phoenician influence, material and cultural:[412] the Punic impetus was commercial, but the Mediterranean world of the great merchants was now confined to the sea lanes to North Africa. Business was in the hands of Spanish barons, workers were mustered in small villages, and food production was the thing.[413] Spain did very well but did not develop.

Cádiz became famous among Greek and Latin authors for the pillars of Hercules associated with its temple,[414] but the pillars did not survive, and the only reference to the God is a second-century Punic inscription on a gold seal, "To the Lord, to the Powerful Milk'astart, and to his servants, to the people of Cádiz (*'gdr = Gadir*)."[415] This God, known from Umm el-'Amed south of Tyre, was a precursor of Melqart, who is the usual counterpart of Greek Heracles, Latin Hercules, and the epithet "The Powerful" (*'zz*) was most likely added to accommodate the labors and the legends. The cult of the God to which this seal attests is also known from a fourth-century inscription at Tas Silg, perhaps by a Carthaginian, and from later Carthaginian inscriptions,[416] and it was probably introduced into Cádiz when Carthage became its most important customer.

Cádiz was important in the fifth and fourth centuries as a distribution center for agricultural products collected from the interior, for its salt production and associated pottery barns for amphorae in which it was stored and shipped, and especially for its tuna fisheries and its salsa (*garum*) factories.[417] There are some signs of new residential construction in the city and in nearby Doña Blanca, where the local Punic pottery became increasingly influenced by native wares.[418] Fifth-century burials were in stone-lined graves, but in the fourth they were in the bare earth and covered with

412. J. M. Blázquez, "El influjo de la cultura semita (Fenicios y Cartagineses) en la formación de la cultura ibérica," *FPI*, 2.163–78; C. Mata Parreño, "Las influencias del mundo feníco-púnico en los orígenes y desarrollo de la cultura ibérica," *Actes* 3, 2.225–44.

413. M. P. García-Gelabert, "Los enterramientos de la alta Andalucía (España): Sus relaciones con el Mediterráneo oriental," *Atti* 2, 2.889–95. I. Grau Mira, "Settlement Dynamics and Social Organization in Eastern Iberia during the Iron Age (Eighth–Second Centuries BC)," *OJA* 22 (2003) 261–79. J. Gran Aymerich and J. R. Anderica, "Populations autochtones et allogènes sur le littoral méditerranéen andalou: Du Málaga à Vélez-Málaga et Frigiliana (VIIIe–VIe s. av. J.-C.)," *Actas* 4, 4.1811–14.

414. W. E. Mierse, "The Architecture of the Lost Temple of Hercules Gaditanus and Its Levantine Associations," *AJA* 108 (2004) 545–76.

415. *KAI* 71.

416. Lipiński, *Dieux et Déesses de l'Univers Phénicien et Punique*, 271–74.

417. M. L. Lavado Florido, "El comercio a través del Guadalquivir en época antigua: El yacimiento de las Monjas (Trebujena-Cádiz)," *Actas* 4, 1.385–93; P. Fernández Uriel, "La industria de la sal," *Actas* 4, 1.345–51; A. Mederos and G. Escribano, "Pesquerías gaditanas en el litoral Atlántico norteafricano," *RSF* 27 (1999) 93–113.

418. D. Ruiz Mata, "Castillo de Doña Blanca (Puerto de Santa María, Prov. Cádiz): Stratigraphische Untersuchung einer orientalisierenden Ansiedlung," *MM* 17 (1986) 87–115, pl. 15c.

stone slabs or pieces of broken amphorae. The dead were buried with their personal possessions, sometimes with unguentaria or *askoi* in the shape of pigeons or roosters.[419] Life in Cádiz worked itself out in fairly plain commercial and industrials routines.

From the mid-fifth century, there are two anthropoid sarcophagi, of a man and a woman,[420] who probably represent the last of the great Phoenician trading families. Both sarcophagi are marble, and in both the skeleton was preserved—his, resting on a cedar bier; hers, wrapped in linen. The coffins and their lids follow the contours of their bodies, and their hands, feet, fingernails, and toenails are carefully sculpted. Both of them have thick, curly hair falling over their ears. Her face is square, her eyes are large and oval, her nose is big, her lips are pursed, and her mouth is severe. His face is long and thin, his lips are full and slightly parted, his moustache is full and his beard falls on his chest, his eyes are like hers, but his nose is small and straight. Her arms are sculpted in the round: her right arm is bent at the elbow to lie across her right thigh (the hand is big and the fingers are spread); her left arm is bent more sharply to rest above the right, and she holds a small alabaster vase in her left hand. His arms are flattened: his right arm is by his side, and his hand is clenched to hold a wreath or garland; his left arm is bent across his chest, and his fingers are bent and separated from his thumb to allow him to hold a pomegranate. The sarcophagi apparently are from the same workshop, perhaps by the same sculptor and, because the faces and gestures have the individuality of portraits, were probably finished in Cádiz from imported materials. The man and woman may have been from the same family (that is, in the same business or maybe husband and wife) and were the last of the Phoenician, or specifically, Sidonian tycoons who had turned Spain into an international destination.

The rest of southern Spain, the future course of which in the Carthaginian Empire had been decided in the sixth century, was inconspicuous in the fifth and fourth. Carteia, at the mouth of the river Guadarranque at the northern end of the Bay of Algeciras, was a safe haven for ships navigating the Straits, and the starting point for pilgrims to Gorham's Cave on the southeast side of Gibraltar.[421] The cave was visited from prehistoric times but became a popular rendezvous again for passengers and crews sailing from North Africa or just along the Spanish coast to and from Cádiz. They left offerings of pottery, jewelry, scarabs, amulets, and terra-cotta figurines in propitiation or in thanksgiving for safe passage to the demon of the Straits who may have devolved (as in the caves at Grotta Regina in Sicily

419. A. Muñoz Vicente and L. Perdigones Moreno, "Estado actual de la arqueología fenício-púnica en la ciudad de Cádiz," *Actas* 4, 2.881–91.

420. H. Richter, "Katalog der Fundgruppen," in *Die Phönizischen Anthropoiden Sarkophage, Teil 1: Fundgruppen und Bestattungskontexte* (ed. S. Frede; Mainz am Rhein: von Zabern, 2000) 65–153, pls. 1–144, ##14:1–2, esp. pp. 147–49, pls. 134–39.

421. M. Bendala Galán, J. Blánquez Pérez, and L. Roldán Gómez, "Nuevas aportaciones sobre la ciudad púnica de Carteia (San Roque, Cádiz)," *Actas* 4, 2.745–58.

W. Culican, "Phoenician Remains from Gibraltar," *Australian Journal of Biblical Archaeology* 2 (1972) 110–45; repr. in *Opera Selecta: From Tyre to Tartessos* (Gothenburg: Åströms, 1986) 685–709; M. Belén and I. Pérez, "Gorham's Cave, un santuario en el Estrecho: Avance del estudio de los materiales ceramicas," *Actas* 4, 2.531–42.

and Es Cuyram on Ibiza) into a familiar and manageable God of the Punic pantheon. Beyond Gibraltar along the Mediterranean coast of Spain, the Punic spirit was manifested in regional commerce, partnership with the indigenous peoples, a common market with standardized storage and transport amphorae, and a sense (visible in separate graveyards and in distinctive burial practices)[422] of being different from their Phoenician predecessors.

Ibiza maintained its commercial links with settlements on the eastern seaboard of Spain in the fifth and fourth centuries. It was not especially prosperous, but the population increased, as is evident from the number of burials in the capital and from the farming communities that began to dot the northern and southern sectors of the island.[423] These were independent estates, or latifundia, with their own graveyards, which were developed around a substantial administrative and storage center and the products of which were shipped to local and mainland markets. By the fifth century, Ibizan merchants had founded trading posts along the coast of Majorca.[424] In the fourth century, entrepreneurs from Ibiza set up shop at Na Guardis, a small island off its southern tip.[425] Here there were residences, a blacksmith shop, stores, and docks where ships on the Ibiza coastal Spain–Balearic route could undergo minor repairs. One of these, which had the misfortune of sinking off the coast of Minorca, was laden with amphorae from Catalonia, with a few from Ibiza, and with rock ballast from southern France.[426]

At the north end of the island of Ibiza, independent of any settlement was the grotto of Es Cuyram, a bipartite cave that was enlarged by adding a vestibule built of hewn stones.[427] This expansion is the subject of a second-century Punic inscription on a small bronze plaque with holes drilled at the four corners so that it could be affixed to the wall:[428]

422. A. Delgado Hervás, A. Fernández Cantos, A. Ruiz Martínez, "Las transformaciones del s. VI a. N. E. en Andalucía: Una visión desde las relaciones entre fenícios e indígenas," *Actas* 4, 4.1781–87.

D. Marzoli, "Ánforas púnicas de Morro de Mezquitilla (Málaga)," *Actas* 4, 4.1631–44.

M. Pellicer Catalán, "Sexi fenicia y púnica," *FPI*, 1.85–107. M. Belén Deamos, "Religious Aspects of Phoenician-Punic Colonization in the Iberian Peninsula: The Stelae from Villaricos, Almería," in *Encounters and Transformations: The Archaeology of Iberia in Transition* (ed. M. S. Balmuth, A. Gilman, and L. Prados-Torreira; Monographs in Mediterranean Archaeology 7; Sheffield: Sheffield Academic Press, 1997) 121–33.

423. J. H. Fernández, "Necrópolis del Puig des Molins (Ibiza): Nuevas perspectives," *FPI*, 1.149–75; B. Costa and J. H. Fernández, "La secuencia cronológica de la necropolis del Puig des Molins (Eivissa): Las fases fenício-púnicas," *Actes* 3, 1.296–310.

C. Gómez Bellard, "Asentamientos rurales en la Ibiza púnica," *FPI*, 1.177–91. N. Benito et al., "Ibiza Púnica: La colonización agrícola. Algunos planteamientos para su estudio," *Actas* 4, 1.305–12.

424. V. M. Guerrero Ayuso, "El impacto de la colonización púnica en la cultura talayótica de Mallorca," *FPI*, 2.339–75.

425. Idem, "Majorque et les guerres puniques: Données archéologiques," in *Punic Wars* (ed. H. Devijver and E. Lipiński; Studia Phoenicia 10; Louvain: Peeters, 1989) 99–114.

426. V. M. Guerrero, J. Miró, and J. Ramón, "L'épave de Binisfuller (Minorque): Un bateau de commerce punique du IIIe siècle av. J.-C.," in ibid., 115–25.

427. M. P. San Nicolás Pedraz, "Interpretación de los santuarios fenícios y púnicos de Ibiza," *Actas* 4, 2.676–89.

428. *KAI* 72.

Made and vowed and restored this stone wall
ʿAbdʾeshmun, son of ʿAzorbaʿal,
the priest, for Our Lady, for Tannit the Almighty.
And he himself, at his own expense, was the engraver and architect.

The plaque is deftly and handsomely inscribed, with some letters shaded to resemble their cursive counterparts, and it is understandable that ʿAbdʾeshmun would want to publish the fact that he did the engraving (*ḥgd*). It may also be true that he built the wall and then repaired it when it became dilapidated and that this was in fulfillment of his vow to Tannit. But it is a little disingenuous that it was at his own expense, because he borrowed and reused the bronze plaque, which had already been inscribed on the other side in the fifth century with a completely different dedication:[429]

For the Lord, for ʾAršupmilqart, this sanctuary
which was vowed by ʾAšʾaddir, the son of Esau,
the son of Birgad, the son of ʾEshmunḥilleṣ.

This sanctuary presumably comprised at least the original vestibule added to the grotto in the fifth century but conceivably included other embellishments as well, to give the cave a cultic character. The first two letters of the God's name and the third letter of the name Birgad ("Chosen by Fortune" [*gd*]) are shaded in the cursive manner, and these inspired the parvenu restorer to do the same. The God is a crasis of the Gods Reshep and Milqart and this syncretism may reflect his Cypriot origin, where combination and identification of the Gods (for example, Reshepmukol and ʾEshmunmilqart) was popular. About three centuries later, when the Western world was Carthaginian, he was replaced by the nearly ubiquitous and almighty Tannit.

Carthage between Greece and Egypt

Carthage became the victim of its privileged upbringing. Its parentage was Cypriot, it grew up among Euboeans,[430] Etruscans, and Western Greeks, and its siblings were the stalwarts of the central Mediterranean and the heroes of the West. It came into its own in the sixth century under a proud aristocracy, adopted a republican constitution and an old-fashioned state religion in the fifth century, then collapsed into a vulgar and abusive nation in the fourth. It envied and resented the Greek world it lived in, displaying its frustrations by trying to wreck Sicily, but survived for awhile because of its command of the seas; it was once commercial and cooperative but became increasingly antagonistic in a Roman world that would gradually replace both of them. Carthage was a beautiful city, well situated, and a great imperial structure admired by all until its cumulative miscalculations cascaded upon it and finally buried it alive.

In the sixth century, under a newly minted wealthy, aristocratic, and aggressive leadership, Carthage entered into some significant commercial

429. Ibid.; J. Ferron, "Las inscripciones votives de la plaqueta de 'Es Cuyram' (Ibiza)," *Trabajos de Prehistoria* 26 (1969) 295–304, pl. 1; M. J. López Grande, "¿Conocimiento y culto de Rašap en el Mediterraneo occidental?" *Actas* 4, 2.619–25.
430. J. Boardman, "Early Euboean Settlements in the Carthage Area," *OJA* 25 (2006) 195–200.

agreements. Around the middle of the century, when Malko᾽ was general, it made a treaty with the Etruscans: its stipulations concerned imports, but there were also guarantees of noninterference in trade and commerce and protocols on eventual mutual assistance.[431] In 508 B.C.E., Mago (*mgn*), then governor of Carthage and the head of the aristocratic family that dominated Carthaginian politics for a century and a half, signed the city's first treaty with Rome.[432]

Carthage, as the stipulations imply, clearly was the superior naval power at the time and controlled a much vaster trade network. The Romans agree that they will not sail west of "the Beautiful Cape," presumably Cap Bon just east of Carthage, and that they will not do business in Libya, east of Cap Bon, except under the supervision of a Carthaginian agent (*mrgl*)[433] or scribe (*spr*). The Carthaginians agree that they will not infringe on Rome's preferential status among the towns of Latium that it controls, interfere with the towns that it does not control, or take up temporary residence or even stay overnight in Latium if it is on a hostile mission. The treaty makes it clear that Carthage monopolized trade and commerce in North Africa and throughout the western Mediterranean and that its ambitions in Italy were not limited to the Etruscan towns in its circle. It also implies that trade was compatible with crime (the Romans agree that, if they are driven west of Cape Bon by a storm or an enemy, neither to buy nor to steal) and could be carried out in raids. The treaty was sealed by an oath which the Romans swore by their primordial Gods, and Mago by the Gods of his fathers.

Early in the fifth century, Carthage began to intervene in the affairs of the Greek cities in Sicily, and its very first engagement ended in the resounding defeat at Himera,[434] a city on the north coast, east of Palermo and Solunto. The attack was planned to coincide with Xerxes' invasion of Europe in order to preoccupy the Greeks in the West and was occasioned by a coup in the city that seemed to justify intervention but probably was driven by the Carthaginian dream of controlling the whole island. Himera, however, was supported by Agrigentum (Akragas), the Carthaginians relied in vain on Selinunte, and the battle was won by Gelon of Syracuse, this in 480 B.C.E., the year of the Greek victory at Salamis. The Carthaginian general Hamilcar (*ḥmlkt*) was killed, according to the Sicilians, or threw himself on the sacrificial pyre in a vain attempt to wrest victory from the Gods, according to the Punic version. But he did die and Carthage was shocked, and Hamilcar's family spent the rest of the century plotting revenge.

But more important things were happening in Carthage during this time and for the same reasons. The invasion of Himera honored the treaty that Carthage, prompted by the family of Mago, made with Xerxes,[435] and the debacle brought the family and its foreign policy into disrepute. Carthage chose a new form of government and new Gods and declared its political

---

431. H. Bengston, *Die Verträge der griechish-römischen Welt von 700 bis 338 v. Chr.* (Die Staatsverträge des Altertums, 2; Munich: Beck, 1962) 13–14 #116.

432. Ibid., 16–20 #121; W. Huss, *Geschichte der Karthager* (Munich: Beck, 1985) 86–92.

433. *CIS* 5933:3–6 ("the vow of Hašiqam the agent [*mrgl*] of ᾽Addirbaʿal").

434. Huss, *Geschichte der Karthager*, 93–99; V. Krings, *Carthage et les Grecs c. 580–480 av. J.-C.* (Studies in the History and Culture of the Ancient Near East 13; Leiden: Brill, 1998) 308–26.

435. Bengston, *Die Verträge der griechisch-römischen Welt von 700 bis 338 v. Chr.*, 28–29 #129.

independence of the Eastern, Phoenician cities that had founded it and to which, especially Tyre, it had enduring ties. However, these cities were by then totally engaged in the politics of the Persian Empire.

The new constitution[436] established a form of republican government that lasted until the destruction of the city and later than that in its territories. Government was in the hands of the magistrates (*šptm*),[437] who were appointed to uphold the constitution, enforce its laws, and determine foreign policy: there were two, appointed for one year, and they were the eponyms of that year. There were two executive officers (*rab*),[438] who were appointed for a fixed term to oversee internal affairs and thus had jurisdiction in times of war and peace. It is possible that the magistrates were chosen from the council of 300 magnates (*'addîrîm*) (these are mentioned twice in Carthaginian texts, and are called "elders" by Aristotle) and that the officers were chosen by the Assembly (*'am*, "the people"). This Assembly represented all the individual citizens (*'dm*) of Carthage as well as civic organizations such as traders and merchants (*mrzḥ*), natural or religious groups called families or clans (*šph*), and ethnic associations (*mzrḥ*). The tight organization left no room for despots or men like Mago and was adopted in all the Carthaginian territories.

The introduction of this new constitution became fixed in the chronology and marked a new beginning in the history of Carthage. This is evident from a damaged but still-legible dedicatory inscription.[439] The introductory dedication is mostly lost: it took up the first four lines, recorded the vow that was made by the man whose name is partly preserved, and the name of the God to whom it was made, Baʿal Ḥamon, who is invoked at the end, alone or with the Goddess Tannit. The last four lines invoke a curse on whoever might remove the stele and its inscription: "May Baʿal Ḥamon judge the mind [*rûḥ*] of that man"—the Carthaginian moral and civil code supposes deliberation and intentionality. The middle two lines are inconspicuous but date the dedication to the "twentieth year of the [magistracy] of the Magistrates in Carthage." Because the inscription can be dated paleograpically to the middle of the fifth century, this implicitly dates the new constitution, which is identified as government by magistrates and the paradigm of which is Baʿal Ḥamon as judge of actions and intentions, to the early fifth century, soon after the willful individualism of Himera.

---

436. Huss, *Geschichte der Karthager*, 458–66; L. J. Sanders, "Punic Politics in the Fifth Century," *Historia* 37/1 (1988) 72–89; F. Gschnitzer, "Phoinikisch-Karthagisches Verfassungsdenken," in *Anfänge politischen Denkens in der Antike: Die nahöstlichen Kulturen und die Griechen* (ed. K. Raaflaub and E. Müller-Luckner; Munich: Oldenbourg, 1993) 187–97.

437. W. Huss, "Der karthagische Sufetat," in *Althistorische Studien Hermann Bengston zum 70. Geburtstag dargebracht von Kollegen und Schülern* (ed. H. Heinen, K. Stroheker, and G. Walser; Wiesbaden: Franz Steiner, 1983) 24–43.

438. W. Huss, "Die Stellung des *rb* im Karthagischen Staat," *ZDMG* 129 (1979) 217–32; A. Ferjaoui, "À propos des inscriptions mentionnant les suffètes et les rabs dans la généalogie des dédicants à Carthage," *Atti* 2, 2.479–83; M. Sznycer, "Les titres puniques des fonctions militaires à Carthage," *HAAN*, 113–21.

439. *CIS* 5632; C. Krahmalkov, "Notes on the Rule of the *šôfṭîm* in Carthage," *RSF* 4 (1976) 153–57; W. Ameling, *Karthago: Studien zu Militär, Staat und Gesellschaft* (Munich: Beck, 1993) 80–83.

The new Gods, patrons of the constitution, were Ba'al Ḥamon (called "genius [*daimōn*] of Carthage" in the oath of Hannibal) and Tannit (who is called his "face," that is, the manifestation or appearance of Ba'al Ḥamon, in innumerable dedications). The Gods were known earlier, but only separately, and the fifth-century innovation is this particular conjunction of their attributes. The Gods, in fact, were old and obsolete, and retrieving them from their Canaanite origins was a deliberate theological archaism and totally consistent with the determination by Carthage to define its ethnicity in the Western world as it abandoned its Eastern, Phoenician identity.

Ba'al Ḥamon[440] was the God El in his manifestation as the resident Lord of the Amanus, one of the four mountains (along with Saphon, Lebanon, and Hermon) that sustained the Canaanite cosmos. In the twelfth century, he was one of the many Gods in the pantheon of Ugarit in North Syria, and in the ninth, he was named the personal God of a petty dynast at Zinjirli in the Amanus Range. In Phoenicia, he is known from personal names once at Byblos in the eleventh century, once at Tyre in the seventh, and from a late sixth-century Tyrian amulet that invokes him and Ba'al Saphon.

In the West, he is mentioned on tombstones: on three late eighth-century steles, two from Malta and one from Carthage, that marked the human and animal sacrifices offered to sacralize the foundation of those colonies; at Motya in Sicily, on sixth-century grave markers of the children who were dedicated to him. At Carthage in the fifth century and later, the God is omnipresent in funerary contexts. The God El whom he represents was the creator of all living things. His abode on a cosmic mountain at the source of the primordial waters of the earth established him as the living link between sky and underworld, between death, life, and transcendence. Phoenician mythology identified him with Greek Chronos, "Time," and similarly, his symbol at Zinjirli was the full moon set within the crescent moon, which marked the phases of endless time.

The Goddess Tannit[441] was the hypostasis of Asherat, the "Goddess" (ʾElat), the wife of El in the epic texts from Ugarit, and the mother of the Gods and of all creatures. In those texts, Asherat is also called "Asherat-of-the-Sea," and her children on whom Ba'al takes revenge for their participation in the attempted coup against him are the "rollers" (*rbm*), "breakers" (*dkym*), and "waves" (*sǧrm*) of the Sea.[442] Her name, Tannit, is from a feminine form of the word for "dragon" or "sea serpent" (*tannîn* + *t*) who, according to biblical texts, is the primordial denizen of the deep and ultimately its personification (Gen 1:21; Isa 27:1, 51:9; Ps 74:13, 148:7; Job 7:12). She appears once in awhile at the mainland Phoenician sites, notably as the theophoric element in personal names from the early cemetery at Tyre, and at Sarepta between Tyre and Sidon where, as Tannit-'aštarot, she was the patroness of a *marzeaḥ* house. But a late inscription from Carthage

440. F. M. Cross, *Canaanite Myth and Hebrew Epic: Essays in the History of the Religion of Israel* (Cambridge: Harvard University Press, 1973) 24–36; Lipiński, *Dieux et Déesses de l'Univers Phénicien et Punique*, 251–64.

441. Cross, *Canaanite Myth and Hebrew Epic*, 28–38; Lipiński, *Dieux et Déesses de l'Univers Phénicien et Punique*, 199–215.

442. *CAT* 1:6:5, 1–4.

that dedicates a building project to her and to Astarte calls her "Tannit of Lebanon."[443]

From the fifth century onward, she is ubiquitous in funerary contexts at Carthage, invoked almost always with Baʿal Ḥamon, but in first place, where she is symbolized by the crescent moon, now inverted over the full moon, which she borrowed from him.[444] In her manifestation as Tannit Face-of-Baʿal, she also borrows his symbol of the full moon: in this appearance, she looks like a woman done in geometric shape, her body an isosceles triangle, sometimes with allusion to her physical form, her arms a long horizontal line sometimes terminating in raised hands, her head a featureless lunar disk resting on the arms at the apex of the triangle, sometimes surmounted by her own symbol the inverted crescent moon (see fig. 6.5). The design might be an astrological sign, an astronomical measurement, or an abstract presentation of the Amanus Mountain with the moon rising over the horizon, but it is fundamentally an expression of the abstract theological notion that Tannit represents in abstract form the person and presence of the God. What is unique about them is this singular conjunction.

Their cult consisted principally of prayer offered by individuals and recorded on steles or tombstones. The written record transcribes a liturgical formality from which the prayer itself must be reconstructed. The inscriptions usually begin, sometimes end, by invoking "The Lady, Tannit Face-of-Baʿal, and the Lord, Baʿal Ḥamon," and the invocation of their titles is an implicit act of praise. Next is the statement that a vow was made, a vow being a form of petition: "If you . . . then I . . . ," arising in a situation of need or distress. Then the individual is identified by name and parentage, perhaps by profession or, when it is a woman who prays, by her familial or marital status.

The next elements are thanksgiving, which is expressed in the confession that the prayer was heard, and petition, expressed in the hope that the Gods will bless the individual. Erecting and inscribing the stele publicizes the accessibility of the Gods and fulfills the vow, and the inscription sometimes ends with a curse on anyone who would disturb, overturn, remove, or steal the stone, which with its text is a "gift" to the Gods: "And anyone who might steal this gift, may Tannit Face-of-Baʿal kill him!"; "Whoever removes this gift, may Tannit Face-of-Baʿal judge the mind of that man!"; "Whoever steals this stone, may Baʿal Ḥamon cut him off!"; "Anyone who might overturn this gift, or disturb it, or destroy it, may his hand wither."[445]

There are many more-or-less significant variations on this basic form of prayer, notably in identifying the situation of distress or in elaborating on the thanksgiving. There is, for instance, a record of manumission that

443. *CIS* 3914; *KAI* 81; P. Bordreuil, "Tanit du Liban (Noveaux documents religieux phéniciens III)," in *Phoenicia and the East Mediterranean in the First Millennium* B.C. (ed. E. Lipiński; Studia Phoenicia 5; Louvain: Peeters, 1987) 79–85, esp. pp. 79–82.

444. C. Picard, "Les représentations de sacrifice *molk* sur les ex-voto de Carthage," *Karthago* 17 (1973–74) 67–138, pls. 6–24, esp. pp. 81–82; T. Redissi, "Étude des empreintes de sceaux de Carthage," in *Karthago III: Die deutschen Ausgrabungen in Karthago* (ed. F. Rakob; Mainz am Rhein: von Zabern, 1999) 4–92, pls. 1–21, esp. pp. 42–45, 84 ##183–85, pl. 16; L. Dubal, "The Riddle of the Protective Crescent in Punic Votive Art," *Actas* 4, 2.583–91.

445. *CIS* 3783:5–7; 4937:2–6; 3784:1–3; 5510:3.

Fig. 6.5. Example of the Symbol of Tannit (from Tunisia, A.O. 5987). © The Louvre Museum/Thierry Ollivier, Paris, 2010.

explains that the prior adverse condition consisted in being apprenticed, and the reason for thanksgiving was in general the fulfillment of the vow and in particular being freed:[446]

446. Ibid., 5522.

> To the Lady, to Tannit Face-of-Baʿal and to the Lord, to Baʿal Ḥamon, the
> vow of Hannibal, maker of potions—when his lord ʾEshmunḥilleṣ, son of
> ʾAdonîbaʿal, son of ʾEshmunḥilleṣ, son of ʾAdonibaʿal, made him a freedman,
> when he was not, gratuitously, without payment, according to a tablet that he
> sealed, by his own decision—because they heard his voice.

The source of this written record was Hannibal's prayer and the answer he
received. The specific reason for thanksgiving is that he was released from
his indenture without having to pay. The release was public, recorded in a
tablet sealed by his master, by an agreement into which he entered "freely"
according to the usual Latin idiom, but in the Punic idiom "deliberately,"
"by his own decision."

The commoner variations on the prayer form occur in texts commemorating the offering of a child to the Gods.[447] Some texts refer to the offering
as a "being brought to Baʿal" (*mlk bʿl*, feminine *mlkt bʿl*), which is commemorated by the inscribed stele (*nṣb*) and is the subject of a vow and the
object of thanksgiving, because the vow has been heard, or of hope that
the prayer will be heard. The pre-fifth-century texts mention only Baʿal
Ḥamon,[448] but the later texts also include Tannit who sometimes is called
"Mother" rather than Tannit:

> Stele of the offering to Baʿal of a boy child [*mlk*] which was vowed by Bodʿaštart,
> son of Bodmilqart, son of Bodʿaštart, son of Bodmilqart, son of Sorbam, to the
> Mother, to the Lady Face-of-Baʿal and to Baʿal Ḥamon. May they hear his
> voice, may they bless him.[449]

There is at least one text in which the man making the offering (it is usually
the father who brings the child to Baʿal) confesses what a difficult decision
it was:

> To the Lady, to Tannit Face-of-Baʿal, and to the Lord, to Baʿal Ḥamon, what
> Magon vowed on behalf of ʾAdonîbaʿal, a stele of a girl child [*mlkt*] in his
> misery [*bmṣrm*].[450]

This kind of offering seems to have been infrequent, but there is other
good evidence for the sacrifice of children in fulfillment of the vow. The
child generally is not named (it had no status) but is referred to as "flesh"
(*bšr*) or, with reference to the child's father or mother, "his flesh" (*bšry* or
bšrm) or "her flesh" (*bšryʾ*). The funerary text often affirms that the sacrifice
is deliberate and intentional (*btm, bntm, bnty*, from the root "understand"
[*byn*]), that is, a religious, moral, and public act and not a personal whim:

> To the Lady, to Tannit Face-of-Baʿal, and to the Lord, to Baʿal Ḥamon, what
> Bodmilqart, son of ʿAbdʾadom vowed—flesh which is of his flesh, deliberately.[451]

The prayer usually ends with this specification of the vow as a deliberate
offering of flesh, and the final thanksgiving and petition for future blessing

---

447. L. E. Stager, "Carthage: A View from the Tophet," *PhWest*, 155–66; S. Moscati and
S. Ribichini, *Il sacrificio dei bambini: Un aggiornamento* (Accademia Nazionale dei Lincei, Quaderno 266; Rome: Accademia Nazionale dei Lincei, 1991) 3–44.
448. *CIS* 5684, 5685.
449. Ibid., 380.
450. Ibid., 198.
451. Ibid., 295.

are rare: when they do occur, sometimes just Tannit (and not both Gods) is thanked for listening and blessing or is asked to listen and bless:

> To the Lady, to Tannit Face-of-Ba'al and to the Lord, to Ba'al Ḥamon, the vow of 'Eshmunḥilleṣ, son of Ger'Ashtart, son of Ḥimilkot, son of 'Addirmilqart—of his flesh, in his deliberation, because she heard his voice. May she bless him. [452]

One of the commemorative texts ends with a quotation of the father's intense plea to Tannit:

> To the Lady, to Tannit Face-of-Ba'al, and to the Lord, to Ba'al Ḥamon, what Bod'aštart, son of Bodmilqart, son of Ba'alshillek vowed: "Take and receive his flesh" [*bšr tqḥ tkblm*]. [453]

Another ends with the father describing his child whom he has vowed to the Gods as "the desired of my flesh" (*'yt 'ršt šry*)—a sad note because 'Arishat, "desired," is also a feminine name (like Désirée), and it may have been hers. A woman might identify herself as a daughter rather than a wife and make an offering of her child, whom she calls "her flesh" (*bšr*), to the Gods: [454] child sacrifice by women is rare, and they do not refer to their devotion as "deliberate." As in all offerings, the stele itself is the material sign of the worshiper's devotion. The child is gone; what remains is the written memory, and so the stele may be protected by a curse on anyone who would think of tipping it over:

> To the Lady, to Tannit Face-of-Ba'al, and to the Lord, to Ba'al Ḥamon, what Kannumiya, servant of 'Eshmun'amas, son of Ba'alyaton vowed of his flesh. May she bless him. And anyone who would overturn this stone, even by my command or by the command of my agent, may Tannit Face-of-Ba'al judge the mind of that man. [455]

The deliberation, the publicity, and the pain [456] were noted by classical writers, who were glad to distance themselves from a rite that they considered at least bizarre. [457] For the Punic faithful, however, to whom the death of any child could be sacramental (the incidental death of an infant became meaningful by association with the sacrifice, immolation, and burial of an animal), the sacrifice of a child confirmed their vow and expressed their deep devotion to the primordial Gods who founded and maintained their city and the world.

Revenge for the defeat and death of Hamilcar waited until the waning of the fifth century, [458] Hannibal, the son of Girsakon (Gisco), and grandson of Hamilcar became the magistrate (*špṭ*) in 410 B.C.E. He intervened in Sicily when Segesta, inland between Eryx and Motya, appealed for help against

---

452. Ibid., 5518.
453. Ibid., 5600.
454. Ibid., 302, 304.
455. Ibid., 3785.
456. H. Bénichou-Safar, "Sur l'incinération des enfants aux tophets de Cartage et Sousse," *RHR* 205 (1988) 57–68.
457. M. Gras, P. Rouillard, and J. Teixidor, "The Phoenicians and Death," *Berytus* 39 (1991) 127–76, esp. pp. 156–57 (citing Plutarch, *On Superstition*, 13).
458. Huss, *Geschichte der Karthager*, 107–23.

Selinunte. He attacked, besieged, and captured Selinunte, which now was allied with Agrigentum, Gela, and Syracuse, but its survivors managed to escape to Agrigentum. Hannibal next attacked and captured Himera and, it is said, sacrificed his prisoners on the very spot where Hamilcar had sacrificed himself for Carthage.[459] When his term as magistrate was over, he and his cousin Himilco, the son of Ḥanno, and grandson of Hamilcar were named commanders in chief (*rab*). They immediately prepared an attack on Agrigentum, but Hannibal died during the siege, and his brother ʾAdonîbaʿal was named co-commander. The capture of the city is recorded in an inscription that places the victory in its contemporary political and religious context:[460]

1. [This monument was dedicated by ʾAdonîbaʿal, son of Girsakon, the commander, and by Ḥimilkot, son of Ḥannoʾ]

2. [the Commander. May] Our Lady Tannit Face-of-Baʿal honor those men [and grant them health and]

3. [inspire] the minds of those men and the minds of their children and [of their whole family].

4. [And anyone] who overturns this monument or defaces it or destroys it, may his hand wither;

5. [and anyone] who does not venerate it, may Our Lady Tannit Face-of-Baʿal and

6. the Lord Baʿal Ḥamon overturn those men in their lives under the sun, along with their children.

7. [But if someone] has called on Melqart, may he grant him health and inspire him

8. from his sanctuary because he venerated him with zeal, and may this man have health and wealth. And this monument

9. was dedicated in the month Paʿulot, the year of ʾEshmunʿamas, the son of ʾAdonîbaʿal, the commander, and of Ḥannoʾ,

10. son of Bodʿaštart, son of Ḥannoʾ, the commander. And the commanders—ʾAdonîbaʿal, son of Girsakon, the commander,

11. and Ḥimilkot, son of Ḥannoʾ, the commander—led an army to ʿAliša, and they captured Agrigentum, and they

12. made peace with the citizens of Naxos. The engraver was Menor, son of ʿAbdmiskar, and Zebug was his assistant.

The inscription, in a frame on a small stone slab, was associated with a monument (*mtnt*, "a gift") that deserved the veneration due to Melqart (lines 5, 8), and it may have been a statue of the God or a victory stele

---

459. L. Maurin, "Himilcon le Magonide: Crises et mutations à Carthage au début du IVe siècle avant J.-C.," *Sem* 12 (1962) 5–43, esp. p. 22.

460. *CIS* 5510; C. Krahmalkov, "A Carthaginian Report of the Battle of Agrigentum 406 B.C. (*CIS* I, 5510, 9–11)," *RSF* 2 (1974) 171–77; A. van den Branden, "L'inscription punique CIS, 5510," in *Al-Hudhud: Festschrift Maria Höfner zum 80. Geburtstag* (ed. R. G. Stiegner; Graz: Karl-Franzens-Universität, 1981) 35–44; P. C. Schmitz, "The Name 'Agrigentum' in a Punic Inscription (*CIS* I, 5510:10)," *JNES* 53 (1994) 1–13.

with his likeness that was placed in his sanctuary (line 8). The first line is missing, but "those men" (lines 2–3) must refer to the heroes of Agrigentum whose names are recorded and whose rank is emphasized (lines 9–11) when the occasion for the dedication (line 7) is narrated.

The inscription is carefully structured and is all about the descendants of Hamilcar and their religion. The first three lines invoke a blessing on the heroes, their children, and their families. It is about political power ("honor"), physical well-being and, as is typical of the Carthaginian mentality, about intentionality, deliberation, and insight. It looks for divine approval of their invasion of Sicily. The next section (lines 4–6) incorporates a traditional curse for physically misusing the monument, but it adds a parallel stipulation requiring a positive mental attitude toward the monument. It obviously anticipates, or acknowledges, serious criticism. Its invocation of Tannit and Baʿal Hamon, rather than just Tannit as in the previous blessing section, suggests that the opposition was some faction or even the government in Carthage, proponents of the constitution and its Gods.

The next part (lines 7–8) is the heart of the matter. It refers to "someone" not to "anyone," to "this man" not to "those men," and to events in past time not to a future action. The introductory "but if" is rhetorical: the conditional keeping the hypothetical style of the preceding section, but the past indicative contrasting with its subjunctives. In the context, "this man" is anyone or each one of the Magonids (Hannibal, for instance, or any of the men named in this text) whose worship of Melqart distinguished this family from the other wealthy and ambitious families of Carthage. The fourth part (lines 8–9) dates the dedication of the monument to the year when the magistrates were family members and close relatives of the heroes of Agrigentum: ʾEshmunʿamas was, in fact, the son of ʾAdonîbaʿal, and Hannoʾ was his cousin and the nephew of Himilkot, the other commander.

The last part (lines 9–12) corresponds to the first section, in which the commanders introduced themselves and sought confirmation of their generosity of spirit. The expedition to Sicily takes two words in Punic, the capture of Agrigentum takes three, and the treaty with Naxos takes five. All the emphasis in the narrative is on the names and the rank of the heroes and on the fact that it was they (*hmt*) who captured one town and made peace with another. The text ends with the names of the professional and his associate who inscribed the monument. They apparently were not embarrassed by the fact that the surface they prepared was not big enough and that this last line had to be written on the frame.

The war ended with a peace treaty between Carthage and Dionysios I (405–367 B.C.E.) of Syracuse.[461] It stipulated that the Carthaginians held the western part of Sicily, that Syracuse belonged to Dionysios, that Himera in north-central Sicily and Agrigentum in the south together with its sister cities could not be fortified and would pay damages to Carthage, and that eastern Sicily remained independent of Dionysios. This was pretty much the pre-Agrigentum situation, and of course it did not last.[462] Dionysios attacked and destroyed Motya, on which the Carthaginian fleet depended

461. Bengston, *Die Verträge der griechisch-römischen Welt von 700 bis 338 v. Chr.*, 152–53 #210.
462. Huss, *Geschichte der Karthager*, 124–45.

for its depredations in Sicily, and Ḥimilkot retaliated by attacking Syracuse. War dragged on until Dionysios died (367 B.C.E.) and the Magonids faded away, and nothing good came of it, except that Carthage, already an imperial power, acquired the reputation of being a persistent and formidable enemy. Sicily was the prize that Carthage could not keep and that after the first Punic War (264–241 B.C.E.) it finally had to relinquish.

In the fifth century before the Sicilian wars, Carthage, to judge from the isolated archaeological evidence,[463] became a worthy metropolis with fine public buildings, new neighborhoods, and improved port facilities— the creation of a wealthy and exuberant society. In the century after the Sicilian wars and before the wars with Rome, according to the inscriptional evidence, there were more modest physical improvements, but these were matched by changes in the social order and by a return to archaic religious practices that together, but in a more settled frame of mind, reflect the same civic pride.

When Ḥimilkot attacked Syracuse, he, whether moved or abandoned by his vaunted divine inspiration, desecrated a suburban graveyard and ransacked the Temple of Demeter and Kore. In order to expiate this great sin, Carthage built a temple for them and introduced their cult into the city.[464] Their cult included burning incense, and hundreds of incense burners have been discovered at Carthage in a depository (*favissa*) of the Temple of Demeter and Kore, in domestic quarters, and in tombs: they are shaped like the heads of pretty, young, Greek or Roman girls (Kore means "girl" and is a title of Persephone) individualized, wearing earrings, and with stylish hairdos, supporting a basket (*calathos*), which would normally contain fruit and was carried in processions for Demeter.[465] It also included the sacrifice of piglets, and excavations have uncovered a fairly dramatic increase in pig bones at Carthage beginning in the fifth century.[466]

Demeter and Kore's cult is attested in an inscription on a statue base:[467] "To the Lady, to her Mother, and to the Lady, Mistress of the burial chamber, what Ḥamilar, son of Baʿalḥannoʾ made." The emphasis in the dedication is on Kore: Demeter is included as "her Mother," and Kore, who is also the bride of Hades, is named as his mistress (*baʿalat*), the mistress of the tomb, which is considered a room (*ḥdrt*) in the infernal mansion. The cult of Kore, not including Demeter, is also known from third-century inscribed tombstones of her priestesses. The earlier ("The Grave of Ḥannibaʿal, priestess of Kore") spells the Goddess's name with a digamma (*waw* in Punic), as it was pronounced in Greek (*krwʾ*).[468] The later spells it phonetically, as

463. M. Vegas, ed., *Cartago fenício-púnica: Las excavaciones alemanas en Cartago 1975–1997* (Cuadernos de Arqueología Mediterránea 4; Barcelona: Universidad Pompeu Fabra—Laboratorio de Arqueología, 1998).

464. Diod. 14.77.5.

465. Z. Chérif, "Les brûles parfums à tête de femme carthaginois," *Atti* 2, 2.733–43; M. J. Pena, "Considerazioni sulla diffusione nel Mediterraneo Occidentale di bruciaprofumi a forma di testa femminile," *Atti* 2, 3.1109–18.

466. Lipiński, *Dieux et Déesses de l'Univers Phénicien et Punique*, 374–80; G. Nobis, "Die Tierreste von Karthago," *Karthago, III: Die Deutschen Ausgrabungen in Karthago* (ed. F. Rakob; Mainz am Rhein: von Zabern, 1999) 574–632, esp. p. 593.

467. *CIS* 177.

468. Ibid., 5987.

the Carthaginians might have said the name.[469] Her temple was just one among many in Carthage, but her story crisscrossed the legends of Adonis, and her cult was inconspicuous in a city charmed by western Greek symbols and fashions.

The sanctuary (*mqm*) of Melqart, which is central in the monument celebrating the victory of Himilkot and ʾAdonîbaʿal at Agrigentum, is mentioned in passing in one other text,[470] a vow to Tannit and Baʿal Ḥamon by a man who identifies himself by name and as "belonging to the people of the Temple of Melqart" (*bʿm bt mlqrt*). But there are inscriptions with allusions to a key ritual in honor of Melqart, and another badly damaged text may describe the liturgy associated with it. The ritual is performed by a man called "The Raiser-of-the-God, the Bridegroom-of-Astronoe" (*mqm ʾlm mtrḥ ʿštrny*)[471] or sometimes identified as just "The Raiser-of-the-God." These are often from the ranks of the magistrates or commanders or children of men with those ranks, and in one instance the man was both a magistrate and the high priest. The texts do not divulge whether they officiated at the time they held the rank, or if they were presenting their credentials.

The God was believed to have died, and his death and rising certainly would have been enacted, with the rising consisting at first of summoning him and then restoring him, his statue, or his emblems to their place of honor in the temple. There is an analogous ritual of the God Shadrapaʾ, the Genius of Healing and a surrogate of the God ʾEshmun, mentioned by a man who identifies himself as "the Awakener of the God through Admonition" (*myqṣ ʾlm bmsr*). The admonition (*msr*) was something such as "Wake up! Why are you sleeping?" because ʾEshmun was the God of the resting (*rpʾm*) of individuals asleep in death.[472] The liturgy for Melqart was the enactment of the marriage of the officiant and Astronoe, "the one who is like Astarte" (*ʿaštarōnāy*), the woman chosen to represent Astarte. The inscription on gold leaf from Pyrgi in Italy associates the king's betrothal to Astarte on the day that the God died with the God's rising and describes the building of a "Holy Chamber" where the marriage rite was celebrated. At Carthage, the marriage rite might have been observed in the Temple of Melqart itself or in the "Holy Chamber" (*ʾšr qdš*) in the Temple of Astarte, which is mentioned twice in contemporary Carthaginian inscriptions.[473]

The text that might describe the actual ceremony or the preparations for it is inscribed in columns on a white marble tablet now broken on all sides.[474] Parts of two columns are preserved: the left column, of which only the beginnings of the lines remain, contains instructions for the fourth

---

469. *RES* 360; *KAI* 70; J. Ferron, "L'inscription punique d'Avignon," *Studi Magrebini* 2 (1968) 89–104, pls. 1–2.

470. *CIS* 264.

471. H.-P. Müller, "Der phönizisch-punische *mqm ʾlm* im Licht einer althebräischen Isoglosse," *Or* 65 (1996) 111–26.

472. *CIS* 3921; *KAI* 77; B. F. Batto, "The Sleeping God: An Ancient Near Eastern Motif of Divine Sovereignty," *Bib* 68 (1987) 153–77; A. Mrozek and S. Votto, "The Motif of the Sleeping Divinity," *Bib* 80 (1999) 415–19.

473. *CIS* 3779:5–6; 5547:7.

474. *CIS* 166; *KAI* 76.

and fifth days; the right column, with only the ends of lines, prescribes preparations for at least two of the earlier days. In both columns, each line is a separate rubric. Beginning with the right column, presumably with the first day, the lines seem to alternate between instructions for food and for clothing: there is something about the mixing and presentation of food, about offering a curtain or covering, about food that is beautiful and rich, about linen and clothing, and again about mixing and presenting food or offerings. The left column, concerning the fourth day, includes the consecration of a branch of beautiful fruit, the consecration of the chamber, and the offering of bread, instructions about the consecrated woman and the bread, about the choice of a beautiful white fig, and about burning finely ground incense. Concerning the fifth day, there is a reference to placing a honeycomb in the chamber, to 200 children, to a veil or covering, and to five unspecified things. There are some echoes in this of ancient love poetry, and if the tablet does describe the preparation of the bridal chamber, it would begin to clarify the role of the bridegroom and Astronoe in raising the God. It would indicate once again a late Carthaginian predilection for reintroducing archaic beliefs and practices—in this instance, from ancient Sumerian, North Syrian, Israelite, and coastal Phoenician codes and customs.[475]

The detailed liturgy, whatever it was, illustrates another Carthaginian trait—a tendency to uniformity and a mania for regulation. Liturgies, of course, are like that, but these characteristics pervade their religious and social thinking. Some of the people, often professionals or from prominent families (a high priestess, priestess of Kore, daughter of a commander and wife of a magistrate, the priest of Baʿalshamem, a *mqm ʾlm*, a maker of pyxides, a commander) were buried in rock-hewn tombs with simple secular grave markers ("the tomb [*qbr*] of. . . .").[476] But almost everybody had a religious burial marked by a gravestone recording his or her vow.

When men made a vow, they followed the prescribed prayer form that ended with thanksgiving to the Gods for having heard their prayer and with a plea for continued blessing. When women made a vow, their prayers stressed the critical situation and concentrated on petition, and thanksgiving and praise were almost always omitted.[477] The crisis seems to have been routine and may have just been their youth (with one exception, the girls are identified as someone's daughter) or perhaps childlessness, but it is striking nevertheless that their divergence from the norm scrupulously follows another set pattern. There are exceptional vows in which the crisis is described. One man prays for his father, a sea captain, and his crew; one man for his children; for his grandchildren,[478] a woman prays for her husband[479]—but even this does not alter the formal pattern of the prayer.

---

475. A. Levin, *Hosea and North Israelite Traditions: The Distinctive Use of Myth and Language in the Book of Hosea* (Ph.D. diss., University of Toronto, 2009).

476. *CIS* 5941–6000.

477. Ibid., 4607–4775, 4988–5015.

478. Ibid., 197; 178; 254.

479. Ibid., 5939.

The elements of public worship at various temples in Carthage are suggested by a variety of texts. The earliest of these, called the Marseille tariff,
is from the second half of the fourth century.[480] It is inscribed in an elegant
semicursive script on a stone tablet but has the structure of an archival
document. The title is in two lines set off from the rest of the document
by leaving the end of the second line blank. It is the catalog of levies on
sacrifices offered in the Temple of Baʿal Saphon that was published by
the 30 men who oversaw these payments. It is dated to the term of two
named commanders, both of them former magistrates, and their unnamed
associates.

The last four lines are the conclusion. This begins by noting that the published document is a précis of rules written at the time stated at the beginning
by the 30 men who oversaw payment to the priests and that the complete
list is available for consultation. "Any levy that is not included on this tablet must be given in accordance with the writings of the men who oversaw
the levies." The rest of the conclusion establishes fines for any priest who
might not follow these rules and some punishment, now lost in a broken
part of the tablet, on anyone who offers a sacrifice and refuses to pay the
set amount. The body of the tariff is a systematic list of sacrificial offerings,
in descending order of size (ox, calf, ram or goat, lamb, kid or fawn, birds)
and value (the amount of money or meat to be paid to the priests) in each
category (whole burnt offering, cooked and eaten) of sacrifice.

Other temples had other rules, customs, and terminology. For instance,
the tariffs could be set by the 10 men who were in charge of the "holy
places" (*mqdšm*), not the 30 in charge of finances, and other items might be
included.[481] However, the cult, temple order, and rituals were established in
writing and may even have been centrally regulated for all the temples in
the city.

There is an epitaph of a servant of the Temple of Isis in Carthage that
illustrates this normative aspect of public worship but that also reveals its
very personal, almost private character:[482]

> Milkpilles, son of Bodmilqart, son of Milkpilles, son of [Bodmilqart, son of]
> Milkpilles, son of Milqartpilles, Raiser-of the-God, son of [Bodmilqart, son
> of] Milkharam—Tombstone of an upright coadjutor I, ʾIšiṣip [.], as a memo-
> rial over the gathering of his bones I dedicated because the spirit of the holy
> things was [his inspiration and] because, like a priest, he in his lifetime ex-
> celled in the holy things and served the Gods with all his strength [in] service
> according to the writings and the law. And I inscribed his name at the top
> of the cornice forever, [and I placed] his coffin beneath it, and I paid respect
> to his bones. The excellent leader of the sodality of the Temple of Isis was
> Sakk[unyaton, son of] ʿAbdyeraḥ, and he wrote the draft of my text on this
> tablet.

---

480. Ibid., 165; *KAI* 69.
481. Ibid., 167 (+ 3915 + 3916 + 3917), 168–70, 3919.
482. Ibid., 6000 bis; A. van den Branden, "Note riguardanti l'iscrizione punica CIS 6000
bis," *Bibbia e Oriente* 23 #129 (1981) 155–59; C. Bonnet, "Le culte d'Isis à Carthage: À propos de
l'inscription funéraire punique CIS I, 6000 bis," in *Ana šadî Labnāni lū allik: Beiträge zu altorientalischen und mittelmeerischen Kulturen—Festschrift für Wolfgang Röllig* (ed. B. Pongratz-Leisten,
H. Kühne, and P. Xella; Neukirchen-Vluyn: Neukirchener Verlag, 1997) 43–56, fig. 1.

The man's name is separated from the following text by a space, and the second sentence in the epitaph ("And I inscribed . . .") indicates that this was intentional. The man was not a priest but a just and upright helper (ʿzr yšr), a faithful sacristan, who acted like a priest in his devotion to the Gods and in his observance of "the writings (mktb) and the law (tʾrt)": for the man who wrote the epitaph, this is what made the dead man upright and his bones worthy of honor. The personal tone is due in part at least to the fact that the men all belonged to the same society or association or "family" (šph), the devotees of the Temple of Isis. The epitaph is dated to the tenure of its excellent (ʾdr) head, and he is credited with writing the first draft (ʾbt, "ghosts," "shadows") of the text—on an ostracon, on a leaf of papyrus, or in chalk on the stone itself—which was then copied by the "engraver." This title may have been included in the damaged spot after his name.

This procedure, carving in stone a text from another medium, is known from two inscriptions in which the engraver was either illiterate or distracted and inscribed his instructions along with the text: (1) A potter was told to inscribe on an urn the name of the man whose ashes it contained and thus began his text with "inscribe on the urn."[483] (2) A man who made a vow to Baʿal Ḥamon added at the end of his text instructions for the engraver to count the number of letters to make sure that he got it right, but instead of counting he just copied the instructions.[484]

Parallel texts from which the monumental inscriptions were copied may also be attested by the bullae found in an archive in a public building in the heart of the city.[485] The building, of which only a bit of the foundations and some of the ground plan and scattered remains of columns and capitals are left, is sometimes thought to have been a temple, and a nearby cemetery where there were about 2,000 tombstones with dedications to Tannit and Baʿal Ḥamon might suggest that it was a temple of these civic Gods. Almost all the bullae have traces of the string that tied the papyrus document, which was sealed twice—once by an individual (21 were sealed by two people and 4 by three individuals) and once by the official or archivist.[486] The archival seals were Egyptian: the most frequently used (there are 2,319 imprints; the seal became worn and had to be replaced five times) bore the cartouche of Thutmosis III (1480–1436 B.C.E.), but there were also seals with the name of a Hyksos pharaoh, with mute hieroglyphic signs, or with a falcon and sphinx—all of them carved in the style of XXVIth Dynasty glyptic.[487] The archive was in use from the fifth to the second century, and the individual seals reflect the changing tastes during this time.

483. *CIS* 6002; J. Ferron, "Epigraphe funéraire punique," *OrAnt* 5 (1966) 197–201, pls. 52–53.

484. *RES* 1543.

485. D. Berges, "Die Tonsiegel aus dem Karthagischen Tempelarchiv," in *Karthago II: Die deutschen Ausgrabungen in Karthago* (ed. F. Rakob; Mainz am Rhein: von Zabern, 1997) 10–214, pls. 6–128; idem, "Los sellos de arcilla del archivo del templo cartaginés," in *Cartago Fenício-Púnica: Las excavaciones alemanas en Cartago 1975–1997* (ed. M. Vegas; Cuaderno de arqueología Mediterránea 4; Barcelona: Universidad Pompeu Fabra—Laboratorio de Arqueología, 1998) 111–32.

486. D. Berges, "Los sellos de arcilla del archivo del templo cartaginés," 112–14.

487. T. Redissi, "Étude des empreintes de sceaux de Carthage," in *Karthago III: Die deutschen Ausgrabungen in Karthago* (ed. F. Rakob; Mainz am Rhein: von Zabern, 1999) 4–92, pls. 1–21, esp. pp. 5–9.

A favorite Egyptianizing theme (of which there are many examples, each from a different seal) was Isis nursing Horus, but the God Bes was also popular, and there are examples of the Horus falcon, the Eye of Horus, the uraeus, and animal-headed Gods.[488] Seals with archaizing Phoenician themes are from the fourth century and feature a God standing, sometimes standing on a lion, or seated on a throne, or a Goddess standing on a lion, or just standing with her right hand raised in benediction, or men standing beside an incense altar or next to the Tree-of-Life.[489] A few imprints have Punic themes, such as the sign of Tannit, but the overwhelming majority of seals were inspired by Greek themes and were influenced by contemporary western Greek, including Sicilian, coinage. We can only conjecture about the purpose of this archive. It was relatively small, lasted a long time, was consistent in its system of individual sealing and official receipt, and close to the cemetery where steles recorded the vows of the people who could afford tombstones, and it may be that the papyri were the official vow and record of sacrifice from which the steles were inscribed. The "deliberation" of which many of these people were proud and which astonished their detractors would have been confirmed by an official and public act of this sort.

Building projects in late Carthage consisted of restoration of the temples or beautification of the city and sometimes creating public or private facilities. Among the latter, there is a housing complex in which one house had a room designed and reserved for performing the *maioumas*, the Festival of the Waters, symbolically the waters of the Flood, in which "water is carried" (*my'ms*), poured out, and then allowed to drain away, rendering the Flood benign.[490] The celebration, without any specifics on its enactment, is mentioned in Carthaginian inscriptions only, but not always, in connection with the manumission of slaves. These inscriptions are the usual vows to Tannit and Ba'al Ḥamon by a man (one time by a woman), whom the most complete formula identifies as "a man of Sidon ['š ṣdn; feminine, 'š ṣdn'] by the authority of his lord [bd 'dny or 'dnm] at the mayumas [lmy'ms], of the people of Carthage ['m qrtḥdšt]."[491] The expression "man of Sidon" is the equivalent of calling someone "Phoenician"; "by the authority of his lord" means that it was done officially and most likely in writing; "at the mayumas" indicates that it was done publicly; and "of the people of Carthage" means that his release from the condition of a servant or slave ('bd) made him a freedman and a full citizen of this city.

The celebration of the mayumas is traditionally associated with the *marzeaḥ*, a professional club or association, and the mayumas discovered

488. Ibid., 5–31.

489. Ibid., 32–40.

490. H. G. Niemeyer and R. F. Docter, "Excavación bajo el Decumanus Maximus de Cartago durante los años 1986–1995: Informe preliminar," in *Cartago Fenício-Púnica: Las excavaciones alemanas en Cartago 1975–1997* (ed. M. Vegas; Cuadernos de arqueología Mediterránea 4; Barcelona: Universidad Pompeu Fabra—Laboratorio de Arqueología, 1998) 47–109, pls. 1–11, esp. pp. 58–65; H. G. Niemeyer, "Un nuevo santuario de la diosa Tanit en Cartago," *Actas* 4, 2.635–42.

R. M. Good, "The Carthaginian *mayumas*," *SEL* 3 (1986) 99–114; H. W. Attridge and R. A. Oden, trans., *De Dea Syria* (Texts and Translations 9; Missoula, MT: Scholars Press, 1976) 18–21 #12–13.

491. *CIS* 269–75, 290, 291, 4908, 4909. *CIS* 4661 = 5638 (the woman's release).

at Carthage, if it was not a public space where the civic rite was performed, may have been a facility of just this sort of club, where from time to time someone graduated to full membership or was released to full citizenship. The room had a black paved waterproof floor and was divided into two equal parts: the western half was a step higher than the eastern and was decorated with the sign of Tannit, with the Evening Star, with the symbol of royalty (*T*), and with the Pleiades, all created by setting pieces of white marble into the pavement. The east part had a depression and a drain near the step and was closed off from the street on the east. The room was roofed and lay south of the entrance courtyard. West of it was a large meeting room, and north of this room off the courtyard was a room the same size, divided into three sections. The house would have been ideal for the meetings of an association, under the auspices of Astarte, as the celestial omens suggest, but proudly Carthaginian, as the Sign of Tannit and the royal symbol urge, with a mayumas room where apprentices could have been promoted to full membership in the profession. Reenacting the Flood, as the traditional story goes, marked the transition from an evil time to a time of divine favor and so, in these manumission texts, "at the mayumas" takes the place of the usual thanksgiving at the end of inscriptions, when the vow has been heard.

The restoration of temples is mentioned mainly in third-century texts, when it seems to have been entrusted to a committee of 10 men appointed by the city. At times the renovations were restricted to a particular furnishing:[492]

> Restored and made this slaughtering block with its feet the ten men who were in charge of the holy places in the year of the magistrates [- - - son of] Girsakkun, and Girʿaštart, son of Yiḥḥanbaʿal, son of ʿAzorbaʿal, son of Šopeṭ. And Bodʿaštart son of [- - - was the designer].

Apparently the slaughtering block was on legs and was where the animals were killed before being brought to the altar. The 10 men (also mentioned in another fragmentary inscription where the renovations are dated to the term of the 2 commanders [*rb*][493] and the designer) did not actually do the work, but still the committee took credit for it. Another inscription, also badly damaged, is dated to the year of the magistrates, to the term of the 2 commanders, to the time of the named men in charge of the work, and to the era of the high priest and seems to record the construction of a purification pool adorned with enthroned cherubim.[494] Another text, this time complete, records the making of a stele and its pedestal for the Temple of Baʿal Ḥamon. This obviously was considered an embellishment and not a renovation and thus escaped the scrutiny of the committee of 10. It is notable for its implicit politics and for its divergence from the standard form:[495]

---

492. Ibid., 175; *KAI* 80.
493. *CIS* 3919.
494. Ibid., 5523; M. Sznycer, "Un texte carthaginois relative aux contructions (C.I.S., I, 5523)," *Sem* 40 (1991) 69–81.
495. *CIS* 3778; *KAI* 78; G. Garbini, "KAI 78 nella lettura di un filologo," *RSF* 19 (1991) 83–88.

> May they bless him and hear his voice for ever! To the Lord, to Baʿalšamem, and to the Lady, to Tannit Face-of-Baʿal, and to the Lord, to Baʿal Ḥamon, and to the Lord, to Baʿal of the Magonids, the carved stele that I consecrated, and under it a broad stone base in the sanctuary of Baʿal Ḥamon, facing the west and its back to the east, according to the vow of Baʿalay- - - -

The man who made the vow traces his lineage through 16 previous generations and, because the inscription belongs paleographically to about the mid-fourth century, probably belonged to one of the founding families of Carthage. The vow and the opening petition are third person, but the actual dedication in fulfillment of the vow is expressed in the first person. The inscription illustrates quite clearly that the object of a vow usually was the stele, and this is exactly what Baʿalay offered, a tall, narrow stele on a broad base. The most striking peculiarity of the dedication is its selection of Gods. The inclusion of the city God and Goddess is no surprise; the mention of Baʿalšamem in first place might suggest that he was the head of the Carthaginian pantheon, as he was in earlier times at Byblos, or it could mean in this particular context that he was the patron God of this illustrious family, perhaps originally from Byblos. The surprise is the inclusion of the God of the Magonids (*mgnm*). According to the memorial of the battle of Agrigentum, this was Melqart, exclusive God of the Tyrians. But this just shows what remarkable influence the family of Mago had in Carthage and the veneration it continued to receive even a century after it lost power. This context suggests that Carthage's political leverage was provided by the old, established, founding families.

There is another text that records the building of twin temples for Tannit and Astarte sometime around the end of the fourth century or the beginning of the third.[496] Because this was not a renovation but a construction project involving "all the people of Carthage," it did not come under the scrutiny of the public works committee either.

> To the Ladies, to Astarte and to Tannit in Lebanon, new sanctuaries as likewise everything in the sanctuaries—the sculptures that are in these sanctuaries, along with their gold work, and along with the individual niches of these statues, and along with all the furnishings of these sanctuaries, and along with the stairs in front of these statues, and along with the stairway that leads up to the precinct of these sanctuaries, as likewise the stairway along the wall retaining this elevation—the people of Carthage made, from the greatest to the least, from the month Hiyar of the magistrates ʿAbdmilqart and Ḥannoʾ and until the month [ ] of the Magistrates Shopet and Ḥannoʾ, when the commanders were - - -, and the high priest was - - -, and the manager was ʿAkboram, the architect.

The Goddesses are mentioned together, without repeating the word "Lady" (*rbt*), and Tannit does not appear as "Face-of-Baʿal" because she is not the Carthaginian but the Lebanese Goddess. They were mentioned together in an inscription on an ivory plaque from Sarepta as "Tannit ʿAštart," but

---

496. *CIS* 3914; *KAI* 81; Bordreuil, "Tanit du Liban (Nouveaux documents religieux phéniciens III)," 79–85; J. Ferron, "Un événement religieux capital à Carthage au début du IIIe siècle avant notre ère," *Mus* 107 (1994) 229–55.

in this inscription they maintain their distinct identities and are honored with separate temples.

The temples were built on a platform (the word is "mountain, hill" (*har*) because the Goddesses are from Lebanon) held by a retaining wall and reached by stairs that led to the temples and by stairways to the precinct itself. The temples are distinguished by their statues, especially by their gold-plated statues, and by their furnishing and can most easily be visualized as columned buildings in a classic Greek style. The building took more than a year, and the date is computed according to the magistrates in each, the terms of the two commanders, and the office of the high priest. The idea of building temples to these Eastern Goddesses fits in with the mood of the time, when Carthage and the Punic world thought it important to summon their ancient Phoenician roots. The competitive attraction of the new temple of Demeter and Kore may have made this especially urgent.

This construction may have been part of a larger building project that included planning a boulevard from the citadel to the port. The inscription describing this work is missing the last third of its seven lines but it has been reconstructed almost entirely:[497]

> [The people of Carthage] opened and built this street to the square at the New Gate, which is in [the wall at the harbor, in the year] of the magistrates Šopeṭ and ʾAdonîbaʿal, during the term of the commanders ʾAdonîbaʿal, son of ʾEshmunḥilleṣ, son of Bo[dbaʿal and - - - son of Bodmil]qart, son of Ḥannoʾ, and their associates. In charge of this work were ʿAbdmilqart, [son of - - -, and - - -, excavators, and] Bodmilqart, son of Baʿalḥannoʾ, son of Bodmilqart, engineer, Yaḥwîʾelon, his brother, [was the builder, and helping with this work] were the prominent stores, the makers of tarpaulins who are in the lower city, the money changers, and the men who [- - - -], the goldsmiths, the shipwrights, the builders of masts, and the makers of anchors, all together. And [any man who would damage this street], our accountants will fine that man a thousand shekels to do whatever is needed [to restore this street].

The street, or boulevard, led from the heights of the citadel to the harbor, precisely to the square in front of the gate built into the new wall, traces of which have been found, separating the port from the city. As usual, the most important information is the date, computed according to the year of the magistrates and the term of the commanders and their associates. Of interest are the three phases of the work assigned to four different men: the only phase preserved is the phase assigned to the engineer, or "leveler," from which it may be conjectured that the first phase was digging and removing obstacles, assigned to two men, and that the last phase was the actual building or paving. These men, presumably, were in charge of work gangs whose members are not named. Of special interest is the variety of stores along the street or around the square at the city gate, which all contributed to the expenses, all of them involved in the shipping business, crafts, or commerce, and all of them working in unison (ʾḥdy) like an association of merchants. The concluding warning might have concerned damage to the monument, as is regularly the case, but the 1,000-shekel fine levied by the accountants suggests that this is what it actually cost to build

---

497. Idem, "L'inscription urbanistique de la Carthage punique," *Mus* 98 (1985) 45–78.

the boulevard. Carthage was built on hills, flowing down to the sea, and the open view provided by this boulevard would have been enchanting.

Conclusion

Carthage reinvented itself in the fifth and fourth centuries. It broke political ties with its founding cities in the East. It changed its constitution and confided it to a civic God and Goddess. It absorbed western Greek culture, evident in its wars and treaties and form of government, in its personal seals, in readily adopting the cult of Demeter and Kore from its Sicilian rival, and gradually in writing its texts with vowels. Its every step forward was shadowed by archaism, by affirming its Phoenician identity, by summoning old Gods, such as Sakkun the "Demiurge," and reviving ancient liturgies. It organized its people in a benign hierarchy, a vast, well-trained, specialized citizenry; slaves (*ʿbd*) and indentured workers who, according to their texts, were proud of the fact; and an aristocracy of professionals. It left nothing to chance, educated its people, centralized authority, introduced a God called "Memory" (*ḥṭrmskr*), but tried to put everything in writing. Its undoing was its forgetfulness.

Conclusion

Phoenicia was a Mediterranean state of mind: it created a world it could fill, mapped it, and outlined it loosely. It inhabited the Asiatic East, swept over Europe, embraced Africa. It grew up among Egyptians, studied in Egyptian schools, learned to cherish the ideals of Egyptian form and movement. It knew Sumerian words, appreciated Akkadian syllabification, graduated in Babylonian literature. It was an associate of the Amorites of Ugarit and acquainted with their Minoan and Mycenean friends. It matured among the Mediterranean Sea Peoples, who challenged the order, while Arameans and Arabs were looking for land and identity. It was innately antiquarian—free to appreciate and peddle the past without ever having to feel responsible for it.

The people lived in cities and towns and outposts along the Levantine coast. They spread from there northward to interior North Syria and Cilicia, and southward from Mount Carmel to Joppa, then inland, and deep into Egypt, to Cyprus, and everywhere overseas. They identified themselves by their city of origin: the Kitian, the Byblian, the Tyrian, the Sidonian, Akkite, Arqite, and Carthaginian. As they traveled from home and, in particular instances, as they were inspired by a common and deliberate purpose, they might identify themselves by their ethnic origin, as Sidonians, descendants of the legendary Ṣid, the Hunter and Fisher and descendant of the original Seafarer. Their Greek friends called them by this name and, because they also invented lovely blue, purple, and crimson dyes, by the name of the murex shellfish that produced these dyes and colored their skin: Phoenicians. The Phoenicians themselves did not use this name but in their last centuries, when they were immersed in Attic culture, sometimes humored their old friends by using the murex as a symbol of their identity.

The Phoenicians, wherever they went, were merchants and traders. They supplied the things that people needed and wanted—some essential, some wanton, and some exotic and extravagant. People who could not compete found them brash or vulgar, but this was only because no one had ever seen business so naturally, humanely, skillfully, and profitably pursued. Nice dishes, everyone learned, made food taste better, and new shapes and near and distant markets inspired a varied diet. Silver had its uses, but money was new, and the Assyrian economy and the Phoenician trade network depended on it. Perfumes, unguents, and scented oils became necessities; class was replaced by sophistication and flaunted in stylish clothes. There was wine from down the coast and around the world. Wealthy clients kept pet monkeys (they show up on witty amulets eating bananas), and cute lion cubs were copied onto shekel weights. Exotica revealed the worldliness of their new owners and their real or imaginary travel. The Phoenicians inspired because they were smart, secular, and secure. They could read, write, and count, tell stories, describe their adventures, and evoke a real world. It was a world of business, where commerce and culture coalesced.

Index of Authors

Index of Biblical Citations

Index of Geographical Names

575